DUGARD'S INTERNATIONAL LAW
A SOUTH AFRICAN PERSPECTIVE

DUGARD'S INTERNATIONAL LAW
A South African Perspective

Fifth edition

By

John Dugard SC
Max du Plessis SC
Tiyanjana Maluwa
Dire Tladi

With contributions by

Anton Katz SC
Arnold Pronto
Andreas Coutsoudis
Eshed Cohen
Jackie Dugard
Rosalind Elphick
Kholofelo Kugler

JUTA

First published 1994
Second Edition 2000
Third Edition 2005
Fourth Edition 2011
Fifth Edition 2018

Juta and Company Ltd, First floor, Sunclare Building,
21 Dreyer Street, Claremont, 7708

ISBN: 9781485128281

Typesetter: Brian Hopking
Cover designer: Matthew Bubear-Craemer

To our families and friends

Preface to the Fifth Edition

Many changes have been made to *International Law: A South African Perspective* in its fifth edition. First, as is to be expected of a new edition, the substance of the work has undergone major changes to take account of new developments both on the international legal scene and in South Africa. Second, the authoring of the book has changed dramatically. Whereas previous editions were largely the work of John Dugard, the fifth edition is the work of a team of authors. Max du Plessis, Tiyanjana Maluwa and Dire Tladi have joined John as authors and editors. In addition, particular chapters have been authored or co-authored by Anton Katz, Arnold Pronto, Eshed Cohen, Andreas Coutsoudis, Jackie Dugard, Rosalind Elphick and Kholofelo Kugler. Jennifer Nettleton-Brom and Shannon Bosch have written sub-sections on the Permanent Court of Arbitration and mercenaries respectively. The third change relates to the title. The editors have decided that the book should now be titled *Dugard's International Law: A South African Perspective,* in recognition of the fact this work is a continuation of the earlier editions by John.

There are many English language treatises on international law. Some reflect a particular national perspective but most claim to be international law treatises not bound to any national jurisdiction. The present work unashamedly presents a South African perspective of international law. The basic principles of international law are described and examined with reference to the principal sources of international law. This examination, however, takes place within the context of South African law. South African state practice, judicial decisions and legislation on international law receive equal treatment with international law as it is practised and taught abroad. This makes the present work one that is designed to assist judicial officers and practitioners, educate students, and guide diplomats in the intricacies of international law both at home in South Africa and abroad.

Many persons have assisted the authors/editors. Not all of them can be named here, but their assistance is gratefully acknowledged. In particular, we wish to thank Ietje Dugard-Barbas who has continued to advise and assist John on matters electronic.

The authors/editors are proud that this book continues to be a Juta publication. We are grateful to Juta for its continued support. Special thanks are due to the publisher, Linda van de Vijver, and the editors, Leila Samodien and Chantelle Hough-Louw, who have guided us in the preparation of this edition.

John Dugard
Max du Plessis
Tiyanjana Maluwa
Dire Tladi

December 2018

Notes on the Authors

John Dugard SC BA LLB (Stellenbosch) LLB LLD (Cantab) has held professorial posts at the Universities of the Witwatersrand, Cambridge, Leiden and Pretoria. He has been a member of the UN International Law Commission (1997 to 2011), judge *ad hoc* of the International Court of Justice (2000 to 2018) and UN Special Rapporteur on the Human Rights Situation in Occupied Palestinian Territory (2001 to 2008). He is a member of the *Institut de Droit International* and an associate member of Doughty Street Chambers, London.

Max du Plessis SC BIuris (SA) LLB (Natal) LLM (Cambridge) PhD (UKZN) is an advocate practising in South Africa (Ubunye Chambers, Durban, and Thulamela Chambers, Johannesburg). He is an associate member of Doughty Street Chambers, London, and an associate fellow (International Law) of Chatham House, London. He is also a senior research associate at the Institute for Security Studies, and honorary research fellow at the University of KwaZulu-Natal.

Tiyanjana Maluwa LLB (Malawi) LLM (Sheffield) PhD (Cantab) is the H. Laddie Montague Chair in Law and Professor of Law and International Affairs at Pennsylvania State University. From 2007 to 2015 he was the founding director of the Penn State School of International Affairs. He was previously Professor of Law at the University of Cape Town, and subsequently served as the Legal Counsel of the OAU and Legal Adviser to the Office of the UN High Commissioner for Human Rights, Geneva.

Dire Tladi BLC LLB (Pretoria) LLM (Connecticut) PhD (Erasmus) is a Professor of international law at the University of Pretoria and an Extraordinary Professor at the University of Stellenbosch. He is a member of the UN International Law Commission and its Special Rapporteur on Peremptory Norms of General International Law (*Jus Cogens*). He is also a member of the *Institut de Droit International*. He is formerly Principal State Law Adviser for International Law at the Department of International Relations and Cooperation and Legal Adviser of the South African Permanent Mission to the United Nations in New York.

Anton Katz SC BSc LLB (UCT) LLM (Columbia) is a member of the Cape Town and New York Bars. He acts as a judge *ad hoc* in the High Court of South Africa. From 2011 to 2018 he was a member of the United Nations Human Rights Council Working Group on

Mercenaries. He has worked as a consultant to the United Nations Office on Drugs and Crime on issues relating to extradition and mutual legal assistance, and to the African Union on the implementation of its Convention on the Prevention and Combating of Terrorism.

Arnold Pronto BProc LLB (Wits) MALD (Fletcher) is a Principal Legal Officer in the Office of Legal Affairs of the United Nations and a member of the Secretariat of the International Law Commission.

Eshed Cohen BA LLB (UCT) is an Advocate of the High Court of South Africa and is a clerk at the Constitutional Court of South Africa (2018 to 2019).

Andreas Coutsoudis BCom LLB (Natal) BCL MPhil (Oxon) is an Advocate of the High Court of South Africa and member of the KwaZulu-Natal Bar. He was a clerk at the Constitutional Court. His practice includes a particular focus on international law.

Jackie Dugard BA (Hons), LLB (Wits) MPhil PhD (Cantab) LLM (Essex) is an Associate Professor in the School of Law, University of the Witwatersrand. She was the co-founder and first executive director of the Socio-Economic Rights Institute of South Africa (SERI) (2010 to 2012) and was the founding director of the Gender Equity Office (GEO) at the University of the Witwatersrand (2014 to 2016).

Rosalind Elphick BA LLB (UCT) MA (University of Sydney) and LLM (University of Michigan) has worked as a legal researcher at the Supreme Court of Appeal of South Africa and as a legal officer at the International Court of Justice.

Kholofelo Kugler BA (UNISA) LLB (Wits) MA (Bern) is Counsel at the Advisory Centre on WTO Law in Geneva, Switzerland and a Visiting Research Fellow at the Olive Schreiner School of Law at the University of the Witwatersrand.

Contents

Abbreviations

1. Law reports and official publications

International

AD	Annual Digest and Reports of Public International Law Cases 1919-1949
BFSP	British and Foreign State Papers
ECHR	European Court of Human Rights Reports
GAOR	General Assembly Official Records
ICJ	International Court of Justice Reports
IHRR	International Human Rights Reports
ILDC	International Law in Domestic Courts (Oxford Reports on International Law)
ILM	International Legal Materials
ILR	International Law Reports
IUSCTR	Iran-United States Claims Tribunal Reports
LNTS	League of Nations Treaty Series
PCIJ	Permanent Court of International Justice Reports
RIAA	Reports of International Arbitral Awards
SCOR	Security Council Official Records
UNTS	United Nations Treaty Series

National

Australia

ALR	Australian Law Reports
CLR	Commonwealth Law Reports
FLR	Federal Law Reports

Canada

DLR	Dominion Law Reports
SCR	Supreme Court Reports

Ireland

IR	Irish Reports

South Africa (including Namibia and Zimbabwe)

(a) Pre-Union

EDC	Reports of the Eastern Districts Court of the Cape of Good Hope (1880–7; 1891–1909)
NLR	Natal Law Reports (1879–1932)
Off Rep	Official Reports of the High Court of the South African Republic (1894–8)
ORC	Orange River Colony Reports (1903–9)
SAR	Reports of the High Court of the South African Republic (1881–92)
SC	Cape Supreme Court Reports (1880–1910)
TS	Transvaal Law Reports (Supreme Court) (1902–9)

(b) 1910–1946

AD	Appellate Division Reports
CPD	Cape Provincial Division Reports
NPD	Natal Provincial Division Reports (1933–46)
OPD	Orange Free State Provincial Division Reports
SWA	Reports of the High Court of South West Africa (1920–45)
TPD	Transvaal Provincial Division Reports
WLD	Witwatersrand Local Division Reports

(c) 1947–present

All SA	All South African Law Reports
BCLR	Butterworths Constitutional Law Reports
ILJ	Industrial Law Journal
PH	Prentice-Hall Weekly Legal Service
SACR	South African Criminal Law Reports
SA	South African Law Reports—These reports, which were introduced in 1947, cover the decisions of the superior courts of South Africa, South West Africa/Namibia and Rhodesia/Zimbabwe. The reports appear in six volumes each year and are cited as follows: 2010 (4) SA 100 (CC). The number in parentheses after the year refers to the volume number and the letter or letters in parentheses at the end of the citation refers to the court which gave the decision.
SAFLII	The Southern African Legal Information Institute (SAFLII) publishes legal information for free public access which comprises mainly South African case law. Its website is *http://www.saflii.org*. Its cases are prefaced by the letters ZA followed by the initials of the relevant division of the High Court. Thus ZANWHC is the citation for a case from the North West High Court.

(d) Government publications

GG	Government Gazette
GGE	Government Gazette Extraordinary
GN	Government Notice

United Kingdom

AC	Appeal Cases
All ER	All England Reports
EWHC	England and Wales High Court
ECWA	English and Wales, Court of Appeal, Civil
ER	English Reports
KB	Kings Bench Division
P	Probate, Divorce & Admiralty Division
QB	Queens Bench Division
UKHL	United Kingdom, House of Lords
WLR	Weekly Law Reports

United States

Cranch Reports	Cranch Reports, United States Supreme Court
F Supp	Federal Supplement
F 2d	Federal Reporter, Second Series
US	Reports of the United States Supreme Court

2. Journals

AHRLJ	African Human Rights Law Journal
AJICL	African Journal of International and Comparative Law
AJIL	American Journal of International Law
AJIL Unbound	American Journal of International Law Unbound
Annual Survey	Annual Survey of South African Law
Aust YIL	Australian Yearbook of International Law
AYIL	African Year Book of International Law
BYIL	British Year Book of International Law
CYIL	Canadian Year Book of International Law
Case W Res JIL	Case Western Reserve Journal of International Law
CILSA	Comparative & International Law Journal of Southern Africa
EJIL	European Journal of International Law
Fordham ILJ	Fordham International Law Journal
GYIL	German Year Book of International Law
Hague Recueil	Recueil des Cours de l'Academie de Droit International
HRLJ	Human Rights Law Journal
HRQ	Human Rights Quarterly
IAR	Investment Arbitration Reporter
ICLQ	International and Comparative Law Quarterly
ICLR	International Criminal Law Review
ICSID	International Centre for the Settlement of International Disputes Review
IJRL	International Journal of Refugee Law
IRRC	International Review of the Red Cross
JAL	Journal of African Law
JEPP	Journal of European Public Policy
JICJ	Journal of International Criminal Justice
LJIL	Leiden Journal of International Law
LQR	Law Quarterly Review
MJIL	Michigan Journal of International Law
Mod LR	Modern Law Review
PER/PELJ	Potchefstroom Electronic Law Journal
NILR	Netherlands International Law Review
NQHR	Netherlands Quarterly of Human Rights
SALJ	South African Law Journal
SAJHR	South African Journal on Human Rights
SAYIL	South African Yearbook of International Law
Stell LR	Stellenbosch Law Review

Texas ILJ	Texas International Law Journal
THRHR	Tydskrif vir Hedendaagse Romeins-Hollandse Reg
TSAR	Tydskrif vir die Suid-Afrikaanse Reg
Virginia JIL	Virginia Journal of International Law
YIILP	Yearbook on International Investment Law and Policy
YJIL	Yale Journal of International Law

3. Other

ACHR	American Convention on Human Rights
ACP	African, Caribbean and Pacific States
AfCFTA	African Contintental Free Trade Area
AGOA	African Growth Opportunity Act
ANC	African National Congress
Anti-Dumping Agreement	Agreement on Implementation of Article VI of the GATT 1994
AU	African Union
BIS	Bank of International Settlements
BIT	Bilateral Investment Treaty
BRICS	Brazil, Russia, India, China, South Africa
CEDAW	Convention on the Elimination of All Forms of Discrimination against Women
CERD	Committee for the Elimination of Racial Discrimination
CESCR	Committee on Economic, Social and Cultural Rights
CETA	European Union—Canada Comprehensive Economic and Trade Agreement
CMA	Common Monetary Area
COMESA	Common Market for Eastern and Southern Africa
CSC	Continental Shelf Convention (1958)
DSU	Understanding on Rules and Procedures Governing the Settlement of Disputes
DTI	Department of Trade and Industry
EAC	East African Community
EC	European Community
ECOSOC	Economic and Social Council
EEZ	Exclusive Economic Zone
EFTA	European Free Trade Area
EFZ	Exclusive Fishing Zone
EPA	European Partnership Agreement
EU	European Union
FET	Free and Equal Treatment
FTA	Free Trade Area
G 20	Group of 20
GATS	General Agreement on Trade and Services
GATT 1947	General Agreement on Tariffs and Trade of 1947
GATT 1994	General Agreement on Tariffs and Trade of 1994
GDP	Gross Domestic Product

HRC	Human Rights Committee
HRW	Human Rights Watch
HSC	High Seas Convention (1958)
IATA	International Air Transport Association
IBRD	International Bank for Reconstruction and Development
ICAO	International Civil Aviation Organization
ICCPR	International Covenant on Civil and Political Rights
ICESCR	International Covenant on Economic, Social and Cultural Rights
ICJ	International Court of Justice
ICRC	International Committee of the Red Cross
ICSID	International Centre for the Settlement of Investment Disputes between States and Nationals of Other States
IDA	International Development Association
IFC	International Finance Corporation
IFI	International Finance Institution
IIA	International Investment Agreement
ILA	International Law Association
ILC	International Law Commission
ILO	International Labour Organization
IMO	International Maritime Organization
IMF	International Monetary Fund
ITAC	International Trade Administration Commission
ITLOS	International Tribunal for the Law of the Sea
LOSC	Law of the Sea Convention (1982)
MERCOSUR	Common Market of the South (*El Mercado Comun de Sud*)
MFN	Most Favoured Nation
MIGA	Multilateral Investment Guarantee Agency
MONUC	United Nations Organization Mission in the Democratic Republic of Congo
NATO	North Atlantic Treaty Organization
NEPAD	New Partnership for Africa's Development
NGO	Non-governmental Organization
NLM	National Liberation Movement
OAS	Organization of American States
OAU	Organization of African Unity
ONUC	United Nations Force in the Congo
PAC	Pan-Africanist Congress
PCA	Permanent Court of Arbitration
PCIJ	Permanent Court of International Justice
PLO	Palestine Liberation Organization
RRO	Refugee Reception Officer
SACU	Southern African Customs Union
SADC	Southern African Development Community
SADC FIP	SADC Protocol on Finance and Investment

SADCC	Southern African Development Coordination Conference
SWAPO	South West African Peoples Organization
TBVC States	Transkei, Bophuthatswana, Venda and Ciskei (South Africa's 'homeland states')
TDCA	Agreement on Trade, Development and Cooperation
TFTA	Tripartite Free Trade Area
TIDCA	Trade, Investment and Development Cooperation Agreement
TPRM	Trade Policy Review Mechanism
TRIPS	Trade Related Aspects of Intellectual Property Rights
TRNC	Turkish Republic of Northern Cyprus
TSC	Territorial Sea and Contiguous Zone Convention (1958)
UN	United Nations
UNAMID	United Nations/African Union Hybrid Operation in Darfur
UNAMIR	United Nations Assistance Mission in Rwanda
UNCLOS	United Nations Convention on the Law of the Sea
UNEF	United Nations Emergency Force in the Middle East
UNESCO	United Nations Educational, Scientific and Cultural Organization
UNFICYP	United Nations Force in Cyprus
UNIFIL	United Nations Interim Force in Lebanon
UNMIK	United Nations Interim Administration in Kosovo
UNOMSA	United Nations Observer Mission in South Africa
UNOSOM	United Nations Operation in Somalia
UNPROFOR	United Nations Protection Force (Yugoslavia)
UNTAC	United Nations Transitional Authority in Cambodia
UNTAET	United Nations Transitional Administration in East Timor
UNTAG	United Nations Transition Assistance Group (Namibia)
WHO	World Health Organization
WTO	World Trade Organization

Table of Cases

Cases decided by the Permanent Court of International Justice and the International Court of Justice

A

B

M

N

O

P

Q

R

S

T

U

Cases decided by other international courts and tribunals

Arbitration Tribunals, International Tribunal for the Law of the Sea, Iran US Claims Tribunal and Others

African Court on Human and Peoples' Rights

European Court of Human Rights

A

B

C

D

G

H

I

J

K

B

C

J

K

L

M

N

R

S

T

U

United States

Table of Statutes

Australia

Namibia

South Africa

A

B

C

D

P

R

S

T

CHAPTER 1

The Nature and History of International Law

John Dugard

International law may be defined as a normative body of rules and principles which are binding upon states in their relations with one another.[1] Rules may broadly be divided into general and particular rules. The rule that the high seas are open to the shipping of all nations is a general rule of international law binding on all states. A particular rule of international law is created by a treaty establishing a relationship between two or a few states only. For instance, the extradition agreement between South Africa and Malawi providing for the reciprocal return of fugitives from justice binds these two states only. Principles reflect the values upon which the international order is based and emphasise that international law is a normative system.

Early international law concerned itself with states only. Now there are other actors on the international stage. Since 1949, it has been accepted that international organisations, such as the United Nations and its specialised agencies, enjoy international legal personality. The recognition of the legal personality of international organisations was the result of an advisory opinion of the International Court of Justice in response to the question whether the United Nations could sue Israel for the death of Count Bernadotte of Sweden, a UN mediator assassinated while on duty in Palestine. The International Court held that the United Nations had the necessary legal personality to bring an action against a state in such circumstances. The Court stated

> [t]hat is not the same thing as saying that it is a state, which it certainly is not, or that its legal personality and rights and duties are the same as those of a state. Still less is it the same thing as saying that it is 'a super-state' . . . . What it does mean is that it is a subject of international law and capable of possessing international rights and duties, and that it has capacity to maintain its rights by bringing international claims.[2]

Since World War II numerous treaties have been signed extending the protection of international law to individuals. These human

[1] See G Simpson (ed) *The Nature of International Law* (2001).

[2] *Reparation for Injuries Suffered in the Service of the United Nations* 1949 ICJ Report 174 at 179.

rights treaties impose obligations of varying kinds upon signatory states to afford protection to their own citizens. In this way, millions of people in the modern world have become the beneficiaries of international law.[3] Individuals benefit from the protection of international law and participate in its processes. They may also be prosecuted for international crimes. They cannot, however, be described as full subjects of international law.

Multinational corporations are busily engaged in international transactions with states. Consequently, new rules of law have been developed to cover these relationships. Although rules of international law may sometimes govern the relationship between states and corporations, these corporations fail to qualify as international subjects.

Other entities play an increasing role in international affairs. Non-governmental organisations (NGOs), such as the International Committee of the Red Cross[4] and Amnesty International, national liberation movements, and indigenous peoples participate in the activities of the international community and appeal to international law to advance their interests.

Although entities other than states participate in the contemporary international legal order, it is essential to recall that states and inter-governmental organisations are the main actors in the international community, the only entities with true international personality and the principal creators of rules of international law.

Much has been written about the sovereignty of states. Unfortunately, the concept of sovereignty conjures up images of supremacy and absolute power which international law seeks to limit in the interests of the community of states. For this reason, it is more accurate, and wiser, to speak of the 'independence' of states rather than of their 'sovereignty'.

Public international law, the subject of this study, must be distinguished from private international law. Public international law governs the relations between states. It comprises a body of rules and principles which seek to regulate relations between states. Private international law concerns the relations between individuals whose legal relations are governed by the laws of different states. If a South African man marries a German woman in India, the question will arise as to which system of law governs the validity of their marriage and their property relations. The system of law that selects or chooses

[3] See Chapter 15.

[4] G Abraham 'Yes, . . . but does it have personality? The International Committee of the Red Cross and sovereign immunity' (2007) 124 *SALJ* 499.

the appropriate law is known as private international law, or conflict of laws.[5]

DIFFERENCES BETWEEN INTERNATIONAL LAW AND MUNICIPAL LAW

International law is generally studied by lawyers with some knowledge of their own national or municipal system of law. They see the existence of a law-making body, an executive or law-enforcement body, and a compulsory system of courts as essential features of any legal system. When they discover that international law lacks developed institutions of this kind, they inevitably question the very existence of international law.[6] At the outset, therefore, it is necessary to address the question whether international law does have a law-making body, an executive power and a judicial system.

1 Legislature

There is no central legislative body in international law with the power to enact rules binding upon all states. The General Assembly of the United Nations is only empowered to adopt recommendations that are not binding upon member states. Although the Security Council may take decisions in terms of article 25 of the UN Charter binding on all member states of the United Nations, action of this kind is limited to situations determined by the Security Council to threaten international peace and security; and in practice the Security Council is seriously restrained from making such determinations by the veto power vested in each of the five permanent member states of the United Nations (China, France, the United Kingdom, Russia and the United States of America). The United Nations therefore cannot be described as an international legislature.[7]

The rules of international law are to be found in agreements between states, known as treaties, and in international custom. These rules are not imposed from above by any central law-making body.

[5] See, on this system of law in South Africa, C Forsyth *Private International Law: The Modern Roman-Dutch Law including the Jurisdiction of the High Courts* 5 ed (2012).

[6] English legal philosopher John Austin preferred to describe international law as 'positive morality' for this reason: see *Province of Jurisprudence Determined* (1954) 133, 201. Criticisms of this kind were prevalent in Grotius's days. In the opening passages of his Prolegomena to *De Jure Belli ac Pacis* (1625) Grotius writes that such a work on international law is 'all the more necessary because in our day, as in former times, there is no lack of men who view this branch of law with contempt as having no reality outside an empty name': para 3 (translation by FW Kelsey in J Brown Scott (ed) *The Classics of International Law* (1925)).

[7] See Chapter 23. Cf P Szasz 'The Security Council starts legislating' (2002) 96 *AJIL* 901.

Instead they are created by the consent of states. Whereas municipal law operates vertically, with rules imposed from above, international law is a horizontal system in which lawmaker and subject are the same legal persona.

2 Executive authority

There is no central executive authority with a police force at its disposal to enforce the rules of international law. Again, the United Nations comes closest to being such an executive body, but it falls short of the domestic model on closer analysis. The United Nations is not a world government: it lacks the power to direct states to comply with the law, and it lacks a permanent police force to punish violators of the law. Where a state's conduct threatens international peace, the Security Council may direct it to comply with its obligations under international law, but during the Cold War period of 1946–1990 this was a rare occurrence, as the veto power was generally exercised to prevent any action being taken against a state for non-compliance. When the Cold War came to an end there was a brief respite, reflected in the Security Council authorisation of collective action by states in the Gulf War of 1991 to force Iraq to withdraw from Kuwait. In more recent times the exercise of the veto power by the United States, Russia or China has in most instances prevented collective action of this kind.

The United Nations is able to raise forces to police certain situations—as in the case of the United Nations Transitional Assistance Group in Namibia (UNTAG), established in 1989/90 to supervise elections in Namibia; the United Nations Protection Force in Yugoslavia (UNPROFOR), created in 1992 to oversee the cease-fire and control disputed areas in the former Yugoslavia; and the United Nations Organization Mission in the Democratic Republic of the Congo (MONUC), established to keep the peace in the Great Lakes region. Alternatively, it may authorise member states to take action on its behalf—as in the case of the Gulf War of 1991 and the civil war in Libya in 2011. But there is no permanent force at the disposal of the Security Council that may be sent to restore peace and order.

Before the Charter system came into existence in 1945, states frequently sought to enforce the rules of international law by means of self-help. An aggrieved state would take the law into its own hands and punish a transgressor state. The Charter of the United Nations in article 2(4) now prohibits the use of force against states, except in the exercise of the right of self-defence or under the authorisation of the United Nations. The result is that international law has lost one of its instruments of law enforcement.[8]

3 International courts

Today there are a number of international courts. The best known is the International Court of Justice in The Hague, which may be used to settle disputes between all states in the world. In addition, there are a number of regional, specialised courts, such as the European Court of Human Rights, which has jurisdiction over disputes arising out of the European Convention on Human Rights. International law therefore does have a judicial system capable of ruling on disputes between states. But there is an important difference between international courts and domestic courts: international courts have jurisdiction only over those states that have consented to their jurisdiction.

The International Court of Justice (known as the Permanent Court of International Justice from 1920 to 1945) was created in 1920, but compared with any domestic tribunal it has heard very few cases. Moreover, disputes which are referred to the Court by consent are often minor disputes that do not threaten relations between states. For instance, in the *Kasikili/Sedudu Island Case*[9] Botswana and Namibia referred a dispute over the boundary between the two countries around Kasikili/Sedudu Island and the legal status of the island—a matter which did not affect the vital interests of either country—to the International Court of Justice. Sometimes disputes involving the vital political interests of states are brought before the International Court of Justice on the basis of consent conferred at an earlier time. In such cases, the Court is seldom able to establish its authority over the parties to the dispute. For instance, when Nicaragua brought a dispute against the United States in 1984, claiming that the United States had mined its harbours and intervened militarily in Nicaragua, the United States refused to appear before the Court—despite the fact that it had consented to disputes between the two states being referred to the International Court of Justice in an earlier treaty—and it repudiated the finding of the Court on the merits of the dispute.[10] The International Court of Justice therefore cannot be seen to be a court suitable for resolving serious political disputes between nations. Moreover, most states refuse to consent to the jurisdiction of the International Court of Justice. Only a

[8] International law does, however, recognise the lawfulness of non-forcible self-help measures—'countermeasures'—taken by an injured state against a wrongdoing state to compel compliance with international law. See Chapter 13.

[9] 1999 ICJ Reports 1045.

[10] See, generally on this subject, 'Appraisals of the ICJ's decision: *Nicaragua v United States (Merits)*' (1987) 81 *AJIL* 77–183.

minority of states in the modern world are prepared to take full advantage of the International Court of Justice for the purpose of settling legal disputes.

The International Court of Justice is also competent to give advisory opinions on matters of concern to the United Nations at the request of the political organs of the United Nations. These opinions carry considerable weight as statements of the law. For example, the International Court gave four opinions on the legal status of South West Africa/Namibia, which established the law to be applied by the international community in its treatment of the dispute with South Africa over this territory.[11] More recently, it rendered an opinion on many of the legal issues concerning the status of the Occupied Palestinian Territory.[12] However significant such opinions might be, they remain advisory and are not binding upon states.

International law therefore differs basically from municipal legal systems in that it has no central legislature or executive authority, and its principal court, unlike domestic courts, lacks compulsory jurisdiction over its subjects.

States are governed by individuals. Consequently, the punishment of state leaders for crimes against the international order (particularly war crimes, genocide, crimes against humanity and aggression) by international courts provides an effective means for the enforcement of international law. After World War II, tribunals were established by the victorious parties to try the Nazi and Japanese war leaders in Nuremberg and Tokyo respectively. Subsequent attempts to create an international criminal court to prosecute state leaders guilty of international crimes failed. However, in 1993/94 two ad hoc tribunals, the International Criminal Tribunal for the Former Yugoslavia and the International Criminal Tribunal for Rwanda, were created to try persons charged with international crimes arising out of the ethnic conflicts in those territories. In July 1998, a diplomatic conference in Rome gave its approval to the establishment of a permanent international criminal court, the International Criminal Court, which came into being in 2002. These courts mark an important development in the enforcement of international law.

THE PROBLEM OF SANCTIONS

The absence of an external central authority with the power to enforce the rules of international law in a regular and consistent manner, if necessary by means of armed force, has prompted much of

[11] See Chapter 22.

[12] *Legal Consequences of the Construction of a Wall in the Occupied Palestinian Territory* 2004 ICJ Reports 136; (2004) 43 *ILM* 1009.

the cynicism about the entitlement of international law to be called 'law'. Critics tend to overlook the fact that domestic law enforcement is not always regular and consistent and that compliance with the law is secured in a variety of ways, of which the threat or use of force is but one. Moreover, international law does have a number of sanctions for breach of a rule of law aimed at securing compliance with the law.

The Charter of the United Nations, in Chapter VII, empowers the Security Council to direct its members either individually or collectively to use force against a delinquent state whose violation of international law constitutes a threat to international peace. There are only two clear precedents[13] for such action. In 1966, the Security Council authorised the United Kingdom to use force on the high seas to prevent oil tankers from reaching the port of Beira when their oil was destined for Rhodesia.[14] In 1990, the Security Council authorised member states 'to use all necessary means' to secure the withdrawal of Iraq's forces from Kuwait,[15] after determining that Iraq's invasion and annexation of Kuwait was illegal.[16] This was the first occasion on which the veto power was not allowed to obstruct the Security Council from taking action against an aggressor.

Since the end of the Cold War in 1990, the United Nations has established peacekeeping forces in many countries plagued by internal strife, such as Somalia, Haiti, the former Yugoslavia and the Democratic Republic of the Congo. On occasion these peace*keeping* forces have engaged in the *enforcement* of the peace by military means. Inevitably, this has resulted in the enforcement of rules of international law relating to human rights, self-determination and humanitarian law. Although, strictly speaking, these are not measures taken against a state for violation of international law, it is in practice difficult to distinguish them from law-enforcement action.

Economic sanctions are another enforcement mechanism at the disposal of the Security Council. A succession of resolutions calling on states to impose comprehensive economic sanctions was adopted to compel Rhodesia to accept majority rule.[17] South Africa too was subjected to a wide range of sanctions over apartheid. In 1977, the

[13] On 27 June 1950, the Security Council recommended to states that they assist South Korea to repel an armed attack by North Korea (SCOR, 5th year, Resolutions and Decisions 5). The absence of the Soviet Union from the Security Council when this resolution was 'passed' raises questions about the validity of this precedent. See Chapter 23.

[14] Resolution 221 (1966).

[15] Resolution 678 (1990).

[16] Resolution 662 (1990).

[17] See, in particular, resolutions 232 (1966) and 235 (1968).

Security Council imposed a mandatory arms embargo on South Africa as a punishment for its discriminatory and repressive laws and practices, and its acts of aggression against neighbouring states.[18] Repeated recommendations of the General Assembly in support of wider economic sanctions prompted states, individually and collectively, to isolate South Africa in the fields of trade, finance, sport and culture. Although the effect of these sanctions was not immediate, they undoubtedly contributed to State President FW de Klerk's decision to abandon apartheid in February 1990.

The end of the Cold War witnessed an increase in the number of Security Council resolutions imposing mandatory sanctions against states. Economic sanctions were imposed on Iraq following the Gulf War in 1991;[19] Libya was subjected to a mandatory arms embargo and to a prohibition on air traffic in 1992 because of its failure to extradite two men suspected of placing a bomb on the ill-fated Pan Am flight 103, which exploded over Lockerbie;[20] the Federal Republic of Yugoslavia (Serbia and Montenegro) was subjected to economic sanctions for its support to the Bosnian Serbs in the Bosnian conflict and its repressive actions in Kosovo;[21] an arms embargo was imposed on Libya in 2011;[22] and economic sanctions have been imposed on North Korea in response to its nuclear and missile activities.[23]

Exclusion from membership in international organisations is another sanction that was effectively employed against South Africa for violating its obligations under the UN Charter. In the 1960s, South Africa was excluded from membership of a number of specialised agencies of the United Nations—such as the International Labour Organization (ILO) and the World Health Organization (WHO)—and in 1974, the General Assembly of the United Nations excluded South Africa from participation in the debates and work of the General Assembly.[24] In 1994, South Africa resumed its membership of these bodies.

Non-recognition of a territorial adjustment must also be seen as a sanction. The Security Council has directed states not to recognise the Turkish Republic of Northern Cyprus as a state on the ground that its creation violated rules of international law.[25] In addition, it has

[18] Resolution 418 (1977). See Chapter 23.

[19] Resolutions 661, 665, 678 (1990).

[20] Resolution 748 (1993).

[21] Resolutions 757 (1992), 820 (1993), 942 (1994).

[22] Resolutions 1970, 1973 (2011).

[23] See, for example, resolution 2375 (2017).

[24] See Chapter 23.

[25] J Dugard *Recognition and the United Nations* (1987) 108–11.

labelled Israel's annexation of the Golan Heights and East Jerusalem illegal acts that should be condemned by non-recognition.[26] During the apartheid era, Transkei, Bophuthatswana, Venda and Ciskei (the 'TBVC states') were subjected to non-recognition at the direction of the Security Council.[27] There is little doubt that non-recognition has seriously obstructed the statehood of the Turkish Republic of Northern Cyprus, and undermined Israel's claims to the Golan Heights and East Jerusalem. It is also clear that non-recognition of the 'TBVC states' played a major part in the delegitimation of the apartheid state.

The punishment of individuals for international crimes, such as war crimes, piracy, hijacking and crimes against humanity, is a sanction of international law in the best tradition of the municipal criminal offence and provides evidence to even the most ill-informed observer that international law is sometimes enforced by punishment.

International law is not, therefore, without sanctions. However, it must be conceded that sanctions of this kind lack the comprehensiveness, regularity and consistency associated with sanctions in domestic law.

IS INTERNATIONAL LAW REALLY LAW?

John Austin's claim that law is the command of a political superior to a political inferior backed by the threat of a sanction is largely discredited today, as is his conclusion that international law fails to qualify as law. His principal 20th century disciple, HLA Hart, has rejected the command theory of law and accepted that international law qualifies as a species of 'law'.[28] Few serious jurists insist on effective sanctions as a requirement for the existence of international law.[29]

The cynic may remain unconvinced and ask what—if not a legislature, executive, compulsory court system and sanctions—are the essential requirements of a system of law? The most satisfactory response to this question is that of Sir Frederick Pollock; namely, that a legal system requires the existence of a political community, and the recognition by its members of settled rules binding upon them.[30]

Judged by these standards, international law certainly qualifies as a system of law. First, there is a political community, namely the

[26] Dugard (n 25) 111–15.

[27] Ibid 98–108.

[28] *The Concept of Law* (1961) ch 10.

[29] R Higgins *Problems and Process: International Law and How We Use It* (1994) 13–16.

[30] *First Book of Jurisprudence* (1929) 28. See, too, R Jennings and A Watts (eds) *Oppenheim's International Law* 9 ed (1992) vol 1 at 9–13.

community of modern states, 'over 193' in number. Although there may be serious political, economic and cultural divisions within this community, it is probably no less divided than many heterogeneous societies. Secondly, there is a body of rules and principles that comprise the international legal order. Thirdly, the members of the international community recognise these rules and principles as binding upon them. This is not to deny that international law is sometimes violated in the most brutal manner and that such violations are sometimes allowed to go unpunished, particularly when committed by a major power. Violations of this kind, however, are the exception and should not be allowed to breed a general cynicism of the role of law in international society.[31] International law is observed and honoured every day in diplomatic and consular relations, trade, air and sea traffic, communications, extradition, etc.[32] On the whole, it is probably observed as much as municipal law is in some societies. Moreover, its binding quality is recognised by international and municipal courts (including those of South Africa)[33] and by statesmen and diplomats in their daily inter-state dealings. No national leader has repudiated the existence of international law since Adolf Hitler. Others may have violated international law, but they have been careful to raise some legal pretext for their action. Saddam Hussein, for example, justified his invasion of Kuwait on 2 August 1990 on the ground that, historically, Kuwait was a part of Iraq as they had both belonged to the Ottoman Empire before World War I. However unfounded such an argument may have been in law and fact [34] it was at least an acknowledgement of the existence of international law.

States acting through their governments recognise and comply with international law for a wide range of reasons. These include an interest, either selfish or altruistic, in the maintenance of peace and good order; an acceptance of the legitimacy of rules of international law;[35]

[31] Both Hans Morgenthau (eg, in 'Positivism, functionalism, and international law' (1940) 34 *AJIL* 260) and George Kennan (*American Diplomacy 1900–1950* (1951) 959) base much of their scepticism about international law on its inability to play a meaningful role in power relations between the major states.

[32] According to Henkin, 'almost all nations observe almost all principles of international law and almost all of their obligations almost all of the time': *How Nations Behave—Law and Foreign Policy* 2 ed (1979) 47.

[33] See Chapter 4.

[34] RV Pillai and M Kumar 'The political and legal status of Kuwait' (1962) 11 *ICLQ* 108.

[35] TM Franck *The Power of Legitimacy among Nations* (1990); TM Franck *Fairness in International Law and Institutions* (1995).

reputation both at home and abroad;[36] anticipated reciprocal treatment; the realisation of the need for co-existence;[37] and fear of economic, political, cultural and sports isolation. Until the Gulf War of 1991, fear of United-Nations-authorised military sanctions probably contributed very little to the decision on the part of states to comply with international law; now, this precedent may act as an additional and cogent reason for compliance.

By and large, states comply with international law for reasons unrelated to the threat of a sanction. This means that international law is not binding because it is enforced but that it is enforced because it is already binding.[38] The basis of the international legal obligation must therefore be found in some source other than the prospect of enforcement. The debate over the identity of this source is a theme that runs like a thread through the history of international law. Essentially this debate, as in municipal law, has taken the form of an exchange over many centuries between naturalists and positivists.

THE HISTORY OF INTERNATIONAL LAW (INCLUDING THEORIES OF INTERNATIONAL LAW)[39]

The roots of international law are to be found in the ancient histories of the Egyptians, Jews, Greeks and Romans, and in the jurisprudence and inter-state practices of the Muslim world. However, it was not until the emergence of the modern state in the wake of the Renaissance and Reformation that the need arose for a law to regulate relations between states. This was confirmed by the Peace of Westphalia of 1648, which brought to an end the Thirty Years War and the authority of the Holy Roman Emperor. Before this time, forces such as feudalism and the Holy Roman Empire, institutionalising the power of the Catholic Church, had obstructed the growth of

[36] Both domestic and international public opinion may induce compliance with international law. South Africa abandoned its policy of apartheid in 1990, in part as a result of hostile international opinion. The United States was compelled to withdraw from Vietnam in 1974, in part as a result of domestic opposition to the war.

[37] G Tunkin 'Co-existence and international law' (1958–III) 95 *Recueil des Cours* 1.

[38] See G Fitzmaurice 'The foundations of the authority of international law and the problem of enforcement' (1956) 19 *Modern LR* 1.

[39] See A Nussbaum *A Concise History of the Law of Nations* (1947); JW Verzijl *International Law in Historical Perspective* 10 vols (1968–1979); M Koskenniemi *The Gentle Civilizer of Nations: The Rise and Fall of International Law 1870–1960* (2002); D Bederman *International Law in Antiquity* (2001); B Fassbender and A Peters (eds) *The Oxford Handbook of the History of International Law* (2012); A Orakhelashvili (ed) *Research Handbook on the Theory and History of International Law* (2011); A Orford and F Hoffman (eds) *The Oxford Handbook of the Theory of International Law* (2016); H Strydom and C Gevers 'Defining Epochs' in H Strydom (ed) *International Law* (2016).

territorial units with strong centralised governments—ie sovereign, independent states—and obviated the need for a law between nations. International law as we know it today is therefore less than five hundred years old.

In both Roman and medieval times the scholarly jurist had played a key role in the development of the law. It was therefore predictable that jurists would be responsible, initially, for the formulation of the principles of law that were to govern states. Neither is it surprising that their main sources in this endeavour would be the *ius gentium* of Roman law, which had exercised a powerful influence on the law of Western Europe and the precepts of natural law that had been absorbed into Canon law under the inspiration of philosopher-theologians such as St Thomas Aquinas.

Early writers on international law came from Spain (Vittoria and Suarez) and Italy (Gentilis, who fled to England to avoid religious persecution). Power then shifted from Spain to the Netherlands, which occupied a key position in the economic and intellectual life of Europe throughout the 17th and early 18th centuries. It was perhaps, therefore, predictable that the Netherlands should produce the 'father' of international law: Grotius, or Hugo de Groot (1583–1645).[40]

Grotius is acclaimed as the 'father of international law' largely in recognition of his monumental treatise *De Jure Belli ac Pacis Libri Tres*. Its commitment to an international legal order, transcending the interests of the nation state, gives it a universal appeal that is lacking in Grotius's earlier works on international law. *Mare Liberum*, published in 1609, and the larger work of which it formed a part, *De Jure Praedae*,[41] is chauvinist in outlook and preoccupied with the advocacy of the maritime interests of the Netherlands.[42]

De Jure Belli ac Pacis was first published in 1625, in the midst of the Thirty Years' War (1618–1648). This work is the starting point of modern natural law as, until its appearance, natural law was so closely coupled with divine law that the two were treated as being almost synonymous. Grotius, himself a devout Christian and recognised theologian, took the extraordinary step—at least for his

[40] J Dugard 'Grotius, the jurist and international lawyer: Four hundred years on' (1983) 100 *SALJ* 213; E Kahn 'Hugo Grotius, 10 April 1583–29 August 1645: A sketch of his life and his writings on Roman-Dutch law' (1983) 100 *SALJ* 192; P van Warmelo 'Hugo Grotius 10th April 1583–28th August 1645' (1983) 9 *SAYIL* 1.

[41] *De Jure Praedae* was not published during Grotius's lifetime. It was discovered in 1864 and published in 1868.

[42] F de Pauw in *Grotius and the Law of the Sea* (1965) accuses Grotius of adapting the 'divine rules of the law of nature to the economic interests of the Dutch East India Company' (at 61).

time—of emancipating natural law from theology. To Grotius '[t]he law of nature is a dictate of right reason',[43] which impels man to seek a peaceful and organised society, and whose validity would hold 'even if we should concede that which cannot be conceded without the utmost wickedness that there is no God, or that the affairs of men are of no concern to Him'.[44]

Drawing on the 'dictate of right reason', as exemplified in the *ius gentium* and the writings of scholars, Grotius sought to construct a just international legal order whose principal aim was the restraint of war. As the first comprehensive and systematic treatment of international law integrated within the structure of a general system of law and jurisprudence, it had immediate success. Today it is still regarded as the bible of international law.

Another Dutch jurist, Cornelius van Bynkershoek (1673–1743), had a profound effect on the development of international law. A distinguished judge, with great experience in maritime and commercial practice, he wrote a number of works on special topics[45] in which he stressed the importance of consent, in the form of custom or treaty, as the basis of international law. Consequently, he was one of the early positivists for whom consent, rather than the principles of natural law, explained the international legal obligation.

Other scholars of this 'classical period' of international law contributed substantially to the growth of international law. Of these, Zouche (1590–1660), Professor of Civil Law at Oxford; Pufendorf (1632–1694), Professor at Heidelberg; and Vattel (1714–1769), a Swiss who served in the diplomatic service of Saxony, are the best known.

The Dutch contribution to the development of international law through Grotius and Van Bynkershoek was significant. Not only did they shape the new international legal order, they also set the scene for the naturalist versus positivist debate that continues today.

International law of this time was in reality an international law of Christian Europe. On the positive side, international law drew on the values and intellect of the scholars of the Renaissance and Enlightenment. On the other hand, there is no doubt that some of the rules of the new legal order were simply rationalisations of the expansionist colonial and imperialist policies of the European powers and their commitment to the slave trade.[46] As late as 1884 the European

[43] *De Jure Belli ac Pacis* 1.1.10.1 (translation by F W Kelsey in J Brown Scott (ed) *The Classics of International Law* (1925)).

[44] *Idem Prolegomena* para 11.

[45] *De Domino Maris* (1702), *De Foro Legatorum* (1721) and *Quaestionum Juris Publici* (1737). See the review of the last treatise in (2010) 23 *Leiden Journal of International Law* 269–71.

[46] See A Anghie *Imperialism, Sovereignty and the Making of International Law* (2005).

colonial powers divided Africa among themselves in the Berlin Conference under the guise of international law. Relics of colonialism's rules persist to this day in international law, particularly in the law governing statehood and the acquisition of territory and in colonial boundaries which have become the frontiers of the modern states of Africa.

It was only in the late 18th century that non-European and later non-Christian nations were admitted to the 'club' of Christian European nations whose relations were governed by the international legal order fathered by Grotius. The admission of the United States and independent South American republics to the European 'club' was followed by the acceptance of Turkey, Japan, China, Persia (Iran) and Siam (Thailand).

The creation of the League of Nations in 1920 saw the extension of membership in the 'club' to other nations, including South Africa. However, the League of Nations was largely Eurocentric in its membership and its concerns, as indeed was the United Nations in its early years. Since the decolonisation of European colonies in Africa, Asia, the Pacific and the Caribbean, the position has changed dramatically. Today, the community of nations is genuinely 'international' and numbers over 193 states, of which nearly all are members of the United Nations. This diversity in the composition of the international community has inevitably given rise to tensions within the international legal order. For some 40 years, the Soviet Union propagated a communist theory of international law,[47] which showed a distrust of bourgeois institutions (such as the International Court of Justice) and some of the rules of 'Western' international law—notably, the rules requiring compensation for the expropriation of foreign investment. Developing states are hostile to those rules of international law most closely associated with colonialism[48] and stress the importance of self-determination. Although different approaches of this kind create difficulties, they should not be exaggerated, as in many respects they resemble the problems faced by multicultural national societies.

Jurisprudentially, the debate between naturalists and positivists remains unresolved. While natural law was pre-eminent during the 17th and 18th centuries, it was replaced in popularity by positivism in the 19th and early 20th centuries. At the national level, positivism took the form of the command theory of law, while in international

[47] G Tunkin *Theory of International Law* (1974); K Grzybowski *Soviet Public International Law* (1970); H Chiu 'Communist China's attitude towards international law' (1966) 60 *AJIL* 245.

[48] See RP Anand 'Attitude of the Asian-African states towards certain problems of international law' (1966) 15 *ICLQ* 55; TO Elias *New Horizons in International Law* (1980).

law, positivists proclaimed consent as its basis. Indeed, under the influence of the German philosopher Hegel, the idea developed that a state was bound only by those rules to which it had clearly consented, and thereby voluntarily restricted its own sovereignty.

The logic of positivism was taken to its extreme form in Nazi Germany. National law became the expression of the will of the Führer and international law was completely subordinated to the will of the state, represented by the Führer. European statesmen educated in the positivist belief that the manner in which a sovereign state treats its own nationals is essentially its own business were legally restrained from intervening to halt the holocaust. This experience starkly illustrated the dangers of legal positivism, and after the war, this philosophy of law was discredited.[49] The trials of Nazi war criminals by the Nuremberg International Tribunal and by post-war German municipal courts testified to the existence of certain basic principles of justice superior to Nazi law. Moreover, the recognition in the Charter of the United Nations of the need for states to promote and respect human rights heralded an abandonment of the notion of the absolute sovereignty of a state over its own nationals. The powerful international human rights movement, which plays a major role in modern international law, is largely inspired by the idealism of natural law.

Today, new theories of law seek to explain the nature of international law and to shape its evolution. In the United States, a sociological movement emerged that draws heavily on the notions of social engineering advocated by Roscoe Pound and the realist movement. This policy-oriented school, associated with the names of Myres McDougal, Harold Lasswell and Michael Reisman of the Yale Law School,[50] sees law as a comprehensive process of authoritative decision-making by a wide range of actors and not as a defined set of rules. The promotion of values, such as power, wealth, enlightenment, skill, well-being, affection, respect and rectitude, plays an important part in this process. More recently, members of the critical legal studies movement have analysed traditional international law

[49] For an illuminating exchange of ideas on this subject, see HLA Hart 'Positivism and the separation of law and morals' (1958) 71 *Harvard LR* 593 and LL Fuller 'Positivism and fidelity to law—a reply to Professor Hart' (1958) 71 *Harvard LR* 630.

[50] See, for example, McDougal, Lasswell and Reisman 'Theories about international law: Prologue to a configurative jurisprudence' (1968) 8 *Virginia Journal of International Law* 188; Higgins (n 29) ch 1.

and highlighted the extent to which international politics dominates the formulation of both rules and theory.[51]

International law has paid little attention to the needs of women and international law institutions have been dominated by men. Only four women have been elected to the International Court of Justice,[52] and women were first elected to the International Law Commission in 2001. This has prompted a feminist appraisal of international law,[53] which has already had an impact on the substance of international law—for instance, in the recognition of sexual crimes in time of war and in the composition of international bodies.

Most theories of international law seek to advance the international legal order by explaining or analysing the nature of international law. However, in the United States, a neo-conservative school has sought to question the value of international law by arguing that international law is subordinate to the national interest.[54] This school, which gained prominence during the presidency of George W Bush and seems to explain the 'America first' policy of Donald Trump, has undermined the commitment of the United States to its international obligations. Significantly, this legal theory 'finds virtually no echo among legal scholars outside the United States'.[55]

None of these schools of jurisprudence on its own can satisfactorily explain the nature of international law and the source of the international legal obligation. While notions of justice and the values of legal idealism associated with natural law form the foundation of much of contemporary international law,[56] particularly the promotion of human rights and the right of self-determination, it cannot be denied that for many states consent remains the basis of their participation in the international community. Consent on its own, however, fails to provide an explanation for the rules and principles that comprise international law. Third World states, for instance, have at no time expressly consented to the rules that shaped international law before they attained independence. Indeed, as consent becomes more difficult to obtain for the creation of new rules

[51] See D Kennedy *International Legal Structures* (1987); M Koskenniemi *From Apology to Utopia* (1989); P Allott *Eunomia* (1990); S Marks *The Riddle of All Constitutions: International Law, Democracy and the Critique of Ideology* (2000).

[52] Rosalyn Higgins was President of the Court from 2006 to 2009.

[53] See H Charlesworth and C Chinkin *The Boundaries of International Law: A Feminist Analysis* (2000); H Charlesworth, C Chinkin and S Wright 'Feminist approaches to international law' (1991) 85 *AJIL* 613.

[54] JL Goldsmith and E Posner *The Limits of International Law* (2005); M Glennon *Limits of Law, Prerogatives of Power: Interventionism after Kosovo* (2001).

[55] TM Franck 'The power of legitimacy and the legitimacy of power: International law in an age of power disequilibrium' (2006) 100 *AJIL* 88, 90.

[56] TM Franck *Fairness in International Law and Institutions* (1995).

of law, consensus in the form of majority decision-making is increasingly adopted. Sociological and critical theories of law have a useful role to play. International law—like municipal law—has no autonomy as a discipline and must be seen as an integral, and important, part of the international political process. Traditionalists ignore this truth at their peril.

The sources of international law are too diverse and the functions it seeks to achieve are too complex to permit a single explanation of its nature and existence. There is a measure of truth in each of the theories advanced to provide an understanding of the nature of international law. Rules and principles of law constitute the flesh, blood, organs and bones of international law. Like physicians, we must study the parts of this body. But the mind of international law is more difficult to comprehend.

THE FRAGMENTATION OF INTERNATIONAL LAW

Today, international law accommodates many branches, each with its own special rules. There are special legal regimes governing, for instance, the sea, trade, environment, human rights, humanitarian law and foreign investment. In addition, many of these branches have their own special courts to pronounce on these special rules. Thus, there is an International Tribunal for the Law of the Sea to adjudicate on maritime disputes, an International Criminal Court to judge issues of humanitarian law, several regional human rights courts to consider violations of human rights law and a Dispute Settlement Body of the World Trade Organization to decide matters of trade. The proliferation of tribunals and the growth of autonomous branches of the law have led to fears that international law is in a process of fragmenting into separate structures, so-called self-contained regimes that threaten the universality of international law. This matter was subjected to careful examination by the United Nations International Law Commission,[57] which concluded that the emergence of special treaty regimes, and the proliferation of tribunals, had not seriously undermined the unity of international law. The present treatise bears this out. While there are undoubtedly special treaty regimes, the general rules of international law remain intact and provide a framework within which the special treaty regimes operate. Moreover, the problem of different rulings from different courts is much exaggerated. Tribunals, in large measure, defer to the jurisprudence of the International Court of Justice.

[57] *Fragmentation of International Law: Difficulties Arising from the Diversification and Expansion of International Law,* Report of the study group of the International Law Commission (finalised by M Koskenniemi) A/CN.4/L682 (2006).

CHAPTER 2

South Africa and International Law: A Historical Introduction

John Dugard

International law is the product of the European state system that came into being in the 16th century.[1] Until the 19th century it was in reality a European law of nations. This system of law, rooted in convictions of European superiority, imperialism and colonialism, accorded little recognition to the political organisms of Africa, whatever their level of sophistication.[2] Indeed, territories occupied by non-European peoples not constituting a social or political aggregation were treated as belonging to no one—as *terra nullius*.[3] The history of international law in southern Africa therefore begins with the first European settlement. This is an unashamedly Eurocentric view, but international law, until the last century, was unashamedly Eurocentric.

The Cape of Good Hope was settled by the Dutch in 1652 when Jan van Riebeeck took possession of the Cape as a refreshment station for the Dutch East India Company, the colonising instrument of the Republic of the United Netherlands.[4] Thus began an association between South Africa and Roman-Dutch law that continues to this day.[5] Between the 16th and 18th centuries, the Netherlands was a major maritime and mercantile power whose lawyers were busily involved in international affairs. It is not surprising therefore that the Netherlands was in the forefront of the development of international law.[6] Several Roman-Dutch jurists wrote on international law topics and two of them—Grotius and Van Bynkershoek—achieved great

[1] See Chapter 1.

[2] Clearly, there were highly developed political structures in Africa at this time. See AJGM Sanders *International Jurisprudence in the African Context* (1979) part 2; TO Elias *Africa and the Development of International Law* (1972) ch 1.

[3] See Chapter 8.

[4] For a description of the government of the Republic of the United Netherlands and its relationship with the Dutch East India Company, see HR Hahlo and E Kahn *The South African Legal System and its Background* (1968) 531–41.

[5] Ibid; JW Wessels *History of the Roman-Dutch Law* (1908).

[6] A Nussbaum *A Concise History of the Law of Nations* (1947) 88, 92, 139.

prominence in this field.[7] Roman-Dutch law and international law consequently evolved together in the Netherlands, and jurists made little attempt to separate the two legal orders.[8]

As a colony, first of the Netherlands (1652–1795, 1803–1806) and then of Britain (1795–1803, 1806–1910), the Cape of Good Hope was not an independent actor in the international community. Acts governed by international law were undertaken on its behalf by the colonial power. Treaties were extended to the Cape,[9] territory was annexed[10] and agreements were signed with native chiefs on a wide range of subjects—including boundaries, sovereignty over conquered lands, the extradition of fugitives and the protection of tribes.[11] Whether these agreements with native chiefs were seen as international agreements at the time is highly doubtful, but today there is support for the view that they were in some cases governed by principles of international law.[12]

The annexation of Natal by Britain in 1843 added another South African colony to the Empire, whose international affairs were conducted along the same lines as those of the Cape of Good Hope. The creation of the Boer Republics introduced a new dimension to the state system of southern Africa. Although Britain recognised the South African Republic (Transvaal) and the Orange Free State as independent states in 1852 and 1854 respectively, it later imposed such severe restraints on the treaty-making power of the Transvaal, after its annexation of that territory from 1877 to 1881, that there were serious doubts about the independence of the South African Republic. While Britain took the view that it was not an independent state, many writers contended that the Pretoria Convention of 1881 and the

[7] See Chapter 1.

[8] See Chapter 4.

[9] For example, extradition agreements were extended to the Cape by Order-in-Council in terms of the British Extradition Act of 1870 (33 & 34 Vict c 52). For a full account of the manner in which treaties were made on behalf of the Cape of Good Hope, see RP Schaffer (née Balkin) *A Critical Analysis of the Treaty-making Powers of the Union of South Africa and the Republic of South Africa* (PhD thesis, University of the Witwatersrand, 1978) 4–8.

[10] For example, Walvis Bay was annexed by the Crown in 1878 and incorporated into the Cape Colony by Act 35 of 1884. See L Berat *Walvis Bay: Decolonization and International Law* (1990) 37.

[11] For references to these agreements, see JA Kalley *South Africa's Treaties in Theory and Practice 1806–1998* (2001). See, in particular, *Treaties entered into by Governors of the Colony of the Cape of Good Hope and other British Authorities with Native Chieftains between 1803 and 1854* (1857).

[12] See MN Shaw *Title to Territory in Africa: International Legal Issues* (1986) 36–45; MF Lindley *The Acquisition and Government of Backward Territory in International Law* (1926) 46; TW Bennett 'Aboriginal title in South Africa' (1993) 9 *SAJHR* 443.

London Convention of 1884 did not deprive the Transvaal of its independent statehood.[13]

Despite doubts about the independence of the South African Republic, the Anglo-Boer War (1899–1902) was viewed by all states—including the United Kingdom—as a war between sovereign independent states.[14] Until the formal annexation of the Orange Free State and Transvaal, in May and October 1900 respectively, the Boer forces were recognised by Britain as lawful belligerents, entitled to be treated as prisoners of war on their capture.[15] Both parties to the conflict claimed to act in accordance with the customs and usages of the law of war, and municipal courts judged many disputes according to the customary laws of war.[16] The annexation of the Boer Republics in 1900 occurred before Britain had established military control over the rural areas of the republics, which gave rise to the claim that Britain's annexation had been premature and contrary to international law.[17] For two years a bitter guerrilla war was waged. Although Britain treated the Boer guerrillas as lawful belligerents, their families were herded into concentration camps and their properties devastated. Serious questions were raised about the legality of the British action under international humanitarian law, then in its infancy.

In 1910 the Union of South Africa was formed. In matters of foreign policy, the Imperial Government continued to act on behalf of the Union.[18] Constitutionally, the South African Parliament remained subject to the authority of Westminster in terms of the Colonial Laws

[13] The 1884 Convention stipulated that the 'South African Republic will conclude no treaty or engagement with any state or nation other than the Orange Free State . . . until the same has been approved by her Majesty'. It was this provision, which seriously limited the independence of the SAR, that gave rise to the debate over its status. See R Jennings and A Watts (eds) *Oppenheim's International Law* 9 ed (1992) vol 1 at 391. T Baty *International Law in South Africa* (1900) provides an excellent contemporary account of the debate. Baty favoured the view that the Transvaal was a 'semi-sovereign' state (45–68). See S Hofmeyr *Die Boere-Republieke en die Volkereg* (1933); DJ Pieterse 'Transvaal en Britse susereiniteit' in *Archives Year Book for South African History* (1940) I ch 6. This issue was discussed in *R v Christian* 1924 AD 101 at 108, 125–6. See further Chapter 5.

[14] Baty (n 13) 45–68; JM Spaight *War Rights on Land* (1911) 14–15.

[15] J Dugard 'The treatment of rebels in conflicts of a disputed character: The Anglo-Boer War and the "ANC-Boer War" compared' in AJM Delissen and GJ Tanya (eds) *Humanitarian Law of Armed Conflict: Challenges Ahead: Essays in Honour of Frits Kalshoven* (1991) 447 at 448–50.

[16] See Chapter 25.

[17] *Oppenheim* (n 13) at 700; Baty (n 13) 92–3.

[18] MM Lewis 'The international status of the British self-governing dominions' (1922–1923) 3 *BYIL* 21.

Validity Act.[19] Consequently, there was no suggestion that South Africa or the other dominions were independent states.[20] In World War I they fought loyally and effectively as part of the Imperial Forces. This contribution did not go unnoticed by the international community and the dominions were substantially rewarded after the War. South Africa, Australia and New Zealand were given responsibility for the mandated territories of South West Africa, New Guinea, Samoa, and Nauru respectively, for whose administration they were directly accountable to the League of Nations.[21] Moreover, South Africa, together with Australia, Canada, New Zealand and India, were admitted to original membership of the League of Nations despite the fact that constitutionally they remained subordinate to the British Crown. Although their precise status was much debated,[22] it is clear that they obtained 'for all League purposes a definite position as, for these matters at least, states of international law'.[23]

The uncertain international status of the dominions did not continue for long. In 1926 an Imperial Conference resolved that Britain and the dominions were 'autonomous communities within the British Empire, equal in status, in no way subordinate one to another in any aspect of their domestic or external affairs though united by a common allegiance to the Crown, and freely associated as members of the British Commonwealth of Nations'.[24] This resolution was given legislative endorsement in 1931 when the British Parliament passed the Statute of Westminster,[25] which repealed the Colonial Laws Validity Act and provided that in future, no Act of the British Parliament would extend to a dominion without the latter's consent. Thus, by 1931 it was clear beyond all doubt that South Africa was a sovereign independent state, a full subject of international law. Domestically, this new status was confirmed by the Status of Union Act[26] and the Royal Executive Functions and Seals Act.[27]

[19] 28 & 29 Vict c 63.

[20] *Oppenheim* (n 13) 257.

[21] For a consideration of some of the constitutional implications of the conferment of the mandate for South West Africa upon South Africa, see J Dugard 'South West Africa and the supremacy of the South African Parliament' (1969) 86 *SALJ* 194.

[22] M Friedlander 'The admission of states to the League of Nations' (1928) 9 *BYIL* 84 at 85.

[23] A Berriedale Keith *The Constitutional Law of the British Dominions* (1933) 47.

[24] See further on this conference G Carpenter *Introduction to South African Constitutional Law* (1987) 205.

[25] 22 Geo v c 4.

[26] Act 69 of 1934.

[27] Act 70 of 1934.

The role played by South Africa in the League of Nations[28] was very different from that which it was later to play in the United Nations from 1946 to 1994. Although the League was largely concerned with European affairs, South Africa made a positive contribution to the maintenance of international peace and gave its full support to the League's collective measures. In fact, South Africa was one of the foremost advocates of collective sanctions against Italy following Italy's invasion of Ethiopia. In recognition of its contribution to the League, a South African—Mr Charles te Water—was elected President of the Assembly of the League of Nations in 1933, and in 1939, in the twilight of the League, South Africa was elected a member of the Council. Despite its close relationship with Britain during the inter-war period, South Africa pursued an independent line in the League of Nations and on occasions seemed to use its position in the League as a means of asserting its independence from Britain.

In 1945 the United Nations was established and in the following year the League of Nations was dissolved. South Africa played a prominent part in the creation of the United Nations. General Smuts, the South African Prime Minister, enjoyed considerable international prestige[29] and was in part responsible for the drafting of the preamble of the United Nations Charter, which reaffirms 'faith in fundamental human rights, in the dignity and worth of the human person, in the equal rights of men and women and of nations large and small'.[30] From the outset, however, South Africa was compelled to play a defensive role as a result of its racial policies.[31] Initially South Africa was attacked for its discriminatory treatment of Indians. Later, after the National Party came to power on the platform of apartheid, South Africa became a symbol of racial injustice in a world committed to racial equality and decolonisation. South Africa's protests that her racial policies were a domestic issue that fell outside the jurisdiction of the United Nations at first received the support of many Western states, but after the police shooting of peaceful demonstrators at Sharpeville in 1960, this support disappeared and apartheid was regarded as a matter of international concern, as a

[28] S Pienaar *South Africa and International Relations between the Two World Wars: The League of Nations Dimension* (1987); N Diederichs *Die Volkebond* (1933).

[29] J Barber and J Barratt *South Africa's Foreign Policy: The Search for Status and Security 1945–1988* (1990).

[30] WK Hancock *Smuts: 2 The Fields of Force 1919–1950* (1968) 428–33. For a more nuanced assessment of Smuts' contribution to the drafting of the preamble, see C Heyns and W Gravett '"To save succeeding generations from the scourge of war": Jan Smuts and the ideological foundations of the United Nations' (2017) 39 *Human Rights Quarterly* 574, 589–94. See, too, C Heyns 'The Preamble of the United Nations' (1995) 7 *African Journal of International and Comparative Law* 329.

[31] See Chapters 15 and 23.

violation of the clauses in the United Nations Charter promoting human rights,[32] and, later, as a crime against humanity. In the ensuing 30 years, South Africa became a pariah state against which a wide range of United Nations sponsored measures were taken, including a mandatory arms embargo in 1977 and exclusion from participation in the General Assembly of the United Nations in 1974.[33]

South Africa's contribution to the development of international law during this period was enormous, although unintended. New rules of treaty and customary law to promote human rights, racial equality and decolonisation evolved as a result of international opposition to apartheid.[34] The prohibition on interference in the domestic affairs of states, enshrined in article 2(7) of the Charter, was substantially weakened by a succession of resolutions condemning apartheid.[35] Notions of statehood were reassessed as a result of the United Nations' refusal to recognise Transkei, Bophuthatswana, Venda and Ciskei as independent states.[36] Humanitarian law was rewritten to confer prisoner-of-war status on combatants belonging to the African National Congress (ANC) and other national liberation movements.[37] In addition, South Africa's six appearances before the International Court of Justice[38] over South West Africa/Namibia enabled the Court to formulate new rules of law on the status of international territories, the powers of the United Nations, human rights and self-determination. While apartheid undermined and discredited the law of South Africa, it succeeded, perversely, in injecting notions of racial equality, self-determination and respect for human rights into an international legal order that in 1945 had few developed rules on these subjects.

While South Africa's negative contribution to international law during the apartheid years was substantial, its positive contribution was minimal. In part the blame for this may be laid at the door of the United Nations, which sought to isolate South Africa by excluding it from international organisations and law-making conferences. But in large measure South Africa itself opted for exclusion and isolation by refusing to accept the primary values of the post-World War II legal

[32] Articles 55 and 56 of the Charter. See further Chapter 15.

[33] See Chapter 23.

[34] See, in particular, the International Convention on the Suppression and Punishment of the Crime of Apartheid of 1973. See Chapter 9.

[35] See Chapter 15.

[36] See Chapter 5.

[37] See Chapter 25.

[38] See Chapter 22.

order—racial equality, respect for human rights and the advancement of self-determination.

Law featured prominently in South African foreign policy before 1994. The men who guided and shaped South Africa's foreign policies—JC Smuts, JMB Hertzog, Eric Louw, Hilgard Muller and RF ('Pik') Botha—were all lawyers. Smuts alone used his talents to advance the international order.[39] At both the Paris Peace Conference of 1919,[40] and the San Francisco Conference of 1945, he worked vigorously to promote his vision of a world in which the rule of law would govern the affairs of states.[41] Louw, Muller and Botha were less concerned with the advancement of a just world order than they were with the sovereign right of South Africa to pursue its racial policies. While international law was for Smuts a sword with which to fashion a new world, for his successors it was a shield, a means of protecting South Africa against the encroaching values of the latter half of the 20th century.[42]

In 1994, South Africa's position in the world changed dramatically following the abandonment of apartheid and the holding of democratic elections, which saw the establishment of a Government of National Unity under the presidency of Nelson Mandela of the African National Congress. South Africa resumed its seat in the General Assembly and was restored to full membership in specialised agencies of the United Nations, from which it had been excluded during the apartheid years. It was readmitted to the Commonwealth of Nations, from which it had withdrawn in 1961, and it became a member of the Organization of African Unity (OAU), the Non-Aligned Movement and the Southern African Development Community (SADC). United Nations sanctions against South Africa were lifted. Diplomatic ties were established with states that had refused

[39] The attitude of Hertzog towards the advancement of an international order was ambivalent. It has been suggested that his support for South Africa's participation in world politics and the League of Nations was motivated mainly by his desire to assert South Africa's independence from Britain (Pienaar (n 28) 7).

[40] In 1918, Smuts published a pamphlet entitled *The League of Nations: A Practical Suggestion*, which served as a foundation for debates at the Paris Peace Conference, particularly on the mandates system.

[41] WK Hancock *Smuts: 1 The Sanguine Years 1870–1919* (1962) ch 21; WK Hancock *Smuts: 2 The Fields of Force 1919–1950* (1968) 428–33. In recent years, much has been written about Smuts' contribution to international peace and human rights. For a critical assessment, see M Mazower *No Enchanted Palace: The End of Empire and the Ideological Origins of the United Nations* (2009) 28–65. For a more favourable assessment, see Heyns and Gravett (n 30).

[42] South Africa's attitude towards international law and the United Nations during this period is well described by JC Heunis *United Nations versus South Africa: A Legal Assessment of United Nations and United Nations Related Activities in Respect of South Africa* (1986).

to have anything to do with South Africa during the apartheid era and new embassies were established abroad, particularly in Africa and Asia. South Africa's identification with the values of the international community was evidenced by its signing of the principal international human rights conventions.

Since its return to the international community, South Africa has played a leading role in the United Nations, the African Union, the Non-Aligned Movement and the Commonwealth. From 2007 to 2009 it held a non-permanent seat on the Security Council of the United Nations and was again elected as a non-permanent member of the Security Council for the periods 2011–2013 and 2018–2019. In 2011 it became a member of BRICS (Brazil, Russia, India, China and South Africa). Within Africa, South Africa has acted as peace broker in the Democratic Republic of the Congo and Burundi. Since it became a democracy, South Africa has therefore progressed from a pariah state into a leader in Africa and the world.

Initially, under President Mandela, South Africa pursued a universalist human rights foreign policy,[43] but under Presidents Mbeki and Zuma the interests of Africa and the African Union have been prioritised.[44] This is reflected in the decision to withdraw from membership of the International Criminal Court rather than hand over President al-Bashir of Sudan to the Court for prosecution—a decision that was later reversed.[45]

* * * * * *

International law comes before national courts in disputes between individuals or between the individual and the state. South African courts have probably entertained more international-law-based arguments than most domestic courts due to the country's vibrant commercial life and conflict-ridden political history.

Early cases demonstrated a clear commitment to international law. In 1894, in *CC Maynard et alii v The Field Cornet of Pretoria*,[46] Chief Justice Kotze of the Transvaal Republic declared that municipal law

> must be interpreted in such a way as not to conflict with the principles of international law. . . . It follows from [this], as put by Sir Henry Maine, 'that the state which disclaims the authority of international law places herself outside the circle of civilized nations'. It is only by a strict adherence to these

[43] In 1995 President Mandela sought the expulsion of Nigeria from the Commonwealth following the execution of Sara Wiwo and eight other environmental activists. This action was much criticised by African states on the ground that it failed to support African solidarity.

[44] For an annual record of South Africa's foreign policy from a legal perspective, see the annual report in the *South African Yearbook of International Law.*

[45] Further on this decision, see Chapters 4 and 10.

[46] (1894) 1 SAR 214 at 223. See, too, the judgment of Jorissen J 232.

> recognized principles that our young state can hope to acquire and maintain the respect of all civilized communities, and so preserve its own national independence.

In the aftermath of the Anglo-Boer War, courts frequently invoked international law to settle claims relating to the confiscation of property.[47] Later disputes, particularly those relating to South Africa's administration of South West Africa,[48] were likewise settled by recourse to international law.

In the apartheid era, wide divisions appeared in the South African population over attitudes towards international law. Whites saw international legal norms as irrelevant, unfair, and characterised by double standards in their implementation, while blacks turned to international law both as a source of redress from the injustices of apartheid and as a standard by which to measure the legitimacy of South African law.[49] The conflict between the two legal orders was highlighted in many court cases. Leaders of the South West Africa Peoples Organization (SWAPO), charged with statutory treason after the revocation of the Mandate for South West Africa by the United Nations, claimed that a South African court had lost its competence to try them under international law.[50] Both Nobel Prize Winner Archbishop Desmond Tutu and the leader of the Pan-Africanist Congress, Robert Sobukwe, invoked international law norms on freedom of movement to challenge administrative restrictions placed upon their right to travel abroad.[51] Laws zoning South Africa's cities along racial lines were challenged on the ground that they violated the Charter of the United Nations' provisions on human rights.[52] Members of the military wings of both SWAPO and the ANC challenged the jurisdiction of the courts to try them on the ground that they were entitled to prisoner-of-war status under contemporary humanitarian law.[53] The leaders of an abortive army coup in Bophuthatswana who were charged with treason argued that the charge was incompetent on the ground that treason was a crime against a 'state', and Bophuthatswana failed to qualify as a 'state' under international law.[54] International law arguments of this kind

[47] See Chapter 25.

[48] See *R v Christian* 1924 AD 101.

[49] J Dugard 'The conflict between international law and South African law: Another divisive factor in South African society' (1986) 2 *SAJHR* 1.

[50] *S v Tuhadeleni and Others* 1969 (1) SA 153 (A).

[51] *Tutu v Minister of Internal Affairs* 1982 (4) SA 571 (T); *Sobukwe v Minister of Justice* 1972 (1) SA 693 (A).

[52] *S v Adams; S v Werner* 1981 (1) SA 187 (A).

[53] *S v Sagarius* 1983 (1) SA 833 (SWA); *S v Petane* 1988 (3) SA 51 (C). See further Chapter 24.

[54] *S v Banda* 1989 (4) SA 519 (B). See further Chapter 5.

did not receive sympathetic consideration before the courts of the apartheid period. On the contrary, judgments of this time showed a hostility to international law resembling that of the executive.[55]

South Africa's new constitutional order gives full recognition to the place of international law in national law[56] and requires courts to interpret all legislation,[57] and particularly the Bill of Rights,[58] to accord with international law. This has led to a renaissance of international law in the jurisprudence of its courts. This will be apparent in the chapters that follow.

[55] J Dugard 'The South African judiciary and international law in the apartheid era' (1998) 14 *SAJHR* 110.

[56] See Chapter 4.

[57] Section 233 of Constitution of the Republic of South Africa, 1996.

[58] Section 39(1) of Constitution of the Republic of South Africa, 1996.

CHAPTER 3

Sources of International Law

John Dugard and Dire Tladi

INTRODUCTION

The sources of international law[1] are described in article 38(1) of the Statute of the International Court of Justice as:

(*a*) international conventions (treaties), whether general or particular;
(*b*) international custom, as evidence of a general practice accepted as law (customary international law);
(*c*) the general principles of law recognised by civilised nations; and
(*d*) judicial decisions and the teachings of the most highly qualified publicists, as subsidiary means for the determination of rules of law.

Article 38 was first drafted in 1920 for the Statute of the Permanent Court of International Justice.[2] It no longer accurately reflects all the materials and forms of state practice that comprise today's sources of international law. Despite this, every effort is made to bring new developments in respect of sources of law within the categories of sources recognised in article 38. Inevitably, this, at times, leads to the expansion of these sources beyond those originally contemplated in 1920.

There is no rule in international law providing for a general hierarchy of sources, particularly between treaty rule and rules of customary international law.[3] Yet, as a matter of practice, there is greater reliance on treaties and customary international law.[4] The

[1] See further on this subject H Thirlway *The Sources of International Law* (2014); J d'Aspremont *Formalism and the Sources of International Law* (2011); C Parry *The Sources and Evidences of International Law* (1965); ME Villiger *Customary International Law and Treaties* (1985); A Cassese *International Law in a Divided World* (1986) 169–99; P Szasz 'General law-making processes' in O Schachter and C Joyner (eds) *United Nations Legal Order* (1995) vol 1 35; A Boyle and C Chinkin *The Making of International Law* (2007); A Pellet 'Article 38' in A Zimmerman & T Thienel (eds) *The Statute of the International Court of Justice: A Commentary* 3 ed (2018).

[2] O Spiermann and M Fitzmaurice 'The history of article 38 of the Statute of the International Court of Justice' in S Besson and J d'Aspremont (eds) *The Oxford Handbook of the Sources of International Law* (2017).

[3] J Pauwelyn *Conflict of Norms in Public International Law* (2003) 133.

[4] In the *North Sea Continental Shelf Cases (Germany/Denmark; Germany/Netherlands)* 1969 ICJ Reports 3, the International Court of Justice adopts a methodical approach of first trying to identify whether there is an applicable treaty rule and then assessing the possibility of a rule of customary international law before, having found no applicable or customary international rule, seeking other applicable sources for the delimitation of the continental shelf.

empirical superiority of these two sources, both of which are founded on the consent of states, emphasises the consensual basis of international law.[5] Modern international law has seen important developments in the hierarchy of norms. Whereas in classical international law all norms and rules enjoyed equal ranking, today, certain norms, known as peremptory norms of general international law (*jus cogens*), enjoy a higher status in the normative hierarchy of sources. Obligations under the UN Charter also enjoy normative superiority over other rules of international law.[6]

TREATIES OR CONVENTIONS

A treaty is an agreement between states or between states and international organisations governed by international law. The rules relating to the capacity to enter into treaties, the procedure to be followed for entering into treaties, the interpretation of treaties, and the termination of treaties are governed by the Vienna Convention on the Law of Treaties of 1969 and the Vienna Convention on the Law of Treaties between States and International Organisations and between International Organisations of 1986.[7] These multilateral conventions define treaties as being written instruments. Many of the provisions of the 1969 Vienna Convention are generally accepted as reflecting rules of customary international law.[8]

Today treaties govern a wide area of international life. Treaties, which may be multilateral in the sense that they bind many states, or bilateral and binding on two states only, are divided broadly into three categories.

1 Contractual

These are treaties of a contractual nature between states governing matters such as trade, extradition, air and landing rights, and mutual defence. Here, two or more states 'contract' with each other to establish a particular legal relationship.

[5] In the *Lotus Case (France v Turkey)* 1927 PCIJ Reports Series A no 10 at 18, the Permanent Court of International Justice stated that '[t]he rules of law binding upon states . . . emanate from their own free will as expressed in conventions or by usages generally accepted as expressing principles of law'.

[6] See article 103 of the UN Charter.

[7] These are discussed in Chapter 20.

[8] See eg *Case Concerning Kasikili/Sedudu Island (Botswana/Namibia)* 1999 ICJ Reports 1045 para 18; *Case Concerning the Territorial Dispute (Libyan Arab Jamahiriya/Chad)* 1994 ICJ Reports 6 para 41; *Case Concerning Oil Platforms (Islamic Republic of Iran v United States of America)* 1996 ICJ Reports 803 para 23.

2 Legislative

A number of treaties have been entered into between states that codify existing rules of customary international law or that create new rules of law. Although these treaties are called legislative or law-making, they are not binding upon non-signatory states. The basic rule governing treaties is *pacta tertiis nec nocent nec prosunt*, ie treaties do not confer obligations or benefits upon non-signatory states.[9]

3 Constitutional

International organisations such as the United Nations are created by multilateral treaties. The Charter of the United Nations is a treaty to which all member states are party and which serves as the constitution of the United Nations. Similarly, the African Union Constitutive Act and the Southern African Development Community (SADC) Treaty serve as the constitution of the African Union and the SADC respectively. The Rome Statute of the International Criminal Court is, likewise, a multilateral treaty that creates a constitution for this court.

CUSTOMARY INTERNATIONAL LAW

Custom plays an important role in undeveloped societies without institutions for law-making or adjudication.[10] When a society develops and establishes a legislature and an effective judicial system, customary rules may be codified, replaced by statute, or formulated with greater precision by judicial decision with the result that statute and judicial decision become the primary sources of law. The international system as yet has no legislature or compulsory judicial system. Consequently, customary international law occupies a significant role in the international legal order.

[9] This was accepted by Conradie J in *S v Petane* 1988 (3) SA 51 (C) 61E–F. See further Y Dinstein 'The interaction between customary international law and treaties' (2006) 322 *Hague Recueil des cours* 247.

[10] For a discussion of customary international law as a source of law, see A D'Amato *The Concept of Custom in International Law* (1971); M Akehurst 'Custom as a source of international law' (1974–1975) 47 *BYIL* 1; HA Strydom 'Customary international law: The legacy of false prophets' (1994) 27 *CILSA* 276; M Byers *Custom, Power and the Power of Rules* (1999); AE Roberts 'Traditional and modern approaches to customary international law: A reconciliation' (2001) 95 *AJIL* 757; MP Scharf *Customary International Law in Times of Fundamental Change* (2013); CA Bradley *Custom's Future: International Law in a Changing World* (2016).

While states give their express consent to be bound by a rule when they enter into a treaty, the 'consent of states' to a customary rule is inferred from their conduct. Inevitably, the question whether a state has consented to a rule by its conduct will raise difficult questions of proof. It is hardly surprising, therefore, that disputes over the existence of customary rules feature prominently in international litigation.

There are two main requirements for the existence of a rule of customary international law: settled practice of states (*usus*) and the acceptance of an obligation to be bound (*opinio juris sive necessitatis*).

1 Elements of customary international law

(a) Settled practice (usus)

In the context of customary international law, practice means the practice of states.[11] The practice of other entities, including that of international organisations and non-governmental organisations, while not irrelevant, does not generally constitute practice for the purposes of establishing customary international law. The practice of other entities is not irrelevant in that it may provide context and may serve as a catalyst for state practice, but it cannot be a substitute for the practice of states in the formation of customary international law.

The practice of one, two or a few states is not a sufficient basis for the establishment of a rule of customary international law. The practice has to be general and widespread.

Evidence of state practice is to be found in a variety of materials, including treaties, the decisions of national courts, national legislation, diplomatic correspondence, policy statements by government officers, opinions of national law advisers, reports of the International Law Commission (ILC) and comments by states on these reports, and resolutions of international organisations, in particular the political organs of the United Nations. There is thus a wide range of materials that can qualify as evidence of state practice. There is, however, a view that only 'real action' or 'action on the ground' can qualify as state practice for the purposes of establishing rules of customary international law. In holding that no customary rule had come into existence in *S v Petane*, Conradie J stated:

> One must . . . look for state practice at what states have done on the ground in the harsh climate of a tempestuous world, and not at what their representatives profess in the ideologically overheated environment of the United Nations where indignation appears frequently to be a surrogate for action.[12]

[11] Draft Conclusion 4 of the Draft Conclusions on the Identification of Customary International Law adopted by the International Law Commission during its Seventieth Session (A/CN.4/L.908).

[12] *S v Petane* (n 9) 61D–E.

According to Conradie J, it is necessary to consider the action or practice of states, and not their promises or rhetoric, as 'customary international law is founded on practice, not on preaching'.[13] Here Conradie J echoed the warning of Mr Justice JT van Wyk, ad hoc judge in the South West Africa legal proceedings of 1960–1966, that *practice* and not political statements are required as evidence of custom.[14] This view, which seeks to exclude political statements by states as well as resolutions of the political organs of the United Nations from the ambit of state practice, is not consistent with the generally held view on the formation of customary international law, which accepts a variety of materials as practice.

Some states provide easy access to their practice by publishing official reports on this subject.[15] In other countries, digests are published by private institutions. Although there is currently no comprehensive record of South Africa's state practice, the *South African Yearbook of International Law* annually publishes a survey of events from the Office of the Chief State Law Adviser for International Law, which, in some instances, provides examples of South Africa's state practice. The *Yearbook* also publishes a list of treaties that have been signed and/or ratified by South Africa, which qualifies as state practice. The United Nations has recently produced a useful compendium of resources where state practice can be found.[16]

Where states actively demonstrate their support for a particular rule, no problem of proof arises. In many cases, however, there will be no clear evidence of this kind. It may, under certain circumstances, be possible to infer consent or acquiescence to a practice from the inaction of some states.[17] According to the ILC only 'deliberate abstention from acting' may count as practice.[18]

According to the International Court of Justice, a practice must constitute 'constant and uniform usage' before it will qualify as custom. This principle was enunciated in the *Asylum Case*,[19] which involved the question whether the practice of granting asylum to

[13] Ibid 59F–G.

[14] *South West Africa Cases (Ethiopia v South Africa; Liberia v South Africa), Second Phase* 1966 ICJ Reports 6 at 169.

[15] See, for discussion, memorandum by the UN Secretariat *Ways and Means for Making the Evidence of Customary International Law More Readily Available* 2018 (A/CN.4/710) paras 26–122.

[16] Ibid. Annexes I–VI.

[17] Draft Conclusion 6, para 1 of the Draft Conclusions on the Identification of Customary International Law (n 11).

[18] Ibid para 3 of the commentary to Draft Conclusion 6.

[19] *Asylum Case (Colombia/Peru)* 1950 ICJ Reports 266.

political refugees in embassies in Latin American countries amounted to a customary rule. After examining state practice in this regard, the Court concluded:

> The facts brought to the knowledge of the Court disclose so much uncertainty and contradiction, so much fluctuation and discrepancy in the exercise of diplomatic asylum and in the official views expressed on various occasions, there has been so much inconsistency in the rapid succession of conventions on asylum, ratified by some states and rejected by others, and the practice has been so much influenced by considerations of political expediency in the various cases, that it is not possible to discern in all this any constant and uniform usage, accepted as law, with regard to the alleged rule of unilateral and definitive qualification of the offence.[20]

Although, as a doctrinal matter, the International Court of Justice has insisted on 'constant and uniform usage'[21] or 'widespread' acceptance of a rule as a prerequisite for *usus*,[22] there have been cases in which the Court has not been rigorous in its application of the rule. In the *Arrest Warrant* case,[23] for example, it was prepared to dispense with evidence of state practice. Here, it held that a Minister of Foreign Affairs is entitled to immunity from the criminal jurisdiction of a foreign court on the ground that the nature and function of his office require such immunity.[24] The Court made no attempt to provide evidence of 'constant and uniform' or 'widespread' practice in support of such a rule.[25] Incidentally, when considering whether there was an exception to the immunity rule in cases of international crimes, the Court did apply a more rigorous search for state practice and, consequently, found that there was no exception.[26] The Court was similarly not rigorous in the search for state practice when it found that there was a customary international law rule obliging states to perform an environmental impact assessment for activities

[20] *Asylum Case* (n 19) 277. The Court seemed to relax this strict approach to settled practice in the *Case Concerning Military and Paramilitary Activities in and Against Nicaragua (Nicaragua v USA)* 1986 ICJ Reports 14 when it stated that a custom did not require 'absolutely rigorous conformity with the rule'. It is sufficient that 'the conduct of states should, in general, be consistent with such rules, and that instances of state conduct inconsistent with a given rule should generally have been treated as breaches of that rule, not as indications of the recognition of a new rule' (at 98).

[21] *Asylum Case* (n 19).

[22] *Fisheries Jurisdiction Case (United Kingdom v Iceland)* 1974 ICJ Reports 3.

[23] *Case Concerning the Arrest Warrant of 11 April 2000 (Democratic Republic of Congo v Belgium)* 2002 ICJ Reports 3.

[24] Ibid paras 53–4.

[25] See the dissenting opinion of Judge ad hoc Van den Wyngaert in this case: ibid 143–51, paras 11–23.

[26] *Arrest Warrant* case (n 23) para 58.

with transboundary impacts.[27] These instances when the Court, for whatever reason, departs from the rigorous search for practice should not detract from the requirement of widespread practice for the establishment of a customary rule. The judgment of the Supreme Court of Appeal in *Minister of Justice v SALC* provides an excellent example of the search for state practice.[28]

In most cases, some passage of time is required for a practice to crystallise into a customary rule. In some cases, however, where little practice is needed to establish a rule, it may come into existence very rapidly. When the General Assembly unanimously approved a resolution in 1963[29] declaring the legal principles governing activities in outer space, there was widespread agreement that a new rule of customary law had been created. In addition to general customary international law, international law also recognises the possibility of regional customary international law, applicable only to certain regions. The *Asylum Case* provides an example of a possible regional customary international law since the case concerned a possible rule of customary international law applicable in Latin America. Although the Court did not find that a rule of regional customary international law existed in that case, it accepted the possibility but held that the practice of granting asylum was not sufficiently 'constant and uniform' to form the basis of a rule of customary international law.

There also exists the possibility for local custom, applicable between two states.[30] The formation of a local customary international law rule, applicable to South Africa and Lesotho alone, was considered in *Nkondo v Minister of Police*,[31] in which the Court was asked to find that custom permitted passengers, who were on board an aircraft en route to Lesotho and were forced to land in South Africa in distress due to bad weather, to exercise a right of transit across South African territory with full immunity from arrest for

[27] *Case Concerning Pulp Mills on the River Uruguay (Argentina v Uruguay)* 2010 ICJ Reports 14 para 203.

[28] *Minister of Justice and Constitutional Development v Southern Africa Litigation Centre* 2016 (3) SA 317 (SCA) ('*Minister of Justice v SALC*') paras 66 et seq. See, for discussion, D Tladi 'Interpretation and international law in South African courts: The Supreme Court of Appeal and the Al Bashir Saga' (2016) 16 *African Human Rights Law Journal* 310.

[29] Resolution 1962 (XVIII). See Chapter 18.

[30] That local customary rules are permissible is clear from the *Case Concerning Right of Passage over Indian Territory* 1960 ICJ Reports 6 at 39.

[31] 1980 (2) SA 894 (O). See J Dugard 'Jurisdiction over persons on board an aircraft landing in distress' (1981) 30 *ICLQ* 902.

crimes against the safety of the state.[32] Relying on the *Asylum Case*,[33] Smuts J held that '[t]he fact that on only four occasions passengers were allowed passage across South African territory without having to comply with immigration formalities' could not serve as evidence of a customary rule.[34] Although the Court does not find that there is sufficient practice in that case, the possibility of a local customary international law rule applicable between two states is accepted.

For a practice to give rise to a rule of customary international law, it must receive 'general' or 'widespread' acceptance.[35] Universal acceptance is not necessary.[36] Although Rumpff CJ suggested that universal acceptance was required in *Nduli v Minister of Justice*,[37] subsequent South African decisions have questioned the correctness of this view and indicated that general acceptance is sufficient.[38] This raises the question whether a dissenting state will be bound by the general acceptance of a rule by other states. One view is that article 38(1)(b) of the Statute of the International Court of Justice 'does not exclude the possibility of a few dissidents for the purpose of the creation of a customary international law'.[39] Another view, approved by Conradie J in *S v Petane*,[40] is that if a state persistently objects to a particular practice while the law is still in the process of development, it cannot be bound by any customary rule that may emerge from such a practice. There is both judicial[41] and academic opinion[42] supporting the view that a 'persistent objector' is not bound in such a

[32] Here, the applicant, a leading member of the outlawed ANC, wanted by the South African Police in connection with the commission of crimes against the state, was arrested in South Africa when the Lesotho Airways flight on which he was travelling was forced to land in Bloemfontein due to bad weather.

[33] *Asylum Case* (n 19).

[34] *Nkondo v Minister of Police* (n 31) 908F–G.

[35] *Fisheries Jurisdiction Case* (n 22) 23–6.

[36] See the *dictum* of Judge Lachs in the *North Sea Continental Shelf Cases (Germany/Denmark; Germany/Netherlands)* 1969 ICJ Reports 3 at 229.

[37] 1978 (1) SA 893 (A) 906D.

[38] See *Inter-Science Research and Development Services (Pty) Ltd v Republica Popular de Mocambique* 1980 (2) SA 111 (T) 124–5; *S v Petane* (n 9) 56–7. Although the Supreme Court of Appeal in *Minister of Justice v SALC* (n 28) para 70 refers to 'an established universal practice', this is likely just an unfortunate choice of words rather than an attempt to establish universal practice as a standard for customary international law.

[39] Dissenting opinion of Judge Tanaka, *South West Africa Cases, Second Phase* (n 14) 291.

[40] *S v Petane* (n 9) 64A–B.

[41] See the *Anglo-Norwegian Fisheries Case (United Kingdom v Norway)* 1951 ICJ Reports 116 at 131; *North Sea Continental Shelf Cases* (n 36) 26–7, 131 (separate opinion of Judge Ammoun); *Asylum Case* (n 19) 277–8; *Nicaragua* case (n 20) 107.

[42] J Crawford *Brownlie's Principles of Public International Law* 8 ed (2012) 28. Cf JI Charney 'The persistent-objector rule and the development of customary international law' (1985) 56 *BYIL* 1.

case. This question has been the subject of debate in the context of apartheid and international law as it is clear that states refused to accept South Africa's persistent objection to treating apartheid as a violation of customary law.[43] This is best explained on the ground that the prohibition on apartheid is a peremptory norm, a norm of *jus cogens*, to which the normal rules relating to persistent objection are inapplicable.

(b) Opinio juris

A settled practice on its own is insufficient to create a customary rule. In addition, there must be a sense of obligation, a feeling on the part of states that they are bound by the rule in question—that the general practice is, in the language of article 38(1)(b), 'accepted as law'. This requirement, sometimes described as the psychological element in the formation of customary international law, was emphasised by the International Court of Justice in the *North Sea Continental Shelf Cases* between West Germany on the one hand, and the Netherlands and Denmark on the other.[44] Here, the Court found that a provision requiring the continental shelf to be divided in accordance with the principle of equidistance contained in the 1958 Geneva Convention on the Continental Shelf had not become a customary rule as, despite some practice in favour of the application of the equidistance principle, there was 'no evidence that [states] so acted because they felt legally compelled to draw [continental-shelf boundaries] in this way by reason of a rule of customary law obliging them to do so'.[45] Elaborating on this requirement, the Court stated:

> Not only must the acts concerned amount to a settled practice, but they must also be such, or be carried out in such a way, as to be evidence of a belief that this practice is rendered obligatory by the existence of a rule of law requiring it. The need for such a belief, ie the existence of a subjective element, is implicit in the very notion of the *opinio juris sive necessitatis*. The states concerned must therefore feel that they are conforming to what amounts to a legal obligation. The frequency, or even habitual character of the acts is not in itself enough.[46]

Proof of *opinio juris* is difficult to produce. Consequently, it is argued by some jurists that *opinio juris* will be presumed when there

[43] JI Charney 'Universal international law' (1993) 87 *AJIL* 529 at 539–40; L Henkin *International Law: Politics and Values* (1995) 39; O Schachter 'International law in theory and practice' (1984 V) 178 *Hague Recueil* 9, 119, 130–1.

[44] *North Sea Continental Shelf Cases* (n 36).

[45] Ibid 45.

[46] Ibid 44.

is evidence of a general practice in support of a particular rule.[47] The judgments of the International Court of Justice in the *North Sea Continental Shelf Cases* and the *Nicaragua* case,[48] however, do not endorse such a presumption. Similarly, the ILC has reconfirmed the continued applicability of both requirements for the establishment of a rule of customary international law.

Evidence of *opinio juris* can be found in the same materials that are used for state practice. The difference is that for *opinio juris* the search is for evidence that states feel bound or entitled to act in a particular way, not just for political or policy reasons but because of the existence of a rule of customary international law. To give a concrete example, the consistent and unanimous adoption of an annual resolution may well constitute practice regarding a rule contained in the resolution. The resolution itself, however, cannot establish a rule of customary international law unless it can be shown, whether by reference to the content of the resolution or by some other acts, that the states adopting the resolution believe the rule in question to be one of customary international law.

As with practice, the question of the 'silent majority'—those states that do not express an opinion as to the legal status of a rule—arises. In these instances, silence can, in certain circumstances, be taken to imply the acceptance of a rule. However, this inference can only be made when those silent states 'were in a position to react and the circumstances called for some reaction'.[49]

2 Resolutions of international organisations

Resolutions of international organisations, in particular political organs of the United Nations, can play an important part in the formation of customary international law, either as practice or as *opinio juris*.[50] Clearly a resolution of either the General Assembly or the Security Council categorised as a recommendation is not binding on states per se. However, an accumulation of resolutions, a repetition of recommendations on a particular subject, may amount to

[47] Crawford (n 42) 26. Dissenting opinion of Judge Tanaka in *North Sea Continental Shelf Cases* 1969 ICJ Reports 176; dissenting opinion of Judge ad hoc Sorensen (246–7).

[48] *Nicaragua* case (n 20) 108–9.

[49] Draft Conclusion 10 of the Draft Conclusions on the Identification of Customary International Law (n 11).

[50] Ibid at Draft Conclusion 12. See, for discussion, I McGibbon 'Means for the identification of international law: General Assembly resolutions: Custom, practice and mistaken identity' in Bin Cheng (ed) *International Law: Teaching and Practice* (1982) 10; and B Sloan 'General Assembly resolutions revisited' (1987) 58 *BYIL* 39. For a critical perspective, see P Weil 'Towards relative normativity in international law' (1983) 77 *AJIL* 413 at 417.

evidence of collective practice on the part of states. Moreover, to the extent that the content of a resolution specifies that a practice is a rule of customary international law, such a resolution may also serve as *opinio juris*.

In some cases, it is accepted that a recommendation of the General Assembly may become a customary rule with very little repetition. As shown above, the Declaration of Legal Principles Governing the Activities of States in the Exploration and Use of Outer Space of 1963 probably became a customary rule upon its adoption by the General Assembly.

More controversial and politically contentious resolutions create problems. In the 1960–1966 legal proceedings between Ethiopia/ Liberia and South Africa over the status of South West Africa (Namibia) it was argued that a customary rule of non-discrimination had been created by repeated General Assembly resolutions condemning apartheid and practices of racial discrimination. South Africa vigorously opposed this on the ground that it would amount to conferring legislative powers upon the General Assembly. In his separate opinion in the *South West Africa Cases, Second Phase*, the South African ad hoc judge, Mr Justice JT van Wyk, rejected this argument that repeated resolutions may establish rules of customary international law, declaring that it 'involved the novel proposition that the organs of the United Nations possessed some form of legislative competence whereby they could bind a dissenting minority'.[51] Although there was support for Judge Van Wyk's view in 1966,[52] today, Judge Tanaka's dissenting opinion[53] in favour of the existence of a customary rule of non-discrimination generated by the political organs of the United Nations prevails.

The Declaration on the Granting of Independence to Colonial Countries and Peoples of 1960 (General Assembly Resolution 1514 (XV)) provides another example of an instance in which a highly controversial resolution has been accepted as evidence of a customary rule. In this resolution the General Assembly asserted the right of all peoples to self-determination and called on colonial powers to take immediate steps to grant independence to their colonial peoples, thereby, in effect, outlawing colonialism. Despite initial resistance to this resolution on the part of colonial powers, it became the basis for the decolonisation of most colonies. The reiteration of this Declaration by large majorities in the General Assembly and the fact of

[51] 1966 ICJ Reports 6 at 170.

[52] See the dissenting opinion of Judge Jessup 432–3.

[53] At 291–4.

decolonisation, which constitutes practice, provide evidence of a settled practice in support of a customary rule outlawing colonialism.

During the apartheid era, South African courts took a conservative approach to the generation of customary rules by resolutions of the General Assembly. In *S v Petane*, involving the question whether Additional Protocol I of 1977, extending prisoner-of-war status to members of national liberation movements, reflected a customary rule as it has been endorsed by resolutions of the General Assembly, Conradie J stated:

> [I]t is doubtful whether resolutions passed by the United Nations General Assembly qualify as state practice at all. . . . They may constitute *opinio juris* which, if expressed with respect to a rule sufficiently delineated through *usus*, may create a customary rule of international law . . . . But, if there is no preceding *usus*, such a declaration cannot give birth to a customary rule, unless, of course, the declaration itself is treated as *usus* at the same time. However, it takes too wide a stretching of the concept of *usus* to arrive at the latter conclusion.[54]

Conradie J accordingly held that there was insufficient evidence of *usus*, in the form of 'material, concrete and/or specific acts of states', to justify a customary rule on this subject. He warned that 'United Nations resolutions cannot be said to be evidence of state practice if they relate, not to what the resolving states take it upon themselves to do, but to what they prescribe for others'.[55]

In reaching this conclusion, Conradie J cast doubt on the validity of the view that certain provisions of the Universal Declaration of Human Rights, adopted by the General Assembly in 1948, had become rules of customary international law. Here, he reasoned that it was difficult to discern a customary rule in abstract statements in support of the Universal Declaration and the incorporation of its provisions into national constitutions when they were contradicted by state practice constituting a flagrant violation of its provisions.[56] A similar approach was adopted by Cooper J in *S v Rudman*.[57]

This cautious judicial approach may be contrasted with that of the United States Second Circuit Court of Appeals in *Filartiga v Pena-Irala*,[58] in which the Court relied on the Universal Declaration of Human Rights and other resolutions of the General Assembly to substantiate the creation of a customary rule of international law prohibiting state torture. Here the Court stated:

[54] *S v Petane* (n 9) 58A–F.

[55] At 59F–G.

[56] At 58G–J.

[57] 1989 (3) SA 368 (E) 376A–B.

[58] 630 F 2d 876 (1980).

> This prohibition has become part of customary international law, as evidenced and defined by the Universal Declaration of Human Rights . . . which states, in plainest of terms, 'no one shall be subjected to torture'. The General Assembly has declared that the Charter precepts embodied in this Universal Declaration 'constitute basic principles of international law'. GA Res 2625 (XXV) (1970) . . . . These UN declarations are significant because they specify with great precision the obligations of member nations under the Charter.[59]

S v Petane, as with many apartheid-era cases, reflected South Africa's aversion and suspicion of international law. This has now given way to what has been termed an 'international law-friendly' constitutional dispensation.[60] As exemplified by the Constitutional Court judgment in *S v Makwanyane*, the South African judiciary now adopts a more open posture towards international law and resolutions adopted by the United Nations, amongst others.[61] This approach is consistent with the approach of the International Court of Justice in the *Nicaragua* case[62] in which the Court was required to decide whether the prohibition on the use of force contained in article 2(4) of the United Nations Charter had acquired the additional status of a customary rule. Without any consideration of *usus* on this subject, the Court held that it

> has however to be satisfied that there exists in customary international law an *opinio juris* as to the binding character of such abstention [from the use of force]. This *opinio juris* may, though with all due caution, be deduced from, inter alia, the attitude of ... states towards certain General Assembly resolutions . . . . The effect of consent to the text of such resolutions . . . may be understood as an acceptance of the validity of the rule or set of rules declared by the resolution.[63]

A cautionary admonition on this subject has, however, been given by the International Court of Justice in its advisory opinion on the *Legality of the Threat or Use of Nuclear Weapons*:[64]

> The Court notes that General Assembly resolutions, even if they are not binding, may sometimes have normative value. They can, in certain circumstances, provide evidence important for establishing the existence of a rule or the emergence of an *opinio juris*. To establish whether this is true of a given General Assembly resolution, it is necessary to look at its content and the conditions of its adoption; it is also necessary to see whether an *opinio juris*

[59] At 882–4.

[60] See N Botha 'Justice Sachs and the interpretation of international law by the Constitutional Court: Equity or expediency?' (2010) 25 *South African Public Law* 235. See D Tladi 'Interpretation of treaties in an international law-friendly framework: The case of South Africa' in Helmut Aust and Georg Nolte (eds) *The Interpretation of International Law by Domestic Courts: Uniformity, Diversity, Convergence* (2016).

[61] *S v Makwanyane* 1995 (3) SA 391 (CC) para 35.

[62] *Nicaragua* case (n 20) 14.

[63] Ibid 99–100.

[64] 1996 ICJ Reports 226.

> exists as to its normative character. Or a series of resolutions may show the gradual evolution of the *opinio juris* required for the establishment of a new rule. . . . Examined in their totality, the General Assembly resolutions put before the Court declare that the use of nuclear weapons would be 'a direct violation of the Charter of the United Nations'; and in certain formulations that such use 'should be prohibited'. The focus of these resolutions has sometimes shifted to diverse related matters; however, several of the resolutions under consideration in the present case have been adopted with substantial numbers of negative votes and abstentions; thus, although those resolutions are a clear sign of deep concern regarding the problem of nuclear weapons, they still fall short of establishing the existence of an *opinio juris* on the illegality of the use of such weapons.[65]

The Security Council is not a legislative body. Its primary function is to maintain international peace and to ensure, if necessary by means of binding resolutions, that states comply with their obligations under the Charter. In recent years, however, the Security Council has passed a number of binding resolutions requiring states to adopt measures to combat terrorism that have a decidedly legislative character.[66] Whether this heralds a new approach to its role remains to be seen.

3 Soft law[67]

Lawyers are accustomed to drawing a clear distinction between law and non-law—hence the importance of rules for identifying the point at which a practice on the part of states becomes a customary rule of law. Today it is suggested that there is 'something' in between that merits the attention of lawyers: 'soft law'. These are imprecise standards, generated by declarations adopted by diplomatic conferences or resolutions of international organisations, that are intended to serve as guidelines to states in their conduct, but which lack the status of 'law'. The Helsinki Final Act of the Conference on Security and Co-operation in Europe of 1975[68] is an example of a non-binding declaration by states which has had a profound effect on the promotion of human rights in Eastern Europe. Another such declaration is the Rio Declaration on the Environment and Development of 1992,[69] which expounds a number of principles, such as the duty on

[65] 1996 ICJ Reports paras 70–1.

[66] See further discussion of this subject in Chapter 23.

[67] JH van Hoof *Rethinking the Sources of International Law* (1983) 179; M Olivier 'Informal agreements under the 1996 Constitution' (1997) 22 *SAYIL* 63 at 69; M Olivier 'Relevance of "soft law" as a source of international human rights' 2002 *CILSA* 289; D Shelton (ed) *Commitment and Compliance: The Role of Non-binding Norms in the International Legal System* (2000).

[68] (1975) 14 *ILM* 1292.

[69] (1992) 31 *ILM* 874.

states to inform states of environmental hazards and the duty on states to carry out an environmental impact assessment for activities likely to have an adverse impact on the environment. The difficulty in securing the consent of states to multilateral treaties governing environmental matters, on which there is a need for urgent action, has prompted this recourse to non-binding standards. Indeed, today environmental international 'law' is heavily dependent on 'soft law'.[70] The passage of time and state practice in support of such a standard may convert it into a customary rule, but until this occurs it serves as a useful guide to state conduct without creating legal obligations for states.

THE RELATIONSHIP BETWEEN CUSTOMARY INTERNATIONAL LAW AND TREATY LAW

Customary international law rules may be embodied in treaty rules. In the *Nicaragua* case,[71] for example, the United States argued that the Court did not have jurisdiction since the case concerned the interpretation of article 2(4) of the UN Charter relating to the prohibition on the use of force. In its declaration accepting the jurisdiction of the Court, the United States had excluded the jurisdiction of the Court in relation to 'disputes arising under a multilateral treaty'.[72] The Court, however, concluding that the reservation cannot bar the Court from exercising jurisdiction because Nicaragua does not only rely on article 2(4) of the UN Charter but also on customary international law, observed that:

> Nicaragua invokes a number of principles of customary and general international law that, according to the Application, have been violated by the United States. The Court cannot dismiss the claim of Nicaragua under principles of customary and general international law, simply because such principles have been enshrined in the texts of the conventions relied upon by Nicaragua. The fact that the abovementioned principles, recognised as such, have been codified or embodied in multilateral conventions does not mean that they cease to exist and to apply as principles of customary law, even as regards countries that are parties to such conventions.[73]

The reasoning by the Court points to the relationship between a treaty and rules and customary international law having the same or

[70] P Birnie and A Boyle *International Law and the Environment* (1992) 26.

[71] *Case Concerning Military and Paramilitary Activities in and Against Nicaragua (Nicaragua v United States)* 1984 ICJ Reports 392.

[72] Ibid para 67.

[73] Ibid para 73. See also *Nicaragua* case (n 20) para 175: '[E]ven if a treaty norm and a customary norm relevant to the present dispute were to have exactly the same content, this would be no reason for the Court to take the view that the operation of the treaty process must necessarily deprive the customary norm of its separate applicability.'

similar content. In the *North Sea Continental Shelf Cases* the International Court of Justice identified three ways that a treaty provision can result in or contribute to a rule of customary international law having the same content.[74] First, a rule of customary international law could be codified into a treaty after the crystallisation of the customary international law rule. Secondly, the process of concluding the treaty could have led to the crystallisation of a rule of customary international law that was emerging. Finally, state practice subsequent to the adoption of the treaty—partly in response to the treaty—led to the emergence of a new rule of customary international law. It should be stressed, however, that in each case it remains necessary to show the existence of a customary international law rule by reference to state practice and *opinio juris*. Moreover, in relation to *opinio juris*, it is necessary to show that state practice is not due to the application of the treaty but rather due to the belief that there exists a 'mandatory rule of customary international law'.[75]

The emergence of a rule of customary international law reflected in a treaty provision was also considered in *S v Petane*,[76] in which the Cape Provincial Division considered the question as to whether a member of the ANC's military wing, *Umkhonto we Sizwe*, was entitled to prisoner-of-war status on the ground that Additional Protocol 1 of 1977 to the Geneva Conventions of 1949, which accords such status to members of national liberation movements, had become part of customary international law and was thus binding upon South Africa. (At this time South Africa was not a party to the Protocol. It became a party in 1995.) The fact that some 60 states had signed the Protocol, said the Court, did not amount to settled practice as there was no evidence that the rule extending prisoner-of-war status to members of national liberation movements had been endorsed by states in their practice. Moreover, the two states at which this aspect of the Protocol was directed, namely Israel and South Africa, had persistently refused to sign the Protocol or to accept its prescriptions in practice.

GENERAL PRINCIPLES OF LAW RECOGNISED BY CIVILISED NATIONS

General principles of law constitute a reserve store of legal principles upon which courts and tribunals may draw when there are no rules of treaty or customary law applicable. In such instances, courts turn to common principles of law found in municipal systems—in so far

[74] *North Sea Continental Shelf Cases* (n 36) paras 60 et seq.
[75] Ibid para 76.
[76] *S v Petane* (n 9).

as they are capable of application to relations between states—in order to fill the gaps in international law. Thus, while international law does not, as a doctrinal matter, recognise hierarchy of sources, general principles are by definition subordinate to treaty and customary international law.

Although sparse use is made of this source, international courts have on occasion invoked the principles of unjust enrichment,[77] reparation for breach of an undertaking,[78] *res judicata*,[79] the limited liability of a corporation,[80] estoppel[81] and *nemo judex in re sua*.[82] As international tribunals, such as the International Court of Justice, comprise judges from different national backgrounds, they are well qualified to draw on general principles of this kind.

An example of the manner in which an international court may draw on general principles of law is provided by the separate opinion of Judge McNair in the *International Status of South West Africa Advisory Opinion*.[83] In considering the nature of the Mandate for South West Africa, Judge McNair stated that it was permissible to have regard to the English system of trusts and to continental institutions of mandate and tutelage in order to ascertain the principles to be applied to the Mandate for South West Africa. He concluded that these institutions indicated that the rights of the trustee were limited and that the trustee was under a legal obligation to administer the property for the benefit of another. In particular, the trustee was not permitted to absorb the trust property into his own estate. Applying these principles to the Mandate for South West Africa, he held that South Africa was unable to alter the status of South West Africa by absorbing the territory into South Africa without first obtaining the consent of the United Nations.

Unlike treaties and custom, general principles of law do not have a consensual basis. Consequently, natural lawyers have claimed that the existence of this source of law confirms the natural law basis of the international legal order. In the 1966 *South West Africa Cases, Second Phase*, Judge Tanaka of Japan stated:

[77] *Lena Goldfields Arbitration* (1930) 5 AD 3.

[78] *Chorzow Factory (Merits)* (1928) PCIJ Reports Series A no 17 at 29.

[79] *Effect of Awards of Compensation Made by the UN Administrative Tribunal* 1954 ICJ Reports 47 at 53; *Case Concerning the Application of the Convention on the Prevention and Punishment of the Crime of Genocide (Bosnia and Herzegovina v Serbia and Montenegro)* 2007 ICJ Reports 43, 89–102.

[80] *Barcelona Traction Light and Power Company, Ltd (Belgium v Spain)* 1970 ICJ Reports 3 at 33–5.

[81] *Case Concerning the Temple of Preah Vihear (Cambodia v Thailand)* 1962 ICJ Reports 6 at 23, 31, 32.

[82] *Mosul Boundary Case* (1925) PCIJ Reports Series B no 12 at 32.

[83] 1950 ICJ Reports 128 at 148.

> [I]t is undeniable that in article 38(1)(c) some natural-law elements are inherent. It extends the concept of the source of international law beyond the limit of legal positivism according to which, the states being bound only by their own will, international law is nothing but the law of the consent and auto-limitation of the state.[84]

States which cling to a positivist approach to international law have difficulty in accepting this source. In the 1966 *South West Africa Cases*, Judge ad hoc Van Wyk rejected the argument that a norm of non-discrimination was binding on South Africa as a general principle of law, stating that article 38(1)(c) of the Statute of the International Court of Justice does not mean that by legislating on particular domestic matters a majority of nations could compel a minority to introduce similar legislation.[85]

Although the natural law basis of this source should not be exaggerated, its influence is clear. This is further evidenced by the manner in which international courts have invoked considerations of humanity[86] and equity[87] under the rubric of general principles of law.

JUDICIAL PRECEDENT

Judicial decisions are a subsidiary means for the determination of rules of law. Judicial decisions in this context refers to both decisions of national and international courts. Article 38(1)(d) of the Statute of the International Court of Justice contains two caveats. First, judicial decisions are only a 'subsidiary means for the determination of the rules of law'. This means that judicial decisions, under article 38(1)(d) of the Statute, do not themselves constitute rules of international law but are only a way of identifying the rules of international law. Since judicial decisions are only a subsidiary means for determining the rules of law, the authority of each decision ultimately depends on the quality of the reasoning.[88]

The second caveat is that judicial decisions as a source of law are subject to article 59 of the Statute, which provides that: 'The decision of the Court has no binding force except between the parties and in respect of that particular case.'

This means that international law, like in the civil-law tradition, knows no doctrine of *stare decisis*. In practice, however, there is a natural tendency for courts to follow their own previous decisions or the decisions of other international tribunals. While the International

[84] *South West Africa Cases* (n 14).

[85] Ibid 170.

[86] *Corfu Channel (Merits)* 1949 ICJ Reports 4 at 22; *Nicaragua* case (n 20) 114.

[87] Crawford (n 42) 44–7.

[88] See para 3 of the commentary to Draft Conclusion 13 of the Draft Conclusions on the Identification of Customary International Law (n 11).

Court of Justice refers to its own previous decisions with caution, other international tribunals and domestic courts charged with international law matters do not hesitate to invoke previous decisions on international law from both international and domestic tribunals.

In recent times—as a result of the increased workload of the International Court of Justice, the proliferation of courts and arbitral tribunals, and the willingness of states to submit to international adjudication—judicial decisions, particularly of international courts, have come to play a more central role in international law. This is a natural development in the evolution of international law from a primitive system in which adjudication was rare to a sophisticated legal order in which courts play a central role.

It is important to draw a clear distinction between the use of judicial decisions under article 38(1)(d), on the one hand, and, on the other, the reliance of judicial decisions as a source of state practice. The former refers to decisions of both domestic and international courts and serves a subsidiary purpose of determining the rules of international law, while the latter refers only to decisions of domestic courts as organs through which the state acts. For the former, the quality of the reasoning is important for its authority while for the latter the quality of the reasoning plays a less important role.

TEXT WRITINGS

The teachings of the most highly qualified publicists are also a subsidiary means for the determination of law. The writings of jurists accordingly provide evidence of rules of law in the same way as writings of Roman-Dutch jurists in South Africa. International tribunals make less use of the writings of jurists today than in the past, as new sources of law have to a large extent made it unnecessary to rely upon the views of jurists for an exposition of the law.

UNILATERAL ACTS OF STATES

Sometimes the unilateral acts of states, particularly in the form of statements by government officials, may create international obligations, and are thus a source of law.[89] In a dispute between Denmark and Norway about the sovereignty over Greenland, Denmark

[89] Crawford (n 42) 416–18; AP Rubin 'The international legal effects of unilateral declarations' (1977) 71 *AJIL* 1; W Fiedler 'Unilateral acts in international law' in R Bernhardt (ed) *Encyclopedia of Public International Law* (2000) vol IV, 1018; E Suy 'Some unfinished new thoughts on unilateral acts of state as a source of international law' (2002) 27 *Tydskrif vir Regswetenskap* 1.

claimed that the Norwegian Foreign Minister, Mr Ihlen, had acknowledged Denmark's claim to sovereignty over Greenland in the course of a minuted conversation with the Danish Minister accredited to Norway. The Permanent Court of International Justice held that in the light of the 'Ihlen Declaration',[90] Norway was under an obligation to refrain from contesting Danish sovereignty over Greenland. In a subsequent dispute between Australia and France over the unlawfulness of French nuclear tests in the atmosphere in the South Pacific Ocean, the International Court of Justice held it was unnecessary for the Court to give a judgment in this matter because statements by the French President at a news conference indicated that France would discontinue atmospheric tests, thereby rendering the dispute moot. In so finding, the Court stated:

> It is well recognized that declarations made by way of unilateral acts, concerning factual or legal situations, may have the effect of creating legal obligations . . . . When it is the intention of the State making the declaration that it should become bound according to its terms, that intention confers on the declaration the character of a legal undertaking, the State being thenceforth legally required to follow a course of conduct consistent with the declaration. An undertaking of this kind, if given publicly and with intent to be bound, even though not made within the context of international negotiations, is binding.[91]

Unilateral acts of this kind do not fall within any of the sources listed in article 38(1) of the Statute of the International Court of Justice. Nevertheless, they do create legal obligations.

CODIFICATION

The uncertainties of customary international law have prompted the international community to resort to codification. Article 13(1) of the United Nations Charter authorises the General Assembly to initiate studies and make recommendations to encourage 'the progressive development of international law and its codification'. To carry out this task the General Assembly has established an International Law Commission consisting of 34 persons of recognised competence in international law, elected by the General Assembly and representing the main legal systems of the world. To date, two South Africans have served on the International Law Commission. John Dugard served on the ILC from 1997 to 2011 while Dire Tladi was first elected in 2011 and continues to serve on the ILC.

Although the constitution of the International Law Commission distinguishes between the progressive development of international

[90] *Legal Status of Eastern Greenland* 1933 PCIJ Reports Series A/B no 53.

[91] *Nuclear Tests Case (Australia v France)* 1974 ICJ Reports 253 at 267–8.

law, ie the exposition of new principles of law, and the codification of law, ie the formulation and systematisation of existing rules of law, it has been difficult to maintain such a distinction in practice. In codifying existing areas of the law, the International Law Commission has been required progressively to develop the law by expounding new principles, with the result that the distinction between progressive development and codification has become blurred.

The ILC prepares reports and draft conventions, which may later be submitted to international conferences for approval. In this way, a number of significant multilateral law-making conventions have come into existence. The Vienna Convention of the Law of Treaties (1969), the Geneva Convention on Diplomatic Relations (1961), the Geneva Convention on Consular Relations (1963), the four Geneva Conventions on the Law of the Sea (1958), the Convention on the Prevention and Punishment of Crimes against Internationally Protected Persons, including Diplomatic Agents (1973), the Convention on the Non-Navigational Use of International Watercourses (1997) and the Convention on Jurisdictional Immunities of States and their Property (2004) are examples of conventions drafted by the ILC.[92] In fact, even the Rome Statute of the International Criminal Court was negotiated on the basis of a draft Statute prepared by the International Law Commission.

The International Law Commission's products goes beyond draft conventions converted into multilateral treaties: it includes draft codes, guidelines, restatements of the law, draft articles that may be transformed into treaties and the reports of the special rapporteurs. The Draft Articles on the Responsibility of States for Internationally Wrongful Acts (2001) and the Draft Articles on Diplomatic Protection (2006) are examples of instruments yet to be translated into treaty form which serve as an authoritative statement of the law.[93] The

[92] The *South African Yearbook of International Law* includes an annual survey of the work of the ILC. See, eg D Tladi 'Progressively developing and codifying international law: The work of the International Law Commission in its sixty-seventh session' (2015) 40 *SAYIL* 432. For a more general overview of the work of the ILC, see R Jennings and A Watts (eds) *Oppenheim's International Law* 9 ed, vol 1 (1992) 103–10; J Dugard 'How effective is the International Law Commission in the development of international law?' (1998) 23 *SAYIL* 34; A Watts *The International Law Commission 1949–1998* (1999) 3 vols; A Pronto and M Wood *The International Law Commission 1999–2009* (2010) vol 4; A Pronto 'Some thoughts on the making of international law' (2008) 19 *EJIL* 601.

[93] *Report of the International Law Commission, General Assembly Official Records* 56th Session, Supplement 10 (A/56/10) 29 (2001); *Report of the International Law Commission, General Assembly Official Records* 58th Session, Supplement 10 (A/61/10) 13 (2006).

work of the ILC is frequently relied on by international tribunals,[94] which suggests that it qualifies as a source of law,[95] either in its own right or as evidence of custom or the expression of views of 'highly qualified publicists'. Sir Arthur Watts states:

> To a considerable extent, debate about the Commission's place in the scheme of things set out in Article 38 of the Statute of the International Court of Justice is artificial. As already noted, that scheme, even if it is about sources at all, is not necessarily exhaustive of the sources of international law; also as noted, the Court has not hesitated to invoke the work of the International Law Commission where it seemed appropriate to do so, without concerning itself with the formal question of how that work might fall within Article 38 of the Court's Statute. It may be more fruitful to think of the Commission's work, and particularly its final draft Articles, in terms of material, rather than formal sources, of international law.[96]

JUS COGENS, OBLIGATIONS *ERGA OMNES* AND A SYSTEM OF HIGHER NORMS

Traditionally, international society is viewed as a horizontal system premised on the sovereign equality of states, while international law is seen as a body of rules based on consent and characterised by their neutrality. A necessary consequence of this is that all legal norms are equal in status.[97] The horizontality of international law means that general rules of international law can be modified or derogated from by states through treaty and customary international law. Two states or more can decide, whether through treaty or local custom, that they will not apply customary international law rules on immunities in their relations with each other. By the same token, two or more states can decide to modify the application of the Vienna Convention on Diplomatic Relations. These general rules of international law that can be modified easily through the agreement of states are referred to as *jus dispositivum.*

In contrast to *jus dispositivum,* there exists a category of norms of international law which cannot be modified or derogated by the mere will of states.[98] This category of norms of international law are

[94] See, for example, the *Case Concerning the Gabcikovo-Nagymaros Project* 1997 ICJ Reports 7 at 39–41 in which the International Court of Justice relied on the ILC's Draft Articles on State Responsibility.

[95] I Sinclair *The International Law Commission* (1987) 121.

[96] Watts (n 92) vol 1, 15.

[97] See P Weil 'Towards relative normativity in international law?' (1983) 77 *AJIL* 413.

[98] *First Report on* Jus Cogens *by Dire Tladi, Special Rapporteur* (2016) (A/CN.4/693) para 64. For more on *jus cogens*, see A Cassese *International Law* 2 ed (2005) 198–212; D Shelton 'Normative hierarchy in international law' (2006) 100 *AJIL* 291; A Bianchi

referred to as peremptory norms of general international law (*jus cogens*).

The notion of *jus cogens* has a long history in international law, dating as far back as Hugo de Groot.[99] However, its position in international law was cemented with its inconclusion in the Vienna Convention on the Law of Treaties of 1969, which, in article 53,[100] provides:

> A treaty is void, if, at the time of its conclusion, it conflicts with a peremptory norm of general international law. For the purposes of the present Convention, a peremptory norm of general international law is a norm accepted and recognized by the international community of states as a whole as a norm from which no derogation is permitted and which can be modified only by a subsequent norm of general international law having the same character.

There is general support for *jus cogens* as a doctrine and much state practice and decisions of international courts in support of it.[101] In the prohibition against South Africa, for example, the Constitutional Court recognised that the prohibition against torture is a peremptory norm of international law.[102] Certain norms are now generally recognised as peremptory. These include the prohibition of aggression, the prohibitions against slavery, genocide, racial discrimination (including apartheid), torture and the denial of self-determination.[103] The International Court of Justice, after studiously avoiding any acknowledgement of peremptory norms, recognised that the prohibitions on genocide and racial discrimination were peremptory norms

'Human rights and the magic of *jus cogens*' (2008) 19 *EJIL* 491; A Orakhelashvili *Peremptory Norms in International Law* (2008).

[99] *First Report on* Jus Cogens (n 98) paras 18 et seq.

[100] CL Rozakis *The Concept of* Jus Cogens *in The Law of Treaties* (1976); J Sztucki Jus Cogens *and the Vienna Convention on the Law of Treaties: A Critical Appraisal* (1974).

[101] See, eg, *Besluß des Zweiten Senats* 7 April 1965, BVerfGE 18, 441 at 449 where the German Constitutional Court upheld a treaty provision because the *jus cogens* norm advanced to impugn a provision in the treaty did not belong to the category of *jus cogens*; *R v Bow Street Metropolitan Stipendiary Magistrate, Ex parte Pinochet Ugarte (No 3)* [1999] 2 All ER 97 (HL); *Ferrini v Federal Republic of Germany (Italian Court of Cassation) 11 March 2004* (reported in (2005) 99 AJIL 242); *Yousuf v Samantar* 699 F.3d 763; *Kenya Section of the International Commission of Jurists v Attorney-General* [2011] *E-Kenyan Law Reports*; *Case Concerning Armed Activities on the Territory of the Congo (Democratic Republic of Congo v Rwanda)* 2006 ICJ Reports 6 para 64. See also the International Criminal Tribunal for the former Yugoslavia in *Furundzija*, Case IT–95–17/1–A (121 ILR 213, 260).

[102] *National Commissioner of Police v Southern African Human Rights Litigation Centre* 2015 (1) SA 315 (CC) para 14.

[103] See, eg, para 5 of the commentary to Draft Article 26 of the Draft Articles on the Responsibility of States for Internationally Wrongful Acts (2001).

in *Democratic Republic of the Congo v Rwanda* in 2006.[104] In that case, John Dugard, sitting as a judge ad hoc, suggested that norms of *jus cogens* had an important role to play in the judicial process:

> The judicial decision is essentially an exercise in choice. Where authorities are divided, or different general principles compete for priority, or different rules of interpretation lead to different conclusions, or State practices conflict, the judge is required to make a choice. In exercising this choice, the judge will be guided by principles (propositions that describe rights) and policies (propositions that describe goals) in order to arrive at a coherent conclusion that most effectively furthers the integrity of the international legal order.
>
> Norms of *jus cogens* are a blend of principle and policy. On the one hand, they affirm the high principles of international law, which recognize the most important rights of the international order—such as the right to be free from aggression, genocide, torture and slavery and the right to self-determination; while, on the other hand, they give legal form to the most fundamental policies or goals of the international community—the prohibitions on aggression, genocide, torture and slavery and the advancement of self-determination. This explains why they enjoy a hierarchical superiority to other norms in the international legal order. The fact that norms of *jus cogens* advance both principle and policy means that they must inevitably play a dominant role in the process of judicial choice.[105]

While there are a core group of norms that are recognised as *jus cogens*, uncertainty still remains about the method of identifying *jus cogens* norms and the consequences that flow from the peremptory status of a norm. To address these and other questions, the International Law Commission decided to appoint a Special Rapporteur to study the topic in 2015. To date, the Special Rapporteur has produced three reports.

In its work thus far, the Drafting Committee of the ILC has adopted conclusions that describe the general characteristics of *jus cogens* as norms that reflect and protect the fundamental values of the international community, that are hierarchically superior to other norms of international law and that are universally applicable.[106] The Drafting Committee has also defined a two-step approach to the identification of *jus cogens* norms.[107] First, it must be a norm of general international law. Secondly, it must be recognised and accepted by the international community of states as a whole as one

[104] *Case Concerning Armed Activities on the Territory of the Congo (Democratic Republic of Congo v Rwanda)* 2006 ICJ Reports 6 para 64 and para 78.

[105] Ibid 611 (para 10).

[106] Draft Conclusion 2 of Draft Conclusions on Peremptory Norms of General International Law (*Jus Cogens*), adopted by the Drafting Committee of the International Law Commission; statement of the Chair of the Drafting Committee on Peremptory Norms of General International Law (*Jus Cogens*) (2017) Annex.

[107] Draft Conclusion 4 of Draft Conclusions on Peremptory Norms of General International Law (*Jus Cogens*).

from which no derogation is permitted. Whether a norm protects the fundamental values of the international community, and is deemed to be universally applicable and hierarchically superior to other norms, must be taken into account in assessing the second element.

The question of the consequences of *jus cogens* has perhaps been the most divisive and controversial.[108] International and regional courts have generally tended to adopt a narrow approach to the consequences of *jus cogens*—sometimes unduly so. This is perhaps most reflected in the current debate on whether there are exceptions to immunity for *jus cogens* crimes.[109] In the *Arrest Warrant* case, the International Court of Justice implicitly concluded that there was no such exception.[110] This conclusion was made more explicit by the Court in *Jurisdictional Immunities of the State*, where the Court drew a somewhat arbitrary distinction between immunities, which it said were procedural in nature, and the more substantive norms of *jus cogens*:[111]

> Assuming for this purpose that the rules of law of armed conflict which prohibit the murder of civilians in occupied territory, the deportation of civilian inhabitants to slave labour and the deportation of prisoners of war to slave labour are rules of *jus cogens*, there is no conflict between those rules and the rules on State immunity. The two sets of rules address different matters. The rules of State immunity are procedural in character and are confined to determining whether or not the courts of one State may exercise jurisdiction in respect of another State. They do not bear upon the question of whether or not the conduct in respect of which the proceedings are brought was lawful or unlawful.

This line of reasoning has generally been followed in regional courts, in particular the European Court of Human Rights.[112] Whatever the merits or demerits of the reasoning of the Court in *Jurisdictional Immunities of the State*, this reasoning should be restricted to immunity from civil proceedings and not extended to immunities in criminal proceedings.[113] The Court itself cautioned that 'the question of whether, and if so to what extent, immunity

[108] See D Costelloe *Legal Consequences of Peremptory Norms in International Law* (2017); *Third Report on Peremptory Norms of General International Law* (Jus Cogens) *by Dire Tladi, Special Rapporteur* (2018) (A/CN.4/714).

[109] See Chapter 9 for more discussion.

[110] *Arrest Warrant* case (n 23).

[111] *Jurisdictional Immunities of the State (Germany v Italy: Greece intervening)* 2012 ICJ Reports 99 paras 92 et seq.

[112] See, for instance, the decisions of the European Court of Human Rights in *Al-Adsani v United Kingdom* (2001) 34 EHRR 273, 123 ILR 24. See also *Naït-Liman v Switzerland*, Judgment of the Grand Chamber of the European Court of Human Rights of 15 March 2018.

[113] *Jurisdictional Immunities of the State* (n 111).

might apply in criminal proceedings against an official of the State' was not an issue in this case.[114] In the South African context, the Supreme Court of Appeal in *Minister of Justice v SALC* took the view that *jus cogens* norms did not establish exceptions to the customary international law immunity of heads of state from foreign criminal jurisdiction.[115] However, two cautionary notes should be made. First, the Court did find that under South African domestic law there was indeed an exception created by statute. Secondly, the conclusion that *jus cogens* did not establish an exception appears limited to the immunity of heads of state, heads of government and ministers for foreign affairs.

A development related to *jus cogens* is the emergence of the concept of obligations *erga omnes*, which developed in response to the *South West Africa Cases* of 1966,[116] in which the International Court of Justice denied legal standing to Ethiopia and Liberia to enforce an obligation owed to the international community—namely the obligation on the part of the South African government to 'promote to the utmost the material and moral well-being and social progress' of the people of South West Africa (Namibia).[117] In 1970, in *Barcelona Traction, Light and Power Company Limited*,[118] the International Court went out of its way to repudiate its finding of 1966 in an *obiter dictum*, which indicated that a litigant state would no longer be required to prove a national interest in the subject matter of its claim where an obligation of concern to all states—an obligation *erga omnes*—was involved. Here, the Court stated:

> [A]n essential distinction should be drawn between the obligations of a state towards the international community as a whole, and those arising *vis-à-vis* another state in the field of diplomatic protection. By their very nature the former are the concern of all states. In view of the importance of the rights involved, all States can be held to have a legal interest in their protection; they are obligations *erga omnes*.
>
> Such obligations derive, for example, in contemporary international law, from the outlawing of acts of aggression, and of genocide, as also from the principles and rules concerning the basic rights of the human person, including protection from slavery and racial discrimination.[119]

[114] *Jurisdictional Immunities of the State* (n 111) para 91. See also *Al-Adsani* (n 112) para 61.

[115] *Minister of Justice v SALC* (n 28).

[116] *South West Africa Cases* (n 14).

[117] See, for discussion, J Allain 'Decolonisation as the source of the concepts of *jus cogens* and obligations *erga omnes*' 2016 *Ethiopian Yearbook of International Law* 35.

[118] 1970 ICJ Reports 3. See further J Dugard '1966 and all that: The *South West Africa* judgment revisited in the *East Timor* case' (1996) 8 *African Journal of International and Comparative Law* 549.

[119] At 32.

As the International Court was itself responsible for first expounding the notion of obligations *erga omnes*, it is not surprising that it was more willing to recognise this concept than it was to recognise the concept of *jus cogens*. In the *East Timor* case, the Court accepted that the right of peoples to self-determination 'has an *erga omnes* character',[120] and, in its advisory opinion on *Legal Consequences of the Construction of a Wall in the Occupied Palestinian Territory*,[121] the Court held that by constructing a wall within Palestinian territory, Israel had violated certain obligations *erga omnes*, notably 'the obligation to respect the right of the Palestinian people to self-determination, and certain of its obligations under international humanitarian law'.[122] It is noteworthy that all these obligations with an *erga omnes* character flow from norms that are recognised as being *jus cogens*.[123] It would thus seem that there is an inextricable link between *jus cogens* norms and obligations *erga omnes* in that the *erga omnes* nature of an obligation flows from the *jus cogens* character of the relevant norm.

In his dissenting opinion in the case *Certain Activities Carried Out by Nicaragua in the Border Area (Costa Rica v Nicaragua)*,[124] Judge ad hoc John Dugard stated that 'the release of carbon into the atmosphere and the loss of gas sequestration services is certainly an obligation *erga omnes*'.[125] In Judge ad hoc Dugard's opinion, the determination that an obligation is one of *erga omnes* must be relevant in assessing the quantum of damages for internationally wrongful acts.[126]

The International Law Commission has given recognition to the concepts of *jus cogens* and obligations *erga omnes* in its 2001 Draft Articles on the Responsibility of States for Internationally Wrongful Acts.[127] The Commission carefully constructs a scheme for the responsibility of states in the case of a breach of higher norms, which recognises both the notion of peremptory norms and the notion that certain obligations are owed to the international community as a whole. It attaches serious consequences to the breach of a peremptory

[120] *East Timor (Portugal v Australia)* 1995 ICJ Reports 90 at 102. See, too, *Application of the Convention on the Prevention and the Punishment of the Crime of Genocide, Preliminary Objections* 1996 ICJ Reports 595 at 616.

[121] 2004 ICJ Reports 136, (2004) 43 *ILM* 1009.

[122] Ibid para 155.

[123] *Third Report on Peremptory Norms of General International Law* (n 108) paras 108 et seq.

[124] Judgment of the International Court of Justice of 2 February 2018 (not yet reported).

[125] Ibid. Dissenting opinion of Judge ad hoc Dugard para 36.

[126] Ibid.

[127] 2001 Draft Articles on the Responsibility of States for Internationally Wrongful Acts, *Report of the International Law Commission, General Assembly Official Records* 56th Session, Supplement 10 (A/56/10) 29 (2001).

norm and recognises the right of non-injured states to institute proceedings and take measures on behalf of the international community as a whole against a state that has violated a 'higher norm'.

Articles 40 and 41 provide that states are obliged to co-operate in bringing to an end, through lawful means, 'serious breaches by a state of an obligation arising under a peremptory norm of a general international law'. They are also obliged to refrain from recognising as lawful a situation created by a serious breach of a peremptory norm. Moreover, in contrast to the decision of the International Court in the 1966 *South West Africa Cases*,[128] a non-injured state is entitled to invoke the responsibility of another state if the other state violates an obligation 'owed to the international community as a whole'.[129] The possibility of such a non-injured state applying measures against a delinquent state 'to ensure cessation of the breach and reparation in the interest of the injured state or of the beneficiaries of the obligation breached' is also contemplated.[130]

The notions of *jus cogens* and obligations *erga omnes* have had a profound effect on international law. Together they have transformed international law from a system in which all rules carried equal weight to a system of 'graduated normativity'[131] in which certain norms enjoy a higher status. Although this development has been challenged on the ground that international society has not evolved to the point where such a two-tier system of norms can be sustained,[132] there can be little doubt that it has transformed the nature and structure of international law.[133]

It is inconceivable that a state committed to compliance with international law, respect for human rights and the promotion of the rule of law under its own constitutional order would tolerate the violation of a norm of *jus cogens*. The *obiter dictum* of the Cape Provincial Division in *Azanian Peoples' Organisation (AZAPO) v Truth and Reconciliation Commission*,[134] that South Africa's constitutional rules 'would, it would seem, enable Parliament to pass a law even if such law is contrary to the *jus cogens*',[135] is therefore unfortunate. The

[128] Above (n 14).

[129] Draft Articles on State Responsibility (n 127).

[130] Ibid article 54.

[131] Weil (n 50).

[132] Ibid.

[133] On the impact of peremptory norms on the international legal order, see A Ferreira-Snyman 'Sovereignty and the changing nature of international law: Towards a world law?' (2007) 40 *CILSA* 395.

[134] 1996 (4) SA 562 (C).

[135] At 574B–C.

failure of the Court to consider the full implications of its *dictum* suggests that it had little understanding of the role of *jus cogens* in the international legal order, and of the importance of ensuring harmony between domestic constitutional norms and the peremptory norms of international law.

CHAPTER 4

The Place of International Law in South African Municipal Law

John Dugard and Andreas Coutsoudis

The relationship between international law and municipal law troubles both theorists and courts. There are two main approaches to this subject—the monist and the dualist.[1]

The monist school, whose leading exponents are Kelsen, Verdross, and Scelle, maintains 'that international and municipal law, far from being essentially different, must be regarded as manifestations of a single conception of law'.[2] Consequently, monists argue that municipal courts are obliged to apply rules of international law directly without the need for any act of adoption by the courts, or transformation by the legislature. For them, international law is incorporated into municipal law without any act of adoption or transformation—hence the fact that the monist position is often described as lending support to a 'doctrine of incorporation'.

Dualists, led by Triepel and Anzilotti, see international law and municipal law as completely different systems of law, with the result that international law may be applied by domestic courts only if 'adopted' by such courts, or transformed into local law by legislation.[3] Lauterpacht portrays the dualist position as follows:[4]

> According to the dualistic view, international and municipal law differ so radically in the matter of subjects of the law, its sources and its substance, that a rule of international law can never *per se* become part of the law of the land; it must be made so by the express or implied authority of the state. Thus conceived, the dualistic view is merely a manifestation of the traditional positivist attitude.

While maintaining that international law is not foreign law,

[1] For an examination of this debate, see JG Starke 'Monism and dualism in the theory of international law' (1936) 17 *BYIL* 66; C Roodt 'National law and treaties' (1987–1988) 13 *SAYIL* 72.

[2] 'International law and municipal law' in E Lauterpacht (ed) *International Law: Being the Collected Papers of Hersch Lauterpacht* vol I *The General Works* (1970) 216 at 217.

[3] For a discussion of the adoption and transformation theories, see F Morgenstern 'Judicial practice and the supremacy of international law' (1950) 27 *BYIL* 42.

[4] Lauterpacht (n 2) 216.

monists have been compelled to accept that the whole body of international law binding on a state cannot be directly applied by municipal courts. This has led to the emergence of the 'harmonisation theory', which qualifies the absolute monist position by acknowledging that in cases of conflict between international law and municipal law the judge must apply his country's own jurisdictional rules.[5] This means that customary international law is to be applied directly as part of the common law, but that conflicting statutory rules and acts of state may prevail over international law. In this way, 'harmony' is achieved between international law and municipal law.

Whatever the jurisprudential basis for the application of international law in municipal law may be, the undeniable fact is that international law is today applied in municipal courts with more frequency than in the past. In so doing, courts seldom question the theoretical explanation for their recourse to international law.[6]

ROMAN-DUTCH LAW

The monist–dualist debate postdates the classical period of Roman-Dutch scholarship. Nevertheless, it is illuminating to examine the attitude of Roman-Dutch law to international law, particularly as it now has constitutional endorsement.

Grotius saw international law and municipal law as components of a universal legal order premised on natural law.[7] He drew no clear distinction between international law and municipal law, and certainly did not regard international law as a foreign legal system. Thus, *De Jure Belli ac Pacis*, which claims to be a treatise on international law, expounds on a number of municipal law topics, such as contract, delict, family relations and criminal law. Although Van Bynkershoek did not share Grotius's faith in natural law, he likewise failed to distinguish between international law and municipal law. Thus, his major work *Quaestionum Juris Publici* contains an integrated study of problems of international law and Dutch public

[5] DP O'Connell *International Law* 2 ed (1970) vol 1 at 44–5; H Booysen *Volkereg en sy Verhouding tot die Suid Afrikaanse Reg* (1989) 68–9.

[6] See S Fatima *Using International Law in Domestic Courts* (2005); Y Shany *Regulating Jurisprudential Relations between National and International Courts* (2007); A Nollkaemper *Domestic Courts and the Rule of International Law* (2009); D Sloss (ed) *The Role of Domestic Courts in Treaty Enforcement: A Comparative Study* (2009); J Nijman and A Nollkaemper (eds) *New Perspectives on the Divide between National and International Law* (2007); International Law Association *Final Report of the Study Group on Principles on the Engagement of Domestic Courts with International Law* (2016).

[7] *De Jure Belli ac Pacis*, Prolegomena paras 16–18; *Inleiding tot de Hollandsche Rechtsgeleertheyd* 1.2.10–13.

law. According to De Louter, in his introduction to Tenney Frank's translation of this work, Van Bynkershoek

> disdains the important demarcation between international and national public law and freely intermingles questions of real international relations with those which only concern the constitution of his country and are ruled by national laws and customs. The result is a medley of materials not always easy to disentangle.[8]

Roman-Dutch law writers generally accepted Grotius's approach to the nature of law and consequently drew no sharp distinction between international law and municipal law.[9] Thus, they did not hesitate to apply international law rules in the municipal law of Holland.[10] The contention that international law and municipal law are inherently different legal orders—to be treated as such—was raised only at the end of the 19th century and, consequently, did not concern the Roman-Dutch jurists. Moreover, it is unlikely that they would have been persuaded by this argument as their loyalty to natural law was largely unquestioning,[11] and, according to the tenets of natural law, international law and municipal law are components of a universal legal order. In these circumstances, it is possible to assert that under Roman-Dutch law international law formed part of municipal law.[12]

After the British occupation in 1806, the Cape retained Roman-Dutch law as its common law, and this common law was in due course accepted by the other colonies and states in southern Africa. This meant that international law remained part of the common law of South Africa and was applied directly by the courts without any statutory incorporation.[13] The extent to which this principle applied in the South African Republic is illustrated by the extravagant comments of Kotzé CJ and Jorissen J in CC *Maynard et alii v The Field*

[8] Cornelis van Bynkershoek *Quaestionum Juris Publici Libri Duo II*, translation in J Brown Scott (ed) *The Classics of International Law* (1930) xl–xli.

[9] Writers use the term 'law of nations' loosely to include both international law and the Roman law *ius gentium*: see Huber *Heedendaegse Rechtsgeleertheyt* 1.2.21, 2; Voet *Commentarius ad Pandectas* 1.1.18, 19.

[10] See, for example, Van der Linden *Rechtsgeleerd Practicaal en Koopmans Handboek* 4.2 (on maritime law). See, too, AJGM Sanders 'The applicability of customary international law in municipal law—South Africa's monist tradition' (1977) 40 *THRHR* 147 at 148.

[11] See JW Wessels *History of Roman-Dutch Law* (1908) 285, 291–3. At 293, he declares that 'natural law . . . was the cornerstone of the whole fabric' of Roman-Dutch law.

[12] This view is challenged by Hercules Booysen: 'Is gewoonteregtelike volkereg deel van ons reg?' (1975) 38 *THRHR* 315 at 316; *Volkereg* (n 5) 77.

[13] One of the earliest reported cases in which principles of international law were invoked was *Ncumata v Matwa* (1881–1882) 2 EDC 272 at 279.

Cornet of Pretoria.[14] After citing with approval a passage from Wharton's *Digest* that 'the Law of Nations makes an integral part of the laws of the land', Kotzé CJ continued that it followed

> as put by Sir Henry Maine 'that the state which disclaims the authority of International Law places herself outside the circle of civilized nations'. It is only by a strict adherence to these recognized principles that our young state can hope to acquire and maintain the respect of all civilised communities, and so preserve its own national independence.[15]

In a similar vein, Jorissen J declared in respect of 'the great principles of modern international law':[16]

> There is no doubt that the laws of this Republic must be viewed and interpreted, in case of ambiguity, with due regard to the higher law, which is accepted in all civilized countries as ideal without further proof.

The Anglo-Boer War (1899–1902) raised a wide range of international law problems,[17] some of which came before the municipal courts of southern Africa. The rights of belligerents,[18] the confiscation of property for war purposes,[19] the seizure of enemy property,[20] and the legality of the annexation of the Boer republics[21] were considered by municipal courts within the context of international law. The views of Roman-Dutch jurists, particularly Grotius, and other publicists were examined in the search for the relevant rule of international law, and in no case was it suggested that international law was a foreign system of law.

ANGLO-AMERICAN LAW

Before 1994, South Africa's constitutional system was modelled on that of Britain. Consequently, South African courts frequently turned to English law, rather than Roman-Dutch law, for guidance on

[14] (1894) 1 SAR 214.

[15] At 223.

[16] At 232.

[17] For a discussion of some of the problems that did not come to court, see T Baty *International Law in South Africa* (1900). He deals with issues such as contraband for neutral ports (Delagoa Bay), the sovereignty of the South African Republic, passage of troops over neutral territory, and the conduct of hostilities. This fair-minded treatise is, surprisingly, singularly lacking in jingoism.

[18] *Mshwakezele v Guduza* (1901) 18 SC 167 at 171; *Van Deventer v Hancke & Mossop* 1903 TS 401 at 419, 424; *Lemkuhl v Kock* 1903 TS 451 at 454; *Olivier v Wessels* 1904 TS 235 at 241; *R v Louw* (1904) 21 SC 36 at 40–1, 46–7.

[19] *Alexander v Pfau* 1902 TS 155 at 159–61, 163–4, 166.

[20] *Du Toit v Kruger* (1905) 22 SC 234 at 237, 239; *Achterberg v Glinister* 1903 TS 326 at 330.

[21] *Van Deventer v Hancke & Mossop* (n 18) 409–10.

questions of public law, including public international law.[22] As English law, like Roman-Dutch law, treats customary international law as part of municipal law,[23] recourse to English law simply confirmed the common-law rule governing the relationship between international law and municipal law. The occasional reference to American law[24] further cemented the position as American law likewise treats customary international law as part of domestic law.[25]

SOUTH AFRICAN LAW BEFORE 1994[26]

International law is essentially made up of treaties, reflecting the *express* agreement of states, and custom, which comprises those rules

[22] See, for example, *Lendalease Finance Co (Pty) Ltd v Corporation de Mercadeo Agricola* 1975 (4) SA 397 (C). See further J Dugard 'The purist legal method, international law and sovereign immunity' in JJ Gauntlett (ed) *JC Noster: 'n Feesbundel* (1979) 36 at 45–9.

[23] For the position in English law, see Lauterpacht (n 2); O'Connell (n 5). The strongest assertion of this position appears in a *dictum* of Lord Denning MR in *Trendtex Trading Corporation v Central Bank of Nigeria* (1977) QB 529 (CA) 553–4: 'A fundamental question arises for decision: what is the place of international law in our English law? One school of thought holds to the doctrine of *incorporation*. It says that the rules of international law are incorporated into English law automatically and considered to be part of English law unless they are in conflict with an Act of Parliament. The other school of thought holds to the doctrine of *transformation*. It says that the rules of international law are not to be considered as part of English law except insofar as they have been already adopted and made part of our law by the decisions of judges, or by Act of Parliament, or long established custom. The difference is vital when you are faced with a change in the rules of international law. Under the doctrine of incorporation, when the rules of international law change, our English law changes with them. But, under the doctrine of transformation, the English law does not change. It is bound by precedent. . . . As between these schools of thought, I now believe that the doctrine of incorporation is correct. Otherwise I do not see that our courts could ever recognise a change in the rules of international law.'

See, too, *R v Jones* [2006] UKHL 16, 132 ILR 668; R O'Keefe 'The doctrine of incorporation revisited' (2008) 79 *BYIL* 7.

[24] *South Atlantic Islands Development Corporation v Buchan* 1971 (1) SA 234 (C) 238B–F.

[25] *The Paquete Habana* 175 US 677 (1900) 700; *Banco Nacional de Cuba v Sabbatino, Receiver, et al* 376 US 398 (1964) 423; ED Dickinson 'The law of nations as part of the national law of the United States' (1952) 101 *Univ of Pennsylvania LR* 26, 792; L Henkin *Foreign Affairs and the Constitution* (1972) 222–3. JF Murphy *The United States and the Rule of Law in International Affairs* (2004).

[26] See RP Schaffer (Balkin) 'The inter-relationship between public international law and the law of South Africa: An overview' (1983) 32 *ICLQ* 277; JW Bridge 'The relationship between international law and the law of South Africa' (1971) 20 *ICLQ* 746; Booysen (n 12) 315 et seq and ch 3 respectively; DJ Devine 'Qualifications on the incorporation of international customary law into South African municipal law' (1973) 1 *Natal Univ LR* 58; J Dugard 'International law is part of our law' (1971) 88 *SALJ* 13; Sanders (n 10); AJGM Sanders 'The applicability of customary international law in South African Law—The Appeal Court has spoken' (1978) 11 *CILSA* 198; G Erasmus

of international conduct to which states have given their *tacit* consent. Different rules applied to the applicability of treaties in South African law before 1994 because treaties were entered into by the executive alone without the endorsement of the legislature.[27]

1 Customary international law

For over 100 years, South African courts simply assumed that the rules and principles of customary international law might be applied by municipal courts as if they were in some way part of South African law. Consequently, they did not require international law to be proved as a foreign legal system. Indeed, in 1971 in *South Atlantic Islands Development Corporation Ltd v Buchan*,[28] the Court refused to admit an affidavit from an expert on international law on the ground that international law was not foreign law and therefore could not be proved by affidavit. South African courts therefore showed strong support for the monist approach (the doctrine of incorporation) in respect of customary international law.

In most cases, courts applied customary international law without questioning its place in the legal order.[29] But in a number of cases, commencing in 1971 with *South Atlantic Islands Development Corporation Ltd v Buchan*,[30] the courts expressly asserted that international law 'forms part of our law' and that it was the duty of a municipal court 'to ascertain and administer the appropriate rule of international law'.

While the Cape Provincial Division in *South Atlantic Islands*[31] found support for the proposition that international law is part of our law in

'The Namibian Constitution and the application of international law' (1989–1990) 15 *SAYIL* 81 at 85–92; N Botha 'The coming of age of public international law in South Africa' (1992–1993) 18 *SAYIL* 36.

[27] In terms of s 6(2)*(e)* of the Republic of South Africa Constitution Act 110 of 1983.

[28] 1971 (1) SA 234 (C) 238B–F. Confirmed in *Southern Africa Litigation Centre v Minister of Justice and Constitutional Development* 2015 (5) SA 1 (GP) para 5. For an early *dictum* that international law need not be proved, see *CC Maynard v The Field Cornet of Pretoria* (n 14) 232.

[29] For example, *Ex parte Belli* 1914 CPD 742 at 745–6; *Marburger v The Minister of Finance* 1918 CPD 183 at 187; (1) *De Howorth v The SS 'India'*; (2) *Mann, George & Co (Delagoa) Ltd v The SS 'India'* 1921 CPD 451 at 457–8; *Crooks and Company v Agricultural Co-operative Union Ltd* 1922 AD 423; *R v Lionda* 1944 AD 348 at 352; *Ex parte Sulman* 1942 CPD 407; *S v Penrose* 1966 (1) SA 5 (N) 10.

[30] Supra (n 28) 283C–D. See, also, *Inter-Science Research and Development Services (Pty) Ltd v Republica Popular de Mocambique* 1980 (2) SA 111 (T) 124H; *Kaffraria Property Co (Pty) Ltd v Government of the Republic of Zambia* 1980 (2) SA 709 (E) 712E–G, 715A; *Yorigami Maritime Construction Co Ltd v Nissho-Iwai Co Ltd* 1977 (4) SA 682 (C) 696E; *Ex parte Schumann* 1940 NPD 251 at 254. Cf *Parkin v Government of the République Démocratique du Congo* 1971 (1) SA 259 (W), which shows support for the adoption theory (261A).

[31] Supra (n 28) 238C–E.

Anglo-American law, the Appellate Division stressed, in *Nduli v Minister of Justice*,[32] that 'the *fons et origo* of this proposition must be found in Roman-Dutch law'.[33] This served as an important reminder that the rule favouring the incorporation of customary international law into South African law is derived from Roman-Dutch law and not English law.

Before 1994, there was one isolated case in which customary international law was transformed into municipal law by legislation. The Prize Jurisdiction Act,[34] which confers prize jurisdiction on all divisions of the Supreme Court of South Africa, defines 'prize' for the purposes of the Act as, inter alia, 'a ship or aircraft captured as prize *jure belli*'. This statutory incorporation of the law of war in prize cases was unnecessary, as the Minister of Justice himself admitted when he explained, in introducing the second reading of the Bill, that '[t]he present position is that our courts have to consult international law in determining what is a prize' and that the purpose of the statutory reference to the law of war was to make it clear that this remained the position.[35] This exceptional case of statutory incorporation *ex abundanti cautela* therefore lends support to the monist position rather than that of the dualists.

As customary international law is a species of common law, it was subordinate to all forms of legislation.[36] There was, however, a statutory presumption that the legislature did not intend to violate international law.[37] Although some decisions asserted that customary international law was subordinate to the common law,[38] there was only one case in which this matter was considered and there the Court gave priority to the rule of customary international law.[39]

[32] 1978 (1) SA 893 (A).

[33] At 906B. The suggestion by Booysen (n 5) 69–70 that the *dictum* in *Nduli* gives support to the dualist adoption theory is discussed and dismissed in the first edition of this work at 43–4.

[34] Act 3 of 1968, s 1.

[35] *House of Assembly Debates* vol 22, col 337 (12 February 1968).

[36] *Alexander v Pfau* (n 19) 159, 164; *Inter-Science Research and Development Services (Pty) Ltd v Republica Popular de Mocambique* (n 30) 124H; *Kaffraria Property Co (Pty) Ltd v Government of the Republic of Zambia* (n 30) 712F, 715A; *Binga v Administrator-General, South West Africa* 1984 (3) SA 949 (SWA) 967F.

[37] GE Devenish *Interpretation of Statutes* (1992) 212; *CC Maynard v The Field Cornet of Pretoria* (n 14) 222–3, 232; *Achterberg v Glinister* (n 20) 334; *Claassens v Wilkens* 1905 ORC 139 141; *R v Lionda* (n 29) 352; *S v Penrose* (n 29) 11E–F; *Hajaree v Ismail* 1905 TS 451 at 456; *Ex parte Adair Properties (Pvt) Ltd* 1967 (2) SA 622 (R) 627B–F.

[38] See cases referred to in n 36.

[39] *Liebowitz v Schwartz* 1974 (2) SA 661 (T) 662A.

2 Treaties and municipal courts[40]

In South Africa,[41] as in the United Kingdom, the power to enter into treaties was entrusted completely to the executive. The legislature played no part in the treaty-making process. Consequently, if treaties were to have become part of South African law without legislative endorsement, wide law-making powers would have been conferred on the executive. This explains why treaties, in most instances, did not become part of municipal law without some act of legislative transformation.[42]

The need for legislation to transform a treaty into South African law was clearly spelled out by Steyn CJ in *Pan American World Airways Incorporated v SA Fire and Accident Insurance Co Ltd*[43] when he stated that it was

> trite law . . . that in this country the conclusion of a treaty, convention or agreement by the South African government with any other government is an executive and not a legislative act. As a general rule, the provisions of an international instrument so concluded, are not embodied in our law except by legislative process . . . In the absence of any enactment giving [its] relevant provisions the force of law, [it] cannot affect the rights of the subject.

The principle of transformation was also extended to resolutions of the General Assembly and Security Council of the United Nations.[44]

Numerous treaties were transformed into South African law by legislative means. But the most important multilateral treaty in the modern world, the Charter of the United Nations, which South Africa signed and ratified in 1945, was not and still has not been enacted into our law.

[40] Roodt (n 1).

[41] See s 6(2)*(e)* of the Republic of South Africa Constitution Act 110 of 1983.

[42] *Minister of the Interior v Bechler; Beier v Minister of the Interior* 1948 (3) SA 409 (A) 447. See, too, *Ex parte Savage* 1914 CPD 827 at 830; *Policansky v Minister of Agriculture* 1946 CPD 860 at 865.

[43] 1965 (3) SA 150 (A) 161C–D. This *dictum* was confirmed by the Appellate Division in *S v Tuhadeleni* 1969 (1) SA 153 (A) 173–5. See, also, *Maluleke v Minister of Internal Affairs* 1981 (1) SA 707 (B) 712; *Binga v Administrator-General, South West Africa* (n 36) 968B–C; *Tshwete v Minister of Home Affairs* 1988 (4) SA 586 (A) 606; *S v Muchindu* 1995 (2) SA 36 (W) 38H–I; *AZAPO v President of the Republic of South Africa* 1996 (4) SA 671 (CC) 688 (para 26).

[44] *Binga v Administrator-General, South West Africa* (n 36) 968E.

THE NEW CONSTITUTIONAL ORDER[45]

1 The 1993 and 1996 Constitutions

In 1993, 26 political groups assembled at Kempton Park to draft a constitution to bring an end to the apartheid legal order. As these groups were in most instances unelected, and simply reflected the political realities of the time, it was considered inappropriate to confer on them the power to draft a final constitution. Instead, the constitution which they fashioned in negotiations that lasted some six months was to serve as an 'interim' constitution, pending the drafting of a constitution by a democratically elected constitutional assembly. As the Interim Constitution represented a political compromise between rival groups, notably the National Party (which had

[45] There is a wealth of literature on the place of international law in the new constitutional order. The following selection takes account of the writings on the Interim Constitution (1993), suggestions for the 'final' Constitution and the 'final' Constitution (1996) itself. N Botha 'International law and the South African Interim Constitution' (1994) 9 *SA Public Law* 245; M Olivier 'The status of international law in South African municipal law: Section 231 of the 1993 Constitution' (1993–4) 19 *SAYIL* 1; T Maluwa 'International human rights norms and the South African Interim Constitution' (1993–4) 19 *SAYIL* 14; N Botha 'Interpreting a treaty endorsed under the 1993 Constitution' (1993–4) 19 *SAYIL* 148; DJ Devine 'The relationship between international law and municipal law in the light of the Interim South African Constitution 1993' (1995) 44 *ICLQ* 1; DJ Devine 'Some problems relating to treaties in the Interim South African Constitution and some suggestions for the definitive Constitution' (1995) 20 *SAYIL* 1; N Botha 'Incorporation of treaties under the Interim Constitution: A pattern emerges?' (1995) 20 *SAYIL* 196; J Dugard 'International law and the final Constitution' (1995) 11 *SAJHR* 241; J Dugard 'The influence of international human rights law on the South African Constitution' (1996) 49 *Current Legal Problems* 305; R Keightley 'Public international law and the final Constitution' (1996) 12 *SAJHR* 405; E de Wet 'The place of public international law in the new South African constitutional order' (1998) 1 *Recht in Afrika* 207; HA Strydom 'The international law openness of the South African Constitution' in G Carpenter and N Botha (eds) *Suprema Lex: Essays on the Constitution Presented to Marinus Wiechers* (1997); J Dugard 'International law and the South African Constitution' (1997) 8 *European Journal of International Law* 77; RC Blake 'The world's law in one country: The South African Constitutional Court's use of public international law' (1998) 115 *SALJ* 668; M Olivier 'Informal international agreements under the 1996 Constitution' (1997) 22 *SAYIL* 63; N Botha 'Treaties after the 1996 Constitution: More questions than answers' (1997) 22 *SAYIL* 95; M du Plessis 'The extra-territorial application of the South African Constitution' (2003) 120 *SALJ* 797; E de Wet 'The friendly but cautious reception of international law in the jurisprudence of the South African Constitutional Court: Some critical remarks' (2005) 28 *Fordham International Law Review* 101; E de Wet 'The status of international law in the South African legal order' in D Shelton (ed) *International Law and Domestic Legal Systems: Incorporation, Transformation and Persuasion* (2011); E Cameron 'Constitutionalism, rights, and international law: The Glenister decision' (2013) 23 *Duke Journal of Comparative & International Law* 389; E de Wet, H Hestermeyer and R Wolfrum (eds) *The Implementation of International Law in Germany and South Africa* (2015).

ruled South Africa since 1948) and the African National Congress (outlawed from 1960 to 1990), it was agreed at Kempton Park that the 'final' constitution would comply with 34 constitutional principles contained in a schedule to the Interim Constitution and that the Constitutional Court created by the 1993 Interim Constitution would be empowered to pronounce on the issue of compliance. This Interim Constitution, approved at Kempton Park, was duly endorsed by the last apartheid Parliament and became the Constitution of the Republic of South Africa Act 200 of 1993.

On 27 April 1994, the Interim Constitution came into effect to govern South Africa's first democratic elections. The Parliament thus served the dual role of legislature and Constitutional Assembly. From January 1995 to May 1996, the Constitutional Assembly met regularly to draft the 'final' constitution in accordance with the 34 constitutional principles agreed upon at Kempton Park. A draft constitution was approved by the required two-thirds majority vote in the Constitutional Assembly on 8 May and was forwarded to the Constitutional Court for certification. The Constitutional Court, however, found fault with a number of provisions in the draft constitution,[46] on the grounds that they failed to comply with the constitutional principles contained in the Interim Constitution, and referred it back to the Constitutional Assembly. After these faults had been remedied by the Constitutional Assembly, the Constitutional Court gave its final approval to the Constitution on 4 December 1996.[47] The new Constitution—the Constitution of the Republic of South Africa, 1996[48]—was signed into law by President Mandela on 10 December 1996.

Previous South African constitutions made no mention of the place of international law in the South African legal order. Both the 1993 and the 1996 Constitutions remedied this omission to ensure that 'international law has a special place in our law'.[49] As the two Constitutions are similar in most respects in their treatment of

[46] *Ex parte Chairperson of the Constitutional Assembly: In re Certification of the Constitution of the Republic of South Africa* 1996 (4) SA 744 (CC).

[47] *Ex parte Chairperson of the Constitutional Assembly: In re Certification of the Amended Text of the Constitution of the Republic of South Africa, 1996* 1997 (2) SA 97 (CC).

[48] While initially the 1996 Constitution bore an Act number (Act 108 of 1996), in terms of s 1(1) of the Citation of Constitutional Laws Act 5 of 2005, 'no Act number is to be associated with the Constitution' from 27 June 2005 (the date of commencement of the Act) and in terms of s 2(2) '[a]ny reference to the "Constitution of the Republic of South Africa, 1996 (Act No 108 of 1996)" contained in any law in force immediately prior to the commencement of that Act, must be construed as a reference to the "Constitution of the Republic of South Africa, 1996"'.

[49] See the comment by Ngcobo CJ in *Glenister v President of the RSA* 2011 (3) 347 (CC) para 97.

international law, the present study will focus attention principally on the 1996 Constitution. Divergences between the two Constitutions will, however, be examined.

2 Customary international law

South African common law treats international law as part of municipal law, as shown above. The common law is given constitutional endorsement by s 232 of the 1996 Constitution, which provides that: 'Customary international law is law in the Republic unless it is inconsistent with the Constitution or an Act of Parliament.'[50]

There can be little doubt that the 'constitutionalisation' of this rule gives it additional weight. Moreover, customary international law is no longer subject to subordinate legislation. Only a provision of the Constitution or an Act of Parliament that is clearly inconsistent with customary international law will trump it. This is emphasised by s 233 of the 1996 Constitution, which provides that:

> When interpreting any legislation, every court must prefer any reasonable interpretation of the legislation that is consistent with international law over any alternative interpretation that is inconsistent with international law.

Common-law rules and judicial decisions are now subordinate to customary international law as it is only the Constitution and Acts of Parliament that enjoy greater legal weight. There can be no suggestion therefore that a new rule of customary international law must give way to South African judicial decisions recognising an earlier rule. Consequently, the doctrine of *stare decisis* cannot be invoked as an obstacle to the application of a new rule of international law. This accords with the *dictum* of Eksteen J in *Kaffraria Property Co (Pty) Ltd v Government of the Republic of Zambia*,[51] in which he applied the principle expounded by Lord Denning MR in the *Trendtex* case[52] that 'international law knows no rule of *stare decisis*'.[53]

3 Proof of customary international law

As noted above, s 232 expressly provides that 'customary international law' (in its totality) is law in South Africa, unless the customary international law in question is inconsistent with the Constitution or an Act of Parliament. This makes clear that s 232 compels courts to undertake a two-stage inquiry. First, a court must determine what the relevant customary international law is in relation to the issue facing

[50] See the remarks of Sachs J on s 232 in *S v Basson* 2005 (1) SA 171 (CC) 216.

[51] Supra (n 30) 715. This matter was deliberately left open by Margo J in *Inter-Science Research and Development Services (Pty) Ltd v Republica Popular de Mocambique* (n 30) 125G–H.

[52] *Trendtex Trading Corporation v Central Bank of Nigeria* [1977] QB 529 (CA).

[53] At 554.

the court. Secondly, having determined the customary international law position, the court must determine whether the relevant customary international law is consistent with the Constitution and domestic legislation. Therefore, it is necessary to turn to both pre-constitutional and post-constitutional judicial precedent in relation to how rules of customary international law are to be determined or proved and then applied.

Since international law is not foreign law, courts may take judicial notice of it as if it were part of our own common law. In practice, this means that courts turn to the judicial decisions of international tribunals and domestic courts, both South African and foreign,[54] and to international law treatises for guidance as to whether a particular rule is accepted as a rule of customary international law on the ground that it meets the twin qualifications of *usus* and *opinio juris*.[55]

Some pre-constitutional South African decisions suggest that our law requires a more stringent test for the acceptance of custom than international law itself demands. In 1905, De Villiers CJ suggested that for a customary rule to be applied, it was necessary that it be 'universally accepted'.[56] Similar language was employed by Rumpff CJ in *Nduli* when he stated:[57]

> It was conceded by counsel for appellants that according to our law only such rules of customary international law are to be regarded as part of our law as are either *universally recognized* or have received the assent of this country . . . . I think that this concession was rightly made.

This test is too strictly formulated. It is therefore necessary to add

[54] See Dugard (n 22). See also *Minister of Justice and Constitutional Development v Southern Africa Litigation Centre* 2016 (3) SA 317 (SCA) ('*Minister of Justice v SALC*'), a case relating to the government's failure to arrest President al-Bashir of Sudan, where Wallis JA, in considering whether there was an exception to the customary international law rule of immunity for heads of state who are alleged to have committed international crimes, held (para 70) that '[i]n the absence of a binding treaty or other international instrument creating such an exception, or an established universal practice in the affairs of nations, one looks to the decisions of international courts for guidance as to the existence of such an exception'.

[55] See Chapter 3.

[56] *Du Toit v Kruger* (n 20). Here, the Chief Justice stated (at 238): 'The modern authorities, to which this court has been referred, on the rights of capture during war do not afford much assistance for the decision of the appeal. The rules which are laid down by some writers for exempting the private property of an enemy from capture have not been so *universally accepted and acted upon as to justify this court in treating them as binding principles of law*' (emphasis added).

[57] Supra (n 32) 906D (emphasis added). For a full examination of this *dictum*, see D Devine 'What international customary law is part of South African law?' (1987–1988) 13 *SAYIL* 119. Support for the *dictum* in *Nduli* is to be found in the judgment of Patel J in *Van Zyl v Government of the RSA* 2005 (11) BCLR 1106 (T) para 91.

the qualification introduced by Margo J in *Inter-Science Research and Development Services (Pty) Ltd v Republica Popular de Mocambique*:[58]

> The concept of universal recognition in this context is obviously not an absolute one, despite the ordinary meaning of the word 'universal', for, 'if a custom becomes established as a general rule of international law, it binds all states which have not opposed it, whether or not they themselves played an active part in its formation'.

This qualification was confirmed by Conradie J in *S v Petane*:[59]

> It is not clear to me whether Rumpff CJ in giving the judgment [in *Nduli*] meant to lay down any stricter requirements for the incorporation of international law usages into South African law than the requirements laid down by international law itself for the acceptance of usages by states. International law does not require universal acceptance for a usage of states to become a custom. . . . Margo J, in giving the judgment of the full Transvaal court in *Inter-Science Research and Development Services (Pty) Ltd v Republica Popular de Mocambique* 1980 (2) SA 111 (T), did not think that the word 'universal', despite its ordinary meaning, was really intended to mean universal. I do not think so either. In the present case, however, the distinction between universal and general recognition makes no difference. *I am prepared to accept that where a rule of customary international law is recognized as such by international law it will be so recognized by our law.*

The correct approach to be adopted is well illustrated by Conradie J's judgment in *S v Petane*, in which he considered the question whether the 1977 Protocol I to the Geneva Conventions of 1949 had become part of customary international law by examining resolutions of the General Assembly, state practice and the writings of jurists. In the course of this judgment, he stated:[60]

> I am . . . prepared to accept that customary international law may . . . be created very quickly, but before it will be considered by our municipal law as being incorporated into South African law the custom, whether created by *usus* and *opinio juris* or only by the latter, would at the very least have to be widely accepted.

Section 231(4) of the Interim Constitution provided that 'the rules of customary international law *binding on the Republic* shall, unless inconsistent with this Constitution or an Act of Parliament, form part of the law of the Republic' (emphasis added). The omission of the word 'binding' from the 1996 Constitution has led one commentator to argue that all rules of customary international law, including those to which South Africa may have 'persistently objected', are part of

[58] Supra (n 30) 125A–B.

[59] 1988 (3) SA 51 (C) 56–7 (emphasis added).

[60] At 57H–I. Another case that affords a good illustration of the manner in which customary international law is to be ascertained is *Nkondo v Minister of Police* 1980 (2) SA 895 (O).

municipal law.[61] This, so it is argued, accords with a 1995 *dictum* of the Constitutional Court that the reference to international law in the Bill of Rights 'includes non-binding law as well'.[62]

The better view is that the word 'binding' was dropped from the 1996 Constitution on the grounds that it was considered to be unnecessary and, indeed, tautologous.[63] As far as South Africa is concerned, a practice to which it has persistently objected is simply not a customary rule. On the other hand, there can be little doubt that the omission of the word 'binding', with its undertones of strict consent, lends support to the proposition that widespread or general acceptance, as opposed to universal acceptance, is sufficient for proof of customary international law. This is the standard set by the International Court of Justice[64] and there is no reason why a South African court should demand a higher standard.

The Supreme Court of Appeal in *Minister of Justice v SALC*[65] (a matter which dealt with the South African government's failure to arrest Sudanese President al-Bashir pursuant to two arrest warrants issued by the International Criminal Court) was required to consider, for the purposes of domestic application, whether there was an international crimes exception to the personal immunity of heads of state as a matter of customary international law. Wallis JA held that one of the factors that a court would consider when seeking to determine whether such an exception existed (together, inter alia, with judgments by international courts) was whether there was an 'established universal practice in the affairs of nations'.[66] It is nevertheless clear from the judgment, read as a whole, that Wallis JA did not intend to suggest that such 'universal practice' was now to be regarded as the necessary standard for South African courts to accept a customary international law rule (or an exception thereto). Wallis JA, in concluding his analysis of the state of customary international law, emphasised that the constitutional role of domestic courts in South Africa was not to develop customary international law, but merely to ascertain the current state of that law and then to 'apply it'. Wallis JA held:

[61] R Keightley (n 45) at 408

[62] *S v Makwanyane* 1995 (3) SA 391 (CC) 413.

[63] N Botha 'International law and the South African Interim Constitution' (1994) 9 *SA Public Law* 245 at 255.

[64] *Fisheries Jurisdiction Case* 1974 ICJ Reports 3 at 23–6. The test of universal acceptance was rejected by Judge Lachs in his separate opinion in the *North Sea Continental Shelf Cases* 1969 ICJ Reports 3 at 229.

[65] Supra (n 54).

[66] *Minister of Justice v SALC* (n 54) para 70.

> *[O]ur task is to assess the state of customary international law as it stands at the present time and apply it*. That is what the Constitution requires us to do. While in other areas of the law the court's function includes the development of the law, in the area of customary international law its task is one of discerning the existing state of the law, not developing it. As Lord Hoffmann said in *Jones*:
>
> > 'It is not for a national Court to develop international law by unilaterally adopting a version of that law which, however desirable, forward-looking and reflective of values it may be, is simply not accepted by other states.'
>
> Development of customary international law occurs in international courts and tribunals, in the contents of international agreements and treaties and by general acceptance by the international community of nations in their relations with one another as to the laws that govern that community. However tempting it may be to a domestic court to seek to expand the boundaries of customary international law by domestic judicial decision, it is not in my view permissible for it to do so.[67]

Wallis JA therefore made it clear that he accepted that if a rule is recognised by international law as part of customary international law, then s 232 makes that rule law in South Africa (save if it is inconsistent with the Constitution or an Act of Parliament). Thus, South African courts are not entitled to include additional, more stringent requirements for the recognition and application of customary international law in South Africa than those accepted by international law itself. Conversely, it is not permissible for a South African court to expand the boundaries of customary international law beyond that recognised by international law. Therefore, s 232, as confirmed by Wallis JA in *Minister of Justice v SALC*, effectively gives the Constitution's imprimatur to Conradie J's statement in *S v Petane* that 'where a rule of customary international law is recognised as such by international law it will be so recognised by our law'[68] (obviously subject to the requirement of constitutional and legislative consistency).

In *National Commissioner v SALC*,[69] a case which dealt with the state's obligation to investigate allegations of torture committed in Zimbabwe by Zimbabwean officials, the Constitutional Court held that since torture is an international crime under customary international law (its prohibition is a peremptory norm of international law) s 232 of the Constitution makes torture a crime in South Africa.[70]

[67] *Minister of Justice v SALC* (n 54) para 74 (emphasis added) with reliance on *Jones v Ministry of the Interior (Saudi Arabia)* [2006] UKHL 26 para 63.

[68] *S v Petane* (n 59) 57.

[69] *National Commissioner of Police v Southern African Human Rights Litigation Centre* 2015 (1) SA 315 (CC) ('*National Commissioner v SALC*').

[70] Paragraphs 35 and 77. As the Court held, torture is also criminalised in South Africa under two domestication acts: the Prevention and Combating of Torture of Persons Act 13 of 2013 and the Implementation of the Rome Statute of the International Criminal Court Act 27 of 2002. Thus, as the Court held at para 39: 'In

4 Treaties[71]

Before 1994, South Africa followed the dualist approach to the incorporation of treaties. Treaties were negotiated, signed, ratified and acceded to by the executive. Only those treaties incorporated by Act of Parliament became part of South African law. Thus, treaty-making fell exclusively within the competence of the executive.

The 1993 Kempton Park negotiators were strongly motivated by considerations of transparency and accountability—which had played little role in the apartheid state. Thus, influenced by the Namibian Constitution,[72] they departed radically from the pre-1993 position in respect of the treaty-making power and incorporation of treaties. While the executive retained its power to negotiate and sign treaties under the Interim Constitution,[73] the National Assembly and Senate were required to 'agree to the ratification of and accession to' treaties.[74] Moreover, where the two houses of Parliament agreed to the ratification of or accession to a treaty, it became part of municipal law, 'provided Parliament expressly so provides'.[75]

The clear purpose of the Interim Constitution was to facilitate the incorporation of treaties into municipal law. The drafters of the Interim Constitution, however, failed to take account of the bureaucratic mind. Government departments, required to scrutinise treaties before they were submitted to Parliament, refused to present treaties to Parliament for its agreement to the ratification until they were completely satisfied that there would be no conflict between the provisions of the treaty and domestic law. The result was that few treaties were presented to Parliament expeditiously. The parliamentary procedures for dealing with treaties further delayed ratification.[76] Consequently, few of the treaties which Parliament agreed to

effect, torture is criminalised in South Africa under s 232 of the Constitution and the Torture Act whilst torture on the scale of crimes against humanity is criminalised under s 232 of the Constitution, the Torture Act and the ICC Act.' This case is further discussed in Chapter 9.

[71] See J Dugard 'South Africa' in D Sloss (ed) *The Role of Domestic Courts in Treaty Enforcement: A Comparative Study* (2009) 448.

[72] See articles 32(3)(e), 63(2)(e) and 144. The text of this Constitution appears in (1989–1990) 15 *SAYIL* 301.

[73] Section 82(1)*(i)* of the Interim Constitution empowered 'the President' to carry out this task, but in practice it was delegated to Ministers of state, particularly the Minister of Foreign Affairs.

[74] Section 231(2) of the Interim Constitution.

[75] Section 231(3) of the Interim Constitution.

[76] The post-apartheid Parliament relies heavily on committees. Thus, a treaty may have to be approved by several parliamentary committees before it is presented for ratification. See J Dugard and I Currie 'Public international law' 1995 *Annual Survey* 76 at 76–9.

ratify were incorporated into municipal law.[77] The hopes of the drafters of the 1993 Interim Constitution were therefore not realised: the ratification of treaties proved to be cumbersome and few treaties were incorporated into municipal law.

In these circumstances, the drafters of the 1996 Constitution elected to return to the pre-1994 position relating to the incorporation of treaties, without abandoning the need for parliamentary agreement to the ratification of or accession to treaties. Section 231 provides:

> (1) The negotiating and signing of all international agreements is the responsibility of the national executive.
> (2) An international agreement binds the Republic only after it has been approved by resolution in both the National Assembly and the National Council of Provinces, unless it is an agreement referred to in subsection (3).
> (3) An international agreement of a technical, administrative or executive nature, or an agreement which does not require either ratification of accession, entered into by the national executive, binds the Republic without approval by the National Assembly and the National Council of Provinces, but must be tabled in the Assembly and the Council within a reasonable time.
> (4) Any international agreement becomes law in the Republic when it is enacted into law by national legislation; but a self-executing provision of an agreement that has been approved by Parliament is law in the Republic unless it is inconsistent with the Constitution or an Act of Parliament.
> (5) The Republic is bound by international agreements which were binding on the Republic when this Constitution took effect.

Although this provision ensures that Parliament will continue to play an active role in treaty-making, it is unfortunate that the realities of the bureaucratic process compelled the Constitutional Assembly to require an Act of Parliament or other form of 'national legislation', in addition to the resolution of approval, for the incorporation of treaties into municipal law. It represents an abandonment of the idealism of 1993 that sought 'to bring international law and domestic law in harmony with each other'.[78]

The Interim Constitution suggested that all treaties signed by the executive were to be agreed to by Parliament before they could be ratified or acceded to on the international plane (by depositing of the necessary instruments with the relevant treaty depositary) or other-

[77] N Botha 'Incorporation of treaties under the Interim Constitution: A pattern emerges' (1995) 20 *SAYIL* 196.

[78] Keightley (n 45) 412.

wise made binding on South Africa.[79] This took no account of the fact that many treaties are intended to come into operation immediately, and that a slow parliamentary approval process would undermine the value of such treaties. Consequently, government departments ignored the letter of the Interim Constitution and distinguished between 'formal' treaties that required parliamentary approval, and less formal treaties that did not.[80] The 1996 Constitution recognises this distinction. While treaties that expressly or by necessary implication require ratification have to be approved by Parliament after signature, agreements of 'a technical, administrative or executive nature' and agreements that do not require ratification or accession do not require parliamentary approval to become binding, but must merely be tabled before Parliament in a reasonable time.[81] In practice, this may give rise to disputes about the precise meaning of the terms 'technical', 'administrative' or 'executive' in the context of treaty law.[82]

The only case that has dealt directly with the question of whether a particular international agreement is technical, administrative or executive in nature is *Earthlife Africa v Minister of Energy*.[83] At issue in the matter was an inter-governmental agreement in relation to nuclear co-operation and procurement between the Russian and South African governments. The agreement had been tabled before Parliament under s 231(3) of the Constitution. A two-judge bench of the Western Cape High Court was required to determine whether the agreement had been lawfully tabled under s 231(3) or whether the government should have tabled it under s 231(2) in order to seek parliamentary approval of the agreement. The parties accepted that the agreement did not make express provision for ratification; therefore, the only issue was whether it could rightly be classified as an agreement of a technical, administrative or executive nature. In finding that it could not be so classified, the Court held as follows:

[79] Section 231(2) of the Interim Constitution provided that 'Parliament shall . . . be competent to agree to the ratification of or accession to an international agreement negotiated and signed' by the executive.

[80] This interpretation was spelt out in a letter from the Minister of Foreign Affairs to other Ministers, titled 'Procedures for the Conclusion of International Agreements' of 13 June 1994.

[81] *Earthlife Africa v Minister of Energy* 2017 (5) SA 227 (WCC) ('*Earthlife Africa*') paras 122–8.

[82] N Botha 'Treaty making in South Africa: A reassessment' (2000) 25 *SAYIL* 69 at 75–8; J Schneeberger 'A labyrinth of tautology: The meaning of the term "international agreement" and its significance for South African law and treaty-making practice' (2001) 26 *SAYIL* 1 at 5–7; W Scholtz 'A few thoughts on s 231 of the South African Constitution' (2004) 29 *SAYIL* 202.

[83] *Earthlife Africa* (n 81).

> The tabling of an IGA under s 231(3) permits the executive to bind South Africa to an agreement without parliamentary approval or the public participation that often accompanies any such parliamentary-approval process. Limiting those international agreements which may be tabled under s 231(3) to a limited subset of run-of-the-mill agreements (or as Prof Dugard puts it, agreements 'of a routine nature, flowing from daily activities of government departments') which would not generally engage or warrant the focused attention or interest of Parliament would give optimal effect to the fundamental constitutional principles of the separation of powers, open and accountable government, and participatory democracy.[84]

The Court's interpretation is consistent with the purpose for referring to agreements of 'a technical, administrative or executive nature' in s 231(3) since it has been noted that '[a]t the constitutional assembly not much weight was attributed to the differences between these terms. It was rather the intention *to provide for an expedited way of dealing with the many minor every-day issues that can be the subject of agreement between two states, and to save Parliament from having to consider technical and departmental matters*.'[85] The approach taken by the Court also accords with that adopted by state international law advisers. They 'understand these terms to refer to agreements of a routine nature, flowing from the daily activities of government departments. The approach suggested by the Office of the President is that where there is any doubt as to whether an agreement falls under s 231(3), the longer, parliamentary route should be followed'.[86]

In *Earthlife Africa*, after considering the contents of the Russia–South Africa inter-governmental agreement, the Court found:

> [T]hree hallmarks of the agreement are its degree of specificity, the frequent use of peremptory language and the scope and importance of key elements which form the bedrock of the agreement. All these factors combine to suggest a firm legal commitment by the contracting parties to the 'strategic partnership' which the agreement establishes between the two countries, as well as in relation to the future steps and developments which the far-reaching agreement clearly foreshadows. . . .
>
> It may well be difficult to delineate the precise line between an agreement relating to the procurement of new nuclear reactor plant as distinct from one dealing with cooperation towards this end. In my view, however, seen as a

[84] *Earthlife Africa* (n 81) para 114, with reference to the fourth edition of this work (at 417).

[85] Schneeberger (n 82) 5, quoting from the Manual on Executive Acts of the President May 1999 (emphasis added). This Manual was revised in 2007. It affirms that the executive views 'technical, administrative agreements' as agreements which are 'not of major political or other significance', 'have no financial consequences and do not affect domestic law'. In short, they deal with 'minor every-day issues' (para 5.5).

[86] Olivier 'Informal international agreements under the 1996 Constitution' (n 45) 64; Botha (n 82) 77–8.

> whole, the Russian IGA stands well outside the category of a broad nuclear cooperation agreement and, at the very least, sets the parties well on their way to a binding, exclusive agreement in relation to the procurement of new reactor plants from that particular country.[87]

The Court therefore held that the inter-governmental agreement was not an agreement of a technical, administrative or executive nature. Accordingly, the Court found that the Minister of Energy's decision to table the agreement under s 231(3) was unconstitutional, and accordingly set the tabling aside.

Whether a treaty requires ratification is ultimately a question of intention. Generally, this will be determined by the express inclusion of a requirement for ratification in the treaty.[88] Where parties intend that an agreement is to come into force immediately, without ratification at the international level, then parliamentary approval for the executive to bind the Republic to the agreement at the international level would only be required if, given the content of the agreement, it would not be a run-of-the-mill agreement (those that are of a technical, administrative, or executive nature). This is so since, whatever the intention of the executive in negotiating an international agreement, the principle of separation of powers, woven into s 231,[89] requires that all but run-of-the-mill agreements (that do not warrant Parliament's attention) must be approved by Parliament. Put differently, it would not be constitutionally permissible for the executive, when negotiating a treaty, to intend to provide for the treaty to immediately bind South Africa on signature if, given its content, the agreement did not fall within the ambit of an agreement of a 'technical, administrative, or executive nature'. This is not surprising. Merely because the executive may desire to bind South Africa to a substantive agreement without first having to obtain Parliament's approval (which could be withheld, and which must generally include a public participation process)[90] does not

[87] *Earthlife Africa* (n 81) paras 109–10.

[88] See article 14 of the Vienna Convention on the Law of Treaties, which emphasises the intention of parties in deciding whether a treaty requires ratification. This principle was approved by the South African Appellate Division in *S v Eliasov* 1967 (4) SA 583 (A). Article 14(1) provides, as one of the means for determining whether a treaty becomes binding on ratification, that '[t]he consent of a State to be bound by a treaty is expressed by ratification when: (a) the treaty provides for such consent to be expressed by means of ratification'.

[89] *Glenister* (n 49) para 89.

[90] See *Earthlife Africa* (n 81) para 114 and *Democratic Alliance v Minister of International Relations and Cooperation* 2017 (3) SA 212 (GP) ('*DA v Minister of International Relations*') paras 61–3. The Constitution obligates both houses of Parliament to facilitate public participation in their legislative and other activities (ss 59(1) and 72(1)).

mean that the executive is constitutionally empowered to do so.[91] Thus, as made clear by *Earthlife Africa*, even in instances where a treaty does not expressly require ratification, whether the executive can dispense with the requirements of s 231(2) will depend on an objective assessment of the nature and terms of the treaty. Thus, s 231 ensures that it will only be a limited subset of agreements that can be made binding absent parliamentary approval. As held by the Court in *Earthlife Africa*, s 231(3) (which allows the requirement for parliamentary approval to be dispensed with) only deals with agreements that would not 'engage or warrant the focussed attention or interest of Parliament'.[92] Similarly, a full bench of the North Gauteng High Court in *DA v the Minister of International Relations* (which dealt with the lawfulness of the government's withdrawal from the Rome Statute of the International Criminal Court) held that when Parliament approves international agreements it does so 'on behalf of the people of South Africa as their elected representative'.[93]

There is some academic debate as to whether an agreement that is expressly subject to ratification might still be tabled under s 231(3) if it could be argued to nevertheless be an agreement that was technical, administrative, or executive in nature.[94] However, without considering the competing academic arguments, the North Gauteng High Court in *DA v the Minister of International Relations*[95] appeared to accept that where an international agreement requires ratification, it must be tabled under s 231(2), since the Court held that 'ratification ... requires prior parliamentary approval in terms of s 231(2)'.[96] In practice, it would be rare for a run-of-the-mill international agreement that would not engage or warrant parliamentary interest and attention (thus constituting an agreement of a technical, administrative or executive nature) to nevertheless make provision for ratification. This is so since the general reason why states parties to an international agreement provide that the agreement will only become binding on ratification is precisely to allow the signatory states to apply their minds to, and comply with, necessary domestic constitutional obligations, prior to agreeing on the international plane to be bound by the agreement.[97]

In *Earthlife Africa*, the Court noted that even if an agreement might

[91] See *DA v Minister of International Relations* (n 90) and *Earthlife Africa* (n 81).
[92] *Earthlife Africa* (n 81) para 114.
[93] *DA v Minister of International Relations* (n 90) para 55.
[94] See Botha (n 82) 76; and compare Schneeberger (n 82) 5.
[95] *DA v Minister of International Relations* (n 90).
[96] Ibid para 47.
[97] MN Shaw *International Law* 8 ed (2017) 691; A Aust *Modern Treaty Law and Practice* 3 ed (2013) 144.

in principle fall within the terms of s 231(3), and therefore not require Parliament's approval, the government would, if it so chose, be entitled to make use of the more onerous procedure in s 231(2) to obtain parliamentary approval in order to make the agreement binding.[98] Therefore, to the extent there is any doubt as to whether an agreement falls within the ambit of s 231(2) or (3), it would be advisable for the government to adopt the more exacting procedure in s 231(2).

In *DA v Minister of International Relations*, the North Gauteng High Court also established that, properly interpreted, s 231 requires that the executive must first obtain parliamentary approval prior to withdrawing from a treaty which Parliament had approved in terms of s 231(2). The Court held that since the depositing of a notice of withdrawal had 'concrete legal effects in international law, as it terminates treaty obligations',[99] prior parliamentary approval was required before the instrument of withdrawal could be deposited by the executive. In this respect, the Court found that the depositing of a notice of withdrawal was the equivalent of depositing an instrument of ratification, which required prior parliamentary approval in terms of s 231(2).[100] The Court held this was so since '[i]f it is Parliament which determines whether an international agreement binds the country, it is constitutionally untenable that the national executive can unilaterally terminate such an agreement'.[101] The Court also found that since the Rome Statute had been domesticated, a notice of withdrawal could not be given, prior to the repeal of the domesticating legislation.[102] The Court therefore held that the national executive's decision to deliver the notice of withdrawal without first obtaining parliamentary approval violated s 231(2) and the separation of powers doctrine underlying that section.[103] In making this finding, the Court rejected the suggestion by government that since it had sought parliamentary approval for the notice of withdrawal after it was deposited, this would cure the unlawfulness. The Court held that '[w]hatever Parliament does about the subsequent request to it by the national executive to approve the notice of withdrawal would not cure its invalidity ... [since] "[a]n invalid act, being a nullity, cannot be ratified, validated or amended"'.[104] Furthermore, the

[98] Paragraph 132.
[99] Paragraph 47.
[100] Paragraphs 47 and 51.
[101] Paragraph 51.
[102] Paragraph 53, read with para 44, and paras 65–6.
[103] Paragraph 57.
[104] Paragraph 59, quoting from C Hoexter *Administrative Law in South Africa* 2 ed (2012) 547.

Court held that the failure to first consult Parliament and obtain its approval prior to depositing the notice of withdrawal also rendered the depositing of the notice procedurally irrational.[105]

While a number of the parties[106] had argued that it was substantively irrational and unlawful for the government to have decided to withdraw from the Rome Statute, the Court found that it was unnecessary to determine any of the substantive challenges since it had already found the notice of withdrawal to be unconstitutional and invalid on procedural grounds.[107] The Court therefore declared the decision to sign and deliver the notice of withdrawal to be unconstitutional and invalid.[108] It also ordered the government to revoke the notice of withdrawal.[109] The government elected not to seek leave to appeal the decision and duly revoked the notice of withdrawal.

Section 231(4) represents a return to the pre-1994 position expounded by the Appellate Division in *Pan American World Airways*.[110] An international agreement or treaty does not become part of domestic law until it is enacted into law by national legislation.[111] An Act of Parliament is 'national legislation' but the term also includes

- *(a)* subordinate legislation made in terms of an Act of Parliament; and
- *(b)* legislation that was in force when the Constitution took effect and that is administered by the national government.[112]

Three principal methods are employed by the legislature to transform treaties into municipal law. In the first instance, the provisions of a treaty may be embodied in the text of an Act of Parliament;[113] secondly, the treaty may be included as a schedule to a

[105] Paragraphs 70 and 71.

[106] In addition to the applicant (the Democratic Alliance, a political party) certain public interest organisations (which had been cited as respondents, and one that had intervened) also challenged the constitutionality of the notice of withdrawal.

[107] Paragraphs 72–7.

[108] Paragraph 84, orders 1 and 2.

[109] Paragraph 84, order 3.

[110] Supra (n 43).

[111] This principle was reaffirmed by the Constitutional Court in *AZAPO v President of the Republic of South Africa* 1996 (4) SA 671 (CC) para 26 and *National Commissioner v SALC* (n 69) para 24; and by the Supreme Court of Appeal in *Progress Office Machines v SARS* 2008 (2) SA 13 (SCA) para 6 (which the Constitutional Court referred to with approval in *International Trade Administration Commission v SCAW* 2012 (4) SA 618 (CC) para 25).

[112] Section 239 of the Constitution.

[113] For example, s 133 of the Civil Aviation Act 13 of 2009 gives municipal effect to the Tokyo Convention on Offences and Certain Acts Committed on Board Aircraft (1963), the Hague Convention for the Suppression of Unlawful Seizure of Aircraft (1970), and the Montreal Convention for the Suppression of Unlawful Acts Against the Safety of Civil Aviation (1971).

statute;[114] and thirdly, an enabling Act of Parliament may give the executive the power to bring a treaty into effect in municipal law by means of proclamation or notice in the *Government Gazette*.[115] Mere publication of a treaty for general information does not constitute an act of transformation.[116] In *S v Tuhadeleni* the Appellate Division refused to accept that the publication of the Mandate for South West Africa for general information in the *Official Gazette* of the territory made the mandate part of the law of the territory.[117]

The place of treaties in our law was summed up in the following terms by Ngcobo CJ in *Glenister v President of the Republic of South Africa*:

> An international agreement that has been ratified by resolution of Parliament is binding on South Africa on the international plane. And failure to observe the provisions of this agreement may result in South Africa incurring responsibility towards other signatory states. An international agreement that has been ratified by Parliament under section 231(2), however, does not become part of our law until and unless it is incorporated into our law by national legislation. An international agreement that has not been incorporated in our law cannot be a source of rights and obligations.[118]

It may have been more accurate for Ngcobo CJ to have said that: 'An international agreement that has been [approved][119] by resolution of Parliament [and thereafter ratified by the executive on the international plane in accordance with the requirements of the agreement (usually by depositing the instrument of ratification with

[114] For example, the Diplomatic Immunities and Privileges Act 37 of 2001 incorporates the Vienna Convention on Diplomatic Relations of 1961 and the Vienna Convention on Consular Relations of 1963 into South African legislation by means of schedules.

[115] For example, s 2(3)*(a)* and (3)*ter* of the Extradition Act 67 of 1962, and s 108 of the Income Tax Act 58 of 1962 (in this regard see the discussions in *Commissioner, South African Revenue Service v Van Kets* 2012 (3) SA 399 (WCC) paras 11–15 and *Commissioner, South African Revenue Service v Tradehold* 2013 (4) SA 184 (SCA) paras 15 and 16).

[116] Morgenstern (n 3) 51.

[117] 1969 (1) SA 153 (A) 173–5. In *Binga v Cabinet for South West Africa* 1988 (3) SA 155 (A) the Appellate Division was asked to reconsider its finding in *Tuhadeleni* that the mandate had not been incorporated into municipal law. Van Heerden JA found it unnecessary to decide on this matter but 'assumed', for the purpose of the appeal, that the mandate had been incorporated (182–3).

[118] Supra (n 49) para 92. Ngcobo CJ made this statement in a minority judgment. See, too, the comments of Moseneke DCJ and Cameron J in the majority judgment in this case at paras 179–81.

[119] Section 231(2) quite appropriately and helpfully refers to 'approval' by Parliament, so as to distinguish it from 'ratification', which is the action on the international plane by the executive once parliamentary approval has been secured. See *DA v Minister of International Relations* (n 90) para 47.

the depositary)][120] is binding on South Africa on the international plane.' Given the wording of s 231(2), and having regard to the relevant domestic constitutional law and international law contexts, once Parliament has approved an international agreement, the executive is then obligated to convey South Africa's agreement to be bound by the treaty to the other states parties, in whatever way provided for in the treaty (usually by depositing an instrument of ratification).[121] Both as a matter of practice and of law, it is the executive and not Parliament that formally conducts South Africa's foreign affairs on the international plane, and it is therefore the executive that takes the necessary international steps (once empowered by Parliament)[122] to advise other countries of South Africa's agreement to be bound by an international agreement.[123] As the North Gauteng High Court held in *DA v Minister of International Relations*, 'prior parliamentary approval is required before instruments of ratification may be deposited with the United Nations'.[124]

5 Self-executing treaties

The proviso to s 231(4) introduces the concept of self-executing treaties—that is, treaties that automatically become part of municipal law, and enforceable by municipal courts, without any act of legislative incorporation—into South African law. The provisions of a treaty approved by Parliament, but not incorporated into municipal law by an Act of Parliament, that are self-executing become part of municipal law unless inconsistent with the Constitution or an Act of Parliament. It is important to emphasise that s 231(4) only provides for self-executing treaties to become municipal law in the absence of legislation if they have been 'approved by Parliament'. This refers to treaties that have been approved by both houses of Parliament in terms of s 231(2). Treaties covered by s 231(3) that have not been

[120] Article 16 of the Vienna Convention on the Law of Treaties provides that: 'Unless the treaty otherwise provides, instruments of ratification, acceptance, approval or accession establish the consent of a State to be bound by a treaty upon:
(a) their exchange between the contracting States;
(b) their deposit with the depositary; or
(c) their notification to the contracting States or to the depositary, if so agreed.'

[121] *DA v Minister of International Relations* (n 90) para 51.

[122] As the Court also pointed out in *DA v Minister of International Relations* (n 90) para 55, '[t]he binding power comes only once parliament has approved the agreement on behalf of the people of South Africa as their elected representative. It appears that it is a deliberate constitutional scheme that the executive must ordinarily go to parliament (the representative of the people) to get authority to do that which the executive does not already have authority to do.'

[123] See *DA v Minister of International Relations* (n 90) paras 51 and 55.

[124] Ibid para 51.

approved by Parliament will not have domestic force even if they could be argued to be self-executing.

Whether the provisions of a treaty are self-executing has troubled the courts of the United States for many years.[125] In 1951, Professor Myres McDougal declared in respect of the position of the United States: '[T]his word self-executing is essentially meaningless, and . . . the quicker we drop it in our vocabulary the better for clarity and understanding.'[126] The soundness of this advice was confirmed by the US Supreme Court in *Medellin v Texas*,[127] in which the Court divided sharply over the meaning of self-executing treaties in a case involving the enforcement of a judgment of the International Court of Justice holding that an alien sentenced to death in the United States was entitled to review of his sentence.[128] American law therefore offers no panacea for the problems that are likely to confront South African courts in the interpretation of s 231(4).

Scholars have expressed divergent views on self-executing treaties. Botha states that s 231(4) was taken over unwisely from US jurisprudence 'with no regard to its suitability to the South African context'.[129] Other writers have described it as 'nonsensical'[130] and 'farcical'.[131] Ngolele[132] and Olivier[133] adopt a different position, in favour of the concept of self-executing treaties, and suggest that human rights treaties, such as the International Covenant on Civil and Political Rights (ICCPR), may be directly applied by South

[125] *Foster v Neilson* 27 US (2 Pet) 253 (1829); *Sei Fujii v California* 242 P 2d 617 (1952), 19 ILR 312. See also Restatement (Third) of the Foreign Relations Law of the United States para 111 (1987); T Buergenthal 'Self-executing and non-self-executing treaties' (1992 IV) *Hague Recueil* 343.

[126] 'Remarks at the annual meeting of the American Society of International Law' (1951) 45 *Proceedings of the American Society of Law* 102.

[127] 128 S Ct 1346 (2008), 170 L Ed 2d 190 (2008).

[128] *Concerning Avena and Other Mexican Nationals (Mexico v US)* 2004 ICJ Reports 12.

[129] N Botha 'Treaty-making in South Africa: A reassessment' (2000) 25 *SAYIL* 69 at 91; Botha in DB Hollis, MR Blakeslee and LB Ederington (eds) *National Treaty Law and Practice* 2 ed (2005) 58.

[130] JD van Vyver 'Universal jurisdiction in international criminal law' (1999) 24 *SAYIL* 107 at 130.

[131] HA Strydom 'The international law "openness" of the South African Constitution' in G Carpenter (ed) *Suprema Lex: Essays on the Constitution Presented to Marinus Wiechers* (1998) 93.

[132] E Ngolele 'The content of the doctrine of self-execution and its limited effect in South African law' (2006) 31 *SAYIL* 153.

[133] M Olivier 'Exploring the doctrine of self-execution as enforcement mechanism of international obligations' (2002) 27 *SAYIL* 99.

African courts as self-executing treaties.[134] Ngolele rejects the view that the adequacy of existing South African law is a condition precedent for self-execution of a treaty. However, in acknowledging that self-execution has limited effect in South Africa, because treaties will be self-executing *only* if consistent with the Constitution and Acts of Parliament, he comes close to accepting that municipal law must be adequate for a treaty to be self-executing, in the sense that it must not obstruct the application of such a treaty. Olivier adopts a more radical position. She argues that in terms of s 231(2), a treaty approved by Parliament has direct application in South African law without the need for incorporation—that is, it is self-executing—provided that it is not inconsistent with the Constitution or an Act of Parliament. Olivier's thesis is based on a false assumption—namely that s 231(2) is designed to give domestic effect to treaties approved by Parliament.[135] Section 231(2) is intended to establish that an international agreement binds South Africa on the international level only after it has been approved by both houses of Parliament. To apply domestically, a treaty must still be 'enacted into law by national legislation', as specified in s 231(4), unless it is self-executing. In addition, it will be self-executing only if the language of the treaty so indicates and existing municipal law, either common law or statute, is adequate in the sense that it fails to place any obstacle in the way of treaty application.

Judicial decisions likewise demonstrate a divergence of opinion. *Nello Quagliani v President of the RSA*[136] concerned the question whether the 1999 extradition agreement between the United States and South Africa was part of South African law, despite the fact that it had not been incorporated into municipal law by national legislation. In considering whether the agreement qualified as a self-executing treaty and was thus part of South African law in terms of the proviso to s 231(4), Preller J stated that he found s 231(4) 'hard to understand',[137] 'at most of academic interest to us' in South Africa,[138]

[134] *Claassen v Minister of Justice and Constitutional Development* 2010 (6) SA 399 (WCC) expressly rejected the suggestion that the ICCPR is a self-executing instrument. Cf *Zealand v Minister of Justice and Constitutional Development* 2008 (4) SA 458 (CC) para 52.

[135] Olivier (n 133) 116.

[136] Unreported, TPD Case No 959/04, 18 April 2008 ('*Quagliani TPD*'). Noted by N Botha in 'Extradition, self-execution and the South African Constitution: A non-event? South African judicial decisions' (2008) 33 *SAYIL* 253 and 'Public international law' 2008 *Annual Survey* 30. See, too, G Ferreira and W Scholtz 'Has the Constitutional Court found the lost ball in the high weeds? The interpretation of section 231 of the South African Constitution' (2009) 42 *CILSA* 269.

[137] *Quagliani TPD* (n 136) 12.

[138] Ibid 13.

and 'foreign to our legal system'.[139] He then found that the agreement in question had not been validly incorporated in terms of s 231(4) and was not part of South African law: that is, it was not self-executing. He stated '[f]rom a reading of the plain words of section 231(4) of the Constitution it is simply not possible to have a statute in terms of which any number of international agreements can subsequently be concluded that will have the force of law in the Republic. What the plain language of the sub-section requires is the enactment into law of every new treaty. In my view that clearly means a new Act of Parliament for every new treaty.'[140] In *Goodwin v Director-General Department of Justice and Constitutional Development*,[141] however, Ebersohn AJ took a completely different line in respect of the same treaty in holding that the treaty 'is a self-executing provision in its totality'[142] and that Preller J's decision in *Quagliani* was 'clearly wrong'.[143]

The Constitutional Court refused to provide any guidance on the meaning to be given to self-executing treaties in the appeals from *Quagliani* and *Goodwin*[144] when it found that it was unnecessary to consider the question whether the extradition agreement between the United States and South Africa should be regarded as self-executing.[145] In making this finding, Sachs J stated on behalf of a unanimous court:

> The question then is whether the Agreement 'becomes law' in South Africa as contemplated by section 231(4) of the Constitution. There are two ways in which this question can be answered. The first is to say that the Agreement itself does not become binding in domestic law, but the international obligation the Agreement encapsulates is given effect to by the provisions in the [Extradition] Act. The second approach is that once the Agreement has been entered into as specified in sections 2 and 3 of the [Extradition] Act, it becomes law in South Africa as contemplated by section 231(4) of the Constitution without further legislation by Parliament.
>
> It is not necessary for the purposes of this case to decide which of these approaches is correct, for their effect in this case is the same. Either the Agreement has 'become law' in South Africa as a result of the prior existence of the [Extradition] Act which constitutes the anticipatory enactment of the Agreement for the purposes of s 231(4) of the Constitution. Or the Agreement

[139] *Quagliani TPD* (n 136).

[140] Ibid 18.

[141] Unreported, TPD Case No 21142/08, 23 June 2008 ('*Goodwin*'). Noted by Botha (n 136).

[142] *Goodwin* (n 141) 13.

[143] Ibid 15.

[144] *President of the Republic of South Africa v Quagliani; President of the Republic of South Africa v Van Rooyen; Goodwin v Director-General, Department of Justice and Constitutional Development* 2009 (4) BCLR 345 (CC).

[145] Ibid 359A–B.

> has not 'become law' in the Republic as contemplated by s 231(4) but the provisions of the Act are all that is required to give domestic effect to the international obligation that the Agreement creates.
>
> I conclude, therefore, that on either of the approaches identified above, no further enactment by Parliament is required to make extradition between South Africa and the United States permissible in South African law.[146]

This *dictum* is incomprehensible.[147] Section 231(4) makes it clear that for a treaty to become law in South Africa it must be enacted into law by national legislation unless it is self-executing. There is no third avenue for the incorporation of treaties. The Constitution makes no exception to s 231(4) for extradition agreements, such as that between the United States and South Africa, which had not been 'enacted into law by national legislation'. The highly convoluted reasoning of the Constitutional Court fails to satisfactorily explain why extradition agreements come into existence by means not contemplated by s 231(4). It is obviously undesirable to have to enact legislation for every extradition agreement. But the solution is either to amend the Extradition Act 67 of 1962 or to consider extradition agreements to be self-executing. Clearly, amending legislation is the most desirable course. Indeed, this was proposed in earlier editions of the present study[148]—a proposal that was not considered by the Constitutional Court. The result of these appeals is that the Court has given an opaque and confusing interpretation of s 231(4) and failed to throw any light on the meaning to be attached to the term 'self-executing'.

South African courts are reluctant to explore the meaning of the term 'self-executing'. This is abundantly clear from the decision of the Constitutional Court in *Quagliani*. It is also clear from the statement of Binns-Ward J in *Claassen v Minister of Justice and Constitutional Development* that:

> The ICCPR is not a self-executing legal instrument, in the sense that this country's formal adoption of its provisions did not, without more, amend our established domestic law. It seems to me that the current case illustrates the need, if unqualified effect is to be given to article 9(5) of the ICCPR, for South Africa to enact legislation . . . .[149]

Courts must, however, address the meaning to be given to self-executing treaties in s 231(4) and not pretend that the proviso to s 231(4) does not exist or argue that treaties can be incorporated into

[146] *President of RSA v Quagliani* (n 144) 363A–E.

[147] Neville Botha describes the judgment of the Constitutional Court in this matter as 'a profoundly unsatisfactory judgment': 'Rewriting the Constitution: The "strange alchemy" of Justice Sachs, indeed!' (2009) 34 *SAYIL* 253.

[148] J Dugard *International Law: A South African Perspective* 3 ed (2005) 213–14.

[149] 2010 (6) SA 399 (WCC) para 36. Critically noted by Magnus Killander in 'Judicial immunity, compensation for unlawful detention and the elusive self-executing treaty provision' (2010) 26 *SAJHR* 386.

municipal law by means other than 'national legislation'—as was done by the Constitutional Court in *Quagliani*. The fact that American courts have had difficulty in satisfactorily defining the term self-executing in *the context of American law* should not deter South African courts from attaching meaning to the term in *the context of South African law*. There is much to be said for identifying an extradition treaty and the ICCPR as 'self-executing' as there is already legislation in place to enable them to be applied in municipal law and they are not inconsistent with the Constitution or an Act of Parliament. But, unfortunately, courts, with the exception of the lower courts in *Quagliani* and *Goodwin*, have refused to address this issue satisfactorily. If full meaning is to be given to s 231(4), it is essential that courts consider this issue in a manner which promotes harmony between South Africa's international obligations and its municipal law.

* * * * * *

A treaty that has been signed and ratified, but not enacted into local law, is binding on South Africa on the international plane. Failure to observe the provisions of such a treaty may result in South Africa incurring responsibility towards other states parties.

6 The national executive and the making of treaties

Section 231(1) confers on the 'national executive' the responsibility for the making of treaties. The President, as head of state and head of the national executive, may be given the power to enter into treaties, such as extradition treaties, in terms of a specific Act, but he is obliged (given s 85(2)*(e)* read with s 231(1) of the Constitution) to act 'in a collaborative manner' with the other members of the Cabinet in exercising this authority.[150]

When the President enters into an agreement he does so as head of the national executive. In the words of the Constitutional Court:

> Given the provisions of section 231 of the Constitution, it is not improper for the President, once the decision to enter into the treaty has been made by the President, to confer other formal aspects relating to the accession to the treaty on other members of the national executive. It is important that these provisions should not be applied in a formalistic manner that will impair the ability of the national executive to function.[151]

In *DA v Minister of International Relations*, the North Gauteng High Court held that s 231(1) only gives the national executive a preliminary power to undertake the 'exploratory work' of negotiating and signing international agreements, but this does not empower the

[150] *President of the Republic of South Africa v Quagliani* (n 144) 355C.
[151] Ibid 356B–C. See, too, *Quagliani TPD* (n 136) 10, noted in Botha (n 136) 257.

executive to bind South Africa to such international agreements; '[t]he binding power comes only once parliament has approved the agreement'[152] (although, the Court was only dealing with treaties that require parliamentary approval in terms of s 231(2)).

7 International agreements or treaties

The 1996 Constitution, like the Interim Constitution, uses the term 'international agreement' instead of the more commonly used term 'treaty'. This creates uncertainty over the meaning of s 231, as there is strong support for the view that the term 'international agreement' is wide enough to include both legally binding agreements (treaties) and non-binding, unenforceable informal agreements.[153] This uncertainty surfaced in the *Harksen* case[154] in which it was argued that s 3(2) of the Extradition Act,[155] authorizing the President to consent to the extradition of a person to a state with which South Africa has no extradition agreement, gives rise to an international agreement if not a treaty. Consequently, the procedure for the adoption of international agreements contained in s 231(2) should be followed in respect of such an undertaking by the President. While the Cape Provincial Division was prepared to contemplate the existence of unenforceable, informal arrangements falling within the scope of an 'international agreement',[156] the Constitutional Court rejected the argument that a presidential undertaking under s 3(2) of the Extradition Act could be categorized as either an international agreement or as an informal agreement.[157] Unfortunately, the Constitutional Court, in a judgment characterized by its brevity and a determination not to consider the broader issues relating to treaty-making, failed to throw light on the meaning to be given to 'international agreement'.[158]

The prevailing view, however, is that the term 'international agreement' in s 231 is synonymous with 'treaty' and refers to legally binding, enforceable agreements as defined in article 2 of the Vienna

[152] *DA v Minister of International Relations* (n 90) para 55.

[153] RR Baxter 'International law in her "infinite variety"' (1980) 29 *ICLQ* 549; A Aust 'The theory and practice of informal international instruments' (1986) 35 *ICLQ* 787; Olivier 'Informal international agreements under the 1996 Constitution' (n 45). *Sed contra* J Klabbers *The Concept of Treaty in International Law* (1996) 63–4, 122–35, 216–17, 243, 245–50. For an overview of the literature, see Schneeberger (n 82).

[154] *S v Harksen; Harksen v President of the Republic of South Africa; Harksen v Wagner NO* 2000 (1) SA 1185 (C); *Harksen v President of the Republic of South Africa* 2000 (2) SA 825 (CC).

[155] 67 of 1962.

[156] *S v Harksen* (n 154) paras 52–4 and 59.

[157] *Harksen v President of the Republic of South Africa* (n 154) para 21.

[158] Schneeberger (n 82) 32.

Convention on the Law of Treaties of 1969.[159] According to this provision, a 'treaty' is

> an *international agreement* concluded between states in written form and governed by international law, whether embodied in a single instrument or in two or more related instruments and *whatever its particular designation* [emphasis added].

'Terminology is not a determinant factor as to the character of an international agreement'—in the words of the International Court of Justice.[160] What is important is that the agreement be between states, in writing, and that the state parties *intend* it to be governed by international law.[161] Once these requirements are met, an international agreement exists between the state parties and it matters not whether it is called an 'international agreement' or 'treaty'—or, for that matter, convention, declaration, act, concordat, protocol, memorandum of understanding or exchange of notes.

No provision is made for the recognition of oral agreements in the Constitution, nor is express provision made for agreements with international organisations.[162]

8 Resolutions of international organisations

Resolutions of international organisations are not treaties and, in most instances, they are not binding on member states. If South Africa wishes to translate such a resolution into municipal law, it must do so by legislation.[163] Resolutions of the Security Council of the United Nations adopted under Chapter VII of the Charter are, however, binding on member states. The Application of Resolutions of the Security Council of the United Nations Act[164] empowers the President to incorporate resolutions of the Security Council into

[159] Olivier 'Informal international agreements under the 1996 Constitution' (n 45) 74; Botha (n 82) 71; Schneeberger (n 82) 32–40.

[160] *South West African Cases, Preliminary Objections,* 1962 ICJ Reports 328 at 331.

[161] See *S v Harksen* (n 154) para 52, in which Van Zyl J stated: 'It is this very intention and consent that distinguishes treaties from informal or ad hoc agreements or arrangements'. The Cape Provincial Division held that an arrangement to extradite a person under s 3(2) of the Extradition Act 67 of 1962 did not qualify as an international agreement because of the absence of an intent to create reciprocal rights and duties (para 59). See, too, the judgment of the Constitutional Court in *Harksen v President of the Republic of South Africa* (n 154) para 21.

[162] See Botha (n 82) 72.

[163] *Binga v Administrator-General, South West Africa* (n 36) 968E; *Welkom Municipality v Masureik and Herman t/a Lotus Corporation* 1997 (3) SA 363 (A) 371; *Masureik and Another (t/a Lotus Corporation) v Welkom Municipality* 1995 (4) SA 745 (O). See further N Botha 'Municipal application of Annex 14 to the Chicago Convention: The role of recommended international practices and procedures in South African municipal law' (1997) 22 *BYIL* 112.

[164] 172 of 1993.

municipal law by proclamation in the *Government Gazette* and to provide for the implementation of such resolutions under South African law. This Act has, however, not yet been brought in force.[165]

9 Statutory (including constitutional) interpretation with special reference to human rights

The 1996 Constitution reveals a clear determination to ensure that the Constitution and South African law are interpreted to comply with international law, particularly in the field of human rights. First, the common-law presumption requiring a court to interpret legislation in compliance with international law[166] is given constitutional form in s 233, which provides:

> When interpreting any legislation, every court must prefer any reasonable interpretation of the legislation that is consistent with international law over any alternative interpretation that is inconsistent with international law.

Secondly, the Bill of Rights, which is modelled on international human rights conventions and on occasion refers directly to international law,[167] is subjected to a special interpretative regime which pays particular attention to international law. Section 39 (s 35 of the Interim Constitution)[168] declares:

> (1) When interpreting the Bill of Rights, a court, tribunal or forum—
> *(a)* must promote the values that underlie an open and democratic society based on human dignity, equality and freedom;
> *(b)* must consider international law; and
> *(c)* may consider foreign law
> (2) When interpreting any legislation, and when developing the common law or customary law, every court, tribunal or forum must promote the spirit, purport and objects of the Bill of Rights.
> (3) The Bill of Rights does not deny the existence of any other rights or freedoms that are recognized or conferred by common law, customary law or legislation, to the extent that they are consistent with the Bill.

Fears that international human rights law might be narrowly construed to cover only clear rules of customary law and those

[165] See Botha (n 82) at 89–90; De Wet in Shelton (ed) *International Law and Domestic Legal Systems* (n 45); H Strydom and T Huarka 'South Africa' in V Gowlland-Debbas (ed) *National Implementation of United Nations Sanctions: A Comparative Study* (2004) 430–2.

[166] See above (n 37) and *S v Basson* (n 50) para 100.

[167] Section 37(4) provides that any legislation enacted in consequence of a declaration of a state emergency may derogate from the Bill of Rights only to the extent that, inter alia, the legislation 'is consistent with the Republic's obligations under international law applicable to states of emergency'. Section 35(3)*(l)* recognises the right 'not to be convicted of an act or omission that was not an offence under either national or international law at the time when it was committed or omitted'.

[168] Section 35(1) of the Interim Constitution required 'a court of law' to 'have regard to public international law'.

human rights conventions to which South Africa is a party have been dispelled.[169] In one of its earliest decisions, in a case involving the constitutionality of the death penalty, the President of the Constitutional Court ruled:

> In the context of s 35(1), public international law would include non-binding as well as binding law. They may both be used under the section as tools of interpretation. International agreements and customary international law accordingly provide a framework within which [the Bill of Rights] can be evaluated and understood, and for that purpose, decisions of tribunals dealing with comparable instruments, such as the United Nations Committee on Human Rights, the Inter-American Commission on Human Rights, the Inter-American Court of Human Rights, the European Commission on Human Rights, and the European Court of Human Rights and, in appropriate cases, reports of specialised agencies such as the International Labour Organisation, may provide guidance as to the correct interpretation of particular provisions of [the Bill of Rights].[170]

Since the establishment of the new constitutional order in 1994, both the Constitutional Court and ordinary courts have shown a great willingness to be guided by international human rights law. Decisions of the European Commission and Court of Human Rights have provided the greatest assistance, but courts have on occasion also considered the 'views' of the United Nations Human Rights Committee, and United Nations reports on human rights matters.[171]

[169] J Dugard 'The role of international law in interpreting the Bill of Rights' (1994) 10 *SAJHR* 208.

[170] *S v Makwanyane* 1995 (3) SA 391 (CC) 413–14. See the comment on this case by N Botha and M Olivier 'Ten years of international law in the South African courts: Reviewing the past and assessing the future' (2004) 29 *SAYIL* 42 at 44–8, 75. The Constitutional Court has confirmed that the principles enunciated in *Makwanyane* in relation to s 35 of the Interim Constitution continue to apply to s 39 of the 1996 Constitution (see, eg, *Government of the Republic of South Africa v Grootboom* 2001 (1) SA 46 (CC) para 26; *Glenister* (n 49) para 178 fn 28). See, too, *Prince v President of the Law Society, Cape of Good Hope* 1998 (8) BCLR 976 (C) 985C–D; *Prince v President, Cape Law Society* 2002 (2) SA 794 (CC) 824A–E, 837E–F, 851B–C, 858–9. Here, the Court considered non-human rights treaties under s 39(1)*(b)*. In practice, human rights treaties will be most frequently invoked but the language of s 39(1)*(b)* does not exclude other treaties.

[171] For instance, the Constitutional Court, in *SATAWU v Garvas* 2013 (1) SA 83 (CC), had regard to a report by the Special Rapporteur on extrajudicial, summary or arbitrary executions to assist it in interpreting the right to freedom of assembly (para 30). In *Rahim v Minister of Home Affairs* 2015 (4) SA 433 (SCA) the Supreme Court of Appeal had regard to the report of the Special Rapporteur of the Human Rights Council of the United Nations on the rights of migrants, a resolution by the Inter-American Commission on Human Rights, and the International Convention on the Protection of the Rights of All Migrant Workers and Members of Their Families (which South Africa was not a party to) in order to establish the considerations that a South African official would have to take into account when deciding whether to arrest and detain an illegal foreigner under the Immigration Act 13 of 2002 (see paras

The manner in which South African courts have invoked international human rights norms is considered in Chapter 15.

While a court must consider treaties to which South Africa is not a party in interpreting the Bill of Rights, no such rule exists in respect of treaties to which South Africa is not a party where the Bill of Rights is not in issue. A treaty to which South Africa is not a party is *res inter alios acta* and may not be considered *qua* treaty, although it may be considered as evidence of a customary rule.[172]

Different considerations apply in respect of a treaty to which South Africa is a party but has not been incorporated into municipal law. In the first instance, a municipal court may have recourse to an unincorporated treaty in order to interpret an ambiguous statute.[173] However, the Constitution's interpretative injunction, contained in s 233, applies to all statutes, not only those that are ambiguous. The Constitutional Court's decision in *S v Okah* makes it clear that s 233 of the Constitution requires courts to favour the interpretation of legislation that is in line with international law (including unincorporated treaties binding on South Africa) even where another reasonable interpretation of the legislation is possible but not in line with

18 and 19). And, in *Glenister* (n 49) the Constitutional Court relied on a report by the Organisation for Economic Co-operation and Development (OECD) in relation to anti-corruption fighting institutions, even though it was not binding. The Court explained that '[t]he OECD report is not itself binding in international law, but can be used to interpret and give content to the obligations in the conventions that we've described' (para 187). See also *Helen Suzman Foundation v President of the Republic of South Africa* 2015 (2) SA 1 (CC) paras 41, 160 and 167.

[172] This is borne out by the judgment in *S v Petane* 1988 (3) SA 51 (C), in which Conradie J considered the question whether the principal provisions of a treaty to which South Africa was not a party—Additional Protocol I of 1977—had been translated into customary law by usage.

[173] *Glenister* (n 49) paras 179–202. See further *Maluke v Minister of Internal Affairs* 1981 (1) SA 707 (B) 713; *Mabuda v Minister of Co-operation and Development* 1984 (2) SA 49 (Ck) 54–5 (discussed in J Dugard 'Public international law' 1984 *Annual Survey* 68 at 82–3). For a discussion of this principle, see J Dugard 'International human-rights norms in domestic courts: Can South Africa learn from Britain and the United States?' in Ellison Kahn (ed) *Fiat Iustitia: Essays in Memory of Oliver Deneys Schreiner* (1983) 221 at 234–6. Cf *Binga v Cabinet for South West Africa* 1988 (3) SA 155 (A) 185F where Van Heerden JA restricted the scope of this argument in an *obiter dictum* in which he found that the presumption in favour of compliance with an international treaty obligation applies only where the statute seeks to give effect to the treaty in question. In limiting this presumption, Van Heerden JA preferred the more restrictive approach of Diplock LJ in *Salomon v Commissioner of Customs and Excise* [1966] 3 All ER 871 (CA) 875–6 to that of Lord Denning MR in *R v Secretary of State for Home Affairs, Ex parte Bhajan Singh* [1975] 2 All ER 1083 (CA). In support of Lord Denning's position, see PJ Duffy 'English law and the European Court of Human Rights' (1980) 29 *ICLQ* 585 at 589.

international law.[174] *S v Okah* involved the state's prosecution of a Nigerian national, who was resident in South Africa, for terrorist activities in Nigeria pursuant to South Africa's domestic anti-terrorism legislation, which provided for extraterritorial jurisdiction. Cameron J held that the Court was required, in terms of s 233 of the Constitution, to interpret the relevant provisions of the Protection of Constitutional Democracy against Terrorist and Related Activities Act[175] in conformity with international law. In determining what the relevant international law was, Cameron J took account of a number of international treaties to which South Africa was party—including treaties which had not been domesticated[176]—that established a duty to prosecute or extradite. Cameron J pointed out that even if the Supreme Court of Appeal's interpretation of the legislation were reasonable, the Court was required by s 233 to interpret the legislation in line with international law. The Court rejected the interpretation adopted by the Supreme Court of Appeal, which 'would create instances in which it would be possible to "prosecute the banker, but not the bomber"',[177] and adopted an interpretation which gave effect to South Africa's international law obligation to prosecute or extradite.

Secondly, an unincorporated treaty may be taken into account in a challenge to the validity of delegated legislation on grounds of unreasonableness.[178] This was confirmed by the Supreme Court of Appeal in *Progress Office Machines CC v SARS*[179] when it held that delegated legislation, in the form of a notice by the Minister of

[174] *S v Okah* 2018 (1) SACR 492 (CC) para 38; see also *Bridon International GmbH v International Trade Administration Commission* 2013 (3) SA 197 (SCA) paras 12, 13 and 26 and *International Trade Administration Commission v SCAW* (n 111) para 43, read with para 25. In *SCAW* the Court held that '[i]n *Progress Office Machines* the Supreme Court of Appeal correctly concluded that the Anti-Dumping Agreement is binding on the Republic in international law, even though it has not been specifically enacted into municipal law', and the Court then went on to hold that 'we are required by the Constitution to interpret domestic legislation governing the duration of anti-dumping duties consistently with these international obligations'.

[175] Act 33 of 2004.

[176] See also *Bridon International* (n 174) paras 12, 13 and 26.

[177] *S v Okah* (n 174) para 26, quoting the oral submissions of counsel for one of the *amici*.

[178] *Molvan v Attorney-General for Palestine* [1948] AC 351 (PC) 365; Morgenstern (n 3) 70.

[179] 2008 (2) SA 13 (SCA) para 11. Cf *Association of Meat Importers v ITAC* [2013] 4 All SA 253 (SCA) paras 56–61 where Nugent JA, writing for the majority, raises questions as to the nature and extent of and the basis for what was decided in *Progress Office Machines* in relation to the indirect application of the WTO Agreement, and, in essence, seeks to qualify the decision (see also the minority judgment by Wallis JA at paras 109–18).

Finance imposing an anti-dumping duty, must be reasonable and that a court might have regard to the state's obligations under an unincorporated treaty—the WTO Agreement of 1995—in making such a determination. (*In casu* the Court found that the notice was unreasonable and, hence, invalid as it violated the WTO Agreement.) Despite earlier failure of the Appellate Division to commit itself on this subject,[180] the finding in *Progress Office Machines* is sound since the concept of reasonableness is inextricably linked with presumptions of legislative intent and there is a presumption that the legislature, in enacting a law, did not intend to violate South Africa's international obligations.

As South African courts are given the power of judicial review of legislation under the 1996 Constitution,[181] it is inevitable that international law will be invoked not only as a guide to statutory interpretation but as a challenge to the validity of legislation. This may take the form of a direct challenge where, for example, it is argued that the procedures for ratification and incorporation of a treaty under s 231 have not been followed. Or it may assume the form of an indirect challenge where international law is invoked to support an interpretation in favour of the unconstitutionality of a statute. The former type of direct challenge in relation to a failure to comply with the procedure in s 231 is illustrated, to an extent, by *Earthlife Africa* (albeit that there had not been any domestic incorporation of the relevant international agreement). As shown above, in this case the Court set aside the tabling of an inter-governmental agreement between Russia and South Africa in relation to nuclear procurement and co-operation under s 231(3) of the Constitution because the international agreement was found, given its substantive content, to be an agreement that fell under s 231(2), which required parliamentary approval to be made binding. The Court also set aside the tabling of inter-governmental agreements with the United States and South Korean governments because of the significant delays (20 years and five years respectively) in tabling them under s 231(3). The Court held that s 231(3) could only be used to table international

[180] In *Winter v Minister of Defence* 1960 AD 194 at 198 and *S v Tuhadeleni* (n 43) 176–7 the Appellate Division left open the question whether proclamations may be tested against the terms of the Mandate for South West Africa, a treaty that was not incorporated into municipal law. In *Binga v Administrator-General, South West Africa* (n 36), especially at 973D–G, the Court wrongly assumed that the *Tuhadeleni* case held that delegated legislation might not be tested against the mandate. See J Dugard 'The revocation of the mandate for South West Africa revisited' (1985) 1 *SAJHR* 154 at 159; G Erasmus 'Mandates, military service and multiple choice' (1985–1986) 11 *SAYIL* 115 at 133.

[181] Section 172 of the Constitution.

agreements to make them binding absent parliamentary approval (as required by s 231(2)) if they were tabled within a 'reasonable time' (as expressly required by s 231(3)) since this was a jurisdictional requirement for the use of s 231(3). Similarly, in *DA v Minister of International Relations* (discussed above) the Court set aside the government's decision to deposit a notice withdrawing South Africa from the Rome Statute (and ordered the government to revoke the notice) since the government, in violation of s 231, had failed to first obtain parliamentary approval for the withdrawal and had failed to repeal the Act that incorporated the Rome Statute into domestic law.

Two major decisions of the Constitutional Court illustrate the indirect type of challenge: *AZAPO v President of the Republic of South Africa*,[182] decided under the Interim Constitution of 1994, which contained no provision equivalent to s 233 of the 1996 Constitution, and *Glenister v President of the Republic of South Africa*.[183]

In *AZAPO* the applicants sought to set aside s 20(7) of the Promotion of National Unity and Reconciliation Act,[184] providing for amnesty from criminal and civil proceedings, on the ground that it was inconsistent with s 22 of the Interim Constitution, which provides that every person shall have the right to have justiciable disputes settled by a court of law or, where appropriate, another independent or impartial forum. In support of this challenge, the applicants argued that the state was obliged by international law, particularly the Geneva Conventions of 1949, to which South Africa is a party but have not been incorporated into domestic law, to prosecute those responsible for gross human rights violations and that the provisions of s 20(7), which authorized amnesty for such offences, constituted a breach of international law.[185]

In an eloquent judgment, written by Mahomed DP, the Constitutional Court held that the epilogue to the Interim Constitution, providing for amnesty, trumped s 22 of the Constitution and that

[182] 1996 (4) SA 671 (CC). For criticisms of this decision, see comments by J Dugard 'Is the truth and reconciliation process compatible with international law? An unanswered question' (1997) 13 *SAJHR* 258; C Braude and D Spitz 'Memory and the spectre of international justice: A Comment on Azapo—*AZAPO v President of the Republic of South Africa* 1996 focus—The Constitutional Court 1996 term—Cases and comments' (1997) 13 *SAJHR* 269; D Moellendorf 'Amnesty, truth and justice: *Azapo* focus—The Constitutional Court 1996 term—Cases and comments' (1997) 13 *SAJHR* 283; Z Motala 'The Constitutional Court's approach to international law and its method of interpretation in the "*Amnesty* decision": Intellectual honesty or political expediency?' (1996) 21 *SAYIL* 29; and De Wet in Shelton (ed) *International Law and Domestic Legal Systems* (n 45).

[183] Supra (n 49).

[184] Act 34 of 1995.

[185] *AZAPO* (n 182) para 25.

s 20(7) of the Promotion of National Unity and Reconciliation Act, authorizing criminal and civil amnesty, was therefore constitutional. From the perspective of international law, the judgment is disappointing because it fails to adequately address the question whether conventional and customary international law oblige a successor regime to punish the officials and agents of the prior regime for international crimes and, thus, gave support to the constitutional challenge advanced by the applicants. From the perspective of the place of international law in the new constitutional order, the judgment is disconcerting because of a strange *dictum* which may be construed as suggesting that a 'proper interpretation' of the Constitution should be sought without recourse to international conventions.

In the course of his judgment, Mahomed DP stated:

> The issue which falls to be determined in this Court is whether s 20(7) of the Act is inconsistent with the Constitution. If it is, the enquiry as to whether or not international law prescribes a different duty is irrelevant to that determination. International law and the contents of international treaties to which South Africa might or might not be party at any particular time are, in my view, relevant only to the interpretation of the Constitution itself, on the grounds that the lawmakers of the Constitution should not lightly be presumed to authorise any law which might constitute a breach of the obligations of the state in terms of international law. . . .[186]
>
> The exact terms of the relevant rules of public international law contained in the Geneva Conventions relied upon on behalf of the applicants would therefore be irrelevant if, on a proper interpretation of the Constitution, s 20(7) of the Act is indeed authorized by the Constitution, but the content of these Conventions in any event does not assist the case of the applicants.[187]

Fortunately, the place of treaties in a challenge to the constitutionality of legislation was clarified in *Glenister v President of the Republic of South Africa*,[188] which considered the constitutionality of legislation that brought into being the Directorate for Priority Crime Investigation (DPCI) (popularly known as the 'Hawks')[189] and disbanded the Directorate for Special Operations (popularly known as the 'Scorpions').[190] Moseneke DCJ and Cameron J, writing for the majority, held that the legislation in question was unconstitutional because the specialized unit it created to combat corruption failed to meet the requirement of independence by not providing for secured conditions of employment and by not removing executive oversight. Parliament was given 18 months to remedy this constitutional defect. The Court held that corruption 'undermines the democratic ethos,

[186] *AZAPO* (n 182) para 26.
[187] Ibid para 28.
[188] Supra (n 49).
[189] South African Police Service Amendment Act 57 of 2008.
[190] National Prosecuting Authority Act 32 of 1998, as amended by Act 56 of 2008.

the institutions of democracy, the rule of law and the foundational values of our nascent constitutional project'.[191] Corruption, said the Court, stunts sustainable development and economic growth and the state becomes unable to fulfil all the rights enshrined in the Bill of Rights, particularly economic and social rights.

In reaching this conclusion, the Constitutional Court relied heavily on international conventions aimed at combating corruption, particularly the United Nations Convention against Corruption,[192] the African Union Convention on Preventing and Combating Corruption[193]and the Southern African Development Community (SADC) Protocol Against Corruption,[194] which South Africa has ratified. These conventions are given effect to by the Prevention and Combating of Corrupt Activities Act 12 of 2004, which in its preamble acknowledges the SADC Protocol against Corruption and expressly declares that South Africa 'desires to be in compliance with and become Party to the UN Convention against Corruption'. The obligation contained in s 7(2) of the Constitution, said the Court, requires the state to respect, protect and fulfil the rights in the Bill of Rights and this creates the duty to create an independent and efficient anti-corruption mechanism. The content of this constitutionally imposed requirement of independence is to be found in the international agreements on corruption that bind South Africa internationally although they have not been incorporated into South African law. The anti-corruption agreements bind South Africa in terms of s 231(2) of the Constitution and this had 'significant impact in delineating the state's obligations in protecting and fulfilling the rights in the Bill of Rights'.[195] The Court continued:

> The obligations in these Conventions are clear and they are unequivocal. They impose on the Republic the duty in international law to create an anti-corruption unit that has the necessary independence. That duty exists not only in the international sphere and is enforceable not only there. Our Constitution appropriates the obligation for itself, and draws it deeply into its heart, by requiring the state to fulfil it in the domestic sphere. In understanding how it does so, the starting point is s 7(2), which requires the state to respect, protect, promote and fulfil the rights in the Bill of Rights .... Implicit in s 7(2) is the requirement that the steps the state takes to respect, protect, promote and fulfil constitutional rights must be reasonable and effective ....[196]

[191] *Glenister* (n 49) para 166.
[192] (2004) 43 *ILM* 37.
[193] (2004) 43 *ILM* 5.
[194] Available at http://www.sadc.int.
[195] *Glenister* (n 49) para 182.
[196] Paragraph 189.

> And it is here where the courts' obligation to consider international law when interpreting the Bill of Rights is of pivotal importance. Section 39(1)*(b)* states that when interpreting the Bill of Rights a court 'must consider international law'. The impact of this provision in the present case is clear, and direct. What reasonable measures does our Constitution require the state to take in order to protect and fulfil the rights in the Bill of Rights? That question must be answered in part by considering international law. And international law, through the interlocking grid of conventions, agreements and protocols we set out earlier, unequivocally obliges South Africa to establish an anti-corruption entity with the necessary independence.
>
> That is the duty this country itself undertook when it acceded to these international agreements. And it is an obligation that became binding on the Republic, in the international sphere, when the National Assembly and the NCOP by resolution adopted them, more especially the UN Convention.
>
> That the Republic is bound under international law to create an anti-corruption unit with appropriate independence is of the foremost interpretive significance in determining whether the state has fulfilled its duty to respect, protect, promote and fulfil the rights in the Bill of Rights, as s 7(2) requires. Section 7(2) implicitly demands that the steps the state takes must be reasonable. To create an anti-corruption unit that is not adequately independent would not constitute a reasonable step. In reaching this conclusion, the fact that s 231(2) provides that an international agreement that Parliament ratifies 'binds the Republic' is of prime significance. It makes it unreasonable for the state, in fulfilling its obligation under s 7(2), to create an anti-corruption entity that lacks sufficient independence.
>
> This is not to incorporate international agreements into our Constitution. It is to be faithful to the Constitution itself, and to give meaning to the ambit of the duties it creates in accordance with its own clear interpretive injunctions. The conclusion that the Constitution requires the state to create an anti-corruption entity with adequate independence is intrinsic to the Constitution itself . . . .[197]
>
> A further provision of the Constitution that integrates international law into our law reinforces this conclusion. It is s 233, which . . . demands any reasonable interpretation that is consistent with international law when legislation is interpreted. There is, thus, no escape from the manifest constitutional injunction to integrate, in a way the Constitution permits, international law obligations into our domestic law. We do so willingly and in compliance with our constitutional duty.[198]

Section 39(2) of the Constitution requires a court, when it develops the common law or customary law, to 'promote the spirit, purport and objects of the Bill of Rights'. In *Carmichele v Minister of Safety and Security (Centre for Applied Legal Studies Intervening)*[199] the Constitutional Court invoked decisions of the European Court of Human Rights,[200] the Convention on the Elimination of All Forms of

[197] *Glenister* (n 49) paras 192–5.
[198] Paragraph 202.
[199] 2001 (4) SA 938 (CC).
[200] Ibid paras 45–8.

Discrimination against Women,[201] and United Nations guidelines ('soft law')[202] to develop a new rule of common law. Commenting on this decision, Neville Botha writes that the Constitutional Court has

> shown clearly that the spirit, purport and objects of the Bill of Rights—which reflects the underlying precepts of the Constitution and the fabric of South African society—are inextricably linked to international law and the values and approaches of the international community and international role players.[203]

The Supreme Court of Appeal later followed the approach of the Constitutional Court.[204]

In *Government of Zimbabwe v Fick and Others*[205] the Constitutional Court had to determine whether a cost order granted by the SADC Tribunal against the Zimbabwean government in favour of certain Zimbabwean farmers could be enforced in South Africa. The cost order had been granted by the Tribunal in a matter where the farmers challenged the Zimbabwean government's expropriation of their land without compensation. The Constitutional Court relied on South Africa's obligations under the SADC Treaty[206] and Tribunal Protocol[207] to develop the common-law rule allowing for the enforcement of foreign court judgments to include the enforcement of judgments by the SADC Tribunal.[208] In particular, Mogoeng CJ, writing for the majority, held that '[t]he Amended [SADC] Treaty, incorporating the Tribunal Protocol, places an international law obligation on South Africa to ensure that its citizens have access to the Tribunal and that its decisions are enforced. Section 34 of the Constitution must therefore be interpreted, and the common law developed, so as to grant the right of access to our courts to facilitate the enforcement of the decisions of the Tribunal in this country. This, as said, will be achieved by regarding the Tribunal as a foreign court, in terms of our common law.'[209]

An increasing number of statutes refer expressly to international

[201] *Carmichele* (n 199) para 62.

[202] Ibid para 73.

[203] 'The role of international law in the development of South African common law' (2001) 26 *SAYIL* 253 at 259.

[204] *Minister of Safety and Security v Carmichele* 2004 (3) SA 305 (SCA) 319–20.

[205] 2013 (5) SA 325 (CC).

[206] Treaty of the Southern African Development Community (which had been amended to incorporate the Tribunal Protocol).

[207] Protocol on Tribunal in the Southern African Development Community.

[208] For a critical discussion of the case, see H Woolaver 'Judicial enforcement of international decisions against foreign states in South Africa: The case of *Government of the Republic of Zimbabwe v Louis Karel Fick and Others*' (2015) 6 *Constitutional Court Review* 217.

[209] *Government of Zimbabwe v Fick* (n 205) para 69.

law and some make it clear that the statute is to be interpreted to accord with international law. For instance, the Promotion of Equality and Prevention of Unfair Discrimination Act[210] provides that any person interpreting the Act may be 'mindful' of international law,[211] and the Implementation of the Rome Statute of the International Criminal Court Act[212] provides that a court applying the Act must consider both conventional and customary international law.[213] Such statutes confirm the principle expounded in s 233 of the Constitution that legislation is to be interpreted in accordance with international law. Of course, given the interpretative obligation imposed by s 233 of the Constitution, the inclusion in statutes of a specific requirement to have regard to international law is, to an extent, unnecessary.

10 Hierarchy of treaties in municipal law

The Constitution is the supreme law of South Africa. A treaty enacted into law by national legislation in accordance with s 231(4) of the Constitution will enjoy the status accorded to it by the act of incorporation: a treaty enacted into law by an Act of Parliament will be treated as an Act of Parliament, whereas a treaty enacted into law by subordinate legislation will be treated as subordinate legislation. A non-self-executing treaty binding on South Africa internationally but not incorporated into municipal law will have no direct force of law. However, *(a)* national legislation must be interpreted in light of and in line with such non-self-executing treaties, as made clear by s 233 of the Constitution and confirmed by the Constitutional Court, inter alia, in *National Commissioner v SALC*[214] and in *S v Okah*;[215] *(b)* such treaties may be used as part of the basis upon which to challenge legislation and government action, along the lines indicated in *Glenister v President of the Republic of South Africa*,[216] *Progress Office Machines CC v SARS*,[217] and *Law Society of South Africa v President of the Republic of South Africa* (discussed below);[218] and *(c)* such non-self-executing treaties may be used as the basis for developing the common law, as was done in *Government of Zimbabwe*

[210] 4 of 2000.
[211] Section 3(2)*(a)*.
[212] 27 of 2002.
[213] Section 2.
[214] 2015 (1) SA 315 (CC) para 24.
[215] *S v Okah* (n 174).
[216] Supra (n 49) paras 192–4.
[217] Supra (n 179) para 11.
[218] 2018 (6) BCLR 695 (GP).

v Fick.[219] A self-executing treaty will obviously, in terms of s 231(4), give way to both the Constitution and an Act of Parliament. Such a self-executing treaty will probably take priority over delegated legislation, in the event of a conflict.

11 The executive certificate[220]

The executive is responsible for the conduct of South Africa's foreign relations, and, in the exercise of this function, it will frequently make decisions on subjects governed by international law. These include[221] the recognition of a foreign state or government,[222] the recognition of territorial acquisitions by another state, the commencement or termination of a state of war with another country,[223] whether or not a person is entitled to diplomatic status,[224] whether any territory is a constituent part of a federation and whether any person is to be regarded as head of state or government of a foreign state.[225] Obviously, it is undesirable that different organs of state should pronounce on the same subject, particularly if their assessment of the legal implications of the matter should differ. As Lord Atkin said in *Government of the Republic of Spain v SS 'Arantzazu Mendi' (The Arantzazu Mendi)*,[226] '[o]ur state cannot speak with two voices . . . the judiciary saying one thing, the executive another'. Consequently, in order to avoid confusion of this kind, the courts have deferred to the judgment of the executive on certain acts or facts of state. The judgment of the executive is generally given in an executive certificate handed in to court, and the effect of such a certificate is 'to substitute the view of the government for an independent judicial investigation into the factual position'.[227] In this way, the executive in effect seeks to usurp the power of a municipal court to apply rules of customary international law to a particular factual situation that comes before it.

[219] Supra (n 205). Neither the SADC Treaty nor the Tribunal Protocol has been domesticated and the Constitutional Court, while not directly considering the issue, did not suggest that either international agreement was self-executing.

[220] See further on this topic, AJGM Sanders 'Our state cannot speak with two voices' (1971) 88 *SALJ* 413; AJGM Sanders 'The courts and recognition of foreign states and governments' (1975) 92 *SALJ* 165; Booysen (n 5) 83–6.

[221] R Jennings and A Watts (eds) *Oppenheim's International Law* 9 ed (1992) vol 1 at 1046–52.

[222] See Chapter 7.

[223] *Minister of Home Affairs v Bickle* 1984 (2) SA 439 (ZS) 450H.

[224] The executive publishes a list of persons entitled to diplomatic immunity in the *Government Gazette* in terms of s 7(2) of the Diplomatic Immunities and Privileges Act 37 of 2001. See *S v Penrose* (n 29); J Dugard 'Consular immunity' (1966) 83 *SALJ* 126.

[225] Section 17 of the Foreign States Immunities Act 87 of 1981.

[226] [1939] AC 256 (HL) 264.

[227] Sanders (n 220) 'Our state cannot speak with two voices' 413–14.

The leading case on the subject of an executive certificate is *S v Devoy* in which the Natal Provincial Division[228] and the Appellate Division[229] considered the continued existence of an extradition agreement between South Africa and Nyasaland (later Malawi) after the dissolution of the Federation of Rhodesia and Nyasaland. Here, the Department of Justice issued a certificate stating that, as far as the South African government was concerned, the treaty continued to be in force after the dissolution of the Federation and that its validity was unaffected by Nyasaland's reversion to colonial status and subsequent emergence as the independent state of Malawi. Although the capacity of Nyasaland to enter into treaties in the pre-independence period was questioned, both the Court *a quo* and the Appellate Division held that they were bound by the executive certificate on this subject and could not 'go behind' it.[230] In the Court *a quo*, James JP stated:[231]

> It is clear from the certificate produced from the Minister of Justice the South African Government recognised the competence of Nyasaland after its secession from the Federation to be a party to an extradition agreement entered into by the government of the Federation. This recognition is a function of the executive branch of government; it is a political act entailing legal consequences. Once that recognition has been granted by the executive branch of any country it is not for the judicial branch to consider whether that recognition was competent.

In *Harksen v President of the Republic of South Africa*,[232] a case decided under the Interim Constitution of 1993, the Cape Provincial Division was confronted with an executive certificate from the Minister of Justice declaring that there was no extradition agreement between South Africa and the Federal Republic of Germany. The Court noted that 'as it is undesirable that different organs of the state should pronounce on the same subject, particularly if their assessments of the legal implications of the matter should differ . . . it may well be that this Court should accept the Minister of Justice's certificate as binding on it'.[233] However, with no consideration of the law governing the conclusiveness or otherwise of an executive certificate, the Court stated:

> Having regard to the view which we take of this matter, it is unnecessary to decide whether the certificate by the Minister of Justice is binding on the

228 1971 (1) SA 359 (N).
229 1971 (3) SA 899 (A).
230 *S v Devoy* (n 228) 363D; *S v Devoy* (n 229) 906–7.
231 *S v Devoy* (n 228) 362H.
232 1998 (2) SA 1011 (C).
233 Ibid 1019–20.

Court and we accordingly proceed on the basis that it is not.[234]

The court then embarked on a thorough examination of extradition treaty relations between South Africa and Germany, and of the law on this subject, from which it concluded that there was indeed no valid treaty in existence.

The source of the executive's power to issue a conclusive (or *prima facie*) certificate has a statutory basis in the case of immunities conferred on foreign diplomats and other foreign state representatives[235] and on foreign states.[236] In other cases, the executive arguably relies on its non-statutory discretionary common-law powers to conduct foreign relations as neither the Interim Constitution[237] nor the 1996 Constitution[238] appear to expressly confer powers on the executive in matters such as the recognition of foreign states or governments or the determination of the existence of treaties between South Africa and foreign states. The continued validity of such powers, sometimes described as prerogative powers, is highly questionable,[239] and the suggestion that the executive retains any of the old prerogative powers other than where those are now provided for in the Constitution or in legislation has been conclusively rejected by the Constitutional Court.[240] However, it is impossible to contemplate the denial of such powers to the executive,[241] as without them it could not carry out its management of the country's foreign relations. Therefore, it is preferable to view these powers, or many of them, as

[234] *Harksen* (n 232) 1020C. See the criticism of this statement by N Botha in 'International law in South African courts' (1999) 24 *SAYIL* 330.

[235] Diplomatic Immunities and Privileges Act 37 of 2001, s 9(3).

[236] Foreign States Immunities Act 87 of 1981, s 17. Unlike s 9(3) of the Diplomatic Immunities and Privileges Act, which merely provides that the certificate is '*prima facie*' proof of any fact in relation to 'any question [which] arises as to whether or not any person enjoys any immunity or privilege under this Act or the [Vienna] Conventions', s 17 of Foreign States Immunities Act provides that the certificate by the Minister of Foreign Affairs (now the Minister of International Relations and Co-operation) is 'conclusive proof', inter alia, of 'whether any foreign country is a state for the purposes of this Act' and 'whether any territory is a constituent part of a federal foreign state for the said purposes'.

[237] Section 82(1) of Act 200 of 1993.

[238] Section 84 of the 1996 Constitution.

[239] *President of the Republic of South Africa v Hugo* 1997 (4) SA 1 (CC) 6–9; G Carpenter 'Prerogative powers in South Africa—Dead and gone at last?' (1997) 22 *SAYIL* 104.

[240] *Mohamed v President of the Republic of South Africa* 2001 (3) SA 893 (CC) paras 31 and 32; *President of the Republic of South Africa v South African Rugby Football Union* 2000 (1) SA 1 (CC) para 144; and *Mansingh v General Council of the Bar* 2014 (2) SA 26 (CC) paras 4–6. Sections 84(1) and 85(2)*(h)* of the Constitution appear to make clear that the executive has no powers outside those provided for in the Constitution or by legislation. See *Mansingh* para 25.

[241] Carpenter (n 239) 108; H Booysen 'Has the act of state doctrine survived the 1993 Interim Constitution?' (1995) 20 *SAYIL* 189 at 191.

now flowing from ss 84(2)*(h)* and *(i)*,[242] 85(2)*(b)*,[243] 92(1)[244] and/or 231[245] of the Constitution when interpreted purposively. This approach has been endorsed by the Constitutional Court.[246] And, as the Supreme Court of Appeal held in *Minister of Justice v SALC*, albeit in the context of statutory interpretation, '[t]he ordinary principle of interpretation is that the conferral of a power conveys with it all ancillary powers necessary to achieve the purpose of that power'.[247]

Yet, outside of the limited situations governed by statute,[248] it is difficult to assert that a certificate issued by the executive on its assessment of an act or fact of state retains its conclusiveness under our new constitutional rules. As shown above, the courts have made clear that all exercises of public power are now subject to constitutional control, and s 232 of the 1996 Constitution provides that 'customary international law is law in the Republic unless it is inconsistent with the Constitution or an Act of Parliament'. This

[242] Section 84(2)*(h)* and *(i)* provide that '[t]he President is responsible for—

. . .

(h) receiving and recognising foreign diplomatic and consular representatives;

(i) appointing ambassadors, plenipotentiaries, and diplomatic and consular representatives'.

[243] Section 85(2) provides that '[t]he President exercises the executive authority, together with the other members of the Cabinet, by—

. . .

(b) developing and *implementing* national policy' (emphasis added).

Such national (as opposed to provincial or local government) policy would evidently include the country's international relations policy.

[244] Section 92(1) provides that '[t]he Deputy President and Ministers are responsible for the powers and functions of the executive assigned to them by the President'. The President evidently can, and does, assign foreign affairs powers and functions to Ministers (see *Von Abo v President of the Republic of South Africa* 2009 (5) SA 345 (CC) paras 43 and 45).

[245] Section 231(1) provides that '[t]he negotiating and signing of all international agreements is the responsibility of the national executive'.

[246] See *Van Abo v The President* (n 244) para 45 where the Constitutional Court held that the source of the executive's power to provide diplomatic protection was 's 85(2) read together with s 92(1) of the Constitution'. In *Kaunda and Others v President of the Republic of South Africa and Others* 2005 (4) SA 235 (CC), O'Regan J pointed out (para 243) that '[i]t is clear, though perhaps not explicit, that under our Constitution the conduct of foreign affairs is primarily the responsibility of the Executive. That this is so, is signified by a variety of constitutional provisions, including those that state that the President is responsible for receiving and recognising foreign diplomatic and consular representatives, appointing ambassadors, plenipotentiaries and diplomatic and consular representatives, and that the national executive is responsible for negotiating and signing international agreements. The conduct of foreign relations is therefore typically an executive power under our Constitution.'

[247] *Minister of Justice v SALC* (n 54) para 95.

[248] The Diplomatic Immunities and Privileges Act 37 of 2001, s 9(3) and the Foreign States Immunities Act 87 of 1981, s 17.

means that an executive certificate issued in terms of any general executive powers in relation to foreign affairs flowing from the Constitution (assuming such power exists) that expresses an opinion on a question of international law—such as whether an entity meets the customary international law requirements of statehood or whether a treaty is in force between South Africa and another state—is now subject to judicial review. The same holds true for executive certificates issued in terms of any statute. Executive certificates issued in terms of a statute, whether the statute provides for them to be conclusive proof (as in the case of the Foreign States Immunities Act) or merely *prima facie* proof (as in the case of the Diplomatic Immunities and Privileges Act), are nevertheless the exercise of public power that will be reviewable, at least on grounds of irrationality or bad faith.[249] In other words, a certificate issued in terms of s 17 of the Foreign States Immunities Act will, as provided for in that section, indeed be conclusive while extant; however, it would always be open to a litigant to seek to review the certificate for failure to comply with the principle of legality, and have it set aside.

In practice, courts will no doubt extend a margin of appreciation to the executive in matters such as the recognition of states and governments in which it is undesirable that the state should 'speak with two voices'. In other cases, such as the continued existence of a treaty, different considerations apply. Sections 232 and 39(1) (where human rights are in issue) require a court to examine whether the statement in an executive certificate correctly reflects customary international law. The court in *Harksen* was therefore correct in declining to accept the Minister's certificate as binding upon it and in making its own determination of the question of customary international law before it.

12 The justiciability of acts of state

Before 1994, the application of international law in South Africa was subject to constitutional rules and prerogative powers derived from English law. The position has now changed dramatically. South Africa is a constitutional democracy in which the principles of executive accountability and transparency feature prominently and the courts are given wide powers of review of executive and administrative action and legislation. Although the Constitution confers on the executive broad powers to enable it to conduct South Africa's foreign relations, these powers are no longer beyond the reach of judicial review.[250]

[249] See *Kaunda* (n 246) para 80; *DA v Minister of International Relations* (n 90) para 44.
[250] Ibid.

This issue is of particular importance in respect of 'acts of state'—that is the acts of foreign states within their own territories and the acts of the South African government in the field of foreign affairs—which have hitherto been beyond judicial scrutiny.

(a) The justiciability of acts of the South African government in foreign relations

The starting point for the doctrine of the non-justiciability of acts of the state to whose structures the courts belong is *Van Deventer v Hancke & Mossop*[251] in which the Transvaal Supreme Court was asked to rule that the British annexation of the South African Republic on 1 September 1900 was premature on the ground that the British forces had not established effective control over the territory—a prerequisite for annexation under customary international law. To this argument, Innes CJ responded:[252]

> It is no doubt correct as a general rule of international law that two circumstances are necessary to create a complete title by conquest: the conqueror must express in some clear manner his intention of adding the territory in question to his dominions, and he must by exercise of military force demonstrate his power to hold it as part of his own possessions. It is also true that in March, 1901, large portions of the Transvaal, including the district of Vryheid, were neither occupied nor dominated by British troops; but on the contrary were under the *de facto* control of the Boer forces. And if this were a foreign court engaged in trying a cause in regard to which the question of when the conquest of the Transvaal was complete became relevant to the inquiry, it is possible that points of considerable intricacy and difficulty would present themselves. But those considerations are not present here. This is a court constituted by the British Crown, exercising powers and discharging functions derived from the Crown. In its dealings with other states the Crown acts for the whole nation, and such dealings cannot be questioned or set aside by its courts. They are acts of state into the validity or invalidity, the wisdom or unwisdom, of which domestic courts of law have no jurisdiction to inquire.

Subsequent decisions adopted a similar approach.[253] The refusal of courts to 'go behind' an executive certificate on a matter of foreign relations was a further manifestation of the non-justiciability of acts of the South African government by domestic courts.[254]

[251] Supra (n 18).

[252] At 409–10. See, to the same effect, *Postmaster-General v Taute; Treasurer-General v Van Vuuren; Postmaster-General v Parsons; Master of Supreme Court v Roth* 1905 TS 582 at 586.

[253] *Ex parte Belli* 1914 CPD 742 at 747; *Verein fur Schutzgebietsanleihen EV v Conradie NO* 1937 AD 113 at 146–7; *Haak v Minister of External Affairs* 1942 AD 318 at 326; *Vereeniging Municipality v Vereeniging Estates Ltd* 1919 TPD 159 at 163.

[254] See above, notes 228–31.

However, over two decades of post-constitutional jurisprudence would appear to confirm that there are now no longer any acts of the South African government in relation to foreign affairs that remain non-justiciable today. First, courts are given the power to apply rules of customary international law not inconsistent with the Constitution or an Act of Parliament. A court therefore has the power to apply a rule of customary international law contrary to an executive decision, which gives it the power to enquire whether an executive act complies with international law. Secondly, s 34 of the 1996 Constitution grants everyone 'the right to have any dispute that can be resolved by the application of law decided in a fair public hearing before a court' without qualification. Thirdly, the Constitutional Court has held that 'every exercise of public power, including every executive act' must comply with the principle of legality,[255] and that the 'exercise of all public power is subject to constitutional control'.[256] The principle of legality requires decisions to be procedurally and substantively rational and lawful (*intra vires* the executive's powers).[257] This applies equally to exercises of public power in relation to foreign affairs, which the Constitutional Court has held are justiciable.[258] In these circumstances, it appears that, in principle, all the executive's decision-making in relation to foreign affairs is now justiciable, and the only question is the standard of review, and the extent to which the Court will give deference to the executive, in light of separation of powers considerations.[259]

[255] *Minister of Defence and Military Veterans v Motau* 2014 (5) SA 69 (CC) para 69; see also *Democratic Alliance v President of the Republic of South Africa* 2013 (1) SA 248 (CC) para 27; *Pharmaceutical Manufacturers Association of SA: In re Ex Parte President of the Republic of South Africa* 2000 (2) SA 674 (CC) paras 51 and 85.

[256] *National Treasury v Opposition to Urban Tolling Alliance* 2012 (6) SA 223 (CC) para 64.

[257] See *DA v Minister of International Relations* (n 90) paras 54 and 64; *Pharmaceutical Manufacturers Association of SA* (n 255) paras 17–20 and 85; *Democratic Alliance v President of the Republic of South Africa* (n 255) para 34; *Mansingh v General Council of the Bar* (n 240 para 25.

[258] *Kaunda* (n 246) paras 78–80. See also the full bench High Court decision of *DA v Minister of International Relations* (n 90) para 44.

[259] Some of the early academic debate and uncertainty appears to have been settled by cases such as *Kaunda* (n 246), *DA v Minister of International Relations* (n 90) and *Law Society v the President* (n 218), as well as others discussed below, which all demonstrate that the courts now view all foreign affairs decisions to be justiciable. For this early academic debate, see Booysen (n 241) who states that acts of state 'have not survived the Interim Constitution unscathed' and that 'an act of state has become justiciable in terms of international law' (196). Carpenter (n 239), however, argues acts of state are 'not subject to judicial scrutiny, in accordance with the doctrine of separation of powers' (111). It is difficult to understand how the doctrine of separation of powers can override ss 232, 34 and, possibly, s 39(1) (if human rights are involved) or the

One of the earlier post-constitutional High Court cases that dealt with the issue is *Kolbatschenko v King NO and Another*.[260] Here, the state sought to prevent judicial review of a decision on the part of the appropriate authorities to request legal assistance from a court in Liechtenstein in a criminal investigation by arguing:

> The respondents' requests for foreign assistance, directed as they are to foreign governments, constitute the conduct of foreign affairs by the Republic. Consequently, neither the decisions to make the requests nor the requests themselves are justiciable in the sense of being susceptible to rescission, review or declaratory proceedings in a South African court.[261]

In support of this argument, it was contended that 'as a general rule, South African courts should exercise judicial restraint when dealing with South Africa's foreign relations with other countries, in particular because of the lack of judicial or manageable standards by which to judge the issue'.[262]

The Court held that there was no absolute rule of non-justiciability in respect of the conduct of foreign relations. It stated:

> [E]ven if one were to accept that the Executive retains certain discretionary non-statutory powers to enable it to conduct foreign relations (such as, for example, the recognition of foreign States and governments or the determination of the existence of treaties between South African and foreign States), it would appear that such powers are no longer *per se* beyond the scrutiny of the South African courts (see, in this regard, Dugard *International Law: A South African Perspective* 2nd ed (2000) at 64–9). Whether or not a court will, in any particular case, sit in judgment upon, and, if necessary, interfere with, a decision or action of the executive depends, in our view, on the nature and subject-matter of the decision or action concerned.[263]

On the one hand, the Court said it should be borne in mind that 'the requirement of accountable, responsive and transparent government is one of the founding values of our constitutional democracy' and that it is 'only in highly exceptional cases that a court will adopt a "hands-off" approach where a discretion has been exercised or an

principle of legality recognised by s 1*(c)* of the Constitution. See further K Lehmann 'The act of state doctrine in South African law: Poised for reintroduction in a different guise' (2000) 15 *SA Public Law* 337; and K Lehmann 'The foreign act of state doctrine: Its implications for the rule of law in South Africa' (2001) 16 *SA Public Law* 68.

260 2001 (4) SA 336 (C). See the comments on this case by N Botha 'The post-Constitution "act of state": The need for further theoretical refinement' (2002) 27 *SAYIL* 295; GN Barrie 'Is the absolute discretionary prerogative relating to the conduct of foreign relations alive and well and living in South Africa?' 2001 (3) *TSAR* 409.

261 *Kolbatschenko* (n 260) 352F–G.

262 Ibid 354C–D.

263 Ibid 355F–H.

executive or administrative decision made which directly affects the rights and interests of an individual applicant'.[264]

On the other hand, the Court acknowledged that:

> South African courts have refused to evaluate decisions or actions in the realm of foreign relations involving issues of a 'high executive nature'. Thus, for example, matters such as the recognition by the South African Government of a foreign State or of a foreign government, or of the status of diplomatic representatives of a foreign State, have generally been regarded as non-justiciable (see, for example, *Inter-Science Research and Development Services (Pty) Ltd v Republica Popular de Mocambique* 1980 (2) SA 111 (T) at 117D–G). Such decisions usually involve the relationship between the South African State and the foreign State concerned, directly affecting the interests of such States *as States*, and are often of so 'political' a nature that the courts have 'no judicial or manageable standards' by which to judge them (*per* Joffe J in *Swissborough Diamond Mines (Pty) and Others v Government of the Republic of South Africa and Others* (1999 (2) SA 279 (T) 334F–G), citing the judgment of Lord Wilberforce in *Buttes Gas and Oil Co v Hammer and Another (Nos 2 and 3); Occidental Petroleum Corp and Another v Buttes Gas and Oil Co and Another (Nos 1 and 2)* [1981] 3 All ER 616 (HL) at 633*a–f*. This type of decision, which falls four-square within the political arena, would include matters such as the making, or the determination of the existence, of treaties between South Africa and foreign States, the declaration of war and the making of peace. In such cases, it is indeed undesirable that the State should 'speak with two voices' and the latitude extended by the Judiciary to the Executive in such matters will be correspondingly large.[265]

The Court held, however, that considerations of this kind did not apply in the present case, as the decision to request foreign legal assistance did '*not* involve the evaluation of social or economic policy among competing claims'.[266] Nor did it concern 'matters of a "high executive nature" directly impacting upon or affecting the relationship between South Africa and the foreign State *as States*'.[267] The Court concluded by stating that it could not be said that in assessing the regularity of a request for foreign legal assistance in a criminal investigation 'a court would be in a "judicial no-man's land" in that it would lack "judicial or manageable standards" by which to judge the issues involved'.[268] Consequently, it held that the request for legal assistance from Liechtenstein was justiciable.

The Constitutional Court adopted a similar approach in *Mohamed v President of the Republic of South Africa (Society for the Abolition of the Death Penalty in South Africa Intervening)*[269] in which it reviewed the

[264] *Kolbatschenko* (n 260) 355C–D.
[265] Ibid 356–7.
[266] Ibid 357C–D (emphasis in the original).
[267] Ibid 357F–G (emphasis in the original).
[268] Ibid 357H–I.
[269] 2001 (3) SA 893 (CC) para 31.

decision of the government to deport a Tanzanian national, who was wanted by the United States in connection with the 1998 bombing of the United States embassy in Dar es Salaam, to the United States. The Court held that the government had acted unconstitutionally by deporting Mohamed without securing an undertaking from the United States that, if convicted, the death penalty could not be imposed on him, and ordered the government to obtain an assurance that such a sentence would not be imposed.[270] The Court stated:

> To stigmatise such an order as a breach of the separation of State power as between the Executive and the Judiciary is to negate a foundational value of the Republic of South Africa, namely supremacy of the Constitution and the rule of law. The Bill of Rights, which we find to have been infringed, is binding on all organs of State and it is our constitutional duty to ensure that appropriate relief is afforded to those who have suffered infringement of their constitutional rights.[271]

That the powers of the executive are not unlimited in foreign affairs was confirmed by the Constitutional Court in *Geuking v President of the Republic of South Africa* when it declared:

> The President . . . must be free to take into account any matter considered relevant to what is a policy decision relating to foreign affairs. It is not for the courts to determine what matters are appropriate or relevant for that purpose. The Court could intervene only if the President were to abuse the power vested in him or use it in a manner contrary to the provisions of the Constitution.[272]

Kaunda and Others v President of the Republic of South Africa and Others (Society for the Abolition of the Death Penalty in South Africa intervening as Amicus Curiae)[273] raised the question whether a court might direct the government to protect its nationals abroad who were threatened with serious human rights violations in Zimbabwe or Equatorial Guinea. Although the Constitutional Court found that the applicants had failed to establish that the government's response to requests for assistance was inconsistent with international law, the Court held that South African nationals facing adverse state action in a foreign country are entitled to request the government to protect them and the government is obliged to consider such requests and to deal with them appropriately. The Court stated:

> *Decisions made by the government in these matters are subject to constitutional control.* Courts required to deal with such matters, will, however, give particular weight to the Government's special responsibility for and particu-

[270] See also *Minister of Home Affairs v Tsebe* 2012 (5) SA 467 (CC).

[271] *Mohamed* para 71.

[272] 2003 (3) SA 34 (CC) para 27.

[273] Supra (n 246). See, too, the judgment of the Transvaal Provincial Division, *Kaunda v President of the Republic of South Africa* 2004 (5) SA 191 (T).

> lar expertise in foreign affairs, and the wide discretion that it must have in determining how best to deal with such matters.[274]

Although the Court recognised that the government should be given a wide margin of appreciation in its decision to extend diplomatic protection to South African nationals, the Court stated:

> If the Government refuses to consider a legitimate request, or deals with it in bad faith or irrationally, a court could require Government to deal with the matter properly. Rationality and bad faith are illustrations of grounds on which a court may be persuaded to review a decision.[275]

Tladi and Dlagnekova are correct in saying:

> The essence of the judgment is, therefore, that while the executive has a broad discretion when conducting foreign affairs, the courts can review such decisions on the grounds of, for example, irrationality and bad faith. Thus, in contrast to the act of state doctrine, the exercise of power by the executive in the conduct of foreign affairs is reviewable by the courts. The courts can declare such exercise to be illegitimate or invalid. Although, the margin of discretion afforded to the state in the exercise of such power is extremely wide, the exercise of the power is nevertheless reviewable.[276]

Von Abo v Government of the Republic of South Africa and Others[277] must be seen in the context of the strictures in *Kaunda* relating to review of executive action taken in bad faith or irrationally. Here, the government failed to provide diplomatic protection to Von Abo, a South African national whose farms were seized without compensation by the Zimbabwe government. Numerous requests for assistance over a period of six years were not taken seriously[278] by the Department of Foreign Affairs. To aggravate matters, when Von Abo initiated legal proceedings against the government arising out of its failure to grant diplomatic protection, the respondent government Ministers, and particularly the Minister of Foreign Affairs, failed to

[274] *Kaunda* (n 246) para 144(6) (emphasis added). See, too, *Van Zyl v Government of the RSA* (n 57) paras 55–7.

[275] *Kaunda* (n 246) para 80. This *dictum* was confirmed in *Von Abo v President of the Republic of South Africa* 2009 (5) SA 345 (CC). See further on the power to review the exercise of the government's discretion, the separate opinions of Judge Ngcobo in *Kaunda* (n 246) (para 172) and Judge O'Regan (paras 243–5, 269–71).

[276] 'The act of state doctrine in South Africa: Has *Kaunda* settled a vexing question?' (2007) 22 *SA Public Law* 444.

[277] 2009 (2) SA 526 (T); 2010 (3) SA 269 (GNP); 2009 (5) SA 345 (CC); 2011 (5) SA 262 (SCA). For a strong criticism of *Von Abo*, see D Tladi 'The right to diplomatic protection, the *Von Abo* decision, and one big can of worms: Eroding the clarity of Kaunda' (2009) 20 *Stellenbosch LR* 14.

[278] According to Prinsloo J, it was 'difficult to resist the conclusion that the respondents were simply stringing the applicant along and never had any serious intention to afford him proper protection. Their feeble efforts, if any, amounted to little more than quiet acquiescence in the conduct of their Zimbabwean counterparts and their "War veteran" thugs' (2009 (2) SA 526 (T) para 112). See, too, para 143.

offer any explanation to the Court by way of affidavit, leaving it to a senior law adviser to attest to the opposing affidavit. This 'shocking dereliction of duty',[279] coupled with the failure to afford protection to Von Abo, led Prinsloo J to conclude that the government had acted irrationally and in bad faith[280] and to issue an order declaring that the failure of the respondents 'rationally, appropriately and in good faith' to consider Von Abo's request for diplomatic protection was inconsistent with the Constitution. He further held that Von Abo had a right to diplomatic protection and that the government had a constitutional obligation to provide diplomatic protection. Prinsloo J accordingly ordered the government to remedy the violation of rights of the applicant by the government of Zimbabwe and to report within 60 days on the steps that had been taken to do so. No appeal was lodged against this order.[281]

The government's response to the above order was remarkable. First, neither the Minister for Foreign Affairs nor any of the other respondent ministers produced an affidavit on steps they had taken to protect Von Abo. Nor was there any explanation as to why they had failed to do so. Instead, the Deputy Director of the Department of Foreign Affairs produced an affidavit that provided information about meetings between relatively junior officials from the Department of Foreign Affairs and the Zimbabwe government at which no serious effort had been made to assert the need to provide relief to Von Abo. (This contrasted with the more assertive and effective actions of other states on behalf of their nationals.)

In these circumstances, Prinsloo J declared the conduct of the Minister of Foreign Affairs to be contemptuous[282] and found that the respondents had failed to comply with the main order.

It is clear that a court cannot instruct the government on how to make diplomatic interventions or on what interventions to make. But it is not true to say that any intervention will suffice. In response to the government's argument that it had discharged its constitutional obligations by making some representations even though they were unsuccessful, Prinsloo J stated:

> I disagree. On this argument . . . it would mean that a government which has the prerogative to decide on the nature of the diplomatic interventions to be made, can opt for the most ineffective and weak measures, which have no prospect of achieving the desired result, and still insist that their feeble efforts

[279] *Von Abo* (n 278) para 41.

[280] Ibid para 143.

[281] In *Von Abo* (n 275) the Constitutional Court held that it was unnecessary for Prinsloo J's order to be confirmed by this Court.

[282] *Von Abo v Government of the Republic of South Africa* 2010 (3) SA 269 (GNP) paras 27 and 56.

> pass constitutional muster because they have the prerogative to decide what measures to adopt . . . . To argue that the measures [adopted by respondents] comply with the court order because it is the prerogative of the government to decide what measures to adopt, is untenable. It does not pass the test as expressed in *Kaunda, Mohamed* and *Fose.* The task must be performed *properly.* The remedy afforded to an aggrieved individual whose fundamental rights have been impaired . . . must be an effective one.[283]

An appeal to the Supreme Court of Appeal in *Von Abo*[284] succeeded on the ground that Von Abo had failed to establish that he was entitled to diplomatic protection and that Prinsloo J had erred in ordering the government to remedy the situation within such a limited time frame and in ordering the government to pay damages to a national in respect of a wrong committed by Zimbabwe in the territory of Zimbabwe. The Court did, however, accept the finding in *Kaunda* that a court may review the decision of government not to exercise diplomatic protection when it had acted irrationally or in bad faith.[285] Here, the SCA held that it was unable to assess the reasonableness and appropriateness of the government's response to Von Abo's request for diplomatic protection because it had not been 'entrusted with the content of the government policy or specific steps taken by particular officials in terms of recognised procedures and protocols'.[286] This led the SCA to state that 'this case is an example of how a government, founded on a constitutional dispensation and a culture of human rights, is not supposed to treat its citizens and its courts'.[287] How, in these circumstances, the Court could fail to make a finding that Von Abo was entitled to diplomatic protection on the grounds of irrationality and bad faith is not clear.

In *DA v Minister of International Relations,* which is discussed in more detail above, a full bench of the North Gauteng High Court found that the government's decision to deposit a notice with the United Nations Secretary-General withdrawing South Africa from the Rome Statute was unconstitutional. In reviewing the government's decision, the Court pointed out that '[i]t is now axiomatic that the exercise of all public power, including the conducting of international relations, must accord with the Constitution. . . . While the notice of withdrawal was signed and delivered in the conduct of international relations and treaty-making as an executive act, it still remained an exercise in public power, which must comply with the

[283] *Von Abo* (n 282) para 58(4).

[284] 2011 (5) SA 262 (SCA). This decision is more fully discussed in Chapter 13 in the section on the discretionary nature of the right to diplomatic protection.

[285] Ibid para 28.

[286] Ibid para 39.

[287] Ibid para 39.

principle of legality and is subject to constitutional control.'[288] The Court ultimately found that the decision should be set aside because it violated s 231(2) of the Constitution and was irrational.

In *Earthlife Africa* the Western Cape High Court was faced with challenges to decisions in relation to the government's entering into of international agreements dealing with nuclear procurement and co-operation (as well as challenges to certain determinations in relation to new energy generation capacity under domestic legislation). One of the challenges the Court was faced with was a challenge to the constitutionality of the Minister of Energy's signature of an inter-governmental agreement (IGA) with Russia relating to nuclear procurement (and the President's authorisation thereof). As shown above, the Court was willing to hold that the international agreement was unlawfully tabled, after being signed, under s 231(3) of the Constitution (avoiding the need for parliamentary approval) when it should have been tabled under s 231(2). However, the Court held that it was premature to determine whether the President and the Minister violated the Constitution by signing the agreement (which would have required the Court to effectively determine that the terms of the agreement were inconsistent with the Constitution).[289] The basis for this finding was that given the relief to be granted due to the unconstitutional tabling (setting aside the tabling under s 231(3)) the international agreement would then still need to be placed before Parliament under s 231(2) (for parliamentary approval) before it became binding on South Africa. The Court therefore held that it was appropriate, in light of the principle of the separation of powers, to refuse, at that stage, to determine whether the President's approval of the signature of the international agreement was irrational and in violation of s 217 of the Constitution (which deals with the requirements for lawful public procurement).[290] The Court explained its decision as follows:

> Should the executive then choose to table the Agreement before Parliament in terms of [s] 231(2), a parliamentary/political process will follow in which the Agreement will be debated in both the NA and the NCOP with a view to its approval or disapproval by Parliament. It may very well also be the subject of a process of public participation conducted through Parliament. The outcome of this process cannot be foreseen nor should it be anticipated. In these circumstances it would be invidious if the Court were, at this stage, to declare that certain of its provisions are inconsistent with the Constitution and, more specifically, [s] 217 thereof. *This is not to suggest, however, that the Court will lack*

[288] *DA v Minister of International Relations* (n 90) para 44.
[289] *Earthlife Africa* (n 81) paras 117–21.
[290] Ibid para 120.

jurisdiction to deal with such a question in future if the need should arise.[291]

In *Law Society of South Africa and Others v President of the Republic of South Africa and Others*[292] the North Gauteng High Court was faced with a challenge arising from the suspension of the SADC Tribunal. The applicants (the Law Society of South Africa and a number of Zimbabwean nationals and companies) sought to have the President's participation in the SADC Summit's decision to suspend the SADC Tribunal in 2011[293] and the President's signature of the 2014 Protocol for the Tribunal (which would replace the extant 2000 Protocol for the Tribunal and limit the Tribunal's jurisdiction to hear only inter-state complaints) declared unconstitutional. Although a number of grounds of review were raised, the President's conduct was challenged primarily on the basis that it was irrational, in bad faith, and violated South Africa's obligations under the SADC Treaty and the 2000 Tribunal Protocol.

The Court held that both the President's participation in the Summit's decision to suspend the Tribunal (effectively failing to object to the consensus decision to suspend the Tribunal) and his signature of the 2014 Protocol were unlawful, irrational and, therefore, unconstitutional.

The Court's finding that the President's participation in the Summit's suspension of the Tribunal was unlawful, irrational and, therefore, unconstitutional was based on a number of grounds (albeit, the judgment does not always clearly delineate between its findings of unconstitutionality in relation to the President's participation in the suspension and those in relation to his signature of the 2014 Protocol). First, the Court found that the President's participation in the suspension was unlawful. The Court held that this was so since it determined that the suspension violated the SADC Treaty (which had been amended to incorporate the 2000 Tribunal Protocol) since '[t]he Tribunal and its jurisdiction lie at the heart of the SADC Treaty and fulfil one of its main purposes. Its emasculation by way of its de facto suspension was therefore similarly in conflict with the Founding Treaty and South Africa's constitutional obligations'.[294] Flowing from the violation of the SADC Treaty, the Court found that the participation in the suspension was also therefore in violation of 'constitutional obligations'. On this point, the judgment is not a picture of clarity. It appears that the Court's finding was based on one

[291] *Earthlife Africa* (n 81) para 120 (emphasis added).

[292] 2018 (6) BCLR 695 (GP).

[293] The President was represented by South Africa's High Commissioner to Namibia.

[294] Paragraph 67.

or more of the following constitutional violations:[295] *(a)* a violation of the rule of law (the Court appeared to accept that an executive action or decision that violated South Africa's international obligations would be in violation of the rule of law enshrined in s 1*(c)*); *(b)* a violation of s 7(2) of the Constitution (the obligation on the state to protect and promote the rights in the Bill of Rights)—although why this section was violated was not explained;[296] or *(c)* a violation of s 231 since there had been no parliamentary approval for the President's conduct in not seeking to prevent the Summit from suspending the Tribunal.[297] Secondly, the Court found that the decision was procedurally and substantively irrational, since the President had not properly explained the reasons for failing to object to the suspension and had not sought to consult with the public in relation to a decision that effectively nullified individuals' vested rights to approach the Tribunal under the existing SADC Treaty and 2000 Protocol (at least while the suspension remained in place).

In relation to the President's signature of the 2014 Protocol, the Court's finding that the decision was irrational and unlawful appears to have been primarily predicated on its acceptance, without clearly determining the issue, that the 2014 Protocol bound South Africa merely on the President's signature. This appears, inter alia, from the fact that the Court held that 'the Tribunal's jurisdiction was simply signed away' by the President[298] and that the President's signature 'severely undermined the crucial SADC institution, the Tribunal'.[299] The difficulty with this finding is that the 2014 Protocol is expressly made subject to ratification. Member states that wish to bind themselves to the Protocol have to ratify it 'in accordance with their constitutional procedures'.[300] The Protocol only comes into force when two-thirds of the member states have deposited their instruments of ratification.[301] While the President signed the 2014 Protocol, the government had not yet sought to ratify the Protocol. Importantly, the 2014 Protocol expressly provided that it is only when it

[295] See paras 66 and 67.

[296] However, the Court did not indicate which rights were violated, since the Court did not find that s 34 provided a right to access international tribunals (as opposed to domestic courts) (see para 21, where the Court records that the Law Society made it clear that it was not arguing that s 34 guaranteed the right of access to international tribunals).

[297] See paras 66 and 67.

[298] Paragraph 69.

[299] Paragraph 71.

[300] Article 52 provides that '[t]his Protocol shall be ratified by Member States who have signed the Protocol in accordance with their constitutional procedures'.

[301] Article 53 provides that '[t]his Protocol shall enter into force thirty (30) days after the deposit of the Instruments of Ratification by two-thirds of the Member States'.

enters into force (after the depositing of the requisite number of instruments of ratification) that it will change the Tribunal's jurisdiction by repealing the 2000 Tribunal Protocol. This is so since article 48 of the 2014 Protocol states that '[t]he 2000 Protocol on the Tribunal in the Southern African Development Community is repealed with effect from the date of entry into force of this Protocol'. Thus, to the extent that the Court's decision was implicitly predicated on accepting that the President bound South Africa to the 2014 Protocol by his mere signature, the Court does not explain how this could be reconciled with the express provisions of the Protocol.

The Court's declarations of unconstitutionality in respect of the President's participation in the suspension of the Tribunal and his signature of the Protocol were, in terms of s 172 of the Constitution, referred by the High Court to the Constitutional Court for confirmation.[302] This was required since the conduct declared unconstitutional amounted to 'conduct of the President', which declarations must, in terms of s 172(2)*(a)*, be confirmed by the Constitutional Court. At the time of writing, the Constitutional Court had not yet determined the matter.

(b) The justiciability of acts of foreign governments

Anglo-American courts, whose decisions have guided South African courts on matters of international law, have produced a substantial body of decisions on the justiciability of acts of foreign states. In South Africa there was no reported decision until 1999.

In the United States the act of state doctrine prohibits a US court from declaring invalid the official act of a foreign sovereign performed within its own territory.[303] Although the doctrine is premised on a policy of judicial restraint, the Supreme Court has held that it 'does not establish an exception for cases and controversies that may embarrass foreign governments'.[304]

The position in England is less clear. Although the term 'act of state' is used, courts prefer to see the refusal to pronounce on acts of

Article 55(1) specifies that 'all instruments of Ratification . . . shall be deposited with the Executive Secretary of SADC who shall transmit certified copies to all Member States'.

[302] Order 3.

[303] *Underhill v Hernandez* 168 US 250 (1897) 252; *Banco Nacional de Cuba v Sabbatino* (n 25) 427–8; J Harrison 'The American act of state doctrine' (2016) 47 *Georgetown Journal of International Law* 507.

[304] *Kirkpatrick v Environmental Tectonics* 493 US 400 (1990) 405. See, too, *Kadic v Karadzic* (1995) 34 *ILM* 1592 at 1612: '[J]udges should not reflexively invoke these doctrines to avoid difficult and somewhat sensitive decisions in the context of human rights.'

foreign governments as the exercise of a policy of judicial restraint. In *Buttes Gas and Oil Co v Hammer (No 3)* Lord Wilberforce declared:

> There exists in English law a more general principle that the courts will not adjudicate upon the transactions of foreign states. Though I would prefer to avoid argument on terminology, it seems desirable to consider this principle, if existing, not as a variety of 'act of state' but one for judicial restraint or abstention.[305]

The existence of a broad principle of judicial restraint in matters affecting the transactions of foreign states has been criticised by scholars[306] and courts in England.[307] Recent decisions, however, suggest that English courts will be prepared to pronounce on the compatibility of foreign law with international law,[308] particularly in the field of human rights.[309]

In the *Belhaj* case the United Kingdom Supreme Court recently had the opportunity to undertake a detailed review of the law in relation to the act of state doctrine and the inter-linked issue of state immunity.[310] In *Belhaj* the claimants sought to bring claims in tort against the United Kingdom government and certain officials for alleged complicity in their rendition and mistreatment at the hands of foreign states. The Supreme Court found that in English law there are three types of foreign acts of state.[311] It held, first, that a court would normally treat a foreign state's legislation as valid in so far as it affects movable or immovable property within the foreign state's jurisdiction, and, secondly, a court would not normally question the validity of a foreign governmental act in respect of property within

[305] [1982] AC 888 at 931. See, too, *Al Jedda v SSD* [2010] EWCA civ 758.

[306] FA Mann in *Foreign Affairs in English Courts* (1986) states: '[T]he great danger, not always avoided, is that by holding a claim non-justiciable the court fails to perform its duty of deciding cases . . . . It is possible that this judicial duty was violated by the most puzzling pronouncement on justiciability that can be found in England' at 69. See, too, JR Crawford 'Public international law' (1982) 53 *BYIL* 253, 267–8; L Collins 'Foreign relations and the judiciary' (2002) 51 *ICLQ* 485.

[307] *Maclaine Watson v Department of Trade and Industry* [1988] 3 All ER 257 (CA) 291 (Kerr LJ); [1989] 3 All ER 523 at 544–5 (Lord Oliver).

[308] *Kuwait Airways Corporation v Iraqi Airways Company* [2002] UKHL 19, [2002] 2 WLR 1353. At para 26, Lord Nichols stated: 'In appropriate circumstances, it is legitimate for an English Court to have regard to the content of international law in deciding whether to recognize a foreign law.' See further paras 28–9, 114–15, 138–40, 148. This decision was cited with approval by Patel J in *Van Zyl v Government of the RSA* (n 57) paras 70–1.

[309] *Abbasi v Secretary of State for Foreign and Commonwealth Affairs* [2002] EWCA Civ 1598, (2003) 42 *ILM* 358 paras 57, 66. See, too, *R v Bow Street Metropolitan Stipendiary Magistrate, Ex parte Pinochet Ugarte* [1998] 3 WLR 1456 (HL) 1480 (Lord Steyn).

[310] *Belhaj and Another v Straw and Others; Rahmatullah v Minister of Defence and Others* [2017] UKSC 3; [2017] 3 All ER 337.

[311] Ibid paras 35–43 (judgment of Lord Mance).

the foreign state's jurisdiction. *It was the scope of the third type of foreign act of state that was principally in issue.* The third type is the rule of non-justiciability or judicial abstention whereby a domestic court will not adjudicate upon sovereign acts committed by a foreign state abroad, which was developed in *Buttes*—and which Lord Sumption, in his separate judgment, styled as an 'international act of state'.[312] Such a situation may arise, inter alia, where a court cannot properly hear a claim due to a lack of judicial or manageable standards, or as a function of the separation of powers, where a court considers that it should not hear a claim since it is outside the proper bounds of its constitutional functions.

Neither the United States act of state doctrine nor the English doctrine of judicial restraint are rules of international law.[313] They are principles of domestic law that limit justiciability in foreign relations in accordance with their own constitutional rules. Consequently, they are not binding on South African courts in terms of s 232 of the Constitution.

A South African court may decide to follow the judicial policies of the United States or the United Kingdom in respect of non-justiciability but it can only do so within the framework of its own constitutional rules in general, and ss 34 and 232 in particular. A court cannot fashion a principle of judicial restraint or non-justiciability for South Africa that takes no account of this framework, particularly when it differs so fundamentally from that of the United States or the United Kingdom.

It is against this background that the decision of the Transvaal Provincial Division in *Swissborough Diamond Mines (Pty) Ltd v Government of the Republic of South Africa*[314] must be viewed. Here, the applicant, a company registered in Lesotho but controlled by South African shareholders, sought to obtain discovery of documents relating to an alleged conspiracy between the South African and Lesotho governments to dispossess the applicant of its rights to diamond leases in Lesotho. With no mention of South Africa's constitutional rules, Joffe J found that the 'true agreement' between South Africa and Lesotho was non-justiciable.[315] Although he found it unnecessary to make any finding on the conduct of the government of Lesotho, he found that the relationship between South Africa and Lesotho 'belonged' to international law and was 'not an area for the

[312] *Belhaj (n 310) paras 234 et seq.*

[313] IA Shearer (ed) *Starke's International Law* 11 ed (1994) 100–1; R Jennings and A Watts (eds) *Oppenheim's International law* 9 ed (1992) vol I at 369; *Banco Nacional de Cuba v Sabbatino* (n 25) 427–8.

[314] 1999 (2) SA 279 (T).

[315] At 330C.

judicial branch of government'. It was therefore 'a matter in respect of which this court should exercise judicial restraint'.[316] In reaching this conclusion, he declared:

> The basis of the application of the act of state doctrine or that of judicial restraint is just as applicable to South Africa as it is to the USA or England. The comity of nations is just as applicable to South Africa as it is to other sovereign states. The judicial branch of government ought to be astute in not venturing into areas where it would be in a judicial no-man's land. It would appear that in an appropriate case, as an exercise of the court's inherent jurisdiction to regulate its own procedure, the court could determine to exercise judicial restraint and to refuse to entertain a matter, notwithstanding it having jurisdiction to do so, in view of the involvement of foreign states therein.[317]

Referring to *Swissborough* as authority, the Supreme Court of Appeal held that '[c]ourts should act with restraint when dealing with allegations of unlawful conduct ascribed to sovereign States'.[318]

More recently, the question of whether a matter should be dismissed on the basis of the act of state doctrine, and the linked basis of state immunity, arose in the case of *Saharawi Arab Democratic Republic and Another v Owners and Charterers of the MV NM Cherry Blossom and Others*.[319] In this case the applicants—the Saharawi Arab Democratic Republic (SADR) (a state recognised by South Africa but regarded by the United Nations as the non-self-governing territory of Western Sahara) and the Polisario Front, a national liberation movement—applied *ex parte* (without notice to the other parties) for an urgent interim interdict to restrain a cargo of phosphate jhat had been mined by a Moroccan mining company, pursuant to Moroccan law, in Western Sahara. (Morocco claims that Western Sahara, which it refers to as the Southern Provinces, forms part of Morocco's territory.) The phosphate mined in Western Sahara was on board the *NM Cherry Blossom*, a ship which had docked in Port Elizabeth to refuel on route to New Zealand. The applicants sought to prevent the phosphate from being removed from the jurisdiction of the Court, pending the determination of an action in which the applicants claimed, inter alia, delivery of the cargo (based on alleged ownership of the phosphate, as a natural resource extracted from Western Sahara, which belonged to the people of Western Sahara). The High Court granted the *ex parte* interim order preventing the cargo from being removed from the Court's jurisdiction pending a return date,

[316] At 334F–H.

[317] At 334D–E. See the criticism of this decision by N Botha 'The foreign affairs prerogative and the 1996 Constitution' (2000) 25 *SAYIL* 265.

[318] *Van Zyl v Government of the Republic of South Africa* 2008 (3) SA 294 (SCA) para 5.

[319] 2017 (5) SA 105 (ECP).

when the Court, after service on the parties, would determine whether to grant an interdict pending the determination of a vindicatory action to be instituted for recovery of the phosphate. In the subsequent opposed hearing, the Moroccan mining company and its subsidiary (collectively 'OCP') opposed the application and sought the dismissal of the interim interdict.

OCP raised two principal legal defences to the applicants' claims. First, that in terms of the act of state doctrine, the issues that must be determined by the Court for the application to succeed were non-justiciable before any South African court. Secondly, that the application indirectly impleaded Morocco (since it required the Court to effectively determine that Morocco's *de facto* administration and law making for Western Sahara, in terms of which OCP conducted its mining, was unlawful and invalid) and thus the Court was barred from hearing the case as a result of Morocco's state immunity.

In considering the act of state defence, the Court found that it was premature to consider whether the doctrine would preclude the applicants' claim to the phosphate. This was so, the Court reasoned, because courts that are dealing with interlocutory proceedings where the issues are of particular complexity should only decide such issues as are strictly necessary to be determined at an interlocutory stage. The Court found that it was only once the issues had been fully and precisely pleaded at the trial stage that it would be appropriate to consider whether the claim made it necessary for the Court to determine the lawfulness of a foreign act of state.[320] However, while not applying the doctrine in the case before it, the Court confirmed a number of features of the doctrine of act of state (or 'foreign act of state') as a matter of South African law. First, it pointed out that '[u]nlike, state immunity, which is a rule of public international law, the doctrine of a foreign act of state is a municipal law rule which derives from common law principles as developed in Anglo-American courts. It is founded upon the principle of mutual respect for equality of sovereign states, the principle of comity.'[321] Secondly, with reference to *Swissborough* and the Supreme Court of Appeal's decision in *Van Zyl v Government of the Republic of South Africa*, it accepted that the act of state doctrine was applicable in South Africa.[322] Thirdly, it pointed out that the guiding principles of the doctrine are that '[a] court which is called upon to exercise restraint or to refrain from adjudicating a matter in respect of which it

[320] Paragraph 92.
[321] Paragraph 86, read with para 95.
[322] Paragraphs 87–8.

otherwise has jurisdiction will do so with caution and then only in circumstances where it is necessary to determine the particular issue engaged by a foreign act of state'.[323] Fourthly, the Court emphasised that the doctrine's application and scope are subject to constitutional discipline. It emphasised that a court 'bound as it is to apply the Constitution as supreme law and to give effect to the spirit, purport and objects of the Constitution, will be mindful of the fundamental rights contained therein, particularly the right of access to the courts enshrined in s 34, in determining the circumstances in which and the ambit of the exercise of its discretion to decline adjudication in circumstances where an act of a foreign sovereign is engaged'.[324]

The Court, in dealing with the issue of state immunity,[325] held that the determination of the applicants' claim would have 'an [e]ffect upon the interests of Morocco but such [e]ffect falls within the realm of political or moral interests and cannot have legal affect. It follows therefore that the claim to state immunity cannot be upheld'. Thus, importantly, the Court accepted that, even though Morocco itself was not directly being sued, if the claim *would* have had an effect on Morocco's legal rights and interests, then state immunity (under the Foreign States Immunities Act 87 of 1981 and customary international law) would preclude the claim. The Court relied on[326] the Supreme Court of Appeal's decision in *Minister of Justice v SALC*, where it accepted that state immunity 'is available when it is sought to implead a foreign state, whether directly or indirectly, before domestic Courts, and also when action is taken against state officials acting in their capacity as such. They enjoy the same immunity as the state they represent'.[327] The Court accepted that the concept of indirect impleading, as articulated in *Minister of Justice v SALC*, was recognised (and precluded by) s 2(2) of the Foreign States Immunities Act.[328] However, the Court noted that since there was no direct South African judicial authority on the principles of indirect implead-

[323] Paragraph 95.

[324] Paragraph 96.

[325] Paragraphs 60–85.

[326] Paragraph 61.

[327] Supra (n 54) para 66. By way of example of what would constitute indirect impleading precluded by state immunity, the Supreme Court of Appeal noted that this would include 'a civil action against an individual in respect of actions on behalf of a foreign state, where permitting an action against the individual would circumvent the state's immunity' (*Minister of Justice v SALC* para 66 fn 41, referencing *Jones v Ministry of the Interior* (n 67) as authority).

[328] Section 2(1) and (2) provide as follows:

'(1) A foreign state shall be immune from the jurisdiction of the courts of the Republic except as provided in this Act or in any proclamation issued thereunder.

ing (presumably other than the brief statement in *Minister of Justice v SALC*) it was necessary to have regard to 'customary international law and, in particular, the manner in which the principle is interpreted and applied'.

The Court, in analysing the customary international law position, relied heavily on the interpretation and application of the principle by the UK Supreme Court in *Belhaj* (discussed above). When one considers the Court's application of the principles of indirect impleading to the facts of the case, it is not entirely clear why the Court suggested that Morocco's interest in the matter was merely 'political', when it had held earlier that '[t]he exercise of administrative control [by Morocco] and the application of Moroccan law to the portion of the territory of Western Sahara under Moroccan control . . . is at the *heart of the dispute as to the exercise of the right to self-determination [which includes the claim to the Cargo] by the Saharawi people*'.[329] The Court partly explained that the reason why it found that the legal rights of Morocco were not affected was that Morocco was not a party to the proceedings and had no proprietary right to the cargo.[330] But neither of these are necessary requirements for indirect impleading (in fact, quite the opposite: in indirect impleading, the foreign state is not a party).[331] And, at a practical level, it is quite easy to see what the effect on Morocco's legal rights would be. The judgment would mean that Morocco could no longer guarantee that OCP would have lawful and enforceable title over the minerals that OCP mined in Western Sahara—thus, effectively rendering Morocco's granting of title and its regulation thereof invalid (at least within South Africa). Conversely, the SADR would henceforth be entitled, as a matter of South African law, to have attached within South Africa's jurisdiction any minerals mined in Western Sahara, notwithstanding the minerals having been mined by entities given legal title to do so by Morocco. This would appear, as a matter of law, at least within South Africa, to render Morocco's laws and the passing of title invalid.

Having found that state immunity did not preclude the Court from determining the matter, and having found that the question of whether the act of state doctrine precluded the claim should be decided at the trial stage, the Court interdicted the removal of the phosphate from the jurisdiction of the Court pending a vindicatory

(2) A court shall give effect to the immunity conferred by this section even though the foreign state does not appear in the proceedings in question.'

329 *Saharawi Arab Democratic Republic* (n 319) para 58 (emphasis added).

330 Ibid para 83

331 Ibid para 74, where the Court quotes with approval from Lord Sumption's judgment in *Belhaj* (n 310).

action for delivery of the cargo, which the applicants were given leave to institute.

13 The extraterritorial application of the Constitution

In *Mohamed v President of the Republic of South Africa (Society for the Abolition of the Death Penalty in South Africa Intervening)*[332] the Constitutional Court held that the deportation of Tanzanian national Mohamed to the United States—with the collusion of US officials, for him to stand trial in that country—violated South Africa's Constitution because the South African government failed to obtain a prior undertaking that, if he were convicted, the death penalty would not be imposed on him. This infringed his constitutional rights to human dignity, life and not to be punished in a cruel, inhuman or degrading manner.[333] The court ordered its judgment to be delivered to the US federal court trying Mohamed in New York. Mohamed was not sentenced to death.

In a thoughtful analysis of the case, Max du Plessis points out that this case did not really constitute an extraterritorial application of the Constitution as the harm to Mohamed in the United States was caused by the action of public officials in South Africa: 'The "extra-territorial" application of the Constitution is thus an application of the Bill of Rights, triggered by effects abroad, which would be the end-result of acts of public officials begun in South Africa.'[334]

This interpretation of *Mohamed* was confirmed by the Constitutional Court in *Kaunda and Others v President of the Republic of South Africa and Others*.[335] In this case, the Court refused to order the South African government to extend the protection offered by the South African Constitution to South African nationals whose rights were threatened in a foreign country (Zimbabwe or Equatorial Guinea). The court stated that 'it is a general rule of international law that the laws of a state ordinarily apply only within its own territory'.[336] It acknowledged that:

> There may be special circumstances where the laws of a State are applicable to nationals beyond the State's borders, but only if the application of the law does not interfere with the sovereignty of other States. For South Africa to

[332] 2001 (3) SA 893 (CC).

[333] The Court relied, inter alia, on *Soering v UK* (1989) 11 EHRR 439 and *United States v Burns* [2001] 1 SCR 283.

[334] 'The extra-territorial application of the South African Constitution' (2003) 120 *SALJ* 797 at 799.

[335] *Kaunda* (n 246) paras 46–57. Cf the dissenting opinion of Judge O'Regan op cit paras 248–56.

[336] Ibid para 38.

> assume an obligation that entitles its nationals to demand, and obliges it to take action to ensure, that laws and conduct of a foreign State and its officials meet not only the requirements of the foreign State's own laws, but also the rights that our nationals have under our Constitution would be inconsistent with the principle of State sovereignty. Section 7(2) should not be construed as imposing a positive obligation on government to do this.[337]

The Court, however, wisely left open the question whether the extraterritorial infringement of a constitutional right by an organ of the South African state in circumstances that do not infringe the sovereignty of a foreign state would be justiciable.[338]

More recently, the question of the extraterritorial effect of the Constitution was indirectly at issue in the case of *Law Society of South Africa v President of the Republic of South Africa*.[339] The applicants challenged the constitutionality of two distinct actions by the President. First, they challenged the President's conduct in relation to the SADC Summit's suspension of the SADC Tribunal in 2011. Secondly, they challenged the President's signature of the new SADC Tribunal Protocol in 2014. The Court held that both the President's actions (his conduct in relation to the suspension and his signature) were irrational and unlawful and therefore unconstitutional. Of relevance to the issue of extraterritoriality is the fact that the Court was prepared to declare that the President's failure—through his representative, the High Commissioner to Namibia, who attended the Summit's meeting on his behalf—to object to the SADC Summit's consensus decision to suspend the Tribunal (taken by the Summit at its May 2011 meeting in Namibia) was unconstitutional. The Court made this declaration of unconstitutionality on a number of grounds, including that the President's conduct was found to be irrational and in violation of constitutional and international law obligations. Notwithstanding that the President, through his representative, was acting as a member of an international organisation (the Summit, SADC's highest policy-making body) not based in South Africa, and was participating in the consensus decision-making process governed by international law and not domestic law (the SADC Treaty governed the decision making in question), the Court was still willing to find that the President's conduct was reviewable in terms of the Constitution. This decision would therefore appear to be authority for the proposition that actions of South Africa's diplomats and other representatives in international organisations, such as the United Nations, remain subject to constitutional control and must

[337] *Kaunda* (n 246) para 44. Confirmed in *Rootman v President of the RSA*, Oxford Reports on International Law ILDC 469 (ZA 2006), [2006] SCA 80 para 11.

[338] Ibid para 45. Cf *R v Cook* [1998] SCR 597.

[339] Supra (n 292).

comply with the Constitution and, in particular, the principle of legality. Thus, these officials' decisions must be rational as a matter of South Africa law and must comply with any relevant constitutional and international law obligations. If their decisions are irrational or unlawful (either violating the Constitution or international law) they would be regarded as violating the principle of legality. The mere fact that a decision or conduct occurred abroad and as part of an international organisation's decision-making process would not preclude a South African court from reviewing the decision.

* * * * * *

The 1996 Constitution includes provisions dealing with succession to treaties, international human rights law, self-determination, humanitarian law and the use of force. These provisions are considered in the appropriate chapters.

CHAPTER 5

States (Including Recognition and Non-recognition)

John Dugard

The state is the centre of the international legal order. Clear rules of customary international law and treaty law proclaim the rights and duties and the privileges and responsibilities of the state. Yet the birth and origins of the state are shrouded in legal uncertainty. There is confusion over whether the creation of a state is a question of fact or of law, whether the fulfilment of certain factual criteria suffices or whether the imprimatur of the law is also required. The death or demise of a state is an area from which international law keeps its distance. States are sovereign, but the notion of sovereignty and its implications are better left for philosophical discourse rather than legal definition. Although the concepts of the state and statehood are central to our understanding of international law, this remains the most unsettled and uncharted branch of international law.

Until recent times only states were subjects of international law. Today other entities, such as inter-governmental organisations, are also accepted as international persons with rights and duties under international law.[1] The state, however, remains the principal actor[2] in the international arena and the *raison d'être* of the international legal system. It is therefore necessary to examine the notion of statehood and to consider how entities claiming to be states are accepted into the community of nations as full subjects of international law.[3]

International law is a product of European, Christian civilisation and was for many centuries a European law of nations.[4] When a new state appeared in Europe, it was received into the community by the old members of the European society of nations. After the decolonisation of the Americas, non-European, Christian states were admitted to the 'club'. With the admission of the Ottoman Empire to the community of nations in 1856, international law ceased to be a law between Christian states only. Thereafter, non-European, non-Chris-

[1] Chapter 1.

[2] R Jennings and A Watts (eds) *Oppenheim's International Law* 9 ed (1992) vol 1 at 16.

[3] See, in particular, on this subject, J Crawford *The Creation of States in International Law* 2 ed (2006).

[4] *Oppenheim* (n 2) 87–91.

tian states such as Japan, China, Siam and Persia were accepted as states. The creation of the League of Nations, and later the United Nations, provided a new mechanism for the collective admission of states to the international community.[5] Although the existing states retained the right to admit new members by unilateral acts of recognition on their part, there is no doubt that the League of Nations and the United Nations have both facilitated and accelerated the process of international acceptance.

The acceptance of new states into the international community is effected mainly by means of 'recognition' on the part of the existing states. Although this process is determined or influenced by political considerations, certain factual criteria for statehood have been adopted to guide the decision to recognise states. Consequently, it is necessary to consider both these criteria and the process of recognition for an understanding of the creation of states.

South African history provides a good illustration of the process of state creation. During the apartheid era, the South African government sought to promote the independent statehood of four Bantustans—Transkei, Bophuthatswana, Venda and Ciskei (the so-called TBVC states)—in order to give legitimacy to the policy of separate development, as the apartheid regime preferred to term apartheid.[6] The refusal of the international community to recognise these entities as states demonstrates how law and politics interact in the creation—or non-creation—of states. More recently, the process of state creation and its hazards have been illustrated by the recognition as states of Palestine and Kosovo by some states but not others and by the manner in which key states have obstructed their admission to the United Nations.

[5] J Dugard *Recognition and the United Nations* (1987); J Dugard 'The secession of states and their recognition in the wake of Kosovo' (2013) 357 *Recueil des Cours* 10 at 57–69. (This lecture series is also published as a pocketbook by the Hague Academy of International Law (2013). References are, however, to the pagination of the *Hague Recueil.*)

[6] J Dugard 'South Africa's independent homelands: An exercise in denationalization' (1980) 10 *Denver Journal of International Law and Policy* 11; GE Norman 'The Transkei: South Africa's illegitimate child' (1977) 12 *New England Law Review* 585; MP Vorster, M Wiechers and DJ van Vuuren (eds) *The Constitutions of Transkei, Bophuthatswana, Venda and Ciskei* (1985).

THE CRITERIA FOR STATEHOOD

The traditional criteria for statehood are described in the Montevideo Convention of 1933,[7] which provides:

> The state as a person of international law should possess the following qualifications: *(a)* a permanent population; *(b)* a defined territory; *(c)* government; and *(d)* capacity to enter into relations with other states.

Although this is a regional convention, signed by 15 Latin American states and the United States, it has come to be accepted as the definitive statement on the criteria for statehood. Its requirements are factual by nature but 'they have been accepted as the normative starting point on state recognition, not only by scholars and lawyers, but also, more importantly, by states'.[8] Consequently, they must be seen as constituting the legal conditions for statehood—conditions that must be considered by third states in deciding whether to grant recognition to a seceding entity.

More recently, since human rights and self-determination have become more important in international law, it has been suggested that for a new entity to succeed in a claim for statehood, it should meet the standards and expectations of the international community on these subjects. This development was given support by Guidelines on the Recognition of New States in Eastern Europe and in the Soviet Union issued by the European Community in 1991,[9] and extended to Yugoslavia, which sought to make recognition of states dependent on compliance with international norms relating to self-determination, respect for human rights and the protection of minorities.

1 Permanent population

No minimum population size is required. Today, more than 50 states have populations of less than one million, and Tuvalu and Nauru have less than 15 000 inhabitants each. The microstate presents problems in the United Nations as it seems unfair that India, with a

[7] The requirements expounded in the Montevideo Convention receive support from Opinion 1 of the Arbitration Commission established in 1991, under the chairmanship of Mr Badinter of France, to advise the European Community on legal problems arising from the dissolution of Yugoslavia. The Commission stated 'that the state is commonly defined as a community which consists of a territory and a population subject to an organized political authority; that such a state is characterized by sovereignty': 92 ILR 162. The Montevideo requirements for statehood were accepted in *Abdi v Minister of Home Affairs* 2011 (3) SA 37 (SCA) 51 para 29.

[8] C Ryngaert and S Sobrie 'Recognition of states: International law or *realpolitik*? The practice of recognition in the wake of Kosovo, South Ossetia and Abkhazia' (2011) 24 *Leiden Journal of International Law* 467 at 472.

[9] (1991) 62 *BYIL* 559; (1992) 41 *ICLQ* 477.

population of 1.3 billion, should have the same voting rights as the Seychelles, with a population of 95 000. Attempts to remedy this inequality in the United Nations, however, have been abandoned and microstates are today accepted as full members of the international community.[10]

2 Defined territory

It is not a necessary prerequisite of statehood that a state has clearly defined and undisputed borders.[11] The borders of Israel and Palestine, for example, have been a subject of dispute for over 50 years. The state, however, should have a stable community within an area over which its government has control. Furthermore, it is not necessary for a state to occupy a single territory. Prior to the creation of Bangladesh in 1971, Pakistan was divided into East and West Pakistan, separated by India; and, Canada separates Alaska from the rest of the United States. It was therefore difficult to argue that Bophuthatswana lacked statehood on the ground that it comprised a number of separate territories.[12]

3 Government

In order to meet this requirement a state must have a government that is in effective control of its territory and that is independent of any other authority.[13] The fact that a government receives substantial financial aid from another state would not in itself appear to affect its formal independence. This was, however, one of the reasons given by the United Kingdom for its refusal to recognise Bophuthatswana.[14]

The requirement of effective government was relaxed in the process of decolonisation, which saw many former colonies recognised as states with governments still heavily dependent on the colonial power. Political considerations, too, have led to a weakening of this requirement. The recognition of Croatia and Bosnia-Herzegovina by the European Community in 1992, and their subsequent admission as 'states' to the United Nations in the same year, cannot be reconciled with this criterion as both were embroiled in a civil war,

[10] See J Duursma *Fragmentation and the International Relations of Micro-States* (1996).

[11] In the *North Sea Continental Shelf Cases*, the International Court of Justice declared that 'there is . . . no rule that the land frontiers of a State must be fully delimited and defined' (1969 ICJ Reports 3 para 46).

[12] *S v Banda* 1989 (4) SA 519 (B) at 540E–F.

[13] Ibid at 540G–H.

[14] *Hansard*, HC, vol 105, col 100 (12 November 1986); vol 126, cols 760–761 (3 February 1988).

in which no authority exercised effective control over either territory, at the time of their recognition.[15]

Difficulties arise when a recognised state degenerates into anarchy or civil war (as in the instances of Yemen and Syria).

Although logic might suggest that such an entity—a 'failed state'—should cease to be a state, the practice of states provides no support for such a view. (The phenomenon of the 'failed state' is considered below.)

A state does not cease to be a state when it is militarily occupied by another state. During World War II, Germany occupied countries such as the Netherlands, Belgium and Denmark, which clearly remained states even though they were subject to the control of German forces. Palestine occupies an unusual position in this respect as it had no government when it was first occupied by Israel in 1967. The subsequent establishment of a government, the recognition of Palestine by some 138 states and its admission to many international institutions reserved for states has remedied this defect and the statehood of Palestine, albeit under Israeli occupation, is today widely recognised.

4 Capacity to enter into relations with other states

The capacity of a state to enter into relations with other states is a consequence of independence.[16] If an entity is subject to the authority of another state in the handling of its foreign affairs, it fails to meet this requirement and cannot be described as an independent state.

The position of the TBVC states illustrates the complexities of this criterion for statehood. Although they enjoyed full constitutional independence under the respective Status Acts, which conferred independence on them,[17] and the formal capacity to enter into treaties[18] and diplomatic relations, they were unable to conduct international relations with states other than South Africa on account of their non-recognition by the international community. In *S v Banda*,

[15] C Warbrick 'Recognition of states' (1993) 42 *ICLQ* 433; M Weller 'The international response to the dissolution of the Socialist Federal Republic of Yugoslavia' (1992) 86 *AJIL* 569.

[16] This explains why the definition of a state, adopted by the Badinter Arbitration Commission (n 7), emphasises 'sovereignty' (independence) rather than 'capacity to enter into relations with other states' (Montevideo) as the fourth requirement of statehood.

[17] The Status of the Transkei Act 100 of 1976 declared that 'the territory known as Transkei . . . is hereby declared to be a sovereign and independent state and shall cease to be part of the Republic of South Africa' (s 1). See above (n 7). Similar statutes were enacted in respect of the other TBVC states.

[18] H Booysen 'The South African homelands and their capacity to conclude treaties' (1982) 8 *SAYIL* 58.

in which the statehood of Bophuthatswana was challenged before a municipal court of that territory in a case of treason, Friedman J held that this requirement of statehood did not apply where the state had 'an infrastructure to implement relations with other states should it be given the opportunity to do so' but was 'precluded from so doing due to political considerations'.[19] 'An entity possessing all the other essentials of being a state', said the judge, 'cannot be regarded as not having the capacity to enter into relations with other states if it is denied the opportunity to demonstrate this capacity in practice.'[20] This view, which ignores the role played by recognition in the creation of states, is out of touch with reality for, as Hedley Bull has written, a community that claims to be sovereign 'but cannot assert this right in practice, is not a state properly so-called'.[21] *Formal* independence does not produce the capacity to enter into relations with other states. In addition, the claimant entity must be recognised by at least some states to make this theoretical capacity a reality to give it *functional* independence. Although recognition may not create a state, it seems it should be taken into account in deciding whether the fourth requirement is met.

The Turkish Republic of Northern Cyprus (TRNC) occupies the same position today as did the TBVC states: it is recognised by no state other than its creator, Turkey. In *Caglar v Billingham (Inspector of Taxes)*, in which the British Special Commissioners of Inland Revenue were concerned with the exemption from liability for income tax for officials of a foreign state, the Commissioners adopted the above reasoning and held that the TRNC failed to qualify as a state:

> In view of the non-recognition of the Turkish Republic of Northern Cyprus by the whole of the international community other than Turkey we conclude that it does . . . not have functional independence as it cannot enter into relations with other states. It does not therefore satisfy the fourth requirement of statehood.[22]

[19] 1989 (4) SA 519 (B) 543C–D. For criticisms of this decision, see R Thomas '"hrough the Looking Glass"—The status of Bophuthatswana in international law' (1990) 6 *SAJHR* 65; DJ Devine '*Banda*'s case 1989: International law implications' (1990) 107 *SALJ* 434; HA Strydom 'Vrae rondom die erkenning van state' (1992) 3 *Stellenbosch LR* 67.

[20] *S v Banda* (n 19) 543G.

[21] *The Anarchical Society* (1977) 8–9. See also G Erasmus 'Criteria for determining statehood' (1988) 4 *SAJHR* 207 at 212, 220.

[22] 108 ILR 510, 545 (para 182). The decision is discussed at some length by C Warbrick 'Unrecognized states and liability for income tax' (1996) 45 *ICLQ* 954. The Commissioners incorrectly attributed these views to J Dugard *Recognition and the United Nations* instead of the present work.

Palestine and Kosovo present no difficulties in this respect. Although neither are members of the United Nations, they are both recognised by over 100 states and conduct relations with these states, thereby demonstrating their capacity to conduct international relations.

The evolving statehood of South Africa and its capacity to enter into relations with other states

In 1910 the four British colonies of the Cape, Natal, Transvaal and the Orange River joined to form the Union of South Africa.[23] This Union met the first three requirements of statehood—population, territory and effective government—but lacked the capacity to enter into relations with other states. The Union was not able to enter into treaties without the assistance of the United Kingdom,[24] to establish diplomatic relations with other states,[25] and to make war or peace.[26] Moreover, constitutionally, the South African Parliament was subordinate to Westminster as a result of the Colonial Laws Validity Act, which recognised the right of the British Parliament to legislate for the Dominions.[27] In these circumstances, South Africa could not claim to enjoy the right to enter into relations with other states or to be independent.

After World War I, South Africa evolved towards a position in which it enjoyed the capacity to enter into relations with other states free from the control of Britain. In 1919 it became an original member of the League of Nations[28] and thereafter asserted its independence from Britain by pursuing independent policies within that organisation.[29] Moreover, in 1920 South Africa was appointed by the League of Nations as Mandatory Power over South West Africa with direct

[23] See LM Thompson *The Unification of South Africa 1902–1910* (1960).

[24] Although Britain allowed South Africa some autonomy in the negotiation of commercial and technical treaties, it retained exclusive control over treaties of a political nature. See MM Lewis 'The international status of the British self-governing dominions' (1922–1923) 3 *BYIL* 21 at 23; RP Schaffer *A Critical Analysis of the Treaty-making Powers of the Union of South Africa and the Republic of South Africa* (PhD thesis, University of the Witwatersrand 1978) 4–8; RB Stewart 'Treaty-making procedure in the British dominions' (1938) 32 *AJIL* 467.

[25] South Africa did not send or receive diplomatic agents before World War I: Schaffer (n 24) 9–12.

[26] RP Schaffer 'The prerogative of war and peace: Its development in South Africa' (1978) 4 *SAYIL* 29.

[27] 28 & 29 Vict c 63.

[28] LM Friedlander 'The admission of states to the League of Nations' (1928) 9 *BYIL* 84 at 85.

[29] S Pienaar *South Africa and International Relations between the Two World Wars: The League of Nations Dimension* (1987).

accountability to the Council of the League.[30] That South Africa was now free to conduct its own foreign policy and to enter into treaties on its own account was confirmed by the Imperial Conference of 1926, which resolved that the Dominions and Britain were 'equal in status, in no way subordinate one to another in any aspect of their domestic or external affairs'.[31] In response, South Africa promptly established its own Department of External Affairs and proceeded to establish diplomatic missions in many parts of the world.[32] Treaties were now entered into by the South African executive on its own.[33] South Africa's constitutional position was brought into line with this state of affairs in 1931 by the Statute of Westminster, which made it clear that Westminster no longer enjoyed the right to legislate for the Dominions.[34] This was confirmed by the South African Parliament in the Status of Union Act[35] and the Royal Executive Functions and Seals Act.[36] By the mid-1930s, only one argument could be seriously advanced to support South Africa's subordination to Britain—namely the alleged right of Britain to declare war on behalf of South Africa.[37] The correctness of this argument was, however, disproved in 1939 when South Africa declared war against Germany independently of Britain.

It is difficult to pinpoint the exact moment at which South Africa became an independent state. Some may point to its admission to the League of Nations as the decisive time, while others may prefer the declaration of war in 1939. The correct view, it seems, is that South Africa acquired full international status at the moment that it acquired the capacity to enter into relations with other states *and* this capacity was recognised by Britain: 1926 therefore appears to be the year in which South Africa became a fully sovereign independent state under international law.[38] Constitutionally, independence was

[30] J Dugard 'South West Africa and the supremacy of the South African Parliament' (1969) 86 *SALJ* 194.

[31] G Carpenter *Introduction to South African Constitutional Law* (1987) 205.

[32] Pienaar (n 29) 6.

[33] Oppenheim states: 'In accordance with the Resolutions of 1926, "full powers" to sign the treaty are issued on the advice of the Dominion Government concerned, not upon the advice of the Government of the United Kingdom in London. Thus, the exercise of the treaty-making power of the Dominions cannot now be regarded as a delegation from any central government; it is derived from their own status' (L Oppenheim *International Law* 8 ed (H Lauterpacht (editor)) 1955 vol 1 at 886).

[34] 22 & 23 Geo v c 4.

[35] Act 69 of 1934.

[36] Act 70 of 1934.

[37] Schaffer (n 26).

[38] See *Harksen v President of the Republic of South Africa* 1998 (2) SA 1011 (C) at 1026–7. *Sed contra*, see Z Motala 'Under international law, does the new order in South

achieved only in 1931, with the passing of the Statute of Westminster, which removed South Africa's legislative subordination to the United Kingdom.

5 Respect for human rights and self-determination

The promotion of human rights has become a concern of international law only since World War II. Before 1945, the manner in which a state treated its own citizens was generally[39] not regarded as a factor to be considered in deciding whether to admit a state to the community of nations. Neither the League of Nations nor any state raised objections to South Africa's racial policies when it became an independent member of the community of states. Since 1945, many new states with poor human rights records have been recognised and admitted to the United Nations. Moreover, there has been no serious suggestion that the recognition of states with outrageous human rights records should be withdrawn.[40]

Despite this, states in recent times have alluded to respect for human rights and self-determination as a precondition for the recognition of statehood. When the Soviet Union dissolved in 1991, the European Community indicated that it would recognise only those parts of the former Soviet Union claiming to be independent states that afforded some evidence of a willingness and capacity to protect and respect human rights.[41] Similar assurances were sought from Slovenia, Croatia, Bosnia and Herzegovina and Macedonia as a precondition for their recognition as states.[42]

The idea that an entity that denied human rights and self-determination would not qualify as a state was initially mooted in the context of the requirement of effective government. A government that denied basic rights, it was suggested, could not be truly

Africa assume the obligations and responsibilities of the apartheid order? An argument for realism over formalism' (1997) 30 *CILSA* 287. Motala argues that South Africa only exercised true self-determination in 1994 and thus achieved statehood in that year.

[39] There were exceptional cases in which human rights issues were considered. In the early 19th century Britain made it clear to Brazil and Mexico that it viewed the abolition of the slave trade as a precondition for recognition: HA Smith *Great Britain and the Law of Nations* (1932) 129–30, 185–7. Britain's recognition of Brazil in January 1826 was followed by a treaty providing for the abolition of the slave trade in November 1826 (197).

[40] On the withdrawal of recognition, see *Oppenheim* (n 2) 176; H Kelsen 'Recognition in international law' (1941) 35 *AJIL* 605 at 611.

[41] (1992) 41 *ICLQ* 477; (1991) 62 *BYIL* 559.

[42] See M Weller 'The international response to the dissolution of the Socialist Federal Republic of Yugoslavia' (1992) 86 *AJIL* 569 at 586; Warbrick (n 15).

organised and effective.[43] But soon this was translated into a new criterion for statehood. Writing on the non-recognition of Rhodesia after its unilateral declaration of independence in 1965, JES Fawcett declared:

> But to the traditional criteria for the recognition of a regime as a new state must now be added the requirement that it shall not be based upon a systematic denial in its territory of certain civil and political rights, including in particular the right of every citizen to participate in the government of his country, directly or through representatives elected by regular, equal and secret suffrage. This principle was affirmed in the case of Rhodesia by the virtually unanimous condemnation of the unilateral declaration of independence by the world community, and by the universal withholding of recognition of the new regime which was a consequence.[44]

Today, support for the linkage of effective government with respect for human rights is to be found in the proposition that there is an emerging norm of democratic entitlement in international law.[45]

Although Fawcett's view has been well received,[46] it is open to a number of criticisms.[47] First, if the systematic denial of human rights, including the right to participate in government by means of free elections, is to become a bar to statehood, it would mean that many states would cease to qualify as states and face withdrawal of recognition. It would hardly be fair to limit this requirement to new states only and to expect a higher moral standard of conduct from them than from the existing members of the international community. Secondly, state practice does not provide support for the proposition that compliance with human rights and self-determination norms is now an additional criterion for statehood. This is particularly true of entities claiming statehood outside the confines of decolonisation, which is the concern of the decolonised world. The expectation that the recognition as states of entities emerging from the dissolution of the former Yugoslavia would be guided by considerations of human rights and respect for minorities was not fulfilled. The European Community failed to implement its own guidelines for recognition, or to follow the advice of the Arbitration Commission it had set up to monitor compliance with its guide-

[43] JES Fawcett *The Law of Nations* (1968) 38–9.

[44] 'Security Council resolutions on Rhodesia' (1964–1965) 41 *BYIL* 102 at 112. See the response to DJ Devine's article on 'The requirements of statehood re-examined' by Fawcett in (1971) 34 *MLR* 417.

[45] TM Franck *Fairness in International Law and Institutions* (1995); JR Crawford 'Democracy and international law' (1993) 64 *BYIL* 113; S Murphy 'Democratic legitimacy and the recognition of states and governments' (1999) 48 *ICLQ* 545.

[46] CN Okeke *Controversial Subjects of Contemporary International Law* (1974) 88.

[47] See DJ Devine 'The requirements of statehood re-examined' (1971) 34 *MLR* 410; 'The status of Rhodesia in international law' 1973 *Acta Juridica* 1 at 84–6.

lines.[48] Croatia was recognised before assurances relating to respect for minorities were given, let alone implemented, while Bosnia was recognised at a time when one of the great human rights tragedies of the 20th century had begun to unfold. In both cases, states preferred to base the decisions to recognise on their perceptions of the political realities of the region.[49]

State practice on this subject is largely confined to the political organs of the United Nations, and from resolutions adopted by these bodies it appears that entities such as Rhodesia, the TBVC states and the Turkish Republic of Northern Cyprus have not been faulted for failure to comply with the requirements of statehood but denounced for violation of certain peremptory norms of international law which result in their 'illegality', 'invalidity' and 'nullity'.[50]

RECOGNITION[51]

This chapter is concerned with the recognition of states as subjects of international law and not with the recognition of the governments in control of states. The latter topic is dealt with separately in Chapter 6. Although a government may be recognised as a *de facto* or *de jure* government, no such distinction is possible in the case of a state. An entity is either recognised as a state or it is not.

Recognition may be either unilateral or collective. In the former case, an individual state, already accepted as a state, recognises that an entity claiming to be a state meets the factual requirement of statehood and is therefore to be regarded as a state, with the rights and duties attached to statehood. Recognition is a precondition for the establishment of diplomatic relations, but it is not essential that the recognising state enter into diplomatic relations with the new state. Collective recognition occurs when a group of states, such as the European Community or the United Nations, recognises the existence of a claimant state directly, by an act of recognition, or

[48] The Opinions of the Arbitration Commission, under the chairmanship of Mr Badinter, may be found in 92 ILR 162–206.

[49] See Warbrick (n 15); Weller (n 42).

[50] See *Accordance with International Law of the Unilateral Declaration of Independence in Respect of Kosovo* 2010 ICJ Reports 403, 437–8 (para 81). See further Dugard *Recognition and the United Nations* (n 5) 86–111.

[51] The two leading treatises on this subject are H Lauterpacht *Recognition in International Law* (1947), re-issued in the Grotius Classic Reprint Series with foreword by James Crawford (2012); T Chen *The International Law of Recognition* (1951). See further Murphy (n 45); TD Grant *The Recognition of States: Law and Practice in Debate and Evolution* (1999); S Talmon *Recognition in International Law: A Bibliography* (1998); M Fabry *Recognizing States: International Society and the Establishment of New States since 1776* (2010); Ryngaert and Sobrie (n 8).

indirectly, by the admission of the state to the organisation in question.

Unilateral recognition is the most orthodox method of recognition. Collective recognition is still relatively uncertain and controversial.

UNILATERAL RECOGNITION

Different views are held about the purpose and consequences of recognition. Two principal schools of thought dominate this debate—the constitutive and the declaratory.[52] According to the *constitutive* school, the recognition of a claimant entity as a state creates or constitutes the state.[53] Recognition therefore becomes an additional requirement for statehood. The *declaratory* school, on the other hand, maintains that an entity becomes a state on meeting the factual requirements of statehood and that recognition by other states simply acknowledges (declares) 'as a fact something that has hitherto been uncertain'.[54]

There are several serious objections to the constitutive view. First, if the claimant state is recognised by state A and not by state B, it becomes in effect both a state and a non-state. Palestine is recognised as a state by 138 states but is not recognised as a state by the United States and some 50 other states. Is it a state only for those states that recognise it but not for other states? Clearly such uncertainty is undesirable. Secondly, if an unrecognised state is not a state, it is not entitled to the rights or subject to the obligations of international law. In practice, this consequence is not real. Many Arab states formally refuse to recognise Israel as a state but they nevertheless accept that they have legal obligations towards Israel. Israel likewise accepts that it has legal obligations towards states that refuse to recognise it.

What Hersch Lauterpacht described as the 'grotesque spectacle'[55] of an entity being a state for some states and not for others could be avoided if states were to recognise entities as soon as they complied with the requirements of statehood set out in the Montevideo Convention. Thus, Lauterpacht contended that once these requirements are met,

> the existing states are under the duty to grant recognition. In the absence of an international organ competent to ascertain and authoritatively to declare

[52] For accounts of this debate and the allegiances of different jurists, see Crawford (n 3) 19–28, Lauterpacht (n 51) ch 4; Chen (n 51) chs 1 and 2; Devine 'The status of Rhodesia in international law' (n 47) 90–145; D Raic *Statehood and the Law of Self-Determination* (2002) 29–38.

[53] For a strong exposition of this view, see H Kelsen 'Recognition in international law: Theoretical observations' (1941) 35 *AJIL* 605.

[54] JL Brierly *Law of Nations* 6 ed (ed H Waldock, 1963) 139.

[55] Lauterpacht (n 51) 78.

> the presence of the requirements of full international personality, states already established fulfil that function in their capacity as organs of international law. In thus acting they administer the law of nations. This legal rule signifies that in granting or withholding recognition states do not claim and are not entitled to serve exclusively the interests of their national policy and convenience regardless of the principles of international law in the matter.[56]

Unfortunately, Lauterpacht's contention is not supported by state practice: states do not regard themselves as being under a legal duty to recognise entities that comply with the requirements of statehood,[57] and political considerations influence their decisions. The notion that recognition is a political act appears in many guises. Sometimes it is claimed that recognition is a matter of policy, not law, while on other occasions it is argued that the facts of a particular case are *sui generis*, which means that they are not governed by law or legal precedent.

In most cases, entities that meet the requirements of the Montevideo Convention are recognised, so the process is not entirely arbitrary. It is, however, necessary to appreciate that political considerations may prompt a state to recognise an entity prematurely or to refuse to grant it recognition. For example, in 1903 the United States immediately recognised Panama when it seceded from Colombia in order to prevent Colombia from asserting its authority over its rebellious province—with the aim of securing for the United States the right to build the Panama Canal.[58] In 1992 member states of the European Community recognised Croatia and Bosnia-Herzegovina before they fulfilled the requirements of statehood for a wide range of political reasons, including the hope that recognition would prevent the escalation of violence.[59] On the other hand, the United States, which is more influenced by political considerations in its recognition practice than other states, refuses to recognise Palestine under the influence of its domestic pro-Israel lobbies.

The political nature of recognition has prompted support for the

[56] *Lauterpacht* (n 51) 6.

[57] In *Madzimbamuto v Lardner-Burke NO* 1968 (2) SA 284 (RA), Beadle CJ stated (319F): 'Few nations (and certainly not the United Kingdom) apply the idealistic "Lauterpacht theory" of recognition, a theory which presupposes that recognition must always depend on an objective legal appraisal of the true facts. Political considerations are frequently the overriding ones and they, too often, depend on no principle other than political expediency.'

[58] The United States did, however, later acknowledge that it had recognised Panama prematurely and paid $25 million to Colombia as reparation.

[59] See Weller (n 42).

declaratory school,[60] which accepts that an entity that meets the requirements of statehood becomes a state regardless of recognition.[61] Inevitably this approach was invoked by supporters of the TBVC states to justify their existence. In *S v Banda*,[62] Friedman J conducted an enquiry into the respective merits of the constitutive and declaratory approaches and found in favour of the latter on the grounds that (i) it is supported by most writers;[63] and (ii) it is more objective and less politically subjective than the constitutive approach.[64] Friedman J is correct in saying that the declaratory approach is less arbitrary than the constitutive and that it enjoys more support. He is wrong, however, to ignore the necessity for at least some recognition by other states. A state without the recognition of any state other than its creator[65] cannot demonstrate its capacity to enter into relations with other states and, from a functional point of view, cannot be described as a state.[66] While it would be ridiculous to deny the statehood of Palestine, which has demonstrated its capacity to enter into relations with other states by entering into diplomatic relations with over 100 states, it would be equally ridiculous to accord statehood to an entity that produces no evidence of such a capacity other than its governmental structure—as was the case with Bophuthatswana and as is the case with the Turkish Republic of Northern Cyprus. In the final resort, therefore, recognition does have a role to play in the creation of a state. This explains the complexity of the constitutive versus declaratory debate. Most declaratorists are

[60] The Badinter Arbitration Commission, charged with the task of monitoring compliance with the European Community's guidelines for the recognition of states following the dissolution of Yugoslavia, found that 'the existence or disappearance of the state is a question of fact; that the effects of recognition by other states are purely declaratory': Opinion 1 in 92 ILR 162.

[61] In *S v Oosthuizen* 1977 (1) SA 823 (N) the Court found that the fact that Rhodesia had not been recognised internationally did not mean it was not a state (825A). For a criticism of this decision, see J Dugard 'Rhodesia: Does South Africa recognise it as an independent state?' (1977) 94 *SALJ* 127.

[62] 1989 (4) SA 519 (B) 531–9.

[63] At 531E, 533–7.

[64] At 531F, 538–9. Although Friedman J is correct in this conclusion, the evidence he adduces does not support his conclusion. Five of the six examples he cites relate to the recognition of *governments* and not states (532–3).

[65] DJ Devine was prepared to accept that as partially recognised states, the TBVC states had some international personality, although it was 'relative and weak': 'Recognition, newly independent states and general international law' (1984) 10 *SAYIL* 18.

[66] See *Caglar v Billingham* above (n 22). *Sed contra*, see MN Shaw *International Law* 8 ed (2017), who states that if an entity were totally unrecognised, 'this would undoubtedly hamper the exercise of its rights and duties . . . but it would not seem in law to amount to a decisive argument against statehood itself' (332).

compelled to acknowledge the need for at least some recognition on the part of existing states as a precondition of statehood.[67]

THE METHOD OF RECOGNITION[68]

No rules are prescribed for the act of recognition. Usually it will take the form of a public declaration by the recognising state which is conveyed to the claimant state. In some cases, it may be implied from the conduct of the recognising state, but such an inference should not be drawn too readily. For conduct to imply recognition it must provide clear evidence of an intention to recognise. Thus, while recognition may be inferred from an exchange of diplomats and the signing of a bilateral treaty between the two states, it should not be inferred from an exchange of consular agents or the fact that both states are parties to a multilateral agreement or are members of the same international organisation.

The question whether South Africa impliedly recognised Rhodesia from 1965 to 1980 was much debated. Despite calls from the United Nations for the isolation of Rhodesia, South Africa maintained diplomatic relations with Rhodesia, continued to trade with the rebellious colony, and sent police to Rhodesia to assist the Rhodesian security forces. Although it was argued in some quarters that this amounted to implied recognition,[69] the South African government persistently denied that it recognised Rhodesia as an independent state and instead maintained an attitude of neutrality in the dispute between Rhodesia and the United Kingdom.[70]

COLLECTIVE RECOGNITION BY THE UNITED NATIONS AND DECOLONISATION[71]

In recent years the European Community (now the European Union) has sought to speak with one voice on the recognition of new states in Europe.[72] This is a wise policy that has helped to produce some consistency in recognition practice in Europe. Here, states have exercised their individual right of recognition collectively in a manner which does not depart substantially from traditional recogni-

[67] See Crawford (n 3) at 93.

[68] *Oppenheim* (n 2) 169.

[69] J Dugard (1969) 86 *SALJ* 113–14; AJGM Sanders 'Die erkenning van state en regerings' (1970) 33 *THRHR* 259 at 264.

[70] See Dugard (n 61); Devine 'The status of Rhodesia in international law' (n 47) and 'Does South Africa recognise Rhodesian independence?' (1969) 86 *SALJ* 438.

[71] See, further, on this subject Dugard *Recognition and the United Nations* (n 5) and 'The secession of states and their recognition' (n 5) 57–69.

[72] For example, in the cases of Croatia, Slovenia, Bosnia and Herzegovina and Macedonia. See Weller (n 42); Warbrick (n 15).

tion practice. More controversial is the question whether admission to the United Nations constitutes recognition.

The Charter of the United Nations provides for two categories of members: original members and those subsequently admitted by the organisation. According to article 3:

> The original Members of the United Nations shall be the states which, having participated in the United Nations Conference on International Organization at San Francisco, or having previously signed the Declaration by United Nations on January 1, 1942, sign the present Charter and ratify it in accordance with Article 110.

Subsequent membership is regulated by article 4, which provides:

> 1. Membership in the United Nations is open to all other peace-loving states which accept the obligations contained in the present Charter and, in the judgment of the Organization, are able and willing to carry out these obligations.
> 2. The admission of any such state to membership in the United Nations will be effected by a decision of the General Assembly upon the recommendation of the Security Council.

Membership in the United Nations is limited to states only. This is clear from articles 3 and 4, but it is reaffirmed by numerous other references to 'state' in the Charter which indicate that the rights and obligations contained in the Charter are linked to statehood.[73]

Fifty-one states, including South Africa, were original signatories to the Charter of the United Nations. During the first decade of the organisation's history only nine new member states were admitted as a result of disagreements between the major powers, but in 1955, following a 'package deal' between the major powers, 16 new states were admitted. Once this impasse was broken, few restraints were placed on the admission of applicant states to the world body, and, as decolonisation swept Asia, Africa, the Caribbean and the Pacific Ocean, the membership of the United Nations multiplied. The dissolution of the Soviet Union, Yugoslavia and Czechoslovakia in the early 1990s added further to the proliferation of states. Today there are 193 members of the United Nations.

In 1955 there were 76 member states of the United Nations. Thirty years later, membership had more than doubled. Of the states admitted since 1955, most are the products of the programme of decolonisation inspired and orchestrated by the United Nations. Some 50 of these post-1955 member states have populations of less than one million.

The Charter of the United Nations, as framed in 1945, implicitly recognised the legitimacy of colonialism, but in Chapter XI it

[73] Articles 2(4)–(7), 11(2), 32, 35(2), 43(3), 50, 52(3), 53(1)–(2), 59, 79, 80(1), 81, 93(2), 107, 110(1)–(4).

introduced the principle of international accountability for colonial administration, for colonial powers undertook to transmit information concerning their territories to the Secretary-General of the United Nations.[74] Moreover, in article 73, administering states undertook to develop self-government (but not independence) in the territories under their administration. Chapter XII, in establishing the International Trusteeship System for mandated territories and the colonies of the vanquished states of World War II, went still further and proclaimed 'development towards self-government or independence'[75] of these trust territories to be an objective of the system. Finally, the Charter affirmed the principle of 'self-determination of peoples'.[76]

The Charter of the United Nations established a dynamic world organisation. Change was foreseen in 1945. But it is unlikely that the founding fathers of the Charter could have foreseen the changes which have been effected in the field of colonialism under the mantle of the Charter's carefully phrased provisions. Within two decades of the San Francisco Conference, with no amendment to the Charter, the position had undergone a complete transformation: the distinction between colony and trust territory had lost its importance, self-determination was widely recognised as a legal right, the legitimacy of colonialism was denied, and organs of the United Nations freely asserted the right to decolonisation.

This transformation was the result of a gradual process, but if one event was to be singled out for special attention, it was the adoption of the Declaration on the Granting of Independence to Colonial Countries and Peoples (Resolution 1514(XV)) by the General Assembly—by 90 votes to none with nine abstentions[77]—on 14 December 1960. This Declaration not only outlawed colonialism but it gave the blessing of the United Nations to the rapid creation of new independent states, with little regard for compliance with the traditional requirements of statehood. In its preamble, Resolution 1514(XV) considers 'the important role of the United Nations in assisting the movement for independence in Trust and Non-Self-Governing Territories', welcomes 'the emergence in recent years of a large number of dependent territories into freedom and independence', and 'solemnly proclaims the necessity of bringing to a speedy and unconditional end colonialism in all its forms and manifestations'. The Declaration then calls for 'immediate steps' to be taken in all

[74] Article 73(e).

[75] Article 76(b).

[76] Articles 1(2) and 55.

[77] The nine abstaining states were Australia, Belgium, the Dominican Republic, France, Portugal, South Africa, Spain, the United Kingdom and the United States.

non-independent territories for the transfer of 'all powers to the peoples of those territories, without any conditions or reservations, in accordance with their freely expressed will and desire, without any distinction as to race, creed or colour, in order to enable them to enjoy complete independence and freedom'. It adds that '[i]nadequacy of political, economic, social or educational preparedness should never serve as a pretext for delaying independence'.

Although Resolution 1541(XV), adopted in the same year, declares that non-self-governing territories may exercise their right of self-determination in one of three ways—by becoming independent, by entering into a 'free association with an independent state' or by integrating with an independent state[78]—United Nations practice shows a definite preference for independence as the ideal form of decolonisation. Evidence of independent statehood would present little difficulty, as this would be provided by admission to the United Nations.

In 1960, the year of Resolution 1514(XV), 17 newly independent states were admitted to membership. Thereafter, the United Nations experienced a steady growth in membership, with the size of its new members growing smaller each year. Few questions were asked about the statehood of the new applicants for membership in the United Nations. In most instances, the colonial power's certification of statehood, demonstrated by the ceremonial act of independence, and the Special Committee on Decolonization's assertion of independence, provided sufficient 'evidence' of statehood for the purposes of admission to the United Nations.

The increase in United Nations membership has largely satisfied the decolonisers and, at the same time, achieved a measure of universality of which the world body may be justifiably proud. But the speed with which this has been accomplished inevitably raises doubts as to whether the traditional criteria for statehood have been observed and still remain intact.[79]

The conclusion seems unavoidable that the self-determination of peoples, which has become a primary value in the contemporary international order, has led to a relaxation of some of the require-

[78] The same options are recognised by Resolution 2625 (XXV) of 1970: the Declaration on Principles of International Law Concerning Friendly Relations and Co-operation among States in Accordance with the Charter of the United Nations.

[79] See WV O'Brien and UH Goebel 'United States recognition policy toward the new nations' in WV O'Brien (ed) *The New Nations in International Law and Diplomacy* (1965) 98 at 212, 223; DP Myers 'Contemporary practice of the United States relating to international law' (1961) 55 *AJIL* 697 at 717; G Kreijen *State Failure, Sovereignty and Effectiveness: Legal Lessons from the Decolonization of Sub-Saharan Africa* (2004), particularly at 49–52.

ments of statehood for the purposes of admission to the United Nations. While the requirements of permanent population and defined territory remain intact, it seems that others, such as effective government and independence, are no longer strictly insisted on where they run counter to developments in international law regarding the right of self-determination.[80] Once a state is admitted to the United Nations, its acceptance as a state for all purposes is assured. This explains the alacrity with which claimant states seek admission to the United Nations. This is well illustrated by the case of South Sudan.

On 9 July 2011 South Sudan declared its independence with the consent of its 'parent' state, Sudan. On 14 July it was admitted to the United Nations. Most states did not have the opportunity to formally declare that they recognised South Sudan. Nor did they bother to do this as their vote for the admission of South Sudan to the United Nations was taken as acceptance of the fact that South Sudan enjoyed international legal personality. It was clear that the admission of South Sudan to the United Nations established its statehood.

Today, apart from Israel, whose statehood is still denied by many Arab states, all members of the United Nations are accepted as states despite the fact that several probably would not have received widespread recognition by individual states had they been left to make a determination of statehood in accordance with the traditional criteria. Thus, it is fair to conclude that many states have achieved statehood by admission to the United Nations and that this procedure for recognition co-exists alongside the traditional method of unilateral recognition.[81] Any description of the law of recognition that fails to take account of this development cannot lay claim to be an accurate reflection of state practice.

The claim that admission to the United Nations constitutes or confirms the existence of a state has important implications for the debate between 'constitutivists' and 'declaratorists'. The main criticisms directed at the constitutive school are, first, the anomalous situation that arises where a state is recognised by state A but not by state B and is therefore both an international person and not an international person at the same time, and, secondly, the fact that the constitutive doctrine gives individual states the arbitrary power to

[80] For example, in 1991, the Federated States of Micronesia and the Republic of the Marshall Islands were admitted to the United Nations despite their strong dependency on the United States.

[81] Christian Hillgruber states that '[o]n admission as a member of the United Nations, the new state then becomes part of the globally organized community of states by way of co-optation' ('The admission of new states to the international community' (1998) 9 *European Journal of International Law* 491 at 492).

recognise an entity as a state or to withhold recognition. Both these weaknesses in the constitutivist position are remedied by the collective recognition of states through the United Nations. If all member states within the United Nations recognise each other's existence as states—with the possible exception of Israel by some of the Arab states—it follows logically that the 'grotesque spectacle'[82] of an entity being a state for some states but not for others is no longer a practical possibility. Furthermore, the arbitrary and subjective individual state decision is replaced by a collective decision of the United Nations.

In 1951, in his *International Law of Recognition*, Chen predicted that when the United Nations had attained complete universality, the notion of recognition would 'wither away' and membership of the United Nations would become the sole standard of relations between states.[83] Unfortunately, this state of affairs has not yet been achieved. Palestine, recognised by 138 states, remains outside of the United Nations largely because of the opposition of the United States, while Kosovo, recognised by 117 states, is kept out of the United Nations by the veto of Russia. The fate of such entities, whether they are described as states or partial states, ensures that unilateral recognition remains a crucial procedure for establishing or confirming the existence of states.

COLLECTIVE NON-RECOGNITION[84]

The United Nations plays an important role in the admission of new states to the international community by the process of collective recognition. Conversely, it may block the acceptance of a state by means of collective non-recognition. The failure of the Bantustan (TBVC) states and the Turkish Republic of Northern Cyprus to qualify as states is better explained in terms of non-recognition than by reference to the criteria for statehood.

The doctrine of non-recognition has its origin in the non-recognition of the puppet state of Manchukuo. When Japan invaded the Chinese province of Manchuria in 1932 and set up the state of Manchukuo, the Secretary of State of the United States, Mr Henry Stimson, declared that the United States would not recognise Manchukuo on the ground that it had been created in violation of the Pact of Paris of 1928, in which states renounced war. This was followed by a resolution of the Assembly of the League of Nations calling upon its members not to recognise Manchukuo. Jurispruden-

[82] Lauterpacht (n 51) 78.

[83] Note 51 at 222.

[84] See Dugard *Recognition and the United Nations* (n 5); 'The secession of states and their recognition' (n 5) 69–72.

tially, the doctrine of non-recognition is founded on the principle of *ex injuria jus non oritur*. According to Hersch Lauterpacht:

> Non-recognition is based on the view that acts contrary to international law are invalid and cannot become a source of legal rights for the wrongdoer. That view applies to international law as one of the 'general principles of law recognised by civilized nations'.[85]

When this doctrine of non-recognition was first expounded, the idea that there were peremptory norms or *jus cogens* was undeveloped. Today it is accepted that there are certain basic norms upon which the international order is founded and that these are peremptory and may not be derogated from under any circumstances.[86] The modern law of non-recognition takes cognisance of this development. An act in violation of a norm having the character of *jus cogens* is illegal, and is therefore null and void. This applies to the creation of states and to the acquisition of territory. States are under a duty not to recognise such acts under customary international law and in accordance with the general principles of law.[87] Resolutions of the Security Council and the General Assembly are, from a jurisprudential perspective, declaratory in the sense that they confirm an already existing duty on states not to recognise such situations. In practical terms, such resolutions are essential as they provide certainty by substituting for the decision of an individual state a collective determination of illegality and nullity.

The above doctrine of non-recognition is endorsed by the International Law Commission's 2001 draft articles on the Responsibility of States for Internationally Wrongful Acts.[88] Articles 40 and 41 provide that no state shall recognise as lawful a situation created by a serious breach of an obligation arising under a peremptory norm of general international law.

The International Court of Justice has given support to this doctrine in the *Kosovo Opinion* by acknowledging that Security Council resolutions on Southern Rhodesia, Northern Cyprus and the Republic of Srpska, determining that resolutions of independence were illegal, were 'connected with the unlawful use of force or other

[85] Op cit (n 51) 420.

[86] Although the concept of *jus cogens* is expressly recognised by the Vienna Convention on the Law of Treaties, which provides that a treaty that violates *jus cogens* is void (article 53), it is not one that should be confined to treaties. See Friedman J in *S v Banda* 1989 (4) SA 519 (B) 544F.

[87] See the *Namibia Opinion* 1971 ICJ Reports 16 at 54.

[88] Report of the International Law Commission, General Assembly Official Records, 56th Session, supplement 10 (A/56/10) (2001).

egregious violations of norms of general international law, in particular those of a peremptory character (*jus cogens*)'.[89]

The following peremptory norms have been recognised by the United Nations for the purposes of non-recognition:

(a) *The prohibition on aggression*. Following the Iraqi invasion of Kuwait in 1990, the Security Council adopted a resolution declaring that the annexation of Kuwait had 'no legal validity' and that states were required not to recognise that annexation.[90] Similar action was taken by the Security Council in respect of the Turkish invasion of Northern Cyprus and the establishment of the Turkish Republic of Northern Cyprus as a consequence of this invasion.[91]

(b) *The prohibition on the acquisition of territory by means of force*. The Security Council has called on states not to recognise Israel's forcible annexation of East Jerusalem and the Golan Heights.[92] The seizure of Palestinian land arising from the construction of Israel's 'security wall' falls into the same category. The International Court of Justice has held that 'all states are under an obligation not to recognise the illegal situation resulting from the construction of the wall'.[93]

(c) *The prohibition of systematic racial discrimination and the suppression of human rights*. This norm, which has its source in the United Nations Charter,[94] convention,[95] and customary international law, and has been recognised by the International Court of Justice,[96] was invoked as a basis for non-recognition of Rhodesia and the Bantustan states.[97]

(d) *The prohibition of the denial of self-determination*. Katanga,[98] Rhodesia,[99] South Africa's administration of Namibia from 1966 to 1990,[100] and the Bantustan states were subjected to non-recognition for violation of this norm.

[89] 2010 ICJ Reports at 438 (para 81).

[90] Resolution 662 (1990).

[91] Resolutions 541 (1983) and 550 (1984).

[92] Security Council resolutions 478 (1980) and 497 (1981).

[93] *Legal Consequences of the Construction of a Wall in the Occupied Palestinian Territory* 2004 ICJ Reports para 163D.

[94] Articles 55 and 56.

[95] International Convention on the Elimination of All Forms of Racial Discrimination (1966), and the International Covenant on Civil and Political Rights (1966) (article 2).

[96] *Barcelona Traction, Light and Power Company Case* 1970 ICJ Reports 3 at 32.

[97] Dugard *Recognition and the United Nations* (n 5) 96–7.

[98] Ibid 86–90.

[99] Ibid 90–8.

[100] Ibid 121.

The non-recognition by the international community of South Africa's Bantustan states of Transkei, Bophuthatswana, Venda and Ciskei (the TBVC states) is best explained in the context of the doctrine of collective non-recognition.[101] When Transkei was granted independence in 1976, the General Assembly of the United Nations immediately condemned the establishment of Bantustans 'as designed to consolidate the inhuman policies of apartheid', rejected Transkei's independence as 'invalid', and called upon all states to 'deny any form of recognition to the so-called independent Transkei'.[102] This call for non-recognition of Transkei was subsequently endorsed by the Security Council.[103] The United Nations responded in similar fashion to the 'independence' of Bophuthatswana,[104] Venda[105] and Ciskei.[106] The resolutions of the Security Council and General Assembly made it clear that the creation of the Bantustan states violated a number of norms in the field of self-determination and human rights and that it was the violation of these norms that prompted the calls for non-recognition. These norms were the unlawfulness of apartheid, systematic racial discrimination and the denial of self-determination.[107]

The collective non-recognition of the Bantustan states on the ground that their creation and continued existence violated peremptory norms of international law resulted in their invalidity. The easy re-absorption of Transkei, Bophuthatswana, Venda and Ciskei into the geographical body of South Africa in 1994, without any transfer agreements,[108] served to confirm the international community's position that they had never become states at all. This experience in failed statehood may rightly be construed as a victory for the United Nations' policy of non-recognition and the principle of *ex injuria jus non oritur*.

[101] See the commentary on draft article 41 in the ILC Report on the *Responsibility of States* (n 88) 289 (para 8).

[102] Resolution 31/6A (1976).

[103] Resolution 402 (1976) and 407 (1997).

[104] General Assembly Resolution 32/105 N (1977).

[105] Statement by Security Council contained in S/13549, 21 September 1979; General Assembly Resolution 34/93 G (1979).

[106] Statement by Security Council S/14794, 15 December 1981.

[107] General Assembly Resolution 1514 (XV) of 1960.

[108] The need for such agreements to return to South Africa was initially advocated by the National Party government. See M Wiechers 'Re-incorporation of the TBVC Countries—International law, practice and constitutional implications' (1990–91) 16 *SAYIL* 119. The present writer advocated the simple repeal of the four South African statutes conferring 'independence' on the Bantustan states: 'Failure of the TBVC states' (1992) 8 *SAJHR* at v (editorial comment). This was the course followed by the Interim Constitution of 1993. See sched 7 of Act 200 of 1993.

SELF-DETERMINATION, TERRITORIAL INTEGRITY AND SECESSION

The right of self-determination features prominently in contemporary international law.[109] This chapter has shown the important role played by the right of self-determination in the process of decolonisation and the creation of states. Before leaving the topic of statehood, the question must be asked: does the right of self-determination have a role to play in the creation of new states in a post-colonial world?[110] Or, put more bluntly, does the right of self-determination give a politically disaffected ethnic minority within a fully independent state the right to determine its destiny by seceding from that state and creating a new state? The problem is illustrated by the claims of Kosovo and Somaliland to separate statehood and by the unsuccessful attempt of Catalonia to secede from Spain in 2017.

The question whether international law recognises secession involves a consideration of the competing claims of two legal titans, self-determination and territorial integrity. Inevitably, any attempt on the part of the population of a state to secede in the exercise of the right of self-determination undermines the territorial integrity of the state in question. The uncertain legal rules and principles governing secession are designed to seek reconciliation between these two principles.

1 Self-determination

That the right of self-determination is a legal right under international law is no longer seriously challenged. It is affirmed in the Charter of the United Nations[111] and given content in Resolution 1514 (XV) of 1960—the Declaration on the Granting of Independence to Colonial Countries and Peoples—and subsequent resolutions of the General Assembly.[112] It has been acknowledged as a 'norm of international law' in the context of decolonisation[113] by the International Court of Justice in the *Namibia Opinion*[114] and the *Western*

[109] R McCorquodale (ed) *Self-Determination in International Law* (2003); K Knop *Diversity and Self-Determination in International Law* (2002); A Cassese *Self-Determination of Peoples: A Legal Appraisal* (1995); C Tomuschat (ed) *Modern Law of Self-Determination* (1993); D Raic (n 52); A Buchanan *Justice, Legitimacy and Self-Determination* (2004).

[110] C Walter, A von Ungern-Sternberg and K Abushov *Self-Determination and Secession in International Law* (2014); M Kohen (ed) *Secession: International Law Perspectives* (2006); Crawford (n 3) ch 9.

[111] Articles 1, 55.

[112] See in particular Resolution 2625 (XXV) of 1970.

[113] Separate opinion of Judge Dillard in the *Western Sahara Case* 1975 ICJ Reports 12 at 121–2.

[114] 1971 ICJ Reports 16, 31.

Sahara Case,[115] confirmed outside the context of decolonisation by the International Covenant on Civil and Political Rights,[116] and recognised as a legal right by many authors.[117] In 1995, in the *East Timor Case*, the International Court of Justice accepted that it has a special status as 'one of the essential principles of contemporary international law' and enjoys 'an *erga omnes* character'.[118] This was confirmed in the advisory opinion on the *Construction of a Wall in the Occupied Palestinian Territory*.[119] In 2017, in *Saharawi Arab Democratic Republic v Owners and Charterers of the Cherry Blossom*, it was recognised as a legal right by a South African court.[120]

Article 1(1) of the International Covenant on Civil and Political Rights contains a broad definition of the right:

> All peoples have the right of self-determination. By virtue of that right they freely determine their political status and freely pursue their economic, social and cultural development.

Article 20(1) of the African Charter on Human and Peoples' Rights likewise declares:

> All peoples shall have the right to existence. They shall have the unquestionable and inalienable right to self-determination. They shall freely determine that political status and shall pursue their economic and social development according to the policy they have freely chosen.

The commitment of these conventions and declarations to self-determination is not matched by clarity. Serious questions remain about whether self-determination is a right that belongs to colonial peoples only, the meaning and content of the right and the identity of the people upon whom the right is conferred.

(a) Self-determination as the right of colonial peoples only

The full implications of the right of self-determination recognised by the UN Charter were unknown but feared by the international community in 1945. Taken to its logical extreme, self-determination threatened the sovereignty and territorial integrity of all states with dissatisfied minorities. It therefore came as a relief to states when self-determination was invoked to further the cause of decolonisation.[121] General Assembly resolutions on the Granting of Indepen-

[115] 1975 ICJ Reports 12, 31–3.

[116] Article 1(1).

[117] Crawford (n 3) 108–28; Cassese (n 109); R McCorquodale 'South Africa and the right of self-determination' (1994) 10 *SAJHR* 4.

[118] 1995 ICJ Reports 90 at 102.

[119] 2004 ICJ Reports 136 para 155.

[120] 2017 (5) SA 105 (ECP) 116 B–C.

[121] See LC Buchheit *Secession: The Legitimacy of Self-Determination* (1978) 7.

dence to Colonial Countries and Peoples[122] and the Declaration on Friendly Relations among States[123] asserted the right of self-determination in the context of decolonisation and decisions of the International Court of Justice gave support to this limitation.[124] The International Covenants on Civil and Political Rights and Economic, Social and Cultural Rights that came into force in 1976, however, recognised the right of self-determination with no restriction to colonial situations[125] and since then, General Assembly resolutions[126] and judicial decisions[127] have acknowledged that the right is not confined to decolonisation. The question arose in the proceedings relating to the *Kosovo Opinion* of 2010, and although the Court declined to pronounce on this matter, most states assumed that the right of self-determination applies outside the colonial context.[128]

(b) External or internal self-determination

Before 1976, when the two International Human Rights Covenants came into force and self-determination was invoked mainly in the context of decolonisation, the right was seen to involve secession or external self-determination. After 1976, however, a distinction was drawn between the right of external self-determination that belonged to colonial peoples and the right of internal self-determination which comprised the right of a population or people within a non-colonial state to choose the government of the state, to participate in a government that represented the whole people of that state and to have the human rights of all persons within the state respected. Although human rights instruments draw no distinction between external and internal self-determination, internal self-determination has become the preferred option in the post-colonial world. This fails to answer the question of whether a right of external self-determination arises in a non-colonial situation when the people of a territory or a people within a territory are denied their right of internal self-determination.[129]

[122] Resolution 1514 (XV).

[123] Resolution 2625 (XXV).

[124] See the *Namibia* Opinion 1971 ICJ Reports 31; and the *Western Sahara* Opinion 1975 ICJ Reports 31–3 and 121 (separate opinion of Judge Dillard).

[125] Article 1(1) in both Covenants.

[126] Vienna Declaration on Human Rights (1993); General Assembly resolution 48/121 of 20 December 1993.

[127] *Reference re Secession of Quebec* (1998) 2 SCR 217 para 138, (1998) 37 *ILM* 1373.

[128] Dugard 'The secession of states and their recognition' (n 5) 84–5.

[129] Ibid 85–8.

(c) *The 'self' in self-determination*

The term 'people' or 'peoples' in the context of self-determination is often interpreted to mean all the people within a state—that is its population—and not the different ethnic groups or 'peoples' that comprise a heterogeneous population.[130] This interpretation, which takes little account of the complexity of the term 'people' or 'peoples',[131] or the ambiguity of the relevant instruments, would ensure that minorities within a state are not accorded the right of secession. Rosalyn Higgins claims that:

> The emphasis in all the relevant instruments and in state practice . . . on the importance of territorial integrity, means that 'peoples' is to be understood in the sense of *all* the peoples of a given territory. Of course, all members of distinct minority groups are part of the peoples of the territory. In that sense they too, as individuals, are holders of the right of self-determination. But minorities *as such* do not have a right of self-determination. That means, in effect, that they have no right to secession, to independence, or to join with comparable groups in other states.[132]

This is not, however, the only interpretation of the term. In *Reference re Secession of Quebec* the Supreme Court of Canada held that 'it is clear that a "people" may include only a portion of the population of an existing state'.[133] Moreover, two decisions of the African Commission on Human and Peoples' Rights accept that a group of persons with a common culture, language and history, occupying a distinct territory, may constitute a people for the purpose of self-determination.[134] Although the International Court of Justice made no finding on this subject in the *Kosovo Opinion*, by necessary implication the Court held that the Albanian population of Kosovo constitutes a people for the purpose of self-determination.[135] It may therefore be accepted that the term 'people' includes a group of persons living within an established state, occupying a distinct

[130] R Higgins *Problems and Process: International Law and How We Use It* (1994) 124.

[131] See J Crawford (ed) *The Rights of Peoples* (1988); R Kiwanuka 'The meaning of "people" in the African Charter of Human and Peoples Rights' (1988) 82 *AJIL* 80.

[132] Higgins (n 130) 124.

[133] (1998) 37 *ILM* 1340 at 1370 (para 124).

[134] *Katanganese Peoples' Congress v Zaire* Communication 75/92, African Commission on Human and Peoples' Rights (1995) 8th Annual Activity Report; (2000) African Human Rights Law Reports 72. *Kevin Mgwanga Gunme v Cameroon* Communication 266/2003, African Commission on Human and Peoples' Rights (2008–2009) 26th Annual Activity Report. F Viljoen *International Human Rights Law in Africa* (2007) 245; D Shelton 'Self-determination in regional human rights law: From Kosovo to Cameroon' (2011) 105 *AJIL* 60 at 67, 69.

[135] Dugard 'The secession of states and their recognition' (n 5) 97.

territory within that state, that shares a common identity, language, religion, culture, history and traditions.[136]

2 Territorial integrity

The principle of territorial integrity equals self-determination in terms of its legal credentials. Article 2(4) of the UN Charter obliges all member states 'to refrain in their international relations from the threat or use of force against the territorial integrity or political independence of any state'. The Constitutive Act of the African Union proclaims as one of its objectives the defence of the territorial integrity of member states.[137] Many General Assembly resolutions of principle expound the principle of territorial integrity. The Declaration on the Granting of Independence to Colonial Countries and Peoples, contained in Resolution 1514 (XV) of 1960, proclaims the right of self-determination but qualifies the right by declaring that:

> Any attempt aimed at the partial or total disruption of the national unity and territorial integrity of a country is incompatible with the Purposes and Principles of the Charter of the United Nations (para 6).

The Declaration on Principles of International Law Concerning Friendly Relations and Co-operation among States in Accordance with the Charter of the United Nations of 1970, contained in Resolution 2625 of 1970, likewise expounds the right of self-determination but adds that nothing in the paragraphs asserting the right of self-determination

> shall be construed as authorizing or encouraging any action which would dismember or impair, totally or in part, the territorial integrity or political unity of sovereign independent states conducting themselves in compliance with the principles of equal rights and self-determination of peoples . . . and thus possessed of a government representing the whole people belonging to the territory without distinction as to race, creed or colour.[138]

In the World Summit Outcome Resolution of 2005, states rededicated themselves to the principle of respect for territorial integrity.[139]

The principle of territorial integrity, guaranteeing respect for existing boundaries, has been invoked by the United Nations to block secession in many situations, including cases in which a minority group within a state has attempted to secede.[140] The Security Council

[136] Dugard 'The secession of states and their recognition' (n5) 98.

[137] Article 3(b).

[138] This provision is endorsed by the Vienna Declaration and Programme of Action (para 2) adopted by the UN World Conference on Human Rights of 1993: (1993) 32 *ILM* 1661, 1663.

[139] General Assembly resolution 60/L.1 of 15 September 2005 para 1(5).

[140] In 1960–1961 the Security Council invoked this principle to block the secession of Katanga from the newly independent Congo: Security Council resolution S/5002

has thus reaffirmed the territorial integrity of Somalia and thereby dismissed the secessionist aspirations of Somaliland and Puntland.[141]

3 State practice and judicial decisions on secession

Secession does not create problems where the parent state consents, however reluctantly, to the creation of a new state by a people occupying part of its territory. In 2011 a referendum was held in South Sudan to determine whether the region would secede from Sudan. After South Sudan voted overwhelmingly in favour of independence, the central government of Sudan accepted the outcome of the referendum. South Sudan became an independent state, with the support of Sudan, and was admitted to the United Nations in July 2011.

Problems arise where the government of a state insists on the maintenance of its territorial integrity and resists, often forcibly, the secession of a region of the state which is dissatisfied with the central government and prepared to take up arms to assert its independence. It is in such situations that the principles of self-determination and territorial integrity come into conflict and the rules of international law for the reconciliation of this conflict are least clear.

In practice, recognition plays a determining role in deciding on the success of a particular secession.[142] If a sufficient number of states recognise a seceding region as an independent state, this will give credibility to its claim to statehood. Admission to the United Nations will place this claim beyond doubt. As shown above, recognition remains the right of each state and many states are guided by political considerations in exercising this right rather than the criteria for statehood of the Montevideo Convention. Consequently, it is difficult to discern clear principles from recognition practice in this field.

Some take the position that secession in the non-colonial context is absolutely prohibited. In 1970, Secretary-General U Thant, speaking at the time of Biafra's attempted secession from Nigeria, declared:

> As far as the question of secession of a particular section of a state is concerned, the United Nations attitude is unequivocal. As an international organization, the United Nations has never accepted and does not accept, and I do not believe will ever accept the principle of secession of a part of its

of 24 November 1961. See, further, Dugard 'The secession of states and their recognition' (n 5) 110.

[141] Security Council resolutions 1766 (2007) and 1772 (2007).

[142] J Dugard and D Raic 'The role of recognition in the law and practice of secession' in M Kohen (ed) *Secession: International Law Perspectives* (2006) 94; Ryngaert and Sobrie (n 8).

member state.[143]

Such a statement is correct in respect of purported secessions that have been denounced by the United Nations as being in violation of peremptory norms of international law.[144] The United Nations has made such determinations in the cases of Katanga,[145] Rhodesia,[146] Transkei, Bophuthatswana, Venda and Ciskei,[147] the Turkish Republic of Northern Cyprus[148] and Republica Srpska[149] on the grounds that such 'states' were created in violation of the prohibitions on denial of the right of self-determination, racial discrimination and the use of force. The suppression of demands for secession in the cases of, for example, Biafra (from Nigeria),[150] Chechnya (from the Russian Federation), the Basque region and Catalonia (from Spain), Kashmir (from India), the Uighur region (from China), Bougainville (from Papua New Guinea), Aceh (from Indonesia) and Kurdistan (from Iraq) give additional credence to the statement of U Thant. This opinion, premised on extreme respect for territorial integrity, is not fully supported by state practice as there are instances in which secessions have succeeded with full recognition and admission to the United Nations.

The cases in which secession has been successful are mainly characterised by two phenomena: first, the separate identity of the seceding region in geographical, historical or constitutional terms; and, secondly, the denial of the right of internal self-determination, accompanied by the violation of human rights, and the exhaustion of attempts to secure internal self-determination. (The secession of Israel from the mandate territory of Palestine in 1948 is an anomaly.)[151]

Secessionist claims made by peoples occupying a distinct area with an identity of its own are more favourably considered by the international community as they do not violate, or violate to a lesser

[143] (1979) *UN Monthly Chronicle* (February) 40.

[144] See advisory opinion of the International Court of Justice in *Accordance with International Law of the Unilateral Declaration of Independence in Respect of Kosovo* 2010 ICJ Reports para 81.

[145] Security Council resolution S/5002 (1961).

[146] Security Council resolution 277 (1970).

[147] General Assembly resolutions 31/6A (Transkei), 32/105N (Bophuthatswana), 34/93G (Venda) and 35/69A (Ciskei); Security Council resolutions 402 (1976), 407 (1977).

[148] Security Council resolutions 541 (1983) and 550 (1984).

[149] Security Council resolution 787 (1992).

[150] DA Ijalaye 'Was Biafra at any time a state in international law?' (1971) 65 *AJIL* 551.

[151] Crawford *The Creation of States in International Law* 2 ed (2006) 434; Dugard 'The secession of states and their recognition' (n 5) 142.

extent, the principle of territorial integrity. This is illustrated by the examples of Bangladesh, Slovenia, Croatia, Bosnia-Herzegovina, Macedonia and Eritrea. Bangladesh,[152] previously East Pakistan, was geographically separated from West Pakistan by India and did not share a common language, history, culture or economy with it. The two parts were united only by a common religion, Islam. In 1971 Bangladesh seceded from Pakistan and, having secured a large number of recognitions, was admitted to the United Nations in 1974. The Socialist Federal Republic of Yugoslavia, before its dissolution, comprised six federal states—Slovenia, Croatia, Bosnia-Herzegovina, Macedonia, Serbia and Montenegro—each with a separate territorial, historical and constitutional identity. Whether Slovenia, Croatia, Bosnia-Herzegovina and Macedonia seceded from the Federal Republic of Yugoslavia in the 1990s or whether the Federal Republic dissolved is disputed.[153] It is, however, instructive that the Badinter Arbitration Commission, established by the European Community to oversee the dissolution of the Federal Republic of Yugoslavia, took the position that the federal boundaries of the constituent federal states within which new states were created complied with the principle of *uti possidetis*[154]—that is, were existing boundaries that might be recognised without offending the territorial integrity of the former Yugoslavia. The secession of Eritrea from Ethiopia in 1993 likewise took place without violation of the principle of *uti possidetis*. Eritrea was an Italian colony from 1890 to 1941, after which it was a trust territory administered by Great Britain until 1952—when it became part of a federation with Ethiopia, and later a province of Ethiopia.[155] Thus, its own separate colonial boundaries were clear before its incorporation into Ethiopia. There is, however, no consistency in respect of secessionist claims made by entities with previously identifiable boundaries. Somaliland, which declared its independence from Somalia in 1991, was previously British Somaliland, and, for a few days in 1960, the independent state of Somaliland. Despite its pre-existing colonial boundaries, no state has yet recognised Somaliland.

Secessionist claims may also be favourably considered when a people in a distinct part of a territory have been denied the right to internal self-determination, subjected to human rights violations, and exhausted all avenues to secure internal self-determination. Such

[152] See Dugard and Raic (n 142) 120–3.

[153] The author prefers to see the dismemberment of Yugoslavia as a case of secession: ibid 123–32.

[154] Opinion 3, 92 ILR 170. See further M Craven 'The EC Arbitration Commission on Yugoslavia' (1995) 66 *BYIL* 333. See further on *uti possidetis*, Chapter 8.

[155] See Cassese (n 109) 218–22.

claims are premised on the paragraph on self-determination in Resolution 2625 (XXV), which declares that the right of self-determination shall not authorise action which would impair the territorial integrity of an independent state conducting itself in compliance with the principles of equal rights and self-determination of peoples 'and thus possessed of a government representing the whole people belonging to the territory without distinction as to race, creed or colour'. Although there is disagreement about the meaning to be given to this paragraph,[156] there is strong support for the view that it recognises that a state loses its right to respect for its territorial integrity if it denies internal self-determination to a people with the result that it is not 'possessed of a government representing the whole people belonging to the territory'. The oppressed people obtain a right to 'remedial secession' in such circumstances, provided they have exhausted all avenues to secure internal self-determination. The secessions of Bangladesh, Bosnia-Herzegovina and Eritrea can also be justified on this ground.

In 1998 the Supreme Court of Canada gave support to remedial secession in *Reference re Secession of Quebec*[157] in which it gave an opinion on the legal right of Quebec to secede from Canada. The Court found that 'international law contains neither a right of unilateral secession nor the explicit denial of such a right',[158] that 'the right to self-determination of a people is normally fulfilled through *internal* self-determination', and that the right to *external* self-determination (secession) 'arises only in the most extreme cases'.[159] Applying this to the case of Quebec, the Court held:

> [T]he international law right to self-determination only generates, at best, a right to external self-determination in situations of former colonies; where a people is oppressed, as for example under foreign military occupation; or where a definable group is denied meaningful access to government to pursue their political, economic, social and cultural development. In all three situations, the people in question are entitled to a right to external self-determination because they have been denied the ability to exert internally their right to self-determination. Such circumstances are manifestly inapplicable to Quebec under existing conditions. Accordingly, neither the population

[156] See the disagreement on this issue among contributors to M Kohen (ed) *Secession: International Law Perspectives* (2006) 10. See further, Cassese (n 109) 118–20; J Dugard 'Secession: Is the case of Yugoslavia a precedent for Africa?' (1993) 5 *African Journal of International and Comparative Law* 163; L Brilmayer 'Secession and self-determination: A territorial interpretation' (1991) 16 *Yale Journal of International Law* 177; L Buchheit *Secession: The Legitimacy of Self-Determination* (1978); Buchanan (n 109) ch 8.

[157] (1998) 37 *ILM* 1340.

[158] Ibid 1369 (para 112).

[159] Ibid 1371 (para 126).

of the province of Quebec, even if characterized in terms of 'people' or 'peoples', nor its representative institutions, the National Assembly, the legislature or government of Quebec, possess (sic) a right, under international law, to secede unilaterally from Canada.[160]

The Supreme Court of Canada inferred a right to external self-determination—remedial secession—in extreme cases of oppression of a 'people' from the paragraph on self-determination in Resolution 2625 (XXV)—the Declaration on Principles of International Law Concerning Friendly Relations and Co-operation among States in Accordance with the Charter of the United Nations of 1970—which protects the territorial integrity of a state only while it conducts itself 'in compliance with the principles of equal rights and self-determination of peoples . . . and [is] thus possessed of a government representing the whole people belonging to the territory without distinction as to race, creed and colour'.

In the *Katangese Peoples' Congress v Zaire*[161] and *Gunme v Cameroon*[162] the African Commission on Human and Peoples' Rights acknowledged the existence of a right of remedial secession but found that the circumstances did not warrant the exercise of this right in the two cases in question. Support for remedial secession premised on Resolution 2625 (XXV) is also to be found in separate opinions in the *Kosovo Advisory Opinion*.[163]

(a) Kosovo opinion

The question of secession came before the International Court of Justice in *Accordance with International Law of the Unilateral Declaration of Independence in Respect of Kosovo.*[164] While expectations that the conundrums of secession might be answered by the Court were not fulfilled, the proceedings before the Court, in which 43 states participated, made it clear that states accept that secession is not simply a political act but rather an act governed by international law.

Kosovo, an autonomous province (but not republic) in the Socialist Federal Republic of Yugoslavia, within the Republic of Serbia, unsuccessfully attempted to assert its independence from Serbia after the dissolution of the Socialist Federal Republic of Yugoslavia in the early 1990s. This resulted in widespread human rights violations and

160 *Secession of Quebec* (n 157) 1373 (para 138).

161 Note 134; F Viljoen *International Human Rights Law in Africa* (2007) 244–5.

162 Note 134.

163 Separate opinions of Judges Concado (paras 177–81) and Yusuf (paras 9–17) *Accordance with International Law of the Unilateral Declaration of Independence in Respect of Kosovo* 2010 ICJ Reports 403.

164 2010 ICJ Reports 403. There is a wealth of literature on this opinion which can be found in the bibliography attached to Dugard 'The secession of states and their recognition' (n 5).

ethnic cleansing by the Serbian government in 1998–1999 and culminated in NATO intervention. After the surrender of Serbia, the United Nations Security Council in Resolution 1244 (1999) established a civil and military presence in Kosovo, known as UNMIK,[165] which governed the territory for 10 years. Attempts to find an acceptable solution failed as Serbia insisted on Kosovo remaining part of Serbia, and Kosovo was not prepared to compromise on independence. In 2008 Kosovo declared its independence from Serbia and to date has been recognised by 117 states, including the United States and most of the member states of the European Union. Membership of the United Nations is impossible as both the Russian Federation and China oppose Kosovo's statehood. (In this respect it resembles Palestine, which has been recognised by over 138 states but cannot hope to be admitted to the United Nations without the approval of the United States.)

Later in 2008 the General Assembly, at the instigation of Serbia, requested the International Court of Justice to give an advisory opinion on the question: 'Is the unilateral declaration of independence by the Provisional Institutions of Self-Government of Kosovo in accordance with international law?'

The question put to the Court was narrow. Unlike the questions put to the Court in the *Namibia*[166] and *Wall*[167] advisory opinions, this question did not ask the Court for an opinion on the legal consequences of Kosovo's unilateral declaration of independence and this allowed the Court to keep its answers within very limited parameters.[168] The Court found that the unilateral declaration of independence issued by the representatives of the people of Kosovo did not violate any general rule of international law[169] or the *lex specialis* created by Security Council resolution 1244 (1999)[170] and expressly declared that its Opinion did not address the issues of Kosovo's

[165] United Nations Interim Administration Mission in Kosovo.

[166] *Legal Consequences for States of the Continued Presence of South Africa in Namibia (South West Africa) notwithstanding Security Council Resolution 276* (1970) 1971 ICJ Reports 16.

[167] *Legal Consequences of the Construction of a Wall in the Occupied Palestinian Territory* 2004 ICJ Reports 136.

[168] *Accordance with International Law of the Unilateral Declaration of Independence in Respect of Kosovo* 2010 ICJ Reports 403, 423 para 51. Cf the criticism of the Court for its failure to adopt a broader approach by Judge Simma in his separate opinion: 2010 ICJ Reports 480. See further on the Court's opinion, R Falk 'Agora: The ICJ's *Kosovo Advisory Opinion*' (2011) 105 *AJIL* 50; '*Kosovo* symposium' (2011) 24 *Leiden Journal of International Law* 71–161, 331–83, 467–90.

[169] *Accordance with International Law of the Unilateral Declaration of Independence in Respect of Kosovo* 2010 ICJ Reports 403 at 436–9 paras 79, 84.

[170] Ibid 451–2 paras 118–19.

statehood or secession, including the notion of remedial secession.[171] The Court took the position that Kosovo's declaration of independence was not illegal as it violated no prohibitory rule of international law and was therefore permitted.[172] (This, despite the fact that Kosovo's declaration was not an abstract statement but the beginning of the process of secession.) The Court did, however, confirm that a unilateral declaration of independence was illegal if it violated a peremptory norm, as had been the case with Rhodesia, the Turkish Republic of Northern Cyprus and the Republic of Srpska.[173]

The most significant feature of the Court's Opinion related to the question of territorial integrity. State practice, reflected in resolutions of the Security Council,[174] had hitherto interpreted respect for territorial integrity broadly to prohibit secessionist actions on the part of disaffected minorities within a state. With scant examination of the subject, the Court held that 'the scope of the principle of territorial integrity is confined to the sphere of relations between states'.[175] This pronouncement takes no account of the fact that the principle of territorial integrity, as pointed out by Judge Koroma in his dissenting opinion,[176] has generally been interpreted as prohibiting non-state actors—that is, would-be secessionist entities—from impairing the territorial integrity of a state, even if this is done in the exercise of the right of self-determination. The Court's *dictum* may be interpreted as meaning that states alone are prohibited from engaging in action that may dismember or impair the territorial integrity of a state and that no such prohibition extends to non-state actors. Such an interpretation has far-reaching consequences for the law of secession as it suggests that the principle of territorial integrity is no obstacle to the exercise of self-determination. At the very least, this matter warranted further consideration on the part of the Court.

(b) Post-Kosovo developments

The failure of the International Court to provide guidance on the law governing secession and the relative success of Kosovo in its bid for independent statehood, with recognition by 117 states despite its non-admission to the United Nations, has inevitably resulted in demands for statehood by other entities.

[171] Ibid 423 para 51; 438–9 paras 82–3.

[172] Ibid paras 56, 79, 84.

[173] Ibid 437–8 para 81.

[174] See above at notes 140, 141.

[175] *Kosovo Opinion* (n 169) 437 para 80.

[176] Ibid 468, 475–476. See further J Dugard 'Abdul Koroma, territorial integrity and the *Kosovo Opinion*' in CC Jalloh and O Elias *Shielding Humanity: Essays in International Law in Honour of Judge Abdul G Koroma* (2015) 50.

In August 2008, Russia and Georgia fought a brief war over South Ossetia which spread to Abkhazia. Both South Ossetia and Abkhazia had previously formed autonomous regions in the Soviet Republic of Georgia and after the dissolution of the Soviet Union had contested Georgian rule. Following the 2008 war, Russia recognised the two entities as independent states, and this was followed by recognition by a handful of states, but with the overwhelming majority of states in the international community withholding recognition.[177]

The will of a people to exercise self-determination is most clearly expressed in a referendum. In recent times referenda have been held to test public opinion on secession in Scotland, the Kurdish autonomous region of Iraq, Catalonia and Crimea. In 2014 the referendum on Scottish independence resulted in 55 per cent of the Scottish electorate rejecting independence, which put an end to demands for Scottish independence. In the Kurdish autonomous region of Iraq, a referendum held in September 2017 revealed tremendous support for independence but the intervention of Iraqi forces shortly afterwards ended this attempt at secession. Catalonian demands for independence drew support from a 90 per cent vote in favour of independence in a low turn-out (43 per cent) referendum in October 2017. A later unilateral declaration of independence was declared illegal by the Spanish central government, which then detained the leaders of the secession movement. All these attempted secessions have involved historical and cultural groups with a distinct identity living in a separate territory claiming a right to self-determination. In none of the societies in question, however, has the central government denied internal self-determination or suppressed human rights to such an extent that the right of remedial secession has become a possibility. This explains why there has been little international sympathy for these secessionist demands.

The secession of Crimea from Ukraine in 2014 and its subsequent annexation by Russia is more complicated.[178] Historically, Crimea was part of Russia from 1783 to 1954 when the General Secretary of the Soviet Communist Party, Nikita Krushchev, awarded it to the Ukraine SSR as a token of friendship. After the dissolution of the USSR, Crimea became an autonomous region within Ukraine. In 2014, 65 per cent of the population of Crimea was Russian. In 2014,

[177] Ryngaert and Sobrie (n 8) 472.

[178] See SF van den Driest 'Crimea's separation from Ukraine: An analysis of the right to self-determination and (remedial) secession in international law' (2015) 62 *Netherlands International Law Review* 329; J Vidmar 'The annexation of Crimea and the boundaries of the will of the people' (2015) 16 *German Law Journal* 365; C Walter 'Postscript: Self-determination, secession and the Crimean crisis' in Walter et al (n 110) 293.

after Ukraine broke its ties with Russia and became pro-European, Russian troops were deployed in Crimea, arguably to protect the Russian Black Sea Fleet at Sevastopol. A referendum was then held in Crimea in which 95 per cent of the voters (with an 83 per cent turn-out) gave their support to independence from Ukraine and to the annexation of Crimea by Russia (which followed shortly after). It is clear that the presence of Russian troops was a factor in this process but whether this interference amounted to an unlawful use of force is debatable. The Security Council was unable to pronounce on this annexation by reason of the Russian veto but the General Assembly did condemn it as a violation of the territorial integrity of Ukraine.[179]

The decision to secede from Ukraine and to seek incorporation within Russia was the result of a referendum in a territory historically closer to Russia than Ukraine, in which a majority, consisting mainly of ethnic Russians, voted in favour of secession. On the other hand, the circumstances did not warrant remedial secession and the Russian military deployment in Crimea constituted a violation of the territorial integrity of the Ukraine within the meaning of the concept as defined by the International Court of Justice in the *Kosovo Opinion*.[180] It has been argued that Russia's intervention was forcible, which means that the annexation of Crimea violated a peremptory norm and is therefore invalid. However, unlike Israel's annexation of East Jerusalem, which has been condemned as illegal by the Security Council,[181] the annexation of Crimea has been condemned only by the General Assembly. Inevitably, this weakens the case against Russia.

4 Conclusion

Although, in the words of the Canadian Supreme Court, 'international law contains neither a right of unilateral secession nor the explicit denial of such a right',[182] it is clear that secession is governed by rules of international law and that these rules guide states in their decision whether to recognise an entity claiming to be a state.[183] The right of self-determination and the principle of territorial integrity remain the most significant principles but both are subject to qualification. It is the task of states and international institutions to balance these rights, rules and principles wisely to ensure fairness and stability in the international legal order.

[179] Resolution 68/262 of 27 March 2014.
[180] See above at n 175.
[181] See resolution 478 (1980).
[182] *Reference Re Secession of Quebec* (1998) 37 *ILM* 1340 at 1369 (para 112).
[183] Dugard 'The secession of states and their recognition' (n 5) 33, 203–4, 214.

5 A South African postscript

Section 235 of the 1996 Constitution provides:

> The right of the South African people as a whole to self-determination, as manifested in this Constitution, does not preclude, within the framework of this right, recognition of the notion of the right of self-determination of any community sharing a common cultural and language heritage, within a territorial entity in the Republic or in any other way, determined by national legislation.

This section should be interpreted in the context of the above rules, practices and principles. The people of South Africa 'as a whole' enjoy the right to self-determination. Communities within the Republic 'sharing a common cultural and language heritage' enjoy a right of internal self-determination, which may by agreement, endorsed by 'national legislation', or take the form of some kind of autonomy 'within a territorial entity in the Republic'. The phrase 'or in any other way' is of uncertain content. Does it mean that all options—including secession—remain open, provided they are determined by 'national legislation'?[184]

FAILED STATES

According to Sir Robert Jennings, a former President of the International Court of Justice, there is a tendency for international lawyers to 'keep away from . . . "black holes" in the system where the basic assumptions, and even the policies of the law, have parted from reality'.[185] The phenomenon of the juridical state or failed state is such a black hole.

An existing, recognised state may descend into anarchy and lawlessness to such an extent that it ceases to meet the requirements of statehood expounded in the Montevideo Convention. It retains its territory and population but lacks an effective, central governmental authority. Warlords control parts of the state. But the state itself, without a central government, is unable to maintain order or to provide the most basic services for its people. Such a state may be described as a 'juridical state'[186] in the sense that it exists only as an international legal person with no substance to back its claim to statehood. Alternatively, it may be described as a 'failed state'.

[184] On the subject of self-determination in the South African context, see McCorquodale (n 117); HA Strydom 'Self-determination, and the South African Interim Constitution' (1993/4) 19 *SAYIL* 43.

[185] Foreword to G Kreijen *State Failure, Sovereignty and Effectiveness* (2004) viii.

[186] RH Jackson *Quasi-States: Sovereignty, International Relations and the Third World* (1990). See further, G Barrie 'Failed states: The new challenge to international law' (2015) 40 *SAYIL* 103.

Yemen, at present, provides an example of a failed state but there are others that come perilously close.

International law cannot be blamed for the breakdown of governmental authority in a state but it can be blamed for maintaining the appearance of statehood by continuing to accept such an entity as a state, and for allowing such an entity to continue to function at the international level through membership in international governmental organisations. Moreover, international law can be blamed for accommodating the failed state by relaxing the requirement of effectiveness—effective government—as a requirement for statehood, and for allowing legality to replace effectiveness. According to Kreijen:

> The failed State merely exists as a normative construction within the texture of international relations—as a separate legal unit without real substance. The failed State's independence exclusively rests on constitutional international principles with a formal-legal character, such as the right to self-determination and the *uti possidetis juris* doctrine, as well as on the recognition of these principles by the international community. As such the failed State's existence rests on comity rather than self-achievement.[187]

The failed state poses a challenge to international law. The withdrawal of recognition, although a logical consequence and a theoretical possibility, is without precedent and is politically unacceptable. Some form of temporary international trusteeship is another avenue that deserves consideration.[188] Unfortunately, the notion of trusteeship is tainted with colonialism and therefore seems an unlikely solution. This leaves informal 'state-building' by the international community as the most viable remedy.[189] Neglect is not a solution as it leaves millions of people without hope for the future and brings international law itself into disrepute.

[187] *Kreijen (n 185) 375.*
[188] Ibid 308–29.
[189] Crawford (n 3) 719–23.

CHAPTER 6

Recognition of Governments

John Dugard

Once an entity becomes a state, it acquires international personality and participates in the affairs of the international community. This participation is conducted by the government of the state, which inevitably will change from time to time, either by democratic means or by revolution. Changes in government do not affect the personality of the state or its rights and obligations. The new government succeeds to the rights and obligations of its predecessor, however it came into existence.[1]

When the change in government is constitutional, no problem arises. Other states continue doing business with the new government and diplomatic relations are unaffected. When the change is unconstitutional, problems arise. The new revolutionary government may have uncertain control over its territory, or it may be unwilling to comply with its international obligations, or it may be challenged by a rival claimant, or it may be controlled by a foreign power, or it may have a poor human rights record, or it may adhere to a different ideology. In these circumstances, other states will have to decide whether the new government really represents the state or whether it is the type of government with which they wish to do business.

Traditionally, the decision is conveyed to the new government by recognition. According to Oppenheim:

> A government which is in fact in control of the country and which enjoys the habitual obedience of the bulk of the population with a reasonable expectancy of permanence, can be said to represent the state in question and as such to be deserving of recognition.[2]

As with the recognition of states, this judgment is left to the governments of other states, which in many instances will be guided by political considerations. For example, the United States refused to recognise the Soviet government of Russia from 1920 to 1933 and the communist government of China from 1948 to 1979.

Recognition by the major powers plays an important legitimating role. Recognition by states such as the United States, the United Kingdom or France will boost the legitimacy of a revolutionary

[1] DP O'Connell *International Law* 2 ed (1970) vol 1 at 394.

[2] R Jennings and A Watts (eds) *Oppenheim's International Law* 9 ed (1992) vol 1 at 150. See further S Talmon *Recognition of Governments in International Law* (1998).

government, while the withholding of recognition by these powers may have serious consequences, both political and economic—hence the importance attached to recognition by the major powers on the part of unconstitutional governments.

The new concern for human rights has created difficulties for the major powers in respect of recognition. Although such a power may recognise a government purely on the ground that it has effective control and appears to be permanent, recognition will inevitably be construed as a form of political approval. Where the newly recognised government has a poor human rights record, such apparent approval may outrage both domestic and international opinion. For this reason, France,[3] the United States,[4] Britain and several other states[5] have officially announced that they will no longer accord recognition to governments (as opposed to states). The British statement of 1980 declares:

> [W]e have decided we shall no longer accord recognition to governments. . . .
>
> Where an unconstitutional change of regime takes place in a recognised state, governments of other states must necessarily consider what dealings, if any, they should have with the new regime, and whether and to what extent it qualifies to be treated as the government of the state concerned. . . . [T]he policy of successive British governments has been that we should make and announce a decision formally 'recognising' the new government. . . . This practice has sometimes been misunderstood, and, despite explanations to the contrary, our 'recognition' interpreted as implying approval. For example, in circumstances where there might be legitimate public concern about the violation of human rights by the new regime, or the manner in which it achieved power, it has not sufficed to say that an announcement of 'recognition' is simply a neutral formality.
>
> We have therefore concluded that there are practical advantages in following the policy of many other countries in not according recognition to governments. Like them, we shall continue to decide the nature of our dealings with regimes which come to power unconstitutionally in the light of our assessment of whether they are able of themselves to exercise effective control of the territory of the state concerned, and seem likely to continue to do so.[6]

[3] MJ Peterson 'Recognition of governments should not be abolished' (1983) 77 *AJIL* 31 at 42–3.

[4] (1977) 77 *US Department of State Bulletin* 462; reproduced in DJ Harris and S Sivakumaran *Cases and Materials on International Law* 8 ed (2015). See further LT Galloway *Recognizing Foreign Governments: The Practice of the United States* (1978). Cf SD Murphy 'Democratic legitimacy and the recognition of states and governments' (1999) 48 *ICLQ* 544 at 566.

[5] In 1988, Australia issued a statement similar to that of Britain—see (1992) 12 *Australian Year Book of International Law* 357.

[6] *Hansard* HL vol 408 cols 1121–2. See, too, S Talmon 'Recognition of governments: An analysis of the new British policy and practice' (1992) 63 *BYIL* 231.

Today it seems that the majority of states adopt this approach.[7]

South Africa's recognition policy is in line with this trend. As a pariah state during the apartheid years, its recognition was not sought after for purposes of approval in the way that claimant governments turned to Britain and the United States for recognition. Only within the southern African region was recognition by South Africa considered to be important. The consistent policy of the South African government during the apartheid era was to adopt a low profile towards revolutionary regimes and to continue diplomatic and trade relations once it was established that the regime had effective control over the territory and seemed likely to continue to do so with some degree of permanency. Explicit statements on recognition were avoided and every effort was made to depoliticise a highly political subject.

The South African approach of this period is illustrated by the response to military coups in Lesotho, Transkei, Ciskei and Venda.

On 30 January 1970, Chief Leabua Jonathan, the Prime Minister of Lesotho, seized power unconstitutionally when he declared a parliamentary election to be invalid and suspended the constitution.[8] Although Britain granted recognition to the new regime only on 12 June, Prime Minister Vorster indicated South Africa's decision to continue normal relations with Lesotho on 6 February in a parliamentary exchange:

> *The Prime Minister:* Now this question has arisen, ie what is our relationship with Lesotho? I want to tell you, Sir, that our relationship with Lesotho is exactly the same as it is with Rhodesia. We are simply carrying on as though nothing has happened. Lesotho is a neighbouring state of ours. We do not interfere with them. We do not dictate to them. We have no hand in their decisions. But it is a neighbouring state with which we have to negotiate, and as far as we are concerned, Chief Jonathan is in effective control of that neighbouring state and we shall continue our negotiations with him as if in fact nothing has happened in Lesotho.
>
> *Sir de Villiers Graaff:* That is official recognition.
>
> *The Prime Minister:* Official recognition or not. Official recognition simply plays no part, just as little as it did in regard to Rhodesia. It is merely a question of our continuing as if nothing has happened. We have our specific relations with them and we are continuing with those specific relations.[9]

When Chief Leabua Jonathan was himself overthrown in a bloodless coup by Major-General JM Lekhanya in 1986, there was no explicit statement on recognition by the South African government. Instead, the Department of Foreign Affairs issued a statement to the

[7] See Galloway (n 4). For a criticism of this trend, see Peterson (n 3).

[8] AJGM Sanders 'Die erkenning van state en regerings' (1970) 33 *THRHR* 259.

[9] *House of Assembly Debates* vol 26 col 454 (6 February 1970).

effect that the Foreign Minister, Mr RF Botha, and a special emissary from the Military Council of Lesotho had agreed on the 'need to work actively for the promotion of good neighbourliness'.[10]

On 30 December 1987, Major-General Bantu Holomisa took over the government of Transkei in a military coup. On 21 January 1988, State President PW Botha stated that the South African government was satisfied that the new administration was in effective control of all functions of government.[11] Later, the State President declared:

> The South African government recognises Transkei as a sovereign independent state and, as it is in the interests of both countries and their peoples to continue the co-operation which has traditionally existed between them, will in future conduct its bilateral relations with the new government.[12]

Military coups in Ciskei[13] and Venda[14] in 1990 were similarly treated.

That the need for continuity and stability continues to guide foreign policy on recognition of governments is clear from South Africa's early recognition of the Kabila government of the Democratic Republic of Congo (formerly Zaire) after the overthrow of the Mobutu regime in 1997. Commenting on this, the Deputy Minister of Foreign Affairs, Mr Aziz Pahad, stated:

> The immediate recognition by South Africa of President Kabila and his government after their military forces took over control of the country appears to have created the impression—especially in the news media—that the South African Government is somehow acting as sponsor of or, 'godfather' to, the Kabila government.
>
> That is not the case at all. The early recognition of the Kabila government was based on the realisation that a power vacuum in Kinshasa would generate chaos and further contribute to the economic collapse of the country.
>
> It was seen as vital that peace and stability be restored to the former Zaire at the earliest possible moment in order to commence the enormous task of bringing about the economic reconstruction of the country.[15]

It would be incorrect, according to Mr Pahad, to infer approval of a government's internal policies from recognition.[16]

[10] ME Muller 'South Africa's foreign policy and international practice as reflected in speeches, parliamentary statements and replies—1986' (1986–1987) 12 *SAYIL* 228 ('South Africa's Foreign Policy').

[11] 1988/89 *Race Relations Survey* 131.

[12] *The Star* 11 February 1988, quoted in M Beukes 'The coup d'etat: "An annual African event"—A South African reading' (1987–1988) 13 *SAYIL* 133.

[13] *The Star* 7 June 1990; H Botha 'South Africa's foreign policy—1990' (1990/91) 16 *SAYIL* 227.

[14] *The Star* 7 June 1990.

[15] *The Star* 19 June 1998 at 9.

[16] Ibid. Mr Pahad stressed that recognition of the Kabila government was 'not in any way inconsistent' with the government's 'commitment to the advancement of human rights in our continent' and that the government would continue to call for the

Although the government's policy is to adopt a low-profile approach towards recognition of governments,[17] resembling that of Britain and the United States, this was not possible when South Africa switched recognition from the government of the Republic of China (Taiwan) to the government of the People's Republic of China (Beijing) in 1998. This was, however, an unusual case made necessary by the need for post-apartheid South Africa to recognise the People's Republic of China as the lawful government of China after it had recognised the government of Taiwan as the government of China for 30 years. Taiwan is not an independent state. However, the government of Taiwan competes with the government of the People's Republic of China in Beijing for recognition as the government of the whole of China. Most states today recognise the Beijing government as the lawful government of China, but a minority, mainly in Central America, persist in recognising Taiwan as the government of China. This was South Africa's position before it recognised the Beijing government in 1998.[18]

The policy of the South African government to support continuity and stability in its recognition of new governments was apparent in its recognition of the new government of Zimbabwe when Robert Mugabe was replaced by Emmerson Mnangagwa.

DE FACTO AND *DE JURE* RECOGNITION

When a new government assumes effective control of a territory with a likely prospect of permanency, it should be given full recognition as a *de jure* government. However, there may be circumstances that warrant some lesser form of recognition; in such a case, the new government will be recognised as a *de facto* government. Such a distinction applies only in the case of recognition of governments. A state cannot be recognised *de facto.*

It has been suggested that *de facto* recognition is appropriate where the government is not firmly established[19] or fails to show a

holding of free and fair elections in the Democratic Republic of Congo. When South Africa entered into diplomatic relations with Iraq, Mr Pahad emphasised that this did not mean that South Africa agreed with its internal policies (*Pretoria News* 6 July 1998).

[17] In an interview with the *Pretoria News* on 6 July 1998, Mr Pahad declared 'you recognise the country but not the government'.

[18] For a discussion of this switch in recognition, see R Henwood 'South Africa's foreign policy—1995–6' (1996) 21 *SAYIL* 256 and R Henwood 'South Africa's foreign policy—1997' (1997) 22 *SAYIL* 151.

[19] See the judgment of Beadle CJ in *Madzimbamuto v Lardner-Burke NO* 1968 (2) SA 284 (RA) 359. In this case, the terms '*de facto*' and '*de jure*' government were invoked in the municipal law context to assess the legal status of the Rhodesian government after 1965. On appeal, the Privy Council indicated that they are terms best confined to

willingness to comply with its international obligations.[20] As *de facto* recognition implies a measure of disapproval, it normally does not include an exchange of diplomats.

De facto recognition has been accorded, in practice, in two situations:

(a) It has been given when the recognising state has doubts about both the stability and the ideology of the new government. Thus, Britain recognised the Soviet government *de facto* in 1921 and *de jure* in 1924.

(b) It has also been accorded when there are two rival governments competing for power. In the Spanish Civil War (1936–1939) Britain continued to recognise the Republican government as the *de jure* government but granted *de facto* recognition to General Franco as he extended his control over the country. The same practice was followed in respect of Italy's conquest of Ethiopia: in 1936 Italy was recognised as the *de facto* government of Ethiopia while Emperor Haile Selassie remained the *de jure* government until 1938.[21]

Today, the distinction between *de facto* and *de jure* recognition is largely discredited and does not seem to have any legal significance.[22]

The present practice of states seems to be to withhold recognition completely where there are doubts about the stability of a new government or where there are two rival powers competing for the government of a country. For instance, during the civil war in Angola between 1975 and 1991, South Africa recognised the state of Angola but did not recognise either the MPLA[23] or UNITA as the *de jure* or *de facto* government of Angola.

international law: *Madzimbamuto v Lardner-Burke* [1968] 3 WLR 1229 (PC) 1249. Cf *Matanzima v President of the Republic of Transkei* 1989 (4) SA 989 (Tk) 998B.

[20] *Oppenheim* (n 2) 156.

[21] O'Connell (n 1) 161.

[22] See AJGM Sanders 'The courts and recognition of foreign states and governments' (1975) 92 *SALJ* 165 at 171.

[23] *House of Assembly Debates* vol 60 cols 112–13 (27 January 1976). In 1985 Mr RF Botha, South Africa's Foreign Minister, stated: 'The government of the Republic of South Africa recognises the People's Republic of Angola as a state but does not recognise the government of President Eduardo Dos Santos as the *de jure* or *de facto* government of the People's Republic of Angola' (certificate issued on 1 May 1985 in *Banco Comercial de Angola v Banco Popular de Angola* WLD; unreported, as the matter was settled out of court).

CHAPTER 7

Recognition in Municipal Law

John Dugard

Only a recognised state or government enjoys *locus standi* in a South African court; only a recognised state or government, or its agents, may plead immunity from the jurisdiction of a South African court; and only the legislative, executive or judicial acts of a recognised state or government will be given legal effect by a South African court.[1] Consequently, when such questions arise, it will be necessary for a municipal court to decide whether the entity has been recognised.

Two questions present problems: first, how is recognition to be proved? Secondly, is the rule that no effect should be given to the acts of an unrecognised state or government absolute? On both these issues South African courts are guided by English law.[2]

PROOF OF RECOGNITION

The recognition of a state or government is a matter that falls within the non-statutory powers of the executive.[3] Consequently, where there is any doubt about the status of a state or government, the court should request the Department of International Relations and Co-operation (DIRCO) for a certificate setting out its views on the subject.[4] If this course is not followed, a situation may arise in which the courts and the executive express different views on matters of foreign policy, which may embarrass the executive in its conduct of foreign affairs.

Our courts have accepted that such an executive certificate is 'conclusive on the matter of recognition',[5] although this may no

[1] *Inter-Science Research and Development Services (Pty) Ltd v Republica Popular de Mocambique* 1980 (2) SA 111 (T) ('*Inter-Science Research v Republica Popular de Mocambique*') 116C–E; AJGM Sanders 'The courts and recognition of foreign states and governments' (1975) 92 *SALJ* 165.

[2] *Inter-Science Research v Republica Popular de Mocambique* (n 1) 117D–E; Sanders (n 1) 166, 168.

[3] Margo J in *Inter-Science Research v Republica Popular de Mocambique* (n 1) 116–17; Sanders (n 1) 165. For an examination of the source of these powers, see Chapter 4 at notes 180–5.

[4] *Inter-Science Research v Republica Popular de Mocambique* (n 1) 118B.

[5] Ibid 118D.

longer be the position under our new constitutional rules.[6] Similarly, the Foreign States Immunities Act provides that a certificate from the Minister of International Relations and Co-operation shall be conclusive evidence on the question 'whether any foreign country is a state' for the purposes of the Act.[7]

Where the question of recognition is 'a matter of judicial cognizance', no certificate is necessary.[8] However, our courts, either out of disregard for the executive's interests or out of ignorance, have accepted entities as states or governments in a number of highly controversial instances. In 1971 a court took judicial notice of the fact that the Congolese government was the 'government of a foreign sovereign state recognised as such by the South African government',[9] despite the fact that there were no diplomatic relations between the two countries. In 1975 the Appellate Division[10] gave effect to the laws of East Germany in a matrimonial dispute without any enquiry into the question whether South Africa recognised East Germany as an independent state. As South Africa had no diplomatic relations with East Germany and the two states were ideologically hostile to each other, it seems more than likely that the executive would have indicated that it did not recognise East Germany.[11] In 1977 the Natal Provincial Division went still further when it pronounced on an issue that the executive had carefully and studiously avoided pronouncing upon for over a decade[12]—Rhodesian independence. In *S v Oosthuizen*,[13] Kriek J took judicial notice of the fact that Rhodesia became a new state in 1965, despite the absence of recognition by states, including South Africa. He accordingly held that an extradition agreement entered into between South Africa and Southern Rhodesia in 1963 had lapsed on the ground that the international personality of Southern Rhodesia had changed.[14]

[6] See Chapter 4 for a discussion of this matter.

[7] Section 17 of Act 87 of 1981.

[8] *Inter-Science Research v Republica Popular de Mocambique* (n 1) 118A; *Bell v S* [1997] 2 All SA 692 (E) 696*a–b*; *The Akademik Fyodorov: Government of the Russian Federation v Marine Expeditions Inc* 1996 (4) SA 422 (C) 441J.

[9] *Parkin v Government of the Republique Democratique du Congo* 1971 (1) SA 259 (W) 259E.

[10] *Sperling v Sperling* 1975 (3) SA 707 (A).

[11] See the valid criticism of this case by H Booysen 'Does South Africa recognise the German Democratic Republic?' (1975) 1 *SAYIL* 132.

[12] DJ Devine 'The status of Rhodesia in international law' 1974 *Acta Juridica* 115–24, 129–31.

[13] 1977 (1) SA 823 (N). See, too, *S v Charalambous* 1970 (1) SA 599 (T).

[14] This case is criticised by J Dugard 'Rhodesia: Does South Africa recognise it as an independent state?' (1977) 94 *SALJ* 127; H Booysen 'Recognition, treaties and the court' (1977) 3 *SAYIL* 179.

In all of the above cases, particularly *S v Oosthuizen*, there was sufficient doubt as to the status of the state or government in question to have warranted a request by the Court for an executive certificate. If such a certificate was necessary to establish that South Africa recognised Mozambique as an independent state and Frelimo as the government of Mozambique in 1979, as held by Margo J in *Inter-Science Research v Republica Popular de Mocambique*,[15] *a fortiori* it was necessary to obtain an executive certificate on the status of Rhodesia. Judicial notice of recognition should be confined to states and governments whose status is a matter of common knowledge—such as the United States, Britain, India, Japan, etc—and not extended to controversial entities, as occurred in *S v Oosthuizen*. Pleas for greater judicial discretion on the subject of recognition are misplaced if they suggest that the judiciary should make findings on recognition with no attempt to first ascertain the view of the executive.[16] Recognition is a highly sensitive subject in international relations and must be left, at least in the first instance, to the body charged with the task of conducting South Africa's foreign relations—the executive. As Lord Atkin warned in *Government of the Republic of Spain v SS 'Arantzazu Mendi'*:[17]

> Our state cannot speak with two voices on such a matter, the judiciary saying one thing, the executive another. Our sovereign has to decide whom he will recognise as a fellow sovereign in the family of states; and the relations of the foreign states with ours in the matter of state immunities must flow from that decision alone.

A court is not excluded from pronouncing on the recognition of a state or government. As suggested in Chapter 4,[18] the 1996 Constitution may permit review of the executive's decision, as reflected in an executive certificate. However, it is submitted that, bearing in mind the words of Lord Atkin in *SS Arantzazu Mendi*,[19] this should be done sparingly and with great circumspection. A court may also intervene when the executive submits a certificate that is ambiguous or non-committal. Indeed, it may treat such a certificate as an invitation to intervene. That unclear certificates are not unusual is demonstrated by the certificates submitted to court by the British government since it abandoned its practice of formally recognising

[15] Supra (n 1) 116–18.

[16] See WJA Brand 'Judisiële onafhanklikheid by kwessies van nie-erkenning' (1974) 37 *THRHR* 329 at 338.

[17] [1939] AC 256 at 264.

[18] See para 11 of Chapter 4.

[19] Supra (n 17).

governments in 1980.[20] In such circumstances, it is incumbent on a court to exercise a discretion that reconciles the interests of the executive with common sense and justice. The *Republic of Somalia v Woodhouse Drake & Carey Suisse*[21] offers a helpful guide to courts on how to proceed in such a case. Here, an English court, in the absence of clear executive certificates, held that in deciding whether a particular political faction was the government of Somalia in 1991, it should have regard to the following factors:

(a) whether it is the constitutional government of the state;
(b) the degree, nature and stability of the control that it exercises over the territory of the state;
(c) whether the British government has any dealing with it and, if so, what is the nature of those dealings; and
(d) in marginal cases, the extent of the international recognition it has as government of the state.

Applying these principles, the Court found that the faction in question did not qualify as the government of Somalia.

LEGAL EFFECT OF ACTS OF UNRECOGNISED STATES AND GOVERNMENTS

For the purposes of municipal law, recognition is constitutive: it creates the state or government. In the absence of recognition, no effect will be given to the legislative, executive or judicial acts of a foreign government. The orthodox view is well illustrated by the leading case on the subject, *Luther v Sagor*.

In 1919, a timber factory owned by the plaintiff was nationalized by the Soviet government of Russia. The plaintiff fled to England. In 1920, the defendant purchased timber from the factory and brought it to England. Britain did not recognise the Soviet government in 1920. The plaintiff sued for the recovery of the timber on the ground that the defendant claimed title from the act of an unrecognised government. The lower court upheld this argument.[22] In 1921, Britain recognised the Soviet government as the *de facto* government of Russia. When the matter went on appeal thereafter, the Foreign Office submitted a certificate to the Court to the effect that it recognised the Soviet government *de facto*, and that the previous government had been overthrown in 1917. The Court of Appeal therefore found for

[20] See the certificates placed before the court in *GUR Corporation v Trust Bank of Africa Ltd (Government of the Republic of Ciskei, Third Party)* [1986] 3 All ER 449 (CA) ('*GUR Corporation v Trust Bank of Africa*'). The texts of the certificates appear below between notes 29 and 30.

[21] [1992] 3 WLR 744 (QB). Cf *Secretary of State for the Home Department v CC and CF* [2012] EWHC 2837 (Admin) paras 122 et seq.

[22] [1921] 1 KB 456.

the defendant[23] on the ground that he had acquired title to the timber as a result of the decrees of a recognised government. The court furthermore held that, first, there was no distinction between *de facto* and *de jure* governments for the purpose of the proceedings, and, secondly, the act of recognition had retrospective effect to 1917 when the Soviet government assumed effective control over Russia.[24]

While the principle expounded in *Luther v Sagor* is justifiable in respect of political acts, such as the nationalisation of property, it can result in great injustices in matters affecting the daily lives of individuals. For instance, in *Adams v Adams*,[25] a divorce decree made by a Rhodesian judge appointed by the Smith government during the UDI period was not recognised by an English court because of the non-recognition of Rhodesia. Hardships of this kind persuaded the International Court of Justice in the *Namibia Opinion* to hold that the consequences of non-recognition of South Africa's administration of Namibia should not extend 'to those acts, such as, for instance, the registration of births, deaths and marriages, the effects of which can be ignored only to the detriment of the inhabitants of the territory'.[26]

Considerations of the above kind, coupled with the fact that recognition on occasion loses sight of political reality, have prompted English courts to qualify the rule in *Luther v Sagor*, usually by imaginative interpretations of the executive certificate. In *Carl Zeiss Stiftung v Rayner & Keeler (No 2)*[27] the House of Lords held that effect could be given to the laws of East Germany—which was not recognised as a state by Britain—on the ground that it was an agent or a subordinate of the recognised authority for the territory—the Soviet Union. It therefore acted for the Soviet Union within the territory of East Germany. In the same case, Lord Wilberforce stated that the rule laid down in *Luther v Sagor* was not absolute and that 'where private rights, or acts of everyday occurrence, or perfunctory acts of administration are concerned . . . the courts may, in the interests of justice and common sense, where no consideration of public policy to the contrary has to prevail, give recognition to the actual facts or realities found to exist in the territory in question'.[28]

[23] [1921] 3 KB 532.

[24] See further, on the subject of the retrospective effect of recognition, DP O'Connell *International Law* 2 ed (1970) vol 1 at 185–92; Sanders (n 1) 172.

[25] [1971] P 188.

[26] 1971 ICJ Reports 16 at 56. In *Emin v Yeldag* [2002] 1 FLR 956 (Fam Div) an English court applied this exception in respect of a divorce granted by a court in the Turkish Republic of Northern Cyprus.

[27] [1967] 1 AC 853 ('*Carl Zeiss*'). See DW Greig 'The *Carl Zeiss* case and the position of an unrecognised government in English Law' (1967) 83 *LQR* 96.

[28] At 954.

The reasoning of the *Carl Zeiss* case was subsequently invoked in respect of Ciskei.

In *GUR Corporation v Trust Bank of Africa*[29] the plaintiff, a Panamanian company, contracted with Ciskei to build a hospital and two schools. Under the contract with the plaintiff, a guarantee of 10 per cent of the contract price was required to be made available to cover claims by Ciskei for the cost of repairing defects in the building. Accordingly, the sum of US $300 000 was lodged with the defendant bank in a deposit account as security for a guarantee given by the bank to Ciskei. Ciskei made a claim on the guarantee, but it was disputed whether the claim had been made in proper form before the guarantee expired. Nonetheless, the defendant bank refused to return the $300 000 to the plaintiff until the question of the validity of the claim was settled. The plaintiff sued the defendant, seeking the return of the deposit; the defendant in turn served a third-party notice on Ciskei, seeking to have the validity of Ciskei's claim determined. Ciskei counter-claimed for a declaration that it was entitled to the deposit.

None of the parties raised the question whether Ciskei, as an unrecognised state, had standing to sue or be sued in an English court, as it was in their interest for the matter to be resolved by an English court. The case came before a South African expatriate, Steyn J (later Lord Steyn), in the Queen's Bench Division, who raised the question himself.

The Foreign and Commonwealth Office submitted two certificates on this subject. In the first, it stated that 'Her Majesty's Government does not recognise the "Republic of Ciskei" as an independent sovereign state, either *de jure* or *de facto*'. In the second, in response to the question '[w]hich state, if any, does Her Majesty's Government recognise as . . . entitled to exercise . . . governing authority in respect of . . . Ciskei?' it stated:

> Her Majesty's Government has not taken and does not have a formal position as regards the exercise of governing authority over the territory of Ciskei. Her Majesty's Government does not have any dealings with the 'Government of the Republic of Ciskei' . . . . Her Majesty's Government has made representations to the South African Government in relation to certain matters occurring in Ciskei and others of the Homelands to which South Africa has purported to grant independence, notably on matters relating to individuals, but has not in general received any positive response from the South African Government.

On the basis of these certificates, Steyn J ruled that Ciskei had no standing before an English court. In upholding the orthodox position, Steyn J dismissed the applicability of either of two possible

[29] Supra (n 20).

exceptions to the rule. First, he held that the qualification suggested by Lord Wilberforce in *Carl Zeiss* was not applicable as this had been a purely commercial matter and not one in which the Court had been 'confronted with the necessity of doing justice to individuals who were caught up in a political situation that was not of their making'.[30] Secondly, he held that the *Carl Zeiss* exception was not applicable as it was not possible to infer from the certificate that Her Majesty's Government viewed South Africa as the governing authority of Ciskei.

On appeal, Sir John Donaldson MR engaged in an ingenious interpretation of the executive certificate, in a manner described by Professor James Crawford as more becoming to a novelist than a judge,[31] in order to reach a different conclusion. He held that the Status of Ciskei Act[32] contained a delegation of legislative power to Ciskei by South Africa which could be revoked subsequently by the South African Parliament. He continued:

> [T]he certified fact that 'Her Majesty's Government has made representations to the South African Government in relation to certain matters occurring in Ciskei and others of the Homelands to which South Africa has purported to grant independence' gives rise to a clear inference that Her Majesty's Government regards the Republic of South Africa as continuing to be *entitled* to exercise sovereign authority over the territory . . . .
>
> It follows that in my judgment the legal status of the Republic of Ciskei and its government is indistinguishable from that which obtained in the case of the GDR and its government at the time with which the *Carl-Zeiss* case was concerned . . . . I would therefore allow the appeal and declare that the government of the Republic of Ciskei has *locus standi* in the courts of this country as being a subordinate body set up by the Republic of South Africa to act on its behalf.[33]

The judgment of the Court of Appeal may be 'strained and artificial',[34] but it does illustrate the determination of the English courts to qualify the rule in *Luther v Sagor* and to pursue a more flexible approach to the acts of unrecognised states and governments. Here the English courts have been influenced by American deci-

[30] *GUR Corporation v Trust Bank of Africa* (n 20) 454H–I.

[31] 'Recent cases' (1986) 57 *BYIL* 405 at 409.

[32] Section 3(1) of Act 110 of 1981.

[33] *GUR Corporation v Trust Bank of Africa* (n 20) 465–6. For comments on this case, see C Warbrick 'Unrecognised states and domestic law' (1987) 50 *MLR* 84; D Lloyd Jones 'Recognition of states and governments—Republic of Ciskei' 1987 *Cambridge Law Journal* 7; N Botha 'From Pimlico to Bisho: Recognition of South African national states in the light of *Carl Zeiss*' (1987–1988) 12 *SAYIL* 156; FA Mann 'The judicial recognition of an unrecognised state' (1987) 36 *ICLQ* 348; A Beck 'A South African homeland appears in the English courts: Legitimation of the illegitimate' (1987) 36 *ICLQ* 350.

[34] *Per* Friedman J in *S v Banda* 1989 (4) SA 519 (B) 549F.

sions[35] which have refused to deny effect to the acts of unrecognised governments when this would fly in the face of reality.[36] For instance, in 1933 a United States court gave legal effect to an oil nationalization decree of the unrecognised Soviet government, commenting that 'to refuse to recognise that Soviet Russia is a government regulating the internal affairs of the country, is to give fictions an air of reality which they do not deserve'.[37]

The agency argument adopted in *Carl Zeiss* and *GUR Corporation v Trust Bank of Africa* does not hold out much hope for a principled qualification of *Luther v Sagor*, as it is dependent on the formulation of the executive certificate in each case. Lord Wilberforce's *obiter dictum* in *Carl Zeiss*, however, does offer some prospect for such a qualification. It has received some support in later decisions[38] and was endorsed by Lord Denning MR in an *obiter dictum* in *Hesperides Hotels v Aegean Holidays Ltd*.[39] In a matter concerning the United Kingdom's non-recognition of the Turkish administration of northern Cyprus, he declared:

> If it were necessary . . . I would unhesitatingly hold that the courts of this country can recognise the laws or acts of a body which is in effective control of a territory even though it has not been recognised by her Majesty's Government *de jure* or *de facto*: at any rate, in regard to the laws which regulate the day-to-day affairs of the people, such as their marriages, their divorces, their leases, their occupations, and so forth; and furthermore that the courts can receive evidence of the state of affairs so as to see whether the body is in effective control or not.[40]

The effect to be given to the acts of unrecognised entities has not been fully considered in South Africa. Nevertheless, there is support for the rule in *Luther v Sagor*. In *Inter-Science Research v Republica Popular de Mocambique*[41] Margo J stated *obiter* that without recognition

[35] *Carl Zeiss* (n 27) 954.

[36] For an examination of these decisions, see O'Connell (n 24) 172–80.

[37] *Salimoff v Standard Oil Company of New York* 262 NY 220 (1933), (1933–1934) AD 22.

[38] Both Steyn J and Sir John Donaldson MR gave implied approval to Lord Wilberforce's *obiter dictum in GUR Corporation v Trust Bank of Africa* (n 20) 454H, 463H–I.

[39] [1978] QB 205. See JG Merrills 'Trespass to foreign land' (1979) 28 *ICLQ* 523.

[40] At 218. See further RD Leslie 'Unrecognised governments in the conflict of Laws: Lord Denning's contribution' (1987) 14 *CILSA* 165. In *Caglar v Billingham (Inspector of Taxes)* 108 ILR 510 (noted by C Warbrick in 'Recent cases on public international law' (1996) 45 *ICLQ* 954) it was held that 'the courts will not acknowledge the existence of an unrecognised state if to do so would involve them acting inconsistently with the foreign policy or diplomatic stance of this country' (534 para 121). See, too, *Kirbis v Türk* (2009) EWHC 1918 (Admin) para 89. Cf *Emin v Yeldag* (n 26).

[41] Supra (n 1).

of the government of Mozambique, its nationalisation decrees could not be acknowledged as governmental acts and 'would have no greater validity than the seizure of . . . assets by some non-governmental body, having no lawful authority or rights in the matter'.[42] In *Standard Bank of SA Ltd v Ocean Commodities Inc*,[43] a case concerning Rhodesia, King J held, without examination of the English authorities, that 'our courts will not recognise the laws of an unrecognised state'.[44]

South African courts have yet to consider whether the rule in *Luther v Sagor* is absolute. South African writers have suggested that the test that should be applied in departing from this rule is whether cognisance can be taken of the acts of unrecognised governments 'without material harm being done to the executive's foreign policy goals'.[45] This is a sensible suggestion. Where laws which regulate the private, day-to-day affairs of ordinary people can be recognised without any embarrassment being caused to the executive's foreign policy interests, the courts should refuse to follow *Luther v Sagor*. In the absence of a clear indication from the executive of its foreign policy interest in a certificate to the court,[46] a court may assume that the executive will raise no objection to the recognition of the laws of an unrecognised government or state affecting the private lives of ordinary people.

[42] At 116D.

[43] 1980 (2) SA 175 (T).

[44] At 181C and 183E.

[45] Sanders (n 1) 170; Brand (n 16) 334, 338–9; HA Strydom 'Vrae rondom die erkenning van state' (1992) 3 *Stellenbosch LR* 67 at 73.

[46] The court should, of course, request an executive certificate in any case where the status of the state or government is in doubt. See *Inter-Science Research v Republica Popular de Mocambique* (n 1) 118B.

CHAPTER 8

Territory

John Dugard and Rosalind Elphick

Territory occupies an important place in international law.[1] A state will not qualify as a 'state' unless it has a defined territory.[2] Moreover, the extent of a state's sovereignty[3] or jurisdiction will in most instances be limited to the extent of its territory. Today the entire land mass of our planet, except Antarctica, where competing claims to exclusive jurisdiction have been 'frozen' by treaty,[4] falls under the exclusive jurisdiction of the states that make up the community of nations. Other forms of 'territory', notably the sea, sea-bed, airspace and outer space, either fall under the exclusive jurisdiction of states or are governed by an international regime that accords them the status of *res communis*, ie territory for communal use.

In previous centuries large portions of the globe were either uninhabited and unclaimed, or inhabited by political communities characterised as 'unorganised', 'primitive', or 'uncivilised' by European states. Such territory was designated as *terra nullius*, land belonging to no one, which could be acquired by means of discovery in the 15th and 16th centuries, and thereafter by means of occupation. Today no *terra nullius* remains, and the concept has come under significant criticism for its historical disregard of the claims of

[1] In Malaysia/Singapore 2008 ICJ Reports (para 122) the International Court of Justice stressed 'the central importance in international law and relations of state sovereignty over territory and of the stability and certainty of that sovereignty'. See, too, MN Shaw *Title to Territory in Africa: International Legal Issues* (1986); M Kohen (ed) *Territoriality and International Law* (2016); RY Jennings (with a new introduction by M Kohen) *The Acquisition of Territory in International Law* (2017) (first published in 1963); MN Shaw *The International Law of Territory* (2018).

[2] See Chapter 5.

[3] The term 'sovereignty' is avoided wherever possible because its meaning varies according to the discipline and context in which it is used. The meaning of the term in international law was accurately described by arbitrator Max Huber in the *Island of Palmas Case*: 'Sovereignty in the relations between states signifies independence. Independence in regard to a portion of the globe is a right to exercise therein, to the exclusion of any other state, the function of a state' (2 RIAA 829 (1928) at 838). See further R Jennings 'Sovereignty and international law' in G Kreijen (ed) *State, Sovereignty, and International Governance* (2002) 27.

[4] See below, notes 164–71.

indigenous peoples.[5] Consequently territory may no longer be acquired by original title, ie by occupation.[6] New states come into existence by recognition, which gives them jurisdiction over a defined territory that previously belonged to another state, as illustrated by the process of decolonisation. Existing states may extend their jurisdiction over territory previously belonging to another state, in which case recognition of the territorial change by other states is essential for a valid change in title.

The acquisition of territory today is therefore governed largely by recognition. The rules that determined the acquisition of territory in earlier days are still important in boundary disputes because such disputes can only be resolved in most instances by an historical examination of the sources of the competing claims, which may go back centuries. Boundary disputes are a common feature of modern international society and are likely to increase. According to Ian Brownlie:

> The pressures of national sentiment, new forms of exploitation of barren and inaccessible areas, the strategic significance of areas previously neglected, and the pressure of population on resources, give good cause for a belief that territorial disputes will increase in significance. This is specially so in Africa and Asia, where the removal of foreign political domination has left the successor states with a long agenda of unsettled problems, legal and political.[7]

In the formative years of international law jurists viewed sovereignty as being similar to ownership in private law. Consequently the methods of acquiring property under Roman private law were

[5] TW Bennett and CH Powell 'Aboriginal title in South Africa revisited' (1999) 15 *SAJHR* 449; R Choudree and G McIntyre 'Resititution of land in two jurisdictions: Australia and South Africa' (1997) 114 *SALJ* 187; U Ozlem 'Developing the doctrine of aboriginal title in South Africa: Source and content' (2002) 46 *Journal of African Law* 131.

[6] The concepts of *terra nullius* and occupation have gained recent attention in the context of the polar regions: PE Steinberg, J Tasch and H Gerhardt *Contesting the Arctic: Politics and Imaginaries in the Circumpolar North* (2015) 18–43; K Dodds, AD Hemmings and P Roberts *Handbook on the Politics of Antarctica* (2017) 54–6; C Collins *Territories beyond Possession? Antarctica and Outer Space* (2017) 7; CR Rossi 'A unique international problem: The Svalbard Treaty, equal enjoyment, and *terra nullius*: Lessons of territorial temptation from history' (2016) 15 *Washington University Global Studies Law Review* 93; W Erlank 'Rethinking *terra nullius* and property law in space' (2015) 18 *Potchefstroom Electronic Law Journal* 2503.

[7] *Principles of Public International Law* 7 ed (2008) 123. See, too, C Anyangwe 'African border disputes and their settlement by international judicial process' (2003) 28 *SAYIL* 29; KH Kaikobad *Interpretation and Revision of International Boundary Decisions* (2012); J Levitt (ed) *Africa: Mapping New Boundaries in International Law* (2008); F Nguendi Ikome 'Africa's international borders as potential sources of conflict and future threats to peace and security' (2012) 223 *Institute for Security Studies Papers* 16.

borrowed and adapted by international law. In classical international law the modes of acquisition of territory were therefore discovery, occupation, accretion, cession, conquest, and prescription. Today claims to territory are based on grounds derived largely from the traditional methods of acquisition, the principle of effectiveness and new expectations based on the right of self-determination.

There are important differences between the acquisition of territory under international law and the acquisition of property in municipal law. In the first instance, changes in territorial title involve a change of sovereignty which usually affects the nationality and allegiance of people living on the territory in question. This may explain why states strongly resist any change in territorial title. Secondly, there is often less clarity about boundaries and the root of title in international law than in municipal law as international law lacks the strict and detailed rules of transfer and registration of ownership known to municipal law.

BACKGROUND CONCEPTS

1 Intertemporal law

Discovery and conquest are no longer accepted as modes of acquisition of territory. The idea that a state might acquire title to territory by discovery alone, without any subsequent act of effective occupation, was suspect during the 15th and 16th centuries.[8] Even if it did exist in this form, it has long since been abandoned as a root of title. Conquest, on the other hand, was an accepted method of acquiring title until after World War I. In 1928, war was outlawed by the General Treaty for the Renunciation of War[9] (also known as the Pact of Paris or the Kellogg-Briand Pact);[10] and in 1945, the Charter of the United Nations prohibited the use of force in international relations.[11] As no right may arise from a wrong (*ex injuria jus non oritur*) it follows that title acquired by the use of force is no longer recognised—as illustrated by the Security Council's non-recognition of Israel's purported annexation of the Golan Heights and East Jerusalem;[12] and the General Assembly's resolution calling upon states not

[8] J Crawford *Brownlie's Principles of Public International Law* 8 ed (2012) 223.

[9] See Chapter 24.

[10] Named after the United States Secretary of State and the French Foreign Minister respectively.

[11] Article 2(4).

[12] See below (n 101).

to recognise a change of status on the territory of Crimea following its annexation by Russia.[13]

Few territorial titles, if any, are today based on discovery alone. On the other hand, a large number are based on conquest, arising out of war or colonial expansion. These titles are to be judged by the law in force at the time the title was first asserted and not by the law of today. This is the principle of intertemporal law.[14]

The leading authority on this subject is the *Island of Palmas Case*.[15] After the Spanish American War of 1898, a defeated Spain ceded the Philippines to the United States by treaty. In 1906 a United States official visited the Island of Palmas, believed to be part of the territory ceded to the United States, and found that the Netherlands had an administration on the small island (with a population of less than 1 000). In a dispute referred to a single arbitrator, Max Huber, the United States claimed that Spain had acquired title to the territory by discovery in the 16th century and that this had been lawfully ceded to the United States by treaty. The Netherlands, on the other hand, based its claim on the continuous and peaceful display of state authority over the island since 1700.

In this case, Huber expounded two principles of intertemporal law.[16] The first principle is that 'a juridical fact must be appreciated in the light of the law contemporary with it, and not of the law in force at the time when a dispute in regard to it arises or falls to be settled'.[17] Consequently, the effect of discovery of the island by Spain was to be determined by the rules of law in force in the 16th century.

The second principle is more controversial. According to Huber:

> As regards the question which of different legal systems prevailing at successive periods is to be applied in a particular case (the so-called intertemporal law), a distinction must be made between the creation of rights and the existence of rights. The same principle which subjects the act creative of a right to the law in force at the time the right arises, demands that the existence of the right, in other words its continued manifestation, shall follow the conditions required by the evolution of law.[18]

On the basis of this principle, Huber held that Spain had failed to maintain or consolidate the title it had acquired by discovery through the effective display of state authority. Conversely, the Netherlands

[13] Resolution 68/262 (27 March 2014); TD Grant *Aggression against Ukraine: Territory, Responsibility and International Law* (2015); J Bering 'The prohibition of annexation: Lessons from Crimea' (2017) 49 *NYUJ Int'l L&Pol* 747.

[14] On the application of this rule in Africa, see M van der Linden *The Acquisition of Africa (1870–1914): The Nature of International Law* (2017) 246 et seq.

[15] *(United States v Netherlands)* 2 RIAA 829 (1928).

[16] TO Elias 'The doctrine of intertemporal law' (1980) 74 *AJIL* 285.

[17] *Island of Palmas Case* (n 15) 845.

[18] Ibid.

had exercised its authority over the island peacefully and continuously since 1700. He therefore awarded the island to the Netherlands.

Huber's second principle of intertemporal law can be interpreted to destroy the first completely.[19] If it means that every territorial title has to be reasserted in accordance with every change in the law, it could produce great instability in the world order. The alarming implications of such an interpretation are illustrated by the disputes over Goa, the Falkland Islands, and Walvis Bay before its cession to Namibia in 1994.

In 1961 India invaded and annexed Goa, a Portuguese colonial enclave on the Indian subcontinent. In justification of its aggression, India argued that Portugal had illegally occupied Goa by means of conquest in the 16th century and that India was simply exercising its right of self-defence against the Portuguese aggressor—some 400 years later.[20] A similar argument was raised by Argentina when it invaded the Falkland Islands (called the Malvinas by Argentina) in 1982. Britain's claim to the islands, argued Argentina, was based on conquest in 1833, which was now unlawful and therefore might be overthrown by the use of force.[21]

Arguments of the above nature were raised in respect of South Africa's occupation of Walvis Bay before 1994.[22] Walvis Bay was proclaimed a British Crown territory in 1878, and annexed to the Cape Colony in 1884, shortly before Germany annexed South West Africa itself. From 1884 to 1910 Walvis Bay was administered as part of the Cape Colony, and after the Union of South Africa was formed in 1910, it became a part of the Union. In 1915 South African forces occupied German South West Africa. After South Africa was granted a mandate over South West Africa by the League of Nations, Walvis Bay was 'administered as if it were part of the mandated territory'.[23] In 1977, as Namibian independence became a possibility, South Africa reasserted its right to Walvis Bay and placed it under the administration of the Cape Province.[24]

According to Lynn Berat, in her study on Walvis Bay,[25] Max

[19] P Jessup 'The Palmas Island arbitration' (1928) 22 *AJIL* 735; Jennings (n 1) 42–5.

[20] SCOR, 16th Year, meetings 987 and 988 (18 December 1961). See further DJ Harris *Cases and Materials on International Law* 8 ed (2015) 355–7.

[21] Ibid 213–17.

[22] For expositions of South Africa's claims to Walvis Bay, see PEJ Brooks 'The legal status of Walvis Bay' (1976) 2 *SAYIL* 187; NJ Botha 'Walvis Bay: Miscellany' (1979) 12 *CILSA* 255; AJ Faris 'The administration of Walvis Bay' (1979) 5 *SAYIL* 63.

[23] Section 1 of the South West Africa Affairs Act 24 of 1922.

[24] Proclamation R202 *GG* 5731 of 31 August 1977 (*Reg Gaz* 2525) issued in terms of the South West Africa Constitution Amendment Act 95 of 1977.

[25] *Walvis Bay: Decolonization and International Law* (1990) 161–7. For a critical review of this study, see J Dugard 'Walvis Bay and international law: Reflections on a recent

Huber's second principle of intertemporal law was applicable to Walvis Bay. She claimed that 'the doctrine of intertemporal law invalidates an original title by applying new rules that affect the root of title'. Consequently, South Africa's claim to Walvis Bay, which was based on 19th century colonialist rules governing the acquisition of territory, was no longer valid as it was in conflict with new peremptory norms of international law which outlaw colonialism and assert the right of self-determination. 'Any right, transaction, or benefit that violates the *jus cogens*,' she maintained, 'is null and void.'[26]

Undoubtedly, the doctrine of *jus cogens* now plays an important part in contemporary international law, but to suggest that peremptory norms should be applied with retroactive effect to territorial titles is positively dangerous. Many boundaries in the modern world have been fixed in violation of what are today regarded as peremptory norms of *jus cogens*, namely the prohibition on the use of force and colonial occupation. To question the validity of these titles on the ground that they violate today's norms of *jus cogens* applied retrospectively is to open Pandora's box. As Professor—later Judge—RY Jennings warned in 1963, '[u]nder these conditions no title would be secure and the supposed aim of the law—stability—would be utterly defeated'.[27]

There are circumstances in which Huber's second principle of intertemporal law should be employed to bring the law into line with reality, as, for example, in the *Aegean Sea Continental Shelf Case*[28] in which the International Court of Justice in 1978 interpreted a 1931 treaty reference to Greece's 'territorial status' as including Greece's continental shelf, despite the fact that the continental shelf was recognised as being part of a state's territory only after 1945. This principle, however, should be used with great caution.[29] As Jennings suggests,[30] it should be invoked only to deny the claim of a party relying on the first principle of intertemporal law, where that party has failed to maintain a minimum degree of sovereign activity over the territory and by its neglect has abandoned its own claim to title or acquiesced in that of the rival claim—as happened in the *Island of*

study' (1991) 108 *SALJ* 82. See further GP Goeckner and IR Gunning 'Namibia, South Africa and the Walvis Bay dispute' (1980) 89 *Yale LJ* 903.

[26] Berat (n 25) 164.

[27] Jennings (n 1) 45.

[28] 1978 ICJ Reports 3 at 33–4.

[29] Elias (n 16) 305–6.

[30] Jennings (n 1) 44–5.

Palmas Case. In such cases, courts will have regard to the *effectivités*—that is, the evidence of the effective display of state functions by a state.

The International Court of Justice has settled a number of territorial disputes by applying the doctrine of intertemporal law,[31] particularly in boundary disputes between African states.[32] The same is true of other tribunals.[33]

2 *Uti possidetis*

Closely related to the principle of intertemporal law is the principle of *uti possidetis*, according to which colonial boundaries, however arbitrarily drawn by the imperial powers, are to be respected.[34] This principle, which has its origins in Latin America and has been endorsed by the Organization of African Unity,[35] is designed to prevent the chaos that inevitably would result from attempts to redraw boundaries to coincide with ethnic groupings.

In the *Frontier Dispute Case*[36] between Burkina Faso and Mali, the International Court of Justice held that this practice was a customary rule of 'general scope'[37] which applied to a new state from the moment it became independent. In effect this 'freezes the territorial title'[38] and confines the right of self-determination of peoples to a territory defined by the colonial power. In the *Frontier Dispute Case* the International Court acknowledged that the principle of *uti possidetis* conflicts with the right of peoples to self-determination.[39] However, said the Court:

[31] *Minquiers and Ecrehos (France v United Kingdom)* 1953 ICJ Reports 47; *Right of Passage over Indian Territory (Portugal v India)* 1960 ICJ Reports 6; *Temple of Preah Vihear (Cambodia v Thailand)* 1962 ICJ Reports 6; *Western Sahara, Advisory Opinion* 1975 ICJ Reports 12; *Land, Island and Maritime Frontier Dispute (El Salvador v Honduras; Nicaragua intervening)* 1992 ICJ Reports 351; *Maritime Delimitation and Territorial Questions between Qatar and Bahrain* 2001 ICJ Reports 40.

[32] *Kasikili/Sedudu Island (Botswana v Namibia)* 1999 ICJ Reports 1045; *Land and Maritime Boundary between Cameroon and Nigeria (Cameroon v Nigeria: Equatorial Guinea intervening)* 2002 ICJ Reports 303.

[33] *Dubai-Sharjah Land Border Arbitration* (1981) 91 ILR 543; *Eritrea and Yemen* (1998) 114 ILR 1 at 32–4.

[34] For a challenge to this principle, see DM Ahmed *Boundaries and Secession in Africa and International Law: Challenging* Uti Possidetis (2015).

[35] In 1964, at the first session of the Conference of African Heads of State and Government, it was resolved that all member states of the OAU 'pledge themselves to respect the borders existing on their achievement of national independence': AGH/Res 16(1).

[36] 1986 ICJ Reports 554.

[37] At 565.

[38] At 568.

[39] See further on this conflict GN Barrie '*Uti possidetis* versus self-determination and modern international law: In Africa the chickens are coming home to roost' 1988

> [T]he maintenance of the territorial status quo in Africa is often seen as the wisest course, to preserve what has been achieved by peoples who have struggled for their independence, and to avoid a disruption which would deprive the continent of gains achieved by much sacrifice. The essential requirement of stability in order to survive, to develop and gradually consolidate their independence in all fields, has induced African states judiciously to consent to the respecting of colonial frontiers, and to take account of it in the interpretation of the principle of self-determination of peoples.[40]

The principle of *uti possidetis* is closely related to that of 'territorial integrity', which is asserted in the Declaration on the Granting of Independence to Colonial Countries and Peoples[41] and other resolutions of the General Assembly on the subject of self-determination.

The principle of *uti possidetis* in the non-colonial context was applied to justify the dissolution of Yugoslavia in 1991–92. Here, the Arbitration Commission—established by the European Community under the chairmanship of Mr Badinter to oversee the guidelines contained in the European Community's Declaration on Yugoslavia—held that the internal federal boundaries of Slovenia, Serbia, Croatia, Bosnia and Herzegovina, Montenegro and Macedonia, which together comprised the Socialist Federal Republic of Yugoslavia, became frontiers protected by international law. 'This conclusion follows,' said the Commission, 'from the principle of respect for the territorial status quo and, in particular, from the principle of *uti possidetis* ... today recognised as a general principle.'[42] This is dangerous reasoning as it undermines the principle of territorial integrity in respect of federal states.[43] Conversely, it is unfair to territorial units such as Kosovo[44] that enjoyed a lower status in the former Yugoslavia but were nevertheless clearly demarcated and granted a certain degree of autonomy.

Although a force for stability in international relations, the principle of *uti possidetis* is highly controversial. It often internationalises as boundaries lines that were simply administrative delimitations in the colonial era and not intended as frontiers.[45] This was acknowledged

TSAR 451; FD Mnyongani 'Between a rock and a hard place: The right of self-determination versus *uti possidetis* in Africa' (2008) 41 *CILSA* 463.

[40] 1986 ICJ Reports 567.

[41] See Chapter 5.

[42] Opinion 3, 92 ILR 170. See, too, Opinion 2, 92 ILR 967. See further M Craven 'The EC Arbitration Commission on Yugoslavia' (1995) 66 *BYIL* 333.

[43] See J Dugard 'Secession: Is the case of Yugoslavia a precedent for Africa?' (1993) 5 *African Journal of International and Comparative Law* 163.

[44] See the Independent International Commission on Kosovo *The Kosovo Report: Conflict, International Response, Lessons Learned* (2000).

[45] SN Lalonde *Determining Boundaries in a Conflicted World: The Role of Uti Possidetis* (2002).

by the International Court of Justice in the *Land, Island and Maritime Frontier Dispute (El Salvador/Honduras) Case* when it stated that '*uti possidetis juris* is essentially a retrospective principle, investing as international boundaries administrative units intended originally for quite other purposes'.[46] The principle is, however, mainly criticized on the ground that it serves the interests of the dominant societal groups at the expense of the right of peoples to self-determination.[47] Despite these criticisms, the principle enjoys continued application. It was recently applied by the International Court of Justice to resolve a boundary dispute in the African context in *Frontier Dispute (Burkina Faso/Niger)*.[48]

3 Original versus derivative title

A traditional distinction is drawn between original and derivative titles of territorial sovereignty. The former, on the one hand, relates to titles that attach to land that has not previously been the subject of any other states title, as in the case of occupation of a *terra nullius* or accretion. Derivative titles, on the other hand, are the result of a transfer of territory from a previous sovereign, as in the case of cession and conquest.

THE MODES OF ACQUISITION OF TERRITORY

1 Discovery

Claims that discovery gave a complete title to territory during the 15th and 16th centuries are today dismissed. The prevailing view is that at that time, discovery created an inchoate title only and that it was necessary for the discoverer to perfect its title by the effective occupation of the territory within a reasonable time.[49]

2 Occupation

Occupation is the method of acquiring territory not belonging to any other state, ie *terra nullius*. Although there is no *terra nullius* left in the modern world, occupation still features prominently in boundary disputes. To succeed in a claim based on occupation, a claimant must prove that it had 'the intention and will to act as sovereign' (*animus occupandi*), that it exercised actual authority over the territory

[46] 1992 ICJ Reports 355 at 388 para 43. See, too, *Frontier Dispute Case* (n 40) 566.

[47] J Castellino and S Allen *Title to Territory in International Law: A Temporal Analysis* (2003).

[48] 2013 ICJ Reports 44 at 73, 84.

[49] *Brownlie* (n 8) 223; *Island of Palmas Case* (n 15) 845.

(*corpus*)[50] and that the territory was *terra nullius*. *Animus occupandi* may be proved by the hoisting of a flag or the placing of a plaque on the territory[51] or by publication of the occupation in a widely distributed newspaper.[52] *Corpus* requires proof of the continuous and effective display of authority over the territory. The degree of authority required varies according to the nature of the territory. Tribunals have been satisfied with very little in the actual exercise of sovereign rights in thinly populated or uninhabitable territories.[53] In *Nicaragua v Colombia*, the International Court held that sovereignty over 'minor' islands could succeed based on very little proof of effective occupation, provided that the opposing claimant was unable to present greater proof.[54]

South Africa's occupation of Marion Island and Prince Edward Island, in order to set up a meteorological station, provides an example of a recent assertion of sovereignty.[55] These islands were first discovered in 1772 by a French navigator, Marion du Fresne, who made no claim to the islands on behalf of France. In 1776 James Cook sailed between the islands and gave them their present names.[56] However, Britain took no steps to establish effective control over the islands. When the South African government decided to claim these islands in 1947 and 1948, it first consulted the British government, which gave an assurance that it laid no claim to the islands.[57] Thereafter, South Africa established its authority over the islands. In 1948 Prime Minister Dr DF Malan made it clear that South Africa had acquired title by occupation. He told Parliament:

> These two islands, though they were discovered so long ago, were practically never occupied. Therefore, because there was no occupation, sovereignty over these islands was really never established by any particular country. The

[50] *Legal Status of Eastern Greenland* 1933 PCIJ Reports Series A/B no 53 at 45–6; *Western Sahara Case* 1975 ICJ Reports 12 at 43.

[51] This was done by the early British settlers of West Falkland.

[52] When Argentina took possession of the Falkland Islands in 1821, it advertised this fact in the *The Times* of London (PJ Beck *The Falkland Islands as an International Problem* (Routledge Revivals) (2014) 89; Harris (n 20) 179.

[53] *Eastern Greenland Case* (n 50) 46; *Island of Palmas Case* (n 15) 840; *Clipperton Island* case (1932) 26 *AJIL* 390.

[54] 2012 ICJ Reports 624 para 80. See also *Sovereignty over Pedra Branca/Pulau Batu Puteh, Middle Rocks and South Ledge (Malaysia/Singapore)* 2008 ICJ Report 12; M Kohen 'Original title in the light of the ICJ judgment on sovereignty over Pedra Branca/Pulau Batu Puteh, Middle Rocks and South Ledge' (2013) 15 *Journal of the History of International Law* 151.

[55] See RP Schaffer 'The extension of South African treaties to the territories of South West Africa and the Prince Edward Islands' (1978) 95 *SALJ* 63.

[56] Prince Edward Island was named after the fourth son of King George III.

[57] This was confirmed by an exchange of notes of February 1949: *Union of South Africa Treaty Series* no 11 of 1950.

nearest to occupation came from the side of England. An application was made to the British Government on one occasion by a company to lease the island to work the guano deposits which they thought were on the island, on another occasion by a whaling company. But these rights which were granted by the British Government were never exercised, and in any case the islands were never occupied. In annexing these two islands I do not think that the Union can in any way be accused or suspected of harbouring aggressive imperialistic designs. These islands practically belong to nobody, so we do not deprive anybody else of his rights.[58]

The Act annexing the islands likewise employs the language of international law in providing in its preamble:

Whereas effective occupation and administration of Marion Island and Prince Edward Island were established on the twenty-ninth day of December, 1947 and the fourth day of January, 1948, respectively, and such occupation and administration will continue permanently.[59]

The concept of *terra nullius* presents difficulties for contemporary international law as it has undergone important changes. During the formative years of international law opinion was divided as to whether international law applied to indigenous peoples: the naturalists argued that all the peoples of the world enjoyed certain inalienable rights, while the positivists denied such rights to indigenous peoples and claimed that international law applied to Christian, civilised nations only.[60] During the 19th century the positivist view prevailed, with the result that indigenous, non-European peoples in loosely organised societies were viewed as having no rights under international law. Consequently, their territory was viewed as *terra nullius*—a designation that gave legal backing to the colonial expansion of that century. Modern international law, determined to erase this mark of imperialist paternalism from the historical record, has sought to minimise the 19th century positivist position. In the *Western Sahara Opinion* of 1975, the International Court of Justice found that the Western Sahara was inhabited by nomadic but socially and politically organised tribes in 1884, at the time of Spanish colonisation of the territory. It held:

Whatever differences of opinion there may have been among jurists, the state practice of the relevant period indicates that territories inhabited by tribes or peoples having a social and political organization were not regarded as *terrae nullius*. It shows that in the case of such territories the acquisition of territory was not generally considered as effected unilaterally through 'occupation' of

[58] *House of Assembly Debates* vol 65 col 3041 (22 September 1948).

[59] The Prince Edward Islands Act 43 of 1948. Section 1(1) of the Act is less elegant as it states that the islands were 'annexed' to South Africa. Clearly, this was a case of occupation and not annexation.

[60] For a description of this jurisprudential debate, see MF Lindley *The Acquisition and Government of Backward Territory in International Law* (1926); Berat (n 25) at 104–9.

> *terra nullius* by original title but through agreements concluded with local rulers . . . [S]uch agreements with local rulers, whether or not considered as an actual 'cession' of the territory, were regarded as derivative roots of title, and not original titles obtained by occupation of *terrae nullius*.[61]

When the first British settlement was established in Australia in 1788, it forcibly displaced a nomadic aboriginal people with a complex social and political organisation. Conquest, rather than occupation, might therefore be seen to be the method by which title was acquired, in which case, under English constitutional law,[62] the laws of the aboriginal people would have remained in force. Judicial decisions held otherwise.[63] In 1889 the Privy Council held that the colony of New South Wales had not been acquired by conquest but had 'consisted of a tract of territory, practically unoccupied, without settled inhabitants or settled law, at the time when it was peacefully annexed to the British Dominions'.[64] Subsequent Australian decisions confirmed this view,[65] but in 1992 it was repudiated by the High Court in *Mabo v State of Queensland*,[66] which approved the approach adopted by the International Court of Justice in the *Western Sahara Opinion*.

This is not an issue in South Africa as the indigenous people constitute the majority and today exercise political power. Despite this, it is interesting to consider the legal basis for Dutch, British and

[61] 1975 ICJ Reports 12 at 39. See further Shaw (n 1) 31–8.

[62] *Campbell v Hall* [1774] 1 Cowper 204; G Carpenter *Introduction to South African Constitutional Law* (1987) 18.

[63] See R Balkin 'International law and sovereign rights of indigenous peoples' in B Hocking (ed) *International Law and Aboriginal Rights* (1988) 19.

[64] *Cooper v Stuart* [1889] 14 AC 286 at 291. In 1979 Justice Murphy declared that this statement 'may be regarded either as having been made in ignorance or as a convenient falsehood to justify the taking of aborigine's land' (*Coe v Commonwealth of Australia* (1979) 24 ALR 118 at 137–8).

[65] *Milirrpum v Nabalco Pty Ltd and the Commonwealth of Australia* (1971) 17 FLR 141 at 242; *Coe v Commonwealth of Australia* (n 64) 129 (*per* Gibbs CJ).

[66] (1992) 107 ALR 1 at 26–9 (Brennan J), 82–3 (Deane, Gaudron JJ), 141–2 (Toohey J). See further A Reilly 'The Australian experience of aboriginal title: Lessons for South Africa' (2000) 16 *SAJHR* 512. In *Alexkor Ltd v Richtersveld Community* 2004 (5) SA 460 (CC) the Constitutional Court, after citing *Mabo*, stated: 'Courts in other jurisdictions have in recent times been faced with complex and difficult problems dealing, after the event, with injustices caused by dispossessions of land, or rights in land, from indigenous inhabitants by later occupiers of the land in question. These later occupiers claimed political and legal sovereignty over the land, and such dispossessions invariably took place in a racially discriminatory manner. They often occurred centuries ago, when the legal norms and principles of later occupiers differed substantially from those of today. In this regard our situation in this country differs substantially from that of the jurisdictions referred to above in that both our Interim Constitution and the Constitution [s 25(7)] have dealt expressly with this problem' (paras 34–5). See, too, *Richtersveld Community v Alexkor Ltd* 2003 (6) SA 104 (SCA).

Boer settlements in South Africa at the expense of the indigenous population.

When the Dutch East India Company first established an outpost at the Cape of Good Hope in 1652, it was not envisaged as a settlement or colony. Over the years, however, this outpost evolved from a refreshment station to a settlement as employees of the company were released to become settlers and began the inevitable process of expansion in search of new lands. In the process, the indigenous inhabitants of the Cape, the San and Khoikhoi, were subjugated. While the socio-political fabric of the San was rudimentary, the Khoikhoi had a developed social organisation. Was the Cape therefore acquired by the Dutch East India Company on behalf of the Republic of United Netherlands by occupation of a *terra nullius* or by conquest?[67]

The African tribes to the east and north were accepted as political societies by the Dutch,[68] the British[69] and the Boers,[70] who all at some stage or another entered into treaties with tribal leaders. While the status of these treaties under international law was uncertain, they did at least make it clear that the African-occupied territories were not viewed as *terrae nullius*. The extension of white settlement into the Eastern Cape,[71]

[67] In 1660 Jan van Riebeeck informed a group of Khoikhoi who had been defeated in a skirmish that they had lost their land in war. It is unlikely, however, that this attitude could be attributed to the Dutch East India Company. See SFN Gie *Geskiedenis van Suid-Afrika* Part I (1928) 77–8; L Marquard *The Story of South Africa* (1955) 39.

[68] TRH Davenport *South Africa: A Modern History* 3 ed (1987) at 32–3.

[69] The British entered into numerous treaties with the African tribes on the eastern frontier. For references to these treaties, see JA Kalley *South Africa by Treaty 1806–1986* (1987). The treaties are published in *Treaties Entered into by the Governors of the Colony of the Cape of Good Hope and Other British Authorities with Native Chieftains between 1803 and 1854* (1857). According to E Brookes *The History of the Native Policy in South Africa from 1830 to the Present Day* 2 ed (1927) the policy of the British in the 1830s was 'to enter into treaties with the various chiefs on the basis of their independent sovereignty' (14). Dr John Philip, the famous missionary, told a Select Committee of the House of Commons in 1836 that in his opinion '[t]he Caffres were quite capable of understanding a system of international law, and of appreciating it' (14). See further TW Bennett 'Aboriginal title in South Africa' (1993) 9 *SAJHR* 443; TW Bennett and CH Powell 'Aboriginal title in South Africa revisited' (1999) 15 *SAJHR* 449.

[70] See S Hofmeyr *Die Boere-Republieke en die Volkereg* (1933) ch 4.

[71] Territories in the Eastern Cape were first annexed by Britain and then incorporated into the Cape Colony. By 1829, the eastern boundary of the Colony extended to the Keiskamma. In 1847 the land between the Keiskamma and the Kei was annexed to the Cape Colony as a separate imperial dependency under the name of British Kaffraria. In 1860 British Kaffraria became a Crown colony and in 1865 it was incorporated in the Cape Colony (Act 3 of 1865 (C)). Griqualand East, Fingoland and Griqualand West were annexed to the Cape Colony in 1877 (Acts 38 and 39 of 1877 (C)). Walvis Bay and certain territories on the St John's River were incorporated in the Cape Colony by Act 35 of 1884 (C); Tembuland, Galekaland and Bomvanaland by Act 3 of 1885 (C); and Pondoland by Act 5 of 1894 (C).

Natal,[72] Orange Free State and Transvaal[73] was therefore based on conquest or cession and not occupation.

South Africa's claim to the enclave of Walvis Bay before 1994 was based on a blend of cession and occupation. In 1876 an agreement was entered into between the special Cape Commissioner, William Coates Palgrave, and Chief Kamaherero of the Herero, establishing a protectorate over a large tract of land that included Walvis Bay.[74] This was not viewed as a treaty of cession but rather as an administrative act over a *terra nullius* by Britain that served notice on European rivals that a particular territory was being occupied.[75] In 1878 Commander Richard Cossantine Dyer RN proclaimed Walvis Bay a British Crown territory and in 1884[76] it was annexed to the Cape Colony.[77] After Dyer's symbolic act of annexation, a resident magistrate was installed and an administration established appropriate to such a small, isolated territory with only a transient indigenous population. Thus, an effective occupation was established over an area viewed as *terra nullius* in accordance with international law of the time.[78]

3 Accretion

A state may acquire sovereignty over territory as a result of natural forces, as occurs when a volcanic island rises within a state's territorial sea or the delta of a river mouth expands. The natural changes in the geomorphology of a river mouth has been the source

[72] The Boer Republic in Natal, established in 1838, was not recognised by Britain, and in 1842 Britain occupied Natal. In 1843 Natal was formally annexed by the British government, and in 1856 it became a separate Crown colony. In 1897 Zululand and Tongaland, annexed by Britain in 1887 and 1895 respectively, were incorporated in Natal.

[73] According to Hofmeyr (n 70) it was clear that 'beide die Republieke die beginsel gehuldig het . . . dat agterlike volke, solang daar maar 'n rudimentêre gesag oor hulle uitgeoefen word, 'n reg het op die soewereiniteit oor hulle gebied, geldig teenoor die meer beskaafde volke. Hierdie beginsel het in die praktyk van die ander state in die reël toepassing gevind, ten minste as teoretiese uitgangspunt. 'n Verkryging van die soewereiniteit oor 'n naturelle-gebied word dan ook by gebreke aan toestemming van die naturelle, deur die state as reël op verowering gegrond' (145). Cf CC Eloff 'Lesotho claims to part of the Orange Free State' (1978) 4 *SAYIL* 108, who states that the Boers acquired title to the triangle of land between the Orange and the Caledon rivers by occupation as it was *terra nullius* (114). The eastern part of the Orange Free State, known as the 'Conquered Territory', was acquired by conquest and cession after wars with the Basuto, confirmed by the Treaty of Aliwal North of 1869.

[74] Berat (n 25) 30–5.

[75] Ibid 115.

[76] Ibid 36–7.

[77] Walfish Bay and St Johns River Annexation Act 35 of 1884 (C).

[78] Berat (n 25) 121. H Booysen supports the view that Walvis Bay was acquired by occupation: *Volkereg en sy Verhouding tot die Suid-Afrikaanse Reg* (1989) 198–9.

of a recent dispute settled by the International Court of Justice between Costa Rica and Nicaragua. In that case, historical agreement between the parties set the boundary between them as running along the course of the San Juan river to its outlet to the sea at 'the extremity of Punta de Castilla'. Over the course of time, however, the mouth of the river drifted north of Punta de Castilla. The Court determined that the boundary between the parties had followed the course of the river as it altered.[79]

4 Cession

Cession is the transfer by treaty of sovereignty over the territory of one state to another state. Before 1945 territory was frequently ceded after a war by the vanquished state to the victorious state. Thus, in 1814, the Cape of Good Hope was ceded by the Netherlands to Britain in the Convention of London at the conclusion of the Napoleonic wars.[80] Cession of territory has also resulted from a gift or sale. In 1866 Austria ceded Venice to France as a gift and shortly thereafter France ceded Venice to Italy. Russia's sale of Alaska to the United States in 1867 for $7.2 million was effected by cession.[81]

South Africa's cession of Walvis Bay and the Off-Shore Islands (better known as the Penguin Islands) to Namibia on 1 March 1994 is a recent example of the transfer of territory from one state to another.[82]

Today, restraints are placed on the cession of territory by the prohibition on the use of force and the right of self-determination. If the acquisition of territory by conquest is no longer permitted, it follows logically that the transfer of territory after a war by cession from the vanquished to the victorious state is also prohibited—in

[79] *Land Boundary in the Northern Part of Isla Portillos (Costa Rica v Nicaragua)* judgment of 2 February 2018.

[80] GW Eybers *Select Constitutional Documents Illustrating South African History 1795–1910* (1918) 19; HR Hahlo and E Kahn *South Africa: The Development of its Laws and Constitution* (1960) 5. Similarly, Alsace-Lorraine was ceded by Germany to France in the Treaty of Versailles (1919). The *Island of Palmas Case* (n 15) concerned a post-war treaty of cession of territory from Spain to the USA.

[81] For further historical examples of cession, see R Jennings and A Watts (eds) *Oppenheim's International Law* 9 ed (2008) vol 1 at 680 et seq.

[82] The text of the treaty is published in GN R951 *GG* 1574 of 20 May 1994 (*Reg Gaz* 5338) and (1994) 33 *ILM* 1526. See, too, Transfer of Walvis Bay to Namibia Act 203 of 1993. See further J Dugard 'Public international law' in 1993 *Annual Survey* 61 at 72 and 1994 *Annual Survey* 98 at 99. The history of Walvis Bay is described above at notes 22 to 25. The Off-Shore islands of Hollams Bird, Mercury, Ichaboe, Long, Seal, Penguin, Halifax, Possession, Albatross Rock, Pomona, Plum-pudding and Roast Beef (or Sinclair's Island) were annexed in 1874 to the Cape, which administered them until 1994. See further Berat (n 25) at 195–208.

accordance with the principle *ex injuria jus non oritur*. This is confirmed by article 52 of the Vienna Convention on the Law of Treaties, which provides that '[a] treaty is void if its conclusion has been procured by the threat or use of force in violation of the principles of international law embodied in the Charter of the United Nations'.

However, by virtue of the principle of intertemporal law, cessions which took place following the use of force at a time when the use of force was not unlawful, remain effective. This is borne out by the submissions of the parties in the case of *Obligation to Negotiate Access to the Pacific Ocean (Bolivia v Chile)* in which Bolivia conceded the validity of the 1904 Peace Treaty between itself and Chile, in terms of which it ceded its coastal territory to Chile (which had conquered that territory) leaving Bolivia land-locked.[83]

The transfer of territory by means of cession without the consent of the people of the ceded territory is today difficult to reconcile with the right of self-determination.[84] When the South African government attempted to cede KaNgwane and the Ingwavuma district of KwaZulu to Swaziland in 1982, in pursuance of the policy of apartheid,[85] it was argued that this proposed cession, on which the affected people were not consulted, violated the right (enshrined in the Declaration on the Granting of Independence to Colonial Countries and Peoples of 1960) of a people to determine their own future. At the same time, it was argued that the proposed cession violated the principle of *uti possidetis* as it sought to tamper with colonial boundaries in Africa. Political opposition to this proposal compelled the South African government to abandon this scheme.[86] Arguments based on international law contributed to this decision, as it was

[83] Written statement of Bolivia on the preliminary objection of Chile (7 November 2014) para 27. See judgment of 1 October 2018.

[84] L Buchheit *Secession: The Legitimacy of Self-Determination* (1978). This view finds support in Grotius *De Jure Belli ac Pacis* 2.6.4.

[85] The obvious goal of this proposed cession was to transfer a substantial portion of the South African black population to a foreign state and thereby reduce the number of black people within South Africa's borders. The Minister of Foreign Affairs, Mr RF Botha, sought, however, to justify it as an historical border readjustment that would consolidate the Swazi people within one territory: *House of Assembly Debates* cols 6252–8 (6 May 1982). See further N Marais 'The Swaziland border dispute' (1982) 8 *SAYIL* 248–59.

[86] When it became clear that both KaNgwane and KwaZulu were opposed to the cession, the matter was referred to two judicial commissions under the chairmanship of Mr Justice FLH Rumpff. The commissions were discontinued in 1984 on the ground that the people in the territories in question were either opposed to the cession or could not freely express their views in the prevailing political climate (1984 *Race Relations Survey* 505–8). The proposal was then abandoned. See further on this: *House of Assembly Debates* cols 145–8 (1 February 1983); M Beukes 'Oor die kwessie van grensaanpassings met Swaziland' (1983) 24 *Codicillus* (May) 19.

made clear to the government that the validity of any agreement of cession in violation of the right of self-determination and *uti possidetis* would be questionable[87] and that the transfer of sovereignty would be subjected to collective non-recognition by the international community along the same lines as the non-recognition of the TBVC states.[88]

5 Conquest

Before the prohibition on the use of force, conquest, annexation and subjugation were accepted methods of acquiring territory. As in the case of occupation, it was necessary to demonstrate both *animus*—the intention to annex the territory—and *corpus*—the physical control of the territory. Consequently, a state did not acquire territory by conquest if it purported to annex territory during the course of a war.

In May and September 1900, Britain purported to annex the Orange Free State[89] and Transvaal[90] respectively, despite the fact that the war, albeit in the form of guerrilla operations, continued until 1902. It was generally accepted that Britain's annexation was premature and that Britain did not obtain title to the Boer Republics under international law until the termination of hostilities.[91]

The lawfulness of the British annexation of the South African Republic came before the Transvaal Supreme Court after the war, in *Van Deventer v Hancke & Mossop*,[92] in which the validity of a Republican decree, issued after the British proclamation of annexation of the Transvaal, was raised. Ironically, counsel for the plaintiff, who had secured title to certain bales of wool as a result of the Republican decree, was JC Smuts, one of the Boer generals who had continued to wage war until 1902.[93] Both Innes CJ and Mason J held that, as judges sitting in a British colonial court, they were obliged to give effect to the British annexation. At the same time, they cast doubt

[87] On the ground that it would violate article 53 of the Vienna Convention on the Law of Treaties, which renders a treaty void if it conflicts with a peremptory norm of international law—a status for which the right of self-determination certainly qualifies. See Chapter 5.

[88] AJGM Sanders 'The "Swaziland Deal" and the international law principle of the self-determination of peoples' (1983) 24 *Codicillus* (Oct) 34.

[89] The text of the annexation proclamation appears in Eybers (n 80) 344.

[90] Ibid 514.

[91] *Oppenheim* (n 81) 700, fn 2; T Baty *International Law in South Africa* (1900) 90–3; Hofmeyr (n 70) 62–8.

[92] 1903 TS 401.

[93] The exchange between Smuts and the Court is fascinating as Smuts carefully refrained from asserting his own personal knowledge of the history of the war (403–7).

on the validity of the annexation under international law. According to Innes CJ:

> It was argued for the plaintiff that the Annexation Proclamation was premature; that at the time when this wool was confiscated the district of Vryheid was subject to the *de facto* control and administration of the Boer forces; that although the Proclamation purported to annex the territory of the Transvaal to the empire, there had, at the time of the annexation, been no effectual occupation of it as a country, and no subjugation of its people; and that therefore the Republic continued to exist as a state, and its government was entitled to exercise legislative and administrative functions. It is no doubt correct as a general rule of international law that two circumstances are necessary to create a complete title by conquest: the conqueror must express in some clear manner his intention of adding the territory in question to his dominions, and he must by the exercise of military force demonstrate his power to hold it as part of his own possessions. It is also true that in March 1901, large portions of the Transvaal, including the district of Vryheid, were neither occupied nor dominated by British troops; but on the contrary were under the *de facto* control of the Boer forces. And if this were a foreign court engaged in trying a cause in regard to which the question of when the conquest of the Transvaal was complete became relevant to the inquiry, it is possible that points of considerable intricacy and difficulty would present themselves. But those considerations are not present here. This is a court constituted by the British Crown, exercising powers and discharging functions derived from the Crown. In its dealings with other states the Crown acts for the whole nation, and such dealings cannot be questioned or set aside by its courts. They are acts of state into the validity or invalidity, the wisdom or unwisdom, of which domestic courts of law have no jurisdiction to inquire.[94]

In 1928 war was outlawed by the Kellogg-Briand Pact and, in 1945, the Charter of the United Nations prohibited the use of force in international relations against the territorial integrity or political independence of any state.[95] Modern customary international law recognises a similar prohibition.[96] In these circumstances, it is clear that territory can no longer be acquired by the use of force, ie by conquest. On the other hand, it is equally clear that titles acquired by conquest before 1928 must be recognised as lawful in accordance with the principle of intertemporal law.[97] Some have argued that the prohibition on the acquisition of territory by force applies only in the case of an aggressive, unlawful war and that a state may lawfully

[94] At 409–10. See, too, the judgments of Mason and Bristowe JJ at 419 and 424, respectively.

[95] Article 2(4).

[96] *Military and Paramilitary Activities in and against Nicaragua (Nicaragua v USA)* 1986 ICJ Reports 14 at 99–100.

[97] See above. Jennings (n 1) 69, 72. See, too, *Bolivia v Chile* (n 83).

obtain title to territory acquired in self-defence.[98] This view is untenable[99] and is rejected by both state practice and resolutions of the United Nations. The General Assembly Declaration on Principles of International Law Concerning Friendly Relations and Co-operation among States in Accordance with the Charter of the United Nations of 1970[100] draws no distinction between the lawful and unlawful use of force in providing:

> The territory of a state shall not be the object of acquisition by another state resulting from the threat or use of force. No territorial acquisition resulting from the threat or use of force shall be recognised as legal.

There have been only a handful of claims of forceful annexation made during the United Nations era. Moreover, the international reaction to these cases has reinforced the customary international law prohibition on annexation. Two examples come to mind.

Although no United Nations resolution has branded Israel as the aggressor in the Six-Day War of 1967, resolutions of both the Security Council[101] and the General Assembly[102] have condemned Israel's purported annexation of East Jerusalem and the Golan Heights on the ground that 'the acquisition of territory by force is inadmissible'—with no distinction drawn between the lawful and the unlawful use of force. The non-recognition of Israel's annexation of East Jerusalem and the Golan Heights[103] supports the view that territory may not be acquired in a war of self-defence. South Africa has supported UN General Assembly condemnations of the Israeli occupation.[104] A more recent case of annexation has been undertaken by a permanent member of the Security Council against a United Nations member. In 2014 the Russian Federation annexed Crimea, part of the territory of Ukraine. This act followed intervention by forces of the Russian Federation, a referendum, and a declaration of independence in Crimea.[105] The United Nations General Assembly rejected the validity of the referendum and does not acknowledge

[98] S Schwebel 'What weight to conquest?' (1970) 64 *AJIL* 344; M Halberstam 'Recognition, use of force and the legal effect of UN resolutions under the revised restatement of the foreign relations law of the United States' (1984) 19 *Israel Law Review* 495 at 503–8. Cf *Oppenheim* (n 81) 703.

[99] Jennings (n 1) 70–2; DW Bowett 'International law relating to occupied territory: A rejoinder' (1971) 87 *LQR* 473.

[100] Resolution 2625 (XXV).

[101] Resolutions 242 (1967), 252 (1968), 298 (1971), 476 (1980), 478 (1980), 497 (1981).

[102] For example, Resolutions 34/70 (1979), ES/72 (1980), 37/123A (1982), 39/146A (1984).

[103] See J Dugard *Recognition and the United Nations* (1987) 111–15, 155–6.

[104] A/RES/71/99 (6 December 2016).

[105] See TD Grant 'Annexation of Crimea' (2015) 109 *AJIL* 68; J Bering 'The prohibition on annexation: Lessons from Crimea' (2017) 49 *NYU JIL&Pol* 747.

any change in status for the territory.[106] South Africa has not voted in favour of any of the resolutions passed in condemnation of Russia's occupation of Crimea: it abstained from the original resolution condemning the annexation in 2014 and voted against the subsequent two resolutions, which characterised Crimea as being subject to 'temporary occupation'.

6 Prescription

Prescription is a concept of uncertain content in international law. Although judicial decisions generally avoid the use of the term, they nevertheless support the conclusion that, by a process analogous to prescription in municipal law, long possession and the exercise of effective control may give rise to a valid title. In the *Kasikili/Sedudu Island Case*,[107] between Botswana and Namibia, both parties agreed that acquisitive prescription was recognised in international law and that the criteria to be satisfied were possession *à titre de Souverain* and peaceful, public and uninterrupted possession that endured for a certain length of time. Although the International Court was not required to apply this test, it did not disagree with the test formulated by the parties.

In theory, the distinction between occupation and prescription is clear. Occupation applies only to a territory that is *terra nullius*. The original occupation must be lawful, and passage of time is irrelevant. Prescription, on the other hand, is 'a portmanteau concept that comprehends both a possession of which the origin is unclear or disputed, and an adverse possession which is in origin demonstrably unlawful'.[108] However, they have much in common for both are rationalisations of effective possession and control. For this reason, tribunals have frequently failed to draw any distinction between the two. In the *Island of Palmas Case* arbitrator Max Huber stressed the importance of sovereign activities (*effectivités*) on the territory of the state on the part of a successful claimant state when he stated that 'the continuous and peaceful display of territorial sovereignty (peaceful in relation to other states) is as good as title'.[109] Similarly, in

[106] GA Res 68/262 (27 March 2014). See also GA Res 71/205 (19 December 2016) and GA Res 72/190 (19 December 2017).

[107] 1999 ICJ Reports 1045 at 1103–4. In this case, Namibia argued that the Masubia tribe of Namibia had continuously and exclusively occupied the island with the full knowledge of Botswana. The Court found it unnecessary to pronounce on the subject of prescription as it had not been established that the members of the tribe had exercised functions of state authority on the island on behalf of Namibia (South West Africa): 1999 ICJ Reports 1101–6.

[108] Jennings (n 1) 36.

[109] *Island of Palmas Case* (n 15) 839.

the *Legal Status of Eastern Greenland Case*, often seen as the leading case on occupation, the Permanent Court of International Justice emphasised that Denmark's claim to Eastern Greenland did not rest on any 'particular act of occupation' but on the peaceful and continuous display of state authority.[110] The International Court of Justice relied on *effectivités* in finding for Malaysia in its dispute with Indonesia in *Sovereignty over Pulau Ligitan and Pulau Sipadan*.[111] Most recently, in *Territorial and Maritime Dispute (Nicaragua v Colombia)*, the Court described relevant acts as 'in particular, but not limited to, legislative acts or acts of administrative control, acts relating to the application and enforcement of criminal or civil law, acts regulating immigration, acts regulating fishing and other economic activities, naval patrols as well as search and rescue operations'.[112]

As a result of this blurring of the distinction between occupation and prescription, some writers have suggested that the two modes of territorial acquisition should be merged into a common source of title[113] or be replaced by a new mode known as the historical consolidation of title.[114]

Questions of source of title commonly arise in disputes in which the original claim to title is lost in an uncertain historical record. In such cases, the court is compelled to decide which of the claimants has effectively exercised sovereignty peacefully and continuously over the disputed territory in recent times.[115] Here, acquiescence plays a major role in the identification of title.[116] Where a state fails to protest over the assertion of sovereignty by another state in a territory that it claims to be its own, it is unlikely to succeed in persuading a court that it has not abandoned its claim to the disputed territory, for, as the International Court of Justice stated in *Malaysia/Singapore*, 'failure to respond to conduct *à titre de Souverain* amounts to acquiescence'.[117] It was essentially on this basis that Huber found in favour of the Netherlands in the *Island of Palmas Case*. Spain failed to protest at the Netherlands' assertion of authority over the island

[110] 1933 PCIJ Reports Series A/B no 53 at 45.

[111] 2002 ICJ Reports 625 paras 134–9.

[112] 2012 ICJ Reports 624 at 655.

[113] MN Shaw treats the two modes of acquisition under the heading 'the exercise of effective control': *International Law* 8 ed (2017) 379.

[114] C de Visscher *Theory and Reality in Public International Law* (1968) 209. See the criticism of this suggestion by Jennings (n 1) 24–8. The International Court of Justice expressed doubts about historical consolidation as a basis of title in territorial disputes in *Land and Maritime Boundary between Cameroon and Nigeria* 2002 ICJ Reports 303 at 352.

[115] *Minquiers and Ecrehos Case* 1953 ICJ Reports 47. *Brownlie* (n 8) 223–6.

[116] *Brownlie* (n 8) 228.

[117] 2008 ICJ Reports 12 paras 120–1.

and was thereby found to have acquiesced in the rival claim.[118] A state that fails to protest over the exercise of sovereignty by its rival remains silent at its peril. This is an issue that has featured in the Falklands/Malvinas dispute where Argentina has protested sporadically and irregularly over Britain's occupation of the islands.[119]

In the southern African context, the issue of protest has been raised in respect of Lesotho's irredentist claims to the eastern part of the Orange Free State (the so-called 'conquered territories'). South African claims to the territory, based on conquest, cession and possibly prescription, appear to be sound.[120] Despite this, Lesotho, since it became independent in 1966, has protested that the territory was unlawfully taken from it by the Orange Free State.[121] While Lesotho may argue that it was unable to protest against the incorporation of the territories during the period that it was a British colony—from 1868 to 1966—it is difficult to reconcile its claims with the principle of *uti possidetis*, which seeks to ensure respect for colonial boundaries.

7 Estoppel

The principle of estoppel or preclusion is part of international law. According to Lord McNair:

> [I]t is reasonable to expect that any legal system should possess a rule designed to prevent a person who makes or concurs in a statement upon which another person in privity with him relies to the extent of changing his position, from later asserting a different state of affairs.[122]

In territorial disputes, the acceptance by one state of another's claim to the territory will preclude it from reasserting its claim. In the *Temple of Preah Vihear Case*,[123] concerning a border dispute between Cambodia and Thailand, the evidence showed that Thailand in its past conduct had accepted that the Temple fell within Cambodia, with the result that it was estopped from later reasserting its claim to that area.

In the late 1980s, as Namibian independence drew near and South Africa showed no sign of including Walvis Bay in an independent

[118] Jennings (n 1) 30.

[119] Harris (n 20) 179–82; PJ Beck *The Falkland Islands as an International Problem* (Routledge Revivals) (2014) 61–84 (detailing the Argentinian claim).

[120] See CC Eloff 'Lesotho claims to part of the Orange Free State' (1978) 4 *SAYIL* 109; I Brownlie *African Boundaries: A Legal and Diplomatic Encyclopaedia* (1979) 1108.

[121] Eloff (n 120) 109–10.

[122] *The Law of Treaties* (1961) 485. See further I Sinclair 'Estoppel and acquiescence' in AV Lowe and M Fitzmaurice (eds) *Fifty Years of the International Court of Justice* (1996) 104.

[123] 1962 ICJ Reports 6 at 30–2.

Namibia, it was argued that South Africa, by administering Walvis Bay as part of the mandated territory of South West Africa from 1922 to 1977, had led the international community to believe that it had integrated Walvis Bay into South West Africa/Namibia, with the result that it was estopped from later asserting that the port remained part of South Africa. According to Berat, estoppel had 'shifted' title from South Africa to Namibia.[124] This claim was questionable for two reasons.

First, it is doubtful whether estoppel can operate to 'shift' a title. Commenting on the judgment of the International Court of Justice in the *Temple of Preah Vihear Case*, RY Jennings states:

> [A]lthough the case confirms that estoppel may assist, and even assist with decisive effect, in the interpretation of facts, and instruments and acknowledgements relative to the vesting of title, it still remains true to say that estoppel is not itself a root of title.[125]

Secondly, it is by no means certain that South Africa's conduct in respect of Walvis Bay met the requirements for the operation of estoppel, which are:

(a) The statement of fact must be clear and unambiguous.
(b) The statement of fact must be made voluntarily, unconditionally, and must be authorised.
(c) There must be reliance in good faith upon the statement either to the detriment of the party so relying on the statement or to the advantage of the party making the statement.[126]

8 Territorial claims based on the right of self-determination

In modern international law, a number of claims to territory are made that are based on the right of self-determination and decolonisation.

(a) Legal ties of a historical nature

In its advisory opinion on *Western Sahara*,[127] the International Court of Justice considered the question whether the Spanish colony of Western Sahara had an identity of its own in 1884, when it was colonised by Spain, which would entitle it to exercise its right to self-determination as a separate entity, or whether its historical 'legal ties' with either of its neighbours, Morocco and Mauritania, were so close that it should be reintegrated with either of these territories. Although the International Court found in favour of the separate identity of Western Sahara, the majority judgment and several of the

[124] Op cit (n 25) 167–73.
[125] Op cit (n 1) 67.
[126] DW Bowett 'Estoppel before international tribunals and its relation to acquiescence' (1957) 33 *BYIL* 176 at 202.
[127] 1975 ICJ Reports 12.

separate opinions elaborated on the notion of 'legal ties' in the context of decolonisation.

The principle of 'legal ties' has its basis in General Assembly Resolution 3292 (XXIX), in which the General Assembly asked the International Court, 'without prejudice to the application of the principles embodied in General Assembly Resolution 1514 (XV)', to give an advisory opinion on, inter alia, the 'legal ties' between Western Sahara and Morocco and Mauritania. That the term 'legal ties' has its origin in a resolution of special application to Western Sahara was stressed by the Court in its opinion when it stated that the term lacked 'a very precise meaning', with the result that its meaning 'has to be found rather in the object and purpose of General Assembly Resolution 3292 (XXIX)'.[128] The concept of 'legal ties' therefore should not be too hastily invoked in other situations,[129] particularly when it is to be used to force integration of one territory into another without first permitting the inhabitants of the disputed territory to express their views on integration by means of a referendum.

That the doctrine of legal or historical ties is not to be considered as a source of territorial title, is evidenced by the clear rejection of Iraq's historical claim to Kuwait,[130] which constituted the basis for its invasion and annexation of Kuwait in 1990.

(b) Colonial enclaves

An enclave is an area totally surrounded by the territory of one state or a 'relatively small area totally surrounded on the landward side by the territory of one other state',[131] a concept that clearly encompassed Walvis Bay before 1994. Contemporary international law contemplates that self-determination, in the case of an enclave classified as non-self-governing, will take the form of automatic reintegration or retrocession into the territory of which the enclave forms a part or the exercise of a free choice by the people of that territory in a plebiscite or referendum.

Where the enclave is small and forms an integral part of the claimant state, the United Nations has dispensed with the need for a

[128] 1975 ICJ Reports 12 at 40. In his separate opinion in the *Western Sahara Case*, Judge Petrén stated: 'The question of the extent to which, and under what conditions, past legal ties may influence the decolonization of a territory seems to me to fall within an as yet inadequately explored area of contemporary international law' (112).

[129] See the attempts to apply this argument to Walvis Bay, Berat (n 25) 155–60, Goeckner and Gunning (n 25).

[130] See, on these claims, RV Pillai and M Kumar 'The political and legal status of Kuwait' (1962) 11 *ICLQ* 108.

[131] MN Shaw *Title to Territory in Africa* (1986) 134.

free choice on the part of the inhabitants of the enclave. In this case, priority is given to para 6 of Resolution 1514 (XV), which insists on the preservation of 'the national unity and territorial integrity' of a decolonised territory.[132] The return of the Spanish enclave of Ifni to Morocco in 1969 provides an example of retrocession without a plebiscite or referendum. This enclave, covering some 1 500 km^2 and with a population of 53 000, was completely surrounded by Morocco on its landward side. Walvis Bay was likewise treated as a colonial enclave to which para 6 of Resolution 1514 (XV) was applicable.[133] This seems to have been the basis of both General Assembly and Security Council resolutions, which stressed that Walvis Bay formed an integral part of Namibia.[134]

9 Concluding comments

International courts do not scrupulously apply the traditional rules relating to the acquisition of territory. In this respect, international law differs from municipal law in which clear rules of acquisition of ownership are strictly applied. Occupation and prescription both require manifestations of effective control with the result that evidence of sovereign activities on a territory (*effectivités*) has come to be regarded as a source of title. This accords with Huber's *dictum* in the *Island of Palmas Case* that 'the continuous and peaceful display of territorial sovereignty (peaceful in relation to other states) is as good as title'.[135] This view has recently been endorsed by the decision in the *Eritrea/Yemen* arbitration in which the tribunal[136] reaffirmed:

> The modern international law of the acquisition (or attribution) of territory generally requires that there be: an intentional display of power and authority over the territory, by the exercise of jurisdiction and state functions on a continuous and peaceful basis.[137]

In territorial disputes, a court will often not look for absolute title on the part of one state but will be satisfied that one party has, on balance, a relatively stronger title than the other. Where one state is able to show some legal title to the territory, the *effectivités* will determine title. Notions of recognition, acquiescence and estoppel

[132] J Crawford *The Creation of States in International Law* 2 ed (2006) 624, 647.

[133] Shaw (n 131) 137–40.

[134] Resolution 432 (1978) of the Security Council declared that 'the territorial integrity and unity of Namibia must be assured through the reintegration of Walvis Bay within its territory'.

[135] *Island of Palmas Case* (n 15) 839.

[136] This tribunal of five arbitrators included three judges who served as President of the International Court of Justice: RY Jennings, S Schwebel and R Higgins.

[137] 22 RIAA 209 (1998) 239, 114 ILR 1 at 69.

will play a role in this process. In *Malaysia/Singapore*[138] the International Court relied heavily on acquiescence and tacit agreement to find that Singapore had a stronger claim to a disputed island than Malaysia and thus had acquired sovereignty over the island. In a dissenting opinion, the present writer, sitting as judge ad hoc,[139] stressed that acquiescence should, as shown in the *Eritrea/Yemen* case, be accompanied by an 'intentional display of power and authority over the territory, by the exercise of jurisdiction and state functions on a continuous and peaceful basis'.[140]

In the case of former colonies, the principle of *uti possidetis* will play an important role in determining title, but where the administrative boundary of the former colony is unclear, recourse will be had to the *effectivités*.[141]

TERRITORIAL DISPUTES IN AFRICA[142]

Before colonial rule, Africa was not delimited into states. This is not to say that there were no boundaries at issue; in fact there were many localised, traditional boundaries established to account for different African peoples, their cultures and traditions. However, these were never formalised.[143]

As a result of colonisation, the continent was demarcated by foreign powers without regard to the peoples' traditional boundaries.[144] These borders divided ethnic groups and the lands to which they were attached, causing significant ethnic tensions. Despite this, most colonially created boundaries have remained intact as a result of the application of the principle of *uti possidetis* which has been endorsed by African leaders.[145]

Ethno-political tensions caused by colonial boundaries continue to beset post-colonial Africa. Many of these disputes have come before the International Court of Justice which in most cases has turned to colonial boundaries to resolve territorial disputes. This is illustrated

138 2008 ICJ Reports 133 paras 120–1, 273–6.

139 Ibid paras 36–43 (dissenting opinion of J Dugard).

140 Supra (n 137).

141 *Land, Island and Maritime Frontier Dispute (El Salvador)/Honduras; Nicaragua Intervening* 1992 ICJ Reports 351 at 389.

142 I Brownlie *African Boundaries: A Legal and Diplomatic Encyclopedia* (1979); N Ikome, 'Africa's international borders as potential sources of conflict and future threats to peace and security' (2012) 223 *Institute for Security Studies Papers* 16.

143 M van der Linden *The Acquisition of Africa (1870–1914): The Nature of International Law* (2017).

144 G Oduntan *International Law and Boundary Disputes in Africa* (2015).

145 OAU Resolution AHG/Res 16 (I) (July 1964); *Constitutive Act of the African Union* article 4(b) (entered into force on 26 May 2001).

by the following cases which have featured prominently in the litigation of the Court.

The *Frontier Dispute* case[146] concerned a boundary dispute between Burkino Faso and Mali arising out the process of decolonisation of French West Africa. In 1960, the colony of French Sudan became the independent state of Mali and the colony of Upper Volta became the independent state of Upper Volta (later renamed Burkina Faso). The Court resolved the dispute by applying the *uti possidetis juris* principle, holding that, upon independence, the two states had succeeded to the territorial boundaries which had delimited the former colonies of Upper Volta and French Sudan in 1932.

In *Territorial Dispute*,[147] involving a dispute between Libya and Chad, the Court rejected Libya's argument that there was no border between them and upheld Chad's submission that a 1955 Treaty of Friendship and Good Neighbourliness concluded between France (which at the time controlled the territory of Chad, known then as French Equatorial Africa) and Libya had created a boundary line between the parties.

In *Land and Maritime Boundary between Cameroon and Nigeria*[148] Cameroon requested the Court to determine the course of the boundary between itself and Nigeria from Lake Chad to the sea. In so doing the Court established the boundary between Lake Chad and the Bakassi Peninsula by examining 17 separate sectors of the boundary, each corresponding to a different historical instrument. In Bakassi, the Court decided that the Anglo-German Agreement of 11 March 1913 applied to delimit the area, and that sovereignty over the peninsula accordingly lay with Cameroon.

In *Kasikili/Sedudu Island*,[149] the Court resolved a dispute between Botswana and Namibia by interpreting and applying a delimitation treaty concluded in 1890 between Great Britain and Germany, in terms of which the boundary between these states' respective spheres of influence in the area of the island was set to run along the 'main channel' of the River Chobe. The Court determined the course of the river's 'main channel' by reference to studies of the depth and width of the channel and its navigability and on this basis concluded that the island formed part of the territory of Botswana.

In *Frontier Dispute (Benin/Niger)*,[150] a Chamber of the International Court resolved a dispute between Benin and Niger on the basis of a boundary inherited from the French administration at the time when

[146] 1986 ICJ Reports 554.
[147] 1994 ICJ Reports 6.
[148] 2002 ICJ Reports 303.
[149] 1999 ICJ Reports 1045.
[150] 2005 ICJ Reports 90.

both Benin and Niger were colonies of France, forming part of French West Africa. The Chamber determined that for one sector of the frontier area there had been a *modus vivendi* between the local authorities of the region during the colonial administration in terms of which the main navigable channel of the River Niger was regarded as constituting the intercolonial boundary. In relation to a second sector of the frontier area the Chamber found that the administrative authorities during the colonial period had considered that the course of the River Mekrou formed the intercolonial boundary. The Chamber accordingly held that the boundary between Benin and Niger followed the median line of that river.

In *Frontier Dispute (Burkina Faso/Republic of Niger)*,[151] the Court again determined the boundary between the two states by reference to the acts and delimitation decisions of the French colonial administration prior to their independence.

At present there are boundary disputes involving Namibia arising out of the colonial era. A secessionist movement in the Caprivi Strip—the Caprivi Liberation Army—argues that the Caprivi Strip, whose people are ethnically different from the people of Namibia, did not become part of the German Protectorate of South West Africa as a result of the 1890 Anglo-German Agreement, which simply provided that the territory would fall within the German sphere of influence. Consequently, the argument goes, the Caprivi Strip did not become part of Namibia on independence in 1990. This dispute is central to the trial of members of the Caprivi Liberation Army for treason at present underway in Namibia.[152] Then there is the dispute with South Africa relating to the boundary along the Orange River. Whereas the Namibian constitution establishes the boundary between Namibia and South Africa as running along the middle of the Orange River,[153] South Africa claims that the boundary runs along the high-water line on the northern bank in terms of the Anglo-German treaty of 1890.[154]

[151] 2013 ICJ Reports 44.

[152] *Munuma v S* (CC 03/2004) [2018] NAHCMD 142 (29 May 2018).

[153] Article 1(4) of the Constitution of the Republic of Namibia.

[154] See G Erasmus and D Hamman 'Where is the Orange River Mouth? The demarcation of the South African/Namibian maritime boundary' (1987–88) 13 *SAYIL* 49.

ANTARCTICA

A number of states[155] have made claims to exclusive sovereignty over different parts of Antarctica. However, these claims,[156] based on discovery, a minimal degree of occupation, and geographic contiguity, are disputed by some of the rival contenders and are not recognised by either the United States or Russia. These facts, coupled with the demand from many quarters that Antarctica should be used for peaceful scientific research and subjected to rigorous conservation measures, resulted in the 1959 Antarctic Treaty,[157] which, in article 4, 'freezes' all territorial claims. It provides that while nothing in the treaty shall be interpreted as prejudicing the prior claims of states to territorial sovereignty:

> [N]o acts or activities taking place while the present treaty is in force shall constitute a basis for asserting, supporting or denying a claim to territorial sovereignty in Antarctica or create any rights of sovereignty in Antarctica. No new claim, or enlargement of an existing claim, to territorial sovereignty in Antarctica shall be asserted while the present treaty is in force.[158]

The treaty provides for the demilitarisation of Antarctica and envisages that the continent will be used for peaceful scientific research, carried out in a spirit of international co-operation with strict regard to ecological protection.

Although South Africa has made no territorial claim to any part of Antarctica, it was one of the original 12 signatory states to the Treaty[159] because of its special interest in the region arising from its geographical situation. South Africa maintains a number of bases in Antarctica for the purpose of scientific research.[160]

It is unlikely that Antarctica will ever become the subject of territorial sovereignty by states as there is strong resistance, particularly among developing nations, to any suggestion that the continent should be made subject to national appropriation. Instead it is suggested either that Antarctica should become a wilderness park,

[155] Argentina, Australia, Chile, France, New Zealand, Norway and the United Kingdom.

[156] See MT De Quintal 'Sovereignty disputes in the Antarctic' (1984) 10 *SAYIL* 161; DR Rothwell 'Polar territorial and maritime sovereignty in the twenty-first century' in C Chinkin and F Baetens *Sovereignty, Statehood and State Responsibility* (2017) 110.

[157] See GN Barrie 'The Antarctic Treaty: Example of law and its sociological infrastructure' (1975) 8 *CILSA* 212; GN Barrie 'The Antarctic Treaty forty years on' (1999) 116 *SALJ* 173.

[158] The text of the treaty appears in 402 UNTS 71.

[159] The seven states listed in n 155 and Belgium, Japan, South Africa, the USSR and the USA.

[160] See Barrie 'The Antarctic Treaty forty years on' (n 157). IJ Ansorge et al 'Exploring South Africa's southern frontier: a twenty year vision for polar research' (2017) 113 *South African Journal of Science* 2.

with natural resource exploitation prohibited and with special environmental protection, or that it should be designated, like the deep seabed, as being the common heritage of mankind, with the consequence that any revenues obtained from the exploitation of the region should be shared with developing countries. In 1991 the Antarctic Treaty members adopted a treaty which prohibits '[a]ny activity relating to mineral resources, other than scientific research'.[161]

The Antarctic Treaties Act of 1996[162] incorporates the Antarctic Treaty, the Protocol on Environmental Protection to the Antarctic Treaty (1991), the Convention for the Conservation of Antarctic Seals (1972) and the Convention on the Conservation of Antarctic Marine Living Resources (1980) into South African law,[163] and confers jurisdiction upon the South African executive and judiciary to exercise jurisdiction in Antarctica over South African citizens and residents and any person 'who is a member of or is responsible for organizing an expedition which has been organized in the Republic to visit Antarctica, but not an expedition organized by the government of another Contracting Party',[164] particularly for the purpose of preventing damage to the Antarctic environment.

[161] Protocol on Environmental Protection to the Antarctic Treaty (1991) 30 *ILM* 1455 (article 7).

[162] Act 60 of 1996.

[163] Section 3.

[164] Section 2.

CHAPTER 9

Jurisdiction and International Crimes

John Dugard, Max du Plessis and Eshed Cohen

JURISDICTION

Jurisdiction is an important aspect of sovereignty.[1] Sovereignty empowers a state to exercise the functions of a state within a particular territory to the exclusion of other states.[2] Jurisdiction is the branch of law that defines these functions. The term therefore refers to the authority that a state has to exercise its governmental functions by legislation, executive and enforcement action, and judicial decrees over persons and property. In most circumstances the exercise of the functions of a state is limited to the territory of the state.[3]

South Africa, like other states, zealously guards against any attempt on the part of other states to exercise their governmental functions within its territorial limits. Foreign police officers may not make arrests in South Africa and foreign governments may not enforce their sovereign acts through South African courts.[4] Any intervention in the domestic affairs of South Africa by other states or international organisations will be resisted as a violation of the prohibition on foreign intervention that receives recognition in article 2(7) of the Charter of the United Nations.[5]

If all states confined the exercise of their governmental functions to their own territories, and jurisdiction was entirely territorial, this topic would require little examination. This, however, is not the case. International trade, migration, travel and crime ensure that states will have an interest in extending their jurisdiction beyond their

[1] C Ryngaert *Jurisdiction in International Law* 2 ed (2015); *Abdi v Minister of Home Affairs* 2011 (3) SA 37 (SCA) 51, fn 8.

[2] *Island of Palmas Case (United States v Netherlands)* 2 RIAA 829 (1928) 838.

[3] In *Kaunda v President of the Republic of South Africa* 2005 (4) SA 235 (CC) the Constitutional Court stated: 'It is a general rule of international law that the laws of a State ordinarily apply only within its own territory' (para 38).

[4] *Commissioner of Taxes, Federation of Rhodesia v McFarland* 1965 (1) SA 470 (W) 474A–B; *Standard Bank of South Africa Ltd v Ocean Commodities Inc* 1980 (2) SA 175 (T) 184G–185D; *Abdi v Minister of Home Affairs* (n 1) para 29.

[5] This article provides that '[n]othing contained in the present Charter shall authorize the United Nations to intervene in matters which are essentially within the domestic jurisdiction of any state'. This provision, which during the apartheid era formed the cornerstone of South Africa's foreign policy, is considered in Chapter 15.

territorial limits to cover persons and property in other countries. The exercise of civil jurisdiction by one state over persons or property in another state, in accordance with the rules of private international law,[6] seldom elicits protest from the state in which the person or property is situated.[7] The same cannot be said about the application of the criminal law to persons, property and events in other countries. This frequently becomes a matter of public debate and the territorial state will be compelled to protest against the exercise of criminal jurisdiction over matters that fall within its exclusive territorial jurisdiction. For this reason, most of the rules relating to the exercise of domestic jurisdiction in international law relate to criminal offences.

The starting point for any discussion of jurisdiction is to distinguish between the two aspects of a state's domestic criminal jurisdiction. First, there is prescriptive jurisdiction.[8] Prescriptive jurisdiction refers to a state's authority to criminalise certain conduct.[9] A state exercises prescriptive jurisdiction when it renders applicable—though it does not necessarily apply—its criminal law to certain conduct by criminalising the conduct concerned. So when state A, in law X, says that murder is a crime, it exercises prescriptive jurisdiction.[10] Secondly, there is enforcement jurisdiction.[11] Enforcement jurisdiction is a state's ability to apply and enforce its criminal laws on certain conduct. This enforcement can occur by (inter alia)

[6] CF Forsyth *Private International Law* 5 ed (2012).

[7] An exception to this rule is to be found in the United States Alien Tort Statute of 1789, which confers civil jurisdiction on a US federal court where an alien sues for a tort committed in violation of the law of nations. (See on this statute *Sosa v Alvarez-Machain* (US Supreme Court) (2004) 43 *ILM* 1390.) In 2004 a US federal district court considered (and dismissed) claims under this statute by victims of apartheid against several multinational corporations that had engaged in business in apartheid South Africa. In finding that doing business in apartheid South Africa had not been a tort committed in violation of the law of nations, the Court heeded the South African government's objection to the litigation on the ground that it would discourage foreign investment in South Africa. *In re South African Apartheid Litigation: Ntsebeza et al v Citigroup et al* 346 F Supp 2d 538. Cf *Khulumani v Barclay National Bank* 504 F 3rd ed 254. Further on this subject, see n 97 below.

[8] It is also known as legislative jurisdiction.

[9] R O'Keefe 'Universal jurisdiction: Clarifying the basic concept' (2004) 2 *Journal of International Criminal Justice* 735 at 736.

[10] Prescriptive jurisdiction is thus important because conduct must be criminalised before it can be prosecuted—otherwise the criminal law in question will be retroactive. Ibid 742. The only exception would be if a state is purely monist and does not need to prohibit an international crime at the domestic level before enforcing it. See C Kress 'Universal jurisdiction over international crimes and the Institut de Droit International' (2006) 4 *JICJ* 561 at 564.

[11] This is also known as executive jurisdiction.

arresting, trying, sentencing and/or punishing a person for engaging in certain conduct.[12] So when state A, by law X, arrests, detains and (assuming conviction) incarcerates person P for murder, then state A exercises enforcement jurisdiction. These two aspects of jurisdiction are independent.[13] A state can exercise prescriptive jurisdiction without exercising enforcement jurisdiction over certain conduct.[14]

The *Lotus Case* is the seminal case on the international law regulating the extraterritorial exercise of prescriptive and enforcement jurisdiction.[15] In this case, a French ship, the *Lotus*, collided with a Turkish ship, the *Boz-Kourt*, on the high seas. The latter ship sank and a number of crew members and passengers lost their lives. The *Lotus* picked up the survivors and put into port in Turkey. Here, the officer of the watch on board the *Lotus* at the time of the collision was arrested, tried and convicted of culpable homicide. France objected to Turkey's exercise of jurisdiction and the dispute was referred to the Permanent Court of International Justice. Before the Court, France argued that only the flag-state had jurisdiction over acts committed on board a vessel on the high seas, while Turkey claimed that it had jurisdiction by reason of the fact that the effects of the collision had been felt on a Turkish ship, which was to be viewed as part of Turkish territory.

In its judgment, the Court expounded the following principles of jurisdiction:

(a) A state 'may not exercise its power in any form in the territory of another state'—unless there is a permissive rule to the contrary.[16]

(b) International law does not prohibit a state 'from exercising jurisdiction *in its own territory*, in respect of any case which relates to acts which have taken place abroad'. States have 'a wide measure of discretion' to extend the application of their

[12] O'Keefe (n 9) at 736.

[13] Some writers refer to a third aspect to jurisdiction: adjudicative jurisdiction. This refers to a national court's competence to adjudge certain matters. In a criminal law context, adjudicative jurisdiction overlaps entirely with prescriptive and enforcement jurisdiction. When a court pronounces on the applicability of the criminal law concerned, that is a manifestation of prescriptive jurisdiction. When a court tries, convicts and/or sentences a person for committing certain conduct, that is enforcement jurisdiction. See O'Keefe (n 9) at 737; Kress (n 10) at 564. See also the Canadian Supreme Court's decision in *R v Hape* [2007] 2 SCR 292, 2007 SCC 26.

[14] The converse is also true in principle, although exercising enforcement jurisdiction without first exercising prescriptive jurisdiction could violate the law of non-retroactivity. O'Keefe (n 9) 741.

[15] 1927 PCIJ Reports Series A no 10.

[16] At 18–19. This principle was referred to with approval by Vieyra J in *Commissioner of Taxes, Federation of Rhodesia v McFarland* (n 4) 473G–H. See, too, *Kaunda v President of the Republic of South Africa* (n 3) para 38.

laws and the jurisdiction of their courts to persons, property and acts outside their territory, 'which is only limited in certain cases by prohibitive rules'.[17]

(c) 'The territoriality of criminal law, therefore, is not an absolute principle of international law.'[18]

The Court held, by the casting vote of the President, that as no rule of international law prohibited Turkey from trying a person for an offence that had produced effects on a Turkish vessel, and hence within Turkey itself, Turkey had not violated international law. In other words, a state can only exercise enforcement jurisdiction extraterritorially if there is an international law allowing it to do so. The default position is that enforcement jurisdiction is territorial only. Hence, the Court explained:

> The first and foremost restriction imposed by international law upon a State is that—failing the existence of a permissive rule to the contrary—it may not exercise its power in any form in the territory of another State. In this sense jurisdiction is certainly territorial; it cannot be exercised by a State outside its territory.[19]

On the other hand, prescriptive jurisdiction can be exercised extraterritorially, unless there is a rule in international law prohibiting a state from doing so.

The *Lotus* decision has been widely criticised,[20] particularly because it empowers states to exercise prescriptive jurisdiction over acts occurring outside their territory—except where there is proof of a rule of international law prohibiting such prescription.

Although the principle of the *Lotus Case* that a state may exercise prescriptive jurisdiction over acts occurring abroad in the absence of a prohibitory rule remains unchanged, in practice states have sought to limit the exercise of extraterritorial prescriptive jurisdiction to cases in which there is a direct and substantial connection between the state exercising jurisdiction and the matter in question.[21] Such connections have been called 'heads' or 'principles' on which a state can extend prescriptive jurisdiction extraterritorially.[22] Presumably,

[17] At 19 (emphasis added).

[18] At 20.

[19] *Lotus Case* (n 15) 18.

[20] See H Lauterpacht *International Law: Collected Papers* (ed E Lauterpacht) (1970) vol 1, 488–9. See, too, the tentative criticism of this *dictum* in *Kaunda v President of the Republic of South Africa* (n 3) para 39. Also see O'Keefe (n 9) fn 12.

[21] See FA Mann 'The doctrine of jurisdiction in international law' (1964) 111 *Hague Recueil* 1 and 'The doctrine of international jurisdiction revisited after twenty years' (1984) 186 *Hague Recueil* 9.

[22] O'Keefe (n 9) 738; H Woolaver 'Prosecuting international crimes in South Africa: Interpreting the requirement of the accused's presence in South African territory under the implementation of the Rome Statute of the ICC Act' (2014) 131 *SALJ* 253 at

states have relied on these heads to confine the exercise of their extraterritorial prescriptive jurisdiction within reasonable limits. So states generally restrict the exercise of jurisdiction to matters committed within their territories or having an effect within their territories, to matters affecting their nationals, or to acts threatening their security. This list is not exhaustive.

So, for example, state A may make it a crime to murder any of its citizens anywhere in the world. This would permissibly extend prescriptive jurisdiction beyond the territory of state A on the basis of passive personality (discussed below). However, should state A proscribe smoking anywhere in the world, it would not be extending its prescriptive jurisdiction in tune with state practice. It would not be relying on any of the principles of extraterritoriality discussed below, although this is, according to the *Lotus Case*, still legal.

In *S v Basson*[23] the Constitutional Court held that a South African court might exercise criminal jurisdiction over a conspiracy entered into in South Africa by members of the South African Defence Force to murder opponents of the South African administration in Namibia during South Africa's occupation of that territory. This was on the ground that there was a 'real and substantial link' between South Africa and the crime—though, this comment was *obiter* because the Court ultimately found that South Africa had jurisdiction on the ground of territoriality because at all relevant times Namibia was under South African occupation.[24]

The various heads on which prescriptive jurisdiction can be extended extraterritorially are discussed below. It must be emphasised that enforcement jurisdiction cannot be extended on any of these grounds extraterritorially. So, for example, even though state A can criminalise murder committed against its nationals anywhere in the world,[25] it cannot unilaterally enforce that law (for example, by attempting to detain the accused) when the accused is in another state's territory. Instead, the state seeking to prosecute the accused should resort to extradition proceedings.[26]

1 Territoriality

'From the standpoint of international law, the jurisdictional competence of a state is primarily territorial,' said the European Court of

256. The status of these principles in international law is far from clear. See O'Keefe (n 9) fn 12.

[23] 2007 (3) SA 582 (CC), 2005 (12) BCLR 1192 (CC) paras 226–30. Here, the Court relied on the decision of the Supreme Court of Canada in *Libman v The Queen* [1985] 2 SCR 178.

[24] Ibid paras 225–7.

[25] On the basis of passive personality, discussed below.

[26] See Chapter 11.

Human Rights in *Bankovic v Belgium*.[27] From this it follows that a state may assert both aspects of its jurisdiction over all criminal acts that occur within its territory and over all persons responsible for such criminal acts, whatever their nationality.[28] In South Africa, as in other countries influenced by the Anglo-American common law, this is the principal basis for the exercise of prescriptive and enforcement jurisdiction. This is reflected in the presumption against the extraterritorial operation of criminal laws.[29]

South African 'territory', for the purposes of criminal jurisdiction, includes South African territorial waters[30] and airspace. Furthermore, any offence committed on board a South African ship[31] on the high seas or in a South African aircraft[32] above the high seas or foreign territory may be tried in a South African court. As theft is a continuing offence under South African law, a court will exercise jurisdiction over a person who possesses property stolen in another state.[33] In *S v Basson*, the Constitutional Court suggested that a territory occupied by South Africa and deemed to be part of South Africa by an Act of Parliament will give South Africa territorial jurisdiction in respect of crimes committed there.[34] In certain circumstances, a South African court will refuse to exercise jurisdiction over a crime committed within South African territory. Foreign diplomats

[27] (2002) 41 *ILM* 517, 123 ILR 94 para 59. In this case, a claim involving injuries resulting from the NATO bombing of Belgrade was rejected as inadmissible because the bombing did not occur in the territories of NATO states.

[28] *R v Holm; R v Pienaar* 1948 (1) SA 925 (A) 929–30; *Commissioner of Taxes, Federation of Rhodesia v McFarland* (n 4) 473F. See in respect of civil jurisdiction *Coin Security Group (Pty) Ltd v Smit NO* 1991 (2) SA 315 (T). In *Stopforth & Veenendal v Minister of Justice* 2000 (1) SA 113 (SCA) the Supreme Court of Appeal held that the Amnesty Committee, established under the Promotion of National Unity and Reconciliation Act 34 of 1995, had no power to grant amnesty 'in respect of offences committed outside South Africa which are not triable in this country but in another country in which any amnesty purportedly conferred by the Amnesty Committee would not be recognised'.

[29] *S v Makhutla* 1968 (2) SA 768 (O); *S v Maseki* 1981 (4) SA 374 (T); GE Devenish *Interpretation of Statutes* (1992) 215. Parliament may expressly provide that a statute is to operate extraterritorially. For example, see s 2(1) of the Prevention of Organised Crime Act 121 of 1998; and s 4(3) of the Implementation of the Rome Statute of the International Criminal Court Act 27 of 2002.

[30] South Africa's territorial waters extend for 12 miles from the low-water line of the coastline. In addition, South Africa has an exclusive economic zone of 200 miles from its coastline, in which it exercises jurisdiction over natural resources: ss 4 and 7 of the Maritime Zones Act 15 of 1994. See, too, s 22(2) of the Defence Act 42 of 2002.

[31] Section 327 of the Merchant Shipping Act 57 of 1951.

[32] Section 150 of the Civil Aviation Act 13 of 2009.

[33] *S v Kruger* 1989 (1) SA 785 (A) 793C–E.

[34] *S v Basson* (n 23) paras 226–7.

are granted immunity from the jurisdiction of municipal courts;[35] a court will not try a person who has been brought before it as a result of an unlawful abduction from another state;[36] and a court will probably refuse jurisdiction over a person wanted for a non-political crime committed in South Africa who is on board a ship or aircraft forced to enter South Africa in distress.[37]

2 Subjective and objective territoriality

A state may exercise jurisdiction where the crime is commenced within its territory and completed in another state (subjective territoriality) or where the crime is commenced within a foreign state and completed within its territory (objective territoriality).[38] Thus, if a gunman standing in state A shoots and kills his victim in state B, both state A (under the principle of subjective territoriality) and state B (under the principle of objective territoriality) will have jurisdiction over the gunman. An extension of objective territoriality is to be found in the 'effects' principle, according to which the state in which the effect or impact of the crime is felt may exercise jurisdiction. This was the basis upon which Turkey exercised jurisdiction in the *Lotus Case*. The effect of the collision was felt on the Turkish ship, which the Court held to be assimilated to Turkish territory.

In Zimbabwe the 'effects' principle was invoked in the bizarre case of *S v Mharapara*[39] in which an ex-Zimbabwean diplomat was convicted of theft from the Zimbabwe government committed while he was in the Zimbabwe diplomatic mission in Belgium. In dismissing the accused's appeal, Gubbay JA said:

> [A] strict interpretation of the principle of territoriality could create injustice where the constituent elements of the crime occur in more than one state or where the *locus commissi* is fortuitous as far as the harm flowing from the crime is concerned . . . A more flexible and realistic approach based on the place of impact, or of intended impact, of the crime must be favoured.[40]

Although this is a necessary extension of the territoriality principle, it may lend itself to abuse—as illustrated by the manner in which

[35] See Chapter 12.

[36] *S v Ebrahim* 1991 (2) SA 553 (A).

[37] *Nkondo v Minister of Police* 1980 (2) SA 894 (O) 898–900.

[38] See *S v Dersley* 1997 (2) SACR 253 (Ck) 255–60, particularly at 260C–E. It is unfortunate that White J, in an otherwise thorough and long overdue examination of the bases for the exercise of criminal jurisdiction in South Africa, saw fit to use the terms 'citizen' (257I) and 'domicile' (258J). The basis for the exercise of criminal jurisdiction is physical presence.

[39] 1986 (1) SA 556 (ZS).

[40] At 563–4. This *dictum* was approved in *S v Dersley* (n 38) 259–60. Cf *Martin v Republic of South Africa* 836 F 2d 91 (2d Cir 1987); M Leigh 'Sovereign immunity' (1988) 82 *AJIL* 583.

the United States has sought to implement its anti-trust legislation, which has both civil and criminal law features.[41]

The United States anti-trust laws, notably the Sherman Act of 1890, seek to ensure competition in commerce by prohibiting monopolistic practices. Relying on the objective territoriality or 'effects' principle, United States courts have given these laws extraterritorial effect[42] to extend to alleged monopolistic agreements governing trade and commerce abroad whose effect, however remote, is felt in the United States. Most countries object strongly to this application of the 'effects' principle to anti-competitive conduct that is not seen as punishable outside the United States. Moreover, it is argued that the United States practice violates international law on the ground that it exceeds the permissible limits of extraterritorial jurisdiction.[43] Although more recent judicial decisions in the United States have sought to modify the impact of the 'effects' doctrine by requiring United States courts to consider the interests of foreign nations,[44] the anti-trust laws continue to intrude on the commercial activities of foreign corporations.[45] In the 1970s the Westinghouse Electric Corporation of the United States filed suit in a United States court against a number of foreign uranium producers in which it alleged that there was price-fixing in violation of the Sherman Act. Included among the defendants were Anglo-American Corporation and Nuclear Fuel Corporation, a subsidiary of Anglo-American. In response to these proceedings, the United Kingdom,[46] Canada, Australia and South Africa enacted legislation aimed at frustrating or blocking the enforcement of the anti-trust laws by prohibiting compliance with

[41] B Cartoon '*The Westinghouse Case*: Collective response to the extraterritorial enforcement of United States anti-trust laws' (1983) 100 *SALJ* 731. See further DW Bowett 'Jurisdiction: Changing patterns of authority over activities and resources' (1982) 53 *BYIL* 1; AV Lowe 'The problems of extraterritorial jurisdiction: Economic sovereignty and the search for a solution' (1985) 34 *ICLQ* 724.

[42] In *United States v Aluminum Company of America (Alcoa)* 148 F 2d 416 (2d Cir 1945) the Court declared that 'any state may impose liabilities, even upon persons not within its allegiance, for conduct outside its borders that has consequences within its borders which the state reprehends' (443).

[43] R Jennings and A Watts (eds) *Oppenheim's International Law* 9 ed (1992) vol 1 at 476.

[44] *Timberlane Lumber Co v Bank of America* 549 F 2d 597 (9th Cir 1976).

[45] See, for example, the manner in which the anti-trust laws were invoked to block an attempt by Minorco SA to obtain control of Consolidated Goldfields: *Consolidated Goldfields Plc v Minorco SA* 871 F 2d 252 (1989); WH Callcott 'Application of US law to foreign transactions' (1989) 87 *AJIL* 923; FA Mann 'The extremism of American extraterritorial jurisdiction' (1990) 39 *ICLQ* 410.

[46] See AV Lowe 'Blocking extraterritorial jurisdiction: The British Protection of Trading Interests Act, 1980' (1981) 75 *AJIL* 257.

United States judicial decrees requesting inspection of documents or evidence located within their territories.

The South African legislation is contained in the Protection of Businesses Act.[47] Section 1 provides that, except with the permission of the Minister of Economic Affairs, 'no judgment, order, direction, arbitration award, interrogatory, commission rogatoire, letters of request or any other request delivered, given or issued or emanating from outside the Republic' shall be enforced in South Africa if it arises from an act 'connected with the mining, production, importation, exportation, refinement, possession, use or sale of or ownership to [*sic*] any matter or material, of whatever nature, whether within, outside, into or from the Republic'. Section 1A prohibits the recognition and enforcement of judgments that provide for multiple or punitive damages—a clear reference to the United States anti-trust legislation, which permits treble damages in anti-trust proceedings. Section 1B provides for the recovery within South Africa by South African residents of the punitive or multiple damages award of a foreign court already paid outside South Africa.

South African law on price fixing extends to acts that have an effect within the Republic. In *American Natural Soda Ash Corporation v Competition Commission*[48] the Supreme Court of Appeal interpreted s 3(1) of the Competition Act,[49] which extends price fixing 'to all economic activity within, or having an effect within, the Republic' to mean both benign and malign effects.[50] It rejected the argument that it extends only to acts with negative or deleterious effects within the Republic.[51]

3 Protection of the state

A state may exercise prescriptive jurisdiction over aliens who have committed acts abroad that are considered prejudicial to its safety and security. The most famous example of a state doing this was in *Attorney-General of the Government of Israel v Eichmann*. There, the District Court of Jerusalem held that Israel had jurisdiction over the crimes committed by Adolf Eichmann because his crimes had, by

[47] 99 of 1978, as amended.

[48] 2005 (6) SA 158 (SCA).

[49] 89 of 1998.

[50] Paragraph 26.

[51] The Supreme Court of Appeal reached this conclusion without any discussion of international law. The Competition Appeal Court, in reaching the same conclusion, made a thorough examination of international law on the subject, citing both the *Lotus Case* (n 15) and the *Barcelona Traction Case* 1970 ICJ Reports 3 in the course of its reasoning. See *American Soda Ash Corporation v Competition Commission of South Africa* 12/CAC/Dec 01; Oxford Reports on International Law ILDC 493.

definition, been prejudicial to the safety and security of the Jewish nation.[52] The House of Lords has also endorsed the protective principle.[53] In *R v Neumann*,[54] Murray J stated, in the trial of an alien resident who had committed acts of treason against South Africa abroad, that as South Africa was a sovereign state, it was 'automatically entitled to punish crime directed against its independence and safety'. Aliens tried in this way must have some connection with South Africa, usually in the form of residence. Were this restraint not adopted, it would give rise to an abuse of extraterritorial powers and to protest from other states.

4 Nationality

Many countries, particularly those with a civil-law tradition, criminalise certain conduct committed by their own nationals abroad. Thus, state A may punish its national for the crime of murder committed in state B, where the victim was a national of state B, once state A's national is within state A's territory. This is known as the exercise of jurisdiction on the ground of 'active nationality'. In some civil-law countries, for example in Germany and Sweden, jurisdiction exists even when the accused became a national after the alleged crime.[55]

Countries influenced by the Anglo-American common law will not exercise prescriptive jurisdiction on this ground unless the municipal law clearly confers jurisdiction.[56] In *S v Mharapara*, described above, the trial judge exercised prescriptive jurisdiction on the ground of nationality, holding that 'a state has jurisdiction with respect to any crime committed outside its territory by a person or persons who is or are its nationals at the time when the offence was committed or

[52] *Attorney-General of the Government of Israel v Eichmann* (1961) 36 ILR 5 para 30. This was confirmed on appeal by the Supreme Court of Israel in *Attorney-General of Israel v Eichmann* (1962) 36 ILR 277 at 304 para 12. This is notwithstanding how, at the time of the Second World War and the Holocaust, Israel did not exist. See D Lasok 'The Eichmann trial' (1962) 11 *ICLQ* 355 at 364.

[53] *Joyce v DPP* [1946] AC 347.

[54] 1949 (3) SA 1238 (Special Ct) 1250. This echoes the decision of the House of Lords in *Joyce v DPP* [1946] AC 347. See, too, *R v Holm; R v Pienaar* (n 28) 930; *Nduli v Minister of Justice* 1978 (1) SA 893 (A) 912–13; *S v Basson* (n 23) para 225.

[55] See the Strafgesetzbuch [StGB] S 4 (FRG) and the Swedish Penal Code Ch 2, s 2. Commentators have argued that this violates the rule of non-retroactivity. See C Bassiouni *International Extradition: United States Law and Practice* 5 ed (2007) 401 and O'Keefe (n 9) 742–3. But see R Cryer *An Introduction to International Criminal Law* 2 ed (2010) 48. Cryer explains that such states require the conduct to be a crime at the *locus delicti* and then that jurisdiction is 'borrowed' by the state exercising jurisdiction. This is also because such civil states refuse to extradite their own nationals and so they extend jurisdiction to ensure prosecution.

[56] The United States rarely relies on it. See Bassiouni (n 55) 401.

when he is or they are prosecuted and punished'.[57] On appeal, while upholding the conviction of the accused in accordance with the 'effects' principle, Gubbay JA rejected nationality as a basis for jurisdiction. He stated:

> [T]here is no rule of international law directing or obliging states to exercise criminal jurisdiction over their nationals for offences committed abroad. International law merely *permits* every state to apply its jurisdiction against its own citizens even when they are situate outside its boundaries. . . . Thus the fact that customary international law is part of the municipal law of a state does not assist, because there is only a permissive principle involved and not a mandatory rule. The permissibility under international law for a state to exercise jurisdiction is not a sufficient basis for the exercise of jurisdiction by a municipal court of that state. A municipal court must be satisfied in addition that the municipal law itself authorises the trial of a national for an offence committed abroad which would be punishable if committed at home.[58]

South Africa, like other common-law countries, treats treason as an exception to the rule that it will not exercise extraterritorial prescriptive jurisdiction on grounds of nationality. In *R v Holm; R v Pienaar*[59] the Appellate Division noted how not all countries criminalise certain conduct of nationals committed abroad. For example, England only prosecutes its nationals for crimes committed abroad if there is legislation specifically providing for this.[60] Watermeyer CJ seemed to incorporate this into South African law when he held that treason is an exceptional crime in the sense that South Africa can prosecute its nationals for it wherever that crime occurred:

> [S]o far as high treason committed by a subject is concerned, there exists no international custom or comity which debars a state from trying and punishing the offender no matter where the offence has been committed. The reason for this is clear, it is because high treason, committed outside of the territory of the state concerned, is an offence only against such state. No other state is interested in punishing the offender and the punishment of the offender by the state concerned does not encroach upon the rights of other states.[61]

Ordinarily, it would seem, crimes committed abroad by South Africans would not fall within South Africa's jurisdiction unless it was treason or authorised by statute.

[57] *S v Mharapara* (n 39) 47D–E.

[58] *S v Mharapara* (n 39) 559E–G. See, too, *R v Holm; R v Pienaar* (n 28) 930; *S v Basson* (n 23) para 224 and para 172, fn 147.

[59] Supra (n 28).

[60] See *R v Page* [1953] 2 All ER 1335 at 1356. Note that s 9 of the British Offences against the Persons Act 1861 asserts jurisdiction over murders committed by British nationals anywhere in the world.

[61] *R v Holm; R v Pienaar* (n 28) 931.

The Constitutional Court in *S v Basson* apparently endorsed this approach.[62] There, the Court held that South Africa could exercise its jurisdiction over South Africans who entered into a conspiracy to commit crimes in Namibia while the latter was under occupation by South Africa. The court said that jurisdiction could be exercised not because of the nationality of the accused but because of a 'real and substantial link' between the two countries on the basis of territoriality.[63]

The Court's express reliance on a real and substantial territorial link,[64] and not on nationality, suggests that South African law does not extend jurisdiction to crimes committed by nationals abroad. Instead, a statute will have to authorise the exercise of jurisdiction in respect of nationality—for example, as in the Implementation of the Rome Statute of the International Criminal Court Act.[65] Hence, the Court accepted that as a general proposition, South African courts 'have declined to exercise jurisdiction over persons who commit crimes in other countries. This, as Dugard points out, is an aspect of sovereignty which has given rise to a presumption against the extraterritorial operation of criminal law'.[66]

5 Passive personality

This principle allows a state to exercise prescriptive jurisdiction over a person who commits an offence abroad that harms one of its own nationals. In the past, Anglo-American countries objected strongly to this basis of jurisdiction.[67] In recent times, however, this jurisdictional ground has been invoked in order to suppress international terrorism.[68] Following the killing of an American national by terrorists on an Italian ship (the *Achille Lauro*) on the high seas in 1985, the United States enacted legislation to give its courts jurisdiction to try anyone

[62] *S v Basson* (n 23).

[63] Paragraphs 225–7.

[64] The Court cited with approval (para 226) La Forest J's finding for the Supreme Court of Canada in *Libman v The Queen* [1985] 2 SCR 178 at 212–3 that 'all that is necessary to make an offence subject to the jurisdiction of our courts is that a significant portion of the activities constituting that offence took place in Canada. As it is put by modern academics, it is sufficient that there be a "real and substantial link" between an offence and this country, a test well-known in public and private international law'.

[65] 27 of 2002, s 4(3)*(a)* and *(b)*.

[66] *S v Basson* (n 23) para 223.

[67] See the separate opinion of Judge Moore of the United States in the *Lotus Case* (n 15) 89–93.

[68] Rome Convention for the Suppression of Unlawful Acts against the Safety of Maritime Navigation (1988) 27 *ILM* 672; International Convention for the Suppression of Terrorist Bombings (1998) 37 *ILM* 249.

who kills or intentionally causes serious bodily injury to a national of the United States outside the United States where the offence 'was intended to coerce, intimidate, or retaliate against a government or a civilian population'.[69] In *United States v Yunis (No 2)*[70] a United States district court invoked passive personality as a basis for exercising jurisdiction over a Lebanese national who hijacked a Jordanian aircraft with United States nationals on board and flew the aircraft over a number of Mediterranean countries.

Although the Rome Statute of the International Criminal Court does not confer jurisdiction on the Court on the basis of passive personality vis-à-vis nationals of state parties, the South African statute implementing this treaty empowers a South African court to exercise jurisdiction in respect of genocide, crimes against humanity and war crimes committed outside South Africa where the accused person has committed the crime 'against a South African citizen or against a person who is ordinarily resident in the Republic'.[71]

6 Universal jurisdiction and international crimes[72]

The principles discussed above empower a state to exercise prescriptive jurisdiction over a crime committed abroad in violation of its own *national* laws. Some conduct violates not only the domestic legal order of a state but also the international order. Such conduct constitutes an international crime. Ideally such crimes should be tried by an international court, but before 1998, a permanent international criminal court seemed impossible. In 1998 a diplomatic conference in Rome gave its approval to the establishment of such a court and in 2002 the International Criminal Court came into being.[73] But the Rome Statute of the International Criminal Court (its founding statute) operates on the basis of complementarity and largely leaves it to the national courts of states to enforce international criminal law, either by trying offenders themselves or by extraditing them to countries that will do so. The principle of *aut dedere aut judicare (punire)*—extradite or try (punish)—is the basis for

[69] Omnibus Diplomatic Security and Anti-Terrorism Act of 1986, Pub L No 99–399 1202*(a)*, 100 Stat 853, 896 (codified at 18 USCA 2331 (Supp 1989)).

[70] 681 F Supp 896 (1988); 82 ILR 344.

[71] Section 4(3)*(d)* of the Implementation of the Rome Statute of the International Criminal Court Act 27 of 2002.

[72] L Reydams *Universal Jurisdiction: International and Municipal Legal Perspectives* (2003); S Macedo (ed) *National Courts and the Prosecution of Serious Crimes under International Law* (2004); 'Editorial comments on universality' (2003) 1 *Journal of International Criminal Justice* 580; JD van der Vyver 'Universal jurisdiction in international criminal law' (1999) 24 *SAYIL* 107.

[73] See Chapter 10.

the enforcement of international criminal law.[74] When a national court exercises prescriptive jurisdiction in this way over an international crime with which it has no jurisdictional link of the kind described above (in sections 1 to 5) it is said that it exercises universal jurisdiction. Here, the national court acts as the agent of the international community in the prosecution of an enemy of all mankind in whose punishment all states have an equal interest.[75]

Seen in this way, universal jurisdiction is defined in the negative. It is when a state exercises prescriptive jurisdiction without there being one of the connections listed above. Defined positively then, universal jurisdiction is prescriptive jurisdiction over offences committed abroad by persons who, at the time of commission, are non-resident aliens, where such offences are not deemed to constitute threats to the fundamental interests of the prescribing state[76] or give rise to effects within the prescribing state's territory.[77]

Some argue that universal jurisdiction cannot exist within a treaty because then jurisdiction is circumscribed by *pacta tertiis* and cannot be exercised by 'any state'.[78] Instead, true universal jurisdiction applies only in the case of crimes under customary international law, in respect of which all states have the right to prosecute. Such crimes are limited to piracy, slave-trading, war crimes, crimes against humanity, genocide and torture. However, in recent years a number of international crimes have been created by multilateral treaties, which confer wide jurisdictional powers upon state parties. These treaties confer universal jurisdiction in that signatory states are required to prosecute or extradite persons who are accused or convicted of the treaty's crimes and who happen to be present in their territory. Because the exercise of prescriptive jurisdiction in such cases does not invoke one of the jurisdictional connections listed above, this is universal jurisdiction.[79] The fact that states not party to the relevant treaty have not proscribed the conduct in question

[74] M Cherif Bassiouni and EM Wise *Aut Dedere Aut Judicare: The Duty to Extradite or Prosecute in International Law* (1995). See *Questions Relating to the Obligation to Prosecute or Extradite (Belgium v Senegal)* 2009 ICJ Reports at 156 and *Questions Relating to the Obligation to Prosecute or Extradite (Belgium v Senegal)* 2012 ICJ Reports 422.

[75] *Attorney-General of the Government of Israel v Eichmann* (1962) 36 ILR 277 298–304.

[76] However, the authors are of the view that criminalising and prosecuting international crimes, given their heinous nature and threat to international peace, will always be in the broader interests of a state.

[77] O'Keefe (n 9) 745.

[78] A Cassese 'Is the bell tolling for universality? A plea for a sensible notion of universal jurisdiction' (2003) 1 *JICJ* 589 at 594.

[79] Of course, the enforcement of the relevant criminal laws is contingent on the accused being present in the state party's territory.

makes no difference to how state parties are criminalising conduct notwithstanding the absence of a jurisdictional nexus.[80]

It must be emphasised that international law *permits* states to exercise jurisdiction over international crimes. It does not compel them to do so in the absence of a treaty obligation.[81] Moreover, most states, including South Africa, will not try a person for an international crime unless the conduct has been criminalised under municipal law.[82]

Universal jurisdiction has in recent times become an issue of controversy.[83] Individual states have enacted legislation to give universal jurisdiction to their own courts to try international crimes recognised by the Rome Statute—genocide, crimes against humanity and war crimes. For example, the Implementation of the Rome Statute of the International Criminal Court Act empowers a South African court to exercise jurisdiction over a person who has committed such crimes outside South Africa if 'that person, after the commission of the crime, is present in the territory of the Republic'.[84] No jurisdictional nexus is required to proscribe the conduct in question.

Some national statutes do not limit universal jurisdiction to the exercise of universal jurisdiction over persons present in their

[80] O'Keefe (n 9) 746–7.

[81] Though some commentators argue that there is a duty in customary international law to extradite or prosecute those accused or convicted of such crimes. See Bassiouni (n 55) 7, 25.

[82] In *S v Basson* 2005 (1) SA 171 (CC) the Constitutional Court appeared to be prepared to permit the extraterritorial prosecution of Dr Basson for crimes under the Riotous Assemblies Act 17 of 1956 on the ground that the conduct in question constituted crimes against humanity and war crimes (paras 34, 37, 119–26). In a later decision in this case, however, the Constitutional Court found it unnecessary 'to consider whether customary international law could be used either as the basis in itself for a prosecution under common law, or, alternatively, as an aid to the interpretation of s 18(2)*(a)* of the Riotous Assemblies Act' (n 23) para 172, fn 147. See further W Ferdinandusse *Direct Application of International Criminal Law in National Courts* (2005). On the other hand, s 232 of the Constitution says that customary international law is law in the Republic unless contrary to the Constitution or legislation. So customary law crimes are domestic crimes in South Africa, so long as they are consistent with the Constitution and legislation.

[83] See H Kissinger 'The pitfalls of universal jurisdiction: Risking judicial tyranny' (2001) 80 *Foreign Affairs* 86. In *S v Basson* (n 23) the Constitutional Court stated that for the purposes of this case 'it is not necessary to enter into controversies surrounding the existence of universal jurisdiction for crimes against humanity and war crimes and a concomitant duty to prosecute' (para 172, fn 147). Most recently, see the African Union's criticism of universal jurisdiction in H van der Wilt 'Universal jurisdiction under attack: An assessment of African misgivings towards international criminal justice as administered by Western states' (2011) 9 *JICJ* 1043.

[84] Section 4(3)*(d)* of Act 27 of 2002.

territory and go further by allowing their courts to issue warrants for the arrest of persons outside their own territory. The question whether international law permits the exercise of universal jurisdiction by national courts over persons *in absentia* arose in a dispute between the Democratic Republic of Congo (DRC) and Belgium in the *Arrest Warrant* case.

In the *Arrest Warrant* case,[85] a Belgian judge issued a warrant *in absentia* for the arrest of the Foreign Minister of the DRC, charging him with crimes against humanity and grave breaches of the Geneva Conventions of 1949 arising out of acts committed in the DRC. The warrant was issued in terms of a Belgian statute conferring jurisdiction on Belgian courts to try such crimes 'wheresoever they may have been committed'. The DRC challenged the legality of the arrest warrant before the International Court of Justice on two grounds: first, that the issue of the warrant constituted an 'exercise of an excessive universal jurisdiction' and, secondly, that the Minister was entitled to immunity from prosecution before a Belgian court.

The International Court upheld the second challenge, which made it unnecessary for the Court to decide on the question of universal jurisdiction.[86] Several judges did, however, give separate opinions which dealt with this topic. Judge Guillaume, President of the Court, found that international law does not recognise universal jurisdiction, except for the crime of piracy, and that universal jurisdiction is 'unknown to international law'.[87] Judges Higgins, Kooijmans and Buergenthal, in a separate but joint opinion, stated that universal jurisdiction may be exercised 'only over those crimes regarded as the most heinous by the international community'[88]—such as piracy, war crimes, crimes against humanity and genocide—and that 'a State may choose to exercise a universal criminal jurisdiction *in absentia*'[89] as there is no rule of international law that prohibits this. Judge ad hoc Van den Wyngaert likewise held that 'there is no conventional or customary international law or legal doctrine in support of the proposition that (universal) jurisdiction for war crimes and crimes

[85] 2002 ICJ Reports 3. See further on this case G Erasmus and G Kemp 'The application of international criminal law before domestic courts in the light of recent developments in international and constitutional law' (2002) 27 *SAYIL* 64; M du Plessis and S Bosch 'Immunities and universal jurisdiction—The World Court steps in (or on?)' (2003) 28 *SAYIL* 346.

[86] See Chapter 12.

[87] *Arrest Warrant* case (n 85) 42, para 12.

[88] Ibid 81, para 60.

[89] Ibid 80, para 59.

against humanity can only be exercised if the defendant is present on the territory of the prosecuting state'.[90]

The Belgian statute conferring universal jurisdiction has since been substantially amended in response to political pressure,[91] particularly from the United States after proceedings had been initiated against Ariel Sharon and former president George HW Bush. It now allows Belgian courts to hear complaints only when the suspect is Belgian or lives in Belgium, the complainant is Belgian or a Belgian resident, or if a treaty requires Belgium to exercise jurisdiction.[92] Other states—such as Spain—retain wide universal jurisdiction statutes, but in practice judges tend to require some connection with the forum state as a precondition for the exercise of jurisdiction.[93]

Universal jurisdiction remains a controversial basis for the exercise of criminal jurisdiction. The political will to exercise universal jurisdiction is seldom forthcoming from states,[94] as illustrated by the manner in which the South African government refused to arrest President al-Bashir, even when South Africa was requested by the International Criminal Court to do so as a state party to the Court.[95] Although universal jurisdiction has not often succeeded in judicial proceedings it has, however, succeeded in deterring persons suspected of international crimes from foreign travel.

Ironically, the United States, which is vehemently opposed to the exercise of universal *criminal* jurisdiction, practises broad *civil* universal jurisdiction over human rights violations committed by non-nationals abroad under the Alien Torts Statute of 1789, which confers civil jurisdiction on a US federal court where an alien sues for a tort committed in violation of the law of nations in any part of the world.[96]

[90] *Arrest Warrant* case (n 85) 173, para 58.

[91] See S Ratner 'Belgium's war crimes statute: A postmortem' (2003) 97 *AJIL* 888; N Roht-Arriaza 'Universal jurisdiction: Steps forward, steps back' (2004) 17 *Leiden Journal of International Law* 375.

[92] S Smis and K Van Der Borght 'Introductory note to Belgium's amendment to the law of June 16, 1993 (as amended by the law of February 10, 1999) concerning the punishment of grave breaches of humanitarian law' (2003) 42 *ILM* 740.

[93] Roht-Arriaza (n 91); *Guatemala Genocide Case* (2003) 42 *ILM* 683; *Peruvian Genocide Case* (2003) 42 *ILM* 1200.

[94] See M Langer 'The diplomacy of universal jurisdiction: The political branches and the transnational prosecution of international crimes' (2011) 105 *AJIL* 1; J Dugard 'International criminal law, the International Criminal Court and civil society' 2016 *Acta Juridica* 3 at 7–8.

[95] See Chapter 10.

[96] See *Sosa v Alvarez-Machain* (n 7). See, too, the joint opinion of Judges Higgins, Kooijmans and Buergenthal in the *Arrest Warrant Case* (n 85) 77, para 48. Recently, however, the US Supreme Court has limited the scope of the Alien Torts Statute. The activities complained of must 'touch and concern' the territory of the United States.

INTERNATIONAL CRIMES[97]

International crimes are crimes that threaten the good order not only of particular states but of the international community as a whole. They are crimes in whose suppression all states have an interest as they violate values that constitute the foundation of the world public order. Some international crimes have their roots in custom while others are the creations of conventions aimed principally at the suppression of human rights violations and international terrorism. Historically, international crimes were largely prosecuted at a domestic level. But since the 1990s, various international legal tribunals have been established to try accused persons for international crimes.[98] Below, various crimes (whether customary or conventional) are explored, with particular emphasis on how (in recent years) states have expanded their domestic prescriptive jurisdiction over these crimes.

1 Customary international law crimes

The earliest international crime was piracy, which is today codified in both the 1958 Geneva Convention on the High Seas[99] and the 1982 United Nations Convention on the Law of the Sea.[100] According to these Conventions, piracy is defined as an illegal act of violence committed for private ends by the crew or passengers of a private ship or aircraft and directed against another ship or aircraft on the high seas. Another crime under customary law is slave trading; indeed, it was at one time classified as a species of piracy. Piracy is a crime under South African law.[101] Piracy is dealt with more fully in Chapter 17 on the Law of the Sea.

War crimes and crimes against humanity are also crimes under customary international law.[102] The London Charter of 1945,[103] which

See *Kiobel v Royal Dutch Petroleum* 133 S Ct 1659 (2013) at 1669. The *Kiobel* limitation was used to reject claims by South African apartheid victims for damages from the United States. See *Balintulo v Ford Motor Co* 796 F 3d 160, 167 (CA2 (NY) 2015). See M Swart 'Requiem for a dream? The impact of *Kiobel* on apartheid reparations in South Africa' (2015) 13 *JICJ* 353.

[97] A Cassese and P Gaeta *Cassese's International Criminal Law* 3 ed (2013); R Cryer, H Friman, D Robertson and E Wilmshurst *International Criminal Law and Procedure* 3 ed (2014); C Stahn and L van den Herik (eds) *Future Perspectives on International Criminal Justice* (2010); A Cassese (ed) *The Oxford Companion to International Criminal Justice* (2009).

[98] See Chapter 10.

[99] Article 15.

[100] Article 101. See, generally, AP Rubin *The Law of Piracy* 2 ed (1998).

[101] Section 24 of the Defence Act 42 of 2002.

[102] M Cherif Bassiouni *Crimes against Humanity in International Criminal Law* (1999); TLH McCormack and GJ Simpson (eds) *The Law of War Crimes* (1997).

[103] 5 UNTS 251, (1945) 39 *AJIL* Suppl 257.

established the Nuremberg Tribunal,[104] defined these crimes for the purposes of the trial held before it; but it is generally accepted that war crimes, and possibly crimes against humanity, were already part of international customary law before 1945. Both are recognised as crimes against the peace and security of mankind by the International Law Commission's 1996 Draft Code of Crimes against the Peace and Security of Mankind.[105] In 1998 these concepts were refined, redefined and expanded to take account of new developments in customary law in the Rome Statute of the International Criminal Court.[106] These crimes are considered more fully in Chapter 10.

Genocide and torture are today also recognised as crimes under customary international law, although both have a basis in a multilateral treaty.

2 International treaty crimes

In recent times, international crimes have been created by multilateral treaties, principally to punish human rights violators or international terrorists. These treaties generally oblige states to try or to extradite offenders. Few recognise universal jurisdiction as a basis for prosecution, while many invoke a combination of traditional bases for the exercise of multiple jurisdiction in order to ensure that all states with some national interest in the prosecution of the offender will have jurisdiction.

(a) Genocide

The Genocide Convention of 1948[107] created the crime of genocide—defined as any act 'committed with the intent to destroy in whole or in part a national, ethnical, racial or religious group'. This crime is now part of customary international law, as evidenced by its inclusion in the International Law Commission's Draft Code of Crimes against the Peace and Security of Mankind[108] and the Rome Statute of the International Criminal Court. South Africa became a party to this Convention on 10 December 1998. Genocide is considered more fully in Chapter 10.

(b) Apartheid

The international crime of apartheid is obviously of special interest to South Africa.

[104] The judgment of this tribunal appears in (1947) 41 *AJIL* 172.

[105] Report of the International Law Commission on the work of its 48th Session, 1996, GAOR, 51st Session Suppl No 10 (A/51/10).

[106] (1998) 37 *ILM* 999, articles 7 and 8. See further Chapter 10.

[107] See WA Schabas *Genocide in International Law: The Crime of Crimes* 2 ed (2009).

[108] See n 105.

In 1973 the General Assembly sponsored the International Convention on the Suppression and Punishment of the Crime of Apartheid,[109] which declares that 'apartheid is a crime against humanity'[110] and criminalises the principal features of apartheid, ranging from murder, torture and arbitrary arrests of members of a racial group to legislative measures calculated to prevent a racial group from participation in the political, social, economic and cultural life of the country, when committed for the purpose of establishing and maintaining domination by one racial group over any other racial group and systematically oppressing its members.[111]

Parties to the Convention undertake to enact legislation to prosecute persons responsible for this international crime. Persons charged with this crime may be tried by the courts of any signatory state 'which may acquire jurisdiction over the person of the accused' or by an international penal tribunal.[112] As far as signatories are concerned, a type of universal jurisdiction is therefore recognised. The offence is also made an extraditable crime. This Convention was not implemented in practice during the apartheid era. The symbolic impact of the Convention was, however, considerable as it portrayed the policies and practices of apartheid as a crime against humanity—a categorisation later confirmed by the Report of the Truth and Reconciliation Commission.[113]

Although the Apartheid Convention is primarily aimed at apartheid as practised in South Africa, it is not limited in time or space. Provisions of the Convention repeatedly refer to the fact that it is to apply not only to apartheid as practised in South Africa but to similar policies of racial discrimination wherever practised. Article I of the Convention declares that 'apartheid is a crime against humanity and that inhuman acts resulting from the policies and practices of racial segregation and discrimination . . . are crimes violating the principles of international law', and in article IV parties agree to punish the crime of apartheid and 'similar segregationist policies or their manifestations'. That apartheid knows no geographical limitation is

[109] (1974) 13 *ILM* 50; RS Clark 'The crime of apartheid' in *International Criminal Law* (ed M Bassiouni) vol I (Crimes) (1987); J Dugard 'L'apartheid' in H Ascensio, E Decaux and A Pellet *Droit International Pénal* (2000) 349. For critical commentaries on this Convention, see H Booysen 'Convention on the crime of apartheid' (1976) 2 *SAYIL* 56; GN Barrie 'The Apartheid Convention after five years' 1981 *TSAR* 280; JC Heunis *United Nations Versus South Africa* (1986) 281; P Eden 'The role of the Rome Statute in the criminalization of apartheid' (2014) 12 *JICJ* 171.

[110] Article I.

[111] Article II.

[112] Article V.

[113] *Truth and Reconciliation Commission of South Africa Report* (1998) vol 1 at 94, vol 5 at 222.

confirmed by the 1977 Additional Protocol I to the Geneva Conventions of 1949,[114] which recognises as a grave breach of the Protocol and the Conventions 'practices of apartheid and other inhuman and degrading practices involving outrages upon personal dignity, based on racial discrimination'.[115]

While the Apartheid Convention remains binding as a convention on more than 100 states that are parties to the agreement, there has been an attempt in recent years to subsume it in the crime against humanity. The 1996 Draft Code of Crimes against the Peace and Security of Mankind recognises institutionalised racial discrimination as a species of crime against humanity and explains in its commentary on this provision that 'it is in fact the crime of apartheid under a more general denomination'.[116] The Rome Statute of the International Criminal Court adopts a similar approach but retains the term 'crime of apartheid' to describe inhumane acts 'committed in the context of an institutionalised regime of systematic oppression and domination by one racial group over any other racial group or groups and committed with the intention of maintaining that regime'.[117]

The precise status of the crime of apartheid is today uncertain. It is a war crime in terms of Additional Protocol I. It is an international treaty crime for states parties to the Apartheid Convention. It is a treaty crime, albeit a species of crimes against humanity, for states that are parties to the Rome Statute of the International Criminal Court.[118] It may be a crime against humanity under customary international law,[119] although an American court has held that it is not a customary law international wrong for the purposes of the Alien Tort Statute on the ground that the convention has not been adopted 'by most world powers'.[120] Although the crime has a life of its own under contemporary international law, it serves as a constant reminder of the racial policies once pursued by the South African government.

(c) Torture

The Torture Convention, to which South Africa became a party in 1998, is considered in Chapter 15. It obliges a state party to make

[114] (1977) 16 *ILM* 1391.

[115] Articles 85(4)(c) and 85(5).

[116] Supra (n 105) 99.

[117] Articles 7(1)(j) and 7(2)(h).

[118] Eden (n 109).

[119] In *S v Basson* (n 82) the Constitutional Court stated that it is 'clear that the practice of apartheid constituted crimes against humanity' (para 37).

[120] *In re South African Apartheid Litigation: Ntsebeza v Citigroup Inc* (n 7).

torture punishable under its domestic law and to take measures to establish jurisdiction over an act of torture committed within its territory when either the offender or victim is a national. Where the offender is 'present' in its territory, a state party is required to either try or extradite him, which in effect establishes universal jurisdiction for parties to the Convention.[121] Torture is a crime under customary international law[122] and is designated as a form of crime against humanity under the Rome Statute of the International Criminal Court.[123]

(d) Hijacking

Three conventions seek to outlaw hijacking and to facilitate the prosecution of hijackers.

The Tokyo Convention of 1963,[124] which applies to acts which jeopardise the safety of an aircraft in flight outside the territory of any state, confers jurisdiction over offences committed on board such an aircraft on the state of registration of the aircraft.[125] A signatory state that is not the state of registration may interfere with an aircraft in flight only in order to exercise its criminal jurisdiction over an offence committed on board an aircraft where 'the offence has effect on the territory of such state', the offence has been committed by or against a national, or the offence is against the security of the state.[126] These clearly represent the jurisdictional connections discussed earlier in this chapter.

The Hague Convention of 1970[127] makes it an offence for any person on board an aircraft unlawfully, by force or intimidation, to

[121] Convention against Torture and Other Cruel, Inhuman or Degrading Treatment (1984) 23 *ILM* 1027, article 5. For more on this subject, see *R v Bow Street Stipendiary Magistrate, Ex p Pinochet Ugarte (No 3)* [1999] 2 All ER 97 (HL). In 1999, South Africa failed to try or extradite to Ethiopia Mengistu Haile Mariam, the former dictator of Ethiopia, who was wanted by that country for torture and other international crimes, despite its obligations under the Torture Convention to which it became a party in 1998. See further J Dugard and CJ Roederer 'Public international law' 1999 *Annual Survey* 99 at 100.

[122] *Furundzija Case* IT-95-17/1-T10 (Trial Chamber of ICTY, Judgment, 10 December 1998) 121 ILR 213 at 260; E de Wet 'The prohibition of torture as an international norm of *jus cogens* and its implication for national and customary law' (2004) 15 *European Journal of International Law* 97.

[123] Article 7(1)(f).

[124] Convention on Offences and Certain Other Acts Committed on Board Aircraft 704 UNTS 219.

[125] Article 3.

[126] Article 4.

[127] Convention for the Suppression of Unlawful Seizure of Aircraft 860 UNTS 105, (1971) 10 *ILM* 133.

seize control of the aircraft while it is in flight.[128] Parties are required to try or to extradite such an offender.[129] A state is permitted to exercise jurisdiction when the offence is committed on board an aircraft registered in that state, when the aircraft on board which the offence is committed lands in the territory of the state with the alleged offender still on board, or when the offence is committed on board an aircraft leased without crew to a lessee who has his principal place of business or residence in that state. In addition, a party to the Convention shall take steps 'to establish its jurisdiction over the offence in the case where the alleged offender is present in its territory' and it does not extradite him.[130]

The Montreal Convention of 1971[131] establishes similar jurisdictional rules for persons who sabotage aircraft on the ground or who place devices on an aircraft in order to endanger its safety in flight.

South Africa is a party to all three Conventions and has incorporated their main provisions into municipal law in the Civil Aviation Act of 2009.[132] In terms of s 133 of this statute, the following acts, inter alia, are criminal offences punishable by a fine or imprisonment not exceeding 30 years:

(a) the unlawful seizure of or exercise of control over an aircraft by force or intimidation;
(b) any act of violence, including an assault on any person on board the aircraft, which is likely to endanger the safety of the aircraft;
(c) the communication of false information that endangers the safety of the aircraft in service;
(d) any damage to an aircraft in service, or the placing of a device likely to cause damage to an aircraft in service, which renders the aircraft incapable of flight or endangers its safety.[133]

South African courts are given competence over offences under the Act committed outside South African airspace when the crime takes place on board a South African aircraft; the aircraft in which the offence is committed lands in the Republic with the offender on

[128] 'Flight' occurs at any time from the moment when all the external doors of an aircraft are closed following embarkation until the moment when the doors are opened for disembarkation: article 3.

[129] Articles 7 and 8.

[130] Article 4.

[131] Convention for the Suppression of Unlawful Acts against the Safety of Civil Aviation (1971) 10 *ILM* 1151. In 1988, a Protocol to the Convention was adopted to bring attacks against people in airports within the scope of the Convention: (1988) 27 *ILM* 627.

[132] Act 13 of 2009.

[133] For judicial interpretations of the predecessor of this provision in the Civil Aviation Offences Act 10 of 1972, see *S v Jeffers* 1975 (4) SA 657 (W); *S v Jeffers* 1976 (2) SA 636 (A); *S v Bergman* 1984 (1) SA 182 (C); *S v Hoare* 1982 (4) SA 865 (N).

board; the act takes place on board an aircraft leased without crew to a lessee who resides permanently in the Republic; the offender is 'present in the Republic'; or the offender is apprehended in the Republic.[134] These last two grounds reflect universal jurisdiction. If the South African government elects not to prosecute the offender, it may extradite him to the state in which the aircraft is registered (or the lessee of the aircraft is permanently resident) or in which the aircraft landed with the offender on board, provided that such state is a party to one of the above-mentioned Conventions.[135]

(e) Offences against the safety of maritime navigation

Piracy, as shown above, involves an act by the crew of one ship against another ship on the high seas, committed for private profit. It does not cover the situation in which passengers on board a ship seize control of the ship by unlawful means on the high seas for a political purpose. This gap in the law was starkly illustrated in 1985 when a group of Palestinian terrorists, who had boarded the *Achille Lauro* luxury liner as passengers, seized control of the ship, held its crew and passengers hostage for the release of prisoners in Israel, and murdered an American national.[136] The result was the adoption of the Rome Convention for the Suppression of Unlawful Acts against the Safety of Maritime Navigation of 1988,[137] which extends the crime of hijacking to ships beyond the outer limits of the territorial sea and requires signatories to try or extradite offenders. Jurisdiction to try offenders is conferred on the flag-state of the ship seized, the state of which the offender is a national, the state whose nationals are victims, and the state at which the seizure is directed 'to compel that state to do or abstain from doing any act' (a combination of the 'effects' and state protection principles). As in the case of aircraft hijacking, signatory states are required to establish jurisdiction over offenders 'present' in their territory when they choose not to extradite.[138]

[134] Sections 150 and 151.

[135] Section 152.

[136] A Cassese *Terrorism, Politics and Law: The* Achille Lauro *Affair* (1989).

[137] (1988) 27 *ILM* 672. See further M Halberstam 'Terrorism on the high seas: The *Achille Lauro* piracy and the IMO Convention on maritime safety' (1988) 82 *AJIL* 269; G Plant 'The Convention for the Suppression of Unlawful Acts against the Safety of Maritime Navigation' (1990) 39 *ICLQ* 27.

[138] Article 6.

(f) Drug-trafficking

The 1988 Convention against Illicit Traffic in Narcotic Drugs and Psychotropic Substances,[139] to which South Africa is a party,[140] is a treaty of co-operation which requires states parties to criminalise the production and distribution of certain narcotic drugs and to exercise jurisdiction over such crimes committed within their territory. It also provides for the extradition of offenders, the confiscation of prohibited drugs and the proceeds of crimes, and mutual legal assistance in the combating of drug-trafficking.

(g) International terrorism

The adoption of a comprehensive agreement to outlaw international terrorism has been on the agenda of the international community for over 70 years.[141] In 1937 a Convention for the Prevention and Punishment of Terrorism[142] was drafted in response to the assassination of King Alexander I of Yugoslavia, which defined acts of terrorism as 'criminal acts directed against a state and intended or calculated to create a state of terror in the minds of particular persons, or a group of persons or the general public'. The Convention, however, was ratified by one state only (India) and never came into force. In more recent times, attempts to draft such a treaty have failed. During the Cold War and, particularly, the period of decolonisation, one state's 'terrorist' was often another's 'freedom fighter'.[143] Wars of national liberation were supported by the Soviet Bloc and developing states, which argued that all methods employed to overthrow colonial, racist or alien regimes were permissible. In this climate, states sought to reach consensus on narrowly defined species of terrorism rather than terrorism itself. Thus, the hijacking of aircraft

139 (1989) 28 *ILM* 493. See further N Boister 'The historical development of international legal measures to suppress illicit drug trafficking' (1997) 30 *CILSA* 1.

140 *Prince v President, Cape Law Society* 2002 (2) SA 794 (CC) 824, 837, 851, 858–9.

141 J Dugard 'Terrorism and international law: Consensus at last?' in E Yakpo and T Boumedra *Liber Amicorum Mohammed Bedjaoui* (1999) 159; Symposium 'A war against terrorism: What role for international law? US and European perspectives' (2003) 14 *European Journal of International Law* 209; J Dugard 'The problem of the definition of terrorism in international law' in P Eden and T O'Donnell (eds) *September 11, 2001: A Turning Point in International and Domestic Law?* (2005) 187; H Duffy *The 'War on Terror' and the Framework of International Law* 2 ed (2015); T Becker *Terrorism and the State* (2006); B Saul *Defining Terrorism in International Law* (2008); B Saul *Terrorism* (2010); G Nesi (ed) *International Co-operation in Counter Terrorism* (2005).

142 The text of the Convention appears in MO Hudson *International Legislation* vol 7, no 499 (1941).

143 J Dugard 'International terrorism and the just war' (1977) 12 *Stanford Journal of International Studies* 21.

and ships was criminalised. The taking of hostages[144] and acts of terrorism aimed at diplomats[145] were also prohibited by treaty.

The end of the Cold War and decolonisation resulted in a radical change of attitude towards international terrorism. The international community no longer showed concern for the causes of terrorism, and the motives of the terrorist, but with the most effective ways of eliminating terrorism. Resolutions of the General Assembly of the United Nations contrasted sharply with the deliberate inaction of this body in the early 1970s. In 1994, in its Declaration on Measures to Eliminate International Terrorism,[146] the General Assembly declared that member states of the United Nations condemn all acts of terrorism wherever and by whomever committed, and that

> criminal acts intended or calculated to provoke a state of terror in the general public, a group of persons or particular persons for political purposes are in any circumstances unjustifiable, whatever the considerations of a political, philosophical, ideological, racial, ethnic, religious or any other nature that may be invoked to justify them.

This new mood resulted in the adoption, in 1997, of the International Convention for the Suppression of Terrorist Bombings,[147] which comes close to a general anti-terrorism convention. This Convention makes it an offence for any person to unlawfully and intentionally place or detonate an explosive device in a place of public use, a state or government facility, or a transportation system with intent to cause serious bodily injury or extensive destruction.[148] A state party is required to exercise criminal jurisdiction over such crimes under domestic law on grounds of territoriality and active nationality and may do so on grounds of passive personality or where 'the offence is committed in an attempt to compel that state to do or abstain from doing any act'.[149] As with similar conventions, a state party is obliged to exercise jurisdiction over an offender 'present' in its territory when it fails to extradite such person.[150] Unlike other conventions, this Convention expressly declares that acts prohibited by this Convention cannot be justified on political, philosophical, ideological, racial, ethnic or religious grounds,[151] and

144 International Convention against the Taking of Hostages (1979) 18 *ILM* 1456.

145 Convention on the Prevention and Punishment of Crimes against Internationally Protected Persons, including Diplomatic Agents (1974) 13 *ILM* 43.

146 Annex to Resolution 49/60 of 9 December 1994.

147 (1998) 37 *ILM* 249.

148 Article 2.

149 Article 6.

150 Article 6(4).

151 Article 5.

that the acts cannot be categorised as political crimes for the purpose of extradition.[152]

This Convention was followed, in 2000, by the International Convention for the Suppression of the Financing of Terrorism,[153] which makes it an offence to fund terrorist offences as defined in the Conventions discussed above, and in 2005 by the International Convention for the Suppression of Acts of Nuclear Terrorism, which makes it an offence to possess nuclear material or make a nuclear device with intent to cause death, bodily injury or damage to the environment. The year 1998 saw the adoption of the Rome Statute of the International Criminal Court, but, despite proposals that this Court be given jurisdiction over terrorist offences, the Court's jurisdiction was confined to aggression (defined only in 2010), genocide, crimes against humanity and war crimes.

The Sixth (Legal) Committee of the General Assembly has, since 2000, been engaged in the task of drafting a comprehensive convention on terrorism which will embrace all forms of terrorism. The outbreak of violence in the Middle East in 2000 has, however, resurrected the debate over the legitimacy of measures taken by those engaged in resistance to military occupation and this has prevented the adoption of such a treaty. This has not, however, deterred regional organisations from adopting general conventions aimed at the suppression of terrorism.[154] In 1999 the Organization of African Unity adopted a Convention of the Prevention and Combating of Terrorism, which defines terrorism in broad terms but provides that

> the struggle waged by peoples in accordance with the principles of international law for their liberation or self-determination, including armed struggle against colonialism, occupation, aggression and domination by foreign forces shall not be considered as terrorist acts.[155]

Since 11 September 2001, when massive acts of terrorism were perpetrated in New York and Washington DC, the combating of international terrorism has become the principal concern of the international community. The Security Council of the United Nations has adopted a number of resolutions, notably resolutions 1373 (2001)

152 Article 11.

153 (2000) 39 *ILM* 268. Over 170 states are party to this Convention.

154 For the texts of such instruments, see United Nations *International Instruments related to the Prevention and Suppression of International Terrorism* (2008); Inter-American Convention against Terrorism (2003) 42 *ILM* 19; Council framework decision of the European Union, 13 June 2002, *Official Journal* L 164 vol 45 (22 June 2002).

155 *International Instruments* (n 154) 222 article 3. See on the adoption and implementation of terrorism conventions in Africa, A Thomashausen 'The "war on terror" in Africa in international law and state practice' (2007) 32 *SAYIL* 85.

and 1566 (2004), under Chapter VII of the Charter, calling upon states to prevent and suppress the financing of terrorist acts, to refrain from providing support to groups involved in terrorist acts, to prevent the commission of terrorist acts, to become parties to international treaties on terrorism, and to enact and enforce domestic legislation to suppress international terrorism. Resolution 1566, adopted on 8 October 2004, is particularly important. It calls upon states to co-operate fully in the fight against terrorism 'on the basis of the principle of extradite or prosecute' (*aut dedere aut judicare*) and attempts a comprehensive definition of terrorism in a paragraph that:

> *Recalls* that criminal acts, including against civilians, committed with the intent to cause death or serious bodily injury, or taking of hostages, with the purpose to provoke a state of terror in the general public or in a group of persons or particular persons, intimidate a population or compel a government or an international organization to do or to abstain from doing any act, which constitute offences within the scope of and as defined in the international conventions and protocols relating to terrorism, are under no circumstances justifiable by considerations of a political, philosophical, ideological, racial, ethnic, religious or other similar nature, and *calls upon* all States to prevent such acts and, if not prevented, to ensure that such acts are punished by penalties consistent with their grave nature.

The Security Council, in Resolution 2253 (2015), recently reaffirmed that member states must hold accountable those responsible for committing, organising or supporting terrorist acts, 'in accordance with their obligations under international law, in order to find and bring to justice, extradite, or prosecute any person who supports, facilitates, participates or attempts to participate in the direct or indirect financing of activities conducted by ISIL, Al-Qaeda and associated individuals, groups, undertakings and entities'.

It is important to note that the main objective of the UN counter-terrorism instruments (being to ensure the apprehension, prosecution, or extradition of persons suspected of committing acts of terrorism) cannot be achieved without the assistance of domestic courts. That is because there are no international tribunals with jurisdictional competence to try acts of terrorism as defined in the counter-terrorism instruments.[156] Accordingly, the duty to bring perpetrators of terrorist acts to justice falls solely on domestic courts.[157]

[156] The Rome Statute of the International Criminal Court, 1998, which created the ICC, would only be applicable to acts of terrorism when committed as a crime against humanity (that is on a widespread or systematic basis).

[157] A Sambei, A du Plessis and M Polaine *Counter-terrorism Law and Practice: An International Handbook* (2009) 2.44 at 35–6. See also the discussion of the Constitutional Court's decision in *S v Okah* below.

No doubt for that reason, in the *Madan* case, the Supreme Court of India was of the view that terrorist violence '*affects society as a whole by terrorising and disturbing the harmony of society*'.[158] Similarly, the Argentinian Supreme Court in the *Clavel* case defined terrorism as a 'crime *jus gentium*, the prosecution of which is not in the exclusive interest of the state injured by it, but ... benefits, ultimately, all civilised nations who are therefore obligated to co-operate in the global fight against terrorism'.[159]

In the light of the above treaties and state practice, it is difficult to resist the conclusion that terrorism is today a crime under customary international law. This was confirmed by an Interlocutory Decision of the Appeals Chamber of the Special Tribunal for Lebanon on 16 February 2011, which ruled that treaties, UN resolutions, and the legislative and judicial practice of states

> evince the formation of a general *opinio juris* in the international community, accompanied by practice consistent with such *opinio*, to the effect that a customary rule of international law regarding the international crime of terrorism, at least *in time of peace*, has indeed emerged. This customary rule requires the following three key elements: (i) the perpetration of a criminal act (such as murder, kidnapping, hostage-taking, arson and so on), or threatening such an act; (ii) the intent to spread fear among the population (which would generally entail the creation of public danger) or directly or indirectly coerce a national or international authority to take some action, or to refrain from taking it; (iii) when the act involves a transnational element.[160]

3 The Protection of Constitutional Democracy against Terrorist and Related Activities Act 33 of 2004

In 2004 the South African Parliament enacted the Protection of Constitutional Democracy against Terrorist and Related Activities Act[161] ('the Act') to give effect to South Africa's obligations in respect of the suppression of terrorism under United Nations conventions, Security Council resolutions and the OAU Convention on the Prevention and Combating of Terrorism of 1999.[162] The Constitutional Court has explained that the purposes of the Act are to create an offence of terrorism that gives effect to international instruments, to extend South African courts' jurisdiction over these offences

[158] *Madan Singh v State of Bihar* (2004) INSC 225 (2 April 2004).

[159] *Enrique Lautaro Arancibia Clavel* 259 (Arg Supreme Court) (2004) 51–2.

[160] Case No STL-11-01/1 para 85. See, too, para 111. For criticisms of this decision, see the Symposium in (2011) 24 *Leiden Journal of International Law* 651–700.

[161] Act 33 of 2004. See A Cachalia's critical comments on this Act in 'Counter-terrorism and international cooperation against terrorism—An elusive goal: A South African perspective' (2010) 26 *SAJHR* 510.

[162] The preamble makes this clear in setting out all the treaties which South Africa is obliged to enforce.

wherever they are committed, to fulfil South Africa's general duty to combat terrorism, and to fulfil South Africa's specific duty to bring to trial perpetrators of terrorism, wherever perpetrated, whom it does not extradite. In *S v Okah*, the Constitutional Court held that '[t]he general duty to combat terrorism is broad. It commands a reading of the Act that enables South Africa to participate, as a member of the international community, in the fight against an international and transnational phenomenon'.[163]

The Act distinguishes between offences constituting 'terrorist activity' and 'convention offences', and confers wide jurisdictional powers on South African courts in respect of both types of terrorism. Although the Act primarily seeks to give effect to United Nations conventions and resolutions, its loyalty to the OAU (now the African Union (AU)) Convention is apparent in its concern to exclude those engaged in wars of national liberation from the ambit of terrorism.

Section 1(1) provides a broad definition of 'terrorist activity', divided into *(a)* the acts constituting terrorism, *(b)* the intent required, and *(c)* the motivation of the perpetrator. 'Terrorist activity' covers any act committed in or outside South Africa which involves the 'systematic repeated or arbitrary use of violence' by any means; 'systematic, repeated or arbitrary' release into the environment of dangerous or harmful substances; endangering the life of any person or persons; causing serious bodily injury to or killing any person or persons; causing serious risk to the health or safety of the public; causing the destruction of or substantial damage to any property, natural resource or environmental or cultural heritage; causing any major economic loss; acts designed to disrupt seriously any essential service; or acts that create a 'serious public emergency situation or a general insurrection in the Republic'. The activity must be intended, or by its nature and context reasonably be regarded as being intended, to:

(i) threaten the unity and territorial integrity of the Republic;
(ii) intimidate, or to induce or cause feelings of insecurity within, the public, or a segment of the public, with regard to its security, including its economic security, or to induce, cause or spread feelings of terror, fear or panic in a civilian population; or
(iii) unduly compel, intimidate, force, coerce, induce or cause a person, a government, the general public or a segment of the public, or a domestic or an international organisation or body or intergovernmental organisation or body, to do or to abstain or refrain from doing any act, or to adopt or abandon a particular standpoint, or to act in accordance with certain principles,

[163] *S v Okah* 2018 (1) SACR 492 (CC) paras 35–7.

whether the public or the person, government, body, or organisation or institution referred to in subparagraphs (ii) or (iii), as the case may be, is inside or outside the Republic . . . .

Finally, the activity must be committed 'for the purpose of the advancement of an individual or collective political, religious, ideological or philosophical motive, objective, cause or undertaking'.

Any person who engages in 'terrorist activity' is guilty of the offence of terrorism (s 2), and any person who commits any act that furthers terrorist activities is guilty of the offence of association with or connection with terrorist activities (s 3).

The offence of terrorism is more widely defined than in any of the international instruments that it seeks to incorporate. It could, for instance, include political protest meetings or industrial action. Hence, s 1(3) excludes from the definition of 'terrorist activity' acts that seriously disrupt essential services or cause major economic loss which are 'committed in pursuance of any advocacy, protest, dissent or industrial action', and which are not intended to cause harm of the kind resulting from any other act constituting a 'terrorist activity'.

Sections 4 to 10 incorporate anti-terrorism conventions to which South Africa is, or intends to become, a party, into municipal law. The International Convention on the Suppression of the Financing of Terrorism (s 4), the International Convention of the Suppression of Terrorist Bombings (s 5), the Protocol for the Suppression of Unlawful Acts against the Safety of Fixed Platforms on the Continental Shelf (s 6), the International Convention against the Taking of Hostages (s 7), the Convention on the Prevention and Punishment of Crimes against Internationally Protected Persons including Diplomatic Agents (s 8), the conventions dealing with the hijacking and sabotage of aircraft (s 9), and the Convention for the Suppression of Unlawful Acts against the Safety of Maritime Navigation (s 10) are incorporated into South African law. Section 9 fails fully to incorporate The Hague[164] and Montreal Conventions[165] on aviation terrorism, and no attempt is made to incorporate the conventions on nuclear terrorism. This is because these conventions are incorporated into South African law by the Civil Aviation Act of 2009[166] and the Nuclear Energy Act of 1999.[167] This is confirmed by the definition of 'convention offence' in s 1 of the Act.

[164] Convention for the Suppression of Unlawful Seizure of Aircraft (n 127).

[165] Convention for the Suppression of Unlawful Acts against the Safety of Civil Aviation (n 131).

[166] Act 13 of 2009.

[167] Section 56(1)*(h)* of Act 46 of 1999, read with ss 34A and 56A inserted by the Schedule to the Protection of Constitutional Democracy against Terrorist and Related Activities Act 33 of 2004 (s 27).

Wide jurisdictional powers are conferred on South African courts in respect of offences under the Act. Jurisdiction may be exercised on grounds of territoriality, active personality, passive personality, protection of the state, or 'any other basis recognized by law'.[168] A person who is 'present' in South Africa may be arrested and subjected to criminal proceedings or extradition if a South African court has jurisdiction or 'any court in a foreign state may have jurisdiction'.[169]

In *S v Okah* the Constitutional Court was faced with the issue of whether the Act confers extraterritorial jurisdiction on South African courts to try alleged offences (beyond the financing of an offence) that occurred outside of South Africa.[170] Okah had been convicted by a South African court of planning and financing various bombings that occurred in Nigeria. In Okah's appeal, the Supreme Court of Appeal held that the Act gives South African courts extraterritorial jurisdiction over the financing of terrorist activities only. Jurisdiction is not extended extraterritorially for the crime of terrorism itself.[171] It therefore overruled the High Court's finding that Okah was guilty of terrorism—he was only found guilty of financing terrorism.

The Constitutional Court rejected the SCA's finding. It held that the proper meaning of 'specified offence', over which South African courts are given extraterritorial jurisdiction, includes the terrorism activity itself and is not limited to the financing thereof. This was because, among other reasons, limiting extraterritorial jurisdiction to financing alone would create absurd instances in which it would be possible to 'prosecute the banker, but not the bomber'.[172] The Constitutional Court held:

> While it is true that territoriality has been the traditional basis on which courts establish jurisdiction, international and South African jurisprudence recognise other methods of asserting jurisdiction. Comity concerns fall away in cases where there is no infringement on the sovereignty of another state. This is particularly true when the crimes over which a court asserts jurisdiction have an international dimension. We should not, through a narrow interpretation of section 15(1), mistakenly perpetuate an historical disinclination to extra-territoriality.[173]

The President is required to give notice by proclamation in the *Gazette* of any Security Council resolution adopted under Chapter VII

[168] Section 15(1)*(b)* and *(c)* of Act 33 of 2004.

[169] Section 15(5) to (8) of Act 33 of 2004.

[170] *S v Okah* (n 163).

[171] The Supreme Court of Appeal's judgment is reported as *S v Okah* 2017 (1) SACR 1 (SCA).

[172] *S v Okah* (n 163) para 26.

[173] Ibid para 43.

of the Charter that identifies a terrorist 'entity' against which states are obliged to take specified actions. Such a proclamation must be tabled in Parliament for consideration and action.[174]

United Nations anti-terrorism conventions and Security Council resolutions make no allowance by way of exception for the actions of national liberation movements. The OAU (now AU) Convention on the Prevention and Combating of Terrorism of 1999, to which South Africa is a party, does, however, exclude from the ambit of terrorism acts committed in the course of 'the struggle waged by peoples in accordance with the principles of international law for their liberation or self-determination, including armed struggle against colonialism, occupation, aggression and domination by foreign forces'. This has clearly put the South African law-maker in a quandary as the Act seeks to accommodate both United Nations conventions and the OAU (now AU) Convention.

First, the Act's preamble asserts that the activities of national liberation movements are exempt from the prohibition on terrorism. Then, s 1(4) provides:

> Notwithstanding any provision of this Act or any other law, any act committed during a struggle waged by peoples, including any action during an armed struggle, in the exercise or furtherance of their legitimate right to national liberation, self-determination and independence against colonialism, or occupation or aggression or domination by alien or foreign forces, in accordance with the principles of international law, especially international humanitarian law, including the purposes and principles of the Charter of the United Nations and the Declaration on Principles of International Law concerning Friendly Relations and Cooperation among States in accordance with the said Charter, shall not, for any reason, including for purposes of prosecution or extradition, be considered as a terrorist activity, as defined in subsection (1).

That the law-maker was aware that the above exemption is highly controversial is demonstrated by s 1(5), which provides:

> Notwithstanding any provision in any other law, and *subject to subsection (4)*, a political philosophical, ideological, racial, ethnic, religious or any similar motive, shall not be considered for any reason, including for purposes of prosecution or extradition, to be a justifiable defence in respect of an offence of which the definition of terrorist activity forms an integral part [emphasis added].

The language of the latter provision is taken from provisions in the International Convention for the Suppression of Terrorist Bombings[175] and the International Convention for the Suppression of the

[174] Sections 25 and 26.
[175] Article 5.

Financing of Terrorism,[176] which are designed to ensure that a political or ideological motive—*including commitment to national liberation*—shall not be a justifiable defence to terrorism. In *Okah*, the Constitutional Court explained:

> Section 1(4) of the Act exempts certain acts from the definition of terrorism, and, thus, prosecution under the Act. To fall under section 1(4), the following criteria must all be met: (1) the act must have taken place within the context of a 'struggle waged by peoples'; (2) that struggle must be 'in the exercise or furtherance of their legitimate right to national liberation, self-determination and independence against colonialism, or occupation or aggression or domination by alien or foreign forces'; and (3) the act must be taken 'in accordance with the principles of international law, especially international humanitarian law'.

On the facts of *Okah*, the bombings orchestrated by Okah violated principles of international humanitarian law. They did not distinguish between combatants and civilians. So Okah's conduct did not qualify for an exemption under s 1(4). That is so, for at least two further reasons (which the Constitutional Court did not consider expressly in its judgment). First, according to articles 25 and 103 of the UN Charter, member states are obliged to carry out Security Council decisions even if they conflict with any 'other international agreements'.[177] Accordingly, even if s 1(4) of the Act is to be understood as modelled on the AU Terrorism Convention,[178] the Security Council resolutions must be understood as imposing overriding obligations on South Africa. Secondly, the AU Terrorism Convention's—and s 1(4)'s—internal limitation, which requires that the struggle 'must be waged in accordance with the principles of international law', means that any acts that are committed contrary to the Security Council's resolutions on terrorism are in any event not in accordance with those principles.

Whether the subjection of sub-s (5) to sub-s (4) of s 1 is effective is placed in doubt by the definition of 'terrorist activity', which in *(c)* requires that 'terrorist activity' be committed for the advancement of a 'political, religious, ideological or philosophical motive, objective, cause or undertaking'. The amendment to the Extradition Act of 1962,[179] contained in the schedule to the Protection of Constitutional

[176] Article 6.

[177] *Questions of Interpretation and Application of the 1971 Montreal Convention arising from the Aerial Incident at Lockerbie (Libyan Arab Jamahiriya v United States of America), Provisional Measures* (order of 14 April 1992) 1992 ICJ Reports 114 para 42.

[178] Article 3(1) of which provides that 'the struggle waged by peoples in accordance with the principles of international law for their liberation or self-determination, including armed struggle against colonialism, occupation, aggression and domination by foreign forces shall not be considered as terrorist acts'.

[179] Act 67 of 1962.

Democracy against Terrorist and Related Activities Act 33 of 2004,[180] adds to the confusion on this subject as it provides that extradition may not be refused 'on the sole ground that it concerns a political offence' in the case of offences under ss 4 and 5 of Act 33 of 2004—that is, offences under the Conventions on Terrorist Bombings and the Financing of Terrorism. At least in this case, there is no exemption for the political offender engaged in a struggle for national liberation.

The exemption of those engaged in a struggle for national liberation from the criminalisation of terrorism cannot be reconciled with the prevailing international approach to terrorism reflected in international conventions and Security Council resolutions. This is made clear, as shown above, in Security Council resolution 1566 of 8 October 2004, which stresses that terrorist acts 'are under no circumstances justifiable by considerations of a political, philosophical, ideological, racial, ethnic, religious or other similar nature'—and which has been reiterated by the Security Council in Resolution 2322 (2016). In its preamble, it reaffirms 'that terrorism in all its forms and manifestations constitutes one of the most serious threats to peace and security' and that any acts of terrorism are criminal and unjustifiable regardless of the motivations, whenever, whoever and by whomsoever committed. Section 233 of the Constitution makes clear that any interpretation of the Act's s 1(4) exemption must be consistent with international law, which includes Security Council resolutions. These resolutions make no allowance by way of exception for the actions of national liberation movements.

The Protection of Constitutional Democracy against Terrorist and Related Activities Act contains provisions dealing with the institution of proceedings, the penalties to be imposed, evidence, investigating powers and preservation orders. These provisions fall largely within the field of domestic law and are consequently not considered.

[180] Section 27.

CHAPTER 10

International Criminal Courts, the International Criminal Court, and South Africa's Implementation of the Rome Statute

Max du Plessis and Eshed Cohen

INTERNATIONAL CRIMINAL COURTS

The idea of a permanent international criminal court was on the international agenda for much of the last century.[1] After World War I, unsuccessful attempts were made to bring the German Emperor to trial before an international tribunal[2] and, later, to try Turks responsible for the genocide of Armenians before a tribunal designated by the Allied powers.[3] In 1937, following the assassination in 1934 of King Alexander of Yugoslavia by Croatian nationalists in Marseilles, treaties were drafted to outlaw international terrorism[4] and to provide for the trial of terrorists before an international tribunal,[5] but states lost interest in this venture as war approached: no state ratified the treaty for an international criminal court and only one ratified the treaty outlawing international terrorism. The aggressive war conducted by Germany, and the atrocities committed by its officials

[1] For an account of this history, see B Ferencz *An International Criminal Court: A Step towards World Peace—A Documentary History and Analysis* (1980).

[2] Article 227 of the Treaty of Versailles (*UK Treaty Series No 1* (1919)) provided for the trial of the Emperor for 'a supreme offence against international morality and the sanctity of treaties' before a special tribunal composed of five judges appointed by the United Kingdom, the United States, France, Italy and Japan. The attempt to bring the Emperor to trial was thwarted when he was granted asylum by the Netherlands.

[3] The 'unratified' Treaty of Sevres of 1920 (*UK Treaty Series No 11* (1920)) provided for the surrender by Turkey of persons 'responsible for the massacres committed during the continuance of the state of war on territory which formed part of the Turkish Empire' (article 230) but in 1923, the Treaty of Lausanne (*UK Treaty Series No 16* (1923), Part VIII) granted amnesty to these persons. See VN Adrian 'Genocide as a problem of national and international law: The World War I Armenian Case and its contemporary legal ramifications' (1989) 14 *Yale Journal of International Law* 221.

[4] See Chapter 9.

[5] Convention for the Creation of an International Criminal Court, in MO Hudson *International Legislation* vol 7 no 500 (1941).

and soldiers during World War II, provided the requisite impetus for the creation by Allied powers of an ad hoc international military tribunal at Nuremberg in 1945.[6] (A similar tribunal was constituted in Tokyo[7] in respect of crimes committed by Japan's leaders.) The establishment of the Nuremberg and Tokyo international military tribunals, which tried the principal leaders of the Nazi and Japanese regimes after World War II for crimes against the peace, war crimes and crimes against humanity, was a natural culmination of the pre-war debate over an international criminal court. Inevitably, however, there was criticism of the fact that these tribunals were established by the victors to try the vanquished.[8] The United Nations was nonetheless energised by the work of these tribunals to adopt, on 9 December 1948, a resolution mandating the International Law Commission to begin work on the draft statute of an international criminal court.[9] The enthusiasm generated by Nuremberg and Tokyo for a permanent court in the immediate post-war period was, however, abandoned during the Cold War. Even the consensus between East and West over apartheid failed to produce the court that had been proposed to try apartheid's criminals in the late 1970s.[10]

By the 1980s, a wide range of factors combined to strengthen the case for the establishment of an international criminal court. These included: the increase in the number of international crimes provided by treaties outlawing hijacking, hostage-taking, torture, seizure of ships on the high seas and attacks on diplomats; the emergence of powerful drug cartels capable of subverting the judicial systems of weak states; and above all, the conviction that international law had progressed sufficiently to enable it to condemn individuals before an international criminal court for violating international norms. The final contributing factor was the end of the Cold War—it was thereafter possible for a more unified United Nations to renew its interest in a permanent international criminal court.

[6] See T Taylor *The Anatomy of the Nuremberg Trials* (1992). The judgment of the Nuremberg Tribunal is published at (1947) 41 *AJIL* 172.

[7] AC Brackman *The Other Nuremberg: The Untold Story of the Tokyo War Crimes Trials* (1989).

[8] For an insightful overview of the criticisms of the Nuremberg trials, see R Overy 'The Nuremberg trials: International law in the making' in P Sands (ed) *From Nuremberg to The Hague—The Future of International Criminal Justice* (2003) 1.

[9] See WA Schabas *An Introduction to the International Criminal Court* (2004) 8.

[10] In 1979 the United Nations Human Rights Commission instructed Professor M Cherif Bassiouni to draft a statute for an international court to try offenders under the 1973 International Convention on the Suppression and Punishment of the Crime of Apartheid. A statute was drafted but no action was taken on the project: see M Cherif Bassiouni *A Draft International Criminal Code and Draft Statute for an International Criminal Tribunal* (1987) 10–11. See further on the crime of apartheid, Chapter 9.

The idea of a permanent criminal court for the world was placed back on the international agenda through a proposal by Latin American states who envisaged such a court as their last resort to prosecute international drug-traffickers.[11]

Thereafter, the International Law Commission was directed by the UN General Assembly to consider the drafting of a statute for an international criminal court. The Commission prepared a draft statute for such a court in the early 1990s, and by 1994, a formal Draft Statute for an International Criminal Tribunal had been adopted by the ILC and forwarded to the General Assembly for consideration.[12] During the time that the Commission was preparing the Draft Statute, events compelled the creation of a court on an ad hoc basis to respond to the atrocities that were being committed in the former Yugoslavia. That tribunal, the International Criminal Tribunal for the Former Yugoslavia (ICTY), was established by the Security Council in 1993 and mandated to prosecute persons responsible for serious violations of international humanitarian law committed in the territory of the former Yugoslavia since 1991.[13] Then, in November 1994, and acting on a request from Rwanda, the Security Council voted to create a second ad hoc tribunal (ICTR), charged with the prosecution of genocide and other serious violations of international humanitarian law committed in Rwanda and in neighbouring countries during 1994.[14] Since they share statutes that are virtually identical, the two tribunals are close relatives.[15]

The Rwanda and Yugoslav tribunals furthered the widespread belief that a permanent international criminal court was desirable and practical. When delegates convened in Rome in 1998 to draft a

[11] See K Kittichaisaree *International Criminal Law* (2001) 27.

[12] See J Crawford 'The ILC's draft statute for an International Criminal Tribunal' (1994) 88 *AJIL* 140 and 'The ILC adopts a statute for an International Criminal Court' (1995) 89 *AJIL* 404.

[13] SC Resolution 808 of 22 February 1993 and SC Resolution 827 of 25 May 1993. For detailed accounts of the creation of the ICTY, see M Cherif Bassiouni and P Manikas *The Law of the International Criminal Tribunal for the Former Yugoslavia* (1996) Chapters I–III. See, too, V Morris and M Scharf *An Insider's Guide to the International Criminal Tribunal for the Former Yugoslavia: A Documentary History and Analysis* (1995).

[14] SC Resolution 955 of 8 November 1994. For details, see C Scheltema and W van der Wolf (eds) *The International Tribunal for Rwanda: Facts, Cases, Documents* (1999).

[15] The ICTR closed on 31 December 2015, and the ICTY closed on 31 December 2017. The essential functions of both tribunals have been preserved through a small and temporary structure (the so-called 'Residual Mechanism') which has the power, inter alia, to prosecute the most senior persons indicted by the Tribunal after the completion of their mandates, and persons who interfere with the administration of justice. See Security Council Resolution 1966 (2010) available at http://www.icty.org/en/press/security-council-adopts-resolution-international-residual-mechanism-criminal-tribunals-irmct.

statute for a permanent international criminal court, the tribunals could provide a reassuring model of how such a court might function. In addition to the example which the tribunals provided of a working criminal justice system, the innovative international criminal law jurisprudence that they had produced—such as the progressive view that crimes against humanity could be committed in peacetime,[16] and the finding that war crimes could be committed during an internal armed conflict[17]—fed into the debates at Rome, and eventually came to be reflected in the Rome Statute.[18]

The Statute of the International Criminal Court was adopted on 17 July 1998 by an overwhelming majority of the states attending the Rome Conference. The conference was specifically organised to secure agreement on a treaty for the establishment of a permanent international criminal tribunal. After five weeks of intense negotiations, 120 countries voted to adopt the treaty. Only seven countries voted against it (including China, Israel, Iraq and the United States) and 21 abstained. By the 31 December 2000 deadline, 139 states had signed the treaty. The treaty came into force upon 60 ratifications. Sixty-six countries—six more than the threshold needed to establish the court—had ratified the treaty by 11 April 2002. This was much sooner than was generally expected. To date, the Rome Statute has been ratified by 124 states[19] and a significant proportion—33—are African.[20] South Africa remains a party to the Statute, although of late its continued membership of the ICC is in doubt (see discussion

[16] At Nuremberg, 'crimes against humanity' were prosecuted as crimes associated with one of the other crimes within the Nuremberg Tribunal's jurisdiction, namely, war crimes and crimes against peace. Since Nuremberg, several variants of crimes against humanity have developed, not all with a nexus to armed conflict. (The most prominent example is genocide—the most egregious form of crime against humanity—which the Genocide Convention of 1948 defines as an offence which can be committed in times of peace and war.) The requirement of a nexus with armed conflict was firmly done away with by the Yugoslavia Tribunal in its celebrated decision in *Prosecutor v Tadic* Case No IT-94-1-AR72 see n 81 below (2 October 1995), (1996) 35 *ILM* 32. Article 7 of the Rome Statute codifies this evolution of crimes against humanity as being crimes committed either in times of peace or war.

[17] See the *Tadic* case (n 16). Interesting developments have also come out of the Rwanda Tribunal's decisions. For instance, in *Prosecutor v Akayesu (Judgment)* ICTR-96-4-Y T Ch 1 (2 September 1998) the Rwanda Tribunal came to the enlightened conclusion that rape could constitute an act of genocide.

[18] Schabas (n 9) 12.

[19] For the latest ratification status, see www.iccnow.org.

[20] For status of African ratification, see https://asp.icc-cpi.int/en_menus/asp/states%20parties/african%20states/Pages/african%20states.aspx. For recent African discontent with the ICC, see discussion further below.

further below). One significant absentee amongst the ratifications is that of the United States.[21]

Along with the ad hoc international criminal tribunals for Rwanda and Yugoslavia, together with, inter alia, the Special Court for Sierra Leone,[22] the International Criminal Court stands as a working model of international criminal justice—one in which an international criminal forum applies rules of international law, is staffed by independent prosecutors and judges, and holds persons individually responsible for crimes against humanity and war crimes, after allowing them a fair trial.

THE INTERNATIONAL CRIMINAL COURT

The International Criminal Court (ICC) is situated in The Hague, in the Netherlands. The ICC is an independent international organisation, and is not part of the United Nations system.[23] The judges for

[21] There is vast literature critiquing the failure by the United States to join the Court. For selected reading, see MP Scharf 'The United States and the International Criminal Court: The ICC's jurisdiction over nationals of non-party states—A critique of the US position' (2001) *Law and Contemporary Problems* 64; M du Plessis 'Seeking an *International* International Criminal Court—Some reflections on the United States opposition to the ICC' (2002) 15 *SACJ* 301; WA Schabas 'United States hostility to the International Criminal Court: It's all about the Security Council' (2004) 15 *EJIL* 710.

[22] On 2 November 2002, the Special Court for Sierra Leone was established pursuant to Security Council Resolution 1315. This tribunal is the result of an agreement between the UN and Sierra Leone to try 'those who bear the greatest responsibility' for crimes against humanity and disrupting the peace process. The Court is a hybrid, staffed by local and international personnel, and has an international prosecutor. Its temporal jurisdiction to prosecute international crimes under its Statute stretches back to crimes committed since 30 November 1996. The case that has attracted the most attention is the trial of former Liberian President Charles Taylor. Taylor was indicted on 7 March 2003 for crimes against humanity, war crimes, and other serious violations of international humanitarian law. These crimes include terrorising the civilian population and collective punishments, unlawful killings, sexual violence, physical violence, use of child soldiers, abductions, forced labour and looting. Due to concerns about regional security if the trial was held in Sierra Leone, the Special Court arranged for the trial to be held at The Hague in the Netherlands. On 26 April 2012 the Trial Chamber found Taylor guilty on all 11 counts, on the modes of liability of planning of crimes and for aiding and abetting of crimes committed by rebel forces in Sierra Leone. On 30 May 2012 the former Liberian president was given a single sentence of 50 years in prison. The conviction and sentence were upheld by the Appeals Chamber. See *Prosecutor v Charles Ghankay Taylor* SCSL-03-01-A (Appeal Chamber Decision) available at http://www.rscsl.org/Taylor.html.

[23] There is a wealth of literature on the ICC. See, for example, A Cassese et al (eds) *The Rome Statute of the International Criminal Court: A Commentary* 3 vols (2002); O Triffterer (ed) *Commentary on the Rome Statute of the International Criminal Court* 3 ed (2016); WA Schabas *The International Criminal Court: A Commentary on the Rome Statute* 2 ed (2016). A number of other books deal with the ICC in the context of general

the Court were sworn in on 11 March 2003 at the Court's inaugural session.[24] In 2018, of the 20 judges, four are from Africa, including the judge president. The current prosecutor is Fatou Bensouda from The Gambia.

The ICC is divided into an Appeals Division, a Trial Division and a Pre-Trial Chamber Division.[25] The Office of the Prosecutor is responsible for receiving and examining referrals and substantiated information on alleged crimes, and conducting investigations and prosecutions before the Court.[26] The Office of the Prosecutor is headed by the prosecutor, who has full authority over the management and administration of the office.[27] In the interests of efficiency and consistency, the prosecutor relies extensively on the registry for administrative services. The registry is responsible for the non-judicial aspects of the administration and servicing of the Court, without prejudice to the functions and powers of the prosecutor. The registry is headed by the registrar, who is elected by the judges and who exercises her functions under the authority of the president of the Court.[28] The work of the Court is overseen by an Assembly of States Parties, which provides management oversight, considers and decides the budget for the Court, conducts elections, and performs other functions. The Assembly meets at least once a year.[29]

ICC CRIMES

The Court can take up only the most serious crimes of concern to the international community as a whole—genocide, crimes against humanity and war crimes—all of which are defined in the Statute.[30] Aggression also falls within the competence of the ICC but an accepted definition of this crime has only recently been added to the

international criminal law: see, for example, A Cassese (ed) *The Oxford Companion to International Criminal Justice* (2010); C Stahn and L van den Herik (eds) *Future Perspectives on International Criminal Justice* (2010); G Boas et al *The International Criminal Law Practitioner* 3 vols (2008–2011); R Cryer et al *An Introduction to International Criminal Law and Procedure* 3 ed (2014).

[24] Judges are elected for terms of office of nine years by the Assembly of States Parties to the Rome Statute, and are not eligible for re-election.

[25] Articles 34 and 39 of the Rome Statute.

[26] Article 42(1). A summary of the submissions received by the Office of the Prosecutor is publicly available. See the ICC's website.

[27] Article 42(2).

[28] Article 43.

[29] Article 112.

[30] Articles 5–8.

Statute.[31] Treaty crimes (such as terrorism or drug trafficking) do not fall within the ICC's jurisdiction but, like the crime of aggression, may be added later after consideration by a review conference.[32] For the purposes of interpreting and applying the definitions of crimes found in the Rome Statute, reference must also be made to the Elements of Crimes, a 50-page document adopted in June 2000 by the Preparatory Commission for the International Criminal Court.[33]

1 Genocide

Genocide is understood as involving the intentional mass destruction of entire groups, or members of a group as members of that group.[34] The first criminal prosecution of 'genocide' took place at the International Military Tribunal at Nuremberg in 1947, when the Nazi leaders were tried for 'crimes against humanity' under the Nuremberg Charter.[35] It took almost half a century, with the establishment of the ICTY and ICTR in 1993/4, before 'genocide' came before an international tribunal once again to be prosecuted at an international level.[36]

[31] Article 5(2). See further, WA Schabas 'The unfinished work of defining aggression: How many times must the cannonballs fly before they are forever banned?' in D McGoldrick, P Rowe and E Donnelly *The Permanent International Criminal Court—Legal and Policy Issues* (2004) 123.

[32] Article 123(1). Consequently, the ICC may only prosecute terrorist acts if the particular acts meet the definitional requirements of the current crimes, the most likely example being crimes against humanity.

[33] See the Finalized Draft Text of the Elements of Crimes (PCNICC/2000/INF/3/Add.2).

[34] The crime of genocide has been committed throughout history, the pre-eminent example being the mass killing of Jews by the Nazis during World War II, and more recently, the slaughter of Tutsis by Hutus in Rwanda. The term 'genocide' is a combination of the Latin words *genus* (kind, type, race) and *cide* (to kill) and was first coined by Raphael Lemkin writing in response to the events of the Second World War. See R Lemkin *Axis Rule in Occupied Europe* (1944) at 79–95; R Lemkin 'Genocide as a crime under international law' (1947) 41 *AJIL* 145. For an historical account of the origins of genocide, see P Sands *East West Street: On the Origins of Genocide and Crimes against Humanity* (2016).

[35] There was no reference to the crime of genocide in the Charter or the judgment of the tribunal, even though it did appear in the indictment and was referred to by the prosecution from time to time.

[36] See Kittichaisaree (n 11) 67. There was at least one *national* prosecution of genocide prior to the ICTY and ICTR's existence; namely, the prosecution of Eichmann before the District Court of Jerusalem (1968). Eichmann was tried for crimes against the Jewish people, an offence under Israeli law which incorporated all the elements of the definition of genocide (see A Cassese *International Criminal Law* (2003) 97).

Article 6 of the Rome Statute, following article IV of the Genocide Convention, defines the underlying conduct that, along with genocidal intent, constitutes the crime of genocide:

(a) killing members of a national or ethnic, racial, or religious group (meaning their 'murder', ie intentional, voluntary killing);[37]

(b) causing serious bodily or mental harm to members of the group (these terms 'do not necessarily mean that the harm is permanent or irremediable');[38]

(c) deliberately inflicting on the group conditions of life calculated to bring about its physical destruction (including, inter alia, 'subjecting a group of people to a subsistence diet, systematic expulsion from homes and the reduction of essential medical services below minimum requirement[s]');[39]

(d) imposing measures intended to prevent birth within the group (such measures consist of 'sexual mutilation, the practice of sterilization, forced birth control [and the] separation of the sexes and prohibition of marriage');[40] or

(e) forcibly transferring children of the group to another group.

The victim of the crime of genocide is the group itself and not the individual.[41] The definition of genocide in the Rome Statute provides that genocide is any one of the enumerated acts committed with intent to destroy, in whole or in part, a national, ethnical, racial or religious group, as such. This chapeau is known as genocidal intent.

The common criterion in the four types of groups protected under the Genocide Convention (national, ethnic, racial or religious) is that 'membership in such groups would seem to be normally not challengeable by its members, who belong to it automatically, by birth, in a continuous and often irremediable manner'.[42] The 'victim' group therefore does not extend to what might be called 'political' and 'social' groups. In respect of the Rome Statute, the drafters have evinced a clear intention to limit the groups to the four identified by the Genocide Convention. The idea of including a 'cultural group' in the ICC Statute was rejected at the Rome Conference. The drafters

[37] *Prosecutor v Akayesu (Judgment)* ICTR-96-4-T TCh 1 (2 September 1998) paras 500–1.

[38] *Akayesu* paras 502–4.

[39] *Akayesu* paras 505–6.

[40] *Akayesu* para 507.

[41] Kittichaisaree (n 11) at 69.

[42] *Akayesu* (n 37) para 511.

were quick to point out that the Genocide Convention was aimed at preventing physical destruction of a group, not cultural destruction.[43]

Genocide is known as the crime of all crimes,[44] as evidenced in the high threshold set for the mental element required for proof of genocide. In the *Jelisic Case*, the ICTY explained that 'it is in fact the *mens rea* which gives genocide its speciality and distinguishes it from an ordinary crime and other crimes against international humanitarian law'.[45] Both customary and conventional definitions of genocide require a prosecutor to establish a form of aggravated criminal intention, or specific intent (*dolus specialis*) in addition to the criminal intent accompanying the underlying offence. The accused must commit the underlying offence with the intent to produce the result charged; that is, the intent to destroy, in whole or in part, a national, ethnic, racial or religious group, as such. Genocide is therefore a crime perpetrated against a 'depersonalised' victim, and carried out for no other reason than that he or she is a member of a specific national, ethnic, racial or religious group.[46]

The intention must be to destroy a group 'in whole or in part'. Genocide can thus be committed through the destruction of a large number of the group (a quantitative attempt at destruction) or the destruction of a limited number of the group who are targeted because of the potential impact of their destruction on the survival of

[43] The same view has been expressed by the ICTY Trial Chamber in its ruling in the *Krstic Case (Judgment)* IT-98-33-T (2 August 2001), (2001) 40 *ILM* 1346. There it confirmed that 'customary international law limits the definition of genocide to those acts seeking the physical or biological destruction of all or part of a group', with the result that an 'enterprise attacking only the cultural or sociological characteristics of a human group in order to annihilate these elements which give to that group its own identity distinct from the rest of the community would not fall under the definition of genocide' (para 580). Genocide appears therefore to be limited to material destruction of a group, rather than the destruction of the national, linguistic, religious, cultural or other identity of that group. It is for this reason that the Australian courts have held that degradation of aboriginal people through confiscation of traditional lands cannot amount to genocide by the responsible Ministers, since the confiscation was not aimed at material destruction of the group as such (see G Robertson *Crimes against Humanity* (2000) at 230).

[44] *The Prosecutor v Jean Kambanda (Judgement and Sentence)* ICTR 97-23-S, International Criminal Tribunal for Rwanda (ICTR) 4 September 1998 para 16.

[45] *Jelisic (Appeal)* ICTY 5 July 2001, IT-95-10-A, (2001) 40 *ILM* 1295 para 66; H Vest 'A structure-based concept of genocidal intent' (2007) 5 *JICJ* 781 at 783.

[46] The specific intention of destroying all or part of the group must have been formed by the accused prior to the commission of the genocidal act. Put differently, the underlying genocidal act (killing, causing serious bodily or mental harm etc) should be done to further the genocidal goal of ensuring the group's destruction (see *Kayishema and Ruzindana (Judgment)*, ICTR-96-1-T, T Ch (21 May 1999) para 91).

the group as a whole (a qualitative attempt at destruction). An example of the latter would be the act of destroying young, fertile women in a group who are of childbearing age. The element of specific intent in the context of genocide 'may, in the absence of direct explicit evidence, be inferred from a number of facts and circumstances, such as the general context, the perpetration of other culpable acts systematically directed against the same group, the scale of the atrocities committed, the systematic targeting of victims on account of their membership of a particular group, or the repetition of destructive and discriminatory acts'.[47] In *Akayesu*, for example, the ICTR Trial Chamber found that the accused had the requisite *mens rea* to commit genocide, and had exhibited that aggravated criminal intention through, inter alia, the systematic rape of Tutsi women. According to the ICTR, the systematic rape of Tutsi women was part of the campaign to mobilise the Hutus against the Tutsi, and the sexual violence was aimed at destroying the spirit, will to live, or will to procreate, of the Tutsi group.[48]

2 Crimes against humanity

The term 'crime against humanity' was first used in its contemporary sense to condemn the atrocities committed by the Turkish forces against their own Greek and Armenian subjects during World War I in 1915. Although no prosecutions ultimately took place, the immediate response of the Allied powers to the massacres was for France, the UK and Russia to proclaim enthusiastically that all members of the Turkish government would be held responsible together with its agents for the 'crimes against humanity and civilization'.[49] At Nuremberg, the idea of a crime against humanity arose again. The crime was the brainchild of Hersch Lauterpacht, a professor of international law in England.[50] Through his influence, the Nuremberg and Tokyo tribunals utilised the technical term 'crime against humanity' to secure, for the first time, the prosecution of individuals for crimes that, by their nature, offended 'humaneness' and thereby became the concern of the international community.[51]

[47] *Jelisic (Appeal)* (n 45) para 47. See also the decision of the ICTR Appeals Chamber in *Kayishema and Ruzindana Case* ICTR Appeals Chamber, Case No ICTR 95-1-A (1 June 2001).

[48] *Akayesu* (n 37) para 732.

[49] See n 3.

[50] See Sands (n 34).

[51] This use of the idea of crimes against humanity—to initiate prosecutions against individuals for atrocities committed within their own territories—led to a measure of discomfort for the Allied powers, who were concerned about the ramifications for their treatment of minorities within their own countries and colonies. As a result, the

At Nuremberg, the notion of crimes against humanity was limited to those acts that occurred only during an international armed conflict.[52] Today, in international criminal law, the nexus between crimes against humanity and war has disappeared, and customary international law prohibits crimes against humanity whether they are committed in times of war or peace.[53]

Crimes against humanity are prohibited under article 7 of the Rome Statute. The term 'crimes against humanity', under the Statute, covers actions that have a common set of features:[54]

(a) The offences are particularly egregious in that they constitute a serious attack on human dignity or a grave degradation or humiliation of one or more human beings.

(b) They are not isolated or sporadic events but are acts that form part of governmental policy, or of a widespread or systematic practice of atrocities tolerated, condoned or acquiesced in by a government or *de facto* authority.

(c) Their prohibition extends regardless of whether they are perpetrated in times of war or peace.

(d) Under the Rome Statute (and the Statutes of the ICTY and the ICTR) the victims of the crimes are civilians or, in the case of crimes committed during armed conflict, persons who do not take part (or no longer take part) in armed hostilities.

Nuremberg notion of 'crime against humanity' had an important rider attached to it: a crime against humanity was committed if it was *associated or linked* with one of the other crimes under the Tribunal's jurisdiction, being war crimes and crimes against the peace (aggression). What this meant is that there had to be a link between crimes against humanity and *international armed conflict*. In part, that is why the Nuremberg trials are spoken of as 'war crimes trials'—since the crimes against humanity there could only be tried if they were attendant on either a crime against peace or war crimes (see Schabas (n 9) 42). See also M Koskenniemi 'Between impunity and show trials' (2002) 6 *Max Planck UNYB* 1.

[52] However, within weeks of the Nuremberg judgment the United Nations expressed its dissatisfaction with this limited scope of crimes against humanity when the General Assembly asserted in the Genocide Convention of 1948 that genocide (the most egregious form of crimes against humanity) could be committed during times of war *and* peace. On that and other developments that gradually led to the link between crimes against humanity and war being dropped, see A Cassese 'Crimes against humanity' in A Cassese et al (eds) *The International Criminal Court: A Commentary* vol I (2002) 73.

[53] Cassese (n 52). The most recent developments relate to the ICTR and ICTY. The establishment of the ICTR—to punish those guilty of crimes committed in an internal conflict—in itself reiterates the point that crimes against humanity do not have to be attendant on an international armed conflict. See, too, the ICTY Appeals Chamber decision in *Prosecutor v Tadic* (1997) 105 ILR 453 para 141.

[54] Cassese (n 52) 64.

The specific acts or classes of offences that make up crimes against humanity under the Rome Statute are those commonly associated with egregious abuses of human rights and include: murder;[55] extermination[56] (involving mass or large-scale killing,[57] or intentional infliction of conditions of life; inter alia, the deprivation of food and medicine calculated to bring about the destruction of part of a population);[58] enslavement;[59] deportation or forcible transfer of population[60] (being the 'forced displacement of the persons concerned by expulsion or other coercive acts from the area in which they are lawfully present, without grounds permitted under international law');[61] imprisonment or other severe deprivation of physical liberty in violation of fundamental rules of international law;[62] torture[63] (being 'the intentional infliction of severe pain or suffering, whether physical or mental, upon a person in the custody or under the control of the accused');[64] sexual violence (which includes 'rape, sexual slavery, enforced prostitution, forced pregnancy, enforced sterilization, or any other form of sexual violence of comparable gravity');[65] persecution[66] (being 'the intentional and severe deprivation of fundamental rights contrary to international law by reason of the identity of the group or collectivity');[67] enforced disappearance[68] (being 'the arrest, detention or abduction of persons by, or with the authorisation, support or acquiescence of, a State or a political organisation, followed by a refusal to acknowledge that deprivation of freedom or to give information on the fate or whereabouts of those persons, with the intention of removing them from the protection of the law for a prolonged period of time');[69] the crime of apartheid[70] (which includes 'inhumane acts of a character similar to [other crimes

[55] Article 7(1)(a).

[56] Article 7(1)(b).

[57] In *Vasiljevic* (ICTY Trial Chamber, 29 November 2002) the Tribunal held that for criminal responsibility to attach for extermination, the accused must have been responsible for a 'large number of deaths'. See also D Mundis 'Current developments at the ad hoc International Criminal Tribunals' (2003) 1 *JICJ* 520 at 521.

[58] Article 7(2)(b).

[59] Article 7(1)(c).

[60] Article 7(1)(d).

[61] Article 7(2)(d)

[62] Article 7(1)(e).

[63] Article 7(1)(f).

[64] Article 7(2)(e).

[65] Article 7(1)(g).

[66] Article 7(1)(h).

[67] Article 7(2)(g).

[68] Article 7(1)(i).

[69] Article 7(2)(i).

[70] Article 7(1)(j).

against humanity], committed in the context of an institutionalized regime of systematic oppression and domination by one racial group over any other racial group or groups and committed with the intention of maintaining the regime';[71] and other inhumane acts[72] that are acts 'of a similar character to [other crimes against humanity] intentionally causing great suffering, or serious injury to body or to mental or physical health').[73]

The Rome Statute then adds a chapeau to these underlying acts to elevate them to the level of crimes against humanity. This chapeau is that any conduct listed in article 7(1) of the Rome Statute must be committed as part of a widespread or systematic attack directed against any civilian population, with knowledge of the attack. An '"[a]ttack directed against any civilian population" means a course of conduct involving the multiple commission of acts referred to in [article 7(1)] against any civilian population, pursuant to or in furtherance of a State or organisational policy to commit such attack'.[74]

The first requirement of the chapeau is that the act complained of must be part of a widespread or systematic attack. Article 7(2) provides elucidation when it says that an attack is 'a course of conduct involving the multiple commission of acts referred to in [article 7(1)] against any civilian population, pursuant to or in furtherance of a state or organizational policy to commit such attack'. The Elements of Crimes say that '"policy to commit such attack" requires that the State or organization actively promote or encourage such an attack against a civilian population'.[75] There is an ongoing debate in international law on whether the requirement of a state or organisational policy to commit an attack in the Rome Statute is at odds with customary international law.[76] The second requirement is that the attack must be directed against a *civilian population*. This distinguishes it from many war crimes which may be targeted at both civilians and combatants, and the requirement also distinguishes the Rome Statute from customary international law, which accepts that a crime against humanity may be committed against civilians and military personnel. Lastly, a crime against humanity cannot be committed unless a specific form of intention is present. Article 7(1)

[71] Article 7(2)(h).

[72] Article 7(1)(k).

[73] Ibid.

[74] Article 7(2)(a).

[75] This can be via a 'deliberate failure to take action'. See fn 6 of the Elements of Crimes.

[76] See, for example, G Werle *Principles of International Criminal Law* 3 ed (2014) 299–300.

provides that a 'crime against humanity' means any of the enumerated acts when committed as part of a widespread or systematic attack directed against any civilian population, 'with knowledge of the attack'. This requirement amounts to a form of specific intent, which sets another threshold that must be crossed before a particular offence can be regarded as a crime against humanity.[77]

3 War crimes

War crimes have an ancient lineage and historically belligerent states took it upon themselves to determine those acts committed in time of war for which they would try the combatants or civilians belonging to the enemy. Of the core crimes in the Rome Statute, 'war crimes' were the first to have been prosecuted at international law. German soldiers were convicted of 'acts in violation of the laws and customs of war' at Leipzig in the early 1920s, pursuant to articles 228 and 230 of the Treaty of Versailles.[78]

Generally speaking, war crimes are crimes committed in violation of international humanitarian law applicable during armed conflicts. The sources of international humanitarian law are vast, and are broadly divided into two categories of substantive rules—'the law of The Hague'[79] and 'the law of Geneva'[80]—and which constitute the

[77] Schabas (n 9) 45; Judgment pursuant to Article 74 of the Statute ICC-01/05-01/08-3343 (21 March 2016): *The Prosecutor v Jean-Pierre Bemba Gombo* paras 166–9; *Prosecutor v Dragoljub Kunarac* ICTY Appeals Chamber, Case No IT-96-23 & 23/1 (12 August 2002) para 102.
Clearly, each of the underlying acts committed (in terms of the greater event—the attack) require their own form of intent. However, overall, these acts must be committed with a specific intention that is associated with the main event—the attack that gives the individual acts their 'crime against humanity' character.

[78] In articles 228–30 of the Treaty of Versailles, Germany recognised the jurisdiction of the Allied powers to try persons accused of violating the laws and customs of war as well as the obligation to hand over such accused persons to the Allies for that purpose. None of these provisions was implemented due to later German pressure. Instead, Germany proposed to try its own nationals accused of war crimes before the Supreme Court of Leipzig, a proposal which produced mock trials which resulted in only 13 convictions out of 901 cases, and with insignificant sentences which ultimately were not executed. See G Abi-Saab 'The concept of "war crimes"' in S Yee and W Tieya (eds) *International Law in the Post-Cold War Area* (2001) 99–118.

[79] The 'law of The Hague' is made up of the Hague Conventions of 1868, 1899 and 1907, which, generally speaking, set out rules regarding the various categories of lawful combatants, and which regulate the means and methods of warfare in respect of those combatants. The Hague Rules also deal with the treatment of persons who do not take part in armed hostilities or who no longer take part in them, but in this respect The Hague Rules have been supplanted by the Geneva Rules, which cover this aspect of humanitarian law in more detail. See further Chapter 25 below on Humanitarian Law.

[80] The 'law of Geneva', so called because it comprises the four Geneva Conventions of 1949 plus the two Additional Protocols thereto of 1977, regulates the

rules concerning behaviour that is prohibited in the case of an armed conflict.

Drawing extensively from these existing sources of humanitarian law, the drafters of the Rome Statute in article 8 have set out an elaborate 'codification' of the rules concerning behaviour that is prohibited in situations of armed conflict. Various preconditions for a war crimes prosecution are built into the Statute. First, in order to constitute a violation of article 8 of the Rome Statute, there must be a nexus between the criminal conduct and the armed conflict. War crimes may be committed during either international or internal armed conflicts,[81] with states parties to the Rome Statute having accepted that responsibility for war crimes can be founded during times of civil war. Secondly, the Rome Statute directs the Court's attention 'in particular' to those war crimes that are 'committed as part of a plan or policy or as part of a large-scale commission of such crimes'.[82] This so-called 'non-threshold threshold' built into article 8 ensures that two jurisdictional triggers—(1) that the war crime is committed as part of a plan or policy, and (2) that the war crime is committed alongside other war crimes on a large scale—should ordinarily be met before the ICC will be seized with the case. Thirdly, article 30 of the Statute provides that to found criminal responsibility for a war crime requires intent and knowledge: intent in relation to the conduct, namely, that the person means to engage in the conduct;

treatment of persons who do not take part in the armed hostilities (such as civilians, the wounded and the sick) and those who used to take part but no longer do (such as prisoners of war). An exception here is the Third Geneva Convention, which, in addition to the focus on treatment of persons no longer involved in the conflict, also regulates the various classes of lawful combatants and thereby updates The Hague Rules. The Hague Rules have been further updated by the First Additional Protocol to the Geneva Convention of 1977, which deals with the means and methods of combat, with a particular emphasis on sparing civilians as far as is possible in an armed conflict. See further Chapter 25 below on humanitarian law.

[81] *Tadic (Appeal) (Decision on the defence motion for Interlocutory Appeal on Jurisdiction)* ICTY Appeals Chamber, case No IT-94-1-AR 72 (2 October 1995) cf n 16 paras 96–136. Until this decision, the scope of international responsibility for war crimes was the subject of much confusion. The two major sources of humanitarian law—war crimes codified in the Geneva Conventions and their Protocols, which addressed the protection of the victims of armed conflict from 'grave breaches', and war crimes as understood under The Hague Convention, which focused on the methods and materials of warfare—did not appear to extend international criminal responsibility to those who committed the prohibited acts during times of internal armed conflicts. In *Tadic*, the ICTY Appeals Chamber stated that international criminal responsibility for war crimes included acts committed during internal armed conflict; that is, during times of civil war.

[82] Article 8(1).

and knowledge in relation to the consequence, namely, that the person means to cause that consequence or is aware that it will occur in the ordinary course of events.

Drawing on the Geneva Conventions and international humanitarian law, the Statute adopts a four-part division to its elucidation of 'war crimes'—the first two divisions cover war crimes committed during an international armed conflict; the last two divisions cover war crimes committed during an internal armed conflict.

(a) War crimes in times of international armed conflict

Grave breaches of the Geneva Conventions (article 8(2)(a))

Article 8(2)(a) of the Rome Statute provides that any of the following acts ('grave breaches') committed during an international armed conflict against persons or property protected under the provisions of the relevant Geneva Convention will amount to a war crime:

- wilful killing;
- torture or inhuman treatment, including biological experiments;
- wilfully causing great suffering, or serious injury to body or health;
- extensive destruction and appropriation of property, not justified by military necessity and carried out unlawfully and wantonly;
- compelling a prisoner of war or other protected person to serve in the forces of a hostile power;
- wilfully depriving a prisoner of war or other protected person of the rights of fair and regular trials;
- unlawful deportation or transfer or unlawful confinement;
- taking of hostages.

The persons protected by article 8(2)(a) are combatants who are considered *hors de combat* because of injury, shipwreck or illness, or because they have been taken as prisoners of war, and civilians. The notion of 'protected property' is not defined in any of the Geneva Conventions but is generally regarded as property found in territories occupied by foreign forces. Such property, which would include medical units and establishments, medical transports, and hospital ships, amongst others, may not be destroyed except in cases of military necessity.[83]

Other serious violations of the laws and customs applicable in international armed conflict, within the established framework of international law (article 8 (2)(b))

Article 8(2)(b) sets out the second category of war crimes and which are limited to international armed conflict. The 'serious violations of

[83] Kittichaisaree (n 11) 41; Cryer et al (n 23) cited 2014 above 302.

the laws and customs applicable in international armed conflict' are generally drawn from the law of The Hague. Unlike the focus of the grave breaches crimes under article 8(2)(a), which aim to protect the innocent victims of war or those who are *hors de combat*, the focus of the crimes under article 8(2)(b) is on the combatants themselves. These crimes are a continuation of ancient rules of chivalry reflecting a code of conduct amongst warriors.[84] As a general overview, article 8(2)(b) of the Rome Statute includes prohibitions on attacks against the civilian population,[85] attacks against civilian objects,[86] as well as attacks that violate the principle of proportionality[87] and attacks against undefended places.[88] Civilians are also protected against 'misuse', for instance, the use of civilians or protected persons as a means to render certain points or areas immune from military operations.[89] The starvation of civilians as a method of warfare is prohibited, as is any attack against objects indispensable to the survival of the civilian population.[90] The 'destruction of property' is outlawed in that the destruction or seizing of the enemy's property is considered a war crime unless such destruction or seizure is imperatively demanded by the necessities of war.[91] The improper use of signs and perfidy is rendered a war crime,[92] and there is a prohibition on killing or wounding persons who are *hors de combat*.[93] Lastly, there is a prohibition placed on declaring that no quarter will

[84] Schabas (n 9) 60; Cryer (n 23) 303–8.

[85] Article 8(2)(b)(i).

[86] Article 8(2)(b)(ii).

[87] Article 8(2)(b)(iii), which prohibits an attack that is intentionally launched in the knowledge that it will cause incidental loss of life or injury to civilians, or damage to civilian objects, or widespread, long-term and severe damage to the natural environment which would be clearly excessive in relation to the concrete and direct overall military advantage anticipated.

[88] Article 8(2)(b)(v), such undefended places being defined as towns, villages, dwellings or buildings that are undefended and that are not military objectives.

[89] Article 8(2)(b)(xxiii), which prohibits utilising the presence of a civilian or other protected person to render certain points, areas or military forces immune from military operations.

[90] Article 8(2)(b)(xxv): intentionally starving civilians 'as a method of warfare by depriving them of objects indispensable to their survival, including wilfully impeding relief supplies as provided for under the Geneva Conventions'.

[91] Article 8(2)(b)(xiii).

[92] Article 8(2)(b)(vii): 'Making improper use of a flag of truce, of the flag or of the military insignia and uniform of the enemy or of the United Nations, as well as of the distinctive emblems of the Geneva Conventions, resulting in death or serious personal injury'.

[93] Article 8(2)(b)(vi).

be given; that is, ordering that there shall be no survivors, threatening an adversary therewith, or conducting hostilities on this basis.[94]

Several of the provisions of article 8(2)(b) deal with prohibited weapons—for example, poison or poisoned weapons,[95] poisonous gases and all analogous liquids, materials or devices,[96] and dum-dum bullets[97]—and render their use a war crime.

In addition to the provisions reflecting The Hague Rules, there are some 'new crimes' under para (b) and which have now been codified by the drafters at Rome. They cover, for instance, the protection of humanitarian and peacekeeping missions[98] and prohibit environmental damage.[99] Another new war crime under the Statute is the conscription or enlistment of children under the age of 15 into the national armed forces or to use them to participate actively in hostilities.[100] Another development relates to 'sexual crimes'. In terms of article 8(2)(b)(xxii) it is a war crime to commit rape, sexual slavery, enforced prostitution, forced pregnancy,[101] enforced sterilisation or any other form of sexual violence also constituting a grave breach of the Geneva Conventions.[102] While the terms rape and enforced prostitution already appear in the Fourth Geneva Convention and Protocol I of 1977, the outlawing of 'sexual slavery', 'forced pregnancy' and 'enforced sterilization' are essentially new crimes.

(b) War crimes in times of non-international armed conflict

Violations of Common Article 3 of the Geneva Conventions (Rome Statute article 8(2)(c) and (d))

The criminal acts proscribed by this section are the Common Article 3[103] crimes of violence to life and person, in particular murder of all

[94] Article 8(2)(b)(xii), as read with article 40 of Additional Protocol I of 1977.

[95] Article 8(2)(b)(xvii).

[96] Article 8(2)(b)(xviii).

[97] Article 8(2)(b)(xix).

[98] See article 8(2)(b)(iii), which prohibits intentionally directing attacks against personnel, installations, material, units or vehicles involved in a humanitarian assistance or peacekeeping mission in accordance with the Charter of the United Nations, as long as they are entitled to the protection given to civilians or civilian objects under the international law of armed conflict.

[99] Article 8(2)(b)(iv).

[100] Article 8(2)(b)(xxvi).

[101] Which is defined in article 7, para 2(f) as 'the unlawful confinement of a woman forcibly made pregnant, with the intent of affecting the ethnic composition of any population or carrying out other grave violations of international law'.

[102] Article 8(2)(b)(xxii).

[103] Common Article 3 to the Geneva Conventions of 1949 proscribes the following acts, even when committed during non-international armed conflicts: '(a) violence to life and person, in particular murder of all kinds, mutilation, cruel treatment and

kinds, mutilation, cruel treatment and torture; committing outrages upon personal dignity, in particular humiliating and degrading treatment; taking of hostages; and the passing of sentences and the carrying out of executions without previous judgment pronounced by a regularly constituted court affording all judicial guarantees that are generally recognised as indispensable. The prohibited acts listed under article 8(2)(c) of the Rome Statute, like the 'grave breaches' in article 8(2)(a), are acts that are committed against 'protected persons'. Such 'protected persons' are described in article 8(2)(c) as 'persons taking no active part in the hostilities [civilians], including members of armed forces who have laid down their arms and those placed *hors de combat* by sickness, wounds, detention or any other cause'.

These standards represent a 'common denominator of core human rights'[104] that must be respected by those engaged in hostilities, whether they are engaged in an international or non-international armed conflict. While the prohibitions apply to armed conflicts 'not of an international character', the ICC Statute provides that these protections do not extend 'to situations of internal disturbances and tensions, such as riots, isolated and sporadic acts of violence or other acts of a similar nature'.[105] Internal disturbances and acts of terrorism that do not amount to an armed conflict are therefore not subject to the laws of armed conflict at all, although the state (but not the rebels) will be subject to the provisions of any human rights treaties to which the state is a party.

Other serious violations of the laws and customs applicable in armed conflicts not of an international nature (Rome Statute article 8(2)(e))

Protocol II of 1977 to the Geneva Conventions largely serves as the inspiration for the prohibitions contained in article 8(2)(e) of the Rome Statute.[106] The article prohibits attacks against the civilian population,[107] 'killing or wounding treacherously a combatant adversary',[108] declaring that no quarter will be given,[109] or destroying or seizing the property of an adversary unless such destruction or

torture; (b) taking of hostages; (c) outrages upon personal dignity, in particular humiliating and degrading treatment; (d) the passing of sentences and the carrying out of executions without previous judgment pronounced by a regularly constituted court, affording all the judicial guarantees which are recognized as indispensable by civilized peoples.'

[104] Schabas (n 9) 65; Cryer (n 23) 276; Cassese et al *International Criminal Law: Cases and Commentary* (2011) 12.

[105] Article 8(2)(d).

[106] See further, on Protocol II, Chapter 25 below on Humanitarian Law.

[107] Article 8(2)(e)(i).

[108] Article 8(2)(e)(ix).

[109] Article 8(2)(e)(x).

seizure is imperatively demanded by the necessities of the conflict,[110] and 'pillaging a town or place, even when taken by assault'.[111]

The following special protections are included under article 8(2)(e): intentional attacks directed against buildings, materials, medical units and transport, and personnel using the distinctive emblems of the Geneva Conventions in conformity with international law, are prohibited;[112] intentional attacks directed against personnel, installations, material, units or vehicles involved in a humanitarian assistance or peacekeeping mission in accordance with the Charter of the United Nations is prohibited so long as they are entitled to the protection given to civilians or civilian objects under the international law of armed conflict;[113] and intentional attacks against buildings dedicated to religion, education, art, science or charitable purposes, historic monuments, hospitals and places where the sick and wounded are collected are prohibited, provided they are not military objectives.

In addition, the following provisions serve to protect against violations of human rights more generally. Article 8(2)(e)(xi) makes it a war crime to subject persons who are in the power of another party to the conflict to physical mutilation or to medical or scientific experiments of any kind which are neither justified by the medical, dental or hospital treatment of the person concerned nor carried out in his or her interest, and which cause death to or seriously endanger the health of such person or persons. Article 8(2)(e)(vi) prohibits rape, sexual slavery, enforced prostitution, forced pregnancy, enforced sterilisation, and any other form of sexual violence also constituting a serious violation of Common Article 3 to the Geneva Conventions, while article 8(2)(e)(vii) outlaws conscripting or enlisting children under the age of 15 years into armed forces or groups or using them to participate actively in hostilities. Article 8(2)(e)(viii) makes it a war crime to order the displacement of the civilian population for reasons related to the conflict, unless the security of the civilians involved or imperative military reasons so demand.

The prohibitions contained in article 8(2)(e) of the ICC Statute apply to armed conflicts not of an international character but not to 'situations of internal disturbances and tensions, such as riots, isolated and sporadic acts of violence or other acts of a similar nature'.[114]

110 Article 8(2)(e)(xii).
111 Article 8(2)(e)(v).
112 Article 8(2)(e)(ii).
113 Article 8(2)(e)(iii).
114 See the limitation contained in article 8(2)(f).

4 Aggression

Although aggression was dubbed the 'supreme international crime' by the Nuremberg Tribunal as far back as 1946,[115] there has only recently been agreement on the definition of the crime of aggression for the purposes of the Rome Statute.

Article 5 of the Rome Statute lists the crime of aggression as one of the core crimes under the Court's jurisdiction. However, in contrast to the other three crimes (genocide, crimes against humanity and war crimes) the Court remained unable to exercise jurisdiction over the crime of aggression as the Statute did not define the crime or set out jurisdictional conditions.[116]

After two weeks of intense debate and years of preparatory work, on 11 June 2010, the Review Conference of the Rome Statute (held in Kampala, Uganda) adopted by consensus amendments to the Rome Statute which include a definition of the crime of aggression.[117] Far more controversially, the Conference also established the conditions under which the Court is empowered to exercise jurisdiction in respect of the crime.[118]

On 14 December 2017, the ICC's jurisdiction over the crime of aggression was activated as of 17 July 2018[119] for ICC member states which have ratified or accepted the amendment to the Rome Statute. It also stipulates that the ICC will not have jurisdiction over ICC member states, or their nationals, that have not ratified or accepted these amendments in the case of a state referral or *proprio motu* (initiated by the ICC prosecutor) investigation.

The Kampala amendment is a complex legal provision which is further complicated by numerous 'understandings' that accompanied its adoption.[120] The 'understandings' of Kampala are purportedly designed to enable the Court to 'dismiss frivolous, or politically

[115] Judgment of the International Military Tribunal for the Trial of German Major War Criminals, Nuremberg, 30 September and 1 October 1946.

[116] Article 5(2) of the Rome Statute prior to amendment by RC/Res 6, 11 June 2010.

[117] For a very insightful account on the negotiation process and the different proposals put forward at Kampala, see the article by the President of the Assembly of States Parties to the Rome Statute, C Wenaweser 'Reaching the Kampala compromise on aggression: The Chair's perspective' (2010) 23 *Leiden Journal of International Law* 883–7. See also N Blokker and C Kress 'A consensus agreement on the crime of aggression: Impressions' (2010) 23 *Leiden Journal of International Law* 890.

[118] RL Manson 'Identifying the rough edges of the Kampala compromise' (2010) 21(3) *Criminal Law Forum* at 417.

[119] Resolution ICC-ASP/16/Res.5, adopted at the 13th plenary meeting on 14 December 2017 by consensus of the Assembly of State Parties.

[120] A du Plessis and C Gevers 'Africa and the codification of aggression: A pyrrhic victory?' (2010) 2 *African Legal Aid Quarterly* 6.

motivated, allegations of aggression and to protect military missions based on self-defence, humanitarian intervention, or other legitimate purposes consistent with the UN Charter'.[121]

It is generally accepted that prosecuting the crime of aggression consists of two parts: the definition of the crime, and the manner in which the Court may exercise jurisdiction over it.

(a) The definition of the crime

Broadly speaking, the conduct prohibited by the crime of aggression is the unlawful and unjustified use of armed force against the territory of another state.[122] According to article 8*bis*(1), the crime of aggression contains an important inbuilt threshold, since it means the planning, preparation, initiation or execution of an act of aggression that, 'by its character, gravity and scale, constitutes a manifest violation of the Charter of the United Nations'. Furthermore, in order to qualify as the crime of aggression, the act of aggression must be performed by a person 'in a position effectively to exercise control over or to direct the political or military action of a State'.[123] This second qualification thus retains the notion, held at Nuremberg, that aggression is a 'leadership crime' that cannot be committed 'by minions and footsoldiers'.[124] An 'act of aggression' means 'the use of armed force by a State against the sovereignty, territorial integrity or political independence of another State, or in any manner inconsistent with the Charter of the United Nations'.[125] Article 8*bis*(2) then lists the various acts, following United Nations General Assembly Resolution 3314 (XXIX) of 14 December 1974, which qualify as acts of aggression:

[121] C Stahn 'The "end", the "beginning of the end" or the "end of the beginning"? Introducing debates and voices on the definition of "aggression"' (2010) 23 *Leiden Journal of International Law* 875 at 879. However, Ferencz argues that determining when military action falls under the exception 'humanitarian intervention' will be difficult since 'what looks to some as humanitarian intervention may appear to others as self-interested adventurism'; see DM Ferencz 'The crime of aggression: Some personal reflections on Kampala' (2010) 23 *Leiden Journal of International Law* 905 at 907.

[122] See also C Kress and L von Holtzendorff 'The Kampala compromise on the crime of aggression' (2010) 8 *JICJ* 1179 at 1190.

[123] Ibid.

[124] See the House of Lords opinion by Lord Bingham in *R v Jones* [2006] UKHL 16 para 16.

[125] Article 8*bis*(2).

(a) the invasion or attack by the armed forces of a state of the territory of another state, or any military occupation, however temporary, resulting from such invasion or attack, or any annexation by the use of force of the territory of another state or part thereof;
(b) bombardment by the armed forces of a state against the territory of another state or the use of any weapons by a state against the territory of another state;
(c) the blockade of the ports or coasts of a state by the armed forces of another state;
(d) an attack by the armed forces of a state on the land, sea or air forces, or marine and air fleets of another state;
(e) the use of armed forces of one state that are within the territory of another state with the agreement of the receiving state, in contravention of the conditions provided for in the agreement, or any extension of their presence in such territory beyond the termination of the agreement;
(f) the action of a state in allowing its territory, which it has placed at the disposal of another state, to be used by that other state for perpetrating an act of aggression against a third state;
(g) the sending by or on behalf of a state of armed bands, groups, irregulars or mercenaries that carry out acts of armed force against another state of such gravity as to amount to the acts listed above, or its substantial involvement therein.

Importantly, the listed acts constitute acts of aggression 'regardless of a declaration of war'. While Resolution 3314 (XXIX) is open-ended, the Court will have to interpret whether the wording of article 8*bis*(2) leaves room for the extension of aggression to other acts of aggression.[126]

Even if the particular conduct is shown to be an 'act of aggression' that accords with one of the listed items, it must meet the further requirement of constituting a 'manifest violation of the Charter of the United Nations' when examining the character, gravity and scale of the act of aggression. Criticism has been levelled at the lack of clear guidance on how criteria such as 'its character, gravity and scale' should be interpreted.[127]

Calls to extend the definition of an act of aggression to include acts by non-state entities (for example, terrorist armed groups, liberation movements and organised insurgents) against a state were not

[126] Stahn (n 121) 876.
[127] Ibid 879.

accommodated by the definition.[128] Accordingly, conduct by non-state entities cannot constitute aggression.

(b) Jurisdiction for the crime of aggression

Perhaps the most controversial issue surrounding aggression has been the jurisdictional triggers of the crime, in particular, the Security Council's role in the prosecution of the crime.[129] Indeed, there had been so much debate around the issue that the Special Working Group on the Crime of Aggression's working document, leading into the Review Conference in Kampala, proposed *six* alternative formulations of how jurisdiction would operate.[130] The version adopted in the Kampala Amendment set up two distinct schemes for the prosecution of aggression.[131] The first allows states and the ICC prosecutor to trigger a prosecution (article 15*bis*) and the second provides for the Security Council to do so (article 15*ter*).

State referral and proprio motu prosecutions

The Court may exercise jurisdiction over a crime of aggression 'arising from an act of aggression committed by a state party, unless that state party has previously declared that it does not accept such jurisdiction by lodging a declaration with the Registrar'.[132] It has been argued that this exclusion provision creates an 'asymmetry' amongst states parties since it allows a state party to displace the Court's jurisdiction over their acts committed against other states parties by making a declaration opting out of jurisdiction. However, it still affords them protection against acts of aggression committed against them by states parties which have not made such a declaration.[133] Ferencz argues that this asymmetry may potentially be at odds with the conventional treaty law notion of a 'contract among consenting states'.[134]

Accordingly, the ICC can prosecute crimes of aggression only if the offending state has consented to the Court's jurisdiction—both by signing the Rome Statute and by subsequently not entering a

[128] Stahn (n 121) 876.

[129] In particular, whether the Security Council would have the exclusive power to determine that an act of aggression had taken place for the purposes of an ensuing prosecution. For instance, article 23(2) of the ILC's 1994 Draft Statute 'suggested making ICC proceedings for the crime of aggression dependant upon a prior determination of the Security Council of an act of aggression'; see Kress and Von Holtzendorff (n 122) at 1194.

[130] Du Plessis and Gevers (n 120) 6.

[131] Blokker and Kress (n 117) 893.

[132] Article 15*bis*(4).

[133] KJ Heller 'The sadly neutered crime of aggression' available at opiniojuris.org.

[134] Ferencz (n 121) 906.

declaration vitiating the Court's jurisdiction over aggression prior to the act in question.[135] The Court also has no jurisdiction over the crime of aggression when committed by nationals of or on the territory of a state that is not a party to the Rome Statute.[136]

Earlier drafts of the amendment proposed that there must have been a 'pre-determination made, of the commission of a state act of aggression, by the United Nations Security Council'.[137] The adopted amendment does not require a Security Council determination for the Court's jurisdiction to be triggered. However, before proceeding with any investigation the prosecutor must first ascertain whether the Security Council has 'made a determination of an act of aggression committed by the State concerned'.[138] If no such determination has been made within six months of the prosecutor informing the Secretary-General of the UN of his intention to launch an investigation, the prosecutor may proceed with such an investigation 'provided that the Pre-Trial Division of the Court (with the approval of six judges) has authorised the commencement of the investigation . . . and the Security Council has not decided otherwise in accordance with article 16'.[139] Some commentators have referred to this mechanism as an 'internal filter' against 'politicized' allegations.[140]

Referral by the Security Council

Article 15*ter* of the Statute provides that the Court 'may exercise jurisdiction over the crime of aggression in accordance with article 13, paragraph (b), subject to the provisions of this article'. However, the only real proviso is the general clause in relation to aggression providing that the Court may only exercise jurisdiction after the amendment has been ratified by 30 states and not before 1 January 2017. This proviso has been satisfied. Accordingly, the Security Council's authority to refer a matter to the Court in respect of aggression will be no different to that which it has in respect of the

[135] Du Plessis and Gevers (n 120) 8. These limits of jurisdiction apply regardless of whether the prosecution of the crime concerned is occasioned by a state party referral under article 14 or the exercise of the Prosecutor's *proprio motu* powers under article 15.

[136] Article 15*bis*(5).

[137] Manson (n 118) 419.

[138] Article 15*bis*(6).

[139] Scheffer notes that the Statute is oddly silent on what the Prosecutor may do if the Security Council determines there has not been aggression: nothing in article 15*bis* 'explicitly prohibits the ICC from forging ahead even if the Security Council renders a negative determination' (D Scheffer 'The complex crime of aggression under the Rome Statute' (2010) 23 *Leiden Journal of International Law* 897 at 901).

[140] Manson (n 118) 419.

other crimes.[141] The Security Council's power to refer an act of aggression to the Court is furthermore not 'conditioned by the requirement of any state's consent to the Kampala amendments'.[142]

Few had thought that consensus in Kampala 'on a comprehensive package on the crime of aggression' was likely or even feasible.[143] Thus, notwithstanding the jurisdictional shortcomings and complexities canvassed above, the attitude of most commentators towards the amendment has been one of 'cautious optimism'.[144]

JURISDICTION

The Rome Statute strictly defines the jurisdiction of the Court. Aside from having jurisdiction only over the most serious crimes of concern to the international community, the temporal jurisdiction of the Court is limited to crimes occurring after the entry into force of the Statute on 1 July 2002.[145] For those states that become party to the Statute after 1 July 2001, the ICC has jurisdiction only over crimes committed after the entry into force of the Statute with respect to that state.[146] Thus, the Court is not a remedy for crimes of the past, which must be addressed by national or other international or hybrid initiatives.

The jurisdictional triggers for the Court to exercise its competence are set out in article 12 of the Statute. This article provides that the Court may exercise jurisdiction if: *(a)* the state where the alleged crime was committed is a party to the Statute (*territoriality*); or *(b)* the state of which the accused is a national is a party to the Statute (*nationality*). In terms of article 14 of the Statute, any state party may refer to the Court a 'situation' in which one or more crimes within the jurisdiction of the Court appear to have been committed, so long as the preconditions to the Court's exercise of jurisdiction have been met, namely, that the alleged perpetrators of the crimes are nationals of a state party or the crimes are committed on the territory of a state

[141] It may, acting under Chapter VII of the UN Charter, refer a situation in which one or more of such crimes appears to have been committed (including aggression) to the Prosecutor for investigation under article 13(b). It may also, by way of a Chapter VII resolution, defer any investigation or prosecution (including for aggression) for a period of 12 months—renewable under the same conditions—under article 16 of the Statute. For more discussion, refer to Du Plessis and Gevers (n 120).

[142] Kress and Von Holtzendorff (n 122) 1211.

[143] Wenaweser (n 117) 887.

[144] Stahn (n 121) 882.

[145] Article 11.

[146] Article 11(2).

party.[147] There has been considerable debate on whether this article allowed a state party to refer alleged crimes committed in its own territory or whether the mechanism was simply intended as an inter-state referral mechanism.[148] However, the decision of the ICC Appeals Chamber in the *Katanga Case* has now clarified that self-referrals are permissible under article 14 of the Statute and that such referrals are indeed consistent with the Rome Statute's 'object and purpose of eradicating impunity for international crimes'.[149] There have been self-referrals of situations to the ICC by Uganda, the Central African Republic, the Democratic Republic of the Congo and, most recently, Mali.[150]

The ICC prosecutor is also authorised by article 15 of the Rome Statute to initiate independent investigations on the basis of information received from any reliable source. The granting to the prosecutor of a *proprio motu* power to initiate investigations was one of the most debated issues during the negotiations of the Rome Statute. In the end, the drafters of the Statute determined that in order for the prosecutor to exercise this power, the alleged crimes must have been committed by nationals of a state party or have taken place in the territory of a state party—the preconditions set out in terms of article 12.[151]

Proposals that the principle of universal jurisdiction should apply in respect of state referrals were rejected at the Rome Conference. That being said, under the Statute, the UN Security Council is empowered to refer to the Court 'situations' in which crimes within the jurisdiction of the Court appear to have been committed.[152] The referral power is a mechanism by which the Court is accorded jurisdiction over an offender, regardless of where the offence took place and by whom it was committed, and regardless of whether the state concerned has ratified the Statute or accepted the Court's

[147] See P Kirsch and D Robinson 'Trigger mechanisms' in A Cassese et al (eds) *The Rome Statute of the International Criminal Court: A Commentary* vol 1 (2002) 623–5.

[148] P Akhavan 'Self-referrals before the International Criminal Court: Are states the villains or the victims of atrocities?' (2010) 21 *Criminal Law Forum* 103 at 103; also see WA Schabas 'First prosecutions at the International Criminal Court' (2006) 27 *HRLJ* 27; MH Arsanjani and WM Reisman 'Law-in-action of the International Criminal Court' (2005) 99 *AJIL* 385.

[149] See Akhavan (n 148) and the ICC Appeals Chamber *Prosecutor v Germain Katanga and Mathieu Ngudjolo Chui* ('Judgment on the appeal of Mr Germain Katanga against the oral decision of Trial Chamber II of 12 June 2009 on the admissibility of the case') ICC-01/04-01/07 OA8 (25 September 2009) para 78.

[150] See the discussion below of situations before the ICC for detail.

[151] See Kirsch and Robinson (n 147) 661–3.

[152] Article 13(b).

jurisdiction.[153] The Statute provides that the Council may only make such a referral by acting under Chapter VII of the United Nations Charter, which means that it must regard the events in a particular country as a threat to the peace, a breach of the peace, or an act of aggression. In determining whether a 'threat to the peace' exists, the Council will be guided by the gravity of the crimes committed, the impunity enjoyed by the crimes' perpetrators and the effectiveness or otherwise of the national jurisdiction in the prosecution of such crimes.[154] Having had regard to these factors, in March 2005 the Security Council referred the atrocities committed in the Darfur region of Sudan to the ICC for investigation.[155] Then, on 26 February 2011, the Security Council unanimously referred the situation in Libya to the ICC.[156] So far, these are the only two Security Council referrals to the Court, both involving African non-members of the ICC. The referrals have helped to heighten critical sentiment of the Court, particularly from African states[157] (as we discuss further below).

ADMISSIBILITY

The International Criminal Court is not expected to supersede national prosecutions of persons guilty of international crimes. Investigations and prosecutions under the Rome Statute are premised on the principle of 'complementarity', whereby the Court is required to rule a case inadmissible when it is being appropriately dealt with by a national justice system.[158] States parties to the Court therefore retain their right and responsibility to investigate offences committed on their territory, or where their nationals stand accused

[153] See Kirsch and Robinson (n 147) 634.

[154] See, in general, Kirsch and Robinson (n 147) 630–1.

[155] SC Resolution 1593, 31 March 2005.

[156] SC Resolution 1970, 26 February 2011. The UN Security Council referred this situation to the ICC, 'condemning the violence and use of force against civilians, deploring the gross and systematic violation of human rights, including the repression of peaceful demonstrators, expressing deep concern at the deaths of civilians, and rejecting unequivocally the incitement to hostility and violence against the civilian population made from the highest level of the Libyan government', then under Muammar Gaddafi.

[157] See further M du Plessis, T Maluwa and A O'Reilly 'Africa and the International Criminal Court' (1 July 2013) Chatham House Report, available at https://www.chathamhouse.org/sites/default/files/public/Research/International%20Law/0713pp_iccafrica.pdf.

[158] Preamble, para 10 article 17. The principle of complementarity was acknowledged by the Constitutional Court in *S v Basson* 2007 (3) SA 582 (CC) when it stated that the establishment of the ICC in no way deprives national courts of responsibility for trying international crimes (para 172).

of committing ICC crimes anywhere else in the world. The ICC will be able to step in only where a national judicial system is unwilling or unable to genuinely investigate.[159] The principle of complementarity ensures that the ICC operates as a system of international criminal justice which buttresses the national justice systems of states parties. It is 'an attempt to balance the principle of state sovereignty and the need to establish an international regime that effectively intervenes when states fail' to do so.[160]

What about amnesties that are accorded by a national state in lieu of prosecution? For centuries, successor regimes have sought to secure peace through the pardoning of their enemies, and modern history is replete with examples where a regime has granted amnesty to officials of the previous regime who were guilty of torture and crimes against humanity, rather than prosecuted them (eg Uruguay, Argentina and El Salvador). So, too, there are examples of outgoing regimes which used their last days of political power to ensure that their members were granted an official 'pardon' from prosecution before the new regime took office (eg Chile). With the advent of truth commissions, it has become possible to channel the grant of amnesty through the commission. So far, only the South African Truth and Reconciliation Commission (TRC) and the recent truth commission in East Timor have been accorded the power to grant amnesty.[161] As the South African experience demonstrates, the prospect of amnesty in exchange for truth is a good incentive to the guilty to provide

[159] See article 17 of the Rome Statute. A country may be determined to be 'unwilling' if it is clearly shielding someone from responsibility for ICC crimes, and may be deemed 'unable' if its legal system has collapsed.

[160] Schabas (n 9) 8; Cassese et al (n 104) 523; R Cryer (n 23) 153. See C Gevers 'Back to the future? Civil society, the "turn to complementarity" in Africa and some critical concerns' 2016 *Acta Juridica* 95, who argues that there is an emerging trend to prosecute international crimes domestically, and that this could be beneficial to the international criminal legal project. For the role civil society has and can play in the domestic prosecution of such crimes, see H Woolaver 'Partners in complementarity: The role of civil society in the investigation and prosecution of international crimes in South Africa' 2016 *Acta Juridica* 129. For discussion on complementarity and the important lessons from African states, see M du Plessis, A Louw and O Maunganidze 'African efforts to close the impunity gap: Lessons for complementarity from national and regional actions' Institute for Security Studies Paper, No 241 (November 2012).

[161] On the South African TRC's amnesty process, see A McDonald 'A right to truth, justice and a remedy for African victims of serious violations of international humanitarian law' (1999) 2 *Law, Democracy and Development* 164–70; P Hayner *Unspeakable Truths* (2002) 98 et seq. On the amnesty process in East Timor, see C Stahn 'Accommodating individual criminal responsibility and national reconciliation: The UN Truth Commission for East Timor' (2001) 95 *AJIL* 962–5.

detailed accounts of the acts they have committed.[162] In any event, the political reality for many transitional governments is that giving a truth commission the power of amnesty rather than criminally prosecuting past offenders is the only realistic and peaceful way in which an existing regime will be persuaded to relinquish power. Whatever the form of amnesty (whether it be granted by a truth commission or by the outgoing or ingoing government as a political act of reprieve) the question to be confronted is how such trumps to prosecution are to be dealt with by the ICC.

The Rome Statute is silent on amnesty, and commentators argue that this is because the Rome Statute was never drafted with the intention of allowing amnesty to trump the Court's jurisdiction.[163] Assuming therefore that the relevant jurisdictional requirements for an ICC prosecution are met, national amnesties granted by a truth commission or by governmental sleight of hand would not per se prevent action by the ICC.[164]

While amnesties do not in principle bar the ICC from exercising criminal jurisdiction over an individual who has been granted amnesty, the political reality is that in some instances it might be expedient or a requirement of justice not to push ahead with the prosecution of such a person. Article 53(2)(c) of the Rome Statute therefore provides the prosecutor with a discretion to refuse prosecution at the instance of a state or the Security Council where, after investigation, he concludes that 'a prosecution is not in the interests of justice, taking into account all circumstances'. Of course, the type of amnesty at issue will play an important role in the prosecutor's decision. No clear rules can be enunciated to distinguish between permissible and impermissible amnesties under international law, but it has been suggested that 'international recognition might be accorded where amnesty has been granted as part of a truth and reconciliation inquiry and each person granted amnesty has been obliged to make full disclosure of his or her criminal acts as a precondition of amnesty and the acts were politically motivated'.[165] The blanket amnesty in Chile passed by the Pinochet regime would

[162] On the importance of the TRC as truth-finder, see *Azapo v President of the Republic of South Africa* 1996 (4) SA 671 (CC) 681–5.

[163] J Dugard 'Conflicts of jurisdiction with truth commissions' in A Cassese et al (eds) *The Rome Statute of the International Criminal Court: A Commentary* (2002) 700–1.

[164] Where a criminal prosecution is instituted by a state under its domestic incorporating legislation, amnesty does not have an extraterritorial effect and the prosecuting state is not required to recognise the amnesty granted to human rights offenders by another state. See Dugard (n 163) 699.

[165] Dugard (n 163) 700.

thus not meet the required standard (in the *Pinochet* case,[166] before the House of Lords, it was not even argued by Pinochet's lawyers that his amnesty in Chile could constitute a bar to his extradition from Britain to Spain)[167] while the South African amnesties, granted by a quasi-judicial amnesty committee functioning as part of a TRC process established by a democratically elected government, may well do so.[168] It is also important to note that the nature of certain offences precludes the grant of amnesty to their perpetrators.[169] It is still open to states to grant amnesty for international crimes without violating a rule of international law, but international lawyers are largely in agreement that states are not permitted to grant amnesty for the crimes of genocide, torture and 'grave breaches' under the Geneva Convention.[170] The preamble of the Statute of the ICC, while binding only in respect of parties to it, confirms this trend when it declares that it is the duty of every state to exercise criminal jurisdiction over those responsible for international crimes.[171]

As a result, whatever form of amnesty the prosecutor is forced to consider, it is clear that she will be more disposed towards those amnesties that have been limited in terms of the nature of the offence

[166] *R v Bow Street Metropolitan Stipendiary Magistrate, Ex p Pinochet Ugarte (No 3)* (1999) 2 All ER 97 (HL).

[167] Dugard (n 163) 699.

[168] Ibid. See, too, R Mani *Beyond Retribution: Seeking Justice in the Shadows of War* (2002) 112–13.

[169] There is a vast body of literature on whether there is an international legal obligation (whether founded in customary or conventional law) obliging states to punish past crimes. See, for example, D Orentlicher 'Settling accounts: The duty to prosecute human rights violations of a prior regime' (1991) 100 *Yale Law Journal* 2537; N Roht-Arriaza 'State responsibility to investigate and prosecute grave human rights violations in international law' (1990) 78 *California Law Review* 449. See also Dugard (n 163) 697.

[170] Dugard (n 163) 699.

[171] It is noteworthy that this trend has been reflected in the mandate of East Timor's truth commission. While the mandate is clearly supportive of individualised amnesty in exchange for truth, the commission may grant 'no immunity' to persons who have committed a 'serious criminal offence', which includes the international crimes of genocide, crimes against humanity, war crimes and torture, as well as the domestic crimes of murder and sexual offences, as defined by the Indonesian Criminal Code. In 1999, pro-Indonesian militia, supported by Indonesian security forces, used violence, threats and intimidation in an attempt to coerce the East Timorese population to support continued integration in Indonesia in the UN-organised 1999 referendum on independence for the island. In apparent revenge for the overwhelming vote in favour of independence, an estimated 1000 supporters of independence were killed and hundreds of thousands fled their homes or were forcibly expelled to Indonesia. After these events, the United Nations took control of East Timor and, through its United Nations Transitional Administration in East Timor, established the Commission for Reception, Truth and Reconciliation in East Timor. See Stahn (n 161) 952–3.

(at the very least it appears that amnesty afforded for the international crimes of torture and genocide will be disregarded) and which have been granted as part of a truth and reconciliation inquiry, in which amnesty recipients have been obliged to make full disclosure of their criminal acts as a precondition of amnesty and to prove that their acts were politically motivated.[172]

SITUATIONS BEFORE THE ICC

Africa is high on the Court's agenda. All of the ICC's convictions have been for crimes committed by Africans in Africa. Ten of the eleven situations before the ICC involve African states and leaders. Of these ten, there have been two important convictions,[173] two acquittals[174] and numerous arrest warrants.

However, the ICC is currently investigating situations around the globe. The Office of the Prosecutor is investigating situations in, for example, Afghanistan, Colombia, Honduras, Iraq/the UK, Mexico, Palestine[175] and Korea.[176] Whether prosecutions will result from these investigations remains to be seen.

A situation that deserves particular mention is the one in Sudan. On 31 March 2005, the UN Security Council passed Resolution 1593, referring the prosecution of those allegedly responsible for the numerous atrocities committed in the Darfur region in Sudan to the ICC.[177] On 4 March 2009, Pre-Trial Chamber I issued a warrant of arrest against Sudanese President Omar al-Bashir for his alleged responsibility under article 25(3)(a) of the Statute for the crimes

[172] See further M du Plessis and J Ford 'Transitional justice: A future truth commission for Zimbabwe' (2009) 58 *ICLQ* 73 at 111–15; M du Plessis 'Truth and reconciliation processes: Lessons for Zimbabwe?' South African Institute of International Affairs, Report 44 (2002).

[173] *Prosecutor v Thomas Lubanga Dyilo* 'Public redacted judgment on the appeal of Mr Thomas Lubanga Dyilo against his conviction' Appeals Chamber, ICC-01/04-01/06-3121-Red (1 December 2014); and *Prosecutor v Germain Katanga* 'Judgment rendu en application de l'article 74 du Statut' Trial Chamber II, ICC-01/04-01/07-3436 (20 March 2014).

[174] *Prosecutor v Mathieu Ngudjolo Chui* 'Judgment on the prosecutor's appeal against the decision of Trial Chamber II entitled "Judgment pursuant to article 74 of the Statute"' Appeals Chamber, ICC-01/04-02/12-271-Corr (7 April 2015); *Prosecutor v Jean-Pierre Bemba Gombo* 'Judgment on the appeal of Mr Jean-Pierre Bemba Gombo against Trial Chamber III's "Judgment pursuant to article 74 of the Statute"' Appeals Chamber, ICC-01/05-01/08-3636-Red (8 June 2018).

[175] In this regard, see J Dugard 'Palestine and the ICC: Institutional failure or bias?' (2013) 11 *JICJ* 563.

[176] For a full account of the current preliminary investigations, see the 2017 report of the Office of the Prosecutor on preliminary investigations, available at https://www.icc-cpi.int/Pages/item.aspx?name=171204-rep-otp-PE.

[177] SC Resolution 1593, 31 March 2005.

against humanity and war crimes alleged by the prosecution.[178] A second warrant of arrest was then issued on 12 July 2010, which included numerous counts of genocide.[179] Al-Bashir is still at large. Various countries have failed to arrest him, including South Africa. The ICC has consistently held that failure to arrest al-Bashir is in contravention of international law.[180]

The Sudan referral has been the subject of much debate and has highlighted numerous contentious issues in international law. Chiefly, it is the first time a sitting president has been investigated for international crimes before the ICC.[181] This has raised the issue of immunity, both before the ICC and domestic tribunals. The issue of immunities is discussed later in this chapter under its own heading.

1 An international criminal court for the 'usual suspects'?[182]

International criminal law has sometimes been criticised for 'providing victors in a conflict with an opportunity to demonise their opponents, sanitise their crimes and perpetuate injustice'.[183] Similarly, since the ICC was established there have been concerns that the

[178] See Warrant of Arrest for Omar Hassan Ahmad al-Bashir, ICC-02/05-01/09 (4 March 2009) available at www.icc-cpi.int/iccdocs/doc/doc639078.pdf.

[179] *Prosecutor v Omar Hassan Ahmad al-Bashir* 'Second decision on the prosecution's application for a warrant of arrest' ICC-02/05-01/09-94 (12 July 2010).

[180] 'Decision under article 87(7) of the Rome Statute on the non-compliance by Jordan with the request by the Court for the arrest and surrender or Omar al-Bashir' Pre-Trial Chamber II, ICC-02/05-01/09-309 (11 December 2017) para 38 (*'Jordan'*); 'Decision under article 87(7) of the Rome Statute on the non-compliance by South Africa with the request by the Court for the arrest and surrender of Omar al-Bashir' Pre-Trial Chamber II, ICC-02/05-01/09-302 (6 July 2017) para 87 (*'South Africa'*); 'Decision on the cooperation of the DRC' ICC-02/05-01/09 (9 April 2014) para 26 (*'DRC'*); 'Decision on the non-compliance by the Republic of Uganda with the request to arrest and surrender Omar al-Bashir to the Court and referring the matter to the United Nations Security Council and the Assembly of State Parties to the Rome Statute' Pre-Trial Chamber II, ICC-02/05-01/09-267 (11 July 2016) para 12 (*'Uganda'*); 'Decision on the non-compliance by the Republic of Djibouti with the request to arrest and surrender Omar al-Bashir to the Court and referring the matter to the United Nations Security Council and the Assembly of the State Parties to the Rome Statute' Trial Chamber II, ICC-02/05-01/09-266 11 July 2016 para 12 (*'Djibouti'*); *Prosecutor v Omar Hassan Ahmad al-Bashir* 'Decision Pursuant to Article 87(7) of the Rome Statute on the Failure by the Republic of Malawi to Comply with the Cooperation Requests Issued by the Court with Respect to the Arrest and Surrender of Omar Hassan al-Bashir' ICC-02/05-01/09 (12 December 2011) para 40 (*'Malawi'*).

[181] S Williams and L Sherif 'The arrest warrant for President al-Bashir: Immunities of incumbent heads of state and the International Criminal Court' (2009) 14 *Journal of Conflict & Security Law* 71 at 71.

[182] M Mandel *How America Gets away with Murder: Illegal Wars, Collateral Damage and Crimes against Humanity* (2004) 207.

[183] Schabas (n 9) 1; see also CS Igwe 'The ICC's favourite customer: Africa and international criminal law' (2008) 40 *CILSA* 294 at 295.

Court has only concentrated on the 'usual suspects', with some arguing that it has illustrated a bias towards prosecuting situations in Africa while neglecting similar violations of the Rome Statute on other continents.[184] They are captured in statements to the effect that the ICC is a 'hegemonic tool of western powers which is targeting or discriminating against Africans'.[185] On the other hand, there are concerns that this 'rhetoric of condemnation' (that the ICC is 'anti-African, and merely an agent of neocolonialism or neo-imperialism') may damage the institution to such an extent that it is simply abandoned.[186]

These concerns are borne out by the reported requests by Kenya to withdraw from the Rome Statute, by Burundi's withdrawal from the ICC, and by South Africa's recent attitude towards its ICC obligations.[187] They are also evidenced in the position adopted within the African Union (AU) in response to the ICC's investigation of President al-Bashir of Sudan. While the ICC warrant of arrest for al-Bashir was welcomed by human rights organisations,[188] the AU called on the Security Council to defer the ICC's investigation into al-Bashir by invoking article 16 of the Rome Statute, which allows for a suspension of prosecution or investigation for a period of up to 12 months.[189] On 3 July 2009, at an AU meeting in Sirte, Libya, the AU

[184] See Igwe (n 183) 294. However, other situations were at the time under preliminary examination by the Office of Prosecutor in Afghanistan, Colombia, Chad, Georgia and Guinea; in this regard, see M Ssenyonjo 'The International Criminal Court arrest warrant decision for President al-Bashir of Sudan' (2010) 59 *International & Comparative Law Quarterly* 205.

[185] M du Plessis 'Recent cases and developments: South Africa and the International Criminal Court' (2009) 3 *SACJ* 441 at 442. See also EO Asaala 'Rule of law or *realpolitik*? The role of the United Nations Security Council in the International Criminal Court processes in Africa' (2017) 17 *AHRLJ* 265; E Keppler 'Challenges for international criminal justice in Africa and the role of civil society' 2016 *Acta Juridica* 66.

[186] N Fritz 'Black–white debate does no justice to a nuanced case' *Business Day* 13 August 2008.

[187] See further discussion below.

[188] See Human Rights Watch 'ICC: Bashir warrant is warning to abusive leaders' 4 March 2009, available at http://www.hrw.org/en/news/2009/03/04/icc-bashir-warrant-warning-abusive-leaders—Human Rights Watch stated that the ICC warrant indicates that '[n]ot even presidents are guaranteed a free pass for horrific crimes'; see also Amnesty International 'ICC Issues Arrest Warrant for Sudanese President al-Bashir' 4 March 2009, available at http://www.amnesty.org/es/node/9632.

[189] Du Plessis (n 185) 443. Article 16 empowers the Security Council to defer an investigation or prosecution for one year if it is necessary for the maintenance of international peace and security under Chapter VII of the UN Charter. The Security Council would need to make a determination that the continued involvement of the ICC is a greater threat to international peace and security than suspending the ICC's work.

took a resolution (the Sirte Resolution) calling on its members to defy the international arrest warrant issued by the ICC for al-Bashir.[190]

This AU decision placed African states party to the Rome Statute in the 'unenviable position of having to choose between their obligations as member states of the AU on the one hand, and their obligations as states party to the Rome Statute, on the other'.[191] To date, even though al-Bashir is the subject of an arrest warrant by the ICC, several states have failed to enforce the warrant after inviting al-Bashir to visit their territory.[192]

The international law questions arising (eg of immunities, commitment to the ICC by African states, Security Council and ICC reform, and the politics of international criminal justice) have generated a plethora of scholarly writing.[193] The issue continues to simmer, with the AU taking a decision in January 2018, inter alia, to 'reiterate its previous decisions on the deferral or termination of proceedings against President Omar Al-Bashir of the Republic of the Sudan in accordance with Article 16 of the Rome Statute' and 'to immediately place on the agenda of the United Nations General Assembly a request to seek an advisory opinion from the International Court of Justice on the question of immunities of a Head of State and Government and other Senior Officials as it relates to the relationship between Articles 27 and 98 and the obligations of States Parties under International Law'.[194]

The friction is of continuing and serious concern, and raises

[190] Du Plessis (n 185) 443. See also African Union Assembly 'Decision on the meeting of African States Parties to the Rome Statute of the International Criminal Tribunal (ICC) (Doc.Assembly/AU/13(XIII))' 3 July 2009, Assembly/AU/Dec. 245(XIII) Rev.1; African Union Assembly 'Decision on the progress report of the Commission on the Implementation of Decision Assembly/AU/Dec.270(XIV) on the second ministerial meeting on the Rome Statute of the International Criminal Court (ICC) Doc.Assembly/AU/10(XV)' 27 July 2010, Assembly/AU/Dec.296(XV); African Union Assembly 'Decision on the implementation of the decisions on the International Criminal Court (ICC) Doc. EX.CL/639(XVIII)' 30–31 January 2011, Assembly/AU/Dec.334(XVI); African Union Assembly 'Decision on the implementation of the assembly decisions on the International Criminal Court—Doc.EX.CL/670 (XIX)' 30 June–1 July 2011, Assembly/AU/Dec.366 (XVII).

[191] D Tladi 'The African Union and the International Criminal Court: The battle for the soul of international law' (2009) 34 *SAYIL* 57 at 57.

[192] See n 180.

[193] See, for example, E Ankumah (ed) *The International Criminal Court and Africa: One Decade On* (2016); C Jalloh and I Bantekas (eds) *The International Criminal Court and Africa* (2017); M du Plessis 'The International Criminal Court that Africa wants' Institute for Security Studies monograph (August 2010).

[194] See the AU decisions, declarations and resolutions at the 30th Ordinary Session of the Assembly, 28–29 January 2018, Addis Ababa, Ethiopia, available at https://au.int/sites/default/files/decisions/33908-assembly_decisions_665_-_689_e.pdf.

debates about the effectiveness of the international criminal justice project more generally, reform of the ICC and the Security Council's relationship with the Court, and a sober reflection of how to resolve the tensions between the AU and the ICC.[195]

SOUTH AFRICA'S IMPLEMENTATION OF THE ROME STATUTE

In order to give effect to its complementarity obligations under the Rome Statute, South Africa incorporated the Rome Statute into its domestic law by means of the Implementation of the Rome Statute of the International Criminal Court Act 27 of 2002 (the 'ICC Act').[196] Prior to the ICC Act, South Africa had no municipal legislation on the subject of war crimes or crimes against humanity,[197] and no domestic prosecutions of international crimes had taken place in South Africa.

Under the ICC Act, a structure is created for national prosecution of crimes in the Rome Statute. The Act takes seriously the 'complementary' obligation on South African courts to domestically investigate and prosecute the ICC offences of crimes against humanity, war crimes and genocide. The preamble, for instance, speaks of South Africa's commitment to bring 'persons who commit such atrocities to justice . . . in a court of law of the Republic in terms of its domestic law where possible'. And s 3 of the Act defines as one of its objects to enable, 'as far as possible and in accordance with the principle of complementarity . . . the national prosecuting authority of the Republic to adjudicate in cases brought against any person accused of having committed a crime in the Republic and beyond the borders of the Republic in certain circumstances'. Like the Rome Statute, the

[195] See further M du Plessis '*Prosecutor v al-Bashir*: Decision under article 87(7) of the Rome Statute on the non-compliance by South Africa with the request by the Court for the arrest and surrender of Omar al-Bashir (Int'l Crim Ct)' (2017) 56 *ILM* 1061.

[196] The ICC Act came into force on 16 August 2002. For further information on the Act, see M du Plessis 'Bringing the International Criminal Court home: The implementation of the Rome Statute of the International Criminal Court Act' (2003) 16 *SACJ* 1.

[197] Although customary international law forms part of South African law, a South African court confronted with the prosecution of a person accused of an international crime would have been hard pressed to convict, since the principle of *nullum crimen sine lege* would probably have constituted a bar to any such prosecution. The same principle would most likely have also put paid to prosecutions under the Geneva Conventions of 1949. South Africa has not incorporated the Geneva Conventions into municipal law nor, prior to the ICC Act, enacted legislation to punish grave breaches. It would therefore have been unlikely for a South African court to try a person for a grave breach of the Conventions in the absence of domestic legislation penalising such conduct. This proposition was challenged before the South African Constitutional Court in *S v Basson* 2007 (3) SA 582 (CC). However, the Court found it unnecessary 'to consider whether customary international law could be used . . . as the basis in itself for a prosecution under the common law' (para 172, fn 147). See Chapter 9 above.

ICC Act does not reach back into the past. The Act provides expressly that '[n]o prosecution may be instituted against a person accused of having committed a crime if the crime in question is alleged to have been committed before the commencement of the Statute'.[198]

1 Incorporation of ICC crimes

The advantage of the Rome Statute of the International Criminal Court is that it brings together in one place a codified statement of the elements which make up the crimes of genocide, war crimes and crimes against humanity. The drafters of the ICC Act, aware of this benefit of codification, incorporated the ICC Statute's definitions of the core crimes directly into South African law through a schedule appended to the Act. In this regard, Part 1 of Schedule 1 to the ICC Act follows the wording of article 6 of the ICC Statute in relation to genocide; Part 2 of the Schedule mirrors article 7 of the Statute in respect of crimes against humanity; and Part 3 does the same for war crimes, as set out in article 8 of the ICC Statute. It is clear that these crimes now form part of South African law through the Act. One of the objects of the Act is 'to provide for the crime of genocide, crimes against humanity and war crimes',[199] and s 4(1) of the Act provides that '[d]espite anything to the contrary in any other law in the Republic, any person who commits a crime [defined as genocide, crimes against humanity and war crimes], is guilty of an offence'. The ICC Act, at this stage, requires amendment in order to provide for the definition and jurisdictional regime for the crime of aggression following the Kampala amendment discussed earlier.

While the Act usefully incorporates the definitions of these crimes into South African domestic law, neither the ICC Act nor Schedule 1 refers specifically to article 9 of the Rome Statute on Elements of Crimes.[200] There is nothing, however, that prevents a South African court from having regard to the Elements of Crimes, were it to be involved in the domestic prosecution of an ICC offence. However, in the interests of clarity and completeness, it is suggested that South

[198] Section 5(2) of the ICC Act.

[199] See s 3*(c)* of the ICC Act.

[200] As mentioned previously in this chapter, for the purposes of interpreting and applying the definitions of crimes found in articles 6, 7 and 8 of the Rome Statute, reference must also be made to the 'Elements of Crimes', a 50-page document adopted in June 2000 by the Preparatory Commission for the International Criminal Court. See the 'Finalized draft text of the elements of crimes' (PCNICC/2000/INF/3/Add.2).

Africa follow the example of other states parties[201] and incorporate, by regulation, the Elements of Crimes.[202]

2 Grounds of jurisdiction

Section 4(1) of the ICC Act creates jurisdiction for a South African court over ICC crimes by providing that '[d]espite anything to the contrary in any other law of the Republic, any person who commits [an ICC] crime, is guilty of an offence and liable on conviction to a fine or imprisonment'. Section 4(3) of the Act goes further and provides for extraterritorial prescriptive jurisdiction.[203] In terms of that section, the jurisdiction of a South African court will be triggered when a person commits an ICC crime outside the territory of the Republic and that person:

(a) is a South African citizen; or

(b) is not a South African citizen but is ordinarily resident in the Republic; or

(c) after the commission of the crime, is present in the territory of the Republic; or

(d) has committed the said crime against a South African citizen or against a person who is ordinarily resident in the Republic.

When a person commits a core crime outside the territory of the Republic in one of these four circumstances, s 4(3) deems that crime to have been committed in the territory of the Republic.

The jurisdictional 'triggers' in the ICC Act are largely uncontroversial. Section 4(1) appears to assert the traditional principle of territoriality; namely, that a state has competency in respect of all acts which occur in its territory. Section 4(3), which provides for extraterritoriality, begins in trigger *(a)* with the recognised nationality basis for prescriptive jurisdiction. That is, international law has long accepted that states have the competency to exercise prescriptive jurisdiction over their nationals for crimes committed anywhere in the world. Trigger *(b)* extends, in similar fashion, prescriptive jurisdiction over South African residents on the basis that they have a close and substantial connection with South Africa at the time of the offence. Trigger *(c)* of the ICC Act extends prescriptive jurisdiction to a person who, 'after the commission of the crime, is present in the

[201] For example, the secretary of state in the United Kingdom has, by regulation, made the Elements of Crimes applicable to proceedings in a service court within the United Kingdom. See The International Criminal Court Act 2001 (Elements of Crimes) Regulations 2001, available at http://www.hmso.gov.uk/si/si2001/20012505.htm.

[202] In terms of s 38 of the ICC Act, the Minister of Justice may make regulations regarding the ICC Act. In terms of s 1 of the Act, such regulations would be included as part of the Act.

[203] See Chapter 9 for a discussion on the different aspects to jurisdiction.

territory of the Republic'. There is no mention here of the person's nationality or residency, and one must assume, given that triggers *(a)* and *(b)* already provide jurisdiction in respect of crimes committed abroad by South African nationals and residents, that trigger *(c)* is referring to individuals who commit a core crime and who do not have a close and substantial connection with South Africa at the time of offence.[204] The jurisdiction in trigger *(c)* is thus grounded on the idea of universal jurisdiction; that is, prescriptive jurisdiction which exists for all states in respect of certain crimes that attract universal prescriptive jurisdiction by their egregious nature, and consequently over the perpetrators of such crimes on the basis that they are common enemies of humankind. This form of prescriptive jurisdiction is to be welcomed because genocide, crimes against humanity and war crimes are among the crimes of most serious concern to the international community as a whole, and as such, are often regarded as giving rise to 'universal jurisdiction'.[205] Trigger *(d)* is founded on the passive personality principle in international law. In terms of that principle, a state has the competency to exercise prescriptive jurisdiction over an individual who causes harm to one of its nationals abroad.

The ICC Act provides that a South African court, charged with the prosecution of a person allegedly responsible for a core crime, shall apply 'the Constitution and the law'.[206] The South African Bill of Rights in s 35 sets out a range of rights for arrested, detained and accused persons. These protections will obviously need to be afforded to any person who is being tried under the ICC Act. In addition, the Rome Statute sets out a comprehensive framework of general principles of liability and defences in Part 3 of the Statute. While the drafters of the ICC Act have not chosen to expressly adopt Part 3, s 2 of the Act says that applicable law for any South African court hearing any matter arising under the Act includes 'conventional international law, and in particular the [Rome] Statute'.[207] Accordingly, the general principles of international criminal law applicable to the prosecution of genocide, war crimes and crimes

[204] The UK's implementing legislation, for example, provides more clearly that, aside from the traditional bases of jurisdiction (territoriality and nationality), the UK courts will have jurisdiction over a person who 'commits acts outside the United Kingdom at a time when he is not a United Kingdom national, a United Kingdom resident or a person subject to UK service jurisdiction and who subsequently becomes resident in the United Kingdom' (see s 68(1) of the United Kingdom's International Criminal Court Act 2001).

[205] See, for example, Cassese et al *The Rome Statute of the International Criminal Court* (n 23) vol 2 at 1862.

[206] Section 2, ICC Act.

[207] See s 2*(a)*.

against humanity (including the available defences contained in the Rome Statute, such as superior orders) ought to find application before a South African court.

3 Complementarity

The ICC Act gives effect to the complementarity scheme by creating the structure necessary for national prosecutions under the ICC Statute. The procedure for the institution of prosecutions in South African courts is set out in s 5 of the Act. This procedure involves different governmental departments and officials. First, the ICC Act requires that the consent of the National Director of Public Prosecutions must be obtained before any prosecution may be instituted against a person accused of having committed a crime.[208] The National Director must, when reaching a decision about a prosecution, recognise South Africa's obligation, in the first instance, under the principle of complementarity in the Rome Statute, to exercise jurisdiction over and to prosecute persons accused of having committed an ICC crime.[209] Given the importance of any such prosecution, it is clear that a specialised court would need to be designated. The Act provides that, after the National Director has consented to a prosecution, an appropriate High Court must be designated for that purpose. Such designation must be provided in writing by the 'Cabinet member responsible for the administration of justice . . . in consultation with the Chief Justice of South Africa and after consultation with the National Director'.[210] The ICC Act does not provide any specific trial procedure or punishment regime for domestic courts. All that the ICC Act provides is for the designation of 'an appropriate High Court in which to conduct a prosecution against any person accused of having committed [an ICC] crime'.[211] Presumably the usual trial procedure for a criminal trial in the High Court will be followed and the High Court will be empowered to issue any of the sentences which it would ordinarily be entitled to impose in terms of its domestic criminal sentencing jurisdiction. Such punishments would include life imprisonment, imprisonment, a fine and correctional supervision.

The expectation under the Act, flowing from South Africa's obligations under the complementarity scheme, is that a prosecution will take place within the Republic. Accordingly, if the National Director declines to prosecute a person under the Act, the Director-

[208] Section 5(1).
[209] Section 5(3).
[210] Section 5(4).
[211] Section 5(5).

General of Justice must be provided with the full reasons for that decision.[212] The Director-General is then obliged to forward the decision, together with reasons, to the Registrar of the International Criminal Court in The Hague.[213]

4 Co-operation with the International Criminal Court

(a) Arrest and surrender

The ICC Act is premised on the understanding that the International Criminal Court will in most circumstances have to rely on the intercession of national jurisdictions to gain custody of suspects. As a result, the ICC Act envisages two types of arrest: one in terms of an existing warrant issued by the ICC, and another in terms of a warrant issued by South Africa's National Director of Public Prosecutions. In both scenarios the warrant (whether endorsed or issued) must be in the form and executed in a manner as near as possible to that which exists in respect of warrants of arrest under existing South African law.[214]

Dealing with the first scenario (an arrest in terms of an existing warrant issued by the ICC), in terms of s 8 of the ICC Act, when South Africa receives a request from the ICC for the arrest and surrender of a person for whom the ICC has issued a warrant of arrest, it must refer the request to the Director-General of Justice with the necessary documentation to satisfy a local court that there are sufficient grounds for the surrender of the person to The Hague.[215] The Director-General must then forward the request (along with the necessary documentation) to a magistrate, who must endorse the ICC's warrant of arrest for execution in any part of the Republic.[216]

Section 9 details the second scenario (an arrest in terms of a warrant issued by the National Director). In this situation, the Director-General of Justice is mandated to receive a request from the ICC for the provisional arrest of a person who is suspected or accused of having committed a core crime, or has been convicted by the ICC. The Director-General is then obliged under the ICC Act to immediately forward the request to the National Director of Public Prosecutions, who must then apply for the warrant before a magistrate.[217]

[212] Section 5(5).
[213] Ibid.
[214] Section 9(3).
[215] Section 8(1).
[216] Section 8(2).
[217] Section 9(1).

After being arrested pursuant to a warrant (whether that warrant was issued by the ICC or by the National Director) the arrestee is to be brought 'before a magistrate in whose area of jurisdiction he or she has been arrested or detained', 'within 48 hours after that person's arrest or on the date specified in the warrant for his or her further detention'.[218]

Having laid their hands on the arrestee, the South African authorities then become engaged in what is known as the 'surrender' of an arrestee to the International Criminal Court—his or her 'delivery' to The Hague. To make a committal order, with a view to the surrender of an arrestee to the International Criminal Court, the magistrate has to be satisfied of three things only. First, the magistrate must be satisfied that the person before court is the individual named in the warrant.[219] Secondly, the person must have been arrested in accordance with the procedures set down by domestic law.[220] Thirdly, the arrestee's rights, as contemplated in the Bill of Rights, must have been respected, if, and to the extent to which, they are or may be applicable.[221] The nature of these three requirements makes it clear that surrender to the ICC is different to extradition in international law. There is no mention of the double criminality rule which has become so central to extradition proceedings; and unlike many extradition proceedings, there is no requirement in the ICC Act that a *prima facie* case be shown against the suspect.[222] Section 10(5) of the ICC Act provides as the primary test that, if, after considering the evidence adduced at the inquiry, the magistrate is satisfied that the three requirements outlined above are met, then the magistrate 'must issue an order committing that person to prison pending his or her surrender to the Court'. Of course, the magistrate also has to be satisfied that the International Criminal Court has a genuine interest in the surrender of the arrestee, and to this end, s 10(5) stipulates that, in addition to the three requirements being met, the magistrate must be content that the person concerned may be surrendered to the Court: *(a)* for prosecution for the alleged crime; *(b)* for the imposition of a sentence by the Court for the crime in respect of which the person has been convicted, or *(c)* to serve a sentence already imposed by the Court.[223] There is little indication in the Act what level of proof must be proffered by the prosecution in respect of these additional requirements, such as whether the court must inquire if there is

[218] Section 10(1).
[219] Section 10(1)*(a)*.
[220] Section 10(1)*(b)*.
[221] Section 10(1)*(c)*.
[222] See Chapter 11 for a full discussion of extradition.
[223] One must assume that the listing of these conditions is in the disjunctive.

evidence to justify the person's trial for the offence he or she is alleged to have committed.[224] Presumably any of these three factual conditions will have been proved by the terms of the International Criminal Court's request, either for the endorsement of its own warrant of arrest within South Africa (in terms of s 8 of the ICC Act) or for South Africa to issue a provisional warrant of arrest pursuant to the Court's request (in terms of s 9 of the ICC Act), such that these additional requirements may be regarded as being satisfied on the strength of the 'material supporting the request' for surrender provided by the International Criminal Court.[225]

(b) *Forms of assistance offered to the Court in fulfilment of article 93 of the Rome Statute*

Article 93 of the Rome Statute requires states parties to assist the ICC by co-operating in relation to investigations and prosecutions. Part 2 of the ICC Act sets out a variety of circumstances in which the relevant competent authorities in the Republic must 'cooperate with, and render assistance to, the Court in relation to investigations and prosecutions'. There are many areas of co-operation (detailed in s 14 of the Act) such as the questioning of suspects, the identification and whereabouts of persons or items, the taking of evidence (including expert opinions), inspections *in loco* (including the exhumation and examination of grave sites) and the execution of searches and seizures, to name but a few.[226] The areas of co-operation must be undertaken in terms of the relevant law applicable to investigations in South Africa, as well as the applicable rules in the Rome Statute,[227] and with the ultimate aim of assisting the ICC.

[224] By contrast, the United Kingdom's ICC Act, for example, makes it clear that a court, when making an order for surrender, 'is not concerned to enquire' whether the warrant was duly issued by the ICC or, where the person to be surrendered is 'alleged to have committed an ICC crime, whether there is evidence to justify his trial for the offence he is alleged to have committed' (see s 5(5) of the International Criminal Court Act 2001; see, too, the commentary on the Act by R Cryer 'Implementation of the International Criminal Court statute in England and Wales' (2002) 51 *ICLQ* 733 at 736).

[225] Article 89 of the Rome Statute, which deals with surrender of persons to the Court, provides that the Court 'may transmit a request for the arrest and surrender of a person, together with the material supporting the request' to a state party, so this material would be before the magistrate. Prior to this, to obtain a warrant of arrest from the ICC, the prosecutor would have had to convince a pre-trial chamber of the Court (consisting of three judges) that there were 'reasonable grounds to believe' the suspect had committed an ICC offence.

[226] The full list of areas of co-operation is set out in s 14*(a)–(l)*. The list is modelled on article 93 of the Rome Statute.

[227] Section 14 reads that the 'relevant competent authorities in the Republic must, *subject to the domestic law of the Republic and the Statute*, cooperate with, and render assistance to, the Court' (emphasis added). The Constitution, where applicable, will no doubt provide the background standards against which the relevant 'co-operation'

Certain acts of co-operation are subject to comprehensive regulation in the ICC Act and others are not. For example, in the context of questioning suspects, the ICC Act stipulates in s 14*(c)* no more than that the competent South African authorities must assist with 'the questioning of any person being investigated or prosecuted'. South African authorities will therefore have to turn to the Rome Statute and South African law for assistance. In this respect, the Bill of Rights in s 35 and the Rome Statute in article 55 equally guarantee certain rights to a person under investigation, such as the right against self-incrimination, the right to remain silent and the right to legal assistance.

Those means of co-operation that are subject to detailed regulation under the ICC Act include the examination of witnesses,[228] the transfer of a prisoner to the ICC for the purposes of giving evidence or to assist in an investigation,[229] the service of process and documents,[230] acts of entry, search and seizure,[231] and the making of forfeiture or confiscation orders.[232]

(c) Specialised units

In order that South Africa's obligations under the ICC Act may be fulfilled, a Priority Crimes Litigation Unit (PCLU) has been established within the National Prosecuting Authority and is headed by a Special Director of Public Prosecutions appointed in terms of s 13(1)*(c)* of the National Prosecuting Authority Act 32 of 1998. Section 13(1)*(c)* provides that the President may, by proclamation in the *Government Gazette*, appoint one or more Directors of Public Prosecutions (referred to as Special Directors) to perform functions assigned to him by the President.

is undertaken. So, for example, when it comes to searches and seizures in terms of s 14*(h)*, read with s 30 of the ICC Act, the relevant provisions of the Act will need to be read in conjunction with ss 10, 12(1)*(a)*–*(d)*, 12(2)*(b)*, 14, 21, 35(5) and 36(1) of the Constitution.

[228] See ss 15, 16, 17, 18 and 19 of the ICC Act. The sections outline the procedure for the examination of witnesses before a magistrate, the rights and privileges of the witness, the offences which a witness might commit, and the procedure by which the attendance of a witness might be secured in proceedings before the International Criminal Court.

[229] See s 20 of the ICC Act.

[230] Ibid s 21.

[231] Ibid s 30. This section is in many respects similar to those provisions of the Criminal Procedure Act 51 of 1977 relating to search and seizure (ss 19–36) but with modifications to reflect the fact that the request for co-operation has been made by the ICC for the purposes of its investigation and not to assist South Africa in criminal investigations unrelated to the ICC.

[232] Sections 14*(k)*, 22(1) and 27(1). For fuller discussion, see Du Plessis (n 196) 10–12.

The Special Director's appointment was confirmed in terms of *Government Gazette* 24876 of 23 May 2003.[233] The Special Director was given two powers: first, to head the PCLU and, secondly, to 'manage and direct the prosecution of crimes contemplated in the Implementation of the Rome Statute of the International Criminal Court Act'. The Unit is thus specifically tasked with dealing with the ICC crimes set out in the ICC Act.

The PCLU has expressed the view that when it comes to the investigation of the alleged perpetrator, it is dependent on the co-operation of the South African Police Services. A Directorate for Priority Crimes Investigation (DPCI) has recently been established within the police, and the crimes under the ICC Act fall within its purview for investigation. In practice, this means that requests by individuals or civil society groups for investigation and prosecution under the ICC Act should be directed jointly to the PCLU and DPCI.

On the assumption that the PCLU, with the assistance of DPCI, takes up the investigation and issues a warrant of arrest (*in camera* or otherwise) and the suspect or suspects are arrested, the matter will then move to the prosecution stage. The ICC Act stipulates that no prosecution may be instituted against a person accused of having committed a core crime without the consent of the National Director of Public Prosecutions. Assuming that such consent is provided, the matter will proceed to court and the PCLU will adopt responsibility for the prosecution of the matter.

(d) Discretionary measures of assistance

In terms of the ICC Act, the President may, at the request of the ICC and by proclamation in the *Government Gazette*, declare any place in the Republic to be the seat of the ICC.[234] Should such a declaration be made, then the ICC Act sets out a variety of privileges and immunities for the Court. First, the Court is accorded such rights and privileges of a South African court of law in the Republic as may be necessary to enable it to perform its functions.[235] Furthermore, the judges, the prosecutor, the deputy prosecutors and the registrar of the Court, while performing their functions in the Republic, enjoy the same immunities and privileges that are accorded to a representative of another state or government in terms of s 4(2) of the South African Diplomatic Immunities and Privileges Act 37 of 2001.[236] Those immunities include immunity from the criminal and civil jurisdiction of the courts of the Republic, and the privileges enjoyed are those

[233] Proclamation 43 of 2003.
[234] Section 6.
[235] Section 7(1).
[236] Section 7(2).

which *(a)* a special envoy or representative enjoys in accordance with the rules of customary international law, or *(b)* are provided for in any agreement entered into with a state, government or organisation whereby immunities and privileges are conferred upon such special envoy or representative.

The deputy registrar, the staff of the Office of the Prosecutor and the staff of the registry of the Court enjoy the privileges and facilities necessary for the performance of their functions in the Republic as may be published by proclamation in the *Government Gazette*, as provided for in s 7(2) of the Diplomatic Immunities and Privileges Act.[237]

The Minister of Foreign Affairs may, after consultation with the Minister of Justice, confer immunities and privileges on any other member of the staff of the Court or any person performing functions for purposes of the ICC Act. Such immunities and privileges are conferred by the Minister of Foreign Affairs publishing a notice in the *Government Gazette*, on such conditions as he or she deems necessary.[238] Any person who is accorded immunities or privileges in terms of the ICC Act must have his or her name entered into a register as contemplated in s 9(1) of the Diplomatic Immunities and Privileges Act.[239]

(e) Enforcement of sentences

The Rome Statute stresses that 'States Parties should share the responsibility for enforcing sentences of imprisonment, in accordance with principles of equitable distribution'.[240] The International Criminal Court has no prison, and states are therefore expected to volunteer their services, indicating their willingness to allow convicted prisoners to serve the sentence within their domestic penal institutions.[241]

After sentencing an offender, the ICC will, in terms of article 103(1)(a) of the Rome Statute, designate the state where the term is to be served. In so doing, the Court must take into account the views of the sentenced prisoner, his or her nationality, and 'widely accepted international treaty standards governing the treatment of prisoners'.[242] In addition, conditions of detention must be neither more nor

[237] Section 7(3).

[238] Section 7(4).

[239] Section 7(5).

[240] See article 103(3)(a) of the Rome Statute as well as rule 201 of the Rules of Procedure and Evidence.

[241] If no state offers its prison services, the host state of the ICC—the Netherlands—will perform the task (see article 103(4) of the Rome Statute).

[242] Article 103(3).

less favourable than those available to prisoners convicted of similar offences in the state where the sentence is to be enforced.[243]

In order to give effect to this enforcement scheme, the ICC Act provides that the Minister of Correctional Services must consult with the Cabinet and seek the approval of Parliament with the aim of informing the ICC whether South Africa can be placed on the list of states willing to accept sentenced persons.[244] If the Republic is placed on the list of states and is designated as a state in which an offender is to serve a prison sentence, then such person must be committed to prison in South Africa.[245] The provisions of the Correctional Services Act[246] and South African domestic law then apply to that individual. However, the sentence of imprisonment may only be modified at the request of the ICC, after an appeal by the prisoner to, or review by, the Court in terms of the Rome Statute.[247]

It is commendable that the ICC Act requires the government to indicate its availability to assist in enforcing the ICC sentences. It is not clear, however, that South Africa will be placed on the list of states available for enforcement duty. The Rome Statute stresses that there can be 'no question of sending a prisoner to a State with prison conditions that do not meet international standards'.[248] This is a particular problem for South Africa, given the poor state of its prisons.[249]

The Rome Statute also enables the ICC to impose a fine, but only '[i]n addition to imprisonment'.[250] On top of this, the ICC is empowered to address the issue of reparations to victims, and may 'make an order directly against any convicted person' specifying reparation.[251] Such an order will no doubt often take the form of monetary compensation. The ICC Act makes provision for the execution of such fines and compensation orders within the Republic.[252] Such orders must be registered with a court in the Republic

[243] Article 106(2).

[244] Section 31.

[245] Section 32.

[246] 111 of 1998.

[247] Section 32(4)*(b)*. This provision is a reflection of the prescription in article 110(2) of the Rome Statute whereby the ICC 'alone shall have the right to decide any reduction of sentence'.

[248] Schabas (n 9) 75.

[249] South African jails are notoriously overcrowded and prisoners are often kept in inhuman conditions. See, for example, *Sonke Gender Justice v Government of South Africa* (unreported, ZAWCHC Case No 24087/15, 22 December 2016 and 23 February 2017) available at http://genderjustice.org.za/publication/pollsmoor-court-order/.

[250] Article 77(2)(a).

[251] Article 75(2).

[252] Sections 25 and 26.

which has jurisdiction.[253] Once the order has been registered, that sentence or order 'has the effect of a civil judgment of the court at which it has been registered' and the Director-General of Justice must pay over to the ICC any amount realised in the execution of the sentence or the order, minus any expenses incurred by the Republic in the execution thereof.[254]

IMMUNITIES

While the ICC Act provides South African courts with potential jurisdiction over persons who may have committed ICC crimes, the issue of immunity from jurisdiction for high-ranking officials remains contentious. The most heated debate has been around the extent to which serving heads of state and other senior government officials can justifiably claim immunity, on the basis of their official status, from proceedings brought against them for allegedly committing international crimes.

This question dramatically rears its head in the al-Bashir case before the ICC. The ICC has issued two warrants of arrest for al-Bashir because of his alleged crimes in Darfur. These were forwarded to South Africa with requests to assist in arresting him.[255] South Africa's obligations under these warrants were also made clear in various communications and consultations with the ICC leading up to al-Bashir's visit.[256] When al-Bashir was present in South Africa in 2015, South Africa did not arrest and surrender him to the ICC. The government's main reason for not doing so was that al-Bashir, as an incumbent head of state, is immune from being arrested and surrendered to—then tried before—the ICC.

The High Court in Pretoria[257] and the Supreme Court of Appeal[258] found that South Africa had violated its obligations under international and domestic law by not arresting and surrendering al-Bashir. The ICC, in its own judgment, reached the same conclusion.[259] This is

[253] Section 25(2) and (3).

[254] Section 26.

[255] 'Decision following the prosecutor's request for an order clarifying that the Republic of South Africa is under the obligation to arrest and surrender Omar al-Bashir' ICC-02/05-01/09 (13 June 2015) para 2.

[256] 'Prosecution's submissions for article 87(7) hearing' ICC-02/05-01/09-289 (17 March 2017) paras 90 et seq.

[257] *Southern Africa Litigation Centre v Minister of Justice and Constitutional Development* 2015 (5) SA 1 (GP).

[258] *Minister of Justice and Constitutional Development v Southern Africa Litigation Centre* 2016 (3) SA 317 (SCA) ('*Minister of Justice v SALC*').

[259] 'Decision under article 87(7) of the Rome Statute on the non-compliance by South Africa with the request by the Court for the arrest and surrender of Omar al-Bashir' Pre-Trial Chamber II, ICC-02/05-01/09-302 (6 July 2017).

not the first or last time the ICC has held that a state breached its obligations under the Rome Statute by relying on immunity to refuse a request to arrest al-Bashir.[260]

Immunity from jurisdiction under international law is discussed elsewhere in this book.[261] The issue of immunity under the ICC Act and the Rome Statute can be divided into four parts that warrant discussion here. First, does South African law, on a domestic level, grant immunity to incumbent heads of state (or other senior state officials) from arrest and surrender to the ICC? Secondly, does South African law grant immunity to incumbent heads of state from prosecution before a South African court? Thirdly, does international law grant immunity to incumbent heads of state from prosecution before the ICC? Fourthly, what are South Africa's international legal obligations regarding incumbent senior officials who are implicated in international crimes, like al-Bashir?

1 Immunity from arrest and surrender to the ICC

South African law does not grant personal or functional immunity to those who are sought for surrender to the ICC.[262] This is for four reasons. First, s 10(9) of the ICC Act provides that the arrested person being a head of state 'does not constitute a ground for refusing to issue an order' for committal and surrender by a magistrate.[263] Tladi explains as follows:[264]

> As du Plessis points out, this provision [s 10(9)] is unambiguous in its effect, ie the mere fact that a person is entitled to inviolability is in itself not a justification for not ordering surrender. This means that even if a South African court itself cannot exercise jurisdiction over a head of state like al-Bashir, this does not apply to the arrest and surrender processes described above. It is noteworthy that while Article 98 of the Rome Statute provides an exception to the duty to cooperate on the basis of immunity as described above, a similar provision does not exist in the Implementation Act. Indeed section 10(9) of the Implementation Act, stating that the status of a person is

[260] After South Africa, the ICC made the same finding in respect of Jordan (although this decision is subject to appeal). Before South Africa, Malawi, Chad, the Democratic Republic of Congo, Djibouti and Uganda were held to have violated their obligations. See n 180.

[261] Chapter 12.

[262] For a discussion of the various sorts of immunity, see Chapter 12 generally and in particular see the discussion there on the important distinction between immunity as a defence or bar to jurisdiction and immunity in respect of a request for judicial assistance.

[263] Read with s 4(2)*(a)* of the Act.

[264] D Tladi 'The duty on South Africa to arrest and surrender President al-Bashir under South African and international law' (2015) 13 *JICJ* 1027 at 1039 (referencing M du Plessis 'South Africa's implementation of the ICC Statute: An African example' (2007) 5 *JICJ* 460).

not a ground for refusing surrender, suggests that the legislator intended to explicitly exclude the effects of Article 98.

Secondly, s 10(1), which lists the factors a magistrate must consider when deciding whether to issue an order of surrender to the ICC, does not include the question whether the arrested person enjoys any immunity.[265]

Thirdly, s 8 provides for the procedure for receiving and executing a warrant of arrest from the ICC. It is silent about immunity. It must be read consistently with s 10(9). To avoid s 10(9) being rendered nugatory, one must read s 8 as not allowing immunity to prevent arrests of persons who stand to be surrendered to the ICC under s 10. An interpretation which renders s 10(9) nugatory is to be avoided.[266]

Finally, not providing immunity against arrest and surrender accords with South Africa's international law obligations.[267] It thus promotes the object of the Act: lawful, effective co-operation between the ICC and South Africa. It also ensures that legislation is reasonably interpreted to be consistent with international law.[268]

Therefore, South African law does not grant immunity from arrest and surrender to the ICC to incumbent heads of state. This election by the South African Parliament to preclude claims to immunity is a progressive step, which is arguably ahead of the international law curve. It accords with the 'prudent approach' advocated by Cassese et al in their leading text on the Rome Statute of the International Criminal Court:

> *To avoid these difficulties* [regarding immunities for officials], *a prudent approach* [for the state's legislature in drafting its ICC implementation legislation] *would be to provide that any issue of immunities will not bar arrest or surrender to the ICC.* In essence, this approach leaves the issue to be decided by the ICC and not by national courts. In this manner, an implementing State can ensure that it will not find itself stuck with a legislative provision—or a judicial interpretation—on international immunities that hinders compliance with an ICC request.[269]

[265] *Minister of Justice v SALC* (n 258) para 99.

[266] Ibid para 101.

[267] Discussed below.

[268] Section 233 of the Constitution.

[269] Cassese et al *The Rome Statute of the International Criminal Court* (n 23) vol 2 at 1857 (emphasis added). And as Wallis JA held in *Minister of Justice v SALC* (n 258) para 103: 'I conclude therefore that when South Africa decided to implement its obligations under the Rome Statute by passing the Implementation Act it did so on the basis that all forms of immunity, including head of state immunity, would not constitute a bar to the prosecution of international crimes in this country or to South Africa cooperating with the ICC by way of the arrest and surrender of persons charged with such crimes before the ICC, where an arrest warrant had been issued and a request for cooperation made. I accept, in the light of the earlier discussion of head of state immunity, that in doing so South Africa was taking a step that many other nations have not yet taken. If

2 Immunity from domestic prosecution

In the groundbreaking *Pinochet* cases, the House of Lords accepted that serving international functionaries (such as current heads of state) retain absolute immunities *rationae personae* (ie personal immunity on account of their status) before domestic tribunals, irrespective of the nature of the crime alleged, unless waived by the sending state. The House of Lords denied immunity to Pinochet in his capacity as a *former* head of state. However, it made it clear that if he had still been an acting head of state, this immunity in international law would have continued to subsist.[270]

The International Court of Justice has affirmed this immunity in its decision in the *Arrest Warrant* case.[271] With regard to the provisions precluding immunity found in the constitutive instruments of a myriad of international criminal tribunals (the most recent being the Rome Statute of the ICC) the Court expressly held that this exception to customary international law was not applicable to national courts.[272] This case law is therefore read as authority for the proposition that there is a dichotomy between immunity for international crimes before international courts and national courts: the personal immunity of an accused person prevents national courts from dealing with allegations of international crimes unless that immunity has been waived, or the senior official has left office.

But what is the position under South African law? In *Minister of Justice v SALC*, the Supreme Court of Appeal said that the ICC Act diverges from the position under customary international law. Wallis JA noted how s 4(2)(a) of the Act provides that the fact that the accused is or was a head of state does not constitute a defence for a crime before a South African court. Because of this, he held, it cannot

that puts this country in the vanguard of attempts to prevent international crimes and, when they occur, cause the perpetrators to be prosecuted, that seems to me a matter for national pride rather than concern. It is wholly consistent with our commitment to human rights both at a national and an international level. And it does not undermine customary international law, which as a country we are entitled to depart from by statute as stated in s 232 of the Constitution. What is commendable is that it is a departure in a progressive direction.'

[270] For instance, Lord Nicholls in the first *Pinochet* case held that 'there can be no doubt that if Senator Pinochet had still been the head of the Chilean state, he would have been entitled to immunity' (see *R v Bow St Magistrate, Ex p Pinochet Ugarte* [1998] 4 All ER (*Pinochet* 1) 938). Lord Millett in the third *Pinochet* case said that 'Senator Pinochet is not a serving head of state. If he were, he could not be extradited. It would be an intolerable affront to the Republic of Chile to arrest him or detain him' (see *R v Bow St Magistrate, Ex p Pinochet (No 3)* [1999] 2 WLR 824 at 905H).

[271] *Arrest Warrant of 11 April 2000 (Democratic Republic of the Congo v Belgium)* 2002 ICJ Reports 3. For criticisms of the decision, see the discussion on immunity in criminal proceedings in Chapter 12.

[272] Paragraph 58.

then be that personal immunity is a procedural bar to domestic prosecution in South Africa. Otherwise s 4(2) is rendered nugatory. The ICC Act would include a defence that no person could rely on, unless South African courts have jurisdiction over heads of state in the first place. Therefore, s 4(2) does not give personal immunity to incumbent heads of state from domestic prosecution in South Africa.[273]

Some commentators have echoed this. Dugard and Abraham argue that s 4(2)*(a)* of the Act represents a choice by the legislature not to follow the 'unfortunate *Arrest Warrant* decision of which it must have been aware'.[274] In effect, the ICC Act simply trumps personal immunity from domestic prosecution.[275]

But there are arguments the other way. For example, some contend that the ordinary meaning of the section does not lift immunity from domestic prosecution, since the provision refers to a 'defence', which is substantive criminal law, while immunity is a procedural matter.[276] Ultimately, though, the Supreme Court of Appeal has put the issue to rest. In *Minister of Justice v SALC*, the Court found as follows at para 103:

> I conclude therefore that when South Africa decided to implement its obligations under the Rome Statute by passing the Implementation Act it did so on the basis that all forms of immunity, including head of state immunity, would not constitute a bar to the prosecution of international crimes in this country.

As a safety net, any decision by the South African authorities not to prosecute entitles the ICC to do so in South Africa's place. Section 5(6) of the ICC Act confirms this in stating that a decision by the National Director of Public Prosecutions 'not to prosecute a person under this section does not preclude the prosecution of that person in the [International Criminal] Court'. In addition, article 98(1) of the Rome Statute entails that states parties have a duty of co-operation with the Court, requiring—as the SCA has now confirmed in *Minister of Justice v SALC*—South Africa to arrest and surrender to the Court persons charged with an ICC crime where those persons are on South African territory and the subject of an arrest warrant from the ICC.

[273] *Minister of Justice v SALC* (n 258) para 95. See further MJ Ventura 'Escape from Johannesburg?: Sudanese President al-Bashir visits South Africa, and the implicit removal of head of state immunity by the UN Security Council in light of *Al-Jedda*' (2015) 13 *JICJ* 995.

[274] J Dugard and C Abraham 'Public international law' 2002 *Annual Survey* 140 at 166.

[275] Du Plessis (n 264) 474.

[276] Tladi (n 264) 1038; Woolaver (n 160) fn 78.

3 Immunity from international prosecution before the ICC

Immunity, including personal immunity from prosecution for international crimes, is waived if states sign up to a tribunal whose charter provides that immunity is not a bar to prosecution.[277] Article 27(2) of the Rome Statute provides that neither functional nor personal immunity can prevent prosecution before the ICC. So, if a state signs up to the Rome Statute, they waive whatever immunity their officials or heads of state would otherwise enjoy as a bar to their prosecution at the ICC.

The issue is that some countries, including Sudan, have not signed the Statute. In multiple decisions, though its reasoning was not always entirely consistent, the ICC has held that al-Bashir's immunity from prosecution before the ICC has been waived by Sudan by means of Security Council Resolution 1593 ('the Resolution')[278] which referred the situation in Sudan to the ICC. Sudan is bound by the Security Council's decision that Sudan is to co-operate fully with the ICC.[279] Moreover, full co-operation necessitates the waiving of al-Bashir's immunity—otherwise the ICC is hampered in prosecuting al-Bashir. Therefore, al-Bashir's immunity has been waived.[280]

Some object that if the Resolution intended to remove al-Bashir's immunity, it would have done so explicitly.[281] However, the Security Council cannot be expected to predict all permutations of 'co-operation'. To do so would have undermined the ICC's judicial independence. The Security Council has subsequently not objected to the issuing of al-Bashir's arrest warrants.[282] And 'cooperate fully' was the term that was used in the resolutions creating the ICTY and ICTR. These resolutions were considered to remove immunities.[283]

Akande has argued, and the ICC has held, that the Resolution entails an actual waiver by Sudan and that it binds Sudan to accept the ICC's jurisdiction in terms of the Statute. The ICC's jurisdiction, as per the Statute, includes article 27(2), which becomes binding on

[277] See *Arrest Warrant* (n 271) para 61. A different reasoning was offered by the Special Court for Sierra Leone in *Prosecutor v Charles Ghankay Taylor* Case No SCSL-2003-1-AR72(E) (31 May 2004). The Court found that customary international law and the international nature of the Court, not state consent, automatically excluded immunity as a procedural bar. For a criticism of this reasoning, see Cryer (n 83) 552. For its support, see P Gaeta 'Does President al-Bashir enjoy immunity from arrest?' (2009) 7 *JICJ* 315 at 317.

[278] See n 180.

[279] Article 25 of the UN Charter.

[280] Ventura (n 273) 1013–14.

[281] Ibid 1018. Jordan made this argument in *Jordan* (n 180) para 16 and South Africa made this argument in *South Africa* (n 180) para 35.

[282] Ventura (n 273) 1021.

[283] Cryer (n 23) 557; *Malawi* (n 180) para 40.

Sudan. This amounts to waiving immunity from prosecution before the ICC.[284]

Gaeta responds to Akande by arguing that the Resolution simply *triggers* the ICC's jurisdiction. It cannot go further and bind Sudan (like a member state) to article 27(2).[285]

Despite this debate, the ICC's reasoning in *DRC* left open the question whether Sudan is, via the SC Resolution, bound to article 27. Akande's argument could explain why the ICC believed that Sudan had actually waived al-Bashir's immunity.[286] However, in *Jordan* and *South Africa*, the ICC made it clear that Sudan is bound to article 27 via the Resolution. Therefore, as things currently stand, al-Bashir does not enjoy immunity in international law from prosecution before the ICC. The Appeals Chamber, in the *Jordan* matter,[287] is currently seized with giving a definitive ruling from the ICC on the issue—and the seriousness of the question moved the Court to make the unprecedented 'Order inviting expressions of interest as *amici curiae* in judicial proceedings (pursuant to rule 103 of the Rules of Procedure and Evidence)'.[288]

4 South Africa's obligations regarding senior officials

Article 98(1) of the Rome Statute provides that member states cannot, when co-operating with the ICC, disregard their obligations to respect the immunities enjoyed by heads of non-member states.[289] So, ordinarily, member states cannot arrest or surrender al-Bashir (or other incumbent heads of state) because of his personal immunity. This is unless the Court can obtain the co-operation of that third state for the waiver of the immunity.

As already indicated, in *DRC*, the ICC found that the Resolution removes al-Bashir's immunity as a bar to member states co-operating with the ICC by arresting and surrendering al-Bashir. The Resolution, which required Sudan to 'cooperate fully' and 'provide any necessary assistance to the Court', constitutes the 'cooperation of that third State [Sudan] for the waiver of the immunity', as required under

[284] D Akande 'The legal nature of Security Council referrals to the ICC and its impact on al-Bashir's immunities' (2009) 7 *JICJ* 333 at 341–2. *Jordan* (n 180) para 38; *South Africa* (n 180) para 91.

[285] Gaeta (n 277) 324.

[286] Cf the *Malawi Decision* Case No ICC-02/05-01/09 (12 December 2011).

[287] See the Hashemite Kingdom of Jordan's appeal against the 'Decision under article 87(7) of the Rome Statute on the non-compliance by Jordan with the request by the Court for the arrest and surrender o[f] Omar al-Bashir' ICC-02/05-01/09-326 (12 March 2018).

[288] See the order of the Appeals Chamber, ICC-02/05-01/09 OA2 (29 March 2018).

[289] *DRC* supra (n 180) para 27.

article 98(1) of the Statute.[290] Therefore, because of the Resolution, South Africa would not have breached its obligation to respect al-Bashir's immunity in international law had South Africa arrested him.

The purpose of article 98(1) is to ensure that immunity is consensually waived by a non-member state.[291] According to the ICC, then, Sudan has given this consent by agreeing to abide by the Resolution. But the ICC's focus on 'co-operation', while it makes al-Bashir's position clear, leaves questions open about the relationship between articles 27 and 98.

Chapter 12 examines the correct position regarding this relationship between articles 27 and 98.[292] An answer to this question from the ICC is expected in the *Jordan* appeal, which at the time of writing is still to be decided.

As things presently stand, the ICC has resolved this uncertainty in *South Africa* and *Jordan* by finding that because Sudan is bound (via the Resolution) to article 27, article 98(1) is inapplicable. There is no immunity to be waived per article 98(1) because it has already been waived through article 27.[293] Therefore, the obligation under article 98(1) does not bar South Africa (or any state party) from arresting al-Bashir.

So, given that South Africa was under an obligation to arrest al-Bashir pursuant to the request from the ICC, South Africa breached its obligation by failing to do so.

SOUTH AFRICA AND THE ICC

South Africa was instrumental in the adoption and drafting of the Rome Statute. Nothing less would be expected from a country that has experienced its own crimes against humanity. But the growing resentment within the AU of the ICC and the recent al-Bashir saga have challenged South Africa's commitment to the Rome Statute. At the time of writing, South Africa is still a party to the Rome Statute and the ICC Act is still in force. But South Africa's withdrawal from the ICC, and a repeal of the ICC Act, are mooted by the government.

On 19 October 2016, about a year after al-Bashir left South Africa, the Zuma government took the decision to withdraw from the Rome Statute and delivered its withdrawal instruments to the UN Secre-

[290] *DRC* supra (n 180) para 29.

[291] Treaty provisions, moreover, are to be interpreted in light of their purpose. See article 31(1) of the Vienna Convention on the Law of Treaties.

[292] See further on this subject, G Mettraux, J Dugard and M du Plessis 'Heads of state immunities, international crimes and President Bashir's visit to South Africa' (2018) 18 *International Criminal Law Review* 1.

[293] *South Africa* (n 180) para 93; *Jordan* (n 180) para 39.

tary-General. An opposition party and various civil society organisations urgently applied to the High Court to review the decision to withdraw from the Statute. A full bench of the High Court granted the order sought and declared the decision invalid.[294] The primary grounds for doing so was that Parliament needed to approve the withdrawal, and that withdrawal could not occur before the ICC Act is repealed.[295]

The government was then forced to reverse itself: on 7 March 2017 it deposited with the UN Secretary-General in New York a document headed 'South Africa: Withdrawal of notification of withdrawal'.

Thereafter, the Minister of Justice, Michael Masutha, announced on 6 December 2017 at the Assembly of States Parties meeting of the ICC in New York that South Africa was attempting for a second time to withdraw from the Court.

He indicated there that he would submit to Parliament South Africa's intention to withdraw from the ICC. To this end, the executive has tabled the International Crimes Bill.[296] Among others, the purpose of the Bill is to repeal the ICC Act. The Bill takes the unfortunate view that the Rome Statute and the ICC Act are inconsistent with international law on immunity. In the first place, the Bill gives effect to South Africa's view that it must withdraw from the ICC. But the arguments in support of its withdrawal have been subjected to withering criticism by many, including a number of retired Justices of South Africa's Constitutional Court.[297] Furthermore, as explained above, while the Supreme Court of Appeal in *Minister of Justice v SALC* expressly rejected the notion that customary international law today recognises an all-encompassing exception to immunities in the case of international crimes, it held that South Africa's ICC Act meant that President al-Bashir was not entitled to immunity while he was in South Africa. As the Court stressed: in adopting this approach 'South Africa was taking a step that many other nations have not yet taken. If that puts this country in the

[294] *Democratic Alliance v Minister of International Relations and Cooperation (Council for the Advancement of the South African Constitution Intervening)* 2017 (3) SA 212 (GP). The government chose not to appeal the decision.

[295] Ibid para 53. See, for a critical discussion, M du Plessis and G Mettraux 'South Africa's failed withdrawal from the Rome Statute: Politics, law, and judicial accountability' (2017) 15 *JICJ* 361.

[296] [B 37–2017].

[297] See 'South Africa should not withdraw from the International Criminal Court: Briefing submitted to the Portfolio Committee on Justice and Correctional Services' International Commission of Jurists (in collaboration with a number of leading jurists), available at http://www.lhr.org.za/sites/lhr.org.za/files/south_africa_icc_briefer_formatted2.pdf?ct=t%28LHR-ICJ+Press+Conference%29&mc_cid=b24c9ee660&mc_eid=%5BUNIQID%5D.

vanguard of attempts to prevent international crimes . . . that seems to me to be a matter for national pride rather than concern. It is wholly consistent with our commitment to human rights, both at a national and at an international level.'[298] Moreover, if South Africa successfully withdraws from the Rome Statute, this will constitute a wasted opportunity to show leadership. The ICC is by no means a flawless institution above reproach. On the contrary, it is in need of constructive engagement from its member states, and South Africa could be playing a leading role in helping improve the ICC and its relationship with many African states who have increasingly become dissatisfied with the Court's case selection and efficiency.[299]

Finally, the ICC has found that al-Bashir lacked immunity because Sudan, via the Security Council resolution, had waived his immunity. For that reason, the Bill changes very little for al-Bashir when it says that the Bill does not apply to anyone who enjoys immunity under customary international law.[300] In any event, repealing the Act and withdrawing from the Rome Statute does not revoke obligations incurred by South Africa while party to the Statute.[301] This means that South Africa will continue to carry its ICC obligations to arrest al-Bashir if he were to arrive in South Africa.[302]

The Bill is in many ways similar to the ICC Act. It domesticates international crimes[303] and sets up the domestic processes for the surrender of a person to an 'entity' that has jurisdiction over the international crimes of which the person is accused.[304] An entity is defined as 'the International Criminal Court, any international organisation, international tribunal, international court, or similar international body which has jurisdiction in respect of an international crime'.[305] Section 12 of the Bill envisages entities making requests for the surrender of sought persons. The obvious difference

[298] *Minister of Justice v SALC* (n 258) para 103.

[299] See M du Plessis 'Ramaphosa can renew South African leadership by recommitting to the ICC' (6 February 2018) Chatham House Expert Comment, available at https://www.chathamhouse.org/expert/comment/ramaphosa-can-renew-south-african-leadership-recommitting-icc.

[300] Section 3(1).

[301] Article 127(2) of the Statute.

[302] See in this regard N Pillay and A Mudukuti 'South Africa and the ICC: Dismantling the international criminal justice system to protect one individual?' *Daily Maverick* 19 June 2018, available at https://www.dailymaverick.co.za/article/2018-06-19-south-africa-and-the-icc-dismantling-the-international-criminal-justice-system-to-protect-one-individual/#.WzdjYy2B2gw.

[303] Chapter 2.

[304] Chapter 4. It also provides for the 'extradition' of persons to foreign states for international crimes.

[305] Section 1, definition of 'entity'.

is that once South Africa withdraws from the Statute, the ICC will not have jurisdiction over future crimes or criminals in South Africa.

At the time of writing, the Bill is still at its early stages. It may well be amended as it progresses through the parliamentary process—and it could face possible legal challenge. There is also the hope that South Africa yet sees its position differently. While there is no question that immunities for heads of state is a thorny issue, the details of those debates, and their importance for the future of the ICC, are precisely where South Africa's strength lies. Instead of its strategy of rejection and withdrawal, South Africa could help work with other African states to improve the ICC from within and to help set the agenda of that institution—the world's first and only permanent international criminal court that is able to ensure accountability for the world's worst crimes.[306]

[306] For details of how that might be done, see Du Plessis and Mettraux (n 295) 369; and M du Plessis 'The Omar al-Bashir case: Exploring efforts to resolve the tension between the African Union and the International Criminal Court' in T Maluwa, M du Plessis and D Tladi (eds) *The Pursuit of a Brave New World in International Law: Essays in Honour of John Dugard* (2017) 431.

CHAPTER 11

Extradition

Anton Katz, Max du Plessis, Eshed Cohen and John Dugard

Extradition[1] may be defined as 'the delivery of an accused or a convicted individual to the state where he is accused of, or has been convicted of, a crime, by the state on whose territory he happens for the time to be'.[2]

International law does not recognise any general duty on the part of states to surrender criminals.[3] In practice, international obligations to return criminals are sourced in extradition agreements between states.[4] These treaties can be bilateral or multilateral.[5] State practice demonstrates a preference for bilateral treaties. The United States, for example, has over 100 such treaties in force.[6] South Africa has eight.[7] But South Africa is also party to the European Convention on Extradition,[8] a multilateral extradition treaty between 50 (mostly European) states.[9]

[1] IA Shearer *Extradition in International Law* (1971); NJ Botha 'Extradition' in *Law of South Africa* vol 10, 2 ed (2008); C and I Stanbrook *The Law and Practice of Extradition* 2 ed (2000); J Dugard and C van den Wyngaert (eds) *International Criminal Law and Procedure* (1996); G Gilbert *Transnational Fugitive Offenders in International Law: Extradition and Other Mechanisms* (1998); C Nicholls, C Montgomery, J Knowles, A Doobay and M Summers *The Law of Extradition and Mutual Assistance* 3 ed (2013); M Cherif Bassiouni *International Extradition: United States Law and Practice* 5 ed (2007).

[2] R Jennings and A Watts (eds) *Oppenheim's International Law* vol 1, 9 ed (1992) 948–9.

[3] Shearer (n 1) 237; N Botha 'The basis of extradition: The South African perspective' (1991–92) 17 *SAYIL* 117 at 131–3. But see Cherif Bassiouni (n 1) 25, who argues that there may be a duty in customary international law to extradite for international crimes.

[4] For an examination of the different bases advanced for the granting of extradition, see Botha (n 3). Botha concludes that 'a duty to extradite arises only in the context of a treaty commitment to do so' (147). In *Attorney-General v Andreson* 1897 Off Rep 287 the Court held that there could be no extradition in the absence of an extradition agreement. Cf the dissent of Ameshoff J at 291–4. See also *Harksen v President of the Republic of South Africa* 2000 (2) SA 825 (CC) para 4.

[5] These treaties, like any other, are regulated by the law of treaties as discussed in Chapter 20.

[6] Cherif Bassiouni (n 1) 24.

[7] For a list of these, including the relevant *Government Gazettes* in which they were published, see the Department of Justice's website at http://www.justice.gov.za/ilr/mla.html.

[8] Paris, 13.XII.1957.

[9] Other than state members of the Council of Europe, the Republic of Korea and Israel have signed and ratified the Convention. See further N Botha 'Strange

Some obligations pertaining to extradition are also sourced in multilateral treaties that do not deal exclusively with extradition. For example, the Convention on the Prevention and Punishment of the Crime of Genocide of 1948, in article 7, obliges countries to grant extradition requests for those accused or convicted of genocide.[10] Conversely, the Convention Against Torture prohibits extradition if the requested state has substantial grounds for believing that the sought person will be subject to torture.[11]

International law does not require extradition treaties to follow a particular form. This means that there are general principles that have emerged from the practice of states which are commonly incorporated into extradition agreements. In 1990 the General Assembly of the United Nations approved a Model Treaty on Extradition containing many of these principles, which aims to provide 'a useful framework' for states in the negotiation and revision of bilateral agreements.[12]

Absent a treaty, a state could still grant an extradition request made by another state. Some states, including South Africa, invoke reciprocity and comity as bases for extradition in the absence of a treaty. Comity describes those actions between states based solely on goodwill or courtesy. Reciprocity is when the request for surrender is accompanied by assurances of reciprocal extradition in comparable circumstances.[13] The primary difference between the two is that comity does not presuppose similar counter-performances by the requesting state at a later stage. Both reflect international principles of friendly co-operation among states.[14] They thus enable a state to extradite a sought person on the request of another state in the absence of a treaty. The conditions under which decisions on the basis of reciprocity or comity are made vary from state to state—it all depends on the domestic empowering provisions for the decision.[15]

bedfellows: South Africa and accession to the European Convention on Extradition 1957' (1998) 23 *SAYIL* 247 at 249–53 in which the author describes the present state of South Africa's extradition relations with European states.

[10] For a further discussion of this Convention, see Chapter 10.

[11] Article 3(1) of the Convention against Torture and Other Cruel, Inhuman or Degrading Treatment or Punishment. South Africa ratified this treaty on 10 December 1998. See *Mohamed v President of the RSA* 2001 (3) SA 893 (CC) para 60.

[12] Resolution 45/116 adopted on 14 December 1990: (1991) 30 *ILM* 1407. See further B Swart 'Refusal of extradition and the UN Model Treaty on Extradition' (1992) 23 *Netherlands Yearbook on International Law* 175.

[13] *Harksen* (n 4); *Geuking v President of the Republic of South Africa* 2003 (3) SA 34 (CC) para 2; *President of the Republic of South Africa v Quagliani, and Two Similar Cases* 2009 (2) SA 466 (CC) para 41.

[14] Cherif Bassiouni (n 1) 25.

[15] Ibid 25–6.

Before 1961, when South Africa became a Republic and left the Commonwealth, extradition between South Africa and other states was governed by two international arrangements. Extradition between South Africa and other Commonwealth countries was regulated by the British Fugitive Offenders Act of 1881,[16] while extradition between South Africa and non-Commonwealth states was governed by the British Extradition Acts of 1870 to 1906,[17] which allowed the British government to extend extradition treaties entered into between the British government and other states to British colonies or dominions. After South Africa acquired full treaty-making power, the South African government was able to enter into treaties with other states on its own behalf, and in this case the treaties were made applicable to South Africa under the Extradition Act of 1870 and the Royal Executive Functions and Seals Act of 1934.[18]

When South Africa left the Commonwealth in 1961, all its extradition arrangements with Commonwealth countries, including the United Kingdom, came to an end. South Africa's departure from the Commonwealth and new Republican status had no effect, however, on its extradition treaties with non-Commonwealth states, which remained in force.[19] In 1962 the Extradition Act 67 of 1962 was enacted to govern the country's extradition relations. This statute, which remains in force, empowered the President to enter into extradition agreements with foreign states.[20]

South Africa's political isolation during the apartheid era made it almost impossible for it to extend its network of extradition agreements.[21] Agreements entered into by the British government on behalf of South Africa under the 1870 to 1906 Extradition Acts were carefully preserved,[22] but new agreements were limited to states

[16] 44 & 45 Vict c 69.

[17] 33 & 34 Vict c 52 (1870), 36 & 37 Vict c 60 (1873), 58 & 59 Vict c 33 (1895), 6 Edw VII c 15 (1906). (The Extradition Act 2003 now governs extradition to and from the United Kingdom.)

[18] Section 7 of Act 70 of 1934.

[19] Section 2(4) of the Extradition Act 67 of 1962. See Chapter 20 on succession to extradition agreements. See, too, Botha (n 9).

[20] Section 2 of Act 67 of 1962.

[21] See Botha (n 3) 118, fn 6.

[22] This was not always possible. In 1968, Denmark terminated its agreement with South Africa: Proc 157 *GG* 2101 of 21 June 1968.

within the southern African region[23] and to fellow pariah states—Israel[24] and the Republic of China (Taiwan).[25]

In these circumstances a special arrangement was made to allow South Africa to return a fugitive to a state with which there was no extradition agreement. The State President was empowered by s 3(2) of the 1962 Extradition Act to consent to the surrender of such a person on an ad hoc basis.

South Africa's return to international respectability has rescued it from isolation in respect of extradition. In 1996, South Africa became covered by the Commonwealth Scheme relating to the Rendition of Fugitive Offenders of 1990,[26] when the Extradition Act was amended to allow extradition to a country designated[27] by the President without the need for an extradition agreement.[28]

The Commonwealth Scheme is not a multilateral treaty but rather an agreed guideline of principles on extradition which forms the basis of reciprocating legislation enacted in Commonwealth states. The Extradition Amendment Act of 1996[29] amends the Extradition Act of 1962, inter alia, to bring South African law in line with the guidelines of the Commonwealth Scheme. In 1998, Namibia, Zimbabwe and the United Kingdom were 'designated' for the purposes of extradition.[30]

In the past decade, South Africa has added considerably to its arsenal of extradition treaties. For instance, in 2001 it entered into a

[23] Swaziland (Proc R292 *GGE* 2179 of 4 October 1968 (*Reg Gaz* 1026)); Botswana (Proc R118 *GG* 2376 of 2 May 1969 (*Reg Gaz* 1128)); and Malawi (Proc 67 *GG* 3424 of 24 March 1972).

[24] Proclamation R14 *GGE* 6362 of 5 February 1960 (*Reg Gaz* 6), amended by Proc R184 *GG* 5283 of 10 September 1976 (*Reg Gaz* 2367).

[25] Proclamation 83 *GG* 11316 of 24 May 1988.

[26] This Scheme, drawn up by Commonwealth law ministers, based on an earlier scheme of 1966 (HMSO, London Cmnd 3008) replaces the Fugitive Offenders Act of 1881 (n 16). The text can be found in Annexure F to the South African Law Commission's *Report on International Co-operation in Criminal Prosecutions* (Project 98, December 1995). See further D McClean *International Judicial Assistance* (1992); N Botha 'The Commonwealth Extradition Scheme and the Law Commission Working Paper 56' (1995) 20 *SAYIL* 40; and D van Zyl Smit 'Developments in criminal law and criminal justice: Re-entering the international community—South Africa and extradition' (1995) 6 *Crim LF* 369.

[27] Although the power to 'designate' a state for the purposes of extradition is primarily intended for Commonwealth countries, it is envisaged that 'designation' may also be extended to a non-Commonwealth country that has the appropriate extradition legislation in place: see the South African Law Commission's *Report on International Co-operation in Criminal Prosecutions* (n 26) at 171 (para 6.105).

[28] Section 2(1)*(b)* of Act 67 of 1962, inserted by Act 77 of 1996.

[29] Act 77 of 1996.

[30] GNR 188 *GG* 18663 of 13 February 1998.

new agreement with the United States and, in 2003, it acceded to the European Convention on Extradition of 1957.[31] It has also entered into treaties with Australia, Canada, India and China.[32] In 2012, South Africa also signed and ratified the SADC Protocol on Extradition, a multilateral treaty dealing with extradition among states in the SADC region.[33]

THE IMPACT OF THE CONSTITUTION

1 Human rights

Extradition has not escaped the impact of human rights law.[34] Some human rights principles have been adopted by extradition agreements; others have been used to obstruct extradition despite their absence from the extradition agreement. In the latter case, it is claimed that international human rights norms, whether based in treaty or custom, 'trump' extradition treaty obligations on the ground that they enjoy a higher status as part of the public order of the international community or of a particular region.

In South Africa, the Constitutional Court has recognised that extradition involves an invasion of fundamental human rights.[35] Because South Africa has a justiciable Bill of Rights, extradition proceedings must protect the rights of those who are accused of crimes by the requesting country.[36] Otherwise the extradition and the relevant law could be invalid.[37]

The two principal human rights norms that have been adopted by extradition treaties and legislation concern the death penalty and

[31] GNR 593 *GG* 22430 of 29 June 2001 (*Reg Gaz* 7100), *GG* 24872 of 13 May 2003, respectively. See further HB van Heerden 'Extradition treaties negotiated since 1994' (2005) 30 *SAYIL* 173.

[32] See GNR 719 *GG* 22542 of 1 August 2001 (Australia); GNR 391 *GG* 22284 of 18 May 2001 (Canada); GNR 312 *GG* 28680 of 7 April 2006 (India); GNR 33 *GG* 27168 of 21 January 2005 (China).

[33] States parties include Angola, Botswana, Lesotho, Malawi, Mauritius, Mozambique, Namibia, Seychelles, Swaziland, Tanzania, Zambia and Zimbabwe. GNR 405 *GG* 35368 of 25 May 2012.

[34] See J Dugard and C van den Wyngaert 'Reconciling extradition with human rights' (1998) 92 *AJIL* 187; GN Barrie 'Human rights and extradition proceedings: Changing the traditional landscape' 1998 *TSAR* 125; M du Plessis 'The extraterritorial application of the South African Constitution' (2003) 120 *SALJ* 796 at 800–13; JMT Labuschagne and M Olivier 'Extradition, human rights and the death penalty: Observations on the process of the internationalization of criminal justice values' (2003) 28 *SAYIL* 130; C Pyle *Extradition, Politics and Human Rights* (2001).

[35] *Geuking* (n 13) para 1.

[36] *Quagliani* (n 13) para 39.

[37] Irish courts have refused extradition where it would violate rights guaranteed by the Constitution. See *Finucane v McMahon* [1990] 1 *IR* 165 (HCt & SC); *Magee v O'Dea* [1994] 1 *IR* 500 (HCt).

non-discrimination. Today it is common practice for extradition agreements to exclude extradition where the crime in respect of which extradition is sought is punishable by death in the state requesting extradition but not the requested state, unless the requesting state provides a satisfactory assurance that the death penalty will not be imposed, or, if imposed, will not be executed.[38] In *Mohamed v President of the RSA (Society for the Abolition of the Death Penalty in South Africa Intervening)*[39] the Constitutional Court held that it was unconstitutional to extradite any person (including undocumented foreigners) to a country where he or she may face the death penalty if put on trial. South Africa can only lawfully extradite a person if the requesting state provides an assurance that the death penalty will not be sought, or, if imposed, will not be carried out. As the Constitutional Court put it in *Minister of Home Affairs and Others v Tsebe and Others*:[40]

> We as a nation have chosen to walk the path of the advancement of human rights. By adopting the Constitution we committed ourselves not to do certain things. One of those things is that no matter who the person is and no matter what the crime is that he is alleged to have committed, we shall not in any way be party to his killing as a punishment and we will not hand such person over to another country where to do so will expose him to the real risk of the imposition and execution of the death penalty upon him. This path that we, as a country, have chosen for ourselves is not an easy one. Some of the consequences that may result from our choice are part of the price that we must be prepared to pay as a nation for the advancement of human rights and the creation of the kind of society and world that we may ultimately achieve if we abide by the constitutional values that now underpin our new society since the end of apartheid.

It is also increasingly the practice for treaties to exclude extradition where the requested state 'has substantial grounds for believing that a request for extradition for an ordinary criminal offence has been made for the purpose of prosecuting or punishing a person on account of his race, religion, nationality or political opinion, or that

[38] This formula, adopted from article 11 of the European Convention on Extradition of 1957 ((1960) 359 UNTS 273), appears in article 5 of the US–South African extradition treaty (n 31). In *United States v Burns* [2001] 1 SCR 283, (2001) 40 *ILM* 1034, the Canadian Supreme Court held that there was an obligation on the Canadian government to seek an assurance from the requesting state (if it applied the death penalty) that the death penalty would not be imposed.

[39] 2001 (3) SA 893 (CC).

[40] 2012 (5) SA 467 (CC) para 67. In *Makwakwa v S* [2011] ZAFSHC 27 (11 February 2011) the request for extradition by Lesotho in respect of conduct that included conspiracy to kill the Prime Minister of the Kingdom of Lesotho included a written assurance that the death penalty would not be carried out should it be imposed.

that person's position may be prejudiced for any of these reasons'.[41] In 1996 the Extradition Act was amended to include such a bar to extradition, extended to cover gender discrimination.[42] The UN Model Treaty on Extradition[43] and the Convention against Torture[44] prohibit extradition where there are substantial grounds for believing that the extradited person will be subjected to torture or to cruel, inhuman or degrading treatment or punishment in the requesting state. The UN Model Treaty on Extradition also prohibits extradition if the extradited person is unlikely to receive a fair trial.[45]

The manner in which an obligation contained in a human rights treaty may trump an extradition treaty obligation is illustrated by the decision of the European Court of Human Rights in the *Soering Case*.[46] Soering, a West German national, murdered his girlfriend's parents in Virginia and fled to the United Kingdom, from which his extradition was requested by the United States. After the United Kingdom ordered his extradition, he petitioned the European Commission of Human Rights, which referred the case to the European Court of Human Rights. The Court held that the United Kingdom was not required, by article 3 of the European Convention on Human Rights, which prohibits torture and inhuman or degrading treatment or punishment, to extradite Soering to the United States, where there was a real risk that he would be subjected to inhuman or degrading treatment by being kept on death row for a prolonged period in the state of Virginia. The Court found that the fact that the actual human rights violation would take place outside the United Kingdom did not absolve the United Kingdom from responsibility for any foreseeable consequence of extradition suffered outside its jurisdiction. The same approach was followed by the United Nations Human Rights

[41] See article 3(2) of the European Convention on Extradition (n 31); article 4(3) of the US–South African Extradition Treaty (n 31).

[42] Sections 11*(b)*(iv) and 12(2)*(c)*(ii) of Act 67 of 1962.

[43] Article 3(f) (n 12).

[44] Article 3 of the Convention against Torture and Other Cruel, Inhuman or Degrading Treatment or Punishment of 1984, (1984) 24 *ILM* 535. For a South African domestic example where the treaty was applied, see *Tantoush v Refugee Appeal Board* 2008 (1) SA 232 (T).

[45] Article 3(f) (n 12) prohibits extradition if the extradited person would not receive the minimum guarantees for a fair trial contained in article 14 of the International Covenant on Civil and Political Rights.

[46] ECHR Series A no 161 (judgment of 7 July 1989), (1989) 28 *ILM* 1063. Cited with approval by Gubbay CJ in *Catholic Commission for Justice and Peace in Zimbabwe v Attorney General* 1993 (4) SA 239 (ZS) 261–4. See further C van den Wyngaert 'Applying the European Convention on Human Rights to extradition: Opening Pandora's box?' (1990) 39 *ICLQ* 757; R Lillich 'The *Soering Case*' (1991) 85 *AJIL* 128.

Committee in *Ng v Canada*.[47] Here, the Committee held that Canada had violated its obligations under article 7 of the International Covenant on Civil and Political Rights prohibiting cruel, inhuman or degrading treatment or punishment by extraditing Ng to the United States when it could reasonably have foreseen that, if sentenced to death in California, he would be executed by gas asphyxiation, a form of punishment in violation of that prohibition.

There are other human rights violations relating to the prohibition against cruel, inhuman or degrading treatment or punishment that may, it has been suggested, obstruct extradition. They are life imprisonment, harsh prison conditions, corporal punishment and brutal pre-trial interrogation methods.[48]

This is a rapidly developing branch of extradition law. The traditional view that the courts of a requested state will not examine the standards of justice applied in the requesting state is no longer followed by many states.[49] Most courts today seriously consider the human rights implications of extradition; and there is increasing practice in favour of making extradition conditional upon the giving of satisfactory assurances by the requesting state that the extradited person's human rights will be respected in that state.[50]

In *Kaunda and Others v President of the Republic of South Africa and Others*,[51] an appeal was made to the above principles in highly peculiar circumstances. The applicants, South African nationals, were arrested in Zimbabwe on suspicion of being mercenaries en route to Equatorial Guinea to stage a coup against the President of that state. Fearing that they might be extradited to Equatorial Guinea, where they anticipated an unfair trial followed by the imposition of the death penalty, they brought proceedings in South Africa to compel the South African government, inter alia, to seek an assurance from the Zimbabwean government that they would not be extradited to Equatorial Guinea, alternatively, if so extradited, to seek assurances that they would receive a fair trial in Equatorial Guinea and not be sentenced to death. The Constitutional Court dismissed the application largely on the ground that it was premature because there was

[47] 98 ILR 479.

[48] Dugard and Van den Wyngaert (n 34) 200–1. The Court in *S v Williams* 1988 (4) SA 49 (W) seemed to recognise this possibility when it stated that it would not extradite a fugitive to a state likely to impose a sentence that 'is wholly inappropriate or unconscionable' (53F–G, 54E–I).

[49] Dugard and Van den Wyngaert (n 34) 189–91.

[50] Ibid 206–8. See *Robinson v Minister of Justice and Constitutional Development* 2006 (6) SA 214 (C) 230F–G.

[51] 2005 (4) SA 235 (CC). For critical discussion, see S Pete and M du Plessis, 'South African nationals abroad and their right to diplomatic protection: Lessons from the "Mercenaries Case"' (2006) 22 *SAJHR* 439.

no clear evidence that the applicants were likely to be extradited to Equatorial Guinea.[52] Moreover, the Court stressed that the arrest of the applicants in Zimbabwe and 'the possibility of their being extradited from Zimbabwe to Equatorial Guinea (were) not the result of any unlawful conduct on the part of the government or of the breach of any duty owed to them'.[53] The Court's judgment does, however, give tentative support to the need to respect human rights in the extradition process. The Court stated:

> [I]f the allegations by the applicants that they will not get a fair trial in Equatorial Guinea prove to be correct, and they are convicted and sentenced to death, there will have been a grave breach of international law harmful to our government's foreign policy and its aspirations for a democratic Africa . . . .
>
> It cannot . . . be said that there is not a risk that the consequences that the applicants fear will happen. Should that risk become a reality the Government would be obliged to respond positively. Given its stated foreign policy, there is no reason to believe that this will not be done.[54]

The Court furthermore stressed that 'decisions made by the government in these matters are subject to constitutional control'.[55]

The extradition agreement between South Africa and the People's Republic of China of 2005 contains a provision that would permit South Africa to deny extradition that might result in the violation of human rights. Article 4(b) permits extradition to be refused where 'the probable penalty that may be imposed in the Requesting State is in conflict with the fundamental principles of the laws of the Requested State'.[56]

Mohamed did not explicitly deal with what would happen if a requesting state refused to give an assurance that the death penalty would not be imposed on a sought person. However, the Constitutional Court in *Tsebe* dealt with precisely this issue.

In *Tsebe* Botswana requested the extradition of Mr Tsebe and Mr Phale, who had fled to and entered South Africa. Both citizens were accused of murder, and the extradition was requested to try the two for murder. However, in Botswana, a person convicted of murder could face the death penalty. The South African Minister of Justice, as per *Mohamed,* thus requested an assurance from Botswana that the

[52] Subsequently, the applicants were tried and sentenced to short jail terms in Zimbabwe. No attempt was made to extradite them to Equatorial Guinea.

[53] *Kaunda* (n 51) para 50.

[54] Ibid paras 126–7.

[55] Ibid para 144(6). See further M du Plessis 'The *Thatcher Case* and the supposed delicacies of foreign affairs: A plea for a principled (and realistic) approach to the duty of government to ensure that South Africans abroad are not exposed to the death penalty' (2007) 20 *SACJ* 143.

[56] See n 32.

two sought persons would not be executed if convicted. Botswana refused to give this assurance because its domestic legislation and the treaty with South Africa did not provide for the giving of such an assurance. Despite all this, the Department of Home Affairs decided to deport the two. The issue therefore was whether South Africa could deport or extradite the two even though Botswana had not given the requested assurance.

The Constitutional Court reiterated the principle in *Mohamed* that the government has no power to extradite or deport or in any way remove from South Africa to a retentionist state any person who, to its knowledge, if deported or extradited to such a state, will face the real risk of the imposition and execution of the death penalty. To do so would be to contravene the government's obligation to fulfil and protect the right to life.[57]

The Court went on to find that extradition or deportation cannot occur where a requesting state refuses to give the assurance regarding the death sentence. That is, the fact that a requesting state refuses to give the assurance does not change South Africa's obligations to protect and fulfil the right to life. And these obligations prevent extradition or deportation without the requisite assurance.[58]

The Court also noted that article 6 of the extradition treaty between South Africa and Botswana allowed either country to refuse extradition 'if under the law of the requesting Party the offence for which extradition is requested is punishable by death and if the death penalty is not provided for such offence by the law of the requested Party'.[59] South Africa, by refusing extradition, was therefore not breaching its duties under international law to Botswana.

Moreover, article 5(c) of the SADC Protocol on Extradition, to which Botswana and South Africa are party, allows for Botswana to make the requisite assurance, and allows South Africa to refuse extradition in the absence of such an assurance.[60] However, South Africa, if it refuses to extradite because there is no assurance, shall, if the other state so requests, 'submit the case to its competent authorities with a view to taking appropriate action against the person for the offence for which extradition had been requested'.

On the facts of *Tsebe*, therefore, Botswana was empowered under international law to give an assurance that neither sought person would be executed if convicted. The Court thus encouraged the South African government to continue to seek a political solution to

[57] *Tsebe* (n 40) para 43.
[58] Ibid para 66.
[59] Ibid para 31.
[60] Ibid paras 34 and 64.

the extradition and acquire the assurance from Botswana.[61] Until then, however, the Court held that neither could lawfully be deported or extradited to Botswana.

2 The relationship between international and municipal law

The Constitution's treatment of international law is discussed in Chapter 4. Given how the Constitution relates international law to the South African municipal system, there are a number of constitutional anomalies arising from the present Extradition Act. In the first place, it is difficult to reconcile the power of the President to consent to an ad hoc extradition under s 3(2)[62] with the requirement in s 231 of the 1996 Constitution that treaties be approved by Parliament to bind the Republic internationally, and that they be incorporated by national legislation to have domestic effect. The President's consent to extradite under s 3(2) is preceded by an exchange of notes between South Africa and the state requesting extradition, which appears to constitute an international agreement, for which s 231 requires approval by Parliament as well as incorporation into domestic law by national legislation. However, in *Harksen v President of the RSA*,[63] the Constitutional Court held that the consent of the President under s 3(2) 'was a domestic act never intended to create international legal rights and obligations',[64] and that the exchange of notes (in this case between South Africa and Germany) did not constitute an agreement and therefore did 'not provide support for the conclusion that the President's consent under s 3(2) was anything more than a domestic act'.[65] The Court further dismissed the argument that the President's

[61] *Tsebe* (n 40) paras 52, 57 and 59. Botswana requested South Africa to try the two accused in South Africa. But South Africa could not accede to this request because there is no legislation authorising South Africa to prosecute people for committing murders outside of the territory of South Africa. Arguably, this could constitute a breach of South Africa's duty under article 5(c) of the SADC Protocol, but the Court did not consider this point.

[62] Ironically this power seems to have been used more frequently since 1990 than before: Botha (n 3) at 137 lists three cases in which this power was used before 1990. Since then it has been used in a number of reported cases: *Hirantner v Minister of Law and Order* 1992 (1) SACR 414 (W); *S v Bell* [1997] 2 All SA 692 (E); *S v Thornhill* 1997 (2) SACR 626 (C); *Harksen v President of the Republic of South Africa* 2000 (2) SA 825 (CC) at 829E–F; *Geuking v President of the Republic of South Africa* 2003 (3) SA 34 (CC).

[63] 2000 (2) SA 825 (CC). For comments on this case and the decision of the Cape Provincial Division in *S v Harksen; Harksen v President of the RSA; Harksen v Wagner* 2000 (1) SA 1185 (C), see J Dugard and G Abraham 'Public international law' 2000 *Annual Survey* 103 at 114; N Botha 'Further questions and answers on extradition in the South African context' (2002) 27 *SAYIL* 311; I Southwood 'Constitutionality of the extradition process' (2000) 25 *SAYIL* 260.

[64] 2000 (2) SA 825 (CC) para 21.

[65] Ibid para 22.

consent under s 3(2) allowed the executive to bypass the requirement of parliamentary approval for treaties laid down in s 231(2) of the Constitution.[66] In *Geuking v President of the Republic of South Africa*, the Constitutional Court dismissed a challenge to s 3(2) on the ground that it does not empower the President to consent to surrender a person to a foreign state.[67] The Court seemed to hold that such a power was necessarily implied in s 3(2).[68]

Secondly, another anomaly arising from the Extradition Act is that the procedure for incorporating extradition agreements entered into after 1996, and 'designation arrangements' made after this date, into domestic law, fails to follow the requirements prescribed by s 231 of the 1996 Constitution. The Act provides, correctly, that such agreements and designations must be approved by Parliament,[69] as required by s 231(2), but it does not provide for the incorporation of the agreement or 'designation' into domestic law by 'national legislation' as required by s 231(4). Instead, it merely provides that the Minister of Justice shall give notice of Parliament's approval of the agreement or 'designation' in the *Government Gazette*,[70] which notice does not qualify as 'national legislation'.[71] This anomaly arises because the Extradition Amendment Act 77 of 1996 was adopted while the Interim Constitution was still in force and before the adoption of the Constitution of the Republic of South Africa, 1996.[72] The Interim Constitution did not require the legislative incorporation of treaties. The failure of the Extradition Act to provide for incorporation as required by s 231(4) of the Constitution was challenged in *President of the Republic of South Africa v Quagliani, and Two Similar Cases*.[73] The Constitutional Court avoided dealing directly with the challenge and held instead—in a form of reasoning that is difficult to follow—that '[e]ither the Agreement has "become law" in South Africa as a result of the prior existence of the [Extradition] Act which constitutes the anticipatory enactment of the Agreement for the purposes of section 231(4) of the Constitution. Or the Agreement has not "become law" in the Republic as contemplated by section 231(4)

[66] *Harksen* 2000 (2) SA 825 (CC) 835–6.

[67] 2003 (3) SA 34 (CC) ('*Geuking v President of the RSA*').

[68] Ibid 44–5.

[69] Section 2(3)*(a)* of Act 67 of 1962.

[70] Section 2(3)*ter*.

[71] See s 239 of the Constitution 1996 for the definition of 'national legislation', which does not include government notices.

[72] This is clear from the report of the South African Law Commission on International Co-operation in Criminal Prosecutions (n 26) 167 (para 6.90).

[73] 2009 (2) SA 466 (CC).

but the provisions of the Act are all that is required to give domestic effect to the international obligation that the Agreement creates.'[74]

The decision in *Quagliani* has been criticised as not having adequately addressed the constitutional difficulty.[75]

3 The rule of law

Most extraditions occur in terms of an extradition agreement. In such a case, extradition proceedings are governed both by the particular extradition agreement in terms of which the foreign state requests extradition and by the Extradition Act 67 of 1962. While the extradition agreement determines the offences in respect of which extradition is possible and the circumstances in which extradition may be refused, the Extradition Act prescribes the procedure to be followed in extradition proceedings and some of the circumstances in which extradition may be refused.

Because the extradition process is regulated by an Act, the process entails the exercise of public power by various actors at different stages. For the most part, there is no issue that the powers given to the Minister of Justice and magistrates by the Extradition Act are public in nature. Although an extradition enquiry before a magistrate is judicial (and not administrative in nature)[76] the Supreme Court of Appeal held in *Zuma v National Director of Public Prosecutions*:[77]

> It is true, as counsel for the appellants reminded us, that the rule of law and the principle of legality require State conduct (which includes the conduct of a judge) to be in accordance with law.

This means that these powers must be exercised lawfully, in good faith and rationally.[78] If not, such decisions can be reviewed and set aside. The review of magistrates' and the Minister's decisions under the Extradition Act are dealt with below. But it is important to note that since the advent of the Constitution, the bases and grounds for reviewing these decisions have been tempered by the Constitution's commitment to the rule of law. In *Fedsure Life Assurance Ltd v Greater Johannesburg Transitional Metropolitan Council*, the Constitutional

[74] Paragraph 46.

[75] Du Toit et al *Commentary on the Criminal Procedure Act* (vol 2) Appendix B16–B17; N Botha 'Rewriting the Constitution: The "strange alchemy" of Justice Sachs, indeed!: South African judicial decisions' (2009) 34 *SAYIL* 253–67. See further Chapter 4.

[76] *Minister of Justice v Additional Magistrate, Cape Town* 2001 (2) SACR 49 (C) 61.

[77] 2008 (1) SACR 298 (SCA) para 15.

[78] See *Fedsure Life Assurance Ltd v Greater Johannesburg Transitional Metropolitan Council* 1999 (1) SA 374 (CC) para 56; *President of the Republic of South Africa v South African Rugby Football Union* 2000 (1) SA 1 (CC) para 148; *Pharmaceutical Manufacturers Association of South Africa: In re Ex parte President of the Republic of South Africa* 2000 (2) SA 674 (CC) para 80.

Court explained that '[t]he rule of law—to the extent at least that it expresses this principle of legality—is generally understood to be a fundamental principle of constitutional law'.[79] The South African Constitution acknowledges this in s 1*(c)*, which mandates that South Africa is a Republic founded on the value of the rule of law.

EXTRADITION DISTINGUISHED FROM OTHER FORMS OF REMOVAL

1 Deportation (disguised extradition) from and to South Africa

'Disguised extradition' may be achieved by deporting a fugitive to a state in which he is accused of a crime, in accordance with deportation procedures. This practice is widely condemned[80] as it deprives the deportee of the rights to which he would be entitled if he were extradited. Inter alia, it deprives him of the right to raise the political offence exception.[81]

The threat posed to human rights by disguised extradition is starkly illustrated by *Mohamed v President of the RSA*.[82] Mohamed, a Tanzanian national, fled to South Africa after participating in the bombing of the US embassy in Dar es Salaam in 1998. He entered South Africa on a false passport and under an assumed name on a visitor's visa. In 1999 Mohamed's whereabouts were discovered by the US Federal Bureau of Investigation (FBI) and it then entered into negotiations with the South African police and immigration authorities for the expeditious transfer of Mohamed to New York, where he had been indicted for murder for the bombing of the US embassy. Although there was an extradition agreement in force between the United States and South Africa, it was decided to declare him to be a prohibited person and deport him immediately to the United States.

[79] *Fedsure Life Assurance* (n 78) para 56.

[80] Shearer (n 1) 76–91; C van den Wyngaert *The Political Offence Exception: The Delicate Problem of Balancing the Rights of the Individual and International Public Order* (1980) 52–63; MG Cowling 'Unmasking "disguised extradition"—Some glimmer of hope' (1992) 109 *SALJ* 241. See, too, the judgment of the European Court of Human Rights in the *Bozano Case* ECHR Series A vol 111 (judgment of 18 December 1986) discussed by Van den Wyngaert (n 46) 774.

[81] In 1962, Britain deported Dr Soblen, a citizen of the United States, to the United States to face a charge of espionage. Had the extradition agreement between the two countries been invoked, Dr Soblen would have been able to rely on the political offence exception. See *R v Brixton Prison (Governor): Ex p Soblen* [1962] 3 All ER 641 (CA); P O'Higgins 'Disguised extradition: The *Soblen Case*' (1964) 24 Mod LR 521.

[82] Supra (n 39). See, on this case, M du Plessis 'The extra-territorial application of the South African Constitution' (2003) 120 *SALJ* 797; N Botha 'Deportation, extradition and the role of the state' (2001) 26 *SAYIL* 227; J Dugard and G Abraham 'Public international law' 2001 *Annual Survey* 128 at 142.

As a result, he was not afforded the opportunity to require the South African government to obtain an assurance from the government of the United States that, if convicted, he would not be sentenced to death and executed. Thus, he was treated differently from a co-accused whose extradition from Germany was made conditional upon an assurance from the United States that he would not be sentenced to death.[83]

The Constitutional Court held that the deportation of Mohamed violated both the Aliens Control Act, 1991 and the Constitution. The former statute permits deportation only to a country of which the person is a national.[84] The Constitution had been violated in that the South African immigration authorities had failed to obtain a prior undertaking from the US government that, if convicted, the death penalty would not be imposed on Mohamed. This failure infringed his rights to human dignity, to life and to not to be punished in a cruel, inhuman or degrading manner. The Court made it clear that a person ought not to be deported or extradited to another state where there was a real risk that his basic human rights would be violated in that state.[85] It stated:

> For the South African government to co-operate with a foreign government to secure the removal of a fugitive from South Africa to a country of which the fugitive is not a national and with which he had no connection other than that he is to be put on trial for his life there, is contrary to the underlying values of our Constitution. It is inconsistent with the government's obligation to protect the right to life of everyone in South Africa, and it ignores the commitment implicit in the Constitution that South Africa will not be a party to the imposition of cruel, inhuman or degrading punishment.[86]

The Court ordered that its judgment be delivered to the Federal Court in New York before which Mohamed stood trial. Mohamed was convicted but not sentenced to death.

The Constitutional Court's decision in *Mohamed* has not always been scrupulously followed by Home Affairs officials. That is best illustrated by the removal of Mr Rashid from South Africa to Pakistan during 2005 on account of his alleged involvement in terrorism, and under circumstances where Rashid appeared to be at risk of torture or inhuman treatment if delivered to Pakistan. Such removals, to what have become known as 'black sites' in the so-called

[83] *Mohamed* (n 39) paras 44 and 52–3.

[84] Ibid 906–9.

[85] Here, the Court relied on *Soering v UK* (1989) 11 EHRR 439 and *Minister of Justice v Burns* [2001] 1 SCR 283, (2001) 40 *ILM* 234.

[86] *Mohamed* (n 39) para 58. The United Nations Human Rights Committee reached a similar conclusion in *Judge v Canada* (2003) 42 *ILM* 1214, where Canada deported a person to the United States without first ensuring that a sentence of death would not be carried out.

war on terror, have been condemned judicially by South African courts and others.[87]

Where a person has been irregularly deported to South Africa in a 'disguised extradition', a South African court should refuse to exercise jurisdiction. In *S v Rosslee*[88] the Cape Provincial Division held otherwise, where an accused person was deported to South Africa by Namibia (with which South Africa at that time had no extradition agreement) after a 'tip off' from the South African police. This decision, which cannot be reconciled with either the English decisions of *R v Bow Street Magistrates, Ex parte Mackeson*[89] and *Bennett v Horseferry Road Magistrates' Court*,[90] or the spirit of *Mohamed*, should not be followed.[91] This applies particularly where the police of the receiving state are themselves complicit in the deportation. Different considerations may, however, apply when the authorities of the receiving state are in no way involved in the deportation.[92]

2 Abduction

One state may not exercise its police powers in the territory of another state. Consequently, the abduction or kidnapping of a person from state 'A' by agents of state 'B' to stand trial in state B is a clear violation of the territorial sovereignty of state A.[93] In such a case, the injured state is entitled to demand the return of the abducted person and may—if there is an extradition agreement—request the extradition of the abductors to stand trial on a charge of kidnapping. The abducted person may, moreover, institute civil proceedings for

[87] For example, Mr Rashid's removal was declared unlawful by the Supreme Court of Appeal in *Jeebhai v Minister of Home Affairs* 2009 (5) SA 54 (SCA). For a discussion of the facts and law, see M du Plessis 'Removals, terrorism and human rights—Reflections on Rashid' (2009) 25 *SAJHR* 353, 360–2. See also the case of *Samotse v Minister of Home Affairs* [2014] ZAGPPHC 1001 (23 December 2014). Most recently, see the decision of the European Court of Human Rights in *Abu Zubaydah v Lithuania* (Application No 46454/11, 31 May 2018) in which the Court strongly condemned Lithuania for its role in the CIA rendition and torture programme.

[88] 1994 (2) SACR 441 (C).

[89] [1982] 75 App R 24. This decision, involving Rhodesia—Zimbabwe—was not followed in *R v Plymouth Magistrates' Court, Ex parte Driver* [1985] 2 All ER 681 DC. This decision was later itself overruled in *Bennett v Horseferry Road Magistrates' Court* [1993] 3 All ER 138 (HL).

[90] [1993] 3 All ER 138 (HL).

[91] See the criticisms of *Rosslee* in J Dugard 'Public international law' 1994 *Annual Survey* 98 at 110–11.

[92] See *S v Beahan* 1992 (1) SACR 307 (ZS).

[93] For the approach of the European Court of Human Rights to abduction, see *Öçalan v Turkey* (2003) 42 *ILM* 257 at 270–97; A Künzli '*Öçalan v Turkey*: Some comments' (2004) 17 *Leiden Journal of International Law* 141.

damages against his abductors.[94] The most effective way to deter territorial violations of this kind is probably for the courts of the abducting state to refuse to exercise jurisdiction over the abductee as this would remove the incentive for the abduction.[95] This, however, has not been the approach of the courts of most countries.[96]

South African courts, relying on Anglo-American authority[97]—and Israel's exercise of criminal jurisdiction over Adolf Eichmann after his kidnapping from Argentina[98]—repeatedly held that they had jurisdiction to try abducted political opponents of the government during the apartheid era.[99] However, in 1991, in a matter that commenced[100] before the abandonment of apartheid in February 1990, the Appellate Division held in *S v Ebrahim*[101] that *under Roman-Dutch law*, a South African court has no competence to try a person

[94] *R v Officer Commanding Depot Battalion RASC, Colchester: Ex p Elliott* [1949] 1 All ER 373 (KB) 376G–H; *S v Ramotse* (1970) cited in *Ex parte Ebrahim: In re Maseko* 1988 (1) SA 991 (T) 1003D. In 1962, an out-of-court settlement was made by the state in a civil action for damages for unlawful arrest instituted by Anderson Ganyile. For a description of this arrest, see E Kahn 'Constitutional and administrative law' 1962 *Annual Survey* 1 at 52, and *Ganyile v Minister of Justice* 1962 (1) SA 647 (E). See, too, *Ebrahim v Minister of Law and Order* 1993 (2) SA 559 (T) in which the plaintiff successfully claimed damages for his abduction by South African governmental agents from Swaziland (commented on in (1992/3) 18 *SAYIL* 142). In *Minister of Law and Order v Thandani* 1991 (4) SA 862 (A) the plaintiff successfully sued the South African police for handing him over to the Ciskei police in breach of the extradition agreement between South Africa and Ciskei.

[95] This was acknowledged by Steyn JA in *S v Ebrahim* 1991 (2) SA 553 (A) 576E. See, too, the *dictum* of Lord Griffiths in *Bennett* (n 90) 151B.

[96] Shearer (n 1) 72–6; Van den Wyngaert (n 80) 50–63.

[97] On the pre-1993 position in England, see *R v Officer Commanding Depot Battalion RASC, Colchester* (n 94); *R v Plymouth Magistrates' Court, Ex parte Driver* [1985] 2 All ER 681 (QB); F Morgenstern 'Jurisdiction in seizures effected in violation of international law' (1952) 29 *BYIL* 265; P O'Higgins 'Unlawful seizure and irregular extradition' (1960) 36 *BYIL* 279. English law has now changed dramatically as a result of *Bennett v Horseferry Magistrates' Court* (n 90) (discussed below). Cf the decision of the European Court of Human Rights in the *Stocké Case* ECHR Series A no 199 (judgment of 19 March 1991).

[98] *Government of Israel v Eichmann* 36 ILR 18 (1961).

[99] *Ganyile* (n 94) 652F–H; *Abrahams v Minister of Justice* 1963 (4) SA 542 (C); *S v Ramotse*, reported in J Dugard 'Foreign affairs and public international law' 1970 *Annual Survey* 69 at 80–2; *Ndhlovu v Minister of Justice* 1976 (4) SA 250 (N); *Nduli v Minister of Justice* 1978 (1) SA 893 (A); *Ex parte Ebrahim: In re S v Maseko* 1988 (1) SA 991 (T). The Rhodesian courts followed the South African decisions: *S v Ndhlovu* 1977 (4) SA 125 (RA).

[100] *Ex parte Ebrahim: In re S v Maseko* 1988 (1) SA 991 (T).

[101] Supra (n 95); (1992) 31 *ILM* 888 (English translation). See on this decision J Dugard 'No jurisdiction over abducted persons in Roman-Dutch law: *Male captus, male detentus*' (1991) 7 *SAJHR* 199; MG Cowling '*S v Ebrahim*' (1991) *SACJ* 384; JHT Labuschagne 'Die volkeregtelike dimensie van staatlike regsnorming of wetsuitleg' (1992) 55 *THRHR* 155.

abducted from another state by agents of the prosecuting state.[102] Consequently, it set aside the conviction and sentence of 20 years' imprisonment imposed on Ebrahim, an ANC operative kidnapped from Swaziland by agents of the South African state and brought to trial before the Transvaal Provincial Division on a charge of treason. The earlier South African decisions were distinguished on the facts[103] or rejected on the ground that they were premised on English law and took no account of Roman-Dutch law. Although the Court made it clear that its decision was based on Roman-Dutch law and not international law,[104] it stated that the rule prohibiting the exercise of jurisdiction over an abducted person was premised on considerations such as the promotion of human rights, good inter-state relations and respect for territorial sovereignty.[105]

Shortly afterwards, the Zimbabwe Supreme Court gave its approval to *S v Ebrahim* in *S v Beahan*.[106] Here, however, Gubbay CJ placed greater emphasis on international law in holding that:

> There is an inherent objection to [exercising jurisdiction over an abductee] both on grounds of public policy pertaining to international ethical norms and because it imperils and corrodes the peaceful coexistence and mutual respect of sovereign nations. For abduction is illegal under international law, provided the abductor was not acting on his own initiative and without the authority or connivance of his government. A contrary view would amount to a declaration that the end justifies the means, thereby encouraging states to become law-breakers in order to secure the conviction of a private individual.[107]

Considerations of this kind were ignored by the Supreme Court of the United States in its much-criticised decision in *United States v Alvarez-Machain*,[108] in which it held that the forcible abduction of a Mexican national from Mexico by US law enforcement agents did not serve as a bar to his trial in the United States. In a dissenting opinion, Justice Stevens invoked *S v Ebrahim* for his conclusion that 'most courts throughout the civilized world . . . will be deeply disturbed by the "monstrous" decision' of the majority.[109]

S v Ebrahim has been followed by the House of Lords in a case of

[102] At 579F–G.

[103] At 568H–J. Here the Court distinguished the Appellate Division decision in *Nduli v Minister of Justice* (n 99).

[104] *S v Ebrahim* (n 95) at 569A–B.

[105] At 582C–E.

[106] 1992 (1) SACR 307 (ZS). See, too, the judgment of the Court *a quo* in *S v Beahan* 1990 (2) SACR 44 (Z).

[107] At 317D–F.

[108] (1992) 31 *ILM* 900.

[109] At 917–18. Justices Blackmun and O'Connor concurred in this dissent. For comments on this case, see 'Agora: International kidnapping' in (1992) 86 *AJIL* 736;

South African origin containing elements of disguised extradition and abduction. In *Bennett v Horseferry Road Magistrates' Court*,[110] a New Zealand national wanted by the English police on charges of fraud committed in the United Kingdom was arrested in South Africa and forcibly returned to the United Kingdom by the South African police, acting in collusion with the English police, under the pretext of deporting him to New Zealand via the United Kingdom. This scheme was devised by the police forces of the two countries as a result of the absence of an extradition agreement between South Africa and the United Kingdom. After examining the judicial precedents on disguised extradition and abduction, including *S v Ebrahim*, the House of Lords held that it would decline to exercise jurisdiction over Bennett as the manner in which his presence had been secured amounted to an abuse of the process of the Court. The Court stressed the importance of refusing to exercise jurisdiction in such a case in order to discourage practices of abduction and unlawful extradition. Lord Griffiths stated:

> Extradition procedures are designed not only to ensure that criminals are returned from one country to another but also to protect the rights of those who are accused of crimes by the requesting country. Thus sufficient evidence has to be produced to show a *prima facie* case against the accused and the rule of speciality protects the accused from being tried for any crime other than that for which he was extradited. If a practice developed in which the police or prosecuting authorities of this country ignored extradition procedures and secured the return of an accused by a mere request to police colleagues in another country they would be flouting the extradition procedures and depriving the accused of the safeguards built into the extradition process for his benefit. It is to my mind unthinkable that in such circumstances the court should declare itself to be powerless and stand idly by.[111]

In approving this approach, Lord Bridge declared:

> There is, I think, no principle more basic to any proper system of law than the maintenance of the rule of law itself. When it is shown that the law enforcement agency responsible for bringing a prosecution has only been enabled to do so by participating in violations of international law and of the laws of another state in order to secure the presence of the accused within the territorial jurisdiction of the court, I think that respect for the rule of law demands that the court take cognisance of that circumstance. To hold that the court may turn a blind eye to executive lawlessness beyond the frontiers of its own jurisdiction is, to my mind, an insular and unacceptable view. Having then taken cognisance of the lawlessness it would again appear to me to be a wholly inadequate response for the court to hold that the only remedy lies in

R Rayfuse 'International abduction and the United States Supreme Court: The law of the jungle reigns' (1993) 42 *ICLQ* 882.

[110] Supra (n 90). *Sed contra*, see the opinion of the Lord Justice-General of Scotland in *Bennett, Petitioner* 1994 SCCR 902.

[111] *Bennett* (n 90) 150–1.

civil proceedings at the suit of the defendant or in disciplinary or criminal proceedings against the individual officers of the law enforcement agency who were concerned in the illegal action taken. Since the prosecution could never have been brought if the defendant had not been illegally abducted, the whole proceeding is tainted.[112]

The philosophy expounded in *S v Ebrahim* was applied to relations between South Africa, Ciskei and Bophuthatswana, which remained nominally independent under South African law until 1994. In *Minister of Law and Order v Thandani*,[113] *S v Wellem*[114] and *S v Buys*,[115] the failure of the police forces of these territories to respect each others' borders, and to follow proper extradition procedures for the rendition of fugitives from justice, was condemned and the exercise of jurisdiction refused. In a number of other extraordinary decisions, however, both the lower courts[116] and the Appellate Division[117] condoned cross-border arrests, police deception and the refusal of the respective police forces of these territories to follow extradition procedures.

The failure of courts, including the Appellate Division in *S v Mahala*[118] and *S v December*,[119] to accept that the 'collection' or 'apprehension' (if not formal 'arrest') of a fugitive by the South African police in the territory of Ciskei or Bophuthatswana had been a violation of another state's territorial sovereignty—and therefore contrary to the fundamental jurisdictional rules proclaimed in the *Lotus Case*[120]—can only be explained on the grounds that these courts did not actually believe that Ciskei and Bophuthatswana were genuine sovereign independent states. While it is possible to sympathise with this judicial cynicism about the 'independence' of the homeland states or Bantustans, particularly as the political decision to re-incorporate them into South Africa had already been made at this time, it is unfortunate that the judges did not fashion a rule premised on the limited sovereignty of Ciskei and Bophuthatswana. Instead, we have a number of unreasoned and uninformed decisions,

[112] Bennett (n 90) 155F–I. See, too, the *dictum* of Lord Lowry at 163.

[113] 1991 (4) SA 862 (A).

[114] 1993 (2) SACR 18 (E).

[115] 1994 (1) SACR 530 (O).

[116] *S v Mahala* 1992 (2) SACR 305 (E); *S v Mofokeng* 1993 (2) SACR 697 (NC); *S v Mabena* 1993 (2) SACR 295 (B); *S v Mahoko* 1993 (2) SACR 509 (B).

[117] *S v Mahala* 1994 (1) SACR 510 (A); *S v December* 1995 (1) SACR 438 (A).

[118] 1994 (1) SACR 510 (A).

[119] 1995 (1) SACR 438 (A).

[120] 1927 PCIJ Reports Series A no 10. See Chapter 9.

which take no account of the basic principles of international law that seek to limit the law and philosophy of *S v Ebrahim*.[121]

The only solution is for the courts of post-apartheid South Africa to repudiate these decisions as judicial aberrations applicable only to the Bantustan states and not to relations between South Africa and foreign states.

3 Surrender to international criminal tribunals

Extradition is to be distinguished from surrender to international criminal tribunals. The latter entails the surrender by a state of a person sought by an international criminal tribunal to that tribunal. There is no requesting state, but a request by an international criminal tribunal.

Under South African law, surrender to the International Criminal Court is regulated by the Implementation of the Rome Statute of the International Criminal Court Act 27 of 2002. This is discussed fully in Chapter 10.

EXTRADITION FROM SOUTH AFRICA TO FOREIGN STATES

The Extradition Act regulates the process for extradition from South Africa to another state. The Act prescribes different processes for extradition depending on whether the requesting state is a foreign state or an associated state.

The Act defines a foreign state as including any foreign territory.[122] An associated state is then defined in s 6 of the Act.[123] There are two requirements for a foreign state to be an associated state. First, the foreign state must be in Africa. Secondly, there must be an extradition treaty between the Republic and that African state that provides for the endorsement for warrants of arrest on a reciprocal basis. We first deal below with the process for a foreign state, while the next section of this chapter deals with the process for requests by an associated state.

The process of extraditing a person from South Africa to a foreign state can be divided into three phases: the administrative phase, the judicial phase and the executive phase.[124]

[121] See the criticisms of decisions such as *S v Mahala* and *S v December* in J Dugard 'Abduction: Does the Appellate Division care about international law?' (1996) 12 *SAJHR* 24; GN Barrie 'The friendly posse and the disregard for territorial jurisdiction' (1996) 113 *SALJ* 576; HA Strydom 'Abductions on foreign soil—again: *S v Mahala*' (1993) 9 *SAJHR* 308; N Botha 'Aspects of extradition and deportation' (1993/94) 19 *SAYIL* 163; JT Schoombie 'A licence for unlawful arrests across the borders' (1984) 101 *SALJ* 713.

[122] Section 1 definition of 'foreign state'.

[123] Section 1 definition of 'associated state'.

[124] *Carolissen v Director of Public Prosecutions* 2016 (2) SACR 171 (WCC) para 69.

1 The administrative phase

A foreign state requesting South Africa to extradite an alleged criminal to it must make its request to the Minister of Justice through diplomatic channels.[125] The Act does not prescribe any form or content for the request, and the Minister is not expected to examine the merits of the request at this stage.[126]

In *S v Thornhill*[127] the Western Cape High Court accepted that the existence of such a request is a jurisdictional fact that must be satisfied before a person can be committed pending surrender.[128] Without a request in terms of s 4, a person is not liable to be surrendered. But a magistrate, when conducting an inquiry under s 10(1), is allowed to presume that such a request has been made unless there is evidence suggesting otherwise.[129] On the facts of *Thornhill*, the Minister had countersigned the President's consent to surrender the sought person.[130] The Minister thus created the impression that he had duly received a request in terms of s 4, and there was nothing to indicate otherwise. The High Court therefore held that the magistrate was justified in finding Mr Thornhill liable for surrender even though the extradition request sent to the Minister via diplomatic channels was not before the magistrate.

If there is an extradition treaty between the requesting foreign state and the Republic, then after receiving a request the Minister has the power to notify a magistrate of such a request.[131] This notification empowers the magistrate to issue a warrant for the arrest of the sought person, regardless of the sought person's whereabouts.[132]

If there is no extradition treaty between the requesting foreign state and the Republic, then the Minister must first forward the request to the President. The President must consent to the surrender of the person. Only thereafter can the Minister notify the magistrate of the request—empowering the latter to issue a warrant of arrest.[133]

[125] Section 4 of Act 67 of 1962.

[126] *Abel v Minister of Justice* 2000 (2) SACR 333 (C) para 55; *Geuking v President of the Republic of South Africa* 2002 (1) SA 204 (C).

[127] 1997 (2) SACR 626 (C).

[128] As per s 10(1). See below.

[129] At 635E–G. This is because of the presumption *omnia praesumuntur rite esse acta*. This presumes in favour of validity on the basis that the necessary formalities for the exercise of power by a functionary had been complied with.

[130] As per s 3(2). The UK had not been designated per s 3(3) at the time, so the President had to consent to the extradition of Mr Thornhill. See below.

[131] The Minister must do so if the extradition treaty obliges South Africa to extradite the sought person. *Abel v Minister of Justice* (n 126) para 66.

[132] Section 5(1)*(a)*.

[133] *Abel v Minister of Justice* (n 126) para 15; *Moti v President of the Republic of South Africa* [2017] ZAGPPHC 501 (18 August 2017) para 26.

The issuing of the notice to the magistrate 'sets in motion' the domestic process of extradition.[134] It is not a decision to extradite the sought person. The Minister's decision under s 11 to surrender the sought person, and his or her consideration of the Act's requirements for extradition, are done only after a committal order by a magistrate.[135] To issue the notice, the Minister only needs to have received the request through diplomatic channels by a person recognised by the Minister as a diplomatic or consular representative.[136] Her decision to issue the notice therefore is not reviewable if she does not consider the merits of the extradition request before issuing such a notice.[137]

In certain circumstances the magistrate may issue a warrant for the arrest or further detention of a person sought to be extradited without notification from the Minister.[138] For this to occur there must be sufficient information before the magistrate to demonstrate that the sought person was accused or convicted of an extraditable offence committed within the jurisdiction of the foreign state.[139] This evidence will be sufficient if it would justify the issuing of the warrant as if the sought person committed an offence in the Republic. If the magistrate issues a warrant without the Minister's notification, then the magistrate must notify the Minister immediately.[140]

Certain extradition treaties provide for the provisional arrest of a sought person. For example, article 9 of the treaty between South Africa and the United States provides that 'in case of urgency, the Requesting State may, for the purpose of extradition, request the provisional arrest of the person sought pending presentation of the documents in support of the extradition request'.[141]

Once the magistrate issues an arrest warrant, the warrant is executed according to the ordinary principles of criminal procedure. If an arrest warrant is issued or executed unlawfully (for example, if the applying officer commits a material non-disclosure) then the subsequent steps in the extradition process (including the hearing) could be unlawful.[142]

[134] Ibid para 38.

[135] This is the executive phase of extraditions. See below.

[136] The request must also state that the person in question is accused (or convicted) of an extraditable offence, or alternatively an offence included in an existing extradition treaty, committed within the jurisdiction of the requesting state. *Abel v Minister of Justice* (n 126) para 60.4.

[137] *Abel v Minister of Justice* (n 126) paras 56–60.

[138] Sections 5(1)*(b)* and 7.

[139] See below for a discussion on extraditable offences.

[140] Section 8.

[141] For example, as in *Carolissen v Director of Public Prosecutions* (n 124).

[142] See *McCarthy v Additional Magistrate, Johannesburg* 2000 (2) SACR 542 (SCA) and *Saliu v S* [2015] ZAGPJHC 179 (25 August 2015). In both cases, there was no material

2 The judicial phase

An arrested person must be brought before a magistrate as soon as possible for the purpose of an enquiry into the extradition of the person.[143] This enquiry is modelled upon a preparatory examination.[144] But the enquiry is not a criminal trial,[145] although the proceedings resemble criminal proceedings in many respects.[146] Importantly, the magistrate can admit the arrested person to bail pending the finalisation of the enquiry.[147]

Section 9(3) regulates the evidence admissible in the enquiry before the magistrate. It prescribes various requirements pertaining to authentication of evidence from the foreign state. These requirements are aimed at ensuring that the relevant evidence submitted by the foreign state 'is what it purports to be'.[148] These authentication requirements apply to any foreign deposition, any statement on oath or affirmation, any record of any conviction, and any warrant issued. They do not apply, for example, to foreign statutes that may be included in the extradition request bundle.[149] At least one of these requirements must be satisfied to authenticate a document.[150]

Section 10 regulates enquiries for extraditions to foreign states.[151] Section 10 empowers the magistrate to commit a sought person to detention pending the Minister's decision to surrender the sought person. That is, the magistrate does not consider whether to extradite or surrender the person before him or her.[152] The decision is only to commit or not to commit.

non-disclosure. But both Courts seem to assume that if there had been, then the subsequent extradition hearing would have been unlawful.

[143] Section 9(1).

[144] Section 9(2). *Garrido v Director of Public Prosecutions, Witwatersrand Local Division* [2004] 4 All SA 110 (SCA) para 24; *S v Mlotshwa* [2009] ZAGPPH 64 (4 March 2009) para 10; *Abel v Minister of Justice* (n 126) para 45. Preparatory examinations are regulated in Chapter 20 of the Criminal Procedure Act 51 of 1977. For a fuller discussion of preparatory examinations, see A Kruger *Hiemstra's Criminal Procedure* (2017) 20-1 et seq.

[145] *S v Bell* [1997] 2 All SA 692 (E) 698F; *Geuking v President of the RSA* (n 67) para 42*(a)*; *Director of Public Prosecutions, Cape of Good Hope v Robinson* 2005 (4) SA 1 (CC) para 33.

[146] See the remarks of Howie JA in his dissenting opinion in *S v McCarthy* 1995 (3) SA 731 (A) 741–2.

[147] Section 65 of the Criminal Procedure Act.

[148] *Benjamin v Additional Magistrate Cape Town* [2014] ZAWCHC 115 (1 August 2014) para 25.

[149] Ibid para 47. They also do not apply to the s 10(2) certificate discussed below. See *Van Rooyen v S* [2014] ZAGPJHC 177 (13 March 2014) para 20.

[150] The section joins the requirement disjunctively ('or'). *Van Rooyen v S* (n 149) para 10; *S v Bell* (n 145) 697.

[151] Section 9(4)*(a)* of the Extradition Act.

[152] *Robinson* (n 145) para 5.

Section 10(1) explains that a magistrate, on the consideration of the evidence before her or him, must be satisfied that two conditions are both fulfilled before a committal order can be made. First, the person must be liable to be surrendered to the foreign state concerned. Secondly, in the case where such person is accused of an offence, there must be sufficient evidence to warrant a prosecution for the offence in the foreign state.[153]

The magistrate does not consider, for example, whether it is unjust or unreasonable to surrender the applicant. This is because the magistrate is not considering surrender to the foreign state but committal pending the final phase of the extradition. This is a narrow and specific issue that does not involve deliberation on human rights issues (for instance). In *Chanthunya v S*,[154] the North West High Court held that the question of whether an assurance not to implement the death penalty had been secured is not a matter to be determined by the magistrate under a s 10 enquiry.

If the magistrate finds that both requirements in s 10(1) are satisfied and issues an order of committal, then the sought person has a right of appeal or review to the provincial or local division of the High Court having jurisdiction before he is surrendered.[155] The sought person can apply for bail pending this appeal.[156] Such a bail application pending appeal is governed by s 65 of the Criminal Procedure Act, and so an appeal against a magistrate's refusal to grant bail can be heard by a single judge.[157]

It is convenient to deal with the second s 10(1) requirement first. For the purpose of satisfying herself or himself that there is sufficient evidence to warrant a prosecution in the foreign state, the magistrate must accept as conclusive proof a certificate issued by the appropriate authority in the requesting state, stating that it has sufficient evidence at its disposal to warrant the prosecution of the person concerned.[158] This test, introduced in 1996, represents an abandonment of the Anglo-American common-law requirement that the requesting state make out a *prima facie* case of guilt against the fugitive before extradition is granted. This was done to overcome difficulties experienced by civil-law systems which do not employ the *prima facie* test and have difficulty in satisfying the requirements inherent in the common-law test. In this

[153] *Geuking v President of the RSA* (n 67) para 15.

[154] [2013] ZANWHC 45 (30 May 2013).

[155] Section 13(1). The grounds for appealing or reviewing the decision are those in s 22 of the Superior Courts Act 10 of 2013. *Abel v Additional Magistrate, Cape Town; S v Abel* 2002 (2) SACR 83 (C).

[156] Section 13(3).

[157] *S v Tucker* 2018 (1) SACR 616 (WCC).

[158] Section 10(2). *Geuking v President of the RSA* (n 67).

respect, South Africa has followed the example of other common-law countries, such as Britain and Australia.[159] As for the first requirement, liability for extradition is regulated in s 3 of the Act. There are three kinds of persons who are liable to be extradited:

(1) Persons who are convicted or accused of an extraditable offence contained in an extradition agreement committed within the jurisdiction of a foreign state. The offence could have been committed before or after the commencement of the Extradition Act or the extradition treaty.[160]

(2) Persons who are accused or convicted of an extraditable offence committed within the jurisdiction of a foreign state that is not party to an extradition treaty with South Africa and the President has consented in writing to their surrender.[161] The power of the President is not to determine whether the person should be extradited but whether the extradition process should be applied to the specific request.[162] The written consent contemplated in s 3(2) of the Act takes the place of a duly concluded extradition treaty with the requesting foreign state.[163] A High Court has held that the President's decision under s 3(2) can be reviewed on the ground of rationality.[164] This means the President cannot consent to an extradition while knowing that the extradition request is spurious and in bad faith.[165] But this review should be launched after the decision is taken.[166]

(3) Persons who are accused or convicted of an extraditable offence committed within the jurisdiction of a designated state. The designation of the state, as per s 2(1)*(b)*, can occur before or after the offence was committed.[167] South Africa has designated Ireland, Zimbabwe, Namibia and the United Kingdom.[168]

[159] See Report of the South African Law Commission on International Co-operation in Criminal Prosecutions (n 26) 153–5, 168–70.

[160] Section 3(1).

[161] Section 3(2).

[162] *Moti v President of the Republic of South Africa* (n 133) para 8.

[163] Ibid para 14.

[164] Ibid para 18.

[165] In *Moti v President of the Republic of South Africa* (n 133) the applicants were accused by Lebanon of fraud committed there, even though, on the common cause facts before the Court, the applicants had never set foot in Lebanon. The applicants approached the Court in an attempt to interdict the President from giving his consent to a request for extradition from Lebanon should Lebanon submit one. The Court accepted that the extradition request, should it be made, would be spurious, and that consenting to it would be irrational. But because no request had been made yet, the application for an interdict was premature.

[166] Ibid paras 19 and 20.

[167] Section 3(3).

[168] GNR 188 *GG* 18663 of 13 February 1998.

All persons liable to be extradited must therefore be *(a)* accused or convicted of an extraditable offence, and *(b)* committed within the jurisdiction of the foreign state. These requirements are considered in turn.

(a) Extraditable offences and double criminality

The principle of double criminality requires that the conduct claimed to constitute an extraditable crime should constitute a crime in both the requesting and the requested state. It is not necessary that the offence should have the same name in both states, provided that it is substantially similar.[169]

In the past it was common practice to list the offences in respect of which extradition is to apply in the extradition treaty. Today the tendency is for parties to provide for extradition in respect of crimes that are punishable in both the requesting state and the requested state with a sentence above a particular severity without naming the crime. For instance, the agreement between South Africa and the People's Republic of China[170] provides:

> For the purpose of this Treaty, extradition shall be granted for conduct which constitutes an offence under the laws of both Contracting States that is punishable by imprisonment for a period of at least one year or by a more severe penalty.

The Extradition Act, as amended in 1996, approves this approach by providing:

> '[E]xtraditable offence' means any offence which in terms of the law of the Republic and of the foreign state concerned is punishable by a sentence of imprisonment or other form of deprivation of liberty for a period of six months or more.[171]

The Extradition Act is silent on the question whether the crime in respect of which extradition is requested must be a crime in South Africa at the time of the extradition request or at the time the alleged

[169] See article 7(2) of UN Model Treaty on Extradition (n 12); articles 2(3) and (5) of the extradition agreement between South Africa and the Peoples' Republic of China (n 32). See, too, *Geuking v President of the RSA* (n 67) para 45; *Abel v Additional Magistrate, Cape Town* 2002 (2) SACR 83 (C) 92; *S v Bell* [1997] 2 All SA 692 (E) 699B–C; *S v Thornhill* 1997 (2) SACR 626 (C) 636E; *Harksen v President of the RSA* 1998 (2) SA 1011 (C) 1038H–I; *Palazzolo v Minister of Justice and Constitutional Development* [2010] ZAWCHC 422 (14 June 2010). See further *M v Federal Department of Justice* (1979) 75 ILR 197 (involving an extradition agreement between Switzerland and South Africa); *R v Governor of Pentonville Prison; Ex p Budlong* [1980] 1 WLR 1110; *Re Nielsen* [1984] AC 606 (HL); *Riley v Commonwealth of Australia* 159 CLR 1, particularly at 15–20. In *S v Bell* (supra) 699–700 the Court held that the principle applied in respect of crimes that had prescribed under South African law.

[170] See n 32, article 2(1).

[171] Section 1 of Act 67 of 1962.

offence was committed. The critical date is that of the extradition request and there is no reason why the term 'extraditable offence' (above) should not be so interpreted. Section 3, which extends the Act to offences committed before the Act or extradition agreement came into operation, supports this interpretation. A South African High Court[172] has, however, followed the interpretation of 'extradition crime' applied by the House of Lords in the *Pinochet Case*,[173] in which it held that the former Chilean dictator could not be extradited to Spain for acts of torture committed in Chile before the United Kingdom enacted the 1984 Torture Convention into municipal law by reason of the principle of double criminality, which it interpreted—in terms of its own statute—to apply only to offences committed abroad that were punishable as crimes in the United Kingdom at the time of their commission.

In *Patel v National Director of Public Prosecutions*,[174] the Supreme Court of Appeal departed from the approach in *Pinochet* and settled the question of when the offence underlying the extradition needs to be a crime under South African law. In *Patel* the offences with which the sought person had been charged in the United States were allegedly committed between 2005 and 2007. That conduct was not criminal in South Africa until 2010, when s 28 of the Financial Intelligence Centre Act 38 of 2001 came into operation.[175] The SCA held that the Act 'unquestionably refers to the present: is the offence an extraditable offence, ie now, at the date of the request for extradition?' Because the sought person was accused of conduct that was criminal at the time of the request by the United States, the requirement of double criminality was satisfied. The Supreme Court of Appeal distinguished the approach in *Pinochet* because the House of Lords based its conclusion on an interpretation of the specific provisions of the UK Extradition Acts that are not mirrored in the South African Extradition Act. In doing so, the Court endorsed the view of one of the authors of this chapter who had stressed that an approach in terms of which the conduct date is decisive for the purpose of double criminality would undermine mutual co-operation between the states and negate the very purpose of a bilateral extradition treaty: the parties enter into reciprocal rights and duties

[172] *Palazzolo* (n 169) para 34.

[173] *R v Bow Street Metropolitan Stipendiary Magistrate; Ex p Pinochet Ugarte (No 3)* [1999] 2 All ER 97 (HL). See, on this decision, A O'Shea '*Pinochet* and beyond: The international implications of amnesty' (2000) 16 *SAJHR* 642 at 653–56; M du Plessis 'The *Pinochet* cases and South African extradition law' (2000) 16 *SAJHR* 669 at 680; C Warbrick 'The extradition law aspects of *Pinochet*' (1999) 48 *ICLQ* 958.

[174] 2017 (1) SACR 456 (SCA).

[175] Ibid para 17.

in order to bring to justice those who have committed serious crimes.[176]

(b) *Within the jurisdiction of the foreign state*

In Chapter 9, the various bases on which states can exercise extraterritorial jurisdiction were discussed. The issue is if the Extradition Act extends liability for extradition to instances when the foreign state exercises extraterritorial jurisdiction. For example, if a Belgian national commits a crime in Venezuela, escapes to South Africa, and then is accused by Belgium on the basis of active personality for the crime committed abroad, is that person accused of an offence 'committed within the jurisdiction' of Belgium?

The Extradition Act is not entirely clear. The starting point will often be South Africa's international legal obligations.[177] Many extradition treaties expressly prevent a requested state from refusing to extradite only because the requesting state exercises extraterritorial jurisdiction.[178] In those instances, the question is whether the Extradition Act can reasonably be interpreted to give effect to that international obligation to extradite in response to extraterritorial exercises of jurisdiction.[179]

There is nothing in the words 'within the jurisdiction' and the structure of the Act to prevent such an extraterritorial interpretation. On the contrary, given the increasingly transnational nature of crimes, and South Africa's exercise of extraterritorial jurisdiction in respect of various crimes,[180] the Extradition Act can reasonably be

[176] *Patel* (n 174) paras 30 and 37 (fn 26) endorsing the views expressed in M du Plessis 'The *Pinochet* cases and South African extradition law' (2000) 16 *SAJHR* 669 at fn 19.

[177] For a full analysis of the problem, see Cherif Bassiouni (n 1) 349–484. For an analysis of the problem under the former UK Extradition Acts, see A Jones *Extradition and Mutual Assistance* (2001) Ch 8.

[178] For example, article 7(2) of the European Convention on Extradition. See also article 2(6) of the treaty with Argentina (GeN 519 *GG* 40978 of 14 July 2017); article 2(5) of the treaty with Canada (n 31); article 2(4) of the treaty with the United States (n 30); article 3(4) of the SADC Protocol on Extradition of 3 October 2002; article 2(4) of the treaty with Australia (n 31); article 2(4) of the treaty with China (n 30); article 2(4) of the treaty with Egypt (GNR 774 *GG* 26497 of 2 July 2004).

[179] As per s 233 of the Constitution. See Chapter 4.

[180] For example, s 4 of the Implementation Act, s 30A of the Films and Publications Act 65 of 1996, s 12(1)*(a)* of the Prevention and Combating of Trafficking in Persons Act 7 of 2013, s 61 of the Criminal Law (Sexual Offences and Related Matters) Amendment Act 32 of 2007, s 11 of the Prohibition of Mercenary Activities and Regulation of Certain Activities in Country of Armed Conflict Act 27 of 2006, s 6 of the Prevention and Combating of Torture of Persons Act 13 of 2013, and s 15 of the Protection of Constitutional Democracy against Terrorist and Related Activities Act 33 of 2004.

interpreted to allow for extraditions in response to extraterritorial exercises of jurisdiction.

The question of extraterritoriality in s 3(1) was touched upon in the High Court by Gamble J and Donen AJ in *Carolissen v Director of Public Prosecutions*.[181] Mr Carolissen was indicted by a grand jury in Maine in the United States for the manufacturing and dissemination of child pornography. At all relevant times, Mr Carolissen was based in Cape Town, South Africa. Yet he had emailed undercover US police officers images and videos of child pornography. The police officers received this pornography while in Maine. They subsequently caused Mr Carolissen's indictment, and the US requested his extradition to the US. Mr Carolissen was arrested and a magistrate ordered his committal pending the Minister's decision to surrender him in terms of s 11. Mr Carolissen appealed this decision.

In the judgment, the High Court found that the United States had jurisdiction over Mr Carolissen. But it required the United States to 'show the necessary *nexus* to its territorial jurisdiction' before extradition could happen.[182] On the facts, 'territorial jurisdiction [was] contained in the assertion [that the agent] was present in Maine when he "chatted" with [Carolissen] and subsequently received the pornographic images which had been manufactured (or possibly sourced elsewhere) by the appellant'.[183] The Court also held that the grand jury 'was satisfied as to territorial jurisdiction' of the United States.[184] It concluded that 'an applicant for extradition must make out a *prima facie* case for its territorial jurisdiction, regardless as to whether the offence relates to cybercrime or otherwise'.[185]

The Court thus, at times, seemed to accept that extradition can only occur if territorial jurisdiction is established. But at other times, the Court made comments to the contrary. It noted:

> [I]t is established law that it is open to a sovereign state to enact legislation permitting it to prosecute within its own jurisdiction suspects who have committed crimes elsewhere in the world, where those crimes might ultimately have a deleterious effect in the territorial jurisdiction of the requesting state.[186]

The Court cited various UK and Canadian authorities for the extraterritorial liability for extradition.[187] Citing *Geuking v President of the RSA*, the Court also emphasised the importance of effective

[181] 2016 (2) SACR 171 (WCC).
[182] Paragraph 48.
[183] Ibid.
[184] Paragraph 49.
[185] Paragraph 50.
[186] Paragraph 37.
[187] Paragraphs 37–41.

extradition for transnational crimes.[188] The Court further made reference to the extraterritorial application of various South African statutes.[189]

It seems then that the Court did not answer the question of extraterritorial jurisdiction generally. It made *obiter* comments regarding extraterritorial jurisdiction and the effectiveness of such jurisdiction for transnational crimes (such as cybercrime). But its ratio is limited to the facts before it. Namely, there was a territorial link to the United States because the child pornography had been sent there. That said, the Court's *obiter* recognition of extraterritorial jurisdiction suggests that s 3(1) would be interpreted extraterritorially if no territorial link had been established.

Recently, the Constitutional Court took a broad interpretation to the extraterritoriality of the Protection of Constitutional Democracy against Terrorist and Related Activities Act 33 of 2004.[190] The Constitutional Court made the following apposite finding at para 43 when interpreting the jurisdiction of the Act:

> While it is true that territoriality has been the traditional basis on which courts establish jurisdiction, international and South African jurisprudence recognise other methods of asserting jurisdiction . . . This is particularly true when the crimes over which a court asserts jurisdiction have an international dimension. We should not, through a narrow interpretation of section 15(1), mistakenly perpetuate an historical disinclination to extra-territoriality.

These comments suggest that courts will interpret 'within the jurisdiction of the foreign state' to include the recognised bases of extraterritorial jurisdiction.

3 The executive phase

When a magistrate issues a committal order, the person is imprisoned pending the Minister's decision to surrender them under s 11. The magistrate cannot grant bail at this stage, although the sought person can apply to the High Court to be admitted to bail pending the s 11 decision.[191]

Under s 11, the Minister has two options. She can decide to surrender the sought person. Or she can refuse to surrender the sought person for various reasons and on certain conditions.[192] These reasons include considerations of fairness, justice and reasonableness. It is at this stage of the extradition process that the merits of the

[188] Paragraph 42.
[189] Paragraph 46.
[190] *S v Okah* 2018 (1) SACR 492 (CC).
[191] *Ex parte Graham: In re United States of America v Graham* 1987 (1) SA 368 (T).
[192] Section 11*(b)* of the Act.

extradition, including human rights concerns, must be considered by the Minister.[193]

The Minister's decision is subject to review.[194]

The Constitutional Court has recently reiterated that if a person is a refugee under South African law, that person cannot be extradited if he or she would be persecuted, lose freedom or be physically harmed as a result of such extradition.[195] Conversely, if South Africa is obliged to extradite someone before he or she is given refugee status, South Africa cannot flout the duty to extradite and grant the sought person refugee status.[196]

The Minister can decide to surrender a citizen of South Africa. Civil-law countries, which exercise personal jurisdiction over their nationals for offences committed abroad, favour the exemption of their own nationals from extradition.[197] Common-law countries, which in most circumstances do not exercise extraterritorial jurisdiction over their nationals, adopt a different approach and allow the extradition of their nationals.[198] These divergent attitudes undermine the important principle of reciprocity. The compromise is for a treaty to include a clause that gives either state discretion to refuse to extradite its own nationals.[199] This allows civil-law countries to refuse extradition of their nationals and to try such nationals themselves, while at the same time permitting common-law countries to extradite their nationals for offences committed abroad beyond their criminal jurisdiction.

[193] The Minister may refuse to surrender the fugitive where proceedings against him are pending in the Republic, where such surrender would in all the circumstances of the case be 'unjust or unreasonable', or where she is satisfied that the person concerned will be prosecuted or prejudiced at his trial in the requesting state by reason of his 'gender, race, religion, nationality or political opinion'.

[194] See, for example, *Tsebe* (n 40) and *Robinson* (n 145).

[195] *Saidi v Minister of Home Affairs* 2018 (4) SA 333 (CC) para 27.

[196] *Mail and Guardian Media Ltd v Chipu NO* 2013 (6) SA 367 (CC) para 23.

[197] The European Convention on Extradition of 1957 ((1960) 359 UNTS 273) recognises the right of a signatory 'to refuse extradition of its nationals' (article 1). The UN Model Treaty on Extradition (n 12) recognises nationality as an optional ground for the refusal of extradition (article 4(a)).

[198] See *Abel v Minister of Justice* (n 126).

[199] See, for example, the Extradition Agreement between South Africa and the People's Republic of China, which provides in article 5: '(1) A Contracting State shall have the right to refuse to extradite its own nationals. (2) If extradition is refused solely on the basis of the nationality of the person sought, the Requested State shall, at the request of the Contracting State, submit the case to its prosecuting authorities.' See GNR 34 *GG* 27168 of 21 January 2005 (*Reg Gaz* 8132). In *S v Pirzenthal* 1969 (2) SA 224 (T) the Court held that the discretion to refuse to extradite a national is one that 'rests with the Minister' and not the Court (225B).

South Africa adheres to the common-law tradition. The Extradition Act of 1962 contains no exemption for nationals. South Africa's attitude towards nationality (citizenship) and extradition was examined by the Constitutional Court in *Geuking v President of the RSA*,[200] in which it was argued that the President, in exercising his power to surrender a person to the Federal Republic of Germany, under s 3(2) of the Extradition Act, had failed to have regard to the fact that the person was a South African national (citizen). The Constitutional Court held:

> In the present case, the President stated in the affidavit he filed in the High Court that in deciding whether to grant his consent under s 3(2) of the Act the citizenship of the appellant would not have been a relevant consideration. I can find no constitutional ground for attacking that policy decision. Unlike the [Federal Republic of Germany] and many other civil law jurisdictions, South Africa does not ordinarily prosecute its citizens for crimes committed beyond its borders. Criminal conduct would go unpunished if South African citizens were not extradited to face prosecution in the country where the crime was committed. The President is therefore entitled to adopt a policy that it is in the interests of the Republic to consent to a request for extradition proceedings against a person, regardless of his or her citizenship.[201]

A crucial factor that should prevent the Minister from ordering surrender is *non bis in idem*. A person may not be extradited in respect of an offence for which he has already been acquitted, or convicted, by the requested state. This principle, which confirms the principle of *autrefois acquit* (or *autrefois convict*), is not expressly included in the Extradition Act but appears in most extradition agreements.[202]

If the Minister does decide to surrender the sought person, then that surrender is regulated by the principle of speciality. According to the principle of speciality, an extradited person may not be tried for an offence other than that for which he was extradited, unless the extraditing state consents to such a prosecution. This principle is confirmed by the Extradition Act[203] and is a common clause in extradition agreements. In terms of the Act, a person may be tried for an offence other than that for which he was extradited if the offence is

[200] Supra (n 67). See, too, *Geuking v President of the RSA* 2002 (1) SA 204 (C).

[201] *Geuking v President of the RSA* (n 67) para 28. See, too, *Abel v Minister of Justice* (n 126) at 342A–C. Cf *Robinson* (n 145) para 20.

[202] See, for example, the Agreement with the United States (n 32) article 6. According to the Law Commission, it is a basic principle of law that must be applied by a magistrate despite its omission from the Act: Report of the SA Law Commission on International Co-operation in Criminal Prosecutions (n 26) 159 (para 6.67).

[203] Sections 2(3)*(c)* and 19 of Act 67 of 1962. In *Harksen v President of the RSA* 1998 (2) SA 1011 (C), the Court 'assumed' without deciding that the principle is part of customary international law (1039–40). In *Harksen v Minister of Justice and Constitutional Development of the RSA* [2002] 4 All SA 642 (C) para 40, the High Court considered speciality to be a principle of customary international law.

one for which he might lawfully have been convicted on a charge of the offence for which extradition was sought.[204] The Supreme Court of Appeal held in *S v Stokes*[205] that the word 'sought' in s 19 of the Act should be read as '*successfully sought*' and the principle of speciality thus respected.

Finally, offences of a political character are of relevance at this stage of the extradition.

(a) Offences of a political character[206]

Extradition law and practice exempt the political offender from extradition. This rule had its origins in the 19th century, when the governments of the new liberal democracies refused to return political dissidents to the despotic states of the *ancien régime*. The principal justifications advanced for the rule are, first, that states should not intervene in the internal political conflicts of other states by assisting in the rendition of political opponents of the government, and, secondly, that political offenders, unlike ordinary criminals, threaten only the criminal justice system of the state from which they have fled and not that of the state granting asylum. Over the years, the romantic image of the political dissident fighting for democracy has been tarnished by the political terrorist fanatically determined to overthrow the regime of his home state by all means, including hostage-taking and hijacking. As a result, the political offence exception has become highly controversial and courts have sought to define the political offence in such a way that it excludes the political terrorist but does not abandon the protection of the genuine political dissident.

South African extradition law recognises the political offence exception. Section 15 of the Extradition Act empowers the Minister of Justice to intervene at any stage during extradition proceedings in order to release a fugitive if he is satisfied that the offence in respect of which extradition is sought is 'an offence of a political character'. Moreover, extradition agreements to which South Africa is a party generally exempt the political offender from extradition. The 1968 agreement with Swaziland,[207] for example, provides in article 3:

> A person claimed shall not be extradited if the offence for which his extradition is requested is regarded by the requested Party as one of a political character, or if he satisfies the requested Party that the request for his

[204] Sections 23*(c)* and 19 of Act 67 of 1962.

[205] 2008 (5) SA 644 (SCA) para 10.

[206] Van den Wyngaert (n 80); Shearer (n 1) 166–93; DP King 'The political offence exception in international extradition' (1980) 13 *CILSA* 247; D Dörfling 'Die "politieke misdryf"—Uitsondering (verweer) in aansoeke om uitlewering' 1996 *TSAR* 475.

[207] Proclamation R292 *GGE* 2179 of 4 October 1968 (*Reg Gaz* 1026).

> extradition has in fact been made with a view to try or punish him for an offence of a political character.

Once an extradition agreement is incorporated into municipal law in accordance with s 2 of the Extradition Act, it becomes part of the law of the land, with the result that a municipal court will be required to consider whether the offence is one of a 'political character'.[208]

Courts throughout the world have experienced great difficulty in deciding when an offence is one of a political character. Clearly treason and sedition are political offences. Problems arise in the case of ordinary crimes, such as murder or robbery, when they are politically motivated. A South African extradition court has not yet been called upon to examine this problem in any detail, but when the occasion arises there is little doubt that guidance will be sought in English law[209] and in the guidelines on 'political offences', laid down in the Promotion of National Unity and Reconciliation Act[210] in order to determine who would qualify for amnesty following the abandonment of apartheid.

English law and the political offence

English decisions have refused to lay down an exclusive definition of 'political offence'. In *Schtraks v Government of Israel*, Lord Radcliffe said: '[N]o definition has yet emerged or by now is ever likely to. Indeed it has come to be regarded as something of an advantage that there is to be no definition.'[211] The decisions do, however, lay down a number of tests or guidelines.

In re Castioni[212] involved a political uprising in Switzerland against the government of one of the cantons in the course of which Castioni killed a member of the government. He then fled to England. His extradition was refused on the ground that the offence was *incidental* to and formed part of a political uprising and was therefore an offence of a political character. This 'incidence test' has been approved by courts in the United States. In a decision involving the extradition of a member of the Irish Republican Army to the United Kingdom, the test was formulated in the following language:

> First there must be an uprising, a political disturbance related to the struggle of individuals to alter or abolish the existing government in their country . . . Second, the charged offence must have been committed in furtherance of the

[208] *S v Bull* 1967 (2) SA 636 (T) at 642E–G.

[209] *Ex parte Rolff* 26 SC 433 at 436, 439; *S v Devoy* 1971 (1) SA 359 (N) 363E–H; *S v Sibanda* 1965 (4) SA 241 (SRA) 243–4.

[210] 34 of 1995.

[211] [1964] AC 556 (HL) 589.

[212] [1891] 1 QB 149 at 166 (Hawkins J) and 156 (Denman J). See, too, *Re Meunier* [1894] 2 QB 415 at 419.

uprising; it must be related to the political struggle or be consequent to the uprising activity.[213]

This test, premised on the presence of a political disturbance or uprising, is too restrictive. In *R v Governor of Brixton Prison, Ex p Kolczynski and Others*,[214] the Court dispensed with the need for a political disturbance where a number of Polish seamen had hijacked a Polish trawler and assaulted a political commissar in order to effect an escape from the oppressive Polish regime. In refusing extradition, Lord Goddard declared that 'reasons of humanity' compelled 'a wider and more generous meaning' of the term 'political offence'—one that went beyond the limited incidence test. A 'wider and more generous' meaning was also given to the term in *Schtraks v Government of Israel*.[215] In this case, Lord Reid stated that political offences were not limited 'to cases of open insurrection' or even to cases of attempts to overthrow a government:

> The use of force, or it may be other means, to compel a sovereign to change his advisers, or to compel a government to change its policy may be just as political in character as the use of force to achieve a revolution. And I do not see why it should be necessary that the refugee's party should have been trying to achieve power in the state. It would be enough if they were trying to make the government concede some measure of freedom but not attempting to supplant it.[216]

In the same case, Lord Radcliffe declared:

> In my opinion the idea that lies behind the phrase 'offence of a political character' is that the fugitive is at odds with the state that applies for his extradition on some issue connected with the political control or government of the country.[217]

English courts have stressed that not every politically motivated crime will qualify as a political offence. In *Cheng v Governor of Pentonville Prison*,[218] Lord Diplock stated:

> But if the accused had killed a dictator in the hope of changing the government of the country, his object would be sufficiently immediate to justify the epithet 'political'. For politics are about government. 'Political' as descriptive of an object to be achieved must, in my view, be confined to the object of overthrowing or changing the government of a state or inducing it to change its policy or escaping from its territory the better so to do.

[213] *Quinn v Robinson* 783 F 2d 776 (9th Cir 1989). See, too, *Eain v Wilkes* 641 F 2d 504 (7th Cir 1981) 518–23, involving the extradition of a member of the PLO to Israel.

[214] [1955] 1 QB 540 at 551.

[215] Supra (n 211).

[216] At 583.

[217] At 591.

[218] [1973] 2 All ER 204 (HL) 209. Cf *Re Gross, Ex p Treasury Solicitor* [1968] 3 All ER 804 (QB) where Chapman J formulated the test as being whether the offender could claim political asylum with any prospect of success (810D).

Although *T v Secretary of State for the Home Department*[219] concerned an application for asylum—by a member of the Front Islamique du Salut (FIS) responsible for placing a bomb at Algiers Airport which killed ten people—the House of Lords made a thorough examination of the political offence exception in extradition. The House of Lords held that the applicant failed to qualify for asylum in terms of article 1F(b) of the Convention Relating to the Status of Refugees of 1951, which denies the granting of asylum to a person who has committed a 'serious non-political crime outside the country of refuge'. Lord Lloyd, for the majority, defined a 'political crime' in language that by necessary implication excluded terrorism as a political offence. He stated:

> A crime is a political crime for the purposes of article 1F*(b)* of the 1951 convention if, and only if: (1) it is committed for a political purpose, that is to say, with the object of overthrowing or subverting or changing the government of a state or inducing it to change its policy; and (2) there is a sufficiently close and direct link between the crime and the alleged political purpose. In determining whether such a link exists, the court will bear in mind the means used to achieve the political end, and will have particular regard to whether the crime was aimed at a military or governmental target, on the one hand, or a civilian target on the other, and in either event whether it was likely to involve the indiscriminate killing or injuring of members of the public.[220]

Amnesty and the political offence

The Promotion of National Unity and Reconciliation Act[221] established amnesty committees which were empowered to grant amnesty to individuals who sought amnesty for acts or 'an act associated with a political objective committed in the course of the conflicts of the past' and who made full disclosure of all relevant facts.[222] The criteria employed for deciding whether the act was one 'associated with a political objective' were drawn from the principles used in extradition law for deciding whether the offence in respect of which extradition was sought was a political offence. The criteria included, inter alia, the motive of the offender; the context in which the act took place and, in particular, whether it was committed 'in the course of or as part of a political uprising, disturbance or event'; the gravity of the act; the objective of the act and, in particular, whether it was 'primarily directed at a political opponent or state property or personnel or against private property or individuals'; whether the act was committed in execution of an order by an organisation; and the

219 [1996] 2 All ER 865 (HL).

220 *T v Secretary of State* (n 219) 899. See, too, the *dictum* of Lord Mustill at 878–86.

221 34 of 1995.

222 Section 20(1). See *Stopforth & Veenendal v Minister of Justice* 2000 (1) SA 113 (SCA) in which the Supreme Court of Appeal held that an amnesty committee had no power to grant amnesty for an offence committed in Namibia.

relationship between the act and the political objective pursued, and 'in particular the directness and proximity of the relationship and the proportionality of the act to the objective pursued'.[223]

This statutory 'codification' of the political offence, and the interpretation of this provision by courts and amnesty committees, may serve as a useful guide to South African courts when they confront the political offence as a defence in extradition proceedings.

International terrorism and the political offence

International terrorism presents a particular problem[224] for extradition, as most transnational acts of terror are politically motivated and fall within the tests laid down for the political offender. There is, however, an important difference between Castioni[225] and the hijacker of an international flight. Castioni's offence threatened the legal order of one state only—Switzerland. Hijacking, on the other hand, threatens the international order and demands an international co-operative response. At present, this response takes the form of extradition or trial by the state with physical control over the offender (*aut dedere aut judicare*)[226] which would be defeated if the political offence exception were to be allowed. Consequently, there is a measure of consensus that the political offence exception should not apply to the extradition of international criminals.

Unfortunately, early multilateral treaties creating international crimes do not expressly exclude the political offence exception. The Hague Convention of 1970 on aerial hijacking,[227] for example, obliges the state with physical control over the hijacker to extradite him, or to submit his case to its competent authorities for the purpose of prosecution in the same manner that it would consider the prosecution 'of any ordinary offence of a serious nature' under its own law. This does not prevent such a state from either deciding that the offence is one of a political nature[228] or pursuing a 'friendly prosecution' of the

[223] Section 20(1).

[224] See, on this subject, Van den Wyngaert (n 80) 139–58; Colloquium 'Terrorism as an international crime' (1989) 19 *Israel Yearbook of International Law*; J Dugard 'Terrorism and international law: Consensus at last?' in E Yakpo and T Boumedra (eds) *Liber Amicorum Mohammed Bedjaoui* (1999) 159; J Dugard 'The problem of the definition of terrorism in international law' in P Eden and T O'Donnell (eds) *September 11, 2001: A Turning Point in International and Domestic Law?* 187; 'Symposium on terrorism' in (2011) 24 *Leiden Journal of International Law* 651–700.

[225] *In re Castioni* (n 212).

[226] See Chapter 9.

[227] Convention for the Suppression of Unlawful Seizure of Aircraft (1971) 10 *ILM* 133, article 7.

[228] In 1975 the Chambre d' Accusation of the Court d' Appel of Paris refused a request from the United States to extradite Holder and Kerkow on hijacking charges

offender.[229] Most other conventions of this kind follow the precedent of the Hague Convention.[230]

The European Convention on the Suppression of Terrorism of 1977[231] adopts a different approach in expressly providing that acts of international terror, including hijacking and hostage-taking, shall not be treated as political offences for the purpose of extradition. This is confirmed by the European Union Extradition Agreement of 1996.[232] The International Convention for the Suppression of Terrorist Bombings of 1998, and the International Convention for the Suppression of the Financing of Terrorism of 1999, unlike other treaties criminalising acts of international terror, expressly exclude the political offence as an obstacle to extradition.[233] Finally, it is today not uncommon for an extradition agreement to exclude from the ambit of the political offence acts declared to constitute an offence under a multilateral treaty which imposes an obligation to prosecute or extradite.[234]

In 2004 the South African Extradition Act of 1962 was amended by the Protection of Constitutional Democracy against Terrorist and Related Activities Act 33 of 2004 to exclude the political offence defence to extradition when a person is charged with 'terrorist activity'.[235]

on the ground of political motive. See McDowell *Digest of United States Practice in International Law* (1976) 168.

[229] Ibid. Arguably, the prosecution in 1982 of the hijackers of an Air India flight following an abortive coup against the government of the Seychelles fell into this category: *S v Hoare and Others* 1982 (4) SA 865 (N).

[230] See, for example, the Convention on the Prevention and Punishment of Crimes against Internationally Protected Persons including Diplomatic Agents of 1973—(1974) 13 *ILM* 43, article 7; the International Convention Against the Taking of Hostages—(1979) 18 *ILM* 1456, articles 8 and 9.

[231] (1976) 15 *ILM* 1272, article 1. The impact of this Convention is weakened by article 13, which permits a state to reserve the right to refuse extradition in respect of a political offence after due consideration of a number of factors relating to the offence. See C van den Wyngaert 'The political offence exception to extradition: How to plug the "terrorists' loophole" without departing from fundamental human rights' (1989) 19 *Israel Yearbook on Human Rights* 297.

[232] *Official Journal of the European Communities* No C313/12 of 23 October 1996. This Agreement goes further than the European Convention on the Suppression of Terrorism as it does not permit states to attach reservations to the obligation to extradite those suspected of offences constituting international terrorism: article 5.

[233] (1998) 37 *ILM* 249; article 11; (2000) 39 *ILM* 268, article 14.

[234] See the extradition treaty between South Africa and the United States of 2001, which excludes not only such crimes from the political offence but also murder and offences against the head of state: GN R593 *GG* 22430 of 29 June 2001 (*Reg Gaz* 7100), article 4.

[235] The Schedule to Act 33 of 2004 amends the Extradition Act by the insertion of s 22, which only excludes the political offence defence in the case of violations of ss 4 and 5 of Act 33 of 2004, dealing with the financing of terrorism and offences relating to

EXTRADITION FROM SOUTH AFRICA TO ASSOCIATED STATES

In order to facilitate extradition between South Africa and its neighbours in Africa, a more expeditious procedure is followed. Here the extradition agreement provides that the requesting state is not required to request extradition through diplomatic channels and may instead submit a warrant for the arrest of the fugitive to the prosecutor having jurisdiction, together with a statement providing details of the offence and *prima facie* evidence of the fugitive's guilt.[236] A magistrate may then simply endorse the warrant for execution in South Africa.[237]

The enquiry before the magistrate then combines the judicial and executive phases discussed above. The magistrate holds an enquiry into questions such as whether the request complies with the terms of the extradition agreement; whether the fugitive will be prosecuted or prejudiced in the associated state by reason of his 'gender, race, religion, nationality or political opinion'; or whether it would in all the circumstances of the case be unjust or unreasonable to extradite the fugitive.[238] In such a case, the magistrate is not required to find that there would be sufficient reason for putting the fugitive on trial had the offence been committed in South Africa.[239] After this enquiry, the magistrate may order the extradition of the fugitive. The Minister is not included in this process. The magistrate decides to extradite—not the Minister. The fugitive has a right of appeal to the provincial or local division of the High Court having jurisdiction before he is surrendered.[240]

INTERNATIONAL CO-OPERATION IN THE SUPPRESSION OF CRIME BY MEANS OTHER THAN EXTRADITION

The internationalisation of crime has made national law enforcement authorities increasingly dependent on international co-operation. Extradition is the oldest and best-known form of such co-operation. However, there is a growing need for international co-operation on the part of both national police forces and judicial authorities in

explosive or lethal devices. Section 1(5) of Act 33 of 2004, however, goes further and excludes the political offence defence in all crimes involving terrorist activity.

[236] Malawi and Botswana qualify as associated states (*S v Bull* (n 208) 640H; *S v Williams* 1988 (4) SA 49 (W) 51B) but not, so it has been held, Swaziland (*Minister of Justice v Bagattini* 1975 (4) SA 252 (T) 256C). Although, compare (regarding Botswana) *S v Khanyisile* [2012] ZANWHC 35 (19 July 2012). The SADC Protocol does not envisage such an endorsement of warrants. See article 6.

[237] Section 6 of Act 67 of 1962.

[238] Section 12. See *S v Bull* (n 208) at 642–3.

[239] *S v Bull* (n 208) 642D, 643B–C.

[240] Section 13.

respect of the collection of evidence, the tracing of the proceeds of crime, money-laundering and the enforcement of judicial orders in criminal proceedings.[241] This has resulted in states entering into both bilateral and multilateral mutual assistance treaties. In 1990 the United Nations gave its approval to a UN Model Treaty on Mutual Assistance in Criminal Matters;[242] there is a Commonwealth Scheme Relating to Mutual Assistance in Criminal Matters;[243] and the 1988 Vienna Convention against Illicit Traffic in Narcotic Drugs and Psychotropic Substances[244] contains a comprehensive set of rules on mutual assistance. Assistance of this kind includes taking evidence or statements from persons, effecting service of judicial documents, executing searches and seizures, tracing the proceeds and instrumentalities of crime, and making persons available to give evidence or assist in investigations.

During the isolation of South Africa under apartheid, there was little incentive to make South African law accord with the requirements relating to mutual assistance in criminal proceedings contained in bilateral treaties or multilateral treaties. Changed circumstances, however, prompted the enactment of the International Co-operation in Criminal Matters Act,[245] which aims to enable South Africa to become a party to such treaties.[246]

This Act provides for the issue of a letter of request to a foreign state for the taking of evidence in the foreign state when an investigation has been instigated into the commission of a crime in South Africa.[247] Parties to the proceedings in South Africa may submit interrogatories attached to the letter of request to the foreign state, or they may appear at the examination to examine and cross-examine witnesses in the foreign state.[248] To permit reciprocal

[241] See D McClean *International Co-operation in Civil and Criminal Matters* (2002). See further N Boister 'Global trends towards the simplification of extradition procedures' in T Maluwa, M du Plessis and D Tladi (eds) *The Pursuit of a Brave New World in International Law: Essays in Honour of John Dugard* (2017).

[242] General Assembly Resolution 45/117 of 14 December 1990, (1991) 30 *ILM* 1421.

[243] McClean (n 241); 1990 *Commonwealth Law Bulletin* 1043.

[244] (1989) 28 *ILM* 493. See further N Boister 'International legal regulation of drug production, distribution and consumption' (1996) 29 *CILSA* 1; N Boister *Penal Aspects of the UN Drug Conventions* (2001).

[245] 75 of 1996. *Reuters Group plc v Viljoen and Others NNO* 2001 (12) BCLR 1265 (C) 1276–7. See, too, HA Strydom and S du Toit 'Transnational crime: The Southern African response' (1998) 23 *SAYIL* 116; J D'Oliveira 'International co-operation in criminal matters: The South African contribution' (2003) 16 *SACJ* 323; G Kemp 'Foreign relations, international co-operation in criminal matters and the position of the individual' (2003) 16 *SACJ* 370.

[246] Section 27.

[247] Section 2. See *Kolbatschenko v King NO* 2001 (4) SA 336 (C).

[248] Section 3.

treatment, a foreign state may request the collection or taking of evidence in South Africa for use in criminal proceedings in the foreign state.[249] In *Thatcher v Minister of Justice*,[250] Mark Thatcher, son of former British Prime Minister Margaret Thatcher, unsuccessfully challenged a request from the government of Equatorial Guinea to the South African government that he be compelled to respond to certain questions relating to his alleged involvement in a failed coup in Equatorial Guinea. The Court dismissed arguments that compelling Thatcher to answer the questions posed to him would violate his right to silence and might have an adverse effect on him in any extradition proceedings against him.[251] In *Thint Holdings (Southern Africa) (Pty) Ltd v National Director of Public Prosecutions; Zuma v National Director of Public Prosecutions*[252] the Constitutional Court, in interpreting s 2(2), held that a letter of request may be issued and sent to a foreign state if the circumstances of the case allow.[253]

The Act also provides for mutual assistance in the enforcement of orders arising from criminal proceedings. These provisions allow a South African court to request a foreign state to assist in the recovery of fines and compensatory orders, and in the enforcement of confiscation and restraint orders.[254] Conversely, provision is made for the enforcement of such orders in South Africa.[255] No provision is made for the execution of foreign prison sentences in South Africa.

An example of a mutual legal assistance treaty entered into in terms of the International Co-operation in Criminal Matters Act of 1996 is that between South Africa and the People's Republic of China of 2005,[256] which provides for mutual legal assistance in matters such as the delivery of documents, the taking of evidence, the locating of persons, the conducting of judicial inspections, the carrying out of searches, the confiscation of the proceeds of crimes and the exchang-

[249] Sections 7 and 8. In *Beheersmaaatschappij Helling I NV v The Magistrate, Cape Town* 2007 (1) SACR 99 (C), the Court held that the authorities had acted irregularly in carrying out searches of premises in South Africa on behalf of the Netherlands. In particular, they had failed to follow the procedure laid down in s 7 of the Act.

[250] 2005 (4) SA 543 (C).

[251] For criticism, see M du Plessis 'The *Thatcher* case and the supposed delicacies of foreign affairs: A plea for a principled (and realistic) approach to the duty of government to ensure that South Africans abroad are not exposed to the death penalty' (2007) 20 *SACJ* 143.

[252] 2009 (1) SA 1 (CC).

[253] See *Mudaly v Gwala* 2011 (1) SACR 302 (KZD).

[254] Sections 13, 19, 23.

[255] Sections 15, 20, 24. *Falk v National Director of Public Prosecutions* 2011 (1) SACR 105 (SCA).

[256] GNR 33 *GG* 27168 of 21 January 2005 (*Reg Gaz* 8132). See, too, the mutual legal assistance treaties with France (R224 *GG* 27371 of 18 March 2005) and Egypt (R775 *GG* 26497 of 2 July 2004).

ing of information on law.[257] Parties may refuse to provide assistance if the offence is not a crime in both states, the request relates to a political offence, or 'the Requested State is of the opinion that the execution of the request would impair its sovereignty, security, public order or other essential public interests, or would be contrary to the fundamental principles of its domestic law'.[258]

This Act must be read with the Prevention of Organised Crime Act,[259] which seeks to suppress racketeering, the financing of terrorism and money-laundering committed in South Africa and elsewhere, inter alia, by confiscation and restraint orders and by the preservation and forfeiture of property used in the commission of such crimes.

[257] Article 1.

[258] Article 3.

[259] 121 of 1998, as amended by the Schedule to the Protection of Constitutional Democracy against Terrorist and Related Activities Act 33 of 2004.

CHAPTER 12

Immunity from Jurisdiction

John Dugard

A state has jurisdiction over all persons within its territory and over all acts that take place within its territory.[1] In certain circumstances, however, it will not exercise its territorial jurisdiction. This occurs where a foreign sovereign, its property or its agents are involved. Although such persons or property are not exempt from legal liability or immune from the observance of the local law,[2] international law exempts them from the exercise of territorial jurisdiction. The non-assertion of jurisdiction in such a case may be ascribed to international comity or to the argument that because 'all sovereigns [are] equal no one of them can be subjected to the jurisdiction of another without surrendering a fundamental right'.[3] In *Liebowitz v Schwartz*,[4] Nicholas J gave his approval to both these explanations when he observed that 'the courts of a country will not by their process make a foreign state a party to legal proceedings against its will', and stated that this principle was 'founded on grave and weighty considerations of public policy, international law and comity'.[5]

The immunity accorded to foreign sovereigns takes two forms: first, sovereign or state immunity, which involves the immunity of the head of a foreign state or government, the government of a foreign state or its senior officials or a department of such a government; secondly, diplomatic and consular immunity, which deals with the immunities and privileges granted to foreign diplomats and consuls.

[1] See, generally, C Ryngaert *Jurisdiction in International Law* (2008). See, too, *Abdi v Minister of Home Affairs* 2011 (3) SA 37 (SCA) 50–1.

[2] In *Dickinson v Del Solar* [1930] 1 KB 379, the Court held that, as diplomats are not immune from legal liability, but merely exempt from being sued where they plead diplomatic immunity, an insurance company could not escape liability where the insured, a diplomat, had chosen not to plead immunity to a claim arising out of a motor accident. This principle was approved in *Portion 20 of Plot 15 Athol (Pty) Ltd v Rodrigues* 2001 (1) SA 1285 (W) 1293 H–I.

[3] DP O'Connell *International Law* 2 ed (1970) vol 2 at 842.

[4] 1974 (2) SA 661 (T).

[5] At 661H, 662A.

SOVEREIGN OR STATE IMMUNITY

Sovereign immunity, which is today more frequently termed 'state immunity', is a 'rule of international law which serves to preclude a state or its representatives from being sued or prosecuted in foreign courts'.[6] It has its origin in the immunity of the person of the foreign sovereign from the jurisdiction of municipal courts.[7] Later, the personification of the sovereign was replaced by the abstraction of the state and its organs. Until the emergence of the socialist state after the Russian revolution in 1917, neither the sovereign nor her government engaged in trade or commercial activities to any appreciable degree. Consequently, states were prepared to grant immunity to all the acts of foreign sovereigns and their governments, including those of their armed forces and state-owned vessels.[8] Sovereign immunity was absolute. The advent of the socialist state and the emergence of state-owned trading corporations altered the situation. Today, many states support a doctrine of restricted or qualified immunity, according to which immunity from the jurisdiction of municipal courts will be granted in respect of acts *jure imperii* (ie governmental public activities) and not in respect of acts *jure gestionis* (ie commercial activities). The reason for this change in attitude is that 'a foreign government which enters into an ordinary commercial transaction with a trader . . . must honour its obligations like other traders: and if it fails to do so, it [should] be subject to the same laws and amenable to the same tribunals as they'.[9]

The doctrine of restricted or qualified immunity in respect of the commercial activities of states has probably acquired the status of customary international law. This appears from the adoption by the General Assembly of the United Nations in 2004 of a United Nations Convention on Jurisdictional Immunities of States and their Property prepared by the International Law Commission. It approves restricted immunity in respect of commercial activities and asserts in its preamble 'that the jurisdictional immunities of States and their

[6] *Saharawi Arab Democratic Republic v Owners and Charterers of the Cherry Blossom* 2017 (5) SA 105 (ECP) para 60. See, too, *Minister of Justice and Constitutional Development v Southern Africa Litigation Centre* 2016 (3) SA 317 (SCA) ('*Minister of Justice v SALC*') para 66. See further H Fox and P Webb *The Law of State Immunity* 3 ed (2015); X Yang *State Immunity in International Law* (2012); C Schreuer *State Immunity: Some Recent Developments* (1988); GN Barrie 'Sovereign immunity of states: Acts *iure imperii* and acts *iure gestionis*—What is the distinction?' (2001) 26 *SAYIL* 156.

[7] In *Mighell v Sultan of Johore* [1894] 1 QB 149, a foreign sovereign was granted immunity in a breach of promise suit.

[8] See the judgment of the United States Supreme Court in *The Schooner Exchange v McFaddon* 7 Cranch 116 (1812).

[9] *Per* Lord Denning in *Thai-Europe Tapioca Service Ltd v Government of Pakistan, The Harmattan* [1975] 1 WLR 1485 at 1491F.

property are generally accepted as a principle of customary international law'.[10]

Among 'Western' states, a restrictive approach has been practised for many years. The United Kingdom was, however, slow to abandon the absolute approach[11] out of respect for the doctrine of *stare decisis*. It was only in 1976 that Lord Denning, in *Trendtex Trading Corporation v Central Bank of Nigeria*,[12] approved the restrictive approach, holding that judicial precedent 'as to what was the ruling of international law 50 or 60 years ago' was no longer binding, as 'international law knows no rule of *stare decisis*'. Since then approval has been given to the restrictive approach by both the House of Lords[13] and Parliament.[14]

The influence of English decisions on South African courts in the field of international law is no more evident than in the field of sovereign immunity, in which South African courts slavishly followed English decisions upholding the absolute doctrine[15] until the abandonment of this approach in *Trendtex*. Thereafter, both the courts and the legislature endorsed the restrictive approach.

Inter-Science Research and Development Services (Pty) Ltd v Republica

[10] Resolution 59/38 of 16 December 2004, (2005) 44 *ILM* 801. See further H Fox 'In defence of state immunity: Why the UN Convention on State Immunity is important' (2006) 55 *ICLQ* 399; R O'Keefe and C Tams (eds) *The United Nations Convention on Jurisdictional Immunities of States and their Property* (2013).

[11] *The Parlement Belge* [1880] 5 PD 197 at 205; *The Porto Alexandre* [1920] P 30; *The Cristina* [1938] AC 485; *Krajina v Tass News Agency* [1949] 2 All ER 274 (CA); *Baccus SRL v Servicio Nacional del Trigo* [1957] 1 QB 438 (CA).

[12] [1977] QB 529 (CA) 554G–H.

[13] *I Congreso del Partido* [1983] 1 AC 244 (HL); *Alcom Ltd v Republic of Colombia* [1984] AC 580 (HL).

[14] State Immunity Act 1978, c 33.

[15] *De Howorth v The SS India* 1921 CPD 451; *Ex Parte Sulman* 1942 CPD 407; *Kavloukis v Bulgaris* 1943 NPD 190; *Parkin v Government of the Republique Democratique du Congo* 1971 (1) SA 259 (W) 262; *Liebowitz v Schwarz* 1974 (2) SA 661 (T); *Lendalease Finance Co Ltd v Corporacion de Mercadeo Agricola* 1975 (4) SA 397 (C) (criticised in J Dugard 'Public international law' 1975 *Annual Survey* 27 at 31; H Booysen 'State immunity' (1975) 1 *SAYIL* 141). In *Lendalease Finance Co Ltd v Corporacion de Mercadeo Agricola* 1976 (4) SA 464 (A) the Appellate Division left open the question whether the restrictive approach had replaced the absolute approach (499D). See, too, *Prentice, Shaw & Scheiss Incorporated v Government of the Republic of Bolivia* 1978 (3) SA 938 (T) in which Goldstone AJ (as he then was) likewise left this matter undecided (940H). (See further J Dugard 'Public international law' 1978 *Annual Survey* 59 at 75; NJ Botha 'State immunity lingers on' (1978) 4 *SAYIL* 179. For a discussion of these South African decisions, see J Dugard 'The "purist" legal method, international law and sovereign immunity' in JJ Gauntlett (ed) *JC Noster: 'n Feesbundel* (1979) 36; BJ Cartoon 'Sovereign immunity in international law: A review of the more important trends and their place in South Africa' (1978) 11 *CILSA* 168.

Popular de Moçambique,[16] decided in 1979, raised the question whether the government of Mozambique could plead sovereign immunity in respect of the commercial activities of a corporation owned by the government. Margo J, delivering the judgment of the Court, acknowledged that there was 'an abundance of South African judicial authority ... in support of the absolute doctrine'.[17] On the other hand, he stated, 'there is good reason to believe that the rule of sovereign immunity has undergone an important change, and that the old doctrine of absolute immunity has yielded to the restrictive doctrine'.[18] In order to demonstrate this change in international law, Margo J examined the movement away from the absolute approach in English law culminating in *Trendtex* and the State Immunity Act 1978; the adoption of the restrictive approach by the United States, Canada and other countries; and the support for the restrictive view on the part of modern writers in South Africa and abroad. On this evidence, he concluded that the restrictive doctrine was a general rule of international law and that a South African court was obliged to apply this rule, in the absence of any statute or principle of South African law in conflict with the doctrine. This left South African precedent, premised on English precedent, as the only obstacle in the way of the application of the restrictive approach. On this subject, Margo J held:

> Were the matter *res nova*, there would be no difficulty in applying the restrictive doctrine. The only remaining question is whether or not, on the principle of *stare decisis*, we should follow the earlier South African decisions. Lord Denning's view in the *Trendtex* case ... is that international law knows no rule of *stare decisis*, but it does not appear to me to be necessary in the present case to adopt that proposition. In South Africa the earlier cases are all founded on the English decisions which laid down and reaffirmed the absolute doctrine of sovereign immunity. ... However, the rule stated in the earlier English decisions no longer represents the rule of international law, and the *ratio* of the earlier South African cases is therefore no longer applicable. To apply the restrictive doctrine would therefore not involve any criticism of or dissent from the earlier South African decisions.[19]

This judgment was endorsed by Eksteen J in the Eastern Cape Division in the following year in *Kaffraria Property v Government of the Republic of Zambia*.[20] Again, the Court directed its attention to the problem caused by precedent in support of the absolute doctrine,

[16] 1980 (2) SA 111 (T). See further J Dugard 'International law in South Africa: The restrictive approach to immunity approved' (1980) 97 *SALJ* 357.

[17] At 119B–C.

[18] At 120C.

[19] At 125G–H.

[20] 1980 (2) SA 709 (E).

particularly *De Howorth v The SS India*,[21] in which Gardiner J had upheld the plea of sovereign immunity in respect of a merchant ship owned by the Portuguese government on the ground that 'any use of a vessel for the purpose of obtaining revenue for the state is a public purpose'.[22] In refusing to follow this precedent, Eksteen J held:

> When that case was decided, however, Gardiner J was merely stating and applying the rules of international law as they existed at the time—as, in fact, we are bound to do today. Customary international law, depending as it does on 'universal recognition by civilized states', is bound to and does change from time to time as a result of changing circumstances, international agreements or treaties, or even by virtue of the force of public opinion; and when it does so change, as it has done on the principle of sovereign immunity, it is the duty of our courts to ascertain the nature and extent of such change and to apply it in appropriate circumstances. Lord Denning has expressed this principle in the *Trendtex* case by his *dictum* that 'international law knows no rule of *stare decisis*' . . . . I therefore see no incongruity in declining today to apply the principles enunciated in the *SS 'India'* case, without in any way reflecting on the correctness of that decision.[23]

Shortly after these judgments were delivered, the legislature gave its approval to the restrictive approach in the Foreign States Immunities Act,[24] which is modelled on the United Kingdom's State Immunity Act.[25]

1 Foreign States Immunities Act 87 of 1981[26]

The Act starts by asserting a general immunity on the part of foreign states (including heads of state, governments and government departments) from the jurisdiction of South African courts in s 2(1). It then proceeds to itemise the circumstances in which sovereign immunity will not prevail in civil cases[27] and, in so doing, gives

[21] 1921 CPD 451.

[22] At 464.

[23] *Kaffraria Property* (n 20) 715B–D.

[24] 87 of 1981.

[25] 1978, c 33. The Australian Foreign States Immunities Act 196 of 1985 is also modelled on the British statute.

[26] See W Bray and M Beukes 'Recent trends in the development of state immunity in South African law' (1981) 7 *SAYIL* 13; G Erasmus 'Proceedings against foreign states—The South African Foreign States Immunities Act' (1982) 8 *SAYIL* 92; N Botha 'Some comments on the Foreign States Immunities Act 87 of 1981' (1982) 15 *CILSA* 334; H Booysen 'Procedural and jurisdictional uncertainties in the Foreign States Immunities Act' (1987–8) 13 *SAYIL* 139.

[27] Section 2(3) makes it clear that the Act is not to be construed as subjecting a foreign state to the criminal jurisdiction of South African courts.

approval to the restrictive approach.[28] Immunity will not be granted in the following cases.

(a) Waiver[29]

A foreign state will have no immunity where it has expressly waived immunity after the dispute has arisen or where it has done so by prior written agreement. A provision in an agreement that it is to be governed by the law of South Africa shall not be regarded as a waiver. A state is deemed to have waived immunity where it has instituted proceedings itself. The waiver extends to any appeal or counter-claim arising out of the proceedings.

(b) Commercial transactions

A foreign state will not be immune from the jurisdiction of municipal courts in proceedings relating to 'a commercial transaction' entered into by the state. 'Commercial transaction', in terms of s 4 of the Foreign States Immunities Act, means:

(i) any contract for the supply of services or goods;

(ii) any loan or other transaction for the provision of finance and any guarantee or indemnity in respect of any such loan or other transaction or of any other financial obligation; and

(iii) any other transaction or activity of a commercial, industrial, financial, professional or other similar character into which a foreign state enters or in which it engages otherwise than in the exercise of sovereign authority,

but does not include a contract of employment between a foreign state and an individual.

In order to determine whether a transaction is commercial, it is therefore necessary to consider its nature[30] and not its purpose.[31] Although most commercial undertakings involving foreign states are covered by this definition, there are still areas of uncertainty in which it will be necessary to have recourse to case law dealing with the

[28] A foreign state does not enjoy immunity if any one of the statutory exceptions contained in ss 3–12 applies to it: *The Akamedik Fyodorov: Government of the Russian Federation v Marine Expeditions Inc* 1996 (4) SA 442 (C) 443B–C.

[29] Section 3.

[30] *The Akademik Fyodorov* (n 28) 447F–H.

[31] The Act repudiates the 'public purpose' test adopted in earlier South African decisions, particularly *De Howorth v The SS India* 1921 CPD 451 at 464 and *Lendalease* (1975) (n 15) 404C–F. According to the UN Convention on Jurisdictional Immunities (n 10): 'In determining whether a contract or transaction is a "commercial transaction" . . . reference should be made primarily to the nature of the contract or transaction, but its purpose should also be taken into account if the parties have so agreed, or if, in the practice of the State of the forum, that purpose is relevant to determining the non-commercial character of the contract or transaction' (article 2(2)).

distinction between *acta jure imperii* and *acta jure gestionis*. As Lord Dyson MR observed in *Benkharbouche v Embassy of the Republic of Sudan*,[32] the 'distinction between sovereign acts and non-sovereign acts is easy to state but notoriously difficult to apply in practice'. The most helpful guidelines are probably those enunciated in *Victory Transport Inc v Comisaria General de Abastecimientos Y Transportes*.[33] According to this decision, *acta jure imperii* are limited to:

(1) internal administrative acts, such as expulsion of an alien;
(2) legislative acts, such as nationalisation;
(3) acts concerning the armed forces;
(4) acts concerning diplomatic activity;
(5) public loans.[34]

Acts concerning the armed forces and diplomatic activity cause particular difficulties. Suggestions[35] that the present law makes it clear that a contract for the purchase of boots for the army or of a battleship for the navy[36] falls clearly within the definition of a commercial transaction, as the purpose of the purchase is no longer relevant, fail to have regard to the fact that courts are likely to be wary in asserting jurisdiction over any matter relating to the armed forces. This is illustrated by *Aerotrade v Republic of Haiti*,[37] in which a United States court granted immunity in respect of a claim for payment for military equipment supplied to the Republic of Haiti for use by its armed forces and for services rendered in connection with the supply of such equipment. The difficulties relating to diplomatic activity are illustrated by two conflicting decisions. In *Prentice, Shaw & Scheiss Incorporated v Government of the Republic of Bolivia*,[38] on the one hand, Goldstone J classified a contract for the erection of an embassy as 'undoubtedly an *actus jure imperii*'. An English court in *Planmount Ltd v Republic of Zaire*,[39] on the other hand, held that 'it is hard to imagine a clearer case of an act or transaction of a private or commercial nature than the repairs to the ambassador's residence'.[40]

The following cases illustrate the complexities of the distinction between acts *jure imperii* and acts *jure gestionis*. In *Littrell v USA (No*

[32] [2015] EWCA Civ 33, para 21.

[33] 336F 2d 354 (2nd Cir 1964), 35 ILR 110. See, too, *Republic of Argentina v Weltover Inc* 504 US 607 (1992).

[34] At 360.

[35] See the judgment of Lord Denning in *Trendtex* (n 12) 558E; FA Mann 'The State Immunity Act 1978' (1979) 50 *BYIL* 43 at 52.

[36] *The Akademik Fyodorov* (n 28) 447H–I; *KJ International v MV Oscar Jupiter* 1998 (2) SA 130 (D) 136B–C.

[37] 376 F Supp 1281 (1974), 63 ILR 41.

[38] 1978 (3) SA 938 (W) 940H.

[39] [1981] 1 All ER 1110 (QB).

[40] At 1114F.

2),[41] the English Court of Appeal held that a claim in tort brought by a United States soldier stationed in the United Kingdom for negligent medical treatment at an American military hospital was 'clearly on the *jure imperii* side of the line'. In *Kuwait Airways Corp v Iraqi Airways Co*[42] the House of Lords considered the question whether Iraqi Airways was entitled to claim immunity in respect of the seizure, retention and use of aircraft belonging to Kuwait Airways following Iraq's invasion of Kuwait in 1990. While it accepted that the initial seizure was *jure imperii*, it held, by three to two, that the subsequent retention and use of the aircraft by Iraqi Airways was *jure gestionis*. The ultimate test, for the majority, as to what constitutes an act *jure imperii* is whether the act in question is of its own character a governmental act or an act that a private citizen can perform. In *Koo Golden East Mongolia v Bank of Nova Scotia*, the English Court of Appeal held that a contract by which a gold mining company deposited gold with the Mongolian Central Bank was entered into 'in the exercise of sovereign authority' as its purpose was to increase Mongolia's currency resources.[43] In *CGM Industrial (Pty) Ltd v KPMG*, the Transvaal Provincial Division held that the seizure of documents by the government of Lesotho for the purpose of criminal investigations was clearly an activity *jure imperii*.[44] The Court held in *Minister of Water Affairs and Forestry v Swissborough Diamond Mines (Pty) Ltd*[45] that the South African government might not be compelled to produce documentation relating to litigation in Lesotho on the ground that the acts in question were acts *jure imperii*.

(c) Contracts of employment

A South African court will have jurisdiction, in terms of s 5(1) of the Foreign States Immunities Act, in proceedings relating to a contract of employment between a foreign state and an individual provided:

(a) the contract was entered into in the Republic or the work is to be performed wholly or partly in the Republic; and

(b) at the time when the contract was entered into the individual was a South African citizen or was ordinarily resident in the Republic; and

(c) at the time when the proceedings are brought the individual is not a citizen of the foreign state.

[41] [1995] 1 WLR (CA) 82. See, too, *Holland v Lampen-Wolfe* [2001] 1 WLR 1573 (HL).

[42] [1995] 1 WLR (HL) 1147.

[43] [2007] EWCA Civ 1443, (2007) 78 *BYIL* 582.

[44] 1998 (3) SA 738 (T) 744D–G, noted in JMT Labuschagne 'Scope of foreign state immunity' (1998) 23 *SAYIL* 262.

[45] 1999 (2) SA 345 (T) 352–4.

This does not apply to proceedings relating to the employment of diplomatic, consular, administrative, technical or service staff of a foreign diplomatic mission or consular post. Nor does it apply to a case in which the parties to the contract have agreed in writing that any dispute arising out of the contract of employment is to be justiciable by the courts of a foreign state.[46]

(d) Personal injury and damage to property

In terms of s 6 of the Foreign States Immunities Act, a foreign state is not immune from the jurisdiction of a municipal court in proceedings relating to the death or injury of any person, or to damage to tangible property caused by its act or omission in the Republic.[47] It has been suggested[48] that one of the purposes of this provision is to permit the victim of a traffic accident to sue the state of the foreign diplomat responsible for the accident, despite the fact that the diplomat could not be sued in person because of the personal immunity from civil actions conferred on diplomats by the Vienna Convention on Diplomatic Relations.

This exception to immunity is wide enough to cover the political or governmental acts of a foreign state. In *Letelier v Republic of Chile*[49] the Court dismissed the argument that Chile could plead sovereign immunity to a claim for damages arising out of the assassination of an opponent of the Chilean government committed by agents of the Chilean government in the United States.

Section 6 makes no exception for the acts of armed forces in providing that a foreign state shall not enjoy immunity in proceedings relating to 'the death or injury of any person' or damage to property occurring in the territory of South Africa. In this respect, it follows the legislation of the United States, the United Kingdom, Australia, Canada, Singapore, Argentina, Israel and Japan, and article 12 of the United Nations Convention on Jurisdictional Immunities of States and their Property. In *Jurisdictional Immunities of the State (Germany v Italy; Greece Intervening)*[50] the International Court of Justice was asked by Italy to find that these instruments provided evidence of a customary rule that armed forces engaged in acts *jure imperii* were not entitled to immunity and hence that Germany was responsible for the acts of its armed forces in Italy in World War II. The Court refused to accept this argument and, in an unconvincing

[46] Section 5(2).
[47] Section 6.
[48] *Letelier v Republic of Chile* 488 F Supp 665 (1980) 671, which deals with the equivalent section in US legislation on this subject.
[49] Ibid 671–3.
[50] 2012 ICJ Reports 99.

judgment, found that 'customary international law continues to require that a state be accorded immunity in proceedings for torts allegedly committed on the territory of another state by its armed forces and other organs of the state in the course of conducting an armed conflict'.[51] This decision does not reflect the law of South Africa as s 6 continues to provide that there shall be no immunity for armed forces in such circumstances.

In *Democratic Alliance v Minister of International Relations and Co-operation; Engels v Minister of International Relations and Co-operation*[52] the Gauteng High Court held that s 6 precluded Grace Mugabe, wife of the then President of Zimbabwe, Robert Mugabe, from claiming immunity in a case involving an assault carried out in Johannesburg. As Robert Mugabe himself would not have been able to succeed in a claim for immunity on account of s 6, it followed that his wife—if she was entitled to immunity as his spouse—would not have been able to claim immunity either.[53]

(e) Miscellaneous

The Foreign States Immunities Act further provides that a foreign state will not enjoy immunity in respect of proceedings relating to immovable property (except where the property is used for a diplomatic mission or a consular post);[54] patents or trade marks;[55] membership of an association;[56] arbitration (where the foreign state has agreed to submit a dispute to arbitration);[57] ships and cargo used for commercial purposes;[58] sales tax, customs or excise duty; and rates in respect of premises used for commercial purposes.[59]

A foreign government may intervene to protect its interests in property that may be affected by the judgment in an action. In such a case, the foreign government must prove that its claim is not illusory or founded on a title that is manifestly defective.[60] It may plead immunity and this will stop the proceedings. Where a foreign state

[51] 2012 ICJ Reports 99 para 78.
[52] [2018] ZAGPPHC 534 (30 July 2018).
[53] Ibid para 40.
[54] Section 7.
[55] Section 8.
[56] Section 9.
[57] Section 10. For an examination of the meaning of this section, see *The Akademik Fyodorov* (n 28) 443–5.
[58] Section 11.
[59] Section 12.
[60] *CGM Industrial (Pty) Ltd v KPMG* (n 44) 745C–E.

intervenes in proceedings, this may be done by an official of that state other than the head of its diplomatic mission.[61]

Any document required to be served for the purpose of instituting proceedings against a foreign state shall be served by transmission through the Department of International Relations and Co-operation to the ministry of foreign affairs of the state.[62]

2 Enforcement[63]

In terms of s 14 of the Foreign States Immunities Act, the property of a foreign state may not be subjected to any process for the enforcement of a judgment or an arbitration award, unless the state gives its written consent to such a process or the property in question is 'in use or intended for use for commercial purposes'.[64]

The equivalent provision in the United Kingdom's State Immunity Act of 1978 allows the head of a state's diplomatic mission to certify that any property is not in use for commercial purposes and this is to be accepted as sufficient evidence of such a fact unless the contrary is proved.[65] In practice, it is extremely difficult for a judgment creditor to discharge the onus of proving that the property is in use for commercial purposes.[66] Fortunately, the South African statute contains no such provision and it is therefore left to the courts to decide this issue.[67]

Waiver of immunity from the jurisdiction of a municipal court by a foreign state does not include consent to the enforcement of an adverse judgment.[68] A separate waiver of immunity for the purpose of judgment is required.

Section 14 was subjected to thorough scrutiny in *The Akademik Fyodorov: Government of the Russian Federation v Marine Expeditions Inc.*[69] Here, the Court held that the warrant for the arrest of a ship for the purpose of providing security for a claim in arbitration constituted a process for the enforcement of an arbitration award. Consequently, the warrant of arrest was to be set aside unless the property

[61] *CGM Industrial* (n 44) 742F–H.

[62] Section 13. See *Portion 20 of Plot 15 Athol (Pty) Ltd v Rodrigues* (n 2) 1290–1.

[63] J Crawford 'Execution of judgments and foreign sovereign immunity' (1981) 75 *AJIL* 820.

[64] Section 14(3). See *Republica Popular de Mocambique v Main Spares Acc (Pty) Ltd* 1986 (4) SA 929 (W).

[65] Section 13(5). Cf the Australian Foreign States Immunities Act 196 of 1985, s 41, which does not give such a certificate the same evidential weight.

[66] *Alcom Ltd v Republic of Colombia* [1984] 1 AC 580 (HL).

[67] For an example of such a judicial enquiry by a US court, see *Letelier v Republic of Chile* 748 F 2d 790 (1984).

[68] Section 14(2).

[69] 1996 (4) SA 422 (C).

was 'in use or intended for use for commercial purposes'. The definition in s 4 of a 'commercial transaction' does not apply to s 14(3), which uses the term 'commercial purposes', said Rose Innes J,

> since the former poses an objective criterion based upon the nature or character of a particular transaction, contract or activity without reference to the purpose with which it was concluded or engaged in, while the latter poses a criterion of the purpose for which property was used or for which it was intended to be used, which introduces a subjective test relating to the purposes or intentions of the foreign state.[70]

The Court then examined the activities in which the ship was engaged and concluded that the polar scientific research for which it was used was a public governmental activity. As it was not used for a commercial purpose, the Court found that it could not be subjected to a warrant for its arrest.

In *Abbott v South Africa*[71] the Spanish Constitutional Court held that bank accounts held by South Africa in Spain to be used for ordinary diplomatic and consular activities were immune from attachment or execution despite the fact that the funds were also used for commercial purposes.

In *Rootman v President of the Republic of South Africa*[72] the Supreme Court of Appeal held that s 14, providing for the execution of a judgment in respect of commercial property belonging to a foreign state (the Democratic Republic of the Congo) could not be re-enforced by an order of the Court directing the South African government to ensure compliance with the execution of the judgment debt.

3 The state, the government and separate entities

For the purposes of the Foreign States Immunities Act, a foreign state includes the head of state, the government and any government department of the state. It does not include a constituent part of a federal foreign state or a 'separate entity', ie 'any entity which is distinct from the executive organs of the government of that foreign state and capable of suing or being sued'.[73] A certificate by the Minister of International Relations and Co-operation will be conclusive proof as to whether any territory is a constituent part of a

[70] At 447F–G. This *dictum* was approved in *KJ International v MV Oscar Jupiter* 1998 (2) SA 130 (D) 136B–C. However, on the facts of this case, the Court held that the ship was used for 'commercial purposes' and that the plea of immunity could not succeed. See further EC Schlemmer 'The immunity of state-owned ships' (2002) 27 *SAYIL* 248.

[71] 113 ILR 411 at 423–4.

[72] Oxford Reports on International Law ILDC 469 (ZA 2006) and [2006] JOL 17547 (SCA). See, too, the decision of the High Court in *Rootman* ILDC 153 (ZA 2005).

[73] Section 1(2).

federation and whether any person is to be regarded as the head of state or government of a foreign state.[74]

When the absolute approach to sovereign immunity prevailed, much of the litigation in this field was aimed at establishing that state-owned corporations or quasi-government departments were not to be assimilated with the state, and were therefore not entitled to immunity.[75] The adoption of the restrictive approach has substantially altered the situation, as today a state-owned corporation will not enjoy immunity for a commercial transaction—even if it can prove that it is to be assimilated with the state.

The Foreign States Immunities Act distinguishes between states and separate entities for the purpose of immunity. A foreign state has immunity in all matters other than the exceptional cases described in the Act. A 'separate entity', however, has immunity only if the proceedings relate 'to anything done by the separate entity in the exercise of sovereign authority' and 'the circumstances are such that a foreign state would have been so immune'.[76] The onus of proof is upon the separate entity to prove that it is entitled to immunity.[77]

In deciding whether an entity qualifies as a government department or 'separate entity', South African courts will be guided by the judgment of Goldstone J in *Banco de Mocambique v Inter-Science Research and Development Services*.[78] Here, the judge held that in order to determine the nature of the relationship between a foreign state and a central bank, it was necessary to have regard to the principles of both South African law and the law of the state in question, namely Mozambique:

> South African law must decide upon the qualities which are necessary or sufficient to confer upon the applicant the status of a department or organ of government. However, Mozambican law is relevant to the issue of whether the applicant in fact possesses those qualities.[79]

Central banks will generally qualify as 'separate entities'. However, they are given preferential treatment in respect of the attachment of their property for the purpose of enforcing judgment debts.

[74] Section 17.

[75] *Lendalease*(n 15) 1975 403; *Krajina v Tass Agency* [1949] 2 All ER 274 (CA); *Baccus SRL v Servicio Nacional Del Trigo* [1957] 1 QB 438 (CA).

[76] Section 15. See *Minister of Water Affairs and Forestry v Swissborough Diamond Mines* 1999 (2) SA 345 (T) 353–4.

[77] H Booysen *Volkereg en sy Verhouding tot die Suid-Afrikaanse Reg* (1989) 302–3. Conversely, if a party seeks to prove that an entity is a separate entity distinct from the government, the onus of proof is on the party so alleging. See *The Akademik Fyodorov* (n 28) 440C–D.

[78] 1982 (3) SA 330 (T), discussed in J Dugard 'Public international law' 1982 *Annual Survey* 57 at 62.

[79] At 335E.

The property of a central bank shall not be regarded as being in use for commercial purposes, with the result that its property will always be immune from execution unless written consent to execution is given.[80]

The Shipping Corporation of India Ltd v Evdomon Corporation[81] concerned a related but different issue—whether a ship owned by a private shipping company, which was a wholly owned subsidiary of the Government of India, could be attached to found jurisdiction by a private company with a claim against the Indian government. Although Corbett CJ considered the case law relating to sovereign immunity, he preferred to see the two situations as 'entirely different'.[82] He held:

> [G]enerally, it is of cardinal importance to keep distinct the property rights of a company and those of its shareholders, even where the latter is a single entity .... And in this regard it should not make any difference whether the shares be held by a holding company or by a government.[83]

Accordingly, he held that there was no reason to pierce the corporate veil in the present case and that the property of the Shipping Corporation of India could not be attached to found jurisdiction.

No reasons are advanced for refusing to distinguish between a non-governmental holding company and a government in the characterisation of the status of a company, despite the fact that sound policy considerations might require a different approach to be adopted. If foreign governments are to be held accountable for their commercial transactions, it is surely desirable that every effort should be made to provide the non-governmental plaintiff with a remedy to enforce its claims—if necessary, by attaching the property of wholly owned subsidiaries of that government in order to found jurisdiction.

4 Indirect impleading and state immunity

The question whether Morocco was indirectly impleaded in proceedings arose in *Saharawi Arab Democratic Republic v Owners and Charterers of the Cherry Blossom*.[84] Here, an application was brought by the Saharawi Arab Democratic Republic for an order restraining the respondents from removing phosphate from the jurisdiction of the Court on the ground that the phosphate had been illegally mined in Western Sahara, which had been unlawfully annexed by Morocco.

[80] Section 15(3). For criticism of this provision, see Erasmus (n 26) 103–4; Mann (n 35) 62.

[81] 1994 (1) SA 550 (A).

[82] At 565I.

[83] At 566C–E.

[84] 2017 (5) SA 105 (ECP). The facts of this case are fully described in Chapter 4.

The respondents opposed the interdict by arguing that the application indirectly impleaded Morocco, under whose laws the phosphate had been mined. They cited the *Monetary Gold*[85] principle expounded by the International Court of Justice to the effect that a court may not exercise jurisdiction in a dispute where the lawfulness of the conduct of a party not before the court (*in casu* Morocco) was in issue. The Court rejected this argument, holding that an order that the phosphate may not be removed from the jurisdiction of the court 'cannot in any legal sense affect the rights of Morocco at international law'.[86] It added that any effect that its order might have on the interests of Morocco 'falls within the realm of political or moral interests and cannot have legal effect'.[87] This meant that the claim to state immunity could not be upheld.

IMMUNITY, HUMAN RIGHTS AND INTERNATIONAL CRIMES

Contemporary international law no longer accepts that a state may treat its nationals as it pleases. Conventions and custom prescribe a wide range of human rights obligations with which states must comply. Moreover, some human rights norms enjoy such a high status that their violation, even by state officials, constitutes an international crime. The doctrine of immunity cannot stand aloof from these developments. International commerce has destroyed the absoluteness of state immunity in respect of commercial transactions. International human rights law and international criminal law may now be poised to weaken it still further.[88]

The conflict between human rights and immunity arises in two situations. First, it arises in *criminal* proceedings, where an incumbent or former head of state or government or senior government official is brought before an international criminal tribunal or domestic court charged with a serious international crime and raises the plea of sovereign immunity as a defence or as bar to the jurisdiction of the court to try him. This also occurs where such a person is present in a foreign state and an international criminal tribunal, or a state with jurisdiction to try him for such a crime, requests the former state to assist in the surrender of such a person to the international criminal

[85] *Monetary Gold Removed from Rome in 1943*, 1954 ICJ Reports 19.

[86] *Cherry Blossom* (n 84) para 84.

[87] Ibid para 85.

[88] See J Foakes *The Position of Heads of State and Senior Officials in International Law* (2014); R van Alebeek *Immunities of States and their Officials in International Criminal Law and International Rights Law* (2008); Y Naqvi *Impediments to Exercising Jurisdiction over International Crimes* (2010); R O'Keefe 'State immunity and human rights: Heads and walls, hearts and minds' (2011) 44 *Vanderbilt Journal of Transnational Law* 999; H Fox and P Webb *The Law of State Immunity* 3 ed (2013).

tribunal, or state with jurisdiction, for the purpose of bringing him to trial. Secondly, it arises in *civil* proceedings, where a government or government agent is sued in civil proceedings in the courts of a foreign state for compensation resulting from an international crime or serious human rights violation, usually committed outside the forum state.

1 Criminal proceedings

The question of the immunity of heads of state or government or senior state officials for serious international crimes such as war crimes, crimes against humanity, torture or genocide is one of the most contested issues of contemporary international law. It is one that has divided judges of both international and national courts, led to fractious debates in the International Law Commission[89] and spawned an acrimonious debate among scholars.[90]

The orthodox formulation of the law of immunity of heads of state or government and of senior state officials, largely inspired by the *Arrest Warrant* case[91] (of which more later), is that there is no immunity for such persons before international criminal tribunals but there is immunity before national courts.[92] A head of state or government or a senior state official does, however, lose immunity after he ceases to hold such office in respect of acts committed in a private capacity before, during or after he assumed office.[93] Immunity persists only in respect of official acts (*acta ratione materiae*)[94] but there is a strong body of opinion that holds that such immunity does not extend to serious international crimes.[95] This formulation, which takes no account of the distinction between immunity as a defence before a court of law or as a bar to the jurisdiction of a court and

[89] See International Law Commission: Sixth Report on Immunity of State Officials from Foreign Criminal Jurisdiction by Concepcion Escobar Hernandez, *GAOR* A/CN.4/722 of 12 June 2018, paras 8–17. See further on the 2017 debate of the International Law Commission, SD Murphy 'Crimes against humanity and other topics: The sixty-ninth session of the International Law Commission' (2017) 111 *AJIL* 970 at 981–8.

[90] See n 88.

[91] *Case Concerning the Arrest Warrant of 11 April 2000 (Democratic Republic of the Congo v Belgium)* 2002 ICJ Reports 3.

[92] Ibid para 58.

[93] Ibid para 61

[94] Ibid para 61.

[95] *R v Bow Street Metropolitan Stipendiary Magistrate: Ex parte Pinochet Ugarte (No 3)* [1999] 2 All ER 97(HL). For the work of the International Law Commission and its decision to exclude immunity *ratione materiae* in respect of serious international crimes, see Murphy (n 89) 981–8, especially at 984.

immunity in respect of judicial assistance, requires careful consideration, particularly as this distinction was in issue in the al-Bashir case before the Supreme Court of Appeal.[96]

The examination of this branch of state immunity that follows describes the manner in which the present law of immunity has developed. At the same time, it argues that an exposition of the law that takes account of the distinction between the different types of immunity described above accords more with contemporary international law's demand that there should be no impunity for international crimes.[97]

The attempt of the Allied powers to try the German Kaiser for international crimes committed during World War I served notice that heads of state were no longer to be seen as immune from prosecution for international crimes.[98] This was confirmed after World War II by the Charters of both the Nuremberg and Tokyo tribunals, which specifically excluded immunities as a defence or as a bar to jurisdiction for those to be tried before the tribunals for war crimes and crimes against humanity. The Nuremberg Tribunal stated unambiguously that '[t]he principle of international law, which under certain circumstances protects the representatives of a state, cannot be applied to acts which are condemned as criminal by international law'.[99] National prosecutions of Nazi war criminals followed a similar course. In 1950 the General Assembly adopted a resolution endorsing the Nuremberg Principles.[100] Principle III declared that '[t]he fact that a person who committed an act which constitutes a crime under international law acted as Head of State or responsible government official does not relieve him from responsibility under international law'. These principles were approved by the Supreme Court of Israel in the trial of Adolf Eichmann[101] and incorporated into the International Law Commission's 1996 Draft Code of Crimes against the Peace and Security of Mankind.[102] The statutes of ad hoc international criminal tribunals for the Former

[96] *Minister of Justice v SALC* (n 6).

[97] For a full exposition of this approach, see G Mettraux, J Dugard and M du Plessis 'Heads of state immunities, international crimes and President Bashir's visit to South Africa' (2018) 18 *International Criminal Law Review* 1.

[98] Ibid 8–10.

[99] *Trial of the Major War Criminals before the International Military Tribunal* vol I (Nuremberg 1947) 223.

[100] Resolution 95(1).

[101] See *Attorney-General of Israel v Adolf Eichmann* 36 ILR 277 at 311.

[102] See article 7 of the Draft Code of Crimes against the Peace and Security of Mankind in *Yearbook of the International Law Commission* (1996) vol II, part 2.

Yugoslavia[103] and Rwanda[104] and the special court for Sierra Leone[105] likewise exclude immunities for heads of state or senior state officials, as does the Rome Statute of the International Criminal Court.[106] In excluding the immunity of heads of state and government for the commission of serious international crimes, the Charters of the Nuremberg and Tokyo tribunals and the statutes of contemporary international criminal tribunals, the jurisprudence of these tribunals, the General Assembly's Principles and the International Law Commission's Draft Code do not in any way suggest that this exclusion of immunities is to be confined to international criminal tribunals. It is the fact that the charges pertain to international crimes which results in the loss of immunities as a defence or bar to jurisdiction and not the character of the court (national or international) in which the person is to be tried. From all of this, it may be concluded that customary international law before the *Arrest Warrant* case of 2002 appeared to recognise a rule that heads of state and government and senior officials were precluded from raising immunity as a defence in their trials or as a bar to jurisdiction, whatever the character of the court before which such person was to be tried and regardless of whether the person acted in a private or official capacity.[107] These developments did not, however, exclude immunity in the case of requests for judicial assistance emanating from another jurisdiction, national or international.

The *Pinochet* case,[108] heard by the House of Lords in the late 1990s, is confusing as six Law Lords gave separate opinions. Nevertheless, it may be seen as giving support to the above view. Although this case involved a request for judicial assistance—the extradition of the former Chilean dictator Pinochet from Britain, where he was receiving medical attention, to Spain for the crime of torture committed in Chile—the House of Lords made it clear that they viewed torture, an international crime, as one not subject to immunity before a national

[103] Article 7(2).

[104] Article 6(2).

[105] Article 6(2).

[106] Article 27.

[107] Article 46A*bis* of the 2014 Malabo Protocol of the African Union, which provides for the immunity of heads of state and government and senior officials, is therefore contrary to customary international law. (This Protocol is discussed in Chapter 26.)

[108] In fact, the House of Lords gave two judgments in this case as the first was set aside because one of the judges (Lord Hoffmann) had failed to disclose his close links with one of the parties to the proceedings. See *R v Bow Street Metropolitan Stipendiary Magistrate: Ex parte Pinochet Ugarte* [1998] 3 WLR 1456 (HL), [1998] 4 All ER 897 (HL); *R v Bow Street Metropolitan Stipendiary Magistrate: Ex parte Pinochet Ugarte (No 2)* [1999] 2 WLR 272 (HL), [1999] 1 All ER 577 (HL) (setting aside the former decision); *R v Bow Street Metropolitan Stipendiary Magistrate: Ex parte Pinochet Ugarte (No 3)* [1999] 2 WLR 872 (HL), [1999] 2 All ER 97 (HL). See, too, *Khurts Bat v German Federal Court* [2011] EWHC 2029 (Admin).

court. The six separate opinions make it difficult to discern the *ratio decidendi* for the refusal of immunity. However, Lord Phillips MR, one of the Law Lords in the *Pinochet* case, later stated that several judges held that the torture alleged against Pinochet could not constitute an official act as required for a former head of state to succeed in a plea of immunity, but that the majority held that he could not assert immunity 'in relation to a criminal prosecution for torture in as much as torture is a breach of *jus cogens* under international law'.[109] In other words, it was the nature of the crime which was to determine the question of immunity. Here, the fact that the matter was before a national court as opposed to an international court did not feature in the reasoning of the Law Lords.

The law of immunity for heads of state or government and foreign ministers was shaken by the *Arrest Warrant* case.[110] Here, the International Court of Justice held that Belgium had violated international law by issuing a warrant for the arrest of the Minister of Foreign Affairs (Mr Yerodia) of the Democratic Republic of Congo (DRC) on charges of crimes against humanity and war crimes committed in the DRC in that it failed to respect the immunity from criminal jurisdiction which the Minister enjoyed under international law before national courts. The Court found that customary international law precluded national courts from trying a Minister of Foreign Affairs, and by implication other senior government officials required to travel in the course of their duties. Although the Court could not find any state practice to support this conclusion, it insisted

[109] *Jones v Ministry of the Interior Al-Mamlaka Al-Arabiya as Saudiya (The Kingdom of Saudi Arabia)* [2004] EWCA Civil 1394 paras 123–4. Cf D Akande 'International law immunities and the International Criminal Court' (2004) 98 *AJIL* 407 at 415; D Akande and S Shah 'Immunities of state officials, international crimes and foreign domestic courts' (2011) 21 *EJIL* 815; R van Alebeek 'The *Pinochet* case: International human rights on trial' (2000) 71 *BYIL* 29; A Bianchi 'Immunity versus human rights: The *Pinochet* case' (1999) 10 *EJIL* 237; CH Powell and A Pillay 'Revisiting *Pinochet*: The development of customary international criminal law' (2001) 17 *SAJHR* 477.

[110] *Case Concerning the Arrest Warrant of 11 April 2000 (Democratic Republic of Congo v Belgium)* 2002 ICJ Reports 3, (2002) 41 *ILM* 536. For comments on this case, see G Erasmus and G Kemp 'The application of international criminal law before domestic courts in the light of recent developments in international and constitutional law' (2002) 27 *SAYIL* 64; K Hopkins 'The International Court of Justice and sovereign immunity: Why the *Yerodia Case* is an unfortunate ruling for the development of public international law' (2002) 27 *SAYIL* 256; M du Plessis and S Bosch 'Immunities and universal jurisdiction—The world court steps in (or on?)' (2003) 28 *SAYIL* 246. See, too, *Case Concerning Certain Criminal Proceedings in France (Republic of Congo v France), Provisional Measures* 2003 ICJ Reports 102, (2003) 42 *ILM* 852 (discontinued 2010); *Case Concerning Certain Questions of Mutual Assistance in Criminal Matters (Djibouti v France)* 2008 ICJ Reports 177.

that the function of a Minister is to travel abroad and engage foreign governments, and this gave rise to a customary rule of immunity.[111]

Even more surprising was the finding of the Court that the Minister was immune from prosecution before national courts for international crimes, including crimes against humanity and war crimes.[112] It acknowledged, however, that this immunity would not apply once he had ceased to hold office 'in respect of acts committed prior or subsequent to his or her period of office, as well as in respect of acts committed during that period of office in a private capacity'.[113] Nor, said the Court, did immunity from prosecution for international crimes extend to international criminal courts.[114]

This decision, premised on a rule of customary international law with little practice to support it, was strongly criticised by Judge ad hoc Van den Wyngaert[115] and Judge Al-Khasawneh[116] as a setback for the law against impunity for the commission of international crimes.

There are several strange features of this decision. The failure of the Court to provide evidence of state practice in support of its decision, the extension of immunity to a foreign minister and the apparent absence of concern for impunity for international crimes have attracted the most criticism. But, in addition, the Court made no attempt to distinguish between immunity as a defence or bar to jurisdiction and immunity in respect of a request for judicial assistance. This case involved a request for judicial assistance for the arrest and extradition of Mr Yerodia to Belgium. It did not concern a plea of immunity as a defence to a charge before a Belgian court by Mr Yerodia when he was present in Belgium. Nor did it involve a plea by Mr Yerodia to bar the jurisdiction of a Belgian court when he was present in Belgium. This was absolutely clear. The Court, however, conflated all three types of immunity in holding that Belgium's circulation of an arrest warrant by Interpol 'constituted a violation of an obligation of Belgium towards the Congo, in that it failed to respect the immunity of an incumbent Minister of Foreign Affairs of the Congo and, more particularly, infringed the immunity

[111] *Arrest Warrant* case (n 110) paras 52–4.

[112] Ibid paras 56–8.

[113] Ibid para 61. The Court fails to define acts committed in 'a private capacity'. Would acts of torture authorised by an official entitled to immunity while in office be subject to prosecution after he leaves office, as held in *R v Bow Street Metropolitan Stipendiary Magistrate: Ex parte Pinochet Ugarte (No 3)* [1999] 2 All ER 97 (HL)?

[114] *Arrest Warrant* case (n 110) para 61.

[115] Ibid paras 24–38.

[116] Ibid para 7.

from criminal jurisdiction then enjoyed by him under international law'.[117]

The Court made it clear that Mr Yerodia's all-encompassing immunity extended only to national courts. In so finding, the Court flatly rejected Belgium's argument that provisions excluding immunity in the charters and statutes of international criminal tribunals and the decisions of these tribunals had created a customary rule excluding immunity in all courts, both national and international.[118] The *Arrest Warrant* case is therefore seen as authority for the proposition that there is a dichotomy between immunity for international crimes before international courts and national courts. This bizarre dichotomy has been seized upon by some scholars and courts to claim that heads of state or government and senior officials are immune from the jurisdiction of national courts in respect of serious international crimes.[119]

The *Arrest Warrant* case has also resulted in a distinction between the acts of senior state officials that are carried out in a private capacity and in an official capacity for the purposes of immunity, and between immunities for incumbent officials and former officials.[120] The latter category distinguishes between immunity *ratione personae* and immunity *ratione materiae*. The former immunity attaches to a person because of his status or office, while the latter form of immunity relates to acts performed in an official capacity.

Immunity *ratione personae* attaches to senior state officials, such as heads of state or government or Ministers of Foreign Affairs, *while they are in office*. This immunity applies even to international crimes, as held by national courts in cases involving Gaddafi,[121] Castro,[122] Sharon,[123] Mofaz[124] and Mugabe[125] while they were still in office. According to Dapo Akande, writing in the wake of the *Arrest Warrant* case:

> Judicial opinion and state practice on this point are unanimous and no case can be found in which it was held that a state official possessing immunity *ratione personae* is subject to the criminal jurisdiction of a foreign state when it

[117] *Arrest Warrant* case (n 110) para 71.

[118] Ibid para 58.

[119] See the cases described in Mettraux, Dugard and Du Plessis (n 97) 8, fn 19.

[120] *Arrest Warrant* case (n 110) para 58.

[121] 125 ILR 456 (France). See S Zappala 'Do heads of state in office enjoy immunity from jurisdiction for international crimes? The *Ghaddafi Case* before the French Cour de Cassation' (2001) 12 *EJIL* 595.

[122] A Cassese *International Criminal Law* (2003) 272 (Spain).

[123] (2003) 42 *ILM* 596 (Belgium).

[124] (2004) 53 *ICLQ* 771 (UK).

[125] (2004) 53 *ICLQ* 769 (UK).

is alleged that he or she has committed an international crime.[126]

Immunity *ratione materiae*, which attaches to official acts, may be invoked not only by serving state officials in respect of their official acts, but also by former officials in respect of official acts performed while they were in office. However, national courts have held that such immunity does not exist when a person is charged with an international crime, either because such acts can never be 'official' or because they violate norms of *jus cogens* and such peremptory norms prevail over immunity. This has recently been confirmed by the International Law Commission.[127]

As the *Arrest Warrant* case is seen as the authority for the distinction between immunity before national courts and international courts and between official acts and private acts, it is necessary to examine the facts of the decision more closely.

'In law context is everything,' said Lord Steyn in *R v Secretary of State for the Home Department, Ex parte Daly*.[128] This means it is necessary to revert to the context of the *Arrest Warrant* case. It concerned a request for judicial assistance by Belgium, that is, a request for the arrest and extradition to Belgium of Mr Yerodia. It did not concern a plea by Mr Yerodia for immunity before a Belgian court or a plea that the court lacked jurisdiction. At no time was Mr Yerodia in Belgium before a Belgian court. This means that the *Arrest Warrant* case is authority only for the proposition that there is immunity in respect of a request for judicial assistance. This is emphasised by the fact that the Court ordered Belgium to cancel the arrest warrant for Mr Yerodia.[129]

The issue of immunity in a request for judicial assistance came before the Supreme Court of Appeal in *Minister of Justice v SALC*,[130] which concerned a visit to South Africa by President al-Bashir of Sudan in 2015 to attend an African Union Summit meeting. President al-Bashir had been indicted by the International Criminal Court on charges of war crimes, crimes against humanity and genocide, which had resulted in a call to South Africa for his arrest and surrender to the ICC in terms of the Rome Statute. The ICC request was confirmed by a decision of the Gauteng High Court, which ordered the government to arrest President al-Bashir and to ensure that he did not leave the country. Despite this order, President al-Bashir was

[126] 'International law immunities and the International Criminal Court' (2004) 98 *AJIL* 407 at 411. See, too, D Akande and S Shah 'Immunities of state officials, international crimes and foreign domestic courts' (2011) 21 *EJIL* 815.

[127] Murphy (n 89) 981–8.

[128] [2001] 2 AC 732.

[129] *Arrest Warrant* case (n 110) para 78.

[130] Supra (n 6).

allowed to leave South Africa. By way of explanation and defence, the South African government argued that it had been faced with two conflicting obligations—the obligation to provide immunity from arrest to all heads of state attending the African Union summit and its obligation to arrest President al-Bashir and surrender him to the ICC.

In essence, this dispute concerned two provisions of the Rome Statute of the ICC dealing with immunities—articles 27 and 98—which *ex facie* appear to contradict each other. Article 27 restates the customary rule espoused in this chapter that immunity is excluded as a defence or bar to jurisdiction, in that the official capacity of a person as head of state or government or other senior official 'shall in no case exempt a person from criminal responsibility'; and immunities that attach to a person under national or international law 'shall not bar the Court from exercising its jurisdiction over such a person'. Article 98 in somewhat convoluted language deals with the question of immunities in the case of judicial assistance. It provides that the Court may not proceed with a request for the surrender of a suspect which would require the requested state to act inconsistently with its obligations under international law with respect to the immunity of a person of a third state unless the Court can first obtain the co-operation of that third state for the waiver of immunity. In effect, article 98 is a blocking mechanism that sets a limit to the ability of the ICC to demand co-operation from a state in relation to the surrender of a suspect where such co-operation would affect the immunities of a third state. This means that the ICC Statute does not give state parties express or implied authority to disregard the immunities of another state. The determination as to whether a request for surrender or assistance from the ICC raises a problem under article 98 is to be made by the state concerned and not the ICC.

Minister of Justice v SALC concerned the question of immunity in a case involving a request for the surrender of President al-Bashir to the ICC, that is, a matter of judicial assistance. It did not involve immunity as a defence or bar to jurisdiction. In this respect, it was like the *Arrest Warrant* case. There was, however, an important difference. In the *Arrest Warrant* case the request for an arrest came from a domestic jurisdiction—Belgium—whereas here the request came from an international tribunal. The Supreme Court of Appeal was acutely aware of this distinction when it stated that there was a difference between saying that an international tribunal with a provision such as article 27 of the ICC Statute excluding immunity 'provides an exception to the customary international law rule that heads of state enjoy immunity *ratione personae*, and saying that a national court asked to provide assistance to that international tribunal is likewise not bound by the customary international law rule. It is the latter proposition with which we are concerned.'[131]

The Supreme Court of Appeal, relying on the *Arrest Warrant* case, rejected the notion that customary international law today recognises an all-encompassing exception to immunities in the case of international crimes.[132] This did not mean, however, that President al-Bashir was entitled to immunity while he was in South Africa.[133] In the case of a request for judicial assistance from the ICC, as was the case here, it was necessary to have regard to domestic law, particularly s 4(2)*(a)* the Implementation of the Rome Statute of the International Criminal Court Act 27 of 2002, which provides that 'despite any other law to the contrary, including customary and conventional international law', the fact that a person is a head of state or government or senior state official is not 'a defence to a crime'. That South Africa was determined not to allow immunity to be raised in its dealings with the ICC was confirmed by ss 8–10 dealing with the procedure for surrendering a suspect to the ICC, which make no mention of immunity. On this basis Wallis JA, speaking for the majority of the Court,[134] declared that when South Africa decided to implement its obligations under the Rome Statute by the Implementation Act 'it did so on the basis that all forms of immunity, including head-of-state immunity, would not constitute a bar to the prosecution of international crimes in this country *or to South Africa cooperating with the ICC by way of the arrest and surrender of persons charged with such crimes before the ICC, where an arrest warrant has been issued and a request for cooperation made*'.[135]

Wallis JA continued that in adopting this approach, 'South Africa was taking a step that many other nations have not yet taken. If that puts this country in the vanguard of attempts to prevent international crimes . . . that seems to me to be a matter for national pride rather than concern. It is wholly consistent with our commitment to human rights, both at a national and at an international level.' The Court therefore found that the government's failure to arrest President al-Bashir and detain him for surrender to the ICC was

[131] *Minister of Justice v SALC* (n 6) para 77.

[132] Ibid para 84. For the reasoning of the Court, see paras 70–84.

[133] Ibid para 85.

[134] A minority comprising Ponnan and Lewis JJA disagreed with the majority's finding that customary international law did not recognise an exception to immunity in the case of international crimes (ibid para 115).

[135] *Minister of Justice v SALC* (n 6) para 103 (emphasis added).

inconsistent with its obligations under the Rome Statute and the Implementation Act and was unlawful.[136]

It is difficult to draw clear conclusions on the present state of international law on the immunities of heads of state or government and of senior state officials. Before the *Arrest Warrant* case there was support for the view that customary international law did not permit immunity to be raised by a head of state or government or senior state official as a defence or bar to jurisdiction when such a person was charged with a serious international crime, such as genocide, crime against humanity, war crime or torture. This portrayal of the law was based largely on the experience of Nuremberg and Tokyo and the instruments which succeeded these trials. The concern of the international community for a world order in which impunity for international crimes no longer prevailed gave support to the notion that immunity had been abolished before both international and national courts where it was raised as a defence or bar to jurisdiction of the court. The idealism of earlier years has been shaken by the *Arrest Warrant* case, which asserts the pre-World War II notion of absolute immunity before national courts. If this decision is confined to its context—judicial assistance—this would go a long way towards restoring faith in this idealism. It is unlikely that the International Law Commission will do this as it is wedded to support for the *Arrest Warrant* case. Whether the International Court of Justice will confine this decision to judicial assistance in the pending advisory opinion on immunities requested by the African Union remains to be seen.

The law governing immunity in respect of requests for judicial assistance is, however, clear. Customary international law does not at this stage exclude immunity in respect of a request for judicial assistance in the arrest and surrender of a head of state or government or senior state official by either the government of another state or an international tribunal, including the ICC. In such a case, it is for the requested state to decide on the basis of its own law and international legal obligations whether to accept a plea of immunity. This is precisely what the Supreme Court of appeal decided in *Minister of Justice v SALC*.

2 Civil proceedings

Courts, both international and national, have held that there is nothing incongruous in denying immunity to senior state officials in criminal proceedings but allowing immunity in civil proceedings against a government or senior state officials for similar conduct. Thus, several judges in *Pinochet* held that Pinochet could successfully

[136] *Minister of Justice v SALC* (n 6) para 113.

have claimed immunity if sued in civil proceedings.[137] This distinction between immunity in criminal and civil proceedings was accepted by the International Court of Justice in *Jurisdictional Immunities of the State (Germany v Italy)*[138] and by the Supreme Court of Appeal in the al-Bashir case.[139] In practice, little turns on this distinction as both national[140] and international courts have accepted the broad formulation of immunity expounded in the *Arrest Warrant* case. Indeed, in *Jurisdictional Immunities of the State* the International Court of Justice stated that the reasoning of the *Arrest Warrant* case 'is applicable to the application of the customary international law regarding the immunity of one State from proceedings in the courts of another'.[141] The blind acceptance of immunity in civil proceedings concerning serious international crimes by both national and international courts on the basis of the *Arrest Warrant* case is unfortunate. In so doing, courts have failed to distinguish between immunity as a defence, bar to jurisdiction or obstruction to judicial assistance. Had they drawn this distinction they might well have reached a different conclusion on the broad scope of immunity in civil proceedings.

Be that as it may, international law now accepts that a plea of immunity will succeed in civil proceedings before a foreign court when a state is sued for damages on the basis that its agents committed international crimes in violation of *jus cogens* norms, such as torture, genocide, crimes against humanity or war crimes. Decisions of both international and national courts attest to this.[142]

In *Jones v Ministry of the Interior Al-Mamlaka Al-Arabiya as Saudiya (the Kingdom of Saudi Arabia)* the House of Lords held that developments in respect of norms of *jus cogens* did not provide an exception to the rule of immunity contained in the State Immunity Act 1978.[143] In so doing, the Court reaffirmed the distinction between civil and criminal proceedings in respect of immunity.[144] And, in so finding, the House of Lords reversed a decision of the English Court of Appeal,[145] which held that 'it can no longer be appropriate to give

[137] [1999] 2 All ER 97 (HL) 157 (Lord Hutton), 179 (Lord Millett) and 182 (Lord Phillips).

[138] 2012 ICJ Reports 99 paras 87, 91.

[139] *Minister of Justice v SALC* (n 6) para 73.

[140] See the decisions cited by the International Court of Justice in *Jurisdictional Immunities of the State* (n 138) paras 85, 96.

[141] *Jurisdictional Immunities of the State* (n 138) para 95.

[142] Ibid paras 85, 96.

[143] *Jones v Ministry of the Interior Al-Mamlaka Al-Arabiya as Saudiya (Saudi Arabia)* [2006] UKHL 26 paras 26–8.

[144] Paragraph 71.

[145] *Jones v Ministry of the Interior Al-Mamlaka Al-Arabiya as Saudiya (The Kingdom of Saudi Arabia)* [2004] EWCA Civil 1394.

blanket effect to a foreign state's claim to state immunity *ratione materiae* in respect of a state official alleged to have committed acts of systematic torture'.[146]

American courts have also applied immunity in civil claims arising out of a breach of a norm of *jus cogens*. In *Siderman de Blake v Republic of Argentina*[147] and *Saudia Arabia v Nelson*,[148] immunity was extended to foreign governments in respect of claims based on torture. In *Princz v Federal Republic of Germany*,[149] Germany succeeded in a plea of immunity in respect of a suit brought by a Holocaust survivor to recover damages for injuries he had suffered in Nazi concentration camps.

The European Court of Human Rights has likewise rejected the argument that immunity does not apply in cases involving the violation of a norm of *jus cogens*. In *Al-Adsani v United Kingdom*[150] the Court held that an English court did not violate article 6 of the European Convention on Human Rights in granting immunity to the government of Kuwait in respect of a claim alleging torture on the part of that government. The Court stated that:

> Notwithstanding the special character of the prohibition of torture in international law, the Court is unable to discern in the international instruments, judicial authorities or other materials before it any firm basis for concluding that, as a matter of international law, a State no longer enjoys immunity from civil suit in the courts of another State where acts of torture are alleged.[151]

This decision was reached by the narrow margin of nine votes to eight. Six judges in a strong dissenting opinion stated:

> The distinction made by the majority between civil and criminal proceedings, concerning the effect of the rule of the prohibition of torture, is not consonant with the very essence of the operation of *jus cogens* rules. It is not the nature of the proceedings which determines the effects that a *jus cogens* rule has upon another rule of international law, but the character of the rule as a peremptory norm and its interaction with a hierarchically lower rule. The prohibition of torture, being a rule of *jus cogens*, acts in the international sphere and deprives the rule of sovereign immunity of all its legal effects in that sphere. The criminal or civil nature of the domestic proceedings is immaterial.[152]

[146] *Jones v Ministry of the Interior Al-Mamlaka* (n 145) paras 92 (Mance LJ) and 131 (Lord Phillips MR).

[147] 965 F 2d 699 (9th Cir 1992); see, too, *Argentine Republic v Amerada Hess Shipping Corp* 488 US 428 (1989).

[148] 100 ILR 544.

[149] 26 F 3d 1166 (DC Cir 1994).

[150] (2001) 34 EHRR 273, 123 ILR 24. See E Voyiakis 'Access to court v state immunity' (2003) 52 *ICLQ* 297.

[151] Paragraph 61. See, too, paras 65–6.

[152] Joint dissenting opinion of Judges Rozakis and Caflisch, joined by Judges Wildhaber, Costa, Cabral Barreto and Vajic (*Al-Adsani* (n 150) para 4).

Support for the above view is to be found in *Prosecutor v Furundzija*[153] in which the International Criminal Tribunal for the Former Yugoslavia held that the prohibition on torture is a peremptory norm which would allow the victim to 'bring a suit for damage in a foreign court'.

The European Court of Human Rights followed its ruling in *Al-Adsani* by upholding a plea of sovereign immunity with regard to civil proceedings for reparation sought by victims of Nazi atrocities in Greece during World War II.[154]

In 2004, in *Ferrini v Federal Government of Germany*, the Italian Court of Cassation held that the Federal Republic of Germany could not succeed in a plea of immunity in a delictual action brought by an Italian citizen for deportation and forced labour during World War II. The Court held that international crimes constituting peremptory norms take priority over immunity.[155]

The *Ferrini* decision resulted in an application by Germany to the International Court of Justice in which it asked the Court to declare that Italy had violated its international law obligations in respect of jurisdictional immunity by allowing such civil claims. In *Jurisdictional Immunities of the State*[156] the International Court held that Italy had violated its obligation to respect the immunity of Germany by allowing civil claims to be brought against it based on violations of international humanitarian law. In so finding, it stated that customary international law does not deprive a state of immunity by reason of the fact that it was accused of serious violations of international human rights or humanitarian law or of *jus cogens* rules.[157]

It is strange that, while courts were prepared to respond to the absolute immunity rule in respect of commercial transactions by fashioning a new rule of customary international law that restricts such immunity, they have been restrained from so doing in respect of the absolute approach to immunity where serious violations of human rights law and international humanitarian law are concerned. Not only have judges refrained from so doing but they have sought to justify their inaction by claiming that it is not the role of national judges to develop new rules of customary international law, pretend-

[153] (1998) 38 *ILM* 317 at 349–50 para 155.

[154] *Kalogeropoulou v Greece and Germany* ECHR Application No 59021/00 (judgment of 12 December 2002), (2003) 42 *ILM* 1030. Here, the European Court of Human Rights overruled a decision of the Greek Supreme Court in *Prefecture of Volotia v Federal Republic of Germany*, noted by M Gavouneli and I Bantekas in '*Prefecture of Voiotia v federal Republic of Germany*' (2001) 95 *AJIL* 198.

[155] *Ferrini v Federal Republic of Germany*, noted by A Bianchi '*Ferrini v Federal Republic of Germany*' (2005) 99 *AJIL* 242.

[156] Supra (n 138).

[157] Ibid paras 91, 97.

ing to be blissfully unaware of the manner in which national courts developed a new rule of international law in respect of commercial transactions.

In *Jones*, Lord Hoffmann acknowledged that the Italian Court in *Ferrini* had 'given priority to the values embodied in the prohibition of torture over the values and policies of the rules of immunity'. He added that if the case had been concerned with domestic law, it

> might have been regarded by some as 'activist' but would have been well within the judicial function . . . . But the same approach cannot be adopted in international law, which is based upon the common consent of nations. It is not for a national court to 'develop' international law by unilaterally adopting a version of that law which, however desirable, forward-looking and reflective of values it may be, is simply not accepted by other states.[158]

This view was endorsed by Wallis JA in the al-Bashir case when he stated that '[h]owever tempting it may be to a domestic court to seek to expand the boundaries of customary international law by domestic judicial decision, it is not in my view permissible to do so'.[159]

These statements are simply wrong. The restrictive approach to sovereign immunity in the case of commercial acts did not come about as a result of treaty or 'the common consent of nations' but as a result of national court decisions from many countries that culminated in a customary law rule. Only much later was the rule converted into national law by legislation, and recognised by treaty in the Convention on Jurisdictional Immunities of States and their Property. Here, national court decisions rejecting absolute immunity provided the necessary evidence of state practice for the formation of a new customary rule.

Foreign states are not immune from litigation in respect of international crimes by virtue of any fundamental sovereign right, but because states, for reasons of policy and comity, decline to exercise jurisdiction.[160] Absolute immunity in respect of commercial transactions has given way to a restrictive approach to accord with changed international expectations and policy. It is not unlikely that absolute immunity in respect of the violation of norms of *jus cogens* will in time change because international policy towards human rights and international crimes has undergone major changes in recent decades. As Judge Yusuf stated in *Jurisdictional Immunities of*

[158] *Jones* (n 143) para 63.

[159] *Minister of Justice v SALC* (n 6) para 74.

[160] See LM Caplan 'State immunity, human rights and *jus cogens*: A critique of the normative hierarchy theory' (2003) 97 *AJIL* 741 at 781. See, too, JMT Labuschagne 'Immunity of the head of state for human rights violations in international criminal law' (2001) 26 *SAYIL* 180.

the State, '[i]mmunity is not an immutable value in international law'.[161]

DIPLOMATIC AND CONSULAR IMMUNITY[162]

The principles governing diplomatic immunity are probably the oldest of all the principles of international law.[163] As all states have an interest in the exchange and protection of diplomats, the rules of diplomatic protection are well settled and strictly observed. This explains the almost universal condemnation of Iran when it held members of the United States embassy in Tehran as hostages from 1979 to 1981, following the admission of the deposed Shah of Iran into the United States for medical treatment. In finding that the government of Iran had violated its obligations under international law, the International Court of Justice declared:

> [T]his case is unique and of very particular gravity because here it is not only private individuals or groups of individuals that have disregarded and set at naught the inviolability of a foreign embassy, but the government of the receiving state itself .... Such events cannot fail to undermine the edifice of law carefully constructed by mankind over a period of centuries, the maintenance of which is vital for the security and well-being of the complex international community of the present day.[164]

Political relations between states are conducted by diplomatic missions, comprising ambassadors and diplomats. Trade relations, on the other hand, are managed by consular officials. Today, the strict distinction between diplomatic and consular services is often blurred in the larger missions, which integrate their political and trade representatives.[165] As the functions of diplomats and consuls differ, special rules of immunity apply to each. Consequently, the law on diplomatic and consular immunities is today contained in two multilateral treaties, both of which are largely declaratory of international law and were drafted by the International Law Commission.

[161] Supra (n 138) para 35, dissenting opinion of Judge Yusuf.

[162] See, generally, C Lewis *State and Diplomatic Immunity* 3 ed (1990); I Roberts (ed) *Satow's Guide to Diplomatic Practice* 7 ed (2017); B Sen *A Diplomat's Handbook of International Law and Practice* 3 ed (1988); E Denza *Diplomatic Law* 4 ed (2016); J Brown 'Diplomatic immunity: State practice under the Vienna Convention on Diplomatic Relations' (1988) 37 *ICLQ* 53; P Behrens *Diplomatic Interference and the Law* (2016).

[163] See the remarks of Schutz J in *S v Muchindu* 1995 (2) SA 36 (W) 37–8.

[164] *Case Concerning United States Diplomatic and Consular Staff in Tehran* 1980 ICJ Reports 3 at 42–3. The decision in this case is endorsed by Schutz J in *S v Muchindu* (n 163) 37–8. This is one of the few occasions on which a South African court has cited a judgment of the International Court of Justice.

[165] DP O'Connell *International Law* 2 ed (1970) vol 2 at 914.

These treaties are the Vienna Convention on Diplomatic Relations of 1961[166] and the Vienna Convention on Consular Relations of 1963.[167]

In 1951 South Africa enacted the Diplomatic Privileges Act,[168] which largely accorded with customary international law.[169] This legislation remained in force, subject to a number of amendments, until 1989 when South Africa finally acceded[170] to the Vienna Conventions on both diplomatic and consular relations and enacted legislation to give effect to its obligations under these treaties.

1 The Diplomatic Immunities and Privileges Act (excluding the Conventions in the schedules)

The Diplomatic Immunities and Privileges Act of 1989[171] was ambivalent as to whether it incorporated the Vienna Conventions on diplomatic and consular relations in full or whether it incorporated only parts of these conventions.[172] In order to remove this uncertainty, a new Diplomatic Immunities and Privileges Act was enacted in 2001,[173] which makes it clear that these two Conventions, together with the Convention on the Privileges and Immunities of the United Nations of 1946 and the Convention on the Privileges and Immunities of Specialized Agencies of 1947, are, subject to the provisions of the Act, to 'have the force of law in the Republic'.[174]

The Act provides that the Vienna Convention on Diplomatic Relations set out in Schedule 1 to the Act, and the Vienna Convention on Consular Relations, set out in Schedule 2 to the Act, are to apply to all diplomatic and consular missions and their members in the Republic.[175]

The Diplomatic Immunities and Privileges Act prescribes the immunities accorded to diplomats, the representatives of international institutions and participants at intergovernmental conferences held in the Republic. Visiting heads of state and special envoys are granted immunity from the criminal and civil jurisdiction of munici-

[166] 500 UNTS 95.

[167] 596 UNTS 261.

[168] 71 of 1951.

[169] *S v Penrose* 1966 (1) SA 5 (N).

[170] On 21 August 1989. See further on this accession the statement by the Deputy Minister of Foreign Affairs, Mr JWH Meiring, in *Debates of Parliament* cols 10196–200 (23 May 1989).

[171] Act 74 of 1989.

[172] See J Dugard and G Abraham 'Public international law' 2001 *Annual Survey* 128 at 135–6. See, too, *Portion 20 of Plot 15 Athol (Pty) Ltd v Rodrigues* (n 2) 1292–3.

[173] Act 37 of 2001.

[174] Sections 1 and 2.

[175] Section 3. Members of a diplomat's family are also entitled to immunity. See s 2*(b)* of Act 37 of 2001 as amended by Act 35 of 2008.

pal courts and enjoy such privileges as 'heads of state enjoy in accordance with the rules of customary international law'. This provision is subject to s 4(2) of the Implementation of the Rome Statute of the International Criminal Court Act 27 of 2002, which provides:

> Despite any other law to the contrary, including customary and conventional international law, the fact that a person—
>
> *(a)* is or was a head of State or government, a member of a government or parliament, an elected representative or a government official;
>
> . . .
>
> is neither—
>
> (i) a defence to a crime; nor
>
> (ii) a ground for a possible reduction of sentence once a person has been convicted of a crime.

This means that a head of state will not be able to plead immunity in respect of the crimes recognised by the Rome Statute—genocide, crimes against humanity and war crimes. This matter is discussed above in the context of *Minister of Justice v SALC*.[176]

The question whether the spouse of a head of state is automatically entitled to immunity under customary international law was considered in *Democratic Alliance v Minister of International Relations and Co-operation*,[177] which concerned a claim to immunity on the part of Grace Mugabe, wife of the former president of Zimbabwe, Robert Mugabe. Vally J held that while customary international law extends immunity *ratione personae* to heads of state and government and foreign Ministers in respect of both their official and private acts, there is no such customary rule in favour of the spouse of such a person. After a thorough examination of the contradictory decisions of national courts on this subject, he concluded that where immunity was granted to a spouse, it 'was on the basis of international comity rather than on the basis of a finding that it is a principle of international customary law'.[178]

The Diplomatic Immunities and Privileges Act extends immunity to the United Nations, specialised agencies and their officials in the Republic in terms of the Convention on the Privileges and Immunities of the United Nations of 1946 and the Convention on the Privileges and Immunities of the Specialized Agencies of 1947.[179] Intergovernmental organisations recognised by the Minister of International Relations and Co-operation, and their officials, may be

[176] Supra (n 6) paras 49–53,92–5,102–3, 116–24.
[177] Supra (n 52).
[178] Paragraph 35.
[179] Section 5(1) and (2).

accorded immunities by means of agreement.[180] Immunities may also be extended to participants in intergovernmental conferences held in the Republic.[181] Agreements are to be published by notice in the *Government Gazette*.[182] In addition, the Minister of International Relations and Co-operation may, in terms of s 7(2), grant immunities and privileges to foreign representatives by notice in the *Government Gazette* in the absence of an agreement.[183] It was under this provision that the Minister conferred immunity, retrospectively, on Grace Mugabe in 2017 in respect of charges of assault on the ground that such immunity was in the interest of South Africa. The Court, however, set aside this decision on the ground that it was inconsistent with the Constitution.[184]

The Minister of International Relations and Co-operation is required to keep a register of all persons entitled to immunity from the civil and criminal jurisdiction of the courts of the Republic.[185] A complete list of such persons is to be published at least once a year in the *Government Gazette* and is kept on the website of the Department of International Relations and Co-operation.[186] If there is any dispute about the entitlement of any person to immunity in legal proceedings in a municipal court, a certificate from the Director-General of International Relations and Co-operation will be *prima facie* evidence on this subject.[187] A waiver of immunity on behalf of any person entitled to immunity is to be express and in writing.[188]

If it appears to the Minister of International Relations and Co-operation that the immunities or privileges accorded to a mission of the Republic in the territory of any state are less than those conferred in the Republic on the mission of that state, the Minister may withdraw so much of the immunities or privileges accorded to that mission as appears to be proper.[189]

All foreign missions or consular posts, the United Nations, and all specialised agencies must submit a written request to the Director-General of International Relations and Co-operation for acquiring, constructing, relocating, renovating, replacing, extending or leasing

[180] Section 5(3).

[181] Section 6.

[182] Section 7.

[183] Section 7(2). See Proc 41 *GG* 14809 of 12 May 1993, for an example of such a notice.

[184] *Democratic Alliance v Minister of International Relations and Co-operation* (n 52) paras 43, 46.

[185] Section 9(1).

[186] Section 9(2) as amended by Act 35 of 2008.

[187] Section 9(3).

[188] Section 8.

[189] Section 10.

immovable property in the name of such mission or its representatives.[190]

As the immunity of diplomats from the jurisdiction of municipal courts extends to motor accidents, a South African citizen may find himself without any legal remedy against a diplomat responsible for such an accident. In order to overcome this problem, the Minister is empowered to compel persons entitled to immunity to insure themselves adequately against claims which may result from motor accidents.[191]

Anyone (including an attorney) who 'wilfully or without the exercise of reasonable care' sues a person entitled to immunity under the Diplomatic Immunities and Privileges Act is guilty of an offence for which the punishment is a fine or imprisonment not exceeding three years.[192]

2 The Vienna Convention on Diplomatic Relations 1961 (Schedule 1)

According to the Diplomatic Immunities and Privileges Act of 2001, the Vienna Convention on Diplomatic Relations is to have 'the force of law in the Republic' and to apply to 'all diplomatic missions and members of such missions in the Republic'.[193] It is therefore necessary to examine its provisions in detail.

There is no right on the part of a state to enter into diplomatic relations with another state and there is no duty to maintain diplomatic relations once they have been entered into.[194] Although the sending state selects its ambassador and diplomatic staff, the receiving state has the right to declare any diplomat to be unacceptable, ie *persona non grata*, before or after he assumes his duties.[195] No explanation is required for such a decision by the receiving state.

The head of a diplomatic mission assumes his duties after he has presented his credentials to the head of the receiving state.[196] Normally the head of a mission will be an ambassador accredited to the head of the receiving state. However, a small mission or one that wishes to adopt a low profile for political reasons may be headed by

[190] Section 12. In *Portion 20 of Plot 15 Athol (Pty) Ltd v Rodrigues* (n 2) the Court held that a plea of diplomatic immunity must fail in respect of property that had been acquired by a diplomat without the submission of a written request to the Director-General.

[191] Section 13.

[192] Section 15.

[193] Sections 2(1) and 3(1).

[194] Article 2 of the Vienna Convention on Diplomatic Relations provides that the establishment of diplomatic relations 'takes place by mutual consent'.

[195] Article 9.

[196] Article 13.

a *chargé d'affaires* accredited to the Minister of Foreign Affairs of the receiving state.[197]

Article 3 describes the functions of a diplomatic mission as, inter alia, representing the sending state, protecting its interests and nationals in the receiving state, negotiating with the government of the receiving state, reporting on conditions in the receiving state, and promoting friendly relations between the sending and receiving state. A diplomatic mission may also perform consular functions.

(a) Inviolability

In order to enable a diplomatic mission to carry out its functions freely, article 22 provides that:

> 1. The premises of the mission shall be inviolable. The agents of the receiving state may not enter them, except with the consent of the head of the mission.
> 2. The receiving state is under a special duty to take all appropriate steps to protect the premises of the mission against any intrusion or damage and to prevent any disturbance of the peace of the mission or impairment of its dignity.
> 3. The premises of the mission, their furnishings and other property thereon and the means of transport of the mission shall be immune from search, requisition, attachment or execution.

Other articles provide that the archives[198] and official correspondence[199] of a mission are inviolable and that a mission may freely communicate with its own government and other missions and consulates of the sending state.[200] The failure of the government of Iran to observe these fundamental principles of diplomatic law in 1979, when it endorsed the seizure of the United States embassy in Tehran by militants, was strongly condemned by the International Court of Justice.[201] In *Democratic Republic of the Congo v Uganda*, the International Court of Justice held that attacks by Congolese armed forces on the Ugandan Embassy in Kinshasa violated article 22.[202]

Diplomatic missions use a diplomatic bag to transport diplomatic

[197] Article 14.
[198] Article 24.
[199] Article 27(2).
[200] Article 27(1).
[201] *Case Concerning United States Diplomatic and Consular Staff in Tehran* (n 164) at 30–1, 42.
[202] 2005 ICJ Reports 168 at 227–8, paras 337–8, 340.

documents or articles intended for official use.[203] This bag may 'not be opened or detained' by the receiving state.[204]

In recent times there have been a number of instances of serious abuse of diplomatic premises and the diplomatic bag by missions. In 1984 persons inside the Libyan mission in London fired shots at demonstrators outside the mission, killing a policewoman. As a result, Britain terminated diplomatic relations with Libya. Diplomatic bags leaving the mission were not searched or scanned. Later a search by the British authorities, accompanied by a representative of the Saudi Arabian embassy, revealed a number of firearms. Although the diplomatic bags were not electronically scanned, the British government took the view that such scanning is permissible as it does not constitute 'opening' or 'detention' of the bag.[205] In the same year an attempt was made to transport a Nigerian political exile in London back to Nigeria in a crate labelled as 'diplomatic baggage'. As the crate was not properly sealed it was opened by customs officials. Two members of the Nigerian High Commission were expelled from Britain as a result of this abuse.[206] These two incidents suggest that the only sanctions for non-observance of the rules of diplomatic law are termination of diplomatic relations and the expulsion of diplomats. It has been suggested, however, that receiving states have the right to enter missions forcibly and to open diplomatic bags in the exercise of the right of self-defence.[207] Considerations of this kind led Pakistan in 1973 to forcibly search the Iraqi embassy, where it discovered large consignments of arms.[208]

(b) Extraterritoriality of missions

The inviolability of the diplomatic mission led to suggestions that it was accorded a special status by the receiving state because it was an extension of the territory of the sending state—that it was extraterritorial. This explanation for the inviolability of the mission is no

[203] During the apartheid era, the diplomatic bag was apparently used by opponents of the regime to transmit sensitive material to persons abroad: see A Wiebalck 'Abuse of the immunity of diplomatic mail' (1984) 10 *SAYIL* 175.

[204] Article 27(3) and (4).

[205] See R Higgins 'The abuse of diplomatic privileges and immunities: Recent United Kingdom experience' (1985) 79 *AJIL* 641. In 1989, the International Law Commission adopted a set of Draft Articles on the Status of the Diplomatic Courier and the Diplomatic Bag Not Accompanied by Diplomatic Courier: *Yearbook of the International Law Commission* (1989) vol II, part 2 at 43. Article 28 provides that the diplomatic bag 'shall be exempt from examination directly or through electronic or other technical devices'.

[206] DJ Harris *Cases and Materials on International Law* 7 ed (2010) 309.

[207] Brown (n 162) 86.

[208] Denza (n 162) 84.

longer accepted.[209] Instead, it is generally agreed that the inviolability of a mission is based on functional necessity; that such inviolability is necessary to enable the mission to perform its functions properly.[210]

The extraterritoriality theory was firmly repudiated by Grosskopf J in *Santos v Santos*[211] when he held that a marriage solemnised in a foreign embassy or consulate by a person (in this case the Portuguese vice-consul) who was not a recognised marriage officer under South African law was invalid. The judge accepted the view of Michael Akehurst[212] that 'diplomatic premises are not extraterritorial; acts occurring there are regarded as taking place on the territory of the receiving state, not on that of the sending state'.[213]

(c) Diplomatic immunities

Diplomats are granted extensive protection and immunities. Article 29 states:

> The person of a diplomatic agent shall be inviolable. He shall not be liable to any form of arrest or detention. The receiving state shall treat him with due respect and shall take all appropriate steps to prevent any attack on his person, freedom or dignity.

The private residence of a diplomat enjoys the same inviolability as the premises of the mission.[214] Article 31 provides:

> 1. A diplomatic agent shall enjoy immunity from the criminal jurisdiction of the receiving state. He shall also enjoy immunity from its civil and administrative jurisdiction, except in the case of:
>   *(a)* a real action relating to private immovable property situated in the territory of the receiving state, unless he holds it on behalf of the sending state for the purposes of the mission;
>   *(b)* an action relating to succession in which the diplomatic agent is involved as executor, administrator, heir or legatee as a private person and not on behalf of the sending state;
>   *(c)* an action relating to any professional or commercial activity exercised by the diplomatic agent in the receiving state outside his official functions.
> 2. A diplomatic agent is not obliged to give evidence as a witness.

[209] See WJ van der Merwe 'Die grondgebied van ambassadepersele' (1987) 28(1) *Codicillus* 20; *Radwan v Radwan* [1972] 3 All ER 967 (Fam) 971; *S v Mharapara* 1986 (1) SA 556 (ZS) 558G–559B.

[210] *Portion 20 of Plot 15 Athol (Pty) Ltd v Rodrigues* (n 2) 1293E.

[211] 1987 (4) SA 150 (W). Discussed by P van Warmelo '*Statum personale, lex loci regi actum* en die beginsel van ekstraterritorialiteit' (1988) 51 *THRHR* 102.

[212] At 152F–G.

[213] *A Modern Introduction to International Law* 4 ed (1982) 115.

[214] Article 30.

In *Portion 20 of Plot 15 Athol (Pty) Ltd v Rodrigues*[215] the Court was faced with a claim to immunity in respect of a real action relating to private property. In finding that the Angolan ambassador did not hold the property in question 'on behalf of the sending state for the purposes of the mission' as required by article 31(1)(a), Hussein J stated:

> [W]hat is contemplated in the Act is that in order to attract immunity the property must be used for the professional, diplomatic purposes of a mission and did not include a diplomatic agent's private residence albeit that the diplomatic agent occasionally carried out official social obligations there.[216]

Members of a diplomat's family enjoy the same immunities,[217] but members of the administrative and technical staff of the mission enjoy immunity from civil jurisdiction only in respect of acts performed within the course of their duties.[218] A diplomat who is a national or permanent resident of South Africa will enjoy immunity only 'in respect of official acts performed in the exercise of his functions'.[219]

As diplomats are not immune from legal liability but only immune from being prosecuted or sued,[220] the sending state may waive immunity on behalf of its diplomat. Such waiver must be express. As in the case of sovereign immunity, a separate waiver is necessary in respect of the execution of a civil judgment.[221]

There is South African authority, albeit in the form of an *obiter dictum*, for the proposition that a diplomat may be arrested and detained for acts which endanger the security of the state. This statement by Smuts J in *Nkondo v Minister of Police*[222] is premised on writings published before the adoption of the Vienna Convention and, in any event, was made before South Africa acceded to the Vienna Convention. Article 29 of the Convention makes it clear that a diplomat is exempt from 'any form of arrest or detention'—presumably including an arrest for an act endangering the security of the state. In such a case, the receiving state's remedy is not arrest but expulsion after declaring the diplomat to be *persona non grata*.

[215] 2001 (1) SA 1285 (W). See further on this case G Abraham '*Portion 20 of Plot 15 Athol*—"Some corner of a foreign field that is forever . . . Angola?"' (2001) 118 *SALJ* 441; JMT Labuschagne 'Diplomatic immunity: A jurisdictional or substantive-law defence?' (2002) 27 *SAYIL* 291.

[216] At 1296C–D.

[217] Article 37(1).

[218] Article 37(2).

[219] Article 38.

[220] *Dickinson* (n 2).

[221] Article 32.

[222] 1980 (2) SA 894 (O) 900–2.

The special status of diplomats does not entitle them to attend legal proceedings from which the public has been excluded. In *S v Mothopeng*,[223] Curlewis J held that diplomats might not attend an *in camera* hearing in the course of a political trial.

3 The Vienna Convention on Consular Relations 1963 (Schedule 2)[224]

The functions of a consul are varied and include the promotion of trade between sending and receiving state, the protection of nationals of the sending state who find themselves in difficulty in the receiving state, the issue of passports to nationals of the sending state, and the issue of visas to non-nationals who wish to travel to the sending state. In port cities consuls deal with the interests of their ships and resolve any disputes that may arise between master and crew.[225] Whereas a state will maintain only one diplomatic mission in a country, it may maintain several consular offices. In South Africa foreign embassies are situated in Pretoria (and Cape Town during the parliamentary session) while consular offices are to be found in Johannesburg, Durban, Cape Town and Port Elizabeth.

As consuls are not responsible for political relations with the receiving state, they enjoy a lower degree of immunity than diplomats.[226] Consular premises are inviolable and may not be entered by the authorities of the receiving state except with the consent of the head of the consular post.[227] The consular archives, correspondence and bag are also protected.[228] A consular officer may not be arrested or detained, 'except in the case of a grave crime',[229] and is immune from the jurisdiction of local courts 'in respect of acts performed in the exercise of consular functions'.[230] This immunity may be waived by the sending state.[231]

Where a state has few interests in another state it may prefer to appoint a local businessman, who may or may not be one of its own nationals, to represent its interests in that state on a part-time basis. Such a representative is known as an honorary consul who, in terms of the Vienna Convention on Consular Relations, has fewer privi-

[223] 1979 (4) SA 367 (T).

[224] LT Lee and J Quigley *Consular Law and Practice* 3 ed (2008).

[225] Article 5 of the Vienna Convention on Consular Relations.

[226] *S v Penrose* 1966 (1) SA 5 (N) 11. See further J Dugard 'Consular immunity' (1966) 83 *SALJ* 126.

[227] Article 31.

[228] Articles 33 and 35.

[229] Article 41.

[230] Article 43. Customary law likewise adopts a functional approach to consular immunity: see Dugard (n 226) 128–30.

[231] Article 45.

leges than a career consul. His immunities are strictly limited to his official functions.[232]

ASYLUM IN DIPLOMATIC AND CONSULAR PREMISES[233]

In 2012 Julian Assange sought and was granted asylum in the Ecuadorian embassy in London. Assange, the founder of WikiLeaks, who had published thousands of classified US cables and documents relating to the US role in armed conflicts in Iraq and Afghanistan, feared that a request for questioning in Sweden in connection with sexual assaults was a pretext for extraditing him to the United States for the publication of classified material. Six years later he remains in the Ecuadorian embassy, unable to leave without being arrested by the British police. This incident starkly illustrates the complexity of the legal problems raised by such asylum. A foreign embassy is inviolable and may not be entered without the consent of the sending state. However, international law does not recognise a right of safe passage out of the country of refuge to the asylum seeker.

Assange's case is not unique. History provides many examples of instances in which the opponents of a regime have sought asylum in foreign embassies and consulates in times of political turmoil. In 1936, thousands of political refugees were granted asylum by diplomatic missions in Madrid during the Spanish Civil War. In 1973, 25 diplomatic missions in Santiago granted asylum to some 8 000 people following the overthrow of the Allende government in Chile. Cardinal Mindszenty was granted refuge in the US embassy in Budapest for 14 years, following the failure of the Hungarian uprising in 1956. In Latin America no less than ten people who at some time in their lives were heads of state found refuge in diplomatic missions.[234]

In the last years of the apartheid era, South Africa added to this historical record.

(a) In 1984, six members of the United Democratic Front threatened with detention under the Internal Security Act took refuge in the British Consulate in Durban.[235] Despite demands for their

[232] Article 58. In *S v Penrose* (n 226) the Court held that the honorary consul for Colombia could not raise a plea of immunity to a charge of negligent driving.

[233] See P Behrens *Diplomatic Interference and the Law* (2016) Ch 11; SP Sinha *Asylum in International Law* (1971); A Jeffery 'Diplomatic asylum: Its problems and potential as a means of protecting human rights' (1985) 1 *SAJHR* 10; F Morgenstern 'Extra-territorial asylum' (1948) 25 *BYIL* 236; R Jennings and A Watts (eds) *Oppenheim's International Law* 9 ed (1992) vol 1 at 1082.

[234] Jeffery (n 233) 23.

[235] For accounts of this asylum, see Jeffery (n 233); J Dugard 'Public international law' 1984 *Annual Survey* 68 at 72–5; W Booyse 'South Africa's foreign policy and

surrender by the South African authorities, the British government refused to compel them to leave. In response to Britain's refusal to surrender the six men, the South African government reneged on an undertaking to return four South Africans to Britain to stand trial on charges arising out of violations of the arms embargo, claiming that this was a lawful act of reprisal.[236]

(b) In 1985, Klaas de Jonge, a Dutch national detained on suspicion of gun-running for the outlawed African National Congress, escaped from police custody and managed to enter the Netherlands embassy in Pretoria. He was immediately re-arrested by the police but released and allowed to return to the Netherlands embassy, following a complaint from the Dutch government that the inviolability of its embassy had been violated by the arrest.[237] There he remained, despite protests from the South African government, until he was allowed to return to the Netherlands as part of an international prisoner exchange in 1987.[238]

(c) In 1988, three prominent leaders of the United Democratic Front—Murphy Morobe, Mohammed Valli Moosa and Vusi Khanyile—detained under the emergency regulations, escaped and took refuge in the American consulate in Johannesburg.[239]

The lawfulness of the granting of asylum in these cases was challenged by the South African government on the following grounds:

(a) The granting of asylum violated South Africa's territorial sovereignty as diplomatic and consular missions are not extra-territorial.

(b) Customary international law does not recognise diplomatic asylum, as evidenced by the *Asylum Case*[240] in which the International Court of Justice denied the right of the Colombian embassy in Peru to grant asylum to a leading political opponent of the government, Haya de la Torre.

international practice as reflected in speeches, parliamentary statements and replies—1984' (1984) 10 *SAYIL* 300–3.

[236] JC Heunis *The Coventry Four* (1985); GN Barrie 'The Durban Six and the Coventry Four: Asylum and reprisal in international law' (1984) 10 *SAYIL* 138. Cf G Erasmus 'Afdwinging van die volkereg deur weerwraak: Wanneer geoorloof?' (1986) 49 *THRHR* 38; JD van der Vyver 'The Coventry Four: Another perspective' (1985–6) 11 *SAYIL* 157.

[237] See D Basson 'Die volkeregtelike beginsels insake diplomatieke asiel en die De Jonge debakel' (1985) 18 *De Jure* 300; J Dugard 'Public international law' 1985 *Annual Survey* 69 at 73.

[238] J Dugard 'Public international law' 1987 *Annual Survey* 74 at 78.

[239] J Dugard 'Public international law' 1988 *Annual Survey* 68 at 72–3.

[240] 1950 ICJ Reports 266.

(c) The Vienna Convention on Diplomatic Relations does not recognise the granting of asylum as a permissible diplomatic function and article 41(3) prohibits the use of the mission 'in any manner incompatible with the functions of the mission'.

(d) The Vienna Convention on Consular Relations likewise fails to recognise asylum as a consular function and not only prohibits the use of consular premises for purposes incompatible with its functions[241] but also obliges consular officials to refrain from interfering in the internal affairs of the receiving state.[242]

Although these arguments are persuasive, they fail to take account of the growing body of support for diplomatic asylum on humanitarian grounds. In all the South African incidents, the fugitives had escaped from detention under arbitrary laws that fell short of minimum standards of criminal justice. It is hardly surprising, therefore, that the foreign states in question refused to surrender the fugitives to the South African authorities. Considerations of humanity were seen to qualify strict compliance with the Vienna Conventions.

The practice of granting diplomatic asylum to political fugitives (as opposed to ordinary criminals) is bound to continue. Although diplomatic and consular premises are not extraterritorial, they are inviolable and may not be entered by the authorities of the receiving state without the consent of the head of the mission. In most cases, receiving states will respect this rule rather than risk an unpleasant diplomatic incident—as illustrated by the De Jonge affair. The receiving state therefore must rely on the government of the sending state to surrender the fugitive, which is unlikely to occur if the receiving state has a poor human rights record and there is popular support for the fugitive in the sending state. Customary law may be evolving in the direction of a rule in favour of diplomatic asylum for fugitives from oppressive regimes. Already there is considerable evidence of *usus* in support of such a rule. Protests from host states against the granting of asylum suggest, however, that the necessary *opinio juris* is still absent.

The position of the post-apartheid South African government is contradictory. In 1999 the South African High Commissioner in Lusaka handed over Zambian secessionist leader Imasiku Mutangelwa to the Zambian authorities after he had spent a week in the High Commission seeking refuge.[243] However, in 2006, the South African government reversed its position when it granted asylum in

[241] Article 5(m).
[242] Article 55. See Booyse (n 235) 301.
[243] *Saturday Star* 7 and 14 August 1999.

the embassy in Kinshasa to Jean-Pierre Bemba, the former Vice-President of the Democratic Republic of the Congo. Deputy Minister of Foreign Affairs Aziz Pahad was reported to have said: 'Bemba is still taking refuge in South African property. He will remain until he sees it fit for him to leave . . . South Africa is bound by international conventions to give him protection.'[244] It is unfortunate that the Deputy Minister failed to specify the 'international conventions' to which he was referring. The Vienna Convention on Diplomatic Relations of 1961 contains no such obligation, but it is possible that the Deputy Minister wished to give South Africa's support to the evolving customary rule of granting asylum to political fugitives in foreign embassies.

[244] *Legalbrief Today* 29 March 2007; *Mail & Guardian* 30 March–4 April 2007 at 16.

CHAPTER 13

State Responsibility, Diplomatic Protection and the Treatment of Aliens

John Dugard

When a state commits an international wrong against another state it incurs international responsibility.[1] In such a case the delinquent state is obliged to make reparation.[2] This responsibility may arise from the violation of a treaty obligation[3] or from the violation of a general obligation owed towards all states. The law of state responsibility[4] in international law resembles the law of delict in domestic law. International law prefers to use the term 'internationally wrongful act' to describe the wrongful act and not the terms 'delict' or 'tort'.

Individuals are criminally responsible for the violation of norms that give rise to international crimes and may be prosecuted before international criminal tribunals,[5] or national courts for international crimes such as genocide, crimes against humanity and war crimes. Whether *states* are subject to criminal responsibility for the violation of norms constituting international crimes is less certain. The International Law Commission (ILC) in its study of state responsibility

[1] According to article 1 of the International Law Commission's Draft Articles on Responsibility of States for Internationally Wrongful Acts: 'Every internationally wrongful act of a State entails the international responsibility of that State' in *Yearbook of the International Law Commission* (2001) vol II, part 2 at 26.

[2] See article 31 of the Draft Articles on State Responsibility (ibid). In the *Chorzów Factory (Indemnity) Case*, the Permanent Court of International Justice stated that 'it is a principle of international law, and even a general conception of law, that any breach of an engagement involves an obligation to make reparation' (1928 PCIJ Reports Series A no 17, 4 at 29).

[3] Case concerning *Gabcikovo-Nagymaros Project (Hungary v Slovakia)* 1997 ICJ Reports 7 at 38.

[4] See J Crawford *State Responsibility: The General Part* (2013); J Crawford, A Pellet and S Olleson (eds) *The Law of International Responsibility* (2010); C Chinkin and F Baetens (eds) *Sovereignty, Statehood and State Responsibility* (2015); A Nollkaemper and D Jacobs (eds) *Distribution of Responsibilities in International Law* (2015); M Ragazzi (ed) *International Responsibility Today: Essays in Memory of Oscar Schachter* (2005).

[5] See Chapter 10.

initially[6] took the position that 'an internationally wrongful act which results from the breach by a state of an international obligation so essential for the protection of fundamental interests of the international community that its breach is recognised as a crime by that community as a whole' gave rise to state criminal responsibility.[7] Examples given by the ILC of such crimes were aggression, colonial domination, slavery, genocide, apartheid and the massive pollution of the atmosphere or the seas. Major objections were raised to the notion of state criminal responsibility, ranging from the impossibility of applying ordinary principles of criminal law and punishment to states to the absence of appropriate machinery for the condemnation of the criminal conduct of states within the existing international institutional structures.[8] Consequently, the ILC dropped the notion of state criminal responsibility from its final Draft Articles on the Responsibility of States for Internationally Wrongful Acts (hereinafter Draft Articles on State Responsibility) and opted instead for a special regime for the violation of peremptory norms not involving state criminal responsibility.[9] This chapter is therefore concerned with state delictual (as opposed to criminal) responsibility for wrongful acts.

A state may incur responsibility directly or indirectly. It incurs responsibility directly when, acting through its organs or agents, it violates its obligations towards another state under a treaty or general international law. Indirect responsibility occurs when a state injures the person or property of a foreign national and in so doing is deemed to have injured the state of nationality of the injured person

[6] The notion of state crime was first raised in 1976 and was retained by the International Law Commission in its first reading of the Draft Articles on State Responsibility of 1996. See Report of the International Law Commission (1996) *GAOR* 51st Session, Supplement No 10 (A/51/10), (1998) 37 *ILM* 440. See further J Dugard 'The criminal responsibility of states' in M Cherif Bassiouni (ed) *International Criminal Law* 2 ed (1999); DW Bowett 'Crimes of states and the 1996 Report of the ILC on State Responsibility' (1998) 9 *European Journal of International Law* 163.

[7] Report of the International Law Commission (n 6) article 19; N Jorgensen *The Responsibility of States for International Crimes* (2003).

[8] See P Weil 'Towards relative normativity in international law?' (1983) 77 *AJIL* 413; K Marek 'Criminalizing state responsibility' (1978–9) 14 *Revue Belge de droit international* 460; L Green 'New trends in international criminal law' (1981) 11 *Israel YB on Human Rights* 9; G Gilbert 'The criminal responsibility of states' (1990) 39 *ICLQ* 345; J Crawford *The International Law Commission's Articles on State Responsibility* (2002) 16.

[9] Crawford (n 8) 35, 242. See articles 40 and 41 of the Draft Articles on State Responsibility (n 1). See also J Crawford 'International crimes of state' in Crawford, Pellet and Olleson (n 4) 405; and the decision of the International Court of Justice in the *Genocide Case (Bosnia v Serbia)* 2007 ICJ Reports 43 at 115 para 170, in which the Court stresses that the obligations for states under the Genocide Convention 'are not of a criminal nature'.

itself. Substantive rules requiring states to act in a particular way or to abstain from certain actions in their relations with other states or rules governing the treatment of the nationals of other states may be termed the 'primary rules' of state responsibility. Rules which govern the attribution of conduct to a state, the circumstances that preclude wrongfulness of such conduct, the invocation of the responsibility of a state and the consequences of a wrongful act are termed the 'secondary rules' of state responsibility.[10]

No attempt is made to examine the primary rules of direct state responsibility in this chapter as they are covered in other chapters. Thus, a state incurs direct responsibility of a primary rule when it violates the territorial sovereignty of another state,[11] fails to respect the immunities of diplomats,[12] interferes with freedom of navigation,[13] pollutes the environment of another state,[14] breaches a treaty obligation[15] or uses force unlawfully.[16] Instead, this chapter will focus

[10] In practice it is difficult to draw a clear distinction between 'primary' and 'secondary' rules. Nevertheless, this distinction has guided the International Law Commission in its approach to state responsibility. See Crawford (n 4) 64–6. There are some similarities between this distinction and that portrayed by HLA Hart in *The Concept of Law* (1961) Ch V, but it is clear that Hart's work did not influence the Commission when it adopted this distinction.

[11] See the *Rainbow Warrior Case (New Zealand v France)* (1987) 26 *ILM* 1346; see further N Botha 'Foreign judicial decisions' (1987–8) 13 *SAYIL* 161. In this case, French secret service agents destroyed a Greenpeace vessel engaged in protests against French nuclear tests in the South Pacific in Auckland harbour. The matter was referred to arbitration by the United Nations Secretary-General who held that France had violated New Zealand's territorial sovereignty and ordered it to pay US$7,000,000 to New Zealand as compensation.

[12] See *United States Diplomatic and Consular Staff in Tehran (United States v Iran) (Hostages Case)* 1980 ICJ Reports 3 at 11. Here, the International Court of Justice found that Iran had violated both its treaty obligations and 'long-established rules of general international law' when it held United States diplomatic and consular staff hostage in Tehran. The Court held that Iran was under an obligation to make reparation to the United States.

[13] See the *Corfu Channel Case* 1949 ICJ Reports 4 (merits) and 1949 ICJ Reports 244 (compensation) in which the International Court of Justice found Albania to be responsible for the mining of British vessels in the Corfu Channel and directed Albania to pay £843 947 as compensation for the damage and loss of life resulting therefrom. (This judgment debt was paid by Albania only in 1992!)

[14] See the *Trail Smelter Case* (1935) 3 UNRIAA 1905 in which Canada was held responsible to the United States for transboundary pollution.

[15] See the *Case Concerning Avena and Other Mexican Nationals (Mexico v United States)* 2004 ICJ Reports 12, (2004) 43 *ILM* 581 in which the International Court of Justice found that the United States had breached its obligation under the Vienna Convention on Consular Relations, article 36(1)(a) and (c), by failing to inform foreign nationals imprisoned in the United States of their right of access to consular officials.

[16] See *Military and Paramilitary Activities in and against Nicaragua (Nicaragua v United States)* 1986 ICJ Reports 14 in which the International Court of Justice held the United

on indirect state responsibility, frequently described as 'diplomatic protection' or the 'treatment of aliens', which constitutes a special regime within the field of state responsibility with its own primary and secondary rules.

Before doing this, however, it is necessary to examine the secondary rules of state responsibility, which apply to both direct and indirect state responsibility, contained in the 2001 Draft Articles on State Responsibility of the International Law Commission.

THE DRAFT ARTICLES ON STATE RESPONSIBILITY[17]

In 1956 the ILC started work under the special rapporteurship of García Amador of Cuba on the subject of state responsibility, one of the major branches of international law and one considered ripe for codification. García Amador focused mainly on state responsibility for injury to aliens and their property, and drew no distinction between primary and secondary rules. In 1963 he was replaced by Roberto Ago of Italy who took the decision to limit the enterprise to the special rules governing state responsibility, that is, secondary rules. Progress under Ago and his successors was slow, and it was not until 1996 that a set of draft articles was completed on first reading.[18] In 2001, under the special rapporteurship of James Crawford of Australia (now a judge of the International Court of Justice), the ILC finally adopted a set of 59 draft articles on second reading. These draft articles largely represent a codification of international law but there are some innovative features, particularly in respect of state responsibility for the violation of peremptory norms. Because of these innovations there has been no rush to refer the draft articles to an international conference for translation into a multilateral treaty, as occurred with similar draft articles prepared by the ILC.[19] Instead it has been considered wise to leave the draft articles as a restatement of the law until there is sufficient support for the draft articles as a whole to make their adoption in treaty form more likely. The draft articles have already been cited with approval by international tribunals and national courts and there is little doubt that they are

States to be responsible for the unlawful use of force against Nicaragua by giving assistance to rebel forces.

[17] See (n 1); Crawford (n 8); 'Symposium: Assessing the work of the ILC on state responsibility' (2002) 13 *European Journal of International Law* 1053; 'Symposium: The ILC's state responsibility articles' (2002) 96 *AJIL* 773.

[18] Draft Articles on State Responsibility, Report of the International Law Commission (1996) *GAOR* 51st Session, Supplement No 10 (A/51/10).

[19] For example, the articles on the law of treaties and diplomatic relations.

viewed by international law practitioners as a restatement of the law.[20] The main features of these draft articles are considered below.

1 Attribution of conduct to a state

'Every internationally wrongful act of a State entails the international responsibility of that State.'[21] An internationally wrongful act occurs when conduct is attributable to the state and constitutes a breach of an international obligation of the state.[22] The draft articles of the International Law Commission take no position on the question whether fault, culpability, negligence or want of due diligence is required for an internationally wrongful act on the ground that the standards of the primary rules differ from one context to another.[23]

It is no defence to a violation of international law that the conduct in question is permitted by the municipal law of the defendant state.[24] As Judge Lauterpacht observed in the *Norwegian Loans Case*:[25]

> National legislation . . . may be contrary . . . to the international obligations of the state. The question of conformity of national legislation with international law is a matter of international law . . . . It is not enough for a state to bring a matter under the protective umbrella of its legislation . . . in order to shelter it effectively from any control by international law.

'One of the cornerstones of the law of state responsibility', declared the International Court of Justice in the 2007 *Genocide Case* (*Bosnia v Serbia*), is 'that the conduct of any state organ is to be considered an act of the state under international law and therefore gives rise to the responsibility of the state if it constitutes a breach of an international obligation of the state'.[26] Article 4(1) of the Draft Articles on State Responsibility elaborates on this principle by providing:

> The conduct of any State organ shall be considered an act of that State under international law, whether the organ exercises legislative, executive, judicial or any other functions, whatever position it holds in the organization of the State, and whatever its character as an organ of the central government or of a territorial unit of the State.

[20] See Report of Secretary-General on Responsibility of States for Internationally Wrongful Acts, Compilation of Decisions of International Courts and Tribunals, *GAOR*, A/71/80 of 21 April 2016.

[21] Article 1 (n 1).

[22] Article 2 (n 1).

[23] Commentary on article 2 at 34 (n 1).

[24] Article 3 (n 1).

[25] 1957 ICJ Reports 9 at 37.

[26] *Application of the Convention on the Prevention and Punishment of the Crime of Genocide (Bosnia and Herzegovina v Serbia and Montenegro)* 2007 ICJ Reports 43 at 202 para 385. See, too, *Bernhard von Pezold v Republic of Zimbabwe* ICSID Case No ARB/10/15, Award of 28 July 2015 para 445.

As a consequence, federal states are responsible for the conduct of their constituent units.

The manner in which a state may incur responsibility through the different organs of the state is illustrated by the *Robert E Brown Claim*, involving a denial of justice and the deprivation of the property rights of an American national by the South African Republic in 1896. Here the arbitral tribunal stated:

> All three branches of the Government conspired to ruin his enterprise. The Executive Department issued proclamations for which no warrant could be found in the Constitution and laws of the country. The Volksraad enacted legislation which, on its face, does violence to fundamental principles of justice recognized in every enlightened community. The judiciary, at first recalcitrant, was at length reduced to submission and brought into line with a determined policy of the Executive to reach the desired result regardless of Constitutional guarantees and inhibitions.[27]

The *La Grand*[28] and *Avena*[29] cases at the beginning of the present century provide further examples of this type of responsibility. Here both the courts and the executive of the United States were held to be responsible for refusing to accord consular rights to foreigners under the Vienna Convention on Consular Relations.

Article 5 of the Draft Articles provides that the conduct of a person or entity not an organ of the state but empowered to exercise elements of governmental authority is considered an act of the state.[30] This includes parastatal entities, public corporations and other subordinate bodies. During the apartheid era the Bantustan states, which were not recognised as states, were treated by states as subordinate bodies set up by South Africa to act on its behalf.[31] Consequently, South Africa was held responsible under international law for the wrongful acts of the Bantustan states.[32]

[27] (1923) 6 RIAA 120; (1923–4) 2 AD 35.

[28] *(Germany v United States)* 2001 ICJ Reports 466 at 472–3.

[29] *(Mexico v United States)* 2004 ICJ Reports 12 at 65–6.

[30] Article 5 (n 1).

[31] *GUR Corporation v Trust Bank of Africa Ltd (Government of Ciskei, Third Party)* [1986] 3 All ER 449 (CA) 466A.

[32] This was demonstrated by a resolution of the Security Council in 1976 holding South Africa and not Transkei responsible for the closure of Transkei borders to Lesotho nationals (Resolution 402 (1976)); a protest made by France in 1987 to the South African government against the imprisonment of a French national in Ciskei (1987/1988 *Race Relations Survey* 573, 891, 915); and the British government's insistence that it held the South African government responsible for the actions of the Bantustan states on 'matters relating to individuals' (*GUR Corporation v Trust Bank* (n 31) 461C–D, 405H–I.) See, too, DJ Devine 'International law tensions arising from the South African situation 1976–1986' 1987 *Acta Juridica* 165 at 171–2.

The question whether a state is responsible for the acts of its military contingent placed under the control of the UN for peacekeeping has resulted in different decisions. In *Behrami and Behrami v France*, the European Court of Human Rights held that the impugned action was attributable to the United Nations and not the states whose military contingents were claimed to have committed internationally wrongful acts.[33] On the other hand, in *Netherlands v Nuhanovic*,[34] the Supreme Court of the Netherlands held that the Netherlands was responsible for the actions and omissions of the Dutch peacekeeping force in Srebenica, which had resulted in the massacre of thousands of Muslims, on the ground that it retained ultimate control.

A state is responsible for acts performed by officials within the scope of their employment. Thus, in the *Union Bridge Company Case*[35] it was held that the British government was liable for the act of an official in the Cape Colony who appropriated neutral property belonging to an American company during the Anglo-Boer War, mistakenly believing that it was not neutral property. The tribunal found that liability was not affected by the fact that it was an error made in good faith. The important factor was that the official had acted within the scope of his duty.

Liability extends beyond official acts performed within the scope of duty to *ultra vires* acts committed by officials. Article 7 of the Draft Articles provides:

> The conduct of an organ of a State or of a person or entity empowered to exercise elements of the governmental authority shall be considered an act of the State under international law if the organ, person or entity acts in that capacity, even if it exceeds its authority or contravenes instructions.[36]

This principle is illustrated by the *Youmans Claim*.[37] Here, the mayor of a Mexican town called out troops to suppress an unruly mob demonstrating outside the house of American employers over a trivial wage dispute. The troops, on arriving at the scene of the riot, instead of dispersing the mob opened fire on the house, as a consequence of which three Americans were killed. The unlawful acts of the troops were imputed to the Mexican government. The tribunal stated:

[33] Application no 71412/01, judgment of 2 May 2007.

[34] Case No 12/03324, judgment of 6 September 2013.

[35] (1924) 6 RIAA 138; (1923–4) 2 AD 170.

[36] See above (n 1).

[37] *United States v Mexico* (1926) 4 RIAA 110 para 14; (1925–6) 3 AD 223. See, too, the *Quintanilla Claim (Mexico v United States)* (1926) 4 RIAA 101; (1925–6) 3 AD 224; *Sandline International Inc/Papua New Guinea Arbitration* (1998) 117 ILR 552 at 561.

> [W]e do not consider that the participation of the soldiers in the murder . . . can be regarded as acts of soldiers committed in their private capacity when it is clear that at the time of the commission of these acts the men were on duty under the immediate supervision and in the presence of a commanding officer. Soldiers inflicting personal injuries or committing wanton destruction or looting always act in disobedience of some rules laid down by superior authority. There could be no liability whatever for such misdeeds if the view were taken that any acts committed by soldiers in contravention of instructions must always be considered as personal acts.

The judgment of the Appellate Division in *Nduli v Minister of Justice*[38] is unsatisfactory in this respect.[39] In this case, Rumpff CJ held that the South African state could not be held responsible for an arrest carried out by the South African police in Swaziland where such an arrest had been carried out contrary to the instructions of their superior officer. This decision is, however, remedied by *S v Ebrahim*,[40] in which the Appellate Division imputed responsibility to the state where a person was abducted from Swaziland by 'instruments' of the state, despite the absence of any evidence of official authorisation for their action.

Article 8 provides:

> The conduct of a person or group of persons shall be considered an act of a State under the international law if the person or group of persons is in fact acting on the instructions of, or under the direction or control of, that State in carrying out the conduct.

As a general principle the conduct of private persons is not attributable to a state under international law, but where there is a special relationship between the persons and the state their conduct is attributed to the state. This includes, for example, the conduct of private individuals who, though not forming part of the army or police force of a state, are employed as auxiliaries or are sent as 'volunteers' to neighbouring states with instructions to carry out missions abroad. Also included is the conduct of groups which act under 'the direction or control' of the state. The degree of control to be exercised by the state in order for conduct to be attributed to it arose in the *Nicaragua Case*.[41] Here, the question was whether violations of international humanitarian law committed by a rebel group operating against the government of Nicaragua—known as the *contras*—might be attributed to the United States. While the

[38] 1978 (1) SA 893 (A).

[39] See NJ Botha 'Municipal application of international law, seizure in foreign territory, terrorism and self defence' (1978) 4 *SAYIL* 170 at 174–5; H Booysen *Volkereg* 2 ed (1989) 253; Devine (n 32) 174.

[40] 1991 (2) SA 553 (AD) 568A–D.

[41] *Military and Paramilitary Activities in and against Nicaragua (Nicaragua v United States)* (merits) 1986 ICJ Reports 14.

International Court of Justice held that the United States was responsible for the 'planning, direction and support'[42] it gave to the *contras*, it rejected Nicaragua's claim that all the conduct of the *contras* was attributable to the United States by reason of its control over them. The Court stated that:

> For this conduct to give rise to legal responsibility of the United States, it would in principle have to be proved that the state had effective control of the military or paramilitary operations in the course of which the alleged violations were committed.[43]

Consequently, only in certain individual instances were acts of the *contras* held to be attributable to the United States, based upon actual directions given by the United States.

The cautious approach of the International Court was criticised by the Appeals Chamber of the International Criminal Tribunal for the Former Yugoslavia (ICTY)[44] when it held that the International Court had set too high a threshold for the test of control. According to the Appeals Chamber, it was sufficient, for attribution to take place, to establish '*overall control* going beyond the mere financing and equipping of such forces and involving also participation in the planning and supervision of military operations'.[45] The International Court of Justice reaffirmed its decision in the *Nicaragua Case* in the *Genocide Case (Bosnia v Serbia)* and held that the 'overall control' test propounded in *Tadic* had 'the major drawback of broadening the scope of state responsibility well beyond the fundamental principle governing the law of state responsibility: a state is responsible only for its own conduct, that is to say the conduct of persons acting, on whatever basis, on its behalf'.[46]

In *Von Pezold v Republic of Zimbabwe* the tribunal held that simple encouragement of private persons by the government did not provide evidence of direction or control.[47]

According to article 9, the conduct of a group of persons may be attributed to a state if the group were in fact exercising elements of governmental authority in default of the official authorities. This

[42] *Nicaragua v United States* (n 41) 51 para 86.

[43] Ibid 64–5 para 115.

[44] *Prosecutor v Tadic* Case No IT-94-1; (1999) 38 *ILM* 1518 at 1541 para 117.

[45] Supra at 1546 para 145 (emphasis in original).

[46] 2007 ICJ Reports 43 at 210 para 406. For criticisms of this aspect of the Court's decision, see R Goldstone and R Hamilton '*Bosnia v Serbia*: Lessons from the encounter of the International Court of Justice with the ICTY' (2008) 21 *Leiden Journal of International Law* 95; J Griebel and M Plücken 'New developments regarding the rules of attribution? The ICJ's decision in *Bosnia v Serbia*' (2008) 21 *Leiden Journal of International Law* 601.

[47] ICSID Case No ARB/10/15, Award 28 July 2015 para 445.

principle is illustrated by *Yeager v Islamic Republic of Iran*[48] in which the acts of the Revolutionary Guards as immigration officials at Tehran airport, in the immediate aftermath of the Iranian revolution, were held to be attributable to Iran on the basis that the Guards, although not actually authorised by the new government,

> at least exercised elements of governmental authority in the absence of official authorities, in operations of which the new Government must have had knowledge and to which it did not specifically object.[49]

The conduct of an insurrectional movement that becomes the new government of a state shall, in terms of article 10, be considered an act of that state under international law. According to the ILC's commentary on this article 'the continuity which . . . exists between the new organization of the state and that of the insurrectional movements leads naturally to the attribution to the state of conduct which the insurrectional movement may have committed during the struggle'.[50]

Increasingly states give aid to other states engaged in either international armed conflicts or non-international armed conflicts with little regard to the question whether the assisted state violates norms of international humanitarian law or human rights law. This aid may, for instance, take the form of military assistance, the provision of arms or participation in the torture of combatants or civilians. Article 16 provides that assistance to a state in the commission of an internationally wrongful act with knowledge of the circumstances of the wrongful act results in the responsibility of the assisting state. Sadly, this is a provision in the Draft Articles which is largely ignored by states.[51]

2 Circumstances precluding wrongfulness

The wrongfulness of conduct that would otherwise be in breach of international law is precluded by consent on the part of the injured state;[52] self-defence taken in conformity with the Charter of the United Nations;[53] countermeasures in response to an illegal act;[54]

[48] (1987) 17 Iran-USCTR 92, 82 ILR 178. See, too, *Hostages Case* 1980 ICJ Reports 3 at 34–5.

[49] *Yeager v Islamic Republic of Iran* (n 48) para 43.

[50] See above (n 1) 50; Crawford (n 8) 117. Cf the decision of the International Court of Justice in *Application of the Convention on the Prevention and Punishment of the Crime of Genocide (Croatia v Serbia)* 2015 ICJ Reports 3 at 51–2.

[51] See further on this provision and the practice of states, E de Wet 'Complicity in violations of human rights and humanitarian law by incumbent governments through direct military assistance on request' (2018) 67 *ICLQ* 287.

[52] Article 20.

[53] Article 21.

[54] Article 22.

force majeure, 'that is the occurrence of an irresistible force or of an unforeseen event, beyond the control of the state';[55] where 'the author of the act in question has no other reasonable way in a situation of distress, of saving the author's life or the lives of other persons entrusted to the author's care';[56] and necessity.[57] None of these circumstances may be relied on if to do so would conflict with a peremptory norm of general international law.[58]

The defence of necessity probably occasions the greatest difficulty in practice as it is most open to abuse. In order to bring it within acceptable limits, article 25 provides:

> 1. Necessity may not be invoked by a State as a ground for precluding the wrongfulness of an act not in conformity with an international obligation of that State unless the act:
>   *(a)* is the only way for the State to safeguard an essential interest against a grave and imminent peril; and
>   *(b)* does not seriously impair an essential interest of the State or States towards which the obligation exists, or of the international community as a whole.
> 2. In any case, necessity may not be invoked by a State as a ground for precluding wrongfulness if:
>   *(a)* the international obligation in question excludes the possibility of invoking necessity;
>   *(b)* the State has contributed to the situation of necessity.[59]

Necessity arises where there is an irreconcilable conflict between an essential interest and an obligation of the state. It will only rarely be available to excuse non-performance of an obligation and is subject to strict limitation to prevent abuse.[60] The defence is most frequently raised in environmental matters. In 1893 Russia prohibited sealing in an area of the high seas in order to prevent the extermination of a fur seal population by unrestricted hunting.[61] In 1967 the British government bombed a Liberian oil tanker, the *Torrey Canyon*, which went aground on submerged rocks off the English coast outside British territorial waters, spilling large amounts of oil which threatened the English coastline. The bombing was designed

[55] Article 23.

[56] Article 24.

[57] Article 25.

[58] Article 26. See *Von Pezold v Republic of Zimbabwe* (n 26) para 657.

[59] In *Gabcikovo-Nagymaros Project (Hungary/Slovakia)* 1997 ICJ Reports 7, the International Court of Justice held that the substantially similar predecessor of article 25 was an accurate reflection of customary international law (40–1 paras 51–2).

[60] In *Von Pezold v Republic of Zimbabwe* (n 26) para 624, the Tribunal warned that the declaration of a state of emergency did not per se give rise to a state of necessity.

[61] The dispute over the 'Russian fur seals' is documented in 86 *British and Foreign State Papers* 220.

to burn the remaining oil.[62] In 1995 Canada seized a Spanish fishing vessel on the high seas in order to conserve straddling stocks and to prevent the overfishing of Greenland halibut.[63]

3 Legal consequences of internationally wrongful acts

In the first instance, the state responsible for an internationally wrongful act is under an obligation to cease that act, if it is continuing, and to offer assurances and guarantees of non-repetition.[64] Secondly, the responsible state is under an obligation to make full reparation for the injury caused by the wrongful act.[65] In the *Chorzów Factory Case* the Permanent Court of International Justice declared:

> The essential principle contained in the actual notion of an illegal act . . . is that reparation must, so far as possible, wipe out all the consequences of the illegal act and reestablish a situation which would in all probability, have existed if the act had not been committed. Restitution in kind, or, if this is not possible, payment of a sum corresponding to the value which restitution in kind would bear.[66]

The Draft Articles on State Responsibility recognise three kinds of reparation: restitution, satisfaction and compensation.[67] Restitution requires the state responsible for committing an internationally wrongful act to re-establish the situation that existed before the wrongful act was committed.[68] 'Satisfaction' consists in an acknowledgment of the breach of international law, an expression of regret or a formal apology.[69] Reparation seldom takes the form of restitution or satisfaction today. In most cases the preferred form of reparation is compensation.

Compensation is to cover 'any financially assessable damage including loss of profits insofar as it is established'.[70] Compensation for personal injury suffered by nationals or officials of a state

[62] *The 'Torrey Canyon'*, Cmnd 3246 (London, Her Majesty's Stationery Office, 1967).

[63] *Fisheries Jurisdiction (Spain v Canada)* 1998 ICJ Reports 431.

[64] Article 30. This obligation was invoked by the applicant states in *La Grand (Germany v United States)* (merits) 2001 ICJ Reports paras 124–5 and *Avena (Mexico v United States)* 2004 ICJ Reports paras 148–50 in order to compel the United States to stop denying foreign nationals access to consular officials and to ensure that the United States would desist from such a practice in future.

[65] Article 31. See, too, the *dictum* in the *Chorzów Factory Case* (n 2).

[66] 1928 PCIJ Reports Series A no 17, 4 at 47. This *dictum* was endorsed by the International Court in the *Genocide Case (Bosnia v Serbia)* 2007 ICJ Reports 43 at 232 para 460.

[67] Articles 34, 35, 36 and 37.

[68] Article 35.

[69] Article 37.

[70] Article 36.

encompasses material losses and non-material damage, such as pain and suffering, mental anguish and humiliation, while compensation reflecting the capital value of property taken or destroyed as a result of an internationally wrongful act is generally assessed on the basis of the 'fair market value' of the property lost.[71]

In recent years the number of reparations awards in the form of compensation has increased sharply. In 1991 the United Nations Compensation Commission was established by the Security Council to process claims and pay compensation for losses resulting from Iraq's invasion of Kuwait (1990–1991).[72] In 2000, Eritrea and Ethiopia established the Eritrea–Ethiopia Claims Commission (EECC) to 'decide through binding arbitration all claims for loss, damage or injury by one Government against the other' resulting from any violations of international law that had occurred during the course of the armed conflict between them.[73] In 2009 the EECC delivered its final awards, compensating each state for material harm on a mass scale.[74] In 2012, the International Court of Justice ordered the Democratic Republic of the Congo (DRC) to compensate Guinea for both material and non-material damages suffered by one of its nationals as a result of his unlawful arrest, detention in and expulsion from the DRC.[75] More recently, in 2018, the International Court of Justice made a compensation award against Nicaragua for environmental damages caused by its unlawful invasion of Costa Rica.[76] Currently pending before the Court is a large claim for compensation for mass harm perpetrated by Uganda during its unlawful invasion and occupation of the DRC (2000–2003).[77]

[71] See the ILC's Commentary on article 36 (n 1) 252–5; Crawford (n 8) 224–5.

[72] UN Doc S/RES/687 (1991) para 16.

[73] Agreement between the Government of the Federal Democratic Republic of Ethiopia and the Government of the State of Eritrea 2138 UNTS 94 (12 December 2000).

[74] Eritrea-Ethiopia Claims Commission, Final Award, Ethiopia's Damages Claims (17 August 2009) UNRIAA vol XXVI at 505–630; Eritrea-Ethiopia Claims Commission, Final Award, Eritrea's Damages Claims (17 August 2009) UNRIAA vol XXVI at 631–770 .

[75] *Case Concerning Ahmadou Sadio Diallo (Republic of Guinea v DRC)* 2012 ICJ Reports 324.

[76] *Certain Activities Carried Out by Nicaragua in the Border Area (Costa Rica v Nicaragua)* 2018 ICJ Reports.

[77] *Armed Activities on the Territory of the Congo (Democratic Republic of the Congo v Uganda)* International Court of Justice press release, unofficial (9 July 2015), available at https://www.icj-cij.org/.

4 Serious breaches of peremptory norms

As shown above,[78] the ILC initially proposed that the Draft Articles on State Responsibility cover both criminal and delictual state responsibility. Although the final Draft Articles are concerned only with delictual responsibility, they recognise that special consequences attach to the breach of peremptory norms of international law (*jus cogens*) and obligations to the international community as a whole (obligations *erga omnes*).[79] Articles 40 and 41 provide that states shall co-operate to bring to an end through lawful means any serious breach of an obligation arising under a peremptory norm of general international law, and shall not recognise as lawful a situation created by such a serious breach. Although the Draft Articles do not identify such peremptory norms, the ILC's Commentary on article 40 provides some examples of such norms: the prohibitions on aggression, slavery, genocide, race discrimination, apartheid and torture, and the obligation to respect the right of self-determination.[80] A breach of an obligation is serious 'if it involves a gross or systematic failure by the responsible state to fulfil the obligation'.[81]

Despite the controversial nature of these provisions there is growing acceptance of them in the jurisprudence of both national and international tribunals.[82]

5 Invocation of the responsibility of a state

The Draft Articles recognise the traditional rule that a state may invoke the responsibility of another state by presenting a claim against such state or instituting legal proceedings against it, if the obligation breached is owed to the injured state itself, or to a group of states including that state and that state is specially affected.[83] However, the Draft Articles go further in providing, in article 48(1), that:

> Any State other than an injured State is entitled to invoke the responsibility of another State if—

[78] See notes 5–8.

[79] See further Chapter 3, section on *jus cogens*, obligations *erga omnes* and a system of higher norms.

[80] ILC's Draft Articles on Responsibility of States for Internationally Wrongful Acts (n 1) 283–4; Crawford (n 8) 246–7.

[81] Article 40(2).

[82] See above, Chapter 3; A Orakhelashvili *Peremptory Norms in International Law* (2006); C Tams *Enforcing Obligations* Erga Omnes *in International Law* (2005); A Cassese 'The character of the violated obligation' in Crawford, Pellet and Ollerson (eds) *The Law of International Responsibility* (n 4) 415.

[83] Article 42.

(*a*) the obligation breached is owed to a group of States including that State, and is established for the protection of a collective interest of the group; or

(*b*) the obligation breached is owed to the international community as a whole.

This article is premised on the notion that a state which is not itself injured by an internationally wrongful act may nevertheless invoke the responsibility of the wrongdoing state when it violates obligations protecting the collective interests of a group of states or of the international community as a whole. This provision repudiates the 1966 decision of the International Court of Justice in the *South West Africa Cases*,[84] which held that Ethiopia and Liberia had no legal standing to bring proceedings against South Africa in respect of its treatment of the people of Namibia because Ethiopia and Liberia were not directly affected themselves; and, international law did not recognise an '"*actio popularis*", or right resident in any member of a community to take legal action in vindication of a public interest'.[85] Moreover, it affirms the *obiter dictum* of the International Court of Justice in the *Barcelona Traction* case that:

> [A]n essential distinction should be drawn between the obligations of a state towards the international community as a whole, and those arising vis-à-vis another state in the field of diplomatic protection. By their very nature the former are the concern of all states. In view of the importance of the rights involved, all states can be held to have a legal interest in their protection; they are obligations *erga omnes*.[86]

6 Countermeasures

The international legal system has no central authority to enforce international law. In these circumstances, states claim the right to enforce compliance with rules of international law by responding to an illegal act with a reciprocal illegal act designed to compel compliance. Self-help of this kind has no place in a developed legal system but, unhappily, international law has not yet reached this stage of development. Although states rely less frequently on self-help measures today than in the past, international law still recognises the right of a state to resort to self-help. Previously, before 1928, when self-help might include the use of force, the term 'reprisal' was used to describe such action.[87] The outlawing of the use

[84] *South West Africa Cases (Second Phase)* 1966 ICJ Reports 6.

[85] Ibid para 88.

[86] *Barcelona Traction Light and Power Company, Limited* 1970 ICJ Reports 3 at 32.

[87] See *Naulilaa Case (Responsibility of Germany for Damage Caused in the Portugal Colonies in the South of Africa) (Portugal v Germany)* (1928) 2 RIAA 1011.

of force has resulted in a need for new terminology.[88] 'Sanctions' is not an appropriate word as this might be confused with action taken by the Security Council to enforce international law in situations constituting a threat to international peace. Instead, the term 'countermeasures' is used to describe self-help measures not involving the use of force.[89] Countermeasures must be distinguished from 'retorsion'—that is, 'unfriendly' conduct which does not violate an international obligation even though it may be a response to an internationally wrongful act. Acts of retorsion may include limitation of normal diplomatic relations, a trade embargo not in violation of a treaty obligation, or termination of an aid programme.

There is a serious danger that countermeasures will be abused. Indeed, some members of the ILC would have preferred not to include any provision on this subject in the Draft Articles on State Responsibility lest this be construed as approval. The ILC ultimately decided to include a section on countermeasures while at the same time making it clear that such measures were to be limited to special circumstances and subjected to strict control.

Article 49 provides:

> 1. An injured State may only take countermeasures against a State which is responsible for an international wrongful act in order to induce that State to comply with its obligations . . .
> 2. Countermeasures are limited to the non-performance for the time being of international obligations of the State taking the measures towards the responsible State.
> 3. Countermeasures shall, as far as possible, be taken in such a way as to permit the resumption of performance of the obligations in question.

Countermeasures are to be proportionate[90] and shall not affect:

(a) the obligation to refrain from the threat or use of force as embodied in the Charter of the United Nations;
(c) obligations for the protection of fundamental human rights;
(d) obligations of a humanitarian character prohibiting reprisals;
(e) other obligations under peremptory norms of general international law.[91]

Moreover, a state taking countermeasures is not relieved from fulfilling its obligations:

[88] Today the term 'reprisals' is still used to describe action taken in international armed conflict ('belligerent reprisals').

[89] See *Gabèikovo-Nagymaros Project (Hungary/Slovakia)* 1997 ICJ Reports 7, 55–7 (paras 82–7); *Air Services Agreement of 27 March 1946 (US v France)* (1979) 18 RIAA 416; OY Elagab *The Legality of Non-Forcible Counter-Measures in International Law* (1988).

[90] Article 51; *Naulilaa Case* (n 87). T Franck 'On proportionality of countermeasures in international law' (2008) 102 *AJIL* 715.

[91] Article 50(1).

(*a*) under any dispute settlement procedure applicable between it and the responsible State;
(*b*) to respect the inviolability of diplomatic or consular agents, premises, archives and documents.[92]

In terms of article 49, which reflects the traditional position, only an injured state may take countermeasures. However, there is some state practice to support the taking of countermeasures by non-injured states where the obligation breached is owed to the international community as a whole. For instance, the United States adopted the Comprehensive Anti-Apartheid Act[93] in 1986 to suspend the landing rights of South African Airways on US territory, in violation of the 1947 US–South Africa Aviation Agreement,[94] in response to the declaration of a state of emergency in South Africa in 1985. This was in order to induce the South African government to establish a non-racial democracy. Similarly, in 1998, Germany, France and the United Kingdom imposed a flight ban on Yugoslavia in violation of bilateral aviation agreements in response to the humanitarian crisis in Kosovo. The Draft Articles take cognisance of this practice and include a saving clause, article 54, which provides that article 49 shall not prejudice the right of a state to take lawful measures against a state that breaches an obligation owed to the international community as a whole 'to ensure cessation of the breach and reparation in the interest of the injured state or of the beneficiaries of the obligation breached'.[95]

DIPLOMATIC PROTECTION[96]

Indirect state responsibility, which is the focus of the present chapter, occurs when a state injures the person or property of a foreign national within its territory. Here, it incurs responsibility because of its failure to treat the foreign national according to the minimum standard of justice required for the treatment of aliens: for instance, by detaining him for an unreasonable period without trial, or by confiscating his property without compensation.

The basis for responsibility in the case of diplomatic protection is that the defendant state has injured the plaintiff state by injuring its national. According to the Permanent Court of International Justice

[92] Article 50(2).
[93] (1987) 26 *ILM* 79 (s 306).
[94] 66 UNTS 233, article VI.
[95] Ibid.
[96] CF Amerasinghe *Diplomatic Protection* (2008); Crawford *State Responsibility* (n 4) 567; J Dugard 'Diplomatic protection' in Crawford, Pellet and Olleson (eds) *The Law of International Responsibility* (n 4) 1051; AHM Vermeer-Künzli *The Protection of Individuals by Means of Diplomatic Protection* (2007).

in the *Mavrommatis Palestine Concession Case*, 'by taking up the case of one of its subjects and by resorting to diplomatic action or international judicial proceedings on his behalf, a State is in reality asserting its own rights—its right to ensure in the person of its subjects respect for the rules of international law'.[97]

The notion that an injury to the individual is an injury to the state itself is not consistently maintained in judicial proceedings. When states bring proceedings on behalf of their nationals, they seldom claim that they assert their own right and often refer to the injured individual as the 'claimant'. Consequently, it has been suggested that when it exercises diplomatic protection, a state acts as agent on behalf of the injured individual and enforces the right of the individual rather than that of the state. Logical inconsistencies in the traditional doctrine, such as the requirement of continuous nationality, the exhaustion of local remedies rule, and the practice of fixing the quantum of damages suffered to accord with the loss suffered by the individual, lend support to this view.[98]

It is difficult to defend the traditional view expounded in *Mavrommatis* as a coherent and consistent doctrine. It is factually inaccurate as it is 'an exaggeration to say that whenever a national is injured in a foreign state, their state as a whole is necessarily injured too'.[99] As a doctrine it is impaired by inconsistencies of the kind mentioned above, which contradict the notion that an injury to the individual is an injury to the state. It is also contradicted by contemporary developments in human rights law and foreign investment law, which empower the individual to bring proceedings in his own right before international tribunals. It cannot therefore seriously be denied that the notion that an injury to a national is an injury to the state is a fiction. Nevertheless, this fiction remains the basis for state intervention on behalf of a national in the exercise of diplomatic protection, and has been accepted as such by South African judicial decisions.[100]

In order to succeed in such a claim, the plaintiff state is required to prove that:

(a) the injured person was its national;

(b) all local remedies have been exhausted; and

[97] 1924 PCIJ Reports Series A no 2 at 12. See, too, *Panevezys-Saldutiskis Railway Case* 1939 PCIJ Reports Series A/B no 76, 4 at 16. This *dictum* has its origin in the statement by the 18th-century jurist Vattel that 'whoever ill-treats a citizen indirectly injures the state' in *The Law of Nations or, Principles of the Law of Nature Applied to the Conduct and Affairs and Nations and Sovereigns* (1758) Ch VI, 136.

[98] These issues are dealt with below.

[99] A Clapham *Brierly's Law of Nations* 7 ed (2012) 256.

[100] *Van Zyl v Government of the RSA* 2008 (3) SA 294 (SCA) 314; *Von Abo v Government of the Republic of South Africa* 2009 (2) SA 526 (T) para 62.

(*c*) the conduct of the defendant state violates the rules of international law relating to the treatment of aliens.[101]

The requirements of nationality and the exhaustion of local remedies comprise the secondary rules of diplomatic protection, while the requirement that the conduct of the defendant state violates the rules of international law relating to the treatment of aliens comprises the primary rules.

In 2006 the ILC agreed on a set of Draft Articles on Diplomatic Protection[102] dealing with the secondary rules of diplomatic protection—that is, nationality and the exhaustion of local remedies. The present author served as Special Rapporteur to the ILC on this subject and produced six reports which resulted in a set of 19 Draft Articles.[103] These Draft Articles have not yet been transformed into a multilateral treaty. However, as the Draft Articles are largely a codification of customary international law, the present chapter will draw heavily on them.

NATIONALITY

The terms 'nationality' and 'citizenship' are used interchangeably and loosely by both politicians and lawyers to indicate a connection between individual and state. South African legislation, in particular, is guilty of failing to draw a clear distinction between the two concepts. The governing statute on this subject, the South African Citizenship Act 88 of 1995, for example, uses the term 'citizenship' where 'nationality' would be more correct.

Nationality is essentially a term of international law and denotes that there is a legal connection between the individual and the state for external purposes. In practice, this means that a South African national may travel on a South African passport[104] and is entitled to protection by the South African government if injured in another

[101] *Van Zyl v Government of the RSA* (n 100) 314.

[102] *Yearbook of the International Law Commission* (2006) vol II, part 2 at 24.

[103] J Crawford 'The ILC Articles on Diplomatic Protection' (2006) 31 *SAYIL* I; J Kateka 'John Dugard's contribution to the topic of diplomatic protection' in T Skouteris and A Vermeer-Künzli *The Protection of the Individual in International Law: Essays in Honour of John Dugard* (special issue of the *Leiden Journal of International Law* (2007)) 193; P Escarameia 'Professor Dugard as an innovator in the work of the International Law Commission' *The Protection of the Individual in International Law: Essays in Honour of John Dugard* 203.

[104] In terms of s 21(4) of the Constitution: 'Every South African citizen has the right to a passport'. The issue of passports is regulated by the South African Passports and Travel Documents Act 4 of 1994. Previously, the granting of a passport was within the discretion of the executive. See *Sachs v Dönges NO* 1950 (2) SA 265 (A); *Fellner v Minister of the Interior* 1954 (4) SA 523 (A); *Tutu v Minister of Internal Affairs* 1982 (4) SA 571 (T); *Boesak v Minister of Home Affairs* 1987 (3) SA 665 (C). During the apartheid era,

country. Citizenship, on the other hand, is a term of constitutional law and is best used to describe the status of individuals internally, particularly the aggregate of civil and political rights to which they are entitled.[105]

A state may provide diplomatic protection to its nationals alone. As the Permanent Court of International Justice observed in the *Panevezys-Saldutiskis Railway Case*, 'it is the bond of nationality between the state and the individual which alone confers upon the state the right of diplomatic protection'.[106]

1 Nationality of natural persons

It is for each state to determine under its own law who are its nationals.[107] There are certain recognised grounds for the conferment of nationality which are followed by most states. These are birth (*jus soli*), descent (*jus sanguinis*) and naturalisation, following upon a period of residence. The South African Citizenship Act[108] accords with international practice for, subject to certain exceptions, it provides that a person becomes a South African national (although it persists in using the term 'citizen') by birth,[109] descent,[110] and naturalisation.[111]

While it is the right of a state to prescribe rules relating to the acquisition of its nationality by means of its own legislation, it is international law that determines whether a state is entitled to exercise diplomatic protection on behalf of a national.[112] This is made clear by article 4 of the ILC's Draft Articles on Diplomatic Protection which provides:

> For the purposes of the diplomatic protection of a natural person, a State of nationality means a State whose nationality that person has acquired, in

the refusal of passports was common: see J Dugard *Human Rights and the South African Legal Order* (1978) 141–3.

[105] See *Tshwete v Minister of Home Affairs (RSA)* 1988 (4) SA 586 (A) in which Nestadt JA examines the distinction between nationality and citizenship (614E–H). See further *Kaunda v President of the RSA* 2005 (4) SA 235 (CC) paras 62–3; *Van Zyl v Government of the RSA* 2005 (11) BCLR 1106 (T) paras 87, 93; and F Venter 'Citizenship and nationality' in W Joubert (ed) *Law of South Africa* 2 ed vol 2, part 2 (2003) 127.

[106] Supra (n 97) 16.

[107] Article 1 of the 1930 Hague Convention on Certain Questions Relating to the Conflict of Nationality Laws: 179 LNTS 89. This Convention came into force in 1937. (It was signed but not ratified by South Africa.)

[108] 88 of 1995. For a clear analysis of this Act, see R Keightley 'The child's right to a nationality and the acquisition of citizenship in South African law' (1998) 14 *SAJHR* 411.

[109] Section 2.

[110] Section 3.

[111] Sections 4, 5.

[112] *Nottebohm Case* 1955 ICJ Reports 4 at 20–1.

accordance with the law of that State, by birth, descent, naturalization, succession of States, or in any other manner, *not inconsistent with international law*.[113]

Marriage to a national is not included in this list as in most circumstances, marriage per se is insufficient for the grant of nationality: it requires in addition a period of residence, following which nationality is conferred by naturalisation. Where marriage to a national automatically results in the acquisition by a spouse of the nationality of the other spouse, problems may arise in respect of the consistency of such an acquisition of nationality with international law.[114]

In most cases, nationality and the right of diplomatic protection will coincide. However, in exceptional cases, international law may refuse to recognise nationality for the purpose of diplomatic protection. This is illustrated by the *Nottebohm Case*.[115]

Mr Nottebohm was born in Germany in 1881. In 1905 he went to Guatemala, where he built up a highly successful business. Thereafter he visited Germany sporadically, but the centre of his business, family and social life was in Guatemala. In 1939, shortly after the start of the war in Europe, Nottebohm visited his brother in Liechtenstein and, fearing that his German nationality might create problems if Guatemala should declare war on Germany, he obtained the nationality of Liechtenstein, a neutral in World War II. Although Liechtenstein law required three years' residence as a condition for the granting of nationality by naturalisation, this requirement was waived in the case of Nottebohm. Nottebohm then immediately returned to Guatemala. In 1943 Guatemala declared war on Germany. Nottebohm was arrested and interned in the United States as an enemy alien. His property was confiscated and he was prohibited from returning to Guatemala after the war.

In 1951 Liechtenstein instituted proceedings before the International Court of Justice in which it claimed compensation from Guatemala on the ground that it had violated its obligations under international law towards Liechtenstein by 'arresting, detaining, expelling and refusing to admit' Mr Nottebohm, a Liechtenstein national, and by 'seizing and retaining his property without compensation'.[116] In reply Guatemala questioned Liechtenstein's right to exercise diplomatic protection on behalf of Nottebohm.

113 Note 102. Emphasis added.

114 Article 9(1) of the Convention on the Elimination of All Forms of Discrimination against Women prohibits the acquisition of nationality in such circumstances.

115 1955 ICJ Reports 4. See further on this case JM Jones 'The *Nottebohm Case*' (1956) 5 *ICLQ* 230; JL Kunz 'The *Nottebohm* judgment' (1960) 54 *AJIL* 536.

116 *Nottebohm Case* (n 112) 6–7.

In its judgment, the Court emphasised the need for real and effective nationality as the basis for diplomatic protection. While it recognised that a state is free to decide on the rules governing the grant of its own nationality, it warned that 'a state cannot claim that the rules it has thus laid down are entitled to recognition by another state unless it has acted in conformity with this general aim of making the legal bond of nationality accord with the individual's genuine connection with the [protecting] state'.[117] Such a bond between state and individual has 'as its basis a social fact of attachment, a genuine connection of existence, interest and sentiments, together with the existence of reciprocal rights and duties. It may be said to constitute the juridical expression of the fact that the individual upon whom it is conferred . . . is in fact more closely connected with the population of the state conferring nationality than with that of any other state'.[118] The facts of this case revealed that while Nottebohm's connections with Liechtenstein were 'extremely tenuous'[119] and failed to constitute a 'bond of attachment', there was a long-standing and close connection between Nottebohm and Guatemala.[120] The Court accordingly held that Liechtenstein was 'not entitled to extend its protection to Nottebohm vis-à-vis Guatemala'.[121]

The Court did not purport to pronounce on the status of Nottebohm's Liechtenstein nationality vis-à-vis all states. It carefully confined its judgment to the right of Liechtenstein to exercise diplomatic protection on behalf of Nottebohm vis-à-vis *Guatemala*. It therefore left unanswered the question whether Liechtenstein would have been able to protect Nottebohm against a state with which he had no close connection. This question is probably best answered in the affirmative as the Court was determined to propound a relative test only,[122] ie that Nottebohm's close ties with Guatemala trumped the weaker nationality link with Liechtenstein.

Article 4 of the ILC's Draft Articles, cited above, does not require a state to prove an effective or genuine link between itself and its national, along the lines suggested in the *Nottebohm Case* as an additional factor for the exercise of diplomatic protection. The ILC took the view that there were certain factors that served to limit *Nottebohm* to the facts of the case in question, particularly the fact that

[117] At 23.
[118] Ibid.
[119] At 25.
[120] At 26.
[121] Ibid.
[122] *Flegenheimer Claim* Italian–United States Conciliation Commission (1958) 25 ILR 91; *Barcelona Traction* (n 86) 1970 ICJ Reports 3 at 42.

the ties between Nottebohm and Liechtenstein were 'extremely tenuous' compared with the close ties between Nottebohm and Guatemala for a period of over 34 years. It concluded that the Court did not intend to expound a general rule applicable to all states but only a relative rule according to which a state in Liechtenstein's position was required to show a genuine link between itself and Nottebohm in order to permit it to claim on his behalf against Guatemala, with whom he had extremely close ties. Moreover, the ILC was mindful of the fact that if the genuine link requirement proposed by the *Nottebohm Case* was strictly applied, it would exclude millions of persons from the benefit of diplomatic protection. This was because in today's world of economic globalisation and migration, there are millions of persons who have drifted away from their state of nationality and made their lives in states whose nationality they never acquire or have acquired nationality by birth or descent from states with which they have a tenuous connection.[123] Despite the refusal of the ILC to treat a 'genuine link' as an additional requirement for the exercise of diplomatic protection, the *Nottebohm Case* constitutes a salutary reminder to states that ultimately it is for international law to decide whether nationality has been conferred in a manner not inconsistent with international law for the purpose of diplomatic protection.

It is in the area of dual and plural nationality that the influence of *Nottebohm* is the greatest. Although many states—including South Africa[124]—disapprove of the exercise of multiple nationality, international law does not prohibit several states from conferring their nationality upon the same individual. A woman born in South Africa of a British father, who marries an Italian and lives for many years in Brazil may qualify for South African, British, Italian and Brazilian nationalities. Which of these states is to protect her if she is injured in Argentina? Or may one of her four national states protect her against another if she is injured by that national state?

The ILC has adopted two rules on this subject, the second of which is premised on the principle expounded in *Nottebohm*.

Article 6 provides that:

> Any State of which a dual or multiple national is a national may exercise diplomatic protection in respect of that national against a State of which that individual is not a national.

Although there is some support for the existence of a 'genuine

[123] Commentary on article 4 (n 102) 33.

[124] See South African Citizenship Act 88 of 1995 as amended by Act 17 of 2004: s 26B.

link', in such a case, the ILC found that the weight of authority does not require such a condition. [125]

The situation is, however, very different when the injured person is a national of both the plaintiff and the defendant state. Early authorities hold that in such circumstances, a rule of non-responsibility applies according to which one state of nationality may not bring a claim against another state of nationality.[126]

Several post-*Nottebohm* arbitral decisions reject this principle and allow the state with which the dual national has an effective and dominant link to sue another state of which the individual is a national.[127] The Iran–United States Claims Tribunal has permitted a dual United States-Iran national whose effective link was with the United States to bring proceedings against Iran. In determining the dominant and effective nationality, said the Tribunal, it would consider 'all relevant factors, including habitual residence, centre of interests, family ties, participation in public life and other evidence of attachment'.[128] The ILC has given approval to these authorities in article 7, which provides:

> A State of nationality may not exercise diplomatic protection in respect of a person against a State of which that person is also a national unless the nationality of the former State is predominant, both at the date of the injury and at the date of the official presentation of the claim.

The practice of states still reveals a reluctance to exercise diplomatic protection on behalf of dual nationals against the other state of nationality. Britain has failed to use diplomatic protection on behalf of predominantly British nationals imprisoned without due process of law by Iran, whose law insists that an Iranian national may never lose her or his Iranian nationality by living abroad and acquiring another nationality.[129]

2 Nationality of corporations and shareholders

Two issues relating to the diplomatic protection of corporations and their shareholders require consideration: first, the question of which

[125] Commentary on article 6 (n 102) 42. See, too, the *Salem Case* (1932) 2 RIAA 1165 at 1188; *Mergé Claim* (1955) 22 ILR 443 at 456; *Dallal v Iran* 3 IUSCTR (1983) 23.

[126] The 1930 Hague Convention on Certain Questions Relating to the Conflict of Nationality Laws (n 107) declares in article 4: 'A State may not afford diplomatic protection to one of its nationals against a State whose nationality such person also possesses.' In 1949, in its advisory opinion on *Reparation for Injuries*, the International Court of Justice described the practice of states not to protect their nationals against another state of nationality as 'the ordinary practice' (1949) ICJ Reports 186.

[127] *Mergé Claim* (n 125).

[128] *Iran-United States, Case No A-18* (1984) 5 IUSCTR 251, (1984) 78 *AJIL* 912 at 914; *Esphahanian v Bank Tejerat* (1983) IUSCTR 157, (1983) 77 *AJIL* 646.

[129] See the case of Mrs Nazanin Zaghari-Ratcliffe whose incarceration in Iran in 2017–2018 has been the subject of a public outcry in the United Kingdom.

state is entitled to protect a company, and, secondly, the question whether the separate legal personalities of the company and shareholders in municipal law preclude a state from protecting its nationals who are shareholders in a company incorporated in another state when damage is inflicted on the company.

In 1970 the International Court of Justice gave an answer to these questions in the *Barcelona Traction* case when it held that the state of registration (or incorporation) of a company may exercise diplomatic protection on behalf of the company and that, subject to certain exceptions, the state of nationality of the shareholders in the company is not entitled to do so.[130] In this case, the Court rejected the argument that a company registered in Canada with an 88 per cent Belgian shareholding might be protected by Belgium, with which the company had a genuine link of the kind expounded in the *Nottebohm* case, against Spain, arising out of an injury inflicted on the company by Spain. Considerations of public policy contributed to this decision. First, when shareholders invest in a corporation doing business abroad, they undertake risks, including the risk that the state of nationality of the corporation may in the exercise of its discretion decline to exercise its right of diplomatic protection.[131] Secondly, many corporations engaged in transnational business have shareholders from several countries; to allow the state of nationality of the shareholders to bring proceedings on behalf of its shareholders may result in a multiplicity of claims by different states, all arising out of injury to the same company.[132]

Article 9 of the ILC Draft Articles on Diplomatic Protection recognises that incorporation confers nationality on a corporation for the purpose of diplomatic protection, but provides an exception for cases where there is no significant connection between the corporation and its state of incorporation. The article provides that:

> For the purposes of the diplomatic protection of a corporation, the State of nationality means the State under whose law the corporation was incorporated. However, when the corporation is controlled by nationals of another State or States and has no substantial business activities in the State of incorporation, and the seat of management and the financial control of the corporation are both located in another State, that State shall be regarded as the State of nationality.

The commentary to article 9 makes clear that there must be some additional tangible connection with the state in which the corporation is formed. It states:

[130] *Second Phase (Belgium v Spain)* 1970 ICJ Reports 3, 42 (para 70); see, too, *Diallo Case (Guinea v DRC) (Preliminary Objections)* 2007 ICJ Reports 582 para 61.

[131] Ibid 35 (para 43), 46 (paras 86–7), 50 (para 99).

[132] Ibid 48–9 (paras 94–6).

> Policy and fairness dictate such a solution. It is wrong to place the sole and exclusive right to exercise diplomatic protection in a State with which the corporation has the most tenuous connection as in practice such a State will seldom be prepared to protect such a corporation.[133]

There are clearly exceptions to the rule expounded in *Barcelona Traction* and article 9—ie cases in which the court will lift the corporate veil in order to allow the state of nationality of the shareholders to exercise diplomatic protection. Where an exception applies, as the shareholders in a company may be nationals of different states, several states of nationality may be able to exercise diplomatic protection.

First, *Barcelona Traction* may be construed to allow the state of nationality of the shareholders to exercise diplomatic protection where the company's national state lacks the capacity to act on its behalf because it fails to have some genuine connection with it.[134] This exception is premised on the fact that the Court in *Barcelona Traction* found that there was 'a close and permanent connection with Canada resulting from over fifty years of incorporation, the holding of board meetings in Canada, and the maintenance of an office in Canada'.[135] *A contrario*, when no such link exists, the state of incorporation of the company may lack the capacity to exercise protection on its behalf.

The second exception is where there is injury to the direct rights of the shareholders, distinct from the company's rights (for instance, in the case of failure to pay dividends, or denial of the right to attend and vote at general meetings or to the right to share in the residual assets of the company on liquidation).[136]

The third exception is where the company has ceased to exist or has lost its capacity to act—for example, where it has gone into liquidation. This exception was accepted by the Court in *Barcelona Traction* although it was not relevant on the facts.[137] The question whether this has occurred is governed by the law of the state of the company's incorporation.[138]

[133] Paragraph 4 of commentary on article 9 (n 102) 38.

[134] FA Mann 'The protection of shareholders' interests in the light of the *Barcelona Traction* case' (1973) 67 *AJIL* 259, 273.

[135] 1970 ICJ Reports 42 (para 71).

[136] Ibid 36 (para 47). See, too, article 12 of the ILC Draft Articles. In the *Diallo Case (Guinea v DRC)* (merits) 2010 ICJ Reports, the International Court acknowledged that a shareholder might be protected where his direct rights in a corporation were infringed but held that Mr Diallo's direct rights had not been infringed: 679–87 (paras 114–48). See, too, *Van Zyl v Government of the RSA* 2005 (11) BCLR 1106 (T) paras 90–1; *Van Zyl v Government of the RSA* (n 100) 319.

[137] 1970 ICJ Reports 40–1 (paras 65–8).

[138] Article 11(a) of ILC Draft Articles.

The fourth exception is where the state of incorporation is itself responsible for inflicting injury on the company, and the foreign shareholders' sole means of protection on the international level is through their state(s) of nationality.[139]

The fourth exception is the most important. It is not uncommon for a developing state to require foreigners wishing to obtain some concession or licence to exploit a resource in that state to establish a company for this purpose, under the laws of that state, with themselves as principal shareholders. If the licence is withdrawn and the assets of the company are confiscated by the government of the state of incorporation, the foreign shareholders are left without a state to protect them unless their own state of nationality is able to exercise protection. There is considerable support for the rule that in such circumstances, the state of nationality of the shareholders may exercise diplomatic protection.[140] Support for such a rule is particularly strong where the injured corporation has been compelled to incorporate in the wrongdoing state. In the *Delagoa Bay Railway Case* the United Kingdom and the United States successfully intervened on behalf of Anglo-American shareholders in a Portuguese company, created in accordance with Portuguese law at the insistence of the Portuguese government, to construct a railway line from Lourenço Marques to Komatipoort in 1889, when the Portuguese government confiscated the assets of the company.[141] In a similar case in which the United Kingdom made a claim on behalf of its nationals, who were shareholders in a Mexican company, the government of the United Kingdom replied as follows to the Mexican argument that a state might not intervene on behalf of its shareholders:

> If the doctrine were admitted that a Government can first make the operation of foreign interests in its territories depend upon their incorporation under local law, and then plead such incorporation as the justification for rejecting foreign diplomatic intervention, it is clear that the means would never be

[139] This exception was acknowledged by the International Court of Justice in the *Barcelona Traction* case: 1970 ICJ Reports 48 (para 92).

[140] Several judges in the *Barcelona Traction* case expressed themselves in support of such a rule in separate opinions: Fitzmaurice at 72–5; Tanaka at 133–4; Jessup at 191–3. (*Sed contra*, see the separate opinions of judges Padilla Nervo at 257–9; Morelli at 240–1; Ammoun at 318). See further JM Jones 'Claims on behalf of nationals who are shareholders in foreign companies' (1949) 26 *BYIL* 225; A Schmulow 'Diplomatic intervention in the event of expropriation of a company without compensation' (1996) 21 *SAYIL* 73.

[141] JB Moore *International Arbitrations* (1898) vol 2 at 1865; JB Moore *Digest of International Law* (1906) vol 6 at 648; (1888–9) 81 *BSFP* 691.

> wanting whereby foreign Governments could be prevented from exercising their undoubted right under international law to protect the commercial interests of their nationals abroad.[142]

This exception has received some support in judicial decisions[143] subsequent to *Barcelona Traction* and has been endorsed by the ILC in its Draft Articles on Diplomatic Protection. Article 11(b) provides:

> A State of nationality of shareholders in a corporation shall not be entitled to exercise diplomatic protection in respect of such shareholders in the case of an injury to the corporation unless:
>
> . . .
>
> *(b)* The corporation had, at the date of injury, the nationality of the State alleged to be responsible for causing the injury, and incorporation in that State was required by it as a precondition for doing businesses there.

In the *Diallo Case (Preliminary Objections)* the International Court of Justice left open the question whether the rule contained in article 11(b) is a rule of customary international law.[144]

Van Zyl v Government of the RSA[145] raised the question whether South Africa might extend diplomatic protection to a national who held shares in and controlled a company registered in Lesotho, where the national had been compelled by the Lesotho authorities to incorporate the company in Lesotho as a condition for obtaining

[142] *Mexican Eagle (El Aguila)* in M Whiteman *Digest of International Law* vol 8 at 1272–4; *Romano-Americano* in GH Hackworth *Digest of International Law* vol 5 at 841. See, too, *El Triunfo* (1902) 15 RIAA 467; *Deutsche Amerikanische Petroleum Gesellschaft Oil Tankers* (1926) 2 RIAA 779 at 790. See further *Yearbook of the International Law Commission* (2006) vol II, part 2 (n 102) 41–2; and the Special Rapporteur's Fourth Report on Diplomatic Protection (*Yearbook of the International Law Commission* (2003) vol II at 3–30).

[143] See the commentary of the ILC on article 11(b) (n 102) 41–2. In the *ELSI Case* 1989 ICJ Reports 15 a Chamber of the International Court of Justice allowed the United States to bring a claim against Italy in respect of damage suffered by an Italian company whose shares were wholly owned by two American companies, without any serious question having been raised as to the lawfulness of the espousal by the United States of its companies' claims. The Chamber avoided pronouncing on the compatibility of its findings with *Barcelona Traction* despite an objection raised by Italy. It is therefore possible to infer support for the exception in favour of the right of the state of shareholders of a corporation to intervene against the state of incorporation when it is responsible for causing injury to the corporation. Cf *Diallo Case (Guinea v DRC) (Preliminary Objections)* 2007 ICJ Reports 582 para 87. See further Y Dinstein 'Diplomatic protection of companies under international law' in K Wellens (ed) *International Law: Theory and Practice: Essays in Honour of Eric Suy* (1998) 505, 512.

[144] *Case Concerning Ahmadou Sadio Diallo (Guinea v DRC) (Preliminary Objections)* 2007 ICJ Reports 582 paras 91–4. See AHM Vermeer-Künzli '*Diallo* and the Draft Articles: The application of the Draft Articles on Diplomatic Protection in the *Ahmadou Sadi Diallo Case*' (2007) 20 *Leiden Journal of International Law* 194. See, too, Vermeer-Künzli in 'The subject matters: The ICJ and human rights, rights of shareholders, and the *Diallo Case*' (2011) 24 *Leiden Journal of International Law* 607.

[145] 2008 (3) SA 294 (SCA).

mining rights there, and these rights and the property of the company had been confiscated without compensation. The Supreme Court of Appeal found it unnecessary to decide this issue but expressed doubts as to whether article 11(b) of the ILC Draft Articles reflected customary international law.[146] In *Von Abo v Government of the Republic of South Africa*[147] Prinsloo J in the Transvaal Provincial Division gave approval to the exception contained in article 11(b), but the Supreme Court of Appeal in this case held that it was unnecessary to decide on this matter.[148]

3 Continuous nationality

A state is entitled to exercise diplomatic protection in respect of a natural person or corporation who was its national continuously from the date of injury to the date of the official presentation of the claim.[149] A suggestion in *Loewen Group Inc v USA*[150] that nationality must extend until the making of the award was rejected by the ILC and was not followed in *Yukos (Isle of Man) v Russian Federation*.[151]

4 Is there a right to diplomatic protection?

A state has the right to exercise diplomatic protection on behalf of a national. It is under no duty or obligation to do so. The internal law of a state may oblige a state to extend diplomatic protection to a national but international law imposes no such obligation. The position was clearly stated by the International Court of Justice in the *Barcelona Traction* case:

> [W]ithin the limits prescribed by international law, a State may exercise diplomatic protection by whatever means and to whatever extent it thinks fit, for it is its own right that the State is asserting. Should the natural or legal person on whose behalf it is acting consider that their rights are not adequately protected they have no remedy in international law. All they can do is resort to municipal law, if means are available, with a view to furthering their cause or obtaining redress .... The State must be viewed as the sole judge to decide whether its protection will be granted, to what extent it is granted, and when it will cease. It retains in this respect a discretionary power the exercise of which may be determined by considerations of a political or other nature, unrelated to the particular case.[152]

A proposal by the Special Rapporteur to the ILC that a limited duty of protection be imposed on the state of nationality was rejected by the

[146] Ibid 319–20.
[147] 2009 (2) SA 526 (T) 544–5.
[148] *Government of the Republic of South Africa v Von Abo* 2011 (5) SA 262 (SCA).
[149] ILC Draft Articles 5 and 10. See, too, *Van Zyl v Government of the RSA* (n 100) 320.
[150] (2003) 42 *ILM* 811 at 847–9.
[151] PCA Case No AA 220 (2010) 199–200 (paras 551–2).
[152] 1970 ICJ Reports 44 (paras 78–9).

ILC as going beyond the permissible limits of progressive development of the law.[153] However, article 19 of the Draft Articles does recommend that a state entitled to exercise diplomatic protection 'should give due consideration to the possibility of exercising diplomatic protection, especially when a significant injury has occurred'.

There is growing support for the proposition that there is some duty on states to afford diplomatic protection to nationals subjected to serious human rights violations in foreign states, albeit under domestic administrative and constitutional rules rather than international law. The constitutions of many states recognise the right of individuals to receive diplomatic protection for injuries suffered abroad, though whether this right is enforceable in the courts of these states is far from clear.[154] Moreover, the courts of several states have seriously entertained claims for diplomatic protection, before dismissing them, mainly on the ground that the state in question had taken some steps to remedy the national's plight.[155] In *Abbasi and Another v Secretary of State for Foreign and Commonwealth Affairs*,[156] in which an order was unsuccessfully sought to compel the British government to provide diplomatic protection to British nationals held by the United States at Guantanamo Bay, the Court held that the executive's decision not to grant diplomatic protection was in principle reviewable but that such review was not justified on the facts before the Court.

This matter was the subject of a decision of the South African Constitutional Court in *Kaunda and Others v President of the Republic of South Africa*,[157] in which an order was sought to compel the South

[153] See First Report on Diplomatic Protection: *Yearbook of the International Law Commission* (2000) vol II, part 1 at 205. Article 4(1) proposed that '[u]nless the injured person is able to bring a claim for such injury before a competent international court or tribunal, the state of his/her nationality has a legal duty to exercise diplomatic protection on behalf of the injured person upon request, if the injury results from a grave breach of a *jus cogens* norm attributable to another state'. For a discussion of this proposal and its rejection, see *Van Zyl v Government of the RSA* (n 100) paras 18–19.

[154] First Report on Diplomatic Protection (n 153) 30–1.

[155] AHM Vermeer-Künzli 'Restricting discretion: Judicial review of diplomatic protection' (2006) 75 *Nordic Journal of International Law* 279.

[156] [2002] EWCA Civ 1598, [2002] All ER (D) 70, (2003) 42 *ILM* 358. In this case, the Court considered the proposal made to the ILC to impose an obligation on states to provide diplomatic protection in the case of serious human rights violations.

[157] 2005 (4) SA 235 (CC). For criticisms of this decision, see ME Olivier 'Diplomatic protection—Right or privilege?' (2005) 30 *SAYIL* 238; S Pete and M du Plessis 'South African nationals abroad and their right to diplomatic protection—Lessons from the *Mercenaries Case*' (2006) 22 *SAJHR* 439; M du Plessis 'John Dugard and the continuing struggle for international human rights' (2010) 26 *SAJHR* 292 at 295. See, too, M Coombs '*Kaunda v President of the Republic of South Africa* Case CCT 23/04, 2004 (10) BCLR 1009' (2005) 99 *AJIL* 681; D Tladi and S Dlagnekova 'The act of state doctrine in South Africa: Has *Kaunda* settled a vexing question?' (2007) 22 *SA Public Law* 444.

African government to intervene diplomatically on behalf of a group of South African nationals who had been arrested in Zimbabwe, allegedly en route to Equatorial Guinea to assist in a coup to overthrow the government of that state. These nationals had been subjected to inhuman and degrading treatment in Zimbabwean prisons and had good cause to fear that they would be denied a fair trial and sentenced to death if extradited to Equatorial Guinea. The majority of the Court dismissed the application, both on the facts and out of deference to the executive in its conduct of foreign affairs. Although the Court, relying on *Barcelona Traction* and the failure of the proposal of the Special Rapporteur to the ILC to compel states to provide diplomatic protection, accepted that international law does not at present oblige states to provide diplomatic protection to its nationals, the majority judgment and the concurring and dissenting opinions recognised that in terms of the 1996 South African Constitution—premised as it is on a commitment to international human rights norms—there is *some* obligation on the part of the government to protect its nationals abroad. Chaskalson CJ, on behalf of the majority, declared that:

> There may . . . be a duty on government, consistent with its obligations under international law, to take action to protect one of its citizens against a gross abuse of international human rights norms. A request to government for assistance in such circumstances where the evidence is clear would be difficult, and in extreme cases possibly impossible to refuse. It is unlikely that such a request would ever be refused by government, but if it were, the decision would be justiciable and a court would order the government to take appropriate action.[158]

The Court stated that if a decision of government on diplomatic protection was irrational it would intervene. It continued:

> If government refuses to consider a legitimate request, or deals with it in bad faith or irrationally, a court could require government to deal with the matter properly. Rationality and bad faith are illustrations of grounds on which a court may be persuaded to review a decision.[159]

In a concurring opinion, Ngcobo J went further, stating that under the Constitution, 'the government has a constitutional duty to grant diplomatic protection to nationals abroad against violations or threatened violations of fundamental international human rights'.[160] In dissent, O'Regan J held that nationals have an 'entitlement to diplomatic protection'[161] and proposed that the government be ordered 'to take appropriate steps to provide diplomatic protection to

[158] *Kaunda* (n 157) para 69.
[159] Ibid para 80.
[160] Ibid para 210.
[161] Ibid para 238.

the applicants to seek to prevent the egregious violation of international human rights norms'.[162]

The question whether South Africa is obliged to provide diplomatic protection to a national was also raised in *Van Zyl v Government of the RSA*.[163] Here, it was argued that the South African government was obliged to exercise diplomatic protection on behalf of Van Zyl, a South African national, against Lesotho as a result of the confiscation of his property interests in Lesotho without compensation. Patel J, in the Transvaal Provincial Division, dismissed the claim, holding that neither international law nor the Constitution recognised a right to diplomatic protection in the circumstances of the case.[164] He distinguished the case from *Kaunda* on the ground that *Kaunda* had involved allegations of gross violations of international human rights, such as torture and physical abuse, whereas *Van Zyl* involved the expropriation of property, and international law does not recognise an international human right to protection of property.[165]

The Supreme Court of Appeal dismissed an appeal against this decision,[166] holding that the government was not entitled to exercise diplomatic protection as no international wrong had been proved, and that local remedies had not been exhausted.[167] At the same time, the Court endorsed *Kaunda* and held that the appellants had no right to diplomatic protection under South African law. 'Nationals have a right,' said the Court, 'to request government to consider diplomatic protection and government has a duty to consider it rationally.'[168]

Von Abo v Government of the Republic of South Africa[169] likewise involved a claim for diplomatic protection—in this case arising out of the expropriation of farms in Zimbabwe belonging to private companies and a trust controlled and owned by a South African national. After failure to obtain redress before the courts of Zimbabwe, Von Abo turned to the South African government for assistance but these requests fell on deaf ears. He therefore applied to court for an order that he had a right to diplomatic protection and that the government had failed rationally, appropriately and in good faith to consider his request for diplomatic protection. His claim was premised on the fact that as principal shareholder in the companies involved, he was entitled to diplomatic protection in terms of the

[162] Ibid para 271.
[163] 2005 (11) BCLR 1106 (T).
[164] Ibid paras 18–31, 64.
[165] Ibid paras 40–2.
[166] *Van Zyl v Government of the RSA* (n 100).
[167] Ibid paras 76, 81, 87–92.
[168] Ibid paras 6, 51–2.
[169] Supra (n 147).

exception contained in article 11(b) of the ILC Draft Articles on Diplomatic Protection (discussed above). Prinsloo J found that the government was guilty of an 'abject failure and dereliction of duty' and had 'done absolutely nothing' to assist Von Abo.[170] Although he accepted that customary international law did not recognise a right to diplomatic protection,[171] he found that *Kaunda* recognised that a court might exercise judicial review where the government had acted in bad faith or irrationally.[172] He therefore made an order declaring that the failure of the government 'to rationally, appropriately and in good faith' consider Von Abo's request for diplomatic protection was inconsistent with the Constitution, that he had a right to diplomatic protection and that the government was under an obligation to provide him with diplomatic protection in respect of the violation of his rights by the government of Zimbabwe. The government was then ordered to report within 60 days on what steps it had taken to secure redress for Von Abo.

After the Constitutional Court ruled that it was not necessary for it to confirm Prinsloo J's order,[173] Von Abo's application returned to the High Court to establish whether the government had complied with the Court's order. At this hearing, it appeared that the government—particularly the Department of Foreign Affairs—had done little to assist Von Abo. The Court held[174] that the 'feeble' and ineffective efforts made did not constitute proper protection and amounted to non-compliance with the Court's order.[175] Prinsloo J declared:

> The internationally recognised forms of diplomatic intervention have been designed to force offending states to toe the line. There is no room for an argument that diplomatic intervention becomes toothless, simply because the offending state exhibits no intention ever to co-operate. It is precisely under those circumstances when the recognised interventions come into play: the strength of the intervention depends on the level of resistance. South Africa is the powerhouse of the region. It is common knowledge that Zimbabwe is dependent on South Africa for almost every conceivable form of aid and assistance. I see no reason why the respondents cannot apply the necessary pressure, under these circumstances, to assist their valuable and long-suffering citizens, such as the applicant. In breach of their constitutional

[170] Ibid paras 91–2.

[171] Ibid para 137.

[172] Dire Tladi has argued that the *Von Abo* decision is inconsistent with *Kaunda*: 'The right to diplomatic protection, the *Von Abo* decision, and one big can of worms: Eroding the clarity of *Kaunda*' (2009) 20 *Stellenbosch LR* 14.

[173] *Von Abo v Government of the Republic of South Africa* 2009 (5) SA 345 (CC). Here, the Court held that diplomatic protection was the responsibility of the government as a whole and not of the President. Consequently, confirmation of Prinsloo J's order was unnecessary in terms of s 172(2)*(a)* of the South African Constitution.

[174] *Von Abo v Government of the Republic of South Africa* 2010 (3) SA 269 (GNP).

[175] Ibid 286–9.

duties, the respondents have refrained from affording such assistance for almost a decade.[176]

The Court held that the appropriate relief in the circumstances was damages arising out of the injury Von Abo had suffered as a result of the violation of his rights by the government of Zimbabwe. These damages were to be determined in a later hearing.

The appeal by the government against this decision to the Supreme Court of Appeal (SCA) succeeded.[177] The SCA held that Prinsloo J had erred in finding that Von Abo had a constitutional right to diplomatic protection as a result of the government's failure to rationally, appropriately and in good faith consider his request for diplomatic protection.[178] This finding is difficult to reconcile with the Court's own finding that 'this case is an example of how government, founded on a constitutional dispensation and a culture of human rights, is not supposed to treat its citizens and its courts'.[179] The Court went on to hold that Prinsloo J had erred in ordering the government to remedy the violation of Von Abo's rights by the Zimbabwe government in 60 days on the ground that such an order ignored the factual situation in Zimbabwe and was unrealistic in prescribing to the government 'the result their diplomatic protection should achieve' for Von Abo in such a limited time frame.[180] The Court stated that the order that the South Africa government pay damages to Von Abo for Zimbabwe's violation of his rights imposed a form of vicarious liability on the South African government. It added:

> It is . . . a completely foreign concept that one state should attract liability in terms of municipal law . . . vis-a-vis its own national for the wrongs of another state, committed by that state in another country vis-a vis the same individual. The only breach that could have occurred in the present case is that the appellants failed to comply with their duty vis-a-vis the respondent to act appropriately to his request for diplomatic protection . . . . The constitutional breach in this case, if there was one, could only have been a failure to have responded appropriately to the respondent's request for diplomatic protection.[181]

EXHAUSTION OF LOCAL REMEDIES

A state may not bring an international claim in respect of an injury to a national before the injured person has exhausted all local reme-

[176] Ibid 292.
[177] *Government of the Republic of South Africa v Von Abo* (n 148).
[178] Ibid para 24.
[179] Ibid para 39.
[180] Ibid para 29.
[181] Ibid paras 31, 33.

dies.[182] This rule was recognised by the International Court of Justice in the *Interhandel Case* as 'a well-established rule of customary international law'[183] and by a Chamber of the International Court in the *Elettronica Sicula (ELSI) Case* as 'an important principle of customary international law'.[184] The exhaustion of local remedies rule ensures that 'the State where the violation occurred should have an opportunity to redress it by its own means, within the framework of its own domestic system'.[185]

'Local remedies' means the remedies that are as of right open to natural or legal persons before the judicial or administrative courts or bodies, whether ordinary or special, of the state responsible for causing the injury.[186] Extra-legal remedies or remedies as of grace or favour do not qualify as remedies to be exhausted.[187] The remedies must, moreover, be available and effective both in theory and in practice.

It is not necessary to exhaust local remedies where there is direct injury to the plaintiff state. Where the claim is mixed, and involves both the direct interests of the state and the interests of its national, the court will apply a preponderance test.[188] In practice, it is often difficult to decide whether the claim is 'direct' or 'indirect' where it is 'mixed'. Many disputes before international courts have presented the phenomenon of the mixed claim. In the *Hostages Case*[189] the International Court found that the claim was preponderantly direct and there was therefore no need to exhaust local remedies where Iran had failed to protect American diplomats and consuls, who were at the same time American nationals. Conversely, in the *Interhandel Case*[190] the International Court found that the claim was preponderantly indirect where Switzerland claimed in the same matter for a direct wrong to itself arising out of a breach of treaty and for an indirect wrong resulting from an injury to a national corporation.

[182] See article 14(1) of the Draft Articles on Diplomatic Protection (n 102).

[183] 1959 ICJ Reports 6 at 27.

[184] 1989 ICJ Reports 15 at 42 (para 50).

[185] *Interhandel Case* (n 183) 27. In the *Ambatielos Claim* the arbitral tribunal declared that 'it is the whole system of legal protection, as provided by municipal law, which must have been put to the test': (1956) 12 RIAA 83 at 120. See further on this subject CF Amerasinghe *Local Remedies in International Law* 2 ed (2004); A Cançado Trindade *The Application of the Rule of Exhaustion of Local Remedies in International Law* (1983); *Van Zyl v Government of the RSA* (n 100) 320–2.

[186] Article 14(2) of ILC Draft Articles.

[187] *Diallo Case (Preliminary Objections)* (n 144) para 47.

[188] See article 14(3) of Draft Articles on Diplomatic Protection (n 102).

[189] *United States Diplomatic and Consular Staff in Tehran* (*US v Iran*) 1980 ICJ Reports 3.

[190] Supra (n 183).

Recently, in the *Avena Case*,[191] in which Mexico brought proceedings against the United States arising out of the maltreatment of Mexican nationals by the United States, the International Court found that it was not necessary to exhaust local remedies where the rights of the state and individual nationals were 'interdependent'.

Where the local remedies are futile or provide no reasonable possibility of effective redress, there is no need to attempt to exhaust them.[192] For instance, if the trial court rules against the alien on the *facts* and an appeal lies to a higher court only on a *question of law*, it is not necessary to exhaust appellate procedures.[193] One of the leading cases on this subject, the *Robert E Brown Claim*,[194] is of South African origin and had a major impact on South African history.

There was a serious constitutional debate in the South African Republic as to whether the laws of the Republic might be tested for validity against the Republic's Constitution (Grondwet). In 1897 in *Brown v Leyds NO*,[195] the precursor to the arbitral proceedings in the *Robert E Brown Claim*, the High Court finally ruled, after a careful examination of the doctrine of judicial review in the United States, that the Grondwet was the supreme law of the land, with the result that legislation enacted contrary to the procedures laid down in the Grondwet was null and void. The Court accordingly set aside executive proclamations and a resolution of the Volksraad, which purported to withdraw a number of mining claims asserted by Brown, an American mining engineer. This led to a confrontation between Chief Justice Kotzé and President Kruger, which culminated in the dismissal of Kotzé, the appointment of a new Chief Justice (R Gregorowski) and the repudiation by President and Volksraad of the 'so-called right of testing'.[196]

In these circumstances, Brown was advised by his counsel, JW Wessels (later to become Chief Justice of the Union of South Africa), that it was pointless to proceed with his claim for damages before the High Court as it was clearly hostile to him. Brown thus invoked the

[191] *Case Concerning Avena and Other Mexican Nationals (Mexico v USA)* 2004 ICJ Reports para 40. See, too, (2004) 43 *ILM* 581 at 599.

[192] See article 15(a) of Draft Articles on Diplomatic Protection (n 102).

[193] *Finnish Ships Arbitration (Finland v UK)* (1934) 3 RIAA 1479, (1933–4) 7 AD 231.

[194] *United States v Great Britain* (1923) 6 RIAA 120, (1923–4) 2 AD 35. See D van der Merwe *Brown v Leyds* (2017); J Dugard 'Toward racial justice in South Africa' in L Henkin and A Rosenthal (eds) *Constitutionalism and Rights: The Influence of the United States Constitution Abroad* (1990) 349 at 352–4; J Dugard *Human Rights and the South African Legal Order* (1978) 21–4.

[195] (1897) 4 Off Rep 17.

[196] For a history of this episode, see Van der Merwe (n 194); J Dugard 'Chief Justice versus President: Does the ghost of *Brown v Leyds NO* still haunt our judges?' 1981 *De Rebus* 421.

protection of his national state on the international plane. However, by the time international proceedings started, the South African Republic had been annexed by Britain, and the United States was obliged to make its claim against Britain as successor to the South African Republic. In proceedings before an arbitration tribunal, Britain raised two objections: first, that Brown had failed to exhaust local remedies by not continuing with his claim for damages before the High Court of the South African Republic, and, secondly, that Britain had not succeeded to the liabilities of the South African Republic arising out of its unlawful treatment of Brown. Although the tribunal ruled in favour of Britain on the second objection, and accordingly dismissed the claim, it rejected the argument that Brown had failed to exhaust local remedies, holding that 'the futility of further proceedings had been fully demonstrated, and that the advice of his counsel was amply justified'. It stressed that a claimant in a foreign state is not required to exhaust justice 'when there is no justice to exhaust'.[197]

The International Law Commission has included two additional species of 'futility' in Draft Article 15. Local remedies need not be exhausted where there is undue delay in the remedial process and where the injured person is 'manifestly precluded' from pursuing local remedies. They need also not be exhausted, in terms of article 15(c), when there is no relevant connection between the injured person and the state alleged to be responsible at the time of the injury. The purpose of the exhaustion of local remedies rule is to give the state in which the injured alien resides, carries on business or owns property an opportunity to provide redress through its own courts. Consequently, where the alien is involuntarily within the territory of the respondent state—or where he has been injured by transboundary environmental harm or some other wrongful act which occurred outside the territory of the respondent state—there is no need for local remedies to be exhausted. This situation is well illustrated by the *Aerial Incident*[198] case in which Israel, in claiming compensation from Bulgaria for the shooting down of an Israeli civilian aircraft over Bulgarian territory, maintained that the exhaustion of local remedies rule was inapplicable because the Israeli nationals killed in the shooting had no voluntary or deliberate connection with Bulgaria. A voluntary link or connection with the respondent state cannot be created by the unlawful act itself.

[197] *Robert E Brown Claim* (n 194) 129. This principle was applied in *Von Abo v Government of RSA* (n 147) paras 82–90.

[198] *Aerial Incident of 27 July 1955 (Israel v Bulgaria) (Preliminary Objections)*—oral Pleadings of Israel, International Court of Justice Pleadings 1959 at 531–2.

Local remedies need not be exhausted where the responsible state has waived compliance with this requirement.[199] Waiver of local remedies must not, however, be readily implied. In the *ELSI Case* a Chamber of the International Court of Justice stated that it was

> unable to accept that an important principle of customary international law should be held to have been tacitly dispensed with, in the absence of any words making clear an intention to do so.[200]

The burden of proof is generally on the respondent state to show that local remedies are available, while the burden of proof is generally on the applicant state to show that there are no effective remedies open to the injured person.[201]

1 Calvo Clause

Dr Calvo, an Argentine jurist, is credited with an ingenious device to obstruct diplomatic intervention by the Western powers. In response to the frequent diplomatic interventions by the Western powers in Latin America, the governments of these states inserted a clause in contracts between state and alien in which the latter agreed to confine himself to the available local remedies and to renounce diplomatic protection. The validity of the 'Calvo Clause' has been questioned by many states, including South Africa, on the ground that the national has no competence to renounce a right that attaches to the state and not to the national.[202]

THE IMPLEMENTATION OF DIPLOMATIC PROTECTION

Diplomatic protection may take the form of 'diplomatic action' or 'judicial proceedings'.[203] Diplomatic action will usually be initiated by an informal complaint by the protecting state or by formal protest, followed by negotiation. If negotiations fail, the protecting state may resort to judicial or arbitral proceedings if the respondent has

[199] Article 15(e) of Draft Articles on Diplomatic Protection (n 102).

[200] 1989 ICJ Reports at 42 (para 150). See M Adler 'The exhaustion of local remedies rule after the ICJ's decision in *ELSI*' (1990) 39 *ICLQ* 641.

[201] The question of burden of proof was considered by the Special Rapporteur in the Third Report on Diplomatic Protection A/CN.4/523 and Add 1 (2002) paras 102–18. The ILC decided not to include a draft article on this subject: *GAOR*, 57th Session, Supplement No 10 (A/57/10) paras 240–52.

[202] D Shea *The Calvo Clause* (1955) 46, 54 (for South Africa's statement on the subject in 1929); R Jennings and A Watts (eds) *Oppenheim's International Law* 9 ed (1992) vol 1 at 930. *North America Dredging Company v Government of* Mexico (1951) 4 UNRIAA 26. The Calvo Clause was considered by the Special Rapporteur in an addendum to the Third Report on Diplomatic Protection A/CN.4/523 Add 1 (2002). The ILC decided not to include a draft article on this subject: *GAOR*; 57th Session, Supplement No 10 (A/57/10) paras 253–73.

[203] See *Van Zyl v Government of the RSA* (n 100) 297.

consented to such proceedings. When there are many complaints involving injury to nationals, states may agree to establish a special arbitral tribunal to adjudicate these complaints. For instance, in 1981, Iran and the United States agreed to establish the Iran–United States Claims Tribunal to consider claims arising from injuries to Iranian and United States nationals in the political turmoil following the overthrow of the Shah of Iran in 1979.[204]

The protecting state may claim reparation from the respondent state in the form of restitution, compensation or satisfaction. In order to induce the respondent state to comply with its obligations, the claimant state may resort to non-forcible countermeasures, such as reprisals, retorsion, severance of diplomatic relations or economic pressure. On some occasions, states have taken forcible measures in order to protect the lives of their nationals abroad, and have sought to justify this as self-defence constituting the ultimate form of diplomatic protection. In 2000 the ILC rejected this argument and decided that the forcible rescue of nationals abroad could not be categorised as diplomatic protection.[205]

THE TREATMENT OF ALIENS[206]

An individual has no right of entry to a state of which she is not a national. If she is admitted, she may be expelled; but mistreatment is not permitted in the process of expulsion.[207] According to article 13 of the International Covenant on Civil and Political Rights, a person facing expulsion is entitled to submit reasons against her expulsion and to have her case reviewed by a competent authority 'except where compelling reasons of national security otherwise require'.[208] Moreover, according to a 1985 resolution of the General Assembly,[209] 'individual or collective expulsion of . . . aliens on grounds of race, colour, religion, culture, descent or national or ethnic origin is prohibited'. In 2014 the International Law Commission adopted a set

[204] (1981) 20 *ILM* 224.

[205] Report of the ILC, 52nd Session, *Yearbook of the International Law Commission* (2000) vol II, part 2 at 74–6 (paras 430–9) (Draft Article 2).

[206] RB Lillich (ed) *International Law of State Responsibility for Injuries to Aliens* (1983); CF Amerasinghe *State Responsibility for Injuries to Aliens* (1967); AV Freeman *The International Responsibility of States for Denial of Justice* (1938); EM Borchard *The Diplomatic Protection of Citizens Abroad* (1915); J Paulsson *Denial of Justice in International Law* (2005).

[207] *Boffolo Case* (1903) 10 RIAA 528; *Rankin v Iran* (1987) 82 ILR 204.

[208] In the *Diallo Case (Guinea v DRC)* (merits) the International Court held that Guinea had violated article 13 in expelling Mr Diallo (2010 ICJ Reports paras 64–74).

[209] Declaration on the Human Rights of Individuals who are not Nationals of the Country in which They Live, Resolution 144(XL) (1985). This resolution was referred to with approval by Friedman J in *Nyamakazi v President of Bophuthatswana* 1992 (4) SA 540 (B) 579G–H.

of Draft Articles on the Expulsion of Aliens,[210] which deals with the rights of a state to expel an alien, the rights of a person subject to expulsion and the procedures to be followed by a state in effecting an expulsion. While a state has the right to expel an alien,[211] a state must treat such a person with humanity and respect for his or her human rights[212] and without discrimination.[213] Collective expulsion is prohibited,[214] and an alien may not be expelled in order to circumvent an ongoing extradition procedure.[215] Provision is also made for procedural rights to be enjoyed by the alien in the process of expulsion.[216]

The right of a state to regulate the admission and removal of aliens within its territory has been asserted by southern African courts.[217] In addition, a number of cases reaffirm the obligation of the authorities to execute deportations in a humanitarian manner.[218] The principal statute governing the admission and expulsion of aliens is the Immigration Act 13 of 2002, which seeks to ensure that the deportation and exclusion of aliens is carried out with due regard for their human rights.[219] Special rules apply to the admission and the expulsion of refugees, which are examined in Chapter 16 below.

An individual admitted to residence in a foreign state may be subjected to certain restrictions to which citizens are not subject. She will usually be denied the right to vote, to hold public office and to be employed (without special permission). But, subject to restrictions of this kind, an alien must be treated decently, in accordance with civilised standards of behaviour. As Nugent JA stated in *Minister of Home Affairs v Watchenuka*, '[h]uman dignity has no nationality. It is inherent in all people—citizens and non-citizens alike—simply

[210] Report of the International Law Commission on its 66th Session A/69/10 at 10; General Assembly Resolution 69/119 of 18 December 2014. See further J Wojnowska-Radziska *The Right of an Alien to be Protected against Arbitrary Expulsion in International Law* (2015).

[211] Article 3.

[212] Articles 13, 16–20.

[213] Article 14.

[214] Article 9.

[215] Article 12.

[216] Articles 26–8.

[217] *Lewis v Minister of Internal Affairs* 1991 (3) SA 628 (B) 639B–F; *Tshwete v Minister of Home Affairs* 1986 (2) SA 240 (E) 243G–H; *Cabinet for the Territory of South West Africa v Chikane* 1989 (1) SA 349 (A) 369F–H, 389C; *Nyamakazi v President of Bophuthatswana* (n 209) 579F–G; *Maluleke v Minister of Internal Affairs* 1981 (1) SA 707 (B) 713; *Xu v Minister van Binnelandse Sake* 1995 (1) SA 185 (T) 192G–H, 193D–E.

[218] *S v Nyimbili; S v Mutembe* 1969 (2) SA 242 (N) (J Dugard 'Foreign affairs and international law' 1969 *Annual Survey* 48 at 62); *S v Mweetwa* 1972 (1) SA 40 (C) 43–4.

[219] See the preamble, para *(l)*; s 2(1); s 34(1)*(e)*. The Act was amended by Act 19 of 2004. See, too, *Lawyers for Human Rights v Minister of Home Affairs* 2004 (4) SA 125 (CC) paras 20, 26.

because they are human.'[220] The position was summarized by Friedman J in *Nyamakazi v President of Bophuthatswana*[221] as follows:

> The international standard relating to the treatment of aliens postulates that if a state admits an alien into its territory, it must conform in its treatment of him to the internationally determined standard. This means that the state should accord treatment to the alien which measures up to the ordinary standards of civilization. The international standard of treatment of aliens applies in respect of fundamental human rights such as the right to life and integrity of persons but not to political rights, in respect of which an alien can only expect equality of treatment or even less than equality with that accorded to the state's own nationals .... There is also a rule of international law which provides that a state may impose restrictions upon the exercise of certain rights by aliens admitted into its territory. A state may thus, therefore, impose restrictions upon the participation by aliens in political or public life, ownership of property by aliens or upon their taking employment.

There is a dispute among states over the standard of treatment to be accorded to aliens. While some (mainly developing states) argue that the standard is a national one, requiring states to treat aliens as well as they treat their own nationals, others (mainly developed states) maintain that there is an international minimum standard, which accords to aliens a higher standard of treatment where the national standard fails to meet international standards. The difference is illustrated by the *Roberts Claim*.[222] Roberts, an American national, was held without trial in Mexico for seven months, in a small cell, together with 30 or 40 Mexicans. Ventilation was poor, sanitary and ablution arrangements primitive, food scarce and coarse, and exercise denied. When sued by the United States for its treatment of Roberts, Mexico responded that he was treated in the same way as his fellow Mexican prisoners. In upholding the claim of the United States, an international tribunal stated:

> Facts with respect to equality of treatment of aliens and nationals may be important in determining the merits of a complaint of mistreatment of an alien. But such equality is not the ultimate test of the propriety of the acts of

[220] 2004 (4) SA 326 (SCA) para 25.

[221] 1992 (4) SA 540 (B) 579C–E. See, too, *Baloro and Others v University of Bophuthatswana* 1995 (4) SA 197 (B) 247E–G. Here, Friedman JP held that the University had violated the constitutional prohibition on discrimination by refusing to promote the applicants because they were not South African nationals. In *Minister of Home Affairs v Watchenuka* (n 220) the Supreme Court of Appeal acknowledged restrictions might be imposed on the right of aliens to choose an occupation (paras 30–1) but not to study (para 36). In *Mahlaule v Minister of Social Development* 2004 (6) SA 505 (CC) the Constitutional Court accepted that, while aliens with permanent residence rights are not entitled to political rights, they are for other purposes (including social benefits) 'in much the same position as citizens' (para 59).

[222] *US v Mexico* (1926) 4 RIAA 77, (1925–6) 3 AD 227.

> authorities in the light of international law. The test is, broadly speaking, whether aliens are treated in accordance with ordinary standards of civilization.[223]

Today, it is accepted that the standard of treatment to be accorded to aliens in respect of their personal rights is an international one, the content of which is to be found in international human rights instruments and customary international law. In the *Diallo Case* the International Court of Justice stated:

> Owing to the substantive development of international law over recent decades in respect of the rights it accords to individuals, the scope *ratione materiae* of diplomatic protection, originally limited to alleged violations of the minimum standard of treatment of aliens, has subsequently widened to include, inter alia, internationally guaranteed human rights.[224]

The content of the international minimum standard in respect of the property rights of aliens is less clear. Indeed, in some quarters the very existence of an internationally accepted standard is disputed.

1 The personal rights of aliens

In 1985 the United Nations General Assembly adopted a Declaration on the Human Rights of Individuals who are not Nationals of the Country in which They Live,[225] which recognises that the human rights expounded in the Universal Declaration of Human Rights and other international instruments should 'also be ensured for individuals who are not nationals of the country in which they live'. Although it is difficult to contend that all the rights of aliens expounded in the 1985 Declaration form part of the minimum standard under customary law, it is clear that those provisions of the Universal Declaration of Human Rights that have become part of international customary law are part of the international minimum standard for the treatment of the persons of aliens. These principles include non-discrimination on grounds of race, the prohibition of torture and of inhuman or degrading treatment or punishment, and the right to a fair trial. In considering the question of whether an alien has been mistreated, international tribunals may accordingly turn to the jurisprudence of human rights tribunals for guidance. In this way, the international minimum standard for the treatment of aliens and the human rights standards for the treatment of a state's own nationals have merged. This was acknowledged by the International Court of Justice in the *Diallo Case* when it declared that the scope of diplomatic protection 'originally limited to alleged violations of the minimum standard of

[223] (1926) 4 RIAA 80.
[224] *Diallo Case (Preliminary Objections)* (n 144) para 39.
[225] Resolution 144 (XL).

aliens, has subsequently widened to include, *inter alia*, internationally guaranteed human rights'.[226]

The international minimum standard is of particular importance in respect of the administration of criminal justice. It is also in this area that there is most consensus on the treatment of aliens. Aliens must be permitted consular visits before trial,[227] must not be subjected to inhuman prison conditions,[228] must be given counsel of their choice,[229] must be brought to trial within a reasonable period of time[230] and must be tried in accordance with fair trial standards.

The right of an alien who has been arrested or detained to be visited by a consular officer of his state of nationality has been codified by the Vienna Convention on Consular Relations of 1963,[231] which obliges states to inform 'without delay' arrested aliens of their right to be visited by and communicate with consular officials of their state of nationality, who may arrange for their legal representation. In two cases the International Court of Justice found the United States to be in breach of this obligation when it failed to inform arrested aliens of their rights to consular access and they were subsequently tried without proper counsel, convicted and sentenced to death. In *La Grand*[232] and *Avena*,[233] Germany and Mexico, respectively, successfully brought legal proceedings against the United States in terms of the Optional Protocol to the Vienna Convention, which confers jurisdiction on the International Court in respect of disputes relating to the application of the Convention. (The United States has since withdrawn from the Optional Protocol to avoid further proceedings being brought against it.) In the *Diallo Case (Guinea v DRC)* (merits) the International Court likewise found that the DRC had violated its obligation to inform the consular authorities of Guinea of Mr Diallo's arrest.[234]

[226] *Diallo Case (Preliminary Objections)* (n 144) 599.

[227] *Chevreau Claim (France v UK)* (1931) 2 RIAA 1113 at 1123 and (1933) 27 *AJIL* 153 at 160.

[228] *Roberts Claim* (n 222).

[229] *Pope Case* in MM Whiteman *Digest of International Law* (1967) vol 8 at 709.

[230] *Roberts Claim* (n 222).

[231] Article 36(1).

[232] *Germany v USA* 2001 ICJ Reports 466, (2001) 40 *ILM* 1069; noted in (2002) 96 *AJIL* 210.

[233] *Mexico v USA* 2004 ICJ Reports 12, (2004) 43 *ILM* 581; noted in (2004) 98 *AJIL* 559. See, too, A Künzli 'Case concerning Mexican nationals' (2005) 18 *Leiden Journal of International Law* 49; GN Barrie 'Reaction of USA courts to the *Avena* judgment' (2006) 31 *SAYIL* 287.

[234] 2010 ICJ Reports paras 90–7. See further A Vermeer-Künzli 'The ICJ and the *Diallo Case*' (2011) 24 *Leiden Journal of International Law* 607.

2 Diplomatic protection and human rights

Diplomatic protection is today an important feature of the arsenal of instruments and procedures designed to protect human rights. It complements human rights instruments of the kind examined in Chapter 15 by providing an effective remedy for the protection of the human rights of aliens. Some argue that diplomatic protection has been replaced by human rights instruments which provide for the protection of both nationals and aliens against oppressive regimes and grant the individual direct access to an international court or monitoring body.[235] Unfortunately, this is only half the truth. Human rights instruments, generally, are weak in remedies. Moreover, not all states are parties to these instruments. This means that diplomatic protection, a procedure recognised by customary international law and binding upon all states, and one that provides for reparation in the form of compensation, restitution and other means of satisfaction, is, if used, a more effective instrument for the redress of human rights violations. There can be little doubt that a claim brought by a government demanding reparation for injury to a national is more effective than individual recourse to an international human rights monitoring body. This explains why nationals injured abroad in the first instance generally appeal to their national state for assistance rather than to the protection afforded by a human rights instrument.[236]

In the final resort, diplomatic protection advances not only the rights of the nationals of the claimant state but also the rights of other aliens in the defendant state and even of the nationals of that state. For by asserting the human rights of its own nationals in a foreign state that oppresses human rights, the protecting state sends out a clear message to that state that its conduct is contrary to international law and must cease.

3 The property rights of aliens—with special reference to expropriation of property[237]

A state incurs responsibility for injury to the property of an alien as well as to her person. If a state arbitrarily confiscates the property of

[235] Tladi (n 172) 29.

[236] R Lillich 'The diplomatic protection of nationals abroad: An elementary principle of international law under attack' (1975) 69 *AJIL* 359.

[237] F Visser 'The principle of permanent sovereignty over national resources and the nationalization of foreign interests' (1988) 21 *CILSA* 76; SKB Asante 'International law and foreign investment: A reappraisal' (1988) 37 *ICLQ* 588; R Higgins 'The taking of property by the state: Recent developments in international law' (1982–3) 176 *Recueil des Cours* 259; R Lillich (ed) *The Valuation of Nationalized Property in International Law* 4 vols (1972–87); G White *Nationalization of Foreign Property* (1961); P Norton 'A law of the future or a law of the past? Modern tribunals and the international law of expropriation' (1991) 85 *AJIL* 474; J Murphy 'Compensation for nationalization in

an alien without paying compensation, it is liable for violation of the international minimum standard. Difficulties arise, however, when an alien's property is seized as part of a policy of nationalisation of the resources of a state, particularly where the 'taking' is on a grand scale involving the nationalisation of an entire industry, such as the oil industry. Here, ideological differences between capitalist and socialist states, historical differences between erstwhile colonial powers and decolonised states, and economic differences between developed and developing states preclude consensus on the rules of state responsibility. While the former group of states insists on an international standard to govern the expropriation of alien property, the latter claims that this matter is governed entirely by the national law of the taking state. This area of law therefore remains unsettled.

There is agreement that international law does not prohibit the expropriation of alien property. Disagreement, however, exists as to the conditions that must be fulfilled to prevent it from becoming unlawful. Traditional international law, as formulated by capital-exporting states, insists that there is an international minimum standard requiring an expropriation to be non-discriminatory, for a public purpose, and accompanied by prompt, adequate and effective compensation. This rule, however, has been brought into question by a number of resolutions of the General Assembly.

The Resolution on Permanent Sovereignty over Natural Resources 1803 (XVII) of 1962 recognises some of these requirements, but in a weaker form, by declaring that:

> Nationalization, expropriation or requisitioning shall be based on grounds or reasons of public utility, security or the national interest which are recognised as overriding purely individual or private interests, both domestic and foreign. In such cases the owner shall be paid appropriate compensation in accordance with the rules in force in the state taking such measures in the exercise of its sovereignty and in accordance with international law. In any case where the question of compensation gives rise to a controversy, the national jurisdiction of the state taking such measures shall be exhausted. However, upon agreement by sovereign states and other parties concerned, settlement of the dispute should be made through arbitration or international adjudication.[238]

This resolution was adopted by 87 votes to 2, with 12 abstentions.[239] France and South Africa were the two dissentient states.

international law' (1993) 110 *SALJ* 79; N Schrijver *Sovereignty over Natural Resources* (1997). See further *Van Zyl v Government of the RSA* (n 163) paras 36–40.

[238] Paragraph 4.

[239] The Soviet bloc, Burma, Cuba and Ghana.

Less accommodating to the interests of developed states is the Charter of Economic Rights and Duties of States, contained in Resolution 3281 (XXIX) of 1974.[240] It declares that each state has the right

> [t]o nationalize, expropriate or transfer ownership of foreign property in which case appropriate compensation should be paid by the state adopting such measures, taking into account its relevant laws and regulations and all circumstances that the state considers pertinent. In any case where the question of compensation gives rise to a controversy, it shall be settled by the domestic law of the nationalizing state and by its tribunals, unless it is freely and mutually agreed by all states concerned that other peaceful means be sought on the basis of the sovereign equality of states and in accordance with the principle of free choice of means.

This resolution was adopted by 120 votes to 6, with 10 abstentions. (In 1974 South Africa was excluded from the General Assembly: hence its absence from the dissentient votes.)

A number of arbitration awards have found that Resolution 1803 (XVII), which retains the international law standard, and not Resolution 3281 (XXIX), accurately reflects customary international law. In *Texaco v Libya*[241] the sole arbitrator, Professor Dupuy, held that the voting on Resolution 1803 (XVII) indicated that it was supported by 'a majority of states belonging to the various representative groups' and was to a large extent 'the expression of a real general will', while the relevant paragraph in Resolution 3281 (XXIX) 'must be analysed as a political rather than a legal declaration concerned with the ideological strategy of development and, as such, supported only by non-industrialized states'. Moreover, ' [t]he absence of any connection between the procedure of compensation and international law and the subjection of this procedure solely to municipal law cannot be regarded by this Tribunal except as a *de lege ferenda* formulation, which even appears *contra legem* in the eyes of many developed countries'.[242]

It is difficult to state with certainty what remnants of the traditional rule can be salvaged from these developments. First, it is accepted that the expropriation must be for a proper public purpose, as is

[240] Paragraph 2(2)(c). This resolution is supported by General Assembly Resolution 3171 (XXVIII) of 1973, and the Declaration on the Establishment of a New International Economic Order contained in Resolution 3201(S-VI) of 1974. See further on Resolution 3281 (XXIX), BH Weston 'The Charter of Economic Rights and Duties of States and deprivation of foreign-owned wealth' (1981) 75 *AJIL* 437.

[241] (1978) 17 *ILM* 1, (1977) 53 ILR 389.

[242] Paragraphs 87–8. See, too, the awards in the *Aminoil Case (Kuwait v American Independent Oil Co)* (1982) 21 *ILM* 976 paras 90, 143–4 and the *Amoco Case (US v Iran)* (1988) 27 *ILM* 1314 para 116.

recognised by Resolution 1803(XVII).[243] However, '[i]t is clear that, as a result of the modern acceptance of the right to nationalize, this term is broadly interpreted, and that states, in practice, are granted extensive discretion'.[244] Secondly, although not specifically mentioned in Resolution 1803 (XVII), the requirement of non-discrimination also appears to remain part of customary international law.[245] Thirdly, international law continues to require the payment of compensation, but the standard to be employed for determining this compensation is unsettled.

It seems clear that the traditional requirement enunciated by United States Secretary of State Cordell Hull in 1938, namely that the compensation be 'prompt, adequate, and effective', is no longer accepted by international law. Although the United States executive and legislative branches still cling to this formula,[246] its judiciary has expressed doubts about the validity of this rule.[247] Today, the standard of 'appropriate' compensation—the phrase employed by Resolution 1803 (XXII)—seems to enjoy the greatest support and has been approved by several arbitral awards.[248] 'Appropriate' compensation will certainly be less than 'prompt, adequate, and effective' compensation, but it has no fixed meaning of its own and will depend upon the circumstances of each case. Thus, in the *Aminoil Case*, the tribunal found that in order to arrive at an 'appropriate' compensation it was necessary to have regard to all the circumstances of the case with special reference to the legitimate expectations of the parties.[249]

Disputes over the expropriation of alien-owned property are often resolved by the states concerned on the basis of 'lump-sum settlements'. In terms of such agreements, the defendant state agrees to pay the plaintiff state a 'lump-sum' in full satisfaction of the claims by the nationals of the plaintiff state. The latter state then distributes the settlement sum among its national claimants.

[243] *Amoco v Iran* (n 242) paras 113, 145–6; *BP Case (UK v Libya)* (1974) 53 ILR 297 at 329. *Sed contra* the *Liamco Case (Libyan American Oil Co v Libya)* (1981) 20 *ILM* 1 at 58–9.

[244] *Amoco v Iran* (n 242) para 145.

[245] *Liamco Case* (n 243) 58–9; *Amoco Case* (n 242) paras 140–2.

[246] See the statement by DR Robinson, Legal Adviser to the Department of State, in (1984) 78 *AJIL* 176.

[247] *Banco Nacional de Cuba v Sabbatino* 376 US 398 (1964) 428–9; *Banco Nacional de Cuba v Chase Manhattan Bank* 658 F 2d 875 at 892 (2nd Cir 1981). See further O Schachter 'Compensation for expropriation' (1984) 78 *AJIL* 121.

[248] *Aminoil Case* (n 242) paras 143–4; *Texaco* case (n 241) para 88. In *Van Zyl v Government of the RSA* (n 100) the Court formulated the test as 'prompt and adequate compensation' (315).

[249] Paragraphs 144–9 (n 242).

Invariably, such a valuation is below the value of the assets concerned and less than adequate compensation.

4 State contracts[250]

States enter into contracts with aliens on a great variety of matters, ranging from contracts for the sale of goods or services to agreements for the exploitation, development and marketing of mineral resources. The latter agreements, known as concession or economic development agreements, play an important role in contemporary international society, as they bring to developing countries investments and technical assistance.[251] On the other hand, they require a substantial initial financial commitment from the alien investor, as they generally involve the construction of permanent installations for the exploitation of the resource in question. For this reason, these agreements will normally seek to provide some guarantee against the risk of nationalisation.

Concession agreements are not treaties because only one contracting party is a state. Consequently, the prevalent view is that a breach of the agreement per se does not incur the responsibility of the state party.[252] When, however, this breach is accompanied by expropriation of the assets of the alien corporation, the state party becomes liable in accordance with the principles of law governing responsibility for expropriation.

Foreign investors generally seek to ensure that the concession agreement protects them against breach of the agreement and expropriation of the assets of the corporation. The methods employed to achieve this purpose have produced great controversy.[253]

First, concession agreements often contain a choice of law clause, which excludes the operation of the municipal law of the host state and substitutes for it a non-municipal system of law such as the 'general principles of law recognised by civilized nations'.[254] Clauses

[250] There is a considerable body of literature on this subject. See in particular CF Amerasinghe 'State breaches of contracts with aliens and international law' (1964) 58 *AJIL* 881; AA Fatouros 'International law and the international contract' (1980) 74 *AJIL* 134; J Kuusi *The Host State and the Transnational Corporation* (1979); FA Mann 'State contracts and state responsibility' (1960) 54 *AJIL* 572; see further *Van Zyl v Government of the RSA* (n 163) para 27.

[251] *Texaco v Libya* (n 241) para 45; *Aminoil Case* (1982) 21 *ILM* 976 paras 97–8.

[252] I Brownlie *Principles of Public International Law* 7 ed (2008) 547. However, RY Jennings has argued that a breach of a state contract gives rise to state responsibility: 'State contracts in international law' (1961) 37 *BYIL* 156.

[253] For a discussion of some of these awards, see C Greenwood 'State contracts in international law—The Libyan arbitrations' (1982) 53 *BYIL* 27.

[254] AD McNair 'The general principles of law recognised by civilized nations' (1957) 33 *BYIL* 1.

of this kind are generally vague as the contracting state is usually unwilling to abandon its own legal system altogether. Thus, the concession agreement between Libya and Texaco, which featured in the *Texaco* case, provided:

> This concession shall be governed by and interpreted in accordance with the principles of law of Libya common to the principles of international law and in the absence of such common principles then by and in accordance with the general principles of law, including such of those principles as may have been applied by international tribunals.[255]

Such clauses, which serve to 'internationalise' an agreement and to remove it from the law of the host state in the event of repudiation, have been held to be lawful by international tribunals.[256] The legal system applied in such cases is a blend of the principles of treaty law and the general principles of contract law and public law recognised in municipal legal systems.[257]

A concession agreement will usually contain an arbitration clause to remove the hearing of any dispute relating to the agreement from the courts of the host state. Such clauses are accepted as valid.[258]

The most controversial contractual device employed in a concession agreement is the 'stabilisation clause', which seeks to prevent the host state from annulling the concession agreement by municipal legislation—particularly by nationalisation legislation. Thus, in the *Aminoil Case,* Kuwait agreed not to annul the agreement 'by general or special legislation or by administrative measures or by any other act whatever' for 60 years.[259]

Although the arbitrator in *Texaco* held that a general stabilisation clause of this kind might prohibit expropriation,[260] the arbitrators in the *Aminoil Case* held that such a clause imposes such severe restraints on the right of a state to exploit its own natural resources that it could not be interpreted to prohibit nationalisation unless it expressly so stated and the period of restriction was of limited

[255] *Texaco v Libya* (n 241).

[256] Ibid para 42. In *Van Zyl v Government of the RSA* (n 100) the Court rejected the appellant's claim that his mining contract with the government of Lesotho had been 'internationalized' (315–17).

[257] Greenwood (n 253) 45–50.

[258] *Texaco v Libya* (n 241) para 44. In *Van Zyl v Government of the RSA* (n 163) the Court held that the absence of such a clause indicated that the agreement was not 'internationalized': paras 27–8, 34, 69, 75, 78.

[259] Paragraph 88 (n 242). The concession agreement in the *Texaco* case (n 241) contained a stabilisation clause valid for 50 years.

[260] Paragraph 73 (n 241).

duration.[261] This latter view enjoys greater support[262] than the *Texaco* decision, as it accords more closely with developments in the law of nationalisation reflected in resolutions of the General Assembly.

Clauses of the above kind are not popular with developing states. Where their bargaining power permits, they insist that concession agreements are to be subjected to the law and courts of the host state.

5 Unlawful nationalisations before foreign municipal courts

If a state nationalises the property of an alien[263] in a manner contrary to international law and sells the confiscated property to a buyer in a foreign state, may the previous owner whose property has been unlawfully seized bring an action in a foreign municipal court to recover the property? Today the weight of authority is against such an action. In rejecting the claim of an American national to sugar confiscated without compensation by the Cuban government, the United States Supreme Court held in *Banco Nacional de Cuba v Sabbatino*[264] that 'the Judicial Branch will not examine the validity of a taking of property within its own territory by a foreign sovereign government, extant and recognised by this country . . . even if the complaint alleges that the taking violates customary international law'.[265] Civil-law systems have reached the same conclusion by applying the *lex rei sitae* to determine the title to the property.[266]

English courts have adopted an approach similar to that of the United States Supreme Court and have held that they will not review the acts of foreign states, including nationalisations, undertaken within their own territories.[267] There is support for the American 'act of state' doctrine expressed in *Sabbatino*[268] and the English doctrine of restraint contained in *Buttes Gas Oil Co v Hammer*[269] in *Swissborough Diamond Mines (Pty) Ltd v Government of the Republic of South Africa*.[270]

[261] Paragraphs 95–102 (n 242). Sir Gerald Fitzmaurice in his separate opinion expressed support for the *Texaco* decision on this issue.

[262] See *Liamco Case (Libyan American Oil Co v Libya)* 62 ILR 140 at 197 (also reported in (1981) 20 *ILM* 1).

[263] This situation is distinguishable from that in *Luther v Sagor* [1921] 3 KB 532 on the ground that the confiscation in that case involved a Russian national and, therefore, did not constitute a violation of international law.

[264] 376 US 398 (1964).

[265] At 428. This ruling was later reversed by Congress in the second Hickenlooper Amendment. For a history of this matter, see DP O'Connell *International Law* 2 ed (1970) vol 2 at 799–802.

[266] O'Connell (n 265) 807–9.

[267] *Buttes Gas and Oil Co v Hammer* [1981] 3 All ER 616 (HL) 628–32; *Williams & Humbert Ltd v W & H Trade Marks (Jersey) Ltd* [1986] 1 All ER 129 at 135–7. *Sed contra*, see *Anglo-Iranian Oil Co Ltd v Jaffrate* [1953] 1 WLR 246.

[268] Supra (n 264).

[269] Supra (n 267).

[270] 1999 (2) SA 279 (T) 330–5.

6 Alternative procedures for the protection of investment and the settlement of investment disputes[271]

The regime of diplomatic protection has not proved to be popular with investors who prefer an investment regime that gives direct access to international arbitration, avoids the uncertainty inherent in the discretionary nature of diplomatic protection, and dispenses with the strict conditions for the exercise of diplomatic protection. Consequently, diplomatic protection in the field of investment has to a large extent been replaced by multilateral and bilateral treaties. In the *Diallo Case (Preliminary Objections)* the International Court of Justice declared:

> In contemporary international law, the protection of the rights of companies and the rights of their shareholders, and the settlement of the associated disputes, are essentially governed by bilateral or multilateral agreements for the protection of foreign investments, such as the treaties for the promotion and protection of foreign investments, and the Washington Convention of 18 March 1965 on the Settlement of Investment Disputes between States and Nationals of Other States, which created an International Centre for Settlement of Investment Disputes (ICSID), and also by contracts between States and foreign investors. In that context, the role of diplomatic protection somewhat faded, as in practice recourse is only made to it in rare cases where treaty regimes do not exist or have proved inoperative.[272]

The Convention on the Settlement of Investment Disputes between States and the Nationals of Other States of 1965[273] establishes an International Centre for the Settlement of Investment Disputes (ICSID) to settle disputes between contracting states and nationals of contracting states, provided both parties consent to submit the dispute to the Centre.[274]

South Africa is not a party to the ICSID Convention, which has 153 contracting states, including most of South Africa's neighbouring states. The reasons for South Africa's failure to become a party to ICSID received substantial attention in *Von Abo v Government of the Republic of South Africa*[275] as the applicant had requested the South African government to become a party to ICSID to enable him to pursue a claim for compensation against the government of Zimbabwe (a contracting state to ICSID) arising out of the seizure of his

[271] S Subedi *International Investment Law: Reconciling Policy and Principle* 3 ed (2016); JW Salacuse *The Law of Investment Treaties* (2015); Z Douglas, J Pauwelyn and JE Vinuales (eds) *The Foundations of International Investment* Law (2014); R Dolzer and CS Schreuer *Principles of Investment Law* (2008); C McLachlan, L Shore and M Weiniger *International Investment Arbitration: Substantive Principles* (2007).

[272] *Diallo Case (Preliminary Objections)* (n 144) para 88.

[273] (1965) 4 *ILM* 532. See WM Tupman 'Case studies in the jurisdiction of ICSID' (1986) 35 *ICLQ* 813; C Schreuer *The ICSID Convention: A Commentary* (2001).

[274] See further the section on 'international investment agreements' in Chapter 21.

[275] Supra (n 147) paras 16, 26–42.

farms in that country. No reasons were given for this refusal to become a party to ICSID despite a strong recommendation in favour of such action by the South African Law Commission in 1998. This decision was taken into account by Prinsloo J in considering whether the government had behaved irrationally in refusing diplomatic protection to Von Abo.

The Multilateral Investment Guarantee Agency (MIGA) was established in 1985 to provide insurance cover against non-commercial risks in respect of foreign investment, including 'expropriation and similar measures . . . which has the effect of depriving the holder of a guarantee of his ownership or control or a substantial benefit from his investment'.[276] MIGA is affiliated to the World Bank. (South Africa is a party to MIGA and has accorded immunities to the Agency in South Africa.[277])

Today foreign investment is largely regulated and protected by bilateral investment treaties (BITs).[278] The number of BITs has grown considerably in recent years and it is estimated that there are about 3 000 such agreements in existence. BITs typically aim to promote foreign investment through the provision of a variety of substantive legal protections to international investors.[279] An important feature of the BIT is its procedure for the settlement of investment disputes. Most BITs provide for the direct settlement of the investment dispute between the investor and the host state, before either an ad hoc tribunal or a tribunal established by ICSID.[280] The dispute settlement procedures provided for in BITs and ICSID offer greater advantages to the foreign investor than the customary international law system of diplomatic protection, as they give the investor direct access to international arbitration and they avoid the political uncertainty inherent in the discretionary nature of diplomatic protection.

Between 1994 and 2009, South Africa entered into several BITs with other states. However, South Africa has subsequently reconsidered the use of BITs in its international investment regime (terminating

[276] See article 11 of the Convention Establishing the Multilateral Investment Guarantee Agency (1989) 28 *ILM* 1233. See further SK Chatterjee 'The Convention establishing MIGA' (1987) 36 *ICLQ* 76.

[277] Proclamation 47 *GG* 15588 of 19 March 1994.

[278] This was acknowledged by the International Court of Justice in the *Barcelona Traction* case (n 86) para 90. See further Chapter 21. See, too, J Kokott *International Report of the Role of Diplomatic Protection in the Field of the Protection of Foreign Investment* (Report of the 70th Conference, International Law Association, New Delhi, 2002) 259; EC Schlemmer 'Bilateral investment treaties, protection of shareholders, and ICSID' (2003) 28 *SAYIL* 292.

[279] See further the section on 'international investment agreements' in Chapter 21.

[280] BITs may also provide for the settlement of investment disputes by means of arbitration between the state of nationality of the investor (corporation or shareholder) and the host state over the interpretation or application of the BIT.

some of its earliest BITs, and introducing investment protection legislation aimed at substituting BIT investment protection). South Africa has also maintained its decision to remain a non-member of ICSID.[281]

[281] See further the sections on 'South Africa's international investment regime' and 'the Protection of Investment Act' in Chapter 21.

CHAPTER 14

Responsibility of International Organisations

Arnold Pronto

International organisations, as subjects of international law, are also capable of committing internationally wrongful acts, thereby incurring international responsibility. The position of international organisations was excluded from the scope of the Draft Articles on State Responsibility, which included the following saving clause:

> These articles are without prejudice to any question of the responsibility under international law of an international organization, or of any State for the conduct of an international organization.[1]

This provision not only preserved the question of the responsibility of international organisations, but also explicitly recognised that the Draft Articles on State Responsibility were incomplete as regarding the responsibility of states that may arise in the context of the conduct of international organisations.

Shortly after the adoption of the Draft Articles on State Responsibility, the International Law Commission (ILC) decided, in 2002, to embark on a second phase of its consideration of the broader topic of international responsibility, this time focusing on the 'responsibility of international organizations'. In 2011 the ILC adopted the Draft Articles on the Responsibility of International Organizations.[2]

Such a two-step approach to the consideration of the topic mirrored the pattern of work followed by the ILC in its consideration of the law of treaties. There a basic distinction had also been drawn between the law regulating treaties between states, and that pertaining to treaties to which international organisations were contracting parties.[3] This distinction recognises that the nature and activities of international organisations raise complex issues of law and policy which cannot easily be dealt with in a text dedicated primarily to the actions of states. Moreover, a continuing problem is the relative

[1] Article 57.

[2] Report of the International Law Commission (2011) *GAOR* 66th Session, Supplement No 10 (A/66/10 and Add 1) para 87.

[3] See Vienna Convention on the Law of Treaties of 1969; and Vienna Convention on the Law of Treaties between States and International Organizations or between International Organizations of 1986.

paucity of international practice concerning the law regulating the activities of international organisations, which presents difficulties for the codification of applicable rules pertaining to the actions of international organisations.[4]

The solution found was for the ILC to draw upon the rules developed for the responsibility of states by way of analogy. This was done on the basic assumption that such rules largely reflect legal propositions not applicable only to states, but also to other subjects of international law. Hence, the Draft Articles on the Responsibility of International Organizations closely follow the structure of the Draft Articles on State Responsibility, with a number of provisions having been transposed verbatim from that text with the necessary modifications. Accordingly, some of the considerations with regard to state responsibility discussed in Chapter 13 also apply, *mutatis mutandis*, to that of the responsibility of international organisations. At the same time, the ILC included a number of provisions unique to the legal position of international organisations.

INTERNATIONAL LEGAL PERSONALITY

The events surrounding the death of Count Bernadotte in Palestine in 1947[5] led to the recognition of the separate legal personality of the United Nations *qua* international organisation, and accordingly the recognition that the class of recognised subjects of international law was not limited to states.

The Draft Articles on the Responsibility of International Organizations are premised on the existence of separate international legal personality. Without such legal recognition, an international organisation is juridically indistinguishable from its members and would not enjoy the capacity to enter into international agreements in its own right, or be able to commit wrongs (delicts) as a matter of international law. Any agreements entered into by it (or wrongs committed by it) would be undertaken in the capacity of 'agent' of the member states, and attributable to them (under the Draft Articles on State Responsibility). It is exactly because international organisations enjoying international personality can incur responsibility separately from their member states that there was a need to develop a distinct set of rules governing such responsibility.

It must be borne in mind, however, that the International Court in the *Reparation for Injuries* advisory opinion qualified its holding with

[4] Moreover, given that few international tribunals enjoy jurisdiction over the actions of international organisations, a large proportion of the (relatively few) judicial pronouncements on the topic emanate from national courts.

[5] See above Chapter 1 at 1.

the general observation that 'subjects of law in any legal system are not necessarily identical in their nature *or in the extent of their rights*, and their nature depends on the needs of the community'.[6] This is the case with international organisations which, contrary to states, do not have a general competence under international law,[7] but instead possess the capacity at the international level to carry out the rights and duties necessary to fulfil the mandates and functions demarcated in their respective foundational documents or 'constituent instruments' (for example, the Charter of the United Nations). As the International Court had occasion to hold a few decades later:

> International organisations are governed by the 'principle of speciality', that is to say, they are invested by the States which create them with powers, the limits of which are a function of the common interests whose promotion those States entrust to them.[8]

DEFINITION OF AN INTERNATIONAL ORGANISATION

International organisations can be defined in at least one of three ways:

1 By analysing their composition

Traditionally the concept of 'international organisation' was synonymous with 'intergovernmental organisation', ie an organisation established by states and whose members are states. This was the approach taken by the ILC in its earlier work on international organisations.[9] It still remains the case that many (if not most) international organisations are intergovernmental in nature. Nonetheless, the ILC recognised that international organisations are not necessarily exclusively established by states and that there are organisations that open their membership to non-state entities, and even to other international organisations. There was no reason to exclude such entities from the scope of the draft articles solely on the basis of their mixed membership. It also found no substantive distinction worth drawing between organisations of a universal

[6] *Reparation for Injuries Suffered in the Service of the United Nations, Advisory Opinion* 1949 ICJ Report 174 at 178 (emphasis added).

[7] *Legality of the Use by a State of Nuclear Weapons in Armed Conflict, Advisory Opinion* 1996 ICJ Report 66 at 78 ('international organisations are subjects of international law which do not, unlike States, possess a general competence').

[8] Ibid. See, too, *Reparation for Injuries* (n 6) 180 ('the rights and duties of an entity such as the Organization must depend upon its purposes and functions as specified or implied in its constituent documents and developed in practice').

[9] See article 2(i) of the Vienna Convention on the Law of Treaties between States and International Organizations or between International Organizations of 1986 ('"international organisation" means an intergovernmental organisation').

character and regional organisations or other such entities enjoying a limited membership.

2 By reference to the method of establishment

Most international organisations are established by treaty, particularly those of the traditional intergovernmental type. For example, the African Union was established by a treaty[10] adopted by the states-members of the former Organization of African Unity. Yet, here too there are exceptions, with entities having been created by other instruments, such as a resolution adopted by a conference of states, for example, in the case of the Organization of the Petroleum Exporting Countries (OPEC).

3 By implication from the existence of separate legal personality

An entity may be considered an international organisation if it is recognised as enjoying separate legal personality under international law. Strictly speaking, such an approach is circular since separate legal personality is a consequence, recognised by law, of the fact that the entity in question is an international organisation. This approach does not describe *how* the organisation came to enjoy separate legal personality, but focuses on the fact of the recognition of such personality as proof of the existence of the organisation as a subject of international law.

The ILC adopted a combination of all three in its definition of an international organisation. It reads:

> 'International organisation' means an organisation established by a treaty or other instrument governed by international law and possessing its own international legal personality. International organisations may include as members, in addition to States, other entities.[11]

While some definitional elements are provided, the requirement of possession of international legal personality is the key threshold requirement. Accordingly, entities such as the International Union for Conservation of Nature (IUCN), whose members include states but which are established under domestic law, are excluded from the scope of the Draft Articles on Responsibility of International Organizations.[12] Similarly, the International Federation of the Red Cross which, in practice, functions like an international organisation, and whose constitution[13] expressly states that it enjoys 'all the rights of a

[10] Constitutive Act of the African Union of 11 July 2000.

[11] Draft article 2(a).

[12] *Yearbook of the International Law Commission* (2011) vol II, part 2 at 50, para 6 of commentary to article 2.

[13] As revised and adopted by the VIth session of its General Assembly in Rio de Janeiro (23–26 November 1987).

corporate body with legal personality',[14] limits its membership to the national societies of the Red Cross to the exclusion of states,[15] and thereby does not qualify as an 'international organisation' for purposes of the Draft Articles. Neither does the Organization for Security and Co-operation in Europe (OSCE), which was established in the context of a series of international instruments (the Helsinki Accords of 1975), and whose membership is intergovernmental in nature, but whose members have traditionally not recognised its separate legal personality.[16] Conversely, the International Labour Organization (ILO) is generally recognised as being an international organisation even though it includes among its members not only states but also representatives of labour movements and employers' organisations.

APPLICABLE LAW AND CONCEPT OF THE 'RULES OF THE ORGANISATION'

The applicable law governing the actions of states is either international law or domestic law (their own and sometimes that of other states). For international organisations there is a third possible set of applicable rules. Collectively known as the 'rules of the organisation', these typically refer to the constituent instrument, as well as any rules developed within the context of the work of the organisation.

The latter include decisions, resolutions, regulations, internal rules and other instruments adopted by its organs in accordance with its constituent instrument and the established practice of the organisation, as well as agreements concluded with third parties and judicial or arbitral decisions binding the organisation.

The Draft Articles on the Responsibility of International Organizations recognise that the rules of the organisation may have a bearing on several issues such as: determining the functions of the organs and agents of an organisation for purposes of establishing the attribution of the acts of such organs or agents to the organisation itself;[17] establishing the existence of an internationally wrongful act owing to the breach of an international obligation arising from the

[14] Article 2.

[15] Article 6.

[16] While such non-recognition limits the application of international law, it does not necessarily affect the recognition of separate legal personality under domestic law. Furthermore, it is possible for an organisation existing under domestic law to become an international organisation upon transformation (for example, through the adoption of an international treaty) into an entity that does satisfy the threshold requirements established by international law.

[17] Article 6(2).

rules of the organisation;[18] and establishing the permissibility of the taking of countermeasures by the organisation.[19] It is also recognised that the rules of the organisation may constitute *lex specialis*, ie special rules which override the draft articles to the extent that they (the special rules) govern in the context of the existence of an internationally wrongful act.[20]

CIRCUMSTANCES UNDER WHICH RESPONSIBILITY MAY ARISE FOR AN INTERNATIONAL ORGANISATION

The Draft Articles on the Responsibility of International Organizations envisage several scenarios under which an international organisation may incur international responsibility. Since an organisation is a legal entity in the sense that it acts in the physical world through its organs and agents, responsibility (as in the case of states) is typically vicarious in that the organisation incurs responsibility through the attribution of the wrongful acts of its organs and agents to it. While attribution is the primary vehicle, the Draft Articles recognise other ways in which an international organisation may incur responsibility.

1 Attribution of conduct to the international organisation

As with state responsibility, the rules on the attribution of conduct lie at the heart of the Draft Articles on the Responsibility of International Organizations. The relevant provisions are transposed almost verbatim from the Draft Articles on State Responsibility since many of the considerations are similar.[21] For an international organisation to be held responsible for an act or omission, the conduct in question must not only be internationally wrongful, but should also be attributable to it.[22] Such questions of attribution of conduct can be complex for large international organisations, such as the United Nations, with a global presence typically carried out in a number of guises (by organs such as the Secretariat, Funds, Programmes etc) and represented by several categories of staff, experts and other individuals through whom the organisation acts, collectively referred to as its 'agents'.[23] In principle, the conduct of one of its organs or agents, in performing their functions as established by the rules of the organisation, is attributable to an international organisation regardless of the position

[18] Article 10(2).

[19] Article 22(2)(b) and (3), and article 51(1)(b) and (2).

[20] Article 64.

[21] See the discussion in the context of state responsibility in Chapter 13 above.

[22] Article 4(a).

[23] See article 2(d). The term 'agent' was employed by the International Court of Justice in *Reparation for Injuries* (n 6) 177.

of the organ or agent in the organisation.[24] It is rare, however, that actions undertaken by organs or agents in conformity with their functions amount to an internationally wrongful act. A more likely scenario is that of an agent acting in excess of his or her authority, or an organ acting contrary to the division of functions within the organisation. While such *ultra vires* conduct may be in contravention of the rules of the organisation, the conduct will nonetheless be attributable to it if it was undertaken by the agent or organ acting in such capacity.[25] As a matter of policy, granting the organisation the ability to deny attribution to it for the conduct of its agents or organs in contravention of its internal rules might deprive third parties of the right of redress. Conversely, acts of an agent not performed in his or her official capacity are not attributable to the international organisation, unless it acknowledges and adopts the conduct in question as its own.[26]

Wrongful conduct may also be attributed to an international organisation where it exercises effective control over an organ of a state or an organ or agent of another international organisation which was placed at its (the controlling organisation's) disposal.[27] While the conduct of organs and agents which have been 'seconded' to an international organisation is attributable to it (and not the lending state or organisation), the position is less clear with regard to entities such as military contingents that are placed at the disposal of an international organisation, but which continue to be subject to the control of their national states. Here the ILC has followed the practice developed by the United Nations of applying the test of the exercise of 'effective control' in determining to which entity the wrongful conduct is to be attributed. This is essentially a factual test turning on the actual control exercised over the specific conduct in question. Accordingly, in peacekeeping missions composed of national military contingents under the exclusive control of the United Nations, the internationally wrongful conduct of such contingents is, in principle, attributable to the organisation and may entail its international responsibility. At the same time, to the extent that the national states retain control over disciplinary and criminal matters of their respective contingents, any such wrongful conduct (to the extent that

[24] Article 6.

[25] Article 8. See *Certain Expenses of the United Nations (Article 17, paragraph 2, of the Charter) Advisory Opinion* 1962 ICJ Reports 151 at 168 ('both national or international law contemplate cases in which the body corporate or politic may be bound, as to third parties, by an *ultra vires* act of an agent'). See also *Trinidad Cement Limited v The Caribbean Community* [2009] CCJ 2 (OJ) para 41.

[26] Article 9.

[27] Article 7.

it amounts to an internationally wrongful act) is attributable to the contributing state and not the United Nations. That effective control is a relative concept, to be ascertained on the facts, becomes evident in the case of joint operations, involving contingents under the exclusive command and control of the United Nations as well as those under the exclusive command of states or other organisations.[28]

The European Court of Human Rights took a different approach in a series of cases[29] relating to the conduct of forces in Kosovo placed at the disposal of the United Nations Interim Administration Mission in Kosovo (UNMIK) or authorised by the United Nations (Kosovo Force (KFOR)), but under the operational command of NATO. In attributing the conduct of KFOR to the United Nations (and not NATO), the Court took the position that the United Nations Security Council, despite delegating operational command to NATO, had retained 'ultimate control'. It is not easy to imagine a scenario where wrongful conduct would not be attributed to the United Nations if the test of ultimate control is be applied, since all of its actions are undertaken on the basis of some authorisation. Such a test does not necessarily accord with the reality of operational command on the ground, especially as regards joint operations. At present, even though the European Court of Human Rights has reaffirmed its position in several subsequent cases,[30] the ultimate control test has by and large been restricted to the jurisprudence of that Court.[31] The ILC

[28] *Yearbook of the International Law Commission* (2011) vol II, part 2 at 58, para 9 of commentary to article 7.

[29] *Behrami and Behrami v France* and *Saramati v France, Germany and Norway* ECHR Decision (Grand Chamber) of 2 May 2007 on admissibility.

[30] See *Kasumaj v Greece* ECHR Decision of 5 July 2007 on admissibility; *Gajić v Germany* ECHR Decision of 28 August 2007 on admissibility; and *Berić v Bosnia and Herzegovina* ECHR Decision of 16 October 2007 on admissibility. However, the European Court took a more nuanced position in *Jaloud v The Netherlands* ECHR Judgment of 20 November 2014, in which the Grand Chamber of the Court applied an analysis closer to the 'effective control' test to hold that the conduct of Dutch troops in Iraq were still attributable to the Netherlands, despite their being under the operational control of the occupying powers operating under an authorisation of the UN Security Council.

[31] The majority in the House of Lords, in a case arising out of the actions of British troops in Iraq, despite seemingly citing the ECHR position with approval, took an approach in line with the effective control test. See *R (on the application of Al-Jedda) (FC) v Secretary of State for Defence* [2007] UKHL 58. The case was subsequently brought before the ECHR, which agreed with the House of Lords that the conduct was attributable to the United Kingdom since in the situation prevailing in Iraq the UN Security Council 'had neither effective control or ultimate authority and control': *Al Jedda v United Kingdom* ECHR Judgment of 7 July 2011 (Grand Chamber) para 84. See also the position taken in *Serdar Mohammed v Ministry of Defence and Mohammed Qasim v Secretary of State for Defence* [2014] EWHC 1369 (QB) para 165, subsequently upheld on appeal in *Serdar Mohammed v Secretary of State for Defence and Yunus Rahmatullah &*

prefers the 'effective control' test, as one more suitable for the attribution of conduct to an international organisation (and hence for the equitable distribution of responsibility).[32] For their part, some national courts, in confronting cases involving such complex arrangements, have proceeded on the basis of the existence of 'dual

the Iraqi Civilian Claimants v Ministry of Defence and Foreign and Commonwealth Office [2015] EWCA Civ 843 para 57. For its part, while the UK Supreme Court, in *Abd Ali Hameed Al-Waheed (Appellant) v Ministry of Defence (Respondent); Serdar Mohammed (Respondent) v Ministry of Defence (Appellant)* [2017] UKSC 1, upheld the outcome of the lower courts on other grounds, the underlying assumption was that the conduct in question could be attributable to the United Kingdom. However, a view closer to the initial ECHR position in the *Behrami* and *Saramati* cases was taken by the UK Court of Appeal in *Kontic v Ministry of Defence* [2016] EWHC 2034 (QB) para 135 ('the relevant acts and omissions complained of are as a matter of law attributable to the United Nations, and not to the United Kingdom'). The matter was also raised in a string of decisions by courts in the Netherlands, considering the attribution of the conduct of the 'Dutchbat' contingent in Srebrenica. In *Mustafić-Mujić v State of the Netherlands*, Case No 265618/HA ZA 06-1672, 10 September 2008, and in *Nuhanović v State of the Netherlands*, Case No 265615/HA ZA 06-1671, 10 September 2008, the District Court of The Hague applied the broader 'under direction and control' test in holding that the acts and omissions of the contingent 'should be attributed strictly, as a matter of principle, to the United Nations' (para 4.11). This finding was reversed on appeal by the Court of Appeal of The Hague, Case No 200.020.173/01 and 200.020.174/01, 5 July 2011, which pointed out that 'the question as to whom a specific conduct of such troops should be attributed, depends on the question which of both parties has "effective control" over the relevant conduct' (ref para 5.8 of each case). It subsequently held that The Netherlands had 'possessed "effective control" over the alleged conduct of Dutchbat that is the subject of Mustafić et al's claim and that this conduct can be attributed to the State' (para 5.20). This position was subsequently upheld by the Supreme Court of the Netherlands, Judgments of 6 September 2013. See also *Stichting Mothers of Srebrenica v State of the Netherlands*, Hague District Court, Case No C/09/295247/HA ZA 07-2973, 16 July 2014 para 4.33. The European Court of Human Rights, in *Jaloud v The Netherlands*, treated the series of decisions in the *Mustać* and *Nuhanović* cases before the Dutch courts as relevant domestic case law (paras 70–4). In Germany, the Higher Administrative Court of North Rhine-Westphalia, in *Anonymous v Federal German Government*, Fourth Chamber, Case No 4 A 2948/11, 18 September 2014 para 1.4.2, in considering the question of whether the transfer of a detained pirate to Kenya conducted as part of the European Union-led naval force (EUNAVFOR) (Operation Atalanta) was attributable to Germany, declined to choose between tests since in its view the application of either test would result in the attribution of the relevant conduct to Germany. See UN document A/72/81 at 16.

[32] See, too, P Bodeau-Livinec, GP Buzzini and S Villalpando '*Behrami & Behrami v France; Saramati v France, Germany & Norway* note' (2008) 102(2) *AJIL* 323; KM Larsen 'Attribution of conduct in peace operations: The "ultimate authority and control" test' (2008) 19 *EJIL* 509; M Milanović and T Papić 'As bad as it gets: The European Court of Human Rights *Behrami and Saramati Decision* and general international law' (2009) 58 *ICLQ* 267.

attribution' to both the state(s) and international organisation involved, on the basis of article 48 of the ILC's Draft Articles.[33]

2 Responsibility in connection with an act of a state or other international organisation

As in the case of state responsibility, the Draft Articles on the Responsibility of International Organizations recognise accomplice liability. Under certain circumstances, an international organisation may incur international responsibility for aiding and assisting a state or another organisation in committing an internationally wrongful act,[34] or for directing and controlling a state or other organisation in the commission of the act.[35] Likewise, an international organisation may be held internationally responsible for coercing a state or other international organisation to commit an internationally wrongful act.[36]

Since an international organisation exists as an entity distinct from its members, it is theoretically possible that it could seek to influence its members 'in order to achieve through them a result that the organisation could not lawfully achieve directly, and thus circumvent one of its international obligations'.[37] The international organisation would thus incur responsibility arising from the adoption of a decision binding or authorising its members to commit an act in violation of its (the organisation's) international obligations.[38]

Finally, international organisations can themselves be members of other international organisations and, under certain circumstances, also incur international responsibility *qua* member of the latter organisation.[39]

THE RESPONSIBILITY OF STATES MEMBERS OF AN INTERNATIONAL ORGANISATION FOR THE ACTS OF AN ORGANISATION

One of the more difficult questions faced by the ILC concerned the issue of whether states members of an international organisation

[33] See, for example, the decisions of the Supreme Court of the Netherlands in *State of the Netherlands v Mustafić-Mujić* and *State of the Netherlands v Nuhanovi* para 3.9.4 ('the possibility of more than one State or organisation being held responsible for the consequences of an internationally wrongful act') and of The Hague District Court in *Stichting Mothers of Srebrenica v State of the Netherlands* para 4.34 ('the same act and/or acts might be attributed to both the State and the UN under what is called *"dual attribution"*').

[34] Article 14.

[35] Article 15.

[36] Article 16.

[37] *Yearbook of the International Law Commission* (2011) vol II, part 2 at 68, para 9 of commentary to draft article 17.

[38] Article 17.

[39] Article 18.

could themselves incur international responsibility arising from the wrongful acts of the organisation. Even though the Draft Articles on the Responsibility of International Organizations focuses on the responsibility of *international organisations*, the ILC felt compelled to also cover the responsibility of *states* for their acts undertaken in connection with internationally wrongful conduct of an international organisation, which had not been directly dealt with in the Draft Articles on State Responsibility.

In the first place a state member incurs international responsibility by seeking to circumvent one of its international obligations by 'causing the organisation to commit an act that, if committed by the State, would have constituted a breach of the obligation'.[40]

The second ground concerns the trickier issue of the possible residual responsibility of the member states of an international organisation for the internationally wrongful acts of the organisation. The ILC took the position that international law did not, in principle, recognise the possibility of 'piercing the veil' so as to allow for such residual responsibility.[41] Nonetheless, it allowed two exceptions to the rule: (1) where a member state has accepted international responsibility for the act of the international organisation, and (2) where the member state gave the third party reason to rely on the responsibility of the member state, for example, where the member state provided an assurance that it would stand in if the responsible organisation did not have the necessary funds.[42] Such responsibility would be subsidiary in character, ie it would be supplementary to that of the organisation that has acted wrongfully.[43]

[40] Article 61(1). See *Luke Munyandu Tembani and Benjamin John Freeth*, African Commission on Human and Peoples' Rights communication 409/12, 30 April 2014 para 134 ('the current trend in International Law is that where states transfer sovereign powers to an International Organisation and in the course of carrying out the functions assigned to it the International Organisation occasions wrongs that would have invoked the international responsibility of the Member States individually had they acted on their own, the States can individually bear responsibility for those wrongful acts and omissions of the International Organisation').

[41] The ILC found support for this proposition in the series of cases relating to the demise of the International Tin Council. See *Maclaine Watson & Co Ltd v Department of Trade and Industry; JH Rayner (Mincing Lane) Ltd v Department of Trade and Industry* (1988) 80 ILR at 109; and *Australia & New Zealand Banking Group Ltd v Commonwealth of Australia; Amalgamated Metal Trading Ltd v Department of Trade and Industry; Maclaine Watson & Co Ltd v Department of Trade and Industry; Maclaine Watson & Co Ltd v International Tin Council* (1990) 29 *ILM* 675.

[42] Article 62(1). See *Arab Organization for Industrialization, Arab British Helicopter Company and Arab Republic of Egypt v Westland Helicopters Ltd, United Arab Emirates, Kingdom of Saudi Arabia and State of Qatar* (1987) 80 ILR 622.

[43] Article 62 (2).

THE FUTURE OF THE DRAFT ARTICLES ON RESPONSIBILITY OF INTERNATIONAL ORGANISATIONS

Upon referring the Draft Articles on Responsibility of International Organizations to the UN General Assembly in 2011, the ILC recommended, inter alia, that the Assembly 'consider, at a later stage, the elaboration of a convention on the basis of the draft articles'. The General Assembly took note of the Draft Articles that year.[44] Their future form has since been discussed by the Sixth Committee of the General Assembly in 2014 and 2017,[45] but no decision has been taken thus far (primarily because their fate is seen as being linked to that of the Draft Articles on State Responsibility).[46]

[44] GA res 66/100, 9 December 2011.

[45] GA res 69/126, 10 Dec 2014 and 72/122, 10 December 2017.

[46] See the discussion in the context of state responsibility in Chapter 13 above.

CHAPTER 15

Human Rights

John Dugard and Jackie Dugard

Today one of the principal aims of international law is the protection of the human rights of the individual against her or his own government.[1] This is a post-World War II development. Before 1945, the concern shown by international law for the treatment of aliens (described in chapter 13) did not extend to the treatment of individuals by their own states. Pre-war international law provided protection to individuals, other than aliens lawfully admitted to the injuring state, in limited situations and circumstances.

Humanitarian law,[2] which seeks to reduce the suffering of combatants and civilians in times of war, began to develop in the 19th century after the adoption of the Geneva Convention for the Amelioration of the Condition of the Wounded in Armies in the Field in 1864, and was well developed by the beginning of the 20th century. Humanitarian intervention,[3] which permits states to intervene forcibly in states whose treatment of their own nationals shocks the conscience of mankind, was recognised by international law as early as the 17th century,[4] although in practice it was used mainly as a pretext for non-altruistic political intervention.[5] The slave trade was abolished largely by collective international action.[6]

The League of Nations period saw three important developments in the international protection of human rights: the mandates system established in 1919 as a sacred trust of civilisation to promote the welfare of 'peoples not yet able to stand by themselves under the

[1] T Meron *The Humanization of International Law* (2006); C Tomuschat *Human Rights: Between Idealism and Realism* 3 ed (2014); H Steiner, P Alston and R Goodman *International Human Rights in Context* 3 ed (2008); R Teitel *Humanity's Law* (2011); D Shelton (ed) *The Oxford Handbook of International Human Rights* Law (2013); S Sheeran and N Rodley (eds) *Routledge Handbook of International Human Rights Law* (2014); I Bantekas and L Oette *International Human Rights Law and Practice* 2 ed (2016); I Nifosi-Sutton *The Protection of Vulnerable Groups under International Human Rights Law* (2017).

[2] See Chapter 25.

[3] See Chapter 24.

[4] Grotius endorsed such a right in 1625 in *De Jure Belli ac Pacis* 2.25.8.

[5] The intervention by Western states in the Ottoman Empire in the 19th century served the dual purpose of protecting Christians against persecution and of weakening the Ottoman Empire.

[6] See DP O'Connell *International Law* vol 2 2 ed (1970) 753–4.

strenuous conditions of the modern world';[7] the International Labour Organization (ILO), created in 1919 to improve the working conditions of employees; and the minority treaties, designed to safeguard the rights of ethnic, religious, and linguistic minorities in the Balkans and Eastern Europe.[8]

Despite these features of international law aimed at promoting the welfare of individuals, minorities, and undeveloped peoples, international law until 1945 was largely concerned with states, at that stage the only subjects of international law, and with the relations between states. The prohibition on intervention in the domestic affairs of states, enshrined in the Covenant of the League of Nations,[9] was respected as a guiding principle. It was this principle that ensured that states failed to intervene in Germany before 1939 despite awareness of the atrocities committed by the Nazis against their own nationals.

The enormity of the atrocities committed by the Nazi regime dramatically changed the nature of international law. This experience compelled statesmen to accept the need for a new world order in which the state was no longer free to treat its own nationals as it pleased. This new order was proclaimed by the Charter of the United Nations (UN Charter), which recognised the promotion of human rights as a principal goal of the new world organisation, and by the London Charter of 1945, which provided for the trial of the major Nazi war leaders.

THE NUREMBERG TRIAL[10]

In 1945, the United States, the Soviet Union, the United Kingdom, and France established an international military tribunal to try the major Nazi leaders for crimes against the peace, war crimes, and crimes against humanity.[11] The Nuremberg trial was followed by the Tokyo trial of the Japanese war leaders on similar charges.[12] The

[7] Article 22 of the Covenant of the League of Nations. See, on the mandates system, J Dugard *The South West Africa/Namibia Dispute* (1973).

[8] M Shaw *International Law* 8 ed (2017) 226.

[9] Article 15(8).

[10] There is a vast literature on this subject. See, for example, R Woetzel *The Nuremberg Trials in International Law* (1962); R Conot *Justice at Nuremberg* (1983); G Ginsburg and V Kudriavtsev (eds) *The Nuremberg Trial in International Law* (1990); T Taylor *The Anatomy of the Nuremberg Trials* (1992); G Mettraux (ed) *Perspectives on the Nuremberg Trial* (2008). The judgment of the Nuremberg tribunal is published in Nuremberg IMT 'Judgment and Sentence' (1947) 41 *AJIL* 172.

[11] See further, Chapter 10.

[12] AC Brackman *The Other Nuremberg: The Untold Story of the Tokyo War Crimes Trials* (1989).

Nuremberg trial has had a major impact on international law. It has inspired the establishment of international criminal courts to try those responsible for the systematic and large-scale violation of human rights[13] and it has contributed substantially to the development of international humanitarian law.[14] From a human rights perspective, the main significance of the Nuremberg precedent is that national leaders and government officials are no longer able to claim immunity before international courts[15] from prosecution for egregious human rights violations by invoking the protection of municipal law or superior orders.

THE CHARTER OF THE UNITED NATIONS

The commitment of the United Nations to human rights[16] was made clear in the preamble to the Charter which reaffirms 'faith in fundamental human rights, in the dignity and worth of the human person, in the equal rights of men and women'. Ironically, the preamble was in part drafted by South Africa's Prime Minister, General Smuts,[17] who, as President of the Commission on the General Assembly, played a leading part in the formation of the United Nations. The Charter itself contains a number of references to human rights. Article 1 includes among the purposes of the United Nations the promotion and encouragement of human rights, while article 13 obliges the General Assembly to initiate studies and make recommendations for promoting human rights. Most important are articles 55 and 56. Article 55 obliges the United Nations to promote 'universal respect for, and observance of, human rights and fundamental freedoms for all without distinction as to race, sex, language, or religion'; and in article 56 '[a]ll members pledge themselves to take joint and separate action in co-operation with the Organization for the achievement of the purposes set forth in article 55'.

The human rights articles of the Charter have several defects. First, they are vague and give no indication of the rights protected, apart from that of non-discrimination. Secondly, no enforcement machin-

[13] See Chapter 10.

[14] See Chapter 25.

[15] See further, Chapter 12.

[16] P Alston and F Megret *The United Nations and Human Rights: A Critical Appraisal* 2 ed (2010).

[17] J Barber and J Barratt *South Africa's Foreign Policy: The Search for Status and Security 1945–1988* (1990) 16–20; C Heyns and W Gravett 'To save succeeding generations from the scourge of war: Jan Smuts and the ideological foundations of the United Nations (2017) 39 *Human Rights Quarterly* 574, 589–94. For a critical assessment of Smuts's role, see M Mazower *No Enchanted Palace. The End of Empire and the Ideological Origins of the United Nations* (2009) 28–65.

ery is provided for, unless the denial of human rights assumes such egregious proportions that it constitutes a threat to international peace under chapter VII of the Charter. Thirdly, it is not clear that the articles create any legal obligations for states, although the pledge to co-operate in promoting human rights in article 56 'at least implies a negative obligation not so to act as to undermine human rights'.[18] Fourthly, there is a conflict between the human rights articles and article 2(7) of the Charter, which provides:

> Nothing contained in the present Charter shall authorize the United Nations to intervene in matters which are essentially within the domestic jurisdiction of any state or shall require the members to submit such matters to settlement under the present Charter; but this principle shall not prejudice the application of enforcement measures under Chapter VII.

South Africa vigorously exploited these weaknesses in the legal status of the human rights articles as it sought to exclude debate, and later action, by the United Nations on its racial policies during the apartheid era.[19]

1 South Africa's racial policies and the human rights clauses of the UN Charter 1949–1994

South Africa's racial policies featured on the agenda of the General Assembly from 1946 to 1994. In 1946, at the request of the Government of India, the General Assembly first considered the question of the treatment of persons of Indian origin in South Africa;[20] and thereafter this item was examined regularly until 1962, when it merged with the question of apartheid.[21] The legal basis for United Nations concern in this matter was the violation of an agreement of

[18] JL Brierly *The Law of Nations* 6 ed (ed H Waldock) (1963) 293. For this reason, wrote Waldock, 'South Africa's racial segregation policies appear to be out of harmony with her obligations under the Charter'.

[19] For the arguments advanced by the South African government, see C Fincham *Domestic Jurisdiction* (1948); HHH Biermann (ed) *The Case for South Africa, As Put Forth in the Public Statements of Eric H Louw, Foreign Minister of South Africa* (1963); JC Heunis *United Nations versus South Africa* (1986); H Booysen *Volkereg* 2 ed (1989) 428–32. *Sed contra*, see J Dugard 'The legal effect of United Nations resolutions on apartheid' (1966) 83 *SALJ* 44; J Dugard 'Apartheid: A case study in the response of the international community to gross violations of human rights' in I Cotler and FP Eliadis (eds) *International Human Rights Law: Theory and Practice* (1992) 301; L Sohn *Rights in Conflict: The United Nations and South Africa* (1994).

[20] See Resolution 44(I) of 8 December 1946 for the first General Assembly Resolution on this subject.

[21] In 1962, the General Assembly considered the question of the treatment of persons of Indian and Indo-Pakistan origin in South Africa, together with the question of the policy of apartheid and adopted a combined resolution on these subjects: Resolution 1761 (XVII) of 6 November 1962. Thereafter, the two subjects were considered together as one item.

1927 between South Africa and India regarding the treatment of persons of Indian origin in South Africa,[22] and the incompatibility of discriminatory laws directed at Indians in South Africa with the human rights articles of the UN Charter. In 1952, the wider apartheid question was raised directly in the General Assembly when 13 countries sought its inclusion on the agenda on the ground that this policy was 'creating a dangerous and explosive situation which constitutes both a threat to international peace and a flagrant violation of the basic principles of human rights and fundamental freedoms which are enshrined in the Charter of the United Nations'.[23] Thereafter the question of apartheid appeared annually on the agenda of the General Assembly. In 1960, following the shooting of blacks at a peaceful demonstration at Sharpeville on 21 March, the question was elevated to the Security Council.[24]

Apartheid was proclaimed at a time when institutionalised (that is, legally authorised) racial discrimination was still to be found in the legal orders of many states in the United States of America and of most colonial regimes. Not surprisingly, therefore, South Africa gained support from many Western governments for its insistence that its racial policies fell within its exclusive domestic jurisdiction. Moreover, the extent to which article 2(7) of the United Nations Charter protected a state's domestic policies from international scrutiny in the new world order was as yet unresolved. Consequently, South Africa's racial policies became the testing ground for the battle between human rights and domestic jurisdiction.

In the early days of the United Nations, South Africa sought to block any discussion of her racial policies on the ground that article 2(7) took precedence over the human rights clauses in the Charter.[25] Encouraged by the support of many Western states, South Africa demanded that an advisory opinion be obtained from the International Court of Justice, but the General Assembly of the United Nations, unsure of the correctness of its interventionist interpretation of article 2(7), preferred to keep the matter away from the Court and refused South Africa's request.[26] Gradually international opinion

[22] MS Rajan *United Nations and Domestic Jurisdiction* 2 ed (1961) 239–40; RP Schaffer 'The legal effect of the Cape Town Agreement' (1976) 93 *SALJ* 441.

[23] 7 UN *GAOR*, Annexes, Agenda Item 66, at 1–3, UN Doc A/2183 (1952).

[24] Resolution 134 of 1960.

[25] R Higgins *The Development of International Law through the Political Organs of the United Nations* (1963) 64–5; Rajan (n 22) 245–55, 282–7; D Prévost 'South Africa as an illustration of the development in international human rights law' (1999) 24 *SAYIL* 211.

[26] Ozdemir A Ozgur *Apartheid, the United Nations and Peaceful Change in South Africa* (1982) 119; DR Gilmour 'The United Nations and apartheid—Certain procedural

changed as apartheid became more brutal, South Africa more intransigent, and decolonisation more widespread. The wisdom of the observation of the Permanent Court of International Justice in the *Nationality Decrees Case* that the question of domestic jurisdiction is 'relative' and 'depends upon the development of international relations'[27] became apparent in respect of apartheid as state after state abandoned its support for the South African position, particularly after the killing of black demonstrators at Sharpeville by apartheid police in 1960. By the early 1960s, only Portugal was prepared to support South Africa's claims under article 2(7).[28] Some states made their concession on article 2(7) reluctantly, and sought to limit their recognition of the precedence of the human rights provisions over domestic jurisdiction to apartheid. Indeed the United Kingdom, when it first abandoned its support for South Africa's position on article 2(7), did so on the ground that apartheid was a special case, *sui generis*.[29] In practice, such a limitation was impossible. Apartheid forced states to choose between the supremacy of domestic jurisdiction and human rights. They chose human rights and, in so doing, took international law into a new era.

Closely related to the debate over domestic jurisdiction was the dispute over the legal status of the human rights provisions in the Charter. Until 1971 South Africa and other states questioned the legal force of the human rights provisions, arguing that they were a mere statement of ideals and failed to impose any legal obligation. This controversy was also resolved in the context of apartheid when the International Court of Justice in the 1971 *Namibia Opinion* held that apartheid—as extended to Namibia—constituted a denial of fundamental human rights and 'a flagrant violation of the purposes and principles of the Charter'.[30] Although this *dictum* was specifically directed at Namibia, a territory with an international status, it was also applicable to apartheid in South Africa. Moreover, it dispelled

aspects of the problem' (1969) 16 *Netherlands International Law Review* 12. On 30 January 1947, General Smuts told the Senate that the refusal of the General Assembly to request an advisory opinion constituted a denial of South Africa's fundamental rights: *Parliamentary Debates*, Senate, cols 4135–37 (30 January 1947).

[27] 1923 PCIJ Reports, Series B No 4 at 24.

[28] For an account of this change in attitude, see Higgins (n 25) 122–3.

[29] UN *GAOR*, 15th Session, Special Political Committee, 242nd meeting (5 April 1961) para 13. See further Ozgur (n 26) 111–12.

[30] *Legal Consequences for States of the Continued Presence of South Africa in Namibia (South West Africa) notwithstanding Security Council Resolution 276 (1970)* 1971 ICJ Reports 16 at 57.

any doubts concerning the legal obligations that were imposed on member states by the human rights provisions in the Charter.[31]

UNIVERSAL DECLARATION OF HUMAN RIGHTS[32]

In 1946, the Economic and Social Council of the United Nations established a Commission on Human Rights, whose first task was to draft an International Bill of Rights, comprising a declaration and a multilateral treaty. The first step in this direction was the drafting of the Universal Declaration of Human Rights (UDHR) by representatives with different cultural and legal backgrounds from all the regions of the world, which was approved by the General Assembly[33] on 10 December 1948, by 48 votes in favour, none against, and eight abstentions. South Africa, now under a National Party government, abstained, together with the Byelorussian SSR, Czechoslovakia, Poland, Saudi Arabia, the Ukrainian SSR, the USSR, and Yugoslavia.

The UDHR proclaims both civil and political rights and economic, social, and cultural rights in the language of aspiration. This is because the Declaration is not a treaty but a recommendatory resolution of the General Assembly and is therefore not legally binding on states. According to its preamble, it is to serve 'as a common standard of achievement for all peoples and all nations'. Although not binding, the UDHR has undoubtedly guided the political organs of the United Nations in their interpretation and application of the human rights clauses in the Charter.[34]

The impact of the UDHR on the development of human rights has been immense. It inspired the International Covenant on Civil and Political Rights (ICCPR), the International Covenant on Economic, Social and Cultural Rights (ICESCR), and several regional human rights conventions; it has served as a model for national Bills of Rights; it has been used by the organs of the United Nations as a

[31] See E Schwelb 'The International Court of Justice and the human rights clauses of the Charter' (1972) 66 *AJIL* 337.

[32] See H Lauterpacht 'The Universal Declaration of Human Rights' (1948) 25 *BYIL* 354; J Humphrey 'The Universal Declaration of Human Rights: Its history, impact and judicial character' in BR Ramcharan (ed) *Human Rights: Thirty Years after the Universal Declaration* (1984); B Weston and S Marks *The Future of International Human Rights. Commemorating the 50th Anniversary of the Universal Declaration of Human Rights* (1999); G Alfredsson and A Eide (eds) *The Universal Declaration of Human Rights: A Common Standard of Achievement* (1999); W Sweet (ed) *Philosophical Theory and the Universal Declaration on Human Rights* (2003); W Schabas (ed) *The Universal Declaration of Human Rights: The Travaux Préparatoires* (2013).

[33] Resolution 217A (III); J Morsink *The Universal Declaration of Human Rights: Origins, Drafting and Intent* (1999).

[34] See the dissenting opinion of Judge Tanaka in the *South West Africa Cases, Second Phase* 1966 ICJ Reports 6 at 293.

standard by which to measure the conduct of states; and it was invoked by the 1975 Final Act of the Conference on Security and Co-operation in Europe (the Helsinki Accord).[35] Consequently, it is argued that the UDHR now forms part of customary international law. In 1968, at an International Conference on Human Rights in Teheran, called by the United Nations to review the progress made since the adoption of the UDHR, a Proclamation of Teheran was adopted by 84 states, which declared:

> The Universal Declaration of Human Rights states a common understanding of the peoples of the world concerning the inalienable and inviolable rights of all members of the human family and constitutes an obligation for the members of the international community.[36]

The Proclamation of Teheran goes too far if it suggests that *all* the rights contained in the UDHR have acquired the status of customary international law. On the other hand, Conradie J goes too far in the other direction in *S v Petane*, where he stressed the need for practice in the establishment of a customary rule of international law:

> The Universal Declaration on Human Rights may be taken as an example in this respect. It has been asserted that in the course of time its provisions have grown into rules of customary international law. This view is often substantiated by citing abstract statements by states supporting the Declaration or references to the Declaration in subsequent resolutions or treaties. Sometimes it is pointed out that its provisions have been incorporated in national constitutions. But what if states making statements like these or drawing up their constitutions in conformity with the Universal Declaration at the same time treat their nationals in a manner which constitutes a flagrant violation of its very provisions, for instance, by not combating large-scale disappearances, by practising torture, or by imprisoning people for long periods of time without a fair trial? Even if abstract statements or formal provisions in a constitution are considered a state practice, they have at any rate to be weighed against concrete acts like the ones mentioned.[37]

The truth lies closer to the centre of the spectrum. Some of the more basic principles of the UDHR, such as that of non-discrimination, the right to a fair trial, and the prohibition on torture[38] and cruel, inhuman or degrading treatment, undoubtedly belong to the *corpus* of customary law today despite the fact that they may not always be observed. Their status as custom is assured by both *opinio juris* and *usus*.

During the apartheid era, both governmental and non-governmental organisations frequently judged South Africa by the standards of the UDHR.[39] Today, the UDHR is an instrument to which South

[35] The text appears in (1975) 14 *ILM* 1293.

[36] UN Doc A/CONF 32/41 at 3 (1968).

[37] 1988 (3) SA 51 (C) 58G–J. See, too, *S v Rudman* 1989 (3) SA 368 at 376A–B.

[38] *Filartiga v Pena-Irala* 630 F 2d 876 (2d Cir 1980); (1980) 19 *ILM* 966.

[39] See M Robertson (ed) *Human Rights for South Africans* (1991).

African courts may turn in their interpretation of the Bill of Rights.[40] As an authoritative statement of the international community, several of whose provisions have acquired the force of customary law, it is eminently suited for such a role.

THE INTERNATIONAL COVENANTS AND CONVENTIONS[41]

Ideological differences between East and West made it impossible to produce a single multilateral treaty giving legal effect to the UDHR. Instead, two Covenants were drafted, the ICCPR and the ICESCR. Together with the UDHR, these two covenants are sometimes referred to as the international bill of human rights. They were adopted by the General Assembly in 1966 but only came into force in 1976 following ratification by 35 states.

Since 1966, seven other core international human rights treaties, along with their associated Optional Protocols, have come into force. These are the International Convention on the Elimination of All Forms of Racial Discrimination (ICERD); Convention on the Elimination of All Forms of Discrimination against Women (CEDAW); Convention against Torture and Other Cruel, Inhuman or Degrading Treatment or Punishment (CAT); Convention on the Rights of the Child (CRC); International Convention on the Protection of the Rights of All Migrant Workers and Members of Their Families (CMW); International Convention for the Protection of All Persons from Enforced Disappearance (CED); and Convention on the Rights of Persons with Disabilities (CRPD).

All these covenants or conventions make provision for individual complaints procedures against one's own state (often via the relevant optional protocol), as long as the state has ratified the relevant covenant or its protocol. The individual complaints procedure for the CMW will only come into force when ten states make the necessary declaration under article 77 (as of early-2018 only three states—Guatemala, Mexico and Uruguay—had made the necessary declaration).

The covenants and conventions and/or their protocols allow for inter-state complaints mechanisms of one kind or another but, as

[40] See s 39(1)*(b)* of the Constitution of the Republic of South Africa, 1996.

[41] The international conventions and their frameworks are sometimes referred to as the international treaty-based system. Only states that have ratified the conventions (known as state parties) have obligations under the treaty-based system. The treaty-based system is distinct from the charter-based system, which is grounded in the United Nations Charter and binds all UN member states, regardless of which treaties they have ratified. The main feature of the charter-based system is the Human Rights Council (formerly the Commission on Human Rights), dealt with under the section on UN Human Rights Bodies, below.

potentially important as this mechanism is, to date, only one of these inter-state complaints mechanisms has been used.[42] Most conventions (all apart from the ICCPR; ICERD; and CMW) provide for inquiry procedures to deal with systemic violations by states, but these are not often engaged.[43] In all these conventions except the CED states can opt out of the inquiry procedure.

A treaty-monitoring committee comprising elected independent experts oversees each convention. The main roles played by the committees are hearing individual complaints, providing clarity on the meaning and scope of the relevant rights through formulating general comments, and receiving and commenting on periodic state reports—the latter mechanism of regular state reporting being the main way through which the compliance of contracting states is monitored.

These mechanisms provide important ways to enforce human rights at the international level. The international human rights system binds state parties (those countries that have ratified or acceded to the conventions) and is complementary to any regional and domestic human rights laws applicable to the specific country. The domestic status of international law in South Africa is governed by section 231(4) of the Constitution, which provides that any international agreement becomes law in the Republic when 'it is

[42] ICERD (see discussion of ICERD below). CAT, CMW and CED along with the Optional Protocol to ICESCR and the Optional Protocol (on a communications procedure) to CRC, set out procedures for the relevant Committee to consider complaints from one state party against another, as long as the states have made a declaration accepting the competence of the Committee in this regard. In addition, ICCPR, ICERD and CRC establish more elaborate procedures for the resolution of disputes between contracting states through the establishment of an ad hoc Conciliation Commission (this applies to all states parties to ICERD but, in relation to the ICCPR and CRC, only to those states parties that have accepted the competence of the relevant committee in this regard). Finally, ICERD, CEDAW, CAT, CMW and CED provide for disputes between contracting states regarding interpretation or application of the relevant convention to be resolved by negotiation or, failing that, by arbitration (states parties can exclude this jurisdiction by making a declaration at the time of ratification/accession—any state that does this is barred, in line with the principle of reciprocity, from bringing cases against other states parties). Interestingly, ICERD provides in article 22 that disputes relating to interpretation of ICERD may be referred to the International Court of Justice in The Hague. This function has been used in several cases, as outlined in the section on ICERD below.

[43] Article 20 of CAT, article 33 of CED, article 11 of the Optional Protocol to ICESCR, article 8 of the Optional Protocol to CEDAW, article 13 of the Optional Protocol (on a communications procedure) of CRC, and article 6 of the Optional Protocol to CRPD.

enacted into law by national legislation; but a self-executing provision of an agreement that has been approved by Parliament is law . . . unless it is inconsistent with the Constitution or an Act of Parliament'. Section 231(5) provides that South Africa is bound by international agreements that were binding at the time of the Constitution taking effect.

While there is clarity around international agreements that have been domesticated through the enactment of national legislation, there is a degree of uncertainty around the issue of self-executing provisions. A treaty provision is self-executing if 'it is capable of direct enforcement [domestically] on the basis of the wording and intention of that particular provision', however many international law scholars argue that the notion of 'self-execution' is inappropriate in the South African context, an unfortunate import from the United States where there is a distinction between an international agreement and an international treaty.[44] Regrettably, especially in the light of the ambiguous status of self-execution, South Africa has domesticated very few international treaties through enacting domestic legislation. There are also no provisions in the Constitution or legislation to establish procedures or principles to give effect to the binding decisions of international (or regional) courts (such as the African Court on Human and Peoples' Rights) or the recommendations of quasi-judicial bodies (such as the African Commission on Human and Peoples' Rights or the UN Committee on Economic, Social and Cultural Rights).[45] Nonetheless, even where they are not directly enforceable domestically, international conventions play a critical role in guiding the interpretation of human rights including by domestic courts. Additionally, in the South African case of *Zimbabwe v Fick*, the Constitutional Court accepted that—in the absence of guidance from the Constitution or legislation—the common-law rule that (where certain requirements are met) a 'foreign judgment' may be enforced domestically, should be developed to include judgments by international courts, including tribunals such as the SADC Tribunal.[46]

[44] F Viljoen 'International protection of human rights' in H Strydom (ed) *International Law* (2016) 363–4. See further, Chapter 4.

[45] Ibid 366.

[46] *Zimbabwe v Fick* 2013 (5) SA 325, especially para 105. See further Chapter 4.

THE TWO CORNERSTONE INTERNATIONAL COVENANTS

1 The International Covenant on Civil and Political Rights (ICCPR)[47]

The ICCPR, which was adopted and opened for signature in 1966 and came into force in 1976, has been ratified by 169 states, including South Africa (in 1998)[48] and the United States (the largest economy in the world). The second largest economy in the world, China is a signatory but has not ratified the ICCPR.

Like the ICESCR, the ICCPR commences with the recognition of the right of self-determination (article 1). Unlike other United Nations instruments which recognise this right in the context of decolonisation, the ICCPR asserts the right of self-determination in general.

Although it proclaims the right to life (article 6), the death penalty is not prohibited except in respect of persons below the age of 18, and pregnant women. In 1989, a Second Optional Protocol was adopted which outlaws the death penalty completely. To date, this Protocol has been accepted by 85 states, including South Africa (in 2002) (but by neither the United States nor China, both of which still have the death penalty).

Torture, cruel, inhuman or degrading treatment (article 7), and slavery (article 8) are prohibited. The right to liberty and security of person is recognised (article 9) and everyone is entitled to a fair and public trial with due regard to a number of minimum guarantees (article 14). The principle of *nullum crimen sine lege* is recognised, except in respect of 'any act or omission which, at the time when it was committed, was criminal according to the general principles of law recognised by the community of nations' (article 15)—such as war crimes, crimes against humanity, and genocide.

The Covenant recognises the freedoms of movement (article 12), thought, conscience and religion (article 18), expression (article 19), assembly (article 21), and association (article 22), but accepts that these rights may be restricted where this is necessary to protect national security, public order, public health or morals, or the rights and freedom of others. Article 20 qualifies the freedom of expression

[47] For an examination of the *travaux préparatoires* of this Covenant, see MJ Bossuyt *Guide to the 'Travaux Préparatoires' of the International Covenant on Civil and Political Rights* (1987). See too L Henkin (ed) *The International Bill of Rights* (1981); M Nowak *UN Covenant on Civil and Political Rights: CCPR Commentary* 2 ed (2005); S Joseph and M Castan *The International Covenant on Civil and Political Rights: Cases, Materials and Commentary* 3 ed (2013).

[48] The Department of Justice and Constitutional Development is responsible for overseeing the implementation of the ICCPR in South Africa.

by prohibiting war propaganda and 'any advocacy of national, racial or religious hatred that constitutes incitement to discrimination, hostility or violence'.

Every citizen is to have the right to vote in periodic elections and to participate in public life (article 25). Privacy (article 17), family life (article 23), and the protection of children (article 24) are recognised.

All persons are to enjoy equality before the law and 'are entitled without any discrimination to the equal protection of the law'. Discrimination on grounds of 'race, colour, sex, language, religion, political or other opinion, national or social origin, property, birth or other status' is prohibited (article 26). Of particular importance for an ethnically and linguistically diverse society such as South Africa, is article 27 which provides:

> In those states in which ethnic, religious or linguistic minorities exist, persons belonging to such minorities shall not be denied the right, in community with other members of their group, to enjoy their own culture, to profess and practice their own religion, or to use their own language.

In time of public emergency threatening the life of the nation, states may derogate from their obligations under the Covenant 'to the extent strictly required by the exigencies of the situation' (article 4). No derogation is permitted, however, from a number of absolute provisions, such as the right to life and the freedom from torture and cruel, inhuman, or degrading treatment or punishment.

Unlike the UDHR,[49] the ICCPR (as well as the ICESCR) is silent on the right to property.

States are obliged to ensure that their legal systems provide effective remedies against violations of the Covenant, including violations committed by government officials (article 2).

International supervision of the ICCPR is entrusted to the Human Rights Committee,[50] a body of 18 experts (mainly lawyers) elected by the contracting states for a renewable four-year term. In the election of the Committee, consideration is to be given to equitable geographical distribution of membership and to the representation of the different forms of civilisation and of the principal legal systems. In June 2016, Christof Heyns (former director of the Centre for Human

[49] Article 17 of the Universal Declaration provides: '(1) Everyone has the right to own property alone as well as in association with others: (2) No one shall be arbitrarily deprived of his property.'

[50] For a comprehensive study on the work of this Committee, see D McGoldrick *The Human Rights Committee: Its Role in the Development of the International Covenant on Civil and Political Rights* (1991). See too J Sisk and A Pronto 'The international human rights norms in South Africa: The jurisprudence of the Human Rights Committee' (1995) 11 *SAJHR* 438; P Alston and J Crawford (eds) *The Future of UN Human Rights Treaty Monitoring* (2000).

Rights at the University of Pretoria) was elected as a member of the Human Rights Committee.

The Committee is not a full-time body and holds three sessions per year. Like all core international human rights treaties, the Human Rights Committee supervises the Covenant in three key ways.

(a) State reports[51]

All contracting states are required to submit reports on the measures they have adopted to give effect to the Covenant. The initial report must be submitted within one year of becoming a contracting state. Thereafter reports must be submitted regularly, at the request of the Committee(usually every four or five years).

The Human Rights Committee considers each report together with any information submitted to it by other sources (for instance by non-governmental organisations such as Amnesty International). The Committee discusses the report with the representative of the reporting state. Article 40(4) permits the Committee to submit appropriate 'general comments', as well as 'concluding observations' regarding any areas of concern to the contracting states.

While many states report as required, some states, including South Africa do not report timeously. South Africa submitted its initial report (due in March 2000) only in November 2014, having also missed, and skipped two subsequent periodic reports that fell due in March 2005 and March 2010. South Africa has also missed the date for its third periodic report (March 2015). In its concluding observations of March 2016 on South Africa's initial report the Committee noted its disappointment over South Africa's very late reporting, as well as South Africa's failure to domesticate the ICCPR. Substantively, the Committee expressed concerns about the high levels of incidents of racism and xenophobia; the vulnerability of protesting activists (including striking miners who were shot dead at Lonmin's Marikana platinum mine on 16 August 2012) and human rights defenders; as well as the government's failure to detain President Omar al-Bashir of Sudan in June 2015, pursuant to an International Criminal Court arrest warrant.[52]

(b) General comments

The Committee also makes general comments on the interpretation and application of the Covenant not specific to particular states. For

[51] See D Fischer 'Reporting under the Covenant on Civil and Political Rights: The first five years of the Human Rights Committee' (1982) 76 *AJIL* 142. Also see the list of state party reports on the UN Human Rights Committee website at: http://tbinternet.ohchr.org/_layouts/treatybodyexternal/TBSearch.aspx?Lang=en&TreatyID=8&DocTypeID=45&DocTypeID=29.

[52] CCPR/C/ZAF/CO/1 (26 April 2016). See further Chapter 10.

example, in General Comment 24, discussed below,[53] it examined the consequences of a reservation to the Covenant that was incompatible with the object and purpose of the Covenant. And in General Comment 18 it elaborated on the meaning and scope of non-discrimination under article 26 of the ICCPR.

(c) Individual complaints

The First Optional Protocol to the ICCPR, which South Africa acceded to in 2002, permits contracting states to recognise the competence of the Committee to receive and consider complaints from individuals who claim to be victims of a violation of the Covenant by a contracting state. The individual must have exhausted all available domestic remedies first and the same matter must not be the subject of any other international investigation (for example, by the African Court of Human and Peoples' Rights acting under the 1998 Protocol to the African Charter on Human and Peoples' Rights (ACHPR) on the establishment of the African Court on Human and Peoples' Rights). The complaint is considered based on written submissions without an oral hearing. The Committee then formulates its 'views', which are forwarded to the defendant state and the complainant. These 'views' are not legally binding and there is no provision for a court to take a binding decision on the matter (as for example under the European Convention on Human Rights).

The workload of the Committee has substantially increased in recent years as a result of the increase in the number of states accepting the Optional Protocol. (At present 116 states, including South Africa, have accepted the First Optional Protocol.) The views of the Committee have become an important part of the jurisprudence of human rights. Notable decisions include *Lovelace v Canada*,[54] in which the Committee found that Canada had violated article 27, dealing with the rights of ethnic minorities, by denying Mrs Lovelace, a Canadian Indian, the right to return to her reserve following the dissolution of her marriage to a non-Indian; *Toonen v Australia*,[55] holding that the Tasmanian Criminal Code, which made private homosexual conduct a criminal offence, violated article 17 guaranteeing the right to privacy; *Ng v Canada*,[56] in which the Committee held that execution by gas asphyxiation (in California) constituted cruel and inhuman treatment, which meant that Canada should not have extradited Ng to the United States; *Roger Judge v Canada*,[57] in which

[53] See Chapter 20.
[54] (1981) CCPR/C/OP/1.
[55] (1994) 1–3 *IHRR* 97; (1994) CCPR/C/46/D/488/1992.
[56] (1994) 1–2 *IHRR* 161; 98 ILR 479 ; (1994) CCPR/C/46/D/469/1991.
[57] (2004) 11–1 *IHRR* 125; (2003) 42 *ILM* 1214; (2004) CCPR/C/78/D/829/1998.

the Committee held that Canada had violated the right to life by deporting a person to the United States where he was under sentence of death, without first obtaining assurances from the United States that the death penalty would not be carried out; and *Mellet v Ireland*,[58] in which the Committee found Ireland's law prohibiting and criminalising abortion to be discriminatory and to amount to cruel, degrading and inhuman treatment.

Since South Africa acceded to the First Optional Protocol in 2002, the Committee has decided two individual complaints against South Africa. In *Prince v South Africa* the Committee held that, although Mr Prince, a Rastafarian, was prohibited from possessing and using cannabis under the country's general laws criminalising drugs, this did not constitute an impermissible limitation of the ICCPR's religious freedom-related rights.[59] However, in *McCallum v South Africa* the Committee found that South Africa had violated article 7 of the ICCPR, the prohibition on torture or cruel, inhuman and degrading treatment or punishment.[60] In this case, following the death of a prison warden, Mr McCallum, who was an inmate in a South African prison, alleged he had been severely assaulted, denied access to a lawyer and his family for more than a month, and had not been granted medical treatment. Here, due to 'the unfortunate failure of the South African government to respond', the Committee based its finding 'on the complainant's uncontested allegations as far as they were adequately substantiated'.[61]

2 The International Covenant on Economic, Social and Cultural Rights (ICESCR)[62]

The ICESCR, which was adopted and opened for signature in 1966 and entered into force in 1976, has been ratified by 166 states including China and, more recently, South Africa. Reflecting the

[58] (2016) CCPR/C/116/D/2324/2013.

[59] (2007) CCPR/C/91/D/1474/2006.

[60] (2010) CCPR/C/100/D/1818/2008.

[61] Viljoen (n 44) 335.

[62] See M Craven *The International Covenant on Economic, Social and Cultural Rights* (1995); A Eide, C Krause and A Rosas *Economic, Social and Cultural Rights* 2 ed (2001); S Liebenberg 'The International Covenant on Economic, Social and Cultural Rights and its implications for South Africa' (1995) 11 *SAJHR* 359; D Brand and C Heyns (eds) *Socio-Economic Rights in South Africa* (2005); S Liebenberg *Socio-Economic Rights: Adjudication under a Transformative Constitution* (2010); B Saul, D Kinley and J Mowbray *The International Covenant on Economic, Social and Cultural Rights. Commentary, Cases and Materials* (2014); M Ssenyonjo *Economic, Social and Cultural Rights in International Law* 2 ed (2016); and B Saul (ed) *The International Covenant on Economic, Social and Cultural Rights: Travaux Préparatoires, 1948–1966* (2016).

original Cold War divide, the United States is a signatory but has not ratified the ICESCR.

Whereas ICCPR rights are usually viewed as individual rights, the ICESCR deals with rights that can be both individual and collective: the rights to work (article 6), to the enjoyment of just and favourable conditions of work—including fair wages and safe and healthy working conditions (article 7), to form and join trade unions (article 8), to social security (article 9), to an adequate standard of living (article 11), to the enjoyment of the highest attainable standard of physical and mental health (article 12), to education—including free and compulsory primary education (article 13), and to participate in cultural life (article 15).

The ICESCR does not contain an explicit right to water or sanitation. However, in July 2010, through Resolution A/RES/64/292, the UN General Assembly recognised the human right to water and sanitation. Moreover, in September 2010 the UN Human Rights Council adopted Resolution A/HRC/RES/15/9 affirming that the rights to water and sanitation as part of existing binding international law.

For many years economic, social and cultural rights (ESCR) were considered non-justiciable, and more aspirational than binding. However, over the past decade these rights have been widely recognised as justiciable and binding across the world and particularly in the global south.[63] Notwithstanding this growing recognition, whereas article 2 of the ICCPR requires states to immediately realise the rights, article 2 of the ICESCR provides that each party to the Covenant should 'take steps . . . to the maximum of its available resources, with a view to achieving progressively the full realization of the rights recognised in the present Covenant by all appropriate means' (article 2).

However, the monitoring body of the Committee on Social and Economic Rights (CESCR), has declared in General Comment 3:

> [T]he Committee is of the view that a minimum core obligation to ensure the satisfaction of, at the very least, minimum essential levels of each of the rights is incumbent upon every State party. Thus, for example, a State party in

[63] E Mureinik 'Beyond a charter of luxuries: Economic rights in the Constitution' (1992) 8 *SAJHR* 464; J Mapulanga-Hulston 'Examining the Justiciability of Economic, Social and Cultural Rights' (2002) 6 *The International Journal of Human Rights* 29; M Dennis and D Stewart 'Justiciability of economic, social and cultural rights: Should there be an international complaints mechanism to adjudicate the rights to food, water, housing and health?' (2004) 98 *AJIL* 462; M Langford (ed) *Social Rights Jurisprudence: Emerging Trends in International and Comparative Law* (2008); M Langford, B Cousins, J Dugard and T Madlingozi (eds) *Socio-Economic Rights in South Africa: Symbols or Substance?* (2013).

> which any significant number of individuals is deprived of essential foodstuffs, of essential primary health care, of basic shelter and housing, or of the most basic forms of education is, prima facie, failing to discharge its obligations under the Covenant. If the Covenant were to be read in such a way as not to establish such a minimum core obligation, it would largely be deprived of its *raison d'être*. By the same token, it must be noted that any assessment as to whether a State has discharged its minimum core obligation must also take account of resource constraints applying within the country concerned. Article 2(1) obligates each State party to take the necessary steps 'to the maximum of its available resources'. In order for a State party to be able to attribute its failure to meet at least its minimum core obligations to a lack of available resources it must demonstrate that every effort has been made to use all resources that are at its disposition in an effort to satisfy, as a matter of priority, those minimum obligations.[64]

Somewhat inexplicably, despite signing the ICESCR in 1994, South Africa ratified this Covenant only in January 2015 (the Department of Justice and Constitutional Development is responsible for overseeing the implementation of the ICESCR in South Africa). The government gave no satisfactory explanation for its failure to ratify the Covenant for the intervening 20 years. This lengthy non-ratification is even more puzzling since the social and economic rights protected by the Bill of Rights were inspired by the ICESCR and ratification requires few changes in the domestic legal order.[65] Moreover, the South African Bill of Rights is seen as a model for the protection of social and economic rights and decisions of South African courts on these rights have been hailed as among the most progressive in the world.

Nonetheless, as a signatory since 1994, South African courts have been empowered to enforce justiciable social and economic rights in the 1996 Constitution.[66] They have used this power cautiously but progressively. However, in a number of decisions, the Constitutional Court has refused to interpret the ESCR in the Constitution to require a 'minimum core obligation' of the kind proclaimed by the Committee on Economic, Social and Cultural Rights and have instead opted for a test of reasonableness. In *Mazibuko v City of Johannesburg*[67] the Constitutional Court refused to quantify the amount of water sufficient for a dignified life. In interpreting s 27 of the Constitution

[64] CESCR General Comment 3 'The nature of states parties' obligations (article 2, para 1)' (1994) 1 *IHRR* 6 para 10; cited in *Minister of Health v Treatment Action Campaign (No 2)* 2002 (5) SA 721 (CC) 737 para 26. See, too, *Government of the RSA v Grootboom* 2001 (1) SA 46 (CC) 63–6.

[65] See L Chenwi and R Hardowar 'Promoting socio-economic rights in South Africa through the ratification and implementation of the ICESCR and its optional Protocol' (2010) 11 *ESR Review* 3.

[66] See D Bilchitz *Poverty and Fundamental Rights: The Justification and Enforcement of Social and Economic Rights* (2007).

[67] 2010 (4) SA 1 (CC).

recognising the right of access to water, the Court affirmed its rejection of the argument that the social and economic rights in the Constitution contain a minimum core which the state is obliged to furnish, the content of which should be determined by the courts[68] and held:

> The positive obligations imposed upon government by the social and economic rights in our Constitution will be enforced by courts in at least the following ways. If government takes no steps to realise the rights, the courts will require government to take steps. If government's adopted measures are unreasonable, the courts will similarly require that they be reviewed so as to meet the constitutional standard of reasonableness. From *Grootboom* it is clear that a measure will be unreasonable if it makes no provision for those most desperately in need. If government adopts a policy with unreasonable limitations or exclusions as described in *Treatment Action Campaign (No 2)*, the court may order that those be removed. Finally, the obligation of progressive realisation imposes a duty upon government continually to review its policies to ensure that the achievement of the right is progressively realised.[69]

It is unclear yet how South Africa's ratification of the ICESCR might change the courts' position on the minimum core content approach and applicable standards of review for the adjudication of ESCR.

Overseeing the ICESCR, is the CESCR. Resembling the ICCPR Human Rights Committee, the ESCR Committee comprises 18 experts elected by the contracting states for four-year terms, which may be renewed. In 2016, Sandra Liebenberg from the Law Faculty at the University of Stellenbosch was elected to serve as a member of the CESCR. The Committee holds two sessions per year and, like the ICCPR, it supervises the Covenant in three key ways: via state reports, general comments and individual complaints.

(a) State reports

All contracting states are required to submit regular reports on the measures they have adopted to give effect to the Covenant. The initial report must be submitted within two years of becoming a contracting state. Thereafter reports must be submitted every five years. South Africa submitted its first report on time, in April 2017. Among the list of issues provided by the CESCR in response to South Africa's initial report, was a query about the measures taken to curb South Africa's

[68] Mazibako (n 67) 18 (para 53), citing *Government of the RSA v Grootboom* 2001 (I) SA 46 (CC) 63–6 (particularly para 32); and *Minister of Health v Treatment Action Campaign (No 2)* 2002 (5) SA 721 (CC) paras 26, 38.

[69] Ibid para 22 (para 67).

very high unemployment rate.[70] The CESCR is due to provide concluding observations on South Africa's initial report in late 2018.

(b) General comments

Among the CESCR's General Comments is General Comment 15 on the right to water,[71] and General Comment 24 on state obligations in the context of business activities.[72]

(c) Individual complaints

In 2008, an Optional Protocol was adopted to provide for individual complaints, which entered into force in May 2013. The Optional Protocol to the ICESCR has been ratified by 23 states, which do not include South Africa, the United States or China. Notwithstanding South Africa's failure to ratify it, the Optional Protocol uses the South African 'reasonableness' standard of review to assess contracting states' violations under the Covenant.

In one of the first individual complaints to be ruled admissible by the CESCR, *I.D.G v Spain*,[73] the Committee found Spain to have violated the petitioner's housing and effective remedy rights by failing to ensure that Spanish banks pursued satisfactory notification processes prior to foreclosing on mortgaged homes. As part of the International Network for Economic, Social and Cultural Rights (ESCR-net), South African experts and the Socio-Economic Rights Institute of South Africa (SERI) played a role in the third party intervention in *I.D.G. v Spain*. In particular, they highlighted South African housing rights jurisprudence including *Gundwana v Steko Development CC* in which the Constitutional Court ruled that South African mortgage foreclosure procedures were unconstitutional.[74] In a subsequent individual complaint, *M.B.D. v Spain*,[75] in which the Committee found Spain to have violated tenants' housing-related rights by not ensuring protection against eviction leading to homelessness, South African experts and NGOs again contributed to the third party intervention, using South African housing jurisprudence including *City of Johannesburg Metropolitan Municipality v Blue Moonlight Properties 39 (Pty) Ltd*.[76]

[70] E/C.12/ZAF/Q/1 (31 October 2017) available at http://tbinternet.ohchr.org/_layouts/treatybodyexternal/Download.aspx?symbolno=E%2fC.12%2fZAF%2fQ%2f1&Lang=en.

[71] CESCR General Comment 15 'The right to water' (2003) E/C.12/2002/11).

[72] CESCR General Comment 24 'State obligations under the ICESCR in the context of business activities' (2017) E/C.12/GC/24.

[73] (2015) *I.D.G. v Spain* E/C.12/55/D/2/2014.

[74] 2011 (3) SA 608 (CC).

[75] (2017) *M.B.D. v Spain* E/C.12/61/D/2015.

[76] 2012 (2) SA 104 (CC).

THE OTHER SEVEN INTERNATIONAL CONVENTIONS

1 International Convention on the Elimination of All Forms of Racial Discrimination (ICERD)[77]

This Convention, which was adopted and opened for signature in 1966 and came into force in 1969, has been ratified by 179 states, including China and the United States. South Africa ratified the ICERD in 1998. The Department of Justice and Constitutional Development is responsible for overseeing the implementation of the ICERD in South Africa.

The Convention defines racial discrimination in article 1(1) as

> any distinction, exclusion, restriction or preference based on race, colour, descent, or national or ethnic origin which has the purpose or effect of nullifying or impairing the recognition, enjoyment or exercise, on an equal footing, of human rights and fundamental freedoms in the political, economic, social, cultural or any other field of public life.

Contracting states condemn racial discrimination and undertake to eliminate it by all appropriate means (article 2). Apartheid receives particular condemnation (article 3). In pursuance of the undertaking to eliminate racial discrimination states agree to guarantee civil and political rights and economic, social, and cultural rights in a non-discriminatory manner (article 5). Furthermore, states undertake to assure to everyone within their jurisdiction effective protection and remedies against acts of racial discrimination (article 6).

The more controversial features of the ICERD are those concerning private or non-governmental discrimination, restrictions on freedom of speech, and affirmative action. Although article 1(1) defines racial discrimination as comprising certain distinctions 'in the political, economic, social, cultural or any other field of *public life*' (emphasis added), article 2(1)(d) obliges states 'to bring to an end, by all appropriate means, including legislation as required by circumstances, racial discrimination by any persons, group or organization', and article 5(f) guarantees equality before the law in '[t]he right of access to any place or service intended for use by the general public, such as transport, hotels, restaurants, cafés, theatres and parks'. All of this indicates that discriminatory action by non-governmental parties

[77] See N Lerner *The UN Convention on the Elimination of All Forms of Racial Discrimination* 2 ed (1980); E Schwelb 'The International Convention on the Elimination of All Forms of Racial Discrimination' (1966) 15 *ICLQ* 966; T Meron 'The meaning and reach of the International Convention on the Elimination of All Forms of Racial Discrimination' (1985) 79 *AJIL* 283; D Keane and A Waughray (eds) *Fifty Years of the International Convention on the Elimination of All Forms of Racial Discrimination: A Living Instrument* (2017).

is prohibited by the Convention.[78] Racist speech is clearly outlawed. Article 4 obliges states to criminalise 'all dissemination of ideas based on racial superiority' and 'incitement to racial discrimination' and to prohibit organisations that 'promote and incite racial discrimination'. Affirmative action is recognised in two ways. First, article 1(4) excludes affirmative action from the ambit of racial discrimination provided 'such measures do not, as a consequence, lead to the maintenance of separate rights for different racial groups and that they shall not be continued after the objectives for which they were taken have been achieved'. On the other hand, article 2(2) obliges states to take affirmative action 'when the circumstances so warrant'.

Enforcement of the Convention is entrusted to the Committee for the Elimination of Racial Discrimination (CERD), which is substantially similar to the ICCPR Human Rights Committee both in its composition and in powers. The principal method of supervision is the submission and consideration of national reports—states must initially report one year after acceding to the Convention and thereafter every two years.

Unfortunately, South Africa has not maintained a good record of ICERD reporting. Having failed to submit its first (January 2000), second (January 2002) and third (January 2004) reports on time, South Africa submitted a consolidated report in December 2004.[79] Among its concluding observations, the Committee noted with regret the delay of almost five years for South Africa's first report.[80] South Africa also missed the due dates for its fourth (January 2006), fifth (January 2008), sixth (January 2010), seventh (January 2012) and eighth (January 2014) reports, submitting a consolidated report in mid-2016.

The ICERD is the only treaty that provides for *compulsory* inter-state complaints[81]—as opposed to the ICCPR's *optional* inter-state claims procedure. States have not utilised this procedure until 2018 when two inter-state complaints were initiated. First, by Palestine against Israel in which Palestine claims that Israel is practising racial

[78] Meron (n 77) 291–5.

[79] See on South Africa's first report, M Olivier 'Compliance with reporting obligations under international law: Where does South Africa stand?' (2006) *SAYIL* 179, 185.

[80] CERD/C/ZAF/CO/3 (19 October 2006) available at http://tbinternet.ohchr.org/_layouts/treatybodyexternal/Download.aspx?symbolno=CERD%2fC%2fZAF%2fCO%2f3&Lang=en; see also L Chenwi 'State of state reporting under international human rights law' Research Paper, Socio-Economic Rights Project, Community Law Centre, University of the Western Cape (September 2010) 31–4 available at http://www.childjustice.org.za/research/South%20Africa%20-%20State%20of%20state%20reporting%20under%20international%20human%20rights%20law.pdf.

[81] ICERD, articles 11–13.

discrimination and apartheid in the occupied Palestinian Territory; and, second, by Qatar against Saudi Arabia, the United Arab Emirates and Bahrain on the ground that their blockades of Qatar constitutes a form of racial discrimination. This procedure envisages a complaint to the CERD which is referred to an ad hoc Conciliation Commission for investigation, report and recommendation.

An optional system of individual complaints, which South Africa has accepted, is also provided for (article 14). And Article 22 of the ICERD provides that disputes relating to the interpretation of the Convention can be referred to the International Court of Justice. This provision has been invoked by states in several cases before the International Court of Justice, including the *Case Concerning Application of the International Convention on the Elimination of All Forms of Racial Discrimination (Georgia v Russian Federation)*.[82]

2 Convention on the Elimination of All Forms of Discrimination against Women (CEDAW)[83]

This Convention was adopted and opened for signature in 1979 and came into force in 1981. A total of 189 states have ratified or acceded to the Convention. The United States, which signed CEDAW in 1980, is the only major country not to have ratified the Convention. South Africa ratified CEDAW in 1995.[84] The Department of Women is responsible for overseeing the implementation of CEDAW in South Africa.

For the purpose of the Convention, discrimination means any distinction made on the basis of sex which 'has the effect or purpose

[82] 2011 ICJ Reports 70.

[83] (1980) 19 *ILM* 33. For a critique of the Convention and patriarchy in the international legal order, see H Charlesworth, C Chinkin and S Wright 'Feminist approaches to international law' (1991) 85 *AJIL* 613. For a guide to the literature, see B Cook 'Bibliography: The international right to non-discrimination on the basis of sex' (1989) 14 *Yale Journal of International Law* 161. See, too, E Evatt 'Eliminating discrimination against women' (1991) 18 *Melbourne University Law Review* 435; R Cook *Human Rights of Women* (1994); F Kathree 'Convention on the Elimination of All Forms of Discrimination Against Women' (1995) 11 *SAJHR* 421; A Hellum and H Aasen *Women's Human Rights: CEDAW in International, Regional and National Law* (2013); S Zwingel *Translating International Women's Rights: The CEDAW Convention in Context* (2016); M Campbell *Using Equality to Address Women's Poverty: The Role of CEDAW* (2018).

[84] In 1993 Parliament adopted the General Law Fourth Amendment Act 132 of 1993, which removed all traces of legislative discrimination against women so as to enable South Africa to ratify CEDAW (see also the Prevention of Family Violence Act 133 of 1993, and the Convention on Consent to Marriage, Minimum Age for Marriage and Registration of Marriages of 1962). And in 1993 South Africa acceded to the Convention on Consent to Marriage, Minimum Age for Marriage and Registration of Marriages of 1962 (the text of this Convention is published in *Human Rights: A Compilation of International Instruments* (2002).

of impairing or nullifying the recognition, enjoyment or exercise by women, irrespective of their marital status, on a basis of equality of men and women, of human rights' in any field (article 1). The Convention condemns discrimination against women and obliges states to ensure that their legal systems guarantee equal rights to women in all spheres of life. Affirmative action is recognised in article 4(1), which permits states to adopt 'temporary special measures aimed at accelerating *de facto* equality between men and women'. Article 4(2) provides that special measures aimed at protecting maternity 'shall not be considered discriminatory'.

Although 'reservations incompatible with the object and purpose' of the Convention are prohibited, no criteria are given for the determination of incompatibility. Consequently, a number of reservations have been made, particularly those that preserve the Islamic Sharia, which seem to defeat the purpose of the Convention.[85]

Enforcement of CEDAW occurs via a 23-person Committee on the Elimination of Discrimination against Women, which receives and considers state reports (to be submitted initially after one year and thereafter every four years or when the Committee requests).

In 1999, an Optional Protocol was adopted to permit the Committee to receive and consider individual petitions relating to violations of the Convention and to investigate systematic violations of the Convention. At present 109 states are parties to this Optional Protocol, including South Africa, which ratified it in 2005, and China (but not the United States).

South Africa delayed its initial report to the Committee, which was due in January 1997, to February 1998. Among the Committee's concluding observations was the need for South Africa to liaise with civil society over the compilation of its reports.[86] South Africa also delayed and consolidated its second (due in January 2001), third (due in January 2005) and fourth (due in January 2009) reports and submitted a consolidated report in July 2009.[87] Among the Committee's concluding observations on this consolidated report was a concern over the government's failure to domesticate CEDAW, as well as concerns over the persistence of patriarchy and stereotypes concerning women's roles and responsibilities in society and the

[85] B Clark 'The Vienna Convention reservations regime and the Convention on Discrimination against Women' (1991) 85 *AJIL* 281.

[86] A/53/58/Rev.1(SUPP) paras100–37 available at http://tbinternet.ohchr.org/_layouts/treatybodyexternal/Download.aspx?symbolno=A%2f53%2f38%2fRev.1(SUPP)&Lang=en; see on South Africa's first report, Olivier 'Compliance with reporting obligations under international law: Where does South Africa stand?' (2006) 31 *SAYIL* 187.

[87] Chenwi (n 80) 37.

family.[88] The South African government has missed the deadline for its fifth and sixth periodic reports.

3 Torture (CAT)[89]

Torture is prohibited by customary international law and is recognised as a norm of *jus cogens*.[90] The Rome Statute of the International Criminal Court also recognises torture as a species of crime against humanity.[91]

The principal anti-torture convention is the Convention against Torture and Other Cruel, Inhuman or Degrading Treatment or Punishment (CAT). CAT was adopted and opened for signature in 1984, came into force in 1987 and has been ratified by 162 states, including South Africa (1998), as well as China and the United States. CAT is the only international human rights treaty to have been properly domesticated, in its entirety, in South Africa through the Prevention and Combating of Torture of Persons Act 13 of 2013. The Department of Justice and Constitutional Development is responsible for overseeing the implementation of CAT.

This Convention defines torture, in article 1, as

> any act by which severe pain or suffering, whether physical or mental, is intentionally inflicted on a person for such purposes as obtaining from him or a third person information or a confession, punishing him for an act he or a third person has committed or is suspected of having committed, or intimidating or coercing him or a third person, or for any reason based on discrimination of any kind, when such pain or suffering is inflicted by or at the instigation of or with the consent or acquiescence of a public official or

[88] CEDAW/C/ZAF/CO/4 (5 April 2011) available at http://tbinternet.ohchr.org/_layouts/treatybodyexternal/Download.aspx?symbolno=CEDAW%2fC%2fZAF%2fCO%2f4&Lang=en.

[89] A Cassese (ed) *The International Fight against Torture* (1991); J Burgers and H Danelius *The United Nations Convention against Torture* (1988); R Keightley 'Torture and cruel, inhuman and degrading treatment or punishment in the UN Convention against Torture and other instruments of international law: Recent developments in South Africa' (1995) 11 *SAJHR* 379; ME Evans 'Getting to grips with torture' (2002) 51 *ICLQ* 365; M Nowak and E McArthur *The UN Convention Against Torture* (2008); 'Special issue: The law of cruelty: Torture as an international crime' (2008) 6 *Journal of International Criminal Justice* 157; M Nowak and E McArthur *The United Nations Convention Against Torture: A Commentary* (2008); N Rodley and M Pollard *The Treatment of Prisoners under International Law* 3 ed (2009); and R Murray and A Hallo de Wolf *The Optional Protocol to the UN Convention Against Torture* (2011).

[90] *Filartiga v Pena Irala* 630 F 2d 876 (2nd Cir 1980); *Prosecutor v Furundzija* 121 ILR 213; *Al-Adsani v UK* 123 ILR 24; E de Wet 'The prohibition of torture as an international norm of *jus cogens* and its implications for national and customary law' (2004) 15 *EJIL* 97; *S v Mthembu* Oxford Reports on International Law, ILDC 958 (ZA 2008) (SCA 2008) paras 30–2.

[91] Rome Statute, article 7.

other person acting in an official capacity. It does not include pain or suffering arising only from, inherent in or incidental to lawful sanctions.

The ban on torture is to be enforced by both municipal criminal-law sanctions and international supervision. First, states undertake either to try or to extradite torturers. Jurisdiction is recognised based on the principles of territoriality, active and passive nationality, and presence (article 5). Secondly, a ten-person Committee against Torture is established with powers similar to those of the other supervisory committees. The Committee receives and considers national reports (states must initially report after one year and thereafter every four years) and there is provision for optional individual complaints procedures for those contracting states that have made a declaration in terms of article 22 of CAT.

When South Africa became a party to the Convention in 1998, it accepted both the inter-state and individual complaints procedures under articles 21 and 22 respectively.[92]

In 2002, an Optional Protocol to the Convention (OPCAT) was adopted, which enables a Subcommittee on Prevention of Torture and other Cruel, Inhuman or Degrading Treatment or Punishment (SPT) to conduct regular visits to places of detention and requires states parties to maintain, at the domestic level, one or several visiting bodies for the prevention of torture.[93] South Africa has signed (2006) but not ratified OPCAT (China and the United States have neither ratified nor signed OPCAT), which has 87 ratifications.

South Africa failed to comply with the date for its initial state report under CAT, January 2000 (as well as the date for its second periodic report, due in January 2004), instead submitting its initial report in June 2005. In its concluding observations on South Africa's initial report the Committee noted its regret at this delay and also that the report did not comply with the guidelines in that it mainly set out statutory provisions rather than examining the implementation of CAT.[94] South Africa missed subsequent reporting deadlines (under CAT state reports are due every four years), submitting its second report in September 2017.[95] The Committee has yet to consider this report.

[92] See on South Africa's first report to the Committee on Torture, Olivier (n 86) 188; L Muntingh 'The betrayal of Steve Biko—SA's initial report to the UN Committee on Torture' (2008) 10 *Law, Democracy and Development* 29.

[93] (2003) 42 *ILM* 26. There are at present 87 state parties to this protocol.

[94] CAT/C/ZAF/CO/1 (7 Dec 2006) available at http://tbinternet.ohchr.org/_layouts/treatybodyexternal/Download.aspx?symbolno=CAT%2fC%2fZAF%2fCO%2f1&Lang=en; see also Chenwi (n 80) 41.

[95] CAT/C/ZAF/2 available at http://tbinternet.ohchr.org/_layouts/treatybodyexternal/Download.aspx?symbolno=CAT%2fC%2fZAF%2f2&Lang=en.

4 Convention on the Rights of the Child (CRC)[96]

The CRC, which was adopted and opened for signature in 1989 and came into force in 1990, has been ratified by 196 states. The United States and Somalia are the only two UN members that are not parties to the Convention (the United States became a signatory in 1995). The Convention protects children against discrimination and asserts their civil and political, economic, social, and cultural rights. The Convention has three Optional Protocols: one dealing with children in armed conflict (OPAC), which has 167 ratifications; one dealing with the sale of children, child prostitution and pornography (OPSC), which has 174 ratifications; and a communications procedure (OPIC) allowing individual children to submit complaints against their state regarding violations of their rights under the Convention and its first two optional protocols, which has 37 ratifications. The CRC and its optional protocols are monitored by an 18-member Committee on the Rights of the Child, which since 2016 has included Professor Ann Skelton from the Centre for Child Law at the University of Pretoria. Contracting states must submit an initial report two years after acceding to the Convention and thereafter every five years.

South Africa ratified the Convention in 1995.[97] South Africa is also a party to OPAC (2009) and the OPSC (2003), but not the OPIC (neither China nor the United States is party to these instruments). The Department of Social Development is responsible for overseeing the implementation of the CRC. South Africa's initial report on the CRC, which was due in July 1997, was submitted in December 1997. Among its concluding observations, the Committee encouraged South Africa to ratify the ICESCR (which it subsequently did in 2015), and to provide adequate support to child-headed households. The Committee also expressed concern over the high incidence of domestic violence, ill-treatment, and abuse of children, including

[96] (1989) 28 *ILM* 1448. See G van Bueren *The International Law on the Rights of the Child* (1995); LJ le Blanc *The Convention on the Rights of the Child* (1995); J Sloth-Nielsen 'Ratification of the United Nations Convention on The Rights of the Child: Some implications for South African law' (1995) 11 *SAJHR* 401; S Detrick *A Commentary on the United Nations Convention on the Rights of the Child* (1999); T Liefaard and JE Doek (eds) *Litigating the Rights of the Child: The UN Convention on the Rights of the Child in Domestic and International Jurisprudence* (2014); T Liefaard and J Sloth-Nielsen (eds) *The United Nations Conventions on the Rights of the Child: Taking Stock after 25 Years and Looking Forward* (2016).

[97] In *Director of Public Prosecutions v P* 2006 (3) SA 515 (SCA) the SCA acknowledged the influence of the Convention on the Rights of the Child on s 28(1)*(g)* of the Constitution.

sexual abuse in the family.[98] South Africa's second, third and fourth reports, due in July 2002, July 2007 and July 2012 respectively, were submitted as a consolidated second report in November 2014. South Africa has not reported since. South Africa also has reporting obligations under the two Optional Protocols to the CRC. South Africa's initial report in terms of the OPSC was due in July 2005, but was submitted in November 2014. South Africa's initial report under OPAC was due in October 2011, but has not yet been submitted.

5 Migrant workers (CMW)[99]

The convention on the Protection of All Migrant Workers and Members of their Families (CMW),[100] which was adopted and opened for signature in 1990 and came into force in 2003, proclaims the rights of migrant workers and provides that there shall be no discrimination against such workers. South Africa is not a party to this convention, which has been ratified by 51 states (not by either China or United States). A 14-member Committee on Migrant Workers supervises the CMW and contracting parties must initially report within a year of acceding to the Convention and every five years thereafter. The individual complaints mechanism for the CMW, which requires ten states parties to make the necessary declaration under article 77, has not yet entered into force.

6 Enforced disappearance (CED)

The CED was adopted by the United Nations General Assembly in 2006, was opened for signature in 2007 and came into force in 2010. It has been ratified by 58 states. South Africa has not ratified the Convention (nor has China or the United States).

Enforced disappearance is defined in article 2 of the Convention as

> the arrest, detention, abduction or any other form of deprivation of liberty by agents of the state or by persons or groups of persons acting with the authorization, support or acquiescence of the State, followed by a refusal to acknowledge the deprivation of liberty or by concealment of the fate or whereabouts of the disappeared person, which place such a person outside the protection of the law.

The Convention, which is substantially modelled on CAT, obliges states parties to investigate acts of enforced disappearance, make enforced disappearance an offence under its domestic law, establish

[98] CRC/C/15/Add.122 available at http://tbinternet.ohchr.org/_layouts/treatybodyexternal/Download.aspx?symbolno=CRC%2fC%2f15%2fAdd.122&Lang=en.

[99] P de Guchteneire, A Pécoud and R Cholewinski (eds) *Migration and Human Rights: The United Nations Convention on Migrant Workers' Rights* (2009).

[100] (1991) 30 *ILM* 1517.

jurisdiction over the offence when the alleged offender is in its territory and co-operate with other states in ensuring that offenders are prosecuted or extradited and assist the victims of enforced disappearance. The Convention which provides an optional individual complaints procedure for contracting states that have made the necessary declaration under article 31, is monitored by a 10-member Committee on Enforced Disappearances. Like torture, the Rome Statute of the International Criminal Court recognises enforced disappearance as a crime.[101]

7 Disabled people (CRPD)[102]

The Convention on the Rights of Persons with Disabilities (CRPD), which was adopted in 2006, opened for signature in 2007 and came into force in 2008, aims to ensure that disabled persons are treated with dignity and that there should be no discrimination against such persons. An 18-member Committee on the Rights of Persons with Disabilities, which in terms of an Optional Protocol allows for individual complaints, monitors it. South Africa is a party to this Convention, which has been ratified by 176 states (including China but excluding the United States, which became a signatory in 2009), as well as the Optional Protocol, which has been ratified by 91 states (neither the United States nor China has ratified the Optional Protocol). In South Africa, the Department for Social Development is responsible for overseeing compliance with CRPD. South Africa's initial state report was due in May 2010 but was submitted in November 2014. The Committee has yet to issue concluding observations on this report and South Africa has not submitted any subsequent reports.

EMERGING RIGHTS

In recent years, several sets of emerging collective rights have begun to be recognised at the international level. The right to self-determination is the most widely recognised of these rights. Others are the right to a satisfactory environment and the right to development. The latter right was proclaimed by the General Assembly in 1986 in the Declaration on the Right to Development,[103] and features prominently in the African Charter on Human and Peoples' Rights discussed in Chapter 26.

[101] Article 7.

[102] V della Fina, R Cera and G Palmisano (eds) *The United Nations Convention on the Rights of Persons with Disabilities: A Commentary* (2017).

[103] Resolution 41/128. See on this right DP Forsythe (ed) *Human Rights and Development: International Views* (1989); TP van Reenen 'The right to development in international and municipal law' (1995) 10 *SA Public Law* 417; D Bradlow 'Differing conceptions of development and the content of international development law' (2005)

1 Business and human rights

Recently, in response to a growing concern about the impact of business activities around the world on human rights and the lack of clarity about the human rights responsibilities of companies, there has been a move to incorporate an international framework to hold private business accountable to human rights standards. In 2005 the UN Commission on Human Rights (now called the Human Rights Council, see below) adopted a resolution requesting the appointment of a special representative of the Secretary-General to identify and clarify standards of corporate responsibility and accountability for transnational corporations and other business enterprises with regard to human rights.[104]

Following extensive research and consultation, the special representative, John Ruggie (a professor at Harvard University's Kennedy School of Government), developed the 2011 UN Guiding Principles on Business and Human Rights.[105] These are a set of 31 principles directed at states and companies that clarify business and governmental obligations to protect and respect human rights in the context of business activities, and to ensure access to effective remedies for individuals and groups adversely impacted by such activities. The Guiding Principles are not a legal agreement to be ratified and are consequently not legally binding. Instead, they highlight best practices for businesses, as well as identifying the already existing obligations on states in respect of business (and other private actor) activities.

Regional organisations such as the Council of Europe, the European Union, and the Organization of America States have expressed support for the Guiding Principles. The Guiding Principles have also informed other relevant global standards, for example, the UN Global Compact, a UN policy initiative for responsible business.[106]

In addition, the Office of the High Commissioner for Human Rights (OHCHR) (see below) has a mandate to lead the business and human rights agenda within the UN system, and to develop guidance and training relating to the dissemination and implementation of the UN Guiding Principles. One of the key ways the Office of the High Commissioner does this is through supporting and advising a five-member Working Group on the issue of human rights and

21 *SAJHR* 47; A Aguirre *The Human Right to Development in a Globalized World* (2008); P Alston and D Robinson *Human Rights and Development: Towards Mutual Reinforcement* (2005).

[104] E/CN.4/RES/2005/69 (20 April 2005).

[105] UN Guiding Principles on Business and Human Rights: Implementing the United Nations 'Protect, Respect and Remedy' Framework (2011) available at http://www.ohchr.org/Documents/Publications/GuidingPrinciplesBusinessHR_EN.pdf.

[106] UN Global Compact available at https://www.unglobalcompact.org.

transnational corporations and other business enterprises (otherwise known as the Working Group on Business and Human Rights).[107]

During 2014 the UN Human Rights Council adopted a resolution proposed by South Africa and Ecuador on the 'Elaboration of an internationally binding instrument on Transnational Corporations and Other Business Enterprises with respect to human rights' to establish an open-ended intergovernmental working group on developing a 'legally binding instrument to regulating, in international law, the activities of Transnational Corporations and other Business Enterprises'.[108] The intergovernmental working group met for its first session between 6 and 10 July 2015 and, at its third session (23 to 27 October 2017) it presented elements for the draft legally binding instrument.[109]

2 UN human rights bodies

(a) Human Rights Council

In 1946, the Commission on Human Rights was created to promote human rights.[110] Situated in Geneva, it was a subsidiary body of the Economic and Social Council (ECOSOC)) and was assisted by a Sub-Commission on the Promotion and Protection of Human Rights, consisting of 26 experts who served in their individual capacities. Initially the Commission confined its activities to standard setting—for instance, it drafted the UDHR and the two Covenants—and the promotion of human rights. However, in the 1960s, largely in response to apartheid, it began to consider situations that revealed a consistent pattern of human rights violations and to make recommendations to ECOSOC on such subjects.

In order to further this activity, it resorted to 'special procedures' consisting of working groups and independent expert special rapporteurs, appointed to report on particular countries—such as Afghanistan, Haiti, Sudan and the Occupied Palestinian Territory or particular themes such as torture, the right to housing, health and education and violence against women. There have been several South African UN special rapporteurs, including John Dugard, the

[107] UN Working Group on Business and Human Rights available at http://www.ohchr.org/EN/Issues/Business/Pages/WGHRandtransnationalcorporationsandotherbusiness.aspx.

[108] A/HRC/26/L.22/Rev.1 (24 June 2014).

[109] UN Human Rights Council Open-ended Intergovernmental working group on transnational corporations and other business enterprises with respect to human rights available at http://www.ohchr.org/EN/HRBodies/HRC/WGTransCorp/Pages/IGWGOnTNC.aspx.

[110] See H Steiner, P Alston and R Goodman *International Human Rights in Context* 3 ed (2008) chapter 9.

Special Rapporteur on the situation of human rights in the Palestinian Territory occupied since 1967 (2001–2008); Rashida Manjoo, the Special Rapporteur on violence against women, its causes and consequences (2009–2015); and Christof Heyns, Special Rapporteur on extrajudicial, summary or arbitrary executions (2010–2016).

Over the years, the Commission became increasingly politicised, in large measure due to the inclusion of states with poor human rights records among its members. Consequently, at the 2005 UN World Summit it was proposed to replace the Commission with a smaller body comprised of member states with good human rights records.[111] This resulted in a new body, the Human Rights Council.

The Human Rights Council,[112] created by General Assembly Resolution 60/251 of 2006, is a subsidiary organ of the General Assembly, and comprises 47 member states elected by simple majority in the General Assembly for three, year terms. Its mandate is to promote the implementation of human rights, to work towards the prevention of human rights violations and to make recommendations to the General Assembly for the further development of international law in the field of human rights. Like its predecessor, it meets at UN headquarters in Geneva.

The Council retains its 'special procedures' with independent country Special Rapporteurs appointed to report on the human rights situation in specific countries (there are currently 14 country mandates) and thematic Special Rapporteurs (there are currently 39 thematic mandates) to report on particular human rights themes. The Sub-Commission on the Promotion and Protection of Human Rights is replaced by an Advisory Committee of 18 experts intended to serve as a think-tank of the Council and with less autonomy and power than its predecessor. Another feature of the Commission—the so-called '1503 complaints procedure'[113]—is retained to allow the Council, assisted by

[111] *A More Secure World: Our Shared Responsibility. Report of the Secretary-General's High-Level Panel on Threats, Challenges and Change, United Nations* (2004) UN Doc A/59/565, at 89 (para 283); World Summit Outcome Document, GA Res of 20 September 2005.

[112] See Steiner, Alston and Goodman (n 110); M Ehrenbeck 'The United Nations Human Rights Council: Establishment and first steps' (2006) 31 *SAYIL* 209; NJ Schrijver 'The UN Human Rights Council: A new "society of the committed" or just old wine in new bottles?' in T Skouteris and A Vermeer-Künzli (eds) *The Protection of the Individual in International Law: Essays in Honour of John Dugard* Special Issue of the *Leiden Journal of International Law* (2007) 81; MO Boyle (ed) *New Institutions for Human Rights Protection* (2009).

[113] In 1970 ECOSOC authorised the Sub-Commission on the Promotion and Protection of Human Rights to investigate situations 'which appear to reveal a consistent pattern of gross and reliably attested violations of human rights' in Resolution 1503 (XLVIII).

the Advisory Committee, to address consistent patterns of gross violations of human rights occurring anywhere in the world.

The most innovative feature of the Human Rights Council is the Universal Periodic Review (UPR) of the fulfilment of each member state of the United Nations of its human rights obligations. This review is carried out by the Council itself in an 'interactive dialogue' based on reports and information submitted by states, the OHCHR, national human rights institutions, and NGOs. UPR assessments are undertaken in four year cycles; the first cycle was 2008–2011, the second was from 2012–2016 and the third is from 2017–2021.

South Africa does not have a good UPR record. It is reported to be the only UN member state not to have submitted a written report ahead of its first cycle UPR (South Africa submitted its report, which was not in the required format, on the same day it was reviewed in Geneva).[114] And although South Africa improved its performance for the second cycle UPR, it was criticised by civil society organisations such as Lawyers for Human Rights and the Consortium for Refugees and Migrants in South Africa for failing to meaningfully consult NGO stakeholders during the compilation of its report.[115]

The Council meets regularly throughout the year in no fewer than three sessions, for a total duration of no less than ten weeks. The Human Rights Council is no less politicised than its predecessor. Indeed the West tends to see it as more politicised than the Commission on Human Rights. In large measure this is due to the fact that membership of the Council is based on an equitable geographical distribution that gives thirteen seats each to Africa and Asia, eight to Latin America, six to Eastern Europe and seven to the Western Europe and Others Group, (the others being the United States, Australia, Canada and New Zealand). This means that the developing world is in most cases able to assemble a majority of votes to support its position. This has been particularly apparent in respect of Palestine which, to the displeasure of the West, has become the litmus test for human rights as far as the developing world is concerned.[116]

South Africa was elected to the Human Rights Council in 2013 but in recent years has played a disappointingly ambivalent role on the

[114] Chenwi (n 80) 64.

[115] Lawyers for Human Rights and the Consortium for Refugees and Migrants in South Africa 'Submission from Lawyers for Human Rights and the Consortium for Refugees and Migrants in South Africa' to the second cycle of the South African Universal Periodic Review 2012' (2012) available at http://www.upr-info.org/sites/default/files/document/south_africa/session_13_-_may_2-12/js5uprzafs132012jointsubmission5e.pdf.

[116] See J Dugard 'The future of international law: A human rights perspective' in *The Protection of the Individual in International Law* (n 112) 1, 5–6.

Council. Despite being the beneficiary of international human rights condemnation of apartheid, South Africa rejects the 'singling out of specific countries for their human rights records', preferring quiet diplomacy to international pressure and 'naming and shaming'.[117]

There are several instances of South Africa's questionable role on the Human Rights Council in relation to human rights abusing states. For example in January 2007, South Africa voted against a UN Security Council resolution condemning human rights abuses in Burma/Myanmar. And South Africa was obstructive of the Council's attempts to address the humanitarian crisis in Darfur (Sudan) between 2006 and 2007.[118]

South Africa has also not acted consistently to protect human rights thematically. For example in 2016 South Africa abstained—on the basis of not wanting to foment 'disunity'—in a vote to establish a mandate on protection against violence and discrimination based on sexual orientation and gender identity;[119] and it voted against a resolution asking states to create and maintain a safe environment for civil society to operate.[120]

(b) The Office of the UN High Commissioner for Human Rights

The OHCHR is part of the secretariat of the United Nations and is led by the High Commissioner for Human Rights, a position created in 1993.[121] The present High Commissioner is Ms Michelle Bachelet of Chili, Ms Navanethem Pillay of South Africa served as High Commissioner from 2008 to 2014. As the United Nations principal human rights official, the High Commissioner acts as a moral authority and a voice for victims of human rights abuses. He guides the mission of OHCHR, makes public statements on human rights issues, and engages in dialogue with governments to strengthen human rights protection.

[117] E Jordaan 'South Africa and the United Nations Human Rights Council' (2014) 36 *Human Rights Quarterly* 90 at 100. See also Statement by South Africa, UN Human Rights Council 5th Sess., 4th plen.mtg., HRC Video Archive (12 June 2007) available at http://www.un.org/webcast/unhrc/archive.asp?go=070612 (cited in Jordaan fn 57).

[118] Ibid at 104–6.

[119] R Bejoy 'South Africa abstains from UN vote to protect human rights' (5 July 2016) *GroundUp*: https://www.groundup.org.za/article/south-africa-shrinks-its-progressive-leadership-un/. See also H Melber 'LGBTI vote at the UN shows battle for human rights is far from won' (18 July 2016) *The Conversation*: https://theconversation.com/lgbti-vote-at-the-un-shows-battle-for-human-rights-is-far-from-won-62307.

[120] K Molander 'Disappointment at South Africa's vote against UN move to strengthen civil society' (7 July 2016) *GroundUp*: https://www.groundup.org.za/article/sa-voted-against-un-move-strengthen-civil-society/.

[121] General Assembly Resolution 48/141. See further, A Clapham 'Creating the High Commissioner for Human Rights: The outside story' (1994) 5 *EJIL* 556; T van Boven 'The United Nations High Commissioner for Human Rights: The history of a contested project' in *The Protection of the Individual in International Law* (n 112) 39.

The OCHR is the powerhouse of the UN human rights enterprise. It works with governments, national human rights institutions, regional and international organisations and civil society to advance the protection of human rights in accordance with international human rights norms. OCHR is headquartered in Geneva and has a staff of about 1000, more than half of whom work in the field in regional and country offices throughout the world, particularly in countries that experience human rights problems.

CONVENTIONS, DECLARATIONS, AND STANDARDS

The multilateral treaties described above constitute the principal universal, as opposed to regional, human rights treaties. There are, however, many other treaties dealing with specific human rights issues. For instance, there are several treaties aimed at the suppression of slavery,[122] which date back to the League of Nations period. Indeed these are the only human rights treaties to which South Africa was a party during the apartheid era. The conventions aimed at the protection of refugees and stateless persons[123] are also an important branch of international human rights law. Refugees and stateless persons are considered in Chapter 16.

The *corpus* of international human rights law extends beyond treaties to include declarations[124] of the General Assembly and other political organs of the United Nations or its specialised agencies, and standards formulated by such bodies. On 25 June 1993, a World Conference on Human Rights, sponsored by the United Nations, adopted the Vienna Declaration on Human Rights and Programme of Action which proclaims the universality of human rights and reaffirms the obligation on all states to promote and respect human rights.[125]

[122] Slavery Convention of 1926, 134 BFSP 355; 1953 Protocol Amending the 1926 Convention, 183 UNTS 378. See too *Human Rights: A Compilation of International Instruments* (n 84).

[123] Convention relating to the Status of Refugees of 1951, 189 UNTS 137; Protocol relating to the Status of Refugees of 1967, 606 UNTS 267 and (1967) 6 *ILM* 78. Convention relating to the Status of Stateless Persons of 1954, 360 UNTS 117; Convention on the Reduction of Statelessness of 1961, UN Doc A/Conf 915 (1961). See, too, *Human Rights: A Compilation of International Instruments* (n 84).

[124] For example, the Declaration on the Right to Development (n 103) and the Declaration on the Elimination of All Forms of Intolerance and Discrimination Based on Religion or Belief, Resolution 36/55 (1981), published in *Human Rights: A Compilation of International Instruments* (n 84).

[125] (1993) 33 *ILM* 1661.

Of particular importance are the standards laid down by the ILO and the Standard Minimum Rules for the Treatment of Prisoners.

1 ILO standards

The ILO has adopted several hundred conventions and recommendations enunciating standards in the field of industrial relations.[126] Conventions are adopted by the General Conference and submitted to member states for ratification. If ratified, such a convention has the same effect as a treaty. Recommendations, on the other hand, are designed to provide guidelines to states. Conventions and recommendations have laid down standards on matters such as freedom of association, conditions of work, social security, health and safety, and acceptable working hours.

2 Standard Minimum Rules for the Treatment of Prisoners

In 1955, the First United Nations Congress on the Prevention of Crime and the Treatment of Offenders adopted a set of Standard Minimum Rules for the Treatment of Offenders, which was subsequently approved by the UN Economic and Social Council in 1957.[127] The Rules have been widely accepted by governments and have influenced judicial decisions in many countries. The South African government, which was represented at the 1955 Congress which adopted the Rules, has sought to incorporate them into its law and practice. In 1990, the General Assembly of the United Nations gave its support to the Standard Minimum Rules.[128]

REGIONAL HUMAN RIGHTS CONVENTIONS

Europe, the Americas, and Africa have adopted regional human rights conventions which complement and reinforce universal human rights conventions. The three regional conventions are arguably more successful than their universal counterparts, because political and cultural homogeneity and shared judicial traditions and institutions within a region provide the basis for confidence in the system, which is necessary for effective implementation.[129] However, each system has in recent years experienced problems regarding

[126] See N Rubin 'International labour law and the law of the new South Africa' (1998) 115 *SALJ* 685.

[127] Resolution 663C (XXIV) of 31 July 1957. The text of the Rules appears in *Human Rights: A Compilation of International Instruments* (n 84). See, further, D van Zyl Smit *South African Prison Law and Practice* (1992) 80–1; NS Rodley and M Pollard *The Treatment of Prisoners under International Law* 3 ed (2009).

[128] Resolution 45/111 of 14 December 1990.

[129] BH Weston, RA Lukes and KM Hnatt 'Regional human rights regimes: A comparison and appraisal' (1987) 20 *Vanderbilt Journal of Transnational Law* 585; C Heyns

enforcement of decisions and legitimacy concerns in the face of increasing resistance from national governments to perceived issues of sovereignty.

Asia is the only region not to have adopted a regional human rights convention, although there are sub-regional human rights systems such as the Arab Charter on Human Rights (which entered into force in 2008) adopted by the League of Arab States and governed by the Arab Human Rights Committee.[130] In addition, in 2009 the South East Asia the Association of Southeast Asian Nations (ASEAN) established the ASEAN Intergovernmental commission on Human Rights (AICHR) as a consultative body overseeing the 2012 ASEAN Human Rights Declaration.[131]

1 The European Convention on Human Rights[132]

The European Convention for the Protection of Human Rights and Fundamental Freedoms (European Convention), which was adopted by the Council of Europe in 1950, came into force in 1953. Today it is an essential component of the political order of the 47-member Council of Europe (not to be confused with the 28-member European Union, which is a distinct organisation), which includes all historically 'Western European' states, Turkey, and erstwhile 'Eastern European' states such as Russia, Hungary, the Czech Republic, and Slovakia. The European Convention is confined to civil and political rights. Economic, social, and cultural rights are protected in a separate convention, the European Social Charter of 1961.[133]

Inspired by the UDHR, the European Convention is similar to the ICCPR. Contracting states are required to 'secure to everyone within their jurisdiction' the rights contained in the Convention (article 1) and to ensure that their municipal law provides 'an effective remedy' (article 13). There is no protection of property rights in the European

'A systematic comparison of regional human rights systems' (2000) 33 *De Jure* 117; D Shelton *Regional Protection of Human Rights* (2008).

[130] For more on the fledgling Arab and Muslim systems see Viljoen (n 44) 341–3.

[131] For more on the nascent South East Asian system see Viljoen (n 44) 343.

[132] 213 UNTS 221. There is a wealth of literature on this Convention. See, for example, W Schabas *The European Convention on Human Rights: A Commentary* (2015); AH Robertson and JG Merrills *Human Rights in Europe* 4 ed (2001); P van Dijk, GJH van Hoof, A van Rijn and L Zwaak (eds) *Theory and Practice of the European Convention on Human Rights* 5 ed (2018); DJ Harris, M O'Boyle, E Bates and C Buckley (eds) *Harris, O'Boyle and Warbrick Law of the European Convention on Human Rights* 3 ed (2014); E Bates *The Evolution of the European Convention on Human Rights* (2009); B Rainey, E Wicks and C Ovey (eds) *Jacobs, White and Ovey: The European Convention on Human Rights* 6 ed (2014).

[133] 529 UNTS 89. This Charter entered into force in 1965. See D Harris *The European Social Charter* 2 ed (2000).

Convention, but this right is guaranteed in the First Protocol to the Convention.[134] The death penalty is not outlawed in the Convention, but this was done in the Sixth Protocol of 1983,[135] which has been ratified by many states.

As treaties form part of the municipal law of most European countries without the need for any act of legislative incorporation, the Convention is part of the local law of most of Europe. Consequently, it is considered and enforced by the domestic courts of these countries in the first instance.[136] Countries that follow a dualist approach to treaties have either incorporated the Convention into municipal law or amended their legislation where appropriate.[137] Furthermore, their courts have used the Convention as an interpretative guide in human rights cases.[138]

The international machinery for the enforcement of the European Convention on Human Rights has undergone a major change. Under the original enforcement scheme, a part-time Commission acted as a filtering body to decide whether applications were admissible and as a mechanism to secure a friendly settlement. Its reports went to the Committee of Ministers of the Council. Where no friendly settlement was achieved, the application was referred to a part-time court to decide the case.

The new system, introduced by Protocol XI of 1994,[139] and first implemented in 1999, is a response to the increased workload imposed on part-time commissioners and judges. The Commission is abolished and there is now only a Court, comprising full-time judges. The Court consists of a number of judges equal to that of the parties to the Convention. They are elected by the Parliamentary Assembly of the Council of Europe and hold office for six years. Judges, sitting

[134] 213 UNTS 262.

[135] Text in (1983) 22 *ILM* 538. This Protocol does not prohibit the death penalty in respect of acts committed in time of war. In 2002 the death penalty was abolished in all circumstances by the Thirteenth Protocol: (2002) 41 *ILM* 515.

[136] A Drzemczewski *European Human Rights Convention in Domestic Law: A Comparative Study* (1983).

[137] The United Kingdom incorporated the Convention in the Human Rights Act 1998.

[138] See J Dugard 'International human rights norms in domestic courts: Can South Africa learn from Britain and the United States?' in E Kahn (ed) *Fiat Justitia: Essays in Memory of Oliver Deneys Schreiner* (1983) 220 at 223–8. The Human Rights Act 1998 directs courts in the United Kingdom to interpret legislation in accordance with the Convention: s 3. See, too, I Cameron 'The Swedish experience of the European Convention on Human Rights since incorporation' (1999) 48 *ICLQ* 20.

[139] (1994) 33 *ILM* 943; see, further, H Schermers 'The Eleventh Protocol to the European Convention on Human Rights' (1994) 19 *European Law Review* 367; R Bernhardt 'Reform of the control machinery under the European Convention on Human Rights: Protocol 11' (1995) 89 *AJIL* 145.

in committees of three, chambers of seven and a Grand Chamber of 17, are responsible for considering the admissibility of complaints and adjudicating on the merits of cases admitted.

Inter-state complaints are, as in the past, mandatory, but this procedure has been used sparingly as states are generally reluctant to disturb relations with their sister European states in this way. The right of individual petition is now mandatory for all states parties to the Convention.

Individuals have brought the majority of cases before both the Commission (before 1999) and the Court. In large measure, this may be ascribed to the fact that the European Convention is so well known to the European people that both individuals and their lawyers see the right of individual petition as a basic legal remedy.

Important decisions have been delivered by the Court on matters such as interrogation as a form of inhuman and degrading treatment;[140] the circumstances in which a state may derogate from its obligations in time of national emergency;[141] contempt of court proceedings as a violation of freedom of expression;[142] the punishment of homosexual conduct between consenting adults in private as an invasion of privacy;[143] corporal punishment as degrading treatment;[144] failure to bring an accused to court within a reasonable time;[145] the right of a prisoner to communicate with his lawyer;[146] separate-language schools and the principle of non-discrimination;[147] the obligation of European states not to extradite persons to the United States for capital crimes where they may be subjected to the 'death-row phenomenon';[148] the excessive use of force by security forces and the right to life;[149] a plea of sovereign immunity in a case involving torture;[150] the question whether member states of NATO might be held responsible for injuries suffered by persons in Serbia as a result of NATO bombings during the Kosovo conflict:[151] and the interpretation of Security Council resolutions that appear to breach

[140] *Ireland v UK* (1979–80) 2 EHRR 25.

[141] *Lawless Case*, ECHR, Series A, vol 3, Judgment of 1 July 1961.

[142] *Sunday Times Case*, ECHR, Series A, vol 30, Judgment of 26 April 1979.

[143] *Dudgeon Case*, ECHR, Series A, vol 45, Judgment of 22 October 1981.

[144] *Tyrer Case*, ECHR, Series A, vol 26, Judgment of 25 April 1978.

[145] *Wemhoff Case*, ECHR, Series A, vol 7, Judgment of 27 June 1968; *Neumeister Case*, ECHR, Series A, vol 7, Judgment of 27 June 1968.

[146] *Golder Case*, ECHR, Series A, vol 18, Judgment of 21 February 1975.

[147] *Belgian Linguistics Case*, ECHR, Series A, vol 6, Judgment of 23 July 1968.

[148] *Soering Case*, ECHR, Series A, vol 161, Judgment of 7 July 1989; (1989) 28 *ILM* 1063.

[149] *McCann v UK*, ECHR Series A, vol 324, 1995.

[150] *Al Adsani v UK* 123 ILR 24.

[151] *Bankovic v Belgium* (2002) 41 *ILM* 517.

human rights obligations.[152] Finally, there have been many cases over the years against various European states related to the treatment of Roma people and Travellers.[153]

In recent years the European regional human rights system has come under pressure from the expanding membership of the Council of Europe (particularly the incorporation of many former Eastern European bloc countries), as well as increasing hostility from some European countries (including the United Kingdom) to human rights as a perceived constraint on national sovereignty. For example, one of the reasons for the 'Leave' victory during the 2016 'Brexit' referendum in the United Kingdom was the judgments of the European Court of Human Rights against the United Kingdom and the perception by many British citizens that European human rights undermine British sovereignty.

2 The Inter-American system[154]

The inter-American system for the protection of human rights was established by the Organization of American States (OAS), which was founded in 1948 in terms of the Charter of the Organization of American States. The OAS comprises all 35 states in Latin America, the Caribbean, the United States, and Canada ('the Americas').

The inter-American human rights system has two sources: the 1948 non-binding American Declaration on the Rights and Duties of Man (American Declaration),[155] and the binding American Convention on Human Rights (ACHR) of 1969. The two instruments overlap and supplement each other. Indeed one of the principal organs, the Inter-American Commission on Human Rights, which was established in 1959,[156] is shared by both regimes.

The ACHR[157] was adopted in 1969 by an intergovernmental conference convened by the OAS and came into force in 1978. Twenty-five states have ratified the Convention (Trinidad and

[152] *Al Jedda v UK*, Judgment of 7 July 2011, para 102.

[153] See European Court of Human Rights 'Factsheet—Roma and Travellers' (February 2018) available at https://www.echr.coe.int/Documents/FS_Roma_ENG.pdf.

[154] C Medina *The Inter-American Convention on Human Rights* (2014); T Buergenthal and D Shelton *Protecting Human Rights in the Americas* 4 ed (1995); DJ Harris and S Livingstone (eds) *The Inter-American System of Human Rights* (1998); JM Pasqualucci *The Practice and Procedure of the Inter-American Court of Human Rights* 2 ed (2013).

[155] Resolution XXX, Final Act of the Ninth International Conference of American States, Bogotá, Colombia; 30 March–2 May 1948.

[156] The Inter-American Commission was incorporated into the Charter of the Organization of American States system only in 1970.

[157] 1144 UNTS 123; (1970) 9 *ILM* 673; (1971) 65 *AJIL* 679. Sometimes this Convention is described as the 'Pact of San José, Costa Rica'—where it was approved.

Tobago, and Venezuela have denounced the Convention, leaving 23 active parties), but the United States and Canada have yet to do so.

The American Convention is devoted, almost entirely, to civil and political rights. However, article 26 obliges states progressively to realise second-generation rights, a matter that is dealt with more fully in a 1988 Additional Protocol. Although the Convention follows broadly the same pattern as the European Convention and the ICCPR, there are several important differences. The right to life commences 'from the moment of conception' (article 4(1)); property is protected (article 21); and special provision is made for the limited application of the Convention in federal states (article 28).

The American Convention provides for a three-tier international enforcement system, by means of the Inter-American Commission on Human Rights, the Inter-American Court of Human Rights, and the General Assembly of the OAS.

The quasi-judicial Inter-American Commission, comprising seven experts, has compulsory jurisdiction over individual petitions (article 44) and optional jurisdiction over inter-state complaints (article 45). It sits in Washington, D.C. in the United States. No use has been made of the inter-state procedure and the system of individual petitions has not been as widely used as it has been in Europe.

The Inter-American Court of Human Rights[158] comprises seven judges and sits in San José, Costa Rica. Only states and the Commission may refer cases to the Court—provided that the states in question have accepted the jurisdiction of the Court (article 62). In addition to these proceedings in contentious cases, the Court may give advisory opinions on the interpretation of the ACHR or any other treaty concerning the protection of human rights in the Americas at the request of any member state of the OAS (article 64).

Although the jurisprudence of the Inter-American Court of Human Rights is limited in comparison with that of its European counterpart, it has given a number of important decisions and opinions.[159] In *Velasquez Rodriquez*,[160] the Court held that Honduras had failed to comply with its obligations under the Convention by failing to investigate disappearances and punish those responsible. In the *Right to Information on Consular Assistance*,[161] the Court gave an opinion at the request of Mexico, in which it held that detained foreign nationals

[158] See LE Frost 'The evolution of the inter-American Court of Human Rights: Reflections of present and former judges' (1992) 14 *Human Rights Quarterly* 171.

[159] S Davidson 'Remedies for violations of the American Convention on Human Rights' (1995) 44 *ICLQ* 405; C Cerna 'The structure and functioning of the Inter-American Court of Human Rights (1979–1992)' (1992) 63 *BYIL* 135.

[160] Series C4, Judgment of 29 July 1988, reported in 95 ILR 259.

[161] Series A 16, OC–16/99, 1999.

had a right to consular assistance, and in the *Barrios Altos Case*[162] the Court found that Peruvian amnesty laws were incompatible with the American Convention.

The Inter-American Commission operates under the Charter of the OAS and not the ACHR when it considers complaints relating to the violation of the American Declaration on the Rights and Duties of Man by member states of the OAS, whether or not such a state has ratified the ACHR. Thus, the Commission was able to investigate the compatibility of the United States' imposition of the death penalty on juveniles with the guarantee of the right to life contained in article 1 of the American Declaration.[163] The Commission, acting under the OAS Charter and with the consent of the defendant state, has the power to conduct inspections *in loco* into human rights violations. This power, which is appropriate for large-scale human rights violations, has been used with some success in states in which there was a consistent pattern of human rights violations.[164] The Inter-American Commission has a promotional role, which it fulfils by means of national reports and studies on subjects such as disappearances, torture, and refugees.

3 The African Charter on Human and Peoples' Rights[165]

The ACHPR, also known as the Banjul Charter, was approved by the Organization of African Unity (OAU) in 1981 and came into force in 1986. South Africa ratified the Charter in 1996. The principal supervisory organ is the African Commission on Human and Peoples' Rights. In 2003, a Protocol establishing an African Court on Human and Peoples' Rights, to which South Africa is a party, came into force. In 2006, judges were elected to the Court and in 2009, the Court handed down its first decision.

The African system for the protection of human rights is examined in Chapter 26.

INTERNATIONAL HUMAN RIGHTS INSTRUMENTS AND SOUTH AFRICAN LAW

Before 1994,[166] there was little that South African courts could—or would—do about international human rights instruments.

[162] (2002) 41 *ILM* 93.

[163] See DT Fox 'Inter-American Commission on Human Rights finds United States in violation' (1988) 82 *AJIL* 601.

[164] Weston, Lukes and Hnatt (n 129) 618–20.

[165] See F Viljoen *International Human Rights Law in Africa* (2007).

[166] See J Dugard 'The South African judiciary and international law in the apartheid era' (1998) 14 *SAJHR* 110.

South Africa was a party to only one instrument with human rights clauses—the UN Charter—and that was not incorporated into municipal law. Consequently, no direct effect could be given to articles 55 and 56 of the Charter. Moreover, attempts to persuade the courts to take these clauses into account as a guide to statutory interpretation fell on deaf ears.[167]

As South Africa was not a party to other human rights conventions, they could not be used even as a guide to statutory interpretation. Suggestions that they might be used as a guide to judicial policy were not viewed favourably. In *S v Khanyile*,[168] Didcott J sought to fashion a right-to-counsel rule for indigent accused by relying on the importance attached to this right in the ICCPR and the European Convention on Human Rights, but this innovative step was rejected by fellow judges and ignored by the Appellate Division.[169] Strangely, ILO standards[170] and the United Nations Standard Minimum Rules for the Treatment of Offenders[171] were given more favourable treatment.

The situation has changed dramatically since 1994. South Africa is a party to the major universal human rights instruments[172] and the ACHPR. Furthermore, the 1996 Constitution, like its predecessor of 1993, requires courts to consider international human rights instruments in their application of the Bill of Rights in the Constitution.

Section 39(1) of the 1996 Constitution,[173] which replaces s 35(1) of the 1993 Constitution,[174] declares:

[167] See *S v Werner* 1980 (2) SA 313 (W); *S v Adams; S v Werner* 1981 (1) SA 187 (A). See, too, *Sobukwe v Minister of Justice* 1972 (1) SA 693 (A).

[168] 1988 (3) SA 795 (N) 801A–D.

[169] *S v Rudman* 1989 (3) SA 368 (E) 376A–B; *S v Rudman* 1992 (1) SA 343 (A).

[170] In a number of decisions, the Industrial Court relied on unincorporated conventions and recommendations of the ILO in giving substance to the term 'unfair labour practice'. See *Metal and Allied Workers Union v Stobar Reinforcing (Pty) Ltd* (1983) 4 *ILJ* 84 (IC); *United African Motor and Allied Workers Union v Fodens SA (Pty) Ltd* (1983) 4 *ILJ* 212 (IC); *National Automobile and Allied Workers Union v Pretoria Precision Castings (Pty) Ltd* (1985) 6 *ILJ* (IC). See, further, DJG Woolfrey 'The application of international labour norms to South African law' (1986–7) 12 *SAYIL* 135.

[171] See the judgments of Conradie J in *S v Staggie* 1990 (1) SACR 669 (C); *S v Daniels* 1991 (2) SACR 403 (C) 405F–I.

[172] The ICCPR, the ICERD, the CEDAW, the CRC, the CAT and the Genocide Convention. See, further, C Heyns and F Viljoen 'The impact of six major UN Human Rights Treaties in South Africa' (2001) 16 *SA Public Law* 28.

[173] Constitution of the Republic of South Africa, 1996.

[174] Act 200 of 1993. Section 35(1) reads: 'In interpreting the provisions of this Chapter [the Bill of Rights] a court of law shall promote the values which underlie an open and democratic society based on freedom and equality and shall, where

When interpreting the Bill of Rights, a court, tribunal or forum—
(a) must promote the values that underlie an open and democratic society based on human dignity, equality and freedom;
(b) must consider international law; and
(c) may consider foreign law.

This provision, together with s 233, which requires a court when interpreting legislation to 'prefer any reasonable interpretation of the legislation that is consistent with international law over any alternative interpretation that is inconsistent with international law', ensures that courts will be guided by international norms and the interpretation placed upon these norms by international courts and other institutions. Fears that international human rights law in this context might be narrowly construed[175] to cover only clear rules of customary law and those human rights conventions to which South Africa is a party, were dispelled by the Constitutional Court in *S v Makwanyane*,[176] where it stated that:

> In the context of s 35(1), public international law would include non-binding as well as binding law. They may both be used under the section as tools of interpretation. International agreements and customary international law accordingly provide a framework within which chap 3 [the Bill of Rights] can be evaluated and understood, and for that purpose, decisions of tribunals dealing with comparable instruments, such as the United Nations Committee on Human Rights, the Inter-American Commission on Human Rights, the Inter-American Court of Human Rights, the European Commission on Human Rights, and the European Court of Human Rights, and, in appropriate cases, reports of specialised agencies such as the International Labour Organisation, may provide guidance as to the correct interpretation of particular provisions of chap 3.[177]

More recently, in *Glenister v President of the Republic of South Africa*,[178] the Constitutional Court underscored the mandatory nature of s 39(1)*(b)*—when 'interpreting the Bill of Rights, a court, tribunal or forum' . . . '*must* consider international law' (emphasis added)—and characterised international law as a critical standard by which to measure state conduct.[179] In this case, finding that 'international law,

applicable, have regard to public international law applicable to the protection of the rights entrenched in this Chapter, and may have regard to comparable foreign case law.'

[175] J Dugard 'The role of international law in interpreting the Bill of Rights' (1994) 10 *SAJHR* 208.

[176] 1995 (3) SA 391 (CC).

[177] At 413–14. See, too, *Prince v President of the Law Society, Cape of Good Hope* 1998 (8) BCLR 976 (C) 985C–D; *Dawood v Minister of Home Affairs* 2000 (1) SA 997 (C) 1033–5; *Kirsh v Kirsh* [1999] All SA 193 (C) 204; *Government of the RSA v Grootboom* 2001 (1) SA 46 (CC) 63.

[178] 2011 (3) SA 347 (CC).

[179] Viljoen (n 44) 365.

through the inter-locking grid of conventions, agreements and protocols . . . unequivocally obliges South Africa to establish an anti-corruption entity with the necessary independence', the Court concluded that the establishment of an independent anti-corruption unit was necessary to fulfil the Bill of Rights.[180]

As a result of the 1996 Constitution, it has now become commonplace for the Constitutional Court and other courts to invoke human rights norms and decisions by international human rights tribunals and supervisory bodies to interpret the Bill of Rights and to set aside laws and administrative practices that violate human rights. It is impossible to examine all the judicial decisions that have invoked international human rights law. The *Annual Survey of South African Law* and academic writings give some indication of the extent of this judicial practice.[181] The following cases provide a glimpse of this new feature of South African law.

In *S v Makwanyane*,[182] involving the constitutionality of the death penalty, several members of the Constitutional Court turned to international human rights instruments to support their reasoning. In *S v Williams*[183] the Court found that corporal punishment was uncon-

[180] *Glenister* (n 178) para 192.

[181] J Dugard 'The influence of international human rights law on the South African Constitution' (1996) 49 *Current Legal Problems* 305; J Dugard 'International law and the South African Constitution' (1997) 8 *EJIL* 77; J Dugard 'The role of human rights standards in domestic law: The southern African experience' in P Alston and J Crawford (eds) *The Future of UN Human Rights Treaty Monitoring* (2000) 269; N Botha 'International law in the Constitutional Court' (1995) 20 *SAYIL* 222; N Botha 'Riding the tide: South Africa's "regular" courts and the application of international law' (1996) 21 *SAYIL* 174; E de Wet 'The place of public international law in the new South African constitutional order: With special reference to international human rights and humanitarian law' (1998) 1 *Recht in Afrika* (published by African Law Association) 207; RC Blake 'The world's law in one country: The South African Constitutional Court's use of public international law' (1998) 115 *SALJ* 668; D Prévost 'South Africa as an illustration of the development in international human rights law' (1999) 24 *SAYIL* 211; M Olivier 'South Africa and international human rights agreements: Procedure, policy and practice' (2003) *TSAR* 293; J Ford 'International and comparative influence on the rights jurisprudence of South Africa's Constitutional Court' in M du Plessis and S Pete (eds) *Constitutional Democracy In South Africa 1994–2004* (2004) 33; H Strydom 'South Africa and international law—From confrontation to co-operation' (2004) 47 *German Yearbook of International Law* 160, 193; N Botha and M Olivier 'Ten years of international law in the South African courts: Reviewing the past and assessing the future' (2004) 29 *SAYIL* 42; F Viljoen 'The relationship between international human rights and humanitarian law in the African human rights system: An institutional approach' (2014) in E de Wet and J Kleffner (eds) *Convergence and Conflicts of Human Rights and International Humanitarian Law in Military Operations* 303; Viljoen (n 44) at 364–6.

[182] 1995 (3) SA 391 (CC).

[183] 1995 (3) SA 632 (CC).

stitutional on the ground that it violated the Constitution's prohibition of 'cruel, inhuman or degrading treatment or punishment'. After stating that '[i]n common with many of the rights entrenched in the Constitution, the wording of this section conforms to a large extent with most international human rights instruments',[184] the Court examined the jurisprudence of the UN Human Rights Committee and the European Commission and Court of Human Rights on the corresponding provisions in these treaties. *Tyrer v United Kingdom*[185] and *Campbell and Cosans v United Kingdom*[186] featured prominently in the judgment. Subsequent decisions of the Constitutional Court have continued this practice. In *Coetzee v Government of the Republic of South Africa*,[187] international human rights norms were used to uphold a constitutional challenge to imprisonment for judgment debts; in *In re Gauteng School Education Bill 1995*,[188] Sachs J examined the practice of the League of Nations and the United Nations on minority rights in a challenge to the validity of an education bill by a minority group; in *National Coalition for Gay and Lesbian Equality v Minister of Justice*,[189] decisions of the European Court of Human Rights and the view of the Human Rights Committee in *Toonen v Australia*[190] were relied on to decriminalise sodomy; in *Christian Education South Africa v Minister of Education*,[191] South Africa's obligations under the Convention against Torture and the CRC were invoked to uphold the prohibition on corporal punishment in independent schools; in *Mohamed v President of the Republic of South Africa*[192] decisions of the European Court of Human Rights were followed in finding that a person might not be deported to a country in which there was a real risk that he might be subjected to cruel, inhuman or degrading treatment; in *Minister of Health v Treatment Action Campaign (No 2)*[193] and in *Mazibuko v City of Johannesburg*[194] the Court examined the concept of a 'minimum core' of economic and social obligations developed by the Committee on Economic Social and Cultural Rights charged with the task of monitoring obligations contained in the International Covenant of Economic, Social and Cultural Rights; and in *Minister of*

[184] At 639.
[185] ECHR, Series A, vol 26, 1978.
[186] ECHR, Series A, vol 48, 1982.
[187] 1995 (4) SA 631 (CC) 660–3.
[188] 1996 (3) SA 165 (CC) 190–204.
[189] 1999 (1) SA 6 (CC) paras 40–4, 45–7.
[190] (1994) 1–3 *IHRR* 97.
[191] 2000 (4) SA 757 (CC) paras 13, 40.
[192] 2001 (3) SA 893 (CC) paras 55–8.
[193] 2002 (5) SA 721 (CC) para 26. See, too, *Government of the RSA v Grootboom* 2001 (1) SA 46 (CC) 63–6.
[194] 2010 (4) SA 1 (CC).

Home Affairs v Fourie; Lesbian & Gay Equality Project v Minister of Home Affairs[195] the Court examined the question whether the UDHR and the ICCPR constituted an obstacle to the Court's finding that the common-law definition of marriage was inconsistent with the Constitution because it unfairly discriminated against same-sex relationships. The Supreme Court of Appeal (SCA) has adopted a similar approach. In *National Media Ltd v Bogoshi*,[196] the SCA considered decisions of the European Court of Human Rights on freedom of expression; in *Minister of Safety and Security v Carmichele*[197] the Court invoked a decision of the European Court of Human Rights in support of its finding that there is a positive duty on the state to protect an individual whose life was at risk from the criminal acts of another individual; and in *Director of Public Prosecutions v P*[198] the Court invoked the CRC to support a finding that a juvenile offender required special consideration. Lower courts have likewise not hesitated to invoke international human rights norms. In *S v Kampher*[199] and *National Coalition for Gay and Lesbian Equality v Minister of Justice*,[200] courts relied on the decision of the European Court of Human Rights in *Dudgeon v UK*[201] for their decision that sodomy, in the sense of sexual acts between consenting male adults, was no longer subject to the criminal sanction; and in *Christian Lawyers Association of South Africa v Minister of Health*,[202] the jurisprudence of the European Court was invoked to dismiss a challenge to the constitutionality of abortion legislation.

More recently, in *National Commissioner of The South African Police Service v Southern African Human Rights Litigation Centre*, the Constitutional Court invoked CAT's obligation on state parties to ensure that acts of torture and attempted torture are offences under criminal law, pointing out that South Africa had achieved this through the enactment of the Torture Act, meaning that South Africa is required to take necessary measures to act against torture including, as in this case, initiating an investigation into the alleged torture of Zimbabweans by Zimbabwe officials.[203] And in *Dladla v City of Johannesburg*, the Constitutional Court drew, inter alia, on submissions from the

[195] 2006 (I) SA 524 (CC) paras 99–105.

[196] 1998 (4) SA 1196 (SCA) 1208, 1210.

[197] 2004 (3) SA 305 (SCA) 319–20.

[198] 2006 (3) SA 515 (SCA) paras 15–16.

[199] 1997 (4) SA 460 (C) 470–6C.

[200] 1998 (6) BCLR 726 (W). Confirmed by the Constitutional Court in 1999 (1) SA 6 (CC) 32–5.

[201] ECHR, Series A, vol 45, 1981; (1981) 4 *IHRR* 149.

[202] 1998 (4) SA 1102 (T) 1125.

[203] *National Commissioner of The South African Police Service v Southern African Human Rights Litigation Centre* 2015 (1) SA 315 (CC)—see especially paras 38–40.

first amicus (Centre for Applied Legal Studies) regarding the international law on the gender dimension of the right to housing to conclude that insofar as they require gender segregation and lock out during the day, the rules of Ekuthuleni housing shelter in Johannesburg 'violate[s] international human rights law' and constitute 'an infringement of the applicants' rights to dignity, freedom and security of the person, and privacy' and, as such, is unlawful.[204]

Recourse to international law under s 39(1)*(b)* may not always advance the rights of the individual. In *Prince v President of the Law Society, Cape of Good Hope* (subsequently referred to the Human Rights Committee as an individual complaint, *Prince v South Africa,* discussed above),[205] the Court found that international norms on religious freedom (in the case of a Rastafarian's use of cannabis for religious purposes) were outweighed by South Africa's international obligations to suppress drug abuse. This shows that a court is not confined to international human rights treaties when it acts under s 39(1)*(b)*.

The Constitution is not the only statute to promote the harmonisation of South African law and international human rights law. The Labour Relations Act 66 of 1995 proclaims as one of the primary objects of the Act 'to give effect to the obligations incurred by the Republic as a member state of the International Labour Organization' and requires the Act to be interpreted in compliance with the public international law obligations of the Republic.[206] The Refugees Act 130 of 1998[207] provides that the Act 'must be interpreted and applied with due regard' to the principal refugees conventions, other relevant conventions and the UDHR.[208]

[204] *Dladla v City of Johannesburg* 2018 (2) SA 327 (CC)—see especially paras 29 and 54.

[205] 1998 (8) BCLR 976 (C) 984–6, 988–9; 2002 (2) SA 794 (CC), paras 104, 116, 141. See further n 59.

[206] Act 66 of 1995, ss 1 and 3. See further N Rubin 'International labour law and the law of the new South Africa' (1998) 115 *SALJ* 685.

[207] See further Chapter 16.

[208] Act 130 of 1998, s 6.

CHAPTER 16

Refugees and Stateless Persons

Anton Katz and Tiyanjana Maluwa*

INTRODUCTION

One of the ways in which international law can be seen at work in South Africa is through its adoption and implementation of international legal protections for asylum seekers and refugees. This chapter therefore has a dual focus: it identifies the international legal obligations applicable to the determination of refugee status and the treatment of refugees, and describes the implementation of these norms in South Africa. First, it considers the key concepts of international refugee law as spelled out in the universal and regional treaties. Secondly, it discusses the specific legislation applicable to refugees, the Refugees Act 130 of 1998 (Refugees Act), and regulations which have been adopted, interpreted and applied by the courts. Thirdly, it offers suggestions on amendments to ameliorate the treatment of asylum-seekers and the asylum process. The discussion in this chapter is, therefore, not intended as an exposé of international refugee law broadly, but is instead focused more specifically on refugee law and refugees in South Africa. These issues are covered in the first part of the chapter.

The second part of the chapter briefly discusses statelessness in South Africa. Although the legal regimes governing refugee status and statelessness are different, they are nevertheless related. Both legal regimes implicate the treatment by states of individuals within their jurisdictions who, though not recognised as citizens or nationals of the state, are entitled to certain protections under international law as refugees or stateless persons. These protections mirror each other to a large degree. However, they are rooted in different treaties and differ in their scope and application.

REFUGEES

South Africa has been a destination for asylum-seekers and refugees throughout its history, and even more so since the end of apartheid in 1994. South Africa's significant population of refugees and asylum-seekers bears testimony to this. Indeed, in the years 2006 to 2011,

* Our sincere thanks to Eshed Cohen for his invaluable research assistance.

South Africa received the highest number of new asylum applications per year of any country in the world.[1] To date it remains one of the world's top ten receiver-states, although the total number of new asylum-seekers has declined progressively over the last two decades.[2]

Refugees in South Africa are governed by a legal regime drawn from international law, on the one hand, and South African municipal law, on the other.[3] The former is based on universal and regional conventions, rules of customary international law, general principles of law and ever-evolving standards in the practice of states and international organisations, in particular the Office of the United Nations High Commissioner for Refugees (UNHCR).[4] On the other side, South African municipal law comprises the Constitution,[5] the Refugees Act and other national laws applicable to all persons within the territory of the Republic, as may be relevant to refugees. Persons that qualify for the status of refugees benefit from the protection of this combined legal regime of international and municipal law.

The international law of refugee protection focuses on the legal tools, treaties, and national laws that prescribe and implement the obligations of states towards refugees. There are two universal treaties: the United Nations Convention Relating to the Status of Refugees of 1951 (1951 UN Convention)[6] and its Protocol Relating to the Status of Refugees of 1967 (1967 Protocol).[7] At the regional level in Africa, the OAU Convention on the Specific Aspects of Refugee Problems in Africa (1969 OAU Convention) has complemented these treaties.[8] The core functions and responsibilities of overseeing the implementation of the United Nations (UN) instruments lies with UNHCR, but there is no equivalent regional agency established under the 1969 OAU Convention. It is the responsibility of each state,

[1] United Nations High Commissioner for Refugees *Global Trends 2012: Displacement—The new 21st century challenge* (June 2013) 26. Available at http://www.unhcr.org/statistics/country/51bacb0f9/unhcr-global-trends-2012.html.

[2] Republic of South Africa, Department of Home Affairs *White Paper on International Migration* (July 2017) 59. See also United Nations High Commissioner for Refugees *Global Trends 2017: Forced displacement in 2017* (2018) 41. Available at http://www.unhcr.org/globaltrends2017/.

[3] See generally, F Kahn and T Schreier (eds) *Refugee Law in South Africa* (2014).

[4] Established by United Nations General Assembly resolution 428 (V) of 14 December 1950. Its mandate is to provide, on a non-political and humanitarian basis, international protection to refugees and to seek permanent solutions for them.

[5] Constitution of the Republic of South Africa, 1996.

[6] 189 UNTS 137. Adopted on 28 July 1951, entered into force on 22 April 1954.

[7] 606 UNTS 267. Adopted on 31 January 1967, entered into force on 4 October 1967.

[8] 1001 UNTS 45. Adopted on 10 September 1969, entered into forced on 20 June 1974.

that is a party to these treaties, to implement its obligations and protect persons who qualify for refugee status within its territory. This requires that states enact the necessary legislation and establish administrative mechanisms to implement the rights of refugees and afford them the protections guaranteed by international law.

International refugee law sets out certain key concepts, including the definition of a refugee, the definition of persecution and grounds for persecution, the principle of *non-refoulement*, and standards of treatment. It is important to bear in mind that the refugee problem is, at heart, a human rights problem.[9] The causes of forced displacement that give rise to the refugee problem are necessarily linked to human rights violations in the country of origin. Thus, the treatment of refugees and asylum-seekers within the state has to be seen not only in terms of the refugee treaties to which the state is a party but also in the broader context of other human rights treaties and customary international law. Because of this, the 1951 UN Convention is often described as a 'human rights treaty', and international refugee law as a species or subset of international human rights law (see Chapter 15). Yet at least three salient features of the 1951 UN Convention distinguish it from standard human rights treaties.[10]

First, unlike most other human rights treaties, the 1951 UN Convention is styled as a convention relating to the *status* of refugee rights, rather than one on the *rights* of refugees. Secondly, it does not frame refugee rights in terms of what 'every refugee shall enjoy' and 'no refugee shall be denied'—language that one might expect in a human rights instrument. This leads to the third salient feature, namely that whereas other human rights treaties focus on the individual as the point of departure, the 1951 UN Convention is state-centric: the 1951 UN Convention focuses on the obligations and undertakings made by states to recognise, respect and protect certain rights and benefits. The same approach is generally followed in the 1969 OAU Convention. Nonetheless, although these treaties were initially adopted as agreements between states on the treatment of refugees, they have subsequently inspired doctrine and practice in which the language of refugee rights has become not only common but also entirely appropriate and acceptable.[11]

[9] B Burson and DJ Cantor *Human Rights and the Refugee Definition* (2013) 1–25.

[10] See, generally, G Goodwin-Gill 'International law, refugees and forced migration' in E Fiddian-Qasimiyeh et al (eds) *The Oxford Handbook of Refugee and Forced Migration Studies* (2014) 36–47. See also G Goodwin-Gill *Refugees and their Human Rights*, RSC Working Paper No 17, University of Oxford (August 2004) 6–7.

[11] Goodwin-Gill ibid; see also, generally, J Hathaway and M Foster *The Rights of Refugees under International Law* 2 ed (2014).

To appreciate the extent to which states abide by their obligations to respect and protect the rights of refugees, it is necessary, at the outset, to examine the judicial and administrative procedures that states have established under their municipal laws for the determination of refugee status, the protection of asylum-seekers pending the outcome of their application for refugee status and the rights accorded to refugees once their status has been determined.

1 The genesis of international refugee law

The notion of a person being a refugee is not of modern origin. The idea of providing refuge and a home to a stranger appeared in the Old Testament and other ancient religious texts. Indeed, it has been argued that the normative character of asylum can be found in its nature as a religious command, as '[a] call for divine protection against human injustice'.[12] It has also been observed that all three monotheistic religions (Christianity, Judaism and Islam), and arguably other religious and secular traditions as well, impose a duty of hospitality and protection to strangers, which has provided the anthropological and historical background to the law and practice of asylum over time. Persons have moved from one country to another throughout history.[13] The movement of persons into the southern African region, and specifically South Africa, is also nothing new. People have sought a home in South Africa—individually or as groups—because of religious and political persecution, war, famine, and economic hardship for a very long time.

However, the modern law of international refugee law can only be traced back as far as a hundred years ago, following the creation of the League of Nations in 1919. The League of Nations took the first legal and institutional initiatives in 1921 with the appointment of the Norwegian diplomat and humanitarian, Fridjof Nansen, as a High Commissioner for Refugees. The following year, the League of Nations issued identity certificates to persons of Russian origin who no longer enjoyed the protection of the Government of the Union of Soviet Socialist Republics and who had not acquired another nationality. During the period of the League of Nations, four other institutions were created to perform all or some of the tasks of the

[12] M–T Gil-Bazo 'Asylum as a general principle of international law' (2015) 27 *IJRL* 3 at 18–20; SP Sinha *Asylum and International Law* (1971) 6. See also S Cheung *Religious Foundations of Asylum and the Challenges of Contemporary Practice* Paper presented at the Fifth International Conference on Peace, Human Rights and Religion, Center for Human Rights Studies, Mofid University, Iran, 13–14 May 2009.

[13] W Olivier 'International refugee law: A reappraisal' (1993) *TSAR* 424 and 667; LA de la Hunt 'Refugees and immigration law in South Africa' in J Crush (ed) *Beyond Control: Immigration and Human Rights in a Democratic South Africa* (1997) 123.

High Commissioner for Refugees. These were the Nansen International Office for Refugees (1931–1938), the Office of the High Commissioner for Refugees coming from Germany (1933–1938), the Office of the High Commissioner of the League of Nations for Refugees (1939–1946), and the Intergovernmental Committee on Refugees (1938–1947).[14] All these were precursors to the developments under the UN.

Europe, in the immediate aftermath of World War II, was confronted with a massive displacement of persons. This resulted in the establishment of the UNHCR in 1950 as the principal UN agency concerned with refugees, and the adoption of the 1951 UN Convention.[15] The agency was tasked with giving effect to article 14(1) of the Universal Declaration of Human Rights (UDHR),[16] which provides that 'everyone has the right to seek and to enjoy in other countries asylum from persecution', and to the 1967 UN Declaration on Territorial Asylum.[17] The 1951 UN Convention was adopted shortly after World War II, and focused on protecting persons fleeing events occurring before 1 January 1951 within Europe. The 1967 Protocol was adopted to remove these limitations and to give the 1951 UN Convention a universal scope. In 1963, the Organization of African Unity (OAU) was established, among other objectives, to promote regional co-operation among African states as they achieved independence. The focus of the OAU was on decolonisation, including the movement of people across borders to escape colonial regimes and wars of independence,[18] and in 1969 it adopted the 1969 OAU Convention.[19]

As South Africa moved out of its international isolation in 1990, it became apparent that the steady flow of persons across Mozambique's borders into South Africa would have to be dealt with.[20] In 1991, South Africa and the UNHCR entered into a basic agreement concerning the presence, role, legal status, immunities, and privileges

[14] G Jaeger 'On the history of the international protection of refugees' (2001) 83 *IRRC* 727 at 729.

[15] V Holzer *Refugees from Armed Conflict* (2015) 32–6.

[16] UNGA Res 217A (III) of 10 December 1948.

[17] UNGA Res 2312 (XXII) of 14 December 1967.

[18] BTM Nyanduga 'Refugee protection under the 1969 OAU Convention Governing the Specific Aspects of Refugee Problems in Africa' (2004) 47 *GYIL* 85, 86.

[19] See M Sharpe 'Organization of African Unity and African Union engagement with refugee protection' (2013) *AJICL* 50, 58 et seq.; J van Garderen and J Ebenstein 'Regional developments: Africa' in A Zimmermann (ed) *The 1951 Convention Relating to the Status of Refugees and its 1967 Protocol* (2011) 188.

[20] C Murray 'Mozambican refugees: South Africa's responsibility' (1986) 2 *SAJHR* 154; JA Faris 'Angolan refugees and South Africa' (1976) 2 *SAYIL* 176 at 185.

of the UNHCR and its personnel in South Africa.[21] South Africa also entered into a tripartite agreement with Mozambique and the UNHCR to deal with the issue of the voluntary repatriations of Mozambicans from South Africa. South Africa became a party to the 1969 OAU Convention in December 1995, and to the 1951 UN Convention and the 1967 Protocol in January 1996.[22]

At this time, South Africa had no specific legislation giving effect to the obligations contained in these conventions. It was only in 1998 that provision was made for these obligations in the Refugees Act, which came into force on 1 April 2000. Before this statute was enacted, persons seeking asylum and refugee status in South Africa were dealt with under the Aliens Control Act 96 of 1991,[23] which was repealed by the Immigration Act 13 of 2002 (Immigration Act).[24] The Minister of Home Affairs is the Minister responsible for all issues relating to citizenship, and she or her delegate has the power to order the deportation of foreigners from South Africa in terms of the Immigration Act.[25]

If a foreigner is recognised as a refugee and granted asylum in South Africa, she is entitled to all the rights set out in the Constitution, except those rights that apply only to South African citizens.[26] Importantly, granting refugee status recognises or declares a person as a refugee, and not vice versa. In the words of the European Court of Human Rights, as endorsed by the South African Constitutional Court, '[a] person does not become a refugee because of recognition, but is recognised because he or she is a refugee'.[27]

2 The definition of a refugee

Under the 1951 UN Convention, there are two elements to refugee status implied in the definition of a refugee. First, the person

[21] GN 2815 in *GG* 13644 of 29 November 1991; J Dugard 'Public international law' 1991 *Annual Survey* 645; J Dugard 'Public international law' 1993 *Annual Survey* 62.

[22] South Africa acceded to the 1969 OAU Convention on 15 December 1995, and to the 1951 UN Convention and the 1967 Protocol on the same day, 12 January 1996.

[23] The Aliens Control Act was amended by the Aliens Control Amendment Act 76 of 1995, which was specifically promulgated to bring the Act into line with constitutional requirements.

[24] See *Minister of Home Affairs v Eisenberg & Associates: In Re Eisenberg & Associates v Minister of Home Affairs* 2003 (5) SA 281 (CC).

[25] *Mohamed v President of the Republic of South Africa* 2001 (3) SA 893 (CC) paras 31–2; *Ulde v Minister of Home Affairs* 2009 (4) SA 522 (SCA) para 6 and *Jeebhai v Minister of Home Affairs* 2009 (5) SA 54 (SCA) para 21.

[26] Section 27 of the Refugees Act. See also *Union of Refugee Women v Director: Private Security Industry Regulatory Authority* 2007 (4) SA 395 (CC). Indeed, all foreigners within the territory of South Africa are entitled to such rights. *Lawyers for Human Rights and Other v Minister of Home Affairs and Other* 2004 (4) SA 125 (CC) para 79.

[27] *Saidi v Minister of Home Affairs* 2018 (4) SA 333 (CC) para 34, quoting *Hirsi Jamaa v Italy* [GC], no 27765/09, ECHR 2012 at 63.

concerned must have a well-founded fear of being persecuted for reasons of race, religion, nationality, membership of a particular social group or political opinion. Secondly, such person is outside the country of her nationality and is unable or, owing to such fear, is unwilling to avail herself of the protection of that country; or not having a nationality and being outside the country of her former habitual residence as a result of such events, is unable or, owing to such fear, is unwilling to return to it. This definition has been widely embraced by legal scholars and commentators.[28]

The definition of a refugee under the 1969 OAU Convention is far broader than that of the 1951 UN Convention. While article I(1) of the 1969 OAU Convention essentially reproduces the 1951 UN Convention's definition, article I(2) broadens this definition in a significant way to include any person who, 'owing to external aggression, occupation, foreign domination or events seriously disturbing or disrupting public order in either a part or the whole of his or her country of origin or nationality, is compelled to leave her place of habitual residence in order to seek refuge elsewhere'.

The 1969 OAU Convention definition was deliberately worded to include people forced into flight from countries still engaged in anti-apartheid and anti-colonial liberation struggles and those fleeing civil wars in their countries, and arguably environmental and other humanitarian disasters as well. The need to respond to the realities of the African continent at the time—armed conflict arising from anti-colonial struggles, internal civil wars and the resulting exoduses—were overriding considerations for the new definition.[29] The 1969 OAU Convention expanded the definition of 'refugee' in the 1951 UN Convention by doing away with the requirement of a 'well-founded fear of persecution' and in introducing objective criteria (dependent only on the prevailing situations in a claimant's country of origin) for determining refugee status. Thus, the 1969

[28] See, generally, G Goodwin-Gill and J McAdam *The Refugee in International Law* 3 ed (2007) 15–20; Hathaway and Foster (n 11) 91–2; D Weissbrodt *Refugees* (2008) 110–33; A Zimmermann and C Mahler 'Article 1 A, para. 2' in A Zimmermann (ed) *The 1951 Convention Relating to the Status of Refugees and its 1967 Protocol: A Commentary* (2011) 280–479; W Worster 'The evolving definition of the refugee in contemporary international law' (2012) 30 *Berkeley Journal of International Law* 94.

[29] T Maluwa *International Law in Post-Colonial Africa* (1999) 180. See also E Arboleda 'Refugee definition in Africa and Latin America: The lessons of pragmatism' (1991) 3 *IJRL* 185 at 195; T Wood 'Expanding protection in Africa? Case studies of the Implementation of the 1969 African Refugee Convention's Expanded Refugee Definition' (2014) 26 *IJRL* 555, 556; T Wood 'The African war refugee: Using IHL to interpret the 1969 African Refugee Convention's Expanded Refugee Definition' in D Cantor and J-F Durieux (eds) *Refuge from Inhumanity? Refugee Protection and the Laws of War* (2014) 177.

OAU Convention 'requires neither the elements of deliberateness nor discrimination inherent in the 1951 Convention'.[30] This development is 'one of the most lauded features of international refugee law today'.[31]

The definition of a refugee in the South African Refugees Act incorporates both the 1951 UN Convention definition and the 1969 OAU Convention definition.[32]

Before turning to deal with the elements of refugee status determination identified in these conventions, it is important to note that there is no 'onus' on a person to prove that they are a refugee. Three South African High Court decisions, with reference to paragraphs 196 and 197 of the *UNHCR Handbook on Procedures and Criteria for Determining Refugee Status*, have held that 'the normal onus in civil proceedings is inappropriate in refugee cases. The inquiry has an inquisitorial element. The burden is mitigated by a lower standard of proof and a liberal application of the benefit of doubt principle'.[33]

(a) Well-founded fear of persecution

The 1951 UN Convention and 1967 Protocol do not provide a definition for, or otherwise clarify what is meant by, the term 'persecution'. The *UNHCR Handbook* provides that:

> There is no universally accepted definition of 'persecution', and various attempts to formulate such a definition have met with little success. From Article 33 of the 1951 Convention it may be inferred that a threat to life or freedom on account of race, religion, nationality, political opinion or membership of a particular social group is always persecution. Other serious violations of human rights—for the same reasons—would also constitute persecution.[34]

Assessments as to whether an individual will face persecution if returned to a particular state must be made on a case-by-case basis taking into account, on the one hand, the notions of individual

[30] R Mandal 'Protection mechanisms outside the 1951 Convention ("Complimentary protection")' (2005) UNHCR Legal and Protection Policy Research Series 13, available at http://www.unhcr.org/435df0aa2.pdf.

[31] See Wood 'Expanding Protection in Africa?' (n 29). See also J Hathaway *The Law of Refugee Status* (1993) 19.

[32] Section 3(b) of the Refugees Act.

[33] *Tantoush v Refugee Appeal Board* (13182/06) [2007] ZAGPHC 191; 2008 (1) SA 232 (T) (11 September 2007) paras 97–8, citing *Fang v Refugee Appeal Board* 2007 (2) SA 447 (T) and *Van Garderen NO v The Refugee Appeal Board* (unreported decision 30720/2006 of 19 June 2007). See however *Kumah v Minister of Home Affairs* 2018 (2) SA 510 (GJ) para 29. See *UNHCR Handbook on Procedures and Criteria for Determining Refugee Status*, HCR/1P/4/Eng/Rev1 (Reissued, Geneva, January 2011). The *UNHCR Handbook* is intended as a guide for government officials dealing with the determination of refugee status.

[34] *UNHCR Handbook* (n 33) para 51.

integrity and human dignity and, on the other hand, the manner and degree to which they stand to be injured.[35] Ordinarily claims involve likely persecution at the hands of the government.[36] The threat of persecution must exist for the claimant in her country as a whole. If there is an area in her own country in which an asylum claimant would be safe from persecution, her claim for asylum may fail.[37] Well-founded fear involves both a subjective and an objective component. The former is based on the applicant's reaction to events that impinge upon her personally; but to make it a well-founded fear, there must be other proof or objective facts that lend support to the applicant's subjective fear.[38] The United States Court of Appeals, in *Pitcherskaia v INS*,[39] was seized with a claim by a Russian national that she had been persecuted on account of her membership of a particular social group, namely, Russian lesbians. She had been forced in the mid-1980s to undergo 'therapy sessions' as she was diagnosed with 'slow-going schizophrenia', a term often used in Russia to label homosexuals. The Court found that the definition of persecution was an objective one and stated that although many asylum cases 'involve actors who had a subjective intent to punish their victims . . . this subjective "punishment or malignment" intent is not required for harm to constitute persecution'. The Court held that the definition of persecution is objective, in that it turns not on the subjective intent of the persecutor, but rather on what a reasonable person would deem 'offensive'. That the persecutor inflicts the suffering or harm in an attempt to elicit information, for his own sadistic pleasure, to cure his victim or to save his soul, is irrelevant. Persecution by any other name remains persecution.

An asylum-seeker who has already suffered persecution in a given state, and who, as a result, is unwilling to return to that state, may qualify as a refugee even if a change in conditions has eliminated any well-founded fear of future persecution,[40] if compelling reasons exist.

The persecution or well-founded fear of persecution must be based on one of five categories: race, nationality, religion, political opinion

[35] Goodwin-Gill and McAdam *(n 28) 49. See also Katshingu v Standing Committee for Refugee Affairs—Western Cape High Court* (19726/10) [2011] ZAWCHC 480 (2 November 2011) 22 et seq and *Harerimana v Chairperson of the Refugee Appeal Board* (10972/2013) [2013] ZAWCHC 209; 2014 (5) SA 550 (WCC) (11 December 2013) paras 36–42.

[36] Cf *INS v Elias-Zacarias* 502 US 478 (1992).

[37] *Etugh v INS* 921 F 2d 36 (3d Cir 1990); Goodwin-Gill and McAdam (n 28) 74–5.

[38] *Melendez v United States Dept of Justice* 926 F 2d 211 (22nd Cir 1991).

[39] 118 F 3d 641 (9th Cir 1997).

[40] *Desir v Ilchert* 840 F 2d 723, 729 (9th Cir 1988). See 1951 Convention on the Status of Refugees, article 1C(6), as interpreted by *UNHCR Handbook* paras 135–6. See, however, *Adan v Secretary of State for the Home Department* [1998] 2 All ER 453.

or membership of a particular group. While race, nationality and religion are comparatively easy to identify as a basis for persecution or a well-founded fear of persecution, the same cannot be said about political opinion or membership of a particular social group.

In terms of the 1951 UN Convention and practice based on the *UNHCR Handbook*,[41] a well-founded fear of persecution based on the specific grounds listed in article 1A(2) of the Convention has been regarded as the only reason for a person to leave a country or to be unwilling to return to it. All other reasons are regarded as irrelevant unless they are used to augment a claim of persecution or to demonstrate the circumstances that the asylum-seeker would face at home.[42] It is for this reason, for example, that asylum status does not ordinarily extend to applicants who are economically oppressed, unless the economic oppression is due to the asylum-seeker's persecuted status.[43] Individuals fleeing other symptoms of state fragility or failure, including widespread insecurity or civil war, will also fall outside the ambit of 1951 UN Convention, as they will usually be unable to establish either an individual risk of persecution or a nexus between that risk and one of the five enumerated grounds for the recognition of refugee status. In Africa, this gap in the protection regime offered by the 1951 UN Convention is filled by its regional counterpart, the 1969 OAU Convention, which expands refugee protection to cover persons who are compelled to leave their homes 'owing to external aggression, occupation, foreign domination or events seriously disturbing public order'.

(b) Political opinion

There is no authoritative definition for the term 'political opinion' under either the 1951 UN Convention or the 1969 OAU Convention, or international law more generally.[44] Political opinion can be understood in the broad sense to include 'any opinion on any matter in which the machinery of state, government, society or policy may be engaged'.[45] The *Michigan Guidelines on Risk for Reasons of Political Opinion* have determined that a 'political' opinion is 'an opinion about the nature, policies, or practices of a state or of an entity that

[41] *UNHCR Handbook* (n 33) para 51.

[42] Ibid para 53.

[43] Ibid para 54.

[44] Colloquium on Challenges in International Refugee Law, 'The Michigan Guidelines on Risk for Reasons of Political Opinion' (2016) 37 *MJIL* 234. On the meaning of 'political opinion', generally, C Dauvergne 'Toward a new framework for understanding political opinion' (2016) 37 *MJIL* 243.

[45] See *UNHCR Handbook* (n 33) para 51. See further Goodwin-Gill and McAdam (n 28) 49; *Canada (Attorney General) v Ward* [1993] (2) SCR 689; (1993) 103 DLR (4th) 1.

has the capacity, legitimately or otherwise, to exercise societal power or authority. A relevant nonstate entity is one that is institutionalised, formalised, or informally systematised and which is shown by evidence of pattern or practice to exercise *de facto* societal power or authority'.[46] A number of domestic decisions have also developed the meaning of 'political opinion'.[47] In *Elias-Zacarias*,[48] the Supreme Court of the United States held that a refusal by Elias-Zacarias to take sides with any political faction in Guatemala was not the affirmative expression of a political opinion. Accordingly, Elias-Zacarias' claim that he would be persecuted on his return to Guatemala on the basis of political opinion failed because of his inability to adduce evidence that he either supported the government or the guerrilla movement in opposition to the government in Guatemala. The Court found that he had failed to show a political motive for his refusal to undergo military service. Courts in the United States, however, have generally concluded that imputed political opinion remains a viable ground for a successful claim to asylum based on political opinion even after the Supreme Court's ruling.[49] In Canada, courts have held that political opinion may be imputed to an individual by his or her government or other agent of persecution. In *Re Inzunza and MEI*,[50] the Court held:

> It should not be whether the Board considers that the applicant has engaged in political activities, but whether the ruling government of the country from which he claims to be a refugee considers his conduct to have been styled as political activity.

The fact that the applicant has committed a politically motivated crime in his own state will not entitle him to refugee status where the crime was a war crime, crime against humanity or act of terrorism.[51]

In *Tshiyombo v Members of the Refugee Appeal Board*, the applicant had been kidnapped and was forced to join a rebellion against the

[46] *Michigan Guidelines* (n 44) 234, 236.

[47] See, for example, *Canada (Attorney General) v Ward* [1993] (2) SCR 689; *Gutierrez Gomez v. Secretary of State for the Home Department* [2001] 1 WLR 549; *Refugee Appeal No 76044* [2008] NZAR 719 (N.Z.); *Refugee Appeal No 76339* [2010] NZAR 386 (R.S.A.A.).

[48] See n 36.

[49] See *Sangha v INS* 103 F 3d 1482, 1488–9 (9th Cir 1997); *Ravindran v INS* 976 F 2d 754, 760 (1st Cir 1992); *Rajaratnam v Moyer* 832 F Supp 1219 (N D III 1993). See TA Aleinikoff *Immigration and Citizenship Process and Policy* 4 ed (1998) 1095.

[50] 103 DLR (3 d) 105.

[51] Convention Relating to the Status of Refugees, article 1F: *T v Secretary of State for the Home Department* [1996] 2 All ER 865 (HL) (discussed in Chapter 11); *INS v Aquirre-Aguirre* 119 SCt 1439 (1999), (1999) 38 *ILM* 786. See, too, s 4 of the Refugees Act 130 of 1998; PJ van Krieken *Refugee Law in Context: The Exclusion Clause* (1999), and *Suresh v Canada (Minister of Citizenship and Immigration)* [2002] 1 SCR 3, 2002 SCC 1.

government. Although he had no 'actual' alliance to the rebel group—his membership having been coerced—he feared persecution on account of his 'perceived association' with it.[52] The Court found that 'it did not matter for the purpose of his asylum application that the applicant did not share the political opinions of the rebel group or had not voluntarily been a member of it'.[53]

(c) Membership of a particular social group

The *UNHCR Handbook* declares that 'membership of a particular social group may be at the root of persecution because there is no confidence in the group's loyalty to the government or because of the political outlook, antecedents or economic activity of its government's policies'.[54]

Membership of a particular social group has been dubbed 'the ground with the least clarity'.[55] It is also a category that has in recent years received growing attention, as the number of refugee claims based on it has 'increased dramatically'.[56]

In the seminal Canadian case of *Canada (Attorney General) v Ward*,[57] a test for this category was developed. In that case, 'a particular social group' was defined variously as: '(i) groups defined by an innate or unchangeable characteristic; (ii) groups defined by a characteristic that is fundamental to human dignity such that a person should not be forced to relinquish it; and (iii) groups defined by a former status, unalterable due to its historical permanence'.[58] This jurisprudence was accepted in South Africa in *Fang v Refugee Appeal Board et al*.[59] In the more recent case of *Tshiyombo v Members of the Refugee Appeal Board*, however, the Court ventured its own definition of the term 'particular

[52] 2016 (4) SA 469 (WCC) para 29.

[53] Ibid. The nature of a political crime for purposes of exclusion from refugee status has also been dealt with by the Constitutional Court in *Gavric v Refugee Status Determination Officer, Cape Town and Others* (CCT217/16) [2018] ZACC 38. The Court concluded that the approach to establishing whether a crime is political should be flexible and also take into account South Africa's historical context.

[54] *UNHCR Handbook* (n 33) para 78.

[55] M Foster 'The "ground with the least clarity": A comparative study of jurisprudential developments relating to "Membership of a Particular Social Group"' UNHCR Legal and Protection Policy Research Series No 25 (2012), available at http://www.unhcr.org/protect; E Feller et al (eds) *Refugee Protection in International Law: UNHCR's Global Consultations on International Protection* (2003) 312 [1]; J Hathaway and M Foster 'Membership of a Particular Social Group' (2003) 15 *IJRL* 477.

[56] A Aleinikoff *Protected Characteristics and Social Perceptions: An Analysis of the Meaning of 'Membership of a Particular Social Group'* (2003).

[57] [1993] 2 SCR 689, 731–2.

[58] This summary of the findings in that case was compiled by Foster (n 55) 7.

[59] 2007 (2) SA 432 (T) para 16 (where the judge stated: 'I associate myself with the categories of particular social groups as enumerated in the Canadian case of Ward').

social group', finding that it 'denote[s] a section of society that is identifiable by the common characteristics of the persons comprising it or of the basis for their mutual coherence'.[60]

South African legislation is unique in the sense that it provides some guidance on the content of the term 'social group'. Section 1(xxi) of the 1998 Refugees Act states that the term '"social group" includes, among others, a group of persons of particular gender, sexual orientation, disability, class or caste'.

The case law is rich with concrete examples of the manifestation of 'particular social groups'. One category that emerges from the case law is women at risk of female genital mutilation (FGM). In *R v Immigration Appeal Tribunal, Ex parte Shah (United Nations High Commissioner for Refugees intervening)*,[61] the House of Lords was called upon to decide whether women in Pakistan constituted a particular social group. Lord Steyn stated that a premise of the 1951 UN Convention was that all human beings shall enjoy fundamental rights and freedoms, and that counteracting discrimination was a fundamental purpose of the Convention.[62] Lord Hoffman rejected the notion that the term 'particular social group' implies an element of cohesiveness, co-operation or interdependence, and accepted that 'social group' could include individuals fearing persecution on 'such basis as gender, linguistic background and sexual orientation'.[63] In *Secretary of State for the Home Department (Respondent) v K (FC) (Appellant); Fornah (FC) (Appellant) v Secretary of State for the Home Department(Respondent)*[64] the House of Lords Appellate Committee held that a woman from Iran who was victimised because of her husband's political activities had a well-founded fear of persecution by virtue of her membership of a particular social group, that is, her husband's family; and that a young woman from Sierra Leone, who feared that if she returned to Sierra Leone she would be at risk of FGM, had a well-founded fear of persecutory treatment because she belonged to a particular social group, namely prospectively adult women in Sierra Leone who had not yet undergone FGM and so remained intact.

The United States Board of Immigration Appeals, in *In Re: Kasinga*,[65] considered the asylum claim of a 19-year-old Togolese

[60] *Tshiyombo* n 52.

[61] [1999] 2 All ER 545 (HL).

[62] Ibid at 551j.

[63] Ibid at 563j.

[64] 2006 UKHL 46; see also note by RMM Wallace 'Secretary of State for the Home Department (Respondent) v K(FC) (Appellant); Fornah (FC)(Appellant) v Secretary of State for the Home Department (Respondent)' (2006) 31 *SAYIL* 263.

[65] (1996) 35 *ILM* 1145.

woman on the basis that, as a member of a social group, namely, the particular tribe to which she belonged, she would be forced to undergo FGM. The Board found that the particular social group of young women in the Tchamba-Kunsuntu tribe who had not undergone FGM as practised by that tribe, and who opposed the practice, fitted the definition of members of a particular social group.[66] The US Court of Appeals for the Second Circuit confirmed this decision in *Abankwah v INS*.[67]

In *Fang v Refugee Appeal Board*,[68] the North Gauteng High Court rejected the notion that Mr Fang was a member of a particular social group in that he had more than one child and if returned to the People's Republic of China he would fall foul of that country's one-child-per-family policy. However, in *Jacob van Garderen NO v The Refugee Appeal Board*[69] the Court held that three young girls from the Democratic Republic of the Congo faced a real risk of persecution on account of their membership of a social group, namely, that of female children.

(d) The expanded refugee definition in the 1969 OAU Convention[70]

The 1969 OAU Convention expands refugee protection to cover persons who are compelled to leave their homes 'owing to external aggression, occupation, foreign domination or events seriously disturbing public order'. The scope of this provision is unclear, particularly insofar as it relates to 'events seriously disturbing public order'.[71]

It is possible to interpret 'events seriously disturbing public order' to include people fleeing non-discriminatory deprivations of their human rights resulting from the complete socio-economic breakdown or failure of a state. However, South Africa has chosen not to accept such an interpretation of the definition. In South Africa, there has been a significant influx of Zimbabwean nationals fleeing

[66] See, also, *Sanchez-Trujillo v INS* 801 F 2d 1571 (9th Cir 1986) and A Helton 'Persecution on account of membership in a social group as a basis for refugee status' (1983) 15 *Columbia Human Rights L Rev* 39, 40–7, 51–2.

[67] (1999) 38 *ILM* 1267.

[68] 2007 (2) SA 432 (T).

[69] Unreported Case No 30720/2006 (T), judgment delivered on 19 June 2007, reported in (2008) 33 *SAYIL* 511.

[70] T Schreier 'An evaluation of South Africa's application of the OAU Refugee Definition' (2008) 25 *Refuge* 53; G Okoth-Obbo 'Thirty years on: A legal review of the 1969 OAU Refugee Convention Concerning the Specific Aspects of Refugee Problems in Africa' (2001) 20 *Refugee Survey Quarterly* 80, 25–32; T Wood 'Fragile states and international protection under the 1969 African Refugee Convention' (2013) 43 *Forced Migration Review* 17; M Sharpe 'The 1969 OAU Refugee Convention: Innovations, omissions and misconceptions' (2012) 58 *McGill Law Journal* 96.

[71] Wood (n 70) 17, 19.

socio-economic breakdown in their home state.[72] However, applications for refugee status made by Zimbabweans claiming refuge from this situation have been almost universally rejected. South African authorities consider these applicants to be 'economic migrants'[73] and that the 'relative stability of law and order in the country means it falls outside the scope of the 1969 Convention'.[74]

One commentator, reviewing the practice of states in the implementation of the OAU's expanded definition of a refugee, suggests that 'states may be more willing to apply the 1969 Convention to persons in situations where the perceived cause of displacement is the existence of armed conflict and a breakdown in law and order. Where persons flee the many other symptoms of state fragility—including poor governance, food insecurity and lack of access to basic services—such application is less straightforward'.[75]

It also remains unclear whether the term 'events seriously disturbing public order' extends to natural disasters. In South Africa, the Supreme Court of Appeal (SCA) was dismissive of a claim to refugee status based on flooding, which the Refugee Appeal Board had dismissed as 'manifestly unfounded'.[76]

(e) 'Bootstrap' refugees or refugees sur place

'Bootstrap' refugees are persons who were not refugees when they left their country of origin, but who became refugees abroad. They are often referred to as refugees *sur place*. The requirement that a person must be outside his country to be a refugee does not mean that he must necessarily have left that country illegally, or even that he must have left it on account of a well-founded fear of persecution. The claimant may have decided to ask for asylum after already having been abroad for some time.[77] A person may become a refugee *sur place* either as a result of his actions or due to circumstances arising in his country of origin during his absence. The profile of refugees *sur place* may thus be considered atypical, but they are nevertheless entitled to the same international protection regime as

[72] Wood (n 70). See, generally, Human Rights Watch *Neighbors in Need: Zimbabweans Seeking Refuge in South Africa* (2008).

[73] *Chihomba v Chairperson: Refugee Appeal Board* (16418/2012) [2015] ZAGPPHC 444 (16 June 2015) paras 32–3 ('The principle of *non-refoulement* addresses bona fide Applicants for asylum and is incapable to cover economic migrants who enter South Africa to benefit financially . . . [M]ost Zimbabwean Nationals who travel to South Africa do so for economic reasons').

[74] Wood (n 70) 18.

[75] Ibid.

[76] *Rahim v The Minister of Home Affairs* (965/2013) [2015] ZASCA 92 (29 May 2015) 2015 (4) SA 433 (SCA) para 26.

[77] The *UNHCR Handbook* recognises a refugee *sur place* at paras 94–6.

other refugees. However, it remains the case that asylum claims *sur place* based on post-departure developments often arouse suspicion, and such suspicion seems to pervade the asylum policies of some countries or the actions of refugee and immigration officials.[78] In examining such claims, courts or asylum determination agencies in host countries would do well to set aside mere suspicions and focus objectively on two factors: the degree to which the asylum-seeker was politically active at home and his motive for leaving his home country. In respect of actions the asylum-seeker may have committed post-departure from his country of origin, regard should be given to whether such actions will come to the attention of the asylum-seeker's home government and what the government's reaction will be.[79]

SOUTH AFRICAN PROCEDURE BEFORE THE REFUGEES ACT[80]

Before South Africa became a party to the 1969 OAU Convention and to the 1951 Refugees Convention and its 1967 Protocol, South Africa recognised no direct obligation to make legal provision for refugees on its territory. Accordingly, migrants to South Africa were dealt with only in terms of the Aliens Control Act, which provided for the control of the admission of persons to, their residence in and their departure from South Africa, but did not provide for the identification or protection of refugees.

The Aliens Control Act provided that, in the first instance, all persons who are not citizens of South Africa are foreigners.[81] There was a general prohibition on foreigners entering or remaining in South Africa *with* a view to permanent residence or temporary residence without the necessary immigration permit or temporary residence permit.[82] Those persons who entered or remained in South Africa without the necessary permit were categorised as illegal foreigners.[83] Every person who applied for refugee status and asylum was immediately granted a temporary permit issued to

[78] See, for example, criticism of EU policy for determination of claims for asylum *sur place* by S da Lomba 'The EU Qualification Directive and refugees sur place' in F Goudappel and H Raulus (eds) *The Future of Asylum in the European Union: Problems, Proposals and Human Rights* (2011) 43–64.

[79] *UNHCR Handbook* (n 33) para 96.

[80] The Refugees Act has been amended on more than one occasion subsequent to its enactment, the most recent of which was by the Refugees Amendment Act 33 of 2008, which has not yet come into operation. The key change is that a Refugee Appeals Authority replaced the Refugee Appeal Board.

[81] Section 1(1) of the Aliens Control Act.

[82] Section 23 of the Aliens Control Act read with ss 25 and 26.

[83] Section 49 of the Aliens Control Act.

prohibited persons, subject to various conditions and valid for a particular period, between three months and six months. The application for asylum was made to an immigration officer, who referred the application to the Refugee Affairs Standing Committee (the Committee), a body established to give effect to the Tripartite Agreement between South Africa, Mozambique, and the UNHCR. The Committee received and considered all applications and granted recognition of refugee status to successful applicants, without providing the asylum-seeker with an interview. In its determination process, it relied on the information provided by the immigration officer who interviewed the asylum-seeker. The Committee advised the applicant of the outcome of the application through an immigration officer and in the event of an unsuccessful application informed the applicant of his right to appeal to the Appeal Board for Refugee Affairs (the Board). The Committee was required to provide all asylum-seekers with reasons in writing for any adverse decisions.[84] Pending the decisions of the Committee and the Board, and the finalisation of his application for asylum, the asylum-seeker was entitled to study and work in South Africa. In *Somali Association of South Africa v Limpopo Department of Economic Development Environment and Tourism* it was held further that asylum-seekers in South Africa have the right to open businesses in South Africa and that, accordingly, the state must allow asylum-seekers to apply for and renew business permits and licences. And, finally, that it is unlawful for the government to close permitted businesses owned by asylum-seekers.[85]

In *Kabuika v Minister of Home Affairs*,[86] asylum-seekers from the former Zaire (now the Democratic Republic of Congo) sought, as a matter of urgency, an interim interdict directing the Minister of Home Affairs to allow them to remain in South Africa pending a judicial review of the decisions by the Committee and the Board. The Court examined the findings of the Committee and the Board and found, after considering reports from Amnesty International and other international bodies concerning the state of affairs in the former Zaire, that the applicants had shown at the very least a *prima facie* right to relief and that they had a well-grounded apprehension of

[84] Until 10 December 1996, the Standing Committee for Refugee Affairs refused to provide reasons for rejections, but, in a case brought before the Cape of Good Hope Provincial Division, an order by consent was granted which required the Standing Committee to provide reasons in writing for any adverse decision. See *Pembele v Appeal Board for Refugee Affairs*, case number 15931/96, unreported.

[85] 2015 (1) SA 151 (SCA).

[86] 1997 (4) SA 341(C).

irreparable harm should they be forced to leave South Africa.[87] The Court found that the relevant decision-making bodies had failed either to consider the reports or to attach adequate weight to them, and that the decision-making bodies had misunderstood the asylum-seekers' version of events regarding their movements in Zaire. The Court therefore ordered the Minister of Home Affairs to allow the applicants to remain in South Africa pending the final determination of the review proceedings instituted in respect of the decisions of the Committee and the Board.

THE REFUGEES ACT

The Refugees Act was enacted to give effect to the relevant international legal instruments and principles relating to refugees within South Africa, and to provide for the reception of asylum-seekers.[88] It was enacted to regulate applications for and recognition of refugee status and to provide for the rights and obligations flowing from such status.[89] The Act must be interpreted and applied with due regard to the 1951 UN Convention, the 1967 Protocol, the 1969 OAU Convention, the UDHR and any other relevant human rights treaty to which South Africa is or becomes a party.[90]

The Act provides that a person qualifies for refugee status if she has a well-founded fear of being persecuted by reason of her race, tribe, religion, nationality, political opinion or membership of a particular social group, and is outside the country of her nationality and is unable or unwilling to avail herself of the protection of that country or, not having a nationality and being outside the country of her former habitual residence is unable or, owing to such fear, unwilling to return to it.[91] The definition mirrors that of the 1951 UN Convention and 1967 Protocol. 'Social group,' as mentioned above, is defined to include a group of persons of particular gender, sexual

[87] At 344J–345A.

[88] See the preamble and *Minister of Home Affairs v Watchenuka* 2004 (4) SA 326 (SCA) para 2; and *Watchenuka v Minister of Home Affairs* 2003 (1) SA 619 (C) 621F–I; *Kiliko v Minister of Home Affairs* 2006 (4) SA 114 (C) para 25 and *Abdi v Minister of Home Affairs* 2011 (3) SA 37 (SCA) para 22. The Refugees Act came into operation on 1 April 2000 pursuant to proc R22, 2000 in *GG* 21075 of 6 April 2000. See FJ Jenkins 'Coming to South Africa: An overview of the application for asylum and an introduction to The Refugees Act' (1999) 24 *SAYIL* 182; S Budhu 'The extent of municipal obligation towards refugees in South Africa (2001) 26 *SAYIL* 246; M Beukes '"Economic refugees": South African reality and international refugee law' (2002) 27 *SAYIL* 206.

[89] *Scalabrini Centre, Cape Town v Minister of Home Affairs* (1107/2016) [2017] ZASCA 126; [2017] 4 All SA 686 (SCA) (29 September 2017) para 35.

[90] Section 6.

[91] Section 3(a).

orientation, disability, class, or caste.[92] The Act provides further that a person may qualify for refugee status if, owing to external aggression, occupation, foreign domination or events seriously disturbing or disrupting public order, in either a part or the whole of her country of origin or nationality, she is compelled to leave her place of habitual residence in order to seek refuge elsewhere.[93] This extended definition is consistent with the provisions of the 1969 OAU Convention.[94] Dependants of a person who qualifies for refugee status are also regarded as refugees.[95]

1 *Non-refoulement* and access to South African territory

International law now recognises the principle of *non-refoulement*, which obliges states to refrain from forcibly returning a refugee to a state where he is likely to suffer persecution or danger to life or freedom.[96] This principle, contained in article 33 of the 1951 UN Convention, read with the 1967 Protocol, has crystallised into a rule of customary international law.[97] The prohibition on *refoulement* is an exception to the international law rule that every sovereign state has the power, inherent in sovereignty, to forbid the entrance of aliens into its territory or to admit them only in such cases and upon such conditions as it may see fit to prescribe.[98]

[92] Section 1(xxi).

[93] Section 3*(b)*.

[94] Article 1(2).

[95] Section 3*(c)*.

[96] The term is derived from the French word *'refouler'*, which means to return or to drive back. See, generally, C Wouters *International Legal Standards for the Protection from Refoulement* (2009); E Feller, V Turk and F Nicholson (eds) *Refugee Protection and International Law* (2003) 87–180. Hugo Grotius, himself a refugee, considered the right to asylum a natural right and asserted that states had a corresponding duty to grant asylum: *De Jure Belli ac Pacis* (1625) 2.2.16. On non-refoulement in Africa specifically, see C d'Orsi *Asylum-Seeker and Refugee Protection in Sub-Saharan Africa* (2015) Chapter 1. As it relates to South Africa, see the discussion by F Khan 'The principle of non-refoulement' in Khan and Schreier (eds) (n 3) 3–19.

[97] C Costello and M Foster 'Non-refoulement as custom and jus cogens? Putting the prohibition to the test' (2015) 46 *Netherlands Yearbook of International Law* 273; *Kabuika* 1997(4) SA 34 at 343; *Saidi v Minister of Home Affairs* (CCT107/17) [2018] ZACC 9 (24 April 2018) para 32.

[98] *Nishimura Ekiu v United States* 142 US 651 (1892) 662. See, also, the *Chinese Exclusion Case* 130 US 581 (1889); *Fong Yue Ting v United States* 149 US 698 (1893); *Xu v Minister van Binnelandse Sake* 1995 (1) SA 185 (T); *Naidenov v Minister of Home Affairs* 1995 (7) BCLR 891 (T); *Parekh v Minister of Home Affairs* 1996 (2) SA 70 (D). See, however, *Foulds v Minister of Home Affairs* 1996 (4) SA 137 (W); *Tettey v Minister of Home Affairs* 1999 (3) SA 715 (D); J Klaaren 'So far, not so good: An analysis of immigration decisions under the Interim Constitution' (1996) 12 *SAJHR* 605; RJ Purshotam 'The right of aliens and migrants to administrative justice and a brief look at the abuse suffered by them in South Africa' (1999) 116 *SALJ* 32; R Pretorius 'Protecting the rights

The principle of *non-refoulement* also operates to ensure that asylum-seekers may not be turned away at the border. Both the UN General Assembly's Declaration on Territorial Asylum and the 1969 OAU Convention declare that asylum-seekers should not face 'measures such as rejection at the frontier',[99] while the 1951 UN Convention protects asylum-seekers who have crossed into the territory of a state without authorisation.[100]

South Africa acknowledges the obligation to allow asylum-seekers entry into its territory in terms of the Refugees Act, which expressly states that asylum-seekers may not be 'refused entry'.[101] Furthermore, South Africa makes two concessions for asylum-seekers, exempting them from its ordinarily applicable standards for migration.

First, asylum-seekers are permitted to enter South Africa without the need for a passport or a valid visa.[102] Section 23 of the Immigration Act[103] provides that immigration officials may 'issue an asylum transit visa to a person who at a port of entry claims to be an asylum-seeker, valid for a period of five days only, to travel to the nearest Refugee Reception Office in order to apply for asylum'. The Immigration Act and its Regulations bestow no authority on border officials to conduct interviews relating to the validity or otherwise of the asylum-seeker's claim.

Secondly, the Refugees Act protects asylum-seekers who enter South Africa irregularly.[104] Refugees are protected from arrest, detention and deportation as illegal immigrants by the provisions of s 2 of the Refugees Act. In terms of this section, no person may be 'expelled, extradited or returned to any other country' if that person may be subjected to persecution on account of his race, religion, nationality, political opinion or membership of a particular social group, or if such person's physical safety or freedom would be threatened on account of external aggression, occupation, foreign domination or other events seriously disturbing public order.

of aliens in South Africa: International and constitutional issues' (1996) 21 *SAYIL* 130; J Nafziger 'The general admission of aliens under international law' (1983) 77 *AJIL* 804.

[99] UN Doc. A/RES/2312(XXII), 14 December 1967, article 3 and article II(3) of the OAU Convention.

[100] 1951 UN Convention, article 31(1).

[101] Section 2 of the Refugees Act; *Abdi v Minister of Home Affairs* 2011 (3) SA 37 (SCA) para 22.

[102] Ibid.

[103] The prescribed procedure for an asylum transit visa is set out in reg 20 of the Immigration Regulations, GN R616 in *GG* 27725 of 27 June 2005.

[104] Section 21(4) of the Refugees Act.

In terms of regulations issued under the Immigration Act in 2014, an asylum transit visa will only be issued to an asylum-seeker who applies 'in person at a port of entry'.[105]

2 Procedure for application for refugee status

The procedure for application for refugee status under the Refugees Act, read with the Refugee Regulations made by the Minister of Home Affairs in terms of s 38,[106] is similar in many respects to the previous procedure under the Aliens Control Act.[107] Accordingly, judicial decisions such as *Kabuika*[108] and *Baromoto*[109] may be used to inform future courts dealing with refugee issues. The Refugees Act is in the process of being amended, although the amended provisions have yet to be enacted into law. The following sections deal with the procedure for application for refugee status under the law as it currently stands.

All applications for refugee status and asylum must be made without delay in person to a Refugee Reception Officer at any Refugee Reception Office.[110]

A Refugee Reception Officer, an official of the Department of Home Affairs, is tasked with ensuring that applications for asylum are properly completed. If necessary, he must assist the applicant in completing the form, and may conduct an enquiry to verify the information contained in the application.[111] In *Kiliko*,[112] the High Court held the Department of Home Affairs has a duty to provide adequate facilities essential for an expeditious handling of applications for asylum-seeker permits.[113] The Refugee Reception Officer must submit applications received by him to a Refugee Status Determination Officer.[114] No proceedings against asylum applicants

[105] GN R413 in *GG* 37679 of 22 May 2014.

[106] GN R366 in *GG* 21075 of 6 April 2000.

[107] Chapters 2 and 3 of the Refugees Act.

[108] 1997 (4) SA 341(C).

[109] 1998 (5) BCLR 562 (W).

[110] Section 21 and reg 2(1)*(a)*.

[111] See *Katshingu v Standing Committee for Refugee Affairs—Western Cape High Court* (19726/10) [2011] ZAWCHC 480 (2 November 2011) 8; *Director-General: The Department of Home Affairs v Dekoba* (224/2013) [2014] ZASCA 71; 2014 (5) SA 206 (SCA); [2014] 3 All SA 529 (SCA) (28 May 2014) para 10.

[112] 2006 (4) SA 114 (C).

[113] See *Intercape Ferreira Mainliner v Minister of Home Affairs* 2010 (5) SA 349 (WCC) paras 14–24; *410 Voortrekker Road Property Holdings CC v Minister of Home Affairs* 2010 (8) BCLR 785 (WCC) paras 1–7.

[114] Section 24.

and those granted asylum may be instituted or continued in respect of their unlawful entry or presence in South Africa.[115]

3 Asylum-seekers

Once a foreigner has made an application for asylum the Refugee Reception Officer must issue to the applicant an asylum-seeker permit allowing the person to sojourn in South Africa temporarily.[116] This permit remains valid while the application to be granted refugee status is finalised.[117] Under Regulations made by the Minister asylum-seekers were prohibited from employment or studying, at least for the first six months of their time in South Africa. In *Minister of Home Affairs v Watchenuka*,[118] the SCA held that the blanket prohibition violated asylum-seekers' constitutional right to dignity. In so finding, the SCA stated that human dignity has no nationality because it is inherent in all people—simply because they are human. Asylum-seekers are thus authorised in general to work or study in South Africa pending the finalisation of their applications for asylum.[119]

(a) Decisions on asylum applications

The Refugee Status Determination Officer, who must be an officer of the Department of Home Affairs with experience and knowledge of refugee matters,[120] must take a decision regarding the application for asylum. The just administrative action provisions of the Constitution[121] apply to the consideration of the application[122] and the applicant must fully understand the procedures, his rights and responsibilities. The Refugee Status Determination Officer may request information or clarification from the applicant or the Refugee Reception Officer, and may consult with a UNHCR representative.

In considering an asylum application, one of four decisions may be made. First, the Refugee Status Determination Officer may grant asylum. Secondly, the application may be rejected as unfounded, in

[115] Section 21(4). This provision is consistent with the provisions of article 31 of the 1951 UN Convention.

[116] Section 22.

[117] *Minister of Home Affairs v Somali Association of South Africa Eastern Cape (SASA EC)* (831/2013) [2015] ZASCA 35; 2015 (3) SA 545 (SCA); [2015] 2 All SA 294 (SCA) (25 March 2015) para 3.

[118] 2004 (4) SA 326 (SCA).

[119] See also *Somali Association of South Africa v Limpopo Department of Economic Development Environment and Tourism* (48/2014) [2014] ZASCA 143; 2015 (1) SA 151 (SCA); [2014] 4 All SA 600 (SCA) (26 September 2014).

[120] Section 8(2).

[121] Section 33 of the Constitution of the Republic of South Africa, 1996.

[122] Section 24(2) of the Refugees Act.

which event the applicant may appeal such rejection to the Refugee Appeal Board. The Refugee Appeal Board may set aside or substitute any decision by a Refugee Status Determination Officer to reject an asylum application.[123] Thirdly, the Refugee Status Determination Officer may reject an application as manifestly unfounded, abusive, or fraudulent. Abusive applications are those made with the purpose of defeating or evading criminal or civil proceedings or repeated applications made without any substantial change in the applicant's personal circumstances or in his country of origin.[124] Fraudulent applications are those made by applicants who know the facts contained in the application to be false and such facts are intended to materially affect the outcome of the application.[125] Manifestly unfounded applications are those made on grounds other than the recognised grounds for granting asylum.[126] The record of applications rejected as manifestly unfounded, abusive or fraudulent must be submitted to the Standing Committee for Refugee Affairs (the Standing Committee).[127] The Standing Committee may confirm or set aside the rejection by the Refugee Status Determination Officer.[128] Fourthly, the Refugee Status Determination Officer may refer any question of law to the Standing Committee. The Standing Committee must refer the application back to the Refugee Status Determination Officer, with such directives as may be necessary, and he must decide the application in terms of such directives. Applications for asylum should be generally adjudicated within 180 days of the filing of a completed asylum application with the Refugee Reception Officer.[129]

The leading case on the substance and process[130] for asylum applications is *Tantoush v Refugee Appeal Board*.[131] The High Court set aside the rejection by the refugee authorities of Mr Tantoush's application for asylum and substituted its own decision, by declaring that he was a refugee and entitled to asylum. In doing so, it held that the appropriate standard to be applied is one of '*a reasonable possibility of prosecution*', used by the US Supreme Court in *Immigration and Naturalization Service v Cardoza-Tonseca*,[132] and not as the Refugee

[123] Section 24(3)*(c)* read with s 26.
[124] Section 1(i).
[125] Section 1(xi).
[126] Section 1(xii).
[127] Section 24(4).
[128] Section 25(3).
[129] Regulation 3(1).
[130] See also *Arse v Minister of Home Affairs* 2010 (7) BCLR 640 (SCA) paras 15–7.
[131] 2008 (1) SA 232 (T).
[132] See *Immigration and Naturalization Service v Cardoza-Tonseca* 480 US 421 (1987) 440.

Appeal Board had held that an applicant was required to prove *'a real risk of persecution on a balance of probabilities'*.[133]

An applicant has the right to review the decisions of the Standing Committee or the Appeal Board to reject their refugee status application to the High Court. The law reports and court rolls are replete with such cases.[134] A Refugee Reception Officer has an obligation to renew the asylum-seeker's permit until the High Court review is finalised.[135]

(b) Detention of failed asylum-seekers[136]

A person whose asylum-seeker permit is withdrawn by the Minister of Home Affairs may be arrested and detained pending the finalisation of his application for asylum, with due regard to human dignity.[137] Detention may be no longer than is reasonable and justifiable and a High Court judge must review any detention exceeding 30 days.[138] Any subsequent period of detention must be reviewed after the expiry of every subsequent period of 30 days.[139] If 30 days elapse and the review of the detention by the High Court has not occurred, the person must be released.[140] In considering the detention of asylum-seekers and refugees, courts will be assisted by decisions concerning the detention of foreigners under the Aliens Control Act and the Immigration Act.[141] Cognisant of the standards of international best practice, according to which illegal immigrant

[133] Emphasis added.

[134] *Tekalign v Minister of Home Affairs* (2774/2015) [2018] ZAECPEHC 23 (22 May 2018); [2018] 3 All SA 291 (ECP) para 1. Many of these review applications are unopposed by the Department of Home Affairs. See *Ngwenya v Minister of Home Affairs* (A3014/2017) [2017] ZAGPJHC 222 (15 August 2017) para 1; *N v Chairperson of the Standing Committee for Refugee Affairs* (15376/16) [2017] ZAWCHC 57 (16 May 2017); *Mubala v Chairperson of the Standing Committee for Refugee Affairs* (10971/2013) [2013] ZAWCHC 208 (8 November 2013).

[135] *Saidi v Minister of Home Affairs* (CCT107/17) [2018] ZACC 9 (24 April 2018); 2018 (4) SA 333 (CC).

[136] See generally C Johnson 'Failed asylum seekers in South Africa: policy and practice' (2015) 1 *African Human Mobility Review* 201.

[137] Section 23.

[138] Section 289.

[139] Compare s 34 of the Immigration Act, and see *Lawyers for Human Rights v Minister of Home Affairs* 2004 (4) SA 125 (CC); *Jeebhai v Minister of Home Affairs* 2009 (5) SA 54 (SCA). See *Johnson v Minister of Home Affairs* 1997 (2) SA 432 (C); *Silva v Minister of Safety and Security* 1997 (4) SA 657 (W); *Fei Lui v Commanding Officer, Kempton Park* 1999 (3) SA 996 (W); and *Abdi v Minister of Home Affairs* 2011(3) SA 37 (SCA) para 20.

[140] *Arse v Minister of Home Affairs* 2010 (7) BCLR 640 (SCA).

[141] For example, *Ulde v Minister of Home Affairs* 2009 (4) SA 522 (SCA); *Aruforse v Minister of Home Affairs* 2010 (6) SA 579 (GSJ); and *Minister of Home Affairs v Rahim* (CCT124/15) [2016] ZACC 3; 2016 (3) SA 218 (CC); 2016 (6) BCLR 780 (CC) (18 February 2016).

detainees should be kept apart from the general prison population, the SCA in *Rahim v The Minister of Home Affairs* determined that failed asylum-seekers who are held in detention pending deportation may not be held in a general prison.[142]

(c) Exclusion from refugee status

Certain persons are excluded from qualifying for refugee status. These include persons whom there is reason to believe have committed a crime against peace, a war crime or a crime against humanity,[143] or a crime which is not of a political nature and which, if committed in South Africa, would be punishable by imprisonment.[144] Similarly, under s 4(1)*(c)* of the Refugees Act, persons who are guilty of acts contrary to the objects and principles of the UN or the OAU are excluded from refugee status. However, it should be noted that in *Gavric v Refugee Status Determination Officer, Cape Town and Others* the Constitutional Court affirmed that non-refoulement applies to those who have been excluded from refugee status and stressed that given the potential consequences resulting from a rejected asylum application, RSDOs must provide adequate reasons for rejection.[145] A person who enjoys the protection of any other state in which she has taken residence will also fail to qualify as a refugee.[146]

(d) Cessation of refugee status

A person recognised as a refugee ceases to qualify as such in five situations.[147] First, if she voluntarily re-avails herself of the protection of her country of nationality; secondly, if she re-acquires her nationality, after she had lost it by some voluntary and formal act; thirdly, if she becomes a citizen of South Africa by naturalisation,[148] or she acquires the nationality of some other country, and enjoys the protection of the country of her new nationality; fourthly, if she voluntarily re-establishes herself in the country which she left; and fifthly, when the circumstances in connection with which she was recognised as a refugee cease to exist and no other circumstances arise which justify her continued recognition as a refugee.

[142] 2015 (4) SA 433 (SCA) para 20, interpreting s 34(1) of the Immigration Act 13 of 2002.

[143] Section 4(1)*(a)*.

[144] Section 4(1)*(b)*; *INS v Aguirre-Aguirre* (1999) 38 *ILM* 786; *T v Secretary of State for the Home Department* [1996] 2 All ER 865 (HL). The exclusion clause contained in the Act is wider than that contained in article 1F of the 1951 UN Convention and may well be unconstitutional. See *Tantoush v Refugee Appeal Board and Other* 2008 (1) SA 232 (T) paras 109–24.

[145] *Gavric v Refugee Status Determination Officer, Cape Town and Others* Supra (n 53).

[146] Section 4(1)*(d)*. See *Abdi v Secretary of State for the Home Department* [1996] 1 All ER 641; *R v Secretary of State for the Home Department, Ex parte Canbolat* [1998] 1 All ER 161.

[147] Section 5(1).

[148] See s 7 of the Citizenship Act 88 of 1995.

4 Amendments to the Refugees Act: New procedures

Since 2008, the legislature has enacted changes to the Refugees Act through four amendment Acts. Except for the 2015 amendment,[149] the amendments have not yet come into force.[150] The amendments will significantly affect the manner in which applications for asylum and refugee status are determined. Originally, the 2008 amendments did away with the Standing Committee. But the 2011 and 2017 amendments reverted to using the Standing Committee, although its role has been altered. The 2017 amendment also substitutes the term 'asylum-seeker permit' with the term 'asylum-seeker visa'.

In terms of the amended Refugees Act, an application for asylum will have to be made in person to a Refugee Status Determination Officer at any Refugee Reception Office.[151] This must be done after reporting to a Refugee Reception Office within five days of entry into the Republic.[152] Prior to making an application for asylum, every applicant must submit their biometrics[153] to an immigration officer at a port of entry or a Reception Office.[154] The applicant must also declare all his or her spouses and dependents (whether in the Republic or elsewhere) when applying for asylum.[155] The biometric data of the applicant, along with her spouse and all dependants, are then submitted again when making an application for asylum.[156] If the applicant wishes for their spouse and dependents to be granted refugee status, then the details of such spouse and dependents must be included in the application.[157]

If the applicant is not in possession of an asylum transit visa as contemplated in s 23 of the Immigration Act, an immigration officer must interview such applicant to ascertain why they are not in possession of such visa.[158] It is also presumed that if an applicant

[149] Refugees Amendment Act 10 of 2015.

[150] Refugees Amendment Act 33 of 2008; Refugees Amendment Act 12 of 2011; Refugees Amendment Act 11 of 2017.

[151] Section 21(1)*(b)* of the Refugees Act 130 of 1998, as amended.

[152] Section 21(1)*(a)*. A compelling reason is required to condone not reporting to an Office within five days. Failure to do so could result in exclusion from refugee status (s 4(1)(i)).

[153] Biometrics is defined as 'any measurable physiological or behavioural characteristics that can be used in verifying the identity of individuals, and may include the use of photographs, fingerprints, hand measurements, signature verification, facial patterns and retinal patterns'.

[154] Section 21(1A).

[155] Section 21(2A).

[156] Section 21(3).

[157] Section 21B.

[158] Section 21(1B).

indicates a language of preference in an application for asylum, then the applicant understands and is proficient in such language.[159]

The Director-General is given the power, by notice in a *Gazette*, to require a category of asylum-seekers to report to a designated Reception Office if the Director-General considers it necessary for the proper administration of the Act.[160] Categories of asylum-seekers include asylum-seekers from a particular country, gender, religion, nationality, political opinion, or social group.[161] If the Director-General exercises this power, she would have to be mindful of not discriminating against a class of asylum-seekers by imposing an additional burden on (or withholding a benefit from) the category of asylum-seekers.

In accordance with the Constitutional Court's judgment in *Chipu*,[162] s 21(5) has been amended to give the Refugee Appeals Authority discretion to allow the media to report on a hearing before it. Before the amendment, the section provided that asylum applications had to be kept confidential at all times. But now the Appeals Authority can grant the media access to hearings if the asylum-seeker gives consent or if the Appeal Authority concludes that such access is in the public interest. This amendment came into effect on 27 September 2015.

The Refugee Status Determination Officer must issue the applicant with an asylum-seeker visa pending the finalisation of the outcome of the application for asylum.[163] The asylum-seeker permit allows the applicant to remain in South Africa pending the finalisation of the application and may be issued subject to conditions.[164] When issued the asylum-seeker visa, all other visas issued to the applicant under the Immigration Act become null and void.[165] The visa holder must then return their visa(s) to the Director-General, and if they fail to do so, they are guilty of an offence.[166] An asylum-seeker is deemed to have abandoned her application for asylum if she does not take steps to renew her asylum-seeker permit within one month after it has expired unless she is able to advance valid reasons for the non-renewal of the permit.[167]

[159] Section 21(7).
[160] Section 21(1C).
[161] Section 21(1D).
[162] *Mail and Guardian Media Ltd v Chipu NO* (CCT 136/12) [2013] ZACC 32; 2013 (11) BCLR 1259 (CC); 2013 (6) SA 367 (CC) (27 September 2013).
[163] Section 22(1).
[164] Section 22(1).
[165] Section 22(2).
[166] Section 22(14).
[167] Section 22(12).

On receipt of an application for asylum, the Refugee Status Determination Officer must take a decision regarding the application for asylum in terms of s 24 of the amended Refugees Act. The provisions of the Promotion of Administrative Justice Act[168] must be applied in the consideration of the application and the applicant must fully understand the procedures, her rights and responsibilities and the evidence presented.[169] The Refugee Status Determination Officer may request information or clarification from the applicant and may consult with a UNHCR representative.[170] The Refugee Status Determination Officer is required to take a decision to either grant the application, reject it as manifestly unfounded, abusive or fraudulent or to reject the application as unfounded.[171] There is no longer a maximum period within which asylum applications are to be determined. If the application is rejected, the applicant must be given written reasons within five working days after the date of the rejection and she must be informed of her right to appeal the decision.[172]

Any decision to reject an application for asylum as unfounded may be appealed to the Refugee Appeals Authority, which has been established in terms of s 8A of the amended Refugees Act.[173] If the Officer rejects her application as unfounded, and unless the applicant lodges an appeal to the Appeals Authority, she will be dealt with under the provisions of the Immigration Act and may be subject to detention and/or deportation procedures.[174] The Refugee Appeals Authority must allow legal representation on the request of the asylum-seeker lodging the appeal.[175] The Refugee Appeals Authority may confirm, set aside, or substitute a decision of the Refugee Status Determination Officer in respect of an application for asylum.[176] If new information, which is material to the asylum application, is presented during the appeal the Refugee Appeals Authority is required to refer the matter back to the Refugee Status Determination Officer to deal with the application afresh, taking into account the new information.[177]

[168] Act 3 of 2000.
[169] Section 24(2)*(a)*.
[170] Section 24(2)*(b)*.
[171] Section 24(3)*(a)*–*(c)*.
[172] Section 24(4).
[173] Section 24B(1).
[174] Section 24(5)*(b)*.
[175] Section 24B(4).
[176] Section 24B(2).
[177] Section 24B(5).

Any decision to reject an application as being manifestly unfounded, abusive, or fraudulent is subject to automatic review by the Standing Committee who may confirm or set aside the decision of the Refugee Status Determination Officer.[178]

If an applicant is granted asylum or refugee status, any children they have in South Africa must be registered under the Births and Deaths Registration Act 51 of 1992. Their birth certificate must then be submitted to a Refugee Reception Office so that the child can be included as a dependant of the asylum-seeker or refugee.[179] They are then accorded the same status as accorded to their asylum-seeker parent.[180] If the child ceases to be a dependant, they can then apply in their own right for asylum in terms of the Refugees Act.[181]

The general rule is that the right to work in South Africa may be endorsed on the asylum-seeker visa. But, under s 22 of the Refugees Act, there are three types of asylum-seekers who are not permitted to have the right to work endorsed on their visa. First, applicants who are able to sustain themselves and their dependants.[182] Secondly, applicants who are offered shelter and basic necessities by the UNHCR or any other charitable organisation or person.[183] Thirdly, applicants who fail to produce letters of employment (or letters of enrolment in the case of studying).[184] Whether this section is constitutional remains to be seen. The SCA in *Watchenuka* explained that being denied the right to work, even when one can sustain oneself, is an unjustifiable limitation of the right to dignity.[185] Yet the amendments prevent those asylum-seekers who can sustain themselves (or are sustained by others) from working.

The Director-General of Home Affairs may withdraw an asylum-seeker visa at any time if the applicant contravenes any conditions endorsed on that visa, the application for asylum has been found to be manifestly unfounded, abusive or fraudulent, the application for asylum has been rejected, or the applicant is or becomes ineligible for

[178] Section 24A(1)–(4).

[179] Section 21B(2).

[180] Section 21B(2A).

[181] Section 21B(5).

[182] Section 22(8)*(a)*. Section 22(6) provides that an applicant may be assessed to determine their ability to sustain themselves and their dependants.

[183] Section 22(8)*(b)*. Section 22(7) provides that if, after assessment, an applicant cannot sustain themselves and their dependents, then they may be offered basic necessities by charitable organisations.

[184] Sections 22(8)*(c)* and (9). Applicants have six months to produce such letters (s 22(11)).

[185] See *Minister of Home Affairs v Watchenuka* (010/2003) [2003] ZASCA 142; [2004] 1 All SA 21 (SCA) (28 November 2003) para 27.

asylum.[186] If the asylum-seeker permit is withdrawn, the asylum-seeker may be arrested and detained pending the finalisation of the application for asylum.[187] Detention may be no longer than is reasonable and justifiable and any detention exceeding 30 days must be reviewed by the High Court.[188] Any subsequent period of detention must be reviewed after the expiry of every subsequent period of 30 days.[189]

The Standing Committee where the refugee status was granted may withdraw such refugee status as a result of fraud, forgery or the provision of false or misleading information, due to a good faith error, omission or oversight committed by the Refugee Status Determination Officer, or if the person ceases to qualify for refugee status in terms of s 5 of the amended Refugees Act.[190] In that event, the Standing Committee is required to inform the affected person before the decision to withdraw the status. The person is then entitled to make representations to the Standing Committee regarding their refugee status and the withdrawal. If the Standing Committee withdraws a person's refugee status, they will be dealt with in terms of the Immigration Act and may be subject to detention and/or deportation.[191]

5 Refugee law and immigration law

Refugee law and immigration law are separate regimes. However, they overlap in some respects, especially at three critical junctures. The first, highlighted above in relation to the principle of *non-refoulement*, relates to the immigration status of an asylum-seeker pending the outcome of their application for refugee status. The second situation is where asylum-seekers or refugees seek to apply for a residence or immigration permit under the Immigration Act while they are in South Africa. The third situation arises when an asylum-seeker receives a final rejection of her asylum claim, or her asylum is withdrawn on the grounds discussed above. In the latter case, she becomes a 'failed asylum-seeker', thereby transitioning from the protection of the refugee law regime to the immigration system. The following subsections will deal with the application of immigration law in the latter two situations.

6 Application for residence or immigration status

Limited provision is made for asylum-seekers and refugees to submit applications for residence or immigration permits in terms of the

[186] Section 22(5).
[187] Section 23.
[188] Section 29(1).
[189] Section 29(2).
[190] Section 36(1).
[191] Section 36(2) and (4).

Immigration Act whilst they are in South Africa. This can cause hardship to both foreigners and citizens. For example, a refugee who lawfully marries a South African citizen in South Africa will not be able to apply for permanent residence (an immigration permit) in South Africa under the existing provisions of the Immigration Act. The Immigration Act will need to be amended to take the provisions of the Refugees Act into account.

A refugee may only apply for permanent residence after five years' continuous residence in South Africa (from the date on which she is granted asylum) and the Standing Committee certifies that she will remain a refugee indefinitely.[192]

Recently, the SCA heard a challenge to a Directive issued by the Director-General of the Department of Home Affairs that prevented all asylum-seekers from applying for visas under the Immigration Act.[193] The SCA dismissed the application to have the Directive declared unconstitutional. Regulation 9(2) of the 2014 Regulations to the Immigration Act requires all visa applications to be made from the applicant's country of origin.[194] Because the asylum-seekers in this case applied from within South Africa, the SCA held that the Department of Home Affairs did not have the power to accept their applications. At the time of writing, the matter has been appealed to the Constitutional Court. Whether reg 9(2) and the Directive are constitutional remains in doubt.

7 Failed asylum-seekers and their eligibility for deportation under immigration law

Both UNHCR and the International Organization for Migration (IOM) define failed asylum-seekers as 'people who, after due consideration of their claims to asylum in fair procedures, are found not to qualify for refugee status, not to be in need of international protection and are not authorized to stay in the country concerned'.[195] In a recent study, Johnson has observed that:

> In South Africa, the state has struggled to implement effective failed asylum-seeker policies in the context of high numbers of asylum-seekers, many without legitimate protection claims, and a lack of [capacity] to administer both refugee and immigrations systems.[196]

[192] Section 27*(c)*, and see *Ruyobeza v Minister of Home Affairs* 2003 (5) SA 51 (C).

[193] *Minister of Home Affairs v Ahmed* (1383/2016) [2017] ZASCA 123; 2017 (6) SA 554 (SCA) (26 September 2017).

[194] GN R413 in *GG* 37679 of 22 May 2014.

[195] Memorandum of Understanding between the United Nations High Commissioner for Refugees (UNHCR) and the International Organization for Migration (IOM), May 1997 para 29. IOM also uses the term 'unsuccessful asylum-seekers'.

[196] Johnson (n 136) 203.

The study assesses South Africa's two failed asylum-seeker return policies, one involving voluntary return with minimal state oversight and the other regarding the more recent attempts to implement a more stringent detention and deportation policy upon receipt of a final rejection of their asylum claim. Johnson concludes that the state's focus has been on the 'removal of failed asylum-seekers regardless of alternative legal options and human rights obligations.'[197] Moreover, the policy shift has also been criticised as amounting to a 'significant reduction of asylum-seekers and refugee protection, culminating in increased danger of *refoulement*.'[198]

It is argued that in order to implement an effective failed asylum-seeker policy, there is a need to reconsider how to increase the effectiveness and efficiency of the individualised refugee status determination system established under the Refugees Act. This system features the right to freedom of movement, the right to work, and local integration as opposed to refugee camp settings. Arguably, alternative immigration options with relaxed conditions for low-skilled migrants might reduce the burden on the asylum system and, ultimately, the high volume of asylum applications and failed asylum-seekers. The challenge for the refugee regime in South Africa is to ensure an effective implementation of the refugee protection framework and its associated human rights protections equally with legally sanctioned but humane immigration control measures. This requires that refugee and immigration officials exercise their discretion with regard to possible detention or deportation of failed asylum-seekers in accordance with the principle of *'in favorem libertatis'*, or in favour of liberty.

INEFFECTIVE PROTECTION IN SOUTH AFRICA

It is widely acknowledged that South Africa 'is struggling to implement the law successfully'.[199] Problems appear to begin at South African border posts, where an African Centre for Migration and Society research report conducted in 2012 documents that state officials had been 'turning away would-be asylum-seekers'.[200]

Once within South Africa, access to Refugee Reception Officers (RROs) has in recent years been reduced by the Minister of Home

[197] Johnson (n 136) 203–4.

[198] TN Polzer *Policy Shifts in the South African Asylum System: Evidence and Implications. Lawyers for Human Rights/ACM Report* (2013) 3.

[199] LA de la Hunt and W Kerfoot 'Due process in South Africa from a practitioners's perspective: Difficulties encountered in the interpretation, application and administration of the Refugees Act' in J Handmaker, LA de la Hunt and J Klaaren (eds) *Advancing Refugee Protection in South Africa* (2008).

[200] R Amit 'All roads lead to rejection' ACMS Research Report (2012) 17.

Affairs' decision to shut two of its five offices. RRO offices are currently located in Musina, Pretoria and Durban. The Refugee Reception offices in Port Elizabeth and Cape Town were closed. However, the SCA has found that '[t]he remaining offices . . . are inadequate'.[201] The decision to shut the RRO Cape Town office was found to be 'irrational' and was accordingly set aside.[202] A similar decision was taken relative to the Port Elizabeth RRO.[203] However, the Department of Home Affairs has yet to comply with these orders.[204]

Asylum-seekers who do lodge their claim at an RRO face a high rate of rejection. In 2016, the Legal Resources Centre and Lawyers for Human Rights reported that the Musina RRO had a zero per cent acceptance rate in 2015, which they took as evidence of 'a failure to take proper decisions'.[205] The judiciary complains of case dockets 'overburdened' with applications for the review of rejected applications for refugee status.[206] Moreover, their review of the decisions of the Refugee Appeal Board and the Standing Committee reveal 'glaring defects in the decision and decision-making process'[207] and 'a systematic dysfunctionality'.[208]

[201] *Scalabrini Centre, Cape Town v Minister of Home Affairs* [2017] 4 All SA 686 (SCA) para 46.

[202] Ibid para 64.

[203] *Minister of Home Affairs v Somali Association of South Africa Eastern Cape (SASA EC)* 2015 (3) SA 545 (SCA).

[204] Republic of South Africa, Department of Home Affairs *Media Statement on the Cape Town Refugee Reception Centre* (17 April 2018), available at http://www.dha.gov.za/index.php/statements-speeches/1093-media-statement-on-the-cape-town-refugee-reception-centre.

[205] Joint Submission by the Legal Resources Centre and Lawyers for Human Rights to the Department of Home Affairs, *Green Paper on International Migration* (2016) para 62, available at https://lrc.org.za/art_external/pdf/2016_09_30_Submission_Green%20Paper_International_Migration_compressed.pdf.

[206] *Tshiyombo v Members of the Refugee Appeal Board* [2016] 2 All SA 278 (WCC); 2016 (4) SA 469 (WCC) (18 November 2015) para 20; *Kumah v Minister of Home Affairs* (n 33) para 1.

[207] *Katshingu v Chairperson of Standing Committee for Refugee Affairs* (19726/2010) [2011] ZAWCHC 480 (2 November 2011).

[208] *Tshiyombo v Members of the Refugee Appeal Board* (n 206) para 14. See further *Dorcasse v Minister of Home Affairs* [2012] 4 All SA 659 (GSJ) (5 October 2012) para 41; *Mubala v Chairperson of the Standing Committee for Refugee Affairs* [2013] ZAWCHC 208 (8 November 2013); *Bolanga v Refugee Status Determination Officer* [2015] ZAKZDHC 13 (24 February 2015) paras 5–7 and 54.

STATELESSNESS[209]

Rosalind Elphick

Under Article 15 of the 1948 UDHR, everyone has the right to a nationality. As with any human right, however, the right to a nationality is not always realised. Where the right to a nationality has failed, human rights law has created a stopgap in the status of 'statelessness'. In 1954, the Convention relating to the Status of Stateless Persons was adopted, defining a stateless person as 'a person who is not considered as a national by any State under the operation of its law'.[210] This instrument further creates a regime for the identification, protection and naturalisation of stateless persons. To a large degree these protections mirror those available to refugees under the 1951 UN Convention. In 1961, a further convention—the Convention on the Reduction of Statelessness—was adopted to set rules for the conferral and non-withdrawal of citizenship in order to prevent cases of statelessness from arising.[211]

South Africa is party to neither of these conventions, despite its 2011 pledge to become a signatory and party to both.[212] This is a significant gap in the statelessness legal regime, as was noted by four of the states in the Working Group on the Universal Periodic Review in their recommendations to South Africa at the Human Rights Council in 2017.[213] That gap is reflected also in South Africa's domestic legal framework, which currently has no mechanism for the identification and documentation of stateless persons.

Without such a mechanism, it is impossible to assess the number of stateless persons or persons at risk of statelessness currently in South Africa. There are however reports of a significant number of cases of statelessness in South Africa and categories of persons who would be affected by the risk of statelessness.[214] Statelessness takes two distinct forms. The first is *de facto* statelessness. This manifests in persons

[209] B Manby *Citizenship and Statelessness in Africa: The law and politics of belonging* (2015); JP George and R Elphick *Promoting Citizenship and Preventing Statelessness in South Africa: A Practitioner's Guide* (2014).

[210] 189 UNTS 137. Adopted on 28 September 1954 and entered into force on 6 June 1960.

[211] 989 UNTS 175. Adopted on 30 August 1961 and entered into force on 13 December 1975.

[212] UNHCR, *Pledges 2011: Ministerial Intergovernmental Event on Refugees and Stateless Persons* (2012) 36. Available at http://www.unhcr.org/4ff55a319.pdf.

[213] UN Doc. A/HRC/36/16 (18 July 2017) paras 139.21–139.23.

[214] See J Sloth-Nielsen and M Ackermann 'Unaccompanied and separated foreign children in the care system in the Western Cape—A socio legal study' (2016) 19 *PER/PELJ* 18–19; JP George and R Elphick *Statelessness and Nationality in South Africa* (2013), available at http://www.refworld.org/docid/519df3594.html.

who have a legal claim to nationality under the law, but have no proof of that claim. In *Nibigira v Minister of Home Affairs*, the South Gauteng High Court describes the circumstances of a *de facto* stateless applicant thus:

> '[T]he Tanzanian Embassy refused to issue him with the requisite one-way travel document which is also referred to as the emergency travel certificate ('ETC') because he was allegedly a Burundian. The Burundian Embassy refused to recognise him as a Burundian national because he failed to speak or rather could not speak their native Kirundi language and they also did not want to listen to or accept his explanation that he could not do so because he left Burundi when he was only 10 years old.'[215]

Another case, *B NO v Minister of Home Affairs*, documents the tale of a minor who was brought to South Africa as a young child and subsequently orphaned—with no apparent family ties elsewhere—by the death of her asylum-seeker mother, whose application for asylum was rejected as 'manifestly unfounded'.[216]

The second type of statelessness is *de jure* statelessness. This manifests in persons who have no legal claim to nationality in any of the states to which that person is connected through either birth or descent. The case of *DGLR and KMRG v Minister of Home Affairs*, for example, dealt with the case of a child born to Cuban parents in South Africa.[217] Subject to certain exceptions, South African nationality is acquired by birth to a South African parent. The Cuban government considers those who work outside of Cuba for a period longer than 11 months to be 'permanent emigrants'.[218] Emigrants with this status are barred under Cuban law from passing their nationality to their children born outside of Cuba.[219] Children born to Cuban 'permanent emigrant' parents in states which do not grant nationality *jus soli*, are stateless at birth.

For persons experiencing either *de facto* or *de jure* statelessness, the effect is the same. Without legal mechanisms for their identification and documentation, stateless persons face enormous practical and legal problems in their everyday lives. Without documentation, stateless persons face difficulties booking flights, opening bank

[215] *Nibigira v Minister of Home Affairs* (41265/2011) [2011] ZAGPJHC 178 (28 November 2011) para 16.

[216] *B NO v Minister of Home Affairs NO* (2665/2017) [2018] ZAECPEHC 24 (29 May 2018) para 8.

[217] *DGLR and KMRG v Minister of Home Affairs* (3 July 2014) ZAGPPHC (unreported), available at http://citizenshiprightsafrica.org/wp-content/uploads/2016/09/Appellants-Heads-of-Argument-Min-of-DHA-v-DGLR-SCA.pdf.

[218] *DGLR and KMRG v Minister of Home Affairs* supra (n 217).

[219] Ibid. The Court's order and the relevant heads of argument are available at http://citizenshiprightsafrica.org/south-africa-dglr-and-another-vs-minister-of-home-affairs-and-others/.

accounts, or registering for health care or education services. As non-citizens of the state in which they are present, they are at constant risk of arrest and detention as an illegal alien. For example, in the case of *Nibigira,* the applicant's petition for release from prolonged immigration detention was denied, inter alia, on the following basis: 'Where would the applicant go if there was a need that he be released from detention? Would that court sanctioned release have meant that he should be allowed to roam South Africa despite the fact that he came in illegally and he has no right or papers to allow him to be here? Must the police or immigration officials not arrest and detain him for deportation again?'[220] Other cases detail difficulties in attaining birth registration for children born stateless or born to stateless parents, making statelessness an intergenerational issue.[221]

Despite the fact that South Africa is not a signatory to the primary international legal instruments related to statelessness, it is nevertheless bound to protect the right to a nationality in terms of a range of other international instruments.[222] Under article 24(3) of the International Covenant on Civil and Political Rights (ICCPR), for example, '[e]very child has the right to acquire a nationality'. In its General Comment No 17 (1989), the Human Rights Committee explained that 'the purpose of this provision is to prevent a child from being afforded less protection by society and the state because he is stateless'.[223] Article 12(4) of the ICCPR also deserves attention. It protects the right of every person to enter 'his own country'—a norm which the Human Rights Committee has interpreted as also being applicable to stateless persons.[224] South Africa is also obliged under the 1965 Convention on the Elimination of all Forms of Racial Discrimination and the 1979 Convention on Elimination of all Forms of Discrimination Against Women not to discriminate against persons on the basis of their 'national origin'.[225]

[220] *Nibigira v Minister of Home Affairs* (n 215) para 76.

[221] *M v Minister of Home Affairs* (6871/2013) [2014] ZAGPPHC 649 (22 August 2014) para 18; *DGLR and KMRG v Minister of Home Affairs* (n 217).

[222] 1957 Convention on the Nationality of Married Women; 1965 Convention on the Elimination of all Forms of Racial Discrimination (ICERD); 1979 Convention on Elimination of all Forms of Discrimination Against Women; 1989 Convention on the Rights of the Child (art 7); the 1966 International Covenant on Civil and Political Rights (art 24(3)); and the 1999 African Charter on the Rights and Welfare of the Child (art 6).

[223] CCPR General Comment No 17 (7 April 1989), reproduced in U.N. Doc. HRI/GEN/1/Rev.6 at 193.

[224] UN Doc. CCPR/C/21/Rev.1/Add.9, General Comment No 27 (2 November 1999).

[225] Article 1(3) of the ICERD.

Some domestic legal protections do exist for stateless persons in South Africa. Section 2(2) of the Citizenship Act 88 of 1995 provides for the granting of South African citizenship to such children born in South Africa. However, it is currently not possible for stateless children to apply for citizenship using this provision, given that the implementing regulations contain no provisions relating to it.[226] As such, at a basic level, there is simply no form to fill out in an application for nationality on this basis at Home Affairs Offices.[227] There are also no rules applicable to guide Home Affairs officials in determining whether or not a child is 'stateless' under the Citizenship Act.[228] This has so far resulted in several successful applications to higher courts, in which cases the Department of Home Affairs has been ordered to register the births of specific children.[229] However, there has been no systemic change.

Stateless persons also have the possibility of relief by making an application in terms of s 31(2*(b)* of the Immigration Act, which entitles the Minister of Home Affairs to grant rights of permanent residence to a foreigner when 'special circumstances' exist which would justify such a decision. In the case of *B NO v Minister of Home Affairs* described above, in the absence of a response from the Minister to an application made under this law, the Court awarded citizenship to the stateless applicant.[230]

[226] *Regulations on the Registration of Births and Death* (GN R128 in *GG* 21075 of 26 February 2014).

[227] Lawyers for Human Rights and Institute on Statelessness and Inclusion *Joint Submission to the Human Rights Council at the 27th Session of the Universal Periodic Review* (22 September 2016) para 20, available at http://www.institutesi.org/SouthAfricaUPR2016.pdf.

[228] Ibid.

[229] *B NO v Minister of Home Affairs NO* (n 216) para 51; *Richard Cathcart NO v Director General of Home Affairs* (993/2017 & 11/2016) ZAECPHC, Unreported, Delivered 3 May 2018; *DGLR and KMRG v Minister of Home Affairs* (n 217).

[230] See n 216.

CHAPTER 17

Law of the Sea

John Dugard and Dire Tladi

INTRODUCTION

The evolution of the law of the sea[1] is the history of international law itself, for since its earliest days, international law has been deeply involved in the regulation of navigation and fishing. The voyages of discovery of the 15th and 16th centuries gave rise to disputes between states which claimed excessive rights over the high seas (notably Spain and Portugal);[2] and states which advocated the freedom of the seas. The Netherlands, as the foremost protagonist of the latter view, invoked the advice of Grotius and this resulted in *Mare Liberum*, written in 1609 at the instance of the Dutch East India Company.[3] In it Grotius asserted that the high seas are open to the shipping of all nations. This principle was gradually accepted and today forms a fundamental principle of the law of the sea. Another basic principle, the right of a coastal state to exclusive sovereignty over its territorial sea, also owes its origin to a Dutch jurist, Cornelius van Bynkershoek.[4]

Since these early days, international law has evolved to take account of developments in navigation and fishing, the exploitation

[1] See in particular, the comprehensive study on the law of the sea from a South African perspective, P Vrancken *South Africa and the Law of the Sea* (2011). See further, DR Rothwell and T Stephens *The International Law of the Sea* 2 ed (2016); Y Tanaka *The International Law of the Sea* 2 ed (2015); DR Rothwell, AG Oude Elferink, KN Scott and T Stephens *The Oxford Handbook on the Law of the Sea* (2015); ED Brown *The International Law of the Sea* 2 vols (1994); DP O'Connell *The International Law of the Sea* (edited by IA Shearer) 2 vols (1982); RR Churchill and AV Lowe *The Law of the Sea* 3 ed (1999); P Vrancken 'Southern Africa and the law of the sea: Problems common, uncommon and unique' 1986 *Acta Juridica* (special issue on the Law of the Sea); P Vrancken 'Post-apartheid South Africa and the sea: First decade legislation (1994–2003)' (2004) 29 *SAYIL* 105; D Anderson *Modern Law of the Sea. Selected Essays* (2007); EWF Couzens 'Sea and seashore' in W Joubert (ed) *LAWSA* 2 ed (2010) 107.

[2] In 1493, Pope Alexander VI divided the newly discovered areas of the globe between Spain and Portugal, which resulted in these two states claiming exclusive rights to the high seas.

[3] R Feenstra (ed) *Hugo Grotius Mare Liberum 1609–2009* with introduction by J Vervliet (2009). For an account of the manner in which Grotius advocated the interests of the Dutch East India Company in this monograph, see F de Pauw *Grotius and the Law of the Sea* (1965).

[4] *De Dominio Maris* II at 7; *Quaestionum Juris Publici 1*, VIII at 2. For a discussion of Van Bynkershoek's views, see *Yorigami Maritime Construction v Nissho-Iwai* 1977 (4) SA 682 (C) 695–6.

of the continental shelf and the deep seabed, the conservation of marine resources, the regulation of marine archaeological research, and the combating of pollution. The sources of the law of the sea are to be found in custom, in four multilateral treaties approved in 1958 to 1960, and in the 1982 United Nations Convention on the Law of the Sea (UNCLOS).

The four conventions adopted by the first and second Geneva conferences on the law of the sea of 1958 and 1960 are the Geneva Conventions on the Territorial Sea and the Contiguous Zone (TSC),[5] the High Seas (HSC),[6] the Continental Shelf (CSC),[7] and the Fishing and Conservation of the Living Resources of the High Seas.[8] These Conventions, which came into force in the mid-1960s, have been ratified by a respectable number of states including South Africa.[9]

Soon after the adoption of the above four Conventions, new issues arose which called for a reassessment of the law of the sea. Of these, the most important were the claims for extended exclusive fishing zones (particularly by Iceland) and for mining rights on the seabed beneath the high seas, known as the deep seabed. In a passionate speech on the peaceful uses of the ocean in 1967, the Ambassador of Malta to the United Nations, Arvid Pardo, called for a new law of the sea treaty. This resulted in the Third United Nations Law of the Sea Conference (UNCLOS III), which met over the course of 11 sessions between 1973 and 1982. South Africa attended the 1973–1974 sessions, with the African National Congress being admitted as an observer.[10] In 1974 South Africa withdrew from the later sessions after some states questioned its credentials. Compromises between the developed and developing states (known as the Group of 77[11]), and coastal and landlocked states ultimately resulted in a comprehensive treaty of 320 articles and nine annexes which reiterate the principles of the 1958 Conventions and expound new rules to govern subsequent developments. This is the UNCLOS.[12] The Convention is sometimes referred to as the 'constitution for the oceans'.[13]

[5] 516 UNTS 205; (1958) 52 *AJIL* 834.

[6] 450 UNTS 82; (1958) 52 *AJIL* 842.

[7] 499 UNTS 311; (1958) 52 *AJIL* 858.

[8] 599 UNTS 285; (1958) 52 *AJIL* 851.

[9] South Africa ratified the four Conventions on 4 September 1963.

[10] For a comprehensive description of South Africa's involvement at UNCLOS III see P Vrancken 'The international law of the sea in South Africa' in E de Wet, H Hestermeyer and R Wolfrum (eds) *The Implementation of International Law in Germany and South Africa* (2015) 148–50.

[11] In fact, there were over 100 member states of this group for most of UNCLOS III.

[12] The text appears in (1982) 21 *ILM* 1261.

[13] E Mann Borgese 'A constitution for the oceans: Comments and suggestions regarding Part XI of the Informal Composite Text' (1977–1978) 15 *San Diego Law*

Shortly before the UNCLOS was to be signed, the United States withdrew its support because of its opposition to the proposed international regime for the deep seabed. This encouraged developed states, concerned about the regime for the deep seabed, to withhold ratification of the UNCLOS. Thus, the UNCLOS failed to secure the required 60 ratifications to bring it into force until 1994.

In 1994, to facilitate the entry into force of the UNCLOS, a compromise was reached on the implementation of Part XI of the UNCLOS dealing with the deep seabed. The compromise was contained in the New York Agreement Relating to the Implementation of Part XI of the United Nations Convention on the Law of the Sea.[14] This Agreement, which is primarily aimed at making the UNCLOS more acceptable to developed states, provides that the Agreement and Part XI of the UNCLOS are to be interpreted as a single instrument and that in the event of inconsistencies between the two instruments, the 1994 Agreement is to prevail.

The 1982 UNCLOS, as modified by the 1994 Agreement, is the principal source of law on the law of the sea. This Convention, to which some 161 states are parties, is to prevail, as between states parties, over the Geneva Conventions on the Law of the Sea of 1958.[15] Only the states parties to the 1958 Conventions remain bound by these Conventions. Customary international law has not remained unaffected by these developments. Many of the rules contained in the 1982 UNCLOS may be seen as a codification of customary international law.[16] Even states that are not party to the UNCLOS, such as the United States, routinely accept the customary status of some of its

Review 371; M Hayashi 'Global governance of deep-sea fisheries' (2004) 19 *International Journal of Marine & Coastal Law* 289.

[14] (1994) 33 *ILM* 1309. See, further, BH Oxman 'Law of the Sea Forum: The 1994 Agreement on the Implementation of the Seabed Provisions of the Convention on the Law of the Sea' (1994) 88 *AJIL* 687; DH Anderson 'Further efforts to ensure universal participation in the UN Convention on the Law of the Sea' (1994) 43 *ICLQ* 886.

[15] Article 311 of the UNCLOS.

[16] The International Court of Justice has already invoked the provisions of the UNCLOS as evidence of customary international law in several cases involving the delimitation of the continental shelf. See *Case Concerning the Continental Shelf (Tunisia/Libya)* 1982 ICJ Reports 18 at 74; *Case Concerning the Continental Shelf (Libya/Malta)* 1985 ICJ Reports 13 at 30; *Case Concerning the Delimitation of the Marine Boundary in the Gulf of Maine Area (Canada/US)* 1984 ICJ Reports 246 at 294; *Case Concerning Maritime Delimitation in the Area Between Greenland and Jan Mayen (Denmark v Norway)* 1993 ICJ Reports 37 at 59; *Case Concerning Maritime Delimitation and Territorial Questions between Qatar and Bahrain (Qatar v Bahrain)* 2001 ICJ Reports 40, paras 167, 175, 176 (discussed by Y Tanaka 'Reflections on maritime delimitations in the *Qatar/Bahrain* case of 16 March 2001 (Merits)' (2003) 52 *ICLQ* 53).

provisions.[17] Already in 1985, before the UNCLOS had even come into force, there was broad support for the view that many parts of the UNCLOS constituted customary international law.

South Africa ratified both the UNCLOS and the 1994 Implementation Agreement on 23 December 1997. In anticipation of ratification, Parliament enacted the Maritime Zones Act 15 of 1994 to bring South Africa's maritime zones into line with the provisions of the UNCLOS. The focus of this chapter will be on the different zones recognised in the UNCLOS. The status of areas of no direct relevance to South Africa, such as archipelagos[18] and straits,[19] will not receive the attention given to them in general treatises.

MARITIME ZONES

1 Internal waters

Internal waters lie to the landward side of the territorial sea.[20] In order to determine the delimitation of internal waters it is necessary to examine the rules relating to the delimitation of the territorial sea. According to the UNCLOS, the territorial sea is measured from the baseline.[21]

Although the territorial sea is normally measured from the low-water line of the coast,[22] this baseline does not always follow the low-water line. In the case of river mouths,[23] harbours[24] and bays[25] a baseline is drawn across the coastal indentation and the water to the landward side is designated as internal water.[26] Where there is a fringe of islands along the coast, straight baselines may be drawn joining appropriate points on these islands and the width of the territorial sea may be measured from this baseline, provided it follows the general direction of the coast[27] (see Fig 1, below). Again,

[17] LB Sohn 'The law of the sea: Customary international law developments—The American University Washington College of Law Edwin A Mooers Lecture' (1985) 34 *American University Law Review* 271.

[18] UNCLOS, articles 46–54.

[19] UNCLOS, articles 37–45.

[20] UNCLOS, article 8.

[21] UNCLOS, article 3.

[22] UNCLOS, article 5; TSC, article 3.

[23] UNCLOS, article 9; TSC, article 13.

[24] UNCLOS, article 11; TSC, article 8.

[25] UNCLOS, article 10; TSC, article 7.

[26] UNCLOS, article 8; TSC, article 5.

[27] UNCLOS, article 7; TSC, article 4. These provisions give approval to the decision of the International Court of Justice in the *Anglo–Norwegian Fisheries Case (United Kingdom v Norway)* 1951 ICJ Reports 116, which upheld a Norwegian decree delimiting Norway's territorial sea by means of a series of straight baselines linking

the water to the landward side will be internal water. The coastal state has full sovereignty over its internal waters.

Figure 1 Baselines and maritime zones (nm = nautical miles)

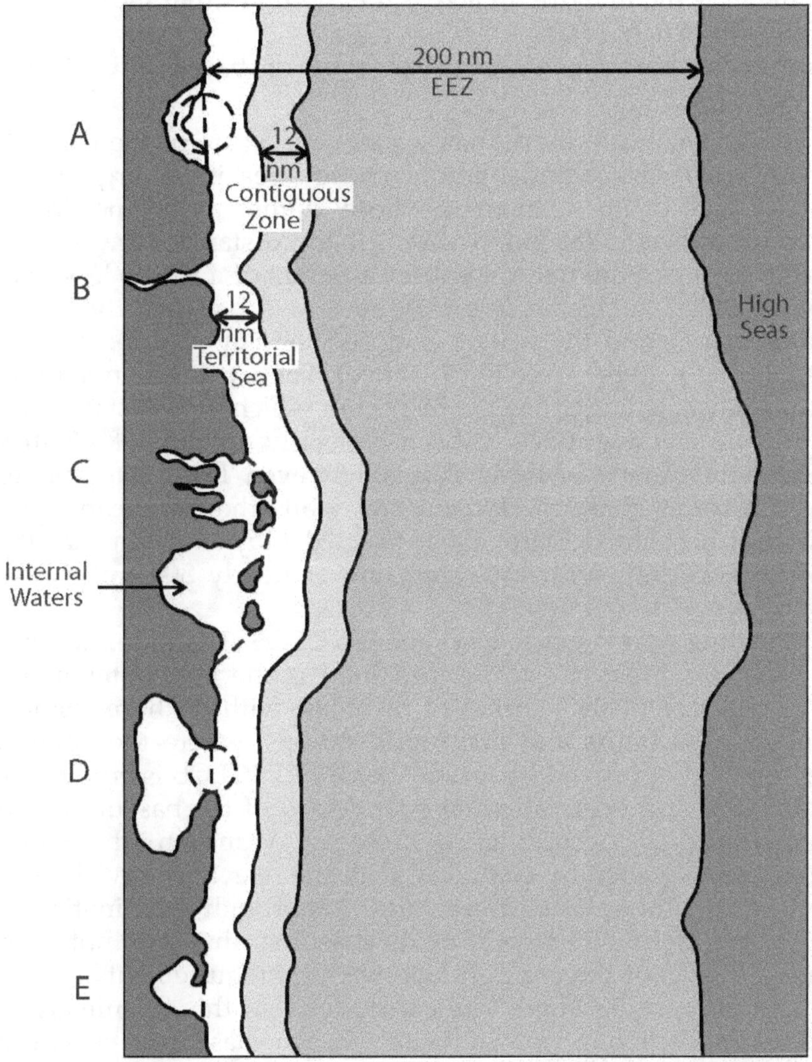

A Not a bay as indentation is smaller than that of area of semi-circle whose diameter is the line drawn across the mouth of that indentation: UNCLOS Article 10(2)

B Baseline drawn across river mouth flowing directly into sea: UNCLOS Article 9

the outermost points of the *skjaergaard*, a fringe of islands and rocks off the Norwegian coast. In *Qatar v Bahrain* (n 16), the International Court of Justice stated that the straight baseline method is exceptional and must be applied restrictively at paras 212–15.

C Straight baselines on deeply indented coast with fringe of islands: UNCLOS Article 7(1)

D A bay as indentation is larger than area of semi-circle whose diameter is the line drawn across the mouth of that indentation: UNCLOS Article 10(2)

E Permanent harbour works form part of baseline UNCLOS Article 11.

A 'bay' must constitute more than a mere curvature of the coast. It must be a well-marked indentation whose 'area is as large as, or larger than, that of the semi-circle whose diameter is a line drawn across the mouth of that indentation'. If the distance between the low-water marks of the natural entrance points of a bay is less than 24 nautical miles, 'a closing line may be drawn between these two low-water marks, and the waters enclosed thereby shall be considered as internal waters'[28] (see Fig 1, above). These rules do not apply to 'historic bays', ie larger bays in respect of which the coastal state's claims to full sovereignty have been generally accepted.[29] Controversy surrounds many of these claims, however. The United States disputes Canada's claim to Hudson Bay, while the European Community and the United States have rejected Libya's claim that the Gulf of Sirte (Sidra), with a closing line of nearly 300 miles, is a historic bay.

The Maritime Zones Act follows the UNCLOS. The baseline from which maritime zones are to be measured is the low-water line,[30] except in the case of those areas of the coast with offshore islands, river mouths, harbours and deep indentations, where the straight baseline method approved by article 7 of the UNCLOS is employed. Internal waters comprise 'all waters landward of the baselines; and ... all harbours'.[31] According to Professor Vrancken, the South African baseline 'generally complies' with the relevant provisions of the UNCLOS. Although he asserts, after a thorough examination of South Africa's claims in respect of its coastline, that it is not clear 'whether all areas of the coast in fact meet the requirements for the drawing of straight baselines', he concludes that this is unlikely to give rise to opposition in view of the fact that the baselines have been drawn conservatively for the purpose of rationalising the measure-

[28] UNCLOS, article 10; TSC, article 7.

[29] UNCLOS, article 10(6); TSC, article 7(6). In *Land, Island and Maritime Frontier Dispute (El Salvador/Honduras: Nicaragua intervening)* 1992 ICJ Reports 351, the International Court accepted that the Gulf of Fonseca was an historic bay.

[30] Section 2(1) of Act 15 of 1994.

[31] Section 3(1).

ment of South Africa's maritime zones and do not prejudice international navigation.[32]

Because internal waters are an integral part of the coastal state's territory,[33] the regime of this maritime zone is not regulated by either the 1958 Conventions or the UNCLOS. There is no right of innocent passage for foreign ships through internal waters,[34] as there is in territorial waters. From this it follows that there is no general right of access for foreign ships to a state's ports.[35] In practice, however, ports are generally open to foreign shipping, subject to regulation by the coastal state. The South African Marine Traffic Act 2 of 1981 permits ships to enter internal waters for the purpose of entering a harbour or fishing harbour,[36] but entry into internal waters may be prohibited in the interests of national security.[37] In the case of foreign warships, notification of the intended visit is customarily given to the coastal authorities.[38]

The coastal state has full criminal and civil jurisdiction over acts on board foreign ships in its internal waters.[39] In practice, however, it generally permits the ship's authorities or the consular agent of the flag state to deal with disputes and minor crimes committed on board a ship. Where the peace and good order of the coastal state are affected, jurisdiction will be exercised. Thus, in the *Wildenhus Case*,[40] the Supreme Court of the United States held that an American court had jurisdiction over a murder committed by a member of the crew on board a Belgian merchant ship in an American port. Different

[32] P Vrancken 'The South African Baseline' (2002) 27 *SAYIL* 158. See further, Vrancken (n 1) ch 3.

[33] See s 3(2) of Act 15 of 1994; *Macard Stein & Co v Port Marine Contractors (Pty) Ltd* 1995 (3) SA 663 (A).

[34] This is confirmed by s 3(3) of Act 15 of 1994.

[35] The assertion of such a general right in *Saudi Arabia v Aramco* (1963) 27 ILR 117 at 212 has been widely criticised: see O'Connell (n 1) vol 2 at 848. In the *Case Concerning Military and Paramilitary Activities in and against Nicaragua (Nicaragua v United States of America)* 1986 ICJ Reports 14 at 111, the International Court of Justice recognised the sovereign right of a coastal state to regulate access to its ports.

[36] Act 2 of 1981, s 4(1). Permission is also granted to foreign sporting vessels and to fishing vessels authorised to operate in internal waters to enter such waters by the Marine Traffic Regulations R194 in *GG* 9575 of 1 February 1985. For a full discussion of the right of foreign ships to enter internal waters and ports, see DJ Devine 'Sea passage in South African maritime zones: Actualities and possibilities' 1986 *Acta Juridica* 203.

[37] Act 2 of 1981, s 7.

[38] According to Devine, warships and submarines have no right of entry or passage rights in internal waters: Devine (n 36) 204–6.

[39] The Defence Act 42 of 2002 authorises a South African military aircraft or warship to enforce South African law in internal waters: s 22(2)*(a)*.

[40] 120 US 1 (1887).

considerations apply in respect of visiting warships: crimes occurring on board such ships fall within the exclusive jurisdiction of the commander and authorities of the flag state.

An exception to the above rules applies in the case of vessels in distress. They may enter internal waters and are not subject to the jurisdiction of the coastal state inside internal waters and ports. This is recognised by both statute[41] and case law[42] in South Africa.

The National Environmental Management: Integrated Coastal Management Act 24 of 2008 gives effect to South Africa's international obligations regarding coastal management and the marine environment.[43]

2 Territorial sea

The first and second conferences on the Law of the Sea, held in Geneva in 1958 and 1960, failed to agree on the width of the territorial sea in the face of strong opposition to the traditional three-mile limit. A compromise proposal for a six-mile territorial sea with a fishing zone of a further six miles failed by one vote to obtain the required two-thirds majority in 1960.[44] The 1982 UNCLOS was able to agree on a territorial sea of 12 nautical miles (one nautical mile is 1852 metres) measured from the baselines described above.[45] The 12-mile limit is accepted by a large majority of states including South Africa and is generally accepted as a customary-law rule today. The Maritime Zones Act of 1994 provides that 'the sea within a distance of twelve nautical miles from the baselines shall be the territorial waters of the Republic'.[46]

The coastal state has sovereignty over its territorial sea, its bed and subsoil, and the airspace above the territorial sea.[47] Sovereignty over the territorial sea vests in the Republic of South Africa[48] and, for

[41] See the definition of 'passage' in s 1 of the Marine Traffic Act 2 of 1981. Cf DJ Devine 'The Cape's False Bay: A possible haven for ships in distress' (1990–91) 16 *SAYIL* 81.

[42] In *Nkondo v Minister of Police* 1980 (2) SA 894 (O), the Court considered the question whether an aircraft forced to land in distress was exempt from the jurisdiction of the court in the same way as a ship. During his reasoning Smuts J accepted 'the established law in regard to the right of ships in distress to enter a port' (898–900, particularly at 900D).

[43] Section 2(*e*) of Act 24 of 2008.

[44] O'Connell (n 1) vol 1 at 161–4.

[45] UNCLOS, article 3.

[46] Section 4(1) of Act 15 of 1994.

[47] UNCLOS, article 2; TSC, articles 1 and 2. See, too, s 3(2) of Act 15 of 1994; and M Ehrenbeck 'South Africa's Maritime Zones Act 1994' (1995) 20 *SAYIL* 213, 217.

[48] *Yorigami Maritime Construction Co Ltd v Nisso-Iwai Co Ltd* 1978 (2) SA 391 (C) at 394G–H; s 4(2) of Act 15 of 1994. See further, Vrancken (n 1) 17–31.

municipal-law purposes, ownership of the territorial sea is vested in the state. The territorial jurisdiction of the maritime provinces includes the territorial sea.[49] Consequently, it was held in *Yorigami Maritime Construction Co Ltd v Nissho-Iwai Co Ltd*, that the Cape Provincial Division had jurisdiction over 'that portion of the territorial sea adjacent to the coastline of its area of jurisdiction'.[50] This decision was confirmed by the Admiralty Jurisdiction Regulation Act 105 of 1983.[51]

Foreign ships have a right of innocent passage through the territorial sea.[52] Passage means 'navigation through the territorial sea for the purpose either of traversing that sea without entering internal waters, or of proceeding to internal waters, or of making for the high seas from internal waters'.[53] Passage must be 'continuous and expeditious' but includes stopping and anchoring in so far as this is incidental to ordinary navigation.[54] Passage is innocent 'so long as it is not prejudicial to the peace, good order or security of the coastal state'.[55] Non-innocent activities include the threat or use of force against the coastal state; practice with weapons of any kind; propaganda directed at the coastal state; the launching, landing, or taking on board of any aircraft or military device; violation of the customs, immigration, or sanitary laws of the coastal state; pollution; fishing; carrying out of research; and interference with the communications system of the coastal state.[56] Submarines must navigate on the surface and show their flag.[57] Neither the 1958 Conventions nor the UNCLOS deal expressly with the right of warships to innocent passage, but customary international law probably supports such a right.[58]

The coastal state must not hamper innocent passage and must give publicity to any danger to navigation within its territorial sea.[59]

[49] DJ Devine 'Performance of provincial functions in maritime zones' (1989) 4 *SA Public Law* 46; Vrancken (n 1) 35–7.

[50] 1978 (2) SA 391 (C) at 395A–B; and 394G. This judgment confirms the decision in *Yorigami Maritime Construction v Nissho-Iwai* (n 4) 694–6. For trenchant criticisms of these decisions, see H Booysen 'Jurisdiction of the South African courts over the South African territorial waters' (1977) 3 *SAYIL* 184; NJ Botha 'Municipal jurisdiction over territorial waters' (1978) 4 *SAYIL* 177.

[51] Act 105 of 1983 s 2.

[52] UNCLOS, article 17; TSC, article 14(1).

[53] TSC, article 14(2). UNCLOS, article 18(1) is substantially similar.

[54] UNCLOS, article 18(2); TSC, article 14(3).

[55] UNCLOS, article 19; TSC, article 14(4).

[56] UNCLOS, article 19(2).

[57] UNCLOS, article 20; TSC, article 14(6).

[58] R Jennings and A Watts (eds) *Oppenheim's International Law* vol 1 9 ed (1992) 618–20; Vrancken (n 1) 133–4.

[59] UNCLOS, article 24; TSC, article 15.

However, it may suspend the right of innocent passage temporarily in specified areas in the interests of security, provided this is done on a non-discriminatory basis.[60] The coastal state may prescribe sea lanes for the regulation of sea traffic.[61]

The coastal state has limited criminal and civil jurisdiction over persons on board foreign ships in the territorial sea. Criminal jurisdiction should not be exercised on board a foreign ship in the territorial sea to arrest any person, except:

- *(a)* if the consequences of the crime extend to the coastal state;
- *(b)* if the crime is of a kind to disturb the peace of the country or the good order of the territorial sea;
- *(c)* if the assistance of the local authorities has been requested by the master of the ship or by a diplomatic agent or consular officer of the flag state; or
- *(d)* if such measures are necessary for the suppression of illicit traffic in narcotic drugs or psychotropic substances.[62]

This rule does not affect the right of the coastal state to arrest a person on board a foreign ship passing though the territorial sea after leaving internal waters. 'The coastal state should not stop or divert a foreign ship passing through the territorial sea for the purpose of exercising civil jurisdiction in relation to a person on board the ship.' Nor should it arrest the ship for the purpose of civil proceedings except where liabilities were incurred by the ship itself in the course of its voyage through the waters of the coastal state. This does not affect the right of the coastal state to arrest a foreign ship in the territorial sea for the purpose of civil proceedings, after it has left internal waters.[63]

South African law[64] recognises the right of innocent passage in the Marine Traffic Act.[65] It makes no distinction between merchant vessels and warships for this purpose.[66] Passage is defined as:

[60] UNCLOS, article 25(3); TSC, article 16(3).

[61] UNCLOS, article 22.

[62] UNCLOS, article 27; TSC, article 19. The Defence Act 42 of 2002 in s 22(2)*(b)* authorises military aircraft and warships to enforce South African law in the territorial sea but makes it clear that this is to be done in accordance with article 27 of the UNCLOS.

[63] UNCLOS, article 28; TSC, article 20. The Defence Act 42 of 2002 in s 22(2)*(b)* makes the power of military aircraft and warships to enforce South African law in the territorial sea subject to article 28 of the UNCLOS.

[64] See Devine (n 36); C Dillon 'Innocent passage in South African territorial waters' (1985) 9(2) *International Affairs Bulletin* 59.

[65] Section 2 of Act 2 of 1981; s 4(3) of Act 15 of 1994.

[66] DJ Devine 'Bays, baselines, passage and pollution in South African waters' (1986) 19 *CILSA* 85 at 93–4.

navigation through the territorial waters in a continuous and expeditious manner for the purpose of

traversing those waters without entering internal waters or calling at a roadstead or offshore installation outside internal waters; or

proceeding to or from internal waters, or a call at any such roadstead or offshore installation, and includes stopping and anchoring, in so far as such stopping or such anchoring is incidental to ordinary navigation or is rendered necessary by *vis major* or distress or is for the purpose of rendering assistance to persons, ships or aircraft in danger or distress.[67]

Passage is innocent if it is 'not prejudicial to the peace, good order or security of the Republic'.[68] Such passage ceases to be innocent if the ship carries or has on board 'cargo or any appliance or apparatus the use of which or persons who may constitute a threat against the sovereignty, territorial integrity or political independence of the Republic'.[69] Innocent passage may be suspended in the interests of national security for a specified period in specified areas.[70] Submarines are required to navigate on the surface and to show their flags.[71]

The South African maritime authorities are given wide powers to stop, detain, seize, or dispose of a ship and its cargo where it is engaged in non-innocent passage[72] or suspected of drug trafficking. These powers do not apply to foreign warships or to foreign government-owned ships operated for non-commercial purposes.[73]

A South African court will not exercise jurisdiction over foreign ships outside territorial waters[74]—except where legislation permits

[67] Section 1 of Act 2 of 1981 as amended by s 19 of Act 23 of 1997.

[68] Section 1.

[69] Section 8. According to Dillon (n 64), this provision goes beyond the meaning of non-innocent passage as recognised by the UNCLOS, article 19. See too G Wardley 'Passage of nuclear powered ships and ships carrying nuclear material: International and South African perspectives' (1995–6) 17 *Sea Changes* 106.

[70] Section 7 of Act 2 of 1981.

[71] Section 3.

[72] This includes the conveyance of munitions: see P Vrancken and E van der Berg 'The South African regulation of the conveyance of munitions by sea' (2005) 30 *SAYIL* 147.

[73] Section 9, read with ss 8 and 8A of Act 2 of 1981.

[74] *South Atlantic Islands Development Corporation v Buchan* 1971 (1) SA 234 (C); *R v Jiouvanni* 1933 SWA 26.

this.[75] But it will exercise both civil[76] and criminal jurisdiction[77] in appropriate circumstances in respect of matters occurring in the territorial sea.[78]

In 2008, a Chinese vessel carrying arms destined for Zimbabwe was interdicted from discharging its cargo at Durban, despite a permit issued in terms of the National Convention Arms Control Act 41 of 2002, on the ground that the arms were to be used for internal repression.[79] Similarly, in 2017 a vessel carrying a cargo of phosphate mined in the territory Western Sahara without the consent of Western Sahara, was interdicted and restrained from taking the cargo from the jurisdiction of the Eastern Cape High Court.[80]

3 Straits

A strait is a narrow passage of water connecting two larger bodies of water which may qualify as high seas or exclusive economic zones (EEZ). Before 1982 straits that fell entirely within the territorial sea of one or more states were governed by the rules of innocent passage, extending to both merchant vessels and warships.[81] The only special privilege accorded to such straits by the 1958 Convention on the Territorial Sea was that the coastal state's right of suspension of passage was prohibited.[82] The recognition of a territorial sea of 12 miles by the 1982 UNCLOS resulted in many straits hitherto classified as high seas becoming territorial sea. The Straits of Gibraltar and the Straits of Dover, both of which are less than 24 miles wide at their narrowest points, illustrate this problem. As a result, the UNCLOS introduced a new form of passage for straits, known as 'transit passage', which confers greater rights on foreign shipping than innocent passage.[83]

[75] The Marine Living Resources Act 18 of 1998 (s 70(1)*(a)*, read with s 1(liv)), provides for jurisdiction over offences committed in South Africa's exclusive economic zone and on its continental shelf. The Marine Pollution (Control and Civil Liability) Act 6 of 1981 likewise gives jurisdiction in respect of pollution activities within the exclusive economic zone.

[76] *Ex parte Gardner Thompson* 1966 (2) PH F99 (D).

[77] BR Bamford *The Law of Shipping and Carriage in South Africa* 3 ed (1983) 202. See too DJ Devine 'Police powers of search without warrant and seizure in maritime zones' 1989–90 *Obiter* 181.

[78] P Vrancken and F Marx 'Birth, marriage and death at sea in South African law' (2015) 4 *SAYIL* 58.

[79] M du Plessis 'A Chinese vessel in Durban with arms destined for Zimbabwe' (2008) 33 *SAYIL* 267.

[80] *Saharawi Arab Democratic Republic v MV NM Cherry Blossom* 2017 (5) SA 105 (ECP).

[81] *Corfu Channel Case (United Kingdom v Albania)* 1949 ICJ Reports 4 at 28.

[82] TSC, article 16(4).

[83] UNCLOS, articles 37–44. See O'Connell (n 1) vol 1 299–337; Jennings and Watts (n 58) 634. DB Hamman *Passage Rights Through Straits* No 5 (Institute of Marine Law, Cape Town 1987).

Passage through straits such as the Bosphorus[84] is governed by treaty. The Suez and Panama canals are likewise open to foreign shipping in terms of special treaties.[85]

4 Contiguous zone

The 1958 Geneva Convention on the Territorial Sea and the Contiguous Zone recognised a contiguous zone of 12 miles from the baseline from which the territorial sea is measured within which a coastal state might exercise the control necessary to prevent and punish infringements of its customs, fiscal, immigration, or sanitary regulations within its territory or territorial sea.[86]

The contiguous zone is retained by the UNCLOS and is extended to 24 miles from the baseline for measuring the territorial sea.[87] This zone has lost much of its purpose as states are now permitted to claim a territorial sea of 12 miles with full sovereign rights and an EEZ of 200 miles. Consequently, many states no longer claim a contiguous zone.

South Africa has a contiguous zone of 24 nautical miles. Within this zone (including the airspace above it) South Africa claims the right to exercise all the powers necessary to prevent contravention of its fiscal, customs, emigration, immigration or sanitary laws.[88]

Although not strictly part of the contiguous zone regime, it is important to note the importance of the 24-mile limit for marine archaeology.[89] Africa's coastline is rich in historical wrecks.[90] The UNCLOS allows a coastal state to claim exclusive jurisdiction over 'objects of an archaeological and historical nature' within the 24-mile contiguous zone.[91] South African legislation recognises a maritime cultural zone, governing objects of an archaeological or historical nature, extending for 24 nautical miles from the baselines used for measuring maritime zones.[92]

5 Exclusive economic zone

At the Third Law of the Sea Conference, there was strong pressure for the recognition of a fishing zone beyond the territorial sea, which

[84] Jennings and Watts (n 58) 641.

[85] Ibid 591.

[86] UNCLOS, article 24.

[87] UNCLOS, article 33.

[88] Section 5 of Act 15 of 1994.

[89] O'Connell (n 1) vol 2 at 908; LH van Meurs 'Legal aspects of marine archaeological research' 1986 *Acta Juridica* 83; GPJ Scheepers 'South African law of shipwrecks: Contemporary and international perspectives' (1989) 10 *Sea Changes* 41.

[90] See those listed in GN 537 *GG* 9134 of 23 March 1984 and GN 641 *GG* 9661 of 29 March 1985.

[91] UNCLOS, articles 303 and 33.

[92] Section 6 of Act 15 of 1994.

would enable developing nations to prevent over-exploitation of their marine resources by the major fishing countries. Moreover, land-locked states also sought to have their fishing rights protected.

At the same time there were several states that claimed a 200-mile territorial sea. The compromise reached was a 12-mile territorial sea and a 200-mile EEZ, measured from the baseline for the territorial sea,[93] within which the coastal state exercised 'sovereign rights for the purpose of exploring and exploiting, conserving and managing the natural resources, whether living or non-living, of the waters superjacent to the sea-bed and of the sea-bed and subsoil'.[94] This means that a state other than the coastal state wishing to exploit the resources of the EEZ of a coastal state can only do so with the agreement of the coastal state.[95] The coastal state also has a duty under the convention to 'ensure through proper conservation and management measures that the maintenance of the living resources in the exclusive economic zone is not endangered by over-exploitation.'[96]

While the coastal state exercises sovereign rights over the natural resources in the EEZ, the UNCLOS provides that land-locked states have 'the right to participate, on an equitable basis, in the exploitation of an appropriate part of the surplus of the living resources of the exclusive economic zones of the same region or subregion.'[97] This right is however, subject to a number of qualifiers. First, it does not apply to all natural resources but only to living resources.[98] Secondly, it applies only if there is a surplus of such living resources.[99] Thirdly, the right is subject to agreement with the coastal state.[100] To date no agreements have been entered into between South Africa and its southern African land-locked neighbours or for that matter amongst any other state anywhere in the world.

The coastal state's sovereign rights are limited to the resources. This means that it does not have the right to enforce its customs or other laws in the EEZ.[101] Although the waters of the EEZ do not enjoy

[93] UNCLOS, article 57.

[94] UNCLOS, article 56. See *M/V 'Virginia' (Panama/Guinea-Bissau)*, Judgment, 2014 ITLOS Reports 4, paras 212–3. E Frankx and P Gautier (eds) *The Exclusive Economic Zone and the United Nations Convention on the Law of the Sea* (2003).

[95] *Advisory Opinion Submitted by the Sub-Regional Fisheries Management Commission*, 2015 ITLOS Reports 4.

[96] UNCLOS, article 61.

[97] UNCLOS, article 69. *Advisory Opinion Submitted by SRFC* (n 95) para 96.

[98] Ibid.

[99] Ibid.

[100] Ibid.

[101] The *M/V 'Saiga' (No 2) Case (Saint Vincent and the Grenadines v Guinea)*, Judgment of ITLOS (1999) 38 *ILM* 1323 at 1351 (para 127).

the status of 'high seas', other states retain the rights of navigation and overflight, and of laying submarine cables and pipelines.[102] The EEZ has been widely accepted by states and in the *Case Concerning the Continental Shelf (Libya v Malta)* the International Court of Justice declared that 'the institution of the exclusive economic zone . . . is shown by the practice of states to have become a part of customary law'.[103]

South Africa has an EEZ of 200 nautical miles from the baselines in which it claims the same rights and powers over all natural resources in the EEZ that it has in respect of its territorial waters.[104] These powers are spelled out in the Marine Living Resources Act 18 of 1998.[105] In pursuit of the goals 'to achieve optimum utilisation and ecologically sustainable development of maritime living resources' and 'to conserve marine living resources for both present and future generations'[106] the authorities are given wide powers to regulate fishing in South African waters[107] by determining a total allowable catch for each year,[108] and by providing for the control of fishing, both local and foreign, by means of licences.[109] A fishing licence will not be granted to a foreign fishing vessel unless there is an agreement between the flag state and the South African government.[110] Certain methods of fishing, for example the use of driftnets, are prohibited[111] and fishing control officers are given wide powers of law enforcement within South African waters[112]—and on the high seas following the hot pursuit of a vessel engaged in unlawful fishing activities in South African waters.[113] South African courts are given jurisdiction over unlawful acts committed by persons on board vessels within South African waters.[114] The factors to be considered in sentencing violators of the rights protected in the EEZ have been considered by

[102] UNCLOS, article 58.

[103] 1985 ICJ Reports 13 at 33. See too *Shooter t/a Shooter's Fisheries v Incorporated General Insurances Ltd* 1984 (4) SA 269 (D) 280H.

[104] Section 7 of Act 15 of 1994.

[105] For the application of this statute, see P Vrancken 'Legal challenges of fisheries management' (2005) 30 *SAYIL* 264. See too CP Wesley 'Fisheries, fishing and sealing' (2005) 10(2) *LAWSA* 2 ed (2005) 2.

[106] Section 2.

[107] Section 1(liv) defines South African waters as including the seashore, internal waters, territorial waters, the EEZ and the continental shelf in respect of sedentary species.

[108] Section 14.

[109] Sections 18–28, 38–41.

[110] Section 39(3).

[111] Sections 44–9.

[112] Sections 51–5.

[113] Section 52.

[114] Section 70.

the courts of Namibia.[115] No doubt these decisions will be of strong persuasive value in South Africa as they are based on South African statute and case law. The authorities are also empowered to provide for the establishment of marine protected areas to allow for the recovery of stocks.[116]

The UNCLOS authorises the coastal state to construct and use installations within the EEZ for the purpose of exercising its rights within this zone.[117] The Maritime Zones Act provides for the application of South African law in respect of such installations.[118]

6 The high seas

The high seas are those parts of the seas not included in the EEZ, the territorial sea, or internal waters.[119] The high seas falls beyond national jurisdiction and no state may acquire sovereignty over them.[120] These seas are open to all states, whether coastal or land-locked. Freedom of the high seas comprises, inter alia, freedom of navigation, overflight, fishing, and scientific research, and the freedom to lay submarine cables and pipelines, and to construct artificial islands.[121]

The freedom of the high seas does not include the freedom to conduct weapons-testing, including the testing of nuclear weapons. The United States hydrogen bomb tests in the North Pacific in 1954, justified as an exercise of the freedom of the high seas, were widely condemned as a violation of international law.[122] France's nuclear tests in the South Pacific in the early 1970s were challenged by Australia and New Zealand before the International Court of Justice, but the Court managed to avoid pronouncing on the legality of

[115] *S v Martinez* 1991 (4) SA 741 (Nm); *S v Curras* 1991 (2) SACR 557 (Nm); *Banco Exterior de Espana SA v Government of the Republic of Namibia* 1992 (2) SA 434 (Nm); *S v Pineiro* 1992 (1) SACR 504 (Nm); *S v Pineiro* 1992 (2) SA 683 (Nm); *S v Redondo* 1993 (2) SA 528 (NmS) 546–52.

[116] Section 43.

[117] UNCLOS, article 60.

[118] Sections 1, 9. See *Schlumberger Logelco Inc v Coflexip SA* 2000 (3) SA 861 (SCA), noted by Vrancken (n 32) 286. See, further, DJ Devine 'South African civil law and offshore installations' (1994) 111 *SALJ* 736; and DJ Devine 'The application of South African law to offshore installations' 1994 *TSAR* 229.

[119] UNCLOS, article 86. Archipelagic waters, whose status is similar to that of internal waters, are also excluded from the high seas by article 86.

[120] UNCLOS, article 89.

[121] UNCLOS, article 87.

[122] E Margolis 'The hydrogen bomb experiments and international law' (1955) 64 *Yale LJ* 629. *Sed contra*, see MS McDougal and NA Schlei 'The hydrogen bomb tests in perspective: Lawful measures for security' (1955) 64 *Yale LJ* 649.

nuclear tests by holding that the issue was moot in the light of a half-hearted undertaking by France to desist from further tests.[123]

Today it is impossible seriously to maintain that such tests are lawful.[124] The UNCLOS declares that the high seas 'shall be reserved for peaceful purposes' and that the freedoms of the high seas 'shall be exercised by all states with due regard for the interests of other states'.[125] Furthermore, the widely accepted Treaty Banning Nuclear Weapons Tests in the Atmosphere, in Outer Space and Under Water of 1963 expressly prohibits the testing of nuclear weapons on the high seas.[126]

The right of land-locked states to gain access to the high seas is of particular importance to many states in the Southern African region. According to the UNCLOS, land-locked states 'shall have the right of access to and from the sea' to enable them to exercise their rights to the high seas. 'To this end, land-locked states shall enjoy freedom of transit through the territory of transit states by all means of transport'.[127] That this right is not absolute is clear from the UNCLOS itself, which recognises that 'the terms and modalities for exercising freedom of transit' are to be agreed on between the land-locked state and the transit state.[128] The UNCLOS therefore appears to be a *pactum de contrahendo* requiring states to enter into negotiations for transit treaties in good faith.[129] An example of this is an agreement between Ethiopia and Djibouti under which Ethiopia can access the

[123] *Nuclear Tests Cases* 1974 ICJ Reports 253; 1974 ICJ Reports 457. See further J Dugard 'The *Nuclear Tests Cases* and the *South West Africa Cases:* Some realism about the international judicial decision' (1976) 16 *Virginia Journal of International Law* 463.

[124] J Frakes 'The common heritage mankind principle and the deep seabed, outer space and Antarctica: Will developed and developing nations reach a compromise?' (2003) 21 *Wisconsin International Law Journal* 409 at 413.

[125] UNCLOS, articles 88 and 87(2).

[126] (1963) 2 *ILM* 889.

[127] UNCLOS, article 125. The HSC, article 3, is less peremptory and declared that land-locked states 'should' have free access to the sea.

[128] Article 125(2). In *Nkondo v Minister of Police* 1980 (2) SA 894 (O) Smuts J held that 'there is no rule of customary international law which grants a right of passage over the territory of a sovereign state' (904–6 at 905E).

[129] See Vrancken (n 1) ch 12; Churchill and Lowe (n 1) 325–6; MA Sulaiman 'Free access: The problem of land-locked states and the 1982 United Nations Convention on the Law of the Sea' (1984) 10 *SAYIL* 144; T Maluwa 'Southern African land-locked states and the rights of access under the new Law of the Sea' (1995) 10 *International Journal of Marine & Coastal Law* 529; V Boloyi 'Access of land-locked states and their interests in the seabed area (2002) 43(1) *Codicillus* 68. See, further, on the subject of transit rights in southern Africa, JD Viall 'The transit of persons to and from Lesotho' (1968) 1 *CILSA* 1, 188, 363.

sea through transit routes in Djibouti.[130] To date, no such agreement has been entered into between South Africa and its regional neighbours.

(a) Jurisdiction over ships on the high seas

Only the state whose flag a ship flies—the flag state—has jurisdiction over a ship on the high seas. Consequently, most municipal-law systems provide that their criminal law will apply on board ships that fly their flags. The Merchant Shipping Act 57 of 1951[131] confers jurisdiction on South African courts to try both citizens and non-citizens for offences committed on board a South African ship on the high seas. The Marine Living Resources Act regulates the fishing of South African ships on the high seas[132] and gives South African courts jurisdiction over citizens and persons ordinarily resident in South Africa in respect of offences relating to such activities on the high seas.[133]

The conferment of nationality on a ship is important, not only for jurisdictional reasons but because every ship is required to fly the flag of one state.[134] Each state is to fix the conditions for the grant of nationality to its ships.[135] In practice, most states require some connection between the owner of the ship and the flag state. South Africa is no exception: The Ship Registration Act of 1998[136] provides that only South African-owned ships,[137] small vessels (other than fishing vessels) owned or operated by South African residents or nationals, and ships on bareboat charters to South African nationals may be registered as South African ships entitled to fly the national flag. This practice is endorsed by the 1958 HSC,[138] the 1982 UNC-

[130] E Bayeh 'The rights of land-locked states in international law: The role of bilateral/multilateral agreement' (2015) 4 *Social Sciences* 27, 29.

[131] Section 327(1) of Act 57 of 1951.

[132] Sections 40–1 of Act 18 of 1998.

[133] Section 70.

[134] Jennings and Watts (n 58) 731.

[135] See *The M/V 'Saiga'* (n 102) paras 63–74.

[136] Act 58 of 1998 ss 3, 4 and 16.

[137] A South African-owned ship means a local fishing vessel as defined in the Marine Living Resources Act 18 of 1998 (s 1(xxxiii)) or any ship, other than a fishing vessel, that is wholly owned by one or more South African nationals; is owned by three or more persons as joint owners where the majority are South African nationals; or is owned by two or more persons as owners in common, where the majority of the shares in the ship are owned by South African nationals (s 1(4) of Act 58 of 1998). The term 'national' includes South African citizens, South African corporations, trusts controlled by South African nationals for the benefit of South African nationals, and the South African government (s 1(1) of Act 58 of 1998).

[138] HSC, article 5. Jennings and Watts (n 58).

LOS,[139] and the 1986 Convention on Conditions for Registration of Ships,[140] which require a 'genuine link' of the kind recognised in the *Nottebohm Case*[141] between the ship and the flag state to ensure that effective control is exercised over the ship. These treaties have thus far failed to curb the granting of 'flags of convenience' by states such as Liberia and Panama, which attract registration of ships by low taxation and the absence of adequate laws on safety standards, and wages and working conditions for the crews. Liberia and Panama each has more registered tonnage than the leading maritime powers. The International Tribunal for the Law of the Sea has, however, held that the 'genuine link' requirement is not intended 'to establish criteria by reference to which the validity of the registration of ships in a flag state may be challenged by other States'.[142] In an advisory opinion that may go some way to reduce flags of convenience, the International Tribunal for the Law of the Sea has held that flag states may be held liable under international law for the illegal, unreported and unregulated fishing by a vessel flying its flag.[143]

In principle, a ship of one state may not interfere with a ship of another state on the high seas. However, a warship may stop and board a foreign ship on the high seas when it is reasonably suspected of engaging in the following activities:[144]

(a) *Piracy*.[145] Both the 1958 Convention on the High Seas and the UNCLOS define piracy as an illegal act of violence committed for private ends by the crew or passengers of a private ship or aircraft and directed against another ship or aircraft on the high seas. Piracy does not include the unlawful seizure of a vessel by passengers or crew for political ends. Such conduct, however, is now subject to the 1988 Rome Convention for the Suppression of Unlawful Acts against the Safety of Maritime Navigation, adopted in the wake of the seizure of the *Achille Lauro*.[146] The Defence Act 42 of 2002 defines piracy as 'any illegal act of

[139] UNCLOS, article 91.

[140] (1987) 26 *ILM* 1229. See Ademuni-Odeke 'The UN Convention on Conditions for Registration of Ships and Flags of Convenience' (1988) 8 *Sea Changes* 63.

[141] 1955 ICJ Reports 4. Discussed in Chapter 13.

[142] *The* M/V *Saiga* (n 102) para 83. See too the *IMCO Case* 1960 ICJ Reports 150.

[143] *Advisory Opinion Submitted by SRFC* (n 96) para 150.

[144] UNCLOS, article 110; HSC, article 22. Section 22(3)*(b)* of Act 42 of 2002 provides that no enforcement of the law may take place outside South Africa's territorial waters 'against foreign ships or those on board them, except in circumstances permitted by international law'.

[145] UNCLOS, articles 100–7; HSC, articles 14–21; AP Rubin *The Law of Piracy* 2 ed (1998); Vrancken (n 1) 428–34; T Potgieter and R Pommerin (eds) *Maritime Security in Southern African Waters* (2009).

[146] See above, Chapter 9.

violence or detention, or any act of deprivation, committed for private ends by the crew' of a ship and directed 'on the high seas, against another ship . . . or against persons or property on board such ship.'[147] An officer of the Defence Force is empowered under the Defence Act, to seize a pirate ship or to arrest any person on board such a ship on the high seas.[148] The Defence Act also confers jurisdiction on courts in the Republic to try any person who commits an act of piracy.[149]

(b) *The slave trade.*[150]

(c) *Unauthorised broadcasting.*[151]

(d) *Failure to show a flag.*[152] A warship may board a ship that flies no flag or one that it suspects of being the same nationality as itself despite the fact that it flies another flag. This is known as 'verification of the flag'. A South African warship is empowered to exercise the right of flag verification in terms of the Defence Act.[153] The Ship Registration Act makes it an offence for the master or owner of a South African ship to conceal the nationality of the ship or to cause the ship to appear not to be a South African ship.[154]

A warship may also interfere with foreign shipping under the Charter of the United Nations or in terms of other treaties. The Security Council may, under Chapter VII, authorise warships to visit or search foreign ships where the interests of international peace and security are threatened. Thus in 1966 the Security Council authorised the Royal Navy to stop tankers carrying oil to the rebellious colony of Rhodesia;[155] and in 1990 it directed states to stop and search ships suspected of violating the sanctions imposed on Iraq.[156] Moreover, in extreme circumstances, a warship may attack a foreign ship on the high seas in the exercise of the right of self-defence under article 51 of

[147] Section 24 of Act 42 of 2002.

[148] Ibid s 25(1).

[149] Ibid s 24(3).

[150] UNCLOS, article 99; HSC, article 13. South Africa might have jurisdiction to try slave-trading. See AV Lansdown and J Campbell *South African Criminal Law and Procedure* vol v (1982) 19–20; South Africa is a party to the 2000 Protocol to Prevent, Suppress and Punish Traffickers in Persons, especially Women and Children, given effect to by the Children's Act 38 of 2005. See further, Vrancken (n 1) 200.

[151] UNCLOS, article 109.

[152] UNCLOS, article 110; HSC, article 22.

[153] Section 26 of Act 42 of 2002.

[154] Sections 4 and 5 of Act 58 of 1998.

[155] Security Council Resolution 221 (1966).

[156] Security Council Resolution 665 (1990).

the Charter.[157] Finally, bilateral or multilateral treaties may confer rights of visit and search on flag ships of the signatories for a particular purpose—such as the suppression of drug trafficking.[158]

(b) *Piracy*

Piracy has for many years been a problem in Asian sea routes, particularly in the Strait of Malacca and the South China Sea. In 2005 this led to the adoption of the Regional Co-operation Agreement in Combating Piracy and Armed Robbery against Ships in Asia.[159] In recent years piracy has become endemic in the waters off Somalia, with acts of piracy occurring as far south as Kenya and the Gulf of Aden in the east.[160] Ships of all kinds have been seized, ranging from oil tankers to fishing vessels and private yachts, and their crews held hostage. Some of those seized have been killed but most of the ships and their crew have been ransomed for large sums of money. Many nations have employed their warships to combat piracy but this has not put an end to this maritime scourge and the methods used by the pirates have become more sophisticated.

The international community has resorted to new and traditional legal procedures to suppress piracy. The Security Council has adopted several resolutions under Chapter VII of the UN Charter[161] authorising states to arrest pirates within the territorial sea and internal waters of Somalia, provided that consent has been obtained from the Somali Federal Government and such permission is reported to the UN Secretary-General. These resolutions make it clear, however, that the authority granted by the Security Council cannot form the basis for a new rule of customary international law. Criminal prosecutions, in the exercise of universal jurisdiction, have been relatively few, and many pirates have simply been released after the recovery of the seized vessel.[162] Most prosecutions have taken place in Kenya which has accepted the transfer of pirates arrested by

[157] The Maritime Zones Act 15 of 1994 (s 11) recognises the right of South Africa to 'take such action in any area of the sea or in the airspace above the sea, as is necessary in the exercise of the principle of self-defence contained in article 51 of the Charter of the United Nations'.

[158] See the United Nations Convention against Illicit Traffic in Narcotic Drugs and Psychotropic Substances article 17 (1989) 28 *ILM* 497.

[159] (2005) 44 *ILM* 829.

[160] See R Geiss and A Petrig *Piracy and Armed Robbery at Sea* (2011).

[161] Security Council Resolutions 1816 (2008), 1846 (2008), 1851 (2008), 1897 (2009), 1950 (2010), 2316 (2016) and 2383 (2017). See further J Ashley Roach 'Countering piracy off Somalia: International law and international institutions' (2010) 104 *AJIL* 397.

[162] See E Kontorovich and S Art 'An empirical examination of universal jurisdiction for piracy' (2010) 104 *AJIL* 436.

warships patrolling the sea off Somalia,[163] but prosecutions have also taken place in the Seychelles, the United States, the Netherlands, Germany and Yemen. A report by the UN Secretary-General proposed a number of options relating to the prosecutions of pirates, including the establishment of a Somali court sitting in a third state or the establishment of an ad hoc international criminal tribunal, either by agreement among states in the region or by resolution of the Security Council under Chapter VII.[164] Although these courts and tribunals were never established, the Security Council has subsequently called upon states with jurisdiction to exercise jurisdiction over pirates operating in Somali waters.[165]

(c) Hot pursuit[166]

A warship or military aircraft may pursue a ship that has violated the laws of its internal waters, territorial sea, contiguous zone, EEZ, or continental shelf. Provided such pursuit is commenced when the foreign ship (or one of its boats) is within internal waters, the territorial sea, contiguous zone, the EEZ, or above the continental shelf (depending upon the nature of the offence), the warship may pursue the delinquent vessel onto the high seas and arrest it there. The pursuit must be uninterrupted and must have been preceded by the giving of a visual or auditory signal to stop.[167] Hot pursuit ceases as soon as the ship pursued enters the territorial sea of its own state or of a third state.

The Defence Act authorises a South African warship or military aircraft to exercise hot pursuit in accordance with the UNCLOS.[168] The Marine Living Resources Act of 1998 also empowers a fishery control officer, 'following hot pursuit in accordance with international law', as reflected in article 111 of the UNCLOS, to stop, board and search outside South African waters, any foreign fishing vessel

[163] JT Gathii 'Kenya's Piracy prosecutions' (2010) 104 *AJIL* 416.

[164] S/2010/394.

[165] See, eg Security Council Resolution 2015 (2011).

[166] UNCLOS, article 111; HSC, article 23. The doctrine of hot pursuit was considered in the *'I'm Alone' Case* (reported in 3 *RIAA* 1609 and (1935) 29 *AJIL* 326), in which a US coastguard vessel sunk a Canadian schooner on suspicion of smuggling liquor during the period of prohibition. The United States was found to have used excessive force in sinking the *'I'm Alone'*. See, too, *S v Pineiro* 1992 (1) SACR 504 (Nm). See further, EJ Molenaar 'Multilateral hot pursuit and illegal fishing in the Southern Ocean: The pursuits of *Viarsa I* and *South Tomi*' (2004) 19 *International Journal of Marine & Coastal Law* 28; Vrancken (n 1) 203–5.

[167] The conditions for the exercise of hot pursuit are cumulative; each of them has to be satisfied for the pursuit to be legitimate: *The M/V 'Saiga'* (n 86). *In casu*, the Tribunal found that the conditions had not been satisfied.

[168] Section 27 of Act 42 of 2002.

which he has reasonable grounds to believe has been used in unlawful fishing in South African waters and to bring such vessel and all persons and things on board to a South African port.[169]

(d) Rescue powers of South African ships

In terms of the Wreck and Salvage Act 94 of 1996, which gives effect to the International Convention on Salvage of 1989, the Master of a South African ship is obliged to render assistance to any ship in distress 'at sea',[170] to any person 'found at sea in danger of being lost, even if that person is a citizen of a country at war with the Republic or with the country in which the ship is registered'[171] and to a ship with which it has collided at sea.[172]

In addition to giving South African warships and military aircraft the right to arrest pirates on the high seas and to exercise the right of flag verification and hot pursuit on the high seas, the Defence Act also provides that such a warship or military aircraft must render assistance to 'any person found at sea in danger of being lost', rescue persons in distress at sea and 'after a collision, render assistance to the other ship'—provided that in time of armed conflict this can be done without serious prejudice to the operation in which it is engaged.[173] The Act also authorises the Defence Force to take action on the high seas to enforce the law of a foreign state with which South Africa has a reciprocal agreement on co-operation in law enforcement at sea.[174]

7 Continental shelf

The continental land mass does not drop sharply where it meets the sea. Instead, it descends gradually to the ocean depths. This submarine rim or ledge off the coast, made up of submerged continental crust, is known as the continental margin, which normally comprises three regions. Nearest the coastline is a platform, usually between 150 and 200 metres beneath the sea, called the continental shelf. Next is a steep incline called the continental slope. Finally, there is the continental rise, consisting of a deposit of sediment, which is normally between 1 500 and 5 000 metres in depth. Beyond this is the deep ocean floor or deep seabed (see Fig 2).

[169] Section 52 of Act 18 of 1998.

[170] Section 5.

[171] Section 6.

[172] Section 7.

[173] Section 28 of Act 42 of 2002. See too the South African Maritime and Aeronautical Search and Rescue Act 44 of 2002.

[174] Section 29 of Act 42 of 2002.

Figure 2

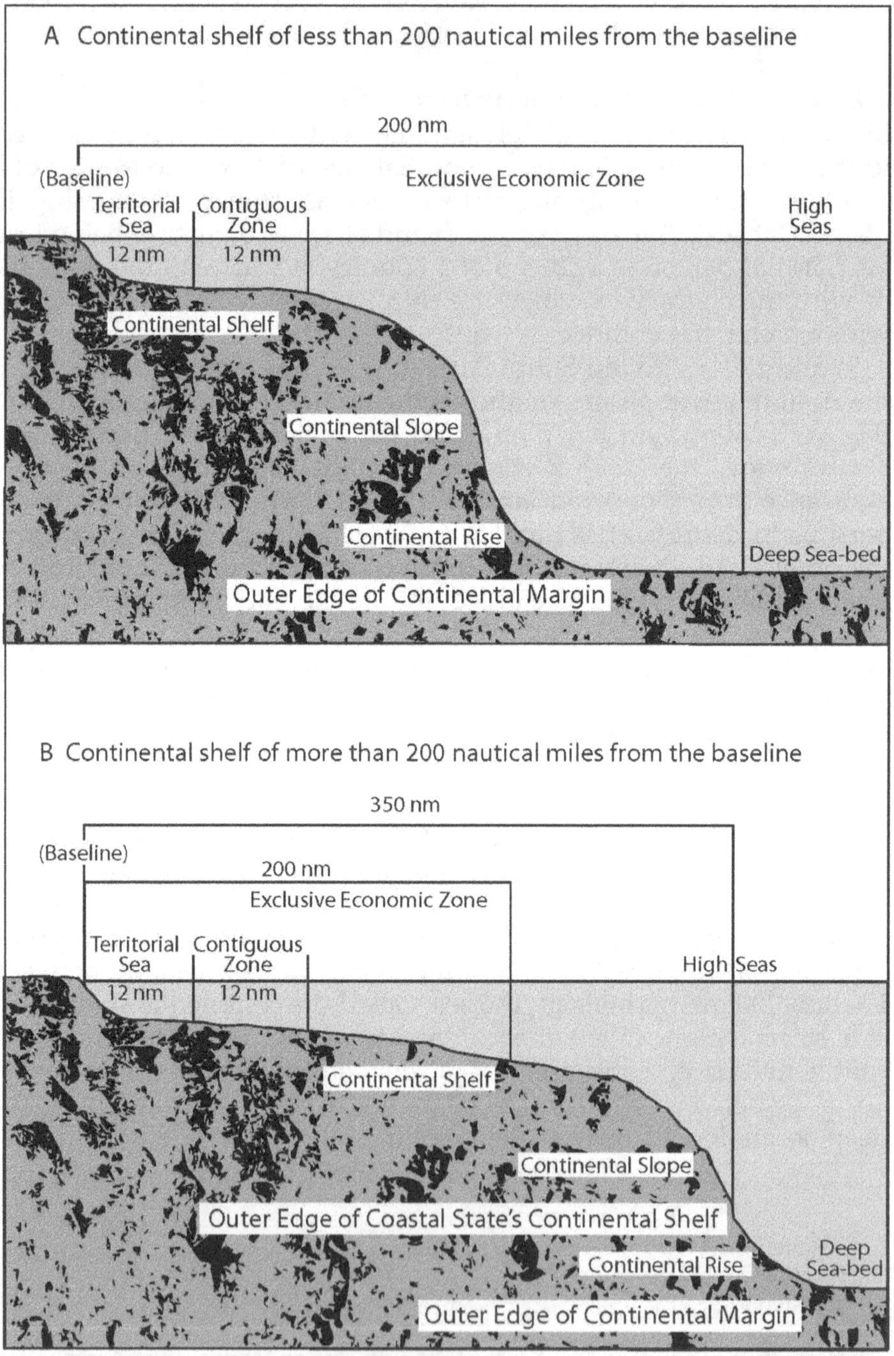
A Continental shelf of less than 200 nautical miles from the baseline
200 nm
(Baseline)
Exclusive Economic Zone
Territorial Sea
Contiguous Zone
High Seas
12 nm
12 nm
Continental Shelf
Continental Slope
Continental Rise
Deep Sea-bed
Outer Edge of Continental Margin
B Continental shelf of more than 200 nautical miles from the baseline
350 nm
(Baseline)
200 nm
Exclusive Economic Zone
Territorial Sea
Contiguous Zone
High Seas
12 nm
12 nm
Continental Shelf
Continental Slope
Outer Edge of Coastal State's Continental Shelf
Continental Rise
Deep Sea-bed
Outer Edge of Continental Margin

The extent of the continental shelf varies considerably. It is less than five miles wide off the west coast of the Americas, while the whole of the North Sea is submerged continental shelf.

Before 1945 international law took little interest in the continental shelf. The situation changed dramatically, however, when technological advances made it possible to drill for oil and natural gas on the continental shelf. Legal recognition was given to these advances in the Truman Proclamation of 1945 in which the United States government declared that 'since the continental shelf may be regarded as an extension of the land-mass of the coastal nation and thus naturally appurtenant to it', the United States government 'regards the natural resources of the subsoil and sea-bed of the continental shelf beneath the high seas but contiguous to the coasts of the United States as appertaining to the United States, subject to its jurisdiction and control'.[175] It added, however, that 'the character as high seas of the waters above the continental shelf and the right to their free and unimpeded navigation are in no way thus affected'. Other states followed the example of the United States and soon there was a substantial body of state practice in support of a rule according exclusive rights of exploration and exploitation on the continental shelf to the coastal state. This practice is reflected in the 1958 Geneva Convention on the Continental Shelf (CSC).

The CSC defines the continental shelf as 'the sea-bed and subsoil of the submarine areas adjacent to the coast but outside the area of the territorial sea, to a depth of 200 metres or, beyond that limit, to where the depth of the superjacent waters admits of the exploitation of the natural resources of the said areas'.[176] The coastal state enjoys 'sovereign rights' for the purpose of exploring and exploiting the natural resources of the continental shelf.[177] These rights are inherent and do not depend on express proclamation[178] because, in the words of the International Court of Justice, the submarine areas comprising the continental shelf 'may be deemed to be actually part of the territory over which the coastal state already has dominion—in the sense that, although covered with water, they are a prolongation or continuation of that territory, an extension of it under the sea'.[179] 'The rights of the coastal state over the continental shelf do not affect the

[175] (1946) 40 *AJIL*; suppl 45.
[176] CSC, article 1.
[177] CSC, article 2(1).
[178] CSC, article 2(3).
[179] *North Sea Continental Shelf Cases (Germany/Denmark; Germany/Netherlands)* 1969 ICJ 3 at 31.

legal status of the superjacent waters as high seas, or that of the airspace above those waters.'[180]

The natural resources of the shelf consist of 'the mineral and other non-living resources of the sea-bed and subsoil together with living organisms belonging to sedentary species, that is to say, organisms which, at the harvestable stage, either are immobile on or under the sea-bed or are unable to move except in constant physical contact with the sea-bed or the subsoil'.[181] The indeterminacy of this definition has resulted in a number of disputes over the status of lobsters, crayfish, and crabs, which are sometimes free-swimming. In 1963, for instance, there was a serious confrontation between Brazil and France as a result of the fishing of lobsters by French fishermen on the Brazilian continental shelf.[182]

Although the UNCLOS reiterates the provisions of the CSC on the nature of the coastal state's rights over the continental shelf,[183] the indeterminate definition of natural resources,[184] and the legal status of the superjacent waters and airspace above those waters,[185] it differs substantially in its demarcation of the outer limit of the continental shelf. The principal reason for the revision of the outer limit of the shelf was the recognition of the 200-mile EEZ by the UNCLOS, which gives all coastal states, irrespective of the extent of their continental shelves, exclusive rights to both the sea and the seabed of the EEZ. Hopes that such a zone would replace the concept of the continental shelf completely were destroyed by the demands of those states with continental shelves in excess of 200 miles that they retain their rights to the full limit of the geographical shelf. To aggravate matters, technological advances after 1958 had made it possible to exploit the resources of the continental slope and margin. The compromise reached at UNCLOS III was that the continental shelf would extend 'to the outer edge of the continental margin, or to a distance of 200 nautical miles from the baselines from which the breadth of the territorial sea is measured where the outer edge of the continental margin does not extend up to that distance'. Where the outer edge of the continental margin exceeds 200 miles, the outer edge of a state's exclusive continental shelf 'either shall not exceed 350 nautical miles from the baselines from which the breadth of the territorial sea is measured or shall not exceed 100 nautical miles from

[180] CSC, article 3.

[181] CSC, article 2(4).

[182] O'Connell (n 1) vol 1 498–503; I Azzam 'The dispute between France and Brazil over lobster fishing in the Atlantic' (1964) 13 *ICLQ* 1453.

[183] UNCLOS, article 77(1) and (3).

[184] UNCLOS, article 77(4).

[185] UNCLOS, article 78(1).

the 2 500 metre isobath, which is a line connecting the depth of 2 500 metres'[186] (see Fig 2 above). The new outer limit of the continental shelf contained in the UNCLOS probably reflects customary law.[187]

The UNCLOS puts in a place the Commission on the Limits of the Continental Shelf (CLCS) to assess the extent of a continental shelf where a state claims that its continental shelf exceeds 200 nautical miles.[188] In 2009, South Africa made two submissions to the CLCS. The first submission pertained to the mainland, consisting of areas to the east, west, and south of South Africa (the mainland submission). The second submission was a joint claim with France, which owns the Crozet archipelago next to South Africa's Prince Edwards Islands (the joint submission). The consideration of the joint submission is ongoing. In 2017, the CLSC approved parts of the mainland submission. It is expected that South Africa will seek to further substantiate those parts of its mainland submission that were not approved.

The system of sharing of the benefits from the exploitation of marine resources, which is a central feature of the deep seabed regime discussed below, applies also to the continental shelf. States with continental shelves in excess of 200 miles are required to make payments in respect of the exploitation of the non-living shelf resources beyond this limit to an International Sea-Bed Authority for distribution to developing states, both coastal and land-locked. Such payments are to commence after five years of production and to increase from 1 per cent to 7 per cent in the following years.[189]

The boundaries of the continental shelf between states adjacent or opposite to each other have given rise to particular problems. The 1958 CSC provides that in the absence of agreement between such states, and unless another boundary line is justified by special circumstances, the boundary line (a) in the case of states opposite to each other is to be 'the median line, every point of which is equidistant from the nearest points of the baselines from which the breadth of the territorial sea of each state is measured' and (b) in the case of states adjacent to each other is to be 'determined by application of the principle of equidistance from the nearest points of the baselines from which the breadth of the territorial sea of each state is measured'.[190] In the first case involving the delimitation of the continental shelf, between the Netherlands/Denmark and West Germany, West Germany challenged the equidistance principle on

[186] UNCLOS, article 76.

[187] See the *Delimitation of the Maritime Boundary in the Gulf of Maine Case (Canada v US)* 1984 ICJ Reports 246 at 294.

[188] UNCLOS, article 76 and Annex II.

[189] UNCLOS, article 82.

[190] UNCLOS, article 6.

the ground that when applied to a concave coastline it would have inequitable results (see Fig 3 below). For this reason, West Germany had not ratified the CSC. In the *North Sea Continental Shelf Cases*[191] the International Court of Justice ruled that the equidistance principle had not become a part of customary international law and that in the absence of such a rule all the circumstances of the particular coastline and shelf should be taken into account to achieve an equitable result. As a result of this decision and others[192] the UNCLOS dropped the equidistance principle and instead simply provides that 'the delimitation of the continental shelf between states with opposite or adjacent coasts shall be effected by agreement on the basis of international law . . . in order to achieve an equitable solution'.[193] Inevitably disagreement over what constitutes an equitable solution has resulted in litigation. Early decisions favoured the result-oriented equity approach approved in the *North Sea Continental Shelf Case*.[194] More recent decisions, however, show support for the drawing of an equidistant line between opposite or adjacent coastlines and then deciding whether any special circumstances exist which would warrant a departure from the equidistant line. Factors to be considered include the configuration of the coastline, the length of the coastline, the presence of islands, security matters and the prior conduct of parties.[195]

In 2017, Ghana and Côte d'Ivoire requested a Special Chamber of the International Tribunal for the Law of the Sea to pronounce on the delimitation of the maritime boundary (including in relation to the

[191] *North Sea Continental Shelf cases* (n 181).

[192] *Anglo-French Continental Shelf Arbitration* 18 *RIAA* 3; (1979) 18 *ILM* 397; 54 ILR 6. See further LDM Nelson 'The roles of equity in the delimitation of maritime boundaries' (1990) 84 *AJIL* 837; Y Tanaka *Predictability and Flexibility in the Law of Maritime Delimitation* (2006).

[193] UNCLOS, article 83.

[194] See *Case Concerning the Continental Shelf (Tunisia Libyan Arab Jamahiriya)* 1982 ICJ Reports 18; *Gulf of Maine Case* (n 189); *Guinea–Guinea Bissau Maritime Boundary Delimitation* (1986) 25 *ILM* 251 (decided by an ad hoc arbitration tribunal comprising three judges of the International Court of Justice); the *Libya–Malta Continental Shelf Case* (n 16).

[195] *Maritime Delimitation in the Area between Greenland and Jan Mayen (Denmark v Norway)* 1993 ICJ Reports 37, 61 (para 51); *Eritrea/Yemen (Phase Two): Maritime Delimitation* 119 ILR 417, 457; *Qatar v Bahrain* (n 16); *Case Concerning the Land and Maritime Boundary between Cameroon v Nigeria* 2002 ICJ Reports, paras 288, 290, 297, 299, 301 (discussed by Y Tanaka in (2004) 53 *ICLQ* 369); *Guyana v Suriname* (2008)102 *AJIL* 119. See, further, JI Charney and LM Alexander (eds) *International Maritime Boundaries* vols I–III (1993–8) and JI Charney and RW Smith op cit vol IV (2002).

territorial sea) between the EEZ and the continental shelf.[196] The Special Chamber recalled that the UNCLOS does not specify any particular methodology for the delimitation of maritime boundaries and declares that the methodology, if the states cannot agree, 'is to be determined through the dispute-settlement mechanism and should achieve an equitable solution, in the light of the circumstances of each particular case'.[197] Nonetheless, consistent with the general trend described, the Special Chamber found that 'the international jurisprudence concerning delimitation of maritime spaces in principle favours the equidistance' methodology and that 'in the absence of any compelling reasons that make it impossible or inappropriate' to apply the equidistance methodology, this methodology should be applied.[198]

South Africa as a party to the 1982 UNCLOS accepts this Convention as the basis for its law governing the continental shelf.[199] The outer limits of the shelf are prescribed in schedule 3 of the Maritime Zones Act of 1994.[200] In 2009 new limits were submitted for consideration to the Commission on the Limits of the Continental Shelf.[201] The Marine Living Resources Act of 1998 adopts the definition of 'sedentary species' contained in the CSC and UNCLOS—that is 'organisms which at the harvestable stage, either are immobile on or under the seabed, or are unable to move except in constant physical contact with the seabed or subsoil'.[202] This Act empowers the South African authorities to enforce its fishing regulatory regime, dealing with the utilisation and conservation of natural

[196] *Dispute Concerning Delimitation of the Maritime Boundary between Ghana and Côte d'Ivoire in the Atlantic Ocean (Ghana/Côte d'Ivoire)*, Judgment of the International Tribunal for the Law of the Sea of 23 September 2017 (not yet reported).

[197] Ibid para 281. See also *Delimitation of the Maritime Boundary in the Bay of Bengal (Bangladesh/Myanmar)*, 2012 ITLOS Reports 4, para 235.

[198] Ibid, para 289. At para 325 the Chamber determined that there were no reasons to depart from the equidistance methodology.

[199] Section 8(1) of the Maritime Zones Act 15 of 1994 provides that the continental shelf as defined in article 76 of the UNCLOS 'shall be the continental shelf of the Republic'.

[200] In introducing this legislation in Parliament the Minister of Transport acknowledged that these limits might be subject to international objections. These limits, which he stressed were 'provisional', had been maximised 'in order to avoid any extensions to them being subject to negotiation with the international seabed authority after the Convention comes into force' (*Debates of the National Assembly* col 3768 (28 October 1994)).

[201] Doc CLCS.31.2009.LOS (Continental Shelf Notification) of 5 May 2009.

[202] Section 1(lii) of Act 18 of 1998.

resources, in respect of the sedentary species of the continental shelf.[203]

Figure 3: Delimitation of continental shelf (Netherlands and Denmark v West Germany)

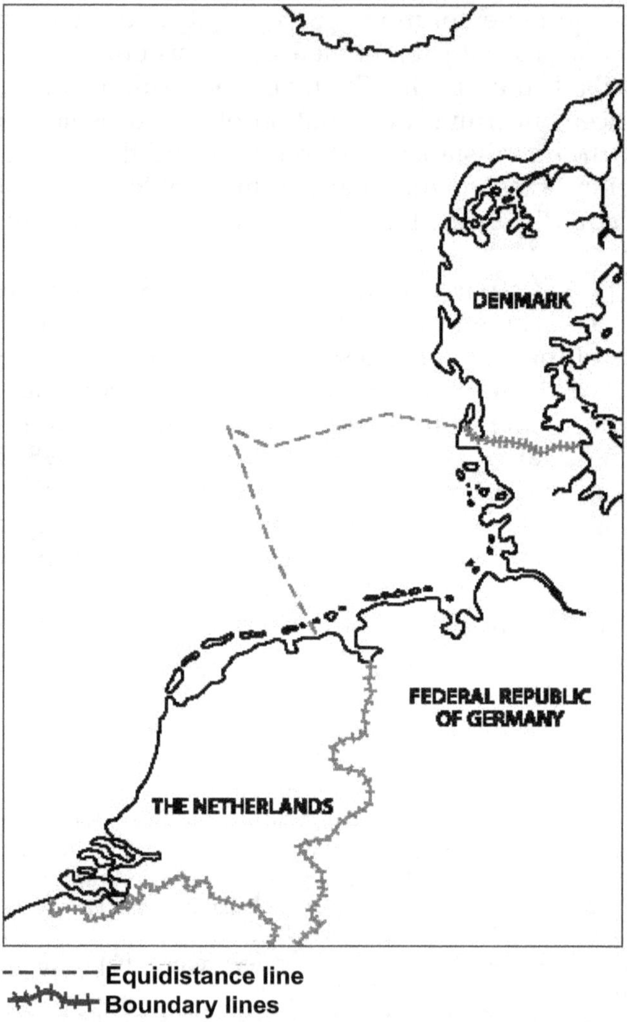

The UNCLOS authorises the coastal state to construct and use installations on the continental shelf for the purpose of exercising its

[203] Section 1(liv) of Act 18 of 1998 defines 'South African waters', in respect of which the Act is to apply, to include the continental shelf in relation to sedentary species. Cf *De Beers Marine (Pty) Ltd v Commissioner SARS* 2002 (5) SA 136 (SCA) (noted by Vrancken (n 32) 305) which dealt with the application of the Customs and Exercise Act 91 of 1964 to activities above the continental shelf. See further, Vrancken (n 1) 176–7.

rights on the shelf.[204] The Maritime Zones Act provides for the application of South African law in respect of such installations.[205]

8 The deep seabed

Technological developments in deep-sea mining after 1960 led to a new interest in the exploitation of the mineral resources of the deep seabed. The question of who might claim title to the deposits of manganese, nickel, copper, and cobalt on the deep ocean floor beyond the continental margin was the most controversial issue before UNCLOS III. The industrialised First World states, with the technical ability to mine the deep seabed, viewed deep seabed mining as a lawful exercise of the freedom of the high seas; while Third World states saw the resources of the deep seabed as the common heritage of mankind which were to be managed by an international body for the benefit of developing nations.

In 1969, before the start of UNCLOS III, Third World states, known as the Group of 77, succeeded in securing the adoption by the General Assembly of a resolution placing a moratorium on the exploitation of the deep seabed pending the establishment of an international regime.[206] In the following year the General Assembly adopted the Declaration of Principles Governing the Seabed and the Ocean Floor, and the Subsoil thereof, beyond the Limits of National Jurisdiction,[207] which declared that the deep seabed (described as 'the Area') and its resources were 'the common heritage of mankind' and not subject to appropriation by any state.

The principles proclaimed in the 1970 Declaration were approved by UNCLOS III and are repeated in Part XI of the UNCLOS. 'The Area' and its resources are to be 'the common heritage of mankind'.[208] 'All rights in the resources of the Area are vested in mankind as a whole.'[209] Resources, however, are defined narrowly as 'solid, liquid or gaseous mineral resources' on or beneath the seabed.[210] This definition has resulted in a heated academic and diplomatic debate about the status of marine biological resources on the seabed.[211] For

[204] UNCLOS, article 80.

[205] Section 9 of Act 15 of 1994.

[206] Resolution 2574 (XXIV), adopted by 62 votes to 28 with 28 abstentions.

[207] Resolution 2749 (XXV), adopted by 108 votes to nil with 14 abstentions; (1971) 10 *ILM* 220.

[208] UNCLOS, article 136.

[209] UNCLOS, article 137(2).

[210] UNCLOS, article 133(a)

[211] For a description of the debate see P Drankier et al 'Marine genetic resources in areas beyond national jurisdiction: Access and benefit sharing' (2012) 27 *International Journal of Marine & Coastal Law* 375; V Germani and C Salpin 'The status of high seas biodiversity in international policy and law' in P Jacquet, RK Pachauri and L Tubiana

some states, this means that Part XI does not apply to biological or living resources. For other states, notably the G77, Part XI, or at least the common heritage of mankind principle, applies to all the resources on the seabed.

The 'common heritage of mankind' principle is said to be composed of several elements, namely that the area is subject to 'non-appropriation', should be under common management, there should be a sharing of benefits from the exploitation of the resources of the area and finally, that the area should be preserved for posterity or future generations.[212] The constituent elements of common heritage of mankind can be seen in the various provisions of UNCLOS. For example, the UNCLOS provides that '[n]o state shall claim or exercise sovereignty or sovereign rights over any part of the Area or its resources, nor shall any state or natural or juridical person appropriate any part thereof. No such claim or exercise of sovereignty or sovereign rights nor such appropriation shall be recognized'.[213] It also provides that '[a]ctivities in the Area shall . . . be carried out for the benefit of mankind as a whole, irrespective of the geographical location of states, whether coastal or land-locked, and taking into particular consideration the interests and needs of developing states'.[214] The legal status of the waters superjacent to the deep seabed and of the airspace above those waters is not affected.[215] They remain free and open to the shipping and aircraft of all nations.

Management of the deep seabed is vested in an International Seabed Authority[216] with headquarters in Jamaica. Its principal

(eds) *Oceans: The New Frontier* (2011) 194; F Millicay 'A legal regime for the biodiversity of the Area' in MH Nordquist, TH Heidar and JN Moore (eds) *Law, Science and Ocean Management* (2007); D Tladi 'Genetic resources, benefit sharing and the law of the sea: The need for clarity' (2007) *Journal of International Maritime Law* 183; D Tladi 'State practice and the making and (re)making of international law: The case of the legal rules relating to marine biodiversity in areas beyond national jurisdiction' (2013) 1 *State Practice and International Law Journal* 97.

[212] D Tladi 'Pursuing a brave new world for the oceans: The place of common heritage in a proposed law of the sea treaty' in T Maluwa, M du Plessis and D Tladi (eds) *The Pursuit of a Brave New World in International Law: Essays in Honour of John Dugard* (2017), 104–8. See also JE Noyes 'The common heritage of mankind: Past, present and future' (2011–12) 40 *Denver Journal of International Law* 447; A Kiss 'The common heritage of mankind: Utopia or reality' (1985) 40 *International Journal* 423, at 423–24; H Singh Rana 'The "common heritage of mankind" and the final frontier: Revaluation of values constituting the international legal regime for outer space activities' (1994) 26 *Rutgers Law Journal* 225 at 231.

[213] UNCLOS, article 137(1).

[214] UNCLOS, article 140.

[215] UNCLOS, article 135.

[216] UNCLOS, articles 156–91.

organs are an Assembly, consisting of the representatives of all states parties, which takes decisions on questions of substance by a two-thirds majority, and a Council, composed of 36 members elected by the Assembly for a four-year term, which takes decisions by either a two-thirds or three-quarters majority, depending on the subject. South Africa has consistently been a member of the Council. The Authority acting through the Assembly and Council may provide for the equitable sharing of benefits derived from activities in the Area.

The operational arm of the Authority, the Enterprise, which is yet to be established, may engage in prospecting and mining, as well as in transporting, processing, and marketing the minerals recovered from the Area.[217] In order to make the Enterprise viable, developed states are expected to transfer technology to it.

The Area is to be exploited by a system of 'parallel access'.[218] A signatory state or commercial operator with the nationality of a signatory state may apply to mine a particular area of the deep seabed. It must specify two sites of substantially the same commercial value in its application. It will be permitted to mine one site, subject to the control of the Authority, while the Enterprise will mine the other 'reserved site'. Contractors will be required to pay licence fees and a percentage of their profits to the Authority. These amounts together with the proceeds from the Enterprise's mining activities will be shared among the developing nations.

Dissatisfaction with the provisions for the management of the deep seabed led to the refusal of the United States to sign the UNCLOS.[219] Other developed states withheld ratification for the same reason. In 1994, the New York Agreement Relating to the Implementation of Part XI of the United Nations Convention on the Law of the Sea[220] was approved within the framework of the United Nations in order to make the UNCLOS acceptable to developed states. The 1994 Agreement, which is to be read with Part XI of the UNCLOS and is to prevail in the event of inconsistency between the two instruments,[221] gives developed states greater powers in the decision-making pro-

[217] UNCLOS, articles 153 and 170.

[218] UNCLOS, article 153. For an account of the highly complicated system of exploitation, provided for both in the UNCLOS and its annexures, see Churchill and Lowe (n 1). See, further, LH van Meurs 'Legal aspects of seabed mining within and beyond areas of national jurisdiction' (1986) 3 *Sea Changes* 79; T Dibb 'Exploitation of the deep seabed: Do land-locked states and the Third World get a look in?' (1987) 6 *Sea Changes* 52.

[219] The reasons advanced by the United States appear in 'Statement by expert panel: Deep seabed mining and the 1982 Convention on the Law of the Sea' (1988) 82 *AJIL* 363.

[220] (1994) 33 *ILM* 1309. Discussed in Oxman (n 14) 687.

[221] Article 2 of the 1994 Agreement.

cesses of the International Seabed Authority.[222] It obliges the Enterprise to conduct its initial deep seabed operations through joint ventures with national undertakings and to act in accordance with 'sound commercial principles'.[223] The 1994 Agreement also provides for the transfer of technology from developed states to the Enterprise on fair and reasonable commercial terms,[224] and requires the Authority to act in accordance with the principle of cost effectiveness.[225] These changes to Part XI of the UNCLOS have had the desired effect and most developed states are today parties to the UNCLOS and the 1994 Agreement.

Little progress has been made in the exploitation of the deep seabed as a result of the decline in the market price of deep seabed minerals and the high cost of underwater mining. The Authority has also made little progress. It has adopted several regulations on the prospecting for and exploration of mineral resources.[226] To date the International Seabed Authority has entered into exploration contracts with 20 contractors, but has not yet entered into any contracts for the actual exploitation of the resources.

In the absence of the Enterprise the Authority is responsible for the exploitation of 'reserved sites' (described above) in association with developing states. Pursuant to this option two developing states in the Pacific Ocean, Nauru and Tonga, made a proposal to exploit reserved areas as the sponsoring states of commercial entities and requested the Authority to seek an advisory opinion from the Seabed Disputes Chamber on the extent of the liability of states sponsoring seabed mining by commercial entities. In its advisory opinion,[227] the Seabed Disputes Chamber held that, while such states did not have strict liability for the activities of sponsored commercial entities, they had an obligation of due diligence, including respect for the precautionary principle and best environmental practices. The Chamber held that there was no distinction in this respect between the obligation of developed and developing nations. To decide otherwise would be to encourage exploitation of the reserved areas by 'States of

[222] Annex to the 1994 Agreement, s 3.

[223] Ibid s 2.

[224] Ibid s 5.

[225] Ibid s 1.

[226] See Regulations on Prospecting and Exploration for Cobalt-rich Ferromanganese Crusts in the Area, 2012 (ISBA/18/A/11); Regulations on Prospecting and Exploration for Polymetallic Sulphides in the Area, 2010 (ISBA/16/A/12); Regulations on the Prospecting and Exploration for Polymetallic Nodules in the Area, 2013 (ISBA/19/C/17).

[227] *Responsibilities and Obligations of States Sponsoring Persons and Entities with Respect to Activities in the Area,* Advisory Opinion, 2011 *ITLOS Reports* 10.

Convenience' and jeopardise the application of the highest standards of protection.

THE MARINE ENVIRONMENT

1 General

The UNCLOS contains many provisions concerning the protection of the marine environment.[228] Different rules apply in different zones. In the territorial sea, because the coastal zone has sovereignty, its domestic environmental protection rules apply. In the EEZ the UNCLOS is obliged to adopt measures for the protection and preservation of the marine environment.[229] With respect to the high seas, the UNCLOS contains a detailed framework for the protection of the marine environment, including limitations on the right to fish,[230] the duty to adopt measures applicable to its nationals relating to the conservation of marine living resources,[231] and the duty on states to conserve marine living resources.[232] Similarly, with respect to the Area, the Convention provides a duty for the protection of the environment in the course of mining activities.[233]

Over and above the maritime zone specific provisions, the UNCLOS contains a part dedicated to the protection and preservation of the marine environment which applies generally across the various maritime zones.[234] The general obligation in Part XII is that 'States have the obligation to protect and preserve the marine environment.'[235] The basic principle in the environmental provisions concerns 'co-operation' for the conservation of the marine environment.[236] The UNCLOS also contains provisions on the duty

[228] See for discussion R Churchill 'The UNCLOS regime for protection of the marine environment—fit for the twenty-first century?' in R Rayfuse (ed) *Research Handbook on International Marine Environmental Law* (2015).

[229] UNCLOS, articles 56, 61 and 62. See also *Advisory Opinion Submitted by SRFC* (n 96) para 96.

[230] UNCLOS, article 116.

[231] UNCLOS, article 117.

[232] UNCLOS, articles 118, 119 and 120.

[233] UNCLOS, article 145. This duty is further elaborated upon in the respective regulations adopted by the International Seabed Authority. See the Regulations (n 226). See for discussion M Lodge 'Protecting the marine environment of the deep seabed' in Rayfuse (n 228).

[234] Part XII of the UNCLOS contains 45 articles.

[235] UNCLOS, article 192.

[236] See, eg UNCLOS, articles 194 and 197.

to conduct impact assessment of planned activities.[237] Part XII has particularly detailed provisions on pollution.[238]

2 Pollution

The ecological damage caused by oil spillage has become a major concern of international law. Both the 1958 Convention on the High Seas,[239] and the 1982 UNCLOS, direct states to take steps to prevent pollution of the seas. The UNCLOS obliges states to ensure that their own ships do not engage in pollution activities and permits them to exercise jurisdiction over foreign ships responsible for pollution in their territorial sea and EEZ.[240]

Other multilateral conventions, to which South Africa is a party, provide for more effective means of combating marine pollution.

(i) The International Convention for the Prevention of Pollution from Ships of 1973 and its 1978 Protocol seek to control and prevent the operational discharge of oil and other hazardous substances from ships. The treaty and its Protocol are incorporated into municipal law by the Marine Pollution (Prevention of Pollution from Ships) Act 2 of 1986.[241]

(ii) The International Convention relating to Intervention on the High Seas in Cases of Oil Pollution Casualties was adopted in 1969 as a result of the *Torrey Canyon* incident, in which a Liberian supertanker negligently became stranded off the Cornwall coast and the United Kingdom bombed the tanker in order to minimise the damage to the coast. Article 1 permits parties to the Convention to take measures on the high seas to prevent or eliminate grave dangers to their coastline from pollution of the sea by oil following upon a maritime casualty. The Convention was incorporated into South African law in 1987.[242] Both the

[237] UNCLOS, article 206: 'When States have reasonable grounds for believing that planned activities under their jurisdiction or control may cause substantial pollution of or significant and harmful changes to the marine environment, they shall, as far as practicable, assess the potential effects of such activities on the marine environment and shall communicate reports of such assessments . . .'. See also R Warner 'Environmental assessment in marine areas beyond national jurisdiction' in Rayfuse (n 228).

[238] UNCLOS, articles 194–7.

[239] UNCLOS, article 24.

[240] UNCLOS, articles 207–22.

[241] The Convention and the Protocol appear in the Schedule to the Act.

[242] By the Marine Pollution (Intervention) Act 64 of 1987. The Convention is set out in the Schedule. See DJ Devine 'Towards an effective implementation of the Intervention Convention in South Africa' (1988) 8 *Sea Changes* 56.

Convention and the South African incorporating statute have been extended to cover substances other than oil.[243]

(iii) The International Convention on Civil Liability for Oil Pollution Damage of 1969[244] imposes strict liability on the owner of any oil tanker registered under the law of a contracting party in respect of pollution damage in the territory or territorial sea of a contracting party. Effect is given to some of the provisions of this treaty by the Marine Pollution (Control and Civil Liability) Act 6 of 1981,[245] which imposes civil and criminal liability on the master of a tanker responsible for the discharge of oil in South Africa's EEZ.

(iv) The Convention on the Prevention of Marine Pollution by Dumping of Wastes and other Matter of 1972,[246] implemented by the National Environmental Management: Integrated Coastal Management Act 24 of 2008, makes it an offence for any person to dump waste at sea.[247]

The Maritime Zones Act contains a general clause authorising action to protect the South African coastline from pollution. It provides that:

> The Republic may, in any area of the sea or the airspace above the sea, take such measures as are necessary against any vessel or aircraft in order to protect the coastline of the Republic or related interests including fishing, from pollution or any threat of pollution resulting from maritime casualty or an act or omission relating to such casualty and which may reasonably be expected to result in major harmful consequences.[248]

3 Conservation and sustainable use of marine biodiversity in areas beyond national jurisdiction

Within areas of national jurisdiction—the territorial sea, EEZ and the continental shelf—the coastal state adopts the rules to protect the marine environment. But there is no mechanism for the establishment of rules for the protection of the environment in areas beyond national jurisdiction. Of course, in respect of the Area, the International Seabed Authority has the mandate to adopt rules, but this is limited to the context of seabed mining. States can also adopt, collectively or unilaterally, measures to be applied to their nationals

[243] Section 5 of Act 64 of 1987, as amended by s 56 of the Shipping General Amendment Act 23 of 1997, gives effect to the Protocol relating to Intervention on the High Seas in Cases of Marine Pollution by Substances other than Oil of 1973.

[244] (1970) 9 *ILM* 45.

[245] See further on this Act, A Stewart 'Civil liability for pollution damage caused by the discharge of oil from vessels—Some aspects of international South African law' (1986) 4 *Sea Changes* 106; DJ Devine 'Statutory offences committed at sea' 1990 *De Rebus* 65.

[246] (1972) 11 *ILM* 1291.

[247] Act 24 of 2008, ss 70 and 79.

[248] Section 10.

or vessels flying their flag. However, such measure cannot apply to non-nationals and are thus ineffective. The governance framework for the protection of the marine environment in areas beyond national jurisdiction has therefore come under severe strain.[249]

The weak governance framework for the protection of the environment in areas beyond national jurisdiction, together with dispute concerning the rules applicable to biological resources on the deep seabed, has prompted an alliance of civil society organisations and some states, including South Africa, to call for a new Implementing Agreement under the UNCLOS for conservation and sustainable use of marine biological diversity in areas beyond national jurisdiction.[250] As a result, the United National Assembly adopted a resolution in 2017 to convene an intergovernmental conference to elaborate an 'international legally binding instrument under the United Convention on the Law of the Sea on the conservation and sustainable use of marine biological diversity in areas beyond national jurisdiction'.[251]

SETTLEMENT OF DISPUTES[252]

The UNCLOS obliges states parties to settle disputes relating to the interpretation or application of the Convention by peaceful means.[253] Where either negotiation or conciliation have failed, states are required to resort to judicial settlement.[254] States have a choice of forum: the International Tribunal for the Law of the Sea (ITLOS) situated in Hamburg (established in 1996); the International Court of Justice; or an arbitral tribunal constituted in terms of Annexes to the UNCLOS.[255] Such a choice is made by a state when it signs or ratifies

[249] KM Gjerde and A Rulska-Domino 'Marine protected areas beyond national jurisdiction: Some practical perspectives for moving ahead' (2012) 27 *International Journal of Marine & Coastal Law* 351. D Tladi 'Conservation and sustainable use of marine biodiversity in areas beyond national jurisdiction: Towards an implementing agreement' in Rayfuse (n 228) 264.

[250] Ibid.

[251] UNGA Res/72/249 of 24 December 2017. See for a discussion of the process and substance, D Tladi 'The proposed implementing agreement: Options for coherence and consistency in the establishment of protected areas beyond national jurisdiction' (2015) 30 *International Journal of Marine & Coastal Law* 654. See also D Tladi 'The common heritage of mankind and the proposed treaty on biodiversity in areas beyond national jurisdiction: The choice between pragmatism and sustainability' (2015) 25 *Yearbook of International Environmental Law* 113.

[252] See DB Hamman 'Implications of ratification of the Law of the Sea Convention for South Africa: Settlement of disputes' (1997) 22 *SAYIL* 1.

[253] UNCLOS, article 279.

[254] UNCLOS, article 287.

[255] See, for example the *Guyana v Suriname* Arbitration Tribunal established under Annex VII: (2008) 102 *AJIL* 119.

the UNCLOS. A special tribunal is also established for disputes relating to the deep seabed: The Seabed Disputes Chamber,[256] which rendered its first advisory opinion in 2011.[257] Subsequently, the Tribunal rendered another important advisory opinion concerning Illegal, Unreported and Unregulated Fishing.[258] Although states may exclude certain disputes from judicial settlement,[259] the UNCLOS goes a long way towards providing for the compulsory settlement of disputes by judicial means.

ITLOS has given judgment in a number of important cases, chief of which is *The M/V 'Saiga', Saint Vincent and the Grenadines v Guinea*[260] in which it dealt with matters such as hot pursuit, 'genuine link', the use of force on the high seas and the protection of ships' crews. In other disputes relating to the law of the sea states have preferred to have recourse to an arbitral tribunal.[261] ITLOS has also given important decisions concerning the delimitation of maritime boundaries.[262]

In 2005 a South African, Albert Hoffmann, was elected as a judge of the International Tribunal for the Law of the Sea.

South Africa has yet to make its choice of forum. When it ratified the UNCLOS in 1997 it declared that it would make such a choice 'at the appropriate time'.

There are a number of issues affecting South Africa that may give rise to disputes. These include South Africa's maritime boundaries with Namibia[263] and Mozambique[264] and the transit rights of land-locked states to the sea. There is no longer any dispute between South Africa and France over the delimitation of the continental shelf between the Prince Edward Islands and the French Crozet Islands.[265]

[256] UNCLOS, article 187.

[257] *Responsibilities and Obligations of Sponsoring States Advisory Opinion* (n 227).

[258] *Advisory Opinion Submitted by SRFC* (n 96),

[259] UNCLOS, articles 299 and 298.

[260] (1999) 38 *ILM* 1323. See, further, G Eiriksson *The International Tribunal for the Law of the Sea* (2000); D Anderson 'The International Tribunal for the Law of the Sea' in M Evans (ed) *Remedies in International Law* (1998).

[261] *The Mox Plant Case (Ireland v UK)* (2002) 41 *ILM* 405; R Churchill and J Scott 'The Mox plant litigation: The first half life' (2004) 53 *ICLQ* 643.

[262] See, eg *Ghana/Côte d'Ivoire* (n 196) and *Bangladesh/Myanmar* (197).

[263] See DB Hamman 'The single maritime boundary—A solution for the maritime delimitation between South Africa and Namibia?' (1995) 10 *International Journal of Marine & Coastal Law* 369; Vrancken (n 1) 180–6.

[264] Vrancken (n 1) 187–8.

[265] M Jacobs 'Treaties' (2008) 33 *SAYIL* 301; Vrancken (n 1) 188–9.

CHAPTER 18

Air and Space Law

John Dugard and Rosalind Elphick

AIR LAW[1]

When aerial navigation became possible at the beginning of the century, lawyers inevitably turned to the law of the sea for guidance on the status of airspace. Four theories were advanced on this basis: first, that airspace, like the high seas, was entirely free; secondly, that there was a lower territorial airspace to which the subjacent state had exclusive rights and a higher zone which was open to all aircraft; thirdly, that the airspace above a state fell within its exclusive sovereignty, subject to a right of innocent passage for foreign civil aircraft; and, fourthly, that a state enjoyed complete sovereignty over the airspace above its land and territorial sea. From the outset it was accepted that the airspace above the high seas was not subject to any state's sovereignty.

World War I brought home to states the importance of control of the skies for military purposes.[2] It was not surprising therefore that the Convention Relating to the Regulation of Aerial Navigation (Paris Convention of 1919)[3] proclaimed that 'every state has complete and exclusive sovereignty over the airspace above its territory'. The International Court of Justice in 1986 confirmed this principle in *Nicaragua v United States* when it stated '[t]he principle of respect for territorial sovereignty is also directly infringed by the unauthorized overflight of a state's territory by aircraft belonging to or under the control of the government of another state'.[4]

[1] IH Diederiks-Verschoor and P Mendes de Leon *An Introduction to Air Law* 9 ed (2012); MS Slabbert 'Aviation and air transport' in WA Joubert (ed) *LAWSA* vol 2 part I 2 ed (2003) 3; PPC Haanappel *The Law and Policy of Air, Space and Outer Space* (2003); PS Dempsey *Public International Air Law* (2008); BF Havel and GS Sanchez *The Principles and Practice of International Aviation Law* (2014); M Milde *International Air Law and ICAO* (2016); R Abeyratne *Convention on International Civil Aviation: A Commentary* (2014).

[2] SJ Fox 'The evolution of aviation in times of war and peace: Blood, tears and salvation' (2014) 31 *International Journal on World Peace* 49.

[3] This convention was incorporated into South African law by the Aviation Act 16 of 1923. On the genesis of the Paris Convention of 1919, see A Dobson *A History of International Civil Aviation* (2017) 1–16.

[4] *Case Concerning Military and Paramilitary Activities in and against Nicaragua (Nicaragua v USA)* 1986 ICJ Reports 14, 128.

Modern air law is largely governed by a number of conventions adopted in Chicago in 1944. The Chicago Convention on International Civil Aviation (Chicago Convention), to which South Africa is a party and which is incorporated into municipal law by the Civil Aviation Act 13 of 2009,[5] lays down the following guiding principles:

(1) Every state has complete and exclusive sovereignty over the airspace above its land areas and territorial waters.[6]

(2) No aircraft on a scheduled flight, ie one that operates according to a published timetable,[7] may overfly another state's territory without special permission.[8]

(3) Aircraft not engaged in scheduled international air service may overfly or land in the territory of another state without permission, subject to the right of the state flown over to require landing, and subject further to the right of the state, for reasons of safety, to require aircraft flying over regions that are inaccessible or without adequate air navigation facilities, to follow prescribed routes or to obtain special permission.[9] If such a non-scheduled flight is engaged in the carriage of passengers, cargo, or mail for reward, the territorial state may impose such conditions as it considers desirable.[10]

(4) Aircraft have the nationality of the state in which they are registered.[11]

Two further treaties were adopted in Chicago in 1944. The International Air Services Transit Agreement, generally known as the 'Two Freedoms Agreement', grants scheduled flights of contracting states (1) the privilege to fly across the territory of another contracting state without landing and (2) the privilege to land for non-traffic purposes (for refuelling and repairs). South Africa is a party to this treaty and has incorporated it into municipal law.[12] The International

[5] It was initially incorporated by the Aviation Amendment Act 42 of 1947, s 1. The text of the Chicago Convention appears in the Third Schedule to Act 13 of 2009.

[6] Chicago Convention (n 5) articles 1 and 2.

[7] According to Slabbert (n 1) para 33: 'The distinction between a scheduled and non-scheduled service is generally similar to that between a regular bus service working to a schedule of times and routes and a taxi plying for ad hoc hire.'

[8] Chicago Convention (n 5) article 6.

[9] Ibid, article 5.

[10] The granting of such permission is regulated in South Africa by the International Air Services Act 60 of 1993. See, further, on the operation of this Act: *Millionair Charter (Pty) Ltd v Chairman, International Air Services Council* [1998] 4 All SA 391 (T).

[11] Chicago Convention (n 5) article 17.

[12] It was initially incorporated by s 2 of the Aviation Amendment Act 41 of 1946. It is now incorporated by the Civil Aviation Act 13 of 2009. The text appears in the Fourth Schedule to this Act.

Air Transport Agreement or 'Five Freedoms Agreement'[13] seeks to add a further three freedoms for scheduled flights to those contained in the 'Two Freedoms Agreement', namely (3) the privilege to put down passengers, mail, or cargo taken on in the territory of the state whose nationality the aircraft possesses; (4) the privilege to take on passengers, mail, and cargo destined for the territory of that state; and (5) the privilege to take on passengers, mail, and cargo destined for the territory of any other contracting state and the privilege to put down passengers, mail, and cargo coming from any such territory. The 'Five Freedoms Agreement' has not been widely ratified and is of little importance today. South Africa is not a party to this Agreement.

In the absence of an accepted multilateral treaty governing scheduled flights, it has been left to states to enter into bilateral treaties providing for the reciprocal operation of scheduled services. Such a bilateral agreement will usually designate a particular airline as the instrument of the state, and determine specific points of departure and arrival, routes, frequency of service, seating, freight-carrying capacity, and tariffs.[14] The regulation of air traffic by bilateral agreement contrasts with the law of the sea, which is regulated by multilateral treaty. The impossibility of examining a multitude of bilateral treaties explains why general international law treatises devote less attention to the law of the air than to the law of the sea.

Two international bodies regulate civil aviation. The International Civil Aviation Organization (ICAO) is a United Nations specialised agency with headquarters in Montreal, which promotes technical and administrative co-operation in the field of civil aviation, including the adoption of safety standards. The International Air Transport Association (IATA) is a non-government organisation comprising most of the airlines and is principally engaged in the setting of fares and tariffs.

In *Welkom Municipality v JP Masureik & HG Herman t/a Lotus Corporation*,[15] the Supreme Court of Appeal (SCA) held that despite the fact that the Chicago Convention of 1944 had been incorporated into municipal law by s 1 of the Aviation Amendment Act 42 of 1947

[13] 171 UNTS 387.

[14] See s 35 of the International Air Services Act 60 of 1993. See, further, Slabbert (n 1) para 70 et seq. For a study on the impact of Bilateral Air Services Agreements in southern Africa, see J Steyn and O Mhlanga 'The impact of international air transport agreements on airline operations in southern Africa' (2016) 5 *African Journal of Hospitality, Tourism and Leisure* 1.

[15] 1997 (3) SA 363 (A) ('*Welkom Municipality v Masureik & Herman*'); overruling *Masureik v Welkom Municipality* 1995 (4) SA 745 (O). See the comment on these cases by N Botha 'Municipal application of annex 14 to the Chicago Convention: The role of recommended international practices and procedures in South African municipal law' (1997) 22 *SAYIL* 112.

(and now the Civil Aviation Act 13 of 2009), recommendations made pursuant to the Convention by ICAO, of which South Africa is a member, 'are not automatically, and without more, invested with the status of a municipal law binding upon the citizenry of South Africa'.[16] The Court added that '[a]part from the fact that they are no more than recommendations, the Convention itself does not impose upon parties to it an absolute obligation to implement them'.[17] Consequently, the SCA upheld an appeal against a judgment holding that the appellant, Welkom Aerodrome, was negligent by reason of its failure to comply with ICAO recommendations on the width of runways of an airport.

The Warsaw Convention for the Unification of Certain Rules Relating to International Carriage by Air of 1929 and its Protocols lay down uniform rules governing the liability of the carrier where damage is sustained to passengers, baggage, and goods during international carriage. Its provisions fall largely within the field of private international law and fall outside the scope of this chapter. The Carriage by Air Act 17 of 1946 incorporates the Warsaw Convention and its Protocols into South African law.[18]

The multilateral treaties dealing with the safety of civil aviation and the prosecution of hijackers are examined in Chapter 9.

1 Distress

Customary international law recognises that a coastal state has no jurisdiction over persons on board a foreign vessel forced to put into port in distress, and scholars have suggested that the same principle should apply to aircraft forced to land in distress.[19] Perhaps the only clear support for this suggestion comes from South Africa. In *Nkondo v Minister of Police*,[20] the Court was called on to decide whether it had jurisdiction to try a member of the ANC military wing whose flight from Mozambique to Lesotho had been forced by adverse weather conditions to land in Bloemfontein. In upholding the applicability of the maritime distress rule to aircraft, Smuts J stated:

> In view of the established law in regard to the rights of ships in distress to enter a port, there appears to be no reason why aircraft in distress should not also enjoy the privileges accorded to ships in distress and it must be accepted

[16] *Welkom Municipality v Masureik & Herman* (n 15) 371.

[17] Ibid.

[18] As amended by the Carriage by Air Amendment Act 15 of 2006. See further on this subject, Slabbert (n 1) 123 et seq. On the subject of aviation insurance, see K Posner, P Chrystal and T Marland *Margo on Aviation Insurance* 4 ed (2014).

[19] B Cheng *The Law of International Air Transport* (1962) 349–51; DP O'Connell *International Law* vol 2 2 ed (1970) 627–9.

[20] 1980 (2) SA 894 (O).

> that international law accords aircraft of one country the right, when in distress, to land on the territory of another country and that as a general rule such aircraft and their occupants may not be subjected to penalties or to unnecessary detention by the territorial sovereign for entering under such circumstances.[21]

Smuts J was not prepared to apply this general principle to a person suspected of crimes against the security of the state in which the aircraft was forced to land and held that Nkondo might be tried under the security laws. The executive proved to be more sensitive (probably realising the advantages attached to such a rule for its own members) and ordered the release of Nkondo and his return to Lesotho.[22]

The South African Maritime and Aeronautical Search and Rescue Act 44 of 2002 incorporates the International Convention on Maritime Search and Rescue of 1979 and Annexure 12 to the Chicago Convention of 1944 into South African law. The Act creates a South African Search and Rescue Organization (SASAR) which is charged with the task of carrying out rescue operations for survivors of aircraft crashes or forced landings, the crew and passengers of vessels in distress and the survivors of any military aircraft or vessel accident if such aircraft or vessel is not engaged in an act of war.[23]

2 Aerial intrusion

Although a state may use force against an unauthorised *military* aircraft in its airspace in the exercise of the right of self-defence, it is not permitted to take such action against trespassing *civilian* aircraft. The shooting down by Soviet jets in 1983 of a Korean Airlines aircraft (Flight 007) which had strayed over militarily sensitive Soviet airspace[24] prompted an amendment to the Chicago Convention. Article 3*bis*, inserted in 1984, provides that, while 'every State, in the exercise of its sovereignty, is entitled to require the landing at some designated airport of a civil aircraft flying above its territory without authority', states 'must refrain from resorting to the use of weapons against civil aircraft in flight and that, in case of interception, the lives of persons on board and the safety of aircraft must not be endangered'.

[21] *Nkondo* (n 20) 900D–E.

[22] See J Dugard 'Jurisdiction over persons on board an aircraft landing in distress' (1981) 30 *ICLQ* 902.

[23] Section 6 of the Aeronautical Search and Rescue Act.

[24] See MN Leich 'Destruction of Korean airliner: Action by international organizations' (1984) 78 *AJIL* 244; F Hassan 'The shooting down of Korean Airlines Flight 007 by the USSR and the future of air safety for passengers' (1984) 33 *ICLQ* 712.

3 Drones[25]

The use of drones/Unmanned Aerial Vehicles (UAVs) by both states and private individuals has become increasingly common. The development of a regulatory framework to govern their nature and use, however, has lagged behind advances in technology. To date there is no international convention governing the use of drones. Whereas the Chicago Convention does apply to 'unmanned aircraft', its application is limited to 'pre-programmed' drones. As such, remotely operated drones—which most are—fall outside the purview of the convention. This problem is not unique to air law. The Special Rapporteur on extrajudicial, summary or arbitrary executions, Christof Heyns, has commented that there is a 'notable lack of consensus on how to apply the rules of international law that regulate the use of force to drones, the fact that drones are now an established technology notwithstanding'.[26]

South Africa is one of the world's first countries to regulate the use of drones. In 2015, it amended the South African Civil Aviation Regulations, adopted in terms of the Civil Aviation Act, to create a comprehensive set of rules governing the use of 'autonomous unmanned aircraft'.[27]

4 Air defence identification zones

An air defence identification zone (ADIZ) is an area of airspace beyond a country's sovereign territory within which the country requires the identification, location, and air traffic control of aircraft in the interest of its national security. There is no international law that specifically governs ADIZs, although various norms are relevant, such as freedom of navigation.[28] The Convention on Civil Aviation also pertains to ADIZs insofar as it directs that all nations must refrain from using weapons against civilian aircraft. The United States established the world's first ADIZ in 1950, during the Cold War with the Soviet Union.[29] The practice has since become contested, given that the extent to which states can impose reporting obligations on aircraft operating outside of their territorial airspace is as yet not defined under international air law. In one particularly

[25] BI Scott *The Law of Unmanned Aircraft Systems: An Introduction to the Current and Future Regulation under National, Regional and International Law* (2016).

[26] Report of the Special Rapporteur on Extrajudicial, Summary or Arbitrary Executions UN Doc A/68/382 (13 September 2013) para 13.

[27] GN 444 *GG* 38830 of 27 May 2015.

[28] CK Lamont 'Conflict in the skies: The law of air defence identification zones' (2014) 39 *Air and Space Law* 187.

[29] IE Rinehart and B Elias *China's Air Defense Identification Zone* Congressional Research Service (2015) 2.

controversial recent incident, on 23 November 2013, China declared an ADIZ over the East China Sea.[30]

OUTER SPACE [31]

Sovereignty over the airspace of a state was accepted as extending for an unlimited distance in accordance with the private law principle *cuius est solum eius est usque ad caelum*. However, when the first satellite—Sputnik—was launched into outer space in 1957, it became clear that this principle could no longer apply. Since then several unanimously adopted General Assembly resolutions[32] (accepted immediately as customary law[33]) and multilateral treaties have expounded a coherent legal regime for outer space. The most important of these is the Treaty on Principles Governing the Activities of States in the Exploration and Use of Outer Space, including the Moon and Other Celestial Bodies of 1967,[34] which proclaims the following principles:

(1) Outer space (which includes the moon and other celestial bodies) is to be free for exploration and use by all states without discrimination (article 1).
(2) Outer space is 'not subject to national appropriation by claim of sovereignty, by means of use or occupation, or by other means' (article 2).[35]
(3) Activities in the exploration and use of outer space are to be conducted in accordance with international law (article 3).
(4) States are not to place in orbit any objects carrying nuclear weapons and no military bases may be established or weapons tested on any celestial body (article 4).
(5) Astronauts are to be treated as 'envoys of mankind in outer space' and are to be given all possible assistance both in outer space and on earth (in the event of 'accident, distress or emergency landing') (article 5). The 1968 Agreement on the

[30] Rinehart and Elias (n 29) 6–7.

[31] C Christol *Space Law* (1991); CJ Cheng (ed) *The Use of Airspace and Outer Space for All Mankind in the 21st Century* (1995); IH Diederiks-Verschoor and V Kopal *An Introduction to Space Law* 3 ed (2008); F von der Dunk and F Tronchetti (eds) *Handbook of Space Law* (2015).

[32] Particularly Resolutions 1721(XVI), 1884 (XVIII) and 1962 (XVIII).

[33] See above, Chapter 3. See further, MP Scharf *Customary International Law in Time of Fundamental Change: Recognizing Grotian Moments* (2013) 136–7.

[34] 610 UNTS 205.

[35] The Agreement Governing the Activities of States on the Moon and other Celestial Bodies (1979) 18 *ILM* 1434 seeks to declare the moon 'the common heritage of mankind' with an international regime similar to that envisaged for the deep seabed. Only a small number of states have signed it. None of the Security Council permanent members has done so.

Rescue of Astronauts, the Return of Astronauts and the Return of Objects Launched into Outer Space supplements this provision.[36]

(6) States are responsible for their national activities in outer space[37] and are liable for damage caused to other states by any object launched into outer space (articles 6 and 7). The Convention on International Liability for Damage Caused by Space Objects of 1972 confirms this principle.[38]

The treaty does not attempt to define the point at which the earth's atmosphere, and hence airspace, ends and outer space begins.[39]

South Africa is a party to the 1967 Treaty on Principles Governing the Activities of States in the Exploration and Use of Outer Space, including the Moon and other Celestial Bodies,[40] the 1968 Agreement on the Rescue of Astronauts, the Return of Astronauts and the Return of Objects Launched into Outer Space,[41] the 1972 Convention on International Liability for Damages Caused by Space Objects[42] and the 1975 Convention on Registration of Objects Launched into Outer Space. South Africa is not a party to the 1979 Agreement Governing Activities of States on the Moon and other Celestial Bodies. In 1993, the Space Affairs Act 84 of 1993 established a South African Council for Space Affairs to promote, manage, and control South Africa's space industry and to ensure that South Africa meets all its international commitments and responsibilities in respect of the peaceful utilisation of outer space 'in order to be recognized as a responsible and trustworthy user of outer space'.[43] The Space Affairs Act defines outer space as 'the space above the surface of the earth from the height at which it is in practice possible to operate an object in an orbit around the earth'.[44]

[36] (1969) 63 *AJIL* 382.

[37] The 1975 Convention on Registration of Objects Launched into Outer Space (1975) 14 *ILM* 43 provides for the identification and registration (in a United Nations registry) of space objects.

[38] (1971) 10 *ILM* 965. Canada invoked this Convention in 1979 when a Soviet satellite powered by a small nuclear reactor broke up over Canada and crashed in its North-West Territories. The Soviet Union agreed to pay compensation of 3 million Canadian dollars. See Canada, Claim Against the USSR for Damage Caused by Soviet Cosmos 954 (1979) 18 *ILM* 899 and Protocol Between the Government of Canada and the Government of the Union of Soviet Socialist Republics (1981) 20 *ILM* 689; CQ Christol 'International liability for damage caused by space objects' (1980) 74 *AJIL* 346.

[39] See, further, on this question R Jennings and A Watts (eds) *Oppenheim's International Law* 9 ed (1992) 839–41.

[40] Ratified on 30 September 1968.

[41] Ratified on 6 October 1969.

[42] Ratified on 14 December 2011.

[43] Space Affairs Act, s 2(1)*(a)*. See, too, s 5(2).

[44] Ibid s 1(xv).

CHAPTER 19

International Environmental Law

John Dugard and Dire Tladi

INTRODUCTION

In April 1986, an explosion occurred at the Chernobyl nuclear power plant near Kiev in the Soviet Union releasing radioactive substances into the atmosphere, which spread as far as Japan and Scandinavia. The Soviet Union took two weeks to acknowledge the disaster. Was this a purely domestic issue or was it governed by international law? Could states affected by the radioactive fall-out bring claims against the Soviet Union? Was the Soviet Union obliged to inform the international community immediately of the disaster?

Questions of this kind can be answered by referring to general principles of international law, particularly those belonging to state responsibility. However, this is not a satisfactory way of dealing with the threats to the land, seas, atmosphere, and life of our planet occasioned by growth in rates of consumption, heavy reliance on fossil fuels, increased urbanisation, modern means of transportation and new technology. Traditional international law, which requires an injured state to prove responsibility for damage caused, may allow a coastal state to recover damages from the owner or flag state of an oil tanker that discharges oil along its coast. Nevertheless, it is inadequate for issues of prevention of harm, particularly of the commons. And, worse still, it fails to deal with damage to the environment caused by pollutants from unidentified sources. The depletion of the ozone by chemical compounds emitted from many states illustrates both the complexity and the gravity of the problem. Threats to our environment, to the very survival of our planet, call for a concerted, co-operative effort which draws on existing rules of treaty and customary international law, but at the same time employs new methods for protecting the environment. This co-operative enterprise is international environment law,[1] a blend of 'hard law' in the form of

[1] M Fitzmaurice and D French *International Environmental Law and Governance* (2015); P-M Dupuy and J Viñuales *International Environmental Law* (2015); A Shawkat et al (eds) *International Environmental Law and the Global South* (2016); P Birnie, A Boyle and C Redgwell *International Law and the Environment* 3 ed (2009); P Sands and J Peel *Principles of International Environmental Law* 3 ed (2012); S Lyster *International Wildlife Law* (1987); J Glazewski *Environmental Law in South Africa* (2000); E Benvenisti *Sharing*

rules of international customary law and treaties, and 'soft law' comprising conference resolutions, guidelines, and programmes of action.

Soft law is to be found in many areas of international law but there is no doubt that it plays a greater role in international environmental law. This is illustrated by the fact that leading instruments setting out fundamental principles of international environmental law are to be found in four soft law sources—the 1972 Stockholm Declaration of the United Nations Conference on the Human Environment (1972 Stockholm Declaration),[2] the 1992 Rio Declaration on Environment and Development (Rio Declaration),[3] the 2002 Declaration of the Johannesburg World Summit on Sustainable Development (Johannesburg Declaration),[4] and the 2012 Rio Plus 20 (The Future We Want). Additionally, instruments such as the Sustainable Development Goals of the United Nations also contain important environmental commitments.[5] All are broadly phrased expositions of principles that avoid employing the language of obligation found in treaties. This is part of a deliberate co-operative strategy. Treaties take long to draft and even longer to ratify. Moreover, there is always the likelihood that the states most likely to cause environmental damage will not ratify the treaty at all. Conference declarations premised on broad consensus rather than consent do not impose obligations on states, but they do reflect a set of principles or standards to guide states, for the violation of which they may be held politically, albeit not legally accountable.

Soft law instruments are not enforceable. But there is little difference in enforceability between Principle 1 of the Stockholm Declaration, which declares:

Transboundary Resources: International Law and Optimal Resource Use (2002); U Beyerlin and T Marauhn *International Environmental Law* (2011); N Schrijver *Development without Destruction: The UN and Global Resource Management* (2010).

[2] (1972) 11 *ILM* 1416.

[3] (1992) 31 *ILM* 874.

[4] Johannesburg Declaration on Sustainable Development (2002) A/CONF.199.L6. See E Bray, D Tladi and I Moodley '2002 World Summit on Sustainable Development—Food and legal thought' (2003) 44 *Codicillus* 10; K Gray 'World Summit on Sustainable Development: Accomplishments and new directions' (2005) 52 *ICLQ* 256.

[5] Transforming Our World: The 2030 Agenda for Sustainable Development, UN Doc A/Res/70/1. See especially Goals 12 (Ensure Sustainable Consumption and Production Patterns), 13 (Take Urgent Action to Combat Climate Change and its Impacts), 14 (Conserve and Sustainably Use the Oceans, Seas and Marine Resources for Sustainable Development) and 15 (Protect, Restore and Promote Sustainable Use of Terrestrial Ecosystems, Sustainably Manage Forests, Combat Desertification, and Halt and Reverse Land Degradation and Halt Biodiversity Loss).

> Man has the fundamental right to freedom, equality and adequate conditions of life, in an environment of a quality that permits a life of dignity and well-being, and he bears a solemn responsibility to protect and improve the environment for present and future generations,

and article 24 of the African Charter on Human and Peoples' Rights which declares, in a legally binding treaty, that:

> All peoples shall have the right to a general, satisfactory environment favourable to their development.

In addition to 'soft law' instruments and the customary international law rules of state responsibility, a growing body of multilateral treaties that seek to protect different features of the environment provide a comprehensive body of law for the protection of the environment. Of the international institutions charged with the task of environmental protection, the most important is the United Nations Environment Programme (UNEP), based in Nairobi, which has done much to develop and promote programmes of action and guidelines.

STATE RESPONSIBILITY AND THE ENVIRONMENT

The Draft Articles on State Responsibility prepared by the International Law Commission (ILC)[6] provide a broad framework for responsibility under international law, which applies to environmental damage caused by an internationally wrongful act. A state commits a wrongful act in terms of these Draft Articles when 'conduct consisting of an action or omission is attributable to the state under international law' and that conduct constitutes a breach of an international obligation of the state.[7] The injured state is entitled to obtain from the state that has committed an internationally wrongful act full reparation in the form of restitution in kind, compensation, satisfaction and assurances and guarantees of non-repetition.[8]

A state commits an internationally wrongful act when it uses, or allows its territory to be used, in such a way as to cause harm or injury to the territory of another state or to persons or property in that state. The leading case on this principle, also known as the *sic utere tuo ut alienum non laedas,* is the *Trail Smelter Arbitration*[9] which concerned a dispute between the United States and Canada over

[6] Report of the International Law Commission *GAOR* 56th Session, Supplement No 10, UN Doc A/56/10. J Crawford *The International Law Commission's Draft Articles on State Responsibility* (2002) ('Draft Articles').

[7] Ibid article 2.

[8] Ibid articles 30, 31, 34–7.

[9] *Trail Smelter Arbitration (United States v Canada)* (1938–1941) 3 *RIAA* 1905.

damage caused to crops in the United States by sulphur dioxide fumes from a smelter in Canada. In holding Canada responsible for the wrongful conduct of the Trail Smelter, the Arbitration Tribunal stated:

> [N]o state has the right to use or permit the use of its territory in such a manner as to cause injury by fumes in or to the territory of another or the properties or persons therein, when the case is of serious consequence and the injury is established by clear and convincing evidence.[10]

This principle is an application of a general principle of international law enunciated by the International Court of Justice in the *Corfu Channel* case.[11] It was reaffirmed by the International Court of Justice in its Advisory Opinion on the *Legality of the Threat or Use of Nuclear Weapons*,[12] when it declared:

> [T]he existence of the general obligation of States to ensure that activities within their jurisdiction and control respect the environment of other States or of areas beyond national control is now part of the corpus of international law relating to the environment.

The principle is found in both the Stockholm Declaration[13] and the Rio Declaration,[14] which recognise the responsibility of states

> to ensure that activities within their jurisdiction or control do not cause damage to the environment of other States or of areas beyond the limits of national jurisdiction.

The 1982 United Nations Convention on the Law of the Sea (UNCLOS) gives treaty force to the principle in article 194, which provides:

> States shall take all measures necessary to ensure that activities under their jurisdiction and control are so conducted as not to cause damage by pollution to other States and their environment.

The obligation imposed upon a state not to engage in activities within its territory that cause harm to other states requires the state to ensure that private persons within its territory act in accordance with this obligation.

The standard of care to be observed by states in activities that may cause environmental harm is, however, unclear. There is some support for strict liability which would make a state liable without fault for damage caused by ultra-hazardous activities within its territory, such as the risk posed by nuclear power plants. For

[10] Trail Smelter (n 9) 1965–6.

[11] See *Corfu Channel Case (Merits)*, 1949 ICJ Reports 4 at 22, where the International Court of Justice declared that a state is obliged 'not to allow knowingly its territory to be used for acts contrary to the rights of other states'.

[12] 1996 ICJ Reports 226 para 29.

[13] Stockholm Declaration (n 2), article 21.

[14] Rio Declaration (n 3), article 2.

instance, the 1972 Convention on International Liability for Damage Caused by Space Objects provides for absolute liability for damage caused by space objects.[15]

The standard of due diligence is, however, more generally accepted than that of strict liability.[16] The UNCLOS, for example, requires states to take

> all measures . . . that are necessary to prevent, reduce and control pollution of the marine environment from any source, using for this purpose the best practicable means at their disposal and in accordance with their capabilities.[17]

Similarly, the Draft Guidelines of the ILC on the Protection of the Atmosphere provides that states 'have the obligation to protect the atmosphere by exercising due diligence . . .'.[18] This standard is, inevitably, flexible and will vary according to the circumstances of the environment-threatening activity in question.

The quantification of damages in respect of environmental harm is not easy. This was emphasised by the United Nations Compensation Commission (UNCC) established in 1991 to consider claims arising out of Iraq's unlawful invasion and occupation of Kuwait. The Panel of Commissioners stressed the 'inherent difficulties in attempting to place a monetary value on damaged natural resources'.[19] The International Court of Justice first considered this matter in 2018 in *Certain Activities Carried Out by Nicaragua in the Border Area (Costa Rica v Nicaragua)*.[20] Here the Court declared that in valuating environmental harm it would make an 'overall assessment' rather than attributing values to specific categories of environmental goods and services, guided in the absence of adequate evidence as to the extent of material damage by equitable considerations and the character of

[15] (1971) 10 *ILM* 965. Canada invoked this Convention in 1979 when a Soviet satellite broke up over Canada and crashed in Canada's North-West Territories. The Soviet Union agreed to pay compensation of 3 million Canadian dollars: Canada, Claim Against the USSR for Damage Caused by Soviet Cosmos 954 (1979) 18 *ILM* 899 and Protocol Between the Government of Canada and the Government of the Union of Soviet Socialist Republics (1981) 20 *ILM* 689.

[16] The principle was approved by the International Court of Justice in the *Case Concerning Pulp Mills on the River Uruguay (Argentina v Uruguay)*, 2010 ICJ Reports 14 paras 187, 197.

[17] United Nations Convention on the Law of the Sea 1833 UNTS 397, article 194(1).

[18] Draft Guideline 3 of the Draft Guidelines on the Protection of the Atmosphere provisionally adopted by the International Law Commission, *Report of the International Law Commission, Sixty-Ninth Session, 2017*, General Assembly Official Records, Supplement No 10, UN Doc A/72/10.

[19] UNCC Governing Council, *Report and Recommendations made by Panel of Commissioners concerning the Fifth Instalment of 'F4' Claims*, UN Doc S/AC.26/2005/10 (30 June 2005) para 81.

[20] 2018 ICJ Reports.

the affected area—an internationally protected wetland[21] Whether the Court succeeded in following this prescription is, however, open to debate as it placed a miniscule monetary compensation on damage to the wetland and refused to have regard to the impact of deforestation on climate change in its quantification of damages.[22]

LIABILITY FOR ACTS NOT PROHIBITED BY INTERNATIONAL LAW

The ILC has for many years been engaged in drafting instruments concerning activities not prohibited by international law, but which involve a risk of causing significant transboundary harm through their physical consequences.[23]

In 2001, the ILC adopted a set of Draft Articles on the Prevention of Transboundary Harm from Hazardous Activities,[24] which deal with risk management, co-operation and consultation by states in respect of activities not prohibited by international law, but which may cause significant transboundary harm. The articles require states to abide by a duty of 'due diligence' in taking preventive or minimising measures. Due diligence, according to the Commentary to the Draft Articles, 'is manifested in reasonable efforts by a State to inform itself of factual and legal components that relate foreseeably to a contemplated procedure and to take appropriate measures in timely fashion, to address them'.[25] Such measures include both formulating policies to prevent significant transboundary harm and implementing those policies.

In 2006, the ILC approved a set of non-binding principles on International Liability for Injurious Consequences Arising out of Acts not Prohibited by International Law (International Liability in Case of Loss from Transboundary Harm Arising out of Hazardous Activities),[26] which aims to ensure 'prompt and adequate compensation to victims of transboundary damage'.[27] Principle 4 requires each state to take all necessary measures to ensure that compensation is available for victims of transboundary damage caused by hazardous

[21] *Costa Rica v Nicaragua* (n 20) paras 78 and 35.

[22] See the dissenting opinion of Judge ad hoc Dugard.

[23] For an account of the early years of this study, see J Barboza 'International liability for injurious consequences of acts not prohibited by international law and the protection of the environment' (1994-III) 247 *Hague Recueil* 291.

[24] Report of the International Law Commission, *GAOR* 56th Session, Supplement No 10 UN Doc A/56/10 370.

[25] Ibid, commentary to article 3, para 10 (393).

[26] Report of International Law Commission, *GAOR* 61st Session, Supplement No 10 UN Doc A/61/10 at 101.

[27] Ibid Principle 3.

activities located within its territory. These measures are to include the imposition of liability upon the person in control of the hazardous activity, in accordance with the 'polluter pays' principle. Such liability does 'not require proof of fault'.[28] Strict liability is justified on the ground that:

> [I]t would be unjust and inappropriate to make the claimant shoulder a heavy burden of proof of fault or negligence in respect of highly complex technological activities whose risks and operation the concerned industry closely guard as secrets.[29]

States should require persons in control of hazardous activities to maintain financial security, such as insurance, to cover claims of compensation.[30] Principle 6 provides that states should provide for appropriate domestic and international procedures to ensure that compensation is paid.

PRINCIPLES OF INTERNATIONAL CO-OPERATION

The general principles of state responsibility provide an inadequate legal system for the enforcement of international standards of environmental protection. Interstate claims premised on wrongful acts, some degree of fault and proof of actual damage are no substitute for environmental regulation. These claims are applicable only when damage has already occurred. It can generally be said that international environmental law is too concerned with *ex post facto* curing of harm and not enough with preventing harm. The prevention principle, which seeks to anticipate and avoid foreseeable risks to the environment, is therefore fundamental to the protection of the environment.[31]

There is thus a need for a community response which focuses on prevention and regulation rather than reparation and adjudication, and which aims at the control and avoidance of environmental harm and at the conservation and sustainable development of natural resources. The need for a co-operative approach to addressing global environmental problems was best captured by Garret Hardin in what has become known as Hardin's Tragedy of the Commons.[32] In his article, Hardin imagined a common grazing land open to all. He postulated that, while users would be aware of the need to preserve the grazing land for the future, there would be no incentive to

[28] ILC Hazardous Activities (n 26) Principle 4(2).

[29] Ibid commentary to Principle 4(2) para 13.

[30] Ibid Principle 4(3).

[31] See L-A Duvic-Paoli *The Prevention Principle in International Environmental Law* (2018).

[32] G Hardin 'Tragedy of the commons' (1968) 162 *Science* 1243.

preserve such land unless there were rules applicable to all, that placed limitations on the right to graze.

Applied in the context of modern international environmental law, states will not have an incentive to protect the global environment unless there are rules that bind other states to the same (or similar) standards. This explains why the emphasis of international environmental law is on the development of supervised treaty regimes to protect the environment. The basis for these treaty regimes is to be found in guidelines, standards and principles expounded at international conferences, of which the Stockholm Declaration,[33] the Rio Declaration,[34] and the Johannesburg Declaration[35] are the most important.

The following are some of the principles that guide and shape international environmental law.

1 Sustainable development[36]

Modern international environmental law is concerned with the conflict between environmental and economic values. Rapid industrialisation, with the consequent sharp increase in economic activity, has led to a significant rise in environmental degradation. Yet economic activity is central to the quest for development. The resulting tension between the demand for development on the part of states (particularly developing states) and the protection and preservation of the environment is addressed by the principle of sustainable development. Sustainable development calls for the integration of environmental, social, and economic concerns.[37] To this end, the Rio Declaration states:

> The right to development must be fulfilled so as to equitably meet developmental and environmental needs of present and future generations (Principle 3).
>
> In order to achieve sustainable development, environmental protection shall constitute an integral part of the development process and cannot be considered in isolation from it (Principle 4).

[33] Stockholm Declaration (n 2).

[34] Rio Declaration (n 3).

[35] Johannesburg Declaration (n 4).

[36] See *Gabcikovo-Nagymaros Project (Hungary/Slovakia)* 1997 ICJ Reports 7, para 140. See essays in MC Cordonier Segger with CG Weeramantry *Sustainable Development Principles in the Decisions of International Courts and Tribunals: 1992–2012* (2017); D Tladi *Sustainable Development in International Law: An Analysis of Key Enviro-Economic Instruments* (2007); P Sands 'International law in the field of sustainable development' (1994) 65 *BYIL* 303; D McGoldrick 'Sustainable development and human rights: An integrated conception' (1996) 45 *ICLQ* 796. A Boyle and D Freestone (eds) *International Law and Sustainable Development: Past Achievements and Future Challenges* (1999).

[37] See Tladi (n 36) 78 et seq.

Sustainable development was famously defined in the Brundtland Commission report as 'development that meets the needs of the present generation without compromising the ability of future generations to meet their own needs.'[38] From this definition, the twin concepts of inter- and intragenerational equity have emerged. Intergenerational equity concerns the idea that there should be equity between generations.[39] This principle requires that the current generation leave the environment in no worse a condition than they found it. In contrast, intragenerational equity requires that there be equity within a generation.[40] Intragenerational equity seeks to enhance the developmental concerns of developing states and communities. In the context of international environmental law, intragenerational equity requires differentiation between developed and developing states, either through different standards of obligations[41] or through the obligation on developed states to transfer financial and technological resources to developing states.[42]

The common but differentiated responsibilities principle reflects intragenerational equity. An example of this principle can be found in principle 7 of the Rio Declaration, which provides:

> In view of the different contributions to global environment degradation, states have common but differentiated responsibilities. The developed countries acknowledge the responsibility that they bear in the international pursuit of sustainable development in view of the pressures their societies-place on the global environment and of the technologies and financial

[38] World Commission on Environment and Development *Our Common Future* (1987) 43.

[39] EB Brown Weiss *In Fairness to Future Generations: International Law, Common Patrimony and Intergenerational Equity* (1989). D Tladi 'Strong sustainability, weak sustainability, intergenerational equity and international law: Using the Earth Charter to redirect the environmental ethics debate' (2003) 28 *SAYIL* 200. L Gundling 'Our responsibility to future generations' (1990) 84 *AJIL* 207. See however, A D'Amato 'Do we owe a duty to future generations to preserve the global environment' (1990) 84 *AJIL* 190.

[40] M Mickelson 'South, North, international environmental law and international environmental lawyers' (2000) 11 *Yearbook of International Environmental Law* 52; J Ntambirweki 'The developing countries in the evolution of international environmental law' (1991) 14 *Hastings International and Comparative Law Review* 906. See, eg, N Schrijver 'De verankering en betekenis van duurzame ontwikkeling in het internationale recht' 2003 *Mededelingen van de Nederlandse Vereniging voor Internationale Recht: Volkenrecht en Duurzame Ontwikkeling* 1, who argues that implicit in sustainable development is the idea that natural resources should not be consumed by a small group of people in industrialised countries.

[41] An example in this regard is the Kyoto Protocol to the United Nations Framework Convention on Climate Change (1998) 37 *ILM* 22, which places emissions reduction commitments on developed states but not on developing states.

[42] See, eg, the Convention on Biological Diversity 1992 1760 UNTS 69.

resources they command (Principle 7).[43]

The emergence of the principle of sustainable development in international law has also had an influence on the South African Constitution. Section 24 of the South African Constitution provides as follows:

> Everyone has the right—
> *(a)* to a environment that is not harmful to their health or well-being; and
> *(b)* to have the environment protected, for the benefit of present and future generations, through reasonable legislative and other measures that—
> (i) prevent pollution and ecological degradation;
> (ii) promote conservation; and
> (iii) secure ecologically sustainable development and use of natural resources while promoting justifiable economic and social development.

For many years, South African courts shied away from relying on this provision, opting instead to rely on just administrative action to address environmental issues.[44] The Constitutional Court, however, examined s 24, and the principle of sustainable development, in *Fuel Retailers Association of Southern Africa v Director-General: Environmental Management, Mpumalanga Province.*[45] The Court stated:

> The principle of integration of environmental protection and socio-economic development is therefore fundamental to the concept of sustainable development. Indeed economic development, social development and the protection of the environment are now considered pillars of sustainable development. [46]

Importantly, the Court relied on the international evolution of sustainable development for its conceptualisation of sustainable development.[47]

2 Notification

There is a duty on states to notify other states timeously of any environmental hazards that are likely to produce harmful effects on

[43] See also Johannesburg Declaration (n 4) para 14 ('The benefits and costs of globalisation are unevenly distributed, with developing countries facing special difficulties in meeting this challenge'), and para 15 ('The benefits and costs of globalisation are unevenly distributed, with developing countries facing special difficulties in meeting this challenge [and] we risk the entrenchment of these global disparities and unless we act in a manner that fundamentally changes their lives, the poor of the world may lose confidence in their representatives.'

[44] L Feris and D Tladi 'Environmental rights' in D Brand and C Heyns (eds) *Socio-Economic Rights in South Africa* (2005).

[45] 2007 (6) SA 4 (CC).

[46] Ibid 24–5 para 53.

[47] L Feris 'Sustainable development in practice: *Fuel Retailers Association of Southern Africa v Director-General Environmental Management, Department of Agriculture, Conservation and Environment, Mpumalanga Province*' (2008) 1 *Constitutional Court Review* 235. D Tladi '*Fuel Retailers*, sustainable development and integration: A response to Feris' (2008) 1 *Constitutional Court Review* 255.

the environment of those states.[48] Related to this is the requirement that a state with knowledge of activities likely to have a significant adverse transboundary environmental effect should consult with states likely to be affected at an early stage.[49]

3 Environmental impact assessment

States are required to undertake an environmental impact assessment (EIA) for proposed activities that are likely to have a significant adverse impact on the environment.[50] In *Pulp Mills on the River Uruguay (Argentina v Uruguay)* the International Court of Justice stated that an EIA 'has gained so much acceptance among states that it may now be considered a requirement under general international law to undertake an environmental impact assessment where there is a risk that the proposed industrial activity may have a significant adverse impact in a transboundary context, in particular, on a shared resource'.[51] Although the Court did not show much state practice in support of this conclusion, the principle has since been accepted in the International Tribunal for the Law of the Sea Advisory Opinion on the *Responsibilities of States Sponsoring Entities*.[52]

The International Court of Justice was again required to examine the question of the need to conduct an EIA in a dispute between Nicaragua and Costa Rica. Nicaragua claimed that Costa Rica's construction of a road along the San Juan River, which falls entirely within the sovereignty of Nicaragua, had taken place without first conducting an EIA and had, in the result, caused significant transboundary harm to Nicaragua.[53] Although the Court found that Nicaragua had failed to prove that the road had caused significant transboundary harm, it found, unanimously, that Costa Rica had 'violated its obligation under general international law' by failing to

[48] Rio Declaration (n 3) Principle 18. See, too, article 8 of the Draft Articles on Prevention of Transboundary Harm from Hazardous Activities (n 24).

[49] Rio Declaration (n 3) Principle 19. See, further, the *Lake Lanoux* Arbitration between Spain and France: (1957) 12 *RIAA* 281; 24 ILR 101.

[50] Rio Declaration (n 3) Principle 17. See, too, the dissenting opinion of Judge Weeramantry in *Request for an Examination of the Situation in Accordance with Paragraph 63 of the Court's Judgment in the 1974 Nuclear Tests* Case *(New Zealand v France)* 1995 ICJ Reports 288 at 344; J Knox 'The myth and the reality of transboundary environmental impact assessment' (2002) 96 *AJIL* 291.

[51] *Pulp Mills case* (n 16) para 204. See for discussion D Tladi 'The principles of sustainable development in the case concerning *Pulp Mills on the River Uruguay*' in Cordonier Segger with Weeramantry (n 36).

[52] *Responsibilities and Obligations of States Sponsoring Persons and Entities with Respect to Activities in the Area*, Advisory Opinion, 2011 *ITLOS Reports* 10.

[53] *Costa Rica v Nicaragua* (n 20) *and Construction of a Road in Costa Rica along the San Juan River (Nicaragua v Costa Rica)* 2015 ICJ Reports 665.

carry out an EIA concerning the construction of the road.[54] The Court stated that 'to fulfil its obligation to exercise due diligence in preventing significant transboundary environmental harm, a State must, before embarking on an activity having the potential to adversely affect the environment of another state, ascertain if there is a risk of significant transboundary harm, which would trigger the requirement to carry out an environmental impact assessment'.[55]

4 Precautionary principle

As described above, there is a general duty on states to prevent damage to the environment. This general duty is reflected in, for example, the *sic utere tuo* principle and the obligation to exercise due diligence. However, both of these rules apply to foreseeable environmental damage. Very often, however, there is no full scientific evidence that particular activities will cause harm. Where the potential environmental harm, though uncertain, is serious or irreversible, there is an expectation that *some* action would be taken to prevent the harm. The precautionary principle emerged to address this issue.[56] There are various formulations of the precautionary principle. Principle 15 of the Rio Declaration, for example, provides that 'where there are threats of serious or irreversible damage, lack of full scientific certainty shall not be used as a reason for postponing cost-effective measures to prevent environmental degradation.'[57] A few things can be noted about the formulation of principle 15. First, the threshold for the application of the precautionary principle is 'serious or irreversible damage', meaning there is no obligation to act if the potential damage is not serious or irreversible. Secondly, even if the potential damage is serious or irreversible, the obligation is only to adopt 'cost-effective measures'.

5 'Polluter pays' principle

Unlike the precautionary principle, the polluter pays principle addresses circumstances where damage has already occurred. It

[54] *Nicaragua v Costa Rica* (n 53) 741 para 229(6). On the meaning of the term 'general international law' see the separate opinion of Judge ad hoc Dugard, ibid 847–849 paras 13–7.

[55] Ibid 706 para 104. In this case Judge ad hoc Dugard carried out a full examination into the content of the obligation to perform an EIA inherent in the Court's finding: ibid 849–60.

[56] D Freestone and E Hey 'Origins and development' in D Freestone and E Hey (eds) *The Precautionary Principle and International Law: Challenges of Implementation* (1996).

[57] Rio Declaration (n 3) Principle 15. See also Bergen Ministerial Declaration on Sustainable Development in ECE Region reprinted in R Churchill and D Freestone (eds) *International Law and Climate Change* (1991); see, too, the Draft Articles on the Prevention of Transboundary Harm from Hazardous Activities (n 24) article 3.

refers to the idea that the costs of pollution are, in principle, to be borne by the polluter.[58] This principle forms the basis of the ILC's Draft Principles on International Liability for Injurious Consequences Arising out of Acts not Prohibited by International Law.[59] It is also captured in Principle 16 of the Rio Declaration, which provides:

> National Authorities should endeavour the internalisation of environmental costs and the use of economic instruments, taking into account the approach that the polluter should, in principle, pay for the costs of pollution . . .

The polluter pays principle, in international law, is an extension of private law remedies relying on market mechanisms to deal with environmental problems.[60]

TRADE AND THE ENVIRONMENT

Some treaties place restrictions on certain forms of trade that are harmful to the environment. The Convention on International Trade in Endangered Species of Wild Fauna and Flora (CITES) of 1973[61] regulates and restricts trade in endangered species, particularly those threatened with extinction; the Basel Convention for the Control of Transboundary Movements of Hazardous Wastes of 1989[62] prohibits the export of hazardous wastes; and the Cartagena Protocol on Biosafety to the Convention on Biological Diversity of 2000 establishes an advanced informed agreement procedure for the trade in living modified organisms (genetically modified organisation).[63] Moreover domestic legislation sometimes places restrictions on the import of certain products in order to persuade supplier nations to comply with conservation measures. Rules of this kind, whether domestic legislation or treaty rules may, however, conflict with trade rules under the World Trade Organization's (WTO) agreements which are designed to promote free trade. This possibility is acknowledged in the preamble of the Cartagena Protocol which, because of the possibility of trade environment conflict, includes three conflicting recitals.[64] First, the preamble recognises that 'trade and environment agreements

[58] See P Sands *Principles of International Environmental Law Vol 1: Frameworks, Standards and Implementation* (1995) 213. Rio Declaration (n 3) Principle 16.

[59] UN Doc A/61/10 (n 26) Principles 3 and 4.

[60] Tladi (n 36) 14.

[61] (1973) 12 *ILM* 1085.

[62] (1989) 28 *ILM* 657. See for discussion D Tladi 'The quest to ban hazardous waste import into Africa: First Bamako and now Basel' (2000) 33 *Comparative and International Law Journal of Southern Africa* 210.

[63] 2226 UNTS 208.

[64] Tladi (n 36) 182–4, especially at 183 ('The Protocol "deals" with the potential conflict between the WTO agreements and the Protocol by including very strange language in the preamble'). See also S Safrin 'The relationship with other agreements:

should be mutually supportive' and secondly emphasises that 'the Protocol shall not be interpreted as implying a change in the rights and obligations' under existing (trade) agreements. Read together, these two preambular recitals suggest that WTO agreements take priority over the Cartagena Protocol. However, the final preambular recital states that the previous recitals should not be read 'to subordinate [the] Protocol to other international agreements.' According to Guruswamy these recitals cancel each other out, leaving the trade and environment conflict unresolved.[65]

Some conflicts between trade and the environment, particularly between national legislation and WTO agreements, have been the subject of international dispute settlement. The *US Tuna Ban Case* illustrates this.[66] Here United States legislation prohibited the import of tuna products from countries that used nets for catching tuna that did not allow dolphin to escape unharmed from these nets. As dolphin regularly swim above schools of tuna, fishermen often cast their nets around dolphin. While some nets permit dolphin to escape, *purse-seine* nets do not. In terms of its legislation aimed at preventing the incidental killing of dolphin, the United States placed an import ban on tuna products from Mexico, which ban Mexico challenged before a General Agreement on Tariffs and Trade (GATT) dispute settlement panel. In finding that the United States' legislation violated the GATT, the panel stated that 'a contracting party may not restrict imports of a product merely because it originates in a country with environmental policies different from its own'.[67]

The Appellate Body of the WTO handed down a similar decision in the *Shrimp Turtle Case*,[68] in which the tribunal held that the United States' ban on the import of shrimp harvested without turtle-excluder devices (which protect sea turtles during shrimp harvesting) violates WTO rules. In holding that the import ban was not

Much ado about savings clause' in C Bail, R Falkner and H Marquard (eds) *The Cartagena Protocol on Biosafety: Reconciling Trade in Biotechnology and Development?* (2002).

[65] LD Guruswamy 'Sustainable agriculture: Do GMOs imperil biosafety' (2002) 9 *Indiana Journal of Global Legal Studies* 461 at 491 ('The Biosafety Protocol, however, makes a travesty of international law. If, as is abundantly clear, the parties to the Biosafety Protocol were unable to agree on the priority or precedence of the Biosafety Protocol over the other trade treaties, they ought to have recognised their disagreement during the negotiations, but refrained from using the Protocol to publicise their differences').

[66] Panel Report on US Restrictions on Imports of Tuna (1991) 30 *ILM* 1594.

[67] Ibid para 6.2.

[68] United States—Import Prohibition of Certain Shrimp and Shrimp Products (1999) 38 *ILM* 118. See also United States—Standards for Reformulated and Conventional Gasoline AB-1996-1 (1996) 35 *ILM* 274.

justified as a natural resource conservation measure under the GATT, because it had been applied in an arbitrary and discriminatory manner, the Appellate Body stated:

> In reaching these conclusions, we wish to underscore what we have not decided in this appeal. We have *not* decided that the protection and preservation of the environment is of no significance to the Members of the WTO. Clearly, it is. We have *not* decided that the sovereign nations that are Members of the WTO cannot adopt effective measures to protect endangered species, such as sea turtles. Clearly, they can and should. And we have *not* decided that sovereign states should not act together bilaterally, plurilaterally or multilaterally, either within the WTO or in other international fora, to protect endangered species or to otherwise protect the environment. Clearly, they should and do.[69]

These decisions, which have been widely criticised by environmentalists, [70] illustrate the conflict between environmentally sensitive laws and policies and the interests of free trade and unrestrained development policies.[71] Clearly, there is a need for reconciliation of the competing interests of international trade and the protection of the environment. A solution must therefore be found that respects the principle of sustainable development by catering for the needs of developing states while at the same time preserving the resources of the planet to provide for the needs of future generations.

ENVIRONMENTAL TREATIES

A network of multilateral treaties seek to protect seas, land, rivers, atmosphere and outer space from environmental degradation; to preserve fauna and flora; and to prohibit ultra-hazardous activities that threaten the environment. Some of the treaties designed to combat marine pollution are described in Chapter 17 on the Law of the Sea. In this section several of the more important environmental treaties are described in order to provide a glimpse of what has already been achieved, and to indicate the enormity of the challenge to set in place an international legal regime that serves effectively to protect our environment.

1 Flora, fauna and biological diversity

As mentioned earlier, CITES[72] regulates trade in endangered species. Appendices list species threatened or likely to be threatened with

[69] Ibid 174 para 185.

[70] See eg D Tladi 'Can the wolf protect the lamb? Free trade regimes as instruments towards sustainable development' (2002) 27 *SAYIL* 149.

[71] See, further, on this subject TJ Schoenbaum 'International trade and protection of the environment: The continuing search for reconciliation' (1997) 91 *AJIL* 268.

[72] (1973) 12 *ILM* 1085. M Cowling and M Kidd 'CITES and the conservation of the African elephant' (2000) 25 *SAYIL* 189.

extinction and prescribe regulations for trade in such species. A Conference of the Parties (COP) meets regularly to review implementation of the Convention. South Africa is a party to the Convention. In 2016, South Africa hosted the 17th COP, which addressed important issues such as the listing of rhino, African elephant and the African lion.

The Convention on Biological Diversity of 1992[73] aims to halt the loss of biological diversity resulting from actions such as deforestation, the destruction of temperate forests, wetlands and coral reefs and the hunting of fauna. According to Sands:

> [T]he destruction and loss of habitats and species brings with it known and unknown ecological consequences: what is ultimately threatened is the ability of ecosystems to purify water, regenerate soil, protect watersheds, regulate temperature, recycle nutrients and waste, and maintain the atmosphere.[74]

The development concerns of developing nations are also taken into account. Article 1 of the Convention describes its objects as

> the conservation of biological diversity, the sustainable use of its components and the fair and equitable sharing of the benefits arising out of the utilization of genetic resources.

South Africa is a party to the Convention. Several protocols have been adopted under the Convention in an attempt to address particular biodiversity issues. The first protocol, the Cartagena Protocol on Biosafety,[75] seeks to address potential environmental damage that may arise from the introduction of genetically modified organisms into the environment. A supplementary protocol, under the Cartagena Protocol, was adopted in 2010 to address liability issues in the event that damage to the environment materialises as a result of the introduction of genetically modified organisms into the environment.[76] In addition to the protocols concerning genetically modified organisms, another protocol under the Biodiversity Convention, addressing access to and the sharing of benefits from genetic resources, was adopted in 2010.[77]

[73] (1992) 31 *ILM* 818.

[74] Sands (n 36) 333.

[75] Cartagena Protocol (n 63).

[76] The Nagoya-Kuala Lumpur Supplementary Protocol on Liability and Redress to the Cartagena Protocol on Biosafety, 15 October 2010, entered into force on 5 March 2018. See A Shibata (ed) *International Liability Regime for Biodiversity Damage: The Nagoya-Kuala Lumpur Supplementary Protocol* (2014). See also D Tladi 'Civil Liability in the context of the Cartagena Protocol: To be or not to be (binding)' (2010) 10 *International Environmental Agreements: Politics, Law and Economics* 15.

[77] The Nagoya Protocol on Access and Benefit-Sharing, 2010, available at http://www.cbd.int/abs.

2 Conservation of marine living resources

In addition to the UNCLOS, a number of conventions seek to conserve marine resources. In 1946, the International Convention for the Regulation of Whaling[78] was adopted to conserve whale stocks and to control the whaling industry. South Africa is party to this Convention. Further, an International Whaling Commission is established to supervise the Convention. In 2014, on the basis of an application by Australia, the International Court of Justice ruled that the Japanese programme which included the catching and killing of whales for scientific purposes was inconsistent with the International Convention for the Regulation of Whaling.[79]

In 1995, a convention was adopted on the Conservation and Management of Straddling Fish Stocks and Highly Migratory Fish Stocks,[80] an implementing agreement under the UNCLOS, which addresses the regulation of stocks of fish that straddle both exclusive economic zones and high seas. In order to ensure that such stocks are not overfished on the high seas, the Convention provides for co-operation, mainly through regional organisations, between coastal states and states fishing on the high seas aimed at conservation and management of the stocks. The Convention requires states parties to prevent overfishing, protect biodiversity in the marine environment and adopt measures to ensure long-term sustainability of straddling fish stocks.[81] Implementation is left largely to the flag state as the Convention requires the flag state to take measures to ensure that its vessels comply with regional conservation measures and to enforce such measures.[82] The Convention includes a number of principles not contained in the UNCLOS such as the precautionary approach[83] and provides for the establishment of Regional Fisheries Management Organisations.[84] The Convention, however, also contains very controversial provisions permitting the vessel of one state party to board the vessels of another state party.[85] The sensitivity of the conservation of straddling stocks is illustrated by an incident in 1995 in which Canadian officers boarded a Spanish vessel fishing for

[78] 161 UNTS 72. See, further, J Glazewski 'The regulation of whaling in international and South African law' (1990–1) 16 *SAYIL* 61.

[79] *Whaling in the Antarctic (Australia v Japan: New Zealand intervening)* 2014 ICJ Reports 226.

[80] (1995) 34 *ILM* 1542. D Anderson 'The Straddling Stocks Agreement of 1995—An initial assessment' (1996) 45 *ICLQ* 463; P Davies and C Redgwell 'The international legal regulation of straddling fish stocks' (1996) 67 *BYIL* 199.

[81] Fish Stocks Agreement (n 80) article 5.

[82] Ibid articles 18 and 19.

[83] Ibid article 6.

[84] Ibid articles 8–10.

[85] Ibid article 21.

Greenland halibut some 245 miles off the Canadian coast in violation of a Canadian law. The law in question had extended Canada's jurisdiction to waters beyond its exclusive economic zone in order to protect straddling stocks from being overfished. Spain protested and instituted legal proceedings against Canada, but the International Court of Justice held that it had no jurisdiction to hear the case. [86]

3 Ozone depletion, global warming and climate change

The Vienna Convention for the Protection of the Ozone Layer of 1985[87] addresses the depletion of the layer of atmospheric ozone above the planetary boundary layer, which allows excessive ultraviolet radiation to penetrate through to the surface of the earth. This framework convention establishes institutions for the adoption of protocols that aim to reduce the production of chlorofluorocarbons (CFCs), the agents principally responsible for the depletion of the ozone layer. The Montreal Protocol on Substances that Deplete the Ozone Layer of 1987[88] provides for the phased reduction of CFCs and similar harmful substances. South Africa is a party to both the Vienna Convention and the Montreal Protocol.

Climate change is caused by the increase of greenhouse gas concentration in the atmosphere.[89] This results from the emission of certain gases, particularly from the combustion of oil, gas and coal, and from the destruction of natural resources such as forests which remove greenhouse gases from the atmosphere. This problem is addressed by the United Nations Framework Convention on Climate Change (UNFCCC) of 1992,[90] which aims to achieve

> stabilization of greenhouse gas concentrations in the atmosphere at a level that would prevent dangerous anthropogenic interference with the climate system. Such a level should be achieved within a time frame sufficient to allow ecosystems to adapt naturally to climate change, to ensure that food production is not threatened and to enable economic development to proceed in a sustainable manner.[91]

Parties commit themselves to take action to mitigate climate change by limiting the emission of greenhouse gases and protecting

[86] *Fisheries Jurisdiction Case* 1998 ICJ Reports 432.

[87] (1987) 26 *ILM* 1529.

[88] (1987) 26 *ILM* 1550. This Protocol has been amended by the Copenhagen Amendment of 1992 (1993) 32 *ILM* 874.

[89] JS Dryzek, R Norgaard and D Schlosberg (eds) *The Oxford Handbook of Climate Change and Society* (2011); J Viñuales 'Balancing effectiveness and fairness in the redesign of the climate change regime' (2011) 24 *Leiden Journal of International Law* 223.

[90] (1992) 31 *ILM* 849. See C Stone 'Beyond Rio: Insuring against global warming' (1992) 86 *AJIL* 445.

[91] UNFCCC (n 90) article 2.

natural resources, particularly forests. Parties undertake to assist developing countries to meet their obligations under the UNFCCC.

The UNFCCC has many provisions couched in discretionary language which weaken its commitments. For instance, the commitment of industrial countries relating to the transfer of technology that reduces the emission of gases is couched in equivocal phrases such as 'as appropriate', 'in so far as possible' and 'all practicable steps'. However, provision is made for the establishment of a COP to review implementation of the Convention. As explained earlier, many of these provisions reflect inter- and intragenerational equity. South Africa became a party to the UNFCCC in 1997.

In 1997, parties to the UNFCCC adopted the Kyoto Protocol,[92] which requires parties to ensure that their aggregate anthropogenic carbon dioxide emissions of greenhouse gases[93] do not exceed assigned amounts.[94] Thus, there are firm obligations on states to either reduce or stabilise their emissions by specific amounts. In addition, the Kyoto Protocol established a number of market mechanisms, such as emissions trading, to decrease the burden of states with emissions commitments.[95] South Africa is a party to this Protocol which only came into force in 2005.

The UNFCCC and the Kyoto Protocol are based on the principle of common but differentiated responsibilities and respective capabilities (CBDRRC), which imposes different obligations in respect of the reduction of greenhouse gases on developed and developing countries. Developed countries are required to reduce their emission of greenhouse gases by approximately 5 per cent below 1990 levels in the period 2008–12. In 2009, a conference was held in Copenhagen to advance the climate change regime but the conference, attended by 125 heads of state and government, was not able to resolve differences and to produce a legally binding agreement. A conference held in Cancun, Mexico, in 2010 recognised that climate change was one of the greatest challenges facing our time; and substantial reduction in greenhouse gas emissions is required. However, the Conference failed to reach agreement on the extension of the Kyoto commitments. In 2012, in Doha, the Kyoto Protocol was amended to provide, inter alia, for a new commitment period to run from 2013 to 2020. The Protocol has yet to enter into force and recent developments, in

[92] Kyoto Protocol (n 41).

[93] The condemned greenhouse gases are carbon dioxide, methane, nitrous oxide, hydrofluorocarbons, perfluorocarbons and sulphur hexafluoride.

[94] Kyoto Protocol (n 41) article 3.

[95] See D Tladi 'Corporates and the flexible mechanisms in the climate change regime: The privatisation of sustainable development' (2007) 32 *SAYIL* 396.

particular the adoption of a new climate change agreement in Paris, suggest that it may never enter into force.[96]

In December 2015, the COP to the UNFCCC adopted the Paris Agreement on Climate under the UNFCCC.[97] Like the UNFCCC, and unlike the Kyoto Protocol, the Paris Agreement does not place firm legal obligations on states to reduce their emissions by a specific amount. The Agreement 'aims to strengthen the global response to threat of climate change' by '[h]olding the increase in the global average temperature to well below 2°C above pre-industrial levels'.[98] The objective will be met by 'nationally determined contributions' which will 'represent progression over time'.[99] As with the UNFCCC, the Paris Agreement is based on the principle of the common but differentiated responsibilities.[100]

South Africa ratified the Paris Agreement in November 2016. The United States is also party to the Paris Agreement, having ratified it in September 2016. However, in August 2017 the United States Department of State sent a formal communication to the United Nations indicating its withdrawal from the Paris Agreement.[101] This withdrawal, however, is invalid since, under the Paris Agreement, a state can only withdraw three years after the entry into force of the Agreement which means that a withdrawal notice can only be submitted as from November 2019.[102]

4 Nuclear activities

Since the accident at the Chernobyl nuclear reactor in 1986, the International Atomic Energy Agency and multilateral treaties have devoted considerable attention to nuclear safety and the protection of the environment from nuclear accidents. The failure of the Soviet Union immediately to provide information to its neighbours of the accident at Chernobyl has prompted states to undertake to provide

[96] Paris Agreement, adopted on 15 December 2015 and entered into force 4 November 2016 (2016) 55 *ILM* 740.

[97] See P Sands 'Climate change and the rule of law: Adjudicating the future of international law' in T Maluwa, M du Plessis and D Tladi (eds) *The Pursuit of a Brave New World in International Law: Essays in Honour of John Dugard* (2017).

[98] Paris Agreement (n 96) article 2(a).

[99] Ibid article 3.

[100] Ibid article 2(2) ('This Agreement will be implemented to reflect equity and the principle of common but differentiated responsibilities and respective capabilities, and in the light of differentiated national circumstances.')

[101] H Zhang et al 'US withdrawal from the Paris Agreement: Reasons, impacts, and China's response' (2017) 8 *Advances in Climate Change Research* 220.

[102] Paris Agreement (n 96), article 28.

such information in bilateral and multilateral treaties.[103] In 1994, the Convention on Nuclear Safety[104] was adopted. It emphasises that the responsibility for nuclear safety rests with the state having jurisdiction over a nuclear installation. Parties are required to account for the safety measures they have taken at periodic review meetings of all parties. South Africa is a party to this Convention and has adopted legislation to give effect to its obligations under the Convention.[105]

Although there exist other nuclear-related treaties, such as the Nuclear Non-Proliferation Treaty and the Treaty on the Prohibition of Nuclear Weapons, these concern nuclear weapons and are not related to the protection of the environment.

5 Hazardous waste

The disposal of toxic and hazardous wastes at sea and on land has led to the adoption of a number of multilateral conventions to prohibit dumping of such substances. The principal convention is the Basel Convention on the Control of Transboundary Movements of Hazardous Wastes and Their Disposal of 1989,[106] to which South Africa is a party. It requires parties to prohibit the export of hazardous and other wastes to parties which have prohibited the import of such wastes and have informed other parties of such prohibitions. Where a state has not prohibited the import of such wastes, parties shall not permit the export of hazardous wastes to that state without its written consent.[107] Parties are required, inter alia, to take appropriate measures to prevent pollution due to hazardous wastes and to ensure that the transboundary movement of hazardous wastes is 'reduced to the minimum consistent with the environmentally sound and efficient management of such wastes'.[108]

The Convention on the Prevention of Marine Pollution by Dumping of Wastes and Other Matter of 1972 makes it an offence for any person deliberately to dump certain substances in the territorial seas of states.[109] In 1991, the Organization of African Unity adopted the Bamako Convention on the Ban of the Import into Africa and the

[103] Convention on Early Notification of a Nuclear Accident of 1986 ((1986) 25 *ILM* 1370); Convention on Assistance in Case of a Nuclear Accident or Radiological Emergency of 1986 ((1986) 25 *ILM* 1377). South Africa is a party to both these conventions.

[104] (1994) 33 *ILM* 1514.

[105] National Nuclear Energy Act 46 of 1999 and the National Nuclear Regulator Act 47 of 1999.

[106] (1989) 28 *ILM* 657. See Z Lipman 'Transboundary movement of hazardous waste: Environmental justice issues for developing countries' 1999 *Acta Juridica* 266.

[107] Article 4(1)(c).

[108] Ibid article 4(2)(d).

[109] See Chapter 17, n 165.

Control of Transboundary Movement and Management of Hazardous Wastes within Africa,[110] which prohibits the import of hazardous wastes into Africa by non-parties.

6 International watercourses

The Helsinki Rules on the Uses of the Waters of International Rivers of 1966,[111] a set of principles produced by the non-governmental International Law Association, has shaped the law on the use of international rivers. Its guiding principle that 'each basin state[112] is entitled, within its territory, to a reasonable and equitable share in the beneficial uses of the waters of an international drainage basin', is complemented by provisions requiring states to prevent pollution in an international drainage basin which would cause substantial injury in the territory of a co-basin state. These principles are given treaty form in the 1997 Convention on the Law of the Non-Navigational Uses of International Watercourses,[113] which obliges states to protect and preserve the ecosystems of international watercourses by preventing pollution and taking measures to preserve the marine environment.[114] This Convention is the model for the Revised Protocol on Shared Watercourses in the Southern African Development Community of 2000.[115] The importance of rules to protect the environment of international watercourses was highlighted in the *Gabcikovo-Nagymaros Project*,[116] in which environmental concerns were expressed about the impact of a canal diverting the Danube River from its original course. Although the International Court of Justice stressed the importance of environmental considerations in its judgment, it made no ruling on the environmental issues raised.[117]

[110] (1991) 30 *ILM* 775. AO Akinnusi 'The Bamako and Basel Conventions on the Transboundary Movement and Disposal of Hazardous Waste: A comparative and critical analysis' (2001) 12 *Stellenbosch LR* 306.

[111] Report of the 52nd Conference of the International Law Association (1966) 484.

[112] A 'basin state' is defined as 'a state the territory of which includes a portion of an international drainage basin' (article 3).

[113] (1997) 36 *ILM* 700.

[114] Articles 20–3.

[115] (2001) 40 *ILM* 317.

[116] 1997 ICJ Reports 7.

[117] Ibid 67–8.

CHAPTER 20

Treaties

John Dugard

INTRODUCTION

Much of international life is regulated by treaty.[1] International organisations are created, peace is made and disputes are settled, air and sea transport is facilitated, trade is conducted, and a wide range of interstate relations are fostered through the medium of the treaty, a written agreement between states. Some treaties are bilateral, creating relations between two states only, others are multilateral, creating relations between many states. They are binding upon states in accordance with the principle of *pacta sunt servanda*,[2] which constitutes the foundation stone of international law.

The rules governing the creation, observance, interpretation, validity, and termination of treaties are to be found in customary law. However, in 1969 the Vienna Convention on the Law of Treaties (Vienna Convention)[3] was signed. Today this multilateral treaty, a blend of codification and progressive development, is viewed as a definitive statement on the law of treaties by both signatories and non-signatories. South Africa is not a party to the Vienna Convention.[4]

[1] See AD McNair *The Law of Treaties* (1961); J Klabbers *The Concept of Treaty in International Law* (2013); M Fitzmaurice and O Elias *Contemporary Issues in the Law of* Treaties (2005); A Aust *Modern Treaty Law and Practice* 3 ed (2013); O Corten and P Klein (eds) *The Vienna Convention on the Law of Treaties. A Commentary* (2011) 2 vols; R Kolb *The Law of Treaties: An Introduction* (2016).

[2] Article 26 of the Vienna Convention on the Law of Treaties reaffirms this principle.

[3] (1969) 8 *ILM* 679.

[4] In *Harksen v President of the Republic of South Africa* 2000 (2) SA 825 (CC) 835–6, para [26] ('*Harksen*'), Goldstone J stated that he was prepared to 'assume in favour of the appellant' that article 46(1) of the Vienna Convention on the Law of Treaties, providing that a state may not invoke its internal law to overrule its consent to be bound by a treaty, reflected customary international law, but at the same time, he warned that 'the extent to which the Vienna Convention reflects customary international law is by no means settled'. Cf *Goodwin v Director-General, Department of Justice* (unreported, TPD Case No 21142/08, 23 June 2008). Here Ebersohn AJ stated (at 12) that the Vienna Convention is part of South African law in terms of s 232 of Constitution of the Republic of South Africa, 1996, and, wrongly, that South Africa is a party to the Vienna Convention (at 16). See further, E Schlemmer 'Die Grondwetlike Hof en die ooreenkoms ter vestiging van die Wêreldhandelsorganisasie' 2010 *TSAR* 749 at 753.

The Vienna Convention[5] defines a treaty as

> an international agreement concluded between states in written form and governed by international law, whether embodied in a single instrument or in two or more related instruments and whatever its particular designation.

This definition calls for several comments. First, while the Vienna Convention is concerned only with agreements between states, agreements between states and international organisations also qualify as treaties. Because special considerations apply to the latter type of treaty, a separate multilateral treaty, the Vienna Convention on the Law of Treaties between States and International Organizations or between International Organizations[6] of 1986, was later drafted, which follows substantially the same pattern as the Vienna Convention. Secondly, although oral agreements between state representatives may create legal obligations for states,[7] they do not qualify as treaties. Thirdly, treaties go by many names.[8] The most commonly used names other than treaty are international agreement, convention, declaration, charter, covenant, pact, protocol, act, statute, concordat, exchange of notes, and memorandum of agreement. In order to give publicity to treaties, and to avoid the dangers of secret treaties, both the Charter of the United Nations[9] and the Vienna Convention[10] require treaties to be registered with the secretariat of the United Nations. They are duly published in the *United Nations Treaty Series*.

It follows therefore that where states, party to an agreement do not intend to create legal obligations or rights under international law, the agreement will not be a treaty. Memoranda of understanding, for instance, are generally not legally binding despite their political significance. It all depends on the intention of parties.

A treaty is not binding on states that are not parties to the agreement. Article 34 of the Vienna Convention states that '[a] treaty does not create obligations or rights for a third state without its consent', a principle that the Supreme Court of Appeal reiterated in *Minister of Justice v SALC* when it stated that a treaty 'cannot impose

[5] Vienna Convention (n 3) article 2(1)(a).

[6] (1986) 25 *ILM* 543.

[7] In the *Legal Status of Eastern Greenland (Denmark v Norway)* (1933) PCIJ Reports, Series A/B, no 53, an oral undertaking by the Norwegian Foreign Minister, Mr Ihlen, that Norway would 'not make any difficulty' in respect of Denmark's claim to Eastern Greenland was held to be binding on Norway and precluded it from contesting Denmark's sovereignty over Eastern Greenland.

[8] There is no essential difference between a 'treaty' and an 'international agreement' (the term employed in s 231 of Constitution of the Republic of South Africa, 1996: see Chapter 4.

[9] Article 102 of the Charter of the United Nations, adopted on 24 October 1945 1 UNTS XVI.

[10] Vienna Convention (n 3) article 80.

obligations on states that are not parties to the treaty and have not consented to the imposition of such obligations'.[11] An exception to this rule occurs, however, when a treaty becomes accepted as customary international law. Arguably the Vienna Convention is today accepted as customary international law.[12]

SOUTH AFRICA'S TREATY-MAKING CAPACITY

Today South Africa is recognised as a sovereign independent state with full treaty-making powers. The exact point in time at which it achieved this status is less clear. In 1919 South Africa was admitted to full membership of the League of Nations despite the fact that constitutionally it remained subordinate to the British Crown, a subordination which was finally removed either in 1926, when an Imperial Conference recognised the independence of the British Dominions, or in 1931, when the Statute of Westminster gave legislative effect to this decision. Whether South Africa acquired full treaty-making capacity in 1919, 1926, or 1931, therefore remains a matter of debate. [13]

THE MAKING OF TREATIES

International law does not prescribe how a state is to exercise its treaty-making power. It is left to the municipal law of each state to determine who may enter into treaties on its behalf. In the United States it is the President and the Senate[14] which have this power while in the United Kingdom the power vests in the executive. South Africa followed the practice of the United Kingdom before 1994. Now, under the 1996 Constitution, the executive and Parliament share this power. In terms of s 231, the national executive[15] has the responsibility of negotiating and signing international agreements. Where an agreement is of 'a technical, administrative or executive

[11] *Minister of Justice and Constitutional Development v Southern Africa Litigation Centre* 2016 (3) SA 317 (SCA) ('*Minister of Justice v SALC*') para 78.

[12] See the statement of Goldstone J to this effect in *Harksen* (n 4) above.

[13] See, further, on the evolution of South Africa's treaty-making power, Chapters 2 and 5. Cf *Harksen* (n 4) 1026–7.

[14] Article II s 2 of the Constitution of the United States.

[15] Section 85 provides that 'the executive authority of the Republic is vested in the President' and that 'the President exercises the executive authority, together with the other members of the Cabinet'. See, further, N Botha 'Treaty-making in South Africa: A reassessment' (2000) 25 *SAYIL* 69, 73–4. The procedure to be followed by the executive is set out in the Manual on Executive Acts of the President of the Republic of South Africa, as revised in 2007.

nature'[16] it binds the Republic on signature without parliamentary approval, but must be tabled in the National Assembly and the National Council of Provinces within a reasonable time.[17] Where, however, the agreement does not fall into one of the above categories it 'binds the Republic only after it has been approved by resolution in both the National Assembly and the National Council of Provinces'.[18]

The 1996 Constitution is premised on the Vienna Convention, which allows final consent to be bound by a treaty to be given by ratification, accession or signature.

Formal agreements, particularly multilateral agreements, normally require ratification in addition to signature. This requires the representative of the state subsequently to endorse the earlier signature. This provides the state with an opportunity to reconsider its decision to be bound by the treaty and, if necessary, to effect changes to its own law to enable it to fulfil its obligations under the treaty. In practice, treaties generally indicate whether ratification is required,[19] but where this is not done, the intention of the parties will have to be ascertained from the surrounding circumstances.[20] Although a state is not bound by a treaty that it has signed but not ratified, it is obliged to refrain from acts that would defeat the object and purpose of such a treaty until it has made clear its intention not to be bound by the treaty.[21] A state may therefore apply a treaty 'provisionally' during the interim period between signature and ratification.[22]

A state may later become a party to a treaty in whose negotiation it did not participate, and which it did not sign, by means of accession, provided that the original parties accept that such states may accede to the treaty. Multilateral law-making treaties that seek to achieve a large measure of universality generally include an accession clause.

[16] See Chapter 4 on the meaning of 'technical, administrative or executive' agreements. In particular see, *Earthlife Africa Johannesburg v Minister of Energy* 2017 (5) 227 (WCC) paras 113–6 (*'Earthlife Africa'*).

[17] Constitution of the Republic of South Africa, 1996, s 231(3). See Botha (n 15) 76, 78.

[18] Constitution of the Republic of South Africa, 1996, s 231(2). See Botha (n 15) 77–8, 79–81.

[19] See eg article 49 of the Vienna Convention on Diplomatic Relations, which states that '[t]he present convention is subject to ratification'.

[20] Vienna Convention (n 3) article 14.

[21] Article 18. In essence, the United States did this in respect of the Rome Statute of the International Criminal Court. In 2000, the Clinton administration signed the Rome Statute, but, in 2002, the Bush administration announced that the United States did not intend to become a party to the Rome Statute, and that it was accordingly absolved from any obligation under this Statute.

[22] Vienna Convention (n 3) article 25; see A Michie 'The provisional application of treaties in South African law and practice' (2005) 30 *SAYIL* 1. This matter is at present being considered by the International Law Commission. See SD Murphy 'Crimes against humanity and other topics: The Sixty-Ninth Session of the International Law Commission' (2017) 111 *AJIL* 978.

For instance, the International Covenant on Civil and Political Rights (ICCPR) provides that it shall be open to accession, inter alia, by any member state of the United Nations.[23]

While it is not difficult to identify an international agreement subject to ratification or accession, in practice, it may prove difficult to identify an agreement of a technical, administrative, or executive nature which comes into force on signature alone. All will depend upon the intention of the parties which must be ascertained from the circumstances surrounding the conclusion of the treaty.[24] The practice of the government law advisers is to treat agreements 'of a routine nature, flowing from the daily activities of government departments' as not requiring parliamentary approval. Where, however, there is any doubt, the agreement is referred to Parliament.[25]

In practice, the government department charged with the responsibility of foreign affairs (in South Africa the Department of International Relations and Cooperation) is principally responsible for the drafting and negotiation of treaties. In order to provide the other party with evidence that the person entering into the treaty has the necessary authority to act on behalf of the state he represents, he must produce appropriate 'full powers'[26]—ie a document designating him as an authorised person[27]—unless it is obvious from his office that he enjoys this power. Thus, heads of state or government, foreign ministers, and heads of diplomatic missions are not required to produce full powers.[28]

RESERVATIONS

When a state has reservations about a provision to be included in a *bilateral* treaty, the appropriate course is for the two parties to renegotiate the provision before the agreement is signed. In such a case, the reservation by one party in effect amounts to a counter-offer. Different considerations apply in respect of *multilateral* treaties.[29] A

[23] ICCPR article 48(3).

[24] Vienna Convention (n 3) article 12; *S v Eliasov* 1967 (4) SA 583 (A), discussed in J Dugard 'The treaty-making process' (1968) 85 *SALJ* 1.

[25] M Olivier 'Informal international agreements under the 1996 Constitution' (1997) 22 *SAYIL* 63 at 64. See further Chapter 4 and *Earthlife Africa* (n 16) paras 113–16.

[26] Vienna Convention (n 3) article 7(1).

[27] Ibid article 2(1)(c).

[28] Ibid article 7(2).

[29] DW Bowett 'Reservations to non-restricted multilateral treaties' (1976–7) 48 *BYIL* 67; JM Ruda 'Reservations to treaties' (1975–III) 146 *Recueil des Cours* 95; F Horn *Reservations and Interpretative Declarations to Multilateral Treaties* (1988); C Redgwell 'Universality or integrity? Some reflections on reservations to general multilateral treaties' (1993) 64 *BYIL* 245; I Ziemele (ed) *Reservations to Human Rights Treaties and the Vienna Convention Regime* (2004); A Pellet 'Art 19' in O Corten and P Klein (eds) *The*

state may become a party to a multilateral treaty while maintaining a reservation which excludes or modifies the legal effect of certain provisions of the treaty in their application to that state, provided that the reservation is compatible with the object and purpose of the treaty.[30] Article 2(1)(d) of the Vienna Convention defines a reservation as

> a unilateral statement, however phrased or named, made by a State when signing, ratifying, accepting, approving, or acceding to a treaty, whereby it purports to exclude or modify the legal effect of certain provisions of the treaty in their application to that State.

A declaration by a state making its acceptance of the treaty conditional upon a particular interpretation—a so-called 'interpretative declaration'—may in fact constitute a reservation.

The present position is the result of a fluctuating history. Early international law required a state wishing to make a reservation to obtain the consent of all parties to a multilateral treaty in order to become a party to the treaty. In 1951, however, the International Court of Justice held, in an advisory opinion on *Reservations to the Convention on the Prevention and Punishment of the Crime of Genocide* that 'a State which has made and maintained a reservation which has been objected to by one or more of the parties to the Convention but not by others, can be regarded as being a party to the Convention if the reservation is compatible with the object and purpose of the Convention'.[31] In this case, a number of states, including the Soviet Union, had entered reservations to a provision in the Convention empowering the International Court of Justice to consider disputes arising out of the Convention,[32] claiming that they might make such reservations in the exercise of their sovereignty.

The Vienna Convention gives its approval to the advisory opinion on *Reservations to the Convention on Genocide*. Article 19 provides:

> A State may, when signing, ratifying, accepting, approving, or acceding to a treaty, formulate a reservation unless:
> *(a)* the reservation is prohibited by the treaty;
> *(b)* the treaty provides that only specified reservations, which do not include the reservation in question, may be made; or
> *(c)* in cases not falling under sub-paras (a) and (b), the reservation is incompatible with the object and purpose of the treaty.

Vienna Convention on the Law of Treaties 405; KL McCall-Smith 'Severing reservations' (2014) 63 *ICLQ* 599.

[30] For an examination of the procedure to be followed in the making of reservations by South Africa, see Botha (n 15) 83–4.

[31] 1951 ICJ Reports 15 at 29.

[32] In terms of article 9 of the Convention on the Prevention and Punishment of the Crime of Genocide of 1948 78 *UNTS* 277 (Genocide Convention).

A reservation requires the acceptance of all the parties 'when it appears from the limited number of the negotiating States and the object and purpose of a treaty that the application of the treaty in its entirety between all the parties is an essential condition of the consent of each one to be bound by the treaty'.[33]

A reservation permitted in accordance with these rules modifies the provisions of the treaty to the extent of the reservation between the reserving state and those states that accept the reservation.[34] A state that objects to the reservation may exclude the operation of the treaty between itself and the reserving state—provided it makes this clear.[35] If it simply objects to the reservation without opposing the entry into force of the treaty between itself and the reserving state, 'the provisions to which the reservation relates do not apply as between the two States to the extent of the reservation'.[36] The reservation 'does not modify the provisions of the treaty for the other parties to the treaty *inter se*'.[37]

The advantage of flexible rules of this kind is that they promote a wide acceptance of multilateral treaties. Conversely, they create confusion over the extent of the obligations between states party to multilateral treaties. The following example illustrates the problem. If state 'A' accepts a reservation to a treaty made by state 'X', but state 'B' objects to such a reservation, the treaty plus the reservation bind A and X, while A and B remain bound by the original treaty *inter se*.

In order to avoid the uncertainty inherent in the system of reservations, some multilateral treaties declare their attitude towards reservations. For example, the 1998 Rome Statute of the International Criminal Court prohibits reservations[38] while the European Convention on Human Rights permits reservations in respect of any particular provision of the Convention, but prohibits 'reservations of a general character'.[39]

The Vienna Convention's regime on reservations has undoubtedly led to more states becoming parties to multilateral treaties. The quest for universality of membership has, however, sometimes been at the expense of the integrity of the treaty. This is particularly evident in the case of human rights treaties where states have entered a wide range of reservations, some of which are difficult to reconcile with the

[33] Vienna Convention (n 3) article 20(2).
[34] Ibid article 21.
[35] Ibid article 20(4)(b).
[36] Ibid article 21(3).
[37] Ibid article 21(2).
[38] Rome Statute of the International Criminal Court article 120.
[39] Ibid article 64.

object and purpose of the treaty.[40] Two reservations illustrate this problem. The United States, when ratifying the ICCPR entered a reservation to article 6(5), which prohibits the imposition of the death sentence 'for crimes committed by persons below eighteen years of age', which reads:

> [T]he United States reserves the right, subject to its Constitutional constraints, to impose capital punishment on any person (other than a pregnant woman) duly convicted under existing or future laws permitting the imposition of capital punishment, including such punishment for crimes committed by persons below eighteen years of age.[41]

Libya, when it acceded to the Convention on the Elimination of All Forms of Discrimination against Women, attached a reservation which reads:

> The accession is subject to the general reservation that such accession cannot conflict with the laws on personal status derived from the Islamic Sharia.[42]

(Several Islamic states have made similar reservations.)

For political reasons, other states parties to these treaties have failed to object to such reservations, or, where they have objected, they have failed to declare that they do not recognise the entry into force of the treaty between themselves and the reserving state.

This has troubled bodies charged with the task of monitoring human rights conventions. The European Court of Human Rights has responded by rejecting reservations that it considers incompatible with the object and purpose of the European Convention on Human Rights. In so doing, it has severed the reservation from the state's acceptance, thereby holding the reserving state bound by the treaty without the offensive reservation.[43] In General Comment 24, the Human Rights Committee declared, in relation to reservations to

[40] JP Gardner and C Chinkin et al (eds) *Human Rights as General Norms and a State's Right to Opt Out: Reservations and Objections to Human Rights Conventions* (1997); Y Tyagi 'The conflict of law and policy on reservations to human rights treaties' (2000) 17 *BYIL* 181; K Korkelia 'New challenges to the regime of reservations under the international covenant on civil and political rights' (2002) 13 *EJIL* 437; GM Ferreira and MP Ferreira-Snyman 'The impact of treaty reservations on the establishment of an international human rights regime' (2005) 38 *CILSA* 148; A Pellet and D Muller 'Reservations to human rights treaties: Not an absolute evil . . .' in U Fastenrath et al (eds) *From Bilateralism to Community Interest: Essays in Honour of Judge Bruno Simma* (2011) 537.

[41] See M Nash 'Contemporary practice of the United States relating to international law' (1995) 89 *AJIL* 109.

[42] Chinkin et al (n 40) 69.

[43] *Belilos v Switzerland* ECHR Series A, vol 132 (1988); *Loizidou v Turkey* ECHR Series A, vol 310 (1995). See too the decisions of the Inter-American Court of Human Rights, examined by T Buergenthal in 'The advisory practice of the Inter-American Human Rights Court' (1985) 79 *AJIL* 20–5.

the ICCPR,[44] that it had the power to determine whether a reservation was incompatible with the object and purpose of the Covenant, and that it would generally make such a finding where the reservation violated a norm of customary international law endorsed by the Covenant or a norm of *jus cogens*. In such a case, it stated that it would (like the European Court of Human Rights) sever the reservation from the state's acceptance and hold it bound without the benefit of the reservation. The Human Rights Committee gave effect to this approach to severance in *Kennedy v Trinidad and Tobago*[45] when it set aside and ignored a reservation to the acceptance of the First Optional Protocol accepting the right of individual petition. The reservation had sought to exclude the jurisdiction of the Committee in respect of prisoners under sentence of death. The Committee found that the reservation discriminated against persons under sentence of death, was contrary to the object and purpose of the Optional Protocol, and, as a result, might be severed from the acceptance of the First Protocol and ignored.

General Comment 24 has provoked a hostile response from states[46] which argue that the Vienna Convention confers the right to object to reservations upon states only. Moreover, any attempt to hold a state bound by a treaty, without the benefit of its reservation, would run counter to the principle that consent is the basis of any treaty obligation.

There are two schools of thought on this subject. The 'permissibility' school, which contends that a reservation contrary to the object and purpose of a treaty is *ipso facto* null and void, irrespective of the reaction of other states; and the 'opposability' school, which maintains that a reservation is valid until other states challenge its validity. The Human Rights Committee's endorsement of the 'permissibility' approach seems both logical and reasonable in a system which fails

[44] CCPR/C/21/Rev 1/Add 6 (1994); reproduced in Chinkin et al (n 40) Appendix I, and (1995) 15 *Human Rights Law Journal* 464. See further C Redgwell 'Reservations to treaties and Human Rights Committee General Comment No 24' (1997) 46 *ICLQ* 390.

[45] CCPR/C/67/D/845/1999; (2000) 7 *IHRR* 315. See, in support of a policy of qualified severance of reservations to human rights treaties, R Goodman 'Human rights treaties, invalid reservations and state consent' (2002) 96 *AJIL* 531.

[46] Notably the United States and the United Kingdom. See Observations by the Governments of the United States and the United Kingdom on Human Rights Committee General Comment No 24 (52) relating to reservations UN Doc A/50/40 (1995); (1995) 16 *Human Rights Law Journal* 422. In May 1998, the South African Department of Justice drafted an opinion on this subject, in which it endorsed the traditional view that reservations should be monitored by states party to the Convention and not by the Human Rights Committee. The South African government itself does not appear to have adopted a position on this subject. See Botha (n 15) 82–3.

to establish an independent arbiter to decide on the compatibility of a reservation with the object and purpose of a treaty, particularly a normative treaty. This view is, however, contested.

The topic of reservations to treaties was the subject of rigorous scrutiny by the International Law Commission from 1995 to 2011. Professor Alain Pellet of France produced 17 reports on the topic and prepared a set of nearly 200 guidelines (accompanied by commentaries on each guideline), which, while not binding, are intended to guide states and international organisations in their treaty practice.[47] While these guidelines cover every aspect of the subject of reservations to treaties, those dealing with the vexed question of reservations to human rights treaties are of particular importance. According to these guidelines, a reservation is invalid if it is incompatible with the object and purpose of the treaty in such a way that it 'affects an essential element of the treaty that is necessary to its general tenor' so as to impair the *raison d'être* of the treaty;[48] and if it is contrary to a peremptory norm of general international law[49] or non-derogable rights.[50] To assess the permissibility of a reservation to a human rights treaty, account must be taken of the interdependence of the rights in the treaty as well as the importance of the right to which the reservation is made 'within the general tenor of the treaty' and 'the extent of the impact the reservation has on the treaty'.[51] A contracting state or organisation, dispute settlement body or treaty monitoring body may assess the permissibility of a reservation.[52] A state that makes an invalid reservation is considered to be a party to the treaty without the benefit of the reservation unless a contrary intention on the part of that state is clear.[53] There is thus a rebuttable presumption that a reserving state will continue to be bound by the treaty to which it has sought to attach an invalid reservation.

Reservations to treaties were considered by the International Court of Justice in the *Case Concerning Armed Activities on the Territory of the Congo (DRC v Rwanda)*.[54] In this case, the International Court of Justice upheld the validity of a reservation by Rwanda to article 9 of the Genocide Convention providing for the referral of disputes over the interpretation and application of the Convention to the Interna-

[47] See Report of the International Law Commission (2011) 63rd Session, *GAOR* 66th Session, Supplement No 10 UN Doc A/66/10.

[48] Guideline 3.1.5.

[49] Guideline 4.4.3.

[50] Guideline 3.1.5.4.

[51] Guideline 3.1.5.6.

[52] Guideline 3.2.

[53] Guideline 4.5.3.

[54] 2006 ICJ Reports 6.

tional Court of Justice. The Court held that while the substantive provisions in the Convention constituted peremptory norms, this did not apply to a procedural provision such as article 9 dealing with dispute settlement.[55] A powerful joint separate opinion authored by five judges[56] explored the validity of reservations of this kind in the context of General Comment 24 of the Human Rights Committee and the decisions of the European Court of Human Rights and the Inter-American Court of Human Rights. It concluded that the 1951 Advisory Opinion of the Court on *Reservations to the Genocide* Convention[57] did not preclude the Court from pronouncing on the validity of a reservation on the grounds of incompatibility with the object and purpose of the Convention. It declared that it is 'not self-evident' that a reservation to article 9 could not be regarded as incompatible with the object and purpose of the Convention and suggested 'that this is a matter that the Court should revisit for further consideration'.[58]

Professor Pellet concluded his guidelines to reservations with a plea to states determined to preserve their right to make reservations to multilateral treaties and to monitoring bodies determined to assert themselves as guardians of the purpose of such treaties, to endeavour to find a solution that reconciled the integrity of the treaty with the universality of participation.[59] Such a reconciliation is essential in a world where multilateral treaties play such a dominant role in the development of international law.

INVALIDITY OF TREATIES

A state may not invoke the fact that it entered into a treaty in violation of its internal law as a ground for invalidating its consent 'unless that violation was manifest and concerned a rule of its internal law of fundamental importance'.[60] Nor may a state invoke an error in a treaty as a ground for invalidity unless the error relates to a fact 'which was assumed by that State to exist at the time when the treaty was concluded and formed an essential basis of its consent to be bound by the treaty'. A state may not rely on an error in this

[55] *DRC v Rwanda* (n 54) 32–3 paras 67–9.

[56] Judges Higgins, Kooijmans, Elaraby, Owada and Simma. Judge Higgins was a party to General Comment No 24 of the Human Rights Committee when she served on that body.

[57] 1951 ICJ Reports 15.

[58] 2006 ICJ Reports 72 para 29.

[59] Pellet Report(n 47) guidelines 3.2 paras 14–15.

[60] Vienna Convention (n 3) article 46. This provision was considered but not decided upon by the Constitutional Court in *Harksen* (n 4) 836 para 27.

way if it contributed to the error by its own conduct or if the circumstances were such as to put it on notice of a possible error.[61]

A treaty will be void where the consent of a state has been secured by means of threats directed at the representative of that state[62]—as has occurred in 1939 when Germany forced the President of Czechoslovakia to sign a treaty creating a German protectorate over Bohemia and Moravia, and again in 1968 when the Soviet Union forced Czechoslovakian representatives to conclude a treaty allowing Soviet troops to be stationed in Czechoslovakia.

Before the prohibition on the use of force in international relations it was not uncommon for a treaty to be procured by the threat or use of force. Indeed, many boundary treaties were concluded after a war in which the victor had expanded its territory. The outlawing of the use of force by the Pact of Paris of 1928 and the Charter of the United Nations[63] has radically altered the situation. Accordingly, article 52 of the Vienna Convention provides:

> A treaty is void if its conclusion has been procured by the threat or use of force in violation of the principles of international law embodied in the Charter of the United Nations.

The emergence of the doctrine of *jus cogens* has had an important impact on the law of treaties. Article 53 of the Vienna Convention declares that a 'treaty is void, if, at the time of its conclusion, it conflicts with a peremptory norm of general international law'. Although there is some dispute over precisely which norms qualify as 'peremptory', there is general agreement that the prohibitions on the use of force, genocide, racial discrimination, slavery, torture, and the suppression of self-determination are part of *jus cogens*.[64]

TERMINATION OF TREATIES

As mentioned above, treaties are to be honoured in accordance with the principle of *pacta sunt servanda*. Consequently, a treaty may not be terminated or suspended unless the treaty contemplates such termination or suspension, or if the parties agree thereto.[65] A material breach of a treaty—ie, the violation of a term essential to the accomplishment of the purpose of the treaty or a repudiation not sanctioned by the Vienna Convention—entitles the other party to

[61] Vienna Convention (n 3) article 48.

[62] Ibid article 51; R Jennings and A Watts (eds) *Oppenheim's International Law* vol 1 9 ed (1992) 1290.

[63] Charter of the United Nations (n 9) article 2(4).

[64] See above, Chapter 3.

[65] Vienna Convention (n 3) articles 54–7. On the procedure to be followed in South Africa for the termination of a treaty, see Botha (n 15) 84–5.

invoke the breach as a ground for terminating the treaty.[66] It was on this basis that the International Court of Justice held that the General Assembly of the United Nations had lawfully terminated the Mandate for South West Africa in 1966 in resolution 2145 (XXI). According to the Court, South Africa had repudiated the Mandate of 1920, by refusing to account to the United Nations for its administration of the territory and had violated its essential provisions by applying apartheid in the territory. Consequently, the General Assembly as successor to the Council of the League of Nations was entitled to terminate the Mandate, 'an international agreement having the character of a treaty', because of South Africa's material breach of the Mandate.[67]

Customary international law recognises the right of a state to terminate a treaty where there has been 'a fundamental change in the circumstances which determined the parties to accept a treaty, if it has resulted in a radical transformation of the extent of the obligations imposed by it'.[68] This principle, known as the doctrine of *rebus sic stantibus*, is codified[69] by article 62 of the Vienna Convention which provides:

> (1) A fundamental change of circumstances which has occurred with regard to those existing at the time of the conclusion of a treaty, and which was not foreseen by the parties, may not be invoked as a ground for terminating or withdrawing from the treaty unless:
> *(a)* the existence of those circumstances constituted an essential basis of the consent of the parties to be bound by the treaty; and
> *(b)* the effect of the change is radically to transform the extent of obligations still to be performed under the treaty.
>
> (2) A fundamental change of circumstances may not be invoked as a ground for terminating or withdrawing from a treaty:
> *(a)* if the treaty establishes a boundary; or
> *(b)* if the fundamental change is the result of a breach by the party invoking it either of an obligation under the treaty or of any other international obligation owed to any other party to the treaty.

The doctrine of *rebus sic stantibus* was debated in South Africa in the late 1960s and early 1970s in the context of the Simonstown Agreement of 1955.[70] In terms of this agreement, the United Kingdom

[66] Vienna Convention (n 3) article 60.

[67] *Legal Consequences for States of the Continued Presence of South Africa in Namibia (South West Africa) Notwithstanding Security Council Resolution 276 (1970)* 1971 ICJ Reports 16 at 46–7.

[68] *Fisheries Jurisdiction (UK v Iceland) Jurisdiction of the Court* 1973 ICJ Reports 3 at 18.

[69] Ibid; *The Gabcikovo-Nagymaros Project (Hungary v Slovakia)* 1997 ICJ Reports 7 at 64–5.

[70] See J Dugard 'The Simonstown Agreement: South Africa, Britain and the United Nations' (1968) 85 *SALJ* 142; GG Lawrie 'The Simonstown Agreement: South Africa,

agreed to transfer control of the Simonstown Naval Base to South Africa on condition that its facilities would be made available to the United Kingdom in any war in which it (but not necessarily South Africa) was involved. Moreover, South Africa undertook to maintain the base for this purpose. At the same time, Britain agreed to supply the South African Navy with a number of naval vessels between 1955 and 1963. In 1964, the British government announced that it would discontinue the supply of any further naval equipment to South Africa in order to give effect to United Nations resolutions calling for an arms embargo against South Africa. Although Britain had by this time supplied the naval vessels expressly provided for in the Simonstown Agreement, it was argued that the Agreement, and particularly South Africa's obligation to maintain the base for the United Kingdom in any war in which it might become involved, was premised on an understanding that Britain would continue to supply South Africa with naval equipment. Consequently, Britain's refusal to do so constituted a fundamental change of circumstance which entitled South Africa to terminate the Agreement. In fact, no such unilateral denunciation occurred because the two parties agreed to terminate the Agreement in 1975[71]—as a result of the changed circumstances. Obviously, this is the preferable course for parties to adopt in a case of this kind as the unilateral invocation of the doctrine of *rebus sic stantibus* can seriously threaten international stability.

The Vienna Convention is silent on the effect of war and armed conflict on treaties.[72] This is an unsettled area of law, as some treaties, such as those dealing with humanitarian law, come into effect on the outbreak of hostilities while others are suspended due to impossibility of performance. Extradition agreements fall into the latter category. This was confirmed in *Harksen v President of the Republic of South Africa*[73] in which the Cape Provincial Division held, relying on American authorities, that:

> [A]n extradition treaty is not abrogated by the outbreak of hostilities between the parties thereto but is merely suspended . . . the suspension of such treaties

Britain and the Commonwealth' (1968) 85 *SALJ* 157; and GG Lawrie 'Britain's obligations under the Simonstown Agreements' (1971) 47 *International Affairs* 708; JC Woodliffe 'White Paper on the legal obligations of the British Government arising out of the Simonstown Agreements' (1971) 20 *ICLQ* 753; J Dugard 'Public international law' 1971 *Annual Survey* 35 at 45–6.

[71] See the statement by the then Minister of Defence, PW Botha, in *House of Assembly Debates* vol 57 col 8489 (16 June 1975); J Dugard 'Public international law' 1975 *Annual Survey* 28; (1975) 1 *SAYIL* 155, 199.

[72] Report of the International Law Commission (2011) 63rd Session, *GAOR* 66th Session, Supplement No 10 UN Doc A/66/10.

[73] 1998 (2) SA 1011 (C).

is ordinarily terminated on and in accordance with a peace treaty between the countries concerned.[74]

INTERPRETATION OF TREATIES[75]

The interpretation of treaties follows the same pattern as the interpretation of statutes in municipal law. There are different approaches that reflect different judicial attitudes towards the nature of the judicial process; and there are different rules, borrowed from municipal law, that judges may invoke to support their decisions.[76]

There are broadly three approaches to treaty interpretation: the textual, the teleological, and the intention of the parties. The first gives effect to the literal or grammatical meaning of words and is the approach favoured by formalists and positivists. The second emphasises the object and purpose of a treaty in the interpretative process. Ambiguities in a treaty are resolved by choosing that interpretation which gives the maximum effect to the main purpose and object of the treaty. The third approach seeks to give effect to the intention or presumed intention of the parties, which the judge infers from the text and the preparatory works (*travaux préparatoires*) or historical record of the treaty. Reliance on the intention of the original signatories to a multilateral treaty to which a considerable number of states have later acceded (as in the case of the Charter of the United Nations) is not satisfactory and for this reason it is argued that regard should be had to the contemporary expectation of parties to a multilateral treaty as evidenced by their subsequent practice rather than to the intention of the original signatories as evidenced by the preparatory works.

The International Court of Justice has approved all these approaches as rules of interpretation at some time or another. Today the Vienna Convention accepts them all. Article 31 recognises both the textual and teleological approaches in providing that a treaty is to be interpreted 'in accordance with the ordinary meaning to be given to the terms of the treaty in their context and in the light of its object and purpose'. The intention-of-the-parties approach receives support

[74] *Harksen* (1998) (n 73) 1023A–B, citing *Argento v Horn* 241 F 2d 258 (6th Cir 1957); *Gallina v Fraser* 177 F Supp 856 (DC, D Conn).

[75] H Lauterpacht 'Restrictive interpretation and the principle of effectiveness in the interpretation of treaties' (1949) 26 *BYIL* 48; R Gardner *Treaty Interpretation* 2 ed (2015); M Fitzmaurice, O Elias and P Merkouris *Treaty Interpretation and the Vienna Convention on the Law of Treaties: 30 Years On* (2010); E Bjorge *The Evolutionary Interpretation of Treaties* (2014).

[76] For example, the rules reflected in the maxims *eiusdem generis, expressio unius est exclusio alterius, contra proferentem, ut res magis valeat quam pereat* and *generalia specialibus non derogant*.

from article 32, which permits recourse 'to supplementary means of interpretation, including the preparatory works of the treaty and the circumstances of its conclusion', while article 31(3) allows consideration of any subsequent agreement between parties relating to the interpretation of the treaty or any subsequent state practice in the application of the treaty that establishes the agreement of the parties regarding its interpretation. (Of course such agreement or practice must be intended to interpret and not to amend the treaty.)

Treaties are living instruments that evolve over time in response to changed circumstances. This matter has been the subject of a study by the International Law Commission into subsequent agreement and practice by states in relation to the interpretation of treaties. The Commission has taken the position that subsequent agreement and practice 'may assist in determining whether or not the presumed intention of the parties on the conclusion of a treaty was to give the terms used a meaning which is capable of evolving over time'.[77]

Like municipal law, international law knows no hierarchy of rules of interpretation. Instead, the judge is allowed to select the rule or approach which he considers most appropriate in the circumstances of the case. This was acknowledged by the International Law Commission in 2018 when it stated that '[t]he interpretation of a treaty consists of a single operation, which places appropriate emphasis on the various means of interpretation indicated respectively in Articles 31 and 32'.[78]

The dispute between South Africa and the international community over South West Africa/Namibia provided a judicial battleground for the different schools of treaty interpretation.[79] In its advisory opinions of 1950,[80] 1955,[81] 1956,[82] and 1971,[83] and in its judgment on preliminary objections in the *South West Africa Cases*

[77] Conclusion 8 of the Draft conclusions adopted by the drafting committee on second reading on subsequent agreement and practice in relation to treaty interpretation, International Law Commission, 70th session, 2018, A/CN.4L 907 of 11 May 2018.

[78] Ibid Conclusion 2.5.

[79] See Chapter 22 below; and J Dugard *The South West Africa/Namibia Dispute* (1973).

[80] *International Status of South West Africa* 1950 ICJ Reports 128.

[81] *Voting Procedure on Questions Relating to Reports and Petitions Concerning the Territory of South West Africa* 1955 ICJ Reports 67.

[82] *Admissibility of Hearings of Petitioners by the Committee on South West Africa* 1956 ICJ Reports 23.

[83] *Legal Consequences for States of the Continued Presence of South Africa in Namibia (South West Africa) Notwithstanding Security Council Resolution 276 (1970)* 1971 ICJ Reports 16.

(Ethiopia and Liberia v South Africa) of 1962,[84] the International Court of Justice adopted a teleological approach by interpreting ambiguities in the Mandate for South West Africa, the Covenant of the League of Nations, and the Charter of the United Nations in such a way as to give effect to the principal object of the mandates system—the 'well-being and development' of the peoples of mandated territories which was to form a 'sacred trust of civilization'.[85] This allowed the International Court of Justice to hold that the United Nations had succeeded to the supervisory powers of the League of Nations over the Mandate despite the absence of any express provision for such a succession;[86] to approve the methods of supervision employed by the United Nations;[87] to find that the mandates system contemplated judicial supervision of a mandatory's administration;[88] and ultimately to hold that the United Nations lawfully terminated the Mandate as a result of South Africa's persistent violation of the Mandate.[89] Only in 1966,[90] when the composition of the Court had been substantially altered by the death, illness, and recusal of three of its members, did a narrow majority reject the teleological method of interpretation and invoke the intention of the signatories to the Covenant of the League of Nations in order to hold (unlike the Court of 1962) that judicial protection of the people of a mandated territory had not been contemplated.

In all its appearances before the International Court of Justice, South Africa pursued a strong anti-teleological approach and instead urged the Court to adopt a textual or original-intention method of reasoning.[91] A similar line of argument characterised the speeches of South African delegates in the political organs of the United Nations during the apartheid era, when they sought to exclude discussion of

[84] *South West Africa Cases, Preliminary Objections* 1962 ICJ Reports 318.

[85] This object is described in article 22 of the Covenant of the League of Nations.

[86] *International Status of South West Africa* (n 80).

[87] *Voting Procedure on Questions Relating to Reports and Petitions Concerning the Territory of South West Africa* (n 81) and *Admissibility of Hearings of Petitioners by the Committee on South West Africa* (n 82).

[88] *South West Africa Cases, Preliminary Objections* (n 84).

[89] *Legal Consequences for States of the Continued Presence of South Africa in Namibia (South West Africa) Notwithstanding Security Council Resolution 276 (1970)* (n 83).

[90] *South West Africa, Second Phase* 1966 ICJ Reports 6, particularly at 48.

[91] See RP Schaffer 'Current trends in treaty interpretation and the South African approach' (1976–7) 7 *Australian Year Book of International Law* 129; AC Cilliers 'Die *Suidwes-Afrika-saak* en die volkereg' (1971) 34 *THRHR* 25; J Dugard 'The *Opinion on South-West Africa (Namibia)*: The teleologists triumph' (1971) 88 *SALJ* 460 and op cit (n 79); JT van Wyk 'The International Court of Justice at the cross-roads' 1967 *Acta Juridica* 201; J Hund 'Positivism and the South African approach to international adjudication: A sociological analysis' (1980) 6 *SAYIL* 1.

apartheid on the ground that it fell within South Africa's exclusive domestic jurisdiction.[92]

Strategically, lawyers representing the South African government had no option but to pursue such a course. Then again, it is probably true to say that the narrow textual-original-intention method of reasoning, which elevated the interest of state sovereignty above the wider community interest and respect for human rights, was one which came naturally to South African government lawyers of this period, for it mirrored the pro-executive, anti-rights decisions of South Africa's municipal courts during the apartheid era.[93]

Constitutional change in South Africa has brought with it changes in respect of judicial approaches to statutory interpretation. Courts do not hesitate to employ purposive methods of interpretation in constitutional matters and this approach has been extended to international matters. In *Abel v Minister of Justice*,[94] *Luxavia (Pty) Ltd v Gray Security Services (Pty) Ltd*,[95] and *Potgieter v British Airways plc*,[96] the Courts expressly approved a purposive interpretation with respect to extradition and aviation treaties incorporated into municipal law.

Courts have invoked the preparatory works (*travaux préparatoires*) of incorporated treaties in the process of interpretation as permitted by article 32 of the Vienna Convention. In *Portion 20 of Plot 15 Athol (Pty) Ltd v Rodrigues*[97] Hussain J considered the preparatory work of the International Law Commission in his interpretation of the Vienna Convention on Diplomatic Relations of 1961, which is incorporated into South African law. In *MV Mbashi Transnet Ltd v MV Mbashi*[98] the Court held that it might have regard to the *travaux préparatoires* of the International Convention on Salvage of 1989. However, in this case, the Court simply gave effect to a provision in the incorporating statute that provided that in interpreting the convention a Court may 'consider the preparatory works to the convention'.[99]

SUCCESSION TO TREATIES[100]

A change in government does not affect the validity of treaties entered into on behalf of a state. The treaties of its predecessor also

[92] JC Heunis *United Nations versus South Africa* (1986).

[93] For a discussion of these decisions, see J Dugard *Human Rights and the South African Legal Order* (1978) parts 4 and 5.

[94] 2001 (1) SA 1230 (C) 1236 para 22.

[95] 2001 (4) SA 211 (W) 222–3 paras 26–8.

[96] 2005 (1) SA 133 (C) 140.

[97] 2001 (1) SA 1285 (W) 1293.

[98] 2002 (3) SA 217 (D) 222–3.

[99] Wreck and Salvage Act 94 of 1996, s 2(5).

[100] DP O'Connell *State Succession in Municipal Law and International Law* 2 vols (1967); Y Makonnen *International Law and the New States of Africa* (1983); R Schaffer

bind the new government. Even if the internal change has been brought about by revolution or involves a change from a monarchy to a republic, the principle of continuity applies. This is because such changes do not alter the international personality of the state that concluded the treaty.[101] The dramatic political change that occurred in South Africa in 1994 must be seen in this context. The transformation from a racist state to a democracy, with full recognition of the principle of self-determination, had profound internal consequences but did not alter South Africa's international personality. It remained a member of the United Nations and continued to be bound by pre-1994 treaties entered into by the National Party government.[102] This is recognised by both the 1993 and the 1996 Constitutions which provide for continuity of treaty obligations.[103]

The position is different when the state itself undergoes a change in legal personality as a result of annexation, decolonisation, the dissolution of one state into several states, or the merger of several states into one state. Here two main theories have been advanced to deal with the question of succession.

Early writers adopted the Roman law principle of 'universal succession' and argued that the new state succeeds to all the treaties of its predecessor. In the late 19th century, the 'clean slate' doctrine, which denies succession completely, replaced this theory. The issue of succession to treaties became important in the 1960's during the process of decolonisation. While doctrine favoured the 'clean slate' approach to treaties entered into on behalf of colonies by the colonial power, the newly independent states adopted a more pragmatic line in many instances and agreed to keep these treaties in force.[104] At this stage, the International Law Association (ILA), under the guidance of

(Balkin) 'Succession to treaties: South African practice in the light of current developments in international law' (1981) 30 *ICLQ* 593; Aust (n 1) ch 22; M Craven *The Decolonization of International Law: State Succession and the Law of Treaties* (2007; I Shearer 'State succession in relation to treaties: Looking back and looking forward' in T Maluwa, M du Plessis and D Tladi *The Pursuit of a Brave New World in International Law. Essays in Honour of John Dugard* (2017) 321.

[101] Jennings and Watts (n 62) 1253. See, too, *Minister of Justice v Bagattini* 1975 (4) SA 252 (T).

[102] Ziyad Motala has argued that South Africa is not bound by its pre-1994 treaties because there has been a change in legal personality. See Z Motala 'Under international law, does the new order in South Africa assume the obligations and responsibilities of the apartheid order? An argument for realism over formalism' (1997) 30 *CILSA* 287. This argument flies in the face of both international law and the 1993 and 1996 Constitutions, which are premised on the continuity of the South African state.

[103] Act 200 of 1993, s 231(1); Constitution of the Republic of South Africa, 1996, s 231(5).

[104] See *Molefi v Principal Legal Adviser* [1971] AC 182 (PC) dealing with the succession of Lesotho to Britain's multilateral treaties.

Professor DP O'Connell, conducted a thorough study of jurisprudence and state practice on this subject and concluded that succession to treaties would occur in the case of newly independent states provided that no contrary action was taken indicating an intention not to be bound by the treaty.[105]

The International Law Commission took up this subject and in 1978, the Vienna Convention on Succession of States in Respect of Treaties (1978 Convention)[106] was adopted. This Convention approves the 'clean slate' doctrine in respect of newly independent states[107] and disavows the methods employed to keep treaties in force after independence.[108] This treaty has been received without enthusiasm by states—only 22 have ratified it to date—which confirms that its prescriptions do not reflect customary law or represent an acceptable progressive development. The Convention's approval of the 'clean slate' rule for newly independent states rather than that of pragmatic continuity, advocated by O'Connell,[109] is particularly questionable.

The Convention has had little, if any, impact on state practice or judicial decisions. Moreover, the 'clean slate' doctrine is subject to important exceptions. The 1978 Convention itself acknowledges that it does not apply to boundary treaties[110] and it has become clear that multilateral human rights treaties are not affected by state succession. In 1997, in General Comment 26 the Human Rights Committee declared that the protection accorded to people under the ICCPR 'devolves with territory and continues to belong to them, notwithstanding change in government or . . . state succession'.[111] In these circumstances it is difficult to discern any clear rules relating to the succession to treaties. Shearer is probably correct in saying that '[i]t may well be that the quest for general rules is illusory in view of the problems posed by issues of identity and continuity of States, and by

[105] For a full account of the work of the ILA, see Shearer (n 100).

[106] (1971) 71 *AJIL* 971. See N Rembe 'The Vienna Convention of state succession in respect of treaties: An African perspective on its applicability and its limitations' (1984) 17 *CILSA* 131.

[107] Vienna Convention (n 3) article 16. This article provides: 'A newly independent state is not bound to maintain in force, or to become a party to, any treaty by reason only of the fact that at the date of the succession of states the treaty was in force in respect of the territory to which the succession of states relates.'

[108] Articles 8 and 9.

[109] Op cit (n 100). See too the criticisms of the 1978 Convention by O'Connell cited in Shearer (n 100) 343–6.

[110] Vienna Convention (n 3) article 11.

[111] A/53/40; MN Shaw *International Law* 8 ed (2017) 743–4.

the exigencies of international relations. For most cases, pragmatic solutions have been found'.[112]

The practice of states in southern Africa has shown a preference for the continuity of treaty obligations. Although the British government took the view that the treaties of the Orange Free State and South African Republic lapsed when they were annexed in 1900,[113] it later took care to ensure that treaties binding on the four colonies continued to bind the Union of South Africa after 1910. The South Africa Act of 1909 provided that '[a]ll rights and obligations under any conventions or agreements which are binding on any of the Colonies shall devolve upon the Union at its establishment'. [114] When South Africa became a Republic in 1961, provision was likewise made for the continuation of treaties in s 112 of the Constitution,[115] which provided:

> All rights and obligations under conventions, treaties or agreements which were binding on any of the Colonies incorporated in the Union of South Africa at its establishment and were still binding on the Union immediately prior to the commencement of this Act, shall be rights and obligations of the Republic, just as all other rights and obligations under conventions, treaties or agreements which immediately prior to the commencement of this Act were binding on the Union.

The 1983 Constitution contained a similar provision.[116]

When South Africa became a democracy, care was taken to ensure that treaties entered into by previous regimes remained in force. The 1993 Constitution provided:

> All rights and obligations under international agreements which immediately before the commencement of this Constitution were vested in or binding on the Republic within the meaning of the previous Constitution, shall be vested in or binding on the Republic under this Constitution, *unless otherwise provided by an Act of Parliament*. [117]

Although this provision recognised the principle of continuity it seemed to contemplate—in the final part—that Parliament might unilaterally divest itself of treaty obligations undertaken by the old regime by an Act of Parliament.[118] This part of the provision, which

[112] Shearer (n 100) 357.

[113] For a discussion of this subject, see Schaffer (n 100) 609–12. See, too, *West Rand Central Gold Mining Co v R* [1905] 2 KB 391 (CA), in which it was held that the British government did not succeed to the financial obligations of the South African Republic.

[114] Section 148(1) of the South Africa Act of 1909; Schaffer (n 100) 612–14.

[115] Act 32 of 1961.

[116] Act 110 of 1983, s 94.

[117] Act 200 of 1993, s 231(1). Emphasis added.

[118] For criticism of this provision, see J Dugard 'International law and the "Final" Constitution' (1995) 11 *SAJHR* 241 at 245.

apparently was inserted to enable South Africa to repudiate suspected secret military agreements with Israel and Taiwan,[119] does not appear in the 1996 Constitution, which provides, without qualification, that:

> The Republic is bound by international agreements which were binding on the Republic when this Constitution took effect.[120]

As the TBVC states were unrecognised, they did not enter into 'treaties' with any state other than South Africa.[121] These agreements were disposed of by internal constitutional arrangements not involving international law.

Successive South African constitutions have therefore sought to ensure that both the treaties entered into on its behalf by the United Kingdom and those entered into by South Africa itself after it achieved treaty-making capacity continue in force despite changes in international and internal constitutional status.[122] Other states have accepted the continued validity of such treaties[123] or have expressly terminated treaties of this kind when they no longer wished them to continue.[124]

Expectations that Namibia would adopt a 'clean slate' policy towards pre-independence treaties entered into on its behalf by South Africa did not materialise when Namibia became independent.[125] Instead, the Namibian Constitution of 1990 provides in article 143:

> All existing international agreements binding upon Namibia shall remain in force, unless and until the National Assembly acting under article 63(2)(d) hereof otherwise decides.

Article 63(2)(d) empowers the National Assembly to decide

[119] See M Olivier 'The status of international law in South Africa municipal law: Section 231 of the 1993 Constitution' (1994/4) 19 *SAYIL* 1 at 4.

[120] Section 231(5) of Act 200 of 1993; *Abel v Minister of Justice* 2001 (1) SA 1230 (C) 1240 para 34. See, too, N Botha 'Treaties after the 1996 Constitution: More questions than answers' (1997) 22 *SAYIL* 95 at 100.

[121] See Schaffer (n 100) 616–20; J Dugard 'Public international law' 1976 *Annual Survey* 26 at 28–31; J Dugard 'Public international law' 1977 *Annual Survey* 49 at 50–2; H Booysen 'The South African homelands and their capacity to conclude treaties' (1982) 8 *SAYIL* 58.

[122] Schaffer (n 100) 614–16.

[123] See *M v Federal Department of Justice and Police* 75 ILR 107, in which the Swiss Federal Tribunal held that an extradition agreement of 1880 between South Africa and Switzerland remained in force. Here the intention of the parties to continue the treaty was confirmed by an exchange of notes.

[124] In 1968, Denmark terminated its extradition agreement of 1873 which had been extended to South Africa by Britain: Proc 157 *GG* 2101 of 21 June 1968.

[125] See PC Szasz 'Succession to treaties under the Namibian Constitution' (1989–90) 15 *SAYIL* 65.

whether or not to succeed to pre-independence treaties entered into by administrations 'in which the majority of the Namibian people have historically not enjoyed democratic representation and participation'.

South African judicial decisions[126] show support for both continuity and non-continuity of treaty obligations on a change of legal personality, but the judicial authority for the former approach is undoubtedly weightier.

In *S v Eliasov*[127] the Transvaal Provincial Division held that Southern Rhodesia did not succeed to an extradition agreement between South Africa and the Federation of Rhodesia and Nyasaland on the dissolution of the Federation. According to Hiemstra J:

> The Federation as a whole was a state with treaty-making capacity. That state was dissolved into three territories and so ceased to exist. With it ceased its treaties. That is the natural and normal sequel.[128]

Later the Natal Provincial Division in *S v Oosthuizen*[129] found that an extradition agreement of 1963 between Southern Rhodesia and South Africa terminated after Rhodesia's unilateral declaration of independence (UDI) in 1965 on the ground that post-UDI Rhodesia was a new state with a different legal personality.

Harksen v President of the Republic of South Africa[130] raised an interesting question of succession to an extradition treaty. The President of South Africa had consented to the extradition of Harksen, an alleged criminal, to Germany in terms of s 3(2) of the Extradition Act 67 of 1962, which gives the President that authority if there is *no extradition agreement* between South Africa and the requesting foreign state. In *Harksen's* case it was argued that the President did not have the necessary authority because an extradition agreement had already been in force between South Africa and Germany, namely, the United Kingdom/Germany agreement of 1872, extended to South Africa during the colonial era. Although this agreement had been suspended during World War II, it was claimed that it had been revived by an exchange of notes between South Africa and the Federal Republic of Germany in 1954. The Court

[126] For a discussion of these decisions, see Schaffer (n 100) 620–7.

[127] 1965 (2) SA 770 (T).

[128] Ibid 773C–D. *Sed contra*, see J Dugard 'Succession to federal treaties on the dissolution of a federation' (1965) 82 *SALJ* 430; N Botha 'The coming of age of public international law in South Africa' (1992/3) 18 *SAYIL* 36 at 38.

[129] 1977 (1) SA 823 (N). The main criticism of this decision is that it decided on the statehood of Rhodesia without recourse to an executive certificate. See J Dugard 'Rhodesia: Does South Africa recognise it as an independent state?' (1977) 94 *SALJ* 127.

[130] 1998 (2) SA 1011 (C) 109–30.

conducted a thorough examination of the vicissitudes of Germany's treaty-making power after World War II and concluded that it had lacked the competence to revive the 1872 agreement without the approval of the Allied High Commission (High Commission for Occupied Germany) before 1955. Thereafter the Federal Republic of Germany could have reactivated the agreement, but in fact this had not been done by the exchange of notes between South Africa and the Federal Republic of 1954: first, because there was no consent on the part of the Allied High Commission as required before 1955; and, secondly, because these notes contained a proposal and counter-proposal which did not constitute an agreement between the two states.

Other decisions point in a different direction. In *S v Bull*,[131] the Transvaal Provincial Division held that Malawi succeeded to the extradition agreement between South Africa and the Federation of Rhodesia and Nyasaland where South Africa's intention to continue to be bound by the treaty was evidenced by an executive certificate. Although the clear evidence of South Africa's intention to be bound by the treaty served to distinguish *Eliasov*, the Court expressed its disagreement with this decision and expressed approval for a rule of succession to treaties where it occurred as a result of an orderly and progressive transfer of constitutional power.[132] The Appellate Division gave its approval to this approach in *S v Devoy*,[133] in which it confirmed Malawi's succession to the Federation's extradition treaty. Here Ogilvie Thompson CJ stated:

> [I]t does not appear to me to be possible to formulate any universal international-law rule regarding the continuation or otherwise of treaties consequent upon the dissolution of the Federation of Rhodesia and Nyasaland. Each case must, I think, be decided on the particular facts relating to it, but, specifically as regards extradition treaties, at the same time bearing in mind the existence of a general tendency in favour of their continuance.[134]

[131] 1967 (2) SA 636 (T).

[132] Ibid 638–40. See J Dugard 'Succession to federal treaties revisited' (1967) 84 *SALJ* 250.

[133] 1971 (3) SA 899 (A). This decision endorsed a finding of the Natal Provincial Division which approved of the approach adopted in *S v Bull: S v Devoy* 1971 (1) SA 359 (N).

[134] *S v Devoy* (n 133) 905H.

CHAPTER 21

International Economic Relations*

Max du Plessis and Kholofelo Kugler[1]

INTRODUCTION

The regulation of international economic relations has evolved from 'gunboat diplomacy' to principles drawn from customary international law, common traditions of municipal law and *lex mercatoria*, or law of the merchant or market place.[2] These sources have influenced the establishment, content and application of principles such as most-favoured nation (MFN) and acquired rights, as well as the application of conceptual cornerstones of the international system such as sovereignty and the principles of non-interference in the internal affairs of states.[3] At a time when the prevailing economic philosophy of international relations was that of *laissez faire* trade[4] and comparative advantage,[5] many of the principles governing international economic relations were principles applicable to the conduct of private persons, rather than to states directly. The development of

* Sir Daniel Bethlehem QC, former Director of the Lauterpacht Research Centre for International Law, University of Cambridge, and Principal Legal Adviser to the Foreign and Commonwealth Office, originally wrote this chapter. It retains some of the original content and structure but has been significantly modified and updated by the named authors to reflect more recent developments.

[1] The views expressed in this chapter do not necessarily reflect the views of any organisations with which Kholofelo Kugler is affiliated.

[2] See generally I Seidl-Hohenveldern *International Economic Law* 3 ed (1999); H Fox *International Economic Law and Developing States: An Introduction* (1992); W Shan, P Simons and D Singh (eds) *Redefining Sovereignty in International Economic Law* (2008). On *lex mercatoria*, see M Mustill 'The new *Lex Mercatoria*: The first twenty-five years' in M Bos and I Brownlie (eds) *Liber Amicorum for Lord Wilberforce* (1987) 149; KP Berger *The Creeping Codification of the* Lex Mercatoria (1999); JW Salacuse *The Law of Investment Treaties* (2015); and S Subedi *International Investment Law: Reconciling Policy and Principle* 3 ed (2016).

[3] See Seidl-Hohenveldern (n 2). On the origins of the MFN clause, see E Ustor 'Report on the Most-Favoured-Nation clause' *Yearbook of the International Law Commission* (1969) vol II, 159–68 and (1970) vol II, 200–37.

[4] The doctrine of *laissez faire* trade, articulated most significantly by Adam Smith, postulates that economic affairs are best guided by the decisions of individuals to the broad exclusion of collective authority.

[5] The doctrine of comparative advantage, generally attributed to David Ricardo, postulates that states (and individuals) should specialise in what they do best and trade with others to meet their outstanding economic needs. It is thus premised on the principle of freedom of trade.

states as organisers and subjects of international law in economic relations, saw much of its refinement in the 20th century.[6]

While sources of international law founded in the practice of states and other economic operators remain important today, the legal regime of international economic relations has changed beyond all recognition in the period since the end of World War II. Perhaps more so than virtually any other area of public international law, economic relations between states and private actors in different states, is regulated by treaty. International organisations today[7] are concerned with the regulation of international economic activity ranging from agriculture to development aid, banking, commodities, post and telecommunications, transport and trade, and virtually all the specialised agencies of the United Nations are engaged in some manner with activity having an economic dimension. This institutionalisation of international economic relations[8] is an important element in what is often dubbed the constitutionalisation of international law.[9]

Other important features of post-war international law dealing with international economic relations have included concerns with the fairness of the international economic order put in place by the Bretton Woods institutions in the immediate aftermath of World War II. There have also been attempts to develop a new international economic order that would more adequately address the needs of developing countries,[10] as well as more general concerns with trade in commodities,[11] development,[12] foreign investment,[13] and the

[6] T Cottier and M Oesch *International Trade Regulation: Law and Policy in the WTO, the European Union and Switzerland Cases, Materials and Comments* (2005) 9–22.

[7] G Schiavone *International Organizations: A Dictionary and Directory* 6 ed (2016); H Booysen 'Globalisation and international trade law' (2001) 26 *SAYIL* 114.

[8] SA Voitovich *International Economic Organizations and the International Legal Process* (1995).

[9] E-U Petersmann *Constitutional Functions and Constitutional Problems of International Economic Law* (1991) and E-U Petersmann 'How to constitutionalize international law and foreign policy for the benefit of civil society?' (1998) 20 *Michigan Journal of International Law* 1.

[10] See, for example, General Assembly Resolution 1803 (XVII) of 14 December 1962 on Permanent Sovereignty over Natural Resources and General Assembly Resolution 3281 (XXIX) of 12 December 1974 on the Charter of Economic Rights and Duties of States. Also, K Hossain (ed) *Legal Aspects of the New International Order* (1980); and C Raghavan *Recolonization: GATT, the Uruguay Round & the Third World* (1990).

[11] See generally T Akiyama et al *Commodity Market Reform in Africa: Some Recent Experience* World Bank Policy Research Working Paper 2995 (2003); BS Chimni *International Commodity Agreements: A Legal Study* (1987).

[12] SR Chowdhury, EMG Denters and PJIM de Waart (eds) *The Right to Development in International Law* (1992).

[13] D Bradlow and A Escher (eds) *Legal Aspects of Foreign Direct Investment* (1999); M Sornarajah *The International Law on Foreign Investment* 2 ed (2004); Subedi (n 2).

regulation of multinational enterprises.[14] A further significant element of the legal regime of international economic relations has been the increasing trend towards regional integration through the establishment of free trade areas, customs unions,[15] and the so-called mega-regional trade agreements that encompass a large number of countries that are not necessarily concentrated in one geographical region. Counter trends to deeper economic integration have also recently emerged with states asserting their sovereign right to regulate in the public interest within the ambit of international investment law;[16] the United Kingdom voting in a national referendum in 2016 to withdraw from the Treaty of Rome establishing the European Union;[17] and the 45th President of the United States, Donald Trump, adopting policies that seek to promote the United States' trade interests,[18] including withdrawing from international free trade treaties.[19]

A body of law generally referred to as international economic law governs current international economic relations. This area of law has been broadly defined to encompass the conduct of sovereign states, as well as that of private actors involved in cross-border economic transactions. This field includes the focus areas of this

[14] See, generally, PT Muchlinski *Multinational Enterprises and the Law* 2 ed (2007).

[15] See, generally et al 'The multilateral system and free trade agreements: What's the strategy?' (2003) 37 *International Law* 805; C Ng'ong'ola 'Regional integration and trade liberalisation in the Southern African Development Community' (2000) 3 *Journal of International Economic Law* 475.

[16] See, generally, C Titi *Right to Regulate in International Investment Law* (2014).

[17] On 24 June 2016, the result of a referendum deciding the United Kingdom's exit from the European Union, referred to as 'Brexit', was announced. See, SB Hobolt 'The Brexit vote: A divided nation, a divided continent' (2016) 23 (9) *Journal of European Public Policy* 12, 59.

[18] On 8 March 2018, the United States announced a 25 per cent and 10 per cent *ad valorem* tariff on steel products and aluminium, respectively. The additional tariffs were adopted pursuant to s 232 of the United States Trade Expansion Act of 1962, as amended, based on national security grounds. Further, on 3 April 2018, the United States Trade Representative announced a list of approximately 1330 Chinese goods that would be subject to an additional duty of 25 per cent pursuant to s 301 of the Trade Act, 1974. This duty would address China's reported policies that coerce foreign companies to transfer technology and intellectual property to domestic Chinese companies as a precondition of establishing a presence or operating in China. See, C Bown 'Chapter 2: The accumulating self-inflicted wounds from Trump's unilateral trade policy' in H Jiming and AS Posen (eds) *PIIE Briefing Part I 18-1 US-China Economic Relations from Conflicts to Solutions* (2018) 8 and 12.

[19] On 30 January 2017, the United States announced its withdrawal from the Trans-Pacific Partnership Agreement.

chapter: the laws and other instruments of financial relations, trade and cross-border investments.

International economic law is also based on the general principles of international law such as *pacta sunt servanda*, freedom, sovereign equality, reciprocity, and economic sovereignty, as well as the more modern tenets of international co-operation, permanent sovereignty over natural resources, and preferential treatment of lesser-developed countries.[20] Each field is disciplined by a complex web of legal instruments; the effectiveness of some have recently been put in question, particularly in the wake of the 2008 global financial crisis.[21]

THE SOURCES OF SOUTH AFRICA'S INTERNATIONAL ECONOMIC LAW COMMITMENTS AND THE KEY OBLIGATIONS

The section below addresses the sources of South Africa's international economic law commitments and the principal obligations that South Africa has undertaken. Some of the following general obligations will be discussed in detail later in the chapter.

The key obligations of parties under international financial law are largely contractual in nature, based on financial debt instruments concluded between the state and the international financial institution (IFI) or private financial institutions. IFIs are international financial organisations and typically include the International Monetary Fund (IMF) and the five multilateral development banks, namely, the World Bank Group, the African Development Bank, the Asian Development Bank, the Inter-American Development Bank, and the European Bank for Reconstruction and Development. The latter four are often referred to as regional development banks.[22] Public international law underpins the contractual debts between the IFI and the state.[23] Within the IMF, this relationship is informed by the financial transactions between the organisation and its members. A member country's quota determines, inter alia, its maximum

[20] Subedi (n 2).

[21] C Manger-Nestler 'Impacts of international law on the restructuring of the global financial system' in A von Bogdandy and R Wolfrum (eds) *Max Planck Yearbook of United Nations Law* 15 (2011) 165–227; C Tietje and M Lehmann 'The role and prospects of international law in financial regulation and supervision' (2010) 13(3) *Journal of International Economic Law* 663–82.

[22] V Bhargava 'The role of the international financial institutions in addressing global issues' in V Bhargava (ed) *Global Issues for Global Citizens: An Introduction to Key Development Challenges* (2006) 394.

[23] RSJ Martha *The Financial Obligations in International Law* (2015) 6.2.2. See also, *Interpretation of the Agreement of 25 March 1951 Between the World Health Organisation and Egypt, Advisory Opinion*, 1980 ICJ Report paras 94–5.

financial commitment to the IMF, its access to financing, and certain mutual financial obligations.[24] International financial law also encompasses the 'soft law' co-operation initiatives that facilitate the engagements of central banks to implement stricter financial regulation.

International trade law obligations are established in the Marrakesh Agreement Establishing the World Trade Organization (WTO Agreement) and its various annexes. The law of the World Trade Organization (WTO) is premised upon the principle of non-discrimination, ie the MFN and the national treatment obligations; progressive trade liberalisation; predictability and transparency; promoting fair competition; and encouraging development and economic reform through special and differential treatment in favour of developing countries and least developed countries.[25]

The basic tenets of international investment law are also memorialised in treaty form. Even for countries that have shirked the treaty model,[26] the following basic principles form the key obligations of the parties: (i) rules on admission and establishment of investments; (ii) the states' right to expropriate and the concomitant restrictions; (iii) standards of treatment of investors such as the states' obligation to grant fair and (iv) equitable treatment (FET) and full protection and security; and the same non-discrimination provisions contained in international trade treaties (MFN and national treatment obligations).[27]

1 International financial agreements

The legal regime of South Africa's international economic relations reflects the range and complexity of the developments discussed in the previous section. At the institutional level, this regime is generally treaty-based and includes a complex set of arrangements of a bilateral, plurilateral, and multilateral nature. These arrangements encompass those that are focused on southern Africa, the African region, as well as those in the broader international arena.

Within the ambit of international financial relations, by virtue of its membership in the United Nations, South Africa is a member of the IMF[28] and four of the five World Bank Group agencies, namely, the

[24] Martha (n 23) 6.1.3.

[25] World Trade Organization available at https://www.wto.org/english/thewto_e/whatis_e/tif_e/fact2_e.htm.

[26] Like South Africa, see below.

[27] See, generally, R Dolzer and C Schreuer *Principles of International Investment Law* 2 ed (2012).

[28] Articles of Agreement of the International Monetary Fund (1945) 1 UNTS 39. Note, the date given in parentheses after the name of this and the other agreements

International Bank for Reconstruction and Development (IBRD),[29] the International Development Association (IDA),[30] the International Finance Corporation (IFC),[31] and the Multilateral Investment Guarantee Agency (MIGA).[32] South Africa is also a member of the African Development Bank Group[33] and the New Development Bank.[34] In the area of international financial regulation, it is a member of the Group of Twenty (G20),[35] while the Reserve Bank of South Africa is a member of the Bank of International Settlements[36] and its Basel Committee on Banking Supervision.[37]

International financial agreements are often in the form of bilateral and syndicated loan agreements between IFIs or private lenders and the sovereign state borrower. Other forms of international financial agreements are sovereign bonds.

At the end of 2017, the South African Reserve Bank estimated South Africa's gross external debt at US$173 billion,[38] approximately 49 per cent of GDP. As at 31 March 2018, South Africa's international indebtedness included IBRD loans, credits, and grants totalling US$4,15 billion, of which US$3,31 billion has been disbursed and US$220 million repaid.[39]

In April 2017, credit ratings agencies Standard and Poor and Fitch downgraded South Africa's sovereign credit rating to default or junk

referred to below is the date of conclusion of the agreement in question. Invariably, this will differ from the date of the agreement's entry into force and, where different, from the date of the agreement's entry into force for South Africa.

[29] Articles of Association of the International Bank for Reconstruction and Development (1945) 2 UNTS 134.

[30] Articles of Agreement of the International Development Association (1960) 439 UNTS 249. The IBRD and the IDA are also commonly described as the World Bank.

[31] Articles of Agreement of the International Finance Corporation (1955) 264 UNTS 117.

[32] Convention Establishing the Multilateral Investment Guarantee Agency (1985) 24 *ILM* 1598 (see also 688).

[33] African Development Bank available at http://www.afdb.org/en/countries/.

[34] Formerly the BRICS Bank.

[35] G20 available at http://www.g20.org/English/index.html. The G20 is an international forum of governments of 20 countries to discuss policies promoting international financial stability.

[36] Bank of International Settlements (BIS) available at https://www.bis.org/about/member_cb.htm?m=1%7C2%t7C601.

[37] BIS available at https://www.bis.org/bcbs/membership.htm.

[38] South African Reserve Bank, Gross External Debt, 29 March 2018.

[39] World Bank 'Country Lending Summaries—South Africa' available at http://web.worldbank.org/WBSITE/EXTERNAL/PROJECTS/0,,pagePK:64392398~piPK:64392037~theSitePK:40941~countrycode:ZA~menuPK:64820000,00.html.

status.[40] Some factors contributing to the downgrade include low economic growth, a fall in commodity prices, the general struggling economy, and political instability arising under the presidency of former president Jacob Zuma. Possible market impacts following such downgrades include increases in inflation and general interest rates, including those at which the government services its debts, an overall decline in bond returns, and the threat of reduced availability of credit.[41]

The impact of rating announcements on emerging-markets like South Africa is significant.[42] As emerging markets are generally considered higher risk, international investors follow such announcements closely and are more likely to respond to negative downgrades by selling their debt and equity instruments, instead of riding out the storms of more developed markets.

While South Africa's membership of, and participation in, IFIs such as the IMF and World Bank are of unquestioned importance, the concomitant commitments invariably impinge on private transactions in a less direct manner because of the nature of agreements that emanate from South Africa's relationships with these organisations. That said, South Africa's sovereign credit rating downgrade to junk status and the potential financial impact on every South African resident highlight that the 'man and woman on the street' are not impervious to even the most remote international economic relationship into which the government enters.

2 International trade agreements

An original Contracting Party to the General Agreement on Tariffs and Trade of 1947 (GATT 1947), South Africa became a founding Member of the WTO in 1995, following the conclusion of the Uruguay Round of Multilateral Trade Negotiations.[43] South Africa is thus party to the Marrakesh Agreement Establishing the WTO, simply known as the WTO Agreement and its four annexes. Annex A contains the Multilateral Agreements on Trade in Goods, including

[40] N Naik, F Bhoola and J Rossouw 'Credit rating agencies: Who are they and do we need them?' (2017) 66 *New Agenda: South African Journal of Social and Economic Policy* 13–6.

[41] G Larraín, H Reisen and J von Maltzan 'Emerging market risk and sovereign credit ratings' *OECD Development Centre*, Working Paper No 124 (April 1997) 8.

[42] Ibid 18–21.

[43] General Agreement on Tariffs and Trade (1947) 55 UNTS 194. Note, the Agreement of 1947 was amended on various occasions subsequent to its entry into force on a provisional basis on 1 January 1948. It is now commonly referred to as GATT 1947. The amended text of GATT 1947 now constitutes the core part of the GATT 1994—the framework agreement: rules and principles applicable to trade in goods that apply under the aegis of the WTO Agreement.

the General Agreement on Tariffs and Trade 1994 (GATT 1994);[44] the General Agreement on Trade and Services (GATS);[45] and the Agreement on Trade-Related Aspects of Intellectual Property Rights (TRIPS).[46] Annex 2 comprises the Understanding on Rules and Procedures Governing the Settlement of Disputes (DSU),[47] while Annex 3 is the Trade Policy Review Mechanism (TPRM).[48] Finally, Annex 4 comprises the Plurilateral Trade Agreements[49] to which South Africa is not a party.

On 30 November 2017, South Africa ratified the Trade Facilitation Agreement,[50] the first agreement concluded by WTO members under the auspices of the WTO. It was concluded at the Bali Ministerial Conference in 2013 and came into force on 22 February 2017.

On the regional front, South Africa is a member of the Southern African Customs Union (SACU),[51] the Common Monetary Area (CMA),[52] and the Southern African Development Community (SADC),[53] the latter being one of South Africa's most significant

[44] Annex 1A of the WTO Agreement also includes Agreement on Agriculture, Agreement on the Application of Sanitary and Phytosanitary Measures, Agreement on Textile and Clothing (no longer in force), Agreement on Technical Barriers to Trade, Agreement on Trade-Related Investment Measures, Agreement on Implementation of Article VI of the GATT 1994 (Anti-Dumping Agreement), Agreement on Implementation of Article VII of the GATT 1994 (Customs Valuation Agreement), Agreement on Preshipment Inspection, Agreement on Rules of Origin, Agreement on Import Licensing, Agreement on Subsidies and Countervailing Measures, and Agreement on Safeguards. We discuss the Anti-Dumping Agreement and its import in South African law later in this chapter.

[45] WTO Agreement, Annex 1B.

[46] WTO Agreement, Annex 1C.

[47] WTO Agreement, Annex 2.

[48] WTO Agreement, Annex 3.

[49] Annex 4 of the WTO Agreement comprises the Agreement on Trade in Civil Aircraft, Agreement on Government Procurement, International Dairy Agreement, and International Bovine Meat Agreement. The latter two agreements are no longer in force.

[50] Trade Facilitation Agreement Facility 'Ratifications List' available at http://www.tfafacility.org/ratifications. South Africa announced its Category A and B commitments. The former are provisions of the Trade Facilitation Agreement that it undertook to implement following the entry into force of the agreement and the latter are provisions that South Africa will implement after a transitional period.

[51] The members of SACU are Botswana, Lesotho, Namibia, South Africa and eSwatini (Swaziland). Established in 1910, SACU is the oldest customs union in the world, SACU available at http://www.sacu.int/show.php?id=394.

[52] The CMA replaced the Rand Monetary Area (RMA) in July 1986. It includes, since the 6 February 1992 conclusion of the Multilateral Monetary Agreement (MMA), Lesotho, Namibia, South Africa, and eSwatini (Swaziland).

[53] The members of SADC are Angola, Botswana, the Democratic Republic of Congo, Lesotho, Madagascar, Malawi, Mauritius, Mozambique, Namibia, the Seychelles, South Africa, eSwatini (Swaziland), Tanzania, Zambia and Zimbabwe.

free-trade partnerships. SADC replaced the Southern African Development Coordination Conference (SADCC) in 1992 with the conclusion of the Treaty of the Southern African Development Community.[54] South Africa became a member of SADC in August 1994. The SADC Secretariat is located in Gaborone, Botswana.

South Africa's bilateral regional arrangements include the Zimbabwe–South Africa Bilateral Trade Agreement.[55] As at the end of April 2018, South Africa had completed negotiations in two regional trade agreements: the SADC–East African Community (EAC)—Common Market for Eastern and Southern Africa (COMESA) Tripartite Free Trade Agreement (TFTA) and the African Continental Free Trade Agreement (AfCFTA). The TFTA seeks to create a Free Trade Area (FTA)[56] within the member regional blocs[57] and the AfCFTA establishes an Africa-wide FTA, a major step in attempting to achieve 'a prosperous Africa based on inclusive growth and sustainable development'[58] by 2063. On 21 March 2018, at the 10th Extraordinary Session of the Assembly on AfCFTA, 44 of 55 members of the African Union countries signed the AfCFTA. This free trade agreement is the second largest trade agreement in the world, after the WTO. While South Africa signed the Kigali Declaration on this occasion, as at the end of June 2018, South African had not yet signed the text of the AfCFTA and the Free Movement Protocol.[59]

Beyond the region, South Africa has concluded a number of trade agreements such as the Agreement on Trade, Development and

[54] M Lee *The Political Economy of Regionalism in Southern Africa* (2003).

[55] The Department of Trade and Industry 'Trade Agreements' available at https://www.thedti.gov.za/trade_investment/ited_trade_agreement.jsp.

[56] The acronym FTA is also interchangeably used for free-trade agreement.

[57] The TFTA encompasses the following 26 countries: Angola, Botswana, Burundi, Comoros, the Democratic Republic of Congo, Djibouti, Egypt, Eritrea, Ethiopia, Kenya, Lesotho, Libya, Madagascar, Malawi, Mauritius, Mozambique, Namibia, Rwanda, Seychelles, South Africa, Sudan, eSwatini (Swaziland), Tanzania, Uganda, Zambia, and Zimbabwe. As at 30 January 2018, it had been signed by 22 of the parties and ratified by Egypt and Uganda. See, TRALAC 'SADC–EAC–COMESA Tripartite Free Trade Area Legal Texts and Policy Documents' available at https://www.tralac.org/resources/by-region/comesa-eac-sadc-tripartite-fta.html.

[58] This is one of the seven key aspirations comprising the Agenda 2063: The Africa We Want that was adopted by the Heads of State and Government at the 24th Ordinary Session of the African Union Assembly that was held in January 2015 in Addis Ababa, see B Vickers *A Handbook on Regional Integration in Africa: Towards Agenda 2063* (2017) 47.

[59] A Parshotam 'Can the African Continental Free Trade Area offer a new beginning for trade in Africa?' (2018) Occasional Paper 280 South African Institute of International Affairs 16.

Co-operation (TDCA) with the EU[60] and the EU–SADC Group Economic Partnership Agreement (EU–SADC EPA).[61] Its other bilateral agreements include the South Africa–US Trade and Investment Framework Agreement and the Memorandum of Understanding between the Government of the Republic of South Africa and the Government of the People's Republic of China on promoting Bilateral Trade and Economic Co-operation.[62] Under the auspices of SACU, South Africa is party to the SACU–US Trade, Investment and Development Cooperation Agreement (TIDCA),[63] *el Mercado Común del Sur* (MERCOSUR)[64]–SACU Preferential Trade Agreement,[65] and the European Free Trade Area (EFTA)[66]–SACU FTA. South Africa is also a beneficiary under the General Preference Schemes of Canada; Japan; Norway; Turkey; the Customs Union between Belarus, Kazakhstan, and Russia; and the Africa Growth and Opportunity Act of 2000 (AGOA), the latter being a preference scheme specifically for African exports to the United States.[67]

3 International investment agreements

South Africa's international investment law relations are currently governed by international investment agreements (IIAs)[68] that comprise the South African Development Community Finance and Investment Protocol and 49 Bilateral Investment Treaties (BITs).[69] South Africa is not a party to the Convention on the International

[60] See also the Cooperation Agreement between the European Community and the Republic of South Africa of October 1994; 1994 *OJ* (L 341) 62 (and the EC Council Decision approving this Agreement at 1994 *OJ* (L 341) 61).

[61] Members of the SADC EPA Group are SACU members plus Mozambique. The EU–SADC EPA has replaced the Trade Chapter of the TDCA.

[62] South African Revenue Services available at http://www.sars.gov.za/legal/international-treaties-agreements/trade-agreements/Pages/default.aspx.

[63] Office of the United States Trade Representative available at https://ustr.gov/countries-regions/africa/southern-africa/south-africa.

[64] Common Market of the South, comprising Argentina, Brazil, Paraguay, and Uruguay.

[65] Organization of American States Foreign Trade Information System, 'MERCOSUR-Southern African Customs Union (SACU)' available at http://www.sice.oas.org/TPD/MER_SACU/MER_SACU_e.ASP.

[66] EFTA is made up of European non-EU states Iceland, Liechtenstein, Norway, and Switzerland.

[67] The preference schemes are inherently unilateral in nature and granted at discretion of the benefactor. Exclusion from such a scheme by a benefactor could be particularly disadvantageous to a beneficiary country that exports significantly to the preference-granting market.

[68] IIAs are a broader category of agreements that include BITs and other international investment arrangements such as investment chapters of FTAs.

[69] The Protection of Foreign Investment Act 22 of 2015 was promulgated on 13 June 2018.

Centre for the Settlement of Disputes (ICSID).[70] ICSID is the dispute settlement arm of the World Bank Group that offers its contracting parties a de-localised dispute-settlement mechanism in the area of international foreign investment.

All BITs are not identical and ultimately they have to be analysed individually. However, many BITs tend to follow a similar basic structure. Usually BITs contain an expropriation clause, which prohibits the host state from directly or indirectly expropriating a protected investment except for a public purpose, in a non-discriminatory manner, in accordance with due process, and upon payment of prompt, adequate and effective compensation (typically benchmarked to fair market value, and without regard to any limitations on compensation as may exist under domestic law).[71] BITs also usually contain a FET clause, which obligates the host state to treat foreign investors and their investments fairly and equitably—this includes duties of transparency, non-arbitrariness, non-discrimination, and reasonableness. BITs further tend to include an MFN clause, which prohibits the host state from treating protected investors and their investments less favourably than investors or investments of other third countries, and a national treatment clause, which prohibits the host state from treating protected investors and their investments less favourably than it treats its own domestic investors and their investments.[72] BITs invariably also contain an Investor–State Dispute Settlement (ISDS) provision, permitting the investor to bring an international arbitration claim against the host state in an international arbitral forum (typically without having to first exhaust domestic remedies) and to obtain compensation from the state for any losses suffered in consequence of the state's non-observance of its BIT obligations.

[70] Convention on the Settlement of Investment Disputes between States and Nationals of Other States (1965) 575 UNTS 159. See further the section on *Is there a right to diplomatic protection?* in Chapter 13.

[71] For instance, article 2(2) of South Africa's BIT with the UK (UK–SA BIT), signed on 20 September 1994 (together with a protocol signed on 25 November 1997) and entered into force on 27 May 1998, provides as follows:

> Investments of national or companies of either Contracting Party shall not be nationalised, expropriated or subjected to measures having effect equivalent to nationalisation or expropriation (hereinafter referred to as 'expropriation') in the territory of the other Contracting Party except for a public purpose related to the internal needs of that Party on a non-discriminatory basis and against prompt, adequate and effective compensation. Such compensation shall amount to the genuine value of the investment expropriated immediately before the expropriation or before the impeding expropriation became public knowledge.

See further LE Peterson 'South Africa's bilateral investment treaties, implications for development and human rights', Occasional Paper, November 2006.

[72] The National Treatment and MFN Treatment clauses are often combined.

Two points are worth noting in respect of these standard BIT protections. First, many BIT provisions have domestic parallels within the South African constitutional context (for example, s 25 protects property rights, s 33 guarantees just administrative action). However, at times the BIT protections may prove more favourable to foreign investors than their constitutional counterparts.

Second, as we discuss further below, in retrospect, it appears that South Africa may not have fully appreciated the effect of entering into BITs as a constraining force upon its policies and legislative goals. A 2009 discussion paper by the Department of Trade and Industry (DTI) suggested that the government had 'a lack of understanding' of 'the dangers inherent in BITs' at the time when they were signed, because the government conducted 'no legal or economic analysis of (their) risk'.[73]

South Africa's current BITs include 11 that are in force,[74] 27 that have been signed but are not yet in force,[75] and 11 that have been terminated.[76] The BITs that were first terminated are the first-generation BITs that South Africa signed with European countries shortly after 1994. Notwithstanding the termination of these agreements, South Africa's BITs typically provide that investments made before the termination of a BIT will continue to be protected for another 10 to 20 years from their date of termination, depending on the provisions of each BIT.[77] They also provide for international dispute settlement at ISDS institutions such as ICSID. As South Africa is not a member of ICSID, its participation in ICSID proceedings is through the aegis of ICSID's Additional Facility Rules (the Rules).[78]

[73] The discussion paper then cautioned that BITs could have a 'severe impact . . . on both constitutional imperatives and government's policy space'. See DTI 'Bilateral Investment Treaty Policy Framework Review' (June 2009).

[74] Those with China, Cuba, Finland, Greece, Italy, Republic of Korea, Mauritius, Nigeria, Russia, Senegal and Sweden. UNCTAD Investment Policy Hub available at http://investmentpolicyhub.unctad.org/IIA/CountryBits/195.

[75] Algeria, Angola, Canada, Chile, Democratic Republic of Congo, Republic of Congo, Czech Republic, Egypt, Equatorial Guinea, Ethiopia, Gabon, Ghana, Guinea, Iran, Israel, Kuwait, Libya, Madagascar, Mozambique, Qatar, Rwanda, Sudan, Tanzania, Tunisia, Turkey, Uganda, and Yemen. Ibid.

[76] Argentina, Austria, Belgium–Luxembourg Economic Union, Denmark, France, Germany, the Netherlands, Spain, Switzerland, and the United Kingdom and Zimbabwe. Ibid.

[77] These clauses are called survival or sunset clauses. The survival clauses of South Africa's BITs with Belgium–Luxembourg Economic Union, Denmark and Spain are 10 years, 15 years with Argentina and the Netherlands, and 20 years with Austria, France, Germany, Switzerland, and the United Kingdom.

[78] The latest version of the Rules was updated in 2006. They were adopted in 1978 and offer arbitration, conciliation, and fact-finding services for disputes that do not

South Africa has maintained its decision not to become a member of ICSID, notwithstanding strong recommendations from the South African Law Commission, which included the following:

> Although South Africa is a developing country, its relatively strong infrastructure and position as the major economic power in the region place South Africa in a somewhat unique position as a country which could get a dual benefit from ICSID membership.[79]

According to the DTI, South Africa's decision to remain a non-member of ICSID continues to be driven by concerns about the ability of international investor-state tribunals to interfere in domestic policymaking, together with the inability of South Africa's domestic courts to review and set aside such arbitral rewards.[80] In this regard, the government's position is aligned with its decision to terminate South Africa's BITs, and to pass the Investment of Protection Act 22 of 2015, which privileges the settlement of investment disputes by foreign investors before South African courts (see discussion further below).

Whilst South Africa is one of seven African countries[81] that are not ICSID members, the questioning of the legitimacy of the ISDS system has seen the likes of Bolivia, Ecuador and Venezuela withdrawing from the ICSID Convention.[82]

4 Conclusion on sources and key principles

As this list of South Africa's international commitments in the field of international finance, trade, and investment illustrates, the legal regime of South Africa's international economic relations is a complex set or 'spaghetti bowl'[83] of treaty arrangements often overlapping in subject matter. And some, like the investment treaties discussed above, are consciously being reconsidered by South Africa.

fall under the scope of the ICSID convention, eg, dispute settlement between a state and foreign national, neither of which are an ICSID member state or a national of an ICSID member state.

[79] South African Law Commission Project 94, 'Arbitration: An International Arbitration Act for South Africa, Report' (1998).

[80] LN Skovgaard Poulsen *Bounded Rationality and Economic Diplomacy* (2015) 187.

[81] Angola, Djibouti, Equatorial-Guinea, Eritrea, Libya, and Western Sahara (a non-self-governing territory). Ethiopia, Guinea-Bissau and Namibia have signed the ICSID Convention but have not yet ratified it.

[82] J Crawford 'The current political discourse concerning international law' (2018) 18(1) *The Modern Law Review* 9.

[83] This term was first used by academic Jagdish Bhagwati to describe the proliferation of free trade agreements where countries extend preferences in different trading arrangements resulting in overlapping and jumbled commitments, See J Bhagwati 'U.S. trade policy: The infatuation with free trade areas' in J Bhagwati and AO Krueger *The Dangerous Drift to Preferential Trade Agreements* (1995) 1–18.

Although each of the three subject areas has its own idiosyncrasies, some commonalities and conclusions can be drawn. First, the majority of South Africa's rights and obligations are in treaty form—indicating a preference for formal and enforceable state-to-state economic relations. Second, the basis of the treaties underpinning South Africa's international finance and trade relations is multilateral in nature. This indicates South Africa's strong preference for multilateral economic relations and rules, as opposed to fragmented disciplines with fewer parties. Third, the principle of non-discrimination (MFN and national treatment obligations) forms the cornerstone of both international investment and trade relations. Finally, South Africa's international economic relations indicates a strong regional and South–South leaning by virtue of its close relationship with its BRICS[84] counterparts. This is in sharp contrast to its former prioritisation of and deference to its relationships with Western economies.

South Africa's overlapping legal regimes and rules also raises the possibility of conflicts of law relating to the hierarchy and application of these rules. Possible conflicts may stem from South Africa's membership of SADC and SACU and its rights and obligations under the larger regional trade agreements. For example, the TFTA does not contemplate the dissolution of the regional trade arrangements; therefore, region-specific carve-outs could erode the negotiated achievements of the TFTA. Such conflicts will have to be managed as between the provisions of the TFTA and the SADC or SACU agreements.[85]

THE SIGNIFICANCE OF SOUTH AFRICA'S INTERNATIONAL OBLIGATIONS IN SOUTH AFRICAN MUNICIPAL LAW

As has been shown,[86] the position under the 1996 Constitution is that a treaty becomes law in South Africa only after it has been incorporated into municipal law by some act of legislative transformation. The exception to this rule is that a self-executing provision of a treaty that has been approved by Parliament becomes law automatically, provided that it is not inconsistent with the Constitution or an Act of Parliament.[87]

[84] An acronym referring to Brazil, Russia, India, China, and South Africa, a group of developing countries that are considered emerging economic and political powers.

[85] For example, article 38(4) of the TFTA provides that in the event of inconsistency or a conflict between the TFTA and the agreements of the regional economic communities, the TFTA will prevail to the extent of the inconsistency or conflict.

[86] See Chapter 4.

[87] In terms of s 231(2)–(4) of the Constitution of the Republic of South Africa, 1996.

In most instances, the economic agreements referred to above to which South Africa is a party have not been enacted into municipal law pursuant to s 231 of the Constitution.[88] Unless particular provisions are construed by the courts to be self-executing,[89] these agreements will not, therefore, be justiciable in domestic courts. The WTO Agreement, for example, while approved by Parliament on 6 April 1995, has not been enacted into municipal law.[90]

Thus, the application of or even applicability of international trade agreements in our domestic law is not a clear-cut matter. While the WTO Agreement as a whole has not been enacted into municipal law, a number of its substantive provisions are reflected in domestic legislation, although frequently without express reference to the related international legal instrument.[91] This is notably the case in respect of legislation in the field of intellectual property which appears to have been drafted with the TRIPS Agreement in mind.[92] Further, the International Trade Administration Commission's (ITAC) regulations[93] that delineate the practice and substance of anti-dumping,[94] countervailing,[95] and safeguards[96] investigations and measures (collectively referred to as trade remedies) also bear a strong resemblance to those contained in the relevant international treaties, but the WTO's Agreement on Implementation of Article VI of the General Agreement on Tariffs and Trade 1994 (Anti-Dumping Agreement), the Agreement on Subsidies and Countervailing Measures, and the Agreement on Safeguards have not been incorporated into South African law.

[88] See further on this subject, *Progress Office Machines CC v SARS* 2008 (2) SA 13 (SCA) and *International Trade Administration Commission v SCAW South Africa* 2010 (5) BCLR 457 (CC).

[89] See Chapter 4.

[90] See GS Eisenberg 'The GATT and WTO Agreements: Comments on their legal applicability to the RSA' (1993–4) 19 *SAYIL* 127; EC Schlemmer 'Die Grondwetlike Hof en die Ooreenkoms ter Vestiging van die Wereldhandelsorganisasie' 2010 *TSAR* 749; *International Trade Administration Commission v SCAW* (n 88).

[91] See further EC Schlemmer 'South Africa and the WTO ten years into Democracy' (2004) 29 *SAYIL* 125.

[92] See, for example, the amendments introduced by the Intellectual Property Laws Amendment Act 38 of 1997 to, inter alia, the Performers' Protection Act 11 of 1967, the Designs Act 195 of 1993 and the Trade Marks Act 194 of 1993.

[93] The trade remedies regulations have been promulgated pursuant to s 59 of the International Trade Administration Commission Act 71 of 2002.

[94] Anti-Dumping Regulations Notice 3197 of 2003.

[95] Countervailing Regulation, 2005.

[96] Amended Safeguards Regulations, 2005.

This does not, however, absolve South Africa of its international obligations. In *Progress Office Machines CC v South African Revenue Services* [97] the Supreme Court of Appeal (SCA) confirmed that the WTO's Anti-Dumping Agreement is binding on South Africa, even though it has not been incorporated into municipal law.[98] The Anti-Dumping Agreement is discussed further below.

Even if trade treaties cannot be directly invoked in South African courts, they can be utilised as interpretative aides. Section 233 of the Constitution requires that when interpreting legislation, the courts must prefer any reasonable interpretation that is in accordance with international law (which includes treaty law). As was highlighted by the SCA's decision in *Progress Office Machines*,[99] it is also possible to contend that the exercise of any power, which is contrary to South Africa's international law obligations, would be an unreasonable and hence unlawful exercise of power.

The courts have a duty to interpret legislation with recourse to the treaties to which South Africa is a party. In addition, South African courts have held that it is incumbent on the administrators to have due regard to South Africa's international obligations—as obviously relevant considerations—when they exercise their decision-making in a field to which the treaty relates. Besides the ability to rely indirectly on international law in domestic courts, any alleged breach of international economic law may be dealt with on the international plane between states party to the relevant agreements. This means that whether or not they are directly applicable as part of South African municipal law, the financial, trade, and investment agreements to which South Africa is a party will constitute an important *corpus* of law in the municipal sphere. Further, any domestic action by South Africa may result in international consequences where alleged breaches of the treaty might be invoked by another state against South Africa.

[97] 2008 (2) SA 13 (SCA) para 6.

[98] This finding was confirmed by the Constitutional Court in *International Trade Administration Commission v SCAW South Africa (Pty) Ltd* 2012 (4) SA 618 (CC); *Association of Meat Importers v ITAC* 2013 (4) All SA 253 (SCA).

[99] Para 11. See further G Erasmus 'The incorporation of trade agreements and rules of origin: The extent of constitutional guidance' (2003) 28 *SAYIL* 157.

THE WORLD TRADE ORGANIZATION AND THE FUNDAMENTAL PRINCIPLES OF INTERNATIONAL TRADE

1 Overview

The WTO Agreement, which entered into force on 1 January 1995, established the WTO[100] and brought into being a diverse body of substantive multilateral trade rules covering trade in goods, services, and principles governing trade-related aspects of intellectual property rights. It also put in place a unique dispute-settlement mechanism that has, in the few years of its operation, become a cornerstone of the integrity of this rules-based system.[101]

The WTO Agreement incorporates its successor agreement the GATT 1947.[102] However, it differs from, and goes beyond, the 1947 arrangements in many important respects. First, the WTO Agreement established, for the first time, an international organisation with responsibilities in the area of international trade.[103] Secondly, whereas the GATT was concerned only with trade in goods, the substantive obligations of the WTO Agreement also include trade in services and trade-related aspects of intellectual property rights. Thirdly, with the advent of the WTO, trade in agriculture,[104] textiles and clothing,[105]

[100] See generally on the GATT/WTO, JH Jackson *The World Trading System: Law and Policy of International Economic Relations* 2 ed (1997) and JH Jackson *The World Trade Organization: Constitution and Jurisprudence* (1998); AH Qureshi *The World Trade Organization: Implementing International Trade Norms* (1996); S Lester and B Mercurio *World Trade Law* (2008).

[101] For details of the workings of this dispute settlement system, see E-U Petersmann (ed) *International Trade Law and the GATT/WTO Dispute Settlement System* (1997) and E-U Petersmann *The GATT/WTO Dispute Settlement System: International Law, International Organizations and Dispute Settlement* (1997).

[102] The General Agreement on Tariffs and Trade 1994 (GATT 1994), the principal framework agreement on trade in goods under the WTO Agreement, provides, inter alia, that it shall consist of the provisions of GATT 1947 as rectified, amended or modified by the terms of legal instruments which had entered into force before the date of entry into force of the WTO Agreement.

[103] The GATT was established after the failure of the US Congress to ratify the Havana Charter of 1948 establishing the International Trade Organisation, the Bretton Wood institution that was meant to govern global trade relations, see P van den Bossche and W Zdouc, *The Law and Policy of the World Trade Organization: Text, Cases, and Materials* (2013) 77–8.

[104] See the Agreement on Agriculture which forms part of the WTO Annex 1A: Multilateral Agreements on Trade in Goods.

[105] See the Agreement on Textiles and Clothing ('ATC') which forms part of the WTO Annex 1A: Multilateral Agreements on Trade in Goods. Pursuant to article 9 of the ATC, the Agreement terminated on 1 January 2005 with the expiry of the 10-year transitional period laid down in the ATC. The expiry of the ATC makes trade in textiles and clothing subject to wider GATT/WTO disciplines.

and other aspects relating to the trade in goods[106] previously effectively outside the GATT arrangements, have been brought within the framework of the WTO's multilateral disciplines. Fourthly, in contrast to the informal and often problematic arrangements that applied to the settlement of disputes under the GATT 1947,[107] the WTO Agreement established a formalised dispute-settlement mechanism designed to address many of the problems of dispute settlement under the previous regime. This includes a two-tier adjudicatory process, involving both ad hoc panels and a standing Appellate Body, governed by a Dispute Settlement Body (DSB) composed of the representatives of WTO Members. The WTO Secretariat is in Geneva, Switzerland and is headed by a Director-General who is currently the former Brazilian diplomat Roberto Azevêdo.[108]

As a contracting party to GATT 1947, South Africa became an original Member of the WTO[109] following parliamentary approval of the Agreement on 6 April 1995.

2 The object, structure and operation of the World Trade Organization

The object of the WTO is to 'provide the common institutional framework for the conduct of trade relations among its Members in matters related to the agreements and associated legal instruments included in the Annexes to this Agreement'.[110] To this end, the functions of the WTO are:[111]

- to facilitate the implementation, administration and operation, and to further the objectives of this Agreement and of the Multilateral Trade Agreements, and to provide the framework for the implementation, administration and operation of the Plurilateral Trade Agreements;
- to provide a forum for negotiations;
- to administer the dispute settlement mechanism;
- to administer the TPRM; and
- to co-operate, as appropriate, with the IMF and with the IBRD and its affiliated agencies.

[106] See, for example, the Agreement on Trade-Related Investment Measures which forms part of the WTO Annex 1A: Multilateral Agreements on Trade in Goods.

[107] For example, as with all GATT decisions, panel reports could only be adopted by consensus. This created the opportunity for the losing party to block or delay the adoption of these reports. See, WTO *A Handbook on the WTO Dispute Settlement System* (2004) 13.

[108] See WTO Agreement, article IV:3 and DSU, article 2.1. Dispute settlement is discussed further below.

[109] See WTO Agreement, article XI:1.

[110] WTO Agreement, article II:1.

[111] WTO Agreement, article III.

The principal decision-making body of the WTO is the Ministerial Conference, composed of representatives of the Members, usually at ministerial level, which meets at least once every two years. The General Council is the WTO's Geneva-based decision-making body. It is generally composed of the representatives of the Members at the level of diplomats and officials who are based in Geneva, which meets as appropriate, usually once a month. The General Council also convenes as the DSB and the Trade Policy Review Body. Beneath the General Council, and operating under its guidance, are the Councils for Trade in Goods, Trade in Services and TRIPS and the various Committees, Working Parties, and Working Groups.

3 Dispute settlement

The Understanding on Rules and Procedures Governing the Settlement of Disputes (DSU) provides for the establishment of ad hoc panels and a standing Appellate Body to assist the DSB in its work.[112] The Secretariat contains various specialised departments including three legal divisions. The Legal Affairs Division is generally responsible for providing legal advice on all matters relating to the WTO agreements, except for the agreements concerning trade remedies (anti-dumping, subsidies, and countervailing measures, and safeguards), trade-related investment measures, and state-trading and civil aircraft, which fall within the purview of the second legal division, the Rules Division. These two legal divisions are tasked with providing support to panel members in various disputes and supporting the negotiation groups of the agreements that are under the scope of their responsibilities.

The third legal division is the Appellate Body, the appellate court of the WTO. This alone is a unique feature of the WTO system, as most international dispute settlement systems do not have an appellate mechanism. The Appellate Body has its own secretariat that provides it with legal and administrative support.[113] The DSU establishes seven Appellate Body members with three members (a division) adjudicating a dispute. Appellate Body members can be appointed for a maximum of eight years, composed of two four-year renewable terms.[114] From 2006 to 2013, South African lawyer David Unterhalter SC was a member of the Appellate Body. Amongst other cases, Unterhalter presided over some of the leading disputes under the Agreement on Subsidies and Countervailing Measures such as

[112] DSU, articles 2, 6 and 17.
[113] See DSU, article 27.
[114] See DSU, article 17.1 and 17.2.

Canada—Feed-In Tariff Programme[115] on renewable energy subsidies in Canada and cases involving subsidies granted to the largest commercial aircraft concerns Airbus[116] and Boeing.[117]

Pursuant to article IX:1 of the WTO Agreement, decision-making in the WTO is usually taken by consensus.[118] While the agreement makes provision for voting procedures, these are never used in practice. Therefore, all WTO decisions, save the establishment of a panel, the adoption of panel and Appellate Body reports, and the authorisation of retaliatory measures, are taken by consensus.[119]

The WTO dispute settlement mechanism is currently facing a crisis. As Members have failed to update the DSU, much of the *lacunae* in WTO law is left to panels and the Appellate Body to interpret. As a result, some members have accused the Appellate Body of judicial overreach. For the past few years, the United States has blocked the appointment of new Appellate Body members as a strategy to force Members to negotiate new rules. If this problem is not resolved soon, the Appellate Body will not have sufficient members[120] to adjudicate appeals and the 'jewel in the crown' of the global trading system could implode.[121]

4 The fundamental principles of international trade

The law governing the multilateral trading system is detailed and complex and cannot be adequately summarised in a brief chapter of this nature. An appreciation of the issues that form the subject matter of negotiation or dispute settlement under the WTO requires a

[115] Appellate Body Report, *Canada—Certain Measures Affecting the Renewable Energy Generation Sector/Canada—Measures Relating to the Feed-in Tariff Program*, WT/DS412/AB/R/WT/DS426/AB/R, adopted 24 May 2013, DSR 2013:I, 7.

[116] Appellate Body Report, *European Communities and Certain Member States—Measures Affecting Trade in Large Civil Aircraft*, WT/DS316/AB/R, adopted 1 June 2011, DSR 2011:I, 7.

[117] Appellate Body Report, *United States—Measures Affecting Trade in Large Civil Aircraft (Second Complaint)*, WT/DS353/AB/R, adopted 23 March 2012, DSR 2012:I, 7.

[118] The footnote to the article provides that '[t]he body concerned shall be deemed to have decided by consensus on a matter submitted for its consideration, if no Member, present at the meeting when the decision is taken, formally objects to the proposed decision'.

[119] DSU, articles 6.1, 16.4, 17.14, and 22.6. These are taken by negative or reverse consensus (see explanation below).

[120] The Appellate Body needs at least three members to function. As from 10 December 2019, there will only be one member left.

[121] T Payosova, GC Hufbauer and JJ Scott '18-5 The dispute settlement crisis in the World Trade Organization: Causes and cures' Peterson Institute for International Economics Policy Brief (2018) 1 available at https://piie.com/system/files/documents/pb18-5.pdf.

familiarity with a wide range of 'black letter' obligations in various WTO agreements and of the jurisprudence of WTO dispute-settlement panels and the Appellate Body as well as of the GATT dispute-settlement panels that operated before 1995.

That said, the legal regime on which these substantive rules are based rests on a number of fundamental principles.[122] These include the principle of non-discrimination, which mostly takes the form of the MFN[123] and national-treatment[124] obligations, market access and the sanctity of the tariff bindings, progressive trade liberalisation, and the general elimination of quantitative restrictions.[125] To this may be added the requirement of transparency in the publication and administration of trade regulations.[126] Most of the agreements contain exceptions to these principles, addressing, for example, circumstances requiring emergency action, balance of payments considerations, security, the protection of human, animal, and plant life and health.

5 The operation of the dispute settlement system and South Africa's participation in World Trade Organizations disputes

The WTO's dispute settlement system is one of the most successful international dispute settlement systems. Since its establishment in 1995, over 550 disputes[127] have been initiated, and over 210 panel reports and over 130 Appellate Body reports have been adopted.[128] One of the major innovations of the Uruguay Round of negotiations was the adoption, as part of the WTO Agreement, of detailed arrangements in respect of dispute settlement. These are now contained in the DSU, which is attached to the WTO Agreement as Annex 2, and which in large measure is a consolidation of the practice that had developed over the years under GATT 1947, together with some important innovations.

As previously mentioned, the principal institution of dispute settlement is the DSB. Pursuant to article 2 of the DSU, 'the DSB shall have the authority to establish panels, adopt panel and Appellate Body reports, maintain surveillance of implementation of rulings and

[122] See JH Jackson, WJ Davey and AO Sykes *Legal Problems of International Economic Relations: Cases, Materials and Text* 4 ed (2002); MJ Trebilcock and R Howse, *The Regulation of International Trade* 3 ed (2004).

[123] GATT 1994, article I; GATS, article II; TRIPS, article 4.

[124] GATT 1994, article III; GATS, article XVII; TRIPS, article 3.

[125] GATT 1994, article XI.

[126] GATT 1994, article X; GATS, article III; TRIPS, article 63.

[127] Not including DSU, Article 21.5 compliance proceedings.

[128] As at June 2018, available at WorldTradeLaw.Netm http://www.worldtradelaw.net/databases/basicfigures.php. These include standard and DSU article 21.5 (compliance proceeding) panel and Appellate Body reports.

recommendations, and authorize suspension of concessions and other obligations under the covered agreements'. Save where otherwise indicated, the DSB operates by consensus.[129] In 2016, the South African Ambassador to the WTO, Xavier Carim, served as the Chair of the DSB.

For purposes of facilitating the settlement of disputes between WTO Members that cannot be settled through consultations or other informal means,[130] the DSB is obliged, at the request of a complaining party, to establish a panel to adjudicate on the matter.[131] The DSU further provides for the establishment of a standing Appellate Body that 'shall hear appeals from panel cases'[132] on 'issues of law covered in the panel report and legal interpretations developed by the panel'.[133]

Although panels operate in a manner akin to other ad hoc arbitration tribunals under international law, their function formally is 'to assist the DSB in discharging its responsibilities under this Understanding and the covered agreements'.[134] Formally, therefore, both panel and Appellate Body reports constitute guidance to the DSB in respect of the matter in issue rather than arbitral decisions binding upon the parties to a dispute directly. In practice, however, the reports invariably amount to decisions with which the parties must comply. Where a panel or the Appellate Body concludes that a measure is inconsistent with a covered agreement, it 'shall *recommend* that the Member concerned bring the measure into conformity with that agreement'.[135]

In keeping with the function of panels and the Appellate Body vis-à-vis the DSB, the DSB must adopt panel and Appellate Body reports before they can be considered binding.[136] In a departure from the usual rule of consensus governing the workings of the DSB, panel and Appellate Body reports 'shall' be adopted by the DSB 'unless the DSB decides by consensus not to adopt' the report in question.[137] This rule, known as the rule of negative or reverse consensus, constitutes perhaps the most important innovation introduced by the DSU in comparison with the pre-WTO dispute settlement arrangements (which required that panel reports be adopted by consensus).

[129] DSU, article 2.4.
[130] See GATT 1994, articles XXII and XXIII and DSU, articles 4–5.
[131] DSU, article 6.
[132] DSU, article 17.1.
[133] DSU, article 17.6.
[134] DSU, article 11.
[135] DSU, article 19.1 (emphasis added).
[136] DSU, articles 16 and 17.14.
[137] DSU, article 14.

This effectively means that all panel and Appellate Body reports, which are put forward for adoption by the parties, will be adopted by the DSB as it is unlikely that all WTO members including the winning party will agree *not* to adopt reports.

South Africa has not, thus far, been a complainant in any WTO proceedings. It has, however, been a respondent in five WTO disputes, all of them relating to South Africa's anti-dumping measures, ie measures taken by South Africa to protect the domestic industry against the introduction of imported goods into the South African market at a price that is less than the normal value of those goods in their country of origin. The practice of dumping gives the imported goods an unfair advantage over those produced domestically and it is common for 'anti-dumping duties' to be levied by the importing countries to neutralise the advantage.

First, on 1 April 1999, India, requested consultations in respect of a recommendation for the imposition of anti-dumping duties by the South African Board on Tariffs and Trade on the import of certain pharmaceutical products from India.[138] Secondly, on 9 April 2003, Turkey requested consultations concerning anti-dumping measures on its imports of blanketing in roll form.[139] Thirdly, on 9 May 2008, Indonesia requested consultations concerning anti-dumping measures on imports of uncoated woodfree white A4 paper.[140] Fourthly, on 21 June 2012, Brazil requested consultations in relation to the preliminary determination and the imposition of provisional anti-dumping duties on imports of frozen meat of fowls of the species *Gallus Domesticus*, whole bird, and boneless cuts.[141] Finally, on 9 November 2015, in what was the 500th dispute initiated at the WTO, Pakistan requested consultations regarding the imposition of provisional anti-dumping measures on the importation of Portland cement products.[142]

In none of these cases has the complaint proceeded to the panel stage. South Africa has been a third party in eight disputes.[143]

6 Anti-dumping legislation and investigations under the World Trade Organization Anti-Dumping Agreement

One particular WTO Agreement deserves special mention given the frequency in which it is used as a trade policy tool, the manner in

[138] *South Africa—Anti-dumping Duties on Certain Pharmaceutical Products from India (DS168).*

[139] *South Africa—Anti-Dumping Measures on Blanketing form Turkey (DS288).*

[140] *South Africa—Anti-Dumping Measures on Uncoated Woodfree Paper (Indonesia) (DS374).*

[141] *South Africa—Anti-Dumping Duties on Frozen Meat from Fowls from Brazil (DS439).*

[142] *South Africa—Anti-Dumping Duties on Portland Cement from Pakistan (DS500).*

[143] As at July 2018.

which it has already featured before South Africa's courts, and the legislation that must be read consistent with it. In *Progress Office Machines*[144] the SCA confirmed that the WTO's Anti-Dumping Agreement is binding on South Africa, 'even though it has not been specifically enacted into municipal law'.[145] The WTO Anti-Dumping Agreement and GATT 1994 are not concerned with dumping *per se*, but with dumping that causes or threatens to cause material injury to the domestic industry of the importing country.[146]

South African anti-dumping law is a complex amalgam of the WTO Anti-Dumping Agreement, the SACU Agreement, the International Trade Administration Act, 71 of 2002 (ITA Act), the Anti-Dumping Regulations, the Board on Tariffs and Trade Act 1986 (BTT Act) and, the Customs and Excise Act, 91 of 1964, as amended (the Customs and Excise Act).

The legislation that deals with anti-dumping is the ITA Act and the Anti-Dumping Regulations promulgated thereunder. The ITA Act should be read together with the Customs and Excise Act. In terms of s 233 of the Constitution, this domestic legislation must be interpreted having regard to the WTO Anti-Dumping Agreement and GATT 1994.[147]

Section 1 of the ITA Act defines 'dumping' as

> the introduction of goods into the commerce of the Republic [of South Africa] or the [combined areas of the Member States of SACU] at an export price . . . that is less than the normal value, of those goods' and Regulation 1 of the Anti-Dumping Regulations defines 'margin of dumping' as 'the extent to which the normal value is higher than the export price, after adjustments have been made for comparative purposes.

The International Trade Administration Commission (ITAC), which was established in terms of s 7 of the ITA Act, is responsible for investigating applications for anti-dumping duties. Section 16(1) of the ITA Act provides that '[t]he Commission must investigate and evaluate—(a) applications in terms of section 26 with regard to

144 *Progress Office Machines* para 6.

145 The Constitutional Court in *International Trade Administration Commission v SCAW South Africa (Pty) Ltd* confirmed this finding (supra n 98). See also *Association of Meat Importers v ITAC* 2013 4 All SA 253 (SCA).

146 In this regard, article VI:1 of the GATT 1994 states that dumping 'is to be condemned if it causes or threatens material injury to an established industry in the territory of a Member or materially retards the establishment of a domestic industry'. Article VI:6(a) also stipulates that no anti-dumping duty shall be levied unless the importing Member 'determines that the effect of the dumping . . . is such as to cause or threaten material injury to an established domestic industry, or is such as to retard materially the establishment of a domestic industry'. Article 11.1 of the Anti-Dumping Agreement further provides that '[a]n anti-dumping duty shall remain in force only as long as and to the extent necessary to counteract dumping which is causing injury'.

147 See Chapter 4.

alleged dumping, or subsidised exports, in or into the Republic or the Common Customs Area'. The Commission may recommend anti-dumping measures, including the imposition of duties on the particular goods that are allegedly being 'dumped' into the South African market.

In terms of s 30 of the ITA Act, ITAC *may* make recommendations to the SACU Tariff Board ((the Tariff Board) contemplated in the SACU Agreement) that the application be approved or rejected. The Tariff Board is then in turn to make recommendations to the Council of Ministers established in terms of article 7 of the SACU Agreement (the Council) on the duty, if any, to be imposed. The Council may, by consensus, approve the imposition of duties, in which event the SACU member states will be required to implement the duties.

Once ITAC has concluded an anti-dumping investigation, it may recommend the imposition of anti-dumping duties. ITAC's recommendation is submitted to the Trade Minister who may accept or reject the recommendation or send it back to ITAC for reconsideration. If the Trade Minister decides to accept ITAC's recommendation to terminate or amend existing anti-dumping duties, or to impose new anti-dumping duties, he will request the Finance Minister to amend Schedule 2 to the Customs and Excise Act accordingly (which the Finance Minister is obliged to do in terms of s 56 of the Customs and Excise Act). If the Trade Minister accepts ITAC's recommendation to maintain existing duties without amendment, then the decision is merely published in the *Government Gazette*.

In practice, the other SACU member states will also amend the relevant schedules to their customs statutes to reflect the duties in Schedule 2 to South Africa's Customs and Excise Act.

GENERAL PRINCIPLES OF INTERNATIONAL INVESTMENT LAW

1 Overview

Unlike the multilateral trade disciplines, there is no multilateral agreement on investment governing foreign direct investment (FDI). The first attempt at an international agreement on investment were articles 11 and 12 of the Havana Charter of 1948.[148] Among the more recent efforts to adopt multilateral instruments on investment are the Guidelines on Foreign Investment proposed by the World Bank in 1992[149] and the Organisation for Economic Co-operation and Devel-

[148] M Sornarajah *The International Law on Foreign Investment* 3 ed (2010) 236; Subedi (n 2); Salacuse (n 2).

[149] Sornarajah (n 148) 38.

opment's negotiations on the Multilateral Agreement on Investment which began in 1994 and were discontinued in 1998.[150] The WTO attempted to take leadership of developing an international FDI code at its Second Ministerial Conference, held in Singapore.[151] WTO Members also failed to come to a consensus on a multilateral FDI agreement,[152] but some of the outcomes of the WTO negotiations are embodied in a piecemeal fashion in WTO agreements such as the Agreement on Trade-Related Investment Measures (TRIMs Agreement) and the FDI disciplines in the GATS (the so-called 'mode 3'). As a result, the body of international investment law is overwhelmingly bilateral and fragmented in nature.

IIAs like BITs have their roots in the first BIT between Germany and Pakistan in 1959.[153] Since then, over 3300 IIAs have been concluded, close to 3 000 of those being BITs.[154] BITs were initially created as an instrument to protect the investments made by colonial powers from expropriation by hostile governments of former colonies in the post-colonial period in the aftermath of World War II.[155] However, at present, over 100 developing countries have entered into these types of agreements with each other—these so-called South–South BITs account for 40 per cent of global BITs.[156]

In accordance with article 38(1) of the International Court of Justice Statute, the principal sources of international investment law are international investment treaties, customary international law, general principles of law, the host state's law, international investment jurisprudence, academic sources, soft law, and other rules of international law.[157] While every IIA governs the specific investment relations between two or more states, there are certain boilerplate provisions that can be found in most agreements. These provisions include: (i) a preamble; (ii) a scope of application clause which delineates, inter alia, the definitional terms of 'investor' and 'investment' and the geographical application of the treaty; (iii) the market access or admission and establishment of investment clauses; (iv) the absolute and relative standards of treatment provisions such as fair

[150] Salacuse (n 2) 241.

[151] WTO, Singapore Ministerial Declaration, adopted on 13 December 1996, WT/MIN(96)/DEC 18 December 1996, para 20.

[152] Sornarajah (n 149) 238.

[153] K Nadavukaren Schefer *International Investment Law: Text, Cases and Materials* 2 ed (2016) 1.

[154] UNCTAD (n 74).

[155] Sornarajah (n 148) 21–4.

[156] See LN Skovgaard Poulsen, 'The politics of South–South Bilateral Investment Treaties' in T Broude, ML Busch and A Porges (eds) *The Politics of International Economic Law* (2011).

[157] Nadavukaren Schefer (n 153) 16–33.

and equitable treatment, and the MFN and national treatment obligations; (v) expropriation; (vi) war and civil disturbance; (vii) transfer of funds; (viii) treaty exceptions; (ix) other specific clauses like performance requirements, umbrella clauses and denial of benefits clauses; and (x) dispute settlement.

2 South Africa's international investment regime

Very few of South Africa's economic policies have been the topic of as much debate as the reform of its foreign investment regime that eventually culminated in the Protection of Investment Act 22 of 2015 (Investment Act), which received presidential assent on 13 December 2015.

Since re-entering international economic relations in 1994, South Africa has concluded 49 BITs.[158] The first BIT that South Africa signed was with the United Kingdom in September 1994. However, since September 2012, South Africa has notified the termination of 11 BITs that it concluded with its European, Argentine and Zimbabwean counterparties in the early years of its post-apartheid regime. The cancellation of the BITs elicited much criticism from the European Union, warning that terminating its BITs will result in the loss of investor confidence in South Africa.[159]

South Africa's actions were informed by, inter alia, its experiences with two cases[160] in which the government found itself embroiled in investment disputes before international arbitral bodies. In 2004, South Africa was reportedly ordered to pay R6,6 million after it failed to provide 'sufficient police protection and security to the Swiss owner of a proposed conference center and game farm located in the north-east of the country'.[161]

[158] See above discussion on South Africa's BITs.

[159] J Marais 'Diplomats break silence on investment bill' *Business Day BDLive* 9 March 2014, available at http://www.bdlive.co.za/business/2014/03/09/diplomats-break-silence-on-investment-bill.

[160] In 2003, there was a confidential BIT arbitration between South Africa and a Swiss investor. It was initiated pursuant to the South Africa–Switzerland BIT and adjudicated under the UNCITRAL Rules. The case is referred to as *Swiss Investor v Republic of South Africa* IA Reporter, 1 July 2003. The claimant owned a conference centre and game reserve in Limpopo province which was subject to vandalism. The investor claimed that South Africa failed to provide, inter alia, full protection and security as required by the BIT. The arbitral tribunal awarded the claimant R6.6 million plus interest for South Africa's failure to uphold its obligations under the BIT. See LE Peterson 'Swiss investor prevailed in 2003 in confidential BIT arbitration over South Africa land dispute' *Investment Arbitration Reporter* 13 (22 October 2008).

[161] The 2003 partial arbitration award (on liability) remains confidential, as does the 2004 final award (on damages). But details surfaced in a 2008 press report by LE Peterson 1 *Investment Arbitration Reporter* 2 (3 June 2008).

The second dispute—*Piero Foresti, Laura De Carli/Republic of South Africa*[162]—involved a claim by a group of European granite mining investors against South Africa. The proceedings were brought under the Italy–SA[163] and BelgoLux–SA BITs.[164] The claim proceeded under the Additional Facility (Arbitration) rules of ICSID. In essence, the claimants complained that the effect of the Mineral and Petroleum Resources Development Act 28 of 2002 was to expropriate their existing mineral rights and replace them with less valuable rights; and to subject them to discriminatory treatment—in violation of the treaties' national treatment guarantees—by operation of the Broad-Based Black Economic Empowerment objectives of the Mining Charter.

The claimants sought compensation in the amount of €266 million (approximately R3 billion) from South Africa. The ICSID Tribunal never issued a decision on the merits of the case as the claimants requested discontinuance on 2 November 2009. The parties reached an agreement in terms of which the claimants were deemed to have complied with the Mining Charter by making a 21 per cent beneficiation offset and providing a 5 per cent employee ownership programme for employees of the Operating Companies.[165] In response to South Africa's request for a default award in respect of the fees and cost, the tribunal directed the claimants to contribute €400 000 in respect of the fees and costs claimed by South Africa.[166] The award was issued on 4 August 2010.

In addition to being the first public international investment dispute case involving South Africa, the matter also made headlines for two reasons. First, there were allegations of corruption against a member of the South African legal team who allegedly solicited a bribe of R5 million from the claimants in order to settle the case.[167] Second, it marked the first time non-disputing parties (NDPs), or amicus curiae, were given such extensive procedural and participatory rights in an ICSID case. The NDPs in question were a coalition of two South African human rights organisations, the Legal Resources Centre (LRC) and the Centre for Applied Legal Studies (CALS) and

[162] ICSID Case No ARB(AF)07/01.

[163] Agreement between the Government of the Republic of South Africa and the Government of the Italian Republic for the Promotion and Protection of Investments, signed in Rome on 9 June 1997.

[164] Agreement between the Republic of South Africa and the Belgo–Luxembourg Economic Union on the Reciprocal Promotion and Protection of Investments, signed in Pretoria on 14 August 1998. Reproduced in Annex B.

[165] *Piero Foresti* (n 162) para 79.

[166] Ibid para 133.

[167] Ibid paras 119–20.

two international organisations, the International Centre for the Protection of Human Rights (INTERIGHTS) and Centre for International Environmental Law (CIEL).[168] The International Commission of Jurists filed a separate petition.[169]

The Tribunal granted the NDPs access to the parties' redacted versions of their memorials and legal opinions and lists of experts and witnesses who provided factual and quantum-related evidence in the case.[170] The Tribunal also requested feedback from the NDPs concerning the 'fairness and effectiveness' of the novel procedures adopted for NDP participation in this case but rejected their request to attend or make oral submissions at the hearing.[171]

Notwithstanding that the matter was settled, the fact that the claim in *Piero Foresti* was brought in the first place, and that the eventual settlement agreement reached beyond just the government and the *Piero Foresti* claimants, demonstrates the legal exposure to which South Africa is subjected under the BITs that it has concluded. The BITs place significant constraints on government in relation to domestic legislative measures that affect foreign investments.

By the time *Piero Foresti* was initiated, the South Africa government had already begun a review of South Africa's FDI regime. The domestic introspection began in 2005 when the DTI initiated the Bilateral Investment Treaty Policy Framework after it was suggested that certain provisions in South Africa's hastily signed BITs prevented the government from implementing public interest policies.[172] However, the review process only formally began in October 2008.[173] South Africa's experiences in *Piero Foresti* were instrumental to the conclusions drawn by the DTI when the BIT review was concluded in 2010. The process culminated in a decision by the South African Cabinet to: (i) impose a moratorium on entering into any further IIAs; (ii) review and renegotiate all South Africa's "first generation" BITs; (iii) implement domestic legislation for the regulation of all investment; (iv) develop a model IIA to serve as a basis for

[168] J Brickhill and M du Plessis 'Two's company, three's a crowd: Public interest intervention in investors-state arbitration (*Piero Foresti v South Africa*)' (2011) 27 *SALJ* 152 at 153.

[169] E Whitsitt 'An ICSID tribunal introduces innovative steps into non-disputing party procedure' *Investment Treaty News* 10 October 2009, available at https://www.iisd.org/itn/2009/11/01/innovative-steps-are-introduced-into-non-disputing-party-icsid-procedure-4/.

[170] *Piero Foresti* (n 162) para 27.

[171] Ibid paras 27 and 29.

[172] DTI (n 55) 12.

[173] *Piero Foresti* (n 162) para. 1.

further renegotiations; and (v) establish an inter-ministerial committee to oversee the process.[174]

Finally, on 1 November 2013, over three years after the conclusion of the BIT policy review, the South African government revealed the result of the almost decade-long deliberations of the future of FDI protection in South Africa when it published the Promotion and Protection of Investment Bill for public comment.[175]

While South Africa's rejection of BITs as an appropriate tool to regulate FDI garnered a fair amount of criticism, South Africa is not the only country that has given second thought to the limitations placed by BITs on its sovereign right to regulate in what it considers the public interest.

In March 2014, Indonesia announced the termination of more than 60 BITs.[176] As at June 2017, Italy, Russia, and India had also unilaterally terminated their investment agreements.[177] The EU and Canada have gone further in their bilateral trade agreement: the European Union–Canada Comprehensive Economic and Trade Agreement (CETA) excludes investor-state dispute settlement altogether in favour of a permanent bilateral investment court.[178]

On the regional front, the SADC heads of state took a decision to terminate the option of natural and legal entities being able to litigate against state parties to the agreement.

In August 2012, the SADC Summit resolved to negotiate the establishment of a new SADC Tribunal that will be limited to hearing disputes between SADC member states only.[179] These negotiations culminated in the adoption of the new SADC Tribunal Protocol at the SADC Summit on 14–15 August 2015. Article 33 thereof confirms the material jurisdiction of the SADC Tribunal as 'on the interpretation of the SADC Treaty and its Protocols relating to disputes *between*

[174] X Carim 'Perspectives on topical foreign direct investment issues by the Vale Columbia Center on sustainable international investment *Columbia FDI Perspectives* No 109 Vale Columbia Center on Sustainable Development (25 November 2013); M Mossallam 'Process matters: South Africa's experience exiting its BITs' *GEG Working Paper 2015/97* University of Oxford The Global Economic Governance Programme (2016) 12; C Vidal-León, 'A new approach to the law of foreign investment: The South African case' in AJ Bjorklund (ed) *Yearbook on International Investment Law and Policy 2014–2015* (2016).

[175] GN 1087 *GG* 36995 of 1 November 2013.

[176] A Crockett 'Indonesia's bilateral investment treaties: Between generations?' (2015) 30 *ICSID Review* 437–48.

[177] Crawford (n 82) 9.

[178] E Sardinha 'Towards a new horizon in investor–state dispute settlement? Reflections on the investment tribunal system in the Comprehensive Economic Trade Agreement (CETA)' (2017) 54 *Canadian Yearbook of International Law* 313.

[179] SADC available at http://www.sadc.int/about-sadc/sadc-institutions/tribun/.

Member States'.[180] This Protocol will come into effect 30 days after the deposit of Instruments of Ratification of two-thirds (ie 10 out of 15) of the member states.[181] The establishment of a state-to-state dispute settlement mechanism will limit the avenues available to private citizens of SADC member states to challenge the actions of their governments outside of domestic courts.

Further, in August 2016, SADC member states agreed to the amendment of Annex 1 to the SADC Protocol on Finance and Investment (FIP). One of the key amendments relates to *locus standi* under this Protocol. Article 26 stipulates that disputes '*between State Parties* shall be resolved in the manner provided under the Protocol on the Tribunal'.[182] This means that only state parties to the SADC Agreement may litigate at the SADC Tribunal. The amendment to Annex 1 of the FIP entered into force in August 2017.

As at June 2018, the SADC Tribunal Protocol had not entered into force. The effect of this, in relation to the SADC FIP, could be that disputes between *state parties* could be resolved as envisaged under the SADC Tribunal Protocol. In other words, the resolution of disputes between SADC member states does not change. Essentially, as the FIP does not expressly exclude private party-state party litigation, non-state parties could still institute proceedings against SADC member states at the Tribunal. However, this remedy is currently not available to private parties as the Tribunal is presently defunct.

The fate of the SADC Tribunal was largely precipitated by Zimbabwe's unwillingness to comply with the rulings in the cases *Mike Campbell (Pvt) Ltd v Republic of Zimbabwe*[183] and *Fick v Government of the Republic of Zimbabwe*.[184] It is unclear when SADC state parties will complete the ratification of the SADC Tribunal Protocol.

3 The Protection of Investment Act

The eventual outcome of the BIT review process is the Protection of Investment Act. The purpose of the Investment Act is to, inter alia, 'protect investment in accordance with and subject to the Constitution, in a manner that balances the public interest and obligations of investors' and 'affirm the Republic's sovereign right to regulate

[180] Emphasis added.

[181] SADC amendment Protocol, article 53.

[182] Emphasis added.

[183] [2007] SADCT 1 (13 December 2007). For a discussion of this case, see M Beukes 'Zimbabwe in the dock; The SADC Tribunal's first decision' (2008) 33 *SAYIL* 228.

[184] *Government of the Republic of Zimbabwe* v *Fick* 2013 (5) SA 325 (CC). See, further, Chapter 4.

investments in the public interest'.[185] In addition to the usual national treatment guarantees,[186] the Investment Act ensures fair administrative treatment in respect of s 33 of the Constitution and applicable legislation[187] such as the Promotion of Administrative Justice Act 3 of 2000.

However, the Investment Act departs from the traditional BIT standard of granting foreign investors full protection and security and instead provides for a 'level of physical security as may be generally provided to domestic investors'.[188] Another departure from the BIT standard is South Africa's dispute resolution clause, according to which, disputes relating to *all* investors in South Africa must be resolved by way of mediation, arbitration, and litigation in *South African domestic courts*. It is only with the consent of the South African government that foreign investors may have recourse to international state-to-state arbitration, on condition that they exhaust domestic remedies.[189]

Pursuant to the International Arbitration Act 15 of 2017, which came into force on 20 December 2017, foreign investors have the option to litigate against South African public bodies through international commercial arbitration, as governed by South African law. This option only applies if the South African public body concludes an arbitration agreement with the private entity, thereby consenting to the jurisdiction of an international commercial arbitral forum.[190]

A further significant departure under the Investment Act is in respect of the standard of compensation following an expropriation. In line with the South African Constitution, the Investment Act specifies that compensation for expropriation must be 'just and equitable', and that market value is but one of several factors to be considered when determining how this standard is to be applied. While this does not mean that compensation for expropriation under the new regime will always be less than market value, or that it will necessarily be significantly less than market value, it is clear that the compensation payable may be less than the 'full market value' that foreign investors had previously been guaranteed by way of protections for their investments under South Africa's BITs.

[185] Investment Act, s 4.

[186] Ibid s 8.

[187] Ibid s 6.

[188] Ibid s 9.

[189] Investment Act, s 13.

[190] Subject to s 13 of the Investment Act, s 5 of the International Arbitration Act binds South African public bodies and applies to any international commercial arbitration in terms of an arbitration agreement to which a public body is a party.

So, too, the Investment Act's definition of expropriation is less extensive than that found under many BITs. The Act expressly suggests that it only applies to 'measures' by the government that have a 'direct' effect on investor's rights,[191] whereas traditional BITs have protected against 'indirect' expropriation through interference by a state in the use of property or with the enjoyment of the benefits even where the property is not seized and the legal title to the property is not affected.[192]

According to the Investment Act's transitional arrangements, existing investments that were made under BITs will continue to be regulated under those BITs until the sunset clauses terminate. Furthermore, the Investment Act must be interpreted in a manner that is consistent with, inter alia, any relevant convention or international agreement to which South Africa is or becomes a party.[193] Accordingly, BITs to which South Africa is a party will be upheld, irrespective of the commencement of the Investment Act.

It is clear that from both a substantive and procedural view, the Investment Act offers a level of protection that is lower than that customarily provided by international investment treaties. It remains to be seen what impact the Investment Act will have on the flow of foreign investment to South Africa,[194] and whether its provisions will come under constitutional scrutiny.

[191] See the definition of 'measure' ('refers to binding governmental action directly affecting an investor or its investment, and includes laws, regulations and administrative action') as read with s 12 (which sets out the government's right to regulate).

[192] In those cases of 'indirect expropriation' the measures taken by the state have a similar effect to expropriation or nationalisation and are generally termed 'indirect', 'creeping', or '*de facto*' expropriation, or measures 'tantamount' to expropriation (see OECD Directorate for Financial and Enterprise Affairs, Working Papers on International Investment, Number 2004/4, Indirect Expropriation and the Right to Regulate in International Investment Law 4).

[193] Investment Act, s 3*(c)*.

[194] See T Gazzini 'Rethinking the promotion and protection of foreign investments: The 2015 South Africa's Protection Investment Act' available at https://ssrn.com/abstract=2960567. See further Mossallam (n 174).

CHAPTER 22

International Adjudication

John Dugard and Rosalind Elphick

INTRODUCTION

International law knows no system of compulsory adjudication. The International Court of Justice and other international courts—such as the International Tribunal for the Law of the Sea—have jurisdiction only where the parties to the dispute have consented to the Court's jurisdiction. The same applies to arbitration tribunals: they, too, are dependent on the consent of states for the exercise of jurisdiction. Inevitably, therefore, the settlement of international disputes by judicial means is the exception and not the rule. Alternative methods of dispute resolution, such as mediation, conciliation, and negotiation, are generally more attractive to states. International adjudication[1] is, however, on the increase: the International Court of Justice is busier today than it has been in its entire history, and more frequent use is made of arbitration tribunals than in past years.

This chapter will focus largely on the International Court of Justice as an institution; and upon its jurisprudence.

A study of the International Court of Justice and its judgments is essential for an understanding of the limitations of international law and of the prospects for an expanded role for international law in the contemporary world order. South Africa has appeared before the International Court of Justice on more occasions than most states, as a result of the legal obligations it assumed in respect of its administration of South West Africa/Namibia. The four opinions and two judgments of the International Court of Justice in this dispute comprise a substantial part of the Court's jurisprudence, and provide a clear illustration of the nature of the international judicial process. A legal chronology of this dispute, which will feature prominently in this chapter, appears as an appendix to this chapter.

This chapter also includes a description of the Permanent Court of Arbitration (PCA) which provides a range of dispute resolution

[1] See G Schwarzenberger *International Law as Applied by International Courts and Tribunals* vol IV (International Judicial Law) (1986); JG Merrills *International Dispute Settlement* 5 ed (2011); E Lauterpacht *Aspects of the Administration of International Justice* (1991); K Oellers-Frahm and A Zimmermann *Dispute Settlement in Public International Law* (2001); J Collier and V Lowe *The Settlement of Disputes in International Law* (1999); F Orrego Vicuna *International Dispute Settlement in an Evolving Global Society* (2004); D French, M Saul and N White (eds) *International Law and Dispute Settlement* (2010).

services to the international community. A study of this intergovernmental organisation and the role it plays in the realm of international dispute resolution is valuable for understanding both the evolution of international adjudication prior to the establishment of the International Court of Justice, as well as the recent revival in the use of arbitration in the adjudication of disputes between states.

A BRIEF HISTORY OF INTERNATIONAL ADJUDICATION

Before a permanent international court was established in 1920, arbitration was the only method for the judicial settlement of disputes. States parties to a dispute would, typically, select suitable arbitrators, who would then choose an umpire. For instance, in the famous *Alabama Claims*[2] Arbitration of 1872, between the United States and Britain arising out of the latter's violation of its duties of neutrality during the American Civil War, a panel of five arbitrators was constituted, comprising jurists from the United States, Britain, Italy, Switzerland, and Brazil. The British arbitrator was the sole dissentient on the finding that Britain had violated its obligations and was obliged to pay $15 500 000 to the United States as compensation.

In 1899, the first Hague Peace Conference was held with the aim of, inter alia, discussing a mechanism for the peaceful resolution of disputes between states.[3] The conference adopted the Convention on the Pacific Settlement of International Disputes (the 1899 Convention) which recognised that for 'questions of a legal nature, and especially in the interpretation or application of International Conventions' arbitration is the 'most effective, and at the same time the most equitable, means of settling disputes which diplomacy has failed to settle'.[4] In order to facilitate 'immediate recourse to

[2] JB Moore *International Arbitrations to which the United States has been a Party* vol 1 (1898) 653. The *Alabama Claims* has an interesting South African link. The *Alabama*, a confederate warship, which was built in British shipyards, was allowed to put into British colonial ports in the course of its marauding aimed at the federal merchant navy. Its arrival at Cape Town was such a major event that it produced one of South Africa's best known songs, 'Daar kom die Alabama'. The arbitration tribunal found that both the building and the refuelling of the *Alabama* were in violation of Britain's obligations as a neutral during the American Civil War. See further, JP van Niekerk 'The story of the CSS ("Daar Kom Die . . .") *Alabama*: some legal aspects of her visit to the Cape of Good Hope, and her influence on the historical development of the law of war and neutrality, international arbitration, salvage and maritime prize' (2007) *Fundamina: A Journal of Legal History* 175.

[3] See BW Daly 'Permanent Court of Arbitration' in C Gioretti (ed) *The Rules, Practice, and Jurisprudence of International Courts and Tribunals* (2012) 37–9.

[4] Article 16 of the 1899 Convention for the Pacific Settlement of International Disputes (1899 Convention). A second Hague Peace Conference, held in 1907, concluded the 1907 Convention for the Pacific Settlement of International Disputes

arbitration', the 1899 Convention established the PCA as a permanent bureau seated in The Hague to operate as a registry for international dispute resolution proceedings.[5] The PCA's member states were empowered to appoint jurists to a panel from which parties might select arbitrators for PCA administered proceedings.[6] This machinery was frequently used before the establishment of an international court in 1920. It has survived the creation of a permanent international court, and continues to provide administrative support for a variety of dispute resolution mechanisms.

The Covenant of the League of Nations contemplated the establishment of a genuine world court,[7] but left it to a later multilateral treaty—the Statute of the Permanent Court of International Justice—to implement this goal. In the result, the Permanent Court of International Justice (PCIJ) was not institutionally linked to the League of Nations, unlike its successor, the International Court of Justice, which was established by the Charter of the United Nations (UN Charter) and which forms an integral part of the United Nations system. The PCIJ was one of the most successful international institutions of the inter-war years. South Africa was a party to the Statute of the Court but did not appear before it in any legal proceedings.

The current International Court of Justice replaced the PCIJ in 1945. As neither the United States nor the Soviet Union, the two superpowers in the post-World War II order, had been signatories to the Statute of the PCIJ, there were sound political reasons for creating a new Court of which they could claim original membership. In addition, the framers of the Charter considered it desirable to integrate the new Court into the United Nations system. This was done by designating the International Court of Justice as the principal judicial organ of the United Nations,[8] and by incorporating the Statute of the International Court of Justice into the Charter.[9] In reality, the International Court of Justice is not a successor to the PCIJ, but rather a continuation of the old Court. It retains its seat at The Hague, under a largely unchanged Statute, and the International Court of Justice has

(1907 Convention). The 1907 Convention was largely a revision of the earlier 1899 Convention.

[5] 1899 Convention, article 20.

[6] Ibid, article 23 and the 1907 Convention, article 44. This panel of potential arbitrators is referred to as the PCA's 'Members of the Court'. The Members of the Court for each PCA member state constitute a 'national group' which is entitled to nominate candidates for the election to the International Court of Justice in terms of the Statute of the ICJ (article 4(1)).

[7] Ibid, article 14.

[8] UN Charter, articles 92–6.

[9] Ibid, article 92.

relied on the jurisprudence of the PCIJ as if it was the same Court. The principal difference between the two Courts is that, whereas only states committed to international adjudication became signatories to the Statute of the PCIJ, all member states of the United Nations automatically become parties to the International Court of Justice's Statute upon signing the Charter.[10]

The increased interest in the judicial settlement of disputes between states has led to the establishment of several international courts with specialised jurisdiction—such as the International Tribunal for the Law of the Sea, the European Court of Human Rights, the Court of Justice of the European Union, the Inter-American Court of Human Rights, the African Court of Human and People's Rights, the African Court of Justice and the Community Court of Justice of the Economic Community of West African States (ECOWAS). The Iran–United States Claims Tribunal has been in existence for 30 years; there are special dispute settlement mechanisms for the World Trade Organization (WTO) and the North American Free Trade Agreement (NAFTA); and the International Centre for the Settlement of Investment Disputes (ICSID) provides machinery for the settlement of investment disputes. To this list, must be added the ad hoc International Criminal Law Tribunals for the Former Yugoslavia (ICTY) and Rwanda (ICTR), and the International Criminal Court (ICC), which apply principles of international law, although they are concerned with the prosecution of individuals, and not the resolution of disputes between states. The proliferation of international tribunals without any recognised hierarchy of authority has given rise to concerns that different tribunals will interpret international law rules in different ways and thereby undermine the unity and universality of international law.[11] These concerns are probably exaggerated 'provided the various tribunals stay within their respective spheres of competence, apply traditional international legal reasoning, show judicial restraint by seeking to avoid unnecessary conflicts, and remain open to reconsider their prior legal pronouncements in order to take account of the case law of other international courts'.[12]

[10] Ibid, article 93(1). Non-members of the United Nations may become parties to the Statute of the International Court of Justice in terms of article 93(2).

[11] The most frequently cited conflict is that between the judgment of the International Court of Justice in the *Nicaragua Case* 1986 ICJ Reports 13 at 64–5 (para 115) and that of the ICTY in the *Tadic Case* (1999) 38 *ILM* 1518 at 1546 (para 145) on the subject of the responsibility of a state for the action of groups under its control.

[12] T Buergenthal 'Proliferation of international courts and tribunals: Is it good or bad?' (2001) 14 *Leiden Journal of International Law* 267. See further, ZB Abebe 'The African Court with a criminal jurisdiction and the ICC: A case for overlapping jurisdiction?' (2017) 25 *African Journal of International and Comparative Law* 418;

THE INTERNATIONAL COURT OF JUSTICE[13]

The International Court of Justice, situated at the Peace Palace, comprises 15 judges 'of recognized competence in international law'[14] who together represent 'the main forms of civilization' and 'the principal legal systems of the world'.[15] They are elected by the General Assembly and United Nations Security Council (UNSC)[16] and hold office for nine years.[17] When the Court was first constituted in 1946, five judges were elected for three years, five for six years, and five for nine years. Consequently, elections to the Court are now held every three years for five judges. In addition, the Court elects the President, who holds office for three years.[18] Nine judges constitute a quorum.[19] A majority of the judges present decides all questions. In the event of an equality of votes, the President has a casting vote.[20] In 1966, Sir Percy Spender of Australia, the President of the Court, secured a 'technical victory' for South Africa in its dispute with Ethiopia and Liberia over South West Africa/Namibia when he exercised both a deliberative and a casting vote in favour of a finding that the applicants lacked the necessary standing to bring the complaint.[21]

Although judges are required to recuse themselves from cases in which they have been personally involved as counsel, or in some

E Karanja and N Muriuki 'The proliferation of international arbitral institutions in Africa and what the future holds for institutional arbitration on the African continent' (2016) 13 *Transnational Dispute Management* 12.

[13] S Rosenne (MN Shaw ed) *The Law and Practice of the International Court 1920–2015* (4 vols) 5 ed (2016); A Zimmermann, C Tomuschat and K Oellers-Frahm (eds) *The Statute of the International Court of Justice: A Commentary* 3 ed (2019); H Thirlway *The International Court of Justice* (2016); H Thirlway *The Law and Procedure of the International Court of Justice* 2 vols (2013); G Hernández *The International Court of Justice and the Judicial Function* (2014); R Kolb *The International Court of Justice* (2014).

[14] Statute of the International Court of Justice, articles 2 and 3.

[15] Ibid, article 9. The present practice is for the Court to comprise five judges from Western states, three from Africa, three from Asia, two from Eastern Europe, and two from Latin America. Although not required by the Statute, nationals of the five permanent members of the UNSC are in practice represented on the Court.

[16] Ibid, articles 4–12. On the process of selection of judges, see R Mackenzie et al *Selecting International Judges: Principle, Process and Politics* (2010).

[17] Statute of the International Court of Justice, article 13.

[18] Ibid, article 21.

[19] Ibid, article 25(3).

[20] Ibid, article 55.

[21] *South West Africa, Second Phase* 1966 ICJ Reports 6; J Dugard *The South West Africa/Namibia Dispute* (1973) 293.

other capacity,[22] they are not required to recuse themselves when their own national state is a party to a dispute. Moreover, if a party to a dispute has no national on the Court, it may appoint a judge ad hoc to sit on the Court for that particular case.[23] In the *South West Africa Cases* of 1960–66, South Africa appointed Mr Justice JT van Wyk, Judge President of the Cape Provincial Division, as its judge ad hoc. In 2002, John Dugard SC was appointed as judge ad hoc by Rwanda, in a dispute with the Democratic Republic of the Congo over armed activities in the territory of the Congo;[24] in 2004, he was appointed as judge ad hoc by Malaysia in a territorial dispute with Singapore;[25] and in 2010 he was appointed as judge ad hoc by Costa Rica in a boundary dispute with Nicaragua.[26] The non-recusal of national judges and the appointment of judges ad hoc are practices, rooted in the composition of early arbitration tribunals, that to some extent undermine the character of the Court—particularly as judges ad hoc and national judges seldom find against their own state or the state that has appointed them.[27]

Article 26 of the Statute of the International Court of Justice permits the creation of chambers composed of three or more judges for dealing with a particular case or category of cases. The International Court of Justice itself determines the composition of a chamber dealing with a particular case after consultation with the parties to the dispute. However, in practice, few disputes are referred to chambers.

The International Court of Justice exercises two jurisdictions. First, it hears disputes between states and gives binding judgments on

[22] Statute of the International Court of Justice, articles 17 and 24. See the controversy surrounding the recusal of Judge Sir Muhammad Zafrulla Khan of Pakistan in the *1966 South West Africa Cases*: Dugard (n 21) 291; V Katan 'There was an elephant in the court room: Reflections on the role of Judge Sir Percy Spender (1897-1985) in the South West Africa cases (1960–1966) after half a century' (2018) 31 *Leiden Journal of International Law* 147; V Kattan 'Decolonizing the International Court of Justice: The experience of Judge Sir Muhammad Zafrulla Khan in the South West Africa cases' (2015) 5 *Asian Journal of International Law* 310.

[23] Statute of the International Court of Justice, article 31.

[24] *Case Concerning Armed Activities on the Territory of the Congo (DRC v Rwanda)*, 2002 ICJ Reports 219; (2002) 41 *ILM* 1175; 2006 ICJ Reports 6.

[25] *Sovereignty over Pedra Branca/Pulau Batu Puteh, Middle Rocks and South Ledge (Malaysia/Singapore)* 2008 ICJ Reports 12.

[26] *Certain Activities Carried Out by Nicaragua in the Border Area (Costa Rica v Nicaragua) and Construction of a Road in Costa Rica along the San Juan River (Nicaragua v Costa Rica)* 2015 ICJ Reports 665 at 673 (para 6).

[27] S Schwebel 'National judges and judges ad hoc of the International Court of Justice' (1999) 48 *ICLQ* 889; Zimmermann et al (n 13) 533; I Scobbie 'Une hérésie en matière judiciaire—The role of the judge ad hoc in the International Court' (2005) 4 *The Law and Practice of International Courts and Tribunals* 421.

such disputes. Such proceedings are described as contentious proceedings. Secondly, the Court may give advisory opinions at the request of designated organs or specialised agencies of the United Nations. The composition of the Court is unaffected by the nature of the proceedings and the same rules of international law are applied in both cases. However, different procedural and jurisdictional rules govern the two proceedings and this makes it necessary to consider these two jurisdictions or competences separately.

CONTENTIOUS PROCEEDINGS

In terms of article 34 of the Statute of the International Court of Justice, only states may be parties to disputes before the Court. The exclusion of international organisations, non-governmental organisations, multinational corporations, and individuals from access to the Court in contentious proceedings may be explained on the basis that states were the only actors in the international legal arena when the Statute was drafted in 1920. This is no longer the case, and today there are calls for an expansion of access to the Court.[28] The weakness of the present rule is illustrated by the *South West Africa Cases* of 1960–66.[29] Here, a dispute developed between the United Nations and South Africa, over the status of South West Africa, after South Africa had refused to accept the United Nations as the successor to the League of Nations in respect of the international supervision of the mandated territory. The United Nations obtained three advisory opinions from the International Court of Justice, holding that South Africa was obliged to account to the United Nations for its administration of the territory, but these were ignored by South Africa. As the United Nations was itself prevented from instituting contentious proceedings against South Africa because of article 34 of the Statute of the International Court of Justice, Ethiopia and Liberia brought proceedings, in effect on behalf of the United Nations, in order to obtain a binding judgment confirming the advisory opinions. This strategy failed when the International Court of Justice, in 1966, held that the two applicant states had no legal interest in the matter,[30]

[28] A Bianchi 'The fight for inclusion: Non-state actors and international law' in U Fastenrath et al (eds) *From Bilateralism to Community Interest: Essays in Honour of Bruno Simma* (2011) 39 (arguing that 'a widespread sentiment exists, among international lawyers, that the traditional subjects doctrine is no longer able to provide a satisfactory account of the social realities underlying international law'). On the extent that non-state actors are permitted to participate: Y Ronen 'Participation of non-state actors in ICJ proceedings' (2012) 11 *The Law and Practice of International Courts and Tribunals* 77.

[29] For a history of these proceedings, see Dugard (n 21) 210–15, 239–375.

[30] *South West Africa, Second Phase* 1966 ICJ Reports 6.

essentially on the ground that the dispute was between South Africa and the United Nations.

1 Jurisdiction

The International Court of Justice is open only to states that are parties to its Statute (ie, members of the United Nations) and states that have been permitted to use the Court under conditions laid down by the UNSC.[31] In spite of the fact that states may have the necessary permission to use the Court, they are not bound to do so: the International Court of Justice does not have compulsory jurisdiction over all such states or over all disputes of international law between these states. It has jurisdiction only over those states which consent to the Court's jurisdiction and only in respect of those disputes which such states consent to be heard by the Court.

Consent, the basis of the Court's jurisdiction, may be given in a number of ways which are provided for in article 36 of the Statute. This provision reads:

> (1) The jurisdiction of the Court comprises all cases which the parties refer to it and all matters specially provided for in the Charter of the United Nations or in treaties and conventions in force.
>
> (2) The states parties to the present Statute may at any time declare that they recognize as compulsory *ipso facto* and without special agreement, in relation to any other states accepting the same obligation, the jurisdiction of the Court in all legal disputes concerning:
>
> *(a)* the interpretation of a treaty;
>
> *(b)* any question of international law;
>
> *(c)* the existence of any fact which, if established, would constitute a breach of an international obligation;
>
> *(d)* the nature or extent of the reparation to be made for the breach of an international obligation.
>
> (3) The declarations referred to above may be made unconditionally or on condition of reciprocity on the part of several or certain states, or for a certain time.
>
> (4) Such declarations shall be deposited with the Secretary-General of the United Nations, who shall transmit copies thereof to the parties to the Statute and to the Registrar of the Court.
>
> (5) Declarations made under Article 36 of the Statute of the Permanent Court of International Justice and which are still in force shall be deemed, as

[31] Statute of the International Court of Justice, article 35. In proceedings brought by Serbia and Montenegro against NATO member states arising out of the Kosovo conflict, the International Court of Justice held that Serbia and Montenegro was not a member of the United Nations and, consequently, was not a state party to the Statute of the International Court of Justice at the time it initiated proceedings against NATO members. It followed that the Court was not open to Serbia and Montenegro under article 35 of the Statute. See, eg, *Case Concerning Legality of Use of Force (Serbia and Montenegro v Portugal)* 2004 ICJ Reports 1160; (2005) 44 *ILM* 299.

between the parties to the present Statute, to be acceptance of the compulsory jurisdiction of the International Court of Justice for the period which they still have to run and in accordance with their terms.

(6) In the event of a dispute as to whether the Court has jurisdiction, the matter shall be settled by the decision of the Court.

A distinction is drawn between the existence of the Court's jurisdiction over a dispute and the compatibility with international law of the acts that are the subject of the dispute.[32] Thus the fact that the subject of the dispute concerns the violation of norms of *jus cogens*, or of obligations *erga omnes*, does not confer jurisdiction on the Court. This was made clear in *Armed Activities on the Territory of the Congo (DRC v Rwanda)* where the Court held that '[j]urisdiction is always based on the consent of the parties'.[33]

Because much of the Court's jurisprudence is devoted to the interpretation of article 36, it is necessary to examine the various ways in which the Court may obtain jurisdiction.

(a) Cases which parties refer to the Court (special agreement)

The International Court of Justice has jurisdiction over a dispute referred to it by states in a special agreement or *compromis*. For example, in 1996, Botswana and Namibia signed a special agreement requesting the Court to resolve a dispute between them concerning the boundary around Kasikili/Sedudu Island, and the legal status of the island.[34]

If one state unilaterally applies to the Court to hear a dispute, and the respondent state conducts itself in such a manner that an agreement to accept jurisdiction may be implied, the Court may exercise jurisdiction in terms of the doctrine of *forum prorogatum*. It was on this basis that the Court held that it had jurisdiction to hear a dispute between the United Kingdom and Albania, arising out of the sinking of British destroyers in the Corfu Channel in 1946. Here the Court inferred consent from an ill-considered letter to the registrar of the International Court of Justice from the Albanian government in which it protested its innocence for the sinking of the destroyers and accepted the jurisdiction of the Court (which it later sought to withdraw) in response to a unilateral application by the United Kingdom.[35] The refusal of Albania to comply with the adverse finding by the Court (ordering it to compensate the United Kingdom for the loss of the destroyers[36]) raised doubts about the wisdom of

[32] *Serbia and Montenegro v United Kingdom* 2004 ICJ Reports 1307 at 1351.
[33] 2006 ICJ Reports 6 at 32, para 64.
[34] *Kasikili/Sedudu Island Case* 1999 ICJ Reports 1045.
[35] *Corfu Channel Case, Preliminary Objection* 1948 ICJ Reports 15.
[36] The International Court of Justice's order was complied with in 1992!

exercising jurisdiction on the ground of implied consent. Despite this, states continue to make unilateral applications to the Court with the hope that the respondent state will consent to the Court's jurisdiction. In 2008, the International Court of Justice exercised jurisdiction in a dispute between Djibouti and France that had been initiated by a unilateral application by Djibouti to which France had consented. Here the Court stated:

> The Court has also interpreted Article 36, paragraph 1, of the Statute as enabling consent to be deduced from certain acts, thus accepting the possibility of *forum prorogatum*. This modality is applied when a respondent State has, through its conduct before the Court or in relation to the applicant party, acted in such a way as to have consented to the jurisdiction of the Court.[37]

(b) *Cases provided for in treaties or conventions in force (compromissory clause)*

Frequently, bilateral or multilateral treaties contain a clause in which parties accept the Court's jurisdiction for any dispute that might in the future arise relating to the treaty in question. Such a clause is known as a compromissory clause. In this respect article 37 of the Statute of the International Court of Justice plays an important role as it provides that a reference in a pre-1946 compromissory clause to the PCIJ shall be construed as a reference to the International Court of Justice. There are nearly 300 bilateral and multilateral treaties with compromissory clauses conferring jurisdiction on the International Court of Justice and many of the cases brought before the Court have invoked such a clause as a basis for jurisdiction.[38]

A compromissory clause gave the International Court of Justice jurisdiction in the *South West Africa Cases*. In this regard, article 7(2) of the Mandate for South West Africa[39] provided:

[37] *Certain Questions of Mutual Assistance in Criminal Matters (Djibouti v France)* 2008 ICJ Reports para 61. See too the dispute between the Republic of Congo (Brazzaville) and France which also involved the doctrine of *forum prorogatum*: *Certain Criminal Proceedings in France Case (Republic of the Congo v France)* 2003 ICJ Reports 102; (2003) 42 *ILM* 852. See S Yee '*Forum prorogatum* returns to the International Court of Justice' (2003) 16 *Leiden Journal of International Law* 701.

[38] See, eg, the *US Diplomatic and Consular Staff in Tehran (Hostages Case)* 1980 ICJ Reports 3; *Case Concerning Military and Paramilitary Activities in and against Nicaragua (Nicaragua v United States of America), Jurisdiction and Admissibility* 1984 ICJ Reports 392; *La Grand (Germany v US)* 2001 ICJ Reports 466; and *Avena (Mexico v US)* 2004 ICJ Reports 12; (2004) 42 *ILM* 581.

[39] Although the Mandate took the form of a resolution of the League of Nations, it was accepted as 'having the character of a treaty or convention' (*South West Africa Cases (Ethiopia v South Africa; Liberia v South Africa), Preliminary Objections* 1962 ICJ Reports 319 at 331).

> The Mandatory [that is, South Africa] agrees that, if any dispute whatever should arise between the Mandatory and another Member of the League of Nations relating to the interpretation or the application of the provisions of the Mandate, such dispute if it cannot be settled by negotiation, shall be submitted to the Permanent Court of International Justice.

The Court, in 1962, upheld the claim of Ethiopia and Liberia, both ex-members of the League of Nations, that there was a dispute between them and South Africa that could not be settled by negotiation. Here the Court found that it had jurisdiction under article 7(2) of the Mandate and article 37 of the Statute, to hear the dispute involving the international status of South West Africa and the compatibility of apartheid with the provision in the Mandate obliging South Africa to 'promote to the utmost' the well-being of the inhabitants of the territory. In so ruling, the Court dismissed a number of preliminary objections raised by South Africa against the continued validity of article 7(2).[40]

(c) Matters specially provided for in UN Charter

Article 36(1) suggests that the UN Charter provides for compulsory jurisdiction in certain cases. In fact, the only provision in the Charter on this subject is article 36(3), which authorises the UNSC to *recommend* to states that legal disputes should be referred to the International Court of Justice. In 1948 in the *Corfu Channel Case*, Britain argued that such a recommendation of the UNSC conferred compulsory jurisdiction on the Court. Although the Court found it unnecessary to consider this argument (as it found that it had jurisdiction on the basis of *forum prorogatum*), seven judges submitted a joint separate opinion denying that such a recommendation could give the Court compulsory jurisdiction.[41] Although the Court itself has yet to decide on this issue, no further attempt has been made to establish the jurisdiction of the Court in this manner.

(d) Optional clause

Article 36(2) of the Statute, known as the 'optional clause', is the most important, and controversial, mechanism for conferring jurisdiction upon the Court. Essentially, it represents a compromise between those states that favour compulsory jurisdiction and those that oppose it, as it allows states to 'opt in' for compulsory jurisdiction by accepting the compulsory jurisdiction of the Court in relation to any other state that likewise accepts such jurisdiction.[42] During the

[40] *South West Africa Cases* (n 39). See too Dugard (n 21) 243–60.

[41] *Corfu Channel Case* (n 35) 31–2.

[42] In *Land and Maritime Boundary (Cameroon v Nigeria), Preliminary Objections* 1998 ICJ Reports 275 the International Court of Justice described a declaration under article

League of Nations[43] period and the first decade of the United Nations,[44] (ie before the expansion of the membership of the United Nations) a substantial majority of states had made declarations under article 36(2) accepting the Court's compulsory jurisdiction. Since then the number of acceptances has greatly diminished and today a third of the states party to the Statute (73 in 2018) have made declarations under article 36(2).[45] Equally disturbing is the fact that Britain is the only permanent member of the UNSC to have done so. South Africa made declarations of acceptance under the Statute of both the PCIJ [46] and the International Court of Justice.[47] In 1967,[48] the South African declaration was withdrawn as the government feared that South Africa might be brought to Court over apartheid and no acceptance has since been made. It is difficult to understand why post-apartheid South Africa has failed to accept the compulsory jurisdiction of the International Court of Justice. The explanation for this, provided by the Minister of Justice and Constitutional Development in the National Assembly on 11 June 2013, is that South Africa believes that every attempt should first be made to settle disputes by negotiation rather than by judicial decision. This is not, however, a valid reason as it would be possible to attach a reservation to an acceptance of the optional clause to the effect that South Africa does not accept the Court's jurisdiction in respect of disputes that have not been the subject of prior negotiation. In these circumstances South Africa's failure to accept the optional clause may be construed as a lack of commitment to the rule of law in international relations.

36(2) as follows: 'Any state party to the Statute, in adhering to the jurisdiction of the Court in accordance with article 36(2), accepts jurisdiction in its relations with states having previously adhered to that clause. At the same time, it makes a standing offer to the other states parties to the Statute which have not yet deposited a declaration of acceptance. The day one of those states accepts that offer by depositing in its turn its declaration of acceptance, the consensual bond is established and no further condition needs to be met' (1998 ICJ Reports 275 at 291 (para 25)).

[43] In 1934, 42 out of 60 states entitled to use the facilities of the Court had accepted compulsory jurisdiction ie, 70 per cent.

[44] In 1955, 33 out of 60 states had made declarations under article 36(2) ie, 55 per cent.

[45] These declarations appear in the *Yearbook of the International Court of Justice* and on the website of the International Court of Justice available at http://www.icj-cij.org/en/declarations.

[46] South Africa made a declaration of acceptance in 1929 for a 10-year period and thereafter until notice of termination was given. In 1940, it was terminated and replaced with a new declaration. See further S Pienaar *South Africa and International Relations between the Two World Wars* (1987) 25–9.

[47] The 1940 declaration was allowed to remain in force until it was terminated and replaced with a new declaration in 1955.

[48] 595 UNTS 363 (1967); 1966–7 *Yearbook of the International Court of Justice* 44.

As of today, some 22 Optional Clause declarations originate from African states, including three of South Africa's immediate neighbours—Botswana, Lesotho and Swaziland. The obvious explanation for the decline in the acceptances of the optional clause is that, unlike the position that pertained under the League of Nations, all member states of the United Nations are automatically parties to the Statute of the International Court of Justice, whether they approve of the judicial settlement of disputes or not. Consequently, a number of states, which are ideologically opposed to international adjudication, are parties to the Statute.

A further reason that has been advanced for this decline is that the manner in which states attach reservations to their declarations of acceptance has effectively undermined the value of the system of compulsory jurisdiction.[49]

Article 36(3) contemplates that reservations may be made on grounds of reciprocity or time. The latter permits a state to limit its acceptance to a specified period. The former ensures that 'jurisdiction is conferred on the Court only to the extent to which the two Declarations coincide in conferring it',[50] which 'enables a Party to invoke a reservation to that acceptance, which it has not expressed in its own Declaration, but which the other Party has expressed in its Declaration'.[51] Thus, in the *Norwegian Loans Case (France v Norway)*[52] Norway, the respondent, successfully invoked a reservation excluding the Court's jurisdiction in domestic disputes as determined by France, contained in France's declaration of acceptance, against France (the applicant state), despite the fact that it had made no such reservation itself.

States have gone beyond the limits of article 36(3) in the reservations attached to their declarations. A common reservation, which was contained in South Africa's 1940–1955 declaration, excludes 'disputes with regard to questions which by international law fall exclusively within the jurisdiction' of the reserving state.[53] No real objection can be raised to such a reservation as it allows *the Court*,

[49] H Waldock 'Decline of the optional clause' (1955/6) 32 *BYIL* 244. See too S Oda 'Reservations in the Declarations of Acceptance of the Optional Clause' (1988) 59 *BYIL* 1; JP Kelly 'The ICJ: Crisis and reformation' (1987) 12 *Yale Journal of International Law* 342. *Sed contra*, see S Alexandrov 'Accepting the compulsory jurisdiction of the International Court of Justice with reservations: An overview of practice with a focus on recent trends and cases' (2001) 14 *Leiden Journal of International Law* 89; Zimmermann et al (n 13) 677.

[50] *Anglo-Iranian Oil Co Case (Jurisdiction) (UK v Iran)* 1952 ICJ Reports 93 at 103.

[51] *Interhandel Case (Switzerland v USA)* 1959 ICJ Reports 6 at 23.

[52] 1957 ICJ Reports 9 at 23–7.

[53] 1946–7 *Yearbook of the International Court of Justice* 215.

acting under article 36(6), to determine whether the dispute is domestic or not.

Some states, inspired by the United States, have gone further and excluded domestic disputes as determined by the reserving state. Thus, South Africa's 1955 Declaration under article 36(2) excluded from the compulsory jurisdiction of the Court

> disputes with regard to matters which are essentially within the jurisdiction of the Government of the Union of South Africa as determined by the Government of the Union of South Africa. [54]

The principal objection to such a reservation, known as the automatic reservation or Connally Amendment (named after the United States Senator responsible for proposing such a reservation), is that it violates article 36(6) by denying the competence of the Court to make such a determination. Despite a number of strong individual judicial opinions, particularly by Judge Lauterpacht,[55] holding that such reservations are invalid, the Court has failed to make such a finding.[56] Its decision in the *Norwegian Loans Case*, however, has discouraged states from persisting with such reservations. If a state that does not include an 'automatic reservation' in its declaration may nevertheless rely on such a reservation in the applicant's declaration because of the principle of reciprocity, it follows that a state with an automatic reservation will seldom be able to bring proceedings against another state.[57] Consequently, most states that maintained such reservations have terminated their declarations of acceptance of the Court's jurisdiction. South Africa did so in 1967, while the United States withdrew its declaration of acceptance in 1985,[58] after the International Court of Justice had exercised jurisdiction over the claims of Nicaragua against the United States arising out of the latter's support for covert military groups (the *Contras*) operating against the Nicaraguan government.[59]

[54] 1955–6 *Yearbook of the International Court of Justice* 184.

[55] *Norwegian Loans Case* (n 52) 34; *Interhandel Case* (n 51) 95. See, too, the separate opinions of Judges Spender (at 54), Klaested (at 75), and Armand-Ugon (at 85) in the *Interhandel Case* (n 51).

[56] The majority of the Court in the *Norwegian Loans Case* (n 52) 27 by implication upheld the validity of the French automatic reservation by allowing Norway to rely on it.

[57] This is illustrated by the *Aerial Incident of July 27, 1955* 1960 ICJ Reports 146, in which the United States was compelled to abandon a claim against Bulgaria arising out of the shooting down of an El Al aircraft, with US nationals on board, over Bulgarian territory when Bulgaria invoked the United States' automatic reservation on domestic jurisdiction.

[58] *Contemporary Practice of the United States* (1986) 80 *AJIL* 163–5.

[59] The United States did not invoke its automatic reservation in this case because the issue—support for military groups in Nicaragua—could not possibly have been

A reservation to a declaration under article 36(2) may be contrary to international law. Thus, in a dispute between Spain and Canada over the arrest of a Spanish fishing vessel on the high seas, the International Court of Justice upheld the validity of a Canadian reservation excluding from the Court's compulsory jurisdiction, disputes over measures taken by Canada against foreign fishing vessels on the high seas. The International Court of Justice stated that there is no rule that requires 'that reservations be interpreted so as to cover only acts compatible with international law . . . this is to confuse the legality of the acts with consent to jurisdiction'.[60]

The International Court of Justice has acknowledged that a declaration under the optional clause constitutes a standing offer by a state to other states that have not yet made such a declaration to do so and to seize the jurisdiction of the Court in respect of that state. As article 36(2) does not require that a period of time must elapse between the deposit of a declaration and the filing of an application, a state may deposit a declaration, immediately file an application against a state that has accepted the optional clause, and then, soon afterwards, terminate its declaration. The International Court of Justice has, unfortunately, allowed this practice known as 'Trial by ambush'.[61] A state that accepts the optional clause may, however, protect itself against such a strategy by requiring in a reservation, as Britain has done, that the declaration of the other party should be deposited no less than a year prior to the filing of an application.[62]

Even in the absence of a reservation to the Optional Clause declaration, the jurisdiction of the Court is not unlimited. Under article 36(2), the Court has jurisdiction over 'all legal disputes' arising between states that have accepted the compulsory jurisdiction of the Court. The Court's jurisdiction is therefore conditional on the existence of a dispute between the parties. Over the years, the Court has developed a significant body of jurisprudence on the matter of identifying the existence of a dispute.[63] The Court determined in the

described as domestic. The United States did, however, raise objections to the validity of Nicaragua's declaration under article 36(2), and it was the Court's rejection of this argument that prompted the United States to withdraw its declaration. *Nicaragua v United States of America*) (n 38).

[60] *Fisheries Jurisdiction (Spain v Canada), Jurisdiction Judgment* 1998 ICJ Reports 432 para 79.

[61] *Right of Passage over Indian Territory, Preliminary Objections (Portugal v India)* 1957 ICJ Reports 125 at 146–7; *Land and Maritime Boundary Case* (n 42) 275, 291 (para 25), 295 (para 34) and 297 (para 39).

[62] See Alexandrov (n 49) 108.

[63] See for example *Application of the International Convention on the Elimination of All Forms of Racial Discrimination Provisional Measures (Georgia v Russian Federation)* 2011 (I) ICJ Reports 84, para 30; *Questions relating to the Obligation to Prosecute or Extradite*

South West Africa Cases that in order for a dispute to exist, '[i]t must be shown that the claim of one party is positively opposed by the other'.[64]

This limit on the Court's jurisdiction recently became the source of controversy in a case brought by the Marshall Islands against the United Kingdom, Pakistan and India. The Marshall Islands claimed that the latter states were in breach of customary international law obligations concerning negotiations relating to the cessation of the nuclear arms race and to nuclear disarmament.[65] The Court determined that it lacked jurisdiction over these applications on the grounds that, prior to the filing of the application, the Marshall Islands had failed to demonstrate that the respondent states were aware that a dispute existed between themselves and the Marshall Islands on the issue of their compliance with their obligations concerning negotiations relating to cessation of the nuclear arms race and to nuclear disarmament.

The Court has been heavily criticised for this decision on the grounds that its decision was overly formalistic, demonstrating a clear will to avoid the politically sensitive issue of nuclear disarmament.[66] One commentator has compared the 'excessive formalism' of the Court in this case to the approach of the Court in the *South West Africa Cases*.[67] This may be true insofar as the very filing of the application, as well as the positions expressed by the parties in the current proceedings, could be taken to demonstrate the existence of a dispute. Moreover, where the respondent state cannot demonstrate that it had been aware of the existence of a dispute as of the date of

(Belgium v Senegal) 2012 (II) ICJ Reports 443-5, paras 50–5; *Alleged Violations of Sovereign Rights and Maritime Spaces in the Caribbean Sea (Nicaragua v Colombia), Preliminary Objections* 2016 (I) ICJ Reports 26, para 50.

64 *South West Africa Cases* (n 39).

65 *Obligations Concerning Negotiations relating to Cessation of the Nuclear Arms Race and to Nuclear Disarmament (Marshall Islands v Pakistan)* 2016 ICJ Reports 552; *Obligations concerning Negotiations relating to Cessation of the Nuclear Arms Race and to Nuclear Disarmament (Marshall Islands v United Kingdom)* 2016 ICJ Reports 833; *Obligations concerning Negotiations relating to Cessation of the Nuclear Arms Race and to Nuclear Disarmament (Marshall Islands v India)* 2016 ICJ Reports 255.

66 V Proulx 'The World Court's jurisdictional formalism and its lost market share: The Marshall Islands decisions and the quest for a suitable dispute settlement forum for multilateral disputes' (2017) 30 *Leiden Journal of International Law* 925; V Proulx 'The Marshall Islands judgments and multilateral disputes at the World Court: Whither access to international justice?' (2017) 111 *AJIL Unbound* 96; A Bianchi 'Choice and (the awareness of) its consequences: The ICJ's structural bias strikes again in the Marshall Islands case' (2017) 111 *AJIL Unbound* 81.

67 I Venzke 'Public interests in the International Court of Justice—A comparison between *Nuclear Arms Race* (2016) and *South West Africa* (1966)' (2017) 11 *AJIL Unbound* 68.

the filing of the application, the fact of the application itself would clearly bring the existence of a dispute to its attention. The Court has responded that, if jurisdiction over disputes were to result only from exchanges in the proceedings before it, a respondent would be deprived of the opportunity to react to the claim made against it before the institution of proceedings against it.[68]

It may be argued that the defect in such an instance could be cured simply by filing a new application and that it was therefore not sensible to make a finding of no jurisdiction in the *Marshall Islands* cases. In fact, however, history has shown that it will not always be possible to cure the defect in the Court's jurisdiction by filing the application anew: soon after the decision of the Court in the *Marshall Islands* cases, the United Kingdom amended its Optional Clause declaration to exclude jurisdiction in any case relating to nuclear disarmament.[69]

(e) Third parties

Strict adherence to the principle of consent to the jurisdiction of the Court has resulted in the International Court of Justice's refusing to pronounce on a dispute between two states which will affect the rights of a third state not party to the proceedings. In the *East Timor Case*,[70] there was a dispute between Portugal and Australia about Australia's exploitation of the continental shelf of the 'Timor Gap', which lies between Australia and East Timor, an island within the Indonesian archipelago. In a treaty of co-operation with Indonesia over the exploitation of the continental shelf of the Gap, Australia had recognised Indonesia's jurisdiction over East Timor, a former Portuguese colony forcibly annexed by Indonesia. When the dispute came before the International Court of Justice, the Court held that it could not pronounce on Australia's recognition of Indonesia's jurisdiction on the ground that this would require a ruling on the lawfulness of Indonesia's occupation of East Timor. Indonesia was not a party to the proceedings before the Court. Portugal's argument, that an obligation *erga omnes*—the right to self-determination—was involved, and that this took precedence over strict observance of the requirement of consent, was dismissed by the Court. The Court held:

[68] *Obligations Concerning Negotiations relating to Cessation of the Nuclear Arms Race and to Nuclear Disarmament (Marshall Islands v Pakistan)* (n 65) 568.

[69] Written statement of the UK Foreign and Commonwealth Office 'Amendments to the UK's Optional Clause Declaration to the International Court of Justice: Written statement—HCWS489' (23 February 2017), available at https://www.parliament.uk/business/publications/written-questions-answers-statements/written-statement/Commons/2017-02-23/HCWS489/; see the text of the amended declaration available at http://www.icj-cij.org/en/declarations/gb.

[70] 1995 ICJ Reports 90.

> Whatever the nature of the obligation involved, the Court could not rule on the lawfulness of the conduct of a state when its judgment would imply an evaluation of the lawfulness of the conduct of another state which is not a party to the case. Where this is so, the Court cannot act, even if the right in question is a right *erga omnes*.[71]

Article 62 of the Statute of the International Court of Justice permits a state that considers that 'it has an interest of a legal nature which may be affected by the decision in the case' between two other states, to request that it be allowed to intervene in the proceedings. In practice, the Court has adopted a strict approach to the granting of intervention to third parties. In 1990 the Court permitted Nicaragua to intervene in a dispute between Honduras and El Salvador over the legal regime of the waters of the Gulf of Fonseca.[72]

2 Admissibility

Preliminary objections[73] that suspend a hearing on the merits are of two kinds: first, pleas to jurisdiction in which the respondent disputes the competence of the Court to hear the case, principally on the ground of some fault in the instrument of consent; secondly, pleas to admissibility in which the respondent objects to the claim on the basis of some defect in the applicant's claim or standing that is unrelated to the competence of the Court. Examples of such pleas are the failure to exhaust local remedies, absence of a legal interest in the issue, and a defective nationality where the applicant state seeks to protect a national.[74]

Both types of pleas are generally raised as 'preliminary objections' with no clear attempt made to distinguish between the two. However, after the Court has satisfied itself that it has jurisdiction or competence to hear the dispute it may either dispose of the pleas of admissibility at the preliminary stage or join them to the issues to be considered at the hearing on the merits. Normally the Court will

[71] *East Timor* Case (n 70) 102. The International Court of Justice reached this decision based on its earlier decision in the *Case of Monetary Gold Removed from Rome in 1943 (Preliminary Question)* 1954 ICJ Reports 19. For a criticism of the Court's judgment in the *East Timor* case, see J Dugard '1966 and all that: The *South West Africa* judgment revisited in the *East Timor Case* (1996) 8 *African Journal of International and Comparative Law* 549.

[72] *Case Concerning the Land, Island and Maritime Frontier Dispute (El Salvador/Honduras) (Nicaraguan Application for Permission to Intervene)* 1990 ICJ Reports 92. This was confirmed in *Land and Maritime Boundary (Cameroon v Nigeria)* 1999 ICJ Reports 1029.

[73] See J Dugard '*South West Africa Cases*, second phase 1966' (1966) 83 *SALJ* 429 at 438–47; and Dugard (n 21) 335–42.

[74] See *Nottebohm Case (Second Phase)* 1955 ICJ Reports 4. Above, Chapter 13.

indicate clearly its decision to defer a finding touching on admissibility to the hearing on the merits.[75]

The controversy surrounding the decision of the International Court of Justice in the *South West Africa Cases* of 1966 essentially involved the question of the categorisation of one of South Africa's preliminary objections. In 1962, at the commencement of the proceedings in the *South West Africa Cases,* South Africa raised several preliminary objections to the claims of Ethiopia and Liberia arising out of the Mandate for South West Africa. Some, which concerned the interpretation of article 7(2) of the Mandate and the competence of the Court to hear the dispute,[76] were clearly pleas to jurisdiction. The third objection, that the dispute did not affect the material interests of the applicants or their nationals, was dismissed by the Court in 1962,[77] without any attempt to categorise it as a plea to jurisdiction or to admissibility. Although this objection certainly had features of admissibility and could have been deferred to the hearing on the merits, the Court declined to do so and rejected it. In 1966, after the Court had heard lengthy argument on the merits of the case—ie on the status of South West Africa and the compatibility of apartheid with the Mandate agreement—it returned to this preliminary issue and, without pronouncing on the merits of the case at all, held that the applicant states had failed to establish any legal interest in the subject matter of their claims.[78] It accordingly dismissed the claims which, in both legal and political terms, constituted a major victory for the apartheid state.[79] The extraordinary reversal of the 1962 judgment can only be explained by changes in the composition of the Court, which saw the thin majority of eight to seven of 1962[80] disappear as a result of the death, recusal, and illness of three judges believed to be well disposed to the applicants. [81] This transformed the minority of 1962 into an eight-to-seven majority in 1966, consisting of the votes of seven judges and the additional casting vote of the President, Sir Percy Spender of Australia. The new majority, in effect, reversed the 1962 finding on the interest of the applicants, which most students of the Court believed had been finally decided in

[75] *Barcelona Traction Case (Preliminary Objections)* (*Belgium v Spain*) 1964 ICJ Reports 6 at 43–7.

[76] *South West Africa Cases* (n 39) 326–7.

[77] Ibid 343.

[78] *South West Africa Cases, Second Phase* 1966 ICJ Reports 6, 51; Dugard (n 21) 293–325.

[79] See Dugard (n 21) 376.

[80] Ibid 243.

[81] Ibid 291–2.

1962.[82] This decision, which undoubtedly bought time for the policy of apartheid, seriously undermined the reputation of the Court, as the unwarranted reversal of the Court's earlier judgment was construed by developing states as a colonialist and racist act. Although the 1971 *Namibia Opinion*[83] went some way towards restoring the reputation of the Court in the eyes of developing states, it was not until the Court ruled in favour of Nicaragua[84] against the United States some 20 years later that the judgment in the 1966 *South West Africa Cases* was at last forgotten.

3 Proceedings[85]

The proceedings before the Court, which are governed by the Statute of the International Court of Justice,[86] and Rules adopted by the Court,[87] broadly resemble the proceedings before municipal courts. There are written and oral proceedings, but judges intervene less than do common-law judges in the oral hearings. On-site visits are possible but rare. The burden of proof lies on the party seeking to establish a fact.[88] Although evidence is usually documentary, it is possible for parties to call witnesses. Indeed, in the *South West Africa Cases* South Africa called 14 expert witnesses to testify on the 'positive' features of apartheid. In recent years the Court has been called upon to resolve disputes with complex factual issues—such as the dispute between the DRC and Uganda over armed activities in the Congo;[89] and that between Bosnia and Serbia over whether Serbia was responsible for acts of genocide committed against Bosnians.[90] The Court has also in recent years taken to hearing evidence from expert witnesses. In the joined cases of *Certain Activities Carried Out by Nicaragua in the Border Area (Costa Rica v Nicaragua) and Construction of a Road in Costa Rica along the San Juan River (Nicaragua v Costa*

[82] See Dugard (n 21) at 332–74 for a selection of academic writings on this subject.

[83] 1971 ICJ Reports 16, discussed below.

[84] *Case Concerning Military and Paramilitary Activities in and against Nicaragua (Nicaragua v United States of America)* 1986 ICJ Reports 14.

[85] For a criticism of the International Court of Justice's practices and procedures, see DW Bowett et al 'The International Court of Justice: Efficiency of procedures and working methods' (1996) 45 *ICLQ* Supplement.

[86] Articles 39–64.

[87] In terms of article 30 of the Statute. The rules appear as Appendix 2 in Zimmermann et al (n 13).

[88] *Nicaragua Case* 1984 ICJ Reports 437 para 101. In the *Case Concerning the Application of the Convention on Genocide (Bosnia v Serbia)* 2007 ICJ Reports 43 at 129 para 209 the Court required a higher standard of proof in cases involving charges of exceptional gravity. Here the evidence must be 'fully conclusive'.

[89] 2005 ICJ Reports 168.

[90] 2007 ICJ Reports 43.

Rica),[91] the Court requested the testimony of the environmental scientists whose work the parties had relied upon in their written pleadings. Further, in the *Whaling Case (Australia v Japan; New Zealand Intervening),* both parties called upon the environmental scientists that had advised them to provide expert testimony.[92] However, serious misgivings have been raised about the manner in which the Court has approached its fact-finding role and about whether it is institutionally equipped to deal with such matters.[93] In the *Case Concerning the Application of the Convention on Genocide (Bosnia v Serbia),* the Court was criticised for both the methods it employed in fact-finding and for its failure to compel Serbia to disclose important evidence in its possession.[94] In 2015, the Court conducted a survey among the counsel which had appeared before it in the previous decade. Their responses demonstrate that there are serious misgivings about the Court's method for and ability to deal with factually complex cases.

English and French are the Court's two official languages.

A majority of judges present decides all questions. The Court delivers a composite majority judgment containing the names of those judges who endorse it. Individual judges are permitted to submit either concurring or dissenting separate opinions.

4 Non-appearance

In a number of controversial cases, the defendant state has refused to appear in Court. France refused to appear in Court when its nuclear tests programme in the South Pacific was challenged by Australia and New Zealand in 1974;[95] Iran adopted a similar approach in respect of the United States' claim for the release of hostages in Iran

[91] *Certain Activities Carried Out by Nicaragua in the Border Area (Costa Rica v Nicaragua) and Construction of a Road in Costa Rica along the San Juan River (Nicaragua v Costa Rica)* 2015 ICJ Reports 677 (para 32).

[92] *Whaling in the Antarctic (Australia v Japan: New Zealand Intervening)* 2014 ICJ Reports 226.

[93] JG Devaney *'Fact-Finding before the International Court of Justice* (2016); L Malintopi, 'Fact finding and evidence before the International Court of Justice (notably in scientific-related disputes)' (2016) 7 *Journal of International Dispute Settlement* 421. See too *Certain Activities Carried Out by Nicaragua in the Border Area (Costa Rica v Nicaragua) and Construction of a Road in Costa Rica along the San Juan River (Nicaragua v Costa Rica),* separate opinion of Judge ad hoc Dugard 2015 ICJ Reports 859.

[94] See *Genocide Case* (n 88) 127–37; dissenting opinion of Judge Al-Khasawneh ibid 241, 254–5; RJ Goldstone and RJ Hamilton '*Bosnia v Serbia*: Lessons from the encounter of the ICJ with the ICTY' (2008) 21 *Leiden Journal of International Law* 95.

[95] *Nuclear Tests Cases (Australia v France)* 1974 ICJ Reports 253.

in 1980;[96] and the United States itself withdrew from proceedings in the *Nicaragua Case*[97] after the Court had ruled that it had jurisdiction. In such a case, the Court may decide in favour of the plaintiff state, after it has satisfied itself that it has jurisdiction and that the claim is well founded in fact and law.[98] Although the practice of non-appearance has since fallen out of fashion at the International Court of Justice, two recent high profile cases of non-appearance before arbitral tribunals—by China in the *South China Sea* case and by Russia in the *MV Arctic Sunrise* case—could be taken to suggest that states do not yet consider the practice to be without legal or political value.[99]

5 Judgment and its enforcement

Pending its final judgment, the Court may 'indicate, if it considers the circumstances so require, any provisional measures which ought to be taken to preserve the respective rights of either party'.[100] In deciding whether to grant provisional measures, the Court does not have to be satisfied that it has jurisdiction to hear the case: it is sufficient if there is a *prima facie* basis for the exercise of jurisdiction.[101] Before 2001, there was no certainty as to whether an order for provisional measures was legally binding. Certainly, states behaved as if such orders were not legally binding, seen from the many instances in which states refused to carry out provisional measures.[102] In 2001, in the *La Grand Case*, the Court finally held that provisional measures are legally binding.[103] Although this decision is

[96] *US Diplomatic and Consular Staff in Tehran (United States of America v Iran)* 1980 ICJ Reports 3.

[97] *Nicaragua v United States of America* (n 84).

[98] See Statute of the International Court of Justice, article 53.

[99] D Guilfoyle and C Miles 'Provisional measures and the MV Arctic Sunrise' (2014) 108 *AJIL* 277–81.

[100] Statute of the International Court of Justice, article 41. For the principles to be applied in such cases, see the *Application of the Convention on the Prevention and Punishment of the Crime of Genocide (Bosnia and Herzegovina v Yugoslavia)* 1993 ICJ Reports 3. See, further, on this case, A Wiebalck 'Genocide in Bosnia and Herzegovina? Exploring the parameters of interim measures of protection at the ICJ' (1995) 28 *CILSA* 83.

[101] *Legality of the Use of Force (Yugoslavia v Belgium) Provisional Measures* 1999 ICJ Reports 132 (para 21).

[102] Interim measures were not complied with in the *Nuclear Tests Cases (Interim Protection) (Australia and New Zealand v France)* 1973 ICJ Reports 99, 135; *US Diplomatic and Consular Staff in Tehran Case (US v Iran)* 1979 ICJ Reports 7; and the *Nicaragua Case (Nicaragua v US), Provisional Measures* 1984 ICJ Reports 169. J Sztucki *Interim Measures in the Hague Court* (1983); JG Merrills 'Interim measures of protection in the recent jurisprudence of the International Court of Justice' (1995) 44 *ICLQ* 90.

[103] *La Grand (Germany v US)* 2001 ICJ Reports 32–41 (particularly para 102).

to be welcomed, it provides a new incentive to states 'to commence proceedings on a shaky jurisdictional foundation in the hope of getting at least the short-term benefit of an order for provisional measures, and this is all the more attractive if the order is immediately binding'.[104] This requires the Court to adopt a strict approach to 'shaky jurisdictional arguments' in requests for provisional measures. Where there is no reasonable possibility that the applicant state will establish jurisdiction in future, the Court should strike the case from its roll in order to discourage futile requests for provisional measures.[105] Recent years have seen a string of provisional measures requests. In 2017 alone, the Court made three provisional measures orders: to ensure the respect for a building used as diplomatic premises in *Equatorial Guinea v France*; to protect minority rights of ethnic Ukrainians in Crimea in *Ukraine v Russia*; and to stay the execution by India of a Pakistani national in *Pakistan v India (the Jadhav Case)*.

The final judgment of the Court, which may take the form of a declaratory judgment or reparation (including assurances of non-repetition or other forms of satisfaction),[106] is binding.[107] Although no appeal is allowed, provision is made for the revision of a judgment if decisive new facts later become available.[108] Article 94 of the Charter empowers the UNSC to enforce the judgment in the event of non-compliance, presumably by economic sanctions in the final resort. This power is subject to the veto of the permanent members, which explains why, in the few instances of non-compliance, no decision on enforcement has been sought from the UNSC.

There has been a high level of compliance with decisions of the International Court of Justice,[109] although there are notable excep-

[104] H Thirlway 'The International Court of Justice' in M Evans (ed) *International Law* (2003) 586.

[105] See the author's separate opinion in the *Case Concerning Armed Activities on the Territory of the Congo (DRC v Rwanda)* 2002 ICJ Reports 265; (2002) 41 *ILM* 1175 at 1204. See, too, the separate opinion of Judge Buergenthal ibid 1201 (para 9) and the note by Chester Brown in MD Evans and C Brown 'Armed activities on the territory of the Congo (New Application: 2002) (*Democratic Republic of the Congo v Rwanda*) Provisional Measures, Order of 1 July 2002' (2003) 52 *ICLQ* 782.

[106] See Chapter 13.

[107] Statute of the International Court of Justice, article 59 and UN Charter, article 94(1).

[108] Statute of the International Court of Justice, articles 60–1. See *Land, Island and Maritime Frontier Dispute (Application for Revision) (El Salvador/Honduras)* 2003 ICJ Reports 392.

[109] See J Charney 'Disputes implicating the institutional credibility of the Court: problems of non-appearance, non-participation, and non-performance' in L Damrosch (ed) *The International Court of Justice at a Crossroads* (1987) 288; C Paulson 'Compliance with final judgments of the International Court of Justice since 1987' (2004) 98 *AJIL*

tions: the *Corfu Channel Case*,[110] in which the judgment debt of 1949 was only paid in 1992; the *Hostages Case*,[111] in which Iran refused immediately to release American diplomats held hostage; the *Nicaragua Case*,[112] in which the United States was found to have unlawfully used force against Nicaragua; the *La Grand Case*,[113] in which the United States failed to provide foreign prisoners in US gaols with consular assistance; and the *Avena Case*,[114] in which the United States failed to prevent the execution of a Mexican national by the state of Texas in defiance of the Court's decision.[115] In recent years, the International Court of Justice has been busier than ever and has heard more cases of high political importance than previously. In these circumstances one might have expected non-compliance to increase. But the contrary is true. Even judgments in controversial land claims cases—such as those between Libya and Chad[116] and Cameroon and Nigeria[117]—have largely been followed. The high level of compliance can be explained by the consensual nature of the Court's jurisdiction. States generally only consent to the Court's jurisdiction in cases in which they are prepared to accept the Court's decision. A good example of this is the boundary dispute between Namibia and Botswana over Kasikili/Sedudu Island.[118] The dispute was referred to the Court by special agreement and, although Namibia did not hide its disappointment over the adverse decision, it did not hesitate to comply with the Court's decision.[119]

State compliance with provisional measures has, however, proven slightly more problematic in recent cases. The clearest example of this is in the *Certain Activities Case (Costa Rica v Nicaragua)*, where Nicaragua acted in breach of a 2011 provisional measures order,

434; K Oellers-Frahm 'Enforcement of the International Court of Justice decisions' in P Wojcikiewicz Almeida and J Sorel *Latin America and the International Court of Justice* (2017) 131.

[110] 1949 ICJ Reports 4 at 244.

[111] *US Diplomatic and Consular Staff in Tehran* 1980 ICJ Reports 7.

[112] 1986 ICJ Reports 14.

[113] 2001 ICJ Reports 466. See Paulson (n 109) 443–8.

[114] 2004 ICJ Reports 12.

[115] In *Avena* the International Court held that Mexican nationals sentenced to death were entitled to have their convictions and sentences reviewed. In *Medellin v Texas* 128 S Ct 1346 the US Supreme Court accepted that the United States was under international law obliged to comply with the International Court's decision but that this obligation did not constitute federal law binding on US State courts. In 2008, Texas executed Medellin.

[116] *Territorial Dispute* 1994 ICJ Reports 6; Paulson (n 109).

[117] *Land and Maritime Boundary between Cameroon and Nigeria* 2002 ICJ Reports 303; Paulson (n 109) 449–54.

[118] 1999 ICJ Reports 1045.

[119] Paulson (n 109) 455.

resulting in significant environmental damages.[120] Nevertheless, in that case, the Court rejected Costa Rica's request to be awarded the costs of having to attend the Court in October 2013 for a second Order on Provisional Measures of Protection.[121] More recently, in the case of *Ukraine v Russia*, Ukraine complained that Russia, by maintaining its ban of the Mejlis, has ignored the 'clear meaning' of the Court's provisional measures order to 'refrain from maintaining or imposing limitations on the ability of the Crimean Tatar community to preserve its representative institutions, including the *Mejlis*'.[122]

Nevertheless, these isolated cases of non-compliance have not affected the popularity of the International Court of Justice as an institution for the settlement of disputes. Whereas in the early years of the Court, it was predominantly used for the settlement of disputes between European states, it is today most frequently used by non-European states.

6 The limits of international adjudication[123]

International adjudication is of relatively recent origin. Many states still refuse to accept adjudication as a method for resolving disputes between states, while those that do, are mostly opposed to the extension of the Court's compulsory jurisdiction. In some quarters, the view that legal disputes with serious political implications affecting the 'vital interests' of states are not appropriate for judicial resolution prevails—they are non-justiciable. Thus, in 1984, in the *Nicaragua Case*, the United States argued that issues relating to the use of force should be dealt with by the political organs of the United

[120] *Certain Activities Carried Out by Nicaragua in the Border Area (Costa Rica v Nicaragua) and Construction of a Road in Costa Rica along the San Juan River (Nicaragua v Costa Rica)* 2015 ICJ Reports 665 at 714 (para 129).

[121] In this regard see the Joint declaration of Judges Tomka, Greenwood, Sebutinde and Judge ad hoc Dugard in *Certain Activities Carried out by Nicaragua in the Border Area (Costa Rica v Nicaragua) and Construction of a Road in Costa Rica along the San Juan (Nicaragua v Costa Rica)*, 2015 (II) ICJ Reports 754.

[122] Ministry of Foreign Affairs of Ukraine 'Statement of the Ministry of Foreign Affairs of Ukraine on the Request for the International Court of Justice to Interpret its Provisional Measures order against the Russian Federation' (24 April 2018), available at https://mfa.gov.ua/en/press-center/comments/8712-zajava-ministerstva-zakordonnih-sprav-ukrajini-shhodo-zvernennya-ukrajini-do-mizhnarodnogo-sudu-oon-stosovno-tlumachennya-nakazu-sudu-pro-zastosuvannya-timchasovih-zahodiv-proti-rosijsykoji-federaciji.

[123] R Higgins 'Policy considerations and the international judicial process' (1968) 17 *ICLQ* 58; L Gross 'Underutilization of the ICJ' (1986) 27 *Harvard Journal of International Law* 571; MA Rogoff 'International politics and the rule of law: The US and the ICJ' (1989) 7 *Boston University International Law Journal* 267.

Nations and not by the Court.[124] This view is contradicted by the increased use of the International Court of Justice to pronounce on highly political disputes—such as the NATO bombing of Yugoslavia;[125] the military intervention of Uganda[126] and Rwanda[127] in the Democratic Republic of the Congo; allegations of genocide against Serbia;[128] and Russia's intervention in Georgia.[129]

No court, municipal or international, can avoid pronouncing on a legal dispute simply because it has political implications. The International Court of Justice was correct, therefore, when it dismissed the United States' arguments of non-justiciability in the *Nicaragua Case*.[130] Then again, courts are inevitably sensitive to the political realities surrounding a dispute and this may prompt them to avoid pronouncing on the merits of a politically contentious dispute by upholding the respondent state's preliminary objections. The International Court of Justice chose this escape route in 1966 in the *South West Africa Cases*;[131] in 1974 in the *Nuclear Tests Cases*,[132] in which Australia and New Zealand sought to restrain France from conducting nuclear tests in the South Pacific; in 1995 in the *East Timor Case*,[133] in which Portugal challenged the lawfulness of Indonesia's occupation of East Timor; and again in the *Marshall Islands* cases.[134] However, it refused to adopt this course in the *Nicaragua Case* in 1986; and found that the United States had violated international law by attacking Nicaraguan territory and by giving military support to

[124] 1984 ICJ Reports 392 at 432–8.

[125] *Case Concerning the Legality of the Use of Force (Serbia and Montenegro v Belgium)* 2004 ICJ Reports 279; (2005) 44 *ILM* 299.

[126] *Case Concerning Armed Activities on the Territory of the Congo (DRC v Uganda)* 2005 ICJ Reports 168.

[127] *Case Concerning Armed Activities on the Territory of the Congo, Preliminary Objections (DRC v Rwanda)* 2006 ICJ Reports 6.

[128] *Genocide Case* (n 88).

[129] *Application of the International Convention on the Elimination of All Forms of Racial Discrimination Provisional Measures (Georgia v Russian Federation)* 2008 ICJ Reports 353, and 2011 ICJ Reports.

[130] 1984 ICJ Reports 392. See the writings on the decision in HW Briggs 'Nicaragua v United States: Jurisdiction and admissibility' (1985) 79 *AJIL* 373–404; 652–63, 992–1004; WM Reisman 'Has the International Court exceeded its jurisdiction? (Editorial comments)' (1986) 80 *AJIL* 128–34.

[131] Dugard (n 21) 374–5.

[132] 1974 ICJ Reports 253; J Dugard 'The *Nuclear Tests Cases* and the *South West Africa Cases:* Some realism about the International Judicial Decision' (1976) 16 *Virginia Journal of International Law* 463, especially at 485–9.

[133] 1995 ICJ Reports 90.

[134] *Obligations concerning Negotiations relating to Cessation of the Nuclear Arms Race and to Nuclear Disarmament (Marshall Islands v United Kingdom)* 2016 ICJ Reports 833.

rebels operating against the government of Nicaragua.[135] Not surprisingly, the judgments in the *South West Africa Cases*, the *Nuclear Tests Cases* and *East Timor Case* were criticised for showing too much caution, while the judgment in the *Nicaragua Case* was condemned for displaying too little caution. The International Court of Justice faces the same challenge as any other court. If it is to survive as a judicial institution, it must temper courage with caution. Conversely, if it is to maintain its credibility, it must on occasion be bold, even at the expense of the major powers.

ADVISORY OPINIONS[136]

The Charter[137] and the Statute of the International Court of Justice[138] authorise the Court to give advisory opinions at the request of the General Assembly, the UNSC, and other organs of the United Nations and specialised agencies that have been so authorised by the General Assembly.[139] The Secretary-General has not been empowered to request an advisory opinion. Neither states nor individuals may request an opinion.

The Court will refuse to give an opinion if answering the question put to it would amount to deciding a dispute between states, as this would undermine the requirement of consent to adjudication. Thus in the *Status of Eastern Carelia Case*,[140] the PCIJ refused to give an opinion in a dispute between Finland and Russia over the status of Eastern Carelia at a time when Russia was not a member of the League of Nations. The International Court of Justice has distinguished this case in several opinions,[141] including the 1971 *Namibia*

[135] 1986 ICJ Reports 14. For a discussion of this decision, see K Highet 'Evidence, the Court, and the *Nicaragua Case*' (1987) 81 *AJIL* 1–183.

[136] See generally on this subject, K Keith *The Extent of the Advisory Jurisdiction of the International Court of Justice* (1971); M Pomerance *The Advisory Function of the International Court in the League and UN Eras* (1973); Zimmermann et al (n 13) 1401; J Dugard 'Advisory opinions and the Secretary-General with special reference to the *2004 Advisory Opinion on the Wall*' in L Boisson de Chazournes and M Kohen (eds) *International Law and the Quest for its Implementation* Liber Amicorum *Vera Gowlland-Debbas* (2010) 403.

[137] UN Charter, article 96.

[138] Statute of the International Court of Justice, article 65.

[139] At present, 22 international bodies are entitled to request advisory opinions.

[140] PCIJ Reports Series B No 5 (1923).

[141] *Interpretation of Peace Treaties Case* 1950 ICJ Reports 65 at 71; *Western Sahara Case* 1975 ICJ Reports 12 at 23–9; *Legal Consequences of the Construction of a Wall in the Occupied Palestinian Territory* 2004 ICJ Reports paras 46–50.

Opinion,[142] in which the UNSC asked the Court for an opinion on 'the legal consequences for states of the continued presence of South Africa in Namibia'. In deciding to give an opinion, the Court held, first, that, unlike Russia, South Africa was a member of the body requesting the opinion (the United Nations) and had participated in the Court's proceedings; and, secondly, that the purpose of the request was not to settle a dispute between states, but to assist the United Nations in respect of its own decisions on Namibia.[143]

The Court will not give an opinion at the request of a specialised agency unless it relates to the activities of the agency. Thus, the Court refused to give an advisory opinion to the World Health Organization on the legality of nuclear weapons.[144] The Court did, however, give an opinion to the General Assembly on this subject, dismissing suggestions that it would go beyond its judicial role in giving its opinion on so controversial a topic.[145]

Although the same Court that gives judgment in contentious proceedings gives an advisory opinion, and it therefore commands the same judicial authority, it is not binding, and consequently is not enforceable under article 94 of the Charter. This does not mean that it is without legal consequences.

In practice, advisory opinions requested by the General Assembly and UNSC are approved by the political organ requesting the opinion, and thus should become the law that guides the United Nations.[146] The history of the South West Africa (Namibia) dispute before the United Nations illustrates how an advisory opinion may achieve such a purpose. In contrast, the treatment of the advisory opinion on the *Legal Consequences of the Construction of a Wall in the Occupied Palestinian Territory*[147] raises serious doubts about the influence an advisory opinion may have upon the political process in the United Nations.

In 1950, the International Court of Justice gave an advisory opinion on the *International Status of South-West Africa*[148] at the request of the General Assembly, in which it rejected South Africa's claim that the Mandate for South West Africa had lapsed on the demise of the

[142] *Legal Consequences for States of the Continued Presence of South Africa in Namibia (South West Africa) notwithstanding Security Council Resolution 276* (1970) 1971 ICJ Reports 16; Dugard (n 21) 446–84.

[143] 1971 ICJ Reports 16 at 23–4.

[144] *Legality of the Use by a State of Nuclear Weapons in Armed Conflict* 1996 ICJ Reports 66.

[145] *Legality of the Threat or Use of Nuclear Weapons* 1996 ICJ Reports 228, para 18.

[146] See the separate opinion of Judge Lauterpacht in *Admissibility of Hearings of Petitioners by the Committee on South West Africa* 1956 ICJ Reports 23 at 46–7.

[147] 2004 ICJ Reports 136.

[148] 1950 ICJ Reports 128; Dugard (n 21) 131–56.

League of Nations. It held that the Mandate continued in force, and that South Africa was obliged to account to the United Nations for its administration of the territory. This opinion was endorsed by two further opinions, dealing with the manner in which the United Nations might exercise its supervisory role. In 1955, the Court held that the General Assembly, in exercising its supervisory role over South West Africa, was not required to follow the unanimity voting rule of the League of Nations when it adopted resolutions, but might instead apply the two-thirds majority voting rule laid down in the UN Charter.[149] In 1956, it held that in order to obtain information on South Africa's administration of South West Africa, the General Assembly's Committee on South West Africa might grant oral hearings to petitioners[150]—a practice not followed by the supervisory body of the League of Nations.

These opinions were approved by the General Assembly, but rejected by South Africa—not because they were merely advisory, but on the ground that, in 1950, the Court had failed to consider certain information concerning debates in the League of Nations in 1946 over the future of mandated territories.[151] This deceptive argument, which was simply a pretext for refusing to comply with the advisory opinions, led to a confrontation with the United Nations which finally turned to contentious proceedings through two nominee states—Ethiopia and Liberia—in order to secure a binding judgment enforceable under article 94 of the Charter.

When the Court put an end to this strategy in 1966, by finding that the applicant states lacked the necessary interest in their claims, the United Nations returned to the advisory opinion route. In 1971, the Court gave an opinion at the request of the UNSC in which it held that the United Nations lawfully terminated the Mandate for South West Africa, that South Africa's presence in Namibia (as South West Africa became known in 1968) was illegal, and that South Africa was obliged to withdraw its administration from Namibia immediately. This opinion was repudiated by South Africa,[152] but approved by the UNSC.[153] As such, it became the basic law of the United Nations on Namibia, culminating in UNSC Resolution 435 (1978) which provided for the establishment of the United Nations Transition Assistance Group (UNTAG) to implement the independence of Namibia

[149] *Voting Procedure Case* 1955 ICJ Reports 67; Dugard (n 21) 176–91.

[150] *Admissibility of Hearings of Petitioners by the Committee on South West Africa* 1956 ICJ Reports 23.

[151] See Dugard (n 21) 164–6.

[152] Prime Minister BJ Vorster dismissed the Court's opinion as politically biased: Dugard (n 21) 490–2, 501–2.

[153] Resolution 301 of 1971; Dugard (n 21) 502.

'through free and fair elections under the supervision and control of the United Nations'. In 1990, full effect was given to the 1971 *Namibia Opinion* when South Africa withdrew its administration and Namibia became independent.[154]

The fact that the UNSC, and not the General Assembly, had requested the 1971 Advisory Opinion was probably the crucial factor in its enforcement. Although the UNSC could not compel South Africa to comply with the Opinion in terms of article 94 of the UN Charter, it succeeded in securing its enforcement, albeit 20 years later, by means of action under its general powers in the Charter.

In 2004, the International Court of Justice gave an advisory opinion at the request of the General Assembly on *Legal Consequences of the Construction of a Wall in the Occupied Palestinian Territory*,[155] in which it held that the wall or barrier being built by Israel, the occupying power, in the Occupied Palestinian Territory, is contrary to international law; that Israel is under an obligation to cease forthwith the construction of the wall and to dismantle sections of the wall that had already been built; that Israel is under an obligation to make reparation for all damage caused by the construction of the wall; that all states are obliged to withhold recognition of the illegal situation resulting from the construction of the wall; and that the United Nations 'should consider what further action is required to bring to an end the illegal situation resulting from the construction of the wall'.[156] In the *Wall Opinion* the International Court of Justice also pronounced on a number of other legal issues. It found that the Fourth Geneva Convention relative to the Protection of Civilian Persons in Time of War of 1949, is applicable to the occupation of Palestine;[157] that, as a consequence, Israeli settlements in the Palestinian territory are unlawful;[158] and that Israel is obliged to comply with international human rights conventions to which it is a party, in its treatment of the people of Palestine.[159] Not unexpectedly, the opinion has been subjected to serious criticism. [160]

[154] See, further, on Namibian independence M Wiechers et al 'The Namibian constitution and independence' (1989–90) 15 *SAYIL* 1–166; J Dugard 'Public international law' (1989) *Annual Survey* 536–43.

[155] 2004 ICJ Reports 136; (2004) 43 *ILM* 1009.

[156] Ibid para 163.

[157] Ibid paras 90–101.

[158] Ibid para 120.

[159] Ibid paras 102–13.

[160] For a critical examination of the *Opinion*, see J Dugard 'Wall Opinion' in E Bjorge and C Miles (eds) *Landmark Cases in Public International Law* (2017) 539; 'Agora: ICJ Advisory Opinion on *Construction of a Wall in the Occupied Palestinian Territory*' (2005) 99 *AJIL* 1–141; A Mangu 'Legal consequences of the construction by Israel of a wall in

Although the *Wall Opinion* has been accepted by the General Assembly,[161] it has not been approved by the UNSC, largely because of opposition to it on the part of the United States. This has resulted in the UNSC, the Secretary-General and, in effect, the General Assembly, ignoring the Opinion.[162] Moreover, it has been completely overlooked by the Quartet, comprising the United Nations, European Union, United States and Russian Federation, which is the body the UNSC has mandated to further the peace process in the region. This response has undermined the authority of the International Court of Justice and brought into question the importance of advisory opinions as a guide to United Nations political decision-making. The 2010 Advisory Opinion on *Kosovo*[163] has done little to reinstate the importance of advisory opinions. By restricting its Opinion to the question whether Kosovo's unilateral declaration of independence had violated international law and by avoiding an examination of the consequences of Kosovo's unilateral declaration of independence—particularly the question whether international law recognises secession—the Court gave an opinion that will probably prove to be of little value. It is not unlikely that the Court has learned from the response to the *Wall Opinion* that it is unwise to pronounce on a contested issue of international law unless absolutely necessary.[164]

Recently, a case of significant importance to the African continent has been referred to the Court for an advisory opinion. This case concerns the legality of the detachment of the Chagos Archipelago from the remainder of the British colony of Mauritius, as it then was.[165] This detachment occurred in 1965, in conjunction with the move toward Mauritian independence.[166] Subsequent to the detachment, Mauritius gained its independence and the Chagos Archipel-

the OPT: South Africa's contribution to the Advisory Opinion of the ICJ' (2005) 20 *SA Public Law* 86.

[161] ES-10/15 (2 August 2004).

[162] See Dugard (n 136).

[163] *Accordance with International Law of the Unilateral Declaration of Independence in Respect of Kosovo* 2010 ICJ Reports.

[164] In the *Legality of the Threat or Use of Nuclear Weapons* Advisory Opinion 1996 ICJ Reports 228, the Court avoided pronouncing on the legality or illegality of the use of nuclear weapons by a state 'in an extreme circumstance of self-defence, in which its very survival would be at stake' (para 105). See GN Barrie and K Reddy 'The International Court of Justice's Advisory Opinion on the Threat or Use of Nuclear Weapons' (1998) 115 *SALJ* 457.

[165] UN Doc A/Res/71/292 (22 June 2017) 2.

[166] British Indian Ocean Territory Order 1965 (S.I. 1965/1920). See generally, J Trinidad *Self-Determination in Disputed Colonial Territories* (2018) 83 et seq.

ago remained under British control.[167] The British government removed the inhabitants of the Chagos Islands from the archipelago after its separation from Mauritius,[168] and Diego Garcia, one of the islands, became the site of a significant United States military installation.[169] The Court has been asked to consider the legal consequences arising from the United Kingdom's continued administration of the Chagos Archipelago.[170] The International Court of Justice has received submissions from the United Nations, its member states (including South Africa) and the African Union.[171] At the time of publication, the decision of the Court is pending.

THE PERMANENT COURT OF ARBITRATION

By Jennifer Nettleton-Brom

The PCA, created in 1899 by the Convention for the Pacific Settlement of International Disputes, is an intergovernmental organisation situated at the Peace Palace in The Hague. It provides administrative support for international dispute resolution proceedings.[172] As of today, the PCA has 121 member states (including South Africa and 23 other African states). The diplomatic representatives of PCA member states accredited to the Netherlands constitute the PCA's 'Administrative Council', which is charged with the 'direction and control' of the organisation.[173]

Although the initial dispute resolution proceedings administered by the PCA were exclusively between states, today the PCA provides its services to arbitrations and other dispute resolution mechanisms 'involving various combinations of states, state-controlled entities, intergovernmental organizations, and private parties'.[174]

[167] See the facts established by the arbitral tribunal in *Chagos Marine Protected Area Arbitration (Mauritius v UK)*, Award, Permanent Court of Arbitration (18 March 2015) paras 69 et seq.

[168] S Allen and C Monaghan *Fifty Years of the British Indian Ocean Territory: Legal Perspectives* (2018) Chapter 7; S Allen *The Chagos Islanders and International Law* (2014).

[169] *R (on the application of Bancoult (No 2)) v Secretary of State for Foreign and Commonwealth Affairs* [2016] UKSC 35 para 86. See further UNGA Resolution 2066 (XX) of 16 December 1965.

[170] 170 General Assembly resolution 71/292 (A/71/L.73) of 22 June 2017.

[171] *Legal Consequences of the Separation of the Chagos Archipelago from Mauritius in 1965 (Request for an Advisory Opinion), Order of 17 January 2018*, 2.

[172] Permanent Court of Arbitration *Introduction to the PCA*, available at https://www.pca-cpa.org/en/about/introduction/.

[173] Article 28 of the 1899 Convention and article 49 of the 1907 Convention.

[174] BW Daly, E Goriatcheva and HA Meighen *A Guide to the PCA Arbitration Rules* (2014) 4. The involvement of private parties in PCA-administered proceedings usually stems from contracts or treaties that contain a reference to arbitration for the settlement of disputes. This chapter only deals with the PCA's services in relation to

The PCA has concluded 'Host Country Agreements' with a number of its member states (including South Africa). These agreements allow the organisation to administer proceedings in the host countries under similar conditions as at its headquarters in The Hague—especially in relation to the privileges and immunities afforded to the participants in those proceedings. In 2010, the PCA opened its first 'overseas office' in Mauritius pursuant to its Host Country Agreement with Mauritius concluded in 2009. The PCA representative in Mauritius assists with capacity-building initiatives in the African region and promotes PCA services and Mauritius as a venue for arbitration. In 2018, the PCA opened a second 'overseas office' in Singapore pursuant to the updated PCA–Singapore Host Country Agreement concluded in 2017 (with a PCA representative in Singapore performing a similar role for that region).[175]

The PCA may administer arbitrations and other forms of dispute resolution under a variety of procedural rules, including its own procedural rules and the procedural rules adopted by the United Nations Commission on International Trade Law (UNCITRAL).[176] In 2012, the PCA adopted its newest set of procedural rules (the PCA Arbitration Rules 2012) which have been tailored to address the particular challenges that may arise in arbitrations that involve a state, state-controlled entity, or intergovernmental organisation.[177] The PCA has also 'devised ad hoc procedural regimes for arbitrations governed by treaties, such as rules of procedure designed for an arbitration pursuant to Annex VII of the United Nations Convention of on the Law of the Sea (UNCLOS)'.[178]

disputes between states. The settlement of disputes between private parties and states that arise out of investment treaties is further dealt with in Chapter 13.

[175] Permanent Court of Arbitration *About us—Structure*, available at https://www.pca-cpa.org/en/about/structure/, read with Permanent Court of Arbitration *Host Country Agreements*, available at https://www.pca-cpa.org/en/relations/host-country-agreements/.

[176] In addition to the PCA administering arbitrations under the various versions of the UNCITRAL Arbitration Rules, the PCA Secretary-General also plays an important role under those rules, in terms of which he may be requested to, inter alia, designate an appointing authority to appoint members of the tribunal.

[177] See Daly et al (n 174) 4, 12.

[178] Ibid. The PCA has administered a number of arbitrations under Annex VII of the United Nations Convention on the Law of the Sea (UNCLOS), in terms of which arbitration is the default means of dispute settlement if a state has not expressed a preference with respect to the dispute resolution mechanisms available under article 287(1) of UNCLOS. The settlement of disputes relating to the interpretation or application of UNCLOS is discussed further in Chapter 17. For a full list of PCA-administered UNCLOS proceedings see the PCA website, available at https://pca- cpa.org/en/services/arbitration-services/unclos/.

The PCA's caseload has increased considerably in recent years. By mid-2018, it had administered over 380 registry cases. The largest growth in the PCA's caseload has been in investor-state arbitrations (which are discussed in more detail in Chapter 13). Since 1996, the PCA has also enjoyed a revival of its role as an administrator of dispute resolution proceedings between states. Between 1902 and mid-2018, the PCA provided administrative assistance in 50 inter-state proceedings, consisting of a variety of arbitration, conciliation, commission of inquiry, claims commission, and review panel proceedings.[179] Recognition of the relative flexibility of arbitration—as compared to judicial adjudication by institutions like the International Court of Justice and the International Tribunal for the Law of the Sea—has led to states returning to the use of arbitration for the adjudication of certain cases. Examples of issues that states may consider when choosing a forum for adjudication include: the ability of parties in arbitration proceedings to appoint arbitrators; the possibility of tailoring arbitral procedural rules and timetables to the needs of a case; and the opportunity to agree on the degree of confidentiality or transparency applicable to each stage of arbitration proceedings.[180]

The PCA has been responsible for facilitating the peaceful resolution of a number of important interstate disputes involving African states. These include proceedings related to boundary disputes, mass claims mechanisms, and law of the sea disputes.[181] For example, a related set of PCA proceedings, involving boundary delimitation and mass claims respectively, were initiated in December 2000 by an agreement between Eritrea and Ethiopia to terminate the military hostilities that had broken out between them in May 1998.[182] The states' peace agreement established the Eritrea–Ethiopia Boundary Commission to delimit and demarcate a common boundary based on

[179] Statistics compiled from PCA Annual Reports, available at https://pca-cpa.org/en/documents/publications/) as well as the PCA Case Repository (available at https://www.pcacases.com/web/allcases/) read with PCA *International Commissions of Inquiry* (available at https://www.pca- cpa.org/wp-content/uploads/sites/175/2016/01/11-Annex-3-en-6440d4.pdf.

[180] See further C Giorgetti 'Between flexibility and stability: Ad hoc procedures and/or judicial institutions?' in P Pazartzis et al (eds) *Reconceptualising the Rule of Law in Global Governance, Resources, Investment and Trade* (2016) 11.

[181] For an analysis of the PCA's broader caseload (both interstate and 'mixed' cases) involving African parties see L Bosman 'The PCA's contribution to international dispute resolution in Africa' (2014) 25 *Stellenbosch LR* 308.

[182] See B MacMahon and F Smith *The Permanent Court of Arbitration* (2010); SD Murphy, W Kidane and TR Snider *Litigating War: Mass Injury and the Eritrea–Ethiopia Claims Commission* (2013); JD Fry 'Ethiopian exceptionalism and the Eritrea–Ethiopia boundary commission' (2017) 25 *African Journal of International and Comparative Law* 35; Bosman (n 181) 315.

colonial treaties and applicable principles of international law.[183] The agreement also established the Eritrea–Ethiopia Claims Commission which was given jurisdiction over all claims for loss, damage or injury related to the armed conflict and resulting from violations of international law.[184] The PCA also served as registry in the arbitration of the boundary dispute between Sudan and South Sudan over the Abyei region, as described further in Chapter 8.[185] Examples of PCA-administered law of the sea disputes that involve African states are: the *Eritrea–Yemen Maritime Delimitation* arbitration; the *Chagos* arbitration (*Mauritius v United Kingdom*), which concerned the establishment by the United Kingdom of a Marine Protected Area around the Chagos Archipelago;[186] and the *Duzgit Integrity* (*Malta v São Tomé and Príncipe*) and *ARA Libertad* (*Argentina v Ghana*) arbitrations, which both concerned the detention of ships.[187]

Appendix: Namibia (South West Africa): A brief legal chronology

1884	Germany declares a protectorate over South West Africa.
1915	South Africa invades and occupies German South West Africa.
1920	South West Africa entrusted to South Africa by the League of Nations in terms of the Mandate for South West Africa.
1946	League of Nations dissolved.
1949	South Africa refuses to account to the United Nations on its administration of South West Africa.
1950	International Court of Justice delivers advisory opinion on the *International Status of South West Africa* 1950 ICJ Reports 128, holding that the Mandate continues in force and that South Africa is obliged to account to the United Nations on its administration of the territory.
1955	International Court of Justice delivers advisory opinion on the *Voting Procedure* to be followed by General Assembly in matters affecting South West Africa, 1955 ICJ Reports 67.

[183] Agreement between the Government of the State of Eritrea and the Government of the Federal Democratic Republic of Ethiopia (12 December 2000) article 4.

[184] Ibid article 5.

[185] See MacMahon and Smith (n 182); M Bockenforde '*The Abyei Award*: Fitting a diplomatic square peg into a legal round hole' (2010) 23 *Leiden Journal of International Law* 555; BW Daly '*The Abyei Arbitration*: Procedural aspects of an intra-state border arbitration' ibid 801.

[186] S Talmon, 'The Chagos Marine Protected Area Arbitration: Expansion of the jurisdiction of UNCLOS Part XV Courts and Tribunals' (2016) 65 *ICLQ* 927.

[187] Bosman (n 181) 315; PCA Case Repository, available at https://www.pcacases.com/web/allcases/.

1956	International Court of Justice delivers advisory opinion on the *Admissibility of Hearings of Petitioners by the Committee on South West Africa* 1956 ICJ Reports 23.
1960	Ethiopia and Liberia institute legal proceedings against South Africa in which they ask the International Court of Justice to find that the Mandate for South West Africa remains in force, that South Africa is obliged to account to the United Nations on its administration of the territory, and that the policy of apartheid violates the Mandate.
1962	South Africa's preliminary objections to the jurisdiction of the International Court of Justice and the admissibility of the applicants' claims are dismissed by Court: *South West Africa Cases, Preliminary Objections* 1962 ICJ Reports 318.
1966	International Court of Justice refuses to pronounce on the merits of the applicants' claims on the ground that the applicants have no legal interest in the subject matter of their claims: *South West Africa, Second Phase* 1966 ICJ Reports 6.
1966	General Assembly of the United Nations revokes the Mandate for South West Africa in Resolution 2145 (XXI).
1968	General Assembly changes the name of South West Africa to Namibia.
1970	UNSC Resolution 276 declares South Africa to be in illegal occupation of Namibia.
1971	International Court of Justice delivers advisory opinion on the *Legal Consequences for States of the Continued Presence of South Africa in Namibia (South West Africa) notwithstanding Security Council Resolution 276 (1970)* 1971 ICJ Reports 16, in which it finds that South Africa is in illegal occupation of Namibia and is obliged to withdraw its administration immediately.
1978	UNSC Resolution 435 proposes an independence plan for Namibia involving the establishment of the UN Transition Assistance Group (UNTAG) to implement free and fair elections under the supervision and control of the United Nations.
1989	UNTAG arrives in Namibia and United Nations-supervised elections are held.
1990	Namibia becomes independent on 21 March.

Bibliography

A comprehensive bibliography on this subject is to be found in J Dugard *The South West Africa/Namibia Dispute* (1973) 543–62.

CHAPTER 23

The United Nations and the Maintenance of International Peace and Security

John Dugard and Tiyanjana Maluwa

INTRODUCTION

The main purpose of the United Nations is the maintenance of international peace and security.[1] To this end it shall take steps to settle disputes that might lead to a breach of the peace 'by peaceful means, and in conformity with the principles of justice and international law'. It is also empowered 'to take effective collective measures for the prevention and removal of threats to the peace'.[2] The organs charged with this task are the Security Council, the General Assembly, and the office of the Secretary-General (Secretariat).[3]

For over 40 years, the racial policies of South Africa, both at home and in South West Africa/Namibia, constituted a major obstacle to the achievement of world peace. Consequently, the political organs of the United Nations devoted more attention to this issue than to any other single item on their agenda during this period. It is appropriate, therefore, in considering the role and powers of the United Nations, to refer to the action taken by the United Nations to persuade and coerce South Africa to abandon apartheid, the system of institutionalised racial segregation and discrimination introduced by the National Party government in 1948.[4]

[1] See the following general works on the United Nations: H Kelsen *The Law of the United Nations* (1951); HG Schermers and N Blokker *International Institutional Law. Unity within Diversity* 5 ed (2011); B Simma et al (eds) *The Charter of the United Nations: A Commentary* 3 ed (2012); P Sands and P Klein (eds) *Bowett's Law of International Institutions* 6 ed (2009); J Klabbers *An Introduction to International Institutional Law* 2 ed (2009); D Sarooshi *The United Nations and the Development of Collective Security* (1999); S Chesterman, I Johnstone and D Malone *Law and Practice of the United Nations* 2 ed (2016); R Kolb *An Introduction to the Law of the United Nations* (2010); R Higgins et al *Oppenheim's International Law: United Nations*, 2 vols (2017).

[2] Article 1(1) of the UN Charter.

[3] The other organs of the United Nations are the Economic and Social Council, the Trusteeship Council, and the International Court of Justice: article 7 of UN Charter.

[4] See, further, on this subject, J Dugard 'The legal effect of United Nations Resolutions on apartheid' (1966) 83 *SALJ* 44; J Dugard 'Apartheid: A case study in the response of the international community to gross violations of human rights' in

GENERAL ASSEMBLY

The General Assembly is the plenary body of the United Nations, with secondary responsibility for the maintenance of international peace and security. It meets annually in ordinary session and provides a forum for the discussion of problems facing the nations of the world. It comprises all 193 member states of the United Nations and each member has one vote.[5] South Africa is a founding member of the United Nations, but was excluded from participation in the debates and work of the General Assembly from 1974 to 1994, as a result of its racial policies.

The exclusion of South Africa from the General Assembly came after the vetoes of France, the United Kingdom, and the United States in the Security Council had saved South Africa from expulsion from the United Nations. Dissatisfied with this decision, the President of the General Assembly ruled that South Africa could no longer participate in the General Assembly, as a result of the finding by the Credentials Committee of the Assembly that the National Party government did not represent the state of South Africa.[6] Subsequent attempts on the part of the South African government to reassert its membership rights failed.[7] The legality of this action on the part of the General Assembly was questioned on the grounds that it interfered with South Africa's rights of membership in the United Nations,[8] and that, in terms of the Charter of the United Nations (UN

I Cotler and FP Eliadis (eds) *International Human Rights Law: Theory and Practice* (1992) 301; L Sohn *Rights in Conflict: The United Nations and South Africa* (1994). For a vigorous defence of South Africa's position, see JC Heunis *United Nations versus South Africa* (1986).

[5] Articles 9 and 18.

[6] J Dugard 'Foreign affairs and public international law' 1974 *Annual Survey* 52–3; (1975) 1 *SAYIL* 217–22. For an account of South Africa's exclusion from a number of UN specialised agencies, see J Dugard 'Sanctions against South Africa' in M Orkin (ed) *Sanctions against South Africa* (1989) 113 at 119; and Heunis (n 4) 148–75, 486–91. The President of the General Assembly was Abdelaziz Bouteflika, the foreign minister of Algeria, who was a fierce critic of the South African government and a champion of the liberation struggle in South Africa.

[7] ME Muller 'Discussions and resolutions on South Africa in the United Nations—1979' (1979) 5 *SAYIL* 164–5; J Dugard 'International law and foreign relations' 1981 *Annual Survey* 39 at 41–2.

[8] D Ciobanu 'Credentials of delegations and representation of member states at the United Nations' (1976) 25 *ICLQ* 351; G Erasmus 'The rejection of credentials: A proper exercise of General Assembly powers or suspension by stealth?' (1981) 7 *SAYIL* 40; JC Heunis (n 4) 189–250. *Sed contra*, see R Suttner 'Has South Africa been illegally excluded from the United Nations General Assembly?' (1984) 17 *CILSA* 279. See, too, CN Patel 'The politics of state expulsion from the United Nations—South Africa a case in point' (1980) 13 *CILSA* 310 and CN Patel 'The legal aspects of state expulsion from the United Nations—South Africa a case in point' (1982–4) *Natal Law*

Charter), only the Security Council and the General Assembly together may suspend a state's membership rights or expel it.[9] South Africa was readmitted to the General Assembly in 1994, following the country's first democratic election.[10]

The General Assembly is authorised to discuss and to adopt resolutions on any question relating to the maintenance of international peace and security or on any question falling within the scope of the UN Charter. Particular disputes may be brought to its attention by member states, non-member states, and the Security Council, and it 'may recommend measures for the peaceful adjustment of any situation . . . which it deems likely to impair the general welfare or friendly relations among nations'.[11] Decisions on 'important questions' are to be made by a 'two-thirds majority of the members present and voting'. Decisions on 'other questions' are to be made by a majority vote. As 'important questions' include recommendations relating to the maintenance of international peace, the admission, suspension, and expulsion of members, and budgetary matters, most resolutions of the General Assembly are adopted by a two-thirds majority vote.[12] An attempt by South Africa to secure a unanimous vote on matters affecting South West Africa, on the ground that voting by unanimity was required by the Covenant of the League of Nations, was dismissed in 1955 by the International Court of Justice.[13]

General Assembly resolutions on its internal management—relating, for instance, to the admission, suspension, and expulsion of members, and to the budget[14]—are legally binding. Conversely, resolutions addressed to member states on matters affecting the maintenance of international peace and the settlement of disputes are not legally binding on states.[15] This does not mean that they are of no value and may be summarily dismissed. Their political weight, particularly if allowed to accumulate over the years, may be considerable—as the history of South Africa's position in the international community during the apartheid era demonstrated. In

Review 197; H Strydom 'South Africa and international law—from confrontation to cooperation' (2004) 47 *GYIL* 160, 172.

[9] Article 5 of the Charter requires the suspension of membership rights to be taken by the General Assembly 'upon the recommendation of the Security Council'. Article 6 lays down a similar procedure for expulsion.

[10] General Assembly Resolution 48/13C of 23 June 1994.

[11] Article 14.

[12] Article 18.

[13] *Voting Procedure on Questions relating to Reports and Petitions Concerning the Territory of South West Africa* 1955 ICJ Reports 67. See Chapter 22 above.

[14] Articles 4–6, 17.

[15] See J Dugard 'The legal effect of UN Resolutions on apartheid' (1966) 83 *SALJ* 44.

addition, General Assembly resolutions have a number of important legal consequences. First, they may provide a legal authorisation for states to engage in action that might otherwise be of questionable legality.[16] Thus, even if economic coercion is to be considered as an unlawful intervention,[17] it could not be argued seriously, in the light of the numerous resolutions of the General Assembly calling for action against South Africa over apartheid, that the economic sanctions imposed by many states against South Africa violated international law.[18] Secondly, if repeated frequently, General Assembly resolutions may acquire the force of a customary rule.[19] In this sense, such resolutions provide evidence of an international consensus relating to the binding nature of an emerging norm.[20] The norm of non-discrimination and the outlawing of apartheid and colonialism appear to fall into this category. Thirdly, resolutions must be considered in good faith with a view to their implementation.[21] Failure to do this, in response to repeated recommendations, may have serious implications for a state. As Judge Lauterpacht observed in the *Voting Procedure Case*, a state

> which consistently sets itself above the solemnly and repeatedly expressed judgment of the [United Nations] Organization, in particular in proportion as that judgment approximates to unanimity, may find that it has overstepped the imperceptible line between impropriety and illegality, between discretion and arbitrariness, between the exercise of the legal right to disregard the recommendation and the abuse of that right, and that it has exposed itself to consequences legitimately following as a legal sanction.[22]

These words, written in 1955 in respect of South Africa's failure to respond to General Assembly resolutions on South West Africa, had a prophetic quality. For there can be little doubt that it was the South

[16] See the *dictum* of Judge Lauterpacht in his separate opinion in the *Voting Procedure Case* (n 13) 115.

[17] See, for example, YZ Blum 'Economic boycotts in international law' (1977) 12 *Texas ILJ* 10. See further Chapter 24.

[18] See Dugard (n 6) 120–2; PC Szasz 'Agora: Is the ASIL policy on divestment in violation of international law?' (1988) 82 *AJIL* 314; WC Maddrey 'Economic sanctions against South Africa: Problems and prospects for enforcement of human rights norms' (1982) 22 *Virginia JIL* 345; K Ferguson-Brown 'The legality of economic sanctions against South Africa in contemporary international law' (1988–9) 14 *SAYIL* 59 at 71–2; A Steenkamp 'Die regmatigheid van ekonomiese sanksies teen Suid-Afrika' (1991) 3 *Stellenbosch LR* 370. *Sed contra*, see GN Barrie 'International law and economic coercion—A legal assessment' (1985–6) 11 *SAYIL* 40 and 'Agora: Is the ASIL policy on divestment in violation of international law?' (1988) 82 *AJIL* 311.

[19] See Chapter 3.

[20] See *Legality of the Threat or Use of Nuclear Weapons* 1996 ICJ Reports 226, para 70.

[21] Dugard (n 15) 50–6.

[22] Supra (n 13) 120.

African government's persistent refusal to consider seriously the repeated calls of the General Assembly for the abandonment of apartheid, that led to the imposition of sanctions against South Africa.

Although the powers of the General Assembly are wide, it must on occasion defer to the Security Council, which enjoys primary responsibility for the maintenance of international peace and security. Article 12 of the UN Charter provides that when a matter is before the Security Council, the General Assembly may not make any recommendation on that matter.[23] More importantly, the General Assembly is precluded from taking enforcement action against a delinquent state. In terms of article 11(2), any question 'on which action is necessary' shall be referred to the Security Council.

In 1950, at the time of the Korean War, the General Assembly attempted to assert a residual power to take action against a state in the Uniting for Peace Resolution.[24] Frustrated by the inaction of the Security Council as a result of the exercise of the veto power, the General Assembly resolved that when this occurred, it might itself recommend 'collective measures, including, in the case of a breach of the peace or act of aggression, the use of armed force, when necessary, to maintain or restore international peace and security'. This resolution was invoked for the establishment of a peacekeeping force in the Middle East,[25] after the 1956 invasion of Egypt by Britain, France, and Israel, and has since been invoked to summon special emergency meetings of the Assembly to consider items of special importance.[26] The frequent use of the veto by the United States to prevent the Security Council from taking action against Israel has

[23] The International Court of Justice has held that article 12 does not preclude the General Assembly from requesting an advisory opinion on a matter that is being considered by the Security Council: *Wall Opinion* 2004 ICJ Reports paras 24–8; *Kosovo Opinion* 2010 ICJ Reports para 23. See further M Cowling 'The relationship between the Security Council and the General Assembly with particular reference to the International Court of Justice Advisory Opinion on the *Israeli Wall Case*' (2005) 30 *SAYIL* 50.

[24] UNGA resolution 377 A (V), adopted on 3 November 1950. South Africa voted in favour of this resolution. See further on this resolution, Higgins et al (n 1), vol 1, paras 2.101–2.104.

[25] The United Nations Emergency Force in the Middle East (UNEF) was established in Egypt with the consent of the Egyptian government in order to maintain peace in that region. It therefore did not involve action *against* a state. See, further, on this force, DW Bowett *United Nations Forces* (1964); R Higgins *United Nations Peace-keeping 1946–1967 (Documents and Commentary)* vol 1 (1969).

[26] In 2003, the General Assembly requested an advisory opinion on the wall Israel was building in Palestinian Territory at that time and is still building at the time of writing. The request was made in terms of a resolution adopted at an Emergency Special Session under the Uniting for Peace Resolution. See, on the procedure

resulted in the General Assembly adopting numerous resolutions in an emergency special session.

More recently, frustrated by the failure of the Security Council to deal with the prolonged war in Syria, some Western and Third World countries, led by Canada, led a push for the President of the General Assembly to convene a plenary session of all member states to explore concerted action, aimed at putting pressure on all parties to the conflict to end it. Instead, following consultations, the President of the General Assembly initially convened an informal meeting at which the Secretary-General and the United Nations Special Envoy to Syria briefed interested member states.[27] However, following that meeting, on 8 December 2016 Canada, Costa Rica, Japan, the Netherlands and Togo, acting on behalf of 74 other member states, requested the convening of a formal plenary meeting of the General Assembly. This meeting took place the following day and resulted in the adoption of a resolution on 'The Situation in the Syrian Arab Republic'.[28] The resolution, inter alia, urged the Security Council 'to further exercise its responsibility for the maintenance of international peace and security by taking additional measures to address the crisis in the Syrian Arab Republic, in particular the devastating humanitarian crisis'. It also stressed, in this regard, article 11 of the Charter.

The Uniting for Peace Resolution has not, however, been used to take action *against* any state, and Canada and the co-sponsors of the resolution on Syria did not invoke it. That action of this kind is the sole prerogative of the Security Council has been accepted by the Assembly, particularly since the ruling of the International Court of Justice in the *Expenses Case*,[29] in 1962, that the term 'action' in article 11(2) means enforcement action *against* a state, and that such action falls exclusively within the powers of the Security Council acting under Chapter VII of the Charter.

South Africa's racial policies featured on the agenda of the General Assembly from 1946 to 1994. In 1946, the General Assembly first considered the question of the treatment of persons of Indian origin

followed *Legal Consequences of the Construction of a Wall in the Occupied Palestinian Territory* 2004 ICJ Reports 136; (2004) 43 *ILM* 1009, paras 29–35.

[27] The Canadian initiative was contained in a letter dated 13 October 2016, sent on behalf of 69 other countries, from the Permanent Mission of Canada to the President of the 71th session of the General Assembly. The letter and the response by the President of the General Assembly, dated 14 October 2016, are available at http;//www.un.org/pga/71/wp-content/uploads/sites/40/2015/08/informal-briefing-on-the-situation-of-syria.pdf.

[28] Resolution A/71/L.39, adopted on 9 December 2016 by a vote of 122 to 13 with 36 abstentions.

[29] 1962 ICJ Reports 151 at 164–5.

in South Africa. In 1952, the policy of apartheid itself was raised in the General Assembly, and thereafter, the question of apartheid appeared annually on the agenda of the Assembly until 1994.[30]

In the 1950s, after a Commission on the Racial Situation in the Union of South Africa had found that apartheid was in conflict with the human rights clauses in the Charter,[31] the General Assembly adopted a number of resolutions calling upon South Africa to reconsider its racial policies.[32] In the 1960s, the mood hardened after the increase in the size of the Afro-Asian bloc, and the change in attitude towards South Africa on the part of many Western states following the shooting of demonstrators by the police at Sharpeville in 1960. In 1962, the General Assembly adopted Resolution 1761 (XVII) in which member states were requested to break off, or refrain from establishing, diplomatic relations with South Africa; to close their ports to all vessels flying the South African flag; to enact legislation prohibiting their ships from entering South African ports; to boycott all South African goods and to refrain from exporting goods, including arms and ammunition, to South Africa; and to refuse landing and passage facilities to all South African aircraft. The measures recommended in Resolution 1761 (XVII) were endorsed and expanded upon each year with larger majorities, until the abandonment of apartheid. Calls for a comprehensive trade boycott were repeated, and states were requested to suspend cultural, educational, and sporting exchanges with South Africa.[33]

Resolution 1761 (XVII) and its successors had their constitutional basis in articles 10–14 of the UN Charter and were thus recommendatory in nature. However, as has been shown above, these resolutions were not without legal consequences. Moreover, these resolutions provided the impetus for the adoption by the United Nations of two treaties relating to the practice of apartheid. First, the International Convention on the Suppression and Punishment of the Crime of Apartheid.[34] Secondly, the International Convention Against Apartheid in Sports.[35] South Africa's argument that the United Nations

[30] See above, Chapter 15

[31] *GAOR*, 8th session (1953), suppl no 16, para 903; *GAOR*, 9th session (1954), suppl no 16, para 358.

[32] General Assembly resolutions 820(IX), 917(X), 1016(XI) and 1178(XII).

[33] For example, Resolution 39/72 of 13 December 1984.

[34] 1015 UNTS 244. Adopted on 30 November 1973; entered into force on 18 July 1976. It may be noted that, significantly, no one was prosecuted for the crime of apartheid while apartheid lasted in South Africa. Equally significantly, no one has been prosecuted for the crime since the end of apartheid, and post-apartheid South Africa has not become a party to the Convention.

[35] 1500 UNTS 177. Adopted on 10 December 1985; entered into force on 3 April 1988.

was precluded from considering its domestic racial policies in terms of article 2(7) of the Charter is considered in Chapter 15.

SECURITY COUNCIL

The Security Council is the executive body of the United Nations and is given primary responsibility for the maintenance of international peace and security.[36] It is composed of 15 members: five permanent members and 10 non-permanent members, elected by the General Assembly for a term of two years. The five permanent members are China, France, Russia, the United Kingdom, and the United States. South Africa was a member of the Council of the League of Nations,[37] but, because of its racial policies, was not elected to serve on the Security Council during the apartheid era. However, South Africa was elected as a non-permanent member of the Security Council for 2007 and 2008 and again for two other two-year terms for 2011 and 2012, and 2018 and 2019.

The Security Council was constituted in 1945, and its permanent members reflect the power relations of that time. Today, states such as Germany and Japan probably have more claim to a permanent seat on the Security Council than the United Kingdom and France. Moreover, states such as India, Brazil, South Africa, Egypt and Nigeria also lay claim to permanent membership. Since 2005, there have been serious discussions and efforts to change the composition of the Security Council by expanding the number of permanent members to include states which contribute most to the United Nations financially, militarily and diplomatically, and to achieve a fairer geographical distribution.[38] To date, none of the competing proposals put forward by different countries or regions has prevailed. Thus, the debate on UN Security Council reform continues, perhaps less earnestly than when it began.[39]

[36] Article 24.

[37] South Africa was elected to the Council of the League in 1939 and, because of the war, attended only one session: S Pienaar *South Africa and International Relations between the Two World Wars: The League of Nations Dimension* (1987) 30–1.

[38] See *A More Secure World: Our Shared Responsibilities: Report of the Secretary-General's High Level Panel on Threats, Challenges and Change* United Nations (2004), A/59/565, at 66, 87; *In Larger Freedom: Towards Development, Security and Human Rights for All* Report of the Secretary-General, *GAOR*, 5th Session (2005) A/59/2005 (21 March 2005) 42; H Strydom 'Chronicles of UN reform' (2006) 31 *SAYIL* 95; Y Blum 'Proposals for UN Security Council reform' (2005) 99 *AJIL* 632.

[39] See B Cox 'United Nations Security Council reform: Collected proposals and possible consequences' (2009) 6 *South Carolina JIL and Bus.* 89; see also M Gould and MD Rablen 'Reform of the United Nations Security Council: Equity and efficiency' (2017) 173 *Public Choice* 145. See also discussion in Chapter 26.

The Security Council is empowered to take decisions binding on all member states of the United Nations.[40] But the price paid for this advance towards world government is high—the veto power vested in the five permanent members. In terms of article 27(3), while decisions on procedural matters in the Security Council are made by an affirmative vote of nine members, decisions on all other matters are to be made 'by an affirmative vote of nine members including the concurring votes of the permanent members'. All the permanent members have invoked this veto when they have perceived their own interests to be threatened, which has deprived the Security Council of much of its effectiveness. After the end of the Cold War the Security Council operated for some years as it was intended to do. However, the recent inability of the permanent members, particularly Russia and the United States, to agree on decisive action on the conflicts in Gaza/Palestine, Syria or Yemen has tempered this optimism. It is not hyperbolic to say that the veto has returned, and some permanent members are not shy to use it to protect their interests or those of their allies.

The severity of the veto has, to some extent, been ameliorated by the practice of abstention. Since the early days of the United Nations, the permanent members have not viewed an abstention from voting in the Security Council as a veto, and this has allowed many resolutions, that one or other of the permanent members was unable to support fully, to be adopted.[41] The lawfulness of this practice was challenged in 1971 by South Africa, when the Security Council requested the International Court of Justice to give an advisory opinion on the legality of South Africa's presence in Namibia in a resolution adopted by 12 votes to none with three abstentions, including abstentions by the Soviet Union and Britain. In rejecting South Africa's argument that an abstention could not be described as a 'concurring' vote, as required by article 27(3), the Court held that states in the Security Council, particularly the permanent members, had 'consistently and uniformly interpreted the practice of voluntary abstention by a permanent member as not constituting a bar to the adoption of resolutions', and that this procedure had been 'generally accepted by Members of the United Nations and evidences a general practice of that Organization'.[42]

An abstention from voting may be regarded as a 'concurring' vote, as the permanent member is present in the Security Council and able

[40] In terms of article 25, member states 'agree to accept and carry out the decisions of the Security Council'.

[41] C Stavropoulos 'The practice of voluntary abstentions by permanent members of the Security Council under article 27(3) of the Charter of the UN' (1967) 61 *AJIL* 737.

[42] *Namibia Opinion* 1971 ICJ Reports 16 at 22.

to make a considered choice on whether to vote or to abstain from voting. It is more difficult to treat the absence of a permanent member from the Council as a 'concurring' vote, despite the fact that permanent members are required to be present at the headquarters of the United Nations at all times.[43] For this reason, serious doubt surrounds the legality of the Security Council resolutions of 1950, recommending that member states of the United Nations provide military assistance to South Korea to repel the armed attack of North Korea. These resolutions were adopted when the Soviet Union was absent from the headquarters of the United Nations, in protest against the United Nations' refusal to accept the communist government of China as the proper representative of China in the United Nations. For this reason, the Soviet Union consistently maintained that these resolutions were invalid.

A dispute or situation likely to endanger the maintenance of international peace and security may be brought to the attention of the Security Council by any member of the United Nations,[44] a non-member state prepared to accept the obligations for pacific settlement provided for in the Charter,[45] the General Assembly,[46] and the Secretary-General.[47] The Security Council may respond by taking action under Chapter VI, Chapter VII, or the general powers contained in article 24.

1 Chapter VI

Chapter VI empowers the Security Council to address disputes that in its judgment do not threaten international peace, within the meaning of Chapter VII, but that, if continued, are '*likely* to endanger the maintenance of international peace and security' (emphasis added).[48] In such a case, the Security Council, acting under article 36(1), may '*recommend* appropriate procedures or methods of adjustment' (emphasis added) for settling the dispute. Article 25, which obliges member states to carry out *decisions* of the Security Council—as opposed to *recommendations*—is not applicable to Chapter VI. In law such recommendations enjoy the same status as recommendations of the General Assembly. Their political weight, however, is greater because of the greater authority vested in the Security

[43] Article 28.
[44] Article 35(1).
[45] Article 35(2).
[46] Article 11(3).
[47] Article 99.
[48] Articles 33, 36.

Council. For example, Resolution 242 of 1967,[49] which lays down several conditions for peace in the Middle East, including the withdrawal of Israeli forces from the occupied territories and recognition of the state of Israel, is widely seen as the blueprint for peace in the region.

Article 36(3) states that the Security Council, in acting under Chapter VI, should bear in mind that legal disputes should 'as a general rule' be referred to the International Court of Justice. In practice,[50] the Security Council seldom follows this advice as there is a clear preference on its part for the political settlement of disputes. Probably the failure of the International Court, in the *Corfu Channel Case*,[51] to accept such a referral as a basis for compulsory jurisdiction has also deterred the Security Council from making use of this power.

The Security Council adopted numerous resolutions on South Africa after it first addressed the question of apartheid in 1960, following the shooting of demonstrators in Sharpeville. On that occasion, the Security Council recognised 'that the situation in the Union of South Africa is one that has led to international friction and if continued might endanger international peace and security', and called upon South Africa to abandon apartheid.[52] Subsequent resolutions included calls for consultation and conciliation,[53] the release of political prisoners,[54] the granting of clemency to political offenders facing execution,[55] the lifting of the state of emergency,[56] and an end to attacks on neighbouring territories.[57] In order to secure the abandonment of racial discrimination, political repression, and military aggression, the Security Council recommended the adoption of a

[49] See J McHugo 'Resolution 242: A legal reappraisal of the right-wing Israeli interpretation of the withdrawal phrase with respect to the conflict between Israel and the Palestinians' (2002) 51 *ICLQ* 851.

[50] There appear to be only two clear instances in which such a recommendation has been made. In 1947, Britain and Albania were advised to take the dispute over the sinking of British naval vessels in the Corfu Channel to the International Court: Resolution 22 (1947). In 1976, it was suggested that the dispute between Greece and Turkey over the Aegean Sea continental shelf be referred to the Court: Resolution 395 (1976).

[51] 1948 ICJ Reports 15 at 31–2.

[52] Resolution 134 (1960).

[53] Resolutions 182 (1963), 191 (1964).

[54] Resolutions 181 (1963), 182 (1963), 191 (1964), 311 (1972), 417 (1977), 473 (1980); 560 (1985).

[55] Resolutions 190 (1964), 191 (1964), 503 (1982), 525 (1982), 533 (1983), 547 (1984).

[56] Resolution 569 (1985).

[57] Resolutions 387 (1976), 393 (1976), 527 (1982), 543 (1983), 546 (1984), 567 (1985), 568 (1985), 602 (1987).

wide range of sanctions. In 1963,[58] an arms embargo was first recommended and, in 1985,[59] the Security Council recommended the suspension of new investment in South Africa, the suspension of guaranteed export loans, the prohibition of all new contacts in the nuclear field, the prohibition of all sales of computer equipment that might be used by the South African army and police, and restrictions in the field of sports and cultural relations. Except for one resolution adopted under Chapter VII,[60] all these resolutions were adopted under Chapter VI. The Security Council determined the South African situation to be one that 'seriously disturbed' international peace or constituted a 'potential threat'[61] to international peace, and not an actual 'threat to the peace' or 'breach of the peace' requiring enforcement action under Chapter VII.

2 Chapter VII

The real power of the Security Council flows from Chapter VII, which permits it to take legally binding decisions under article 25 directing member states to impose economic sanctions or to use force to maintain international peace.[62] Because of the serious consequences of such action, the permanent members of the Security Council have not hesitated to use their veto power to obstruct action of this kind where their interests have been involved. During the Cold War, both the Soviet Union and the United States used their vetoes liberally to protect their interests. China, France, and the United Kingdom have also made use of their vetoes on occasion. This explains why most of the forcible interventions of doubtful legality, threatening the peace of the world between 1945 and 1990, were not acted upon by the Security Council. Soviet intervention in Hungary (1956), Czechoslovakia (1968), and Afghanistan (1979) was not met with action by the United Nations any more than was the United States intervention in the Dominican Republic (1965), Vietnam (1965–73), Grenada (1983), or Panama (1989).

After the end of the Cold War, the Security Council found it possible to achieve consensus on the need for intervention to secure

[58] Resolutions 181 (1963); 182 (1963). The call for an arms embargo was repeated in resolutions 191 (1964), 282 (1970), 311 (1972), 473 (1980).

[59] Resolution 569 (1985).

[60] Resolution 418 (1977), discussed below.

[61] See, for example, resolutions 181 (1963), 191 (1964), 311 (1972), 473 (1980), 282 (1970).

[62] E de Wet *The Chapter VII Powers of the United Nations Security Council* (2004); V Lowe and A Roberts *The UN Security Council and War* (2008). See also H Nasu 'Chapter VII Powers and the rule of law: The jurisdictional limits' (2007) 26 *Aust YIL* 87.

international peace in certain situations. Thus, action of some kind was taken under Chapter VII in response to Iraq's invasion of Kuwait (1990–1991);[63] the conflicts in the former Yugoslavia,[64] Somalia,[65] Liberia,[66] Rwanda[67] and East Timor;[68] the failure of Libya to extradite the persons alleged to have been responsible for the bombing of Pan Am Flight 103 over Lockerbie in 1992;[69] the uprising against Colonel Gaddafi's regime in 2011;[70] the refusal of former President Gbagbo of Côte d'Ivoire to leave office;[71] and the use of chemical weapons in Syria.[72] On the other hand, the Security Council was unable to reach agreement on action to be taken against Yugoslavia in respect of Kosovo (1999), and against Saddam Hussain's Iraq (2003), which resulted in action taken by some Western states without the authorisation of the Security Council. As already noted above, more recently the Security Council has been prevented from taking action in respect of Syria, Yemen and Gaza/Palestine because of the veto of either Russia or the United States.

In order to trigger action under Chapter VII, it is necessary for the Security Council to determine, under article 39, that the situation in question constitutes a 'threat to the peace, breach of the peace, or act of aggression'. This is a political decision made by a political body subject to the possibility of a veto by one of the permanent powers. For this reason, none of the above forcible interventions on the part of the Soviet Union or the United States was found to constitute a threat to international peace. Where the interests of the permanent members of the Security Council are not involved, the Security Council has, particularly in recent years, had less difficulty in making such a determination.

There is a dispute as to whether the Security Council may adopt a resolution under article 39, determining that a situation constitutes a threat to the peace justifying action under Chapter VII, when it involves a serious violation of human rights within a particular territory. Some argue that there must be some external element, which affects a neighbouring state or has 'the potential of provoking

[63] Resolution 678 (1990).
[64] Resolutions 733, 743, 757, 787 (1992); 827 (1993).
[65] Resolution 794 (1992).
[66] Resolution 788 (1992).
[67] Resolution 955 (1994).
[68] Resolution 1264 (1999).
[69] Resolution 748 (1992).
[70] Resolution 1973 (2011).
[71] Resolution 1975 (2011).
[72] Resolution 2011 (2013).

armed conflict between states',[73] while others maintain that a serious violation of human rights within a single state permits a determination of threat to the peace under article 39.[74] The practice of the Security Council is inconsistent. On occasion the Security Council has responded to an internal pattern of human rights violations but linked this to the effect on neighbouring states. For instance resolution 418 (1977), in which the Security Council responded to a massive crackdown on internal political opposition in South Africa by imposing an arms embargo, referred not only to the violation of human rights in South Africa itself, but also to South Africa's attacks on neighbouring states and to South Africa's acquisition of arms and related material as the reason for the finding under article 39.[75] Other resolutions are less clear on the need for some external element. In 1992, the Security Council made a finding under article 39 that the internal humanitarian crisis in Somalia constituted a threat to the peace.[76] During the liberation struggle in South Africa, the ANC persistently argued that apartheid per se constituted a threat to the peace. It was therefore surprising that during its tenure of a non-permanent seat on the Security Council in 2007/8 the ANC government of South Africa should have adopted a different position. In 2007 South Africa, together with China and Russia, voted against a proposed resolution condemning the military junta in Myanmar (Burma) for its violation of human rights on the ground that an internal human rights situation 'does not fit with the Charter mandate conferred on the Security Council which is to deal with matters that are a threat to international peace and security'.[77]

Similar considerations appear to have guided the South African government in its approach to Zimbabwe during the Robert Mugabe regime.

Security Council resolution 1970 of 26 February 2011 on Libya confirms that the Security Council may take action under Chapter VII on an internal situation with no potential for provoking an armed conflict between states. In this unanimously adopted resolution the Security Council, acting under Chapter VII, deplored the violation of

[73] De Wet (n 62) 138–44, 149–77.

[74] BG Ramcharan *The Security Council and the Protection of Human Rights* (2002) 211; C Tomuschat *Human Rights; Between Idealism and Realism* (2003) 130; Higgins et al (n 1) vol 2, 738, para 22.20.

[75] See De Wet (n 62) 140, 150–1.

[76] Resolution 794. See De Wet (n 62) 155–8.

[77] D Tladi 'Strict positivism, moral arguments, human rights and the Security Council: South Africa and the Myanmar vote' (2008) *AHRLJ* 23. See further D Tladi 'Reflections on the rule of law in international law: The Security Council, international law and the limits of power' (2006) 31 *SAYIL* 231; D Tladi 'South African lawyers, values and the new vision of international law' (2008) 33 *SAYIL* 167.

human rights by the Gaddafi regime, expressed concern over the use of violence against civilians and imposed an arms embargo on the regime and a travel ban on its leaders. No determination was made under article 39 and the Security Council simply asserted that in so acting it was 'mindful of its primary responsibility for the maintenance of international peace and security'. South Africa's support for this resolution in the Security Council suggests that it no longer adheres to the position it adopted on Myanmar (Burma) in 2007. Further support for the view that the Security Council may take measures under Chapter VII in respect of an internal situation threatening human rights is provided by Security Council resolution 1973 of 17 March 2011 imposing a 'no fly zone' over Libya and authorising states to take 'all necessary measures' to protect civilians. This resolution, adopted under Chapter VII, is premised on the Responsibility to Protect Resolution of 2005[78] and determines that the situation in Libya 'continues to constitute a threat to international peace and security'. There is no suggestion that the situation in Libya poses a threat to the peace in any other state. Again, South Africa voted in favour of the resolution.

Three types of responses to a 'threat to the peace' are provided for in the Charter. A fourth—legislation—is in the process of emerging in the practice of the Security Council.

(a) Provisional measures

Article 40 provides for the adoption of provisional measures, such as a cease-fire or withdrawal of forces, before enforcement action is taken. Over the years, since 1950, the Security Council has adopted decisions containing provisional measures that the Council called upon the parties to a conflict to comply with in order to prevent the aggravation of the situation. Some decisions have specifically mentioned measures falling under article 40, while in other instances article 40 was not explicitly mentioned in the deliberations of the Security Council. In practice, where relevant, provisional measures have been imposed in parallel to the adoption of measures under articles 41 and 42.[79]

(b) Non-forcible measures

Article 41 authorises the Security Council to direct member states to take measures not involving the use of force to implement its

[78] 2005 World Summit Outcome, General Assembly Resolution 60/1, discussed in Chapter 24.

[79] See United Nations *Repertoire of the Practice of the Security Council, Part VII: Actions with Respect to Threats to Peace, Breaches of the Peace, and Acts of Aggression (Chapter VII of the Charter)*, 19th suppl (2014–2015) 26, available at http://www.un.org/en/sc/repertoire.

decisions.[80] 'These may include complete or partial interruption of economic relations and of rail, sea, air, postal, telegraphic, radio and other means of communication, and the severance of diplomatic relations.'

Little use was made of this power during the Cold War outside southern Africa. Comprehensive economic sanctions were imposed on Rhodesia from 1966 to 1979.[81] In 1977 the Security Council responded to the suppression of political opposition in the wake of the killing of anti-apartheid activist Steve Biko by state security officers by adopting a limited and cautiously worded resolution under article 41 directing states to impose an arms embargo on South Africa. In resolution 418, adopted on 4 November 1977, the Security Council

> *[a]cting* . . . under Chapter VII of the Charter of the United Nations,
>
> 1. *Determines*, having regard to the policies and acts of the South African government, that the acquisition by South Africa of arms and related *matériel* constitutes a threat to the maintenance of international peace and security;. *Decides* that all states shall cease forthwith any provision to South Africa of arms and related *matériel* of all types, including the sale or transfer of weapons and ammunition, military vehicles and equipment, para-military police equipment and spare parts for the aforementioned, and shall cease as well the provision of all types of equipment and supplies and grants of licensing arrangements for the manufacture or maintenance of the aforementioned.[82]

Since 1990, greater use has been made of article 41. In 1990, economic sanctions were imposed against Iraq following its invasion of Kuwait.[83] In 1992, the Security Council imposed a mandatory arms and air embargo on Libya as a result of its failure to extradite the

[80] See V Gowlland-Debbas (ed) *United Nations Sanctions and International Law* (2001); De Wet (n 62) 178–256; HA Strydom 'Reassessing the appropriateness of sanctions' (1999) 24 *SAYIL* 199; V Gowlland-Debbas (ed) *National Implementation of United Nations Sanctions: A Comparative Study* (2004).

[81] Resolutions 232 (1966), 253 (1968), 277 (1970). See, further on this subject, HR Strack *Sanctions: The Case of Rhodesia* (1978); R Zacklin *The United Nations and Rhodesia: A Study in International Law* (1974); J Nkala *The United Nations, International Law, and the Rhodesian Independence Crisis* (1985); DJ Devine 'The status of Rhodesia in international law' 1973 *Acta Juridica* 1 and 1974 *Acta Juridica* 109; J Dugard *Recognition and the United Nations* (1987) 90–8; V Gowlland-Debbas *Collective Responses to Illegal Acts in International Law* (1990).

[82] See on this historic resolution, Higgins et al (n 1) vol 2, 984, paras 26.51–54. Some South African writers have questioned the lawfulness of this resolution. See MP Vorster and NJ Botha 'Security Council resolution 418 (1977)' (1978) 4 *SAYIL* 130; GN Barrie 'International law and economic coercion—A legal assessment' (1985–6) 11 *SAYIL* 40; JC Heunis (n 4) 334–92; H Booysen *Volkereg* 2 ed (1989) 440. See, too, NC Crawford and A Klotz (eds) *How Sanctions Work: Lessons from South Africa* (1999).

[83] Resolutions 661, 665 (1990), 687 (1991).

suspected bombers of Pan Am Flight 103.[84] In 1991–1992, an embargo was imposed on the supply of arms to the territories formerly comprising Yugoslavia[85] and later economic and diplomatic sanctions were imposed on Serbia and Montenegro.[86] In 2005, economic sanctions were imposed on Sudan in response to human rights violations committed in the Darfur region;[87] and in 2011 an arms embargo was imposed on Libya[88] and economic sanctions on the regime of former President Gbagbo of Côte d'Ivoire.[89] That the measures listed in article 41 are not exhaustive is shown by the establishment of international criminal tribunals for the former Yugoslavia[90] and Rwanda[91] under this provision.[92] The Security Council also adopted resolutions under article 41 establishing international civil administrations for Kosovo,[93] East Timor[94] and Iraq.[95] In the case of Kosovo and East Timor, civil administration was transferred to bodies functioning under the control of a Special Representative of the UN Secretary-General, the United Nations Interim Administration Mission in Kosovo (UNMIK)[96] and the United Nations Transitional Administration in East Timor (UNTA-ET),[97] respectively. In the case of Iraq, civil administration was, in terms of the Security Council resolution, vested in the United States and the United Kingdom (the 'Authority').[98]

[84] Resolution 748 (1992).
[85] Resolutions 713, 724, 727 (1992).
[86] Resolutions 757 (1992), 820 (1993), 942 (1994), 1160 (1998).
[87] Resolutions 1556 (2004), 15911 (2005).
[88] Resolution 1970 (2011).
[89] Resolution 1975 (2011).
[90] Resolution 827 (1993).
[91] Resolution 955 (1994).
[92] For confirmation of the fact that their tribunals were established under article 41, see *Prosecutor v Tadic* (1996) 35 *ILM* 32.
[93] Resolution 1244 (1999).
[94] Resolution 1272 (1999).
[95] Resolution 1483 (2003).
[96] Resolution 1244 (1999) was adopted on 10 June 1999. On 17 February 2008, the Assembly of Kosovo declared independence and adopted a new constitution. UNMIK has continued to exist notwithstanding this declaration of independence. It operates alongside the European Union Rule of Law Mission in Kosovo (EULEX Kosovo), a deployment of the European Union police and civilians, which was approved by the Security Council in late 2008 as an assistance mission to UNMIK rather than its replacement.
[97] The UN Transitional Administration in East Timor operated as an interim civil administration and peacekeeping mission in the territory of East Timor from 25 October 1999 until its independence on 20 May 2002.
[98] De Wet (n 65) 311–19.

(c) Forcible measures

Article 42 provides that, should the Security Council decide that the measures provided for in article 41 would be inadequate or have proved to be inadequate, 'it may take such action by air, sea or land forces as may be necessary to maintain or restore international peace and security'.

In 1945, it was contemplated that such action would be taken by a United Nations force set up by agreements entered into between the Security Council and member states, in terms of article 43, making military contingents available to the Security Council. This force would be placed under the command of a Military Staff Committee provided for in article 47. This scheme has failed to materialise because, as a result of the Cold War, no force has been established under article 43.

Consequently, the only enforcement action taken against states under article 42 has been action *authorised* by the United Nations and not action taken by the United Nations itself. Although this practice is not explicitly approved by article 42, it constitutes the exercise of an acceptable implied power.[99] Authorisation by the Security Council to states to use force legitimises the use of force under the Charter, but it results in operations that are not kept under the strict control of the United Nations.

In 1950, at the time of North Korea's invasion of South Korea, the Security Council was able to adopt three resolutions as a result of the fortuitous absence of the Soviet Union from United Nations headquarters. These resolutions determined the invasion to be a breach of the peace and recommended that member states 'furnish such assistance to the Republic of Korea as may be necessary to repel the armed attack', and that such forces should be made available 'to a unified command under the United States'.[100] South Africa was one of 16 states to send armed forces to Korea. Although under the command of the United States, the various contingents did fly the United Nations flag together with their own flags.

The next instance of United Nations-authorised force occurred in 1966, shortly after Rhodesia's unilateral declaration of independence, when the Security Council called on the British government to enforce an oil boycott against Rhodesia by preventing 'by the use of force if necessary the arrival at Beira of vessels reasonably believed to

[99] N Blokker 'Is the authorization authorized? Powers and practice of the UN Security Council to authorize the use of force by "coalitions of the able and willing"' (2000) 11 *EJIL* 541; T Franck *Recourse to Force: State Action against Threats and Armed Attacks* (2002) 20–31.

[100] These resolutions were adopted on 25 June, 27 June, and 7 July 1950, respectively. See Higgins et al (n 1) vol 2, 1010, paras 26.99–100.

be carrying oil destined for Rhodesia'.[101] Shortly afterwards a British warship intercepted a Greek tanker on the high seas and forced it to divert its course from Beira. Thereafter British warships maintained a patrol in the area to prevent oil tankers from entering the port of Beira.

The most dramatic, and effective, action taken with United Nations authorisation was that against Iraq in 1991. After Iraq's invasion of Kuwait in August 1990, the Security Council adopted several resolutions directing states to impose economic sanctions on Iraq. When this appeared to have no effect, the Security Council adopted resolution 678, authorising member states, in co-operation with the government of Kuwait, 'to use all necessary means' to ensure the withdrawal of Iraqi forces from Kuwait. Consequently, 22 states under the leadership of the United States sent forces to the Gulf, and within five days of the start of the ground offensive, Iraqi forces were removed from Kuwait. United Nations involvement in this action, after the adoption of resolution 678, was even more limited than in the case of Korea. In these circumstances, it has been argued by commentators that the operation in the Gulf War was an exercise in collective self-defence rather than an example of United Nations action under article 42.[102]

On 17 March 2011, the Security Council adopted a resolution imposing a no-fly zone on the forces of Libyan leader Muammar Gaddafi and authorising states to take 'all necessary measures' to protect civilians.[103] This authorisation resulted in forcible action being taken by NATO against the Gaddafi regime. The action by NATO not only ended in the toppling of the Gaddafi regime, but in his killing by members of one of the armed groups. Subsequently there were accusations among some UN member states, including South Africa, which had voted in favour of the resolution as a non-permanent member of the Security Council, that some Western countries had pushed for the adoption of the resolution in bad faith, using the pretext of enforcement action to effect regime change in Libya. The question of what exactly resolution 1973 permitted NATO to do—the prevention of gross violations of human rights based on

[101] Resolution 221 (1966); Higgins et al (n 1) vol 2, 1012, paras 12.104–26.107.

[102] See EV Rostow 'Agora: The Gulf Crisis "Until what? Enforcement action or collective self-defense?"' (1991) 85 *AJIL* 506. See, further, on the Gulf War, the other contributors to 'Agora: The Gulf Crisis' (1991) 85 *AJIL* 63–109, 516–35; O Schachter 'United Nations law in the Gulf Conflict' (1991) 85 *AJIL* 452; C Greenwood 'New world order or old?' (1992) 55 *Modern LR* 153; Higgins et al (n 1) vol 2, 1011 paras 26.101–3.

[103] Resolution 1973 (2011).

the responsibility to protect or a licence for regime change?—was also the subject of subsequent scholarly debate.[104]

(d) Legislation[105]

The Security Council is not a world parliament. It is empowered by Chapter VII and article 25 of the Charter to adopt legally binding decisions in situations that it determines threaten international peace, but its role is 'not to create or impose new obligations having no basis in the Charter, but rather to identify the conduct required of a Member State because of its pre-existing Charter obligations'.[106] Consequently, the Security Council does not legislate; rather, it enforces Charter obligations. In recent years, however, the Security Council has adopted resolutions under Chapter VII that have all the appearances of legislation: they are general and abstract in character; they are phrased in neutral language, apply to an indefinite number of cases and are not limited in time; they do not name states; and although triggered by a particular situation they are not restricted to it.[107] Three resolutions illustrate this development: first, resolution 1373 (2001),[108] adopted in the wake of the terrorist attacks in the United States on 11 September 2001, which decides that states shall 'prevent and suppress the financing of terrorist acts', freeze the funds of terrorists, take steps to prevent the commission of terrorists acts and criminalise the perpetration of terrorist acts; secondly, resolution 1540 (2004),[109] which imposes obligations on states to prevent

[104] See, for example, PR Williams and C Popken 'Security Council resolution on Libya: A moment of legal & moral clarity' (2011) 44 *Case W Res JIL* 225; T Hostovsky-Brandes and A Zemach 'Controlling the execution of a Security Council mandate to use force: Does the Council need a lawyer?' (2013) 36 *Fordham ILJ* 657; A de Waal 'African roles in the Libyan conflict' (2013) 89 *International Affairs* 365; Higgins et al (n 1) vol 2, 1023, para 26.120.

[105] P Szaz 'The Security Council starts legislating' (2002) 96 *AJIL* 901; M Happold 'Security Council Resolution 1373 and the Constitution of the United Nations' (2003) 16 *Leiden Journal of International Law* 593; S Talmon 'The Security Council as world legislature' (2005) 99 *AJIL* 175; I Johnstone 'Legislation and adjudication in the Security Council: Bringing down the deliberative deficit' (2008) *AJIL* 275; CH Powell 'The role and limits of global administrative law in the Security Council's anti-terrorism programme' 2009 *Acta Juridica* 32.

[106] DW Bowett 'Judicial and political functions of the Security Council and the International Court of Justice' in H Fox (ed) *The Changing Constitution of the United Nations* (1997) 70–80.

[107] Talmon (n 105) 176–7. On the 'legislative' function of the Security Council, see further, Talmon (n 105); Johnson (n 105).

[108] Adopted on 28 September 2001.

[109] Adopted on 28 April 2008. See too Resolution 2118(2013) which 'determines that the use of chemical weapons anywhere constitutes a threat to international peace and security.'

non-state actors from acquiring weapons of mass destruction; and thirdly, resolution 1566 (2004),[110] which in condemning 'all acts of terrorism' and calling upon states 'to co-operate fully in the fight against terrorism' provides a comprehensive definition of terrorist acts. All three resolutions were adopted unanimously.

The Security Council is using its enforcement powers to adopt normative resolutions that are legally binding on all members of the United Nations. In so doing, it has assumed the role of international law-maker. Such a legislative role may be justified if it is restricted to action taken under Chapter VII, designed to maintain international peace and security and confined to subjects that threaten international peace, as this would seem to serve the objects and purposes of Chapter VII. Resolutions 1373, 1540 and 1566 fall into this category of action. Clearly this legislative role, in which a 15-member Council takes decisions that bind 193 states, must be exercised with care—as consent is still seen by many states to be the foundation of international law.

3 Article 24

The practice of the Security Council suggests that it sees itself as a body operating either under Chapter VI, when it acts by recommendation, or under Chapter VII, when it acts by binding 'decision' in terms of article 25. In the 1971 *Namibia Opinion*,[111] the International Court of Justice was faced with the task of deciding whether Resolution 276 (1970), in which the Security Council declared South Africa's continued presence in Namibia to be illegal, was a legally binding decision under article 25, despite the fact that it was not preceded by a finding under article 39, and thus clearly did not fall under Chapter VII. The Court held that resolution 276 had been adopted under article 24, which confers general powers on the Council to discharge its responsibilities for the maintenance of international peace, in addition to the specific powers referred to in article 24(2). In order to decide whether article 25 applied to a resolution adopted under this 'general power', it was necessary to consider the language and context of the resolution. After examining the language and background of resolution 276, the Court concluded that it was legally binding under articles 24 and 25, and that South Africa was, therefore, under a legal obligation to withdraw its administration from Namibia.[112]

[110] Adopted on 8 October 2008.

[111] 1971 ICJ Reports 16.

[112] At 52–4. See, too, R Higgins 'The Advisory Opinion on Namibia: Which United Nations Resolutions are binding under Article 25 of the Charter?' (1972) 21 *ICLQ* 270.

Although the ruling of the Court that article 25 is not limited to decisions under Chapter VII may be correct as a matter of interpretation, it does not accord with the expectation of states in the Security Council, where the practice is still to confine binding decisions under article 25 to Chapter VII.[113]

4 Review of Security Council action

The powers of the Security Council under Chapter VII are far-reaching. Article 25 of the Charter obliges states to accept and carry out 'decisions' adopted under Charter VII and article 103 provides:

> In the event of a conflict between the obligations of the members of the United Nations under the present Charter and their obligations under any other international agreement, their obligations under the present Charter shall prevail.

These powers have been exercised widely since the end of the Cold War. The Security Council has adopted a large number of resolutions under Chapter VII, and has, in addition, begun to legislate under Chapter VII. The Security Council has always played a quasi-judicial role in the course of dispute settlement but since 1999 this role has become more pronounced. In that year, the Security Council adopted resolution 1267,[114] in the wake of the bombing of US embassies in Kenya and Tanzania, which provides for the listing of individuals associated with the Taliban and Al-Qaeda and the imposition of financial and travel sanctions upon such persons. Later, after the attack on the World Trade Centre on 9/11, the Security Council adopted resolution 1373, mentioned earlier, which created a Counter-Terrorism Committee (CTC) charged with the task of monitoring actions adopted by states to suppress terrorism. Thus, today the Security Council is heavily engaged in surveillance of, and action against, individuals it identifies as supporting or associated with international terrorism.[115]

This new activity on the part of the Security Council has given rise to the question of judicial review of the Security Council actions that

[113] The British government rejected the Court's finding that article 25 applied to resolutions outside Chapter VII. See J Dugard *The South West Africa/Namibia Dispute* (1973) 505.

[114] Adopted on 15 October 1999.

[115] For an examination of the activities of the Security Council sanctions committees on terrorism and the compatibility of these activities with international law, see Higgins et al (n 1) vol 2, 749–753, paras 22.35 –37; H Strydom 'Counter—Terrorism Sanctions and Human Rights' in T Maluwa, M du Plessis and D Tladi *The Pursuit of a Brave New World in International Law. Essays in Honour of John Dugard* (2017) 395.

exceed the limits of its powers,[116] violate norms of *jus cogens* or transgress fundamental human rights.[117] The International Court of Justice has considered the review of Security Council decisions in several cases, notably *Lockerbie*,[118] but has not yet questioned the discretion of the Security Council.[119] The European Court of Justice has, however, done so in respect of the 'listing' of individuals in terms of resolution 1267. In *Kadi*[120] the European Court of Justice annulled a regulation of the Council of the European Union, implementing a decision of the Security Council Sanctions Committee. The decision had listed Kadi and the Al Barakaat International Foundation as being associated with Al-Qaeda and subject therefore to the freezing of their funds, on the ground that it violated their fundamental rights under the law of the European Communities, including the right to be heard, the right to effective judicial review and the right to property.

PEACEKEEPING FORCES[121]

Despite the failure to set up a United Nations force under article 43 of the Charter, both the General Assembly and the Security Council have undertaken peacekeeping operations in many trouble spots of the world. These include the United Nations Emergency Force in the Middle East (UNEF), set up to supervise the cease-fire in that region after the Suez invasion of 1956; the United Nations Force in the Congo (ONUC), established in 1960 to maintain order in the Congo shortly after independence; the United Nations Force in Cyprus (UNFICYP), set up in 1964 to keep the peace between Greek and

[116] Article 24 provides that the Council is to 'act in accordance with the purposes and principles of the United Nations'. By necessary implication action that does not accord with the purposes and principles of the United Nations is *ultra vires*.

[117] See De Wet (n 65); D Akande 'The International Court of Justice and the Security Council: Is there room for judicial control of decision of the political organs of the United Nations?' (1997) 46 *ICLQ* 309; Higgins et al (n 1) vol 1, 355 paras 9.68-70.

[118] *Questions of Interpretation and Application of the 1971 Montreal Convention Arising from the Aerial Incident at Lockerbie (Libya v US & UK), Provisional Measures* 1992 ICJ Reports 3. See V Gowlland-Debbas 'The relationship between the International Court of Justice and the Security Council in the light of the *Lockerbie Case*' (1994) 88 *AJIL* 643.

[119] In the *Genocide Convention, Provisional Measures (Bosnia v Serbia)* 1993 ICJ Reports 325 Judge ad hoc Lauterpacht raised the interesting question of the priority of norms in the case of a conflict between a Security Council resolution and a norm of *jus cogens* (the prohibition on genocide): ibid 440.

[120] *Kadi & Al Barakaat International Foundation v Council & Commission* (European Court of Justice, Grand Chamber) 8 September 2008, noted in (2009) 103 *AJIL* 305.

[121] R Higgins *United Nations Peacekeeping 1946–1967 (Documents and Commentary)* 4 vols (1969–81); H McCoubrey and N White *International Organizations and Civil Wars* (1995); Higgins et al (n 1) vol 2, 1025 et seq, chapter 27.

Turkish Cypriots; the United Nations Interim Force in the Lebanon (UNIFIL), created in 1978 to patrol the Israeli–Lebanese border; the United Nations Protection Force (UNPROFOR), established in 1992 for certain parts of the former Republic of Yugoslavia, whose mandate was to create the conditions of peace and security required for an overall settlement of the Yugoslav crisis; the United Nations Transitional Authority in Cambodia (UNTAC), set up in 1992 to supervise transition to a new administration after multi-party elections; the United Nations Operation in Somalia (UNOSOM), created in 1992 to facilitate a cessation of hostilities in Somalia and to promote a political settlement; the United Nations Assistance Mission for Rwanda (UNAMIR), established in 1994 to provide humanitarian assistance in Rwanda; the United Nations Mission in Sierra Leone (UNAMSIL), established in 1998 to monitor a cease-fire and to provide assistance; the United Nations Interim Administration in Kosovo (UNMIK), established in 1999 to provide a civil administration for Kosovo; the United Nations Transitional Administration in East Timor (UNTAET), established in 1999 to administer the territory until independence; the United Nations Organization Mission in the Democratic Republic of the Congo (MONUC), established in 1999 to keep the peace in the Great Lakes region; and the United Nations-African Union Hybrid Mission in Darfur (UNAMID) established in 2007 to implement the Darfur Peace Agreement. Peacekeeping operations have also been established in southern Africa. In 1989, the United Nations Transition Assistance Group (UNTAG), established by the Security Council in resolution 435 (1978), played a major role in the supervision of the elections preceding Namibian independence.[122] In 1992, the Security Council authorised the Secretary-General to deploy United Nations observers in South Africa to assist the structures set up under the National Peace Accord, charged with the task of promoting peace in South Africa in anticipation of elections for a democratic South Africa.[123] This group, known as the United Nations Observer Mission in South Africa (UNOMSA), was enlarged from some 100 observers to nearly 3 000 in 1994 to enable it to monitor South Africa's first democratic elections.

[122] See on the role of UNTAG in the Namibian independence process, J Dugard 'Public international law' 1989 *Annual Survey* 536–43.

[123] Resolution 772 of 17 August 1992. The Security Council endorsed the suggestion to this effect made by Mr Cyrus Vance, who visited South Africa in July 1992 as special representative of the Secretary-General. See the Report of the Secretary-General on the Question of South Africa to the Security Council: S/24389 of 7 August 1992. See, further, on UNOMSA, J Cassette 'UN Observer Mission in South Africa' (1993) 18 *SAYIL* 1. See, too, Security Council Resolution 894 of 14 January 1994.

These operations, involving contingents from different countries, have been established in terms of ad hoc agreements between the United Nations and the states contributing the contingents. Where United Nations forces or observers are stationed in a territory, the United Nations enters into an agreement with the host state providing for privileges, immunities and facilities for the United Nations.[124] The Charter does not expressly provide for such operations, which, with the exception of UNEF (established by the General Assembly in terms of the Uniting for Peace Resolution[125]), have been created by the Security Council, acting either under Chapter VI or under its general powers in article 24. In the *Expenses Case*, the International Court of Justice upheld the lawfulness of such operations, in terms of implied powers in the Charter.[126] The Court held that, provided peacekeeping forces operate with the consent of the host state, they do not constitute enforcement action. Any action directed *against* a non-consenting state, however, would constitute enforcement action and require compliance with the provisions of Chapter VII.

In recent years, the distinction between peacekeeping, not involving the use of force, and enforcement action has become blurred, causing some to say that peacekeeping has its legal basis in Chapter VI. United Nations operations designed to maintain some semblance of peace in civil wars have increasingly resorted to force in self-defence, or in order to provide humanitarian assistance to civilians caught up in the conflict. Peacekeeping has therefore become peace-enforcement. This is illustrated by the history of UNPROFOR in Bosnia–Herzegovina between 1992 and 1995. Although originally intended as a traditional peacekeeping mission, stationed in the territory with the consent of the government and committed to the principles of impartiality and non-use of force, circumstances compelled it to assume a different role as the conflict between Muslims, Croats and Serbs within the territory intensified. Largely for humanitarian reasons the United Nations prohibited military flights over Bosnia and designated certain areas as 'safe areas'. These prescriptions were enforced by military means by the United Nations, with the assistance of NATO, in terms of Chapter VII resolutions calling for their enforcement by 'all necessary measures'.[127] In 1999, acting under Chapter VII, the Security Council established a 'multinational

[124] See, for example, the agreement between the United Nations and South Africa according immunities and privileges to members of UNOMSA; GN 114 *GG* 15470 of 4 February 1994; Proc 72 of 1994 *GG* 15697 of 26 April 1994.

[125] See supra n 24.

[126] 1962 ICJ Reports 151 at 168, 177.

[127] See resolutions 770 (1992), 816 (1993).

force' to restore peace and security in East Timor.[128] This followed the violence that ensued after the territory had overwhelmingly voted for independence from Indonesia. The 'multinational force' was authorised 'to take all necessary measures to fulfil this mandate'. Nowhere is the new role of the United Nations in peacekeeping more apparent than in the Democratic Republic of Congo, where UN peacekeepers have engaged in aggressive operations in the eastern regions of the country. This transformation of peacekeeping into peace-enforcement in the interests of humanity is a necessary evolution of the exercise of the implied powers conferred on the Security Council by the Charter. The veto power in the Council ensures that the exercise of these implied powers will not exceed acceptable limits.

The involvement of United Nations forces in violent civil conflicts has inevitably had consequences for their personal safety. In response to this new phenomenon the United Nations, in 1995, promoted the Convention on the Safety of United Nations and Associated Personnel[129] which requires states to criminalise, under their national law, murder, kidnapping and violent attacks directed at United Nations personnel and to exercise criminal jurisdiction over such offences on the basis of territoriality and active nationality or to extradite offenders to a state having jurisdiction.

South Africa has been involved in international peacekeeping for a relatively short time. Its participation in international peacekeeping commenced with the deployment of military personnel in 1998 in what was claimed to be a Southern African Development Community (SADC) intervention in Lesotho (see below). The following year, South Africa took part in a United Nations peacekeeping operation for the first time as part of MONUC, mentioned above. However, its first major troop contribution was to the African Union Mission in Burundi (AMIB) in 2004, which later became the UN Operation in Burundi (ONUB). Since then, South African forces have been deployed in 15 international peacekeeping missions, including eight UN peacekeeping operations in Burundi, Central African Republic, Eritrea/Ethiopia, Darfur (Sudan), Côte d'Ivoire, Democratic Republic of Congo (twice) and Liberia. The Defence Act 42 of 2002 regulates participation of members of the South African Defence National Force in international peacekeeping operations.[130]

[128] Resolution 1264 (1999).

[129] (1995) 34 *ILM* 482.

[130] Act 42 of 2002, ss 92–6. See T Neethling 'The SANDF as an instrument of peacekeeping in Africa: A critical analysis of three main challenges' (2011) 36 *Journal for Contemporary History* 134; L Heinecken and R Ferreira 'Fighting for peace: South Africa's role in peacekeeping in Africa (Part I)' (2012) 21 *African Security Review* 20.

SECRETARY-GENERAL[131]

The Secretary-General, who is appointed by the General Assembly on the recommendation of the Security Council,[132] is more than simply an international bureaucrat responsible for the management of the Secretariat of the United Nations. In terms of article 99 of the Charter, he is authorised to bring to the attention of the Security Council any matter that threatens international peace, a competence that carries with it the implied power to carry out investigations on his own initiative in order to inform the Security Council properly. Moreover, the Secretary-General is frequently instructed by the Security Council to act as mediator in disputes, a role pursued by successive Secretary-Generals in respect of South Africa's racial policies. The extent to which the Secretary-General becomes actively involved in the promotion of international peace will depend largely on his personality and perception of his office. Dag Hammarskjöld of Sweden (1953–1961) was an activist, who in effect directed the United Nations peacekeeping operation in the Congo (ONUC) when the Security Council was unable to give him instructions because of rivalry between the permanent members. Opposition to this activist approach among the permanent members led to the appointment of successor Secretary-Generals—U Thant of Burma (1961–1971) and Kurt Waldheim of Austria (1972–1981)—who adopted a more neutral stance and saw themselves largely as the bureaucratic servants of the permanent members of the Security Council. Pérez de Cuéllar of Peru (1982–1991) and Boutros Boutros-Ghali of Egypt (1992–1996) played a more active role, particularly in the promotion of peace-keeping operations. Kofi Annan of Ghana (1997–2006) brought a new independence and commitment to the office of Secretary-General but his successor, Ban Ki-moon, of South Korea (2007–2016), returned to the low-profile, bureaucratic style of earlier Secretary-Generals. Ban Ki-moon's successor, Antonio Guterres, a former Portuguese Prime Minister and former UN High Commissioner for Refugees, signalled his intention to play a more activist role, putting international peace as a priority, on assuming office on 1 January 2017.

REGIONAL ARRANGEMENTS[133]

The United Nations Charter contemplates that the United Nations will be assisted by regional arrangements in the quest for interna-

[131] See L Gordenker *The UN Secretary-General and the Maintenance of Peace* (1967); S Chesterman (ed) *Secretary or General? The UN Secretary-General in World Politics* (2007); J Dugard 'Advisory Opinions and the Secretary-General with special reference to the 2004 Advisory Opinion on the Wall' in L Boisson de Chazournes and M Kohen (eds) *International Law and the Quest for its Implementation: Liber Amicorum Vera Gowlland-Debbas* (2010) 403; Higgins et al (n 1) vol 1, 525 et seq.

[132] Article 97.

[133] See, generally, Sands and Klein (n 1).

tional peace, provided that their activities are consistent with the purposes and principles of the Charter. Indeed article 52(2) declares that members of the United Nations should make every effort to achieve pacific settlement of local disputes through regional arrangements before referring them to the Security Council.

The main regional arrangements are the Organization of American States (OAS), the African Union (AU) (previously the Organization of African Unity (OAU)), the Arab League (formally the League of Arab States, LAS), and the European Union (EU). The status of NATO, a regional collective security alliance, is considered in Chapter 24.

The Security Council may use regional arrangements for enforcement action under its authority. Thus, in Bosnia–Herzegovina, the United Nations made use of NATO to enforce 'no fly' prohibitions and to protect 'safe areas'. Moreover the Dayton Peace Agreement of 1995[134] envisaged that peace in Bosnia–Herzegovina would be maintained by a NATO multinational implementation force (IFOR), authorised by the Security Council acting under Chapter VII.[135] Following NATO's bombing of the Federal Republic of Yugoslavia in 1999, in order to compel it to desist from human rights violations in Kosovo, the Security Council, acting under Chapter VII, adopted Resolution 1244 on 10 June in which it authorised an 'international security presence' in Kosovo, 'with substantial NATO participation' to establish 'a safe environment for all people in Kosovo and to facilitate the safe return to their homes of all displaced persons and refugees'. As mentioned earlier, the Security Council's 2011 authorisation to states to take 'all necessary measures' to protect civilians in Libya[136] resulted in NATO taking military action against the Gaddafi regime.

Article 53 makes it clear that 'no enforcement action shall be taken under regional arrangements or by regional agencies without the authorisation of the Security Council'. For this reason, the attempt on the part of the United States to justify its naval 'quarantine', or blockade, of Cuba, in 1962, as regional action taken under the authority of the OAS, despite the failure of the Security Council to approve it, was misplaced. It may well have been an exercise in anticipatory self-defence,[137] but it could not be justified under article 53 of the Charter without clear authorisation from the United

[134] (1996) 35 *ILM* 75.

[135] Resolution 1031 (1995); (1996) 35 *ILM* 251. In 1996, IFOR gave way to SFOR (stabilisation force), which is also NATO led.

[136] Resolution 1973 (2011).

[137] See Chapter 24 below.

Nations.[138] The NATO bombing of the Federal Republic of Yugoslavia from March to June 1999, without Security Council authorisation, was likewise illegal regional action. NATO did not seriously argue that prior decisions of the Security Council condemning Yugoslavia for its repressive action against the people of Kosovo[139] constituted authorisation. Instead it sought to justify its action as humanitarian intervention.[140] Clearly, article 53 requires *prior* authorisation by the Security Council for any regional action involving the use of force. However, forcible interventions by the Economic Community of West African States (ECOWAS) in Liberia (1990–1991) and Sierra Leone (1997–1999), in response to humanitarian disasters, were endorsed by the Security Council after the interventions had occurred.[141]

South Africa became a member of the Southern African Development Community (SADC) in 1994.[142] Although SADC is principally aimed at promoting regional economic development, it also concerns itself with issues of regional security.[143] Suggestions that South Africa's intervention in Lesotho, in September 1998, was permissible regional action directed at the restoration of order in a fellow member state (Lesotho) were misguided as no prior—or subsequent—authorisation for military intervention was obtained from the Security Council. (This issue is considered further in Chapter 24.)

[138] See Q Wright 'The Cuban quarantine' (1963) 57 *AJIL* 546; *sed contra*, see LC Meeker 'Defensive quarantine and the law' (1963) 57 *AJIL* 515.

[139] Resolutions 1199 (1998) and 1203 (1998).

[140] See, further, Chapter 24.

[141] See T Franck *Recourse to Force: State Action against Threats and Armed Attacks* (2002) 155–62.

[142] The text of the Treaty establishing SADC appears in (1993) 32 *ILM* 116. South Africa became a member on 30 August 1994.

[143] In 1997, SADC adopted a Protocol on Politics, Defence and Security in the SADC Region: see (1999) 11 *AJICL* 197.

CHAPTER 24

The Use of Force by States

Dire Tladi and John Dugard

INTRODUCTION

The prohibition on the use of force is the cornerstone of the Charter of the United Nations (UN Charter) and one of the most fundamental rules of modern international law. Yet, international law did not outlaw war or the use of force[1] by states before 1928. Although, the distinction in doctrine, between 'just war' and 'unjust war' was quite prevalent,[2] the notion that recourse to war was permissible only when the cause was just, was not accepted by states.[3] Despite this, if only for reasons of political expediency, states did seek to justify their military actions. The right of self-defence, for instance, was frequently invoked as a ground for military intervention for political expediency and in order to secure the moral high ground. The Covenant of the League of Nations did not outlaw war. Instead, it set up settlement procedures designed to delay recourse to war, in the hope that this would restrain states from going to war.

In 1928, the General Treaty for the Renunciation of War,[4] also known as the Pact of Paris or the Kellogg-Briand Pact,[5] was signed. In this treaty, adopted outside the framework of the League of Nations, states 'condemn recourse to war for the solution of international controversies, and renounce it as an instrument of national policy in their relations with one another'. It was also agreed that

[1] See further on the use of force, I Brownlie *International Law and the Use of Force by States* (1963); Y Dinstein *War, Aggression and Self-Defence* 5 ed (2011); C Gray *International Law and the Use of Force by States* 3 ed (2008); T Franck *Recourse to Force: State Action against Threats and Armed Attacks* (2002); G Barrie 'Forcible intervention and international law: Legal theory and realities' (1999) 116 *SALJ* 791; M Byers *War Law* (2005); D Kennedy *Of Law and War* (2006); O Corten *The Law against War* (2012). For a comprehensive collection of articles on the use of force, see T Ruys and O Corten (with A Hofer) (eds) *The Use of Force in International Law: A Case-Based Approach* (2018).

[2] See, eg, MW Janis *International Law* (2016). For a history of the debate over just and unjust war, see Brownlie (n 1) ch 1. For a brief discussion of Grotius' advocacy of the just war doctrine, see J Dugard 'Grotius, the jurist and international lawyer: Four hundred years on' (1983) 100 *SALJ* 212 at 217–19.

[3] A Randelzhofer and O Dörr, 'Article 2(4)' in B Simma et al (eds) *The Charter of the United Nations: A Commentary* vol 2 (2012) 204.

[4] Treaty between the United States and other Powers Providing for the Renunciation of War as an Instrument of National Policy, Paris, 1928, 94 LNTS 57.

[5] Named after the US Secretary of State and the French Foreign Minister, respectively.

disputes were to be settled by 'pacific means'. The Kellogg-Briand Pact was accepted by over 60 states, including all the Great Powers of that period. South Africa, like many other states, became a party to the agreement subject to the right to go to war in self-defence, and to be released from the obligations of the treaty in respect of a party that violated the treaty.[6] Without any machinery for collective action against a state that violated its provisions, the Kellogg-Briand Pact was powerless to halt the aggressive wars that followed the advent of dictatorships in the 1930s. After World War II, however, it formed the basis for the prosecution of the Nazi and Japanese war leaders in the Nuremberg and Tokyo trials respectively, for 'crimes against peace' defined, inter alia, as the waging of a war in violation of international treaties.[7]

The Kellogg-Briand Pact remains in force, although its prohibition has now been subsumed by that of the UN Charter, which outlaws both war and the use of force.

THE PROHIBITION ON THE USE OF FORCE

The principal source on the prohibition against the use of force can be found in Article 2(4) of the Charter of the United Nations, which provides:

> All members shall refrain in their international relations from the threat or use of force against the territorial integrity or political independence of any state, or in any other manner inconsistent with the Purposes of the United Nations.

In 1986, this prohibition on the use of force was found to be a rule of customary law by the International Court of Justice in the *Nicaragua Case*.[8] Although, the Court was reluctant to explicitly declare the prohibition a norm of *jus cogens*, it implicitly endorsed the *jus cogens* status of the norm when it observed that

> it is frequently referred to in statements by state representatives as being not only a principle of customary international law but also a fundamental or cardinal principle of such law. The International Law Commission, in the course of its work on codification of the law of treaties, expressed the view that 'the law of the Charter concerning the prohibition of the use of force in itself constitutes a conspicuous example of a rule of international law having the character of *jus cogens*'.[9]

[6] S Pienaar *South Africa and International Relations between the Two World Wars: The League of Nations Dimension* (1987) 96.

[7] Brownlie (n 1) chs 9 and 10.

[8] *Military and Paramilitary Activities in and against Nicaragua (Nicaragua v USA) Merits* 1986 ICJ Reports 14 paras 98–100.

[9] Ibid para 190.

Like the prohibition on murder in domestic society, the prohibition on the use of force in international society is not always observed. However, it is recognised by states as a fundamental principle of the contemporary international legal order, as a norm with the status of *jus cogens*. States that violate this norm often seek to justify their action under one of the exceptions to the use of force. None denies the existence of such a rule.

The South African Constitution recognises the rules of international law governing the use of force. Section 200(2) provides:

> The primary object of the defence force is to defend and protect the Republic, its territorial integrity and its people in accordance with the Constitution and the principles of international law regulating the use of force.

The Defence Act of 2002, likewise, provides:

> The Defence Force must perform its functions in accordance with the Constitution and international law regulating the use of force.[10]

1 The forms of force prohibited

Article 2(4) is clear on a number of issues. Both the use and threat[11] of the use and threat of force are prohibited. Also, both declared and undeclared wars are outlawed. This extension of the prohibition contained in the Kellogg-Briand Pact is essential, as today few conflict situations are formally categorised as 'war' by the parties to the conflict. The prohibition on the use of force in article 2(4) is limited to force used in 'international relations'. International law prohibits neither recourse to revolution nor the suppression of an internal revolution. This traditional rule is now subject to developments in human rights and self-determination.

While the text of article 2(4) of the Charter seems relatively clear, questions have been raised about the qualifier 'against the territorial integrity or political independence of any state'. Some have suggested that this language narrows the scope of the prohibition. In other words, do these words suggest that actions aimed at 'noble' causes fall outside the prohibition since they are not directed at the territorial integrity or political independence of the state. In reality, however, these 'qualifiers' do not qualify the prohibition, but merely describe it. In other words, any use of force by one state against another state involves a breach of the territorial integrity or political independence of that state.

[10] Section 2*(c)* of Act 42 of 2002.

[11] On the prohibition on the threat of the use of force, see *Legality of the Threat or Use of Nuclear Weapons* 1996 ICJ Reports 226, para 47; N Stürchler *The Threat of Force in International Law* (2007).

Furthermore, the text of Article 2(4) does not provide a complete picture of the force that is prohibited. For such a picture, it is necessary to consider the subsequent practice of states and of the political organs of the United Nations, to the extent that the latter is reflective of or gives rise to the practice of states. Of particular importance is the General Assembly's Declaration on Principles of International Law concerning Friendly Relations and Co-operation among States in Accordance with the Charter of the United Nations of 1970,[12] (hereinafter referred to as the Declaration on Principles of International Law), which seeks to provide an authoritative interpretation of a number of key Charter provisions. From this, it is apparent that rules relating to the use of force have been modified in order to promote the interests of peoples struggling for self-determination against colonial regimes and alien subjugation.

Two issues relating to the meaning of the term, 'force' have given rise to debate. First, is the prohibition in article 2(4) limited to 'armed force'? Secondly, is the indirect use of force through surrogate forces outlawed?

(a) Economic force

The traditional view is that article 2(4) prohibits the use of *armed* force alone. This view is supported by the negotiating history of article 2(4),[13] and by the qualification of the term 'force' as 'armed force' in the preamble and article 46 of the Charter. Despite this, some states maintain that, as economic coercion may destroy the political independence of a state as effectively as armed force, it is essential to interpret article 2(4) to encompass all forms of force. This interpretation received little support from Western nations until the 1973 Arab oil boycott shook the economies of the West.[14]

Although the argument that article 2(4) prohibits economic coercion is generally not accepted, there is support for the view that economic coercion violates the principle of non-intervention unless authorised by the Security Council acting under Chapter VII of the Charter.[15] Here, reliance is placed on the 1970 Declaration on Principles of International Law, which prohibits the use of economic measures that aim 'to coerce another state in order to obtain from it

[12] Resolution 2625 (XXV).

[13] A Brazilian proposal to extend the prohibition of article 2(4) to include economic force was rejected during the drafting of the Charter: *United Nations Conference on International Organization, Documents* (1945), VI, 334–40.

[14] J Paust and AP Blaustein 'The Arab-Oil Weapon—A threat to international peace' (1974) 68 *AJIL* 410.

[15] See YZ Blum 'Economic boycotts in international law' (1977) 12 *Texas International Law Journal* 5 at 10.

the subordination of the exercise of its sovereign rights'.[16] On this basis, it has been argued that the economic sanctions imposed by states[17] on South Africa in order to coerce it to abandon apartheid were unlawful.[18] There was no substance in this argument. Even if it is accepted that economic coercion is an unlawful intervention under international law, it is clear that it is illegal only if it seeks to 'subordinate' the exercise of the target state's sovereign rights for some purpose inconsistent with the principles of the Charter. In the case of South Africa under apartheid, numerous recommendations of the General Assembly and Security Council designated the imposition of economic sanctions against South Africa as action designed to ensure compliance with the principles of the Charter.[19]

The uncertainty of the rules relating to the prohibition of economic coercion is illustrated by the *Nicaragua Case*,[20] in which the International Court of Justice found that the cessation of US economic aid to Nicaragua, the reduction in the sugar quota for US imports from Nicaragua, and a US trade embargo against Nicaragua, did not constitute a violation of the principle of non-intervention.

(b) Indirect force

If state 'A' gives active support to rebels of state 'B', such as permitting them to establish bases in its territory for attacks on state B, it makes itself a party to an unlawful use of force. Encouraging the organisation of armed bands for incursion into the territory of another state is a prohibited use of force, and this is confirmed by the 1970 Declaration on Principles of International Law, as well as by the International Court of Justice's decision in the *Nicaragua* case.[21] Here the Court held that the United States had violated the prohibition on the use of force by arming and training rebels but not by supplying funds to rebels. In recent times, this principle has been confirmed by Security Council resolutions condemning acts of terrorism which have reminded states of their obligation not to allow armed bands to use their territories for the commission of terrorist acts against other states.[22] The United States justified its 2001 invasion of Afghanistan

[16] Resolution 2625 (XXV).

[17] See, for instance, the United States Comprehensive Anti-Apartheid Act of 1986 (1987) 26 *ILM* 111.

[18] GN Barrie 'International law and economic coercion—A legal assessment' (1985–1986) 11 *SAYIL* 40.

[19] See K Ferguson-Brown 'The legality of economic sanctions against South Africa in contemporary international law' (1988–9) 14 *SAYIL* 59; above, Chapter 23 n 18.

[20] *Nicaragua* (n 8) paras 244–5.

[21] Ibid 118–19 (especially para 228).

[22] Resolutions 1373 (2001), 1566 (2004).

on the ground that the Taliban government of that country had allowed Al-Qaeda to operate from its territory and had thereby made itself a party to the unlawful use of force against the United States.[23]

Whether this prohibition extends to support for armed bands belonging to a national liberation movement seeking to assert the right to self-determination, is not so clear. The Court was careful, in the *Nicaragua Case*, to leave undecided the question whether support for armed bands in the 'process of decolonization' was prohibited,[24] while the 1970 Declaration on Principles of International Law suggests that there is no prohibition in such a case.[25]

Suggestions during the apartheid era that neighbouring states were permitted to allow the ANC and PAC to operate from their territories, on the ground that the prohibition on support for armed bands did not extend to forces engaged in the struggle to overthrow apartheid, led the apartheid regime to enter into non-aggression pacts with Swaziland and Mozambique. The pacts reiterated the prohibition on support for armed bands.[26] The Nkomati Accord[27] of 1984, between South Africa and Mozambique, provided in article 3:

> The High Contracting Parties shall not allow their respective territories . . . to be used as a base . . . by another state, government, foreign military forces, organizations or individuals which plan or prepare to commit acts of violence, terrorism or aggression against the territorial integrity or political independence of the other or may threaten the security of its inhabitants.

Mozambique had as much to gain from this Accord as South Africa, as the South African government had secretly permitted the Mozambique rebel group RENAMO to operate from its territory.

[23] See M Byers 'Terrorism, the use of force and international law after 11 September' (2002) 51 *ICLQ* 401, 408. For a repudiation of this justification, see G Abraham and K Hopkins 'Bombing for humanity: The American response to the 11 September attacks and the plea of self-defence' (2002) 119 *SALJ* 783.

[24] *Nicaragua* case (n 8) para108. In his dissenting opinion Judge Schwebel strongly criticised the approach of the Court on this issue. He held that the prohibition on support for armed bands extended to the 'process of decolonization' as well: 350–1.

[25] Resolution 2625 (XXV). This resolution declares that peoples pursuing their right to self-determination 'are entitled to seek and to receive support in accordance with the purposes and principles of the Charter' from other states. Whether military support accords with the principles of the Charter is highly debatable.

[26] South Africa–Swaziland Agreement Concerning Security (1984) 23 *ILM* 286.

[27] The text appears in 'Documentation: Nkomati Accord' (1984) 10 *SAYIL* 317; J Dugard 'Public international law' 1984 *Annual Survey* 68; (1984) 23 *ILM* 282. See, further, on the Nkomati Accord, G Erasmus *The Accord of Nkomati: Context and Content* (South African Institute of International Affairs 1984); T Stein 'South Africa's non-aggression agreements with the Frontline States' (1984) 10 *SAYIL* 1; M Beukes 'Nkomati: The Accord and its background' (1983) 9 *SAYIL* 116.

Similar non-aggression agreements were entered into between South Africa and the Bantustan states.[28]

CIRCUMSTANCES IN WHICH FORCE IS PERMITTED WITHOUT THE AUTHORISATION OF THE UNITED NATIONS

The UN Charter permits states to use force in only two circumstances: first, under the authority of the Security Council,[29] and, secondly, in the exercise of the right of individual or collective self-defence under article 51. The use of force by states under the authority of the United Nations is examined in Chapter 23.[30] This chapter will consider only the possible justifications for the use of force without the authorisation of the United Nations.

1 Self-defence

(a) General

The right of self-defence in international law exists to allow states to defend themselves against the unlawful use of force. It exists in tandem with the prohibition on the use of force. Although the Kellogg-Briand Pact did not include an express reference to 'self-defence',[31] it can be read to include the right of self-defence since it is the use of force 'as an instrument of national policy' that is renounced and the use of force in self-defence is not the same as the use of force as 'as an instrument of national policy'. It has been argued that the right to use force in self-defence as a matter of international law was formulated during the *Caroline* incident.[32] However, the *Caroline*

[28] See the pacts with Transkei (GN 1976 *GG* 5320 of 22 October 1976 (*Reg Gaz* 2384)), J Dugard 'Public international law' 1976 *Annual Survey* 27; Bophuthatswana (GN 2496 *GG* 5823 of 6 December 1977 (*Reg Gaz* 2569)), J Dugard 'Public international law' 1977 *Annual Survey* 50; Venda (GN 2014 *GG* 6652 of 12 September 1979 (*Reg Gaz* 2861)); and Ciskei (GN 691 *GG* 8204 of 14 May 1982 (*Reg Gaz* 3427)). In 1978 Transkei unilaterally suspended its non-aggression pact with South Africa: J Dugard 'Public international law' 1978 *Annual Survey* 59 at 64.

[29] Under Chapter VII, or article 53.

[30] Other exceptions to the prohibition, however, should be seen in the context of the framework of the Charter, grounded in the system of collective security. See in this regard D Tladi 'The use of force in self-defence against non-state actors, decline of collective security and the rise of unilateralism: Whither international law?' in D Tladi, C Tams and ME O'Connell *The Trialogues on the Use of Force against Non-State Actors* (2018).

[31] Above n 4.

[32] The *Caroline* incident of 1837 involved a dispute between the United States and Britain over the destruction by British forces in American waters of an American ship, the *Caroline*, used for transporting rebels to assist a rebellion against British rule in Canada. The US Secretary of State, Daniel Webster, informed the British government that for a plea of self-defence to succeed it would be necessary 'to show a necessity of

incident could not have reflected a formulation of self-defence under international law since international law did not, at that time, prohibit the use of force.[33] Self-defence, as a legal rule, does not make sense without the contemporaneous existence of the prohibition on the use of force.

The right of self-defence requires action taken in self-defence to be an immediate and necessary response to a situation threatening a state's security and vital interests. The response was to be kept within the bounds of proportionality. The right to self-defence can be exercised whether on land or the sea, including the high seas. To this end, the Maritime Zones Act of 1994 affirms this right in asserting that

> the Republic may take such action in any area of the sea or in the airspace above the sea, as is necessary in the exercise of the principle of self-defence contained in Article 51 of the Charter of the United Nations.[34]

Article 51 of the UN Charter is less generous. It provides:

> Nothing in the present Charter shall impair the inherent right of individual or collective self-defence if an armed attack occurs against a member of the United Nations, until the Security Council has taken measures necessary to maintain international peace and security. Measures taken by members in the exercise of this right of self-defence shall be immediately reported to the Security Council and shall not in any way affect the authority and responsibility of the Security Council under the present Charter to take at any time such action as it deems necessary in order to maintain or restore international peace and security.

The International Court of Justice has suggested that the content of the right to self-defence under the Charter and under customary

self-defence, instant, overwhelming, leaving no choice of means and no moment for deliberation' and that the action was neither 'unreasonable nor excessive'. The exchange between the United States and United Kingdom governments is reproduced in full in JB Moore *Digest of International Law as Embodied in Diplomatic Discussions, Treaties and Other International Agreements: Volume II* (Washington: U.S. Government Printing Office 1906) 409–13. See RY Jennings 'The *Caroline* and *McLeod Cases*' (1938) 32 *AJIL* 82; AC Arend 'International law and preemptive use of military force' (2003) 26 *The Washington Quarterly* 89, 90; C Richter 'Pre-emptive self-defence, international law and US policy' (2003) 1 *Dialogue* 55, 57; J Paust 'Self-defence targeting of non-state actors and permissibility of U.S. use of drones in Pakistan' (2010) 19 *Journal of Transnational Law and Policy* 237, 241; SD Murphy 'Self-defence and the Israeli Wall Advisory Opinion: An *ipse dixit* from the ICJ?' (2005) 99 *American Journal of International Law* 62, 65. The right of self-defence under customary international law is not to be equated with self-preservation. For this reason, the comment of Smuts J, that 'the right of national security and of self-preservation is superior to all other rights' in *Nkondo v Minister of Police* 1980 (2) SA 894 (O) 903C–D, is unfortunate.

[33] See D Tladi 'The use of force in self-defence against non-state actors in international law: Recalling the foundational principles of international law' (2012) 2 *Zanzibar Yearbook of Law* 71.

[34] Section 11 of Act 15 of 1994.

international law is not exactly the same.[35] The Court pointed to the fact that the article 51 did not contain the requirements of proportionality and necessity, which were part of customary international law on self-defence.[36] Yet, in reality, these requirements must be seen, through the operation of the rules of interpretation,[37] as forming part of article 51 of the Charter.

For a state to resort to self-defence it must be able to show that it has been the victim of an 'armed attack'. What constitutes an 'armed attack' is a difficult question and must be decided on the facts of each case. The International Court of Justice has, however, made it clear that not every act constituting an unlawful use of force constitutes an armed attack. In the *Nicaragua Case* the Court distinguished the 'most grave forms of the use of force (those constituting an armed attack) from other grave forms'.[38] In the *Oil Platforms Case*[39] the Court reaffirmed this *dictum* and held that a number of acts carried out by Iran involving the use of force did not constitute armed attacks justifying action in self-defence by the United States.

Some writers argue that article 51 contains a complete and exclusive formulation of the right of self-defence,[40] while others maintain that the phrase 'inherent right' in article 51 preserves the pre-Charter customary right.[41] In the *Nicaragua Case*, the International Court gave support to the latter view, when it held that 'article 51 of the Charter is only meaningful on the basis that there is a "natural" or "inherent" right of self-defence, and it is hard to see how this can be other than of a customary nature, even if its present content has been confirmed and influenced by the Charter'.[42] The International Court confirmed this approach in its Advisory Opinion on the *Legality of the Threat or Use of Nuclear Weapons* when it declared that some of the constraints on the resort to self-defence 'are inherent in the very concept of self-defence', while others are specified in article 51. Moreover, said the Court:

> The submission of the exercise of the right of self-defence to the conditions of necessity and proportionality is a rule of customary international law.[43]

[35] *Nicaragua* case (n 8) para 175.

[36] Ibid 176.

[37] See Chapter 21.

[38] *Nicaragua* (n 8) para 191.

[39] Case *Concerning Oil Platforms (Islamic Republic of Iran v United States of America)* 2003 ICJ Reports, paras 51, 76.

[40] Brownlie (n 1) 272–5; H Kelsen *Law of the United Nations* (1950) 914.

[41] D Bowett *Self-Defence in International Law* (1958) 184–6.

[42] *Nicaragua* case (n 8) para 94.

[43] *Nuclear Weapons* Advisory Opinion (n 11) paras 40–1. The Court confirmed this *dictum* in the *Oil Platforms* case (n 39) para 76.

At any rate, since the content of self-defence under customary international law is similar to the rule in article 51, not much flows from this debate.[44]

Because article 51 provides the only escape from the prohibition on the use of force, states have sought to expand its terms generously to permit recourse to force in a wide range of situations. Some of the arguments raised in support of actions taken in self-defence are considered below.

One of those most controversial issues in contemporary international law, is the question whether, a state is permitted to use force against non-state actors in the territory of third states.[45] This issue is considered separately in section 8 of this chapter.

(b) *Anticipatory self-defence and pre-emptive action*

Legal scholars are divided as to whether article 51 allows anticipatory self-defence. One school argues that article 51 permits force to be used in self-defence if, and only if, an armed attack occurs.[46] Another argues that the customary-law right of anticipatory self-defence is preserved by the phrase 'inherent right' in article 51, and that in the context of modern weaponry it is ridiculous to argue that the drafters of the Charter could have intended to exclude such a right.[47]

On a number of occasions, states have invoked anticipatory self-defence to justify their actions. Israel justified its attack on Egypt, at the start of the Six-Day War in 1967, as anticipatory self-defence on the grounds that the mobilisation of Egyptian forces on the Israeli border, the closure of the Straits of Tiran, and the conclusion of a military pact between Egypt and Jordan, provided evidence of an

[44] C Tams 'Self-defence against non-state actors: Making sense of the 'armed attack' requirement' in Tladi, Tams and O'Connell (n 30), advocates a slightly different view. He suggests that that both customary international law and treaty law apply, but any potential controversy should be addressed by 'according primacy to [the] treaty rules'. Thus, he argues, we should expect the 'customary self-defence to "recede" behind the Charter rule'.

[45] For literature on this issue see: Tladi, Tams and O'Connell (n 30), Murphy (n 32), Paust (n 32), A Ozubide 'How the use of force against non-state actors transformed the law of self-defence after 9/11' (2016) 41 *SAYIL* 1.

[46] Brownlie (n 1) 275–8; Dinstein (n 1) 166–8; L Henkin *How Nations Behave* 2 ed (1979) 141–5.

[47] Bowett (n 41) 187–93; M McDougal 'The Soviet Cuban quarantine and self-defense' (1963) 57 *AJIL* 597; dissenting opinion of Judge Schwebel in the *Nicaragua Case* 1986 ICJ Reports 347–8. For a survey of the literature, see CJ Botha 'Anticipatory self-defence and reprisals re-examined, South African attacks on ANC bases in neighbouring states' (1985–6) 11 *SAYIL* 138 at 145–57. See, further, K Motshabi 'International law and the US raid on Libya' (1987) 104 *SALJ* 669.

imminent attack.[48] Again, in 1981, Israel justified its destruction of an Iraqi nuclear reactor as anticipatory self-defence.[49] Although the United States government preferred to justify its blockade, or 'quarantine', of Cuba in 1962 as regional action under the authority of the OAS,[50] many lawyers argued that it would have been more appropriate to justify it as anticipatory self-defence. As none of these arguments were approved by the Security Council[51] it is difficult to maintain that state practice supports a right of anticipatory self-defence. The International Court of Justice carefully avoided pronouncing on this issue in the *Nicaragua Case*,[52] but its endorsement of the view that article 51 preserves the customary right of self-defence[53] lends support to the argument that the right of anticipatory self-defence is still a part of international law. For anticipatory self-defence, however, an attack, though not yet commenced, must be imminent.

In recent years, an even wider notion of self-defence has appeared in the practice of states: pre-emptive action. In 2002, in the wake of 9/11, President Bush issued a new National Security Strategy, which declared:

> For centuries, international law recognised that nations need not suffer an attack before they can lawfully take action to defend themselves against forces that present an imminent danger of attack. Legal scholars and international jurists often conditioned the legitimacy of pre-emption on the existence of an imminent threat—most often a visible mobilization of armies, navies, and air forces preparing to attack.
>
> We must adapt the concept of imminent threat to the capabilities and objectives of today's adversaries. Rogue states and terrorists do not seek to attack us using conventional means. They know such attacks would fail. Instead they rely on acts of terror and, potentially, the use of weapons of mass destruction—weapons that can easily be concealed, delivered covertly, and used without warning.

[48] See M Oren *Six Days of* War (2002). Cf J Quiqley 'The six day war—1967' in Ruys, Corten and Hofer (n 1); J Quigley *The Six-Day War and Self Defence. Questioning the Legal Basis for Preventive War* (2013).

[49] T Ruys 'Israel's airstrikes against Iraq's Osirag Nuclear Reactor—1981' [. . .]; WT Mallison and SV Mallison' The Israeli aerial attack of June 7, 1981, upon the Iraqi Nuclear Reactor: Aggression or self-defense?' (1982) 15 *Vanderbilt Journal of Transnational Law* 417.

[50] See for discussion, A Orakhelashvili 'The Cuban Missile Crisis—1962' in Ruys, Corten and Hofer (n 1). LC Meeker 'Defensive quarantine and the law' (1963) 57 *AJIL* 515.

[51] The Security Council took no resolution on either the 1967 Six-Day War or the Cuban missile crisis. It did, however, unanimously condemn Israel's attack on the Iraqi nuclear reactor: Resolution 487 (1981) (text in (1981) 75 *AJIL* 724).

[52] *Nicaragua* case (n 8) para 103.

[53] Ibid, para 94.

> . . .
>
> The United States has long maintained the option of pre-emptive actions to counter a sufficient threat to our national security. The greater the threat, the greater is the risk of inaction—and the more compelling the case for taking anticipatory action to defend ourselves, even if uncertainty remains as to the time and place of the enemy's attack. To forestall or prevent such hostile acts by our adversaries the United States will, if necessary, act pre-emptively.[54]

Whereas a state that relies on anticipatory self-defence will be able to point to a 'palpable and imminent threat', the state that claims to act in pre-emptive self-defence will point only to an attack as a possibility. Inevitably, in such a case the evidence of a possible attack will be ill defined and speculative.[55]

The International Court of Justice has interpreted article 51 strictly[56] and given no support to the notion of pre-emptive action. In the *Legal Consequences of the Construction of a Wall in the Occupied Palestinian Territory* the Court held that the construction of a 'security wall' in Palestinian territory could not be justified on grounds of self-defence against possible attacks by Palestinian militants.[57] Moreover, in *Armed Activities in the Territory of the Congo* the Court rejected claims by Uganda that it had intervened in the Democratic Republic of the Congo in self-defence, holding that Uganda's actions were 'essentially preventative' and that article 51 'does not allow the use of force by a state to protect perceived security interests'.[58]

In 2004, a High-Level Panel on Threats, Challenges and Change, appointed by the Secretary-General of the United Nations to make proposals for the reform of the institutions for collective security, submitted a report,[59] in which it gave approval to the right of a state to take unilateral military action 'as long as the threatened attack is *imminent*, no other means would deflect it, and the action is proportionate'. The High-Level Panel stated that, while a state might act 'pre-emptively' against an imminent or proximate threat, it could not act 'preventively' without approval from the Security Council. This indicates support for a moderate form of anticipatory self-defence but falls short of approval for pre-emptive action.

[54] (2002) 41 *ILM* 1478.

[55] WM Reisman and A Armstrong 'The past and future of the claim of preemptive self-defense' (2006) 100 *AJIL* 525.

[56] J Green *The International Court of Justice and Self-Defense in International Law* (2009).

[57] *Legal Consequences of the Construction of a Wall in the Occupied Palestinian Territory*, 2004 ICJ Reports 136 para 139.

[58] *Case Concerning the Armed Activities in the Territory of the Congo (Democratic Republic of the Congo v Uganda)*, 2005 ICJ Reports 168 paras 143 and 148.

[59] *A More Secure World: Our Shared Responsibility* United Nations, 2004, UN Doc A/59/565 at 54 (emphasis original).

(c) *Self-defence and accumulation of events*

An unresolved aspect of the debate over anticipatory self-defence concerns the question of whether a state, subjected to a series of cross-border guerrilla raids from a neighbouring territory, is entitled to retaliate in self-defence. Here, the target state does not respond to each raid which is often small, involving only a handful of guerrillas and causing little injury to life and property in the target state, and not in itself constituting an 'armed attack'. Instead, it allows the raids to accumulate and then retaliates by attacking guerrilla bases at what it considers to be the opportune time. The delay in the response gives such action a punitive appearance, which would suggest that it is an act of reprisal, but its purpose is protective—to protect the target state against further, predictable, attacks. Action of this kind, described as the response to an 'accumulation of events', has been justified as anticipatory self-defence[60] in both the Middle East[61] and southern Africa.[62]

In 1982, the South African Defence Force (SADF) attacked houses in Maseru, which were claimed to be occupied by members of the ANC.[63] Forty-two persons were killed, including women and children. According to the Chief of the Defence Force, this raid was 'a pre-emptive strike aimed at forestalling attacks on South Africa during the festive season'.[64] In 1986, the SADF carried out simultaneous military raids against ANC bases in Zimbabwe, Zambia, and Botswana, in which people were killed and extensive damage was done to property.[65] On this occasion, State President PW Botha justified the action as follows:

> [I]t is a particularly serious transgression of international law for states to provide sanctuary to elements which plan, instigate and execute acts of terror against other states, as is happening in Southern Africa. It is an established principle of international law that when this occurs, the state against which such acts are perpetrated, has the right to resort to acts of self-defence and to carry out pre-emptive strikes.[66]

[60] See DW Bowett 'Reprisals involving recourse to armed force' (1972) 66 *AJIL* 1.

[61] Ibid 5–6; YZ Blum 'The Beirut raid and the international double standard' (1970) 64 *AJIL* 73.

[62] See Botha (n 47); JC Heunis *United Nations versus South Africa* (1986) 393–436.

[63] T Reinold 'South African incursion into Lesotho—1982' in Ruys, Corten and Hofer (n 1).

[64] G Carpenter 'The South African raid on terrorist bases in Lesotho' (1982) 8 *SAYIL* 154.

[65] E Kwakwa 'South Africa's May 1986 military incursions into neighbouring African states' (1987) 12 *Yale Journal of International Law* 421.

[66] *House of Assembly Debates* 20 May 1986 (cols 6032–4).

During the 1980s, many such raids on ANC bases in neighbouring states were undertaken.[67] An even greater number were undertaken against SWAPO bases in Angola from South African military bases in Namibia.[68]

Neither Israel[69] nor South Africa[70] succeeded in persuading the Security Council that their actions were undertaken in self-defence. Most of these raids were strongly condemned by the Security Council and the 'accumulation of events' version of anticipatory self-defence was repudiated.[71]

Bowett[72] has suggested that if such raids are not to be classified as anticipatory self-defence, they should be treated as permissible reprisal action. Like self-defence, reprisal action requires a prior unlawful act against the claimant state by the target state, a failed attempt to secure redress by other means, and a proportionate response. Despite their similarities, the Charter permits self-defence, while article 2(4) outlaws forcible reprisals.[73] The reason for this is that the former is protective in purpose, while the latter are punitive.

(d) Collective self-defence

The UN Charter distinguishes between collective security, which is to be undertaken by the Security Council acting under Chapter VII, and collective self-defence, which may be exercised by states under article 51 without United Nations authorisation. From this, it follows that a state may only assist an attacked state in collective self-defence when the attack, in its context, also threatens the security—the 'self'—of the assisting state.[74] If there is no such threat to the assisting state, it is

[67] See Botha (n 47) 138–41; K Motshabi 'South Africa's actions against neighbouring states' in M Orkin (ed) *Sanctions against Apartheid* (1989) 123; FM Higginbotham 'International law, the use of force in self-defense and the southern African conflict' (1987) 25 *Columbia Journal of Transnational Law* 529, 561–72.

[68] These attacks were condemned by the Security Council, inter alia, on the ground that South Africa used the international territory of Namibia 'as a springboard' for perpetrating the armed attacks: see resolutions 387 (1976), 428 (1978), 447 (1979), 475 (1980), 543 (1984), 546 (1984), 567 (1985).

[69] Bowett (n 60) at 7–9.

[70] The 1982 Maseru raid was condemned in resolution 527 (1982) ((1982) 8 *SAYIL* 211–12). See, too, resolution 568 (1985) condemning a SADF attack on a civilian target in Gaborone in which 12 people were killed (J Dugard 'Public international law' 1985 *Annual Survey* 69). See, further, Higginbotham (n 67).

[71] Bowett (n 60) 7–9.

[72] Ibid.

[73] The 1970 Declaration on Principles of International Law declares that 'states have a duty to refrain from acts of reprisal involving the use of force' (General Assembly resolution 2625 (XXV)).

[74] Bowett (n 41) 206–7; See, too, the dissenting opinion of Judge Jennings in the *Nicaragua* case (n 8) paras 545–6.

required to request the Security Council to take the necessary action under Chapter VII.

The breakdown of the United Nations system of collective security during the Cold War led to the abandonment of this distinction.[75] The North Atlantic Treaty Organization (NATO) was founded in 1949 to provide for a system of regional collective self-defence. In terms of article 5 of the NATO Treaty,[76] states in Western Europe and North America agreed that 'an armed attack against one . . . shall be considered an attack against them all' requiring a collective armed response under article 51 to assist the victim. The Warsaw Pact,[77] founded by the Soviet Bloc in 1955, contained a similar provision designed to protect states in Eastern Europe from Western aggression. Whereas an attack by the Soviet Union on West Germany no doubt would have threatened the security of all NATO members, it could hardly be suggested that an attack by Syria on Greece (a member of NATO) would have threatened the security of Canada (a member of NATO). Thus, it appears that both the NATO and Warsaw Pacts extended beyond the permissible limits of true collective self-defence and, instead, sought to usurp the collective security function of the Security Council of the United Nations.

Today, the abandonment of the distinction between collective security and collective self-defence seems complete. In the *Nicaragua Case*, the International Court of Justice failed to insist on any self-interest on the part of the assisting state and only required that the victim state should declare that it had been attacked and request the assistance of other states.[78] Furthermore, in 1990, the Security Council itself recognised the right of third states to aid Kuwait against Iraq—at Kuwait's request—even though those states had not been attacked and had no treaty or special links with Kuwait.[79]

The Warsaw Pact was dissolved when the Cold War came to an end. NATO has been expanded to include some former member states of the Warsaw Pact and no longer sees itself as an organisation whose only aim is the defence of the North Atlantic region. Instead, it appears to view itself as an organisation committed to the defence of the world against rogue states with weapons of mass destruction

[75] Brownlie (n 1) claims that state practice has never supported such a distinction. He argues that '[t]here is a customary right . . . to aid third states which have become the object of an unlawful use of force. It is immaterial whether this right is called a sanction, collective defence or collective self-defence' (330–1).

[76] 4 UNTS 243.

[77] (1955) 49 *AJIL* Suppl 194.

[78] *Nicaragua* case (n 8) para 105.

[79] Resolutions 661 and 678 (1990); O Schachter 'United Nations law in the Gulf Conflict' (1991) 85 *AJIL* 452 at 457.

(Iraq) and to the advancement of human rights and good governance within Europe (Kosovo). Neither NATO's own constitution, founded on the principle that an attack against one member state is an attack on all, nor the UN Charter provides a basis for NATO's new role. Collective security involving the use of force remains the responsibility of the Security Council. So does humanitarian assistance involving the use of force.

2 Hot pursuit

On some occasions, the SADF justified its cross-border raids during the apartheid era as 'hot pursuit'.[80] Although it is not uncommon to describe 'follow-up' operations into another state's territory as hot pursuit,[81] this is an unfortunate misuse of the term. Hot pursuit is a doctrine belonging to the law of the sea that permits a warship to pursue and arrest a ship on the high seas if it has violated the laws applicable in the maritime zones of the coastal state. It ceases as soon as the pursued ship enters its own territorial waters or those of another state.[82] As hot pursuit on land results in the violation of the territorial sovereignty of another state, it is not analogous to the doctrine of hot pursuit known to the law of the sea. For this reason, hot pursuit on land is not recognised by international law.[83] If a state wishes to justify cross-border raids, it must do so in terms of the right of self-defence. In the Southern African context, such pursuits were frequently a pretext for the unlawful violation of a neighbour's territorial sovereignty. In 1985, the Security Council condemned a South African raid on Gaborone in which 12 people were killed, and rejected 'South Africa's practice of "hot pursuit" to terrorize and destabilize Botswana and other countries in southern Africa'.[84]

3 Defence of nationals

Customary international law recognised the right of a state to use force to protect its nationals abroad. Today this right is asserted by

[80] AJ Luttig 'The legality of the Rhodesian military operations inside Mozambique—The problem of hot pursuit on land' (1977) 3 *SAYIL* 136 at 145.

[81] Luttig (n 80); RP Pace 'Word die spontane agtervolgingsleerstuk misbruik?' (1976) 39 *THRHR* 66.

[82] Above, Chapter 17.

[83] Bowett (n 41) 38–41; NM Poulantzas *The Right of Hot Pursuit in International Law* (1969); TM Kühn 'Terrorism and the right of self-defence' (1980) 6 *SAYIL* 42 at 49–50; DJ Devine 'International law tensions' 1987 *Acta Juridica* 165 at 185; Motshabi (n 68) 127.

[84] N Hajjami 'The intervention of the United States and other Eastern Caribbean states in Grenada—1983' in Ruys, Corten and Hofer (n 1).

those who take a broad view of article 51,[85] and denied by those who see article 51 as excluding the customary-law right.[86] This is a species of self-defence that lends itself to serious abuse, as illustrated by the numerous occasions on which the United States has invoked it as a pretext for military intervention in Latin-American states, including Grenada in 1983,[87] and Panama in 1989.[88] On the other hand , the fact that a right may be abused should not result in its denial. That there are circumstances in which this form of intervention is justified, is illustrated by the Entebbe incident,[89] in which Israeli commandos intervened forcibly to rescue Israeli nationals held hostage by Palestinian terrorists in Entebbe, Uganda, after their flight from Tel Aviv to Paris had been hijacked, and the Ugandan authorities had failed to secure their release. On this occasion, the three conditions required by customary international law for intervention were present: first, an imminent danger of injury to nationals; secondly, a failure or inability on the part of the territorial sovereign (Uganda) to protect the nationals; and, thirdly, the measures of protection taken by Israel were confined to protecting its nationals against injury.[90] In February 2011, the British government, by means of an airlift, intervened in Libya to rescue British oil workers whose lives were at risk in the chaos that followed the overthrow of the Gaddafi regime in eastern Libya. Here too the requirements of customary international law for such an intervention were met.

It is generally accepted that this right applies to the protection of persons only, and not to property.[91]

Sometimes the right of self-defence of nationals is portrayed as the ultimate form of diplomatic protection of nationals. The International Law Commission has, however, dismissed this argument, deciding

[85] Bowett (n 41) 87–105; R Lillich, T Wingfield and J Meyen (eds) *Lillich on the Forcible Protection of Nationals Abroad* (2002); Franck (n 1) 76–96.

[86] Brownlie (n 1) 289–301; N Ronzitti *Rescuing Nationals Abroad through Military Coercion and Intervention on Grounds of Humanity* (1985).

[87] Hajjami (n 1).

[88] Ved P Nanda 'The validity of United States intervention in Panama under international law' (1990) 84 *AJIL* 494; Franck (n 1) 91. N Tsagouris 'The US intervention in Panama—1989' in Ruys, Corten and Hofer (n 1).

[89] C Kreß and BN Nußberger 'The Entebbe Raid—1976' in Ruys, Corten and Hofer (n 1); RD Margo 'The legality of the Entebbe raid in international law' (1977) 94 *SALJ* 306; Franck (n 1) 82.

[90] H Waldock 'The regulation of the use of force by individual states in international law' (1952-II) 81 *Recueil des Cours* 455 at 466–7.

[91] Bowett (n 41) 100–5.

that the use of force cannot be justified as an exercise of diplomatic protection.[92]

4 Humanitarian intervention[93]

On several occasions before 1945, states intervened in other states to protect non-nationals where their treatment was so outrageous that it 'shocked the conscience of mankind'.[94] Inevitably, such 'humanitarian interventions' often masked an ulterior political purpose. Since 1945 arguments have been raised in support of the continuance of this right. Indeed, it has been suggested that India's intervention in East Pakistan (now Bangladesh) in 1971 and Tanzania's invasion of Uganda in 1979 were examples of humanitarian intervention, despite the fact that in neither of these cases did the invading power justify its action on this ground, preferring instead to justify their actions as self-defence.[95]. However, humanitarian intervention falls within the scope of the prohibition in article 2(4) of the Charter;[96] there is little state practice to support it and it is objected to by a large number of states, in particular the Non-Aligned Movement;[97] and the danger of abuse of such a right outweighs its benefit to humanity. At best 'it cannot be said to be unambiguously illegal'.[98]

As the Security Council is not bound by the prohibition contained in article 2(4), when it acts under Chapter VII, it may recommend intervention on humanitarian grounds by United Nations forces (as in Bosnia–Herzegovina)[99] or by individual states in appropriate circumstances. For instance, in 1991, the Security Council, in an

[92] *Report of International Law Commission GAOR* 55th session, supplement No 10 (A/55/10) 148–52.

[93] F Teson *Humanitarian Intervention: An Inquiry into Law and Morality* 2 ed (1997); J Holzgrefe and R Keohane (eds) *Humanitarian Intervention: Ethical, Legal and Political Dilemmas* (2003); Franck (n 1) 135–73; A Roberts 'The so-called "right" of humanitarian intervention' (2000) 3 *Yearbook of International Humanitarian Law* 3; GN Barrie 'Humanitarian intervention in the post-cold war era' (2001) 118 *SALJ* 155; S Chesterman *Just War or Just Peace. Humanitarian Intervention and International Law* (2001); N Wheeler *Saving Strangers: Humanitarian Intervention in International Society* (2002); R Goodman 'Humanitarian intervention and pretexts for war' (2006) 100 *AJIL* 107.

[94] The most frequently cited example is France's intervention in Syria in 1860–61 to protect the Maronite Christians from further massacres.

[95] See Franck (n 1) 139–45.

[96] Ibid 136–7.

[97] See, eg 17 Summit of Heads of State and Government of the Non-Aligned Movement, 16–17 September 2016, where it was stated that the humanitarian intervention 'has no basis either in the UN Charter or international law'.

[98] See UK Foreign Policy Document No 148 published in (1986) 57 *BYIL* 614 (para II 22).

[99] Resolution 752 (1992).

ambiguously phrased resolution,[100] approved (or at least tolerated) the intervention of the United States, the United Kingdom and France in Northern Iraq to protect Kurds against the savagery of Saddam Hussein's forces in the wake of the Gulf War.[101]

NATO's recourse to the use of force against the Federal Republic of Yugoslavia in 1999, in order to resolve a humanitarian crisis caused by Yugoslavia's violation of human rights in its province of Kosovo, is, possibly, an example of humanitarian intervention. That there was a humanitarian crisis in Kosovo that threatened international peace and security in terms of Chapter VII of the Charter was recognised by the Security Council in two resolutions adopted in 1998.[102] The Council warned of the 'impending humanitarian catastrophe' in Kosovo and demanded that measures be taken by Yugoslavia and the Kosovo Albanian leadership to avert such a catastrophe. The Security Council failed, however, to authorise the use of force to avert the catastrophe. When the situation deteriorated, and it became clear that Russia would veto a Security Council resolution for the authorisation of the use of force, NATO resorted to military action without Security Council authorisation.

The NATO intervention in Kosovo was not based on self-defence and nor was it authorised by the UN Security Council. It was initiated because of an ongoing humanitarian crisis which had been acknowledged by the Security Council. Whether such a determination provided a legal basis for NATO's action is debatable.[103] One school argued that NATO's action was a clear violation of the Charter, while another contended that the gravity of the human calamity in Kosovo, coupled with the Security Council resolutions designating the situation as a humanitarian catastrophe, justified NATO intervention. The United Kingdom sought to argue that the intervention was legally justified on the basis of humanitarian

[100] Resolution 688 (1991). See for discussion E de Wet 'The Gulf War—1990–1991' in Ruys, Corten and Hofer (n 1).

[101] Franck (n 1) 152.

[102] Resolutions 1199 (1998) and 1203 (1998).

[103] There is a wealth of literature on this subject. See B Simma 'NATO, the UN and the use of force: Legal aspects' (1999) 10 *EJIL* 1; A Cassese '*Ex Injuria Jus Oritur*: Are we moving towards legitimation of forcible humanitarian countermeasures in the world community?' (1999) 10 *EJIL* 23; 'Symposium: The International Legal Fall-out from Kosovo' (2001) *EJIL* 391–537; D Kritsiotis 'The Kosovo Crisis and NATO's application of armed force against the Federal Republic of Yugoslavia' (2000) 49 *ICLQ* 330; A Boyle 'Kosovo: House of Commons Foreign Affairs Committee 4th Report, June 2000' (with memoranda submitted by I Brownlie, C Chinkin, C Greenwood and V Lowe) (2000) 49 *ICLQ* 876–943; 'Editorial comments: NATO's Kosovo intervention' (with comments by L Henkin, R Wedgwood, J Charney, C Chinkin, RA Falk, T Franck and WM Reisman) (1999) 93 *AJIL* 824–62.

intervention.[104] This view had limited support in international scholarship.[105] Other participating states, however, though justifying the necessity of the action never claimed it was legally justified. The US, for example, stated that the actions of NATO were 'necessary to respond to Belgrade's brutal persecution of Kosovar Albanians, violations of international law, excessive and indiscriminate use of force' and that these actions by Belgrade 'foreshadow[ed] a humanitarian catastrophe of immense proportions,' but never claimed that the actions were legal.[106] Moreover, other states, including Russia,[107] China,[108] India,[109] Malaysia,[110] and Ukraine[111] questioned the legality of the intervention. Russia attempted to persuade the Security Council to condemn NATO aggression, but this proposal was defeated by three votes in favour and 12 against.[112]

The International Court of Justice avoided pronouncing on this issue in proceedings brought against NATO member states by Yugoslavia on the ground that it lacked jurisdiction.[113] Probably the most satisfactory solution is that given by the Independent International Commission on Kosovo, chaired by South African Constitutional Court judge and former prosecutor for the International Criminal Tribunal for the Former Yugoslavia, Richard Goldstone, which found:

> [T]he NATO campaign was illegal, yet legitimate. Such a conclusion is related to the controversial idea that a 'right' of humanitarian intervention is not consistent with the UN Charter if conceived as a legal text, but that it may, depending on context, nevertheless, reflect the spirit of Charter as it relates to

[104] United Nations Security Council, 3988th Meeting on 24 March 1999 (UN Doc} S/PV.3988), 12. Sir Jeremy Greenstock on behalf of the UK stated: 'The action being taken is legal. It is justified as an exceptional measure to prevent an overwhelming humanitarian catastrophe.' He further stated that 'Every means short of force has been tried to avert this situation. In these circumstances, and as an exceptional measure on grounds of overwhelming humanitarian necessity, military intervention is legally justifiable.'

[105] FR Teson 'Kosovo: A powerful precedent for the doctrine of humanitarian intervention' (2009) 1 *Amsterdam Law Forum* 42; C Greenwood *Humanitarian Intervention: The Case of Kosovo* (2002) 12 *Finnish Yearbook of International Law* 141.

[106] United Nations Security Council, 3988th Meeting, 24 March 1999 (UN Doc S/PV.3988), 4.

[107] Ibid 2

[108] Ibid 12

[109] Ibid 15

[110] Ibid 9

[111] Ibid 10

[112] Franck (n 1) 167–9.

[113] *Cases concerning the Legality of the Use of Force (Serbia and Montenegro v Belgium et al)* 2004 ICJ Reports; (2005) 44 *ILM* 299.

the overall protection of people against gross abuse.[114]

This view seems to liken humanitarian intervention to euthanasia: it remains unlawful but is tolerated in genuine cases.

In 2000 the Constitutive Act of the African Union was adopted, which, in article 4(h), recognises the right of the African Union 'to intervene in a member state pursuant to a decision of the Assembly in respect of grave circumstances, namely: war crimes, genocide and crimes against humanity.' Surprisingly, the drafters of the Constitutive Act did not consider the apparent conflict between this provision and article 2(4) of the UN Charter or the need for Security Council authorisation for regional action involving the use of force.[115] To date, despite a number of situations involving grave human rights violations on the African continent, such as Darfur, Zimbabwe, Côte D'Ivoire and Libya, there has been no attempt to invoke article 4(h).

In 2005, following intense discussion of humanitarian intervention and the responsibility of the international community to protect societies subjected to grave human rights violations,[116] the General Assembly of the United Nations adopted resolution 60/1, titled the World Summit Outcome Document, which after declaring that states have a 'responsibility to protect' (now referred to as 'R2P') their population from genocide, war crimes, ethnic cleansing and crimes against humanity, declares:

> The international community, through the United Nations, also has the responsibility to use appropriate diplomatic, humanitarian and other peaceful means, in accordance with Chapters VI and VII of the Charter, to help protect populations from genocide, war crimes, ethnic cleansing and crimes against humanity. In this context we are prepared to take collection action, in a timely and decisive manner, through the Security Council, in accordance with the Charter, including Chapter VII, on a case-by-case basis and in cooperation with relevant regional organizations as appropriate, should peaceful means be inadequate and national authorities are manifestly failing to protect their populations from genocide, war crimes, ethnic cleansing and crimes against humanity.

[114] *The Kosovo Report* (2000) 186. See, too, Franck (n 1) 180, 184. See for discussion, including criticism and dangers of the 'unlawful but legitimate' language D Franchini and A Tzanakopoulos 'The Kosovo crisis—1999' in Ruys, Corten and Hofer (n 1).

[115] M Kunschak 'The African Union and the right to intervention: Is there a need for Security Council authorization?' (2006) 31 *SAYIL* 195, 205–6. See too, S Africa and R Pretorius 'South Africa, the AU and the responsibility to protect' (2012) 12 *African Human Rights Law Journal* 394; D Kuwali and F Viljoen *Africa and the Responsibility to Protect* (2013).

[116] For an examination of these debates and the reports they engendered, see C Stahn 'Responsibility to protect: Political rhetoric or emerging legal norm?' (2007) 101 *AJIL* 99.

The language of this resolution, by qualifying the right to intervene 'through the Security Council, in accordance with the Charter,' makes it clear that it cannot serve as a justification of humanitarian intervention.[117] This resolution has been invoked by the Security Council in resolutions 1970 (26 February 2011) and 1973 (17 March 2011) on Libya, which together impose an arms embargo and 'no fly zone' on Libya and authorise states to take 'all necessary measures' to protect civilians.[118] The preambles to both these resolutions, adopted under Chapter VII, emphasise the responsibility of the Libyan authorities 'to protect its population'. They also emphasise that military intervention on the basis of responsibility to protect requires Security Council authorisation.

5 The invasion of Iraq in 2003

In March 2003, the United States and the United Kingdom invaded Iraq. The invasion occurred without clear Security Council authorisation and could not seriously be justified as an exercise in self-defence. This event has been widely construed as a violation of the Charter's prohibition on the use of force and as a threat to the legal order that has governed the world since 1945.

Although it has been suggested that the United States and the United Kingdom in engaging in this action 'all but discarded the fig leaf of legal justification,'[119] a sophisticated legal argument in defence of the action was presented by the British Attorney-General,[120] which was later endorsed by the Legal Adviser of the United States Department of State.[121]

According to the British Attorney-General, Lord Goldsmith, the United Kingdom justified its intervention in Iraq on the basis of three Security Council resolutions adopted under Chapter VII—resolutions 678 (1990), 687 (1991) and 1441 (2002). Resolution 678 (1990), adopted after Iraq's invasion of Kuwait in 1990, authorised states to 'use all necessary means' to restore international peace and security.

[117] See D Tladi 'The intervention in Côte d'Ivoire—2011' in Ruys, Corten and Hofer (n 1); M Vashakmadze 'Responsibility to protect' in Simma et al (n 3). For a contrary view see Stahn (n 116), 120.

[118] D Tladi 'Security Council, the use of force and regime change: Libya and Côte d'Ivoire' (2012) 37 *SAYIL* 22.

[119] T Franck 'What happens now? The United Nations after Iraq' (2003) 97 *AJIL* 607, 608.

[120] See the statement by Lord Goldsmith published in (2003) 52 *ICLQ* 810.

[121] See WH Taft and TF Buchwald 'Pre-emption, Iraq, and international law' (2003) 97 *AJIL* 557. At the time this article was written, Mr Taft was legal adviser to the US Department of State, and Mr Buchwald was assistant legal adviser for Political-Military Affairs of the US Department of State. See, too, J Yoo 'International law and the war in Iraq' (2003) 97 *AJIL* 563 at 571.

This formula was understood to authorise the use of force and provided the legal basis for the use of force against Iraq in 1991. This resolution was suspended by resolution 687 (1991), which provided for a cease-fire following the forcible eviction of Iraq from Kuwait, on condition that Iraq destroyed all weapons of mass destruction and agreed to the inspection of its weaponry by United Nations inspectors. In 2002, following 12 years of failure on the part of Iraq to fully comply with resolution 687, the Security Council adopted resolution 1441, in which it found that Iraq was in material breach of its obligations under resolution 687 by reason of its failure to co-operate with United Nations' weapons inspectors. The resolution gave Iraq a 'final opportunity' to comply with its disarmament obligations and warned it of the 'serious consequences' it would face if it failed to comply with these obligations. Failure to comply with this resolution revived resolution 678 and allowed states to use force against Iraq in terms of this resolution without further authorisation from the Security Council.

The above argument is open to several objections. First, resolution 678 authorised states to use force only for the purpose of evicting Iraq from Kuwait. It did not provide states with a general licence to use force against Iraq for any reason relating to the maintenance of international peace and security.[122] Secondly, there is nothing in the Charter or the resolutions cited by the British government to suggest that states may use force unilaterally against a state that is in material breach of Security Council resolutions. It is for the Security Council to determine that a material breach has occurred and to decide upon the action to be taken in response to such a breach.[123] Thirdly, resolution 1441 neither expressly nor impliedly authorises states to use force against Iraq. That it is impossible to interpret resolution 1441 as impliedly authorising the revival of resolution 678 is borne out by the failure of the United States and the United Kingdom to gain support for a resolution in February 2003 authorising the use of force. The majority of members of the Security Council were clearly opposed to such a resolution.[124] The better view, in the circumstances, is that the United States and the United Kingdom acted unlawfully in invading Iraq in March 2003. In the words of Vaughan Lowe:

> It is simply unacceptable that a step as serious and important as a massive military attack upon a state should be launched on the basis of a legal

[122] See the memorandum of the Legal Department of the Ministry of Foreign Affairs of the Russian Federation (hereinafter 'Russian memorandum') in (2003) 52 *ICLQ* 1059; V Lowe 'The Iraq crisis: What now?' (2003) 52 *ICLQ* 859, 865.

[123] Russian memorandum (n 122) 1060; Frank (n 119) 613.

[124] D McGoldrick *From 9/11 to the Iraq War* (2004) 78–86; Russian memorandum (n 122) 1062.

argument dependent upon dubious inferences drawn from the silences in resolution 1441 and the muffled echoes of earlier resolutions, unsupported by any contemporary authorisation to use force.[125]

The general view that the invasion of Iraq was illegal confirmed by a British inquiry into the Iraq war conducted by Lord Chilcot which reported in 2016 that 'the circumstances in which it was decided that there was a legal basis for the military action were far from satisfactory' and that the action of the United States and United Kingdom had undermined the authority of the Security Council.[126]

6 Intervention in civil strife and civil wars[127]

(a) Intervention where the rebels are not externally assisted

A sovereign independent state is permitted to choose its own political system and government.[128] Some countries exercise this choice by means of the ballot, others by means of the bullet. In either case, it is an internal affair, an exercise in self-determination. Other states may not interfere in this process even if it degenerates into civil war.[129] This is confirmed by the 1970 Declaration on Principles of International Law,[130] which obliges states not to 'interfere in civil strife in another state'. Although past state practice appeared to recognise a rule permitting support by other states for the incumbent government in a civil war, this rule is no longer accepted where the rebels constitute an organised movement with the political object of replacing the government.

Difficulties arise where a state is requested by an incumbent friendly government to assist in the restoration of law and order

[125] Lowe (n 122) 865–6. See, too, MG Cowling 'The Iraqi war and collective security' (2003) 28 *SAYIL* 225; P Shiner and A Williams (eds) *The Iraq War and International Law* (2008). See also P Sands *Lawless World: America and the Making and Breaking of Global Rules—From FDR's Atlantic Charter to George W Bush's Illegal War* (2005), 174 et seq.

[126] House of Commons *The Report of the Iraq Inquiry* (2016) (Chilcot Report). See for discussion J Seaton 'Chilcot report: Introduction' (2016) 87 *Political Quarterly* 476; P Robinson 'Learning from the Chilcot report: Propaganda, deception and the "War on Terror"' (2017) 11 *International Journal of Contemporary Iraqi Studies* 47.

[127] See for discussion E de Wet 'The modern practice of intervention by invitation in Africa and its implications for the prohibition of the use of force' (2015) 26 *European Journal of International Law* 979.

[128] *Nicaragua* case (n 8) para 108.

[129] See generally on this subject JN Moore (ed) *Law and Civil War in the Modern World* (1974); Brownlie (n 1) 321–7; JC Stassen 'Intervention in internal wars: Traditional norms and contemporary trends' (1977) 3 *SAYIL* 65.

[130] Resolution 2625(XXV). See too the 1965 Declaration on the Inadmissibility of Intervention in the Domestic Affairs of States and the Protection of their Independence and Sovereignty, General Assembly resolution 2131(XX), which contains an identical provision (text in (1966) 60 *AJIL* 662).

resulting from a disturbance unconnected with the choice of government or political system. Here there is support for the view that a state may intervene at the invitation of the incumbent government.[131] Thus, South Africa would be entitled to accept an invitation from the government of Botswana to assist in the restoration of order when there had been widespread looting following a strike by the police force for higher wages; but it would not be permitted to accept an invitation from the King of Swaziland to assist in the suppression of a revolt against the monarchy. The latter would interfere with the right of self-determination; the former would not. South Africa's intervention in Lesotho in September 1998[132] falls between these two extremes. Undoubtedly, there was a breakdown of law and order in Lesotho. But it was caused by political disaffection arising from electoral fraud and accompanied by demands for the removal of the government. South Africa's intervention was therefore of dubious legality. Nor did the fact that South Africa acted on behalf of the Southern African Development Community (SADC) cure this illegality. A regional organisation may not use force against a member state without authorisation from the Security Council of the United Nations, acting under article 53 of the Charter. No such authorisation had been sought or given.

(b) Intervention where the rebels are externally assisted

A state may intervene to assist the incumbent government if the rebels are supported by another state and such support is sufficiently substantial to amount to an armed attack.[133] In such a case, the intervening state acts in support of the incumbent government in the exercise of the right of collective self-defence against foreign aggression. The post-World War II period has seen a number of interventions justified on this ground. In 1956, the Soviet Union intervened in Hungary at the request of a puppet regime to suppress an uprising that it alleged was supported by foreign forces.[134] From 1965 to 1973, the United States gave support to the government of South Vietnam because it claimed that the rebels, the Vietcong, were supported by North Vietnam.[135] In 1979, the Soviet Union intervened in Afghani-

[131] R Jennings and A Watts (eds) *Oppenheim's International Law* 9 ed vol 1 (1992) 435–8.

[132] See (1998) 23 *SAYIL* 320–31. GN Barrie 'South Africa's intervention in Lesotho: What does international law say?' (1999) 372 *De Rebus* 46.

[133] On the meaning of 'armed attack', see the *Nicaragua* case (n 8) paras 103–4, 118–19.

[134] D Harris *Cases and Materials on International Law* 7 ed (2010) 743.

[135] See *Memorandum on the Legality of United States Participation in the Defense of Vietnam* prepared by the Legal Adviser of the US State Department (1966) 60 *AJIL* 565.

stan to protect an incumbent puppet government against foreign-supported rebels.[136] In 1983, the United States intervened in Grenada to protect the government against Cuban-supported revolutionaries.[137] All these interventions were founded on shaky factual foundations. The evidence of foreign support for the rebels in the cases of Hungary, Afghanistan, and Grenada was not substantiated, while the United States' argument that Vietnam comprised two separate states, instead of one unit in which a civil war was fought between North and South, was highly suspect.[138] In these circumstances, the conclusion is inescapable that the great powers have frequently used the right of collective self-defence in civil wars as a pretext in order to advance their own ideological interests.

South Africa's intervention in Angola in 1975/6 was, likewise, of doubtful legality.[139] Shortly before Angola became independent in November 1975, South African troops entered southern Angola and were stopped only some 200 km from Luanda. The SADF withdrew in March 1976. The South African government justified this exercise on the ground that the MPLA[140] government of Angola was supported by Cuba and the Soviet Union. On 30 January, Prime Minister BJ Vorster told Parliament:

> Our involvement was the effect of Russian and Cuban intervention. If they did not enter Angola, if they did not take part in this affair, if they did not try to subvert the whole of Angola and to suppress its people, South Africa would never have entered Angola at all. We were not involved in the civil war. We had nothing to do with it whatsoever; it was not our affair. I therefore say that we were not a party to the civil war.[141]

South Africa's defence was widely rejected, and its intervention condemned by the Security Council,[142] on the ground that the evidence tended to support the MPLA government's claim that it had invited Cuba to send troops to Angola to assist it against South African aggression.

The conflict in the Democratic Republic of the Congo in 1999 and thereafter illustrates the complexity of intervention in civil wars.

[136] Harris (n 134) 744.

[137] CC Joyner et al 'The United States action in Grenada' (1984) 78 *AJIL* 131–75.

[138] There is a wealth of literature on this topic. Most articles appear in RA Falk (ed) *The Vietnam War and International Law* 4 vols (1968–76).

[139] For accounts of this intervention, see M Horrell et al 'Angola' 1976 *Survey of Race Relations* 410–32; C Legum and T Hodges *After Angola: The War over Southern Africa* (1976).

[140] People's Movement for The Liberation of Angola.

[141] *House of Assembly Debates* vol 60, col 368 (30 January 1976). For further statements of this kind, see P Pauw 'Buys and Another v Lennox Residential Hotel' (1976) 2 *SAYIL* 279–82.

[142] Resolution 387; 1976 *Annual Survey* (n 29) 38.

Uganda and Rwanda intervened initially in the DRC in order to suppress rebel movements operating against them from the territory of the DRC but then remained to assist rebel groups fighting against the Congolese government. Zimbabwe, Namibia, and Angola then intervened to assist the Congolese government. Repeated Security Council resolutions[143] and the establishment of a peacekeeping mission (MONUC) eventually resulted in the withdrawal of foreign forces.

Two recent examples in the Middle East illustrate the complexity of applying the rules of intervention by invitation. In Yemen, when a rebel group called the Houthis sought to overrun the government, forcing the President to flee from Yemen, a coalition led by Saudi Arabia and supported by the United States and the United Kingdom, launched what was termed Operation Decisive Storm.[144] At the time the Yemeni President requested assistance, while in neighbouring Saudi Arabia, he had clearly lost control of the territory. At face value, therefore, this intervention appeared to be an unlawful use of force.[145] Yet, for the most part, other states expressed support for the intervention.[146] It has been suggested that the involvement of Iran with the rebels made this intervention acceptable. However, it is doubtful whether the Iranian involvement was sufficiently substantial to justify the intervention by third states.

As in the case of the Saudi-led intervention in Yemen, the intervention of US-allied forces in Iraq and the Russian-led intervention against ISIS, at the invitation of Syria,[147] were met with support by other states.[148] Even more than in the case of Yemen, no argument was made that ISIS had the support of a third state. Although, the argument of collective self-defence was often raised, it is not clear that requirements of self-defence were met, in particular the requirement that there must be an armed attack. The best justification for these two sets of intervention is the invitations by Iraq and Syria

[143] Resolutions 1234 (1999), 1291 (1999), 1304 (2000).

[144] L Ferro and T Ruys 'The Saudi-led military intervention in Yemen's Civil War' in Ruys, Corten and Hofer (n 1); Nathalie Weizmann 'International law on the Saudi-led military operations' March 2017 *Just Security*.

[145] See, for discussion, Z Vermeer 'The *jus ad bellum* and the airstrikes in Yemen: Double standards for decamping presidents?' *EJIL: Talk!* April 2015.

[146] Ferro and Ruys (n 144) 902.

[147] O Corten 'The military operation against Islamic State (ISIL or Da'esh)—2014' in Ruys, Corten and Hofer (n 1).

[148] The US-led intervention in Syria against ISIS is discussed separately below in Section 8.

respectively,[149] even though there was no suggestion of a third state supporting ISIS.[150] Bannelier-Christakis adds further that where the target of the intervention is a 'UN-designated terrorist group' like ISIS, the invitation is legitimate.[151] Syria and Iraq were thus entitled to invite third states to come to their assistance.

7 Wars of national liberation[152]

Many of the prohibitive rules relating to the use of force have been relaxed, and possibly amended, in wars of self-determination involving national liberation movements (NLMs) recognised by the United Nations—as were SWAPO, ANC, PAC, and PLO. Such wars are no longer viewed as purely internal civil wars, but as international wars to which the laws of war are to apply.[153] Moreover, states are encouraged to give support to NLMs despite the prohibition on military aid to armed bands operating from neighbouring territories. This is evidenced by a number of generously phrased General Assembly resolutions that called upon states to provide the necessary 'moral, political and material assistance' to the ANC and PAC in their legitimate struggle against the South African apartheid regime,[154] which many states interpreted as authorisation for military support.

This development, which resurrects the notion of the just war,[155] has not been accepted by Western states, and finds no support in resolutions of the Security Council.[156] In his dissenting opinion in the *Nicaragua Case*, Judge Schwebel stated:

> [I]t is lawful for a foreign state ... to give to a people struggling for self-determination moral, political and humanitarian assistance; but it is not lawful for a foreign state ... to intervene in that struggle with force or to provide arms, supplies and other logistical support in the prosecution of armed rebellion.[157]

[149] See, for discussion, K Bannelier-Christakis 'Military interventions against ISIL in Iraq, Syria and Libya, and the legal basis of consent' (2016) 29 *Leiden Journal of International Law* 743.

[150] Corten (n 148), 887.

[151] Bannelier-Christakis (n 149), 774.

[152] HA Wilson *International Law and the Use of Force by National Liberation Movements* (1988).

[153] Protocol I to the Geneva Conventions of 1949, adopted in 1977, extends the protection of the Geneva Conventions on the laws of war to wars of self-determination: see Chapter 25 below.

[154] See, for example, resolution 38/39A of 5 December 1983; and 39/72A of 13 December 1984.

[155] See J Dugard 'SWAPO: The *Jus ad Bellum* and the *Jus in Bello*' (1976) 93 *SALJ* 144; EB Firmage 'The "war of national liberation" and the Third World' in JN Moore (ed) *Law and Civil War in the Modern World* (1974) 304.

[156] Wilson (n 152), 136.

[157] *Nicaragua* case (n 8) para 351.

Attempts by the supporters of NLMs to bring their military actions under the rubric of self-defence are unconvincing. The argument that colonialism is a continuing aggression, dating back to the start of the colonial occupation, which may legitimately be resisted in the second half of the 20th century, was raised by India in justification for its seizure of Goa in 1961, and by Argentine to justify its invasion of the Falklands Islands in 1982. It has not been taken seriously, however, as it ignores the principle of intertemporal law according to which titles acquired by force when this method of acquisition was lawful are recognised as valid today.[158] A second argument construes colonialism as an assault on the colonial *people*, constituting an 'armed attack' within the meaning of article 51 of the Charter, which permits third states to assist the colonial people in the exercise of the right of collective self-defence. This argument is likewise untenable as it is based on a rewriting of article 51, and not on an interpretation. Article 51 requires an 'armed attack' against a 'member of the United Nations'—ie a *state* and not a people—as a precondition for the exercise of the right of individual or collective self-defence.[159]

It may have been difficult to justify the military support given by South Africa's neighbours and other states to the ANC and PAC in their struggle against apartheid in terms of the strict letter of the Charter of the United Nations. On the other hand, it should be borne in mind that the Charter created a dynamic world organisation which is required to evolve to meet new conditions. This evolution has been particularly pronounced in the field of self-determination. The institution of colonialism has been denounced by numerous United Nations resolutions[160] and is generally considered to be unlawful today. Two important General Assembly resolutions—the 1970 Declaration on Principles of International Law[161] and the 1974 Resolution on the Definition of Aggression[162]—have recognised the right of peoples under colonial and racist regimes, and alien subjugation, to receive support from other states in pursuit of the forcible exercise of their right to overthrow such regimes. Moreover, these majorities have been endorsed by large majorities in the General Assembly. In 1977, the First Protocol to the Geneva Conventions of 1949 extended the protective principles of the laws of

[158] See J Dugard 'The Organization of African Unity and colonialism: An inquiry into the plea of self-defence as a justification for the use of force in the eradication of colonialism'(1967) 16 *ICLQ* 157 at 169.

[159] Dugard (n 156), 172. Cf Wilson (n 152) 130–5.

[160] Particularly the General Assembly's Declaration on the Granting of Independence to Colonial Countries and Peoples, resolution 1514 (XV).

[161] Resolution 2625 (XXV).

[162] Resolution 3314 (XXIX).

international war to combatants engaged in wars of national liberation against colonial domination, racist regimes, and alien occupation.[163] Numerous resolutions of the General Assembly have called on states to give 'material' assistance to NLMs;[164] and the target states of armed attacks launched by NLMs from bases in foreign territory have been condemned by the Security Council for their forcible response.[165] It is hardly surprising therefore that the International Court of Justice in the *Nicaragua Case* excluded wars of self-determination when it condemned support for armed bands as an unlawful use of force.[166]

Wars of national liberation have lost much of their relevance since the decolonisation of Africa, the abandonment of apartheid in South Africa and the creation of the Palestinian Authority by the Oslo Accords in the Occupied Palestinian Territory. Nevertheless, NLMs and the lawfulness of their military actions remain an important feature of South African history.

8 Self-defence against non-state actors: the case of terrorism[167]

A recent controversy that has arisen concerns the question whether a state is entitled to use force against non-state actors in the territory of third states without the territorial state's consent.[168] This controversy arises because of the increase, both in terms of the frequency and intensity, of acts of terrorism committed by non-state actors, often operating in the territory of third states.

As a general rule, the use of force against non-state actors in the territory of third states without the latter's consent would appear to violate article 2(4) of the UN Charter. Yet, in recent times, a number of authors have asserted the use of force in a third state in response to

[163] See Chapter 25 below.

[164] See (n 154).

[165] Ibid (n 68).

[166] *Nicaragua* case (n 8).

[167] See T Becker *Terrorism and the State* (2006); L Moir *Reappraising the Resort to Force. International Law,* Jus ad Bellum *and the War on Terror* (2010); H Duffy *The 'War on Terror' and the Framework of International Law* 2 ed (2015).

[168] For a selection of reference on the debate see: Paust (n 32); Murphy (n 32); D Tladi 'The nonconsenting innocent state: The problem with Bethlehem's Principle 12' (2013) 107 *AJIL* 570; K Trapp 'Back to basics: Necessity, proportionality, and the right of self-defence against non-state actors' (2007) 56 *ICLQ* 141; C Tams 'The use of force against terrorists (2009) 20 *European Journal of International Law* 359; O Corten 'The "Unwilling or unable test": Has it been, and could it be, accepted?' (2016) 29 *Leiden Journal of International Law* 777; V Kattan 'Furthering the "war on terrorism" through international law. How the US and UK resurrected the Bush Doctrine on using preventive military force to combat terrorism' (2018) 5 *Journal on the Use of Force and International Law* 97; See for a comprehensive assessment Tladi, Tams and O'Connell (n 30).

acts of terrorism from non-state actors is permitted under international law.[169] This view has also been propagated in three widely discussed policy-oriented documents, namely the Chatham Principles,[170] the Leiden Recommendations[171] and the Bethlehem Principles which have advanced the idea that the use of force is permitted when the territorial state is 'unwilling or unable' to effectively curb the activities of the non-state actor concerned.[172] This view, which on its face is incorrect, is advanced on the basis of three arguments.

First, it is suggested that despite the rules under the UN Charter, customary international law permitted the use of force in self-defence in the territory of third states. For this argument reliance is placed on the *Caroline* incident which concerned the use of force against non-state actors. However, as Brownlie noted, to rely on the *Caroline* incident as a statement of customary international law in the 21st century is 'anachronistic and indefensible'.[173]

Secondly, it is argued that the ordinary meaning of the words in article 51 require only an 'armed attack' and not an 'armed attack from a state'. However, this view ignores the rule that in treaty interpretation, the ordinary words must be understood in their context and in light of the object and purpose of the treaty.[174] Moreover, in a consistent line of cases, the International Court of Justice has interpreted 'armed attack' as referring to an armed attack by one state against another state. This interpretation began with the *Nicaragua* case where the Court stated that there is

> general agreement on the nature of the acts which can be treated as constituting armed attacks. In particular, it may be considered to be agreed that an armed attack must be understood as including not merely action by

[169] See Murphy (n 32); Paust (n 32); Tams (n 168); M Wood 'International law and the use of force: What happens in practice?' (2013) 53 *Indian Journal of International Law* 345; O Schachter 'The extraterritorial use of force against terrorist bases' (1989) 11 *Houston Journal of International Law* 11 (1989) 309; T Reinold 'State weakness, irregular warfare and the right to self-defence post 9/11' (2011) 105 *American Journal of International Law* 244.

[170] Principles of International Law on the Use of Force by States in Self-Defence (2005) adopted by a group of British international lawyers consisting of Frank Berman, Daniel Bethlehem, Christopher Greenwood, Vaughn Lowe, Philippe Sands, Malcolm Shaw, Elizabeth Wilmshurst and Michael Wood.

[171] Leiden Policy Recommendations on Counter-Terrorism and International Law (2010), prepared by a group of European and American experts: Andrea Bianchi (Italy), Michael Wood (United Kingdom), Steven Ratner (United States), Elizabeth Wilmshurst (United Kingdom), Christian Tams (Germany) and Claus Kreß (Germany).

[172] D Bethlehem 'Principles relevant to the scope of a state's right of self-defense against an imminent or actual armed attack by nonstate actors' (2012) 106 *AJIL* 769.

[173] *Brownlie's Principles of Public International Law* (ed J Crawford) 8 ed (2012) 751.

[174] See Chapter 20. For an application of these rules of interpretation to article 51 see Tladi (n 30) and Tams (n 44).

> regular armed forces across an international border, but also 'the sending by or on behalf of a State of armed bands, groups, irregulars, or mercenaries, which carry out acts of armed force against another State of such gravity as to amount to' an actual armed attack conducted by regular forces, 'or its substantial involvement therein.' This description . . . may be taken to reflect customary international law.[175]

Similarly, in its advisory opinion on *Legal Consequences of the Construction of a Wall in the Occupied Palestinian Territory*,[176] the Court rejected the Israeli argument that the construction of the Wall was justified in terms of article 51 of the UN Charter as interpreted by Resolutions 1368 and 1373. It stated:

> Article 51 of the Charter . . . recognises the existence of an inherent right of self-defence in the case of an armed attack by one state against another state. However, Israel does not claim that the attacks against it are imputable to a foreign state.

The Court also notes that Israel exercises control in the Occupied Palestinian Territory and that, as Israel itself states, the threat which it regards as justifying the construction of the Wall originates within, and not outside, that territory. The situation is thus different from that contemplated by Security Council Resolutions 1368 (2001) and 1373 (2001), and therefore Israel could not in any event invoke those resolutions in support of its claim to be exercising a right of self-defence.[177]

In *Armed Activities in the Territory of the Congo*[178] the Court adopted a similar stance when it held that Uganda could not justify its action in the Congo as self-defence when it responded to an armed attack emanating, not from armed bands acting on behalf of the Democratic Republic of the Congo, but, from the Allied Democratic Force (ADF), comprising Ugandan forces opposed to the Ugandan government.

The third pillar of the proposition that the use of force against terrorists in the territory of a third state is lawful is that state practice recognises such a right and, consequently, by virtue of article 31(3) of the Vienna Convention on the Law of Treaties, article 51 of the Charter must be interpreted as permitting the use of force against

[175] *Nicaragua* case (n 8) para 195.

[176] *Wall* Advisory Opinion (n 58) para 139. See the comment by J Dugard in 'The Wall' in E Bjorge and C Miles (eds) *Landmark Cases in International Law* (2017) 556: 'The real reason that resolutions 1368 and 1373 do not apply, unfortunately not mentioned by the Court, is that Israel is essentially engaged in a policing operation as occupying power of the OPT. Israel is not the victim of an armed attack that allows it to invoke Article 51 and the sympathy of the world. It is an occupying power that is building a wall to maintain its occupation.'

[177] Ibid para 139. This aspect of the Court's opinion was strongly criticised by Judges Higgins (para 33), Kooijmans (para 35) and Buergenthal (para 6).

[178] *Armed Activities in the Territory of Congo* (n 58) para 146.

non-state actors in the territory of third.[179] Examples of practice that have been advanced in support of this contention include, amongst others, US strikes against a pharmaceutical plant in 2008 in response to Al-Qaeda bombings of US Embassies; Turkish incursions into Northern Iraq in response to the attacks by the Kurdistan Workers Party; and Israeli attacks in Lebanon against Hezbollah. Yet, in all of these cases, without exception, the use of force was met with criticism from other states, with the result that it cannot form the basis of either new law or a new interpretation of the law.[180]

A more recent example of the use of force against terrorists in the territory of a third state is the US-led strikes against ISIS in Syria.[181] Although there was a UN Security Council resolution encouraging states 'to take all necessary measures' to address the threat posed by ISIS, this resolution did not authorise the use of force.[182] While there have been many states using force against ISIS in Syria, they have all advanced different justifications.[183] Moreover, even the acts against ISIS in Syria have come under criticism from different states and can therefore not form the basis of new law or a new interpretation of law.[184]

Without question, the terrorist attacks committed by Al-Qaeda in

[179] Article 31(3)(b) of the Vienna Convention on the Law of Treaties provides that when interpreting treaties 'subsequent practice in the application of the treaty which establishes the agreement of the parties regarding its interpretation' shall be taken into account.

[180] See Tladi (n 33).

[181] See for discussion D Tladi and M Shaqra 'Assessing the legality of the coalition air strikes targeting the Islamic State in Iraq and the Levant (ISIS) in Syria under International Law' (2015) 40 *SAYIL* 281; Corten (n 147).

[182] UN Security Council Resolution 2249 (2015), para 5. D Akande and M Milanovic 'The constructive ambiguity of the Security Council's ISIS Resolution' *EJIL: Talk!* 21 November 2015.

[183] See discussion of these in Corten (n 147). See also Tladi (n 30).

[184] See, eg Final Document of the 17th Summit of Heads of State and Government of the Non-Aligned Movement, 17–18 September 2016, Island of Margarita, Venezuela, para 5. See also UN Doc S/PV.8175, 6 February 2018 in which Mexico stated that it was concerned by the 'continuous references to Article 51 of the Charter of the United Nations by some States to address threats to international peace and security with military action, especially against non-State actors. Mexico is troubled that such a practice, coupled with the ambiguous language of recent Council resolutions, runs the risk of a de facto broadening of exceptions to the general prohibition on the use of force, as set out in Article 2, paragraph 4, of the Charter of the United Nations, in an irregular manner'). See also statement of Brazil at Security Council debate on upholding international law within the context of the maintenance of international peace and security of 17 May 2018 (S/PV.8262) ('A few States have been arguing that self-defence could be applied as a response to "non-state actors", sometimes adding as a condition the criterion of "unwillingness" or "inability of the territorial state to respond" to those "non-State actors". Brazil does not agree with such an interpretation . . .').

the United States on 11 September 2011 have given the impetus for those arguing for an expanded approach to self-defence. Judge Simma's observation in *Armed Activities in the Territory of the Congo* is apposite:

> Such a restrictive reading of Article 51 might well have reflected the state, or rather the prevailing interpretation, of the international law on self-defence for a long time. However, in the light of more recent developments not only in State practice but also with regard to accompanying *opinio juris*, it ought urgently to be reconsidered, also by the Court. As is well known, these developments were triggered by the terrorist attacks of September 11, in the wake of which claims that Article 51 also covers defensive measures against terrorist groups have been received far more favourably by the international community than other extensive re-readings of the relevant Charter provisions, particularly the 'Bush doctrine' justifying the pre-emptive use of force. Security Council resolutions 1368 (2001) and 1373 (2001) cannot but be read as affirmations of the view that large-scale attacks by non-State actors can qualify as 'armed attacks' within the meaning of Article 51.[185]

However, it is not clear that these events led to the types of changes suggested by Judge Simma. Following these acts of terrorism the Security Council adopted Resolutions 1368 (12 September 2001) and 1373 (28 September 2001), in which it recognised the inherent right of self-defence of states, before proceeding to condemn the terrorist acts in question. While some have argued these resolutions endorse the right to use of force against non-state actors in the territory of third states, a good faith interpretation does not support such a view.

On 7 October 2001, the United States and the United Kingdom began bombing Afghanistan on the ground that the Taliban government of that country had allowed Al-Qaeda terrorists to operate from its territory and thereby made itself a party to the unlawful use of force against the United States.[186] This attack might be explained in terms of the traditional right of self-defence: the Taliban government had allowed Al-Qaida terrorists to train on its territory and operate from its territory; Al-Qaeda's unlawful acts might therefore be attributed to the government of Afghanistan permitting the United States to use force against the Taliban.

It is therefore difficult to argue that the law of self-defence has shifted to permit the use of force against terrorists on the territory of third states. What may indeed be shifting is the strict test of attribution advanced in the *Nicaragua* case, where the Court required 'effective control' of the non-state actor by the territorial state in order to justify the use of force in self-defence.

[185] *Armed Activities in the Territory of Congo* (n 58), para 11.

[186] For an account of these events, see Abraham and Hopkins (n 23).

A second objection is more serious. Self-defence against terrorism involves punitive action against terrorist bases or the state that harbours terrorists after the act of terrorism has occurred with the intention of preventing further such action.[187] This clearly goes beyond anticipatory self-defence which is limited to a response to an imminent threatened attack that cannot be deflected by other means.[188] For this reason, it is probably best to see self-defence against terrorism, where it amounts to preventive action against future attacks, as permissible only with prior Security Council's approval—as happened in the case of the invasion of Afghanistan, which was preceded by Security Council Resolutions 1368 and 1373 approving the exercise of the right of self-defence.

Terrorism is a serious threat to international peace and security, but it is one that must be contained and confronted by multilateral action under the auspices of the Security Council and not by unilateral action under the guise of self-defence.

[187] Abraham and Hopkins (n 23) 796, 800.

[188] See the formulation of anticipatory self-defence by the Secretary-General's High-Level Panel on Threats, Challenges and Change (n 59).

CHAPTER 25

Humanitarian Law

John Dugard

INTRODUCTION

International law distinguishes between the *jus ad bellum*—the right to go to war—and the *jus in bello*—the law governing the waging of war and the treatment of combatants and civilians in time of war. The former was dealt with in Chapter 24 on the Use of Force by States. This chapter examines the *jus in bello*, previously known as the laws of war but today called international humanitarian law (IHL).

THE SOURCES AND SCOPE OF HUMANITARIAN LAW[1]

The protective principles of humanitarian law extend to all combatants and civilians in an international armed conflict, irrespective of the justice or legality of the war. No distinction is made between the forces or civilian population of the aggressor and those of the victim for the purposes of humanitarian law. IHL covers the treatment of prisoners of war, sick and wounded military personnel, civilians in armed conflict and in occupied territory, and the limits imposed by the law on methods and weaponry of warfare. Whereas the laws of war were concerned only with international armed conflict—that is, interstate conflicts—contemporary IHL covers both international armed conflicts and non-international armed conflicts.

The starting point of modern humanitarian law was the battle of Solferino in 1859 between Austrian and Franco-Italian forces, in which thousands of wounded combatants were left to die without medical attention. Appalled by this sight, a young Swiss banker, Henry Dunant, started a movement which led to the creation of the

[1] A Clapham and P Gaeta (eds) *Oxford Handbook of International Law in Armed Conflict* (2014); E Crawford and A Pert *International Humanitarian Law* (2015); K Watkin *Fighting at the Legal Boundaries: Controlling the Use of Force in Contemporary Conflict* (2016); N Melzer *International Humanitarian Law: A Comprehensive Introduction* (2016); S Sivakumaran *The Law of Non-International Armed Conflict* (2012); A Roberts and R Guelff (eds) *Documents on the Laws of War* 3 ed (2000); D Fleck (ed) *The Handbook of Humanitarian Law* 2 ed (2008); T Meron *The Humanization of International Law* (2006); F Kalshoven *Reflections on the Law of War* (2007); Y Dinstein *The Conduct of Hostilities under the Law of Armed Conflict* 2 ed (2010); M Osiel *The End of Reciprocity, Terror, Torture and the Law of* War (2009); R Kolb and R Hyde *An Introduction to the International Law of Armed Conflicts* (2008); O Ben-Naftali (ed) *International Humanitarian Law and International Human Rights* Law (2011). See, too, the comments on humanitarian law in *S v Basson* 2007 (3) SA 582 (CC) paras 171–83.

Geneva-based International Committee of the Red Cross (ICRC), a non-governmental organisation (NGO) committed to providing relief to the victims of armed conflict, and to the first multilateral humanitarian treaty—the Geneva Convention on the Amelioration of the Condition of the Wounded in Armies in the Field of 1864. Since then a host of multilateral treaties have been adopted. These treaties, together with a body of customary rules,[2] comprise modern humanitarian law.

Important treaties were adopted at The Hague in 1899 and 1907, dealing primarily with the 'laws and customs of war'. More modern treaties were concluded in Geneva in 1949 and 1977, concerned largely with the protection of persons from the effects of armed conflict. IHL is therefore sometimes described as comprising 'the law of The Hague' and 'the law of Geneva'. However, in its advisory opinion on the *Legality of the Threat or Use of Nuclear Weapons*, the International Court of Justice stated that the two systems 'have become so closely inter-related that they are considered to have gradually formed one single complex system, known today as international humanitarian law'.[3]

In recent years, international criminal tribunals have been created with the power to enforce IHL. These tribunals have contributed substantially to the development of IHL.

According to the International Court of Justice:

> The cardinal principles contained in the texts constituting the fabric of humanitarian law are the following. The first is aimed at the protection of the civilian population and civilian objects and establishes the distinction between combatants and non-combatants; states must never make civilians the object of attack and must consequently never use weapons that are incapable of distinguishing between civilian and military targets. According to the second principle, it is prohibited to cause unnecessary suffering to combatants; it is accordingly prohibited to use weapons causing them such harm or uselessly aggravating their suffering. In application of that second principle, states do not have unlimited freedom of choice of means in the weapons they use.[4]

1 Law of The Hague

The Law of The Hague determines the rights and duties of belligerents in the conduct of their military operations and limits the choice

[2] Customary law is specifically recognised in a paragraph in the preamble to The Hague Convention (IV) Respecting the Laws and Customs of War on Land of 1907, known as the Martens Clause. See the study of the ICRC on this subject, JM Henckaerts and L Doswald Beck (eds) *Customary International Humanitarian Law (ICRC)* 3 vols (2005); T Meron 'Revival of customary humanitarian law' (2005) 99 *AJIL* 817. See, too, the comments of Sachs J in *S v Basson* 2005 (1) SA 171 (CC) 216; and *S v Basson* (n 1) paras 174, 177.

[3] 1996 ICJ Reports 226, 256.

[4] *Legality of the Threat or Use of Nuclear Weapons* 1996 ICJ Reports 226, 257.

of the means of doing harm. It seeks to strike a balance between military necessity and humanitarian considerations. This body of law is founded on the Hague Conventions of 1899, as revised in 1907. The most important of these conventions is the Fourth Convention of 1907 Respecting the Laws and Customs of War on Land, to which is attached an annexure known as the Hague Regulations.[5] These Regulations deal with the status of belligerents, the conduct of hostilities, the prohibition of weapons 'calculated to cause unnecessary suffering', the termination of hostilities, and the rules governing military occupation. Article 22 declares that 'the right of belligerents to adopt means of injuring the enemy is not unlimited'. The Hague Regulations, to which South Africa is a party,[6] are today generally accepted as forming part of customary law.[7]

2 The prohibition of weapons that cause unnecessary suffering

Since 1907, other treaties have been adopted to limit the use of weapons designed to cause unnecessary suffering. In 1925, the Geneva Protocol prohibiting the use in war of poisonous gases and bacteriological methods of warfare was adopted.[8] This treaty is supplemented by a 1972 Convention that prohibits the production and stockpiling of bacteriological weapons[9] and a 1993 Convention on the prohibition of the use of chemical weapons.[10] South Africa is a party to all three conventions and in 1993 adopted legislation to give domestic effect to its obligations under these conventions.[11] South Africa is also a party to a convention prohibiting booby-traps, incendiary weapons and the use of laser weapons designed to cause permanent blindness.'[12]

In 1997, a convention, known as the Ottawa Convention, was adopted to ban the use, production, and transfer of anti-personnel

[5] The texts of the Hague Regulations and other Hague Conventions of 1907 appear in Roberts and Guelff (n 1).

[6] For a list of the Hague Conventions to which South Africa is bound, see CHD Smart 'The municipal effectiveness of treaties relevant to the executive's exercise of belligerent powers' (1987–8) 13 *SAYIL* 23 at 27.

[7] See the judgment of the Nuremberg International Military Tribunal (1947) 41 *AJIL* 172. See, too, *Legal Consequences of the Construction of a Wall in the Occupied Palestinian Territory* 2004 ICJ Reports 136 para 89.

[8] (1975) 14 *ILM* 49. See *S v Basson* (n 1) paras 180–3.

[9] (1972) 11 *ILM* 309.

[10] (1993) 32 *ILM* 800.

[11] Non-proliferation of Weapons of Mass Destruction Act 87 of 1993.

[12] Protocol IV to the Convention on Prohibitions or Restrictions on the Use of Certain Conventional Weapons which may be deemed to be Excessively Injurious or to have Indiscriminate Effects (1998) 35 *ILM* 1218.

landmines.[13] South Africa played a major role in the adoption of this convention, to which it is a party. The Ottawa Convention, which according to its preamble, aims 'to put an end to the suffering and casualties caused by anti-personnel mines that kill or maim hundreds of people every week', is founded on three principles: that the right of the parties to an armed conflict to choose methods of warfare is not unlimited; the prohibition of the employment in armed conflicts of weapons that cause unnecessary suffering; and the need to distinguish between civilians and combatants in armed conflicts. In article 1, states undertake 'never under any circumstances' to use, develop, produce, or acquire anti-personnel mines and to destroy all anti-personnel mines in areas under their control. Municipal effect is given to this treaty by the Anti-Personnel Mines Prohibition Act 36 of 2003,[14] which prohibits the use, stockpiling, production, or development of anti-personnel mines, requires the destruction of such mines and criminalises the violation of the prohibition of such weapons. According to the preamble to this Act, South Africa 'has unilaterally destroyed all the Republic's stockpiled anti-personnel mines'.

Two weapons that cause great suffering in an indiscriminate manner are cluster bombs and white phosphorus. Cluster bombs, unlike ordinary bombs, do not explode all at once but break up into smaller units which fall over a wide area and then explode. They leave explosive remnants on the ground after use and may thus cause human suffering after the cessation of hostilities. In 2010, the Convention on Cluster Munitions (CCM) came into force. Modelled on the Ottawa Convention on landmines, this convention prohibits states parties from using, developing, or producing cluster munitions.[15] White phosphorus is a toxic incendiary weapon that causes chemical burns. It is not illegal when used as an obscurant for creating a smokescreen in military operations, but it is illegal when used in a densely populated area because it violates the prohibition on indiscriminate and disproportionate attacks on civilians[16] and causes unnecessary and superfluous harm to civilians.[17] Israel's use

[13] Convention on the Prohibition of the Use, Stockpiling, Production and Transfer of Anti-Personnel Mines and on their Destruction (1997) 36 *ILM* 1507. See, too, the Schedule to the Anti-Personnel Mines Prohibition Act 36 of 2003.

[14] Particularly ss 2–6 and 13.

[15] N Woudenberg and W Wormgoor 'The Cluster Munitions Convention: Around the world in one year' (2008) 11 *Yearbook of International Humanitarian Law* 391; G Nystuen and S Casey-Maslen *The Law on Cluster Munitions: A Commentary* (2010).

[16] See article 51(4) of Additional Protocol I to the Geneva Conventions.

[17] Article 51 of Additional Protocol I; IJ MacLeod and APV Rogers 'The use of white phosphorus and the law of war' (2007) 10 *Yearbook of International Humanitarian Law* 75 at 94–5.

of this weapon in its attack on Gaza in 2008–2009, codenamed Operation Cast Lead, was widely condemned for this reason.[18]

It is difficult to reconcile nuclear weapons with the norms of humanitarian law, particularly the prohibition on weapons that cause unnecessary suffering. There are therefore cogent reasons to support their illegality.[19] A number of treaties seek to limit the testing and proliferation of such weapons, notably the 1963 Treaty Banning Nuclear Weapons Tests in the Atmosphere, in Outer Space and Under Water,[20] the 1971 Treaty on the Prohibition of the Emplacement of Nuclear Weapons and Other Weapons of Mass Destruction on the Sea-bed and the Ocean Floor and in the Subsoil Thereof,[21] and the 1996 Comprehensive Test Ban Treaty.[22] In 1968, the Treaty on the Non-Proliferation of Nuclear Weapons (NPT)[23] was adopted to prevent the spread of nuclear weapons and to further the goal of nuclear disarmament. While 191 states are parties to the treaty, four states with nuclear weapons—India, Pakistan, North Korea and Israel—are not. In 1961 and 1972, the General Assembly adopted resolutions[24] that seek to outlaw nuclear weapons. Most recently, on 7 July 2017, 122 states endorsed a Treaty on the Prohibition of Nuclear Weapons that prohibits the development, production, testing, stockpiling, or transfer of nuclear weapons and the threat or use of such weapons. Sadly, neither the nuclear powers nor the NATO states gave their support to this treaty. It will come into force when ratified by 50 states.

South Africa occupies a significant place in the evolution of the opposition to nuclear weapons. During the apartheid era, it secretly

[18] *Amnesty International: Rain of Fire: Israel's Unlawful Use of White Phosphorus in Gaza* (March 2009).

[19] There is an extensive literature on this subject. See, eg, G Schwarzenberger *The Legality of Nuclear Weapons* (1958); N Singh *Nuclear Weapons and International Law* (1959); AS Miller and M Feinrider (eds) *Nuclear Weapons and the Law* (1984); M Cohen and ME Gouin *Lawyers and the Nuclear Debate* (1988); N Singh and E McWhinney *Nuclear Weapons and Contemporary International Law* 2 revised ed (1989).

[20] (1963) 2 *ILM* 889.

[21] (1971) 10 *ILM* 146.

[22] (1996) 35 *ILM* 1439.

[23] (1968) 7 *ILM* 811; J Dugard 'Public international law' 1991 *Annual Survey* 647. See, too, above, n 11.

[24] Resolution 1653 (XVI): Declaration on the Prohibition of the Use of Nuclear and Thermo-Nuclear Weapons UN Doc A/RES/1653 (XVI) (24 November 1961); Resolution 2936 (XXVII): Resolution on the Non-Use of Force in International Relations and Permanent Prohibition of the Use of Nuclear Weapons UN Doc A/RES/2936 (XXVII) (29 November 1972).

acquired nuclear weapons[25] and opposed resolutions prohibiting nuclear weapons, but in 1991 the National Party Government under President de Klerk abandoned its role as a nuclear state and destroyed six nuclear fission devices.[26] In 1991, South Africa became a party to the NPT and in 1993 Parliament adopted the Non-Proliferation of Weapons of Mass Destruction Act 87 of 1993, which commits the government to taking 'initiatives to prevent the proliferation and development of weapons of mass destruction' and to prohibiting all nuclear explosions and tests.[27] A council is established which is empowered, inter alia, to ensure that South Africa's international obligations with regard to the non-proliferation of nuclear weapons are fulfilled. In 1997, it became a party to the African Nuclear-Weapon-Free Zone Treaty (the Treaty of Pelindaba).[28] South Africa is a party to the treaties prohibiting nuclear tests and on 20 September 2017 it signed the Treaty on the Prohibition of Nuclear Weapons.

In 1996, the International Court of Justice gave an advisory opinion on the *Legality of the Threat or Use of Nuclear Weapons*[29] at the request of the General Assembly. Arguments raised against the legality of nuclear weapons were founded on the prohibition of the use of force in the Charter of the United Nations, conventional and customary rules of IHL governing the law of armed conflict and neutrality, human rights and environmental conventions, and treaties and General Assembly resolutions restricting the use and testing of nuclear weapons. The principal thrust of these arguments is reflected in the following passage in the Court's Opinion:

> Another view holds that recourse to nuclear weapons could never be compatible with the principles and rules of humanitarian law and is therefore prohibited. In the event of their use, nuclear weapons would in all circumstances be unable to draw any distinction between the civilian population and combatants, or between civilian objects and military objectives, and their effects, largely uncontrollable, could not be restricted, either in time or in

[25] See on the co-operation between Israel and South Africa in order to obtain a nuclear capacity, S Polakow-Suransky *The Unspoken Alliance: Israel's Secret Relationship with Apartheid South Africa* (2010).

[26] See the statement by President FW de Klerk in *Debates of Parliament* cols 3465–72 of 24 March 1993.

[27] Act 87 of 1993, s 2(1)*(a)* and *(f)*.

[28] *National Assembly Debates*, col 6075 (6 Nov 1997).

[29] 1996 ICJ Reports 226. See, further, L Boisson de Chazournes and P Sands *International Law, the International Court of Justice and Nuclear Weapons* (1999); GN Barrie and K Reddy 'The ICJ's Advisory Opinion on the legality of the threat or use of nuclear weapons' (1998) 115 *SALJ* 457; RA Falk 'Nuclear weapons, international law and the World Court: An historic encounter' (1997) 91 *AJIL* 64; MJ Matheson 'The Opinion of the ICJ on the threat or use of nuclear weapons' (1997) 91 *AJIL* 417.

> space, to lawful military targets. Such weapons would kill and destroy in a necessarily indiscriminate manner, on account of the blast, heat and radiation occasioned by the nuclear explosion and the effects induced; and the number of casualties which would ensue would be enormous. The use of nuclear weapons would therefore be prohibited in any circumstance, notwithstanding the absence of any explicit conventional prohibition. That view lay at the basis of the assertions by certain States before the Court that nuclear weapons are by their nature illegal under customary international law, by virtue of the fundamental principle of humanity.[30]

In an unsatisfactory Opinion, the Court failed to answer the question whether the threat or use of nuclear weapons was prohibited in all circumstances. It held:

(a) unanimously, that neither customary nor conventional international law specifically authorises the threat or use of nuclear weapons;

(b) by 11 votes to three, that neither customary nor conventional international law comprehensively and universally prohibits the threat or use of nuclear weapons;

(c) unanimously, that a threat or use of force by means of nuclear weapons that is contrary to article 2(4) of the UN Charter and that fails to meet all the requirements of article 51 is unlawful;

(d) unanimously, that a threat or use of nuclear weapons should be compatible with the requirements of the international law applicable in armed conflict (particularly international humanitarian law) and specific obligations under treaties and other undertakings expressly dealing with nuclear weapons;

(e) by seven votes to seven, by the President's casting vote, that the threat or use of nuclear weapons would generally be contrary to the rules of international law applicable in armed conflict, and, in particular, the principles and rules of humanitarian law, but that in view of the current state of international law and the facts before the Court, it could not conclude definitively whether the threat or use of nuclear weapons would be lawful or unlawful in an extreme circumstance of self-defence, in which the very survival of a state would be at stake; and

(f) unanimously, that there exists an obligation to pursue in good faith and conclude negotiations leading to nuclear disarmament in all its aspects under international control.[31]

In 2016 the International Court of Justice missed another opportunity to add its voice to the opposition to nuclear weapons when a divided court held, by the casting vote of the President, that it lacked jurisdiction by reason of the absence of a proven 'legal dispute' to

[30] 1996 ICJ Reports 262 para 92.

[31] Ibid 265 para 105.

pronounce on an application of the Marshall Islands to find that the United Kingdom, India and Pakistan had failed to pursue negotiations in good faith leading to nuclear disarmament as required by Article VI of the NPT.[32] Sadly, this much-contested technical decision included the votes of all judges from states with a nuclear capacity.

3 Law of Geneva

The Law of Geneva aims to protect combatants no longer engaged in the conflict, and civilians not involved in the hostilities, and is founded on the principle that persons not actively engaged in armed conflict should be treated humanely. It has its roots in the Hague Regulations of 1907 and in the Geneva Conventions of 1929, providing for the protection of prisoners of war and of the wounded and sick. South Africa was a party to the 1929 Conventions, which applied to most belligerents during World War II—but not between Germany and the Soviet Union. These Conventions have been replaced by four Geneva Conventions of 1949,[33] which seek

(i) to ameliorate the condition of the wounded and sick in armed forces in the field, and
(ii) of the wounded, sick, and shipwrecked members of armed forces at sea;
(iii) to regulate the treatment of prisoners of war; and
(iv) to protect civilians in time of war.

In 1977, two Additional Protocols supplemented these conventions.[34] Protocol I deals with the protection of victims of *international* armed conflicts, while Protocol II seeks to expand the protection accorded to the victims of *non-international* armed conflicts, provided for in article 3, common to the four Geneva Conventions of 1949. In 2018, the four Geneva Conventions of 1949 had been accepted by 196 states, while 174 states were party to Protocol I and 168 to Protocol II. South Africa became a party to the four Conventions of 1949 in 1952 and to the 1977 Protocols in 1995. The Implementation of Geneva Conventions Act 8 of 2012 incorporated the Geneva Conventions and its Protocols into South African law in 2012.

While nearly all states are parties to the 1949 Conventions, some important states—India, Indonesia, Iran, Israel, Malaysia, Pakistan, Sri Lanka, Turkey, and the United States—are not parties to the

[32] *Obligation Concerning Negotiations relating to Cessation of the Nuclear Arms Race and to Nuclear Disarmament (Marshall Islands v UK), Preliminary Objections* 2016 ICJ Reports 833.

[33] GNs R749–752 *GGE* 2064 of 3 May 1968 (*Reg Gaz* 953).

[34] (1977) 16 *ILM* 1391 at 1442.

Additional Protocols. Many of the principles contained in these Protocols are, however, rules of customary international law.[35]

4 Principles of humanitarian law

(a) Combatants and prisoners of war

Humanitarian law is premised on the distinction between combatants and civilians. Combatants are legitimate targets in armed conflicts; civilians are not. Combatants are entitled to engage in armed conflict and, if captured, to be treated as prisoners of war. Civilians who engage in armed hostilities are unprotected by the law of armed conflict and are not entitled to prisoner-of-war status if captured. On the contrary, they may be tried and punished for their belligerent acts.

The Third Geneva Convention of 1949 governs the status and treatment of prisoners of war. This Convention is founded on the principle that a prisoner of war is neither a criminal nor a hostage but someone who is held for the sole purpose of preventing him from rejoining the enemy's armed forces. The detaining state is under a strict obligation not to ill-treat prisoners of war and to release and repatriate them immediately after the cessation of hostilities.[36]

When regular armies fought wars, it was not difficult to distinguish between combatants and civilians. Resistance movements of the kind that operated in occupied countries during World War II and guerrilla groups engaged in wars of national liberation have, however, resulted in the blurring of this distinction. Article 44(3) of Additional Protocol I of 1977 largely assimilates regular and irregular forces. It provides that combatants are obliged to distinguish themselves from the civilian population while they are engaged in an attack or in a military operation preparatory to an attack. When an armed combatant cannot so distinguish himself, the status of combatant may be retained provided that arms are carried openly during each military engagement, and during such time as the combatant is visible to the adversary while engaged in a military deployment preceding the launching of an attack.

Furthermore, a person who takes part in hostilities and falls into the power of an adverse party 'shall be presumed to be a prisoner of war' entitled to be protected by the Third Convention until such time as his status has been determined by a competent tribunal'.[37] The refusal of the United States to treat Taliban combatants captured in Afghanistan as prisoners of war and instead to detain them indefi-

[35] See Henckaerts and Doswald Beck (n 2).

[36] Third Convention, article 118.

[37] First Protocol, article 45; Third Convention, article 5.

nitely in Guantanamo Bay is contrary to humanitarian law, as they were members of the Afghan armed forces of an effective government of Afghanistan who took part in an international armed conflict against the United States. Members of Al-Qaeda, on the other hand, may be regarded as civilians engaging in criminal activities who may be tried and punished, in accordance with the procedural guarantees contained in article 75 of Protocol I.[38]

Great difficulties arise in respect of civilians who take up arms for limited action and then return to civilian life. In terms of article 51(3) of Additional Protocol I, civilians lose the protection accorded to civilians 'for such time as they take a direct part in hostilities'. There is no precise definition of the term 'direct participation in hostilities'[39] but care should be taken not to extend this term to cover civilians whose activities merely support the adverse party's war or military effort as article 50 of Additional Protocol I warns that 'in case of doubt whether a person is a civilian, that person shall be considered to be a civilian'. The subject has received considerable attention as a result of Israel's practice of 'targeted assassinations', that is the killing of Palestinian militants at a time when they are not participating in hostilities.[40] The Israeli Supreme Court has attempted to place restraints on this practice,[41] but the practice still continues. In many cases, the killing of militants constitutes the extrajudicial execution of militants who should be arrested and brought to trial rather than summarily executed under the pretext that they have taken a direct part in hostilities and thereby lost the protection accorded to civilians under humanitarian law.

This issue arose in connection with the killing of Osama bin Laden in a private house in Pakistan by US Navy Seals in May 2011. While the United States defended its action as an act taken in national defence, the UN Special Rapporteur on extrajudicial, summary and arbitrary executions, Professor Christof Heyns of the University of Pretoria, pointed out that 'the norm should be that terrorists be dealt

[38] See G Aldrich 'The Taliban, Al Qaeda, and the determination of illegal combatants' (2002) 96 *AJIL* 891. See too 'Agora: Military commissions' (2002) 96 *AJIL* 320–64; H Strydom 'The case of the Guantanamo detainees in United States (and other) courts' (2004) *TSAR* 294.

[39] Henckaerts and Doswald Beck (n 2) vol 1, 22–3.

[40] M Sfard *The Wall and the Gate. Israel, Palestine and the Legal Battle for Human* Rights (2018) 410; N Melzer *Targeted Killings in International Law* (2008); P Alston 'Using international law to combat targeted killings' in U Fastenrath et al (eds) *From Bilateralism to Community Interest: Essays in Honour of Judge Bruno Simma* (2011).

[41] *Public Committee against Torture in Israel v Government of Israel* HCJ 769/02. See further, E Crawford *Identifying the Enemy Civilian Participation in Armed Conflict* (2015).

with as criminals, through legal processes of arrest, trial and judicially decided punishment'.[42]

(b) Occupation and protection of civilians[43]

Humanitarian law contains special rules for the treatment of civilians in occupied territories. These rules are to be found in the Fourth Geneva Convention of 1949, which provides a highly developed set of rules for the protection of civilians in an occupied territory, including the right to respect for person and religious practices, and the prohibition of torture and other cruel, inhuman, or degrading treatment, hostage-taking, reprisals, intimidation and collective punishment. The wounded and sick shall be the object of particular protection and respect and there are various judicial guarantees as to due process. The destruction of property is prohibited, except where 'absolutely necessary' by military operations. The deportation of civilians from the occupied territory to the territory of the occupying power is prohibited and the occupying power is prohibited from transferring parts of its own civilian population to the territory it occupies.[44]

The occupying power has the authority to administer an occupied territory but does not acquire sovereignty. Accordingly, the occupying power may not annex the occupied territory or parts of this territory. Moreover, no attempt on the part of the occupying power to annex the territory or to change its status shall affect the application of the Fourth Convention.[45] Article 43 of the Hague Regulations provides that, 'unless absolutely prevented', the occupying power shall respect the laws in force in the territory at the commencement of the occupation. The law of belligerent occupation is not dependent on the status of the territory before occupation, even where the occupied territory was not subject to the sovereignty of any state. Thus, Israel's claim that the Fourth Geneva Convention does not apply to East Jerusalem, the West Bank and Gaza on the ground that Jordan and Egypt respectively had no valid claim to these territories prior to the 1967 conflict was rejected by the International Court of Justice in its advisory opinion on the *Legal Consequences of the Construction of a Wall in the Occupied Palestinian Territory*.[46]

[42] News release, Office of the High Commissioner for Human Rights, Geneva, 6 May 2011.

[43] See E Benvenisti *The International Law of Occupation* 2 ed (2012); Y Dinstein *The International Law of Belligerent Occupation* (2009).

[44] Fourth Geneva Convention, article 49.

[45] Ibid article 47.

[46] 2004 ICJ Reports paras 90–101.

The question whether a territory is occupied, and therefore subject to the rules governing occupation, gives rise to difficulties. In the *Case Concerning Armed Activities on the Territory of the Congo*[47] the International Court of Justice held that Uganda occupied parts of the Democratic Republic of the Congo on the ground that under customary international law 'territory is considered to be occupied when it is actually placed under the authority of the hostile army, and the occupation extends only to the territory where such authority has been established and can be exercised'. Judged by this test, Western Sahara is occupied by Morocco, Northern Cyprus by Turkey, and Palestine by Israel.[48] Israel denies that it remains the occupying power of Gaza, but, although it has not had a permanent military presence in the territory since 2005, it continues to maintain a tight control over the territory's land and maritime boundaries and airspace, and to conduct military incursions into the territory, which seems to meet with the test for occupation.[49]

The prohibition on the transfer of civilians of the occupying power into the occupied territory contained in article 49(6) of the Fourth Geneva Convention was introduced because of Germany's practice during World War II of colonising occupied territories by settling them with German civilians. This explains the firm response of the international community to Israel's settlement of some 800 000 Israeli civilians in the West Bank and East Jerusalem which has been condemned by the International Court of Justice[50] and the United Nations Security Council (UNSC)[51] as illegal. Israel is not, however, the only occupying power to engage in this practice of neo-colonisation. Turkey has transferred citizens into occupied Northern Cyprus and Morocco has likewise transferred its citizens into occupied Western Sahara.

'Conceptually, occupation is neutral. It connotes an authority and a responsibility.'[52] This means that, at least conceptually, it is a fact that is neither lawful nor unlawful. The prolonged nature of Israel's occupation of the Palestinian territories, coupled with its *de jure* or *de*

[47] 2005 ICJ Reports 168, 229 para 172.

[48] *Wall Opinion* (n 7) 167 para 78.

[49] Dinstein (n 43) 276–86.

[50] *Wall Opinion* (n 7) para 120. See, generally, *Occupation, Colonialism, Apartheid? A Re-assessment of Israel's Practices in the Occupied Palestinian Territories under International Law*, a study sponsored by the South African Human Sciences Research Council (2009), available at http://sro.sussex.ac.uk/43295/1/Occupation_Colonialism_Apartheid-FullStudy_copy.pdf.

[51] See Security Council Resolution 2334 of 23 December 2016. See further T Meron 'The West Bank and International Humanitarian Law on the eve of the fiftieth anniversary of the Six-Day War' (2017) 111 *AJIL* 357.

[52] Benvenisti (n 43) 15.

facto annexation of Palestinian territory, illegal settlement of Israeli citizens in Palestinian territory, failure to act in the best interests of the occupied people and application of a policy of apartheid,[53] have, however, led to argument that Israel's occupation is illegal.[54]

(c) *Distinction and proportionality*

Two fundamental principles of humanitarian law govern the question of who may be targeted and what may be attacked in the conduct of hostilities. These are the principles of distinction and proportionality.[55]

The principle of distinction is codified in article 48 of Protocol I which provides:

> [T]he Parties to the conflict shall at all times distinguish between the civilian population and combatants and between civilian objects and military objectives and accordingly shall direct their operations only against military objectives.[56]

As shown above, in practice it is often difficult to make such a distinction, particularly when civilians assume the role of combatants and then revert to civilian status. Article 50 of Additional Protocol I describes a civilian as a person who is not a member of the armed forces, but article 31(3) recognises that civilians lose their civilian status and hence protection 'for such time as they take a direct part in hostilities'. There is no clear definition of the term 'direct participation in hostilities' and each case must be examined on its own circumstances,[57] bearing in mind the presumption in favour of retention of civilian status.[58]

The principle of proportionality requires that even military objectives may not be attacked if an attack is likely to cause civilian

[53] J Dugard and J Reynolds 'Apartheid, international law and the Occupied Palestinian Territory' (2013) 24 *EJIL* 867.

[54] O Ben-Naftali, A Gross and K Michaelis 'Illegal occupation; Framing the Occupied Palestinian Territory' (2005) 23 *Berkeley Journal of International Law* 551. See too the report of the UN Special Rapporteur on the Human Rights situation in the Occupied Palestinian Territory, Michael Lynk, *General Assembly Official Records*, UN Doc A/72/556, 23 October 2017.

[55] See the *dictum* of the International Court of Justice in *Legality of the Threat or Use of Nuclear Weapons* 1996 ICJ Reports at 257 para 78.

[56] See, too, article 52(2) of Protocol I which provides that 'Attacks shall be limited strictly to military objectives. In so far as objects are concerned, military objectives are limited to those objects which by their nature, location, purpose or use make an effective contribution to military action and whose total or partial destruction, capture or neutralization, in the circumstances ruling at the times offers a definite military advantage.'

[57] See the decision of the Israeli Supreme Court in the *Targeted Killings Case* HCJ 769/02 para 40.

[58] See Additional Protocol I, article 50(1).

casualties or damage which would be excessive or disproportionate in relation to the concrete or direct military advantage which the attack is expected to produce.[59]

These two principles impose important duties on the commander who orders an attack. He must balance the likely civilian casualties and damage to civilian property against the concrete and direct military advantage anticipated from an attack. Particular difficulties arise in respect of military targets situated near to hospitals, schools, and residential areas. Article 58 of Protocol I requires states 'to avoid locating military objectives within or near densely populated areas' but in practice, states often fail to comply with this obligation and in such cases, the commander is not absolved from complying with the obligations inherent in the principles of distinction and proportionality.

The principles of distinction and proportionality assumed an important role in the evaluation of Israel's conduct during its assaults on Gaza in 2008–2009 (Operation Cast Lead) and 2014 (Operation Protective Edge). While Israel maintained that it had faithfully observed these principles, several investigations found that the Israel Defense Force had committed war crimes due to its indiscriminate and disproportionate assault on the civilian population of Gaza.[60]

The principles of distinction and proportionality are put to the test by targeted assassinations conducted by drones.[61] Increasingly technologically advanced states choose to assassinate or 'liquidate' hostile actors by means of rockets fired from unmanned drones. Inevitably, such actions are frequently taken against persons taking no direct part in hostilities and result in substantial collateral loss of life on the part of innocent civilians. Although opinions are divided on the legality of such operations it is clear that the existing rules of IHL are ill-equipped to deal with the methods employed by modern technology to cause human suffering.

(d) International and non-international armed conflicts

In the past wars generally followed a declaration that the states in question were at war. Today such declarations are highly unusual

[59] Additional Protocol I, articles 51(5)(b) and 57.

[60] See N Finkelstein *Gaza. An Inquest into its Martyrdom* (2018). Two international fact finding missions were conducted on Operation Cast Lead under the chairpersonship of South African jurists: *Human Rights in Palestine and Other Occupied Arab Territories: Report of the United Nations Fact Finding Mission on the Gaza Conflict* A/HRC/12/48 (15 September 2009) (Judge Richard Goldstone, the chair of this mission subsequently retracted part of the findings of the report); *No Safe Place: Report of the Independent Fact Finding Committee on Gaza* (presented to the League of Arab States 30/4/2009) (This investigation was chaired by the present author).

[61] See C Heyns et al, 'The international law framework regulating the use of armed drones' (2016) 65 *ICLQ* 791; CH Heyns 'Autonomous weapons in armed conflict and the right to a dignified life: An African perspective' (2017) 33 *SAJHR*.

with the result that the Geneva Conventions of 1949, in terms of common article 2, apply 'to all cases of declared war or of any other armed conflict' which may arise between states, 'even if the state of war is not recognised by one of them'. According to the International Criminal Tribunal for the former Yugoslavia:

> [A]n armed conflict exists whenever there is a resort to armed force between states or protracted armed violence between governmental authorities and organised armed groups or between such groups within a state. International humanitarian law applies from the initiation of such armed conflicts and extends beyond the cessation of hostilities until a general conclusion of peace is reached; or, in the case of internal conflicts, a peaceful settlement is achieved. Until that moment, international humanitarian law continues to apply in the whole territory of the warring states or, in the case of internal conflicts, the whole territory under the control of a party, whether or not actual combat takes place.[62]

The above-cited passage makes it clear that humanitarian law applies to both international and internal conflicts.[63] This is a recent development, as early humanitarian law applied only to armed conflicts involving two or more states—that is, international armed conflicts—and not to civil wars or internal conflicts. In terms of the Geneva Conventions of 1949 the only protection for those engaged in hostilities against government forces within a state—that is, 'in the case of armed conflict not of an international character'—is to be found in common article 3 of the four conventions. This provides that, in such conflicts, each party to the conflict, is bound to accept, 'as a minimum', that persons taking no active part in hostilities are to be treated humanely without any adverse distinction based on race, colour, religion or faith, sex, birth or wealth. To this end, the following acts are prohibited:

(a) violence to life and person, in particular murder, cruel treatment and torture;
(b) hostage-taking;
(c) outrages upon human dignity, in particularly, humiliating and degrading treatment;
(d) the passing of sentences and the carrying out of executions in the absence of due process.

The wounded and sick are also to be cared for.

In *S v Basson*[64] the Constitutional Court held that common article 3 established 'a basic yardstick' for evaluating the manner in which a

[62] *Tadic Case*, Appeals Chamber (Jurisdiction), Decision of 2 October 1995, Case No IT-94-1-AR 72 para 70; 105 ILR 453 at 488; (1996) 35 *ILM* 32 at 54. Cited with approval by the Constitutional Court in *S v Basson* (n 1) paras 175, 178.

[63] See L Moir *The Law of Internal Armed Conflict* (2002).

[64] *S v Basson* (n 1) paras 181–4.

medical officer was to treat the wounded and sick and non-combatants in an armed conflict. To subject such persons to poisoning clearly violated the obligation contained in article 3.

Rebels engaged in an internal civil war are not entitled to the privileges accorded to combatants in international armed conflicts; in particular, they enjoy no right to be treated as prisoners of war.

The concern for human rights manifested in the post-World War II legal order,[65] together with the prevalence of wars of decolonisation—that is, wars of national liberation[66]—led to demands for the revision of humanitarian law to include armed conflicts not of an international character. This led, in 1977, to the inclusion of article 1(4) in Additional Protocol I and to the adoption of Additional Protocol II on non-international armed conflicts.

Article 1(4) of Additional Protocol I extends the application of the Geneva Conventions of 1949 to

> armed conflicts in which people are fighting against colonial domination and alien occupation and against racist regimes in the exercise of their right of self-determination.

To benefit from this provision, a national liberation movement (NLM) is required to deposit a declaration accepting the obligations under the law of Geneva with the Swiss Federal Council.[67] Members of the NLM then become entitled, inter alia, to be treated as prisoners of war by the colonial/racist power (if it accepts Protocol I) and not as criminal rebels or terrorists. This controversial provision was directed largely at apartheid South Africa and Israel, the states then engaged in hostilities against NLMs. For this reason, South Africa refused to ratify the Additional Protocols until 1995. Despite its controversial nature, which has resulted in both the United States and Israel refusing to sign Additional Protocol I, the practical impact of article 1(4) has been small. Indeed, it has yet to be applied.

Additional Protocol II on the Protection of Victims of Non-International Armed Conflicts develops and supplements common article 3 of the 1949 Geneva Conventions. It contains more detailed

[65] In the *Tadic Case* (n 62) para 83, the ICTY stated that 'recent trends of State practice and the whole doctrine of human rights tend to blur in many aspects the traditional dichotomy between international wars and civil strife'. See, too, *S v Basson* (n 1) para 179.

[66] See H Wilson *International Law and the Use of Force by National Liberation Movements* (1988); GM Abi-Saab 'Wars of national liberation in the Geneva conventions and protocols' (1979-IV) 165 *Recueil des Cours* 353; A Borrowdale 'The law of war in southern Africa: The growing debate' (1982) 15 *CILSA* 41; J Dugard 'SWAPO: The *jus ad bellum* and the *jus in bello*' (1976) 93 *SALJ* 44; FR Ribeiro 'International humanitarian law: Advancing progressively backwards' (1980) 97 *SALJ* 42.

[67] Additional Protocol I, article 96(3).

provisions on fundamental guarantees, treatment of the wounded and sick and protection of the civilian population. However, it is more restricted than common article 3. Whereas common article 3 applies to any armed conflict within a state, Protocol II applies only to armed conflicts which take place in a party to Protocol II between its armed forces and dissident armed forces which, under responsible command, 'exercise such control over a part of its territory as to enable them to carry out sustained and concerted military operations and to implement this Protocol'. Moreover, the Protocol does not apply to internal disturbances, including riots and sporadic acts of violence.[68] This means that its provisions apply only to civil wars in which both sides to the armed conflict control parts of the territory of a state; whereas common article 3 comes into operation when the conflict qualifies as an 'armed conflict', without the requirement that rebel forces control territory.

The traditional dichotomy between international armed conflicts and non-international armed conflicts was manifested in the punishment of those who violated humanitarian law. The 1949 Geneva Conventions[69] and Additional Protocols[70] provide for the punishment of those who commit 'grave breaches' of these conventions—that is war crimes[71]—in international armed conflicts only. Here too, state practice has changed. In *The Prosecutor v Tadic*,[72] the Appeals Chamber of the International Criminal Tribunal for the Former Yugoslavia carefully examined this practice and concluded that customary international law today imposes criminal liability for the violation of the laws and customs of war in both internal and international armed conflicts. The Rome Statute of the International Criminal Court confirms the blurring of the distinction between international and non-international armed conflicts in the field of the punishment of violations of humanitarian law. Genocide and crimes against humanity may be committed in time of peace and war.[73] Some war crimes, mainly those designated as 'grave breaches' of the Geneva Conventions and Additional Protocol I, may still only be

[68] Additional Protocol I, article 1.

[69] See First Convention, articles 49 and 50 and Second Convention, articles 50 and 51. The Third Convention, articles 129 and 130 and Fourth Convention, articles 145 and 147 contain substantially similar provisions.

[70] Article 85.

[71] Article 85(5) declares that 'grave breaches' of the 1949 Conventions and Protocol I 'shall be regarded as war crimes'.

[72] *Tadic Case* (n 62) paras 84–137.

[73] Rome Statute, articles 6 and 7. There is no threshold for genocide. In the case of crimes against humanity, the act must be 'committed as part of a widespread or systematic attack directed against any civilian population, with knowledge of the attack' (article 7).

committed in time of international armed conflict;[74] but others may be committed in armed conflicts not of an international character, provided the conflict has advanced beyond the level of 'internal disturbances and tensions, such as riots, isolated and sporadic acts of violence or other acts of a similar nature'.[75]

(e) Human rights and international humanitarian law

Humanitarian law and human rights law have different sources and rules but they are both premised on respect for human dignity and therefore are separate parts of a single order committed to respect for human rights in armed conflicts.[76] This is borne out by the jurisprudence of the ad hoc criminal tribunals for the former Yugoslavia[77] and Rwanda, the International Criminal Court (ICC) and the International Court of Justice. In its advisory opinion on the *Legal Consequences of the Construction of a Wall in the Occupied Palestinian Territory*[78] the International Court of Justice rejected Israel's argument that humanitarian law as *lex specialis* alone was applicable to its administration of the occupied Palestinian territory. Instead, it held that Israel's conduct in the occupied Palestinian territory was to be judged in accordance with norms of both humanitarian law and human rights law.

(f) Enforcement of international humanitarian law

In 1952, Hersch Lauterpacht wrote, with the enforcement of humanitarian law in mind, that:

> If international law is in some ways at the vanishing point of law, the law of war is, perhaps even more conspicuously, at the vanishing point of international law.[79]

Ongoing conflicts in Syria, Yemen, Palestine and central Africa resulting in widespread suffering on the part of civilian populations testify to the correctness of Lauterpacht's comment. However, the weak enforcement of humanitarian law, and in many cases its complete non-enforcement, is not the result of an absence of international law-enforcement procedures and mechanisms but of the absence of a political will on the part of states and international institutions to take action to ensure compliance with humanitarian law.

Both the 1949 Geneva Conventions and Protocol I[80] oblige states 'to

[74] Ibid, article 8(2)(a) and (b).
[75] Ibid, article 8(2)(c)–(f).
[76] R Provost *International Human Rights and Humanitarian Law* (2002).
[77] See, eg, *Prosecutor v Anto Furundzija* 121 ILR 213 at 271.
[78] 2004 ICJ Reports paras 102–13.
[79] H Lauterpacht 'The problem of revision of the law of war' (1952) 20 *BYIL* 382.
[80] Common article 1.

respect and to ensure respect' for the Conventions 'in all circumstances' and to disseminate knowledge of the principles contained therein.[81] All four Geneva Conventions[82] and Protocol I[83] oblige states to exercise universal jurisdiction to prosecute persons responsible for the commission of 'grave breaches' of the Conventions and Protocol but this procedure is hardly ever used. Article 90 of Protocol I establishes an International Fact-Finding Commission to investigate violations of the Protocol and Conventions but it may only act when a complaint is initiated by a state that has recognised its competence and against a state that has likewise recognised its competence. In practice, this mechanism is therefore not used by states. States that violate the Conventions may be held responsible in accordance with the rules of state responsibility, and claims have been brought before the International Court of Justice based on violations of humanitarian law.[84] Far more use could, however, have been made of this enforcement mechanism.

The establishment of ad hoc international criminal tribunals and the ICC with jurisdiction over serious violations of IHL[85] gave rise to expectations that the prosecution of offenders would result in the enforcement of IHL and deter military and political leaders in conflict situations from violating IHL. The failure of the ICC to prosecute more than a handful of offenders has, however, resulted in scepticism about this method of enforcement. Moreover, the evidence suggests that the establishment of the ICC has had little deterrent effect. Finally, the UNSC has predictably been constrained by the veto power of permanent members to take action in serious conflict situations.

The failure of states and institutions to respond to violations of IHL has placed a heavy burden on civil society to aid victims of armed conflict and to conduct fact-finding missions to expose wrongdoers. The pre-eminent NGO body remains the ICRC which monitors the conduct of belligerents in armed conflict and is empowered to visit prisoners of war.

[81] See eg Third and Fourth Geneva Conventions articles 127 and 144, Protocol I, article 83 and Protocol II, article 19.

[82] First Convention, articles 49 and 50, Second Convention, articles 50 and 51, Third Convention, articles 129 and 130 and Fourth Convention, articles 146 and 147.

[83] Protocol I, article 85.

[84] See, eg, *Nicaragua v United States (Merits)* 1986 ICJ Reports 14; *Armed Activities on the Territory of the Congo (DRC v Uganda)* 2005 ICJ Reports 168.

[85] See Chapter 10.

HUMANITARIAN LAW AND SOUTH AFRICAN MUNICIPAL LAW

1 The Anglo-Boer War

The Anglo-Boer War[86] occurred at a time when humanitarian law was in its infancy. As the Boer Republics were not parties to any of the humanitarian conventions, customary international law governed the hostilities. Both parties to the conflict claimed to act in accordance with the customs and usages of the laws of war: at times both parties accused each other of violations of these customs;[87] and municipal courts judged many disputes, particularly relating to the seizure and forfeiture of the property of belligerents, in accordance with the customary laws of war.[88]

Despite the fact that Britain did not recognise the Transvaal as a fully sovereign state, and despite the failure of the Boer forces to wear distinctive uniforms, the forces of both Republics were treated as combatants and not as rebels. After the annexation of the Boer Republics in 1900 and the transformation of the war into a guerrilla war, Britain continued to treat the forces of the Boer Republics as lawful belligerents. The families and property of these forces were not accorded the same treatment after 1900. Wives and children were forced into concentration camps, where thousands died from disease, farmhouses were burnt, and lands devastated. In this respect the Boer forces were treated as rebels whose families and property were not entitled to the respect accorded to lawful belligerents. Boers resident in the Cape and Natal, who joined the Republican forces, were treated as rebels[89] and, in some instances, were executed without fair trial.[90]

[86] See J Dugard 'The treatment of rebels in conflicts of a disputed character: The Anglo-Boer War and the "ANC-Boer War" compared' in AJM Delissen and GJ Tanya (eds) *Humanitarian Law of Armed Conflict: Challenges Ahead: Essays in Honour of Frits Kalshoven* (1991) 447 at 448–50; AWG Raath and HA Strydom 'The Hague Conventions and the Anglo-Boer War' (1999) 24 *SAYIL* 149.

[87] See T Baty *International Law in South Africa* (1901).

[88] See *Van Deventer v Hancke and Mossop* 1903 TS 401; *Lemkuhl v Kock* 1903 TS 451; *Olivier v Wessels* 1904 TS 235; *R v Louw* (1904) 21 SC 36; *Alexander v Pfau* 1902 TS 155; *Du Toit v Kruger* (1905) 22 SC 234; *Acterberg v Glinster* 1903 TS 326.

[89] See 'Cape treason trials' reported in (1901) 18 *SALJ* 164; *R v De Jager* (1901) 22 NLR 65; *R v Boers* (1900) 21 NLR 116; *R v Gowthorpe* (1900) 21 NLR 221; *R v Venter* (1901) 22 NLR 185.

[90] JH Snyman 'Rebelle—Verhoor in Kaapland gedurende die Tweede-Vryheidsoorlog met spesiale verwysing na die Militêre Howe (1899–1902)' (1962) 25 *Archives Year Book for South African History* 1.

2 The status of humanitarian treaties

The Constitution makes it clear that South Africa intends to honour its IHL obligations.[91] Section 198*(c)* declares that 'national security must be pursued in compliance with the law, including international law' and s 199(5) provides that:

> The security services must act, and must teach and require their members to act, in accordance with the Constitution and the law, including customary international law and international agreements binding on the Republic.

Moreover, s 37(8) provides that the law governing detention without trial during a state of emergency shall not apply to non-South African citizens detained in consequence of an international armed conflict. Here the state 'must comply with the standards binding on the Republic under international humanitarian law in respect of the detention of such persons'.

Although South Africa became a party to the four Geneva Conventions in 1952 and to the Additional Protocols in 1995, they were only incorporated into municipal law in 2012.[92] Prior to the incorporation of the Conventions, it was suggested that as they affected belligerent rights, they might be applied by municipal courts without any legislative act of incorporation.[93] Support was found for this argument in judicial decisions applying The Hague Regulations[94] and 1929 Geneva Conventions[95]—predecessors of the 1949 Conventions. This argument was premised on the existence of prerogative powers which gave the executive the competence to legislate in certain areas of foreign relations, particularly affecting belligerency. Whatever the merits of this argument, it is not valid today, as the Constitution no longer recognises the executive prerogative.[96]

[91] H Strydom '*Jus ad bellum* and *jus in bello* in the South African Constitution' (2004) 29 *SAYIL* 78 at 88–9.

[92] Implementation of Geneva Conventions Act 8 of 2012. See M du Plessis 'The Geneva Conventions and South African Law' (2013) 43 *ISS Policy Brief*. Prior to this, the Geneva Conventions had been published for 'general information' in the *Government Gazette*. See J Dugard 'Foreign affairs and public international law' 1968 *Annual Survey* 49 at 56–8.

[93] See CHD Smart 'The municipal effectiveness of treaties relevant to the executive's exercise of belligerent powers' (1987–8) 13 *SAYIL* 23 at 39; H Booysen 'Treaties, enemy aliens and prisoners of war in South African law' (1973) 90 *SALJ* 386 at 387–8.

[94] *Labuschagne v Maarburger* 1915 CPD 423 at 431–3. See, too, *Lieben's Estate v Custodian of Enemy Property* 1925 TPD 232; *Eschenburg's Estate v Custodian of Enemy Property* 1926 TPD 132.

[95] *R v Giuseppe* 1943 TPD 139; *R v Werner* 1947 (2) SA 828 (A) 832. In *S v Petane* 1988 (3) SA 51 (C) Conradie J assumed the correctness of *R v Giuseppe* (54G–H).

[96] *President of the Republic of South Africa v Hugo* 1997 (4) SA 1 (CC) 6–9; G Carpenter 'Prerogative powers in South Africa—Dead and gone at last?' (1997) 22 *SAYIL* 104. Cf

The four Conventions of 1949 and the two Protocols are attached as schedules to the Implementation of the Geneva Conventions Act and incorporated in this manner. Section 2 declares that the objects of the legislation are to enact the Conventions and Protocols into domestic law as required by s 231(4), to ensure South African compliance and to ensure the prevention of, and punishment for, breaches of the Conventions and Protocols.

The Implementation of the Geneva Conventions Act must be read in conjunction with the Implementation of the Rome Statute of the International Criminal Court Act 27 of 2002—which makes 'grave breaches' of the 1949 Conventions and violations of common article 3 of these conventions and prohibitions contained in the Additional Protocols punishable under South African law.[97]

3 Mercenaries

By Shannon Bosch

In the past, wars were fought by mercenaries.[98] Today international law has turned against mercenaries, largely as a result of their involvement in conflicts in Africa. Additional Protocol I of 1977 denies mercenaries 'the right to be a combatant or a prisoner of war';[99] and in 1989, the International Convention against the Recruitment, Use, Financing and Training of Mercenaries[100] was adopted to criminalise the recruitment and use of mercenaries, as well as participation in hostilities as a mercenary. Although South Africa is not a party to the 1989 Convention, the Regulation of Foreign Military Assistance Act 15 of 1998 (FMA Act) gave effect to the main provisions of the Convention by making it an offence for anyone to 'recruit, use or train persons for or finance or engage in mercenary activity'.[101]

Curiously the FMA Act goes much further than the 1989 Convention and prohibits a range of activities that typically characterise the private security industry, and are not perceived with mercenary

the comments of Sachs J in *S v Basson* (n 2) 216 suggesting that the provisions in the 1949 Geneva Conventions requiring states to punish 'grave breaches' of the Conventions had the force of law in South Africa.

[97] See Chapter 10.

[98] See C Botha 'From mercenaries to "private military companies": The collapse of the African State and the outsourcing of state security' (1999) 24 *SAYIL* 133; C Walker and D Whyte 'Contracting out of war? Private military companies, law and regulation in the UK' (2005) 54 *ICLQ* 651.

[99] Additional Protocol I, article 47.

[100] (1990) 29 *ILM* 89.

[101] FMA Act, ss 2 and 8.

intent.[102] This move to regulate the participation of South African nationals in the private security industry through the extraterritorial application of domestic legislation was peculiar and not widely supported.[103] The rest of the international community had elected instead to regulate the private security industry through codes of conduct,[104] a Draft Convention on Private Military and Security Companies[105] and more recently accreditation with the International Organization for Standardization (ISO).[106]

The political climate which prevailed in 1998, when the FMA Act was drafted, sheds some light on why the South African government perceived any unauthorised foreign military assistance with mercenary suspicion.[107] Post 1994, after the South African armed forces were reorganised, many ex-South African National Defence Forces' special operations personnel were forced into early retirement.[108] Their expertise and experience in nonconventional conflicts made them highly sought after by foreign private military and security companies (PMSCs) and foreign militaries.[109] The ANC government was concerned that their credibility amongst their fellow African states would be undermined if they were seen as a haven for mercenaries and complicit in the activities of PMSCs like Executive Outcomes.[110] Moreover, the activities of these PMSCs began to attract the attention of the United Nations Special Rapporteur for the Working group on the use of mercenaries as a means of violating

[102] Included in the list is the provision of general equipment, advice and training to other militaries. See D Avant *The Market for Force: The Consequences of Privatizing Security* (2005) 162.

[103] The only other state to have adopted a similar approach is India. See S Bosch, M Maritz and M Kimble 'Mercenaries or legitimate actors' in G Schaub and R Kelty (eds) *Private Military and Security Contractors: Controlling the Corporate Warrior* (2016) 62.

[104] International Committee for the Red Cross *The Montreux Document on Pertinent International Legal Obligations and Good Practices for States Related to Operations of Private Military and Security Companies During Armed Conflict* (2009); International Code of Conduct Association *International Code of Conduct for Private Security Service Providers* (2010).

[105] Office of the High Commissioner for Human Rights *Draft Convention on Private Military and Security Companies* A/HRC/15/25 (2010).

[106] International Organization for Standardization *Management System for Private Security Operations—Requirements with Guidance for Use* ISO 18788 and ISO 28007; R DeWinter-Schmitt 'A new twist to management standards, bringing in human rights' *Private Security Monitor* (Summer 2014).

[107] Bosch, Maritz and Kimble (n 103) 65.

[108] R Taljaard 'Implementing South Africa's Regulation of Foreign Military Assistance Act' in A Bryden and M Caparini (eds) *Private Actors and Security Governance* (2006) 169.

[109] Bosch, Maritz and Kimble (n 102) 47.

[110] Avant (n 102) 161.

human rights and impeding the exercise of the right of peoples to self-determination, who questioned their influence and particularly their access to the continent's natural resources.[111]

Initially several foreign PMSCs retrenched their South African personnel when the FMA Act entered into force, and it appeared as if the Act was curtailing the booming PMSC industry.[112] Some domestic PMSCs quietly re-incorporated themselves and moved offshore, charter shopping for states where the domestic legislation was less draconian.[113] Others continued to operate within South Africa's borders on a more clandestine level.[114] All were at pains to avoid the vagaries of the National Conventional Arms Control Committee (NCACC), and very few applications for authorisation to offer foreign military assistance were lodged by South African nationals or corporations.[115] Despite the wide ambit of the FMA Act, only a handful of high-profile instances of alleged mercenary activities have ever been prosecuted under the FMA Act.[116] Many of those prosecutions have ended in plea bargains, suspended jail terms and insignificant fines (ranging from R10 000 to R200 000).[117] In court the FMA Act faced legal challenges on the grounds that the unfettered discretionary powers given to the NCACC rendered its provisions unconstitutional.[118] Domestic courts did not see PMSCs and PSCs with mercenary suspicion and questions arose whether the FMA Act was specifically drafted with the intention of de-legitimising the

[111] S Franklin 'SA and international attempts to regulate mercenaries and private military companies' (2008) 17 *Transnational Law and Contemporary Problems* 247; F Mathieu and N Dearden 'Corporate mercenaries: The threat of private military and security companies' (2007) 34 *Review of African Political Economy* 747.

[112] UK-based Erinys retrenched 100 South African security contractors: N Hodge 'Army for hire' *Slate* (31 August 2006).

[113] Saracens, Security Control Systems and Lifeguard moved off shore, and Executive Outcomes were forced to cease operating under that name, but several of their operatives reportedly moved across to Lifeguard and continued to work in Sierra Leone: B Perrin *Modern Warfare: Armed Groups, Private Militaries, Humanitarian Organizations, and the Law* (2012) 228.

[114] Frederick, Nicholas and Duncan went underground: see, C Holmqvist 'Private security companies: The case for regulation' *Stockholm International Peace Research Institute* Policy Paper 9 (2005) 42.

[115] Concern arose around whether applications would be unfairly denied (in terms of s 9), or withdrawn at a later stage (in terms of ss 4(3) and 5(3)) of the FMA Act (Bosch, Maritz and Kimble (n 103) 59; S Gumedze 'In the absence of a legally binding instrument for private security actors, the need for the implementation of the international code of conduct for private security service providers in Africa cannot be gainsaid' *Institute for Security Studies* 2012.

[116] S Bosch 'South Africans offering foreign military assistance abroad: How real is the risk of domestic prosecution?' (2018) 21 *PER/PELJ* 4.

[117] Bosch, Maritz and Kimble (n 103) 54.

[118] Bosch (n 116) 5; Avant (n 102) 162.

private security industry rather than prohibiting mercenarism.[119] South Africa remained a prolific supplier of personnel to the private security industry, and it was business as usual for an estimated 1.7 million-plus, deployed abroad as private security contractors (PSCs).[120] Ironically, the hard-line stance taken by the FMA Act, has resulted in the industry going underground, off-shore, and effectively circumventing any government regulation.[121]

In response to the challenges that the FMA Act was facing, the Prohibition of Mercenary Activities and Regulation of Certain Activities in Country of Armed Conflict Act 27 of 2006 (PMA Act) was adopted.[122] The scope of application of the PMA Act once again expanded the term mercenary well beyond what was envisaged in the 1989 Convention to include 'other forms of involvement in the security sector that might only destabilise states, irrespective of whether the situation rose to the level of an armed conflict and even without an armed conflict being declared'.[123] The definition also included within the PMA Act's ambit 'advice, logistical support, training, security services or personnel recruitment',[124] including supportive or financial assistance in a conflict, where private gain was shown. The jurisdictional scope of the PMA Act[125] makes it possible for the National Prosecuting Authority to prosecute South African citizens, residents and locally registered companies performing these activities without NCACC authorisation, even outside of South Africa's borders, in the employ of foreign PMSCs and even at the invitation of the territorial state.[126] The PMA Act attained the necessary presidential assent in November 2007, however it has yet to receive the necessary presidential proclamation and regulations required to make it binding law.

[119] Avant (n 102) 167; Bosch (n 116) 5.

[120] E Gaston 'Mercenarism 2.0? The rise of the modern private security industry and its implications for international humanitarian law enforcement' (2008) 49 *Harvard International Law Journal* 241.

[121] Taljaard (n 108) 169.

[122] See C Botha 'If you can't be with one you love, love the one you're with: A critical analysis of the latest South African anti-mercenary legislation' (2006) 31 *SAYIL* 224; M Cowling 'Outsourcing and the military: Implications for international humanitarian law' (2007) 32 *SAYIL* 312.

[123] Security and Constitutional Affairs Select Committee Report 2006.

[124] Franklin (n 111) 251. This would include a South African company selling anything from backpacks to tents to a foreign military or any armed group.

[125] PMA Act, s 11.

[126] Bosch (n 116) 8. This encompasses the more than 800 South Africans who currently serve in the British armed forces, and all those who serve in the Israeli Defense Force.

The 2012 and 2015 *South African Defence Review* hints at why the PMA Act has stalled and the FMA Act is seldom the basis for prosecutions. In 2012, the *Review* noted that African private security contractors provide essential force-multiplying services and that 'PSCs with links to South Africa will continue to feature in defence transformation, peacekeeping and peace building in conflict and post-conflict for the foreseeable future'.[127] In 2015 the *South African Defence Review* acknowledged that mercenarism was not to be confused with '[t]he legal activities of private security companies,' but that the issue 'remains the effective regulation of South African Private security companies'.[128] This indicates a new willingness to revisit the South African government's view of the PMSC industry, and explains why the PMA Act appears to have been shelved.

4 The treatment of members of national liberation movements

The status of members of NLMs in southern Africa became a matter of legal controversy in the 1980s. The extension of the privileges of the Geneva Conventions to NLMs by Protocol I of 1977, coupled with the ANC's purported acceptance of the obligations under Protocol I,[129] gave rise to expectations on the part of NLMs that their forces would be accorded privileged treatment as prisoners of war.[130] The South African government, which had refused to sign the 1977 Protocols, rejected this development in humanitarian law and continued to treat the escalating conflict[131] as an internal war to which, at most, common article 3 of the Geneva Conventions applied.[132] Consequently, those members of NLMs captured in border conflicts

[127] Department of Defence *South African Defence Review*—Draft Document for Public Engagement (2012) chapter 3 para 48.

[128] Ibid para 48.

[129] In 1980, Oliver Tambo, President of the ANC, deposited a declaration with the President of the Red Cross (and not the Swiss Federal Council) in which the ANC stated that it intended 'to respect and be guided by the general principles of international humanitarian law applicable in armed conflicts' and to respect the rules contained in the Geneva Conventions of 1949 and Additional Protocol I of 1977 'wherever practically possible' (1981) 220 *International Review of the Red Cross* 20. See too Borrowdale (n 66) 41.

[130] See J Dugard 'The conflict between international law and South African law: Another divisive factor in South African society' (1986) 2 *SAJHR* 1 at 17–19.

[131] In *End Conscription Campaign v Minister of Defence* 1989 (2) SA 180 (C), Selikowitz J held that the conflict in South Africa itself did not constitute 'war' justifying the application of martial law. He acknowledged the existence of such a 'war' in northern Namibia (203D).

[132] N Boister 'The legal regulation of the South African "armed conflict" by Common Article 3 of the 1949 Geneva Conventions' (1988–9) 14 *SAYIL* 129. In 1975 Booysen argued that the conflict in South Africa did not amount to an 'armed conflict' of either an internal or international character and that the Geneva Conventions were

or apprehended for acts of violence in South Africa were treated as ordinary criminals and not as prisoners of war. The issue was raised before the courts of South Africa and South West Africa (Namibia) on several occasions.[133]

Attempts to persuade the courts that Protocol I had become part of customary international law,[134] with the result that they were barred from trying combatants belonging to NLMs on the ground that they were entitled to prisoner-of-war status, were unsuccessful. In *S v Petane*,[135] Conradie J dismissed such a plea raised by a member of the military wing of the ANC, *Umkhonto we Sizwe*, charged with terrorism arising out of an attempt to place a bomb in a shopping centre, holding that there was insufficient state practice (*usus*) to support such a rule.[136] Trengove AJ approved this finding in the Namibian case of *S v Mule*.[137]

In several decisions, however, courts were prepared to find that developments in IHL, culminating in Protocol I, and the belief on the part of NLM members that they were engaged in an international conflict and entitled to prisoner-of-war status, constituted mitigating factors for the purpose of punishment.[138] In this way, courts were able to avoid passing sentence of death on SWAPO and ANC

accordingly inapplicable: 'Terrorists, prisoners of war and South Africa' (1975) 1 *SAYIL* 14.

133 J Dugard 'Human rights, humanitarian law and the South African conflict' (1989) 2 *Harvard Human Rights Yearbook* 101; N Boister 'The *ius in bello* in South Africa: A postscript?' (1991) 24 *CILSA* 72; C Murray 'The status of the ANC and SWAPO and international humanitarian law' (1983) 100 *SALJ* 402 and C Murray 'The ANC in court: Towards international guidelines in sentencing' (1987) 14 *Journal of Southern African Studies* 140.

134 For an early argument to this effect, see A Borrowdale 'The future of the law of war: The place of the Additional Protocols of 1977 in customary international law' (1981) 14 *CILSA* 79.

135 1988 (3) SA 51 (C). See further on this case, H Booysen 'Protocol I tot die Geneefse Konvensies van 1949—Gewoonteregtelike volkereg?' (1988) 51 *THRHR* 244.

136 See above, Chapters 3 and 4. In 2001, a South African court refused an opportunity to reconsider issues of the kind raised in *Petane: Lombo v the ANC* (unreported, DCLD Case No 9006/93, 20 April 2001)—noted by M Cowling 'International humanitarian law and the armed struggle in South Africa' (2001) 26 *SAYIL* 221.

137 1990 (1) SACR 517 (SWA) 527*f*–*g*. See too *S v Mapumulo* (unreported, NPD Case No CC 93/85) noted in Dugard (n 86) 453–4.

138 *S v Sagarius* 1983 (1) SA 833 (SWA) 836—discussed by C van der Schijff 'Considerations of international humanitarian law in [the] sentencing of members of SWAPO—*S v Sagarius* 1983 1 SA 833 (SWA)' (1983) 9 *SAYIL* 112 and MG Cowling 'The effect of international law on municipal law in times of armed conflict—*S v Sagarius* 1983 (1) SA 833 (SWA)' (1983) 7 *SACC* 79; *S v Mule* 1990 (1) SACR 517 (SWA) 529–30; *S v Masina* 1990 (4) SA 709 (A) 717–19.

combatants. This approach was not uniform. In two cases,[139] judges dismissed this argument as irrelevant and sentenced ANC members to death. The accused in one case were executed, despite pleas for mercy from the UNSC,[140] while the accused in the other case were released in 1992 as part of the amnesty accorded to political prisoners.

5 The Truth and Reconciliation Commission Report and international humanitarian law

During the apartheid era the South African army and police were involved in major military operations in Angola and Northern Namibia; in counter-insurgency operations in pre-independence Zimbabwe; in cross-border raids into Lesotho, Botswana, Swaziland, Mozambique, Zimbabwe and Zambia; and in covert operations in the Seychelles and Comores. South African security forces killed more people in the maintenance of the apartheid state *outside* South Africa than within. In 1978, for instance, over 600 men, women, and children were killed in a raid on the SWAPO base/refugee camp at Kassinga in Angola, 198 kilometres north of the Namibian border.

During this period, it is not clear how the South African security forces saw their obligations under the Geneva Conventions. No clear policy statement was made on this subject in respect of external conflicts. The Angolan conflict, particularly in its initial phases when the South African army advanced to the outskirts of Luanda in 1975, could be described as an international armed conflict. In contrast, the war in northern Namibia and southern Angola probably qualified as a non-international armed conflict to which common article 3 of the Geneva Conventions applied. The low intensity conflict on South Africa's own northern borders, on the other hand, probably failed to meet the threshold of article 3. The South African government consistently treated members of SWAPO arrested in Namibia (and southern Angola), and members of the ANC and PAC arrested in South Africa (or neighbouring territories), as 'terrorists' and criminals who were not entitled to treatment as prisoners-of-war.[141]

[139] *S v Mogoerane* (unreported, TPD judgment, 6 August 1982), reprinted in (1983) 1 *Lawyers for Human Rights Bulletin* 118; *S v Mncube and Nondula* (unreported, TPD Circuit Court (Messina) Case No 449/87, 5 May 1988), discussed in J Dugard 'Public international law' 1988 *Annual Survey* 76 and J Dugard 'Soldiers or terrorists? The ANC and the SADF compared' (1988) 4 *SAJHR* 221). The judgment of the Appellate Division in the latter case is reported in *S v Mncube en 'n Ander* 1991 (3) SA 132 (A); criticised in J Dugard 'Public international law' 1991 *Annual Survey* 645 at 656. See further P Harris *In a Different Time* (2007).

[140] Resolution 533 (1983); Dugard (n 130) 18–19.

[141] See above (notes 135–140).

The Truth and Reconciliation Commission Report of 1998[142] makes no attempt to identify the nature of the conflicts in southern Africa from the perspective of IHL. However, it makes it clear that in its assessment of the responsibility of both government and ANC forces for gross human rights violations in their military operations that it was guided by the principles of IHL contained in the Geneva Conventions and Additional Protocols.

Although the Truth and Reconciliation Commission acknowledges the distinction between international and non-international armed conflicts, and the distinction between grave breaches and common article 3 protection, it makes no attempt to evaluate the conflicts in question because:

> This distinction between international and internal armed conflicts is less relevant today, as the laws of war have evolved to regulate more closely the use of force in all situations of armed conflict.[143]

Guided by these principles it found that the attack on Kassinga in 1978 resulted in the commission of gross human rights violations against the civilian occupants of Kassinga camp by reason of the use of fragmentation bombs in the initial air assault which constituted an indiscriminate use of force, and the failure to take adequate care to protect the lives of civilians.[144] The Truth and Reconciliation Commission further found that the South African security forces were responsible for gross violations of human rights on a vast scale in their military campaigns in Namibia and Angola.[145]

The Truth and Reconciliation Commission accepted that the liberation movements had been engaged in a 'just war' in their struggle against apartheid. But it distinguished between the 'justice of war' and 'justice in war' and declared that 'the fact that the apartheid system was a crime against humanity did not mean that all acts carried out in order to destroy apartheid were necessarily legal, moral and acceptable'. Torture, abduction and the killing and injuring of defenceless persons (both civilians and soldiers out of combat) could not be regarded 'as morally or legally legitimate, even where the cause was just'. 'Apartheid as a system was a crime against humanity' but acts carried out by *any* of the parties to the conflict in southern Africa could be classified as human rights violations.[146]

142 *Truth and Reconciliation Commission Report*, 5 volumes (1998).
143 Ibid vol 1 at 75.
144 Ibid vol 2 at 46–55.
145 Ibid vol 2 at 60–1, 84.
146 Ibid vol 1 at 66–9.

CHAPTER 26

The African Union

Max du Plessis and Tiyanjana Maluwa

INTRODUCTION

Africa was not part of the move to multilateral institutions that unfolded at the international level at the turn of the last century. The reason for this was obvious. The emergence of this phenomenon occurred shortly after an earlier, more debilitating and less civilising, phenomenon: the European colonisation of African peoples and territories. Thus, with the exception of four states that had either never been colonised (Ethiopia and Liberia) or had become formally independent or were regarded as autonomous dominions of the colonial empire (Egypt and South Africa), the colonised African territories were not members of the League of Nations, the first truly international organisation in the history of humankind. Africa's participation in the move to multilateral institutions had to wait for the establishment of the United Nations (UN) in 1945, and the emergence of the erstwhile colonies into independent states in the early and mid-1960s.

Two developments accompanied the emergence of independent African states from the ashes of colonialism. The first was the more or less automatic admission of these new states to UN membership. Secondly, the establishment of a continental organisation whose membership was open to all independent African states as a forum for the pursuit of common objectives.

THE ORGANIZATION OF AFRICAN UNITY

The Organization of African Unity (OAU) was established on 25 May 1963 with the adoption of the OAU Charter by 32 African states in Addis Ababa, Ethiopia. By the time it was formally replaced by the African Union (AU) on 9 July 2002, its membership comprised 53 countries, namely all the independent African states, with the sole exception of Morocco.[1] Under the apartheid government, South

[1] Morocco had formally withdrawn from the organization in 1984 in protest against the admission of the Sahrawi Arab Democratic Republic (SADR). Morocco opposes SADR's claim to independent statehood and sovereignty over the territory of the former Spanish colony of Western Sahara, which it regards as part of its own national territory. See GJ Naldi *The Organization of African Unity: An Analysis of its Role* (1989) 59–68.

Africa had remained excluded from the OAU. On 23 May 1994, South Africa acceded to the OAU Charter. The OAU Council of Ministers, meeting in its 60th ordinary session in Tunisia from 6 to 11 June 1994, adopted a resolution in which the Council welcomed 'South Africa as the 53rd member of the OAU' and expressed 'confidence that it will play a significant role in strengthening the African family of nations'.[2]

The OAU was designed as a regional intergovernmental organisation with the aim of promoting unity and solidarity among African states.[3] The provisions of the OAU Charter reflected the overriding concerns of Africa in the late 1950s and 60s. These included the need to ensure the rapid decolonisation of Africa and resultant self-determination for those African peoples that were still being ruled by colonial powers,[4] and to protect newly acquired statehood by stressing sovereign equality of states[5] and the principle of non-interference in internal affairs.[6] The Charter's focus was thus on the protection of the state, rather than the individual.[7] To the extent that the OAU had concern for the question of human rights, such concern was largely focused on the right of self-determination of peoples in the context of decolonisation and apartheid.[8] South Africa came to be a priority for the OAU. Thus, in relation to the apartheid regime the OAU at its very first session adopted resolutions condemning South Africa's policy of racial segregation as a 'serious threat to peace and international security', 'incompatible with its political and moral obligations as a member state of the United Nations' and a 'grave danger to stability and peace in Africa and in the world'.[9] Over the years, the OAU condemned a range of actions by the apartheid government on human rights grounds. It also, inter alia, called for: the non-recognition of South African Bantustans;[10] expressed its deep concern at the treatment of political prisoners in gaol and called for

[2] See OAU Council of Ministers, 'Resolution on South Africa', OAU Doc CM/Res 1515 (LX).

[3] On the OAU generally, see K Mathews 'The Organization of African Unity' in D Mazzeo (ed) *African Regional Organizations* (1984) 49 et seq. See also Z Cervenka *The Unfinished Quest for Unity: Africa and the Organization of African Unity* (1977); COC Amate *Inside the OAU: Pan-Africanism in Practice* (1986).

[4] Preamble of the OAU Charter; article 3(3).

[5] Article 3(1).

[6] Article 3(1) and (2).

[7] See R Murray *Human Rights in Africa: From the OAU to the African Union* (2004) 7.

[8] Ibid 7–8.

[9] Resolution on Apartheid in South Africa, CM/Res 13 (II).

[10] Resolution on Non-Recognition of South African Bantustans, CM/Res 492 (XXVII).

their release;[11] condemned the aggressive policies of the South African government towards its neighbours, Namibia, Angola and Zambia;[12] and criticised South Africa for the killing of demonstrators,[13] and for holding unfair trials.[14]

During its 37-year existence, apart from numerous resolutions, the OAU adopted 23 multilateral law-making treaties, thereby contributing towards the development of international law.[15] Eighteen of the 23 treaties are still in force. Included in these 18 is the African Convention on the Conservation of Nature and Natural Resources.[16] Article 2 of this Convention articulates the principles of sustainable development, and respect for the environment as a common heritage of humankind or public good.[17] Subsequently, the Bamako Convention on the Ban of the Import into Africa and the Control of Transboundary Movement and Management of Hazardous Waste within Africa[18] reaffirmed a number of international environmental law principles; for example: state responsibility for transboundary pollution, the 'polluter pays' principle, and obligations relating to sustainable management and resource utilisation.[19] The OAU also

[11] Resolution on South Africa, CM/Res 538 (CCVIII); Resolution on the Abduction and Detention of Victor Matlou of ANC by South African Police, CM/Res 767 (XXXIV); Resolution on South Africa, CM/Res 554 (XXIX), paras 11–12; Resolution on South Africa, CM/Res 120 (L); Resolution on South Africa, CM/Res 1244 (LI). See also supra n 9.

[12] Resolution on Namibia, CM/Res 629 (XXXI), para 10; Resolution on the Current Situation in South Africa, CM/Res 956 (XLI).

[13] Resolution on South Africa, CM/Res 636 (XXXI), preamble.

[14] See, eg, resolution on South West Africans on Trial in South Africa, AHG/Res 50 (IV).

[15] See T Maluwa 'The African Union, the Southern African Development Community, and the New Partnership for Africa's Development: Some observations on South Africa's contribution to international law-making and institution building in Africa, 1994–2004' (2004) 29 *SAYIL* 5.

[16] African Convention on the Conservation of Nature and Natural Resources, adopted on 15 September 1968, entered into force on 16 June 1969, OAU Doc BAB/LEG/24.1; available at https://au.int/sites/default/files/treaties/ See, also, 1001 UNTS 3. South Africa is not, to date, a party to this Convention. For criticism of South Africa's failure to ratify the Convention, see Maluwa (n 15) 27–8.

[17] As Maluwa (n 15) notes at 12, what is particularly remarkable about this treaty is that African states were elaborating these principles before they became more commonly acknowledged, even within the UN context.

[18] Bamako Convention on the Ban and the Import into Africa and Control of Transboundary Movement and Management of Hazardous Waste within Africa, adopted on 30 January 1991, available at https://au.int/sites/default/files/treaties/. See also 2101 UNTS 177. South Africa is not, to date, a party to the Convention. For criticism of South Africa's failure to ratify the Convention, see Maluwa (n 15) 28–9.

[19] See, further, Chapter 19 on International Environmental Law.

adopted the African Nuclear Weapon-Free Zone Treaty (Treaty of Pelindaba).[20]

The African Charter on Human and Peoples' Rights of 1981[21] (discussed further below) became the first international instrument to recognise explicitly the right to a general satisfactory environment as a human right.[22] The Charter also recognised the notion of 'peoples' rights' as distinct from, or as a subset of, 'human rights' and highlighted the notion of third generation rights, including the right to development, the right to peace, and the aforementioned right to a satisfactory environment. Another OAU treaty aimed at the protection of human rights is the African Charter on the Rights and Welfare of the Child.[23]

The OAU Convention Governing the Specific Aspects of Refugee Problems in Africa[24] is also worthy of mention. The Convention is credited with enriching the debate on the concept of 'refugeehood', for example, by broadening the definition of a refugee and the scope of the principle of *non-refoulement* in international refugee law.[25] In response to the problem of terrorism, in 1999 the OAU adopted the OAU Convention on the Prevention and Combating of Terrorism.[26] Twenty-two years earlier, due to the scourge of mercenarism on the African continent, the OAU had adopted the Convention for the Elimination of Mercenarism in Africa.[27] These are only a few examples of the various areas in which the OAU provided a forum

[20] The final text of the treaty was approved by the OAU Assembly of Heads of State and Government on 23 June 1995. However, it was formally opened for signature at a special summit of the OAU in Cairo, Egypt, on 11 April 1996, where it was signed by 47 of the OAU's 53 member states; available at https://au.int/sites/default/files/treaties/. See also UNGA Doc A/50/426. It entered into force on 15 July 2009; ratified by South Africa on 13 March 1998.

[21] African Charter on Human and Peoples' Rights, adopted on 27 June 1981 (1982) 21 *ILM* 58; also available at https://au.int/sites/default/files/treaties/; acceded to by South Africa on 9 July 1996.

[22] See article 24.

[23] Adopted on 11 July 1990 and entered into force on 19 November 1999; OAU Doc CAB/LEG/24.9/49, available at https://au.int/sites/default/files/treaties/; ratified by South Africa on 7 January 2000.

[24] OAU Convention Governing the Specific Aspects of Refugee Problems in Africa, adopted on 10 September 1969, 1001 UNTS 45; available at https://au.int/sites/default/files/treaties/; acceded to by South Africa on 15 December 1995.

[25] Maluwa (n 15) 13. See also Chapter 16 on Refugees and Stateless Persons.

[26] Adopted on 14 July 1999 and entered into force on 6 December 2002; available at https://au.int/sites/default/files/treaties/ ratified by South Africa on 7 September 2002. See also Chapter 9 on Jurisdiction and International Crimes.

[27] Adopted on 3 July 1977 and entered into force on 22 April 1985; available at https://au.int/sites/default/files/treaties/; South Africa has not become a party to the Convention. For criticism, see Maluwa (n 15) 29–30.

for its members to develop common legal norms through multilateral treaties to govern their relations. Following its assumption of OAU membership, South Africa became a party to some of these treaties, including through accession to treaties that had been adopted prior to 1994.[28]

FROM THE OAU TO THE AFRICAN UNION

In 2000, responding to both internal and global changes and challenges, the OAU underwent a transformation to become the AU.[29] The AU was established by the Constitutive Act of the African Union, adopted at the 36th ordinary session of the Assembly of Heads of State and Government of the OAU on 11 July 2000, in Lomé, Togo.[30] In terms of article 33(1) of the Constitutive Act, the OAU remained operational for a transitional period of one year, following the entry into force of the Constitutive Act on 26 May 2001. The AU was formally inaugurated in Durban, South Africa, on 9 July 2002, at the 37th ordinary session (and last summit) of the OAU. Its headquarters is in Addis Ababa, Ethiopia, at the former seat of the OAU. By the time the AU was inaugurated in Durban, all the 53 former OAU member states, except the Democratic Republic of Congo and Madagascar, had ratified the Constitutive Act and deposited instruments of ratification with the Secretary-General of the OAU.[31] The Democratic Republic of Congo deposited its instrument of ratification on the day of the inauguration itself, and Madagascar followed suit almost a year later, on 10 June 2003. South Sudan, which seceded from Sudan on 9 July 2011 following a referendum, joined the AU on 27 July 2011. Morocco, which as noted above had withdrawn from the OAU in 1984, joined the new organisation on 30 January 2017, thereby becoming its 55th member.

[28] See, generally, 'South Africa in Africa: Assessing South Africa's participation in Organization of African Unity and African Union treaties' in T Maluwa, M du Plessis and D Tladi (eds) *The Pursuit of a Brave New World in International Law: Essays in Honour of John Dugard* (2017) 264.

[29] See, generally, KD Magliveras and GJ Naldi 'The African Union—A new dawn for Africa?' (2002) 51 *ICLQ* 415; and M Cowling 'The African Union—An evaluation' (2002) 27 *SAYIL* 193. For critical discussion of the African Union, see H Richardson 'The danger of oligarchy within the Pan-Africanist authority of the African Union' (2003) 13 *Transnat'l L & Contemp Probs* 255. See also T Maluwa 'The transition from the Organization of African Unity to the African Union' in A Yusuf and F Ouguergouz (eds) *The African Union: Legal and Institutional Framework—A Manual on the Pan-African Organization* (2012) 25.

[30] See Decision on the Establishment of the African Union, OAU Doc. AHG/Dec 143 (XXXVI). Text of the Constitutive Act available at https://au.int/sites/default/files/treaties/; see also 2158 UNTS 3.

[31] South Africa ratified the Constitutive Act on 3 March 2001.

Why the transformation from OAU to AU? A number of reasons might be identified.[32] By the end of the 1980s, there was a widespread perception that the OAU was in serious need of reform. For one thing, the original motivation for the OAU's creation—the pan-Africanist ideals of securing independence for African peoples and uniting against colonial subjugation—no longer sustained the organisation following the period of decolonisation that Africa witnessed in the 1960s, 1970s and into the 1980s.[33] Similarly, its agenda of championing the struggle against apartheid and racist minority rule in southern Africa had been fulfilled with the attainment of a post-apartheid democratic dispensation in South Africa. A new *raison d'être* was needed to unite the organisation. One goal would have been to focus on securing peace amongst Africa's newly independent states—a goal that would have been consistent with the OAU's function as a pan-African body constituted to improve the lives of Africa's people. However, increasingly the OAU came to be criticised for its failure to respond to serious conflicts between member states.[34] In addition, several of Africa's leaders in the fight for independence led their newly liberated nations into totalitarianism, with an ineffectual OAU doing little to put a stop to this African malaise.[35] It did not help that the OAU found itself caught between superpower rivalries during the Cold War; that ideological clashes led to debilitation of the OAU as it failed adequately to respond to civil wars that were fueled by East/West interests (such as in Angola and Mozambique); and that development and reform programmes initiated by the OAU became characterised by lofty words and promises at OAU summits and little or no meaningful follow-up action.[36] Matters did not improve after the end of the Cold War as the OAU suffered from under-funding by member states, and an unwieldy Assembly structure, in which the 53 members inclined towards

[32] See, generally, CA Packer and D Rukare 'The New African Union and its Constitutive Act' (2002) 96 *AJIL* 365 especially at 365–9. See also T Maluwa 'Re-imagining African unity: Some preliminary observations on the Constitutive Act of the African Union' (2001) 9 *African Yearbook of International Law* 3–38.

[33] Ibid 366.

[34] See Y El-Ayouty 'An OAU for the future: An assessment' in Y El-Ayouty (ed) *The Organization of African Unity after Thirty Years* (1994) 180; A Mangu 'What future for human and peoples' rights under the African Union, New Partnership for Africa's Development, African Peer Review Mechanism and the African Court' (2004) 29 *SAYIL* 136–40. As regards criticisms of the OAU's failures in protecting human rights, see generally C Nwanko 'The OAU and human rights' (1993) 4 *Journal of Democracy* 50; O Ojo and A Sesay 'The OAU and human rights: Prospects for the 1980s and beyond' (1986) 1 *Human Rights Quarterly* 86.

[35] See Packer and Rukare (n 32) 367.

[36] Ibid.

preserving national interests and sovereignty at the expense of a true commitment to regional co-operation and finding 'African solutions for African problems'.[37] These developments generated a sense that there was a need not only to review the objectives and work of the OAU, but to put in its place a new mechanism or institutional structure that would reinvigorate the project of African unity and integration.

1 The objectives, principles and organs of the AU

Due to the problems that beset the OAU, at the end of the 20th century African leaders chose to start afresh with the AU. The Constitutive Act consists of a preamble and 33 dispositive articles. It enumerates a rather expansive list of 14 objectives that go well beyond those previously enshrined in the OAU Charter. The objectives, or purposes, stipulated in the OAU Charter were limited to the following: promotion and achievement of unity and solidarity of African states; co-ordination and intensification of co-operation and efforts to achieve a better life for African peoples; defence of the sovereignty, territorial integrity and independence of African states; eradication of colonialism; and the promotion of international co-operation within the context of the Charter of the United Nations (UN Charter) and the Universal Declaration of Human Rights. The core objectives of the AU expand on these, and evidence a commitment by African leaders not only to tackle the key economic and social issues facing the continent, but also to improve the AU relative to the weaknesses that had come to cripple the OAU.

The objectives of the AU are set out in article 3 of the Constitutive Act. They are designed to enhance political co-operation and economic integration amongst African states, and include the promotion of sustainable development at the economic, social and cultural levels;[38] promotion and defence of African positions on issues of common interest; promotion of peace, security and stability; promotion of democratic principles and institutions, popular participation

[37] See El-Ayouty (n 34) 179.

[38] This objective builds on earlier initiatives that began under the OAU for the development, mobilisation, and utilisation of African human and material resources in an effort to achieve self-sufficiency for the continent. The framework was set in place by the OAU's adoption of the Lagos Plan of Action and Final Act in which the intention was expressed to create an African Economic Community. This intention came to be realised with the Abuja Treaty Establishing the African Economic Community, which entered into force in 1994 (for the text of the treaty, see (1991) 30 *ILM* 1241). On the African Economic Community, see K Danso 'The African Economic Community: Problems and prospects' (1995) *Africa Today* 4th Quarter 31; See, also, Chapter 21 on International Economic Relations. See also M Mbenge and O Illy 'The African Economic Community' in Yusuf and Ouguergouz (n 29) 187–202.

and good governance; promotion and protection of human rights in accordance with the African Charter on Human and Peoples' Rights and other relevant instruments; and the advancement of research in all fields, in particular science and technology, and the eradication of preventable diseases and the promotion of good health. Also included among the new objectives are the establishment of the necessary conditions for the continent to play its rightful role in the global economy and in international negotiations, and the co-ordination and harmonisation of policies between the various African Regional Economic Communities.[39] While these objectives focus on inter-African co-operation, together they point to a general theme of upgrading Africa's position on the international plane so that African states might play a greater role in the world economy and in global negotiations.[40]

More significantly, perhaps, article 4 of the Constitutive Act incorporates new, radically expanded principles with potentially far-reaching implications. These may be roughly classified into two categories. The first category consists of principles that are more or less generally recognised in international law. These include the prohibition of the use of force among member states; peaceful coexistence among member states and their right to live in peace and security; respect for democratic principles, human rights and the rule of law, and good governance. The second category of principles reflects the new thinking and approaches among African states on how to co-ordinate common responses to present-day political and socio-economic challenges: the principles of participation by African peoples in the activities of the organisation; the establishment of a common defence policy for the African continent; the right of the AU to intervene in member states under certain conditions where war crimes, genocide and crimes against humanity have been committed; the right of member states to request intervention from the AU in order to restore peace and security; promotion of self-reliance, social

[39] The AU recognises eight Regional Economic Communities, which are regarded as the building blocks of the African Economic Community (n 38): Arab Maghreb Union (UMA), Common Market for Eastern and Southern Africa (COMESA), Community of Sahel-Saharan States (CENSAD), East African Community (EAC), Economic Community of Central African States (ECCAS), Economic Community of West African States (ECOWAS), Intergovernmental Authority on Development (IGAD) and Southern African Development Community (SADC). See U Uzodike 'The role of regional economic communities in Africa's economic integration: Prospects and constraints' (2009) 39 *Africa Insight* 26; S Karangizi 'The Regional Economic Communities' in Yusuf and Ouguergouz (n 29) 231–39. See also Chapter 21 on International Economic Relations.

[40] See KD Magliveras and GJ Naldi (n 29) 416.

justice and gender equality; and the condemnation and rejection of unconstitutional changes of government.

The Constitutive Act has established various new organs and bodies, notably the Assembly, the Executive Council and the Commission. These organs are responsible for initiating and translating into concrete actions the objectives, vision and mission of the organisation. The supreme body of the OAU—the Assembly of Heads of State and Government—has been remodelled to become the AU Assembly. The AU Assembly retains supremacy within the overall structures of the AU and continues to be composed of heads of states and government or their duly accredited representatives.[41] The Assembly meets at least once a year in ordinary session, and may meet more than that in extraordinary session.[42] Its functions include determining the common policies of the Union, receiving, considering and taking decisions on reports and recommendations from other organs of the Union, considering requests for membership of the Union, monitoring the implementation of policies and decisions of the Union and ensuring compliance therewith by all member states, and adopting the budget of the Union.[43] The Assembly is thus the ultimate custodian and repository of the collective authority shared by the member states. Articles 13 and 15 of the Constitutive Act outline how the Executive Council and the Specialised Committee can facilitate the work of the Assembly in exercising its authority.

The Executive Council, which is in turn subordinate to the Assembly,[44] is composed of Ministers of Foreign Affairs or other government designates,[45] and is expected to engage in policy-making in areas of common interest to the member states across a broad range of sectors such as foreign trade, energy, industry and mineral resources, water resources and irrigation, transport and communications, education, and social security.[46]

The Constitutive Act established several Specialised Technical Committees, such as committees on rural economy and agriculture, monetary and financial affairs, trade, customs and immigration matters, industry, science, technology, energy, natural resources and environment, and on health, labour and social affairs in order to

[41] See Constitutive Act, article 6(1) and (2).

[42] Article 6(3).

[43] See article 9.

[44] It meets at least twice a year in ordinary session but may convene an extraordinary session, (see article 10(2)).

[45] Article 10(1).

[46] For details regarding the functions of the Executive Council, see article 13.

provide technical assistance to the Executive Council in its policy decision-making.[47]

The AU Commission is the Secretariat of the AU.[48] The Commission is entrusted with executive functions, such as representing the AU and defending its interests,[49] implementing decisions taken by other organs,[50] promoting integration and social development,[51] and promoting peace, security, democracy and stability.[52] The Secretariat is composed of a Chair, Deputy Chair and eight other Commissioners. Each Commissioner is responsible for a particular portfolio.[53] The Commission is, therefore, the only body that deals with the operational matters of the AU on a daily basis servicing all the other organs. In executing its mission, the Commission deploys its conferred authority and mandate and performs at a higher level than a mere secretariat, as was previously the case with the OAU General Secretariat. In practice the AU Commission (along with the Peace and Security Council, discussed below) has taken centre-stage in shaping the agenda of the AU, including the human security agenda.[54]

Other bodies established under the Constitutive Act include a Pan-African Parliament which, by article 17, is intended 'to ensure the full participation of African peoples in the development and economic integration of the continent'. The Pan-African Parliament was inaugurated on 18 March 2004 at its seat in Midrand, South Africa. Its powers are set out in its founding instrument, the Protocol to the Treaty Establishing the African Economic Community relating to the Pan-African Parliament.[55] To an extent, it is modelled on the European Union's (EU) Parliament, which plays a central role in ensuring the democratic nature of the EU.[56] Like its European counterpart, the Pan-African Parliament has as one of its objectives

[47] See article 14 for a full list of the Specialised Technical Committees.

[48] Article 20 of the Constitutive Act.

[49] See Statutes of the Commission, ASS/AU/2(I)–d (2002), article 3(2)(a).

[50] Ibid article 3(2)(c).

[51] Ibid article 3(2)(p).

[52] Ibid article 3(2)(r).

[53] The portfolios are Peace and Security, Political Affairs, Infrastructure and Energy, Social Affairs, Human Resources, Science and Technology, Trade and Industry, Rural Economy and Agriculture and Economic Affairs.

[54] T Tieku 'African Union promotion of human security in Africa' (2007) 16 *African Security Review* 28.

[55] See Protocol to the Treaty Establishing the African Economic Community relating to the Pan-African Parliament, Doc EAHG/3 (V), EAHG/DEC2 (V). Adopted on 2 March 2001, and entered into force on 14 December 2003; ratified by South Africa on 3 July 2002.

[56] See Murray (n 7) 35. See, also, T Demeke 'The new Pan-African Parliament: Prospects and challenges in view of the experience of the European Parliament' (2004) 4 *AHRLJ* 53 and S Mpanyane 'Transformation of the Pan-African Parliament: A path

the promotion of 'the principles of human rights and democracy', and it is required to 'encourage good governance, transparency and accountability in member states'.[57] The Parliament is composed of five representatives from each state, which should include at least one woman in their delegations, and 'must reflect the diversity of political opinions in each National Parliament or other deliberative organ'.[58] In its first term of five years, the Parliament was to exercise consultative and advisory powers only, but thereafter it would have legislative powers. However, at the time of writing, the Pan-African Parliament still only exercised advisory and consultative powers.[59]

The Constitutive Act also established the Court of Justice of the African Union. While the Pan-African Parliament is envisaged as something akin to a legislature for Africa, the African Court of Justice is intended to play a role similar to that of the Court of Justice of the European Communities.[60] It will act as the regional adjudicator, staffed by judges whose charge under article 26 is that they 'be seized with matters of interpretation arising from the application or implementation of the Constitutive Act [of the AU]'. The Protocol of the Court of Justice of the African Union was adopted in July 2003 in Maputo, Mozambique and entered into force on 11 February 2009.[61] However, the Court has not been operationalised. In fact, on 1 July 2008 it was merged with the African Court of Human and Peoples' Rights to become what is now known as the African Court of Justice and Human Rights. The Protocol on the Statute of the African Court of Justice and Human Rights will replace the existing Protocol of the African Court of Justice.[62] (The African Court of Human and Peoples' Rights is discussed below.)

Another notable body of the new organisation is its Peace and Security Council,[63] which is modelled on the UN Security Council. It

to a legislative body?' Institute for Security Studies Paper No 181, March 2009, available at http://www.iss.co.za.

[57] See Protocol on the Pan-African Parliament, article 11(1).

[58] Ibid article 4.

[59] Ibid article 11. A Protocol to the Constitutive Act of the African Union relating to the Pan-African Parliament giving the Pan-African Parliament legislative powers, was adopted by the AU Assembly on 27 June 2014. To date, only six countries have ratified the Protocol, which requires 28 ratifications to enter into force.

[60] On the work of the European Court of Justice, see P Sands and P Klein *Bowett's Law of International Institutions* 5 ed (2001) 404–12.

[61] See www.au.int/en/sites/default/files/protocol_of_the_court_of_justice_of_the_ african_union.pdf.

[62] Article 1 of the Protocol on the Statute of the African Court of Justice and Human Rights (2008).

[63] Established by the Protocol Relating to the Establishment of the Peace and Security Council of the African Union, adopted on 9 July 2002 and entered into force

has been tasked with taking decisions on conflict prevention, management and resolution, and is described as a 'collective security and early warning arrangement to facilitate timely and efficient response to conflict and crisis situations in Africa'.[64] Aside from its emergency powers, the Council has a general mandate to develop a common defence policy and 'promote and encourage democratic practices, good governance and the rule of law, protect human rights and fundamental freedoms, respect for the sanctity of human life and international humanitarian law, as part of efforts for preventing conflicts'.[65] The Council is composed of 15 states reflecting the geographical regions of the continent and which, notably, are to be committed to principles of democratic governance, the rule of law and human rights, as a requirement for membership of the Council.[66] The Council generally takes its decisions by consensus, but where consensus cannot be reached, then, on substantive matters, the Council adopts its decision by a two-thirds majority vote.[67] The work of the Council is discussed further below.

Article 19 of the Constitutive Act creates three Pan-African financial institutions—the African Central Bank, the African Monetary Fund and the African Investment Bank. The overall objectives of these institutions are to foster economic growth and accelerate economic integration in Africa. Of these, instruments establishing the African Investment Bank and the African Monetary Fund have been adopted (in 2009 and 2014, respectively), but neither of them has entered into force. None of these institutions is, therefore, yet in actual existence or operational.

The last organ of the AU that requires mention is the Economic, Social and Cultural Council (ECOSOCC). It is described as being 'an advisory organ composed of different social and professional groups of the member states of the Union',[68] and is composed of 150 civil society organisations covering such diverse interests as those of women, children, the elderly, the disabled, professional groups, non-governmental organisations, workers, employers, traditional leaders, academics, and religious and cultural organisations, and the

on 16 December 2003; ratified by South Africa on 15 May 2003. For discussion, see H Strydom 'Peace and security under the African Union' (2003) 28 *SAYIL* 59.

[64] Article 1 of the Protocol Relating to the Establishment of the Peace and Security Council of the African Union.

[65] Ibid article 3(f).

[66] Ibid article 5(2)(g).

[67] Ibid article 8(13).

[68] Constitutive Act of the AU, article 22(1).

African diaspora.[69] With the advice and encouragement of these diverse interest groups, the Council aims to fulfil its function of promoting human rights, the rule of law, good governance and gender equality.[70] The First Permanent General Assembly of ECOSOCC was elected on 8 September 2008, in Dar es Salaam, United Republic of Tanzania.

2 The New Partnership for Africa's Development and the African Peer Review Mechanism

The transition of the OAU to the AU must be understood against the backdrop of another development: The establishment of the New Partnership for Africa's Development (NEPAD). In January 2001, President Thabo Mbeki of South Africa unveiled a programme (then known as the Millennium Partnership for the African Recovery Programme, or MAP) for Africa's 'recovery' at the World Economic Forum meeting in Davos, Switzerland. The MAP was jointly finalised in February 2001 by Presidents Mbeki, Olusegun Obasanjo of Nigeria and Abdelaziz Bouteflika of Algeria. During the fifth extraordinary summit of the OAU/Africa Economic Community (AEC) held in Sirte, Libya, in March 2001, the MAP was integrated with another initiative, the Omega Plan for Africa, which had been proposed separately by President Abdoulaye Wade of Senegal to the same summit. The combined programme was subsequently renamed NEPAD.[71] NEPAD has been described as a 'holistic, comprehensive and integrated strategic framework for the socioeconomic development of Africa, with a programme of action that embraces initiatives on peace and security, democracy and political governance, as well as economic and corporate governance'.[72] The importance of NEPAD is

[69] See Murray (n 7) 37; K Sturman and J Cilliers 'ECOSOCC bringing people's power back to the African Union?' (2003) 12 *African Security Review* 71; see, too, article 4 of the Statutes of the Economic Social and Cultural Council, available at http;//www.africa-union.org/ecosoc/statutes-en.pdf. The ECOSOCC Statutes were adopted before South Sudan and Morocco became members of the AU and have not been amended with regard to the total number of civil society organizations (CSO) members. Given that the current membership of the AU is now 55, in practice, the total number of CSO members would be 154.

[70] ECOSOCC Statutes, articles 2 and 7.

[71] See the NEPAD website at http://www.nepad.org. See also, generally, R Kanpur 'The New Partnership for Africa's Development (NEPAD): An initial commentary' (2002) 29 *SA Journal of Political Studies* 87–100; A de Waal 'What's new in the "New Partnership for Africa's Development"?' (2002) 78 *International Affairs* 463.

[72] See Maluwa (n 15) 4 fn 10. See also J Akokpari 'The AU, NEPAD and the promotion of good governance in Africa' (2004) 13 *Nordic Journal of African Studies* 243; P Chabal 'The quest for good government and development in Africa: Is NEPAD the answer?' (2002) 78 *International Affairs* 447; K Amuwo 'Globalization, NEPAD and the governance question in Africa' (2002) 6 *African Studies Quarterly* 65.

that it is 'an African-led, African-owned and African-managed initiative underpinned by an agreed set of principles to which the participating countries commit themselves'.[73]

NEPAD was formally adopted as a programme of the OAU at a summit on 11 July 2001, and is a 'pledge by African leaders' to achieve certain goals.[74] In terms of NEPAD's founding document, African leaders 'recognise that failures of political and economic leadership in many African countries impede the coherent mobilisation of resources into productive areas of activity in order to attract and facilitate domestic and foreign investment'.[75] To that end, various strategies are adopted in the document to which the leaders commit themselves, with the ultimate goal to 'consolidate democracy and sound economic management on the continent' and a 'pledge to promote peace and stability, democracy and sound economic management and people-centred development and to hold each other accountable in terms of the agreements outlined in the programme'.[76] The implementation of NEPAD's commitments was previously undertaken through a Head of State and Government Implementation Committee, chaired by Nigeria, with Senegal and Algeria as vice-chairs, and 17 other African states making up the remainder of the 20-strong Committee. In February 2010, the AU established the NEPAD Planning and Coordinating Agency as a technical body of the AU to replace the NEPAD Secretariat as an implementation agency.[77] The Chairperson of the Heads of State and Government Orientation Committee reports to the AU Assembly on its activities and makes recommendations for its consideration and adoption, the AU Assembly being the highest tier of the NEPAD governance structure.[78]

[73] See Maluwa (n 15) 4 fn 10.

[74] 'A new African initiative: Merger of the Millennium Partnership for the African Recovery Programme (MAP) and Omega Plan' July 2001 para 1.

[75] Ibid para 34.

[76] Ibid para 73. NEPAD's monitoring mechanism has come to be known as the APRM. For detail, see *Objectives, Standards, Criteria and Indicators for the African Peer Review Mechanism (APRM)* NEPAD/HSGIC-03-2003/APRM/Guideline/OSCI, 9 March 2003. See, also, C Stals 'The African Peer Review Mechanism as an integral part of the New Partnership for Africa's Development: Recent developments' (2004) 4 *AHRLJ* 130; R Herbert 'The survival of NEPAD and the African Peer Review Mechanism: A critical analysis' (2004) 11 *SA Journal of International Affairs* 21.

[77] Decision Assembly/AU/Dec. 283 (XIV).

[78] A resolution of the Heads of State and Government Implementation Committee recommended in February 2004 that NEPAD, which had until then functioned independently, should be incorporated into the AU structures. The AU Heads of State and Government endorsed this resolution in July 2004 (Assembly/AU/ Dec.38 (III). For more on this see A Mangu (n 34) 144–56.

The mainstay of NEPAD's plan for the promotion of democracy and human rights is its African Peer Review Mechanism (APRM) in terms of which African states hold each other accountable to agreed principles of good governance. With the creation of the AU, peer review is now placed under the direct control of the AU.[79] The APRM is an instrument voluntarily acceded to by member states of the AU as an African self-monitoring mechanism.[80] Participating in the APRM entails an undertaking to submit to periodic peer reviews, facilitate reviews and adhere to agreed standards of good political, economic and corporate governance. Peer review takes place under the auspices of the AU's Conference on Security, Stability, Development and Cooperation in Africa (CSSDCA) Unit.[81] The potential advantage of this move is that the obligations for the 55 member states under the AU are mandatory whereas the APRM is a voluntary arrangement (other than for those states—significantly smaller in number than compared with the 55 member states of the AU[82]—that have chosen to be bound). Implementation of the CSSDCA review process is thus mandatory for AU member states. Amongst other measures, implementation of the CSSDCA process is to be achieved by the designation of focal points in states to co-ordinate and monitor their implementation of the CSSDCA core values,[83] and through the

[79] Ibid. As a further sign of NEPAD's subsidiary role to that of the AU, the NEPAD secretariat, currently based in Pretoria, South Africa, will in future relocate to Addis Ababa, Ethiopia, or will constitute a satellite office of the AU Commission. There is, however, ongoing confusion and flux between the various institutions within the NEPAD and CSSDCA processes—for critical comment, see A Lloyd and R Murray 'Institutions with responsibility for human rights protection under the African Union' (2004) 48 *Journal of African Law* 165 at 180–6. See also J Akokpari 'Policing and preventing human rights abuses in Africa: The OAU, the AU and the NEPAD peer review' (2004) 2 *International Journal of Legal Information* 461.

[80] NEPAD Declaration on politics, democracy, economics and corporate governance. See further A Mangu 'Assessing the effectiveness of the African Peer Review Mechanism and its impact on the promotion of democracy and good political governance (2007) 7 *AHRLJ* 354.

[81] See J Cilliers 'NEPAD's Peer Review Mechanism' (Institute for Security Studies Paper No 64, November 2004) 2, available at http://www.iss.co.za. While the CSSDCA mechanism is now an AU process, the initiative for its establishment was taken by the OAU Assembly of Heads of State and Government at its Fourth Extraordinary Session in Sirte, Libya, in September 1999; see AHG/Decl.4 (XXXVI). It was formally adopted by the 36th Ordinary Session of OAU Assembly in Lomé, Togo, in July 2000. The CSSDCA process, therefore, predates NEPAD.

[82] As of June 2018, 36 AU member states had acceded to the APRM's Memorandum of Understanding and 20 had been peer-reviewed after completing their self-assessments. For the latest status, see http://www.aprm-au.org/.

[83] States are expected to implement the CSSDCA values through, inter alia, the promulgation of Constitutions with Bills of Rights, and a commitment to free and fair elections, separation of powers, and protection of human rights. See the Draft

creation of national co-ordinating committees.[84] Member states' performance is to be monitored by a standing conference of the CSSDCA every two years. To assist in the monitoring process, the national units set up by member states co-ordinate with the CSSDCA Unit and civil society and others to produce country reports.[85] The CSSDCA unit was restructured and is now the Citizens' Directorate, within the Bureau of the Chairperson of the AU Commission.

By June 2018, 20 member countries had been peer reviewed. Nevertheless, peer review has been painfully slow and political will and commitment to APRM implementation remains an ongoing concern.[86]

THE AFRICAN UNION AND PEACE AND SECURITY IN AFRICA

No single factor has contributed more to the social economic decline of the African continent and the suffering of the civilian population than conflict within and between the states.[87] Peace and security has now been acknowledged as one of the key priorities of the AU.[88] The Peace and Security Council is intended to provide a more robust mechanism than its predecessor, the OAU's Central Organ of the Mechanism for Conflict Prevention, Management and Resolution, whose performance was regarded as unimpressive.[89] The Peace and

Memorandum of Understanding on Security, Stability, Development and Cooperation in Africa, paras 26–8, available at http://www.au2002gov.za/docs/background/cssdca.htm.

[84] Murray (n 7) 30.

[85] Ibid.

[86] On the challenges of implementing the APRM see, eg, NM Stultz 'African states experiment with peer reviewing: The APRM' (2007) *Brown Journal of World Affairs* 247; R Herbert and S Gruzd 'Taking stock of the African Peer Review Mechanism' (2009) 14 *SA Journal of International Affairs* 5; A Babington-Ashaye 'The African Peer Review Mechanism at ten: From lofty goals to practical implementation' (2011) 19 *African Yearbook of International Law* 21.

[87] Preamble to the Protocol Relating to the Establishment of the Peace and Security Council of the African Union. For further discussion see T Murithi 'Institutionalising Pan-Africanism' (Institute for Security Studies Paper No 143, June 2007) available at http://www.iss.co.za. See also K Kindiki 'The normative and institutional framework of the African Union relating to the protection of human rights and maintenance of peace and security' (2003) 3 *AHRLJ* 97.

[88] In July 2005, the AU Assembly at Sirte, Libya, optimistically set a goal for a conflict-free Africa by 2010.

[89] Created pursuant to the Protocol Relating to the Establishment of the Peace and Security Council of the African Union, adopted by the AU Assembly at its inaugural summit in Durban, South Africa, on 11 July 2002; entered into force on 16 December 2003, and ratified by South Africa on 15 May 2003. C Powell 'The African Union's emerging peace and security regime' Institute for Security Studies Paper No 119, May 2005, available at http://www.iss.co.za 9 and Murithi (n 87) 3. However, despite

Security Council may authorise peace missions, and recommend to the Assembly that the AU intervene in certain situations where grave crimes (such as crimes against humanity, war crimes and genocide) are being perpetrated, as provided for in article 4(h) of the AU Constitutive Act.[90] In February 2003, the AU Heads of State and Government adopted the Protocol on Amendments to the Constitutive Act of the African Union. The Protocol, not yet in force at the time of this writing, amends a number of provisions in the Constitutive Act, including article 4(h).[91] The amended article 4(h) extends the right to intervene to situations that pose a 'serious threat to legitimate order to restore peace and stability to the Member State of the Union upon the recommendation of the Peace and Security Council'.[92] The establishment of the Peace and Security Council of the AU thus provides a clearly defined mechanism for determining situations representing a serious threat to legitimate order and the steps necessary to restore peace and stability to the member states, in close

criticisms of its performance, the OAU did enjoy some success on account of its mediation in the Democratic Republic of Congo. For a further discussion see J Sarkin 'The role of the United Nations, the African Union and the Africa's Sub-regional Organization in dealing with Africa's human rights problem: connecting humanitarian intervention and the responsibility to protect' (2009) 53 *Journal of African Law* 1.

[90] Article 7 of the Protocol Relating to the Establishment of the Peace and Security Council of the African Union. Article 4(h) of the AU Constitutive Act provides for the right of the African Union to intervene in a member state, pursuant to a decision of the Assembly, in respect of grave circumstances, namely war crimes, genocide and crimes against humanity. This is a welcome development, and one that conflicts with the well-established principles of 'sovereign equality and interdependence among Member States', 'prohibition on the use of force or threat to use force among Member States' and 'non-interference by any Member State in the internal affairs of another'. The AU's emerging peace and security regime draws on elements of a protection framework as set out in the 2006 UN General Assembly resolution on 'The Responsibility to Protect' (R2P). (See further on this resolution, Chapter 24.) This resolution recasts sovereignty, at least rhetorically, from being an absolute, intrinsic right of statehood, to being a 'responsibility' to protect one's citizens from crimes against humanity, genocide and war crimes. If this responsibility is deliberately flouted, the R2P doctrine stipulates that the offending state becomes vulnerable to intervention from the international community. It is premised on the understanding that sovereignty is conditional and is defined in terms of a state's willingness and capacity to protect its citizens.

[91] Somewhat unusually, the Protocol was in fact adopted twice: first, by the First Extraordinary Session of the AU Assembly in Addis Ababa, Ethiopia on 3 February 2003; and again by the Second Ordinary Session of the AU Assembly in Maputo, Mozambique on 11 July 2003. See T Maluwa 'Fast-tracking African unity or making haste slowly? A note on the amendments to the Constitutive Act of the African Union' (2004) 51 *NILR* 195.

[92] See, further, S Gumedze 'The African Union and the responsibility to protect' (2010) 10 *AHRLJ* 138; B Kioko 'The right of intervention under the African Union's Constitutive Act: From non-interference to non-intervention' (2003) 85 *IRRC* 807.

co-operation with the UN Security Council.[93] It is, however, unclear whether UN authorisation is required prior to the undertaking of regional intervention by the AU.[94] The AU's March 2005 document 'The Common African Position on the Proposed Reform of the United Nations', known as the Ezulwini Consensus, acknowledges that intervention by regional organisations should be under UN Security Council approval, but that such approval could be granted after the intervention had already begun in cases where immediate action was required.[95]

Complementing the peace and security architecture of the AU is the African Standby Force which has been created for deployment on the instructions of the Peace and Security Council as a rapid-response standby force.[96] The African Standby Force comprises troops, military observers, police units, and civilian specialists.[97] Regional

[93] See article 7(r) of the Protocol Relating to the Establishment of the Peace and Security Council of the African Union. On co-operation with the UN Security Council, see article 17(1) and (3) of the Peace and Security Protocol. For further discussion, see Gumedze (n 92).

[94] Concerning the limits of the use of regional force, see Z Deen-Racsmany 'A redistribution of authority between the UN and regional organizations in the maintenance of peace and security' (2000) 13 *LJIL* 297–331. See also Sarkin (n 89).

[95] Arguments put forward for empowering the AU to intervene in regional conflicts have been that the United Nations has historically failed to act, and with enough force and speed, in cases of serious human rights violations in Africa. Rwanda is a prime example of such a failure to act. That being said, the AU failed to act decisively in respect of the violence in Libya in January 2011 and it was left to the UN Security Council to authorise military action in Libya (to establish a 'no-fly zone' and to protect civilians in Security Council resolution 1973). See M du Plessis and C Gevers 'Libya crisis a lost opportunity for ineffectual African Union' *Business Day* 28 March 2011. On the implications of article 4(h) of the AU Constitutive Act for the requirement of prior UN Security Council authorisation, see, generally, J Allain 'The true challenge to the United Nations system of the use of force: The failures of Kosovo and Iraq and the emergence of the African Union' (2004) *8 Max Planck Yearbook of UN Law* 237 at 264; J Levitt 'The law on intervention: Africa's pathbreaking model' (2005) 7 *Global Dialogue* 48, available at http://www.worlddialogue.org/content.php?id+330; S Paliwal 'The primacy of regional organizations in international peacekeeping: The African example' (2011) 51 *Virginia Journal of International Law* 185; and D Kuwali and F Viljoen (eds) *Africa and the Responsibility to Protect: Article 4(h) of the African Union Constitutive Act* (2014).

[96] See article 13 of the Protocol Relating to the Establishment of the Peace and Security Council of the African Union and the Policy Framework for the Establishment of the African Standby Force and Military Staff Committee, Submitted by African Military Experts to African Chiefs of Defence Staff, 12–14 May 2003, Exp/ASF-MSC/2(I).

[97] The African Standby Force was originally intended to be in place by 2010, but due to lack of support and capacity, it was declared operationally ready only in 2016. As of June 2018, it still has not been deployed in its originally designed form, not because of lack of opportunities but rather a demonstration of the power of the

Economic Communities, which were initially created for economic integration, have taken on an important role in peacekeeping, peace enforcement and post-conflict activities.[98] Further, a Continental Early Warning System has been put in place in order 'to facilitate the anticipation and prevention of conflicts' through the establishment of a Conflict Management Directorate which collects and analyses data used to advise the Peace and Security Council on potential conflicts and appropriate responses.[99] A Panel of the Wise (made up of 'five highly respected African personalities from various segments of society who have made outstanding contributions to the cause of peace, security and development on the continent'[100]) has been constituted to advise the Peace and Security Council 'on all issues pertaining to the promotion, and maintenance of peace, security and stability in Africa'.[101] The Panel was inaugurated on 18 December 2007. A Peace Fund was also established to ensure that there would be sufficient resources for post-conflict reconstruction efforts.[102] In accordance with its protective mandate, the AU has undertaken several regional interventions in Africa, briefly discussed below.

(a) The African Mission in Burundi (AMIB)

In April 2003, the AU deployed its first peace operation, wholly initiated and executed by the AU, during the Burundian civil war. The mission was deployed after the signing of individual ceasefire agreements between the government and different rebel groups, under the Arusha Peace and Reconciliation Agreement for Burundi signed in Arusha, Tanzania, on 28 August 2000, which provided the

Regional Economic Communities (see above n 39 and below n 98). See L Darkwa 'The African Standby Force: The African Union's tool for the maintenance of peace and security' (2017) 38 *Contemporary Security Policy* 471.

[98] Some of the Regional Economic Communities (n 39) have increasingly taken on regional security roles, creating Regional Standby Forces, which form the building blocks of the African Standby Brigade. An example of this is ECOWAS's formation of the Economic Community of West African States Monitoring Group (ECOMOG), a sub-regional brigade consisting of police, military and civilians. For further discussion see G Segell 'A decade of African Union and European Union trans-regional security relations' (2010) 38 *Scientia Militaria: SA Journal of Military Studies* 25.

[99] Powell (n 89); article 12 of the Protocol Relating to the Establishment of the Peace and Security Council of the African Union.

[100] Article 11(2) of the Protocol Relating to the Establishment of the Peace and Security Council of the African Union. See A Jegede 'The African Union peace and security architecture: Can the panel of the wise make a difference?' (2009) 9 *AHRLJ* 409.

[101] Article 11(3) of the Protocol Relating to the Establishment of the Peace and Security Council of the African Union.

[102] Ibid article 21.

basis for the establishment of AMIB. In essence, AMIB was launched as a substitute for an absent UN force, and was tasked with four objectives: overseeing the implementation of the ceasefire agreement; supporting disarmament, demobilisation and reintegration (DDR) initiatives; creating enabling conditions for a follow-on UN peacekeeping force; and contributing to economic and political stability in Burundi.

A total of 3 335 peacekeepers and observers, consisting of both military and civilian components, mainly from South Africa, Ethiopia and Mozambique were deployed to Burundi for one year, with the possibility of an extension, pending the deployment of a UN peacekeeping force. As the AU's first peace operation, it can be seen as a test case for the AU's initial capability to conduct peace operations. In this respect, it can also be said to have been the result of the AU's ambition to take on peace operations when the UN was not willing to do so, despite its limited resources and the reality that the mechanisms for such a task were not in place.

(b) Peace Operation in Burundi (ONUB)

The AMIB was generally regarded as successful in restoring relative peace and stability in most provinces in Burundi. However, it failed in its other objective of achieving DDR. AMIB's challenges and failures resulted from a combination of factors, including the lack of political will by AU member states, with the exception of South Africa, to commit adequate resources—both financial and material—to the operation and the unwillingness of the international community to support the mission. South Africa was the largest force on the ground, contributing approximately 1 500 troops. As a result, although on paper this was an AU mission, it was effectively dependent on one troop-contributing country. Yet the stabilisation that AMIB brought to Burundi was regarded as successful enough to warrant the involvement of the UN, which absorbed AMIB after 14 months of operations.

The UN mission was known as the United Nations Peace Operation in Burundi (ONUB). Under the Security Council resolution, adopted unanimously, the mission was to be deployed from 1 June 2004 in order to support and help to implement the efforts undertaken by Burundians to restore lasting peace and bring about national reconciliation. The resolution also authorised the UN Secretary-General to ensure the transfer of authority from the AU to the Secretary-General's Special Representative.[103] ONUB ended its mission on 31 December 2006.

[103] United Nations Security Council Resolution 1545 of 21 May 2004. For a discussion and analysis of the AU's peacekeeping missions in Burundi, Somalia and

(c) *The African Mission in Sudan (AMIS)*

The African Mission in Sudan (AMIS) operated in Sudan's western region of Darfur from 2004 to 2007. The AU's involvement in Darfur followed the outbreak of the conflict in 2003. The origins of the conflict lay in sporadic attacks involving armed tribal groups and militias called the *Janjaweed*. Later it widened into a conflict between forces of the Government of Sudan and two major rebel groups, the Sudan Liberation Movement/Army (SLM/A) and the Justice and Equality Movement (JEM), with innocent civilians increasingly becoming victims of targeted attacks by both the *Janjaweed* and government forces. These attacks and resultant deaths affecting thousands of lives have been widely described as amounting to gross violations of human rights and genocide. The AU assisted in brokering a Humanitarian Ceasefire Agreement (HCFA) between the Government of Sudan and the two rebel groups in April 2004. This entailed the establishment of AMIS and the deployment of 7 000 troops to the Darfur region. A major aspect of the mission's mandate was to monitor, verify, investigate, and report on violations of the ceasefire.[104] However, the number of troops—drawn from Gambia, Kenya, Nigeria, Rwanda, South Africa and Senegal—was insufficient for the vast territory covered by its mandate. And, as with AMIB, AMIS was inadequately resourced.

While AMIS struggled to discharge its mandate effectively, lengthy negotiations continued at the UN aimed at overcoming the Sudanese Government's opposition to the deployment of a UN force. Eventually, a compromise was reached in November 2006 between Sudan, the AU and the UN Security Council to set up a hybrid AU–UN force. But due to further obstruction by the Government of Sudan, it was not until 31 July 2007 that the UN Security Council was able to authorise the establishment of the hybrid force, the United Nations–African Union Mission in Darfur (UNAMID), consisting of over 20 000 personnel.[105] AMIS formally ceased to exist on 31 December 2007. On that day, the UNAMID Joint Special Representative of the UN and the AU took up his command at a solemn ceremony at the

Darfur, see I Badmus, *The African Union's Role in Peacekeeping: Building on Lessons Learned from Security Operations* (2015).

[104] The HCFA was signed by the Government of Sudan, the Sudan Liberation Movement/Army (SLM/A) and the Justice and Equality Movement (JEM) on 8 April 2004. Among other things, the parties agreed to establish a Joint Commission (JC) and a Ceasefire Commission (CFC), which would implement the HCFA.

[105] UNSC Res 1769 (2007) on the establishment of the AU/UN Hybrid Operation in Darfur (UNAMID), adopted on 31 July 2007.

AU headquarters in Addis Ababa. UNAMID thereby formally commenced its operation on 1 January 2008. The AU intervention in Darfur was not entirely successful, partly because of its narrow and insufficient mandate, which did not include civilian protection, as well as serious logistical and capacity constraints due to fragmented international assistance and donor rigidity. An additional factor was the Sudanese government's reluctance to co-operate fully with the mission for most of its existence.

(d) The African Mission in Somalia (AMISOM)

In March 2007, the AU deployed a regional peacekeeping mission into Somalia. It was created by the African Union's Peace and Security Council on 19 January 2007 with an initial six-month mandate. The mission, based on the AMIB model, was deployed with UN Security Council authorisation.[106] The AU originally undertook to send 8 000 peacekeepers to respond to the crisis but initially was only able to send 1 200 Ugandan soldiers due to lack of funds, transport, and communication equipment. Although as many as 20 AU member states had at one point reportedly considered contributing to AMISOM, only six have contributed troops over the decade since its establishment. These are Uganda (2007), Burundi (2007), Djibouti (2011), Kenya (2012), Sierra Leone (2013) and Ethiopia (2014), with Uganda remaining by far the major player and contributor.

The initial high number of AU member states willing to consider participating in AMISOM suggests that a number of countries wanted to be seen to be joining the AU's efforts to assist the fledgling Somali government to defeat the terrorist threat posed by *Al Shabaab*. This thinking fits into the narrative that Somalia represented the region's frontline in the US-led 'global war on terrorism'. In particular, leaders of some of these countries, namely Ethiopia, Kenya and Uganda, were keen to burnish their reputations as regional leaders and allies of the US in the fight against terrorism. One aspect of AMISOM's mandate was to create the conditions necessary for the withdrawal of Ethiopian troops in Somalia. Ethiopia, and subsequently Kenya, had initially deployed their forces unilaterally into Somalia to address national security and political problems raised by the instability in the country and contain *Al Shabaab* away from their territories. Both countries only joined the multilateral force afterwards. The intractability of the political and security situation in Somalia has turned AMISOM into the longest-running peacekeeping force ever undertaken by the AU. The mission has also witnessed the

[106] UNSC Res 1744 (2007) on the Situation in Somalia, adopted on 21 February 2007.

largest number of AU peacekeepers killed by terrorists or armed groups involved in the conflict. The UN Security Council has authorised the AU Peace and Security Council to renew AMISOM's mandate several times since its establishment. The latest authorisation was adopted under Security Council resolution 2372 on 30 August 2017.

THE AFRICAN UNION AND HUMAN RIGHTS

One of the major criticisms of the OAU over the 37-years of its existence was its failure to address systematic violations of human rights in the continent.[107] While article 2(1)(e) of the OAU Charter declared as one of the OAU's goals that member states should 'promote international cooperation, having due regard to the Charter of the United Nations and the Universal Declaration of Human Rights', it took almost two decades before the Assembly of Heads of State and Governments adopted, in 1981, a human rights instrument for the region, already mentioned above, the African Charter on Human and Peoples' Rights.[108] The African Charter—or Banjul Charter[109] as it is also known—established the normative framework for the promotion and protection of human rights in Africa. Two other instruments adopted subsequently by the OAU have expanded this normative framework: the African Charter on the Rights and Welfare of the Child[110] and the Protocol to the African Charter on Human and Peoples' Rights on the Rights of Women in Africa.[111] In addition to these, the Protocol to the African Charter on Human and Peoples' Rights on the Establishment of the African Court on Human and Peoples' Rights, adopted in 1998,[112] established the judicial

[107] For discussions of human rights under the OAU in the pre-1981 period, see, eg, LO Adegbite, 'African attitudes to the international protection of human rights' in A Eide and A Schou (eds) *International Protection of Human Rights* (1968). See also A Aluko 'The Organization of African Unity and human rights' (1981) 283 *The Round Table* 234; OC Eze 'The prospects for international protection of human rights in Africa' (1974) 1 *African Review* 79. See also n 34.

[108] See n 21.

[109] This is in recognition of the fact that the draft Charter that had been adopted by a meeting of independent experts convened in Dakar, Senegal from 28 November to 8 December 1979 at the request of the OAU Assembly was considered and adopted by an OAU Ministerial Conference in Banjul, Gambia, from 9 to 15 June 1980. The text adopted in Banjul was formally adopted by the OAU Assembly at its summit in Nairobi the following June; see OAU Doc. CAB/LEG/67/9.

[110] OAU Doc CAB/LEG/24.9/49. See n 23.

[111] Adopted on 1 July 2003, entered into force on 25 November 2005; ratified by South Africa on 17 December 2004.

[112] OAU Doc CAB/LRG/AFCHPR/PROT(III). Adopted on 10 July 1998, entered into force on 25 January 2004; ratified by South Africa on 3 July 2002.

mechanism to complement the African Commission on Human and Peoples' Rights (ACHPR) established under the African Charter (see below). Taken together, these treaties provide for the substantive norms and institutional mechanisms of the African regional human rights system. To these core African human rights treaties may be added other OAU and AU treaties that have an indirect bearing on human rights, although not adopted as human rights treaties as such.[113]

The provisions of the AU Constitutive Act suggest that human rights will play an important role in the work of the Union.[114] For instance, the preamble speaks of states being 'determined to promote and protect human and peoples' rights, consolidate democratic institutions and culture and to ensure good governance and the rule of law'. As one of its central objectives, the AU recognises the need to 'encourage international co-operation, taking due account of the Charter of the United Nations and the Universal Declaration of Human Rights' and to 'promote and protect human and peoples' rights, in accordance with the African Charter on Human and Peoples' Rights and other relevant human rights instruments'.[115]

Member states are accordingly expected to promote gender equality and to have 'respect for democratic principles, human rights, the rule of law and good governance', and to respect the sanctity of life.[116] Of obvious importance, given the peer review mechanism that exists under the AU, is the principled commitment by the Union under its Constitutive Act to condemn and reject 'unconstitutional changes of governments'.[117] There is thus a clear trend in the Act towards limiting the sovereignty of member states and, in appropriate circumstances, permitting the involvement of the Union in the domestic affairs of African countries notwithstanding the principle of non-interference by any member state in the internal affairs of another.[118]

[113] These include the OAU Convention Governing the Specific Aspects of Refugee Problems in Africa (1969), OAU Convention on the Prevention and Combating of Terrorism (1999), African Union Convention on Preventing and Combating of Corruption (2003), African Charter on Democracy, Elections and Governance (2007), and African Union Convention for the Protection and Assistance of Internally Displaced Persons (2009).

[114] See, generally, F Viljoen *International Human Rights Law in Africa* (2007); R Murray *Human Rights in Africa: From the OAU to the African Union* (2004), and Lloyd and Murray (n 79).

[115] Constitutive Act of the AU, article 3(e) and (h).

[116] Ibid article 4(l), (m), and (o).

[117] Ibid article 4(p).

[118] Ibid article 4(g).

1 African Charter on Human and Peoples' Rights

The African Charter on Human and Peoples' Rights has been in force since 21 October 1986. Today, all AU member states have ratified the Charter, with the sole exception of Morocco, which only joined the AU in January 2017. An oversight body provided for under Part II (articles 30 to 59) of the Charter, the ACHPR, was established on 2 November 1987. The African Charter is explicitly recognised in the AU Constitutive Act as one of the means by which the Union aims to 'promote and protect human and peoples' rights'.[119] Together, the African Charter and the ACHPR have come to be regarded as the principal means by which human rights might be promoted and protected on the continent, along with other relevant human rights instruments, such as those mentioned above.[120]

Although the Charter was inspired by other human rights conventions, it was intended to be a uniquely African document on human rights. This is clear from the Charter's preamble, which highlights certain defining characteristics of the African regional system for the protection of human rights:

> Taking into consideration the virtues of their historical tradition and the values of African civilisation which should inspire and characterise their reflection on the concept of human and peoples' rights . . .
>
> Considering that the enjoyment of rights and freedoms also implies the performance of duties on the part of everyone;
>
> Convinced that it is henceforth essential to pay particular attention to the right to development and that civil and political rights cannot be dissociated from economic, social and cultural rights in their conception as well as universality and that the satisfaction of economic, social and cultural rights is a guarantee for the enjoyment of civil and political rights.

Accordingly, and in line with other conventions, the Charter recognises the basic first and second generation rights; civil and political and social, economic and cultural rights. In addition, recognition is accorded to third-generation collective rights such as the rights to development, self-determination and a satisfactory environment. Unlike other conventions, the Charter recognises the duties of the individual—towards family, society, and state.

In respect of the Charter's civil and political rights protections,[121] one finds the standard international human rights guarantees, such

[119] Article 3(e) and (h).

[120] See n 113. For a comprehensive analysis of the Charter, see F Ouguergouz *The African Charter on Human and Peoples' Rights: A Comprehensive Agenda for Human Dignity and Sustainable Democracy in Africa* (2003).

[121] See, generally, C Heyns 'Civil and political rights in the African Charter' in M Evans and R Murray (eds) *The African Charter on Human and Peoples Rights: The System in Practice, 1986–2000* (2001) 137.

as equality before the law (article 3), respect for life and the integrity of the person (article 4), the right to freedom of conscience and religion (article 8), and the right of assembly (article 11). However, while the Charter contains no derogation clause for emergency situations, the proclaimed rights are undermined by so-called 'claw-back clauses' that confine the Charter's protection to the rights defined in national law. For example, article 6 provides that 'no one may be deprived of his freedom *except for reasons and conditions previously laid down by law*' (emphasis added), and article 9 limits a person's freedom to express opinions *'within the law'*. The difficulty with claw-back clauses is that, arguably, rights may be made subject to municipal law. These claw-back clauses have been severely criticised.[122] The ACHPR has recently gone some way towards ameliorating their effect by interpreting clawback clauses restrictively, and by suggesting that phrases such as 'within the law' and 'subject to law', when used as part of claw-back clauses, should be understood to refer to international law, not domestic law. For instance, in *Media Rights Agenda and Constitutional Rights Project v Nigeria*[123] the Commission was concerned with the banning of a number of periodicals critical of the Nigerian regime's annulment of the results of elections held in 1993. The Commission found that governments should avoid restricting rights and should have special regard to those rights protected by constitutional or international human rights law, one such right being the right to freedom of expression in article 9 of the Charter. According to the Commission,

> '[t]o allow national law to have precedent over the international law of the Charter would defeat the purpose of the rights and freedoms enshrined in the Charter. *International human rights standards must always prevail over contradictory national law. Any limitation on the rights of the Charter must be in conformity with the provisions of the Charter*'.[124]

The Commission stressed that possible limitations must be founded in a legitimate state interest, and the evils of limitations of rights must be strictly proportionate to and absolutely necessary for the advantages that are to be obtained.[125]

[122] See, eg, EA Ankumah *The African Commission on Human and Peoples' Rights* (1996) 176.

[123] *Media Rights Agenda and Constitutional Rights Project v Nigeria* (2000) 7 *IHRR* 265.

[124] Paragraph 66 (emphasis added).

[125] See, also, *Amnesty International v Zambia* (2000) 7 *IHRR* 286, where the African Commission warned against a facile resort to the limitation clauses in the African Charter to restrict Charter rights. Importantly, the Commission held that the onus is on the state to prove that it is justified to resort to the limitation clause (para 50).

Regarding socio-economic rights,[126] the African Charter includes the right to property (article 14), the right to work and equal pay (article 15), the right to the best attainable standard of physical and mental health (article 16), the right to education (article 17), and the right to the protection of the family (article 18). There is no mention of the right to food and social security, nor of the right of access to adequate housing. However, the ACHPR has engaged in generous interpretation to ensure that these unwritten socio-economic rights are protected through the means of other socio-economic rights that are codified in the Charter. For example, the Commission has found that the starvation of prisoners violated article 16's guarantee of the right to enjoy the best attainable state of physical and mental health, and it has decided that forcibly evicting persons from their homes amounted to a violation of the right to property guaranteed in article 14.[127] Depriving persons of basic services such as drinking water, electricity and basic medicine has also been characterised by the Commission as a violation of article 16.[128]

In respect of the collective rights of peoples, the Charter includes a range of important protections, including the right to a satisfactory environment favourable to development (article 24), the right to economic, social and cultural development (article 22), and the right to existence and self-determination (article 20). The meaning of the term 'peoples' in the Charter is not clear.[129] In the light of the earlier

[126] See, in general, CA Odinkalu 'Analysis of paralysis or paralysis by analysis? Implementing economic, social and cultural rights under the African Charter on Human and Peoples' Rights' (2001) 23 *Human Rights Quarterly* 327; CA Odinkalu 'Implementing economic, social and cultural rights under the African Charter on Human and Peoples' Rights' in Evans and Murray (n 121) 178; P de Vos 'A new beginning? The enforcement of social, economic and cultural rights under the African Charter on Human and Peoples' Rights' (2004) 8 *Law, Democracy and Development* 1. For perhaps its most extensive decision on socio-economic rights, see the decision of the African Commission on Communication 155/96 *The Social and Economic Rights Action Center and the Center for Economic and Social Rights v Nigeria*. See, too, the discussion of the decision in F Coomans 'The *Ogoni* case before the African Commission on Human and Peoples' Rights' (2003) 52 *ICLQ* 749.

[127] See Communications 54/91, 61/91, 98/93, 164/97 and 210/98 against Mauritania, cited by Odinkalu ibid ('Analysis of Paralysis . . .') 364.

[128] See Communications 25/89, 47/90, 56/91 and 100/93; *World Organization Against Torture et al v Zaire*, cited in Odinkalu (n 126) ('Analysis of Paralysis. . .') 365.

[129] N Kiwanuka 'The meaning of "people" in the African Charter on Human and Peoples' Rights' (1988) 82 *AJIL* 80. See, further, R Murray and S Wheatley 'Groups and the African Charter on Human and Peoples' Rights' (2003) 25 *Human Rights Quarterly* 213. For a discussion of the rights of peoples generally, see W Benedek 'The rights of peoples: The main issues' in J Crawford (ed) *The Rights of Peoples* (1988) 71–9; FN Fanana 'The "peoples' rights" under the African Charter on Human and Peoples' Rights' (1997) 1 *Lesotho LJ* 37.

commitment by the OAU to the preservation of colonial borders, it would be wrong to interpret the right of a people to self-determination to include a right to secession, despite the fact that a literal reading of the Charter's article 20 permits such an interpretation.[130]

Through the preamble's reference to 'the virtues of [African states'] historical tradition and the values of African civilisation', the African Charter highlights cultural distinctiveness as an important feature within the continent. This uniqueness of its character is exemplified in the Charter's inclusion of duties. For instance, article 27 provides that every individual shall have duties towards his family and society, the state, and other legally recognised communities and the international community, and article 28 speaks of an individual's duty to respect and consider his fellow beings without discrimination, and to maintain relations aimed at promoting, safeguarding and reinforcing mutual respect and tolerance. Article 29 particularises these principles by providing that the individual has a duty, inter alia, to respect his parents at all times and to maintain them in case of need, to serve his national community by placing his physical and intellectual abilities at its service, to preserve and strengthen the national independence and the territorial integrity of his country and to contribute to its defence in accordance with law, and to pay taxes imposed by law in the interests of the society. The Charter therefore stresses 'solidarity' and attempts to highlight a specific structure of the African society—one in which the individual owes something to his society and state. The inclusion of duties in the Charter is not without its problems, however. For one thing, some duties impinge on rights within the Charter itself. For instance, article 8 provides that '[freedom] of conscience, the profession and free practice of religion shall be guaranteed', but it is not clear how one reconciles this right with article 29(5) which places a duty on the individual 'to preserve and strengthen the national independence and the territorial integrity of his country and to contribute to its defence in accordance with the law'. Where, for example, does that leave conscientious objection to military service on religious grounds? A further problem is that

[130] This is confirmed by the ruling of the African Commission in *Katangese Peoples' Congress v Zaire*, Communication 74/92, reported in (1996) 3 *IHRR* 136 and (1995) 13 *Netherlands Quarterly of Human Rights* 478, which holds that self-determination is to be exercised within existing borders. (See further Chapter 5). The Commission has also provided some interpretation and clarification of the notion of 'peoples' rights' in other cases: *Kevin Mgwana Gunme et al v Cameroon*, Communication 266/03, available at http://caselaw.ihrda.org/doc/266.03/; *Sudan Human Rights Organization and Centre on Housing Rights and Evictions v Sudan*, Communication 279/03-296/05, available at http://caselaw.ihrda.org/doc/279.03-296.05/; and *Centre for Minority Rights Development (Kenya) and Minority Rights Group (on behalf of Endorois Welfare Council) v Kenya*, Communication 276/03, available at http://caselaw.ihrda.org/doc/276.03/.

many of the duties do not appear to be capable of meaningful enforcement. At best, perhaps, is to conceive of the duties as hortative: a reminder for African societies to contemplate the complex web of individual and community duties and rights and to seek a balance between the competing claims of the individual and society.[131]

2 African Commission on Human and Peoples' Rights

The supervisory organ of the African Charter is the ACHPR, situated in Banjul in The Gambia. Its establishment, mandate and methods of work are provided for in Part II of the Charter (articles 30 to 59). The Commission is comprised of 11 members who serve in their personal capacities and who are elected for a six-year period.[132] The Commission's members are expected to promote, protect and interpret the rights in the African Charter,[133] and they meet twice a year in fortnight-long sessions.

The principal function of the Commission is to promote human rights in Africa by means of public education.[134] The Commission has a mandate in terms of article 45 of the African Charter to collect documents, undertake research, organise seminars, disseminate information, collaborate with relevant organisations, lay down principles and give recommendations to governments. To this end, the Commission has adopted a Programme of Action and has organised a number of conferences, seminars and workshops in collaboration with NGOs or other institutions such as the United Nations Centre for Human Rights.[135] It has also passed a number of resolutions and recommendations (eg, encouraging governments to establish national commissions for human rights and to incorporate human rights into teaching curricula at all levels).[136] It has adopted over 100

[131] See, generally, M Mutua 'The Banjul Charter and the African cultural fingerprint: An evaluation of the language of duties' (1995) 35 *Virginia Journal of International Law* 339.

[132] See, further, R Murray *The African Commission on Human and Peoples' Rights and International Law* (2000) 11; Viljoen (n 114) 310.

[133] Article 45 of the African Charter.

[134] On the promotional role of the African Commission, see V Dankwa 'The promotional roles of the African Commission on Human and Peoples' Rights' in Evans and Murray (n 121) 335.

[135] See, further, Murray (n 114) 15. See, also, VOO Nmehielle *The African Human Rights System: Its Laws, Practice, and Institutions* (2001) 176–80.

[136] See Recommendations and Resolutions of the African Commission, Banjul, The Gambia, December 1998. In recent times, the Commission has moved to issue robust criticism of ongoing human rights violations in particular African states. See, eg, the African Commission's Resolution on the Human Rights Situation in Darfur, Sudan, adopted at its 37th Ordinary Session held from 27 April to 11 May 2005 in Banjul, The

resolutions on thematic, procedural and country-specific issues.[137] Through these resolutions, the ACHPR defines the content of rights in the African Charter, condemns human rights violations and addresses administrative and procedural issues relevant to its work. The Commission has furthermore assigned to each commissioner a number of missions into member states in terms of the Commission's promotional and protective mandate.[138]

The African Charter is enforced by way of state-reporting and individual/NGO complaints. In respect of the reporting procedure, state parties are expected to submit country reports every two years. These are considered by the Commission, which may adopt general observations.[139] State parties are required to report on the legislative and other measures that they have taken to implement the Charter.[140] There is unfortunately a poor record of submission, with 12 states having never submitted any report to the Commission,[141] and most states are behind in their obligations in this regard.[142] Aligned with this difficulty is the fact that the Commission does not have a well-developed follow-up system. The Commission's approach is to engage in 'constructive dialogue' with the state by way of questions put to state representatives who attend the meetings.[143] While the sessions involve open discussions between commissioners, NGOs

Gambia (ACHPR/Res 74 (XXXVII) 05; text available at http;//www.achpr.org/english/resolutions/resolution79_en.html).

[137] J Biegon and M Killander 'Human rights developments in the African Union during 2009' (2009) 9 *AHRLJ* 212.

[138] Commissioners are expected to organize lectures and seminars in collaboration with domestic institutions with the aim of promoting the African human rights mechanisms in the country concerned. See Nmehielle (n 135) 179.

[139] On the Reporting Procedure, see article 62 of the African Charter on Human and Peoples' Rights. See, generally, M Evans, T Ige and R Murray 'The Reporting Mechanism of the African Charter on Human and Peoples' Rights' in Evans and Murray (n 121) 36 and Biegon and Killander (n 137) 300.

[140] See eg the discussion in F Viljoen 'Examination of state reports at the 27th session of the African Commission on Human and Peoples' Rights: A critical analysis and proposal for reform' (2000) 16 *SAJHR* 576. See also K Quashigah 'The African Charter on Human and Peoples' Rights: Towards a more effective reporting mechanism' (2002) 2 *AJHRL* 261.

[141] Comoros, Cote D'Ivoire, Djibouti, Equatorial Guinea, Eritrea, Gabon, Guinea-Bissau, Liberia, Malawi, Sao Tome and Principe, Sierra Leone, Somalia. For the latest list see http://www.achpr.org/english/_info/statereport_considered_en.html.

[142] http://www.achpr.org/english/_info/statereport_considered _en.html.

[143] Viljoen argues that the procedure adopted by the Commission, which consists of a series of questions posed in quick succession followed by a statement in defence, is hardly conducive to true dialogue: see n 140. For further discussion, see J Biegon 'Towards the adoption of guidelines for state reporting under the African Union Protocol on Women's Rights: A review of the Pretoria Gender Experts Meeting, 6–7 August 2009' (2009) 9 *AHRLJ* 620.

and governments,[144] the Commission only at its 29th session in 2001, made public its comments about the reports, and the responses to the questions.[145]

The Commission has developed a quasi-judicial approach in dealing with communications from individuals or NGOs alleging violations of rights in the Charter.[146] The state against which the communication is directed is informed and sent a copy of the allegations for its comments on admissibility. The Commission considers the admissibility question in the light of the information received from the parties. The admissibility requirements are set out in article 56 of the African Charter:[147] authors must not be anonymous; communications must not be submitted in disparaging language, or be based exclusively on news from the media; local remedies must have been exhausted;[148] the communication must be submitted in a reasonable time and the matter must not have been settled by other international organs. If the matter is declared admissible, the parties are invited to submit their arguments on the merits.[149] The implicated state party has three months within which to do so, and any comments received will be sent by the Commission to the author of the communication for a response. The Commission will then hear the matter on the merits and its decision is sent to the parties and published in the Commission's *Annual Activity Report*. This publication of decisions is a significant move by the Commission, not least of all because the Commission has thereby accorded itself a freedom not to observe the constraints of confidentiality imposed by the Charter. The political organs have accepted this transparency, with the result that the individual complaints proce-

[144] Murray (n 114) 163.

[145] The Commission today continues this practice of providing 'concluding comments' on the reports. See, further, M Evans, T Ige and R Murray in Evans and Murray (n 121) 56.

[146] See articles 55–9 of the African Charter dealing with 'Other Communications'. These communications relate to any non-state communication, including communications from groups/NGOs as well as individuals (for details see CA Odinkalu and C Christensen 'The African Commission on Human and Peoples' Rights: The development of its non-state communication procedures' (1998) 20 *Human Rights Quarterly* 235). Under articles 47 to 54 of the Charter states parties are provided with a procedure for interstate complaints—this procedure has never been invoked.

[147] On admissibility generally, see F Viljoen 'Admissibility under the African Charter' in Evans and Murray (n 121) 61. See also Viljoen (n 114) 331.

[148] Only effective local remedies need be exhausted. See, further, on local remedies, NJ Udombana 'So far, so fair: The local remedies rule in the jurisprudence of the African Commission on Human and Peoples' Rights' (2003) 97 *AJIL* 1.

[149] Rule 119(1) of the Rules of Procedure of the African Commission on Human and Peoples' Rights.

dure has begun to resemble that of other monitoring bodies. This development has been accompanied by an increase in the number of complaints received by the Commission from non-state parties.

Aside from state reporting and individual communications, the Charter may be enforced through the Commission's article 58 power to investigate 'massive violations' of human rights.[150] For instance, in *Lawyers Committee for Human Rights v Zaire* (1990),[151] the Commission held that allegations of torture, detention and arbitrary arrests proved the existence of a series of serious or massive violations. In cases where the Commission concludes that 'one or more communications apparently relate to special cases which reveal the existence of a series of serious or massive violations of Human and Peoples' Rights', the Commission, under article 58(1) is to refer the cases to the Assembly of the African Union for that body's consideration. The Assembly may in turn request the Commission to undertake an in-depth study of these cases and to make a factual report, accompanied by its findings and recommendations.[152] In addition to the Commission's power to deal with serious or massive human rights violations, it has also developed a special mechanism, involving the appointment of special rapporteurs, to deal with thematic human rights issues, notably human rights defenders, refugees, asylum seekers and internally displaced persons, freedom of expression, conditions of detention, and women's rights.[153]

While the ACHPR has stated on more than one occasion that it considers its decisions as an authoritative interpretation of the Charter, and thus binding on states,[154] the extent to which the recommendations are legally binding depends largely on the goodwill of states.[155] In November 2006, the ACHPR adopted a Resolution

[150] The requirement that a communication meet admissibility requirements will be waived if there is '*prima facie* evidence' of a series of serious or massive violations in relation to article 58 of the Charter—see R Murray 'Serious or massive violations under the African Charter on Human and Peoples' Rights: A comparison with the Inter-American and European mechanisms' (1999) 17 *Netherlands Quarterly of Human Rights* 109.

[151] Communication 47/90, 16 October 1990; ruling delivered at the 18th Ordinary Session of the African Commission on Human and Peoples' Rights, held in Praia, Cape Verde, 2–11 October 1995.

[152] Article 58(2). The Assembly, however, has not responded to any of the submissions forwarded to it by the African Commission: see Murray (n 7) 60.

[153] See, generally, Murray (n 114) 22–4.

[154] Ibid 54–5.

[155] See, however, F Viljoen and L Louw 'The status of the findings of the African Commission: From moral persuasion to legal obligation' (2004) 48 *Journal of African Law* 1. The authors argue that there is a movement towards the decisions being viewed as legally binding, one reason being that under the new AU structures, when the Assembly adopts, after consideration, the Commission's *Annual Activity Report*,

on the Importance of Implementation of the Recommendations of the African Commission, during its 20th ordinary session in order to highlight the importance of observance of these recommendations.[156]

The OAU policy organs did little to ensure that member states complied with their reporting obligations or with adverse decisions of the Commission.[157] There is, accordingly, an urgent need for the AU to consider how the Commission's position may be strengthened within the new structures of the AU, and for the Commission to urge the AU policy organs to take its supervisory role under the African Charter more seriously.[158]

3 African Court on Human and Peoples' Rights

In June 1998, the OAU adopted the Protocol on the African Court on Human and Peoples' Rights,[159] which entered into force on 25 January 2004 upon receiving the required 15 ratifications.[160] The Court 'complements the protective mandate' of the Commission.[161] The Court is staffed by 11 judges, the same number as the members of the ACHPR, elected in an individual capacity and by secret ballot, who hold office for a six-year renewable term. The first group of judges of the African Court was elected on 22 January 2006. Despite the

'[t]he Assembly, as "parent" institution, takes legal responsibility for the findings of the Commission by way of its act of "adoption"' (10). See too F Viljoen and L Louw 'State compliance with recommendations of the African Commission on Human and Peoples Rights 1994–2004' (2007) 101 *AJIL* 1.

[156] See further, M du Plessis and L Stone 'A court not found' (2007) 7 *AHRLJ* 533.

[157] For full discussion of the relationship between the OAU/AU and the African Commission, see Murray (n 7) 49–72. For a discussion on the marginalisation of the African system in general and its jurisprudence, see R Murray 'International human rights: Neglect of perspectives from African institutions' (2006) 55 *ICLQ* 193.

[158] To this end, the African Commission has established working groups on indigenous populations and communities, economic, social and cultural rights, the death penalty, the Robben Island Guidelines (which has subsequently been renamed the Committee for the Prevention of Torture and Cruel, Inhuman or Degrading Treatment or Punishment in Africa), the environment and human rights violations in Africa.

[159] See, generally, Viljoen (n 114) 418–78; See also J Harrington 'The African Court on Human and Peoples' Rights' in Evans and Murray (n 121) 305; GJ Naldi and K Magliveras 'Reinforcing the African system of human rights: The Protocol on the establishment of a regional court of human and peoples' rights' (1998) 16 *Netherlands Quarterly of Human Rights* 431; JC Mubangizi and A O'Shea 'An African court of human and peoples' rights' (1999) 24 *SAYIL* 257; M Matua 'The African human rights court: A two-legged stool?' (1999) 21 *Human Rights Quarterly* 342; N Pityana 'Reflections on the African Court on Human and Peoples' Rights' (2004) 4 *AHRLJ* 121; RW Eno 'The jurisdiction of the African Court on Human and Peoples' Rights' (2002) 2 *AHRLJ* 223.

[160] See n 112.

[161] Article 2 of the Court's Protocol.

requirement of gender balance, only two female judges were elected.[162] The Court officially commenced its operations in Addis Ababa in November 2006, but in August 2007 it moved its seat to Arusha, Tanzania.

The Court has competence to decide 'all cases and disputes submitted to it concerning the interpretation and application of the Charter, this Protocol and any other relevant Human Rights instrument ratified by the states concerned,'[163] and to provide an opinion on any legal matter relating to the Charter or any other relevant human rights instrument.[164]

Cases may be submitted to the Court by the Commission, a state party which has lodged a complaint with the Commission, a state party against whom a complaint has been lodged, a state party whose citizen is a victim of human rights violations, and African Intergovernmental Organizations.[165] In exceptional cases, the Court may allow individuals or NGOs to bring cases before the Court without first having to refer the matter to the Commission.[166] In terms of article 5 of the Protocol '[t]he Court may entitle relevant non-governmental organizations (NGOs) with observer status before the Commission, and individuals to institute cases directly before it, in accordance with article 34(6) of this Protocol'. Article 34(6) of the Protocol provides as follows:

> At the time of the ratification of this Protocol or any time thereafter, the State shall make a declaration accepting the competence of the Court to receive cases under article 5(3) of this Protocol. The Court shall not receive any petition under article 5(3) involving a State Party which has not made such a declaration.

Articles 5 and 34(6) thus create two conditions for individuals to have direct access to the Court. The first is that the state party concerned must have made a declaration pursuant to article 34(6) of the Protocol. The second is that the Court itself must choose to exercise its discretion to hear the case. Normally, it may only consider such cases once the Commission has considered the matter and has prepared a report or taken a decision.[167] The declaration required from a state under article 34(6)—allowing an individual or NGO to bring a complaint against it to the Court—is an unfortunate condition imposed under the Protocol. Certainly, it will do little to help

[162] Article 14(3) of the Court's Protocol.

[163] Article 3 of the Court's Protocol.

[164] Ibid article 4.

[165] Ibid article 5(1). See IB Elsheik 'The future relationship between the African Court and the African Commission' (2002) 2 *AJHRL* 252 at 256.

[166] Ibid article 5(3) read with article 34(6) of the Court's Protocol.

[167] Ibid article 8.

build the reputation of the Court in the eyes of the countless African victims of human rights violations who, in the absence of an article 34(6) declaration by their state, will be unable to access the African Court on Human and Peoples' Rights.[168] As one commentator has rightly noted, '[o]ne need not be extensively versed in African politics to gauge the likelihood of African states making an extra effort to provide their citizens and civil society groups with avenues through which to hold them accountable'.[169] For reasons that remain unclear, it is accordingly disappointing to note that South Africa has to date not played a leading role by making an article 34(6) declaration.[170]

The proceedings of the Court will usually be in public and oral hearings are envisaged.[171] Where the interests of justice require it, those appearing before the Court may be entitled to free legal representation.[172] If the Court finds a violation of a protected right, it shall order an appropriate measure to remedy the violation.[173] This may include compensation,[174] and provisional measures may also be adopted.[175] The judgment of the Court is final and without appeal.[176] In a significant improvement on the ACHPR's procedures, states parties undertake to comply with the judgment of the African Court in any case to which they are parties.[177] Of special significance—and

[168] See, further, Matua (n 159) 355.

[169] Harrington (n 159) 319.

[170] A possible reason for South Africa's unwillingness to make a declaration is because it is influenced by the unhelpful suggestion of its State Law Advisers that the future African Court might act as something of a court of appeal with the power 'to overrule the highest court in the domestic jurisdiction of a state party'. (See the views of the State Law Adviser (International Law), A Stemmet 'A future African Court for Human and Peoples' Rights and domestic human rights norms' (1998) 23 *SAYIL* 233–6.) For reasons explaining this suggestion to be overblown, see NB Pityana 'Hurdles and pitfalls in international human rights law: The ratification process of the Protocol to the African Charter on the establishment of the African Court on Human and Peoples' Rights' (2003) 28 *SAYIL* 110 especially at 116–27.

[171] Article 10 of the Court's Protocol.

[172] Article 10(2) however, the article does not say who must bear the burden of providing this representation.

[173] Article 27.

[174] Article 27(1).

[175] Article 27(2).

[176] Article 28.

[177] Article 30. The enforcement of the Court's Order was discussed by Allehone Mulugeta Abebe with regard to the case of *African Commission on Human and Peoples' Rights v Great Socialist People's Libyan Arab Jamahiriya* (discussed further below) in which he states that, although the Order is binding, it 'can only be implemented through diplomatic pressure'. See AM Abebe 'A landmark provisional ruling of the African Court on Human and Peoples' Rights on Libya' *International Law Observer*, 2 April 2011, available at http://www.internationalobserver.edu. See also M Swart

mirroring the European system in this respect—is that implementation of the Court's decisions will be monitored by the political bodies of the AU. In this regard, article 29(2) of the Court's Protocol provides that the Council of Ministers shall be notified of the judgment and shall monitor its execution on behalf of the Assembly of the African Union. In addition, Article 30 of the Court's Statute states: 'The States parties to the present Protocol undertake to comply with the judgment in any case to which they are parties within the time stipulated by the Court and *to guarantee its execution*.'[178]

The Court has to date handed down judgments in both contentious and advisory cases. For example, the decision of *Yogogombaye v The Republic of Senegal*[179] concerned an application by a Chadian national residing in Switzerland brought against the Republic of Senegal, with a view to obtaining suspension of the ongoing proceedings against Hissène Habré, former head of state of Chad, who had been granted political asylum in Dakar, Senegal. The Court found that in order for it to hear a case brought by an individual against a state party, there must be compliance with articles 5(3) and 34(6), requiring the deposit by the state of a special declaration authorising such a case to be brought against it. Senegal had not made a declaration pursuant to article 34(6) and accordingly the Court concluded that it did not have jurisdiction to hear the matter. The second case heard by the Court, *African Commission on Human and Peoples' Rights v Great Socialist People's Libyan Arab Jamahiriya*,[180] concerned an Order for Provisional Measures in respect of the violence that shook Libya in early 2011.[181] Libya was ordered by the Court to 'immediately refrain from any action that would result in loss of life or violation of physical integrity of persons' and to report to the Court within 15 days on

'Can regional and sub-regional African courts strengthen the rule of law in Africa? Questions of impact and enforcement' in CC Jalloh and O Elias (eds) *Shielding Humanity: Essays in International Law in Honour of Judge Abdul G Koroma* (2015) 706 at 719–21.

[178] However, see R Cole 'The African Court on Human and Peoples' Rights: Will political stereotypes form an obstacle to the enforcement of its decisions?' (2010) *CILSA* XLIII.

[179] Application No 001/2008. For further discussion see Biegon and Killander (n 137) 228.

[180] Application No 004-2011. See further on this and the subsequent default judgment by the African Court against Libya in *African Commission on Human and Peoples' Rights v Libya*, App No 002/2013, (Judgment: June 3, 2016) M Ayissi 'African Commission on Human and Peoples' Rights v. Libya' (2017) 111 *AJIL* 738.

[181] The violations complained of related to, inter alia, the detention of an opposition lawyer in Benghazi; random shooting of demonstrators by security forces; and 'excessive use of heavy weapons and machine guns against the population'. See further M du Plessis and C Gevers 'Human rights court provides some light in African tunnel' *Business Day* 15 April 2011.

'measures taken to implement the Order'. The ACHPR brought this application. The Court made this Order *proprio motu* (of its own accord) in the course of its consideration.

More recently, the Court has issued a steady number of judgments.[182] In probably one of its most consequential judgments, the Court offered a substantive interpretation of the normative content of the notion of peoples' rights under the Charter in its judgment in the *African Commission on Human and Peoples' Rights v Republic of Kenya* (the *Ogiek* case), delivered on 26 May 2017.[183] The case involved a claim over ownership of traditional land by a group of indigenous people in Kenya, the *Ogiek*, which had been lodged against the Government of Kenya. After an eight-year battle, the African Court found that the Kenyan government had violated seven articles of the African Charter (including Articles 21 and 22) in a land rights case that dates back to colonial times.[184] This is the first time that the African Court has ruled on an 'indigenous peoples' case. The *Ogiek* case was first lodged as a complaint before the ACHPR. The ACHPR, for the first time in its history, referred the case to the African Court on the basis that it evinced serious human rights violations. Through this historic judgment, the African Court has validated the approach and understanding of the ACHPR on the meaning of peoples' rights enshrined in the African Charter.

On 1 July 2008, the Assembly of Heads of State and Government of the AU adopted the Protocol on the Statute of the African Court of Justice and Human Rights to merge the African Court on Human and Peoples' Rights with the African Court of Justice of the African Union (Merger Protocol).[185] The Protocol will enter into force 30 days after

[182] For a list of judgments in contentious matters and advisory opinions by the Court, see http://www.acthprmonitor.org/case-archive/.

[183] African Court on Human and Peoples' Rights, *African Commission on Human and Peoples' Rights v Republic of Kenya,* App No 006/2012, (Judgment: May 26, 2017), available at http://www.african-court.org/en/index.php/55-finalised-cases-details/864-app-no-006-2012-african-commission-on-human-and-peoples-rights-v-republic-of-kenya-details.

[184] Overall, the Court found that there was a violation of the following Articles: 1, 2, 8, 14, 17(2) and (3), 21 and 22 of the Charter.

[185] The arguments for the merged court were both financial and organisational. The expense associated with funding two courts made it impractical. Further, African leaders wanted to avoid the overlap that exists in the European system between the European Court of Human Rights and the European Court of Justice. (This 'overlap' is sometimes misunderstood because the former is a court established under the auspices of the European Convention on Human Rights for all the 47 members of the Council of Europe; the latter court is an organ of the EU and has jurisdiction only over its members. Thus, the two courts are not related. However, since all EU states, currently 28, are members of the Council of Europe and are parties to the European Convention on Human Rights, there are concerns about consistency in case law

the deposit of the instrument of ratification by 15 member states of the AU. The African Court of Justice and Human Rights will be the main judicial organ of the AU.[186] It will have jurisdiction over all cases and legal disputes that relate to 'the interpretation and application of the Constitutive Act, Union treaties and all subsidiary legal instruments, the African Charter and any question of international law'.[187] The Protocol Establishing the Court will replace the existing protocols establishing, on the one hand, the African Court of Justice, and on the other hand, the African Court of Human and Peoples' Rights.

The African Court of Justice and Human Rights will have its seat in Arusha, Tanzania, the current seat of the African Court of Human and Peoples' Rights. Article 16 of the Protocol provides for two sections of the African Court of Justice: A general affairs section and a human rights section with eight judges in each.[188] However, the AU Assembly adopted another protocol amending the Merger Protocol at its 23rd ordinary session in Malabo, Equatorial Guinea, on 27 June 2014. The Protocol on Amendments to the Protocol on the Statute of the African Court of Justice and Human Rights (Malabo Protocol) creates a third division of the Court: the International Criminal Division. It expands the jurisdiction of the yet-to-be established African Court of Justice and Human Rights to crimes under international law and transnational crimes. Quite apart from questions about the wisdom of adopting a protocol to amend another protocol that has not yet entered into force, and which is itself aimed at amending an earlier treaty that is also not yet in force, other concerns have been raised about expanding the Court's jurisdiction. These relate to both the political motivations behind the development and the implications for the integrity of international criminal justice, and the extent to which the future merged court can play a positive role in a continent persistently afflicted with the scourge of conflict and impunity for international crimes.[189] Moreover, there has been

between the two courts). This contrasts with an earlier decision taken, after much debate, by a meeting of African Ministers of Justice which had been convened to finalise the Protocol on the Court of Justice of the African Union (see AU Doc Assembly/AU/Dec 45 (III)).

[186] Article 2 of the Statute of the African Court of Justice and Human Rights.

[187] Ibid article 28.

[188] Ibid article 16.

[189] The Malabo Protocol has already attracted a significant amount of scholarly commentary and literature, both positive and critical, within the relatively short time since its adoption, especially for an instrument that has not yet entered into force. See, eg, M Sirleaf 'The African justice cascade and the Malabo Protocol' (2017) 11 *International Journal of Transnational Justice* 71; CC Jalloh 'The nature of the crimes in the African Criminal Court' (2017) 15 *Journal of International Criminal Justice* 799;

particular criticism over the inclusion of article 46A bis in the protocol, which states: '[N]o charges shall be commenced or continued before the court against any serving AU Head of State of Government, or anybody acting or entitled to act in such capacity, or other senior state officials based on their functions, during their tenure of office.'[190]

These questions arise in the context of ongoing tensions between some African states and the International Criminal Court (ICC), discussed in the section below.

In any case, under the protocol, the only entities that will be entitled to submit cases to this merged court will be state parties to the present Protocol; the Assembly, Parliament and authorised organs of the AU; and a staff member of the AU acting within the staff rules and regulations of the Union.[191] Individuals and NGOs accredited to the AU or its organs may only have access to the Court in respect of a state party that has made a declaration accepting the jurisdiction of the Court over cases submitted by NGOs or individuals.[192] It is important to note that article 46 of the Protocol on the Statute of the African Court of Justice and Human Rights gives the African Court of Justice and Human Rights, like the African Court of Human and Peoples' Rights, the power to issue final and binding decisions.[193] Further, the Protocol provides that 'parties shall comply with the judgment made by the Court, within the time stipulated by the Court and shall guarantee its execution'.[194] The Executive Council of the AU will be tasked with the responsibility of monitoring the execution of the Court's decision. In the event of a failure to

G Werle and M Vormbaum (eds) *The African Criminal Court: A Commentary on the Malabo Protocol* (2017); and M du Plessis 'Implications of the AU decision to give the African Court jurisdiction over international crimes' Institute for Security Studies Paper No 235, June 2012, available at https://issafrica.s3.amazonaws.com/site/uploads/Paper235-AfricaCourt.pdf; and M du Plessis 'A case of negative regional complementarity? Giving the African Court of Justice and Human Rights jurisdiction over international crimes' *EJILTalk*, August 2012, available at https://www.ejiltalk.org/a-case-of-negative-regional-complementarity-giving-the-african-court-of-justice-and-human-rights-jurisdiction-over-international-crimes/.

[190] For critical comment, see M du Plessis 'Shambolic, shameful and symbolic implications of the African Union's immunity for African leaders' Institute for Security Studies Paper No 278, November 2014, available at https://www.files.ethz.ch/isn/185934/Paper278.pdf.

[191] Ibid article 29. This provision confers upon staff members capacity to sue the Organization on administrative or employment-related disputes. Currently, as is common with other international organizations, AU staff members may file cases before the AU's own internal judicial mechanism, the Administrative Tribunal.

[192] Ibid article 30(f) read with article 8(3).

[193] Ibid article 46(1) and (2) of the Protocol to the Statute.

[194] Ibid article 46(3).

comply with a judgment, the African Court of Justice and Human Rights may refer the matter to the Assembly, which will decide upon measures to be taken to give effect to that judgment, including the imposition of sanctions.[195]

4 Tension between African states, the UN Security Council and the International Criminal Court[196]

On 31 March 2005, the UN Security Council for the first time used its discretion under article 13 of the Rome Statute of the International Criminal Court to refer a matter to the newly created ICC for possible prosecution. It did so by adopting resolution 1593 in which it referred the situation in Darfur, Sudan to the ICC.[197] The ICC pre-trial chamber thereafter issued arrest warrants for four Sudanese officials, including Sudan's President Omar al-Bashir for war crimes, crimes against humanity and genocide. The Government of Sudan has objected to the indictment, arguing that Sudanese sovereignty is being violated. Further, the AU has called on the UN Security Council to invoke article 16 of the Rome Statute to suspend the processes initiated by the ICC against al-Bashir. The UN Security Council has failed to act on the request. In 2009, the African Union Assembly expressed deep concern at the indictment, stating that 'in view of the delicate peace process underway in The Sudan, the application could seriously undermine peace efforts'.[198] It further directed all AU member states to withhold co-operation from the ICC in respect of the arrest and surrender of al-Bashir.[199] In November 2009 the AU presented a proposal for an amendment to article 16

[195] In fall article 46(5).

[196] For a thorough discussion of the issue see D Akande, M du Plessis and C Jalloh 'An African expert study on the African Union concerns about article 16 of the Rome Statute of the ICC' Institute for Security Studies, (2010), available at http://www.iss.co.za. See also OC Imoedemhe 'Unpacking the tension between the African Union and the ICC: The way forward' (2015) 23 *AJICL* 74; and, generally, C Jalloh and I Bantekas (eds) *The International Criminal Court and Africa* (2017).

[197] The referral was made under article 13(b) of the Rome Statute of the International Criminal Court 2187 UNTS 3; adopted on 17 July 1998, entered into force on 1 July 2002. South Africa ratified it on 27 November 2000.

[198] Decision on the application by the ICC prosecutor for the indictment of the President of the Republic of the Sudan Assembly/AU/Dec 221(XII). For further discussion see D Tladi 'The African Union and the International Criminal Court: The battle for the soul of international law' (2009) 34 *SAYIL* 57.

[199] Article 16 grants the Security Council the power to 'defer' an ongoing investigation or prosecution for one year if the Security Council determines it is necessary for the maintenance of international peace and security under chapter VII of the UN Charter. It would be necessary to show that the continued involvement of the ICC is a greater threat to international peace and security than suspending the ICC's work. It has been argued that the request for the Article 16 deferral is baseless in

giving the General Assembly the authority to defer an investigation should the Security Council 'fail to act' on such a request within six months.[200] In July 2010, AU heads of state reiterated this decision, and further suggested that the indictment displays selectivity and double standards in respect of the prosecution of war crimes, especially in Africa.[201] The saga highlights a growing attitude within the AU that African leaders should not be held to account to a non-African Court,[202] with the AU Assembly requesting the ACHPR and the African Court on Human and Peoples' Rights to examine the implications of the African Court being empowered to try international crimes.[203]

This has strained relations between the ICC and the AU.[204] The tension was exacerbated when in 2010 the ICC prosecutor asked the Court's pre-trial chamber to issue summons for six people on the grounds that they had committed crimes against humanity in the post-election violence in Kenya in 2007 and 2008. The indicted individuals included the President Uhuru Kenyatta and Deputy President William Ruto. The backlash against the ICC was considerable, with Kenya's Parliament passing a resolution calling for Kenya's withdrawal from the Rome Statute and the AU agreeing to

law and motivated by a desire to further alienate the ICC from Africa. Both the United States and the United Kingdom have publicly stated that they will veto such a request.

[200] Article 16, in its current formulation, gives the UN Security Council the exclusive power to request deferral of ICC investigations and prosecutions. Africa's proposed article 16 amendment faces the political obstacle of garnering support for a provision which implicates the relationship between the General Assembly and the Security Council regarding the maintenance of international peace and security. For more on this see M du Plessis and C Gevers 'Making amend(ment)s: South Africa and the International Criminal Court from 2009 to 2010' (2009) 34 *SAYIL* 1.

[201] Assembly/AU/Dec 296(XV). This decision clearly creates a *prima facie* obligation on African states not to do so. With respect to member states of the African Union that are also states parties to the Rome Statute, this would appear to create a conflict between the obligations imposed by the Rome Statute and those imposed by the decisions of the African Union.

[202] In July 2008, the AU stated that 'abuse of the principle of universal jurisdiction is a clear violation of sovereignty' and 'indictments against African leaders have had a negative impact on international relations'. Al-Bashir's subsequent visits to Kenya and Chad, both states parties to the Rome Statute, in defiance of an ICC arrest warrant has further strained the relationship between Africa and the ICC. See Gumedze (n 92) 152; and Biegnon and Killander (n 137) 231.

[203] Decision on the Implementation of the Assembly Decision on the Abuse of the Principle of Universal Jurisdiction Doc. Assembly/AU/Dec.213 (XII) and Assembly/AU/Dec 271 (XIV). This decision led to the adoption of the Malabo Protocol discussed above (n 189).

[204] See generally M du Plessis 'The International Criminal Court and its work in Africa: Confronting the myths' (Institute for Security Studies Paper No 173, November 2008). See also Imoedemhe (n 196).

transmit a request to the UN Security Council asking it to defer the ICC's investigation into the Kenyan violence.[205] The ICC subsequently dropped (or 'suspended') the cases in 2014 and 2016, respectively, and declared a mistrial due to the 'troubling incidence of witness interference and intolerable political meddling'. However, the indictment against President al-Bashir still stands. Both the al-Bashir and Kenyatta cases, and the fact that to date all the other cases before the ICC have involved African countries, strengthened the views and suspicions of the critics of the Court, who have accused it of practising selective justice and targeting African states and their leaders.[206]

Furthermore, the apparent failure and unwillingness of the UN Security Council to address the AU's concerns led to repeated calls at successive AU summits, since 2009, for AU members that are parties to the Rome Statute not to co-operate with the ICC and to withdraw from it.[207] So far, only three countries have followed or attempted to follow this course: Burundi, South Africa and Gambia notified the UN Secretary-General of their intentions to revoke their ratifications of the Rome Statute and thereby terminate their membership of the Court. In their respective announcements made in quick succession in October 2016, all three countries claimed that their decisions reflected sovereign choices consistent with their national constitutions and the Rome Statute itself.[208] Subsequently, Gambia and South Africa revoked their notifications of withdrawal. In Gambia's case, this followed the election of a new government that opposed the previous government's position on membership of the ICC. South Africa's revocation was forced upon the government by a decision of the South African High Court in Pretoria on 22 February 2017, which

[205] See Decision on the Implementation of the Decisions on the International Criminal Court (ICC): Assembly/AU/Dec.334(XVI), adopted by the Sixteenth Ordinary Session of the AU Assembly held in Addis Ababa from 30–31 January 2011.

[206] See, eg, M deGuzman 'Is the ICC targeting Africa inappropriately? A moral, legal, and sociological assessment' in RH Steinberg (ed) *Contemporary Issues Facing the International Criminal Court* (2016) 333.

[207] These calls culminated in the adoption of the 'Withdrawal Strategy' by the AU Assembly at its 28th Ordinary Session in Addis Ababa on 31 January 2017. See Assembly/AU/Dec.622(XXVIII), para. 8. The decision also welcomed and fully supported the 'sovereign decisions' taken by Burundi, South Africa and The Gambia as pioneer implementers of the withdrawal strategy' (para 2).

[208] The announcements by Burundi, South Africa and Gambia were made in quick succession on 18 October, 24 October, and 21 October 2016, respectively, through notifications to the UN Secretary-General.

ruled that the decision to withdraw from the ICC was unconstitutional and invalid.[209]

THE QUEST FOR A PERMANENT SEAT FOR AFRICA ON THE UN SECURITY COUNCIL

Articles 52, 53 and 54 of the UN Charter, which provide for regional arrangements and their co-operation with the world body, presuppose the existence of regional organisations, such the AU. Since its creation, the AU (as with the OAU before it), has co-operated with the UN within the purview of the UN Charter. One aspect of this co-operation has been the creation of joint AU–UN peacekeeping operations in Burundi and Sudan, as seen above. These have been undertaken within the purview of article 53 of the UN Charter, which allows the UN to utilise regional arrangements and agencies for enforcement action for the maintenance of peace and security.

As an organisation whose members comprise the largest regional block of the UN membership (54 of the 193 members[210]), the AU has pushed for greater visibility, influence, and recognition of its interests within the UN. In part, this is reflected in the demand for at least one permanent seat for the Africa region on the United Nations Security Council. The AU regards the inclusion of African states as necessary in order to make the Security Council more representative and legitimate and give Africa a place in the balance of power in a reformed Security Council. African states, including South Africa, have repeatedly voiced concern about the unjust composition of the Security Council whose permanent membership still mirrors the immediate post-World War II power relations.[211] Reform of the Security Council, specifically, has been an on-and-off item on the agenda of the UN for some time, but especially since 21 March 2005 when former Secretary-General Kofi Annan put forward his plan for a comprehensive reform of the UN.[212] The reconfiguration of the fossilised permanent membership of the Security Council has been

[209] *Democratic Alliance v Minister of International Relations* 2017 (3) SA 212 (GP). See further M du Plessis and G Mettraux 'South Africa's failed withdrawal from the Rome Statute: Politics, law, and judicial accountability' (2017) 15 *Journal of International Criminal Justice* 361.

[210] One of the 55 AU member states, Sahrawi Arab Democratic Republic, is not a member of the UN. It has never formally sought admission to the UN. Given its contested statehood, even within the AU, it is unlikely that it would obtain the required support if it applied for UN membership.

[211] See W Okumu 'Africa and the UN Security Council Permanent Seats' (2005) 2 *African Renaissance* 16.

[212] UNGA Doc A/59/2005: *In Larger Freedom: Towards Development, Security and Human Rights for All.*

one of the major demands of not only the African states, but other states from the various regional groups as well. However, without agreement among member states on the various competing proposals that have been tabled, this has also proved to be the sticking point that has stalled the entire UN reform project. The African common position on this issue, reached after a series of deliberations at ministerial and summit levels, is encapsulated in the document known as '*The Ezulwini Consensus*'.[213] The AU proposal calls for the allocation of two permanent seats to Africa, with veto power, and five non-permanent seats. There is no doubt that most UN member states support the call for reform of the organisation, in particular the Security Council. These include all the five permanent members of the Security Council, at least on paper. Yet although these states continue to profess their support for reform, because of obvious self-interest there does not appear to be any prospect of a quick consensus on what that reform should look like. Rather, it is likely that for the foreseeable future states that have a stake in maintaining the status quo will prefer to guard jealously their coveted positions and veto power in the Security Council, and effectively resist any change that threatens their hegemony.[214] For the AU, therefore, UN Security Council reform appears to have receded beyond the horizon and serious debate on the issue remains in limbo.

[213] Ext/EX.CL/2 (VII): The Common African Position on the Proposed Reform of the United Nations: The 'Ezulwini Consensus', adopted by the Executive Council at its seventh extraordinary session, 7–8 March 2005, Addis Ababa, Ethiopia. The 'Ezulwini Consensus' was reaffirmed by the AU Assembly at its 10th Ordinary Session in Addis Ababa, Ethiopia, on 2 February 2008. See Assembly/AU/Dec. 184(X), Decision on the Reform of the United Nations Security Council. Although the AU has not proposed any countries as its candidates for a permanent seat, it is generally thought that Algeria, Egypt, Ethiopia, Nigeria and South Africa would be the main contenders.

[214] For example, in her testimony to the US House Foreign Affairs Committee on 28 June 2017, Ambassador Nikki Haley, in response to a question from Congressman Ami Bera, reiterated that the US supported UN Security Council reform as long as it did not take away its veto. These remarks are not included in her opening statement, available at http://www.unus.state.gov. But her response to Congressman Bera, reported in the media, is available at https://www.outlookindia.com/newsscroll/us-supports-un-security-council-reforms-nikki-haley/1086924.

Index

H

M

N

U

www.ingramcontent.com/pod-product-compliance
Lightning Source LLC
LaVergne TN
LVHW060007210926
848481LV00013B/3663

* 9 7 8 1 4 8 5 1 2 8 2 8 1 *